Organisation development and change

by

Dianne M. Waddell
Thomas G. Cummings
Christopher G. Worley

NELSON
★
™
THOMSON LEARNING

Australia · Canada · Mexico · Singapore · Spain · United Kingdom · United States

NELSON

THOMSON LEARNING

102 Dodds Street
South Melbourne Victoria 3205

Email nelson@nelson.com.au
Website http://www.nelson.com.au

First published in 2000
10 9 8 7 6 5 4 3 2
07 06 05 04 03 02 01

Copyright © 2000 Nelson Thomson Learning

National Library of Australia
Cataloguing-in-Publication data

Waddell, Dianne, 1949–.
Organisation development and change
Includes index.
ISBN 0 17 010278 5.

1. Organizational change. 2. Organizational innovation. I.
Cummings, Thomas G. II. Worley, Christopher G. III.
Title.

302.35

Edited by Susan Lawrence and Diane Fowler
Text and cover designed by Gail McManus
Typeset by Susan Lawrence
Typeset in 9.5/11 pt Sabon
Printed in Singapore by MarKono Print Media Pte Ltd.

Nelson Australia Pty Limited ACN 058 280 149 (incorporated in Victoria)
trading as Nelson Thomson Learning.

CONTENTS

Preface ix
Acknowledgements x

Chapter 1 What is organisation development? 1
Why study organisation development? 3
    Application 1.1 Supermarkets engage in performance-improving activities 5
A short history of organisation development 6
    Application 1.2 Team-building weekends 7
    Application 1.3 Participatory action research to empower Aboriginal health workers 8
    Application 1.4 Benchmarks fuel improvements..10
    Application 1.5 All change, says ANZ boss...12
    Application 1.6 An example of autonomous work groups at Westrail...................14
    Application 1.7 MLC merger chief: how to build a financial giant 15
Evolution in organisation development..16
Overview of the book 17
Summary 20
Activities 20
Notes 21

PART 1 Overview of organisation development 25
Chapter 2 The nature of planned change 26
Theories of planned change..26
    Application 2.1 Action learning—the subtle organisation transformer 31
General model of planned change 32
Different types of planned change 34
    Application 2.2 Planned change: radical approach to education 34
Critique of planned change...37
Summary 41
Activities 42
Notes 42

Chapter 3 The organisation development practitioner 45
Who is the organisation development practitioner? 45
Skills and knowledge of an effective organisation development practitioner 46
    Application 3.1 Consultant styles matrix..47
The professional organisation development practitioner 51
    Application 3.2 Personal view of an external consultant 52
    Application 3.3 Personal views of internal and external consultants 54
Professional values...57
Professional ethics 58
    Application 3.4 Former manager banks on new career 61
Summary 62
Activities 63
Notes 63
Appendix: Professional codes of practice for accounting organisations 65

PART 2 The process of organisation development..............67

Chapter 4 Entering and contracting 68
Entering into an OD relationship 68
   Application 4.1 St Andrew's total care ethos 71
Developing a contract...72
   Application 4.2 Organisational learning in practice.................73
Summary 76
Activities..76
Notes 77

Chapter 5 Diagnosing organisations.............................78
What is diagnosis?...78
The need for diagnostic models...79
Open systems model...80
Organisation-level diagnosis 82
   Application 5.1 Nike's strategic orientation............................87
   Application 5.2 How NEC went back to school and won kudos on the world stage..........90
Summary 93
Activities 94
Notes 94

Chapter 6 Diagnosing groups and jobs 96
Group-level diagnosis..96
   Application 6.1 The evolution of industrial relations in a changing environment.............99
Individual-level diagnosis...101
   Application 6.2 Breaking down the 'them' and 'us' attitude at GEMCo 103
Summary 106
Activities..106
Notes 106

Chapter 7 Collecting and analysing diagnostic information.........................108
The diagnostic relationship 108
Methods for collecting data...110
   Application 7.1 A benchmarking intervention into an executive team...................116
Sampling 118
Techniques for analysing data...119
Summary 125
Activities 125
Notes 125

Chapter 8 Feeding back diagnostic information 127
Determining the content of the feedback 127
Characteristics of the feedback process..................................129
   Application 8.1 Dulux Australia Ltd......................................130
Survey feedback 131
   Application 8.2 Changing business culture: information is the key...............133
Summary 136
Activities 137
Notes 137

Chapter 9 Designing interventions..............................139
What are effective interventions?...139
How to design effective interventions 140
Overview of interventions..144
Summary 148
Activities...149
Notes 149

Chapter 10 Managing change 150
Overview of change activities 150
Motivating change 152
    Application 10.1 Lessons from a leader 154
Creating a vision 155
    Application 10.2 Commonwealth Handling Equipment Pool (CHEP) 157
    Application 10.3 Griffith University 158
Developing political support 159
    Application 10.4 Using social networks to implement change in a consumer goods
    company 162
Managing the transition 162
    Application 10.5 Tubemakers Australia's Yennora plant 163
Sustaining momentum 164
    Application 10.6 Nally (WA) Pty Ltd 165
Summary 167
Activities 167
Notes 167

Chapter 11 Evaluating and institutionalising OD interventions 169
Evaluating OD interventions 169
Institutionalising interventions 179
    Application 11.1 Evaluating an outdoor workshop for team building in an MBA
    programme 180
    Application 11.2 Institutionalising structural change at Hewlett-Packard 185
Summary 188
Activities 188
Notes 189

PART 3 Human process interventions 191
Chapter 12 Interpersonal and group process approaches 192
T-Groups 192
    Application 12.1 Unstructured strangers' T-group 193
Process consultation 195
    Application 12.2 Process consultation at Apex Manufacturing Corporation 199
Third-party intervention 202
    Application 12.3 Cultural change: its effect on the University of Hong Kong
    estates office 204
Team building 206
    Application 12.4 Towards a team-based approach 211
Summary 215
Activities 216
Notes 216

Chapter 13 Organisation process approaches 219
Organisation confrontation meeting 219
    Application 13.1 A Work-Out meeting at General Electric's Medical Systems business ... 220
Inter-group relations interventions 222
    Application 13.2 A culture of conflict 226
Large-group interventions 229
    Application 13.3 Implementation of delivery modes 231
Grid® Organization Development: a normative approach 232
    Application 13.4 Organisation development at the Sigma plant 236
Summary 238
Activities 238
Notes 238

PART 4 Technostructural interventions 241

Chapter 14 Restructuring organisations 242
Structural design..242
  Application 14.1 Liverpool City Council—decentralised reform in
    local government...251
  Application 14.2 Emtech International—forming business networks 255
Downsizing 256
  Application 14.3 TQM and downsizing in large organisations 259
Re-engineering 262
  Application 14.4 Inland Revenue Authority of Singapore—business
    process management 265
Summary 268
Activities 269
Notes 269

Chapter 15 Employee involvement 272
Employee involvement: what is it? 272
Employee involvement applications 276
  Application 15.1 Work restructuring and employee relations—Mobil Adelaide refinery..281
  Application 15.2 Quality circles in Reckitt & Colman's Pharmaceutical Division 286
  Application 15.3 JAL and employee involvement 290
  Application 15.4 Total quality management at Glaxo India 296
Summary 299
Activities 300
Notes 300

Chapter 16 Work design..304
The engineering approach 304
The motivational approach 305
  Application 16.1 Managing the linkage with primary producers 310
The socio-technical systems approach 313
  Application 16.2 A break with the old 319
Designing work for technical and personal needs................................323
Summary 327
Activities 328
Notes 328

PART 5 Human resource management interventions 333

Chapter 17 Performance management 334
A model of performance management 335
Goal setting 336
  Application 17.1 The performance enhancement process at Monsanto.............340
Effects of goal setting and MBO 341
Performance appraisal 342
  Application 17.2 Performance appraisal at Dulux, Clayton 345
Reward systems 347
  Application 17.3 Pay-for-performance systems: experiences in the Australian
    public sector 350
Summary 359
Activities 360
Notes 360

Chapter 18 Developing and assisting members **364**

Career planning and development interventions 365

    Application 18.1 Playing the regional game...367

    Application 18.2 Linking career planning, human resource planning

        and strategy at Colgate-Palmolive..371

    Application 18.3 Succession planning at AGL..374

    Application 18.4 Work equality in 'phase two', maybe...377

Work force diversity interventions 383

    Application 18.5 Denny's diversity turnaround 387

Employee wellness interventions...389

    Application 18.6 Johnson & Johnson's employee assistance and

        Live for Life programmes 392

    Application 18.7 Dealing with stress at Melbourne Water Corporation 400

Summary 401

Activities 402

Notes 402

PART 6 Strategic interventions **407**

Chapter 19 Organisation and environment relationships **408**

Organisation and environment framework 408

Open systems planning 412

    Application 19.1 Open systems planning at Seaside Hospital 414

Integrated strategic change..419

    Application 19.2 Research design and shop floor practice:

        the CSIRO-Holden collaboration 421

Transorganisational development 423

    Application 19.3 A new strategic alliance for PDL Electronics 426

Summary 427

Activities 428

Notes 428

Chapter 20 Organisation transformation...**431**

Characteristics of transformational change..431

Culture change 434

    Application 20.1 Yakka devises a service that imports could not match 442

Self-designing organisations 444

    Application 20.2 Walking the talk pays off in Knox 447

Organisation learning 447

    Application 20.3 BHP management school will nurture new leadership style....................455

Summary 456

Activities 457

Notes 457

PART 7 Special applications of organisation development **461**

Chapter 21 Organisation development in global settings **462**

International organisation development...462

    Application 21.1 Job enrichment in an Egyptian organisation 468

Worldwide organisation development..473

    Application 21.2 Globalisation and a new human resource policy in Korea........................479

Global social change...481

    Application 21.3 Building global social change organisations in South Africa 485

Summary 489

Activities 490

Notes 490

PART 8 Case studies 495

Introduction to the case studies...496

Case study A   Changing HR practices in China—CableCo 499

Case study B   Managing strategic change at Energize.............................510

Case study C   Employee relations at Centrelink 518

Case study D   World Vision Australia: a not-for-profit organisation 529

Case study E   Pilkington: an organisation in transition 541

Case study F   Water industry reform—stopping the leaking tap? 548

Case study G   The acquisition of Heatane by Elgas..............................558

Case study H   Self-managed work teams as a management tool..............568

Case study I   Call centre relocation: Advantage Credit Union 577

Case study J   Melbourne City Parking and Traffic 583

Case study K   Changes in Telstra's field workforce 591

Case study L   Guardian Pharmacies Australia Limited.........................599

Case study M   Stanley Australia 607

Case study N   Quenos: The Kemcor–Orica joint venture 614

Case study O   Disability Service: inevitable structural change 620

Index..625

PREFACE

For the past 25 years, with seven editions, the textbook by Thomas Cummings and Christopher Worley has been used as a medium of teaching change management. I feel privileged at being able to contribute to their work, by placing a 'South-East Asian' perspective on the theories presented. They are experts in the field and have provided an opportunity to present readers with a set of change theories that explore the complex issues in the management of change.

In this book the case studies and illustrative material from the US have been replaced by examples of local situations and practices. More recent change models by Australian researchers have also been included where appropriate. From a critical learning perspective, review questions have been added at the end of each chapter in order to stimulate questioning, analysis and application. The new case studies have been placed after the content chapters so that students do not categorise change processes by treating them in isolation. They should appreciate that changes within organisations are holistic and inclusive of many factors, and do not follow a prescriptive or predictable scenario.

It would be remiss of me to not acknowledge the many people who have assisted me these last months. I would particularly like to thank those organisations that have co-operated in the development of the cases about themselves. I would also like to thank the authors of those cases who have so enthusiastically developed, analysed and critiqued the cases in their own time.

The support and professionalism of the staff at Nelson Thomson Learning were essential. I am particularly grateful to Glen Sheldon and Melissa Traverso who were very encouraging throughout the process. Also Sue Lawrence and Jo Tayler for their diligence and patience in editing of the publication drafts.

I would like to thank many people, including my associates Deb Stewart, Nell Kimberley and Richard Winter and many other academics who gave valuable feedback during the draft stages. I hope to continue my association with all of them.

Of course it would not have been possible without my 'unofficial boss' and daughter Suzy, who did all the hard work.

This of course is not the end but the beginning. Hopefully the next edition will have your contribution—otherwise the book cannot be called a success.

Di Waddell
Melbourne
August 2000

ACKNOWLEDGEMENTS

The publishers would like to thank the following publishers, journals, organisations and institutions for permission to reproduce diagrams, quotes, tables or other material:

© *The Australian*, pp. 71–2, 13 November 1997; B. Benedict Bunker & B. Alban, pp. 220–1, *Journal of Applied Behavioural Science*, 28 (4, 1992): 579–91; R. Blake & A. Adams McCanse, p. 243, *Leadership Dilemmas Grid Solutions*, Gulf Publishing, Houston, 1991, p. 29; R. Blythe, H. Rao & N. Shahani, pp. 296–8, 'TQM in Glaxo India – a step-by-step implementation process. *The TQM Magazine*', Vol. 9, Iss. 2, 1997, pp. 98–105 (MCB University Press); A. Brown, pp. 165–6, *Asia Pacific Journal of Quality Management*, 1993, 2(3), pp. 67–76; R. Callahan, p. 284, 'Quality circles: a programme for productivity improvement through human resource development', Unpublished paper, Albers School of Business, Seattle University, 1982, p. 16; K. Cameron, S. Freeman & A. Mishra, p. 257, *Academy of Management Executive*, 1991, 5(3): 62; CHEP Australia, p. 157, http://www.chep.com.au/profile.html; L. Corbett, pp. 231–2, *Production & Inventory Management Journal*, 1992, 33(3), pp. 74–9; T. Cummings, pp. 324, 326, *Outlook*, 6, 1982, pp. 39, 40; D. Davis & T. Fisher, pp. 163–4, 'The Pace of Change: A Case Study of the Development of a Total Quality Organization', *International Journal of Quality & Reliability Management*, Vol. 11, Iss. 8, 1994, pp. 5–18 (MCB University Press); P. Dawson, pp. 281–2, 'Redefining human resource management: work restructuring and employee relations at Mobil Adelaide Refinery', *International Journal of Manpower*, Vol. 16, No. 12, 1995, pp. 47–5 (MCB University Press); G. Donavan, p. 574, *Self Managed Work Team Global Network*, Perth, 1997, p. 3; Michael Duncan & V. Nilakant, pp. 510–17, Department of Management, University of Canterbury, New Zealand; R. Dunford & P. McGraw, pp. 286–7, *Work and People*, 1986, 12:2, pp. 22–5; W. Dyer, pp. 207, 213, *Team Building*, ©1995. Reprinted by permission of Prentice-Hall, Inc., Upper Saddle River, NJ; Executive Enterprises, pp. 277, 277, *National Productivity Review*, Winter, 1981–82, 1:1. All rights reserved; R. Fells, p. 99, *Work and People*, Vol.12, No. 2, 1986, pp. 13–18; J. Flint, pp. 12–13, *Sydney Morning Herald*, 20 November 1997; Anonymous, p. 5, *Foodweek*, 9 June 1998, Vol. 7, Ian Huntly Pty Ltd, Cremorne; P. Glass, pp. 116–118, *Total Quality Management*, Abingdon; R. Gottliebsen, p. 43, *Business Review Weekly*, 26 January 1998; L. Greiner & V. Schein, pp. 160, 162, *Power and Organization Development*, ©1988. Reprinted by permission of Prentice-Hall, Inc., Upper Saddle River, NJ; M. Griffen, p. 7, *The Sunday Age*, 19 April 1998, pp. 16–19; D. Grose & A. Clark, pp. 130–1, *Work and People*, Vol.11, No. 1, 1985; J. Hackman & G. Oldham, p. 306, *Work Redesign*, ©1980. Reprinted by permission of Prentice-Hall, Inc., Upper Saddle River, NJ; C. Handy, pp. 531, 532, *The Age of Paradox*, Paradox, Mass: Harvard Business School Press, 1994; D. Harvey & D. Brown, pp. 47–8, *An Experiential Approach to Organization Development* 5/E., 1996, pp. 94–6. Reprinted by permission of Prentice-Hall, Inc, Upper Saddle River, NJ; S. Hoyle, p. 15, *Australian Financial Review*, 20 February 1998:1; R. Helker, pp. 8–9, *ANZ Journal of Public Health*, Curtin, 21, 7:784–8, 1997; David James, pp. 90–3, 442–4, 455–6, *Business Review Weekly*, 29 September 1997, 17 March, 1997, 10 Febuary 1997; R. Jones, pp. 251–2, 'Implementing decentralised reform in local government: Leadership from the Australian experience', *The International Journal of Public Sector Management*, Vol. 12, No. 1, pp. 63–76 (MCB University Press); T. Jones, pp. 340–1, *Human Resource Management*, 34(3), 1995, pp. 425–42; L. Jorgensen, pp. 103–104, *Work and People*, Vol.14, No.1, 1991, pp. 28–33; S. Kim & D. Briscoe, pp. 479–80, 'A new human resource policy in Korea: transformation to a performance-based HRM', *Employee Relations*, Vol. 19, No. 4, 1997, pp 298–308; Kluwer Academic Publishers, p. 59, M. White & L. Rhodeback, 'Ethical dilemas in organization development: a cross-cultural analysis', *Journal of Business Ethics*, 11, 1992, pp. 663–70, Fig. 11. © By kind permission from Kluwer Academic Publishers; J.Kotter & J. Heskett, p. 595, *Corporate Culture and Performance*, The Free Press, New York, 1992; R. Kriegel & D. Brandt, p. 596, *Sacred Cows Make the Best Burgers*, Harper Collins Publishers, Australia, 1996; E.E. Lawler III, p. 288, *Change in Organizations*, Jossey-Bass, San Fransisco, 1982, pp. 298–9; E. Lawler III, p. 353, *Improving Life at Work*, eds. J. Hackman & J. Suttle, Goodyear, Santa Monica, 1977; E. Lawler, S. Mohrman & T. Cummmings, p. 112, *Center for Effective Organizations*, University of California; D. Lewis,

E. French & P. Steane, pp. 226–7, 'A Culture of Conflict', *Leadership & Organization Development Journal*, Vol 18, No. 6, 1997, pp. 275–82 (MCB University Press); R.Likert, p. 12, *New Patterns of Management*, New York: McGraw-Hill, 1961, p. 113. With permission of The McGraw-Hill Companies; J. Luft, p. 196, *Human Relations Training News*, 5, (1961): 6–7; B. Macy & P. Mirvis, pp. 174, 175, *Evaluation Review*, (6), 1982, pp. 301–72, 308–9; N. Marshall, pp. 350–2, *Public Productivity & Management Review*, 1998, 21(4), pp. 403–18; Maribyrnong City Council, p. 570, internal document; C. Massey & R. Walker, pp. 73–6, *The Learning Organization*, 6, 1, 1999, pp. 38–44; p. 14, *Public Personnel Management*, 1997, Vol. 26, No. 2, pp. 257–72; P. Mazany, S. Francis & P. Sumich, p. 180, 'Evaluating the effectiveness of an outdoor workshop for team building in an MBA programme', *Team Performance Management*, Vol. 3, No. 2, 1997, pp. 97–115; J. McCann & J.R. Galbraith, pp. 244, 246, 248, *Handbook of Organizational Design: Remodelling Organizations and Their Environment*, eds. P.C. Nystrom & W.H. Starbuck, Oxford University Press, New York, 1981, Vol. 2, p. 61; Melbourne City Council, p. 586, *Annual Review1996-1997*, Melbourne, September 1997, p. 88; B. Miles, pp. 319–321, *Work and People*; S. Mohrman & T. Cummings, p. 445, *Self-Designing*, ©1989. Reprinted by permission of Prentice-Hall, Inc., Upper Saddle River, NJ; K. Murrell & M. Wahba, pp. 468–70, adapted from *Organization Development Journal*, 1987, 5(1), pp. 57–63. The *Organization Development Journal*, c/o The O.D. Institute, 11234 Walnut Ridge Road, Chesterland, OH 44026 USA; D. Nadler, pp. 111, 108, 128, *Feedback and Organization Development*, ©1977, p. 119, 43, 146. Reprinted by permission of Prentice-Hall, Inc., Upper Saddle River, NJ; D. Nelms, pp. 290–2, *Air Transport World*, 1992, 29(3), pp. 92–4; T. Nitschke & M. O Keefe, pp. 310–11, 'Managing the linkage with primary producers: experiences in the Australian grain industry', *Supply Chain Management*, Vol. 2, No. 1, 1997, pp. 4–6 (MCB University Press); J. Preston & L. DuTroit, pp. 485–8, *International Journal of Public Administration*, 16, 1993: 1767-91; J. Preston & T. Armstrong, pp. 485–8, *Public Administration Quarterly*, 15, 1991, pp. 65–82; C. Rance, p. 447, *The Age*, 14 March 1998, p. 36; R. Rowe, pp. 211–13, *Career Development International*, 1996, 1/2, pp. 19–24; E. Schein, pp. 199–200, *Process Consultation*, Vol 1, 2/E, ©1999, pp. 18–26. Reprinted by permission of Prentice-Hall, Inc., Upper Saddle River, NJ; C. Scott & D. Jaffe, p. 596, *Managing Organizational Change*, Crisp Publications California, 1989. ; K. Shepard & A. Raia, p. 49, *Training and Development Journal 35*, April 1981: 93. Reprinted with permission. All rights reserved; W. Schmidt & A. Johnson, p. 56, *A continuum of consultancy styles*, unpublished manuscript, July 1970, p. 1; F. Shiel, pp. 61–2, *The Age*, 24 March 1998; S. K. Sia & B. S. Neo, pp. 265–268, 'Transforming the tax collector re-engineering the Inland Revenue Authority of Singapore', *Journal of Organisational Change Management*, Vol. 11, No. 6, 1998, pp. 496–514 (MCB University Press); S. Siksna & F. Broadbent, p. 31, *Action Learning—the subtle transformer: the University of Queensland's action learning programme*, The University of Queensland; C. Singh & M. Hart, pp. 133–4, *Australian Accountant*, 68(8): 50–52; W. Snyder & T. Cummings, p. 450, 'Organization learning disorders: conceptual model and intervention guidelines', Working paper, School of Business, University of Southern California, 1996; K. Tang, pp. 158–9, *Total Quality Management*, 1998, 9:7, pp. 539–52; N. Tichy & S. Sherman, pp. 220–1, from *Control Your Destiny or Someone Else Will*, ©1993 by Noel M. Tichy and Stratford Sherman. Used by permission of Doubleday, a division of Random House, Inc.; University of California, p. 253, reprinted from the *California Management Review*, Vol. 28, No. 3 ©1983, by permission of the Regents of the University of California; C. Vardon, pp. 521, 522, *Reforming the Public Sector: Problems and Solutions*, eds. C. Clark & D. Corbett, Allen and Unwin, Sydney, 1999, pp. 178–9; G. Vasilash, pp. 154–5, *Production*, January 1993, 105(1), pp. 32–8; K. Walters / ABIX, pp. 255–6, "Teamwork helps to light the way", reproduced in *BRW*, 4 May 1998, p. 60; R.G. Walton, p. 203, *Managing Conflict*, 2E, ©1987. Adapted by permission of Prentice-Hall, Inc., Upper Saddle River, NJ; D. Wheatley, pp. 10–11, *Business Queensland*, Qld, 23 March 1998; C. Wilson & J. Wilson, pp. 204–5, *Facilities*, 1999, Vol. 17, No. 3/4, pp. 79–85; *Work and People*, pp. 345–7, October 1993, 14(3), pp. 19–21; C. Zanetti, p. 522, *Australian Journal of Public Administration*, 57:4, pp. 3–13.

Every effort has been made to trace the copyright owners. Should any material have been inadvertently missed, the copyright owner is asked to contact Nelson Thomson Learning for rectification in future editions.

Finally, the publishers would like to sincerely thank those organisations that have been the subjects of applications and case studies for so willingly allowing the material to be published.

General introduction to organisation development

This is a book about *organisation development* (OD), a process that applies behavioural science knowledge and practices to help organisations achieve greater effectiveness, including increased financial performance and improved quality of work life. Organisation development differs from other planned change efforts, such as technological innovation, training and development or new product development, in that the focus is on building the organisation's ability to assess its current functioning and to achieve its goals. Moreover, OD is oriented to improving the total system—the organisation and its parts in the context of the larger environment that impacts on them.

This book reviews the broad background of OD and examines assumptions, strategies and models, intervention techniques, and other aspects. This chapter provides an introduction to OD, describing the concept of OD itself, and explains why OD has expanded rapidly in the past 45 years, both in terms of people's needs to work with and through others in organisations and in terms of organisations' needs to adapt to a complex and changing world. It briefly reviews the history of OD and describes its evolution into its current state. This introduction is followed by an overview of the rest of the book.

What is organisation development?

Organisation development is both a professional field of social action and an area of scientific inquiry. The practice of OD covers a wide spectrum of activities, with seemingly endless variations upon them. Team building with top corporate management, structural change in a local council, and job enrichment in a manufacturing firm are all examples of OD. Similarly, the study of OD addresses a broad range of topics, including the effects of change, the methods of organisational change, and the factors that influence OD success.

A number of definitions of OD exist and are presented in Table 1.1. Each definition has a slightly different emphasis. For example, Burke's description focuses attention on culture as the target of change; French's definition is concerned with OD's long-term interest in, and use of, consultants; Beckhard's and Beer's definitions address the process of OD; while Dunphy and Stace refer to the 'soft' approaches. The following definition incorporates most of these views and is used in this book:

> *Organisation development is a systemwide application of behavioural science knowledge to the planned development and reinforcement of organisational strategies, structures and processes for improving an organisation's effectiveness.*

This definition emphasises several features that differentiate OD from other approaches to organisational change and improvement, such as technological innovation, training and development, and organisation evolution.

First, OD applies to an entire system, such as an organisation, a single plant of a multi-plant firm, or a department or work group. This contrasts with approaches that focus on one or few aspects of a system, such as training and development or technological innovation. In these approaches, attention is narrowed to individuals within a system or to the improvement of particular products or processes.

TABLE 1.1	Definitions of organisation development

- Organisation development is a planned process of change in an organisation's culture through the utilisation of behavioural science technology, research and theory. (Warner Burke)[1]

- Organisation development refers to a long-range effort to improve an organisation's problem-solving capabilities and its ability to cope with changes in its external environment with the help of external or internal behavioural-scientist consultants, or change agents, as they are sometimes called. (Wendell French)[2]

- Organisation development is an effort (1) *planned*, (2) *organisation-wide*, and (3) *managed from the top* to (4) increase *organisation effectiveness and health* through (5) planned *interventions* in the organisation's 'processes', using *behavioural science* knowledge. (Richard Beckhard)[3]

- Organisation development is a system-wide process of data collection, diagnosis, action planning, intervention and evaluation aimed at: (1) enhancing congruence between organisational structure, process, strategy, people and culture; (2) developing new and creative organisational solutions; and (3) developing the organisation's self-renewing capacity. It occurs through the collaboration of organisational members working with a change agent using behavioural science theory, research and technology. (Michael Beer)[4]

- Organisation development is a 'soft' approach that describes a process of change undertaken in small incremental steps managed participatively. (Dexter Dunphy and Doug Stace)[5]

Second, OD is based on behavioural science knowledge and practice, including microconcepts, such as leadership, group dynamics and work design, and macro-approaches, such as strategy, organisation design and international relations. These subjects distinguish OD from such applications as technological innovation, which emphasise the technical and rational aspects of organisations. These approaches tend to neglect the personal and social characteristics of a system. In addition, the behavioural science approach to change acknowledges the individual's influence over an organisation's destiny. More deterministic perspectives, such as organisation evolution, discount the influence of organisation members on effectiveness.

Third, whereas OD is concerned with planned change, it is not, in the formal sense, typically associated with business planning or technological innovation nor, in the deterministic sense, often associated with organisation evolution. Instead, OD is more an adaptive process for planning and implementing change than a blueprint for how things should be done. It involves planning to diagnose and solve organisational problems, but such plans are flexible and often revised as new information is gathered about the progress of the change programme. If, for example, the performance of international managers were seen to be a concern, a reorganisation process might begin with plans to assess the current relationships between the international divisions and the corporate headquarters, and to redesign them if necessary. These plans would be modified should the assessment discover that most of the international managers' weak performance could be attributed to poor cross-cultural training prior to their international assignment.

Fourth, OD involves both the creation and the subsequent reinforcement of change. It moves beyond the initial efforts to implement a change programme to a longer-term concern for stabilising and institutionalising new activities within the organisation. For example, the implementation of self-managed work teams might focus on ways by which supervisors could give workers more control over work methods. After the workers had been given more control, attention would shift to ensuring that supervisors continued to provide that freedom; including the possible rewarding of supervisors for managing in a participative style. This attention to reinforcement is similar to training and development approaches that address maintenance of new skills or behaviours, but differs from other change perspectives that do not address how a change can be institutionalised.

Fifth, OD encompasses strategy, structure and process changes, although different OD programmes may focus more on one kind of change than another. A change programme aimed at modifying organisation strategy, for example, might focus on how the organisation relates to a wider environment and on how those relationships can be improved. It might include changes in both the grouping of people to perform tasks (structure) and the methods of communicating and solving problems (process) used to support the changes in strategy. Similarly, an OD programme directed at helping a top-management team become more effective might focus on interactions and problem-solving processes within the group. This focus might result in the improved ability of top management to solve company problems in strategy and structure. Other approaches to change, such as training and development, typically have a narrower focus on the skills and knowledge of organisation members.

Finally, OD is oriented to improving organisational effectiveness. This involves two major assumptions. First, an effective organisation is able to solve its own problems and focus its attention and resources on achieving key goals. OD helps organisation members gain the skills and knowledge necessary to conduct these activities by involving them in the process. Second, an effective organisation has both high performance, including quality products and services, high productivity and continuous improvement, and a high quality of work life. The organisation's performance is responsive to the needs of external groups, such as stockholders, customers, suppliers and government agencies, that provide the organisation with resources and legitimacy. Moreover, it is able to attract and motivate effective employees who then perform at high levels.

This definition helps to distinguish OD from other applied fields, such as management consulting, operations management, or new product development. It also furnishes a clear conception of *organisation change*, a related focus of this book. Organisation change is a broad phenomenon that involves a diversity of applications and approaches, including economic, political, technical and social perspectives. Change in organisations can be in response to external forces, such as market shifts, competitive pressures and radical new product technologies, or it can be internally motivated, such as by managers trying to improve existing methods and practices. Regardless of its origins, change does affect people and their relationships in organisations and so can have significant social consequences. For example, change can be resisted, sabotaged or poorly implemented. The behavioural sciences have developed useful concepts and methods for helping organisations deal with these problems. They help managers and administrators to manage the change process. Many of these concepts and techniques are described in this book, particularly in relation to managing change.

Organisation development can be applied to managing organisational change. However, it is primarily concerned with change that is oriented to transferring the knowledge and skills needed to build the capability to achieve goals, solve problems and manage change. It is intended to change the organisation in a particular direction, toward improved problem solving, responsiveness, quality of work life and effectiveness. Organisation change, in contrast, is more broadly focused and can apply to any kind of change, including technical, managerial and social innovations. These changes may or may not be directed at making the organisation more developed in the sense implied by OD.

Why study organisation development?

In each of the previous editions of this book we have argued that organisations must adapt to increasingly complex and uncertain technological, economic, political and cultural changes. We have also argued that OD can help an organisation create effective responses to these changes and, in many cases, proactively influence the strategic direction of the firm. The rapidly changing conditions of the past few years confirm these arguments and accent their relevance. According to several observers, organisations are in the midst of unprecedented uncertainty and chaos, and nothing short of a management revolution will save them.[6] Three major trends are shaping change in organisations: globalisation, information technology and managerial innovation.[7]

First, *globalisation* is changing the markets and environments in which organisations operate as well as the way they function. New governments, new leadership, new markets and new countries are emerging and creating a new global economy. The falling of the Berlin Wall symbolised the reunification of Germany; entrepreneurs are appearing in Russia, the Balkans and Siberia as the former Soviet Union evolves, in fits and starts, into separate, market-oriented states; China's emergence as an open market and the governance mechanism over Hong Kong, together with financial turmoil in South-East Asia that began with the fall of the Thai baht, represent a powerful shift in global economic influence.

Second, *information technology* is changing how work is performed and how knowledge is used. The way an organisation collects, stores, manipulates, uses and transmits information can lower costs or increase the value and quality of products. Electronic data interchange, for example, directly connects two organisations, allowing instantaneous exchange of sales data, pricing, inventory levels and other information. This can be used to adjust manufacturing scheduling, service delivery, new product development activities and sales campaigns. In addition, the ability to move information easily and inexpensively throughout and between organisations has fuelled the down-sizing, delayering, and restructuring of firms. High-speed modems and laptop computers have allowed for a new form of work known as telecommuting; organisation members can work from their homes or cars without ever going to the office. Finally, information technology is changing how knowledge is used. Information that is widely shared reduces the concentration of power at the top of the organisation. Decision making, once the exclusive province of senior managers who had key information, is shared by organisation members who now have the same information.

Third, *managerial innovation* has both responded to the globalisation and information technology trends and accelerated their impact on organisations. New organisational forms, such as networks, strategic alliances and virtual corporations, provide organisations with new ways of thinking about how to manufacture goods and deliver services. The strategic alliance, for example, has emerged as one of the indispensable tools in strategy implementation. No single organisation—not even BHP, Lend Lease or Western Mining Corporation, can control the environmental and market uncertainty it faces. Many CEOs of Australian companies share this viewpoint. For example, Hugh Morgan of WMC believes that resource companies need a geographic spread of assets and is investigating mergers and alliances. Qantas and Ansett have extended their Australian operations into the global market with alliances with Oneworld and Star respectively. In addition, new methods of change, such as down-sizing and re-engineering, have radically reduced the size of organisations and increased their flexibility, while new large group interventions, such as the search conference and open space, have increased the speed with which organisational change can take place.

Managers, OD practitioners and researchers argue that these forces are not only powerful in their own right, but interrelated. Their interaction makes for a highly uncertain and chaotic environment for all kinds of organisations, including manufacturing and service firms and those in the public and private sectors. There is no question that these forces are profoundly impacting on organisations. Application 1.1 illustrates how one organisation responded to these chaotic conditions.[8]

Fortunately, a growing number of organisations are undertaking the kinds of organisational changes needed to survive and prosper in today's environment. They are making themselves more streamlined and nimble, and more responsive to external demands. They are involving employees in key decisions and paying for performance rather than time. They are taking the initiative in innovating and managing change, rather than simply responding to what has already happened.

APPLICATION 1.1

Supermarkets engage in performance-improving activities

Coles Supermarkets engaged in performance-improving activities, such as its relationship with suppliers, in the two years prior to 1998, according to Alan Williams. He points out that performance-based indicators for stakeholders involve strong communication between staff, suppliers and customers. Review and feedback processes have been formally embarked upon, and activities such as annual workshops that involve suppliers facilitate this process. Staff also provide valuable advice, and the Coles Express stores are a result of teamwork within the Coles organisation, without external consultation. Late night and weekend service has been developed in conjunction with the Shop Distributive & Allied Employees Association. Coles spent A$10m on staff training during 1997 and 1998, and employed 2500 people during that period.

Organisation development is playing an increasingly important role in helping organisations change themselves. It is helping organisations to assess themselves and their environments and to revitalise and rebuild their strategies, structures and processes. OD is helping organisation members go beyond surface changes to transform the underlying assumptions and values that govern their behaviours. The different concepts and methods discussed in this book are increasingly finding their way into government agencies, manufacturing firms, multi-national corporations, service industries, educational institutions and not-for-profit organisations. Perhaps at no other time has OD been more responsive and practically relevant to organisations' needs if they are to operate effectively in a highly complex and changing world.

Organisation development is obviously important to those who plan a professional career in the field, either as an internal consultant employed by an organisation or as an external consultant practising in many organisations. A career in OD can be highly rewarding, providing challenging and interesting assignments, which involve working with managers and employees to improve their organisations and their work lives. In today's environment, the demand for OD professionals is rising rapidly. For example, consulting has been the biggest area of growth for Australia's 'Big Five' accounting practices, and it now represents 25–30% of their total worldwide billings. Firms such as Arthur Andersen and PricewaterhouseCoopers expect the growth in strategic consulting and management consulting to grow. The owners of fast-growing companies are making more use of consultants, and 58% increased the use of their services in 1998. This would indicate that career opportunities in OD should continue to expand in Australia.

Organisation development is also important to those who have no aspirations to become professional practitioners. All managers and administrators are responsible for supervising and developing subordinates and for improving their departments' performance. Similarly, all staff specialists, such as accountants, financial analysts, engineers, personnel specialists or market researchers, are responsible for offering advice and counsel to managers, and for introducing new methods and practices. Finally, OD is important to general managers and other senior executives as it can help the whole organisation be more flexible, adaptable and effective.

Organisation development can help managers and staff personnel perform their tasks more effectively. It can provide the skills and knowledge necessary for establishing effective interpersonal and helping relationships. It can show personnel how to work effectively with others in diagnosing complex problems and devising appropriate solutions. It can help others become committed to the solutions, thereby increasing the chances of their successful implementation. In short, OD is highly relevant to anyone who has to work with and through others in organisations.

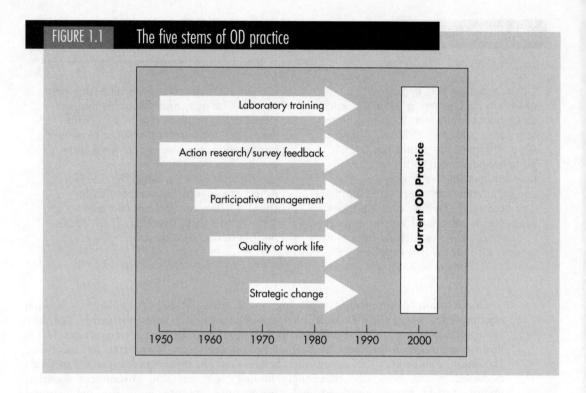

FIGURE 1.1   The five stems of OD practice

A short history of organisation development

A brief history of OD will help to clarify the evolution of the term as well as some of the problems and confusions that have surrounded its development. As currently practised, OD emerged from five major backgrounds or stems, as shown in Figure 1.1. The first was the growth of the National Training Laboratories (NTL) and the development of training groups, otherwise known as sensitivity training or *T-groups*. The second stem of OD was the classic work on action research conducted by social scientists who were interested in applying research to the management of change. An important feature of action research was a technique known as survey feedback. Kurt Lewin, a prolific theorist, researcher and practitioner in group dynamics and social change, was instrumental in the development of T-groups, survey feedback and action research. His work led to the initial development of OD and still serves as a major source of its concepts and methods. The third stem reflects the work of Rensis Likert and represents the application of participative management to organisation structure and design. The fourth background is the approach that focuses on productivity and the quality of work life. The fifth stem of OD, and the most recent influence on current practice, involves strategic change and organisational transformation.

Laboratory training background

This stem of OD pioneered laboratory training, or the T-group—a small, unstructured group in which participants learn from their own interactions and evolving dynamics about such issues as interpersonal relations, personal growth, leadership and group dynamics. Essentially, laboratory training began in the summer of 1946, when Kurt Lewin and his staff at the Research Center for Group Dynamics at the Massachusetts Institute of Technology (MIT) were asked by the Connecticut Interracial Commission and the Committee on Community Interrelations of the American Jewish Congress for help in research on training community leaders. A workshop was developed, and the community leaders were brought together to learn about leadership and discuss problems. At the end of each day, the researchers discussed privately what behaviours and group dynamics they had observed. The community leaders asked permission to sit in on these feedback sessions, to which the researchers finally gave their assent. Thus, the first T-group was formed, in which people reacted to data about their own behaviour. The researchers drew two conclusions about this first T-group experiment: (1) feedback about group interaction was a rich learning experience, and (2) the process of 'group building' had potential for learning that could be transferred to 'back-home' situations.[9]

A new phenomenon arose in 1950 when an attempt was made to have T-groups in the morning and cognitive-skill groups (A-groups) in the afternoon. However, the staff found that the high level of carry-over from the morning sessions turned the afternoon A-groups into T-groups, despite the resistance of the afternoon staff members, who were committed to cognitive-skill development. This was the beginning of a decade of learning experimentation and frustration, especially in the attempt to transfer skills learned in the T-group setting to the 'back-home' situation.

Three trends emerged in the 1950s: (1) the emergence of regional laboratories, (2) the expansion of summer programme sessions to year-round sessions, and (3) the expansion of the T-group into business and industry, with NTL members becoming increasingly involved with industry programmes. Notable among these industry efforts was the pioneering work of Douglas McGregor at Union Carbide, of Herbert Shepard and Robert Blake at Esso Standard Oil (now Exxon), and of McGregor and Richard Beckhard at General Mills. Applications of T-group methods at these three companies introduced the term 'organisation development' and led corporate personnel and industrial relations specialists to expand their roles to offer internal consulting services to managers.[10]

Applying T-group techniques to organisations gradually became known as 'team building'—a process for helping work groups become more effective in accomplishing tasks and satisfying member needs. Application 1.2 presents an example of the importance of team building in an insurance company.[11]

APPLICATION 1.2

Team-building weekends

Team-building weekends in Australia are no longer just the province of executives, as employers are now including more general employees in these exercises. AIG Insurance (the American International Group) has sent its customer service/call centre employees away to such a weekend, organised by Peregrine Corporate Training. These team-building programmes are also considered to be good training programmes for the companies. It is unwise of employees to rebel against the programme while it is being held, as the corporate trainers usually prepare individual reports on the employees at the end of the programme. The University of New South Wales' John Toohey says that team-building exercises will be mere window-dressing unless employees are allowed to make a contribution.

Action research and survey feedback background

Kurt Lewin was also involved in the second movement that led to OD's emergence as a practical field of social science. This second background refers to the processes of action research and survey feedback. The action research contribution began in the 1940s with studies conducted by social scientists John Collier, Kurt Lewin and William Whyte, who discovered that research needed to be closely linked to action if organisation members were to use it to manage change. A collaborative effort was initiated between organisation members and social scientists to collect research data about an organisation's functioning, analyse it for causes of problems and devise and implement solutions. After implementation, further data were collected to assess the results, and the cycle of data collection and action often continued. The results of action research were twofold: members of organisations were able to use research on themselves to guide action and change, while social scientists were able to study that process to derive new knowledge that could be used elsewhere.

Among the pioneering action research studies was the work of Lewin and his students at the Harwood Manufacturing Company,[12] and the classic research by Lester Coch and John French on managing resistance to change.[13] This latter study led to the development of participative management as a means of getting employees involved in planning and managing change. Some more recent Australian contributions include Chenhall and Langfield-Smith's case studies on the development of performance measurement systems,[14] and Singh and Hart's experience of managing resistance through action research at Bethesda Hospital, Melbourne.[15] These studies do much to establish action research as being integral to organisation change. Today, it is the backbone of most OD applications. Application 1.3 provides an example of action research being used to empower Aboriginal health workers.[16]

APPLICATION 1.3　　　Participatory action research to empower Aboriginal health workers

In an attempt to increase Aboriginal health workers' ability to gain greater control and responsibility within the Aboriginal-controlled health service in South Australia, and to address the concerns regarding their disillusionment and consequent resignations, the workers were encouraged to actively undertake research into the study of their situation.

The Aboriginal health worker programme is a Federal Government key strategy to improve Aboriginal health and is considered to be one of the most important factors for improving the status of Aboriginal health as recognised throughout Aboriginal communities.

However, the Aboriginal health workers, who are the key point of entry for their communities into the Western health care system and who act as mediators between Western and traditional medical systems, were at a distinct disadvantage in their role, for three main reasons:

- the standard of training received
- their low literacy and numeracy levels
- a lack of participation in decision making within the health service.

Previous attempts to research these issues had been seen as unsuccessful by the Aboriginal health workers because of the way in which the research had been conducted. In those studies, it was asserted that the health workers had no input, researchers taking their findings with them when they left. Considering that one of the health workers' main concerns was a lack of control and responsibility in their own work, this means of research was far from empowering.

So, to address the issue of empowerment, Commonwealth, state and territory ministers recommended in 1992 that health workers should undertake research and receive the appropriate training in research skills. This type of participatory action research has 'an explicit focus on who defines the research problems and who generates and analyses the information sought'. It begins with the concerns of the people involved, and during the research process there is an emphasis on action and change.

The research took place mostly within the communities of Ernabella and Amata on the Anangu Pitjantjatjara Lands in South Australia. The principle researcher was well known to the study participants as she had been a community health nurse at Ernabella in 1989–90, and was therefore able to work from a position of trust. The broad objectives of the study were determined by the researcher, but specific issues were generated by the Aboriginal health workers. These objectives were to enable the Aboriginal health workers to:

- reflect on their work situation without non-Aboriginal intervention
- identify problem areas within their work
- bring about action for change in at least one of these problem areas
- develop work skills.

The process centred on Aboriginal health worker meetings where data was collected. In order to ensure the validity of the study, data was also collected from interviews with non-Aboriginal health staff, community members, past Aboriginal health workers and education workers from Ernabella and Amata, and from interviews with the Nganampa Health Council health committee. By sorting and collating the data to produce their own 1993 health worker report, the Aboriginal health workers further confirmed the study's validity.

The Aboriginal health workers responded enthusiastically to the process and began to take action in organising meetings, which was significant in terms of empowerment—the workers were taking control, on their own terms and to their own agenda.

Other positive actions resulted from the recommendations of the Aboriginal health workers. All workers were tested, graded and then paid accordingly, and the first two-week training block took place.

The study produced two reports, one decided upon by the Aboriginal health workers and the other a historical background written by the principal researcher. Positive change occurred as a result of the participatory action research, which acted as a catalyst for greater empowerment. The health workers were able to present their concerns directly and to see change implemented on their recommendations.

A key component of most action research studies was the systematic collection of survey data, which was subsequently fed back to the client organisation. Following Lewin's death in 1947, his Research Center for Group Dynamics at MIT moved to Michigan and joined with the Survey Research Center as part of the Institute for Social Research. The institute was headed by Rensis Likert, a pioneer in the development of scientific approaches to attitude surveys. Likert's doctoral dissertation at Columbia University, 'A technique for the measurement of attitudes', was the classic study in which he developed the widely used, five-point 'Likert Scale'.[17]

In an early study of the institute, Likert and Floyd Mann administered a companywide survey of management and employee attitudes at Detroit Edison.[18] Over a two-year period beginning in 1948, three sets of data were developed: (1) the viewpoints of 8000 non-supervisory employees about their supervisors, promotion opportunities and work satisfaction with fellow employees; (2) similar reactions from first- and second-line supervisors; and (3) information from higher levels of management.

The feedback process that evolved was an 'interlocking chain of conferences'. The major findings of the survey were first reported to the top management and then transmitted throughout the organisation. The feedback sessions were conducted in task groups, with supervisors and their immediate subordinates discussing the data together. Although there was little substantial research evidence, the researchers intuitively felt that this was a powerful process for change.

In 1950, eight accounting departments asked for a repeat of the survey, and this generated a new cycle of feedback meetings. Feedback approaches were used in four departments, but the method varied, with two of the remaining departments receiving feedback only at the departmental level. Because of changes in key personnel, nothing was done in two departments.

A third follow-up study indicated that more significant and positive changes, such as job satisfaction, had occurred in the departments that were receiving feedback than in the two departments that did not participate. From these findings, Likert and Mann derived several conclusions about the effects of survey feedback on organisation change, and this led to extensive applications of survey-feedback methods in a variety of settings. The common pattern of data collection, data feedback, action planning, implementation and follow-up data collection in both action research and survey feedback can be seen in these examples. Application 1.4 presents a current example of the utilisation of survey feedback.[19]

APPLICATION 1.4

Benchmarks fuel improvements

Caltex-Ampol's Lytton refinery is reaping benefits from a human resource management system that allows management to link its employee development programmes with its wider business objectives. The programme, *Investors in People*, was developed in England and is marketed in Australia through the Australian Institute of Management (AIM). Caltex-Ampol, together with Toowoomba's Pacific Seeds, took part in an AIM pilot that began in 1996.

Eighteen months after receiving accreditation, Alan Snell, the refinery's employment development manager, believed that the real benefits of taking part in the pilot were only just beginning to be appreciated by management.

'It has allowed us to much more easily incorporate the training and development required for change and has thus given us a significant advantage over our competitors,' Snell said.

'And even within our own company, we are enjoying an advantage. Our sister refinery at Kurnell, for example, is doing the hard yards more than we are.'

Investors in People is an accreditation scheme for organisations that operate human resource development schemes at a 'benchmark' level of performance.

The standard provides a framework for improving business performance and competitiveness through a planning approach that links the process of setting and communicating business objectives

with training programmes that develop people to meet those objectives.

Before coming to Australia, *Investors in People* had operated in the UK for six years. Aimed at providing a comprehensive best practice benchmark against which an organisation could audit its policies and practice in the development of people, it makes effective use of all resources by developing a culture of continuous improvement.

The standard is a cyclical process based on four key points:
- a commitment to develop all employees to achieve business goals and targets
- regularly reviewing training and development needs in the context of the business
- taking relevant action to meet training and development needs for all staff
- evaluating outcomes of training and development for individuals and the organisation.

These four principles are broken down into 24 indicators, and it is against these that organisations produce evidence for assessment.

Snell believed that achieving accreditation was far from the end of the process.

'I feel we only just got there. There was some evidence that we hadn't reaped the full benefits of *Investors in People*, and there were further strategies we needed to put into place,' he said.

The refinery embarked upon the pilot in the belief that it would help achieve business goals by making the optimum use of its best strategic advantage—its people.

The aim was, therefore, to develop people in a climate in which the individual's contribution to the business needs were maximised, thereby establishing a highly trained and efficient workforce that was proactive in its approach to jobs and self-improvement.

Snell says that at the time there was strong *employee feedback* that emphasised the need of the company to improve in the areas of training and development.

'There were lots of subtleties in *Investors* that we are now recognising as being beneficial, particularly in the development of positive linkages between managers and employees,' Snell said. 'This has made it easier to introduce new initiatives into the company.'

Snell said that, as a result of the programme, the company is now more discerning about the training it offers employees.

'We evaluate our training and development along the lines of what is needed to implement changes that will give us significant advantages over our competitors,' he said.

Participative management background

The intellectual and practical advances from the laboratory training and action research/survey-feedback stems were closely followed by the belief that a human relations approach represented a one-best-way to manage organisations. This belief was exemplified in research that associated Likert's participative management (System 4) style with organisational effectiveness.[20] This framework characterised organisations as having one of four types of management systems:[21]

- *exploitive authoritative* systems (System 1) exhibit an autocratic, top-down approach to leadership. Employee motivation is based on punishment and occasional rewards. Communication is primarily downward, and there is little lateral interaction or teamwork. Decision making and control reside primarily at the top of the organisation. System 1 results in mediocre performance.
- *benevolent authoritative* systems (System 2) are similar to System 1, except that management is more paternalistic. Employees are allowed a little more interaction, communication and decision making but within limited boundaries defined by management.
- *consultative* systems (System 3) increase employee interaction, communication, and decision making. Although employees are consulted about problems and decisions, management still makes the final decisions. Productivity is good, and employees are moderately satisfied with the organisation.
- *participative group* systems (System 4) are almost the opposite of System 1. Designed around group methods of decision making and supervision, this system fosters high degrees of member involvement and participation. Work groups are highly involved in setting goals, making decisions, improving methods and appraising results. Communication occurs both laterally and vertically, and decisions are linked throughout the organisation by overlapping group membership. Shown in Figure 1.2, this linking-pin structure ensures continuity in communication and decision making across groups by means of people who are members of more than one group—the groups they supervise and the higher-level groups of which they are members. System 4 achieves high levels of productivity, quality and member satisfaction.

Likert applied System 4 management to organisations, using a survey–feedback process. The intervention generally started with organisation members completing the *profile of*

FIGURE 1.2   The linking pin

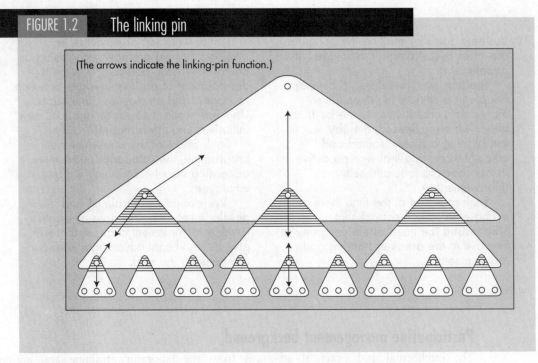

(The arrows indicate the linking-pin function.)

Source: Reproduced by permission of the publisher from R. Likert, *New Patterns of Management* (New York: McGraw-Hill, 1961), p. 113.

organisational characteristics.[22] The survey asked members for their opinions about both the present and ideal conditions of six organisational features: leadership, motivation, communication, decisions, goals and control. In the second stage, the data were fed back to different work groups within the organisation. Group members examined the discrepancy between their present situation and their ideal, generally using System 4 as the ideal benchmark, and generated action plans to move the organisation toward System 4 conditions.

Application 1.5 presents an Australian example of how a form of participative, and holistic, programme is adapted and implemented.[23]

APPLICATION 1.5   All change, says ANZ boss

If one word were to be used to describe Mr John McFarlane's seven-week reign at ANZ, it would be 'change'.

He gives every indication that he's a man in a hurry to take ANZ where he thinks it should go, and that means changing everything from the corporate culture to his predecessor's approach to acquisitions.

He calls the strategy 'ANZ 2000', and the most telling sign is that the new boss wants to see a greater proportion of women and managers from other parts and sectors of the bank's 42-country network represented in senior management.

Banks are notorious for resisting cultural change. Among the majors, only Westpac has made significant progress in promoting women.

Similarly, the bank's retired chief executive, Mr Don Mercer, kept ANZ well out of the market for an Australian acquisition, based on the not unreasonable reckoning that the prices were just too high.

However, McFarlane said yesterday that ANZ was back on the prowl if it could find a target that offered an entry point to high-growth markets or provided a strategic opportunity, possibly with new technology.

He also took the opportunity to unveil the new reporting lines for the ANZ global project, confirming suspicions that he was not totally satisfied with the plan's original design.

The key changes are the increased importance given to funds management and private banking—the high-net-worth segment of ANZ's customer base, both of which now become direct reports.

It is also clear that the new head of human resources, Ms Elizabeth Proust, will be a key figure in the change management process at the bank, which precludes external hiring of staff in other than exceptional circumstances.

From a financial perspective, ANZ 2000 sets a 15% hurdle rate of return for all the bank's activities, while the aim is to increase revenue streams at better than country growth rates.

Mr McFarlane has also put a lid on some of the bank's riskier activities, reportedly an ANZ synonym for the investment bank, saying that those businesses will only be allowed to expand at the same rate as the group as a whole.

However, the arguably most ambitious task he's set ANZ is to make dealing with the bank 'an enjoyable customer experience'. A big ask in a country where bank bashing is a national sport.

Productivity and quality-of-work-life background

Projects to improve productivity and the quality of work life (QWL) were originally developed in Europe during the 1950s. Based on the research of Eric Trist and his colleagues at the Tavistock Institute of Human Relations in London, this approach examined the technical and human sides of organisations and how they interrelated.[24] It led to the development of the sociotechnical systems methods of work design that underlie many of the employee involvement and empowerment efforts occurring in Australia today.

Early practitioners in Great Britain, Ireland, Norway and Sweden developed work designs that were aimed at better integrating technology and people. These QWL programmes generally involved joint participation by unions and management in the design of work and resulted in work designs that gave employees high levels of discretion, task variety, and feedback about results. Perhaps the most distinguishing characteristic of these QWL programmes was the development of self-managing work groups as a new form of work design. These groups were composed of multi-skilled workers who were given the necessary autonomy and information to design and manage their own task performances.

In Australia today, top management keeps employees motivated by a combination of good financial rewards, an interesting environment and challenging projects. The staff are also given feedback about their own work and kept informed about the company's situation. The change programme at James Hardie, for instance, involved the development of a culture based on teamwork and driven by the principles that underpin the company's strategic intent. Their programme to introduce and implement a new Environment Health and Safety System is well advanced in Australia and New Zealand, and, in recognition of their commitment to implementing such procedures and practices, the James Hardie Building Boards facility at Rosehill was awarded the first New South Wales WorkCover Techsource Safety Management Award.[25]

Gradually, QWL programmes expanded beyond individual jobs to include group forms of work and other features of the workplace that can affect employee productivity and satisfaction, such as reward systems, work flows, management styles and the physical work environment. This expanded focus resulted in larger-scale and longer-term projects than the early job enrichment programmes and shifted attention beyond the individual worker to work groups and the larger work context. Equally importantly, it added the critical dimension of organisational efficiency to what had been up to that time a predominant concern for the human dimension. The economic and human resource problems that faced Australia during the 1980s have further reinforced this focus upon organisational efficiency.

At one point, the productivity and QWL approach became so popular that it was called an ideological movement. International conferences were aimed at identifying a coalition of groups from among unions and management that supported QWL ideals of employee involvement, participative management and industrial democracy. Some Australian companies adopted the Japanese method of management and employee participation, which involved the spread of quality circles. Ford was one such company. Popularised in Japan, *quality circles* are groups of employees trained in problem-solving methods who meet regularly to resolve work environment, productivity, and quality-control concerns and to develop more efficient ways of working.

Finally, the productivity and QWL approach has gained new momentum by joining forces with the total quality movement advocated by W. Edward Deming[26] and Joseph Juran.[27] In this approach, the organisation is viewed as a set of processes that can be linked to the quality of products and services, modelled through statistical techniques and continuously improved.[28] Quality efforts at Toyota, Sheraton and Ericssons, along with federal government support through the establishment of the Business Excellence Awards, have popularised this strategy of organisation development.

Application 1.6 presents an example of staff taking responsibility for, and managing, assigned work, resulting in increased productivity and quality of work life.[29]

APPLICATION 1.6 — An example of autonomous work groups at Westrail

Westrail is a government-operated railway service that controls much of the railway system in Western Australia. Maintenance along its extensive system is undertaken by maintenance groups operating within different geographical divisions. Each group is assigned a particular portion of the system that it must maintain. Maintenance refers to a variety of scheduled duties that range from the laying of new tracks and upkeep of old sections to unscheduled emergency work caused by events such as derailments, and repairs stemming from environmentally-related damage.

A system was implemented in the mid-1980s that re-organised the maintenance groups along the lines of autonomous work groups. Previously, the groups had been organised along traditional lines with all duties being directly assigned by supervisors and with no opportunity for autonomy about the designation of tasks among individuals, or the opportunity for scheduling work and designing work plans. Generally, an autocratic style limited opportunities for innovation and problem solving, and feedback and support systems were poor.

The new system compensated for most of these drawbacks by granting workers much greater autonomy over the scheduling and designation of tasks. A system was introduced that used scheduling forms, enabling thorough work plans to be developed. The forms also serve as a source of feedback for the groups as they are used by upper management to provide direct comparative data about the effectiveness of the group's performance. In addition, the traditional first-line supervisory position was replaced by a trackmaster who acted in the role of facilitator and coordinator, rather than as a traditional supervisor who controls most aspects of the job.

Strategic change background

The strategic change background is a recent influence on OD's evolution. As organisations and their technological, political and social environments became more complex and more uncertain, the scale and intricacies of organisational change increased. This trend has produced the need for a strategic perspective from OD and has encouraged planned change processes at the organisation level.[30]

Strategic change involves improving the alignment in an organisation's environment, strategy and organisation design.[31] Strategic change interventions include efforts to improve both the organisation's relationship to its environment and the fit between its technical, political and cultural systems.[32] The need for strategic change is usually triggered by some major disruption to the organisation, such as the lifting of regulatory requirements, a technological breakthrough or a new CEO from outside the organisation.[33]

One of the first applications of strategic change was Richard Beckhard's use of open systems planning.[34] He proposed that an organisation's environment and its strategy could be described and analysed. Based on the organisation's core mission, the differences between what the environment demanded and how the organisation responded could be reduced and performance improved. Since then, change agents have proposed a variety of large-scale or strategic change models.[35] Each of these models recognises that strategic change involves multiple levels of the organisation and a change in its culture, is often driven from the top by powerful executives and has important impacts on performance.

The strategic change background has significantly influenced OD practice. For example, the implementation of strategic change requires OD practitioners to be familiar with competitive strategy, finance and marketing, as well as team building, action research and survey feedback. Together, these skills have improved OD's relevance to organisations and their managers.

Application 1.7 provides an example of the strategic change process that changes culture and improves performance. Note that this was written in 1998.[36]

APPLICATION 1.7	MLC merger chief: how to build a financial giant

David Clarke is approaching the task of engineering the largest financial services merger this country has ever seen as though it were a building project.

As befits an organisation with its roots firmly in the property industry, his description of the job is littered with phrases such as 'design teams' and 'project managers'.

The 42-year-old Mr Clarke has been chief executive of Lendlease Corporation Ltd subsidiary MLC Ltd since he joined the company from Lloyds merchant bank in 1993.

And he is chief executive designate of the entity that will be created by the merging of the Australian and New Zealand life insurance and funds management businesses of MLC and National Mutual Holdings Ltd.

At the end of the National Mutual/ MLC merger process, be that in a year's time or 18 months, an entity will have been created with a value of about $5 billion. It will command at least $50 billion of funds under management and enjoy a dominant position in both the life insurance and funds management markets in Australia and New Zealand.

It will be 49% owned by Lend Lease and 51% by National Mutual.

Mr Clarke oversees more than 100 people, divided into project management and project design groups, a range of 'functional teams' and numerous 'business leaders'.

He is setting a cracking pace. Even as the teams assess both businesses, decide which bits to keep, which to fix and which to discard, they remain on target to produce a comprehensive three-year business plan for the new entity by the end of March.

Mr Clarke laughs when asked if he's actually having fun.

'It's terrific,' he said. 'It's extraordinarily exciting. That excitement runs right through both organisations.'

'Sure there are people who are nervous about what this may mean for them personally, but the feeling in the place is terrific. The feeling is genuine that we have a real opportunity to create something new and different in the Australian and New Zealand financial service market.'

'People know what sort of challenge that is going to be and they are not shirking it.'

Evolution in organisation development

Current practice in organisation development is strongly influenced by these five backgrounds, as well as by the trends that shape change in organisations. The laboratory training, action research and survey feedback and participative management roots of OD are evident in the strong value focus that underlies its practice. The more recent influences, the quality-of-work-life and strategic change backgrounds, have greatly improved the relevance and rigour of OD practice. They have added financial and economic indicators of effectiveness to OD's traditional measures of work satisfaction and personal growth.

Today, the field is being influenced by the globalisation and information technology trends described earlier. OD is being carried out in many more countries and in many more organisations that operate on a world-wide basis, and this is generating a whole new set of interventions as well as adaptations to traditional OD practice.[37] In addition, OD must adapt its methods to the technologies now being used in organisations. As information technology continues to influence organisational environments, strategies and structures, OD will need to manage change processes in cyberspace as well as face-to-face. The diversity of this evolving discipline has led to tremendous growth in the number of professional practitioners, in the kinds of organisations involved with OD and in the range of countries within which OD is practiced.

The expansion of the OD network is one indication of this growth. OD divisions have been set up by many training and development organisations and courses are being taught at Australian universities at postgraduate and undergraduate levels—for example, the Australian Graduate School of Management (University of Sydney), which offers the Graduate Certificate in Change Management.[38]

In addition to the growth of professional societies and educational programmes in OD, the field continues to develop new theorists, researchers and practitioners who are building on the work of the early pioneers and extending it to contemporary issues and conditions. Included among the first generation of contributors are Chris Argyris, who developed a learning and action–science approach to OD;[39] Warren Bennis, who tied executive leadership to strategic change;[40] Edgar Schein, who continues to develop process approaches to OD, including the key role of organisational culture in change management;[41] Richard Beckhard, who focused attention on the importance of managing transitions;[42] and Robert Tannenbaum, who continues to sensitise OD to the personal dimension of participants' lives.[43]

Among the second generation of contributors are Warner Burke, whose work has done much to make OD a professional field;[44] Larry Greiner, who has brought the ideas of power and evolution into the mainstream of OD;[45] Edward Lawler III, who has extended OD to reward systems and employee involvement;[46] Newton Margulies and Anthony Raia, who together have kept our attention on the values underlying OD and what they mean for contemporary practice;[47] and Peter Vaill and Craig Lundberg, who continue to develop OD as a practical science.[48]

Included in the newest generation of OD contributors are Dave Brown, whose work on action research and developmental organisations has extended OD into community and societal change;[49] Thomas Cummings, whose work on sociotechnical systems, self-designing organisations and transorganisational development has led OD beyond the boundaries of single organisations to groups of organisations and their environments;[50] Max Elden, whose international work in industrial democracy draws attention to the political aspects of OD;[51] William Pasmore and Jerry Porras, who have done much to put OD on a sound research and conceptual base;[52] and Peter Block, who has focused attention on consulting skills, empowerment processes and reclaiming our individuality.[53] Other newcomers who are making important contributions to the field include Ken Murrell and Joanne Preston, who have focused attention on the internationalisation of OD;[54] Sue Mohrman and Gerry Ledford, who have focused on team-based organisations and compensation;[55] and David Cooperrider, who has turned our attention toward the positive aspects of organisations.[56] In Australia there are such centres as the Centre for Corporate Change in the Australian Graduate School of Management at the University of New South Wales and the Centre for Workplace Culture Change at RMIT University, both of which are actively contributing to the body of current research. These academic contributors are joined by a large number of internal OD practitioners and external consultants who lead organisational change, such as the Australian Institute of Training and Development.[57]

Many different organisations have undertaken a wide variety of OD efforts. Many organisations have been at the forefront of innovating new change techniques and methods, as well as new organisational forms. Larger corporations that have engaged in organisation development include General Electric, General Motors, Ford, Corning Glass Works, Intel, Hewlett-Packard, Polaroid, Procter & Gamble and IBM. Traditionally, much of this work was considered confidential and not publicised. Today, however, organisations have increasingly gone public with their OD efforts, sharing the lessons with others.

Organisation development work is also being done in schools, communities and local, state and federal governments. A system that encourages staff at Casey Institute of TAFE to learn from one another has won its designer, Stuart Williams, a prestigious individual achievement recognition award from the Australian Human Resources Institute (AHRI). It requires all departments to provide six hours of training to fellow staff members annually.[58] The University of Technology in Sydney is awarding testamurs to employees of AMP who sign up for its workplace-based programme. Described as a revolutionary step by AMP management, the initiative is designed to assess work performance in terms of academic criteria. The award courses, from the faculties of business or mathematical and computer sciences, are based on performance agreements negotiated between AMP, UTS and the employee.[59]

Organisation development is increasingly international. As well as in South-East Asia, it has been applied in the United States, Canada, Sweden, Norway, Germany, Japan, Israel, South Africa, Mexico, Venezuela, the Philippines, China, Hong Kong, Russia and the Netherlands. These efforts have involved such organisations as Saab (Sweden), Norsk Hydro (Norway), Imperial Chemical Industries (England), Shell Oil Company, Orfors (Sweden) and Alcan Canada Products.

Although it is evident that OD has vastly expanded in recent years, relatively few of the total number of organisations in Australia are actively involved in formal OD programmes. However, many organisations are applying OD approaches and techniques without knowing that such a term exists.

Overview of the book

This book presents the process and practice of organisation development in a logical flow, as shown in Figure 1.3. Part I provides an overview of OD that describes the process of planned change and those who perform the work. It consists of two chapters. Chapter 2 discusses the nature of planned change and presents some models that describe the change process. Planned change is viewed as an ongoing cycle of four activities: entering and

FIGURE 1.3   Overview of the book

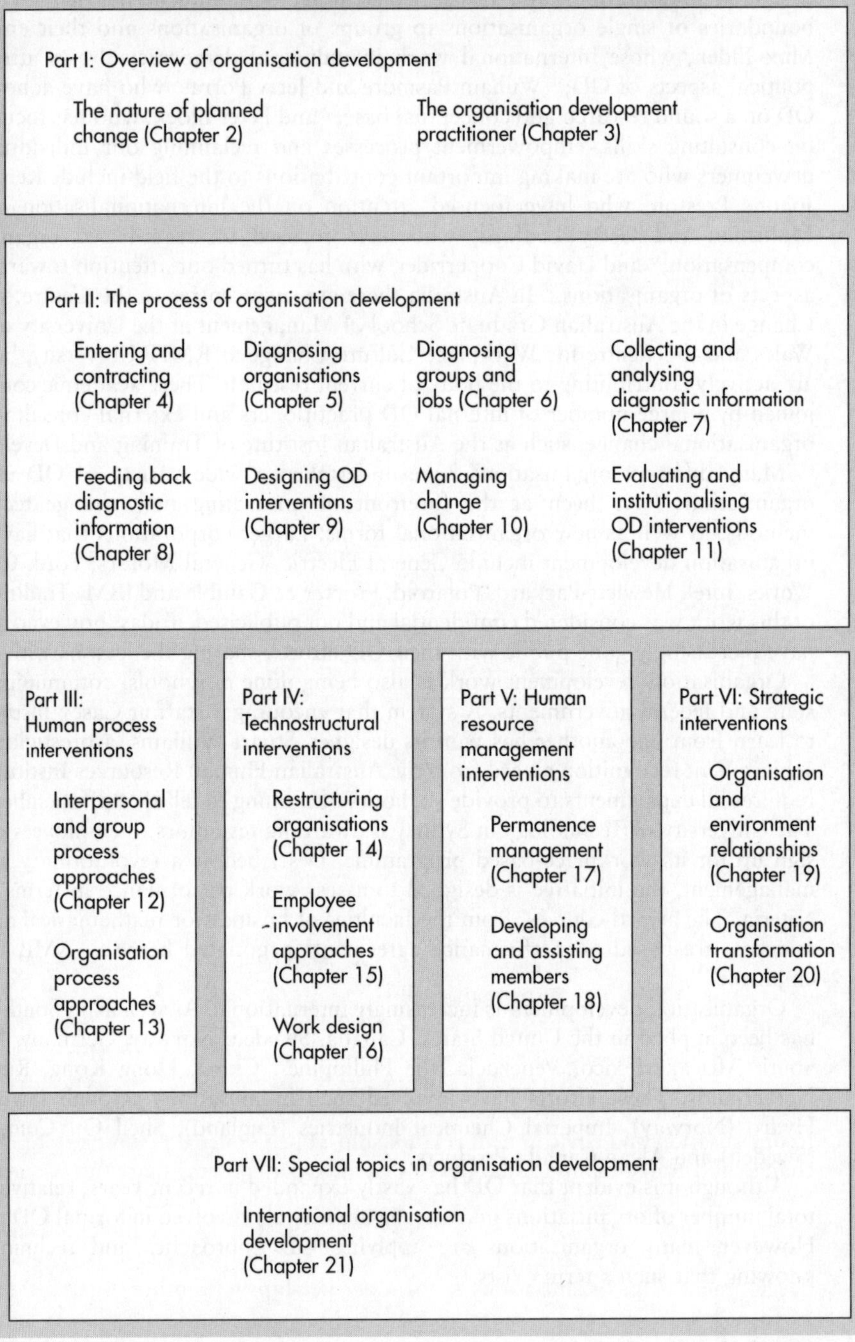

Part I: Overview of organisation development

The nature of planned change (Chapter 2)

The organisation development practitioner (Chapter 3)

Part II: The process of organisation development

Entering and contracting (Chapter 4)

Diagnosing organisations (Chapter 5)

Diagnosing groups and jobs (Chapter 6)

Collecting and analysing diagnostic information (Chapter 7)

Feeding back diagnostic information (Chapter 8)

Designing OD interventions (Chapter 9)

Managing change (Chapter 10)

Evaluating and institutionalising OD interventions (Chapter 11)

Part III: Human process interventions

Interpersonal and group process approaches (Chapter 12)

Organisation process approaches (Chapter 13)

Part IV: Technostructural interventions

Restructuring organisations (Chapter 14)

Employee -involvement approaches (Chapter 15)

Work design (Chapter 16)

Part V: Human resource management interventions

Permanence management (Chapter 17)

Developing and assisting members (Chapter 18)

Part VI: Strategic interventions

Organisation and environment relationships (Chapter 19)

Organisation transformation (Chapter 20)

Part VII: Special topics in organisation development

International organisation development (Chapter 21)

contracting, diagnosing, planning and implementing, and evaluating and institutionalising. Chapter 3 describes the OD practitioner and provides insight into the knowledge and skills needed to practice OD, and the kinds of career issues that can be expected.

Part II consists of eight chapters that describe the process of organisation development.

Chapter 4 characterises the first activity in this process—entering an organisational system and contracting with it for organisation development work. Chapters 5, 6, 7 and 8 present the steps associated with the next major activity of the OD process: diagnosing. This involves helping the organisation to discover causes of problems and suggesting areas for improvement. Chapters 5 and 6 present an open systems model to guide diagnosis at three levels of analysis: the total organisation, the group or department and the individual job or position. Chapters 7 and 8 review methods for collecting, analysing and feeding back diagnostic data. Chapters 9 and 10 address issues concerned with the third activity: planning and implementing change. Chapter 9 presents an overview of the intervention design process. Major kinds of interventions are identified, and the specific approaches that make up the next four parts of the book are introduced. Chapter 10 discusses the process of managing change and identifies key factors that contribute to the successful implementation of change programmes. Chapter 11 describes the final activity of the planned change process—evaluating OD interventions and stabilising or institutionalising them as a permanent part of organisational functioning.

Parts III to VI present the major interventions used in OD today. Part III (Chapters 12 and 13) concerns human process interventions aimed at the social processes within organisations. These are the oldest and most traditional interventions in OD. Chapter 12 describes interpersonal and group process approaches—T-groups, process consultation and team building. Chapter 13 presents more system-wide process approaches, such as organisational confrontation meetings, inter-group relations and large-group interventions.

Part IV (Chapters 14, 15 and 16) reviews technostructural interventions that are aimed at organisation structure and at better integrating people and technology. Chapter 14 is about restructuring organisations; it describes the alternative methods of organising work activities as well as processes for downsizing and re-engineering the organisation. Chapter 15 presents interventions for improving employee involvement. These change programmes increase employee knowledge, power, information and rewards through parallel structures, high-involvement organisations and total quality management. Chapter 16 describes change programmes directed at work design, both of individual jobs and of work groups, for greater employee satisfaction and productivity.

Part V (Chapters 17 and 18) presents human resource management interventions that are directed at integrating people into the organisation. These interventions are traditionally associated with the personnel function in the organisation and have increasingly become a part of OD activities. Chapter 17 concerns the process of performance management. This is a cycle of activities that helps groups and individuals set goals, appraise work and reward performance. Chapter 18 discusses three interventions—career planning and development, work force diversity and employee wellness—that develop and assist organisation members.

Part VI (Chapters 19 and 20) is concerned with strategic interventions that focus on organising the firm's resources to gain a competitive advantage in the environment. These change programmes are generally managed from the top of the organisation and take considerable time, effort and resources. Chapter 19 presents three interventions that relate to organisation and environment relationships: open systems planning, integrated strategic change and transorganisational development. Open systems planning is aimed at helping an organisation to assess its environment and develop strategies for relating to it more effectively. Integrated strategic change infuses strategy formulation and implementation with the OD perspective to improve organisation performance. Transorganisational development helps organisations to form partnerships with other organisations in order to perform tasks that are too complex and costly for them to undertake alone. Chapter 20 describes three interventions for radically transforming organisations: culture change, self-designing organisations and organisation learning. Culture change is directed at changing the values, beliefs, and norms shared by organisation members. Self-designing organisational interventions are concerned with helping organisations gain the internal capacity to fundamentally alter themselves. Finally, organisation learning is a change process aimed at helping organisations develop and use knowledge to continually change and improve themselves.

Part VII (Chapter 21) is concerned with special topics in OD. Chapter 21 describes the practice of OD in international settings. OD can be applied internationally, but needs to be modified to fit each country's cultural context and environment. Organisation development in world-wide organisations is aimed at improving the internal alignment of strategy, structure and process so as to achieve global objectives. Finally, the practice of OD in global social change organisations promotes sustainable development and the improvement of human potential in emerging countries.

Summary

This chapter introduced OD as a planned change discipline concerned with applying behavioural science knowledge and practice to help organisations achieve greater effectiveness. Managers and staff specialists must work with and through people to perform their jobs, and OD can help them form effective relationships with others. Organisations are faced with rapidly accelerating change, and OD can help them cope with the consequences of change. The concept of OD has multiple meanings. The definition provided here resolved some of the problems with earlier definitions. The history of OD reveals its five roots: laboratory training, action research and survey feedback; participative management; productivity; quality of work life and strategic change. The current practice of OD goes far beyond its humanistic origins by incorporating concepts from organisation strategy and structure that complement the early emphasis on social processes. The continued growth in the number and diversity of OD approaches, practitioners and involved organisations attests to the health of the discipline and offers a favourable prospect for the future.

 ACTIVITIES

Review questions

1 What is the definition of organisation development?
2 Organisation development attempts to help an organisation cope with what aspects of the organisation's environment?
3 What is the meaning of 'T-group', and when was one first formed?
4 What is the assumption that underlies the use of survey feedback in OD?
5 What is the most distinguishing characteristic of QWL?
6 What factors have an effect on productivity?
7 With what functional considerations do practitioners need to be familiar if they are to create strategic change?

Discussion and essay questions

1 Discuss the value of planned change and discuss why it is necessary.
2 Compare and contrast the five 'stems' of organisation development — laboratory training, action research/survey feedback, participative management, quality of work life and strategic change.
3 Outline the key events in the history and evolution of organisation development. What do you predict will be the future directions of the field?

Notes

1 W. Burke, *Organization Development: Principles and Practices* (Boston, Mass.: Little Brown, 1982).
2 W. French, 'Organization development: objectives, assumptions, and strategies', *California Management Review*, 12 (February 1969): 23–34.
3 R. Beckhard, *Organization Development: Strategies and Models* (Reading, Mass.: Addison-Wesley, 1969).
4 M. Beer, *Organization Change and Development: A Systems View* (Santa Monica, Calif.: Goodyear Publishing, 1980).
5 D. Dunphy and D. Stace, *Beyond the Boundaries* (Sydney: McGraw Hill, 1994).
6 J. Naisbitt and P. Aburdene, *Re-inventing the Corporation* (New York: Warner Books, 1985); N. Tichy and M. Devanna, *The Transformational Leader* (New York: John Wiley and Sons, 1986); R. Kilmann and T. Covin, eds, *Corporate Transformation: Revitalizing Organizations for a Competitive World* (San Francisco: Jossey-Bass, 1988); T. Peters, *Thriving on Chaos: Handbook for a Management Revolution* (New York: Alfred A. Knopf, 1987); J. Kotter, *Leading Change* (Cambridge, Mass.: Harvard Business School Press, 1996).
7 T. Stewart, 'Welcome to the revolution', *Fortune* (13 December 1993): 66–80; C. Farrell, 'The new economic era', *Business Week* (18 November 1994).
8 Anonymous, 'New relationship fuels success', *Foodweek* (9 June 1998): 7.
9 L. Bradford, 'Biography of an institution', *Journal of Applied Behavioural Science*, 3 (1967): 127; A. Marrow, 'Events leading to the establishment of the National Training Laboratories', *Journal of Applied Behavioural Science*, 3 (1967): 145–50.
10 W. French, 'The emergence and early history of organization development with reference to influences upon and interactions among some of the key actors' in *Contemporary Organization Development: Current Thinking and Applications*, ed. D. Warrick (Glenview, Ill.: Scott, Foresman, 1985): 12–27.
11 M. Griffin, 'Another day at the office', *The Sunday Age* (19 April 1998): 16–19.
12 A. Marrow, D. Bowers and S. Seashore, *Management by Participation* (New York: Harper and Row, 1967).
13 L. Coch and J. French, 'Overcoming resistance to change', *Human Relations*, 1 (1948): 512–32.
14 R. Chenhall and K. Langfield-Smith, 'Factors influencing the role of management accounting in the development of performance measures within organizational change programs', *Management Accounting Research*, 4 (1998): 361–86.
15 C. Singh and M. Hart, 'Changing business culture: information is the key', *Australian CPA*, 8:8 (1998): 50–52.
16 R. Helker, 'Participating action research as a strategy for empowering Aboriginal health workers', *ANZ Journal of Public Health*, 21:7 (1997): 784–88.
17 W. French, 'The emergence and early history of organization development with reference to influences upon and interactions among some of the key actors' in *Contemporary Organization Development: Current Thinking and Applications*, ed. D. Warrick (Glenview, Ill.: Scott, Foresman, 1985): 19–20.
18 F. Mann, 'Studying and creating change' in *The Planning of Change: Readings in the Applied Behavioural Sciences*. eds W. Bennis, K. Benne and R. Chin (New York: Holt, Rinehart and Winston, 1962): 605–15.
19 D. Wheatley, 'Benchmarks fuel improvements', *Business Queensland* (23 March 1998).
20 R. Likert, *The Human Organization* (New York: McGraw-Hill, 1967); S. Seashore and D. Bowers, 'Durability of organizational change', *American Psychologist*, 25 (1970): 227–33; D. Mosley, 'System Four revisited: some new insights', *Organization Development Journal*, 5 (Spring 1987): 19–24.
21 *Ibid.*
22 *Ibid.*
23 J. Flint, 'All change, says ANZ boss', *Sydney Morning Herald*, (20 November 1997).
24 A. Rice, *Productivity and Social Organisation: The Ahmedabad Experiment* (London: Tavistock Publications, 1958); E. Trist and K. Bamforth, 'Some social and psychological consequences of the longwall method of coal-getting', *Human Relations*, 4 (January 1951): 1–38.
25 http://www.jameshardie.com.au
26 M. Walton, *The Deming Management Method* (New York: Dodd, Mead and Company, l986).
27 J. Juran, *Juran on Leadership for Quality: An Executive Handbook* (New York: Free Press, 1989).

28 'The quality imperative', *Business Week*, Special Issue, 25 October 1991.

29 D. Elloy and A. Randolph, 'The effect of superleader behaviour on autonomous work groups in a government operated railway service', *Public Personnel Management*, 26 (1997): 257–72.

30 M. Jelinek and J. Litterer, 'Why OD must become strategic' in *Research in Organizational Change and Development*, 2, eds W. Pasmore and R. Woodman (Greenwich, Conn.: JAI Press, 1988): 135–62; P. Buller, 'For successful strategic change: blend OD practices with strategic management', *Organizational Dynamics* (Winter 1988): 42–55; C. Worley, D. Hitchin and W. Ross, *Integrated Strategic Change* (Reading, Mass.: Addison-Wesley, 1996).

31 Worley, Hitchin, and Ross, *Integrated Strategic Change, ibid.*

32 R. Beckhard and R. Harris, *Organizational Transitions: Managing Complex Change*, 2nd ed. (Reading, Mass.: Addison-Wesley, 1987); N. Tichy, *Managing Strategic Change* (New York: John Wiley and Sons, 1983); E. Schein, *Organizational Culture and Leadership* (San Francisco: Jossey-Bass, 1985); C. Lundberg, 'Working with culture', *Journal of Organization Change Management*, 1 (1988): 38–47.

33 D. Miller and P. Freisen, 'Momentum and revolution in organisation adaptation', *Academy of Management Journal*, 23 (1980): 591–614; M. Tushman and E. Romanelli, 'Organizational evolution: a metamorphosis model of convergence and reorientation' in *Research in Organizational Behaviour*, 7, eds L. Cummings and B. Staw (Greenwich, Conn.: JAI Press, 1985): 171–222.

34 Beckhard and Harris, *Organizational Transitions, op. cit.*

35 T. Covin and R. Kilmann, 'Critical issues in large scale organization change', *Journal of Organization Change Management*, 1 (1988): 59–72; A. Mohrman, S. Mohrman, G. Ledford Jr, T. Cummings, and E. Lawler, eds, *Large Scale Organization Change* (San Francisco: Jossey-Bass, 1989); W. Torbert, 'Leading organizational transformation' in *Research in Organization Change and Development*, 3, eds R. Woodman and W. Pasmore (Greenwich, Conn.: JAI Press, 1989): 83–116; J. Bartunek and M. Louis, 'The interplay of organization development and organization transformation' in *Research in Organizational Change and Development*, 2, eds W. Pasmore and R. Woodman (Greenwich, Conn.: JAI Press, 1988): 97–134; A. Levy and U. Merry, *Organizational Transformation: Approaches, Strategies, Theories* (New York: Praeger, 1986).

36 S. Hoyle, 'MLC merger chief: how to build a financial giant', *The Australian Financial Review* (20 February 1998): 1.

37 A. Jaeger, 'Organization development and national culture: where's the fit?' *Academy of Management Review*, 11 (1986): 178; G. Hofstede, *Culture's Consequences: International Differences in Work-Related Values* (London: Sage, 1980); P. Sorensen Jr, T. Head, N. Mathys, J. Preston and D. Cooperrider, *Global and International Organization Development* (Champaign, Ill.: Stipes, 1995).

38 http://www2.agsm.edu.au

39 C. Argyris and D. Schon, *Organizational Learning* (Reading, Mass.: Addison-Wesley, 1978); C. Argyris, R. Putnam and D. Smith, *Action Science* (San Francisco: Jossey-Bass, 1985).

40 W. Bennis and B. Nanus, *Leaders* (New York: Harper and Row, 1985).

41 E. Schein, *Process Consultation: Its Role in Organization Development* (Reading, Mass.: Addison-Wesley, 1969); E. Schein, *Process Consultation, 2: Lessons for Managers and Consultants* (Reading, Mass.: Addison-Wesley, 1987); E. Schein, *Organizational Culture and Leadership*, 2nd ed., (San Francisco: Jossey-Bass, 1992).

42 Beckhard and Harris, *Organizational Transitions, op. cit.*

43 R. Tannenbaum and R. Hanna, 'Holding on, letting go, and moving on: understanding a neglected perspective on change' in *Human Systems Development*, eds R. Tannenbaum, N. Margulies and F. Massarik (San Francisco: Jossey-Bass, 1985): 95–121.

44 W. Burke, *Organization Development: Principles and Practices* (Boston: Little, Brown, 1982); W. Burke, *Organization Development: A Normative View* (Reading, Mass.: Addison-Wesley, 1987); W. Burke, 'Organization development: then, now, and tomorrow', *OD Practitioner*, 27 (1995): 5–13.

45 L. Greiner and V. Schein, *Power and Organizational Development: Mobilizing Power to Implement Change* (Reading, Mass.: Addison-Wesley, 1988).

46 E. Lawler III, *Pay and Organization Development* (Reading, Mass.: Addison-Wesley, 1981); E. Lawler III, *High-Involvement Management* (San Francisco: Jossey-Bass, 1986).

47 A. Raia and N. Margulies, 'Organization development: issues, trends, and prospects' in *Human Systems Development*, eds R. Tannenbaum, N. Margulies and F. Massarik (San Francisco: Jossey-Bass, 1985): 246–72; N. Margulies and A. Raia, 'Some reflections on the values of organizational development', *Academy of Management OD Newsletter*, 1 (Winter 1988): 9–11.

48 P. Vaill, 'OD as a scientific revolution' in *Contemporary Organization Development: Current Thinking and Applications* (Glenview, Ill.: Scott, Foresman, 1985): 28–41; C. Lundberg, 'On organisation development interventions: a general systems–cybernetic perspective' in *Systems Theory for Organisational Development*, ed. T. Cummings (Chichester, England: John Wiley and Sons, 1980): 247–71.

49 L. Brown and J. Covey, 'Development organizations and organization development: toward an expanded paradigm for organization development' in *Research in Organizational Change and Development*, l, eds R. Woodman and W. Pasmore (Greenwich, Conn.: JAI Press, 1987): 59–87.

50 T. Cummings and S. Srivastra, *Management of Work: A Socio-Technical Systems Approach* (San Diego: University Associates, 1977); T. Cummings, 'Transorganizational development' in *Research in Organizational Behaviour*, 6, eds B. Staw and L. Cummings (Greenwich, Conn.: JAI Press, 1984): 367–422; T. Cummings and S. Mohrman, 'Self-designing organizations: towards implementing quality-of-work-life innovations' in *Research in Organizational Change and Development*, 1, eds R. Woodman and W. Pasmore (Greenwich, Conn.: JAI Press, 1987): 275–310.

51 M. Widen, 'Sociotechnical systems ideas as public policy in Norway: empowering participation through worker managed change', *Journal of Applied Behavioural Science*, 22 (1986): 239–55.

52 W. Pasmore, C. Haldeman and A. Shani, 'Sociotechnical systems: a North American reflection on empirical studies in North America', *Human Relations*, 32 (1982): 1179–204; W. Pasmore and J. Sherwood, *Sociotechnical Systems: A Source Book* (San Diego: University Associates, 1978); J. Porras, *Stream Analysis: A Powerful Way to Diagnose and Manage Organizational Change* (Reading, Mass.: Addison-Wesley, 1987); J. Porras, P. Robertson and L. Goldman, 'Organization development: theory, practice, and research' in *Handbook of Industrial and Organizational Psychology*, 2nd ed., ed. M. Dunnette (Chicago: Rand McNally, 1990).

53 P. Block, *Flawless Consulting* (Austin, Tex.: Learning Concepts, 1981); P. Block, *The Empowered Manager: Positive Political Skills at Work* (San Francisco: Jossey-Bass, 1987); P. Block, *Stewardship* (San Francisco: Berrett-Koehler, 1994).

54 K. Murrell, 'Organization development experiences and lessons in the United Nations development program', *Organization Development Journal*, 12 (1994): 1–16; J. Vogt and K. Murrell, *Empowerment in Organisations* (San Diego: Pfeiffer and Company, 1990); J. Preston and L. DuToit, 'Endemic violence in South Africa: an OD solution applied to two educational settings', *International Journal of Public Administration*, 16 (1993): 1767–91; J. Preston, L. DuToit and I. Barber, 'A potential model of transformational change applied to South Africa' in *Research in Organizational Change and Development*, 9 (Greenwich, Conn.: JAI Press, in press).

55 S. Mohrman, S. Cohen, and A. Mohrman, *Designing Team-Based Organizations* (San Francisco: Jossey-Bass, 1995); S. Cohen and G. Ledford Jr, 'The effectiveness of self-managing teams: a quasi-experiment', *Human Relations*, 47 (1994): 13–43; G. Ledford and E. Lawler, 'Research on employee participation: beating a dead horse?' *Academy of Management Review*, 19 (1994): 633–36; G. Ledford, E. Lawler and S. Mohrman, 'The quality circle and its variations' in *Productivity in Organizations: New Perspectives from Industrial and Organizational Psychology*, eds J. Campbell, R. Campbell and associates (San Francisco: Jossey-Bass, 1988); A. Mohrman, G. Ledford Jr, S. Mohrman, E. Lawler III and T. Cummings, *Large Scale Organization Change* (San Francisco: Jossey-Bass, 1989).

56 D. Cooperrider and T. Thachankary, 'Building the global civic culture: making our lives count' in *Global and International Organization Development*, eds P. Sorensen Jr, T. Head, N. Mathys, J. Preston and D. Cooperrider (Champaign, Ill: Stipes, 1995): 282–306; D. Cooperrider, 'Positive image, positive action: the affirmative basis for organising' in *Appreciative Management and Leadership*, eds S. Srivastva, D. Cooperrider and associates (San Francisco, Calif.: Jossey-Bass, 1990); D. Cooperrider and S. Srivastva, 'Appreciative inquiry in organizational life' in *Organizational Change and Development*, 1, eds R. Woodman and W. Pasmore (Greenwich, Conn.: JAI Press, 1987): 129–70.

57 S. Marinos, 'Getting down to business beyond 2000', *The Age* (24 February 1998): 6.

58 C. Rance, 'Recognition for Casey learning system', *The Age* (20 September 1997): 12.

59 A. Hepworth, 'Yearning for more learning', *The Australian Financial Review* (5 June 1984): 4.

PART 1

OVERVIEW OF ORGANISATION DEVELOPMENT

CHAPTERS

2   The nature of planned change

3   The organisation development practitioner

The nature of planned change

The increasing pace of global, economic and technological development makes change an inevitable feature of organisational life. However, change that happens to an organisation can be distinguished from change that is planned by organisation members. In this book, the term 'change' will refer to planned change. Organisation development is directed at bringing about planned change in order to increase an organisation's effectiveness. It is generally initiated and implemented by managers, often with the help of an OD practitioner, either from inside or outside the organisation. Organisations can use planned change to solve problems, to learn from experience, to adapt to external environmental changes, to improve performance and to influence future changes.

All approaches to OD rely on some theory about planned change. These theories describe the different stages through which planned change may be effected in organisations and explain the temporal process of applying OD methods to help organisation members manage change. In this chapter, we first describe and compare three major theories of organisation change: Lewin's change model, the action research model and contemporary adaptations to action research. These three approaches, which have received considerable attention in the field, offer different concepts of planned change. Next we present a general model of planned change that integrates the earlier models and incorporates recent conceptual developments in OD. This model has broad applicability to many types of planned change efforts and serves to organise the chapters in this book. We then discuss different types of change and how the process can vary according to the change situation. Finally, several critiques of planned change are presented.

Theories of planned change

Conceptions of planned change have tended to focus on how change can be implemented in organisations.[1] Called 'theories of changing', these frameworks describe the activities that must take place in order to initiate and carry out successful organisational change. In this section, we describe and compare three different theories of changing: Lewin's change model, the action research model and contemporary approaches to change. These frameworks have received widespread attention in OD and serve as the primary basis for a general model of planned change.

Lewin's change model

One of the early fundamental models of planned change was provided by Kurt Lewin.[2] He conceived of change as a modification of those forces that keep a system's behaviour stable. Specifically, the level of behaviour at any moment in time is the result of two sets of forces—those striving to maintain the *status quo* and those pushing for change. When both sets of forces are about equal, current levels of behaviour are maintained in what Lewin termed a state of 'quasi-stationary equilibrium'. To change that state, one can increase those forces pushing for change, decrease those forces that maintain the current state or apply some combination of both. For example, the level of performance of a work group might be stable because group norms maintaining that level are equivalent to the supervisor's pressures for change to higher levels. This level can be

FIGURE 2.1   Comparison of planned change models

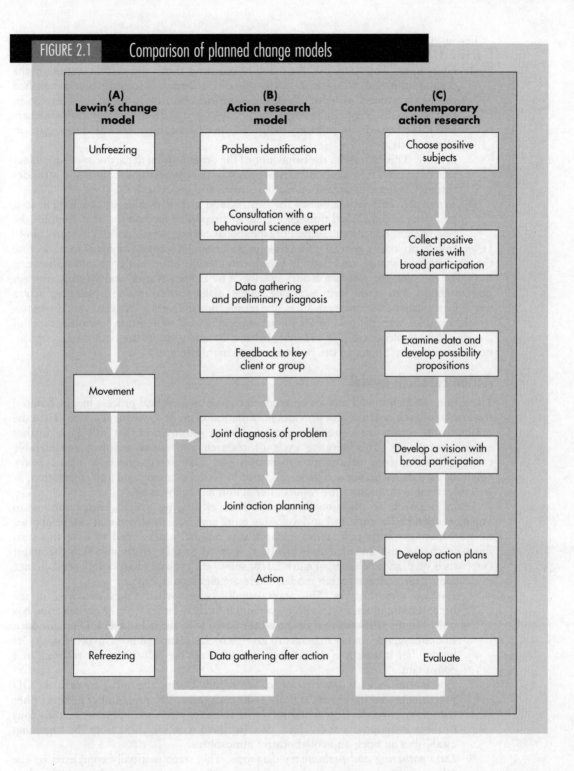

(A)
Lewin's change model

Unfreezing

Movement

Refreezing

(B)
Action research model

Problem identification

Consultation with a behavioural science expert

Data gathering and preliminary diagnosis

Feedback to key client or group

Joint diagnosis of problem

Joint action planning

Action

Data gathering after action

(C)
Contemporary action research

Choose positive subjects

Collect positive stories with broad participation

Examine data and develop possibility propositions

Develop a vision with broad participation

Develop action plans

Evaluate

increased either by changing the group norms to support higher levels of performance or by increasing supervisor pressures to produce at higher levels. Lewin suggested that modifying those forces that maintain the *status quo* produces less tension and resistance than increasing forces for change, and consequently is a more effective strategy for change.

Lewin viewed this change process as consisting of three steps, which are shown in Figure 2.1(A):

1 *Unfreezing*. This step usually involves reducing those forces that maintain the organisation's behaviour at its present level. Unfreezing is sometimes accomplished through a process of 'psychological disconfirmation'. By introducing information that shows discrepancies between the behaviours desired by organisation members and those behaviours currently exhibited, members can be motivated to engage in change activities.[3]

2 *Moving*. This step shifts the behaviour of the organisation, department or individual to a new level. It involves the development of new behaviours, values and attitudes through changes in organisational structures and processes.

3 *Refreezing*. This step stabilises the organisation at a new state of equilibrium. It is frequently accomplished through the use of supporting mechanisms that reinforce the new organisational state, such as organisational culture, norms, policies and structures.

Lewin's model provides a general framework for understanding organisational change. Because the three steps of change are relatively broad, considerable effort has gone into elaborating them. For example, the planning model, developed by Lippitt, Watson and Westley, arranges Lewin's model into seven steps: scouting, entry, diagnosis (unfreezing), planning, action (movement), stabilisation and evaluation, and termination (refreezing).[4] Lewin's model remains closely identified with the field of OD, however, and is used to illustrate how other types of change can be implemented. For example, Lewin's three-step model has been used to explain how information technologies can be implemented more effectively.[5]

Action research model

The action research model focuses on planned change as a cyclical process in which initial research about the organisation provides information to guide subsequent action. Then the results of the action are assessed to provide further information that will guide further action, and so on. This iterative cycle of research and action involves considerable collaboration between organisation members and OD practitioners. It places heavy emphasis on data gathering and diagnosis prior to action planning and implementation, as well as careful evaluation of the results after action has been taken.

Action research is traditionally aimed both at helping specific organisations to implement planned change and at developing more general knowledge that can be applied to other settings.[6] Although action research was originally developed to have this dual focus on change and knowledge, it has been adapted to OD efforts in which the major emphasis is on planned change.[7] Figure 2.1(B) shows the cyclical phases of planned change as defined by the action research model. There are eight main steps:

1 *Problem identification*. This stage usually begins when a key executive in the organisation, or someone with power and influence, senses that the organisation has one or more problems that might be alleviated with the help of an OD practitioner. In one case, the quality manager of an electronics plant had been involved with OD before, but it took her almost a year to persuade the plant manager to bring in a consultant.

2 *Consultation with a behavioural science expert*. During the initial contact, the OD practitioner and the client carefully assist each other. The practitioner has his or her own normative, developmental theory or frame of reference and must be conscious of those assumptions and values.[8] Sharing them with the client from the beginning establishes an open and collaborative atmosphere.

3 *Data gathering and preliminary diagnosis*. This stage is usually completed by the OD practitioner, often in conjunction with organisation members. It involves gathering appropriate information and analysing it to determine the underlying causes of organisational problems. The four basic methods of gathering data are interviews, process observation, questionnaires and organisational performance data (unfortunately, often overlooked). One approach to diagnosis begins with observation, proceeds to a semi-structured interview and concludes with a

questionnaire to measure precisely the problems identified by the earlier steps.[9] When gathering diagnostic information, it is possible that OD practitioners may influence members from whom they are collecting data. In OD, 'every action on the part of the ... consultant constitutes an intervention' that will have some effect on the organisation.[10]

4 *Feedback to key client or group*. Because action research is a collaborative activity, the diagnostic data are fed back to the client, usually in a group or work-team meeting. The feedback step, in which members are given the information gathered by the OD practitioner, helps them to determine the strengths and weaknesses of the organisation or the department under study. The consultant provides the client with all relevant and useful data. Obviously, the practitioner will protect those sources of information and, at times, will withhold data if the group is not ready for the information or if the information would make the client overly defensive.

5 *Joint diagnosis of problem*. At this point, members discuss the feedback and explore with the OD practitioner whether they want to work on identified problems. A close interrelationship exists among data gathering, feedback and diagnosis as the consultant summarises the basic data from the client members and presents the data to them for validation and further diagnosis. An important point to remember, as Schein suggests, is that the action research process is very different from the doctor–patient model, in which the consultant comes in, makes a diagnosis and prescribes a solution. Schein notes that the failure to establish a common frame of reference in the client–consultant relationship may lead to faulty diagnosis or to a communications gap whereby the client is sometimes 'unwilling to believe the diagnosis or accept the prescription'. He believes 'most companies have drawers full of reports by consultants, each loaded with diagnoses and recommendations which are either not understood or not accepted by the "patient"'.[11]

6 *Joint action planning*. Next, the OD practitioner and the client members jointly agree on further actions to be taken. This is the beginning of the moving process (described in Lewin's change model), as the organisation decides on how best to reach a different quasi-stationary equilibrium. At this stage, the specific action to be taken depends on the culture, technology and environment of the organisation; the diagnosis of the problem and the time and expense of the intervention.

7 *Action*. This stage involves the actual change from one organisational state to another. It may include installing new methods and procedures, reorganising structures and work designs, and reinforcing new behaviours. These actions typically cannot be implemented immediately, but require a transition period as the organisation moves from the present to a desired future state.[12]

8 *Data gathering after action*. Because action research is a cyclical process, data must also be gathered after the action has been taken in order to measure and determine the effects of the action and to feed the results back to the organisation. This, in turn, may lead to rediagnosis and new action.

Contemporary adaptations to action research

The action research model underlies most current approaches to planned change and is often identified with the practice of OD. Action research has recently been extended to new settings and applications, and consequently researchers and practitioners have made the requisite adaptations to its basic framework.[13]

Trends in the application of action research include the movement from smaller sub-units of organisations to total systems and communities.[14] In these larger contexts, action research is more complex and political than in smaller settings. Therefore, the action research cycle is co-ordinated across multiple change processes and includes a diversity of stakeholders who have an interest in the organisation. (We describe these applications more thoroughly in Chapters 19 and 20.)

Action research is also increasingly being applied in international settings, particularly in developing nations in the southern hemisphere.[15] Embedded within the action research model, however, are 'northern hemisphere' assumptions about change. For example, action research traditionally views change more linearly than Eastern cultures, and it treats the change process more collaboratively than Latin American and African countries.[16] To achieve success in these settings, action research needs to be tailored to fit their cultural assumptions. (This is described in more detail in Chapter 21.)

Finally, action research is increasingly being applied to promote social change and innovation.[17] This is demonstrated most clearly in community-development and global social-change projects.[18] These applications are heavily value-laden and seek to redress imbalances in power and resource allocations across different groups. Action researchers tend to play an activist role in the change process, which is often chaotic and conflictual. (Chapter 21 reviews global social-change processes.)

In view of these general trends, action research has undergone two key adaptations. First, contemporary applications have substantially increased the degree of member involvement in the change process. This contrasts with traditional approaches to planned change where consultants carried out most of the change activities, with the agreement and collaboration of management.[19] Although consultant-dominated change still persists in OD, there is a growing tendency to involve organisation members in learning about their organisation and how to change it. Referred to as 'participatory action research',[20] 'action learning',[21] 'action science'[22] or 'self-design',[23] this approach to planned change emphasises the need for organisation members to learn about it at first hand if they are to gain the knowledge and skills to change the organisation. In today's complex and changing environment, some argue that OD must go beyond solving particular problems to helping members gain the necessary competence to continually change and improve the organisation.[24]

In this modification of action research, the role of OD consultants is to work with members to facilitate the learning process. Both parties are 'co-learners' in diagnosing the organisation, designing changes and implementing and assessing them.[25] Neither party dominates the change process. Rather, each participant brings unique information and expertise to the situation, and together they combine their resources to learn how to change the organisation. Consultants, for example, know how to design diagnostic instruments and OD interventions, while organisation members have 'local' knowledge about the organisation and how it functions. Each participant learns from the change process. Organisation members learn how to change their organisation, to refine and improve it. OD consultants learn how to facilitate complex organisational change and learning.

Application 2.1 gives a brief description of an action learning programme that is regarded as a major vehicle for change and innovation by the senior executive staff at the University of Queensland. The programme plays an important role in changing the way complex problems and issues are perceived and addressed. The programme has fostered these changes through its design and by promoting action learning as an effective model for addressing new and complex issues.[26]

The second adaptation to action research is the promotion of a 'positive' approach to planned change.[27] Referred to as 'appreciative inquiry', this application of planned change suggests that all organisations are to some degree effective and that planned change should focus on the 'best of what is'.[28] This assumption challenges the dominant metaphor that organisations are problems to be solved.[29] Rather, appreciative enquiry helps organisation members understand and describe their organisation when it is working at its best. That knowledge is then applied to creating a vision of what the organisation could be. Because members are heavily involved in creating the vision, they are committed to changing the organisation in that direction. Considerable research on expectation effects supports this positive approach to planned change.[30] It suggests that people tend to act in ways that make their expectations occur; a positive vision of what the organisation can become can energise and direct behaviour to make that expectation come about.

These contemporary adaptations to action research are depicted in Figure 2.1(C). Planned change begins with choosing positive aspects of the organisation to examine, such as a particularly effective work team or a new product that has been developed and brought to market especially fast. If the focus of inquiry is real and vital to organisation members, the change process itself will take on these positive attributes. The second step

APPLICATION 2.1

Action learning — the subtle organisation transformer

The University of Queensland's action learning programme is a staff development programme that uses action learning methodology to initiate, implement and evaluate projects undertaken by teams from across the University. It has been consistently successful at bringing groups of diverse staff together to work on projects that the University considers important and that also meet participants' learning goals.

The programme has funded ten or eleven projects each year since 1992. Projects are proposed by potential participants or sponsors and selected by a University committee. Teams are often inter-disciplinary and include both academic and general staff. The emphasis is on collegiality and learning from others through frequent and open reflection. Teams are sponsored by senior members of staff (often pro-vice-chancellors, deans and heads of department) who provide the organisational support necessary to initiate and maintain a project's goals. The sponsor's advocacy keeps the highest levels of the organisation informed of the programme and the projects' outcomes.

The programme continues to be supported and funded by the University, not only because of the learning and staff development it facilitates, but also because of the many valuable concrete outcomes produced. Since the programme began, more than 80 projects have achieved solutions, new ideas and innovations in widely varying areas, but particularly in teaching and learning and quality management. Many projects begin investigation and improvement and, while they achieve much in their first year, they form the networks to continue and advance their project into the realms of real and lasting change. Their sponsors encourage them to approach change proactively and this support for taking initiatives has no doubt made it possible for real change to occur.

The changes brought about through programme design include value systems, recognising the action learning process in inter-disciplinary teams as a useful way of tackling complex problems, appreciation of context planning and increased creativity and lateral thinking in problem solving. These changes are not at the macro level, but instead are occurring within and across departments as cultural changes. The networks and temporary structures that were established by a team are extended beyond the completion of the project. That is, collaboration between departments has increased, and non-traditional and non-hierarchical structures are being established and utilised. Another indicator of organisational change is that broad and complex issues that previously would have been left untouched are now being addressed.

involves gathering data about the 'best of what is' in the organisation. A broad array of organisation members are involved in developing data-gathering instruments, collecting information and analysing it. In the third stage, members examine the data to find stories, however small, that present a picture of the future that is truly exciting and possible. From these stories, members develop 'possibility propositions'—statements that bridge the organisation's current best practices with ideal possibilities for future organising.[31] This re-directs attention from 'what is' to 'what might be'. In step four, all relevant stakeholders are brought together to construct a vision of the future and to devise action plans for moving in that direction. Finally, implementation of those plans proceeds similarly to the action and evaluation phases of action research described previously. Members make changes, assess the results, make necessary adjustments and so on as they attempt to move the organisation towards the vision.

Comparisons of change models

All three models—Lewin's change model, the action research model and contemporary adaptations to the action research model—describe the phases by which planned change occurs in organisations. As shown in Figure 2.1, the models overlap in that their emphasis on action to implement organisational change is preceded by a preliminary stage (unfreezing, diagnosis or examining positive aspects of the organisation) and is followed by a closing stage (refreezing or evaluation). Moreover, all three approaches emphasise the application of behavioural science knowledge, involve organisation members in the change process and recognise that any interaction between a consultant and an organisation constitutes an intervention that may affect the organisation. However, Lewin's change model differs from the other two in that it focuses on the general process of planned change, rather than on specific OD activities.

Lewin's model and the action research model differ from contemporary approaches in terms of the level of involvement of the participants and the focus of change. The first two models emphasise the role of the consultant with limited member involvement in the change process. Contemporary applications, on the other hand, treat both consultants and participants as co-learners who are heavily involved in planned change. In addition, Lewin's model and action research are more concerned with fixing problems than with focusing on what the organisation does well, and leveraging those strengths.

General model of planned change

The three theories of planned change in organisations described above—Lewin's change model, the action research model and contemporary adaptations to the action research model—suggest a general framework for planned change, as shown in Figure 2.2. The framework describes the four basic activities that practitioners and organisation members jointly carry out in organisation development. The arrows connecting the different activities in the model show the typical sequence of events, from entering and contracting, to diagnosing, to planning and implementing change, to evaluating and institutionalising change. The lines connecting the activities emphasise that organisational change is not a straightforward, linear process, but involves considerable overlap and feedback among the activities. Because the model serves to organise the remaining parts of this book, Figure 2.2 also shows which specific chapters apply to the four major change activities.

Entering and contracting

The first set of activities in planned change concerns entering and contracting. These events are described in Chapter 4. They help managers decide whether they want to engage

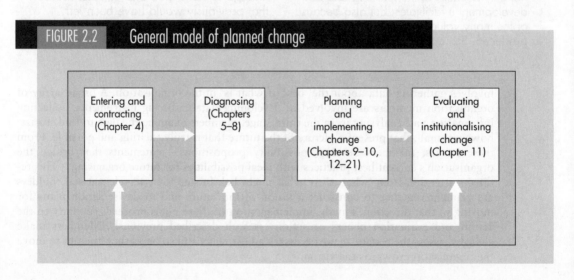

FIGURE 2.2   General model of planned change

further in a planned change programme and commit resources to such a process. Entering an organisation involves gathering initial data to understand the problems or opportunities facing the organisation. Once this information has been collected, the problems are discussed with managers and other organisation members in order to develop a contract or agreement to engage in planned change. The contract spells out future change activities, the resources that will be committed to the process, and how OD practitioners and organisation members will be involved. In many cases, organisations do not get beyond this early stage of planned change, because disagreements about the need for change surface, resource constraints are encountered or other methods for change appear more feasible. When OD is used in non-traditional and international settings, the entering and contracting process must be sensitive to the context in which the change is taking place.

Diagnosing

In this stage of planned change, the client system is carefully studied. Diagnosis can focus on understanding organisational problems, including their causes and consequences, or on identifying the organisation's positive attributes. The diagnostic process is one of the most important activities in OD. It includes choosing an appropriate model for understanding the organisation and gathering, analysing and feeding back information to managers and organisation members about the problems or opportunities.

Diagnostic models for analysing problems (described in Chapters 5 and 6) explore three levels of activities. Organisation problems represent the most complex level of analysis and involve the total system. Group-level problems are associated with departmental and group effectiveness, and individual-level problems involve how jobs are designed.

Gathering, analysing and feeding back data are the central change activities in diagnosis. Chapter 7 describes how data can be gathered through interviews, observations, survey instruments or archival sources, such as meeting minutes and organisation charts. It also explains how data can be reviewed and analysed. In Chapter 8, the process of feeding back diagnostic data is described. Organisation members, often in collaboration with an OD practitioner, jointly discuss the data and their implications for change.

Planning and implementing change

In this stage, organisation members and practitioners jointly plan and implement OD interventions. They design interventions to improve the organisation and make action plans to implement them. As discussed in Chapter 9, there are several criteria for designing interventions, including the organisation's readiness for change, its current change capability, its culture and power distributions and the change agent's skills and abilities. Depending on the outcomes of diagnosis, there are four major types of interventions in OD. Chapters 12 and 13 describe human process interventions at the individual, group and total system levels. Chapters 14, 15 and 16 present interventions that modify an organisation's structure and technology. Chapters 17 and 18 address human resource interventions that seek to improve member performance and wellness. Chapters 19 and 20 describe strategic interventions. These change programmes involve managing the organisation's relationship to its external environment and the internal structure and process necessary to support a business strategy. Finally, Chapter 21 contains specialised information for carrying out OD in international settings and in non-traditional organisations, such as schools, health-care organisations and the public sector.

Implementing interventions is concerned with managing the change process. As discussed in Chapter 10, it includes motivating change, creating a desired future vision of the organisation, developing political support, managing the transition towards the vision and sustaining momentum for change.

Evaluating and institutionalising change

This last stage in planned change involves an evaluation of the effects of the intervention and management of the institutionalisation of successful change programmes. These two activities are described in Chapter 11. Feedback to organisation members about the intervention's results provides information about whether the changes should be continued, modified or suspended. Institutionalising successful changes involves reinforcing them through feedback, rewards and training.

Application 2.2 describes how the different phases of planned change have been applied.[32] It demonstrates how traditional planned change activities, such as entry and contracting, survey feedback and change planning, can be combined with contemporary methods, such as large-group interventions and high levels of participation.

Different types of planned change

The general model of planned change describes how the OD process typically unfolds in organisations. In actual practice, the different phases are not nearly as orderly as the model implies. OD practitioners tend to modify or adjust the stages to fit the needs of the situation. Steps in planned change can be implemented in a variety of ways that depend on the client's needs and goals, the change agent's skills and values and the organisation's context. Therefore, it is clear that planned change can vary enormously from one situation to another.

APPLICATION 2.2

Planned change: radical approach to education

Schools and universities ... must provide courses that foster executive independence and develop world-ranking skills. I do not know anybody who knows exactly how the Australian university system will develop in the next five years. Along with those changes will come new teaching methods as the merits of continuing to have an actual student presence on campus are evaluated against the benefits of electronic communication. Our universities will certainly need to be globally competitive. The Asian students that are an essential underpinning of Australian university finances will be much harder to attract. Perhaps we can poach students from US universities.

Most universities have innovative plans for adapting to change and are seeking to consolidate their place in the Asian market with a variety of responses, including setting up overseas campuses. But probably the most unusual approach is one devised by the vice-chancellor of Melbourne University, Professor Alan Gilbert. Gilbert is saying that Australia's future prosperity depends on being a world-ranking generator of what he calls

'knowledge workers'—people who can prosper in a globalised information and service-oriented community. Companies will set up operations in areas with a good supply of knowledge workers trained to global standards. He believes that in this environment, university education, certainly postgraduate education, is too important to be left to non-profit organisations alone. So he is setting up a postgraduate university that aims to make a profit and pay good dividends to its shareholders. It will be linked with overseas universities and will offer globally competitive remuneration contracts to its academic staff.

A university in Australia that breaks the mould and pays salaries that will attract the best available professors and other staff while integrating itself into a globalised network will be vastly different from what we have come to expect. The aim is to provide training equal to the world's best. The existing university will gain fees from the new project and some of its staff may find lucrative jobs.

The Gilbert model is not the only approach to change but it represents a new style of thinking. Therefore it is exciting.

To understand these differences better, planned change can be contrasted across situations on two key dimensions: the magnitude of organisational change and the degree to which the client system is organised.

Magnitude of change

Planned change efforts can be characterised as falling along a continuum, ranging from *incremental* changes that involve fine-tuning the organisation to *quantum* changes that entail fundamentally altering how it operates.[33] Incremental changes tend to involve limited dimensions and levels of the organisation, such as the decision-making processes of work groups. They occur within the context of the organisation's existing business strategy, structure and culture, and are aimed at improving the *status quo*. Quantum changes, on the other hand, are directed at significantly altering how the organisation operates. They tend to involve several organisational dimensions, including structure, culture, reward systems, information processes and work design. They also involve changing multiple levels of the organisation, from top-level management through departments and work groups to individual jobs.

Planned change has traditionally been applied in situations that involve incremental change. Organisations in the 1960s and 1970s were mainly concerned with fine-tuning their bureaucratic structures by resolving many of the social problems that emerged with increasing size and complexity. In these situations, planned change involves a relatively bounded set of problem-solving activities. OD practitioners are typically contacted by managers to help solve specific problems in particular organisational systems, such as poor communication among members of a work team or high absenteeism among shop floor employees in a production facility. Diagnostic and change activities tend to be limited to these issues, although additional problems may be uncovered and may need to be addressed. Similarly, the change process tends to focus on those organisational systems that have specific problems, and it generally ends when the problems are resolved. Of course, the change agent may contract to help solve additional problems.

In recent years, OD has increasingly been concerned with quantum change. As described in Chapter 1, the greater competitiveness and uncertainty of today's environment have led a growing number of organisations to drastically alter the way in which they operate. In these situations, planned change is more complex, extensive and long-term than when applied to incremental change.[34] Because quantum change involves most features and levels of the organisation, it is typically driven from the top of the organisation, where corporate strategy and values are set. Change agents help senior managers create a vision of a desired future organisation and energise movement in that direction. They also help executives develop structures for managing the transition from the present to the future organisation. This may include, for example, a variety of overlapping steering committees and redesign teams. Staff experts may also redesign many features of the firm, such as performance measures, rewards, planning processes, work designs and information systems.

Because of the complexity and extensiveness of quantum change, OD professionals often work in teams that consist of members with different yet complementary expertise. The consulting relationship persists over relatively long time periods and includes a great deal of renegotiation and experimentation among consultants and managers. The boundaries of the change effort are more uncertain and diffuse than in incremental change, making diagnosis and change seem more like discovery than problem solving. (Complex strategic and transformational types of change are described in more detail in Chapters 19 and 20.)

It is important to emphasise that quantum change may or may not be developmental in nature. Organisations may drastically alter their strategic direction and way of operating without significantly developing their capacity to solve problems and achieve both high performance and quality of work life. For example, firms may simply change their marketing mix, dropping or adding products, services or customers; they may drastically downsize by cutting out marginal businesses and laying off managers and workers or they may tighten managerial and financial controls and attempt to squeeze more out of the labour force. On the other hand, organisations may undertake quantum change from a developmental perspective. They may seek to make themselves more competitive by developing their human resources, by getting managers and employees more involved in problem solving and innovation, and by promoting flexibility and direct, open communication. This OD approach to quantum change is particularly relevant in today's rapidly changing and competitive environment. To succeed in this setting, organisations such as Australia Post, Australian Taxation Office and the Department of Defence are transforming themselves from control-oriented bureaucracies to high-involvement organisations capable of continually changing and improving themselves.

Degree of organisation

Planned change efforts can also vary according to the degree to which the organisation or client system is organised. In over-organised situations, such as in highly mechanistic, bureaucratic organisations, various dimensions, such as leadership styles, job designs, organisation structure and policies and procedures are too rigid and overly-defined for effective task performance. Communication between management and employees is typically suppressed, conflicts are avoided and employees are apathetic. In under-organised organisations, on the other hand, there is too little constraint or regulation for effective task performance. Leadership, structure, job design and policy are ill-defined and fail to control task behaviours effectively. Communication is fragmented, job responsibilities are ambiguous and employees' energies are dissipated because of lack of direction. Under-organised situations are typically found in such areas as product development, project management and community development, where relationships among diverse groups and participants must be co-ordinated around complex, uncertain tasks.

In over-organised situations where much of OD practice has historically taken place, planned change is generally aimed at loosening constraints on behaviour. Changes in leadership, job design, structure and other features are designed to liberate suppressed energy, to increase the flow of relevant information between employees and managers and to promote effective conflict resolution. The typical steps of planned change—entry, diagnosis, intervention and evaluation—are intended to penetrate a relatively closed organisation or department and make it increasingly open to self-diagnosis and revitalisation. The relationship between the OD practitioner and the management team attempts to model this loosening process. The consultant shares leadership of the change process with management, encourages open communication and confrontation of conflict and maintains flexibility when relating to the organisation.

When applied to organisations that face problems because of being under-organised, planned change is aimed at increasing organisation by clarifying leadership roles, structuring communication between managers and employees, and specifying job and departmental responsibilities. These activities require a modification of the traditional phases of planned change and include the following four stages:[35]

1 *Identification*. This step identifies the relevant people or groups that need to be involved in the change programme. In many under-organised situations, people and departments can be so disconnected that there is uncertainty about who should be included in the problem-solving process. For example, managers of different departments who have only limited interaction with each other might disagree or be confused about which departments should help to develop a new product or service.

2 *Convention*. In this phase, the relevant people or departments in the company are brought together to begin organising for task performance. For example, department managers might be asked to attend a series of organising meetings to discuss the division of labour and the co-ordination required to introduce a new product.

3 *Organisation*. Different organising mechanisms are created to structure the newly required interactions among people and departments. They might include creating new leadership positions, establishing communication channels and specifying appropriate plans and policies.

4   *Evaluation.* In this final step the outcomes of the organisation phase are assessed. The evaluation might signal the need for adjustments in the organising process or for further identification, convention and organisation activities.

By carrying out these four stages of planned change in under-organised situations, the relationship between the OD practitioner and the client system attempts to reinforce the organising process. The consultant develops a well-defined leadership role, which might be autocratic during the early stages of the change programme. Similarly, the consulting relationship is clearly defined and tightly specified. In effect, the interaction between the consultant and the client system supports the larger process of bringing order to the situation.

Critique of planned change

Despite their continued refinement, the models and practice of planned change are still in a formative stage of development, and there is considerable room for improvement. Critics of OD have pointed out several problems with the way planned change has been both conceptualised and practised.

Conceptualisation of planned change

Planned change has typically been characterised as involving a series of activities for carrying out effective change in organisations. Although current models outline a general set of steps that need to be followed, considerably more information is needed to guide how those steps should be performed in specific situations. In an extensive review and critique of planned change theory, Porras and Robertson argued that planned change activities should be guided by information about: (1) the organisational features that can be changed, (2) the intended outcomes from making those changes, (3) the causal mechanisms by which those outcomes are achieved and (4) the contingencies upon which successful change depends.[36] In particular, they noted that the key to organisational change is change in the behaviour of each member and that the information available about the causal mechanisms that produce individual change is lacking. Overall, Porras and Robertson concluded that the information necessary for guiding change is only partially available and that a good deal more research and thinking are needed to fill the gaps. Chapters 12 to 20 on OD interventions review what is currently known about change features, outcomes, causal mechanisms and contingencies.

A related area where current thinking about planned change is deficient is knowledge about how the stages of planned change differ across situations. Most models specify a general set of steps that are intended to be applicable to most change efforts. The previous section of this chapter showed, however, how change activities can vary, depending on such factors as the magnitude of change and the degree to which the client system is organised. Considerably more effort needs to be expended on identifying situational factors that may require modification of the general stages of planned change. This would probably lead to a rich array of planned change models, each geared to a specific set of situational conditions. Such contingency thinking is sorely needed in planned change.

Planned change also tends to be described as a rationally-controlled, orderly process. Critics have argued that, although this view may be comforting, it is seriously misleading.[37] They point out that planned change has a more chaotic quality, often involving shifting goals, discontinuous activities, surprising events and unexpected combinations of changes. For example, managers often initiate changes without clear plans that clarify their strategies and goals. As change unfolds, new stakeholders may emerge and demand modifications that reflect previously unknown or unvoiced needs. These emergent conditions make planned change a far more disorderly and dynamic process than is customarily portrayed, and conceptions need to capture this reality.

Finally, the relationship between planned change and organisational performance and effectiveness is not well understood. OD has traditionally had problems assessing whether interventions are, in fact, producing observed results. The complexity of the change situation, the lack of sophisticated analyses and the long time periods for producing results have all contributed to a weak evaluation of OD efforts. Moreover, managers have often accounted for OD efforts with *post-hoc* testimonials, reports of possible future benefits and calls to support OD as the right thing to do. In the absence of rigorous assessment and measurement, it is difficult to make resource-allocation decisions about change programmes and to know which interventions are most effective in certain situations.

Practice of planned change

Critics have suggested that there are several problems with the way planned change is carried out.[38] These concerns are not with the planned change model itself, but with how change takes place and with the qualifications and activities of OD practitioners.

A growing number of OD practitioners have acquired skills in specific techniques, such as team building, total quality management, large-group interventions or gain sharing, and have chosen to specialise in those methods. Although such specialisation may be necessary, given the complex array of techniques that make up modern OD, it can lead to a certain myopia. Some OD practitioners favour particular techniques and ignore other OD strategies that might be more appropriate. They tend to interpret organisational problems as requiring the favoured technique. Thus, for example, it is not unusual to see consultants pushing such methods as diversity training, re-engineering, organisation learning or self-managing work teams as solutions to most organisational problems.

Effective change depends on a careful diagnosis of how the organisation is functioning. Diagnosis identifies the underlying causes of organisational problems, such as poor product quality and employee dissatisfaction. It requires both time and money, and some organisations are not willing to make the necessary investment. They rely on preconceptions about what the problem is and hire consultants with appropriate skills for solving it. Managers may think, for example, that work design is the problem and hire an expert in job enrichment to implement a change programme. The problem, however, may be caused by other factors, such as poor reward practices, and job enrichment would be inappropriate. Careful diagnosis can help to avoid such mistakes.

In situations that require complex organisational changes, planned change is a long-term process involving considerable innovation and learning on site. It requires a good deal of time and commitment and a willingness to modify and refine changes as the circumstances require. Some organisations demand more rapid solutions to their problems and seek 'quick fixes' from experts. Unfortunately, some OD consultants are more than willing to provide quick solutions. They sell prepackaged programmes, which tend to be appealing to managers as they typically include an explicit recipe to be followed, standard training materials and clear time and cost boundaries. The quick fixes, however, have trouble gaining wide organisational support and commitment. They seldom produce the positive results that have been advertised.

Other organisations have not recognised the systemic nature of change. Too often, they believe that intervention into one aspect or unit of the organisation will be sufficient to ameliorate the problems. They are unprepared for the other changes that may be necessary to support a particular intervention. For example, at Mono Pumps in Melbourne, the positive benefits of an employee involvement programme did not begin to appear until after the organisation had redesigned its reward system to support the cross-functional collaboration necessary for solving highly complex problems. Changing any one part or feature of an organisation often requires adjustments in other parts in order to maintain an appropriate alignment. Thus, although quick fixes and change programmes that focus on only one part or aspect of the organisation may resolve some specific problems, they generally do not lead to complex organisational change, or increase members' capacity to carry out change.[39]

The contingency approach to change management

Australian researchers Dexter Dunphy and Douglas Stace argue that change management should be approached from a situational perspective. Their argument for contingency is as follows: 'dramatically different approaches to change can work in different circumstances

... turbulent times create varied circumstances and demand different responses according to the needs of the situation. What is appropriate for one organisation may not be appropriate for another. So we need a model of change ... that indicates how to carry change strategies to achieve optimum fit with the changing environment.'[40]

As a result of some seven years' research into change management techniques in Australia, Dunphy and Stace have derived a model of change that incorporates both 'soft' and 'hard' approaches. The model is a two-dimensional matrix that categorises the scale of change (from fine-tuning OD to corporate transformation CT) and the style of management that needs to be employed to facilitate the change (from collaborative to coercive). Four process change strategies or topologies may be identified from these dimensions.[41]

Scale of change

- *Fine tuning:* Organisational change, which is an ongoing process characterised by fine tuning of the 'fit' or match between the organisation's strategy, structure, people and processes. Such effort is typically manifested at departmental/divisional levels.
- *Incremental adjustment:* Organisational change, which is characterised by incremental adjustments to the changing environment. Such change involves distinct modifications (but not radical change) to corporate business strategies, structures and management processes.
- *Modular transformation:* Organisational change, which is characterised by major re-alignment of one or more departments/divisions. The process of radical change is focused on these sub-parts rather than on the organisation as a whole.
- *Corporate transformation:* Organisational change, which is corporation-wide, characterised by radical shifts in business strategy, and revolutionary changes throughout the whole organisation.

FIGURE 2.3   Organisational change strategies

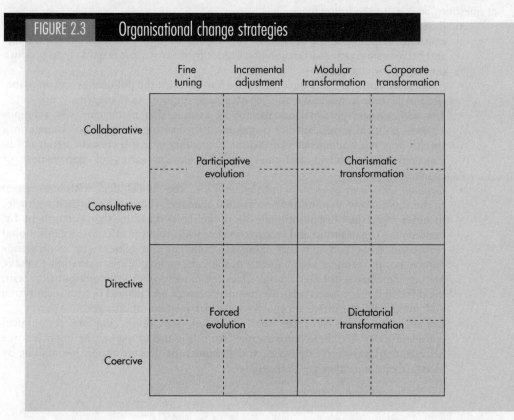

Style of management

- *Collaborative:* This involves widespread participation by employees in important decisions about the organisation's future, and about the means of bringing about organisational change.
- *Consultative:* This style of leadership involves consultation with employees, primarily about the means of bringing about organisational change, with their possible limited involvement in goal setting that is relevant to their area of expertise or responsibility.
- *Directive:* This style of leadership involves the use of managerial authority and direction as the main form of decision making about the organisation's future, and about the means of bringing about organisational change.
- *Coercive:* This style of leadership involves managers/executives or outside parties forcing or imposing change on key groups in the organisation.

Typology of change strategies and conditions for their use

- *Participative evolution:* Use when organisation is 'in fit' but needs minor adjustment, or is 'out of fit' but time is available and key interest groups factor change.
- *Charismatic transformation:* Use when organisation is 'out of fit' and there is little time for extensive participation, but there is support for radical change within the organisation.
- *Forced evolution:* Use when organisation is 'in fit' but needs minor adjustment, or is 'out of fit', but time is available. However, key interest groups oppose change.
- *Dictatorial transformation:* Use when organisation is 'out of fit', there is no time for extensive participation and no support within the organisation for radical change, but radical change is vital to organisational survival and fulfilment of the basic mission.

As with any model, Dunphy and Stace's model has created considerable debate, and questions arise as to the following:

- *Resistance to change:* Does it deal with the powerful and painful impact that resistance has on the organisation's capacity to deal with 'discontinuous' change and become innovative? Managing resistance by destroying it is unlikely to produce the hoped-for changes.
- *Political dimension:* Does the model take into account the political processes associated with trade union and employee actions in response to management decisions?
- *The management group:* Does the model assume that management is a homogeneous political group, in that a management decision to introduce change in a specific way is a homogeneous decision? The reality is that there exist variations in managerial commitment and this can influence the successful management of change.
- *Dealing with unforeseen circumstances:* Does the model deal with unforeseen circumstances and assume that individual managers have the information to let them see when their organisation is 'out of fit'? Does it assume that a congruent 'fit' between the organisation and its environment leads to more effective organisational performance; or consider that there are inherent difficulties with contingency approaches in defining what constitutes the environment. Does it attempt to make predictable what is not predictable? Does the model avoid dealing responsibly with the difficult issues associated with turbulent change and instead opt for a simplistic and potentially aggressive approach to the management of change?
- *Ethical considerations:* Does the model, at any point, explore the ethical considerations? Are there consequences from 'the use of explicit or implicit force between managers and employees, and an autocratic process of decision making by management and other key stakeholders'?

Summary

Theories of planned change describe the activities that are necessary in order to modify strategies, structures and processes to increase an organisation's effectiveness. Lewin's change model, the action research model and more recent adaptations of action research offer different views of the phases through which planned change occurs in organisations. Lewin's change model views planned change as a three-step process of unfreezing, movement and refreezing. It provides a general description of the process of planned change. The action research model focuses on planned change as a cyclical process involving joint activities between organisation members and OD practitioners. It involves eight sequential steps that overlap and interact in practice: problem identification, consultation with a behavioural science expert, data gathering and preliminary diagnosis, feedback to key client or group, joint diagnosis of the problem, joint action planning, action and data gathering after action. The action research model places heavy emphasis on data gathering and diagnosis prior to action planning and implementation, as well as on the assessment of results after action has been taken. In addition, change strategies are often modified on the basis of continued diagnosis, and termination of one OD programme may lead to further work in other areas of the firm. Recent trends in action research include the movement from smaller to larger systems; from domestic to international applications and from organisational issues to social change. These trends have led to two key adaptations of action research: increased involvement of participants in the change process and a more appreciative approach to organisational change.

These theories can be integrated into a general model of planned change. Four sets of activities—entering and contracting, diagnosing, planning and implementing, and evaluating and institutionalising—can be used to describe how change is accomplished in organisations. These four sets of activities also describe the general structure of the chapters in this book. The general model has broad applicability to planned change. It identifies the steps that an organisation typically moves through in order to implement change and specifies the OD activities necessary for effecting the change.

Although the planned change models describe general stages of how the OD process unfolds, there are different types of change according to the situation. Planned change efforts can vary in terms of the magnitude of the change and the degree to which the client system is organised. When situations differ on these dimensions, planned change can vary greatly. Critics of OD have pointed out several problems with the way planned change has been conceptualised and practised. They point out specific areas where planned change can be improved.

ACTIVITIES

Review questions

1 Identify the people generally responsible for carrying out planned change efforts.
2 In Lewin's model of change, what brings about the proposed change?
3 Describe the three sequential steps in Lewin's change model.
4 What is action research and what is the 'first step'?
5 What happens when an organisation is over-organised?
6 When an action researcher is dealing with an organisation that is under-organised, what are the steps in the change process?
7 What are the major problems associated with planned change efforts?
8 How useful is the Dunphy and Stace model when considering transformational change?

Discussion and essay questions

1 What is 'planned change' as compared to 'unplanned change'? Give current examples.
2 What are the key features of Lewin's change model? Describe its strengths and weaknesses.
3 Describe the major differences between under-organised and over-organised organisations.
4 What problems associated with planned change should the OD practitioner be aware of? How might such problems be overcome?
5 What are the positive and negative aspects of Dunphy and Stace's model? How does it take into account such things as: resistance, politics, dealing with unforeseen circumstances, ethics, particular group characteristics, etc?
6 Compare and contrast the various models of planned change. Discuss the advantages and disadvantages of each.

Notes

1 W. Bennis, *Changing Organizations* (New York: McGraw-Hill, 1966); J. Porras and P. Robertson, 'Organization development theory: a typology and evaluation' in *Organizational Change and Development*, 1, eds R. Woodman and W. Pasmore (Greenwich, Conn.: JAI Press, 1987): 1–57.

2 K. Lewin, *Field Theory in Social Science* (New York: Harper and Row, 1951).

3 E. Schein, *Process Consultation*, 1 and 2 (Reading, Mass.: Addison-Wesley, 1987).

4 R. Lippitt, J. Watson, and B. Westley, *The Dynamics of Planned Change* (New York: Harcourt, Brace and World, 1958).

5 R. Benjamin and E. Levinson, 'A framework for managing IT-enabled change', *Sloan Management Review* (Summer 1993): 23–33.

6 A. Shani and G. Bushe, 'Visionary action research: a consultation process perspective', *Consultation*, 6 (Spring 1987): 3–19; G. Sussman and R. Evered, 'An assessment of the scientific merit of action research', *Administrative Science Quarterly*, 12 (1978): 582–603.

7 W. French, 'Organization development: objectives, assumptions, and strategies', *California Management Review*, 12 (1969): 23–34; A. Frohman, M. Sashkin and M. Kavanagh, 'Action research as applied to organization development', *Organization and Administrative Sciences*, 7 (1976): 129–42; E. Schein, *Organizational Psychology*, 3rd ed. (Englewood Cliffs, N.J.: Prentice-Hall, 1980).

8 N. Tichy, 'Agents of planned change: congruence of values, cognitions, and actions', *Administrative Science Quarterly*, 19 (1974): 163–82.

9 M. Beer, 'The technology of organization development' in *Handbook of Industrial and Organizational Psychology*, ed. M. Dunnette (Chicago: Rand McNally, 1976): 945.

10 E. Schein, *Process Consultation: Its Role in Organization Development* (Reading, Mass.: Addison-Wesley, 1969): 98.

11 *Ibid*, 6.

12 R. Beckhard and R. Harris, *Organizational Transitions*, 2nd ed. (Reading, Mass.: Addison-Wesley, 1987).

13 M. Elden and R. Chisholm, 'Emerging varieties of action research: introduction to the special issue', *Human Relations*, 46:2 (1993): 121–42.

14 G. Ledford and S. Mohrman, 'Self-design for high involvement', *Human Relations*, 46:2 (1993): 143–168; B. Bunker and B. Alban, 'The large group intervention—a new social innovation?' *Journal of Applied Behavioral Science*, 28:4 (1992): 473–80.

15 R. Marshak, 'Lewin meets Confucius: a review of the OD model of change', *Journal of Applied Behavioral Science*, 29:4 (1993): 393–415; K. Murrell, 'Evaluation as action research: the case of the Management Development Institute in Gambia, West Africa', *International Journal of Public Administration*, 16:3 (1993): 341–56; J. Preston and L. DuToit, 'Endemic violence in South Africa: an OD solution applied to two educational settings', *International Journal of Public Administration*, 16:11 (1993): 1767–91.

16 D. Brown, 'Participatory action research for social change: collective reflections with Asian nongovernmental development organizations', *Human Relations*, 46:2 (1993): 208–27.

17 D. Cooperrider and S. Srivastva, 'Appreciative inquiry in organizational life' in *Organizational Change and Development*, 1, eds R. Woodman and W. Pasmore (Greenwich, Conn.: JAI Press, 1987): 129–70.

18 D. Cooperrider and W. Pasmore, 'Global social change: a new agenda for social science?' *Human Relations*, 44:10 (1991): 1037–55.

19 W. Burke, *Organization Development: A Normative View* (Reading, Mass.: Addison-Wesley, 1987).

20 D. Greenwood, W. Whyte, and I. Harkavy, 'Participatory action research as process and as goal', *Human Relations*, 46:2 (1993): 175–92.

21 J. Enderby and D. Phelan, 'Action learning groups as the foundation for cultural change', *Asia Pacific Journal of Human Resources*, 32:1.

22 C. Argyris, R. Putnam, and D. Smith, *Action Science* (San Francisco: Jossey-Bass, 1985).

23 S. Mohrman and T. Cummings, *Self-designing Organizations: Learning How to Create High Performance* (Reading, Mass.: Addison-Wesley, 1989).

24 P. Senge, *The Fifth Discipline* (New York: Doubleday, 1990).

25 M. Weisbord, *Productive Workplaces* (San Francisco: Jossey-Bass, 1987).

26 M. Siksna and F. Broadbent, 'Action learning—the subtle transformer: the University of Queensland's action learning programme', The Teaching and Educational Development Institute, The University of Queensland, St Lucia, Qld.

27 D. Cooperrider, 'Positive image, positive action: the affirmative basis for organizing' in *Appreciative Management and Leadership*, eds S. Srivasta, D. Cooperrider and associates (San Francisco, Calif.: Jossey-Bass, 1990); D. Cooperrider, lecture notes, Presentation to the MSOD Chi Class, October 1995, Monterey, Calif.

28 D. Cooperrider and S. Srivastva, 'Appreciative inquiry in organizational life', *op. cit.*

29 D. Cooperrider and T. Thachankary, 'Building the global civic culture: making our lives count' in *Global and International Organization Development*, eds P. Sorensen Jr, T. Head, N. Mathys, J. Preston, and D. Cooperrider (Champaign, Ill.: Stipes, 1995): 282–306.

30 D. Eden, 'Creating expectation effects in OD: applying self-fulfilling prophecy' in *Research in Organization Change and Development*, 2, eds W. Pasmore and R. Woodman (Greenwich, Conn.: JAI Press, 1988); D. Eden, 'OD and self-fulfilling prophesy: boosting productivity by raising expectations', *Journal of Applied Behavioral Science*, 22 (1986): 1–13; D. Cooperrider, 'Positive image, positive action', *op. cit.*

31 F. Barrett and D. Cooperrider, 'Generative metaphor intervention: a new approach for working with systems divided by conflict and caught in defensive perception', *Journal of Applied Behavioral Science*, 26 (1990): 219–39.

32 R. Gottliebsen, 'Comment', *Business Review* (26 January 1998):4.

33 D. Nadler, 'Organizational frame-bending: types of change in the complex organization' in *Corporate Transformation*, eds R. Kilmann and T. Covin (San Francisco: Jossey-Bass, 1988): 66–83; P. Watzlawick, J. Weakland and R. Fisch, *Change* (New York: W.W. Norton, 1974); R. Golembiewski, K. Billingsley and S. Yeager, 'Measuring change and persistence in human affairs: types of change generated by OD designs', *Journal of Applied Behavioral Science*, 12 (1975): 133–57; A. Meyer, G. Brooks and J. Goes, 'Environmental jolts and industry revolutions: organizational responses to discontinuous change', *Strategic Management Journal*, 11 (1990): 93–110.

34 A. Mohrman, G. Ledford Jr, S. Mohrman, E. Lawler III and T. Cummings, *Large-Scale Organization Change* (San Francisco: Jossey-Bass, 1989).

35 L. Brown, 'Planned change in underorganised systems' in *Systems Theory for Organisation Development*, ed. T. Cummings (Chichester, England: John Wiley and Sons, 1980): 181–203.

36 J. Porras and P. Robertson, 'Organization development theory, practice, and research' in *Handbook of Industrial and Organizational Psychology*, 3, 2nd ed., eds M. Dunnette and M. Hough (Palo Alto, Calif: Consulting Psychologists Press, 1992).

37 T. Cummings, S. Mohrman, A. Mohrman and G. Ledford, 'Organization design for the future: a collaborative research approach' in *Doing Research That Is Useful for Theory and Practice*, eds E. Lawler III, A. Mohrman, S. Mohrman, G. Ledford and T. Cummings (San Francisco: Jossey-Bass, 1985): 275–305.

38 A. Frohman, M. Sashkin and M. Kavanagh, 'Action research as applied to organization development', *Organization and Administrative Sciences* 7 (1976): 129–42; S. Mohrman and T. Cummings, *Self-designing Organizations: Learning How to Create High Performance* (Reading, Mass.: Addison-Wesley, 1989); M. Beer, R. Eisenstat and B. Spector, 'Why change programs don't produce change', *Harvard Business Review*, 6 (November–December 1990): 158–66.

39 Beer, Eisenstat and Spector, 'Why change programs don't produce change', *op. cit.*

40 D. Dunphy and D. Stace, *Under New Management: Australian Organisations in Transition* (Sydney, McGraw Hill, 1990): 82.

41 D. Dunphy and D. Stace, 'Strategies for organisational transition', Centre for Corporate Change, Paper 002, 1991, AGSM, University of New South Wales.

The organisation development practitioner

Chapters 1 and 2 provided an overview of the field of organisation development and a description of the nature of planned change. This chapter extends that introduction by examining the people who perform OD in organisations. A closer look at OD practitioners can provide a more personal perspective on the field, and help us to understand the essential character of OD as a helping profession, involving personal relationships between OD practitioners and organisation members.

Much of the literature about OD practitioners views them as internal or external consultants who provide professional services: diagnosing problems, developing solutions and helping to implement them. More recent perspectives expand the scope of OD practitioners to include professionals in related disciplines, such as industrial psychology and organisation theory, as well as line managers who have learned how to carry out OD in order to change and develop their departments.

A great deal of opinion and some research studies have focused on the necessary skills and knowledge of an effective OD practitioner. Studies provide a comprehensive list of basic skills and knowledge needed by all OD practitioners if they are to be effective.

Most of the relevant literature focuses on people who specialise in OD as a profession and addresses their roles and careers. The OD role can be described in relation to the position of OD practitioners: internal to the organisation, external to it or in a team composed of both internal and external consultants. The OD role can also be examined in terms of its marginality in organisations and of where it fits along a continuum from client-centred to consultant-centred functioning. Finally, organisation development is an emerging profession that provides alternative opportunities for gaining competence and developing a career. The stressful nature of helping professions, however, suggests that OD practitioners must cope with the possibility of professional burnout.

As in other helping professions, values and ethics play an important role in guiding OD practice and minimising the possibility of clients being neglected or abused.

Who is the organisation development practitioner?

Throughout this text, the term 'organisation development (OD) practitioner' refers to at least three kinds of people. The most obvious group of OD practitioners consists of those people who specialise in OD as a profession. They may be internal or external consultants who offer professional services to organisation clients, including top managers, functional department heads and staff groups. OD professionals have traditionally shared a common set of humanistic values, promoting open communications, employee involvement and personal growth and development. They tend to have common training, skills and experience in the social processes of organisations (e.g. group dynamics, decision making and communications). In recent years, OD professionals have expanded those traditional values and expertise to include more concern for organisational effectiveness, competitiveness and bottom-line results, and greater attention to the technical, structural and strategic parts of organisations. This expansion is mainly in response to the highly competitive demands that face modern organisations. It has resulted in a more diverse set of OD professionals geared to helping organisations cope with those pressures.[1]

Second, the term 'OD practitioner' applies to people who specialise in fields related to OD, such as reward systems, organisation design, total quality management, information technology or business strategy. These content-oriented fields are increasingly becoming integrated with OD's process orientation, particularly as OD projects have become more comprehensive, involving multiple features and varying parts of organisations. A growing number of professionals in these related fields are gaining experience and competence in OD, mainly through working with OD professionals on large-scale projects and through attending OD training sessions. For example, Australia's 'Big 5' accounting firms have diversified into management consulting and change management. In most cases, these related professionals do not fully subscribe to traditional OD values, nor do they have extensive training and experience in OD. Rather, they have formal training and experience in their respective specialities, such as industrial relations, management consulting, control systems, health care and work design. They are OD practitioners in the sense that they apply their special competence within an OD-like process, typically by having OD professionals and managers help to design and implement change programmes. They also practise OD when they apply their OD competence to their own specialties, thus diffusing an OD perspective into such areas as compensation practices, work design, labour relations and planning and strategy.

Third, the term 'OD practitioner' applies to the increasing number of managers and administrators who have gained competence in OD and who apply it to their own work areas. Various reviewers of change management argue that OD applied by managers, rather than OD professionals, has grown rapidly.[2] It has been suggested that the faster pace of change affecting organisations today is highlighting the centrality of the manager in managing change. Consequently, OD must become a general management skill. Along these lines, the Centre for Corporate Change at the Australian Graduate School of Management has studied a number of firms such as the NSW State Library and Woolworths, where managers and employees have become 'change masters'.[3] They have gained the expertise to introduce change and innovation into the organisation.

Managers tend to gain competence in OD by interacting with OD professionals in actual change programmes. This on-the-job training is frequently supplemented with more formal OD training, such as the variety of OD workshops offered by the Australian Institute of Management (AIM), Institute of Engineers (IE), Australian Production and Inventory Control Society (APICS) and others. Line managers are increasingly attending such external programmes. Moreover, a growing number of organisations, including Ernst and Young and Ericcson, have instituted in-house training programmes for managers to learn how to develop and change their work units. As managers gain OD competence, they become its most basic practitioners.

In practice, the distinction between the three kinds of OD practitioners is becoming blurred. A growing number of managers have moved, either temporarily or permanently, into the OD profession. For example, companies such as Budget trained and rotated managers into full-time OD roles so that they could gain the skills and experience necessary for higher-level management positions. Also, it is increasingly common to find managers (e.g. David Mallen from MCS Management Consultants and Ann Boland, an Independent Consultant and Psychologist, formerly from Ernst and Young) using their experience in OD to become external consultants, particularly in the employee involvement area. More OD practitioners are gaining professional competence in related specialties, such as business process re-engineering, reward systems, and career planning and development. Conversely, many specialists in these related areas are achieving professional competence in OD. Cross-training and integration are producing a more comprehensive and complex kind of OD practitioner, who has a greater diversity of values, skills and experience than does the traditional OD practitioner.

Skills and knowledge of an effective organisation development practitioner

Much of the literature about the skills and knowledge of an effective OD practitioner claims that a mixture of personality traits, experiences, kinds of knowledge and skills can be assumed to lead to effective practice. For example, research on the characteristics of successful change practitioners yields the following list of attributes and abilities: diagnostic ability, basic knowledge of behavioural science techniques, empathy, knowledge of the theories and methods within the consultant's own discipline, goal-setting ability, problem-solving ability, ability to do self-assessment, the ability to see things objectively, imagination, flexibility, honesty, consistency and trust.[4] Although these qualities and skills are certainly laudable, there has been relatively little consensus about their importance in effective OD practice.

Many consulting styles or approaches have been suggested, but each style usually varies according to its underlying character—shaped by the kinds of skills and techniques that the consultants use, the values they bring to their clients and the manner in which they carry out their assignments. Other research also examines the degree of emphasis that the consultant places upon two inter-related goals or dimensions of the change process. Application 3.1 describes a classification that involves the consultant's orientation to the two inter-related dimensions:

1 the degree of emphasis upon effectiveness or goal accomplishment
2 the degree of emphasis upon relationships, morale and participant satisfaction.[5]

APPLICATION 3.1   Consultant styles matrix

Based upon two dimensions, an emphasis on morale and an emphasis on effectiveness, five different types of consultant styles or roles may be identified.
The stabiliser style: The goal of the stabiliser style consultant is neither effectiveness nor participant satisfaction. Rather, the consultant is trying to refrain from rocking the boat, and to maintain a low profile. The underlying motivation is often survival, or merely following the directives of top management. Such a role is usually found in large organisations where development

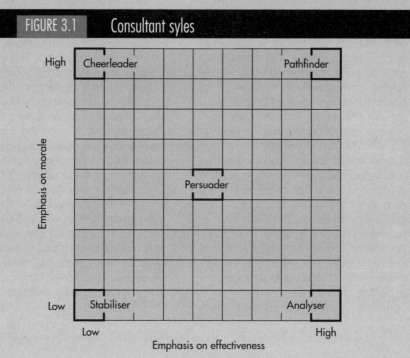

FIGURE 3.1   Consultant syles

programmes may be part of the staff function and are not highly regarded by top management. This style is usually regarded as having been forced upon the individual by organisation pressures, so that the individual has learned to conform and suppress internal motivations.

The cheerleader style: The cheerleader style places an emphasis on the satisfaction of organisation members and is chiefly concerned with employee motivation and morale. The cheerleader seeks warm working relationships and in general is more comfortable in non-confrontational situations. Effectiveness *per se* is not emphasised, the assumption being that if member satisfaction is high, effectiveness will also be high. Unfortunately, there is a great deal of evidence that contradicts this assumption. The cheerleader strongly pushes for improved morale, and open conflict or locking horns is avoided by attempts to smooth over differences and maintain harmony.

The analyser style: The analyser style places the greatest emphasis on efficiency with little emphasis being given to member satisfaction. The analyser feels most comfortable with a rational assessment of problems and assumes that the facts will lead to a solution. This type of consultant may be quite confrontational, usually relying on authority to resolve conflict, and on rational problem-solving processes. The analyser has a background of specialised expertise, knowledge and experience applicable to the solution of specific problems. The client needs to have a problem solved, a service performed or a study made; the analyser consultant takes responsibility for providing these functions. This type of consultant is based on the belief that the client does not need to know, or cannot learn the skills to solve its problems. The success of the consultant is largely dependent on the client having properly diagnosed its problem and having called in the right kind of consultant.

The persuader style: The persuader style focuses on both dimensions, effectiveness and morale, yet optimises neither. Such a style provides a relatively low-risk strategy, yet avoids direct confrontation with other forces. This approach may be used when the consultant's power or leverage is low relative to other participants. This style is motivated primarily by a desire to satisfy, i.e. to achieve something that is 'good enough'. A great deal of effort is applied in attempting to satisfy the differing forces, thus gaining a majority block of support for prepared changes. The resulting change programme may often be watered down or weakened to the point where organisation improvement is unlikely.

The pathfinder style: The pathfinder style seeks both a high degree of effectiveness and a high degree of member satisfaction, believing that greater effectiveness is possible when all members are involved and problem solving is done through teamwork. There is an awareness that confrontation and conflict are often a means to a more effective organisation and to more satisfied individual members. The pathfinder approach uses collaborative problem solving and challenges the underlying patterns of member behaviour.

Most organisation problems are complex situations and may not be neatly solved by any one particular change, but will depend upon the particular consultant, the nature of the problem and the type of organisation climate that exists. The styles are not mutually exclusive. All consultant styles can be effective and are inter-related. A consultant may use different styles at different times to meet changing client system needs and deal with diverse situations. Frequently, some combination of the types may be applied.

TABLE 3.1	Core and advanced skills for the future OD practitioner

General consultation skills
Organizational diagnosis
Designing and executing an intervention
Process consultation
Entry and contracting
Interviewing
Designing and managing large change processes
*Management development
*Assessment of individual competence

Intrapersonal skills
Conceptual and analytical ability
Integrity (educated moral judgment)
Personal centering (staying in touch with one's own purpose and values)
Active learning skills
Rational-emotive balance
Personal stress management skills (maintaining one's own health and security)
*Entrepreneurial skills

Organization behavior/organization development knowledge and intervention skills
Group dynamics (team building)
Organization development theory
Organization theory
Organization design
Communication
Intergroup dynamics
Open systems
Reward systems
Conflict
Large-system change theory
Leadership
Power
Motivation
Theories of learning
Sociotechnical analysis
Job design
*Adult development/career and stress management
*Personality theory (individual differences)
*Transorganization theory
*Cross-cultural theory

Interpersonal skills
Listening
Establishing trust and rapport
Giving and receiving feedback
Aptitude in speaking the client's language
Ability to model credible behaviours
Counseling and coaching
Negotiation skills

*Languages and nonverbal cross-cultural skills
*Telephone intervention skills
*Communication theory-based skill, such as T.A., neuro-linguistic programming, etc.
*Suggestion skills (metaphors and hypnosis)

Research and evaluation knowledge and skills/research design
Action research
Diagnostic research
Evaluation research
*Theory-building research
*Case method research and writing methods

Data collection
Research interviewing
Participant-observation methods (from anthropology)
Questionnaire design and use
*Unobtrusive measures
*Job measurement

Data analysis
Elementary statistics
*Computer skills
*Advanced statistics

Presentation skills
Training skills
Public speaking and lecturing
Political influence and selling skills
Writing proposals and reports
*Graphic and audiovisual skills

Experience as a line manager/major management knowledge areas
Human resource management
Management policy and strategy
*Information systems
*Legal and social environment
*Quantitative methods
*Production (operations management)
*Finance
*Operation research
*Economics
*Marketing
*International business
*Accounting

Collateral knowledge areas
Social psychology
*Industrial psychology
*Cultural anthropology
*Policy analysis
*Psychopathology and therapy
*Systems engineering and analysis
*Manufacturing research and development

*Indicates advanced skills

Source: Reproduced by permission of the publisher from K. Shepard and A. Raia, 'The OD training challenge', *Training and Development Journal* 35 (April 1981): 93. Copyright April, 1981, Training and Development, American Society for Training and Development. All rights reserved.

The experts' opinions about the importance of different skills and knowledge for an effective OD practitioner appear in Table 3.1. It lists 84 items for the future OD practitioner: 50 core skills that all OD practitioners should possess and 34 advanced skills that are ideal or desirable for the mature OD practitioner. The skills and knowledge are arranged in order of importance, with general consultation skills scoring highest and collateral knowledge areas scoring lowest. Within each category, the individual items are also ranked in order of importance.

The information in Table 3.1 applies primarily to people who specialise in OD as a profession. For those people, the list of skills and knowledge seems reasonable, especially in the light of the growing diversity and complexity of interventions in OD. Gaining competence in those areas may take considerable time and effort, and it is questionable whether the other two types of OD practitioners—managers and specialists in related fields—also need this full range of skills and knowledge. It seems more reasonable to suggest that some sub-set of the items listed in Table 3.1 should apply to all OD practitioners, whether they are OD professionals, managers or related specialists. These items would constitute the basic skills and knowledge of an OD practitioner. Beyond this background, the three types of OD practitioners would probably differ in areas of concentration. OD professionals would extend their breadth of skills across the remaining categories in Table 3.1; managers would focus on the major management knowledge areas; and related specialists would concentrate on skills in their respective areas, such as those included in the major management and collateral knowledge areas.

Based on the data in Table 3.1, as well as on more recent studies of OD skills,[6] all OD practitioners should have the following basic skills and knowledge if they are to be effective:

1 *Intrapersonal skills:* Despite the growing knowledge base and sophistication of the field, organisation development is still a human craft. The practitioner is the primary instrument of diagnosis and change. The core intra-personal skills listed in Table 3.1 can help practitioners to be effective in the service of planned change. Practitioners must often process complex, ambiguous information and make informed judgments about its relevance to organisational issues. This requires considerable conceptual and analytical ability.

   They must also have the personal centring to know their own values, feelings and purposes and the integrity to behave responsibly in a helping relationship with others. Bob Tannenbaum, one of the founders of OD, argues that self-knowledge is the most central ingredient in OD practice and suggests that practitioners are becoming too enamoured with skills and techniques.[7] Some recent data support his view. A study of 416 OD practitioners found that 47% agreed with the statement: 'Many of the new entrants into the field have little understanding of or appreciation for the history or values underlying the field'.[8] Because OD is a highly uncertain process that requires constant adjustment and innovation, practitioners need to have active learning skills and a reasonable balance between their rational and emotional sides. Finally, OD practice can be highly stressful and can lead to early burnout, so practitioners need to know how to manage their own stress.

2 *Interpersonal skills:* Practitioners must create and maintain effective relationships with individuals and groups within the organisation to help them gain the competence necessary to solve their own problems. The core inter-personal skills listed in Table 3.1 promote effective helping relationships. Such relationships start with a grasp of the organisation's perspective and require listening to members' perceptions and feelings in order to understand how they see themselves and the organisation or department. This understanding provides a starting point for joint diagnosis and problem solving. Practitioners must establish trust and rapport with organisation members so that they can share pertinent information and work effectively together. This requires being able to converse in the members' own language and to exchange feedback about how the relationship is progressing.

   To help members learn new skills and behaviours, practitioners must serve as concrete role models of what is expected. They must act in ways that are credible to organisation members and provide them with the counselling and coaching necessary for development and change. Because the helping relationship is jointly determined, practitioners need to be able to negotiate an acceptable role and to manage changing expectations and demands.

3   *General consultation skills:* All OD practitioners should have the first two of the general consultation skills listed in Table 3.1: organisational diagnosis and designing and executing an intervention. OD starts with diagnosing an organisation or department to understand the causes of its problems and to discover areas for further development. OD practitioners need to know how to carry out an effective diagnosis, at least at a rudimentary level. They should know how to engage organisation members in diagnosis, how to help them ask the right questions and how to collect and analyse information. A manager, for example, should be able to work with subordinates to jointly find out how the organisation or department is functioning. The manager should know basic diagnostic questions (see Chapters 5 and 6), some methods for gathering information, such as interviews or surveys and some techniques for analysing it, such as force-field analysis or statistical means and distributions (see Chapters 7 and 8).

In addition to diagnosis, OD practitioners should know how to design and execute an intervention. They need to be able to lay out an action plan and to gain commitment to the programme. They also need to know how to tailor the intervention to the situation, using information about how the change is progressing in order to guide implementation (see Chapter 11). For example, managers should be able to develop action steps for an intervention with subordinates. They should be able to gain their commitment to the programme (usually through participation), sit down with them and assess how it is progressing, and make modifications if necessary.

4   *Organisation development theory:* The final basic tool that OD practitioners should have is a general knowledge of OD, as presented in this book. They should have some appreciation for planned change, the action research model and contemporary approaches to managing change. They should have some familiarity with the range of available interventions and the need for assessing and institutionalising change programmes. Perhaps most important is that OD practitioners should understand their own role in the emerging field of organisation development, whether as managers, OD professionals or specialists in related areas.

The professional organisation development practitioner

Most of the literature about OD practitioners has focused on people specialising in OD as a profession. In this section, we discuss the role and typical career paths of OD professionals.

The role of organisation development professionals

Position

Organisation development professionals have positions that are either internal or external to the organisation. *Internal consultants* are members of the organisation, and are usually located in the Human Resources department. They may perform the OD role exclusively, or they may combine it with other tasks, such as compensation practices, training or labour relations.[9] Many large organisations, such as Mayne Nickless, have created specialised OD consulting groups. Their internal consultants typically have a variety of clients within the organisation, serving both line and staff departments.

Internal consultants have certain advantages because they are insiders. They can typically save time identifying and understanding organisational problems as they have intimate knowledge of the organisation and its dynamics. They know the organisation's culture, informal practices and sources of power. They have access to a variety of information, including rumours, company reports and direct observations. Internal consultants are also usually accepted more quickly by organisation members. They are more familiar and less threatening to members than outsiders and so can more readily establish rapport and trust.

The major disadvantages of internal consultants include a possible loss of objectivity because of their strong ties to the organisation. These links may also make them overly cautious, particularly when powerful others can affect their careers. Internal consultants may also lack certain skills and experience in facilitating organisational change, and they may not have the clout that is often associated with external experts.

External consultants are not members of the client organisation; they typically work for a consulting firm, a university or themselves. Organisations generally hire external consultants to provide a particular expertise that is unavailable internally, and to bring a different and potentially more objective perspective into the organisation development process. External consultants also have the advantage of being able to probe difficult issues and to question the *status quo*, particularly when they are not overly dependent on one client.[10] They are often afforded some deference and power because of their perceived expertise and objectivity, and they can use this influence to mobilise resources for change.

Application 3.2 gives the view of Doug Marsh, Chairman of a New Zealand-based company, who is also a director and business adviser.

APPLICATION 3.2

Personal view of an external consultant

The wonderful thing about entering the new millennium is the exciting prospect of sharing with inspired managers the very notion of creating or reinventing the enduring great company.

There is also the opportunity for partnering executives who have learned that the enduring great companies of the twenty-first century will probably be those that need to have radically different structures, strategies, practices and attitudes towards change than those in the twentieth century.

The world's most successful visionary companies are those that distinguish core values and purpose (which should never change) from operating practices, business strategies and tactical actions, which should be constantly scrutinised and reinvented/adapted in response to a rapidly changing world.

There needs to be a philosophy of preserving the core while simultaneously stimulating progress and 'change'.

The reality is, however, that there are companies that do not have clearly-defined core ideology (purpose and values) and who are uncertain as to who they are, what they stand for and why they exist.

The question is not necessarily 'how should we change', but rather 'what do we stand for and why do we exist'.

The external consultant in the context of organisation development is not so much concerned with 'what', but rather with the process. Creating alignment between organisation outcomes, management attitude and staff aspirations, as well as ideology and strategy, is fundamental for successfully transforming any organisation, and a challenge for many consultants to boards and management.

Consultants to management now recognise that corporate bonding, collegiality (glue) is becoming ideological, more than at any time in the past. Employees are demanding operating autonomy, while also demanding a sense of purpose, involvement and the knowledge that the organisation stands for something.

Misalignments come in many forms. There are those that promote behaviour and possible outcomes that are inconsistent with core ideology. There are often attitudinal misalignments—between the board and stakeholders, management and staff—giving lip service to creating 'change' (dictatorial power) over, instead of empowerment and power, with.

External consultants deploy best practice models, analytical and creative processes as well as the genius of 'not necessarily either/or; but both', leading to the reinvention of mechanisms, processes and strategies that bring core values and purpose to life. They represent a catalyst for change toward the envisioned future.

Like the eye of the General, external consultants must concentrate on identifying the misalignments, impediments and cancer cells that need to be obliterated from inside the organisation if they are to preserve the core and inclusively stimulate progress.

Contributor: Doug. G. Marsh FNZIM (Life), New Zealand-based company chairman, director and and business adviser.

A major disadvantage of external consultants is the extra time that it takes them to enter the organisation and gain a working knowledge of it. Organisation members may be wary of outsiders, and may not trust them enough to give them pertinent information. External consultants may also be viewed negatively because they are seen as having relatively little invested in the organisation and the outcomes of change efforts. Organisation members may believe that, should problems arise, external consultants can simply walk away with little negative consequence to themselves.

A promising approach to having the advantages of both internal and external OD consultants is to include them both as members of an *internal–external consulting team*.[11] External consultants can combine their special expertise and objectivity with the inside knowledge and acceptance of internal consultants. The two parties can provide complementary consulting skills, while sharing the workload and possibly accomplishing more than either would by operating alone. Internal consultants, for example, can provide almost continuous contact with the client, while their external counterparts can periodically provide specialised services, perhaps on two or three days each month. External consultants can also help train their organisation partners, thus transferring OD skills and knowledge to the organisation.

Although little has been written on internal–external consulting teams, recent studies suggest that the effectiveness of such teams depends on the members developing strong, supportive, collegial relationships. They need to take time to develop the consulting team, confronting individual differences and establishing appropriate roles and exchanges. Members need to provide each other with continuous feedback and to make a commitment to learning from each other. In the absence of these team-building and learning features, internal–external consulting teams can be more troublesome and less effective than consultants working alone.

Application 3.3 provides personal accounts of the internal and external consulting positions, as well as interactions between them.[12]

Marginality

A promising line of research on the professional OD role centres on the issue of marginality.[13] The *marginal person* is one who successfully straddles the boundary between two or more groups that have differing goals, value systems and behaviour patterns. In the past, the marginal role has always been seen as dysfunctional. Now marginality is seen in a more positive light; there are many examples of marginal roles in organisations: the salesperson, the buyer, the first-line supervisor, the integrator and the project manager.

Evidence is mounting that some people are better at taking marginal roles than others. Those who are good at marginal roles seem to have personal qualities of low dogmatism, neutrality, open-mindedness, objectivity, flexibility and adaptable information-processing ability. Rather than being upset by conflict, ambiguity and stress, they thrive on it.

The internal consultant's view

An instrument of change—that's what I am. I live in the organisation, trying to work with two levels of concern at the same time: those on the surface and those that lurk just below.

I try to use my mind and body to sense the existing data, to diagnose problems and to develop strategies for change. I absorb all that I encounter: the excitement of a new project, the struggle to get it started and the reactions of the organisation. Some reactions are positive, many are not. The fear, anger and frustration are around, even if they aren't directed toward me.

Of course I understand these reactions. They mean that change is occurring. The system is unfreezing. I'm patient, working with the process, helping it along, working through the stuck places, working with people who are critical of the project's success, working with groups to help them adapt, etc., etc.

Sometimes my body aches and I feel depressed. I know how to take care of myself—deep breathing, meditation and exercise. Gradually, I become adept at analysing the situation, building models to explain behaviour and learning to cope personally. But still the emotions of others regarding the changes bombard me. I seal my body off fairly well. I don't feel as much, or as intensely, as before, but I still feel. On the other hand, I sometimes get so excited about all the possibilities, the risks I see people taking, their commitment to a difficult change effort—the adrenaline flows and I feel fulfilled.

I feel isolated, even from my staff. But that's what an internal feels—never quite in or like anyone else in the organisation, a little apart but still showing loyalty and commitment. But I know how to manage. You call on your friendly external consultant. Over the years, I have called on many of them. I needed them for training events, team building, design work, strategising, etc.

However, underneath each piece of work, I needed them for professional and personal support. I educated each of them about my organisation and its idiosyncrasies. The smart ones listened, did the job they were hired to do and in some way managed to meet my unspoken request for support. Through them, I learned the valuable lessons necessary for developing an effective external–internal consulting team. Eventually, I even learned to ask for personal support directly, not always couched in terms such as 'what is good for the organisation?'

The external consultant's view

I am also an agent of change. I spend most of my time helping internal consultants and managers initiate and manage changes that they have stimulated. In that process I too am the recipient of others' feelings. Fortunately, most of these feelings are positive. I am appreciated for my assistance, applauded for my knowledge, and liked for my interpersonal skills. Finally, I am rewarded handsomely for my time and effort. Thus, for the most part, I feel pleased and rewarded for my work as a consultant.

In my role, I may leave an organisation while the time-consuming and important work of nursing a change along is being done. So, while I experience the risk and excitement at the beginning of a change, I do not always experience the difficult day-to-day maintenance that the internal person experiences. When I tire of a particular person or project (or they tire of me), I have several others to provide my emotional and financial sustenance. However, there are still times when I feel exhausted. The work has taken its toll and no amount of positive support takes away the weariness. I rest, play tennis and practise better health habits—aware that in a few days I will be working with another client on another problem.

I get asked by clients to perform a wide variety of tasks, ranging from being a content expert to listening to them as might a therapist. However, regardless of the request, I am usually aware of an unspoken need on the part of the internal consultant to have me support his or her project, position or person. When the request is to support a project, it is usually clear. When the request is to support a position, it is less clear but often shown by the selection of me as the consultant. However, when the request is to support the individual personally, the request is almost never overt.

Often comments such as 'You seem very concerned about this situation' or 'You must feel pretty unsupported right now' go unanswered. Perhaps the relationship isn't at a point where we can discuss personal needs. Maybe that wouldn't be professional. Perhaps we are still maintaining 'face' for each other.

Individuals with marginal orientations are more likely than others to develop integrative decisions that bring together and reconcile viewpoints between opposing organisational groups, and are more likely to remain neutral in controversial situations. Thus, the research suggests that the marginal role can have positive effects when it is filled by a person with a marginal orientation. Such a person can be more objective and better able to perform successfully in linking, integrative or conflict-laden roles.[14]

A study of 89 external OD practitioners and 246 internal practitioners (response rates of 59% and 54%, respectively) showed that external OD professionals were more comfortable with the marginal role than were internal OD professionals. Internal consultants with more years of experience were more marginally oriented than were those with less experience.[15] These findings, combined with other research on marginal roles, suggest the importance of maintaining the OD professional's marginality, with its flexibility, independence and boundary-spanning characteristics.

Use of knowledge and experience

The professional OD role has been described in terms of a continuum ranging from client-centred (using the client's knowledge and experience) to consultant-centred (using the consultant's knowledge and experience), as shown in Figure 3.2. Traditionally, OD consultants have worked at the client-centred end of the continuum. OD professionals, relying mainly on sensitivity training, process consultation and team building (see Chapter 12), have been expected to remain neutral, refusing to offer expert advice on organisational problems. Rather than contracting to solve specific problems, the consultant has tended to work with organisation members to identify problems and potential solutions, to help them study what they are doing now and to consider alternative behaviours and solutions, and to help them discover whether in fact the consultant and they can learn to do things better. In doing this, the OD professional has generally listened and reflected upon members' perceptions and ideas and helped to clarify and interpret their communications and behaviours.

With the recent proliferation of OD interventions in the structural, human resource management and strategy areas, this limited definition of the professional OD role has expanded to include the consultant-centred end of the continuum. In many of these newer approaches, the consultant may have to take on a modified role of expert, with the consent and collaboration of organisation members. For example, if a consultant and managers were to try to bring about a major structural redesign (see Chapter 14), managers may not have the appropriate knowledge and expertise to create and manage the change. The consultant's role might be to present the basic concepts and ideas and then to struggle jointly with the managers to select an approach that might be useful to the organisation

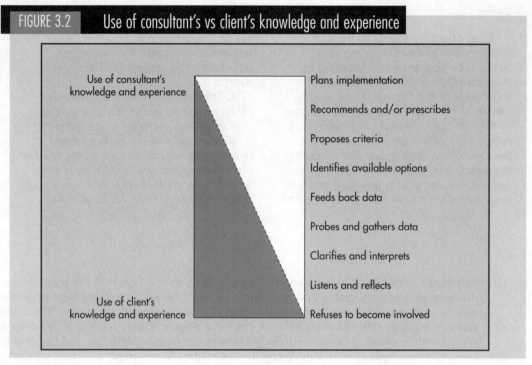

FIGURE 3.2 Use of consultant's vs client's knowledge and experience

Source: Adapted by permission of the authors from W. Schmidt and A. Johnson, 'A continuum of consultancy styles' (Unpublished manuscript, July 1970), p. 1.

and decide how it might be best implemented. In this situation, the OD professional recommends or prescribes particular changes and is active in planning how to implement them. However, this expertise is always shared rather than imposed.

With the development of new and varied intervention approaches, the role of the OD professional needs to be seen as falling along the entire continuum from client-centred to consultant-centred. At times, the consultant will rely mainly on organisation members' knowledge and experiences to identify and solve problems. At other times, it may be more appropriate for the OD professional to take on the role of expert, withdrawing from this role as managers gain more knowledge and experience.

Careers of organisation development professionals

Unlike such occupations as medicine and law, OD is an emerging practice. It is still developing the characteristics of an established profession: a common body of knowledge, educational requirements, accrediting procedures, a recognised code of ethics and rules and methods for governing conduct. This means that people can enter professional OD careers from a variety of educational and work backgrounds. They do not have to follow an established career path, but rather have some choice about when to enter or leave an OD career and whether to be an internal or external consultant.[16]

Despite the looseness or flexibility of the OD profession, most OD professionals have had specific training in OD. This training can include relatively short courses (one day to two weeks), programmes or workshops conducted within organisations or at outside institutions, such as TAFE's 'Train the Trainer' programmes. OD training can also be more formal and lengthy, including master's programmes (for example, Swinburne University of Technology's Master of Organisation Dynamics) and doctoral training.

As might be expected, career choices widen as people gain training and experience in OD. Those with rudimentary training tend to be internal consultants, often taking on OD roles as temporary assignments on the way to higher managerial or staff positions. Holders of master's degrees are generally evenly split between internal and external consultants. Those with doctorates may join a university faculty and consult part-time, join a consulting firm or seek a position as a relatively high-level internal consultant.

External consultants tend to be older, to have more managerial experience, and to spend more of their time in OD than do internal practitioners. Perhaps the most common career path is to begin as an internal consultant, gain experience and visibility through successful interventions or publishing and then become an external consultant. A field study found that internal consultants acquired greater competence by working with external consultants who deliberately helped to develop them. This development took place through a tutorial arrangement of joint diagnosis and intervention in the organisation, which gave the internal consultants a chance to observe and learn from the model furnished by the external consultants.[17]

There is increasing evidence that an OD career can be stressful, sometimes leading to burnout.[18] Burnout comes from taking on too many jobs, becoming over-committed, and, in general, working too hard. OD work often requires six-day weeks, with some days running up to 14 hours. Consultants may spend a week working with one organisation or department and then spend the weekend preparing for the next client. They may spend 50–75% of their time on the road, living in planes, cars, hotels, meetings and restaurants. Indeed, one practitioner has suggested that the majority of OD consultants would repeat the phrase 'quality of work life for consultants' as follows: 'Quality of work life? For consultants?'[19]

Organisation development professionals are increasingly taking steps to cope with burnout. They may shift jobs, moving from external to internal roles to avoid travel. They may learn to pace themselves better and to avoid taking on too much work. Many are engaging in fitness and health programmes and are using stress-management techniques, such as those described in Chapter 18.

Professional values

Values have played an important role in OD from its beginning. Traditionally, OD professionals have promoted a set of humanistic and democratic values. They have sought to build trust and collaboration; to create an open, problem-solving climate; and to increase the self-control of organisation members. More recently, OD practitioners have extended those humanistic values to include a concern for improving organisational effectiveness (e.g. to increase productivity or to reduce turnover) and performance (e.g. to increase profitability). They have shown an increasing desire to optimise both human benefits and production objectives.[20]

The joint values of humanising organisations and improving their effectiveness have received widespread support in the OD profession, as well as increasing encouragement from managers, employees and union officials. Indeed, it would be difficult not to support these joint concerns. But, increasingly, questions have been raised about the possibility of simultaneously pursuing greater humanism and organisational effectiveness.[21] More practitioners are experiencing situations in which there is conflict between the employees' needs for greater meaning and the organisation's need for more effective and efficient use of its resources. For example, expensive capital equipment may run most efficiently if it is highly programmed and routinised; yet people may not derive satisfaction from working with such technology. Should efficiency be maximised at the expense of people's satisfaction? Can technology be changed to make it more humanly satisfying yet remain efficient? What compromises are possible? These are the value dilemmas often faced when trying to optimise both human benefits and organisational effectiveness.

In addition to value issues within organisations, OD practitioners are dealing more and more with value conflicts with powerful outside groups. Organisations are open systems and exist within increasingly turbulent environments. For example, hospitals are facing complex and changing task environments. Australia has long had privately-owned hospitals and now public hospitals are being offered to private operators. This means a proliferation of external stakeholders with interests in the organisation's functioning, including patients, suppliers, health insurance funds, employers, the government, shareholders, unions, the press and various interest groups. These external groups often have different and competing values for judging the organisation's effectiveness. For example, shareholders may judge the firm in terms of price per share, the government in terms of compliance with equal employment opportunity legislation, patients in terms of quality of care, and ecology groups in terms of hazardous waste disposal. Because organisations must rely on these external groups for resources and legitimacy, they cannot simply ignore these competing values. They must somehow respond to them and try to reconcile the different interests.

Recent attempts to help firms manage external relationships suggest the need for new interventions and competence in OD.[22] Practitioners must not only have social skills like those proposed in Table 3.1, but also political skills. They must understand the distribution of power, conflicts of interest and value dilemmas inherent in managing external relationships and be able to manage their own role and values in respect to those dynamics. Interventions promoting collaboration and system maintenance may be ineffective in this larger arena, especially when there are power and dominance relationships between organisations, and competition for scarce resources. Under these conditions, OD practitioners may need more power-oriented interventions, such as bargaining, coalition forming and pressure tactics.

For example, firms in the tobacco industry have waged an aggressive campaign against efforts of groups such as the Australian Medical Association, the Royal Australasian College of General Practitioners, the Australian Cancer Society and the Federal and State Governments, to limit or ban the smoking of tobacco products. They have formed a powerful industry coalition to lobby against anti-smoking legislation; they have spent enormous sums of money sponsoring leading sporting and culture events, conducting public relations and refuting research that purportedly show the dangers of smoking. These power-oriented strategies are intended to manage an increasingly hostile environment. They may be necessary for the industry's survival. People practising OD in such settings may need to help organisations implement such strategies if they are to manage their environments effectively. This will require political skills and greater attention to how the OD practitioner's own values fit with those of the organisation.

Professional ethics

Ethical issues in OD are concerned with how practitioners perform their helping relationship with organisation members. Inherent in any helping relationship is the potential for misconduct and client abuse. OD practitioners can let personal values stand in the way of good practice; they can use the power inherent in their professional role to abuse organisation members (often unintentionally).

Ethical guidelines

To its credit, the field of OD has always shown concern for the ethical conduct of its practitioners. There have been several articles and conferences about ethics in OD. The School of Management and the Australian Business Ethics Network at RMIT and the St James Ethics Centre conducted a successful one-day symposium on teaching and training in business ethics.[23] In addition, statements of ethics governing OD practice have been sponsored by many professional associations, e.g. the Australian Association for Professional and Applied Ethics (AAPAE) is comprised of academics and professionals across a range of disciplines in a non-partisan and non-profit association, while Corporate Ethics is committed to helping business develop a strategic system that incorporates value and ethics.[24] The accounting industry is just one of many professions that has codes of ethics: the Code of Professional Conduct (the Australian Society of Certified Practising Accountants—ASCPA) and the Rules of Ethical Conduct (the Institute of Chartered Accountants in Australia—ICAA)[25] The ethical guidelines issued by these associations appear in the appendix to this chapter.

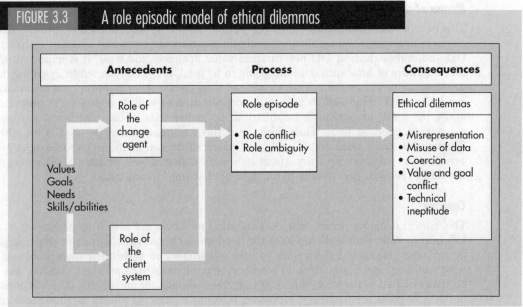

FIGURE 3.3   A role episodic model of ethical dilemmas

Source: L. White and M. Rhodeback, 'Ethical dilemmas in organization development: a cross-cultural analysis,' Figure 1 *Journal of Business Ethics* 11 (1992): 663–70. With kind permission from Kluwer Academic Publishers.

Ethical dilemmas

Although adherence to statements of ethics helps prevent ethical problems from occurring, OD practitioners can still encounter ethical dilemmas. Figure 3.3 is a process model that explains how ethical dilemmas can occur in OD. The antecedent conditions include an OD practitioner and a client system with different goals, values, needs, skills and abilities. During the entry and contracting phase, these differences may or may not be addressed and clarified. If the contracting process is incomplete, the subsequent intervention process or role episode is subject to role conflict and role ambiguity. Neither the client nor the OD practitioner is clear about their respective responsibilities. Each is pursuing different goals, and each party is using different skills and values to achieve those goals. The role conflict and ambiguity can lead to five types of ethical dilemmas: (1) misrepresentation, (2) misuse of data, (3) coercion, (4) value and goal conflict and (5) technical ineptitude.

Misrepresentation

This occurs when OD practitioners claim that an intervention will produce results that are unreasonable for the change programme or the situation. The client can contribute to this problem by portraying inaccurate goals and needs. In either case, one or both parties is operating under false pretences and an ethical dilemma exists. For example, in an infamous case called 'The undercover change agent,' an attempt was made to use laboratory training in an organisation whose top management did not understand it and was not ready for it. The OD consultant sold 'T-groups' as the intervention that would solve the problems that faced the organisation. After the chairman of the firm made a surprise visit to the site where the training was being held, the consultant was fired. The nature and style of the T-group was in direct contradiction to the chairman's concepts about leadership.[26] Misrepresentation is likely to occur in the entering and contracting phases of planned change when the initial consulting relationship is being established. To prevent misrepresentation, OD practitioners need to be very clear about the goals of the change effort and to explore openly with the client its expected effects, its relevance to the client system and the practitioner's competence in executing the intervention.

Misuse of data

This occurs when information gathered during the OD process is used punitively. Large amounts of information are invariably obtained during the entry and diagnostic phases of OD and, although most OD practitioners value openness and trust, it is important that they be aware of how such data are going to be used. It is a human tendency to use data to enhance a power position. Openness is one thing, but leaking inappropriate information can be harmful to individuals and to the organisation as well. It is easy for a consultant, under the guise of obtaining information, to gather data about whether a particular manager is good or bad. When, how or if this information can be used is an ethical dilemma not easily resolved. To minimise misuse of data, practitioners should agree with organisation members up front about how data collected will be used. This agreement should be reviewed periodically in the light of changing circumstances.

Coercion

This ethical dilemma occurs when organisation members are forced to participate in an OD intervention. People should have the freedom to choose whether or not to participate in a change programme if they are to gain self-reliance to solve their own problems. In team building, for example, team members should have the option of deciding not to become involved in the intervention. Management should not unilaterally decide that team building is good for members. However, freedom to make a choice implies knowledge about OD. Many organisation members have little information about OD interventions, what they involve and the nature and consequences of becoming involved with them. This makes it imperative for OD practitioners to educate clients about interventions before choices are made as to whether or not to implement them.

Coercion can also pose ethical dilemmas for the helping relationship between OD practitioners and organisation members. Inherent in any helping relationship are possibilities for excessive manipulation and dependency, two facets of coercion. Kelman pointed out that behaviour change 'inevitably involves some degree of manipulation and control, and at least an implicit imposition of the change agent's values on the client or the person he [or she] is influencing'.[27] This places the practitioner on two horns of a dilemma: (1) any attempt to change is in itself a change and thereby a manipulation, no matter how slight, and (2) there exists no formula or method to structure a change situation so that such manipulation can be totally absent. To attack the first aspect of the dilemma, Kelman stressed freedom of choice, seeing any action that limits freedom of choice as being ethically ambiguous or worse. To address the second aspect, Kelman argued that the OD practitioner must remain keenly aware of her or his own value system and alert to the possibility that these values are being imposed upon a client. In other words, an effective way to resolve this dilemma is to make the change effort as open as possible, with the free consent and knowledge of the individuals involved.

The second facet of coercion that can pose ethical dilemmas for the helping relationship involves dependency. Helping relationships invariably create dependency between those who need help and those who provide it.[28] A major goal in OD is to lessen the clients' dependency on consultants by helping them gain the knowledge and skills to address organisational problems and manage change themselves. In some cases, however, achieving independence from OD practitioners can result in the clients being either counter-dependent or over-dependent, especially in the early stages of the relationship. To resolve dependency issues, consultants can openly and explicitly discuss with the client how to handle the dependency problem, especially what the client and consultant expect of one another. Another approach is to focus on problem finding. Usually, the client is looking for a solution to a perceived problem. The consultant can redirect the energy to improved joint diagnosis so that both are working on problem identification and problem solving. This moves the energy of the client away from dependency. Finally, dependency can be reduced by changing the client's expectation—from being helped or controlled by the practitioner— to focusing on the need to manage the problem. This helps to reinforce the concept that the consultant is working for the client and offering assistance at the client's discretion.

Value and goal conflict

This ethical dilemma occurs when the purpose of the change effort is not clear or when the client and the practitioner disagree over how to achieve the goals. The important practical issue for OD consultants is whether it is justifiable to unilaterally withhold services from an organisation that does not agree with their values or methods. G. Lippitt suggested that the real question is the following: Assuming that some kind of change is going to occur anyway, doesn't the consultant have a responsibility to try to guide the change in the most constructive fashion possible?[29] The question may be of greater importance and relevance to an internal consultant or to a consultant who already has an ongoing relationship with the client.

Argyris takes an even stronger stand, maintaining that the responsibilities of professional OD practitioners to clients are comparable to those of lawyers or doctors, who, in principle, are not permitted to refuse their services. He suggests that the very least the consultant can do is provide 'first aid' to the organisation as long as the assistance does not compromise the consultant's values. Argyris suggests that if the Ku Klux Klan were to ask for assistance and the consultant could at least determine that the KKK was genuinely interested in assessing itself and willing to commit itself to all that a valid assessment would entail concerning both itself and other groups, the consultant should be willing to help. If the Klan's objectives later prove to be less than honestly stated, the consultant would be free to withdraw without being compromised.[30]

Technical ineptitude

This final ethical dilemma occurs when OD practitioners attempt to implement interventions for which they are not skilled or when the client attempts a change for which it is not ready. Critical to the success of any OD programme is the selection of an appropriate intervention, which depends, in turn, on careful diagnosis of the organisation. Selection of an intervention is closely related to the practitioner's own values, skills and abilities. In solving organisational problems, many OD consultants tend to emphasise a favourite intervention or technique, such as team building, total quality management or self-managed teams. They let their own values and beliefs dictate the change method.[31] Technical ineptitude dilemmas can also occur when interventions do not align with the ability of the organisation to implement them. Again, careful diagnosis can reveal the extent to which the organisation is ready to make a change and possesses the skills and knowledge to implement it.

Application 3.4 presents an example of an ethical dilemma that arises frequently in 'change' situations.[32]

APPLICATION 3.4 — Former manager banks on new career

Without warning, Christian Van Deur started crying while out walking the dog one evening before his long career with the ANZ Bank ended in a nervous breakdown a year ago.

Mr Van Deur's bewilderment over what had occurred turned to acute embarrassment soon afterwards when he had the first of many crying fits at the bank branch he managed in Ringwood.

The 47-year-old Scoresby father of two says his breakdown was clearly a product of work-related stress, but at the time he hated to admit what was happening.

'You had to hide your feelings and look positive, in essence to live a lie, because if you showed any negativity it was just contagious,' Mr Van Deur said yesterday.

Mr Van Deur's job was one of about 40 000 cut in banking since 1991. Most of those retrenched have found work again, but the changes have, nevertheless, caused enormous turmoil.

Mr Van Deur said customer complaints grew as the bank centralised its branch services, and the pressure grew further with the new drive to sell financial services.

'Nine out of ten customers came in with a problem to be solved and the problem was usually caused by us. I just hated customer complaints. I hated not meeting their expectations,' he said.

'In the past, if there was a problem to be solved, you solved it quickly within the branch because that's where the staff were and the problem was caused.'

'Under the new system, where services were centralised, you never found the person that messed up. You just got told eventually that it would be sorted out and it wouldn't happen again. Yeah, right.'

As more was demanded of him, Mr Van Deur said his working week stretched to 60 hours, but still his anxieties about performance grew. 'You take it very personally when you have had a very good banking career with good reports and good promotions over the years,' he said.

At the start of his 28-year career with the bank, he felt certain it would be a career for life, Mr Van Deur said. Now he can barely stand to enter a bank. He said the ANZ had provided him with a generous retrenchment package and, his health now restored, he hoped to become a bus driver and to leave unmanageable pressures ...

Summary

This chapter examined the role of the OD practitioner. This term applies to three kinds of people: individuals specialising in OD as a profession, people from related fields who have gained some competence in OD and managers who have the OD skills necessary to change and develop their organisations or departments. Comprehensive lists exist of core and advanced skills and knowledge that an effective OD specialist should possess, but a smaller set of basic skills and knowledge is applicable for all practitioners, regardless of whether they are OD professionals, related specialists or managers. These include four kinds of background: intrapersonal skills, interpersonal skills, general consultation skills and knowledge of OD theory.

The professional OD role can apply to internal consultants who belong to the organisation undergoing change, to external consultants who are members of universities and consulting firms or are self-employed and to members of internal–external consulting teams. The OD role may be aptly described in terms of marginality. People with a tolerance for marginal roles seem especially adapted for OD practice because they are able to maintain neutrality and objectivity and to develop integrative solutions that reconcile viewpoints between opposing organisational departments. Whereas, in the past, the OD role has been described as falling at the client end of the continuum from client-centred to consultant-centred functioning, the development of new and varied interventions has shifted the role of the OD professional to cover the entire range of this continuum.

Although OD is still an emerging profession, most OD professionals have specific training in OD, ranging from short courses and workshops to graduate and doctoral education. No single career path exists, but internal consulting is often a stepping-stone to becoming an external consultant. Because of the hectic pace of OD practice, OD specialists should be prepared to cope with high levels of stress and the possibility of career burnout.

Values have played a key role in OD, and traditional values promoting trust, collaboration and openness have recently been supplemented with concerns for improving organisational effectiveness and productivity. OD specialists may face value dilemmas in trying to jointly optimise human benefits and organisation performance. They may also encounter value conflicts when dealing with powerful external stakeholders, such as the government, stockholders and customers. Dealing with these outside groups may take political skills, as well as the more traditional social skills.

Ethical issues in OD involve how practitioners perform their helping role with clients. OD has always shown a concern for the ethical conduct of practitioners, and several ethical codes for OD practice have been developed by the various professional associations in OD. Ethical dilemmas in OD tend to arise around the following issues: misrepresentation, misuse of data, coercion, value and goal conflict and technical ineptitude.

ACTIVITIES

Review questions
1 Distinguish between an internal and an external change agent.
2 What are the core skills of an OD practitioner?
3 What are the advantages and disadvantages of an internal change agent? Compare this to an external change agent.
4 What is meant by the 'professional ethics' of a change agent?

Discussion and essay questions
1 Discuss the role of the OD practitioner in depth.
2 Which would be more beneficial for an organisation—an external or internal change agent? Explain your answer.
3 What type of ethical considerations would confront an OD practitioner and how may they be addressed?
4 Why is burnout prevalent among change agents? What can be done, if anything, to avoid it? Can you be effective and cautious at the same time? Why?

Notes

1 A. Church and W. Burke, 'Practitioner attitudes about the field of organization development' in *Organization Change and Development*, eds W. Pasmore and R. Woodman (Greenwich, Conn.: JAI Press, 1995).
2 Centre for Corporate Change in the Australian Graduate School of Management, The University of NSW and The University of Sydney, http://www.ccc.agsm.edu.au
3 Centre for Corporate Change, *Working Papers*, Nos 005 and 028.
4 B. Glickman, 'Qualities of change agents', (Unpublished manuscript, May 1974); R. Havelock, *The Change Agent's Guide to Innovation in Education* (Englewood Cliffs, N.J.: Educational Technology, 1973): 5; R. Lippitt, 'Dimensions of the consultant's job' in *The Planning of Change*, eds W. Bennis, K. Benne and R. Chin (New York: Holt, Rinehart and Winston, 1961): 156–61; C. Rogers, *On Becoming a Person* (Boston: Houghton Mifflin, 1971); N. Paris, 'Some thoughts on the qualifications for a consultant', (unpublished manuscript, 1973); 'OD experts reflect on the major skills needed by consultants: with comments from Edgar Schein', *Academy of Management OD Newsletter* (Spring 1979): 1–4.
5 D. Harvey and D. Brown, *An Experiential Approach to Organization Development*, 5th ed., (New Jersey: Prentice Hall, 1996): 94–96.
6 J. Esper, 'Core competencies in organization development', (independent study conducted as partial fulfilment of the MBA degree, Graduate School of Business Administration, University of Southern California, June 1987); E. Neilsen, *Becoming an OD Practitioner* (Englewood Cliffs, N.J.: Prentice-Hall, 1984); S. Eisen, H. Steele and J. Cherbeneau, 'Developing OD competence for the future' in *Practicing Organization Development*, eds W. Rothwell, R. Sullivan and G. McLean (San Diego: Pfeiffer, 1995).

7 B. Tannenbaum, 'Letter to the editor', *Consulting Practice Communique*, Academy of Management Managerial Consultation Division, 21:3 (1993): 16–17; B. Tannenbaum, 'Self-awareness: an essential element underlying consultant effectiveness', *Journal of Organizational Change Management* 8:3 (1995): 85–86.

8 A. Church and W. Burke, 'Practitioner attitudes about the field of organization development' in *Organization Change and Development*, eds W. Pasmore and R. Woodman (Greenwich, Conn.: JAI Press, 1995).

9 M. Lacey, 'Internal consulting: perspectives on the process of planned change', *Journal of Organizational Change Management* 8:3 (1995): 75–84.

10 *Ibid.*

11 E. Kirkhart and T. Isgar, 'Quality of work life for consultants: the internal–external relationship', *Consultation*, 5 (Spring 1986): 5–23; J. Thacker and N. Kulick, 'The use of consultants in joint union/management quality of work life efforts', *Consultation*, 5 (Summer 1986): 116–26.

12 Confirmed in interviews with two change consultants, David Mallen and Anne Boland.

13 R. Ziller, *The Social Self* (Elmsford, N.Y.: Pergamon, 1973).

14 R. Ziller, B. Stark and H. Pruden, 'Marginality and integrative management positions', *Academy of Management Journal*, 12 (December 1969): 487–95; H. Pruden and B. Stark, 'Marginality associated with interorganizational linking process, productivity and satisfaction', *Academy of Management Journal* 14 (March 1971): 145–48; W. Liddell, 'Marginality and integrative decisions', *Academy of Management Journal*, 16 (March 1973): 154–56; P. Brown and C. Cotton, 'Marginality, a force for the OD practitioner', *Training and Development Journal*, 29 (April 1975): 14–18; H. Aldrich and D. Gerker, 'Boundary spanning roles and organizational structure', *Academy of Management Review*, 2 (April 1977): 217–30; C. Cotton, 'Marginality—a neglected dimension in the design of work', *Academy of Management Review*, 2 (January 1977): 133–38; N. Margulies, 'Perspectives on the marginality of the consultant's role' in *The Cutting Edge*, ed. W. Burke (La Jolla, Calif.: University Associates, 1978): 60–79.

15 P. Brown, C. Cotton and R. Golembiewski, 'Marginality and the OD practitioner', *Journal of Applied Behavioural Science*, 13 (1977): 493–506.

16 D. Kegan, 'Organization development as OD network members see it', *Group and Organization Studies*, 7 (March 1982): 5–11.

17 J. Lewis III, 'Growth of internal change agents in organizations', (PhD Dissertation, Case Western Reserve University, 1970).

18 G. Edelwich and A. Brodsky, *Burn-Out Stages of Disillusionment in the Helping Professions* (New York: Human Science, 1980); M. Weisbord, 'The wizard of OD: or, what have magic slippers to do with burnout, evaluation, resistance, planned change, and action research?' *The OD Practitioner*, 10 (Summer 1978): 1–14; M. Mitchell, 'Consultant burnout' in *The 1977 Annual Handbook for Group Facilitators*, eds J. Jones and W. Pfeiffer (La Jolla, Calif: University Associates, 1977): 145–56.

19 T. Isgar, 'Quality of work life of consultants', *Academy of Management OD Newsletter* (Winter 1983): 2–4.

20 A. Church and W. Burke, 'Practitioner attitudes about the field of organization development' in *Organization Change and Development*, eds W. Pasmore and R. Woodman (Greenwich, Conn.: JAI Press, 1995).

21 T. Cummings, 'Designing effective work groups' in *Handbook of Organisational Design*, eds P. Nystrom and W. Starbuck (Oxford: Oxford University Press, 1981): 250–71.

22 J. Schermerhorn, 'Interorganizational development', *Journal of Management*, 5 (1979): 21–38; T. Cummings, 'Interorganisation theory and organisation development' in *Systems Theory for Organisation Development*, ed. T. Cummings (Chichester, England: John Wiley and Sons, 1980): 323–38.

23 http://www.bf.rmit.edu.au/Aben

24 http://www.arts.unsw.edu.au/aapae; http:/corporate-ethos.com.au

25 D. Grace and S. Cohen, *Business Ethics, Australian Problems and Cases*, 2nd ed. (Melbourne: Oxford University Press, 1998): 124–126.

26 W. Bennis, *Organization Development: Its Nature, Origins, and Prospects* (Reading, Mass.: Addison-Wesley, 1969).

27 H. Kelman, 'Manipulation of human behaviour: an ethical dilemma for the social scientist' in *The Planning of Change*, 2nd ed., eds W. Bennis, K. Bennie and R. Chin (New York: Holt, Rinehart and Winston, 1969): 584.

28 R. Beckhard, 'The dependency dilemma', *Consultants' Communique*, 6 (July–August–September 1978): 1–3.

29 G. Lippitt, *Organization Renewal* (Englewood Cliffs, N.J.: Prentice-Hall, 1969).
30 C. Argyris, 'Explorations in consulting-client relationships', *Human Organizations*, 20 (Fall 1961): 121–33.
31 J. Slocum, Jr, 'Does cognitive style affect diagnosis and intervention strategies?' *Group and Organization Studies*, 3 (June 1978): 199–210.
32 F. Shiel, 'Former manager banks on new career', *The Age* (Tuesday, 24 March 1998).

Appendix: Professional codes of practice for accounting organisations

There are two accrediting bodies for accountants in Australia: the Australian Society of Certified Practising Accountants (ASCPA) and the Institute of Chartered Accountants in Australia (ICAA).

Code of the ASCPA

In Section B of its Code of Professional Conduct, the ASPCA identifies eight 'fundamental principles of professional conduct':

- *the public interest:* 'Members must at all times safeguard the interests of their clients and employers provided that they do not conflict with the duties and loyalties owed to the community, its laws and social and political institutions'.
- *integrity:* 'Members must not breach public trust in the profession or the specific trust of their clients and employers. Observance of accepted norms of honesty and integrity must underlie all their professional decisions and actions'.
- *objectivity and independence:* 'Members must be objective, impartial and free of conflicts of interest in the performance of their professional duties. They must be independent and be seen to be independent when providing auditing and other reporting or attestation services'.
- *competence and due care:* 'Members must strive continually to improve their technical services and to keep their knowledge up-to-date. They must bring due care and diligence to bear upon the discharge of their duties to clients and employers. Members must not undertake professional work which they are not competent to perform and, when in doubt, must obtain such advice and assistance as will enable them to carry out the work competently'.
- *compliance with accounting and auditing standards:* 'Conscious of the professional accountant's responsibility for the integrity of financial information and the public interest involved therein, members must comply with the Accounting and Auditing Standards of the profession and Approved Accounting Standards issued under Statute'.
- *compliance with other standards and the guidance given by the society:* 'Members must comply with the Standards issued or guidance given by the Society on Taxation, Insolvency, Management Consultancy and any other matters of a technical or professional nature'.
- *confidentiality:* 'Members must not disclose information acquired in the course of their professional work except where consent has been obtained or where there is a legal or professional duty to disclose. Members must not use such information for their personal advantage or that of a third party'.
- *image of the profession and the society:* 'Members must refrain from any conduct or action in their professional role which may tarnish the image of the accounting profession or unjustifiably detract from the good name of their professional body'.

Code of the ICAA

In paragraph eight of its Rules of Ethical Conduct (REC), the ICAA identifies six fundamental principles that should govern the conduct of the institute's members' professional relationships with others:

- *integrity:* 'They should be straightforward, honest and sincere in their approach to professional work.'
- *objectivity:* 'They must be fair and must not allow prejudice or bias to override their objectivity. When reporting on financial matters which come under their review they should maintain an impartial attitude.'
- *independence:* 'They should both be and appear to be free of any interest which might be regarded, whatever its actual effect, as being incompatible with integrity and objectivity.'
- *confidentiality:* 'They should respect the confidentiality of information acquired in the course of their work and should not disclose any such information to a third party without specific authority or unless there is a legal or professional duty to disclose it.'
- *technical standards:* 'They should carry out their professional work in accordance with the technical and professional standards relevant to that work.'
- *professional competence:* 'They should have a duty to maintain their level of competence throughout their professional career. They should only undertake work they can expect to complete with professional competence.'

PART 2

THE PROCESS OF ORGANISATION DEVELOPMENT

CHAPTERS

4 Entering and contracting

5 Diagnosing organisations

6 Diagnosing groups and jobs

7 Collecting and analysing diagnostic information

8 Feeding back diagnostic information

9 Designing OD interventions

10 Managing change

11 Evaluating and institutionalising OD interventions

4

Entering and contracting

The planned change process described in Chapter 2 generally starts when one or more key managers or administrators sense that their organisation, department or group could be improved or has problems that could be alleviated through organisation development. The organisation might be successful, yet has room for improvement. It might be facing impending environmental conditions that necessitate a change in how it operates. The organisation could be experiencing particular problems, such as poor product quality, high rates of absenteeism or dysfunctional conflicts between departments. Conversely, the problems might appear more diffuse and consist simply of feelings that the organisation should be 'more innovative,' 'more competitive' or 'more effective'.

Entering and contracting are the initial steps in the OD process. They involve defining in a preliminary manner the organisation's problems or opportunities for development and establishing a collaborative relationship between the OD practitioner and members of the client system about how to work on those issues. Entering and contracting set the initial parameters for carrying out the subsequent phases of OD: diagnosing the organisation, planning and implementing changes and evaluating and institutionalising them. They help to define what issues will be addressed by those activities, who will carry them out and how they will be accomplished.

Entering and contracting can vary in complexity and formality according to the situation. In those cases where the manager of a work group or department serves as his or her own OD practitioner, entering and contracting typically involve the manager and group members meeting to discuss what issues they should work on and how they will jointly accomplish this. Here, entering and contracting are relatively simple and informal. They involve all relevant members directly in the process without a great deal of formal procedures. In situations where managers and administrators are considering the use of professional OD practitioners, either from inside or outside the organisation, entering and contracting tend to be more complex and formal.[1] Organisation development practitioners may need to collect preliminary information to help define the issues to be worked on. They may need to meet with representatives of the client organisation, rather than with the total membership: they may need to formalise their respective roles as well as how the OD process will unfold.

This chapter discusses the activities that are involved in entering into, and contracting for, an OD process. The main focus of attention will be the complex processes that involve OD professionals and client organisations. However, similar entering and contracting issues need to be addressed in even the simplest OD efforts, where managers serve as OD practitioners for their own work units. Unless there is clarity and agreement about what issues need to be worked on, who will address them and how this will be accomplished, subsequent stages of the OD process are likely to be confusing and ineffective.

Entering into an OD relationship

An OD process generally starts when a member of an organisation or unit contacts an OD practitioner about potential help in addressing an organisational issue.[2] The organisation member may be a manager, staff specialist or some other key participant, and the practitioner may be an OD professional from inside or outside the organisation. Determining whether the two parties should enter into an OD relationship typically involves clarifying the nature of the organisation's problem, the relevant client system for that issue and the appropriateness of the particular OD practitioner.[3] In helping to assess these issues, the OD practitioner may need to collect preliminary data about the organisation. Similarly, the organisation may need to gather information about the practitioner's competence and experience.[4] This knowledge will help both parties determine whether they should proceed to develop a contract for working together.

This section describes the following activities that are involved in entering an OD relationship: (1) clarifying the organisational issue, (2) determining the relevant client and (3) selecting the appropriate OD practitioner.

Clarifying the organisational issue

When seeking help from OD practitioners, organisations typically start with a *presenting problem*—the issue that has caused them to consider an OD process. It may be specific (decrease in market share, increase in absenteeism) or general ('we're growing too fast', 'we need to prepare for rapid changes'). The presenting problem often has an implied or stated solution. For example, managers may believe that, because members of their teams are in conflict, team building is the obvious answer. They may even state the presenting problem in the form of a solution: 'We need some team building'.

In many cases, however, the presenting problem is only a symptom of an underlying problem. For example, conflict among members of a team may result from several deeper causes, including ineffective reward systems, personality differences, inappropriate structure and poor leadership. The issue facing the organisation or department must be clarified early in the OD process so that subsequent diagnostic and intervention activities are focused on the right issue.[5]

Gaining a clearer perspective on the organisational issue may require the collection of preliminary data.[6] OD practitioners often examine company records and interview a few key members to gain an introductory understanding of the organisation, its context and the nature of the presenting problem. These data are gathered in a relatively short period of time, typically from a few hours to one or two days. They are intended to provide rudimentary knowledge of the organisational issue that will enable the two parties to make informed choices about proceeding with the contracting process.

The diagnostic phase of OD involves a far more extensive assessment of the organisational issue than occurs during the entering and contracting stage. The diagnosis might also discover other issues that need to be addressed, or it might lead to redefining the initial issue that was identified during the entering and contracting stage. This is a prime example of the emergent nature of the OD process, where things may change as new information is gathered and new events occur.

Determining the relevant client

A second activity involved in entering an OD relationship is the definition of who is the relevant client for addressing the organisational issue.[7] Generally, the relevant client includes those organisation members who can directly impact on the change issue, whether it be solving a particular problem or improving an already successful organisation or department. Unless these members are identified and included in the entering and contracting process, they may withhold their support for, and commitment to, the OD process. In trying to improve the productivity of a unionised manufacturing plant, for example, the relevant client may need to include union officials as well as managers and staff personnel. It is not unusual for an OD project to fail because the relevant client was inappropriately defined.

Determining the relevant client can vary in complexity according to the situation. In those cases where the organisational issue can be addressed in a particular organisation unit, client definition is relatively straightforward. Members of that unit constitute the relevant client. They or their representatives would need to be included in the entering and contracting process. For example, if a manager asked for help in improving the decision-making process of his or her team, the manager and team members would be the relevant clients. Unless they are actively involved in choosing an OD practitioner and defining the subsequent change process, there is little likelihood that OD will improve team decision making.

Determining the relevant client is more complex when the organisational issue cannot readily be addressed in a single organisation unit. Here, it may be necessary to expand the definition of the client to include members from multiple units, from different hierarchical levels and even from outside the organisation. For example, the manager of a production department may seek help in resolving conflicts between his or her unit and other departments in the organisation. The relevant client would transcend the boundaries of the production department because it alone cannot resolve the organisational issue. The client might include members from all departments involved in the conflict as well as the executive to whom all the departments report. If this interdepartmental conflict also involved key suppliers and customers from outside the firm, the relevant client might also include members of those groups.

In these complex situations, OD practitioners may need to gather additional information about the organisation in order to determine the relevant client. This can be accomplished as part of the preliminary data collection that typically occurs when clarifying the organisational issue. When examining company records or interviewing personnel, practitioners can seek to identify the key members and organisational units that need to be involved in addressing the organisational issue. For example, they can ask organisation members such questions as: 'Who can directly impact the organisational issue?' 'Who has a vested interest in it?' 'Who has the power to approve or reject the OD effort?' Answers to these questions can help determine who is the relevant client for the entering and contracting stage. The relevant client may change, however, during the later stages of the OD process as new data are gathered and changes occur. If so, participants may have to return to this initial stage of the OD effort and modify it.

Selecting an OD practitioner

The last activity involved in entering an OD relationship is selecting an OD practitioner who has the expertise and experience to work with members on the organisational issue. Unfortunately, little systematic advice is available on how to choose a competent OD professional, whether from inside or outside the organisation. Perhaps the best criteria for selecting, evaluating and developing OD practitioners are those suggested by the late Gordon Lippitt, a pioneering practitioner in the field.[8] Lippitt listed areas that managers should consider before selecting a practitioner, including the ability of the consultant to form sound interpersonal relationships, the degree of focus on the problem, the skills of the practitioner relative to the problem, the extent that the consultant clearly informs the client as to his or her role and contribution and whether the practitioner belongs to a professional association. References from other clients are highly important. A client may not like the consultant's work, but it is critical to know the reasons for both pleasure and displeasure. One important consideration is whether the consultant approaches the organisation with openness and an insistence on diagnosis or whether the practitioner appears to have a fixed programme that is applicable to almost any organisation.

Certainly, OD consulting is as much a person specialisation as it is a task specialisation. The OD professional must not only have a repertoire of technical skills but also the personality and interpersonal competence to be able to use himself or herself as an instrument of change. Regardless of technical training, the consultant must be able to maintain a boundary position, co-ordinating various units and departments and mixing disciplines, theories, technology and research findings in an organic rather than a mechanical way. The practitioner is potentially the most important OD technology available.

Thus, in the selection of an OD practitioner, perhaps the most important issue is the fundamental question, 'How effective has the person been in the past, with what kinds of organisations, using what kinds of techniques?' In other words, references must be checked. Interpersonal relationships are tremendously important, but even con artists have excellent interpersonal relationships and skills.

The burden of choosing an effective OD practitioner should not, however, rest entirely with the client organisation.[9] Organisation development practitioners also bear a heavy responsibility for seeking an appropriate match between their skills and knowledge and what the organisation or department needs. Few managers are sophisticated enough to detect or understand subtle differences in expertise among OD professionals. They often do not understand the difference between consultants who specialise in different types of interventions. Thus, practitioners should help to educate potential clients. Consultants should be explicit about their strengths and weaknesses and about their range of competence. If OD professionals realise that a good match does not exist, they should inform managers and help them find more suitable help.

Application 4.1 describes the process at St Andrew's War Memorial Hospital, Brisbane.[10] It highlights the importance of clarifying the organisational issue and identifying the relevant people when entering and contracting.

APPLICATION 4.1　St Andrew's total care ethos

St Andrew's War Memorial Hospital in Brisbane is an acute-care private hospital with a commitment to compassionate quality care that stems from the Christian ideals of the Uniting and Presbyterian churches. The hospital has been highly recommended in the AHRI Awards for Leadership and Excellence in Human Resources for its leadership.

The hospital has achieved a considerable reputation for cardiac care. It pioneered the use of laser surgery in gynaecology and is well known in the fields of orthopaedics and ophthalmology. It is the first Queensland hospital to achieve accreditation by the Australian Council of Health Care Standards. It describes its dedication to patient care as total personal care.

This is a concept, it says, that goes beyond the traditional boundaries of patient/doctor/hospital relations. Its total personal care ethos extends to staff, and is a major component of the hospital's strategic plan. The hospital employs about 850 people from a wide range of professional and educational backgrounds.

Unlike other Queensland hospitals that separate nursing and non-nursing personnel functions and services, St Andrew's has the only fully-integrated organisation-wide human resource function—the *organisation development team* (ODT). This provides advisory support services and resources focused on assisting all managers and staff to achieve organisational and individual performance goals. The ODT is responsible for designing, introducing and evaluating organisational management processes for improved efficiency and performance.

The team encompasses human resources, workplace health and safety/infection control, staff development, library services, accreditation and quality/management/process improvement. Some of the ODT's greatest achievements have been in its role in change management projects. It has taken a facilitation and leadership role in these projects, as well as in the more conventional aspects of human resource management.

The hospital's view is that the external health care environment is facing rapid change, and in many ways is following American trends. Health care organisations need to be able to respond flexibly to the changes, which are unpredictable. After analysing the environment and anticipating the changes, a review of the organisation was conducted by the ODT and the management team, headed by the chief executive officer, Vaughan Howell.

This review incorporated mission, vision, values, core business, structure and organisation design, culture and management processes and led to significant changes planned in stages. The ODT was established to combine the skills of many personnel whose roles were initiating, leading and facilitating change.

The planned change process began with the clarification of the hospital's mission and vision, following through to the strategic planning process. This incorporated all stakeholders. Major organisational redesign affected 90% of staff, linking the planning process to performance management, 'quality management process' and individual goal setting. The creation of the ODT provided a pool of specialist advisers who had an organisation-wide focus and who could work with all managers to develop staff, without having any allegiance to a particular divisional area.

It also meant re-orientating the team from the traditional HR mindset to the concept of organisation development, which has brought HR issues to the forefront of decision making and strategic planning.

Developing a contract

The activities of entering an OD relationship—clarifying the organisational issue, determining who is the relevant client, and deciding whether the practitioner is appropriate for helping the organisation—are a necessary prelude to developing an OD contract. They define the major focus for contracting, including the relevant parties. Contracting is a natural extension of the entering process and clarifies how the OD process will proceed. It typically establishes the expectations of the parties, the time and resources that will be expended, as well as the ground rules under which the parties will operate.

The goal of contracting is to make a good decision about how to carry out the OD process.[11] It can be relatively informal and involve only a verbal agreement between the client and OD practitioner. A team leader with OD skills, for example, may voice his or her concerns to members about how the team is functioning. After some discussion, they might agree to devote one hour of future meeting time to diagnosing the team with the help of the leader. Here, entering and contracting are done together in an informal manner. In other cases, contracting can be more protracted and result in a formal document. This typically occurs when organisations employ outside OD practitioners. Government agencies, for example, generally have procurement regulations that apply to contracting with outside consultants.[12]

Regardless of the level of formality, all OD processes require some form of explicit contracting that results in either a verbal or written agreement. Such contracting clarifies the client's and the practitioner's expectations about how the OD process will take place. Unless there is mutual understanding and agreement about the OD process, there is considerable risk that someone's expectations will be unfilled.[13] This can lead to reduced commitment and support, to misplaced action or to premature termination of the process.

The contracting step in OD generally addresses three key areas:[14] (1) what each party expects to gain from the OD process; (2) the time and resources that will be devoted to OD and (3) the ground rules for working together.

Mutual expectations

This part of the contracting process focuses on the expectations of the client and the OD practitioner. The client states the services and outcomes to be provided by the OD practitioner and describes what the organisation expects from the OD process and the consultant. Clients can usually describe the desired outcomes of the OD process, such as decreased turnover or higher job satisfaction. Encouraging them to state their wants in the form of outcomes, working relationships and personal accomplishments can facilitate the development of a good contract.[15]

The OD practitioner should also state what he or she expects to gain from the OD process. This can include the opportunity to try new OD interventions, report the results to other potential clients and receive appropriate compensation or recognition.

Time and resources

To accomplish change, the organisation and the OD practitioner must commit time and resources to the effort. Each must be clear about how much energy and resources will be dedicated to the change process. Failure to make explicit the necessary requirements of a change process can quickly ruin an OD effort. For example, a client may clearly state that the assignment involves diagnosing the causes of poor productivity in a work group. However, the client may expect the practitioner to complete the assignment without talking to the workers. Typically, clients want to know how much time will be necessary to complete the assignment, who needs to be involved, how much it will cost and so on.

Block has suggested that resources can be divided into two parts.[16] *Essential* requirements are things that are absolutely necessary if the change process is to be successful. From the practitioner's perspective, they can include access to key people or information, enough time to do the job right and commitment from certain people. The organisation's essential requirements might include a speedy diagnosis or assurances that the project will be conducted at the lowest price. Being clear about the constraints on carrying out the assignment will facilitate the contracting process and improve the chances for success. *Desirable* requirements are the things that would be nice to have but are not absolutely necessary. They may include access to special resources and written, as opposed to verbal, reports.

Ground rules

The final part of the contracting process involves specifying how the client and the OD practitioner will work together. This includes such issues as confidentiality, if and how the OD practitioner will become involved in personal or interpersonal issues, how to terminate the relationship and whether the practitioner is supposed to make expert recommendations or help the manager to make decisions. For internal consultants, organisational politics make it especially important to clarify issues of how to handle sensitive information and how to deliver 'bad news'.[17] These process issues are as important as the substantive changes to take place. Failure to address these concerns can mean that the client or the OD practitioner has inappropriate assumptions about how the process will unfold.

Application 4.2 compares two organisations and identifies how they used consultants in response to certain circumstances.[18]

In both the following cases the client brief is similar: there is an identified (but not well-defined) development opportunity. The mechanism that has been selected to take advantage of the opportunity is also the same; a consultant has been selected to facilitate a process of change. However, there are also differences. While organisational learning has a contribution to make in both cases, the exact part it plays differs. For example, in Organisation A the stated objective is a change in employee behaviour, but organisational learning emerges as an outcome of the process. This contrasts with Organisation B, where increasing the organisation's ability to learn is an objective. In both cases the consultant facilitating the process uses learning as a developmental technique.

Organisation A

Organisation A is a consulting engineering firm employing some 20 people. The current CEO who owns all of the company's shares and acts as managing director established the business.

When the CEO initially contracted the consultant, Organisation A had recently completed the documentation of operational procedures and the preparation of manuals. Staff were ignoring these and the CEO felt that the solution to this problem was to have the staff introduced to the content and purpose of the manuals within a training programme. The selection of a firm specialising in training followed the CEO's preliminary assessment (as stated to the consultant) that Organisation A was facing a particular problem that could be solved with the assistance of an 'expert'; in this case a trainer who could achieve a change in employee behaviour.

However, during the preliminary stages of the assignment negotiation, the consultant concluded that the issues within the client organisation were broader than those identified by the CEO. As a result the consultant's response was to propose a broad-based development process for the company, which encompassed the initial brief and stressed the value of working simultaneously on different aspects of the company (culture, systems, planning and personal development). The CEO quickly accepted the revised brief as it corresponded with his unstated feelings about the complexity of the challenge facing the company. From his perspective, the company could already be described as 'successful', and yet

there were also changes that he wanted to make. While he had focused on the 'non-conformance' aspect of his employees' behaviour in identifying the source of a 'problem', he was equally aware of the company's current achievements and future potential. In retrospect he described his feelings in the following way:

We knew there were a lot of things we needed to know, but didn't know what they were. So we started with training, which exposed us to new ideas and we were then able to see the project more holistically.

By the time work started on the assignment, both the consultant and the client recognised that the focus would be broader than the delivery of training. The modified assignment implied an alteration of roles; whereas the original brief had meant that the consultant could validly take a 'resource/expert' role (using her expertise in training and development to change employee behaviour), the revised brief suggested the 'process' role as being more appropriate. The reciprocal role taken by the client also changed—from an 'information supplier' to a 'participant'. As the assignment continued, the focus continued to expand and, as a result, the consultant and the client renegotiated roles a number of times. Factors that guided this process included the current task focus, the stage of the assignment and the developing levels of trust between the two parties.

The final outcome was a co-operative relationship that established the conditions for an outcome that was far beyond the scope of that which had originally been planned. As the CEO later commented:

Find a company that's good at what it does and develop a partnership with it. At the beginning the consultant just provided training, then we formed a relationship. They educated us and became our corporate development arm.

These and other similar comments reflect his growing realisation that, had his original brief been followed, it might have limited the consultant's potential to contribute to the company. He recognised that, while the initial role that he had asked the consultant to play (that of trainer) was useful, the role of educator was more valuable. His flexibility in allowing the consultant to modify roles in the context of the developing assignment (and to indicate to him the appropriate client role) was a critical factor in the assignment's success.

Organisation B

Organisation B is an educational institution undergoing considerable change. The impact of increased student numbers; a rising level of expectations of financial accountability and the development of competition within the education market were all creating pressure on operational systems and the people who operate them. Within the organisation, a number of teams had been working on change processes, with the help of an external facilitator, and the subject of this case was one of those teams.

At this time, the team in question was having to respond to the changing environment with new systems that would increase their ability to process work quickly. The philosophy of the organisation meant that individual learning was also seen as a positive outcome for team members. As a result, the project manager (a senior manager) contracted a consultant to facilitate a change process that would effect positive system changes while simultaneously involving the team responsible for implementing the changes.

The context for the assignment suggested a 'process' role and a broadly defined development programme. In response to this brief, the consultant entered into a structured set of activities that involved all parties in determining the scope of the assignment and the primary role that each party would take. The project manager became the assignment sponsor, the

organisation became the ultimate client and the team became the primary client, these last descriptions drawing on Schein's typology of contact clients, intermediate clients, primary clients and ultimate clients.[19]

The emphasis placed on clarifying roles and expectations meant that there was very little role renegotiation during the course of the assignment. The focus of the assignment also remained constant once the collaborative scoping exercise had been completed. This focus encompassed both aspects of the original brief—the employee team to be involved (and developed), while positive system changes were being effected. The need for individual learning to occur during the process ensured that organisational learning functioned as a consulting technique in Organisation B, as well as an organisation goal.

Organisational learning in a consulting assignment

At first sight the cases appear to represent quite different examples of a consultancy assignment. In Organisation A the CEO had undertaken a preliminary assessment and had selected a consultant according to his perception of the task that needed to be undertaken. The role implied by his assessment was that of 'resource' consultant or expert. However, during the course of the assignment, the consultant's role changed from resource consultant (in the shape of a trainer) to organisational educator. Her relationship with the organisation also widened, and as the assignment concluded, she was carrying out multiple roles, including educator to the organisation. As a consequence of this role, Organisation A became a 'learning partner', complementing the consultant's role of educator. In Organisation B, the situation prompted the project manager to approach a process consultant to facilitate the assignment with the participation of those members of the unit under focus. The consultant clearly defined the roles of the participants, including the project manager, the employee team and the organisation undergoing change, and involved them in defining the terms of the assignment.

The different approaches provide an insight into how organisations and their consultants can integrate the concept of organisational learning into the wider context of organisational development: in both cases the development of organisational learning was seen as a valuable goal, even if it was not initially identified (as in Organisation A). In this organisation the consultant was crucial in helping the organisation recognise the value of learning, as well as guiding it through the learning process.

It is this ultimate recognition of the value of organisational learning that provides the link between the two cases. Despite the differences at the start of the process, by the time the scope of the assignment was agreed both

organisations had identical goals— organisational development with a focus on individual learning. From this point of similarity, the two assignments diverged again in practice, with the consultants taking different approaches to the selection of appropriate roles. Consultant A allowed role modification to occur naturally, in response to the developing relationship between the consultant and the client, and Consultant B clarified roles as a deliberate and integral part of the change. However, while the process of role selection differed, the roles played by the consultants were similar and, as a consequence, the two sets of clients also played similar roles in their respective contexts. In a final point of similarity, both assignments produced an improved level of learning as one of the assignment outcomes.

Summary

The entering and contracting processes constitute the initial activities of the OD process. They set the initial parameters for the phases of planned change that follow: diagnosing, planning and implementing change and evaluating and institutionalising it. Organisational entry involves clarifying the organisational issue or presenting problem, determining the relevant client and selecting an OD practitioner. Developing an OD contract focuses on making a good decision about whether or not to proceed, and allows both the client and the OD practitioner to clarify expectations about how the change process will unfold. Contracting involves setting mutual expectations, negotiating time and resources and developing ground rules for working together.

 ACTIVITIES

Review questions

1 What is the process of entering a client system?
2 What problems may be encountered when entering a client system?
3 Who has the burden of responsibility for selecting an OD consultant?
4 What is the goal of the contracting process and what are the steps involved?

Discussion and essay questions

1 Describe the process of entering an organisational system from an internal OD practitioner's perspective.
2 How would you explain the contracting process to someone who had never heard of OD? Why is it important?

Notes

1 M. Lacey, 'Internal consulting: perspectives on the process of planned change', *Journal of Organization Change Management*, 8:3 (1995): 75–84; J. Geirland and M. Maniker-Leiter, 'Five lessons for internal organization development consultants', *OD Practitioner* 27 (1995): 44–48.

2 C. Margerison, 'Consulting activities in organizational change', *Journal of Organizational Change Management*, 1 (1988): 60–67; P. Block, *Flawless Consulting: A Guide to Getting Your Expertise Used* (Austin, Tex.: Learning Concepts, 1981); R. Harrison, 'Choosing the depth of organizational intervention', *Journal of Applied Behavioural Science*, 6:11 (1970): 182–202.

3 M. Beer, *Organization Change and Development: A Systems View* (Santa Monica, Calif.: Goodyear, 1980); G. Lippitt and R. Lippitt, *The Consulting Process in Action*, 2nd ed. (San Diego: University Associates, 1986).

4 L. Greiner and R. Metzger, *Consulting to Management* (Englewood Cliffs, N.J.: Prentice-Hall, 1983): 251–58; Beer, *Organization Change and Development, op. cit.*, 81–83.

5 Block, *Flawless Consulting, op. cit.*

6 J. Fordyce and R. Weil, *Managing WITH People*, 2nd ed. (Reading, Mass.: Addison-Wesley, 1979).

7 Beer, *Organization Change and Development, op. cit.*; Fordyce and Weil, *Managing WITH People, op. cit.*

8 G. Lippitt, 'Criteria for selecting, evaluating, and developing consultants', *Training and Development Journal*, 28 (August 1972): 10–15.

9 Greiner and Metzger, *Consulting to Management, op. cit.*

10 News, 'St Andrew's total care ethos', *The Australian*, (13 November 1997), 37, Reuters Business Briefing.

11 Block, *Flawless Consulting, op. cit.*; Beer, *Organization Change and Development, op. cit.*

12 T. Cody, *Management Consulting: A Game Without Chips* (Fitzwilliam, N.H.: Kennedy and Kennedy, 1986): 108–16; H. Holtz, *How to Succeed as an Independent Consultant*, 2nd ed. (New York: John Wiley and Sons, 1988): 145–61.

13 G. Bellman, *The Consultant's Calling* (San Francisco: Jossey-Bass, 1990).

14 M. Weisbord, 'The organization development contract', *Organization Development Practitioner*, 5:11 (1973): 1–4; M. Weisbord, 'The organization contract revisited', *Consultation*, 4 (Winter 1985): 305–15; D. Nadler, *Feedback and Organization Development: Using DataBased Methods* (Reading, Mass.: Addison-Wesley, 1977): 110–14.

15 Block, *Flawless Consulting, op. cit.*

16 *Ibid.*

17 Lacey, 'Internal consulting', *op. cit.*

18 C. Massey and R. Walker 'Aiming for organizational learning: consultants as agents of change', *The Learning Organization*, 6:1 (1999): 38–44, MCB University Press.

19 E. Schein, *Process Consultation: Its Role in Organization Development*, 2 (2nd ed.) (Reading, Mass.: Addison-Wesley, 1987): 118.

Diagnosing organisations

Diagnosing organisations is the second major phase in the model of planned change described in Chapter 2 (Figure 2.2). It follows the entering and contracting stage (Chapter 4) and precedes the planning and implementation phase. When it is done well, diagnosis clearly points the organisation and the OD practitioner towards a set of appropriate intervention activities that will improve organisation effectiveness.

Diagnosis is the process of assessing the functioning of the organisation, department, group or job to discover the sources of problems and areas for improvement. It involves collecting pertinent information about current operations, analysing those data and drawing conclusions for potential change and improvement. Effective diagnosis provides the systematic understanding of the organisation necessary for the design of appropriate interventions. Thus, OD interventions derive from diagnosis and include specific actions that are intended to resolve problems and improve organisational functioning. (Chapters 12 to 20 show the major interventions used in OD today.)

This chapter is the first of four chapters that describe different aspects of the diagnostic process. It presents a general definition of diagnosis and discusses the need for diagnostic models in guiding the process. Diagnostic models derive from conceptions about how organisations function and tell OD practitioners what to look for when diagnosing organisations, departments, groups or jobs. They represent a road map for discovering current functioning. A general, comprehensive diagnostic model is presented, based on open systems theory. The chapter concludes with a description and application of an organisation-level diagnostic model. Chapter 7 describes and applies diagnostic models at the group and job levels. Chapters 8 and 9 complete the diagnostic phase by discussing the processes of data collection, analysis and feedback.

What is diagnosis?

Diagnosis is the process of understanding how the organisation is currently functioning: it provides the information necessary for designing change interventions. It generally follows from successful entry and contracting. The preliminary activities in planned change set the stage for successful diagnosis. They help OD practitioners and client members jointly determine organisational issues to focus on, show how to collect and analyse data to understand them and how to work together to develop action steps from the diagnosis.

Unfortunately, the term 'diagnosis' can be misleading when applied to organisations. It suggests a model of organisation change analogous to medicine: an organisation (patient) experiencing problems seeks help from an OD practitioner (doctor); the practitioner examines the organisation, finds the causes of the problems and prescribes a solution. Diagnosis in organisation development is, however, much more collaborative than such a medical perspective implies. The values and ethical beliefs that underlie OD suggest that both organisational members and change agents should be jointly involved in discovering the causes of organisational problems. Similarly, both should be actively involved with developing appropriate interventions and implementing them.

For example, a manager might seek OD help to reduce absenteeism in his or her department. The manager and an OD consultant might jointly decide to diagnose the cause of the problem by examining company absenteeism records and by interviewing selected employees about possible reasons for absenteeism. Analysis of these data could uncover causes of absenteeism in the department, thus helping the manager and the practitioner develop an appropriate intervention for reducing the problem.

The medical view of diagnosis also implies that something is wrong with the patient and that one needs to uncover the cause of the illness. In those cases where organisations do have specific problems, diagnosis is problem-oriented. It seeks reasons for the problems. However, many managers involved with OD are not experiencing specific organisational problems. Rather, they are interested in improving the overall effectiveness of their organisation, department or group. Here, diagnosis is development-oriented. It assesses the current functioning of the organisation to discover areas for future development. For example, a manager might be interested in using OD to improve a department that already seems to be functioning well. Diagnosis might include an overall assessment of both the task-performance capabilities of the department and the impact of the department upon its individual members. This process seeks to uncover specific areas for future development of the department's effectiveness.

In organisation development, diagnosis is used more broadly than a medical definition would suggest. *It is a collaborative process between organisation members and the OD consultant to collect pertinent information, analyse it and draw conclusions for action planning and intervention.* Diagnosis may be aimed at uncovering the causes of specific problems; or it may be directed at assessing the overall functioning of the organisation or department to discover areas for future development. Diagnosis provides a systematic understanding of organisations so that appropriate interventions may be developed for solving problems and enhancing effectiveness.

The need for diagnostic models

Entry and contracting processes can result in a need to understand a whole system or some part or feature of the organisation. To diagnose an organisation, OD practitioners and organisational members need to have some idea as to what information to collect and analyse, which can be based on intuitive hunches right through to scientific explanations of how the organisations function. Conceptual frameworks that people use to understand organisations are referred to as *diagnostic models*.[1] They describe the relationships between different features of the organisation, its context and its effectiveness. As a result, diagnostic models point out what areas to examine and what questions to ask when assessing how an organisation is functioning.

However, all models represent simplification of reality and therefore choose certain features as critical. Focusing attention on those features, often to the exclusion of others, can result in a biased diagnosis. For example, a diagnostic model that relates team effectiveness to the handling of interpersonal conflict would lead an OD practitioner to ask questions about relationships among members, decision-making processes, and conflict-resolution methods. Although relevant, these questions ignore other group issues such as the composition of skills and knowledge, the complexity of the tasks performed by the group and member inter-dependencies. Thus, diagnostic models must be carefully chosen to address the organisation's presenting problems as well as to ensure comprehensiveness.

Potential diagnostic models are everywhere. Any collection of concepts and relationships that tries to represent a system or explain its effectiveness can potentially qualify as a diagnostic model. Major sources of diagnostic models in OD are the literally thousands of articles and books that discuss, describe and analyse how organisations function. They provide information about how and why certain organisational systems, processes or functions are effective. These studies often concern a specific facet of organisational behaviour, such as employee stress, leadership, motivation, problem solving, group dynamics, job design and career development. They can also involve the larger organisation and its context, including the environment, strategy, structure and culture. Diagnostic models can be derived from that information by noting the dimensions or variables that are associated with organisational effectiveness.

Another source of diagnostic models is the OD practitioner's own experience in organisations. This field knowledge is a wealth of practical information about how organisations operate. Unfortunately, only a small part of this vast experience has been translated into diagnostic models. These more clinical models represent the professional judgments of people with years of experience in organisational diagnosis. They generally link diagnosis with specific organisational processes, such as group problem solving, employee motivation or communication between managers and employees. The models list specific questions for diagnosing such processes.

This chapter presents a general framework for diagnosing organisations rather than attempting to cover the diversity of OD diagnostic models. The framework describes the systems perspective prevalent in OD today and integrates several of the more popular diagnostic models. The systems model provides a useful starting point for diagnosing organisations or departments. (Additional diagnostic models that are linked to specific OD interventions are given in Chapters 12 to 20.)

Open systems model

This section introduces systems theory, a set of concepts and relationships that describes the properties and behaviours of things called *systems*—organisations, groups and people, for example. Systems are viewed as unitary wholes composed of parts or sub-systems; they serve to integrate the parts into a functioning unit. For example, organisation systems are composed of departments such as sales, manufacturing and research. The organisation serves to co-ordinate the behaviours of its departments so that they function together. The general diagnostic model based on systems theory that underlies most of OD is called the 'open systems model'.

Systems can vary in how open they are to their outside environments. *Open systems*, such as organisations and people, exchange information and resources with their environments. They cannot completely control their own behaviour and are influenced in part by external forces. Organisations, for example, are affected by such environmental conditions as the availability of raw material, customer demands and government regulations. Understanding how these external forces affect the organisation can help to explain some of its internal behaviour.

Open systems display a hierarchical ordering. Each higher level of system is composed of lower-level systems. Systems at the level of society are composed of organisations; organisations are composed of groups (departments); groups of individuals; and so on. Although systems at different levels vary in many ways—such as in size and complexity, for example—they have a number of common characteristics by virtue of being open systems. These properties can be applied to systems at any level. The following key properties of open systems are described: (1) inputs, transformations and outputs; (2) boundaries; (3) feedback; (4) equifinality and (5) alignment.

Inputs, transformations and outputs

Any organisational system is composed of three related parts: inputs, transformations and outputs, as shown in Figure 5.1. *Inputs* consist of human or other resources, such as information, energy and materials, coming into the system. They are acquired from the system's external environment. For example, a manufacturing organisation acquires raw materials from an outside supplier. Similarly, a hospital nursing unit acquires information about a patient's condition from the attending doctor. In each case, the system (organisation or nursing unit) obtains resources (raw materials or information) from its external environment.

Transformations are the processes of converting inputs into outputs. In organisations, transformations are generally carried out by a production or operations function that is composed of social and technological components. The social component consists of people and their work relationships, whereas the technological component involves tools, techniques and methods of production or service delivery. Organisations have developed elaborate mechanisms for transforming incoming resources into goods and services. Banks,

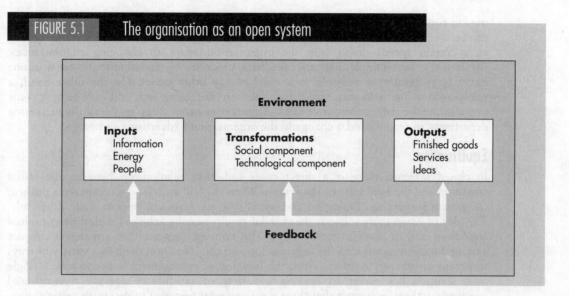

FIGURE 5.1 The organisation as an open system

for example, transform deposits into mortgage loans. Schools attempt to transform students into more educated people. Transformation processes can also take place at the group and individual levels. For example, research and development departments can transform the latest scientific advances into new product ideas.

Outputs are the result of what is transformed by the system and sent to the environment. Thus, inputs that have been transformed represent outputs ready to leave the system. Health insurance funds, such as HCF and Medibank Private, receive money and medical bills, transform them through the operation of record keeping and export payments to hospitals and doctors.

Boundaries

The idea of boundaries helps to distinguish between systems and environments. Closed systems have relatively rigid and impenetrable boundaries, whereas open systems have far more permeable ones. Boundaries—the borders, or limits, of the system—are easily seen in many biological and mechanical systems. Defining the boundaries of social systems is more difficult as there is a continuous inflow and outflow through them. For example, where are the organisational boundaries in this case? Call centres for various companies may be positioned offshore (e.g. mail order services are being centralised and established in India and will be able to service companies based in Australia and elsewhere). The emergence of the information superhighway and worldwide information networks will continue to challenge the notion of boundaries in open systems.

The definition of 'boundary' is arbitrary, as a social system has multiple sub-systems and one sub-system's boundary line may not be the same as that of another. As with the system itself, arbitrary boundaries may have to be assigned to any social organisation, depending on the variable to be stressed. The boundaries used for studying or analysing leadership may be quite different from those used to study inter-group dynamics.

Just as systems can be considered to be relatively open or closed, the permeability of boundaries also varies from fixed to diffuse. The boundaries of a community's police force are probably far more rigid and sharply defined than are those of the community's political parties. Conflict over boundaries is always a potential problem within an organisation, just as it is in the world outside the organisation.

Feedback

As shown in Figure 5.1, *feedback* is information about the actual performance or the results of the system. However, not all such information is feedback. Only information used to control the future functioning of the system is considered to be feedback. Feedback can be used to maintain the system in a steady state (e.g. keeping an assembly line running at a certain speed) or to help the organisation adapt to changing circumstances. McDonald's, for example, has strict feedback processes for ensuring that a meal in one outlet is as similar as possible to a meal in any other outlet. On the other hand, a salesperson in the field may report that sales are not going well and may suggest some organisational change to improve sales. A market research study may lead the marketing department to recommend a change in the organisation's advertising campaign.

Equifinality

In closed systems, there is a direct cause-and-effect relationship between the initial condition and the final state of the system. When the 'on' switch on a computer is pushed, the system powers up. Biological and social systems, however, operate quite differently. The idea of *equifinality* suggests that similar results may be achieved with different initial conditions and in many different ways. This concept suggests that a manager can use varying forms of inputs into the organisation and can transform them in a variety of ways to obtain satisfactory outputs. Thus, the function of management is not to seek a single rigid solution but rather to develop a variety of satisfactory options. Systems and contingency theories suggest that there is no universal best way to design an organisation. Organisations and departments providing routine services, such as Telstra and Optus's long-distance phone services, should be designed differently from pharmaceutical development groups at F. H. Faulding & Co. Ltd or Glaxo Wellcome Australia.

Alignment

A system's overall effectiveness is determined by the extent to which the different parts are aligned with each other. This alignment or fit concerns the relationships between inputs and transformations, between transformations and outputs and among the sub-systems of the transformation process. Diagnosticians who view the relationships between the various parts of a system as a whole are taking what is referred to as a 'systemic perspective'.

Fit and alignment refer to a characteristic of the relationship between two or more parts. Just as the teeth in two wheels of a watch must mesh perfectly for the watch to keep time, so too do the parts of an organisation need to mesh for it to be effective. For example, Southcorp attempts to achieve its goals through a strategy of diversification, and a divisional structure is used to support that strategy. A functional structure would not be a good fit with the strategy as it is more efficient for one division to focus on one product line than for one manufacturing department to try to make many different products. The systemic perspective suggests that diagnosis is the search for misfits among the various parts and sub-systems of an organisation.

Organisation-level diagnosis

When viewed as open systems, organisations can be diagnosed at three levels. The highest level is the overall organisation and includes the design of the company's strategy, structure and processes. Large organisation units, such as divisions, subsidiaries or strategic business units, can also be diagnosed at this level. The next lowest level is the group or department, which includes group design and devices for structuring interactions among members, such as norms and work schedules. The lowest level is the individual position or job. Diagnosis of these include ways in which jobs are designed in order to elicit required task behaviours.

Diagnosis can occur at all three organisational levels, or it may be limited to problems that occur at a particular level. The key to effective diagnosis is to know what to look for at each level, as well as how the levels affect each other.[2] A basic understanding of organisation-level issues is important in diagnosis at any level of analysis as these issues are important inputs to understanding groups and individuals.

The organisation level of analysis is the broadest systems perspective typically taken in diagnostic activities. The model shown in Figure 5.2 is similar to other popular

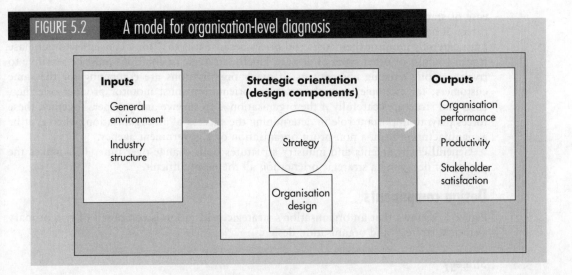

FIGURE 5.2   A model for organisation-level diagnosis

organisation-level diagnostic models. These include Weisbord's six-box model,[3] Nadler and Tushman's congruency model,[4] and Kotter's organisation dynamics model.[5] Figure 5.2 proposes that an organisation's strategy and organisation design, as well as its design components, represent the way the organisation positions and organises itself within an environment (inputs) to achieve specific outputs. The combination of strategy and organisation design is called a 'strategic orientation'.[6]

Inputs

To understand how a total organisation functions, it is necessary to examine particular inputs and design components and to examine the alignment of the two sets of dimensions. Figure 5.2 shows that two key inputs affect the way an organisation designs its strategic orientation: the general environment and industry structure.

The *general environment* represents the external elements and forces that can affect the attainment of organisational objectives.[7] It can be described in terms of the amount of uncertainty present in social, technological, economic, ecological and political forces. The more uncertainty there is in how the environment will affect the organisation, the more difficult it is to design an effective strategic orientation. For example, the technological environment in the watch industry has been highly uncertain over time. The Swiss, who built precision watches with highly-skilled craftspeople, were caught off-guard by the mass production and distribution technology of Timex in the 1960s. Similarly, many watch manufacturers were surprised by, and failed to take advantage of, digital technology.

The increased incidence of AIDS in the work place (social environment) and the implementation of the Equal Opportunity and Anti-Discrimination Acts (political environment) have also forced changes in the strategic orientations of organisations.

An organisation's *industry structure* or task environment is another important input into strategic orientation. As defined by Michael Porter, an organisation's task environment consists of five forces: suppliers, buyers, threats of substitutes, threats of entry and rivalry among competitors.[8] First, strategic orientations must be sensitive to powerful suppliers who can increase prices (and therefore lower profits) or force the organisation to pay more attention to the supplier's needs than to the organisation's needs. For example, unions represent powerful suppliers of labour that can affect the costs of any organisation within an industry. Second, strategic orientations must be sensitive to powerful buyers. Aeroplane purchasers, such as Qantas Airlines or country governments, can force Airbus, McDonnell-Douglas or Boeing to lower prices or appoint the planes in particular ways. Third, strategic orientations must be sensitive to the threat of new firms entering into competition. Profits in the restaurant business tend to be low because of the ease of starting a new restaurant. Fourth, strategic orientations must be sensitive to the threat of new products or services that can replace existing offerings. Ice cream producers must carefully monitor their costs and prices because it is easy for a consumer to purchase frozen yoghurt or other types of dessert. Finally, strategic orientations must be sensitive to rivalry among existing competitors. If many organisations are competing for the same customers, for example, then the strategic orientation must monitor product offerings, costs and structures carefully if the organisation is to survive and prosper. Together, these forces play an important role in determining the success of an organisation, whether it be a manufacturing firm, a non-profit organisation or a government agency.

General environments and industry structures both change over time. This makes the process of designing a strategic orientation all the more difficult.

Design components

Figure 5.3 shows that an organisation's strategic orientation is composed of two primary elements: strategy and organisation design.

Strategy

A strategy represents the way an organisation uses its resources (human, economic or technical) to gain and sustain a competitive advantage.[9] It can be described by the organisation's mission, goals and objectives, strategic intent, and functional policies. A *mission statement* describes the long-term purpose of the organisation, the range of products or services offered, the markets to be served and the social needs served by the organisation's existence. *Goals and objectives* are statements that provide explicit

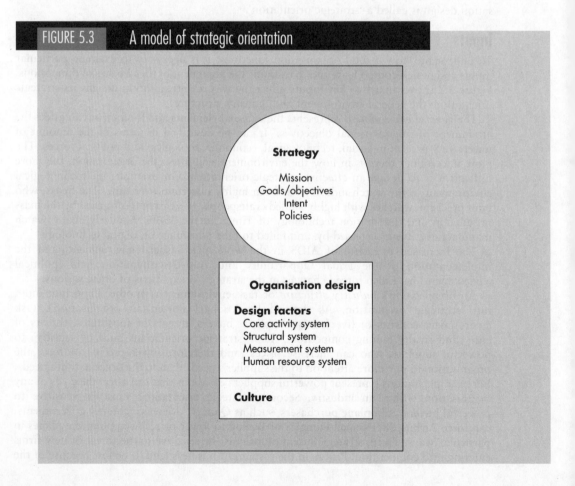

FIGURE 5.3 A model of strategic orientation

direction, set organisational priorities, provide guidelines for management decisions and serve as the cornerstone for organising activities, designing jobs and setting standards of achievement. Goals and objectives should set a target of achievement, such as 50% gross margins, an average employee satisfaction score of four on a five-point scale or some level of productivity; provide a means or system for measuring achievement; and provide a deadline or time frame for accomplishment.[10] A *strategic intent* is a succinct label that describes *how* the organisation intends to achieve its goals and objectives. For example, an organisation can achieve goals through differentiation of its product or service, by achieving the lowest costs in the industry or by growing the organisation. Finally, *functional policies* are the methods, procedures, rules or administrative practices that guide decision making and convert plans into actions. In the semi-conductor business, for example, Intel has a policy of allocating about 30% of revenues to research and development in order to maintain its lead in microprocessors.[11]

Organisation design

The organisation's design is comprised of four design factors and culture. *Design factors* are organisational sub-systems or change levers that support the business strategy. To implement a strategy successfully, the design factors must be aligned with the strategic intent and with each other. The four design factors are the core activity system, the structural system, the measurement system and the human resource system.

The core activity system is concerned with the way in which an organisation converts inputs into products and services. It represents the heart of the transformation function and includes production methods, work flow and equipment. Automobile companies have traditionally used an assembly-line technology to build cars and trucks. Two features of the technological core have been shown to influence other design components: interdependence and uncertainty.[12] *Technical interdependence* involves ways in which the different parts of a technological system are related. High interdependence requires considerable co-ordination between tasks, such as might occur when departments must work together to bring out a new product. *Technical uncertainty* refers to the amount of information processing and decision making required during task performance. Generally, when tasks require high amounts of information processing and decision making, they are difficult to plan and create routines for. The technology of car manufacturing is relatively certain and moderately interdependent. As a result, car manufacturers specify in advance the tasks that workers should perform and how their work should be co-ordinated.

The structural system describes how attention and resources are focused on task accomplishment. It represents the basic organising mode chosen to (1) divide the overall work of an organisation into subunits that can assign tasks to individuals or groups and (2) co-ordinate these subunits for completion of the overall work.[13] Structure, therefore, needs to be closely aligned with the organisation's core activity systems.

Two ways of determining how an organisation divides work are to examine its formal structure and to examine its level of differentiation and integration. Formal structures divide work by function (accounting, sales or production), by product or service (Fairlane, LTD or Falcon) or by some combination of both (a matrix composed of functional departments and product groupings). These are described in more detail in Chapter 14. The second way to describe how work is divided is to specify the amount of differentiation and integration in a structure. Applied to the total organisation, differentiation refers to the degree of similarity or difference in the design of two or more subunits or departments.[14] In a highly-differentiated organisation, there are major differences in design between the departments. Some departments are highly formalised with many rules and regulations, others have few rules and regulations and still others are moderately formal or flexible.

The way an organisation co-ordinates the work across subunits is called integration. Integration can be achieved in a variety of ways—for example, by using plans and schedules; using budgets; assigning special roles, such as project managers, liaison positions or integrators; or creating cross-departmental task forces and teams. The amount of integration required in a structure is a function of (1) the amount of uncertainty in the environment, (2) the level of differentiation in the structure and (3) the amount of interdependence between departments. As uncertainty, differentiation and interdependence increase, more sophisticated integration devices are required.

Measurement systems are methods of gathering, assessing and disseminating information on the activities of groups and individuals in organisations. Such data tell how well the organisation is performing and are used to detect and control deviations from goals. Closely related to structural integration, measurement systems monitor organisational operations and feed data about work activities to managers and organisational members so that they can better understand current performance and co-ordinate work. Effective information and control systems are clearly linked to strategic objectives; provide accurate, understandable and timely information; are accepted as legitimate by organisational members; and produce benefits in excess of their cost.

Human resource systems include mechanisms for selecting, developing, appraising and rewarding organisation members. These influence the mix of skills, personalities and behaviours of organisation members. The organisation's strategy and core activities provide important information about the required skills and knowledge that need to be present if the organisation is to be successful. Appraisal processes identify whether those skills and knowledge are being applied to the work, while reward systems complete the cycle by recognising performance that contributes to goal achievement. Reward systems may be tied to measurement systems so that rewards are allocated on the basis of measured results. (Specific human resource systems, such as rewards and career development, are discussed in Chapters 15 and 16.)

Organisation *culture* is the final element in an organisation's design. It represents the basic assumptions, values and norms shared by organisation members.[15] These cultural elements are generally taken for granted and serve to guide members' perceptions, thoughts and actions. For example, McDonald's culture emphasises 'efficiency', 'speed' and 'consistency'. It orients employees to company goals and suggests the kinds of behaviours necessary for success. In Figure 5.3, culture is separated from, and beneath, the design factors as it represents both an outcome of prior choices made about the strategy and the design factors and a foundation that can either hinder or facilitate change. In diagnosis, the focus is on understanding the current culture well enough to determine its alignment with the other design factors. Such information may partly explain current outcomes, such as performance or effectiveness. (Culture is discussed in more detail in Chapter 18.)

Outputs

The outputs of a strategic orientation can be classified into three components. First, organisation performance refers to financial outputs such as profits, return on investment and earnings per share. For non-profit and governmental agencies, performance often refers to the extent to which costs were lowered or budgets met. Second, productivity concerns the internal measurements of efficiency such as sales per employee, waste, error rates, quality or units produced per hour. Third, stakeholder satisfaction reflects how well the organisation has met the expectations of different groups. Customer satisfaction can be measured in terms of market share or focus group data; employee satisfaction can be measured in terms of an opinion survey; investor satisfaction can be measured in terms of share price.

Alignment

Assessing the effectiveness of an organisation's current strategic orientation requires that knowledge of the above information be acquired in order to determine the alignment among the different elements.

1 Does the organisation's strategic orientation fit with the inputs?
2 Do the elements of the strategy fit with each other?
3 Do the elements of the organisation design fit with each other?
4 Do the elements of the organisation design support the strategy?

For example, if the elements of the external environment (inputs) are fairly similar in their degree of certainty, then an effective organisation structure (design factor) should have a low degree of differentiation. Its departments should be designed similarly because each faces similar environmental demands. On the other hand, if the environment is complex and each element presents different amounts of uncertainty, a more differentiated structure is warranted. Esso's regulatory, ecological, technological and social environments differ greatly in their amount of uncertainty. The regulatory environment is relatively slow paced and detail oriented. Accordingly, the regulatory affairs function within Esso is formal and bound by protocol. In the technological environment, on the other hand, new methods for discovering, refining and distributing oil and oil products are changing at a rapid pace. These departments are much more flexible and adaptive, very different from the regulatory affairs function.

Analysis

Application 5.1 describes the Nike organisation and provides an opportunity to perform an organisation-level analysis.[16]

APPLICATION 5.1

Nike's strategic orientation

In 1993, Nike was the leader in US domestic-brand athletic footwear with more than 30% market share. It also produced sports apparel, hiking boots, and upscale men's shoes. But after six years of solid growth, international sales were falling, sales of basketball shoes were down, and the firm's stock price had dropped 41% since November 1992. Analysts were projecting declines in both total revenues and profits for the next fiscal year. In addition, Nike had been the focus of attack from several stakeholder groups. Organized labor believed that Nike exploited foreign labor; the African American sector noted the lack of diversity in Nike's work force; and the general public was getting tired of sensationalizing athletes.

Nike's traditional strategy was built around high-performance, innovative athletic shoes, aggressive marketing, and low-cost manufacturing. Using input from athletes, Nike developed a strong competence in producing high-quality athletic shoes, first for running, then for basketball and other sports. By contracting with well-known and outspoken athletes to endorse the product, a Nike image of renegade excellence and high performance

emerged. Other consumers who wanted to associate with the Nike image could do so by purchasing their shoes. Thus, a large market of weekend warriors, people pursuing a more active lifestyle, serious runners and anyone wanting to project a more athletic image became potential customers. Nike contracted with low-cost, foreign manufacturing plants to produce its shoes.

An athletic shoe retailer places orders with Nike representatives, who are not employees of Nike but contract with Nike to sell its shoes, for delivery in six to eight months. The Futures program, as it is called, offers the retailer 10 percent off the wholesale price for making these advanced orders. The orders are then compiled and production scheduled with one of Nike's Asian manufacturing partners. Nike doesn't actually make shoes. Instead, it develops contract relationships with Taiwanese, Korean, Japanese and other low-cost sources. On-site Nike employees guarantee that the shoes meet the Nike standards of quality.

Nike's culture is distinctive. The organization, built by athletes, for athletes, is very entrepreneurial, and the 'Just Do It' marketing campaign aptly describes the way things are done at

Nike. As one senior executive put it, 'It's fine to develop structures and plans and policies, if they are viewed, and used, as tools. But it is so easy for them to become substitutes for good thinking, alibis for not taking responsibility, reasons to not become involved. And then we'd no longer be Nike.'

What emerged, by the mid-1980s, was a way of working that involved setting direction, dividing up the work, pulling things together, and providing rewards.

Although Phil Knight, founder and chairman of Nike, sets the general direction for Nike, he rarely sets clear goals. For example, Knight views Nike as a growth company. The athletic drive pushes employers to achieve bigger sales and put more shoes on more feet than anyone else. Others are concerned that the decision to go public in the early 1980s produced pressures for profitability that sometimes work against growth. Implementation of the general direction depends on people being tuned into the day-to-day operations. 'You tune into what other people are doing and, if you're receptive, you start to see the need for something to be done', Knight says.

Nike changed from a functional organization in 1985 to a product division structure in 1987. In addition, 1993 brought additional structural change. The new president, Tom Clark, was busy implementing stronger communication and collaboration among manufacturing, marketing and sales. This description, however, belies the informality of the organization. In essence, the aim of the Nike structure is to fit the pieces together in ways that best meet the needs of the product, the customers and the market.

In pulling things together, Nike relies on meetings as the primary method for co-ordination. The word 'meeting' connotes more formality than is really intended. Meetings, which occur at all levels and in all parts of the organization, range from an informal gathering in the hallway, to a three-day off-site, to formal reviews of a product line. Membership in a meeting is equally fluid, with the people who need to be involved invited and those who don't, not invited. Although more formal systems have emerged over the years, their use is often localized to the people or groups who invented them and is met with resistance by others. Thus, with the exception of Futures, there is little in the way of formal information systems.

Finally, Knight favors an annual performance review system with annual pay increases tied to performance. In actuality, however, the system is fairly unstructured and some managers take time to do the reviews well while others do not. And although no formal compensation policy exists, most employees and managers believe that Nike is a 'great place to work.' For most people, rewards come in the form of growth opportunities, autonomy and responsibility.

Organisation-level dimensions and relationships may be applied to the diagnosis of Nike, as an example. A useful starting point is to ask how well the organisation is currently functioning—to examine the organisation's outputs yields measures of market share, financial performance and stakeholder satisfaction. Nike's string of solid annual increases over six years was followed by real or predicted declines. Discovering the underlying causes of these problems begins with an assessment of the inputs and strategic orientation and then proceeds to an evaluation of the alignments among the different parts. In diagnosing the inputs, two questions are important:

1 *What is the company's general environment?* Nike's environment is uncertain and complex. Technologically, Nike is dependent on the latest breakthroughs in shoe design and materials to keep its high-performance image. Socially and politically, Nike's international manufacturing and marketing operations require that it be aware of a variety of stakeholder demands from several countries, cultures and

governments, including the US government, which might view Nike's foreign manufacturing strategy with some concern about US jobs. Other stakeholders are pressuring Nike for changes to its human resource practices.

2 *What is the company's industry structure?* Nike's industry is highly competitive and places considerable pressure on profits. First, the threat of entry is high. It is not difficult or expensive to enter the athletic shoe market. Many shoe manufacturers could easily offer an athletic shoe if they wanted. The threat of substitute products is also high. Nike's image and franchise depend on people wanting to be athletic. If fitness trends were to change, then other footwear could easily fill the need. This possibility clearly exists because Nike's marketing has sensationalised professional athletes and sports, rather than emphasising fitness for the average person. The bargaining power of suppliers, such as providers of labour, shoe materials and manufacturing, is generally low because the resources are readily available and there are many sources. The bargaining power of buyers is moderate. At the high-performance end, buyers are willing to pay more for high quality, whereas at the casual end, price is important and the purchasing power of large accounts can bid down Nike's price. Finally, rivalry among firms is severe. A number of international and domestic competitors exist, such as Reebok, Adidas, New Balance, Puma, Converse and Tiger. Many of them have adopted similar marketing and promotion tactics to Nike and are competing for the same customers. Thus, the likelihood of new competition, the threat of new substitute products and the rivalry among existing competitors are the primary forces creating uncertainty in the environment and squeezing profits in the athletic shoe industry.

The following questions are important in assessing Nike's strategic orientation:

1 *What is the company's strategy?* Nike's strategy is clear on some points and nebulous on others. First, although the company has no formal mission statement, it has a clear sense about its initial purpose in producing high-quality, high-performance athletic footwear. That focus has blurred somewhat as Nike has ventured into apparel, hiking boots and casual shoes. Its goals are also nebulous because Phil Knight does not set specific goals, only general direction. The tension between growth and profits is a potential source of problems for the organisation. On the other hand, its strategic intent is fairly clear. It is attempting to achieve its growth and profitability goals by offering a differentiated product—a high quality, high-performance shoe. Informal policies dominate the Nike organisation.

2 *What is the company's organisation design?* First, the core activities of Nike are moderately uncertain and interdependent. For example, developing high-quality, state-of-the-art shoes is uncertain, but there is no evidence that research and development is tightly linked to production. In addition, the Futures programme creates low interdependence between manufacturing and distribution, both of which are fairly routine processes. Second, Nike's product division structure appears moderately differentiated, but the new president's emphasis on communication and co-ordination suggests that it is not highly integrated. Moreover, although Nike appears to have a divisional structure, its contract relationships with manufacturing plants and sales representatives give it a fluid, network-like structure. Third, human resource and measurement systems are under-developed. There is no compensation policy, for example, and formal control systems are generally resisted. The one exception to this is the Futures programme that tracks orders (which are really advance revenues). Finally, Nike's culture is a dominant feature of the organisation design. The organisation appears driven by typical athletic norms of winning, competition, achievement and performance.

Now that the organisation outputs, inputs and throughputs have been assessed, it is time to ask the crucial question about how well they fit together.

The first concern is the fit between inputs and strategic orientation. The complex and uncertain environment suits Nike's focus on differentiation and a generally flexible organisation design, which explains its incredible success during the 1970s, 1980s and into the 1990s. The alignment between its strategic orientation and its environment appears sound.

The second concern is the alignment of the elements within strategy and organisation design. The elements of Nike's strategy are not aligned. It clearly intends to differentiate its product by serving the high-end athlete with high-performance shoes. However, this small group of athletes may have trouble communicating its needs to a large, diversified organisation. Growth goals and a diversified mission quite obviously do not align with Nike's differentiation intent. This hypothesis is supported by the lack of clear goals in general, and policies that support neither growth nor profitability.

Within the organisation design, the core activity systems appear to be well supported and aligned with the structure. Product development, market development, and manufacturing development are inherently unprogrammable tasks that require flexibility and adaptability from the organisation. Although a product structure overlays most of Nike's activities, the structure is not rigid, and there appears to be a willingness to create structure as and when it is required to complete a task. In addition, the Futures programme is important for two reasons. First, it reduces uncertainty from the market by getting retailers to take the risk that a shoe will not do well. For the retailer, this risk is mitigated by Nike's tremendous reputation and marketing clout. Second, knowing in advance what will be ordered provides Nike with the ability to schedule production and distribution far in advance. This is a powerful device for integrating Nike's activities. Finally, the lack of a formal human resources system supports the fluid and flexible design, but creates problems in that there is no direction for hiring and development, a point noted by the various stakeholders at the beginning of the application.

Obviously, any discussion of Nike's organisation design has to recognise the powerful role its culture plays. More than any design factor, the culture promotes co-ordination of a variety of tasks, serves as a method for socialising and developing people and establishes methods for moving information around the organisation. Clearly, any change effort at Nike will have to acknowledge this role, and design an intervention accordingly. The strong culture will either sabotage or facilitate change, depending on how the change process aligns with the culture's impact on individual behaviour.

The last element of alignment is the extent to which the organisation design supports the strategy. In this case, there appears to be a good fit. The differentiated strategic intent requires an organisation design that focuses on the creation of new ideas in products, marketing and manufacturing. The flexible structure, informal systems and driving culture would seem well suited for that purpose.

Based on this diagnosis of the Nike organisation, at least two intervention possibilities are suggested. First, the OD practitioner could suggest increasing Nike's clarity about its strategy. In this intervention, the practitioner would want to avoid talking about formalising Nike's strategy because the culture would resist such an attempt. However, there are some clear advantages to be gained from a clearer sense of Nike's future, its businesses and the relationship between them. Second, Nike could focus on increasing the integration and co-ordination of its organisation design. Although the culture provides a considerable amount of social control, the lack of any human resource systems and the relatively underdeveloped integration mechanisms suggest that finding ways to co-ordinate activities without increasing formalisation would be a value-added intervention.

Application 5.2 describes the NEC Australia organisation and provides an opportunity for performing an organisation-level analysis.[17]

APPLICATION 5.2   How NEC went back to school and won kudos on the world stage

Faced with becoming just an agency for head office, NEC Australia decided on a complete makeover. Now it is a benchmark model for the rest of the company.

Australians are not good at making quality products and the Japanese lead the world. Right? Not necessarily. NEC Australia is being examined by the company's headquarters in Japan because it is considered to have some areas in which it has the highest quality standards of any part of the company. The Australian division believes it has developed a world-leading approach to forming knowledge teams.

Developing Australian managers to compete globally is becoming one of the nation's most important economic challenges, especially if unemployment is to be reduced. Transnational companies are increasingly dominating world commerce, to the extent that they produce almost a quarter of world economic output and their inter-company movement of goods and services is able to distort world trade figures. In a sense, a new kind of comparative advantage is being created: not between firms in different countries but between national management groups within the same company.

NEC Australia seems to have risen to the challenge. Certainly, the immediate evidence is impressive enough. NEC Australia won the Australian Quality Award in 1994, achieved ISO 9000 and 14000 accreditation in 1994–5, won the Australian Human Resources Institute Award in 1995 and the Australian Customer Service Award in 1996. The company exports to Indonesia, Brazil, China, Italy and Fiji.

This is the result of NEC Australia's management undertaking a complete change of the $300m company's culture and strategic position.

In 1989, management at the company's headquarters in Mulgrave, Melbourne, had to make a decision: either they would get out of manufacturing back-office computer and communications technology altogether and become just an agency, or they would position themselves to compete on the global stage. Clearly, the second course was preferable but it meant change. Most of the managers had at best a local, state-based orientation, and were ill-equipped to enter the regional, much less the global, arena.

Hilton Ludekens, senior general manager, corporate services, for NEC Australia, says staff numbers were cut from 1300 to 900, but those who remained were not of a high enough standard for global competition. He says: 'What we would have had to do is replace local managers with managers who have international experience. That would have cost at least 40% more, based on the expatriate expenses alone.'

NEC management decided to link up with Monash University's Mt Eliza Business School. What was to be avoided was a training exercise that managers would find interesting but which would have little effect on their subsequent behaviour. The chosen approach was to combine school and work to create an interplay between theoretical and practical learning.

The intention was to do something similar to apprenticeship training: in this case, for managing in a global context. It required a shift away from the traditional liberal arts emphasis of the university, by which learning for its own sake is considered to have priority. Instead, the emphasis was on pragmatic learning that is judged on how it can be applied in action.

Traditionally, industry formation for workers has been undertaken by civic bodies such as chambers, apprenticeship systems, associations, unions and guilds (many of which have been allowed to wither in Australia). For managers hoping to prepare themselves for global competition, the equivalent formation role is increasingly being performed by business schools.

Ted James, national credit manager for NEC Australia, who ultimately earned an MBA from the process, says the intellectual leap was significant. 'I have had to move from considering work in terms of Mulgrave, to looking at the state, then the regional environment, then the global context.' Some of the projects he did as part of the course, he says, were both an academic test and something that could be directly applied within the company. 'Management consultants quoted us $100 000 to do a benchmarking study over two weeks. The document I produced (for the course) would probably be worth $30–40 000 to the company.'

The first step in the programme was to select 20 managers to go on a middle-management course. From that group, 17 were selected to go to the next level on an executive training programme. When this group was first assessed, they were slightly above average; after the course they were at the top of the range.

Determining why there was such an improvement is one of the issues challenging Graeme Pocknee, a lecturer at the Mt Eliza Business School's global-strategy centre, who headed the programme. He says that, although NEC Australia produces only 3% of NEC's global output, the company is benchmarked by 90% of NEC's world-wide operations in the areas of competency and marketing.

He believes the main requirement is 'momentum': developing an integrated approach that takes into account the needs and incentives of all staff, and creates volition across the organisation. 'What they seem to have done is generate this momentum consciously', he says. 'That is what separates them out.'

Usually, change is addressed piecemeal, he says, because of an external event, such as a change in the market, capital risk or a merger. 'Very rarely does it happen that an organisation says, "We are going to change the nature of our business, which requires a holistic review of our future, our competencies and strategies and the relationship between those elements."' Usually what happens is that they focus on what is important first, and are under enormous time pressures to get early results.'

Pocknee says that NEC had been losing money for ten years and was not in manufacturing 'with their hearts and their minds'. Moreover, there was a cultural divide between the strongly individualistic Australian managers and the consensus-driven Japanese management. Japan was sceptical about using Australia as a base for exports and

Australian management knew the company either had to get to international level quickly or get out of manufacturing altogether and become an agency. There was no middle ground.

That such a change was possible at all is due to NEC's use of a federalist structure internationally, which allows it to encourage local innovation while retaining control of strategy at the regional level, and strong central financial control at the company's headquarters. Reporting, however, is complex. The company uses a matrix structure that requires senior managers to report to at least four people in Australia, (as well as reporting internationally).

The key was Ludekens, who had rapport with both the Australian and Japanese management. Pocknee says: 'Both groups trusted him enough to use him for passing messages back and forth.'

With the senior managers, the focus was on providing a contextual understanding of global imperatives, developing modern tools and techniques, and adopting a common business language. Leadership simulations were also used.

The 17 high-performing middle-managers who were at the centre of the company's repositioning were selected from different divisions of the company and formed into an elite group. This group fostered the sharing of knowledge and developed a cross-disciplinary understanding through their study and their exposure to each other (other middle managers were put through a parallel but less intensive process, and line managers were trained in more technical areas).

The educational process, which concentrated mainly on quality and strategy, was linked throughout to specific company outcomes and academically assessed. The time period set for the 17 elite managers was three years, and each manager spent 26 days a year at school (only 12 of which were contributed by the company). School-fee and lost-time costs were about the same. In two years, the group achieved best national practice; in three years, best international practice.

Pocknee believes the result was a 'learning team', an effective example of the type of 'knowledge organisation' that most management theorists believe is essential in modern businesses. What was different was not so much the individual elements (most of which were well-known methods of quality implementation, strategy development, stakeholder analysis and change management) but the integration of training with specific company outcomes and the aligning of the managers' personal motives and incentives with company objectives.

Pocknee says: 'They measured everything. What is occurring is a knowledge process that combines internal and external knowledge.'

NEC Australia is merging with the two other Australian subsidiaries: NEC Information Systems and NEC Home Electronics—'boxes in, boxes out' companies, agencies for overseas product operating on fine profit margins. The combined company, with a revenue of $600m aimed for $1b by the year 2000. The methods used in NEC Australia were to be adopted across the merged company.

Ludekens believes that NEC Australia proved that Australian management can shine on the international stage. One reason has been psychological: 'They (the elite managers) felt bloody important.'

Summary

This chapter presented background information for diagnosing organisations, groups and individual jobs. Diagnosis is a collaborative process, involving both managers and consultants in collecting pertinent data, analysing them and drawing conclusions for action planning and intervention. Diagnosis may be aimed at discovering the causes of specific problems, or it may be directed at assessing the organisation or department to find areas for future development. Diagnosis provides the practical understanding that is necessary in order to devise interventions for solving problems and improving organisation effectiveness.

Diagnosis is based on conceptual frameworks about how organisations function. Such diagnostic models serve as road maps in that they identify areas to examine and questions to ask when determining how an organisation or department is operating.

The comprehensive model presented here views organisations as open systems. The organisation serves to co-ordinate the behaviours of its departments. It is open to exchanges with the larger environment and is influenced by external forces. As open systems, organisations are hierarchically ordered—they are composed of groups, which in turn are composed of individual jobs. Organisations also display five key systems properties: (1) inputs, transformations and outputs; (2) boundaries; (3) feedback; (4) equifinality and (5) alignment.

An organisation-level diagnostic model is described and applied. It consists of environmental inputs, a set of design components called a strategic orientation and a variety of outputs, such as performance, productivity and stakeholder satisfaction. Diagnosis involves understanding each part in the model and then assessing how the elements of the strategic orientation align with each other and with the inputs. Organisation effectiveness is likely to be high when there is good alignment.

ACTIVITIES

Review questions
1 What are the possible symptoms of an organisational problem?
2 What is diagnosis? Explain its multi-faceted aspects.
3 What does proper diagnosis involve?
4 When is it appropriate to seek an organisation-level diagnosis?

Discussion and essay questions
1 Outline some of the key issues in open systems theory.
2 Discuss the relationship between the type of task environment faced by the organisation and how design components such as technology, structure, measurement systems and human resource systems must be adapted.
3 Describe an effective diagnostic model at the organisation-level. Discuss its major inputs, outputs and strategic orientation.
4 Name and discuss four key systems properties of an organisation.

Notes

1 D. Nadler, 'Role of models in organizational assessment', in *Organizational Assessment*, eds E. Lawler III, D. Nadler and C. Cammann (New York: John Wiley and Sons, 1980): 119–31; R. Keidel, *Seeing Organizational Patterns* (San Francisco: Berrett-Koehler, 1995); M. Harrison, *Diagnosing Organizations*, 2nd ed. (Thousand Oaks, Calif.: Sage Publications, 1994).

2 D. Coghlan, 'Organization development through interlevel dynamics', *The International Journal of Organizational Analysis*, 2 (1994): 264–79.

3 M. Weisbord, 'Organizational diagnosis: six places to look for trouble with or without a theory', *Group and Organizational Studies*, 1 (1976): 430–37.

4 D. Nadler and M. Tushman, 'A diagnostic model for organization behaviour', in *Perspectives on Behaviour in Organizations*, eds J. Hackman, E. Lawler III and L. Porter (New York: McGraw-Hill, 1977): 85–100.

5 J. Kotter, *Organizational Dynamics: Diagnosis and Intervention* (Reading, Mass.: Addison-Wesley, 1978).

6 M. Tushman and E. Romanelli, 'Organization evolution: a metamorphosis model of convergence and reorientation' in *Research in Organization Behaviour*, 7, eds L. Cummings and B. Staw (Greenwich, Conn.: JAI Press, 1985); C. Worley, D. Hitchin and W. Ross, *Integrated Strategic Change: How OD Builds Competitive Advantage* (Reading, Mass.: Addison-Wesley, 1996).

7 F. Emery and E. Trist, 'The causal texture of organizational environments', *Human Relations*, 18 (1965): 21–32; H. Aldrich, *Organizations and Environments* (Engle-wood Cliffs, N.J.: Prentice-Hall, 1979).

8 M. Porter, *Competitive Strategy* (New York: Free Press, 1980).

9 M. Porter, *Competitive Advantage* (New York: Free Press, 1985); C. Hill and G. Jones, *Strategic Management*, 3rd ed. (Boston: Houghton Mifflin, 1995).

10 C. Hofer and D. Schendel, *Strategy Formulation: Analytical Concepts* (St Paul, Minn.: West Publishing Company, 1978).

11 R. Hoff, 'Inside Intel', *Business Week* (1 June 1992): 86–94.

12 J. Thompson, *Organizations in Action* (New York: McGraw-Hill, 1967); D. Gerwin, 'Relationships between structure and technology', in *Handbook of Organisational Design*, 2, eds P. Nystrom and W. Starbuck (Oxford: Oxford University Press, 1981): 3–38.

13 J. Galbraith, *Organization Design* (Reading, Mass.: Addison-Wesley, 1977); D. Robey and C. Sales, *Designing Organizations*, 4th ed. (Homewood, Ill.: Irwin, 1994).

14 P. Lawrence and J. Lorsch, *Organization and Environment* (Cambridge: Harvard University Press, 1967).

15 V. Sathe, 'Implications of corporate culture: a manager's guide to acting', *Organizational Dynamics* (Autumn 1983): 5–23; E. Schein, *Organizational Culture and Leadership*, 2nd ed. (San Francisco: Jossey-Bass, 1990).

16 Adapted from material in G. Willigan, 'High performance marketing: an interview with Nike's Phil Knight', *Harvard Business Review* (July–August, 1992); D. Yang and M. Oneal, 'Can Nike just do it?' *Business Week* (18 April 1994): 86–90; D. Rikert and C. Christensen, 'Nike (A)' 9-395-025 (Boston: Harvard Business School, 1984); D. Rikert and C. Christensen, 'Nike (B)' 9-385-027 (Boston: Harvard Business School, 1984).

17 James, D. 'How NEC went back to school and wound up winning kudos on the world stage', *Business Review* (29 September 1997), 82.

Diagnosing groups and jobs

Chapter 5 introduced diagnosis as the second major phase in the model of planned change. Based on open systems theory, an organisation-level diagnostic model was described and applied. After the organisation level, the next two levels of diagnosis are the group and job. Many large organisations have groups or departments that are themselves relatively large, like the operating divisions at BHP and Pacific Dunlop. Diagnosis of large groups can follow the dimensions and relational fits applicable to organisation-level diagnosis, because large groups or departments essentially operate much like organisations, and diagnosing them as organisations can assess their functioning.

However, small departments and groups can behave differently from large organisations. Therefore, they need their own diagnostic models to reflect these differences. In the first section of this chapter, we discuss the diagnosis of work groups. Such groups generally consist of a relatively small number of people working face-to-face on a shared task. Work groups are prevalent in all sizes of organisations. They can be relatively permanent and perform an ongoing task, or they can be temporary and exist only to perform one particular task or to make a specific decision.

Finally, we describe and apply a diagnostic model of individual jobs—the smallest unit of analysis in organisations. Individual jobs are constructed to perform specific tasks or sets of tasks, but their design can affect individual and organisational effectiveness.

Group-level diagnosis

Figure 6.1 shows the inputs, design components, outputs and relational fits for group-level diagnosis.[1] The model is similar to other popular group-level diagnostic models, such as Hackman and Morris's task group design model[2] and Ledford, Lawler and Mohrman's participation group design model.[3]

Inputs

Organisation design is clearly the major input in group design. It consists of the design components that characterise the larger organisation within which the group is embedded. These include core activity, structural, measurement and human resource systems, as well as organisational culture. Core activity systems can determine the characteristics of the group's task; structural systems can specify the level of co-ordination required between groups. The human resource and measurement systems, such as performance appraisal and reward systems, play an important role in determining team functioning.[4] For example, individually-based performance appraisal and reward systems tend to interfere with team functioning as the members may be more concerned with maximising their individual performance to the detriment of team performance. Collecting information about the group's organisation design context can greatly improve the accuracy of diagnosis.

Design components

Figure 6.1 shows that groups have five major components: (1) goal clarity, (2) task structure, (3) group composition, (4) group functioning and (5) performance norms.

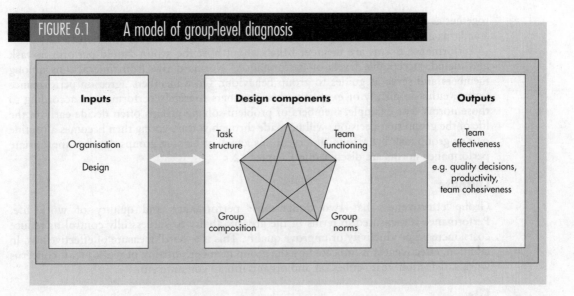

FIGURE 6.1   A model of group-level diagnosis

Inputs	Design components	Outputs
Organisation Design	Task structure / Team functioning / Group composition / Group norms	Team effectiveness e.g. quality decisions, productivity, team cohesiveness

Goal clarity involves how well the group understands its objectives. In general, goals should be moderately challenging; there should be a method for measuring, monitoring and feeding back information about goal achievement; and the goals should be clearly understood by all members.

Task structure is concerned with how the group's work is designed. Task structures can vary along two key dimensions: co-ordination of members' efforts and regulation of their task behaviours.[5] The co-ordination dimension involves the degree to which group tasks are structured to promote effective interaction among group members. Co-ordination is important in groups who perform interdependent tasks, such as surgical teams and problem-solving groups. It is relatively unimportant, however, in groups composed of members performing independent tasks, such as a group of telephone operators or salespeople. The regulation dimension involves the degree to which members can control their own task behaviours and be relatively free from external controls, such as supervision, plans and programmes. Self-regulation generally occurs when members can decide on such issues as task assignments, work methods, production goals and membership. (Interventions for designing group task structure are discussed in Chapter 16.)

Composition concerns the membership of groups. Members can differ on a number of dimensions that have relevance to group behaviour. Demographic variables, such as age, education, experience and skills and abilities, can affect how people behave and relate to each other in groups. Demographics can determine whether the group is composed of people who have task-relevant skills and knowledge, including interpersonal skills. People's internal needs can also influence group behaviours. Individual differences in social needs can determine whether group membership is likely to be satisfying or stressful.[6]

Group functioning is the underlying basis of group life. How members relate to each other is important in work groups as the quality of relationships can affect task performance. In some groups, for example, interpersonal competition and conflict between members result in their providing little support and help for each other. Conversely, groups may become too concerned about sharing good feelings and support, and spend too little time on task performance. In organisation development, considerable effort has been invested to help work groups develop healthy interpersonal relations, including an ability and a willingness to openly share feelings and perceptions about the members' behaviours so that interpersonal problems and task difficulties can be worked through and resolved.[7] Group functioning therefore involves (1) task-related activities, such as giving and seeking information and elaborating, co-ordinating and evaluating activities; and (2) the group-maintenance function, directed toward holding the group together as a cohesive team and includes encouraging, harmonising, compromising, setting standards and observing.[8] (Interpersonal interventions are discussed in Chapter 12.)

Performance norms are member beliefs about how the group should perform its task and include acceptable levels of performance.[9] Norms derive from interactions among members and serve as guides to group behaviour. Once members agree on performance norms, either implicitly or explicitly, then members routinely perform tasks according to those norms. For example, members of problem-solving groups often decide early in the life of the group that decisions will be made through voting; voting then becomes a routine part of group task behaviour. (Interventions aimed at helping groups develop appropriate performance norms are discussed in Chapter 12.)

Outputs

Group effectiveness has two dimensions: performance and quality of work life. Performance is measured in terms of the group's ability to successfully control or reduce costs, increase productivity or improve quality. This is a 'hard' measure of effectiveness. In addition, effectiveness is indicated by the group member's quality of work life. It concerns work satisfaction, team cohesion and organisational commitment.

Fits

The diagnostic model in Figure 6.1 shows that group design components must fit inputs if groups are to be effective in terms of performance and the quality of work life. Research suggests the following fits between the inputs and design dimensions:

1   Group design should be congruent with the larger organisation design. Organisation structures with low differentiation and high integration should have work groups that are composed of highly-skilled and experienced members performing highly interdependent tasks. Organisations with differentiated structures and formalised human resource and information systems should spawn groups that have clear, quantitative goals and support standardised behaviours. Although there is little direct research on these fits, the underlying rationale is that congruence between organisation and group designs supports overall integration within the company. When group designs are not compatible with organisation designs, groups often conflict with the organisation.[10] They may develop norms that run counter to organisational effectiveness, such as happens in groups that are supportive of horseplay, goldbricking and other counter-productive behaviours.

2   When the core activity system of organisation design results in interdependent tasks, co-ordination among members should be promoted by task structures, composition, performance norms and group functioning. Conversely, when technology permits independent tasks, the design components should promote individual task performance.[11] For example, when co-ordination is needed, task structure might physically locate related tasks together; composition might include members with similar interpersonal skills and social needs; performance norms would support task-relevant interactions; and healthy interpersonal relations would be developed.

3   When the core activity system is relatively uncertain and requires high amounts of information processing and decision making, group task structure, composition, performance norms and group functioning should promote self-regulation. Members should have the necessary freedom, information and skills to assign members to tasks, to decide on production methods and to set performance goals.[12] When technology is relatively certain, group designs should promote standardisation of behaviour, and groups should be externally controlled by supervisors, schedules and plans.[13] For example, when self-regulation is needed, task structure might be relatively flexible and allow the interchange of members across group tasks; composition might include members with multiple skills, interpersonal competencies and social needs; performance norms support complex problem solving; and efforts made to develop healthy interpersonal relations.

Analysis

Application 6.1 presents an example of how the processes of consultation and negotiation were used by management and the work force at BP's Kwinana refinery to adapt to major changes in their working environment.[14]

The evolution of industrial relations in a changing environment

It became increasingly apparent in 1985 that the Kwinana refinery was facing a serious economic situation, with production costs making it cheaper to refine oil in Singapore and ship it to Western Australia. At a management seminar to develop a strategy to handle the situation it was decided that a major investment programme was necessary to modernise the refinery; without this the future of the refinery was uncertain. However, funds would not be forthcoming for such a programme unless there were clear evidence of an ability to introduce change and reduce costs in all the refinery's operations.

The company began formal negotiations with the unions on the question of redundancies in August 1985. The view of the company was that there was a need for about 220 retrenchments. The company had negotiated a redundancy agreement for the closure of another refinery and this agreement had become the standard for retrenchments in the organisation.

To manage the redundancies, the central decisions relating to the HRM dimension of the redundancy that focuses attention on achieving an efficient labour utilisation, were the subject of negotiation rather than unilateral decision by management. The union stance was also an indication that further negotiation on the redundancy package already on offer would be necessary, thus extending the joint decision making to all aspects of the implementation of the redundancy.

One example was in the tank farm area where ideas emerged through discussion and negotiation, enabling changes to be made to the work carried out by the operators. These changes increased the proportion of day work and resulted in greater savings by reduced shift working. Similarly in the fabrication shop, work was reorganised and some of the distinctions between trades lowered. In some cases the workers and local representatives were more willing to accept the change and consequent reduction in staffing than were the union officials.

The five months of negotiation resulted in major and widespread changes in the operation of the refinery and created the basis for more change. These negotiations were concluded to the satisfaction of both parties and without recourse to industrial action or to the industrial tribunal. All parties recognised that the refinery's commercial viability was central. More important, it was widely acknowledged that a key element in the success of the negotiations was the involvement of line management and the employees. This involvement took place in the context of the good negotiating relations that existed at the refinery between the industrial relations specialists and local union representatives. Because of the involvement at the work group level, the proposals for change were developed at the point where they would be implemented, and this raised the quality of the agreement in its substance and acceptance. This factor is important not only in terms of maintaining a high level of labour utilisation, which was the object of the staff/redundancy exercise, but also in terms of the development of relationships between management, workers and the unions on site. The basis of the continuing relationship between the parties was the agreement to develop formal procedures on occupational health and safety, and on technological change, both in the context of an industrial democracy framework.

This case shows the complexity of the industrial relations system at the plant. It can be seen that no one issue can be compartmentalised as each issue takes place in a context of continuing relationships and prior agreements and because each issue has a variety of consequences. For example, the negotiations on work practices were in the context of the redundancy package. Similarly, the introduction of new technology held implications for recruiting and training, for the development of the employee relations climate and for the role of the union in the place of work.

The key issue in diagnosing group inputs is the design of the larger organisation within which groups were embedded. BP's design is relatively differentiated. Each plant, like Kwinana, is allowed to set up its own organisation design. Similarly, although no specific data are given, the company's technology, structure, measurement systems, human resource systems and culture appear to promote flexible and innovative behaviours at the plant level. Indeed, freedom to innovate in the manufacturing plants is probably an outgrowth of the firm's OD activities and participative culture.

In the case of decision-making groups, such as Occupational Health and Safety, organisation design also affects the nature of the issues that are worked on. A single Refinery Safety and Health Committee (RS&HC) was established as 'an independent body accountable to the refinery manager'. Only the chief fire and safety officer and a safety inspector are *ex-officio* members: all of the 14 other representatives are elected by work groups that cover the whole of the refinery. The committee exists to 'ensure that arrangements exist for joint consultation with all employees on health and safety matters and to encourage effective participation by employees in accident prevention, consistent with policies laid down by the RS&HC'. Although the committee's terms of reference are not as explicit as the union's draft document that formed part of its claim in the negotiations, the essential elements of establishing an effective joint approach to safety are present, reflecting the common ground between management and unions on this issue.

The issue of health and safety can be addressed in three broad areas—in policy formulation, in plant design and in the operation of the plant, e.g. in the operation of the refinery any BP employee has the authority to shut down a process if he or she considers that it is becoming unsafe. In essence, the committee has been concerned with correctly channelling the information made available by management, but which had not been getting through to where it was needed, when it was needed.

There are determinants of safe performance, such as design, the level of training, work pressures, management commitment and so on. The joint approach adopted by management, employees and unions at BP is part of achieving a safe working environment at the refinery. Management commitment is evident. Employee involvement takes place in a variety of ways: in the development of work procedures and in the activity of the committee itself. Employee control, rather than just participation in decision making, is at two levels. First, at the point of production, if it is considered that the operation is unsafe. Second, control can be exercised collectively where the union membership is prepared to make safety an industrial issue. It is the integration of all these aspects that will determine the long-term success of the safety programme at BP.

The committee meetings appear to be devoted to problems that affect all the functional departments. This suggests that the problems entail high interdependence among the functions; consequently, high co-ordination among members is needed to resolve them. The team meetings also seem to include many issues that are complex and not easily solved. This implies that there is a relatively high amount of uncertainty in the core activity system. The causes of the problems or acceptable solutions are not readily available. Members must process considerable information during problem solving, especially when there are different perceptions and opinions about the issues.

Diagnosis of the team's design components answers the following questions:

1   How clear are the group's goals?
2   What is the group's task structure?
3   What is the composition of the group?
4   What are the group's performance norms?
5   What is the nature of team functioning in the group?

The issues that the team deals with are highly interdependent and often uncertain. The meetings are intended to resolve plant-wide problems that affect the various functional departments. Those problems are generally complex and require the members to process considerable information and create innovative solutions. The team's task structure and composition appear to fit the nature of team issues. The face-to-face meetings help to co-ordinate problem solving among the department managers. Team members seem to have the necessary task-relevant skills and experience, apart from the interpersonal skills, that could help the problem-solving process. However, there may be a conflict in the priority between the problems chosen by the team to be solved and the problems facing individual managers.

The key difficulty seems to be a mismatch between the team's performance norms and interpersonal relations and the demands of the problem-solving task. Complex, interdependent problems require performance norms that support the sharing of diverse and often conflicting kinds of information. The norms must encourage members to generate novel solutions and assess the relevance of problem-solving strategies in the light of new issues. Members need to explicitly address how they are using their knowledge and skills and how they are weighing and combining members' individual contributions.

In this example, the team's performance norms fail to support complex problem solving; rather, they promote a problem-solving method that is often superficial, haphazard and subject to external disruptions. Members' interpersonal relations reinforce adherence to the ineffective norms. Members do not confront personal differences or dissatisfaction with the group process. They fail to examine the very norms that contribute to their problems. In this case, diagnosis suggests the need for group interventions aimed at improving performance norms and developing healthy interpersonal relations.

Individual-level diagnosis

The lowest level of organisational diagnosis is the individual job or position. An organisation consists of numerous groups; a group, in turn, is composed of several individual jobs. This section discusses the inputs, design components and relational fits for diagnosing jobs. The model shown in Figure 6.2 is similar to other popular job diagnostic frameworks, such as Hackman and Oldham's job diagnostic survey and Herzberg's job enrichment model.[15]

Inputs

Three major inputs affect job design: (1) organisation design, (2) group design and (3) the personal characteristics of jobholders.

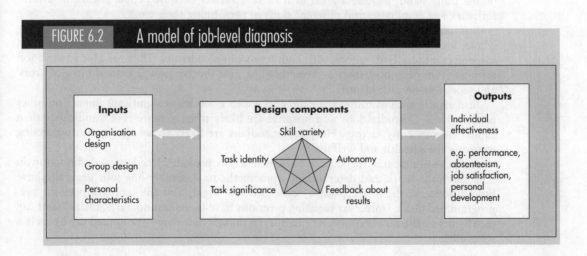

FIGURE 6.2   A model of job-level diagnosis

Inputs	Design components	Outputs
Organisation design	Skill variety	Individual effectiveness
Group design	Task identity — Autonomy	e.g. performance, absenteeism, job satisfaction, personal development
Personal characteristics	Task significance — Feedback about results	

Organisation design is concerned with the larger organisation within which the individual job is the smallest unit. Organisation design is a key part of the larger context surrounding jobs. Core activity systems, structure, measurement systems, human resource systems and culture can have a powerful impact on the way jobs are designed and on people's experiences in jobs. For example, company reward systems can orient employees to particular job behaviours and influence whether people see job performance as fairly rewarded. In general, core activity systems composed of relatively uncertain tasks and low interdependency are likely to support job designs that allow employees flexibility and discretion in performing tasks. Conversely, low uncertainty work systems are likely to promote standardised job designs requiring routinised task behaviours.[16]

Group design concerns the larger group or department containing the individual job. Like organisation design, group design is an essential part of the job context. Group task structure, goal clarity, composition, performance norms and group functioning serve as inputs to job design. They typically have a more immediate impact on jobs than the larger, organisation-design components. For example, group task structure can determine how individual jobs are grouped together—as in groups that require co-ordination among jobs or in ones comprising collections of independent jobs. Group composition can influence the kinds of people that are available to fill jobs. Group performance norms can affect the kinds of job designs that are considered acceptable, including the level of jobholders' performances. Goal clarity helps members to prioritise work, and group functioning can affect how powerfully the group influences job behaviours. When members maintain close relationships and the group is cohesive, group norms are more likely to be enforced and followed.[17]

Personal characteristics of individuals occupying jobs include their age, education, experience, and skills and abilities. All of these can affect job performance as well as how people react to job designs. Individual needs and expectations can also affect employee job responses. For example, individual differences in growth need—the need for self-direction, learning and personal accomplishment—can determine how much people are motivated and satisfied by jobs with high levels of skill variety, autonomy and feedback about results.[18] Similarly, work motivation can be influenced by people's expectations that they can perform a job well, and that good job performance will result in valued outcomes.[19]

Design components

Figure 6.2 shows that individual jobs have five key dimensions: (1) skill variety, (2) task identity, (3) task significance, (4) autonomy and (5) feedback about results.[20]

Skill variety identifies the degree to which a job requires a range of activities and abilities to perform the work. Assembly-line jobs, for example, generally have limited skill variety because employees perform a small number of repetitive activities. Most professional jobs, on the other hand, include a great deal of skill variety because people engage in diverse activities and employ several different skills in performing their work.

Task identity measures the degree to which a job requires the completion of a relatively whole, identifiable piece of work. Skilled craftspeople, such as tool-and-die makers and carpenters, generally have jobs with high levels of task identity. They are able to see a job through from beginning to end. Assembly-line jobs involve only a limited piece of work and score low on task identity.

Task significance identifies the degree to which a job has a significant impact on other people's lives. Custodial jobs in a hospital are likely to have more task significance than similar jobs in a toy factory. Hospital custodians are likely to see their jobs as affecting someone else's health and welfare.

Autonomy indicates the degree to which a job provides freedom and discretion in scheduling the work and determining work methods. Assembly-line jobs generally have little autonomy: the work pace is scheduled and rigid, and the workers perform pre-programmed tasks. University teaching positions have more autonomy: academic staff can usually determine how a course is taught, even though they may have limited say over class scheduling.

Feedback about results involves the degree to which a job provides employees with direct and clear information about the effectiveness of task performance. Assembly-line jobs often provide high levels of feedback about results, whereas academics must often contend with indirect and ambiguous feedback about how they are performing in the classroom.

The five job dimensions can be combined into an overall measure of *job enrichment*. Enriched jobs have high levels of skill variety, task identity, task significance, autonomy and feedback about results. They provide opportunities for self-direction, learning and personal accomplishment at work. Many people find enriched jobs internally motivating and satisfying. (Job enrichment is discussed more fully in Chapter 16.)

Fits

The diagnostic model in Figure 6.2 suggests that job design must fit job inputs to produce effective job outputs, such as high quality and quantity of individual performance, low absenteeism and high job satisfaction. Research reveals the following fits between job inputs and job design:

1   Job design should be congruent with the larger organisation and group designs within which the job is embedded.[21] Both the organisation and the group serve as a powerful context for individual jobs or positions. They tend to support and reinforce particular job designs. Highly differentiated and integrated organisations and groups that permit members to self-regulate their behaviour fit enriched jobs. These larger organisations and groups promote autonomy, flexibility and innovation at the individual job level. Conversely, bureaucratic organisations and groups relying on external controls are congruent with job designs that score low on the five key dimensions. Both organisations and groups reinforce standardised, routine jobs. As suggested earlier, congruence across different levels of organisation design promotes integration of the organisation, group and job levels. Whenever the levels do not fit each other, conflict is likely to emerge.

2   Job design should fit the personal characteristics of the job holders if they are to perform effectively and derive satisfaction from work. Generally, enriched jobs fit people with strong growth needs.[22] These people derive satisfaction and accomplishment from performing jobs that involve skill variety, autonomy and feedback about results. Enriched jobs also fit people possessing moderate to high levels of task-relevant skills, abilities and knowledge. Enriched jobs generally require complex information processing and decision making; people must have comparable skills and abilities in order to perform effectively. Jobs scoring low on the five job dimensions generally fit people with rudimentary skills and abilities and with low growth needs. Simpler, more routine jobs require limited skills and experience; they fit better with people who place a low value on opportunities for self-direction and learning. In addition, because people grow through education, training and experience, job design must be monitored and adjusted from time to time.

APPLICATION 6.2   Breaking down the 'them' and 'us' attitude at GEMCo

GEMCo, a BHP subsidiary, mines and exports manganese ore, an essential element for steelmaking, as it gives steel its hardness. The company is based on Groote Eylandt in the Gulf of Carpentaria in Australia's north. It operates one of the world's largest high-grade manganese ore deposits from its mining leases on the island, producing much of the world's manganese ore. Each year the company mines about two million tonnes of total products. It built the port, township and treatment plant on Groote Eylandt, together with associated services. About 540 people work for the company.

The manager of GEMCo, Mr Bob Wunder, sees that the only way that restructuring will succeed is with the co-operation of workers and managers. Often, though, people need to acquire the skills to work together. 'To help discover ways of working together, GEMCo ran several training courses on industrial participation for all levels of employees,' Mr Wunder said.

GEMCo used the Industrial Participation Unit of the Royal Melbourne Institute of Technology (RMIT) to run a series of workshops on Groote Eylandt. 'The workshops have been successful because they have shown that everyone can work together; common goals emerged for managers and workers on the island, and this established a common base on which to develop the teamwork needed to achieve change in the work place. Everyone has to work together, and can work together to solve common problems. And everyone can work together as a team. The key to

problem resolution is negotiation. Give and take are crucial. The original position will rarely be the final position. Through team building, and by developing a joint understanding and commitment, a win–win outcome can be achieved. Both managers and the work force will benefit,' says Mr Wunder.

'The RMIT workshops have achieved a greater trust between managers and workers; the engrained "them" and "us" attitude is starting to break down. Since the workshops, employees who attended have the skills and the desire to sit down and solve problems together without confrontation, to find participative solutions. Confrontation isn't good for anyone. The workshops also developed people's communication skills and this is important in redesigning their jobs. Managers are now listening to the people doing the work, and workers are now participating, having their say, and determining how they do their jobs.'

Analysis

Application 6.2 presents an example of an Australian industry facing the most extensive overhaul of work arrangements in the country's history, but one enterprise—on remote Groote Eylandt—feels that it is well prepared to face the challenge of restructuring.[23]

To implement restructuring, Mr Bob Wunder sees that GEMCo will need to balance training with production; eliminate restrictive work practices; and produce more with the same number of people. 'This company—and all enterprises—have to take care of the people who help make the profit. People also have to see that the harder they work the more benefits they get. More money is one way, but that's only part of the answer. In another way, people want to have satisfying jobs and be recognised for a job well done. GEMCo can train its employees, and increase their job skills, but those skills will need to be recognised elsewhere. They really need the assurance that skills they acquire, and the tickets they get through restructuring, will be transportable to other work sites. The increase of skills will then be of benefit to Australia,' says Mr Wunder.

GEMCo has begun to determine how best to reduce the number of job classifications at the company, which currently stands at 95. As GEMCo is self-supporting on Groote Eylandt, there is a wide range of traditional mining jobs—scrapers, excavators, truck drivers, labourers, mill attendants, operators, controllers, maintenance workers, tradespeople, stackers, shiploaders, ship and port gangs—as well as 'town jobs' such as gardeners, mess hands, retail and administrative staff, electricians, fire and ambulance officers and so on.

Four unions were originally represented at GEMCo: Transport Workers Union, Amalgamated Metal Workers Union, Federated Miscellaneous Workers Union and Electrical Trades Union. Since then GEMCo has set up a Joint Consultative Committee (JCC) and working parties to discuss the restructuring process. The JCC is made up of one representative from each union, two managers (mining and human resources) and a training co-ordinator. The working parties are made up of supervisors and representatives of the work group from each department involved in award restructuring.

These committees play a major role in reducing the number of job classifications and are helping people take part in the decisions of change. The working parties identify the skills required to do certain jobs and the training that may be required. Part of the process is to determine how to assess people's skills. Wages do not necessarily reflect skills and this issue is addressed through restructuring. A system introduced by another mine allocates a number of points to particular job skills. Workers have to acquire job skills to gain the points that will take them to a higher pay level. Whatever reclassification structure GEMCo introduces, workers will be able to move up the structure by acquiring new skills and training, and GEMCo will be providing training so that people can progress along a career path in parallel with the company's needs.

The most positive thing that can occur with award restructuring is that it causes people to become more interested in their jobs. It provides more interesting work with more input from everyone on the way they perform. However, it is also two-sided. It benefits the workers because jobs are more interesting and this will benefit GEMCo because it is creating a more productive work force.

GEMCo's managers would admit that there is no blueprint for restructuring, that people are understandably cautious and apprehensive of it and of making mistakes during the process of work place change. At the same time, GEMCo managers and employees want to get restructuring right, and are trying to build change into their work so that restructuring will evolve, in different stages, and change the work place.

Creating the climate for change has set the scene. Establishing the JCC and the working parties, and holding courses such as the RMIT industrial participation workshop and job redesign seminars have created an air of enthusiasm. Developing a training programme is seen as a priority in two areas: personal development and job skills. Their training programme includes:
- identifying the skills required for each job and assessing the value of skills
- upgrading workers' skills, rather than deskilling
- holding developmental courses, such as presentation skills, facilitator skills, supervisory courses, meeting procedures courses, communication skills, team building, job redesign and participation courses
- developing language courses for non-English speakers
- introducing a familiarisation tour of Groote Eylandt, of the mine and township, for employees and their families so that families learn about the mine.

Having a plan for restructuring and what needs to be done has given the company employees an idea of how restructuring will work. It has also given employees a goal on which to focus.

Examination of inputs and job design features, and how the two fit, can help explain the causes of these problems and anticipate their remedy.

Diagnosis of individual-level inputs answers the following questions:

1 What is the design of the larger organisation within which the individual jobs are embedded?
2 What is the design of the group containing the individual jobs?
3 What are the personal characteristics of job holders?

Diagnosis of individual jobs involves the following job dimensions:

1 How much skill variety is included in the jobs?
2 How much task identity do the jobs contain?
3 How much task significance is involved in the jobs?
4 How much autonomy is included in the jobs?
5 How much feedback about results do the jobs contain?

Summary

In this chapter, diagnostic models associated with groups and individuals were described and applied. Each of the models derive from the open systems view of organisations developed in Chapter 5. Diagnostic models include the input, design component and output dimensions necessary for understanding groups and individual jobs.

Group diagnostic models take the organisation's design as the primary input; examine goal clarity, task structure, group composition, performance norms and group functioning as the key design components; and list group performance and member quality of work life as the outputs. As with any open systems model, the alignment of these parts is the key to understanding effectiveness.

At the individual job level, organisation design, group design and characteristics of each job are the salient inputs. Task variety, task significance, task identity, autonomy and feedback work together to produce outputs of work satisfaction and work quality.

 ACTIVITIES

Review questions
1 What does 'group-level' diagnosis examine?
2 Explain your understanding of QWL.
3 What design components are appropriate for individual-level diagnosis?
4 How would you describe team effectiveness?

Discussion and essay questions
1 Discuss the similarities and differences among the organisation, group and individual levels in open systems theory.
2 Discuss team effectiveness as an output at the group level.
3 What are the key components of group level diagnosis? Discuss how the absence of any one of these components can impact on outputs.
4 Choose any two major design components in groups and describe how they can be adapted to different organisational designs.

Notes

1 S. Cohen, 'Designing effective self-managing work teams' in *Advances in Interdisciplinary Studies of Work Teams*, 1, ed. M. Beyerlein (Greenwich, Conn.: JAI Press, 1995).
2 J. Hackman and C. Morris, 'Group tasks, group interaction process, and group performance effectiveness: a review and proposed integration' in *Advances in Experimental Social Psychology*, 9, ed. L. Berkowitz (New York: Academic Press, 1975): 45–99; J. Hackman, ed., *Groups That Work (And Those That Don't): Creating Conditions for Effective Teamwork* (San Francisco: Jossey-Bass, 1989).
3 G. Ledford, E. Lawler and S. Mohrman, 'The quality circle and its variations', in *Productivity in Organizations: New Perspectives from Industrial and Organizational Psychology*, eds J. Campbell, R. Campbell and associates (San Francisco: Jossey-Bass, 1988): 255–294.
4 D. Ancona and D. Caldwell, 'Bridging the boundary: external activity and performance in organizational teams', *Administrative Science Quarterly*, 37 (1992): 634–65; S. Cohen, 'Designing effective self-managing work teams', *op. cit.*; S. Mohrman, S. Cohen and A. Mohrman, *Designing Team-Based Organizations* (San Francisco: Jossey-Bass, 1995).
5 G. Susman, *Autonomy at Work* (New York: Praeger, 1976); T. Cummings, 'Self-regulating work groups: a socio-technical synthesis', *Academy of Management Review*, 3 (1978): 625–34; J. Slocum and H. Sims, 'A typology for integrating technology, organization, and job design', *Human Relations*, 33 (1980): 193–212.

6   J. Hackman and G. Oldham, *Work Redesign* (Reading, Mass.: Addison-Wesley, 1980).
7   E. Schein, *Process Consultation*, I–II (Reading, Mass.: Addison-Wesley, 1987).
8   W. Dyer, *Team Building*, 3rd ed. (Reading, Mass.: Addison-Wesley, 1994).
9   Hackman and Morris, 'Group tasks, group interaction process, and group performance effectiveness', *op. cit.*; T. Cummings, 'Designing effective work groups', in *Handbook of Organisational Design*, 2, eds P. Nystrom and W. Starbuck (Oxford: Oxford University Press, 1981): 250–71.
10 Cummings, 'Designing effective work groups', *ibid.*
11 Susman, *Autonomy at Work*; Cummings, 'Self-regulating work groups'; Slocum and Sims, 'A typology for integrating technology, organization, and job design', all *op. cit.*
12 Cummings, 'Self-regulating work groups'; Slocum and Sims, 'A typology for integrating technology, organization, and job design', both *op. cit.*
13 *Ibid.*
14 R. Fells, 'The evolution of industrial relations in a changing environment', *Work and People*, 12:2 (1986): 13–18.
15 Hackman and Oldham, *Work Redesign*, *op. cit.*; F. Herzberg, 'One more time: how do you motivate employees?' *Harvard Business Review*, 46 (1968): 53–62.
16 J. Pierce, R. Dunham and R. Blackburn, 'Social systems structure, job design, and growth need strength: a test of a congruence model', *Academy of Management Journal*, 22 (1979): 223–40.
17 Susman, *Autonomy at Work*; Cummings, 'Self-regulating work groups'; Slocum and Sims, 'A typology for integrating technology, organization, and job design', all *op. cit.*
18 Hackman and Oldham, *Work Redesign*; Pierce, Dunham and Blackburn, 'Social systems structure, job design, and growth need strength: a test of a congruence model', both *op. cit.*
19 E. Lawler III, *Motivation in Work Organizations* (Monterey, Calif.: Brooks/Cole, 1973).
20 Hackman and Oldham, *Work Redesign, op. cit.*
21 Pierce, Dunham, and Blackburn, 'Social systems structure, job design, and growth need strength: a test of a congruence model'; Susman, *Autonomy at Work*; Cummings, 'Self-regulating work groups'; Slocum and Sims, 'A typology for integrating technology, organization, and job design', all *op. cit.*
22 Hackman and Oldham, *Work Redesign*; Pierce, Dunham, and Blackburn, 'Social systems structure, job design, and growth need strength: a test of a congruence model', both *op. cit.*
23 L. Jorgensen, 'Breaking down the "them" and "us" attitude at GEMCo', *Work and People*, 14:1 (1991): 28–33.

Collecting and analysing diagnostic information

Organisation development is vitally dependent on organisation diagnosis: the process of collecting information that will be shared with the client when jointly assessing how the organisation is functioning and determining the best change intervention. The quality of the information gathered is, therefore, a key part of the OD process. In this chapter, we discuss several key issues associated with collecting and analysing diagnostic data on how an organisation or department functions.

Data collection involves gathering information on specific organisational features, such as the inputs, design components, and outputs presented in Chapters 5 and 6. The process begins by establishing an effective relationship between the OD practitioner and those from whom data will be collected, and then choosing data-collection techniques. Four methods can be used to collect data: questionnaires, interviews, observations and unobtrusive measures. Data analysis organises and examines the information to make clear the underlying causes of an organisational problem or to identify areas for future development. The next step in the cyclical OD process is the feedback of data to the client system, an important process described in Chapter 8. The overall process of data collection, analysis and feedback is shown in Figure 7.1.

The diagnostic relationship

In most cases of planned change, OD practitioners play an active role in gathering data from organisation members for diagnostic purposes. For example, they might interview members of a work team about causes of conflict among members; they might survey employees at a large industrial plant about factors that contribute to poor product quality. Before collecting diagnostic information, practitioners need to establish a relationship with

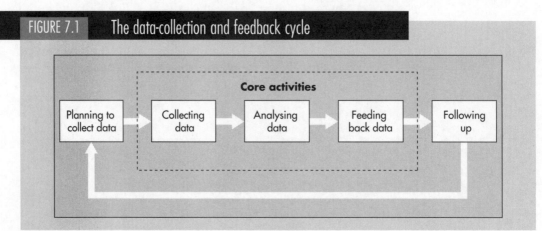

FIGURE 7.1 The data-collection and feedback cycle

Source: D. Nadler, *Feedback and Organization Development* © 1977 by Addison-Wesley Publishing Company, Inc., p. 43. Reprinted by permission of Addison-Wesley Publishing Co., Inc. Reading, Mass.

those who will provide and subsequently use it. Because the nature of that relationship affects the quality and usefulness of the data collected, it is vital that OD practitioners provide organisation members with a clear idea of who they are, why the data are being collected, what the data gathering will involve and how the data will be used.[1] Answers to these questions can help to allay people's natural fears that the data might be used against them. Such answers also help to gain members' participation and support, which is essential for developing successful interventions.

Establishing the diagnostic relationship between the consultant and relevant organisation members is similar to forming a contract. It is meant to clarify expectations and to specify the conditions of the relationship. In those cases where members have been directly involved in the entering and contracting process described in Chapter 4, the diagnostic contract will typically be part of the initial contracting step. However, in situations where data will be collected from members who have not been directly involved in entering and contracting, OD practitioners will need to establish a diagnostic contract as a prelude to diagnosis. The answers to the following questions provide the substance of the diagnostic contract:[2]

1 *Who am I?* The answer to this question introduces the OD practitioner to the organisation, particularly to those members who do not know the consultant, but will be asked to provide diagnostic data.

2 *Why am I here, and what am I doing?* These answers are aimed at defining the goals of the diagnosis and data-gathering activities. The consultant needs to present the objectives of the action research process and to describe how the diagnostic activities fit into the overall developmental strategy.

3 *Who do I work for?* This answer clarifies who has hired the consultant, whether it be a manager, a group of managers or a group of employees and managers. One way to build trust and support for the diagnosis is to have such persons directly involved in establishing the diagnostic contract. Thus, for example, if the consultant works for a joint labour–management committee, representatives from both sides of that group could help the consultant build the proper relationship with those from whom data will be gathered.

4 *What do I want from you, and why?* Here the consultant needs to specify how much time and effort people will need to give in order to provide valid data, and subsequently to work with these data in solving problems. Because some people may not want to participate in the diagnosis, it is important to specify that such involvement is voluntary.

5 *How will I protect your confidentiality?* This answer addresses member concerns about who will see their responses and in what form. This is especially critical when employees are asked to provide information about their attitudes or perceptions. OD practitioners can either assure confidentiality or state that full participation in the change process requires open information sharing. In the first case, employees are frequently concerned about privacy and the possibility of being punished for their responses. To alleviate concern and to increase the likelihood of getting honest responses, the consultant may need to assure employees of the confidentiality of their information. This may require explicit guarantees of response anonymity. In the second case, full involvement of the participants in their own diagnosis may be a vital ingredient in the change process. If sensitive issues arise, assurances of confidentiality can restrict the OD practitioner and thwart meaningful diagnosis. The consultant is bound to keep confidential the issues that are most critical for the group or organisation to understand.[3] OD practitioners must think carefully about how they want to handle confidentiality issues.

6 *Who will have access to the data?* Respondents typically want to know whether or not they will have access to their data and who else in the organisation will have similar access. The OD practitioner needs to clarify access issues and, in most cases, should agree to provide respondents with their own results. Indeed, the collaborative nature of diagnosis means that organisation members will work with their own data to discover causes of problems and to devise relevant interventions.

7 *What's in it for you?* This answer is aimed at providing organisation members with a clear assessment of the benefits they can expect from the diagnosis. This usually entails describing the feedback process and how they can use the data to improve the organisation.

8 *Can I be trusted?* The diagnostic relationship ultimately rests on the trust that is established between the consultant and those providing the data. An open and honest exchange of information depends on such trust, and the practitioner should provide ample time and face-to-face contact during the contracting process in order to build this trust. This requires the consultant to actively listen and openly discuss all questions raised by respondents.

Careful attention to establishing the diagnostic relationship helps to promote the three goals of data collection.[4] The first and most immediate objective is to obtain valid information about organisational functioning. Building a data-collection contract can ensure that organisation members provide information that is honest, reliable and complete.

Data collection can also rally energy for constructive organisational change. A good diagnostic relationship helps organisation members to start thinking about issues that concern them, and it creates expectations that change is possible. When members trust the consultant, they are likely to participate in the diagnostic process and to generate energy and commitment for organisational change.

Finally, data collection helps to develop the collaborative relationship necessary for effecting organisational change. The diagnostic stage of action research is probably the first time that most organisation members meet the OD practitioner. It can provide the basis for building a longer-term relationship. The data-collection contract and the subsequent data-gathering and feedback activities provide members with opportunities for seeing the consultant in action and for getting to know her or him personally. If the consultant can show employees that she or he is trustworthy, is willing to work with them and is able to help improve the organisation, then the data-collection process will contribute to the longer-term collaborative relationship so necessary for carrying out organisational changes.

Methods for collecting data

The four major techniques for gathering diagnostic data are questionnaires, interviews, observations and unobtrusive methods. Table 7.1 briefly compares the methods and lists their major advantages and problems. No single method can fully measure the kinds of variables important to OD; each has certain strengths and weaknesses.[5] For example, perceptual measures, such as questionnaires and surveys, are open to self-report biases, such as the respondents' tendency to give socially desirable answers rather than honest opinions. Observations, on the other hand, are susceptible to observer biases, such as seeing what one wants to see rather than what is really there. Because of the biases inherent in any data-collection method, we recommend that more than one method be used when collecting diagnostic data. The data from the different methods can be compared, and if they are consistent, it is likely that the variables are being validly measured. For example, questionnaire measures of job discretion could be supplemented with observations of the number and kinds of decisions that the employees are making. If the two kinds of data support one another, job discretion is probably being accurately assessed. If the two kinds of data conflict, then the validity of the measures should be examined further—perhaps by employing a third method, such as interviews.

Questionnaires

One of the most efficient ways of collecting data is through *questionnaires*. Because they typically contain fixed-response questions about various features of an organisation, these paper-and-pencil measures can be administered to large numbers of people simultaneously. Also, they can be analysed quickly, especially with the use of computers, thus permitting quantitative comparison and evaluation. As a result, data can easily be fed back to

TABLE 7.1	Different methods of data collection

Method	Major advantages	Major potential problems
Questionnaires	1 Responses can be quantified and easily summarized 2 Easy to use with large samples 3 Relatively inexpensive 4 Can obtain large volume of data	1 Non-empathy 2 Pre-determined questions missing issues 3 Over-interpretation of data 4 Response bias
Interviews	1 Adaptive—allows data collection on a range of possible subjects 2 Source of 'rich' data 3 Empathic 4 Process of interviewing can build rapport	1 Expense 2 Bias in interviewer responses 3 Coding and interpretation difficulties 4 Self-report bias
Observations	1 Collects data on behavior, rather than reports of behavior 2 Real time, not retrospective 3 Adaptive	1 Coding and interpretation difficulties 2 Sampling inconsistencies 3 Observer bias and questionable reliability 4 Expense
Unobtrusive measures	1 Non-reactive—no response bias 2 High face validity 3 Easily quantified Interviews	1 Access and retrieval difficulties 2 Validity concerns 3 Coding and interpretation difficulties

Source: D. Nadler, *Feedback and Organization Development* ©1977 by Addison-Wesley Publishing Company, Inc., p. 119. Reprinted by permission of Addison-Wesley Publishing Co., Inc., Reading, Mass.

employees. Numerous basic resource books on survey methodology and questionnaire development are available.[6]

Questionnaires can vary in scope, some measuring selected aspects of organisations and others assessing more comprehensive organisational characteristics. They can also vary in the extent to which they are either standardised or tailored to a specific organisation. Standardised instruments are generally based on an explicit model of organisation, group or individual effectiveness. These questionnaires usually contain a pre-determined set of questions that have been developed and refined over time. For example, Table 7.2 presents a standardised questionnaire for measuring the job design dimensions identified in Chapter 6: skill variety, task identity, task significance, autonomy and feedback about results. The questionnaire includes three items or questions for each dimension; a total score for each job dimension is computed simply by adding the responses for the three relevant items and arriving at a total score from 3 (low) to 21 (high). The questionnaire has wide applicability. It has been used in a variety of organisations with employees in both blue-collar and white-collar jobs.

TABLE 7.2   Job design questionnaire

Here are some statements about your job. How much do you agree or disagree with each?

My job:	Strongly disagree	Disagree	Slightly disagree	Undecided	Slightly agree	Agree	Strongly agree
1 provides much variety	[1]	[2]	[3]	[4]	[5]	[6]	[7]
2 permits me to be left on my own to do my own work	[1]	[2]	[3]	[4]	[5]	[6]	[7]
3 is arranged so that I often have the opportunity to see jobs or project through to completion	[1]	[2]	[3]	[4]	[5]	[6]	[7]
4 provides feedback on how well I am doing as I am working	[1]	[2]	[3]	[4]	[5]	[6]	[7]
5 is relatively significant in our organization	[1]	[2]	[3]	[4]	[5]	[6]	[7]
6 gives me considerable opportunity for independence and freedom in how I do my work	[1]	[2]	[3]	[4]	[5]	[6]	[7]
7 gives me the opportunity to do a number of different things	[1]	[2]	[3]	[4]	[5]	[6]	[7]
8 provides me with an opportunity to find out how well I am doing	[1]	[2]	[3]	[4]	[5]	[6]	[7]
9 is very significant or important in the broader scheme of things	[1]	[2]	[3]	[4]	[5]	[6]	[7]
10 provides an opportunity for independent thought and action	[1]	[2]	[3]	[4]	[5]	[6]	[7]
11 provides me with a great deal of variety at work	[1]	[2]	[3]	[4]	[5]	[6]	[7]
12 is arranged so that I have the opportunity to complete the work I start	[1]	[2]	[3]	[4]	[5]	[6]	[7]
13 provides me with the feeling that I know whether I am performing well or poorly	[1]	[2]	[3]	[4]	[5]	[6]	[7]
14 is arranged so that I have the chance to do a job from the beginning to the end (i.e., a chance to do the whole job)	[1]	[2]	[3]	[4]	[5]	[6]	[7]
15 is one where a lot of other people can be affected by how well the work gets done.	[1]	[2]	[3]	[4]	[5]	[6]	[7]

Scoring:
Skill variety . . . . .questions 1, 7, 11
Task identity . . . . .questions 3, 12, 14
Task significance . . . . .questions 5, 9, 15
Autonomy . . . . .questions 2, 6, 10
Feedback about results . . . . .questions 4, 8, 13

Source: Reproduced by permission of E. Lawler, S. Mohrman and T. Cummings, Center for Effective Organizations, University of Southern California.

Several research organisations have been highly instrumental in developing and refining surveys. Australian Council for Educational Research is a prominent example. Two of the institute's most popular measures of organisational dimensions are 'Changing your management style' and 'Team climate inventory'.[7] Other examples of packaged instruments include 'Organisational change: orientation scale' available from the Australian Institute of Management.[8] In fact, so many questionnaires are available that rarely would an organisation have to create a totally new one. However, because every organisation has unique problems and special jargon for referring to them, almost any standardised instrument will need to have organisation-specific additions, modifications or omissions.

Customised questionnaires, on the other hand, are tailored to the needs of a particular client. Typically, they include questions composed by consultants or organisation members, receive limited use and do not undergo longer-term development. Customised questionnaires can be combined with standardised instruments to provide valid and reliable data focused on the particular issues that face an organisation.

Questionnaires, however, have a number of drawbacks that need to be taken into account when choosing whether to employ them for data collection. First, responses are limited to the questions asked in the instrument. They provide little opportunity to probe for additional data or ask for points of clarification. Second, questionnaires tend to be impersonal, and employees may not be willing to provide honest answers. Third, questionnaires often elicit response biases, such as the tendency to answer questions in a socially acceptable manner. This makes it difficult to draw valid conclusions from employees' self-reports.

Interviews

A second important measurement technique is the *individual* or *group interview*. These probably represent the most widely-used technique for collecting data in OD. They permit the interviewer to ask the respondent direct questions, and so further probing and clarification is possible as the interview proceeds. This flexibility is invaluable for gaining private views and feelings about the organisation and for exploring new issues that emerge during the interview.

Interviews may be highly structured, resembling questionnaires, or highly unstructured, starting with general questions that allow the respondent to lead the way. Structured interviews typically derive from a conceptual model of organisation functioning; the model guides the types of questions that are asked. For example, a structured interview based on the organisation-level design components identified in Chapter 5 would ask managers specific questions about organisation structure, measurement systems, human resource systems and organisation culture.

Unstructured interviews are more general and include broad questions about organisational functioning, such as:

- What are the major goals or objectives of the organisation or department?
- How does the organisation currently perform with respect to these purposes?
- What are the strengths and weaknesses of the organisation or department?
- What barriers stand in the way of good performance?

Although interviewing typically involves one-to-one interaction between an OD practitioner and an employee, it can be carried out in a group context. Group interviews save time and allow people to build on others' responses. A major drawback, however, is that group settings may inhibit some people from responding freely.

A popular type of group interview is the focus group or sensing meeting.[9] These are unstructured meetings conducted by a manager or a consultant. A small group of 10 to 15 employees is selected, representing a cross-section of functional areas and hierarchical levels or a homogeneous grouping, such as minorities or engineers. Group discussion is frequently started by asking general questions about organisational features and functioning, an intervention's progress or current performance. Group members are then encouraged to discuss their answers in some depth. Consequently, focus groups and sensing meetings are an economical way of obtaining interview data and are especially effective in understanding particular issues in some depth. The richness and validity of that information will depend on the extent to which the manager or consultant develops a trust relationship with the group and listens to member opinions.

Another popular unstructured group interview involves assessing the current state of an intact work group. The manager or consultant generally directs a question to the group, calling its attention to some part of group functioning. For example, group members may be asked how they feel the group is progressing on its stated task. The group might respond and then come up with its own series of questions about barriers to task performance. This unstructured interview is a fast, simple way of collecting data about group behaviour. It allows members to discuss issues of immediate concern and to engage actively in the questioning and answering process. This technique is, however, limited to relatively small groups and to settings where there is trust among employees and managers, and a commitment to assessing group processes.

Interviews are an effective method of collecting data in OD. They are adaptive, allowing the interviewer to modify questions and to probe emergent issues during the interview process. They also permit the interviewer to develop an empathetic relationship with employees, frequently resulting in frank disclosure of pertinent information.

A major drawback of interviews is the amount of time required to conduct and analyse them. They can consume a great deal of time, especially if the interviewers take full advantage of the opportunity to hear respondents out, and change their questions accordingly. Personal biases can also distort the data. Like questionnaires, interviews are subject to the self-report biases of respondents and, perhaps more importantly, to the biases of the interviewer. For example, the nature of the questions and the interactions between the interviewer and the respondent may discourage or encourage certain kinds of responses. These problems suggest that interviewing takes considerable skill to gather valid data. Interviewers must be able to understand their own biases, to listen and establish empathy with respondents and to change questions to pursue issues that develop during the course of the interview.

Observations

One of the more direct ways of collecting data is simply to *observe* organisational behaviours in their functional settings. The OD practitioner may do this by casually walking through a work area and looking around or by simply counting the occurrences of specific kinds of behaviours (e.g. the number of times a phone call is answered after three rings in a service department). Observation can range from complete participant observation, in which the OD practitioner becomes a member of the group under study, to more detached observation, in which the observer is clearly not part of the group or situation itself and may use film, videotape or other methods to record behaviours.

Observations have a number of advantages. They are free of the biases inherent in self-report data. They put the practitioner directly in touch with the behaviours in question, without having to rely on others' perceptions. Observations also involve real-time data, describing behaviour that is occurring in the present rather than the past. This avoids the distortions that invariably arise when people are asked to recollect their behaviours. Finally, observations are adaptive in that the consultant can modify what she or he is observing according to the circumstances.

Among the problems with observations are difficulties in interpreting the meaning that underlies the observations. Practitioners may need to code the observations to make sense of them, and this can be expensive, take time and introduce bias into the data. Because the observer is the data-collection instrument, personal bias and subjectivity can distort data unless the observer is trained and skilled in knowing what to look for, how to observe, where and when to observe and how to record data systematically. Another problem concerns sampling. Observers must not only decide which people to observe; they must also choose the time periods, territory and events in which observations will be made. Failure to attend to these sampling issues can result in highly biased samples of observational data.

When used correctly, observations provide insightful data about organisation and group functioning, intervention success and performance. For example, observations are particularly helpful in diagnosing the interpersonal relations of members of work groups. As discussed in Chapter 6, interpersonal relations are a key component of work groups; observing member interactions in a group setting can provide direct information about the nature of those relationships.

Unobtrusive measures

Unobtrusive data are not collected directly from respondents but from secondary sources, such as company records and archives. These data are generally available in organisations and include records of absenteeism or tardiness, grievances, quantity and quality of production or service, financial performance and correspondence with key customers, suppliers or governmental agencies.

Unobtrusive measures are especially helpful in diagnosing the organisation, group and individual outputs presented in Chapters 5 and 6. At the organisation level, for example, market share and return on investment can usually be obtained from company reports. Similarly, organisations typically measure the quantity and quality of the outputs of work groups and individual employees. Unobtrusive measures can also help to diagnose organisation-level design components—structure, work systems, control systems and human resource systems. A company's organisation chart, for example, can provide useful information about organisation structure. Information about control systems can usually be obtained by examining the firm's management information system, operating procedures and accounting practices. Data about human resource systems are often included in a company's personnel manual.

Unobtrusive measures provide a relatively objective view of organisational functioning. They are free from respondent and consultant biases and are perceived by many organisation members as being real. Moreover, unobtrusive measures tend to be quantified and reported at periodic intervals, permitting statistical analysis of behaviours occurring over time. Examination of monthly absenteeism rates, for example, might reveal trends in employee withdrawal behaviour.

The major problems with unobtrusive measures occur when collecting such information and drawing valid conclusions from it. Company records may not include data in a form that is usable by the consultant. If, for example, individual performance data are needed, the consultant may find that many firms only record production information at the group or departmental level. Unobtrusive data may also have their own built-in biases. Changes in accounting procedures and in methods of recording data are common in organisations; such changes can affect company records independently of what is actually happening in the organisation. For example, observed changes in productivity over time might be caused by modifications in methods of recording production, rather than by actual changes in organisational functioning.

Despite these drawbacks, unobtrusive data serve as a valuable adjunct to other diagnostic measures, such as interviews and questionnaires. Archival data can be used in preliminary diagnosis, indicating those organisational units that have absenteeism, grievance or production problems. Interviews can then be conducted or observations made in those units to discover the underlying causes of the problems. Conversely, unobtrusive data can be used to cross-check other forms of information. For example, if questionnaires reveal that employees in a department are dissatisfied with their jobs, company records might show whether that discontent is manifested in heightened withdrawal behaviours, in lowered quality work or in similar counterproductive behaviours.

Application 7.1 describes the use of OD intervention methods to collect diagnostic data on employee performance and perceptions.[10]

A benchmarking intervention into an executive team

The restructuring of the Australian economy since the mid-1980s and the recommendations towards corporatisation and privatisation of government-owned enterprises have resulted in extraordinary challenges for management. In 1993–94, the Victorian government commenced a drive in all sectors of government service to reduce expenditure, rein in public sector debt and increase revenue. This requirement placed pressure on the executive teams of statutory authorities (semi-government agencies), which were major contributors to state government revenues, to cut costs and increase productivity levels. Decisions about asset sales, restructuring, downsizing, new technology, retraining and outsourcing became major and urgent agenda items. Targets with short lead times were set, and the government expected individual agencies to deliver.

Background

Prior to 1990, statutory authorities, in the main, were bureaucracies of paternalism, ever swelling in response to more demand for their services. But since then, these statutory authorities have been required to operate in an external environment of dramatic and constant change. So it was with the organisation here. This resulted in a continual process of redesign in order to streamline the business and satisfy increasing community expectations of the quality of service delivery and financial performance of public businesses, and accountability to government. Competition became the key word. Constant external change resulted in an internal environment of turbulence. Although the organisation in which this project was conducted was performing well in the context of the Australian environment, the executive team proposed to follow a process of internal reform in order to become competitive to international standards.

To become more commercial, the executive team set out the desired directions for change in values and culture.

This project was conducted against that background in 1993–94.

The choice of a technique for intervention in a turbulent environment must be on the basis of the possibilities and limitations of that technique, and the chosen technique must be adapted to the kind of data and conditions with which it will be used.[11]

Issues of time availability and timing, personal sensitivity and interpersonal factors that highlighted difficulties in relationships within the executive team suggested the use of an instrument that would provide a measure of 'whole team' performance.

The instrument selected was the team performance index (TPI). This is a diagnostic tool measuring the key factors required by effective teams, which were described after many years of research by Margerison and McCann.[12] An important feature was the opportunity to give 360° feedback about the performance of the team, whereby the results of the survey process were returned to the team for their subsequent critique and confirmation of results. Respondents could include board members, managers who reported directly to the executive team and other individuals or groups with whom the team was required to interact.

The TPI is a multi-survey instrument that compares perceptions of how well the team is performing on the team performance factors. The team performance factors—advising, innovating, promoting, developing, organising, producing, inspecting, maintaining and team linking—form the basis of the types of work model designed to improve individual and team performance.

At a normal scheduled meeting of the executive team, the tool was introduced.

A presentation:
- outlined the development of the TMS instruments
- highlighted aspects of the research base
- introduced the TPI, the option of anonymity and 360° feedback by co-workers.

The 54 questions comprise six for each of the nine team performance factors. Particular note was made of the use of simple undisguised questions with a structured response. For each question, respondents are asked to rate to what extent the activity listed should occur (not at all, to a little, to some extent, to a great extent or to a very great extent), given the mission and objectives of the team.

Having assessed the importance of the activity, the respondent is then asked to what extent the team actually does perform that activity. In this way, the instrument measures the gap between what 'is' and what 'should be'. In order to allow for variability there is the flexibility for rating from 0 to 4 the importance of each activity for the team.

In discussion, the option of anonymity was preferred by one member of the executive, so this was adopted for all respondents. The respondents to be asked to take part in the survey and complete a TPI were ten executive team members, 52 managers who reported directly to the executive team and three members of the board.

The opportunity for benchmarking the executive team's performance, together with the possibility of focused improvement, all helped to gain commitment from all team members.

A memo from the managing director set out in detail the purpose of the questionnaire (the TPI), why respondents had received it, what was requested and a timetable for feedback.

The memo highlighted the importance of a high level of response in order to ensure the comprehensiveness of the data, and stressed that the responses would be presented in such a way as to guarantee confidentiality.

In this project, it was necessary to provide feedback that was structured and valid and could be accepted in a non-defensive manner by an executive team.

The TPI and the resulting profile appeared to satisfy the requirement to measure a team's performance in an acceptable, non-threatening manner using 360° feedback. At an executive team meeting, the components of the profile were discussed and overview provided. Discussion centred on the importance rankings and the nature of the executive team and the way its work was perceived. Top management's role has changed, but the supervisor and the co-workers' perception appears to have been coloured by their past experience in the 'old' bureaucratic system.

On the other hand, there was overwhelming agreement that the three areas where the team needed to be strong in order to meet the challenges of the business were innovating, promoting and team linking.

Where were they now?

Innovating. Although the governmental pressure for corporatisation was known and a timetable proposed, the team had been slow to pursue world-best practice. The organisation immersed itself in a sea of special projects managed internally with some external assistance. Small incremental steps, rather than massive change, was the strategy pursued. It was happening, but too little was taking too long.

Promoting. The executive team met on a regular basis. The work of the team had been largely secretive, and generally involved crises of political and operational matters. Little discussion about the content or results of executive team meetings occurred with the co-workers. Teams at the top were increasingly required to create and sell powerful new visions, but the process of vision-making was subsumed by changing government priorities, which often forced an atmosphere of crisis. The work of the executive team was not directed towards actions associated with promoting, but rather towards the fighting of immediate organisational fires.

Team linking. The executive team was under constant pressure to perform by increasing the revenue dividend to government. This was to occur by restructuring, operating commercially, contracting out, developing staff capabilities, quality management, culture change and reform of work and management practices. Many programmes were introduced in parallel, and the subsequent overlap caused a high level of stress among the executive team members who were buffeted by the turbulence and demands of changes. They had competed for diminishing resources. Hostility among team leaders caused power cliques to form.

The executive team had been unable to develop a high level of respect, understanding and trust with each other. But that was what the team and their co-workers wanted. The realities of the data presented by the TPI responses reflected their unspoken perceptions.

Conclusions

Confronted with the diagnosis and the rationale, the executive team moved quickly to discuss remedial actions. An action plan included:
- all senior managers to receive detailed feedback from the TPI at the next meeting by each executive team member and his direct reports
- selling the changes that were occurring more persuasively to all staff in an effort to increase their understanding of the urgency of the government's agenda
- openly communicating the vision of a more commercial and leaner organisation
- encouraging and listening carefully to new ideas within their own executive team and within the operational areas
- identifying each team members' linking skills need and supporting the development of greater capability
- encouraging more unified external linking
- planning for regular meetings together with workshops off-site to work together on improving the executive team's performance
- repeating the TPI within 12 months and review progress.

This action plan was agreed upon as being useful and practical. Most of the executive team members embarked enthusiastically on a process for improvement. All commented positively on the diagnostic and remedial usefulness of the TPI and the resulting team performance profile.

Sampling

Before discussing how to analyse data, the issue of sampling needs to be emphasised. Application of the different data-collection techniques invariably raises the following questions: 'How many people should be interviewed and who should they be?' 'What events should be observed and how many?' or 'How many records should be inspected and which ones?'[13]

In many OD cases, sampling is not an issue. Practitioners simply collect interview or questionnaire data from all members of the organisation or department in question, and so do not have to worry about whether the information is representative of the organisation or unit because all members of the population are included in the sample.

Sampling becomes an issue in OD, however, when data are collected from *selected* members, behaviours or records. This is often the case when diagnosing organisation-level issues or large systems. In these cases, it may be important to ensure that the sample of people, behaviours or records adequately represents the characteristics of the total population. For example, a sample of 50 employees might be used to assess the perceptions of all 300 members of a department. A sample of production data might be used to evaluate the total production of a work group. OD practitioners often find that it is more economical and quicker to gather a sampling of diagnostic data than to collect all possible information. If done correctly, the sample can provide useful and valid information about the entire organisation or unit.

Sampling design involves considerable technical detail, and consultants may need to become familiar with basic references in this area or to obtain professional help.[14] The first issue to address is *sample size*, or how many people, events, or records are needed to carry out the diagnosis or evaluation. This question has no simple answer: the necessary sample size is a function of size of the population, the confidence desired in the quality of the data and the resources (money and time) available for data collection.

First, the larger the population (e.g. number of organisation members or total number of work outcomes) or the more complex the client system (e.g. the number of salary levels that must be sampled or the number of different functions), the more difficult it is to establish a 'right' sample size. As the population increases in size and complexity, the less meaning one can attach to simple measures, such as an overall average score on a questionnaire item. Because the population is composed of such different types of people or events, more data are needed to ensure an accurate representation of the potentially different subgroups. Second, the larger the proportion of the population that is selected, the more confidence one can have about the quality of the sample. If the diagnosis concerns an issue of great importance to the organisation, then extreme confidence may be needed, indicative of a larger sample size. Third, limited resources constrain sample size. If resources are limited but the required confidence is high, then questionnaires will be preferred to interviews because more information can be collected per member per dollar.

The second issue to address is *sample selection*. Probably the most common approach to sampling diagnostic data in OD is a simple random sample in which each member, behaviour or record has an equal chance of being selected. For example, assume that an OD practitioner would like to randomly select 50 people out of the 300 employees at a manufacturing plant. Using a complete list of all 300 employees, the consultant can generate a random sample in one of two ways. The first method would be to use a random number table in the back of almost any statistics text; the consultant would pick out the employees corresponding to the first 50 numbers under 300 beginning anywhere in the table. The second method would be to pick every sixth name ($\frac{300}{50} = 6$) starting anywhere in the list.

If the population is complex, or many sub-groups need to be represented in the sample, a *stratified sample* may be more appropriate than a random one. In a stratified sample, the population of members, events or records is segregated into a number of mutually exclusive sub-populations. Then, a random sample is taken from each sub-population. For example, members of an organisation might be divided into three groups: managers, white-collar workers and blue-collar workers. A random sample of members, behaviours or records could be selected from each grouping in order to make diagnostic conclusions about each of the groups.

Adequate sampling is critical when gathering valid diagnostic data, and the OD literature has tended to pay little attention to this issue. OD practitioners should gain rudimentary knowledge in this area and use professional help if necessary.

Techniques for analysing data

Data analysis techniques fall into two broad classes: qualitative and quantitative. Qualitative techniques are generally easier to use because they do not rely on numerical data. This also makes them easier to understand and interpret. Quantitative techniques, on the other hand, can provide more accurate readings of the organisational problem.

Qualitative tools

Of the several methods for summarising diagnostic data in qualitative terms, two of the most important are content analysis and force-field analysis.

Content analysis

A popular technique for assessing qualitative data, especially interview data, is *content analysis*. Content analysis attempts to summarise comments into meaningful categories. When done well, a content analysis can reduce hundreds of interview comments into a few themes that effectively summarise the issues or attitudes of a group of respondents. The process of content analysis can be quite formal and specialised references describe this technique in detail.[15] In general, however, the process can be broken down into three major steps. First, responses to a particular question are read to gain familiarity with the range of comments made and to assess whether some answers are occurring over and over again. Second, based on this sampling of comments, themes are generated that capture these recurring comments. Themes consolidate different responses that say essentially the same thing. For example, in answering the question 'What do you like most about your job?' different respondents might list their co-workers, their supervisors, the new machinery and a good supply of tools. The first two answers concern the social aspects of work, and the second two address the resources available for doing the work. Third, the respondents' answers to a question are then placed into one of the categories. The categories with the most responses represent those themes that are most often mentioned.

Force-field analysis

A second method of analysing qualitative data in OD derives from Kurt Lewin's three-step model of change. Called 'force-field analysis', this method organises information pertaining to organisational change into two major categories: forces for change and forces for maintaining the *status quo* or resisting change.[16] Using data collected through interviews, observation or unobtrusive measures, the first step in conducting a force-field analysis is to develop a list of all the forces that promote change and all those that resist change. Then, based on either personal belief or perhaps on input from several members of the client organisation, a determination is made of which of the positive and which of the negative forces are most powerful. One can either rank the order or rate the strength of the different forces.

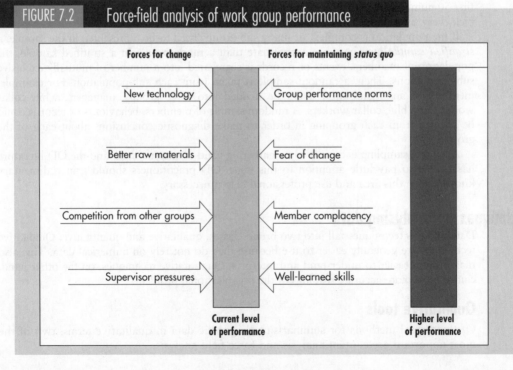

FIGURE 7.2   Force-field analysis of work group performance

Forces for change | Forces for maintaining *status quo*

New technology → | ← Group performance norms

Better raw materials → | ← Fear of change

Competition from other groups → | ← Member complacency

Supervisor pressures → | ← Well-learned skills

Current level of performance   Higher level of performance

Figure 7.2 illustrates a force-field analysis of the performance of a work group. The arrows represent the forces, and the length of the arrows corresponds to the strength of the forces. The information could have been collected in a group interview in which members were asked to list those factors maintaining the current level of group performance and those factors pushing for a higher level. Members could also have been asked to judge the strength of each force, with the average judgment shown by the length of the arrows.

This analysis reveals two strong forces pushing for higher performance: pressures from the supervisor of the group and competition from other work groups performing similar work. These forces for change are offset by two strong forces for maintaining the *status quo*: group norms supporting present levels of performance and well-learned skills that are resistant to change. According to Lewin, efforts to change to a higher level of group performance, shown by the darker band in Figure 7.2, should focus on reducing the forces that maintain the *status quo*. This might entail changing the group's performance norms and helping members to learn new skills. The reduction of forces maintaining the *status quo* is likely to result in organisational change with little of the tension or conflict that typically accompanies change caused by increasing the forces for change.

Quantitative tools

Methods for analysing quantitative data range from simple descriptive statistics of items or scales from standard instruments to more sophisticated, multivariate analysis of the underlying instrument properties and relationships among measured variables.[17] The most common quantitative tools are means, standard deviations, frequency distributions, scattergrams, correlation coefficients and difference tests. These measures are routinely produced by most statistical computer software packages. Therefore, mathematical calculations are not discussed here.

Means, standard deviations and frequency distributions

One of the most economical and straightforward ways of summarising quantitative data is to compute a mean and standard deviation for each item or variable measured. These represent the respondents' average score and the spread or variability of the responses, respectively. These two numbers can easily be compared across different measures or subgroups. For example, Table 7.3 shows the means and standard deviations for six questions asked of 100 employees about the value of different kinds of organisational rewards. Based on the five-point scale ranging from one (very low value) to five (very high

TABLE 7.3	Descriptive statistics of value of organisational rewards	
Organisational rewards	**Mean**	**Standard deviation**
Challenging work	4.6	.76
Respect from peers	4.4	.81
Pay	4.0	.71
Praise from supervisor	4.0	1.55
Promotion	3.3	.95
Fringe benefits	2.7	1.14

Number of respondents = 100
1 = very low value; 5 = very high value

| TABLE 7.4 | Frequency distribution of responses to 'Pay' and 'Praise from supervisor' items |

Pay (mean = 4.0)

Response		Number checking each response	Graph*
1	Very low value	0	
2	Low value	0	
3	Moderate value	25	XXXXX
4	High value	50	XXXXXXXXXX
5	Very high value	25	XXXXX

Praise from supervisor (Mean = 4.0)

Response		Number checking each response	Graph*
1	Very low value	15	XXX
2	Low value	10	XX
3	Moderate value	0	
4	High value	10	XX
5	Very high value	65	XXXXXXXXXXXX

Each X = 5 people checking the response

value), the data suggest that challenging work and respect from peers are the two most highly valued rewards. Monetary rewards, such as pay and fringe benefits, are not as highly valued.

But the mean can be a misleading statistic. It only describes the average value and so provides no information on the distribution of the responses. Different patterns of responses can produce the same mean score. Therefore, it is important to use the standard deviation along with the frequency distribution to gain a clearer understanding of the data. The frequency distribution is a graphical method for displaying data that shows the number of times a particular response was given. For example, the data in Table 7.3 suggest that both pay and praise from the supervisor are equally valued with a mean of 4.0. However, the standard deviations for these two measures are very different at 0.71 and 1.55, respectively. Table 7.4 shows the frequency distributions of the responses to the questions about pay and praise from the supervisor. Employees' responses to the value of pay are distributed toward the higher end of the scale, with no one rating it as being of low or very low value. In contrast, responses about the value of praise from the supervisor fall into two distinct groupings: 25 employees felt that supervisor praise has a low or very low value, whereas 75 persons rate it high or very high. Although both rewards have the same mean value, their standard deviations and frequency distributions suggest different interpretations of the data.

In general, when the standard deviation for a set of data is high, there is considerable disagreement over the issue posed by the question. If the standard deviation is small, the data are similar on a particular measure. In the example described above, there is disagreement over the value of supervisory praise (some people think it is important but others do not), but there is fairly good agreement that pay is a reward with high value.

Scattergrams and correlation coefficients

In addition to describing data, quantitative techniques also permit OD consultants to make inferences about the relationships between variables. Scattergrams and correlation coefficients are measures of the strength of a relationship between two variables. For example, suppose the problem being faced by an organisation is increased conflict between the Manufacturing and the Engineering Design departments. During the data-collection

TABLE 7.5	Relationship between change orders and conflicts	
Month	**Number of change orders**	**Number of conflicts**
April	5	2
May	12	4
June	14	3
July	6	2
August	8	3
September	20	5
October	10	2
November	2	1
December	15	4
January	8	3
February	18	4
March	10	5

phase, information about the number of conflicts and change orders per month over the past year is collected. The data are shown in Table 7.5 and plotted in a scattergram in Figure 7.3.

A scattergram is a diagram that visually displays the relationship between two variables. It is constructed by locating each case (person or event) at the intersection of its value for each of the two variables being compared. For example, in the month of August, there were eight change orders and three conflicts, and their intersection is shown on Figure 7.3 as an X.

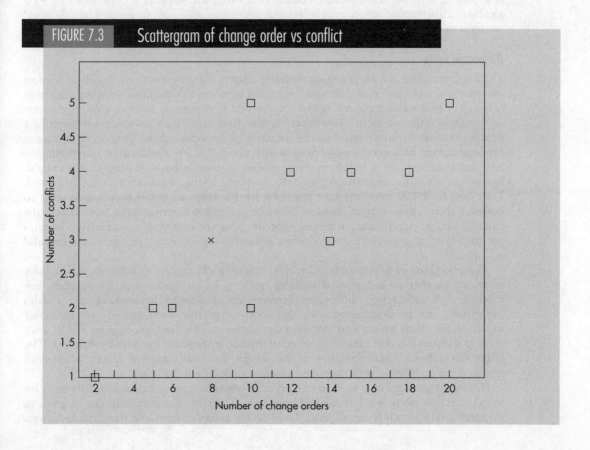

FIGURE 7.3   Scattergram of change order vs conflict

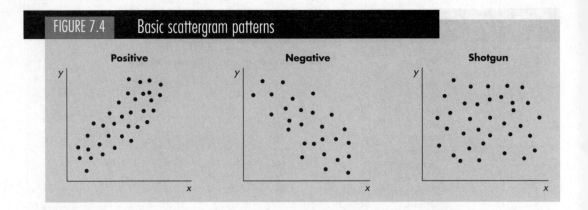

FIGURE 7.4   Basic scattergram patterns

Three basic patterns can emerge from a scattergram, as shown in Figure 7.4. The first pattern is called a positive relationship, because, as the values of x increase, so do the values of y. The second pattern is called a negative relationship, because as the values of x increase, the values of y decrease. Finally, there is the 'shotgun' pattern. Here, no relationship between the two variables is apparent. In the example shown in Figure 7.3, an apparently strong positive relationship exists between the number of change orders and the number of conflicts between the Engineering Design and the Manufacturing departments. This suggests that change orders may contribute to the observed conflict between the two departments.

The correlation coefficient is simply a number that summarises data in a scattergram. Its value ranges between +1.0 and –1.0. A correlation coefficient of +1.0 means that there is a perfect, positive relationship between two variables, whereas a correlation of –1.0 signifies a perfectly negative relationship. A correlation of 0 implies a 'shotgun' scattergram where there is no relationship between two variables.

Difference tests

The final technique for analysing quantitative data is the difference test. It can be used to compare a sample group against some standard or norm to determine whether the group is above or below this standard. It can also be used to determine whether two samples are significantly different from each other. In the first case, such comparisons provide a broader context for understanding the meaning of diagnostic data. They serve as a basis for determining 'how good is good or how bad is bad'.[18] Many standardised questionnaires have standardised scores based on the responses of large groups of people. It is critical, however, to choose a comparison group that is similar to the organisation being diagnosed. For example, if 100 engineers take a standardised attitude survey, it makes little sense to compare their scores against standard scores representing married males from across the country. On the other hand, if industry-specific data are available, a comparison of sales per employee (as a measure of productivity) against the industry average would be valid and useful.

The second use of difference tests involves assessing whether two (or more) groups differ from one another on a particular variable, such as job satisfaction or absenteeism. For example, job satisfaction differences between an accounting department and a sales department can be determined with this tool. Given that each group took the same questionnaire, their means and standard deviations can be used to compute a difference score (t-score or z-score) indicating whether the two groups are statistically different. The larger the difference score relative to the sample size and standard deviation for each group, the more likely that one group is more satisfied than the other.

Difference tests can also be used to determine whether a group has changed its score on job satisfaction or some other variable over time. The same questionnaire can be given to the same group at two points in time. Based on the group's means and standard deviations at each point in time, a difference score can be calculated. The larger the score, the more likely that the group actually changed its job satisfaction level.

The calculation of difference scores can be very helpful for diagnosis but requires the OD practitioner to make certain assumptions about how the data were collected. These assumptions are discussed in most standard statistical texts, and OD practitioners should consult them before calculating difference scores for purposes of diagnosis or evaluation.[19]

Summary

This chapter has described several different methods of collecting and analysing diagnostic data. Because diagnosis is an important step that occurs frequently in the planned change process, a working familiarity with these techniques is essential. Methods of data collection include questionnaires, interviews, observation and unobtrusive measures. Methods of analysis include qualitative techniques, such as content and force-field analysis, and quantitative techniques, such as the mean, standard deviation, correlation coefficient and difference tests.

 ACTIVITIES

Review questions
1 What is the meaning, and basis, of 'diagnostic relationship'?
2 What are the goals of data collection?
3 Under what circumstances would a questionnaire be used?
4 What value is 'observation' when diagnosing?
5 Which method of gathering data is the most objective and why?

Discussion and essay questions
1 Describe the advantages and disadvantages of the various methods of data collection.
2 Under what conditions are quantitative and/or qualitative tools useful in analysing data?

Notes

1 S. Mohrman, T. Cummings and E. Lawler III, 'Creating useful knowledge with organizations: relationship and process issues' in *Producing Useful Knowledge for Organizations*, eds R. Kilmann and K. Thomas (New York: Praeger, 1983): 613–24; C. Argyris, R. Putnam and D. Smith, eds, *Action Science* (San Francisco: Jossey-Bass, 1985); E. Lawler III, A. Mohrman, S. Mohrman, G. Ledford, Jr and T. Cummings, *Doing Research That Is Useful for Theory and Practice* (San Francisco: Jossey-Bass, 1985).
2 D. Nadler, *Feedback and Organization Development: Using Data-Based Methods* (Reading, Mass.: Addison-Wesley, 1977): 110–14.
3 W. Nielsen, N. Nykodym and D. Brown, 'Ethics and organizational change', *Asia Pacific Journal of Human Resources*, 29 (1991).
4 Nadler, *Feedback and Organization Development*, op. cit., 105–7.
5 W. Wymer and J. Carsten, 'Alternative ways to gather opinion', *HR Magazine* (April 1992): 71–78.
6 Examples of basic resource books on survey methodology include: S. Seashore, E. Lawler III, P. Mirvis and C. Cammann, *Assessing Organizational Change* (New York: Wiley Interscience, 1983); J. Van Mannen and J. Dabbs, *Varieties of Qualitative Research* (Beverly Hills, Calif.: Sage Publications, 1983); E. Lawler III, D. Nadler and C. Cammann, *Organizational Assessment: Perspectives on the Measurement of Organizational Behaviour and the Quality of Worklife* (New York: Wiley Interscience, 1980); R. Golembiewski and R. Hilles, *Toward the Responsive Organization: The Theory and Practice of Survey/Feedback* (Salt Lake City:

Brighton Publishing, 1979); Nadler, *Feedback and Organization Development, op. cit.*; S. Sudman and N. Bradburn, *Asking Questions* (San Francisco: Jossey-Bass, 1983).

7 http://www.acer.edu.au/index3.html/

8 J. Jones and W. Bearley, 'Organization change: orientation scale', *HRDQ*, (King of Prussia, Pennsylvania, 1986).

9 J. Fordyce and R. Weil, *Managing WITH People*, 2nd ed. (Reading, Mass.: Addison-Wesley, 1979); W. Wells, 'Group interviewing' in *Handbook of Marketing Research*, ed. R. Ferder, (New York: McGraw-Hill, 1977); R. Krueger, *Focus Groups: A Practical Guide for Applied Research*, 2nd ed. (Thousand Oaks, Calif.: Sage Publications, 1994).

10 P. Glass, 'A benchmarking intervention into an executive team', *Total Quality Management* (Abingdon, 1998).

11 J. McGrath, 'Towards a theory of method for research organisations' in W. Cooper, H. Leavitt and M. Shelly (eds), *New Perspectives in Organization Research* (New York, Wiley, 1964).

12 C. Margerison and D. McCann, *Team Management: Practical New Approach* (Mercury, 1990).

13 C. Emory, *Business Research Methods* (Homewood, Ill.: Richard D. Irwin, 1980):146.

14 W. Deming, *Sampling Design* (New York: John Wiley, 1960); L. Kish, *Survey Sampling* (New York: John Wiley, 1965); S. Sudman, *Applied Sampling* (New York: Academic Press, 1976).

15 B. Berelson, 'Content analysis' in *Handbook of Social Psychology*, ed. G. Lindzey (Reading, Mass.: Addison-Wesley, 1954); O. Holsti, 'Content analysis', *Handbook of Social Psychology*, 2nd ed., eds G. Lindzey and E. Aronson (Reading, Mass.: Addison-Wesley, 1968).

16 K. Lewin, *Field Theory in Social Science* (New York: Harper and Row, 1951).

17 More sophisticated methods of quantitative analysis are found in the following: W. Hays, *Statistics* (New York: Holt, Rinehart and Winston, 1963); J. Nunnally, *Psychometric Theory*, 2nd ed. (New York: McGraw-Hill, 1978); F. Kerlinger, *Foundations of Behavioral Research*, 2nd ed. (New York: Holt, Rinehart and Winston, 1973); J. Cohen and P. Cohen, *Applied Multiple Regression/Correlation Analysis for the Behavioral Sciences*, 2nd ed. (Hillsdale, N.J.: Lawrence Erlbaum Associates, 1983).

18 A. Armenakis and H. Field, 'The development of organizational diagnostic norms: an application of client involvement', *Consultation*, 6 (Spring 1987): 20–31.

19 Cohen and Cohen, *Applied Multiple Regression/Correlation Analysis for the Behavioral Sciences, op. cit.*

Feeding back diagnostic information

Perhaps the most important step in the diagnostic process is feeding back diagnostic information to the client organisation. Although the data may have been collected with the client's help, the OD practitioner is usually responsible for organising and presenting them to the client. Properly analysed and meaningful data can have an impact on organisational change only if organisation members can use the information to devise appropriate action plans. A key objective of the feedback process is to be sure that the client has ownership of the data.

As shown in Figure 8.1, the success of data feedback depends largely on its ability to arouse organisational action and to direct energy towards organisational problem solving. Whether or not feedback helps to energise the organisation depends on the content of the feedback data and on the process by which they are fed back to organisation members.

In this chapter we discuss criteria for developing both the contents of feedback information and the processes for feeding it back. If these criteria are overlooked, the client may not take responsibility for the problems that face the organisation. A special version of data feedback that has arisen out of the wide use of questionnaires in OD work is known as 'survey feedback'. Its central role in many large-scale OD efforts warrants a special look at this flexible and potentially powerful technique.

Determining the content of the feedback

Large amounts of data are collected in the course of diagnosing the organisation. In fact, there is often more information than the client needs or could interpret in a realistic period of time. If too many data are fed back, the client may decide that changing is impossible. Therefore, OD practitioners need to summarise the data in ways that are useful for clients, so that they can both understand the information and draw action implications from it. The techniques for data analysis described in Chapter 7 can inform this task. Additional criteria for determining the content of diagnostic feedback are described below.

Several characteristics of effective feedback data have been described in the literature.[1] They include the following nine properties:

1 *Relevant*. Organisation members are more likely to use feedback data for problem solving if they find the information meaningful. Including managers and employees in the initial data-collection activities can increase the relevance of the data.

2 *Understandable*. Data must be presented to organisation members in a form that is readily interpreted. Statistical data, for example, can be made understandable through the use of graphs and charts.

3 *Descriptive*. Feedback data need to be linked to real organisational behaviours if they are to arouse and direct energy. The use of examples and detailed illustrations can help employees gain a better feel for the data.

4 *Verifiable*. Feedback data should be valid and accurate if they are to guide action. Thus, the information should allow organisation members to verify whether the findings really describe the organisation. For example, questionnaire data might include information about the sample of respondents as well as frequency distributions for each item or measure. This kind of information can help members

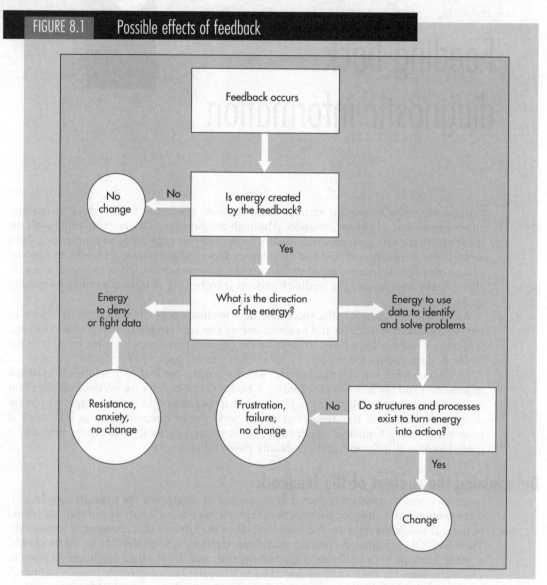

FIGURE 8.1 Possible effects of feedback

Source: D. Nadler, *Feedback and Organization Development*, p. 146, © 1977 by Addison-Wesley Publishing Company, Inc. Reprinted by permission of Addison-Wesley Publishing Company, Inc., Reading, Mass.

verify whether the feedback data accurately represent organisational events or attitudes.

5 *Timely*. Data should be fed back to members as quickly as possible after being collected and analysed. This will help ensure that the information is still valid and is linked to members' motivations to examine it.

6 *Limited*. Because people can easily become overloaded with too much information, feedback data should be limited to what employees can realistically process at any one time.

7 *Significant*. Feedback should be limited to those problems that organisation members can do something about. This will help energise them and direct their efforts toward realistic changes.

8 *Comparative*. Feedback data without some benchmark as a reference can be ambiguous. Whenever possible, data from comparative groups should be provided in order to give organisation members a better idea of how their group fits into a broader context.

9 *Unfinalised*. Feedback is primarily a stimulus for action and should, therefore, spur further diagnosis and problem solving. Members should be encouraged, for example, to use the data as a starting point for more in-depth discussion of organisational issues.

Characteristics of the feedback process

In addition to providing effective feedback data, it is equally important to attend to the process by which that information is fed back to people. Typically, data are provided to organisation members in a meeting or series of meetings. Feedback meetings provide a forum for discussing the data, drawing relevant conclusions and devising preliminary action plans. Because the data might include sensitive material and evaluations of organisation members' behaviours, people may come to the meeting with considerable anxiety and fear about receiving the feedback. This anxiety can result in defensive behaviours aimed at denying the information or providing rationales. More positively, people can be stimulated by the feedback and the hope that desired changes will result from the feedback meeting.

Because people are likely to come to feedback meetings with anxiety, fear and hope, OD practitioners need to manage the feedback process so that constructive discussion and problem solving will occur. The most important objective of the feedback process is to ensure that organisation members own the data. Ownership is the opposite of resistance to change and refers to people's willingness to take responsibility for the data, its meaning and the consequences of using the data to devise a change strategy.[2] If the feedback session results in organisation members rejecting the data as invalid or useless, then the motivation to change is lost and members will have difficulty in engaging in a meaningful process of change.

Ownership of the feedback data is facilitated by the following five features of successful feedback processes:[3]

1 *Motivation to work with the data*. People need to feel that working on the feedback data will have beneficial outcomes. This may require explicit sanction and support from powerful groups so that people feel free to raise issues and identify concerns during the feedback sessions. If they have little motivation to work with the data or feel that there is little chance to use the data for change, the information will not be owned by the client system.

2 *Structure for the meeting*. Feedback meetings need some structure, or they may degenerate into chaos or aimless discussion. An agenda or outline and a discussion leader can usually provide the necessary direction. If the meeting is not kept on track, especially when the data are negative, ownership can be lost in conversations that become too general. When this happens, the energy gained from dealing directly with the problem is lost.

3 *Appropriate membership*. Generally, people who have common problems and can benefit from working together should be included in the feedback meeting. This may involve a fully intact work team, or groups made up of members from different functional areas or hierarchical levels. Without proper representation in the meeting, ownership of the data is lost because the participants cannot address the problem(s) suggested by the feedback.

4 *Appropriate power*. It is important to clarify the power possessed by the group. Members need to know to which issues they can make necessary changes, on which they can only recommend changes and on which they have no control. Unless there are clear boundaries, members are likely to have some hesitation about using the feedback data for generating action plans. Moreover, if the group has no power to make changes, the feedback meeting will become an empty exercise, rather than a

real problem-solving session. Without the power to address change, there will be little ownership of the data.

5 *Process help.* People in feedback meetings need help to work together as a group. When the data are negative, there is a natural tendency to resist the implications, deflect the conversation onto safer subjects and the like. An OD practitioner with group process skills can help members stay focused on the subject and improve feedback discussion, problem solving and ownership.

When combined with effective feedback data, these features of successful feedback meetings enhance member ownership of the data. They help to ensure that organisation members fully discuss the implications of the diagnostic information and that their conclusions are directed toward organisational changes that are relevant and feasible.

In Application 8.1, it is shown how Dulux Australia introduced a programme that resulted in a significant shift towards a more participative climate and developed specific mechanisms for learning how to share decision making and solve organisational problems.[4]

APPLICATION 8.1   Dulux Australia Ltd

Dulux Australia Ltd manufactures and distributes a large range of surface coatings, some 6000 different products, for domestic and industrial use. It employs 2100 people and has facilities in all Australian states, with its head office in Melbourne. Its major shareholder is ICI Australia Ltd, but it operates as an independent company. It was established in 1918 and since then has absorbed a number of other companies with similarly long histories.

In its first 48 years, Dulux had five managing directors, averaging about ten years in office, who provided stable and predictable, even though traditional, leadership. However, in the 17 years between 1967 and 1984, it had four managing directors, averaging four years in office. The rapid changes of leadership and various reorganisations, together with recent tough trading conditions and more militant unions, led to feelings of insecurity among employees. These feelings were reinforced by staff reductions and the threatened and eventual closure of a long-established plant.

The new managing director, appointed in 1981, had experienced social science-based change programmes as a senior manager in an Australian division of the British holding company. He decided that the organisational climate should be shifted towards increasing participation of all staff in decision-making processes as a means of increasing organisational effectiveness.

Superordinate values
The guiding value here was that of democracy, including the notions that individuals at all levels had a right to participate in decisions that affected them, and that they had information and skills that would improve the quality of the decisions. An associated value was that a rational scientific method was as applicable in decision making as it was to the technical side of the enterprise. Thus, all problems should be tackled by a repeated cycle of operations composed of problem appreciation, theory building, data collection, experimental change and evaluation of consequences.

These two superordinate values were seen as requiring the collaborative efforts of interested parties who may have previously seen themselves as independent of, or even in conflict with, one another. These values were somewhat vague at first. They became more clearly articulated as the programme developed and as attempts were made to translate them from 'motherhood' statements into concrete guides for specific action capable of implementation.

The process of building sanction and ownership

The managing director's intentions and approach were shared by senior members of the head office personnel department. They suggested that an external consultant be commissioned to help with a programme that was to be directed towards making the organisation climate more participative. After some discussions, the consultant was asked to plan and conduct a two-day seminar for senior managers.

The broad purpose of the seminar was to provide an opportunity for a representative group of senior managers to review the company's effectiveness in the management of its human resources and to identify areas for improvement.

As a result of the seminar, senior managers agreed that there was a need to develop a more participatory organisational climate. It was also agreed that more systematic survey evidence was needed, both to assess the current climate and to provide a bench-mark against which to measure change.

Thus, the seminar achieved the critical conditions for the developing programme by obtaining top-level sanction for it and by broadening ownership beyond the initiating managing director and the internal and external consultants.

A steering committee was set up to plan and manage the programme, which was directed to changing the organisational climate towards increased participation by all members. The committee's first task was to conduct and report on the survey of the current organisational climate.

The results of the survey confirmed many of the perceptions expressed by senior managers in their seminar about there being room for increased participation by people at the lower levels of the organisation. The results also identified the strength of the organisation in being seen as one that desired harmonious relations with its people and wished to provide the conditions for them to use their abilities fully.

The steering committee faced the task of what to do with the information gathered in the survey. It decided to establish four strategy groups to build on the strengths of the organisation and to further the goal of increased participation. These groups would have access to the results of the survey as a basis for their own activities and would act as immediate reinforcers of the general dissemination of the results through the usual chain of command and the company newspaper.

Four months after they were established, the strategy groups met over two days with members of the executive and the steering committee in order to review their progress. They were asked to report on their experiences in identifying problems, collecting data and canvassing possible solutions. They were also asked to report on their experiences in their groups, and in their relationships with people outside the groups.

Bringing the four groups together allowed cross-fertilisation of ideas. It also gave the group the protection of being members of a larger collective when facing members of the executive and the steering committee. More positively, the presence of the managing director and other senior managers showed them that their efforts were considered to be both important and sanctioned.

Survey feedback

Survey feedback is a process of collecting data from an organisation or department through the use of a questionnaire or survey. The data are analysed, fed back to organisation members and used by them to diagnose the organisation and to develop interventions to improve it. Because questionnaires are often used in organisation diagnosis, particularly in OD efforts that involve large numbers of participants, survey feedback is discussed here as a special case of data feedback. It is both an integral part of diagnostic feedback and a powerful intervention in its own right.

As discussed in Chapter 1, survey feedback is a major technique in the history and development of OD. Originally, this intervention included only data from questionnaires about members' attitudes. However, attitudinal data can be supplemented with interview data and more objective measures, such as productivity, turnover and absenteeism.[5] Another trend has been to combine survey feedback with other OD interventions, including work design, structural change and inter-group relations. These change methods are the outcome of the planning and implementation phase that follows on from survey feedback, and are fully described in Chapters 12 to 20.

What are the steps?

Survey feedback generally involves the following five steps:[6]

1 *Members of the organisation, including those at the top, are involved in preliminary planning of the survey.* In this step, it is important that all parties are clear about the level of analysis (organisation, department or small group) and the objectives of the survey itself. Because most surveys derive from a model about organisational or group functioning, organisation members must, in effect, approve that diagnostic framework. This is an important initial step in gaining ownership of the data and in ensuring that the right problems and issues are addressed by the survey.

   Once the objectives have been determined, the organisation can use one of the standardised questionnaires described in Chapter 7, or it can develop its own survey instrument. If the survey is developed internally, pre-testing the questionnaire is important in order to be certain that it has been constructed properly. In either case, the survey items need to reflect the objectives established for the survey and the diagnostic issues being addressed.

2 *The survey instrument is administered to members of the organisation or department.* Ideally, the survey could be administered to all members, but, because of cost or time constraints it may be necessary to administer it to a sample of members. If so, the size of the sample should be as large as possible to improve the motivational basis for participation in the feedback sessions.

3 *The OD consultant usually analyses the survey data, tabulates the results, suggests approaches to diagnosis and trains client members to lead the feedback process.*

4 *Data feedback usually begins at the top of the organisation and cascades downward to groups reporting to managers at successively lower levels.* This waterfall approach ensures that all groups at all organisational levels involved in the survey receive appropriate feedback. Most often, members of each organisation group at each level discuss and deal with only that portion of the data that involves their particular group. They, in turn, prepare to introduce data to groups at the next lower organisational level, if appropriate.

   Data feedback can also occur in a 'bottom-up' approach. Initially, the data for specific work groups or departments are fed back and action items proposed. At this point, the group addresses problems and issues within its control. The group notes any issues that are beyond its authority and suggests actions. This information is combined with information from groups that report to the same manager. These combined data are then fed back to the managers who review the data and the recommended actions. Problems that can be solved at this level are addressed. In turn, their analyses and suggestions about problems of a broader nature are combined, and feedback and action sessions proceed up the hierarchy. In this way, the people who are the most likely to carry out recommended action get the first chance to propose suggestions.

5 *Feedback meetings provide an opportunity to work with the data.* At each meeting, members discuss and interpret their data, diagnose problem areas and develop action plans. OD practitioners can play an important role during these meetings.[7]

They can facilitate group discussion to produce accurate understanding, focus the group on its strengths and weaknesses and help to develop effective action plans. Although these steps can have a number of variations, they generally reflect the most common survey feedback design.[8] Application 8.2 gives an example of how staff and managers at Bethesda Private hospital are fed back data they have generated.[9]

Changing business culture: information is the key

Bethesda, a major private surgery and rehabilitation hospital, was faced with uncertainty about the real source of its operating surplus and the way in which costs and income were shifting over time between different service areas and products. It assigned a research firm, Australian Best Practice Consulting, to develop a new business model and system that would clearly indicate how each product was actually performing.

The first step was to conduct research into the percentage of time that various service providers put into the hospital's different 'products' over a typical month. Instead of producing a consultant's report, the data was fed back directly to staff and management groups in open fora. Working teams were spontaneously formed from these groups to ensure that each identified issue (costs exceeding income, reliability of cost estimates arising from the time percentages and so on) would be addressed. The time-based data gave a reasonably good initial indicator of where the cost pressures were, in terms of the direct costs of providing services to both inpatients and outpatients. More importantly, it allowed an interim, total cost model to be constructed, of which a set of monthly activity-based cost reports could be built for all departments and wards.

New model

The costs model was refined through successive monthly report cycles. Although income could be identified against individual products, most costs were paid through the centralised finance area and had been distributed to rehabilitation departments and wards only when actually generated by them.

The new model allowed all costs to be distributed on a basis acceptable to all areas. However, the model remained flexible for the first year while the reporting media were being built. Successive meetings with staff and managers refined the cost percentages allocated to different products and to different medical and allied health departments and wards.

A completely new business model was designed, discussed and adopted. This saw business managers appointed from among the existing clinical specialists to manage the profitability, marketing, pricing and service levels provided against each product. This business-based structure for reporting was a complete departure from the earlier organisation-based structure. The previous reporting arrangements had identified only those costs that were directly expended by medical and allied health department or nursing unit managers, who might provide services to three or more patients at a time. This, in turn, had allowed no identification of product profitability, since costs had not been able to be tracked against products.

The only basis for estimating costs before the time-based study had been the percentage of income—which is often a quite misleading basis on which to estimate costs. As reports from the new model were used month by month, the four new business team managers, each with a group of related products, began to see and suggest ways in which cost identification and allocation could be shifted to a real-time, rather than estimated, basis.

The culture at that point had 'turned the corner' to a true business focus.

Strategic planning based on a realistic assessment of product profitability and life cycle became possible. A number of sessions were held with business managers, medical, allied health and nursing unit managers. These created new product marketing approaches, revised operating procedures and service arrangements that would create longer-term stability in product income. An enormous added benefit of the new business model and its subsequent refinements was the capacity to accurately identify real costs against individual product income on a per hour and per bed-day basis.

The new model enabled business managers to identify unprofitable products and go directly to health funds or compensating bodies with strong arguments for increasing funding levels for particular products. This strategy also created a pre-emptive advantage for the hospital. It allowed the hospital to begin to plan realistic 'episodes of care' (standardised packaging) of particular products with which it could go to health funds, offering services that were based on what would be a profitable and realistic mix of cases within that product range. This facility allowed the hospital and the funds to develop a common vision that creates 'win–win' outcomes for the funds, the hospital and their joint customer.

The benefits of the new model include:

- business teams and managers are now fully aware of, and responsible for, product/service success
- staff have increased awareness of costs and participate readily in cost-reduction measures
- comprehensive decision-support information is now available to improve both income and cost controls
- performance criteria are established for all managers
- performance is monitored on a monthly basis at all levels
- monthly business meetings ensure that synergies are harnessed for problem solving when addressing business and performance issues such as performance against budget, resource utilisation, financial viability, variations in statistics, strategic marketing and profitability
- an ability to separately track inpatient and outpatient costs, and income by product
- full electronic automation of management reporting in user-friendly formats on a well-known platform, allowing easy user extraction and manipulation of data to generate one-off reports
- training of all management staff to ensure computer literacy and use of the report suite to assist analysis and decision making.

Survey feedback and organisational dependencies

Traditionally, the steps of survey feedback have been applied to work groups and organisational units with little attention to dependencies among them. Recent studies, however, suggest that the design of survey feedback should vary according to how closely linked the participating units are with one another.[10] When the units are relatively independent and have little need to interact, survey feedback can focus on the dynamics that occur within each group and can be applied to the groups separately. When there is greater dependency among units and they need to co-ordinate their efforts, survey feedback must take into account relationships among the units, paying particular attention to the possibility of inter-group conflict. In these situations, the survey-feedback process needs to be co-ordinated across the interdependent groups. Special committees and task forces representing the groups will typically manage the process. They will facilitate the inter-group confrontation and conflict resolution generally needed when relations across groups are diagnosed.

Limitations of survey feedback

Although the use of survey feedback is widespread in contemporary organisations, the following limits and risks have been identified:[11]

1 *Ambiguity of purpose.* Managers and staff groups responsible for the survey feedback process may have difficulty reaching sufficient consensus about the purposes of the survey, its content and how it will be fed back to participants. This confusion can lead to considerable disagreement over the data collected and the probability that nothing will be done with it.

2 *Distrust.* High levels of distrust in the organisation can render the survey feedback ineffective. Employees need to trust that their responses will remain anonymous and that management is serious about sharing the data and solving problems jointly.

3 *Unacceptable topics.* Most organisations have certain topics that they do not want examined. This can severely constrain the scope of the survey process, particularly if the neglected topics are important to employees.

4 *Organisational disturbance.* The survey feedback process can unduly disturb organisational functioning. Data collection and feedback typically infringe on employee work time. Moreover, administration of a survey can call attention to issues with which management is unwilling to deal. It can create unrealistic expectations about organisational improvement.

Results of survey feedback

Survey feedback has been used widely in business organisations, schools, hospitals, federal and state governments and branches of the military. The United States Navy used survey feedback in more than 500 navy commands. More than 150 000 individual surveys were given, and a large bank of computerised research data was generated. Promising results were noted between survey indices and non-judicial punishment rates, incidence of drug abuse reports and the performance of ships undergoing refresher training (a post-overhaul training and evaluation period).[12] Positive results have been reported in such diverse areas as an industrial organisation in Sweden and the Israeli Army.[13]

One of the most important studies of survey feedback was done by Bowers, who conducted a five-year longitudinal study (the Inter-company Longitudinal Study) of 23 organisations in 15 companies, involving more than 14 000 people in both white- and blue-collar positions.[14] In each of the 23 organisations studied, repeat measurements were taken. The study compared survey feedback with three other OD interventions: interpersonal process consultation, task process consultation and laboratory training. The study reported that survey feedback was the most effective of the four treatments and the only one 'associated with large across-the-board positive changes in organisation climate'.[15]

These findings have been questioned on a number of methodological grounds and, since then, a more critical and comprehensive study has provided alternative explanations for the findings of the original study.[16] Although pointing to the original study as a seminal piece, the critique discovered methodological problems in the research itself. It did not question the original conclusion that survey feedback is effective in achieving organisational change, but it did question the fairness of the procedure employed for the evaluation of the other intervention techniques. It suggested that any conclusions to be drawn from action research studies should be based, at least in part, on objective operating data.

Comprehensive reviews of the literature present differing perspectives on the effects of survey feedback. In one review, survey feedback's biggest impact was on attitudes and perceptions of the work situation. The study suggests that survey feedback might best be viewed as a bridge between the diagnosis of organisational problems and the implementation of problem-solving methods, because there is little evidence to suggest that survey feedback alone will result in changes in individual behaviour or organisational output.[17] Another study suggests that survey feedback has positive effects on both outcome variables (e.g. productivity, costs and absenteeism) and process variables (e.g. employee openness, decision making and motivation) in 53% and 48%, respectively, of the studies measuring those variables.[18] When compared with other OD approaches, survey feedback was only bettered by interventions that used several approaches together, e.g. change programmes involving a combination of survey feedback, process consultation and team building. On the other hand, another review found that, in contrast to laboratory training and team building, survey feedback was least effective, with only 33% of the studies that measured hard outcomes reporting success.[19] The success rate increased to 45%, however, when survey feedback was combined with team building. Finally, a meta-analysis of OD process interventions and individual attitudes suggested that survey feedback was not significantly associated with overall satisfaction or attitudes about co-workers, the job or the organisation. Survey feedback was only able to account for about 11% of the variance in satisfaction and other attitudes.[20]

Studies of specific survey-feedback interventions in the US have suggested conditions that improve the success of this technique. One study in an urban school district reported difficulties with survey feedback and suggested that its effectiveness depends partly on the quality of those leading the change effort, members' understanding of the process, the extent to which the survey focuses on issues important to participants and the degree to which the values expressed by the survey are congruent with those of the respondents.[21] Another study in the military concluded that survey feedback works best when supervisors play an active role in feeding data back to employees and helping them to work with it.[22] Similarly, a field study of funeral co-operative societies concluded that the use and dissemination of survey results increased when organisation members were closely involved in developing and carrying out the project and when the consultant provided technical assistance in the form of data analysis and interpretation.[23] Finally, a long-term study of survey feedback in an underground mining operation suggests that continued, periodic use of survey feedback can produce significant changes in organisations.[24] The feedback process can guide the change programme.

Survey feedback is widely used in OD. It enables practitioners to collect diagnostic data from a large number of organisation members and to feed that information back to them for purposes of problem solving. Organisations can use any of several pre-designed surveys, or they can develop their own. Evidence supporting the effectiveness of survey feedback is mixed, in part because it is difficult to separate the effects of collecting and feeding back information from the subsequent problem-solving interventions based on those data. The available evidence also suggests that survey feedback is most effective when used in combination with other OD techniques. More systematic and rigorous research is needed to assess the impact of survey feedback.

Summary

This chapter has described the process of feeding back data to a client system. It is concerned with identifying the content of the data to be fed back and designing a process of feedback that ensures ownership of the data. Feeding back data is a central activity in almost any OD programme. If members own the data, they will be motivated to solve organisational problems. A special application of the data-collection and feedback process is called survey feedback, and is one of the most accepted processes in organisation development. Survey feedback highlights the importance of contracting appropriately with the client system, establishing relevant categories for data collection, and feeding back the data as necessary steps for diagnosing organisational problems and developing interventions for resolving them.

ACTIVITIES

Review questions
1 What is most important in designing data feedback?
2 Describe some features of a successful feedback meeting.

Discussion and essay questions
1 Discuss the major diagnostic activities of an OD practitioner.
2 Discuss the usefulness and limitations of survey feedback.
3 Explain the key issues/problems that the OD practitioner has to be aware of when feeding back data.

Notes

1   S. Mohrman, T. Cummings and E. Lawler III, 'Creating useful knowledge with organizations: relationship and process issues' in *Producing Useful Knowledge for Organizations*, eds R. Kilmann and K. Thomas (New York: Praeger, 1983): 61–24.

2   C. Argyris, *Intervention Theory and Method: A Behavioral Science View* (Reading, Mass.: Addison-Wesley, 1970); P. Block, *Flawless Consulting* (Austin, Texas: Learning Concepts, 1981).

3   D. Nadler, *Feedback and Organization Development: Using Data-Based Methods* (Reading, Mass.: Addison-Wesley, 1977): 156–58.

4   D. Grose and A. Clark, 'Using strategy groups to build sanction and ownership in organizational development', *Work and People*, 11:1 (1985).

5   D. Nadler, P. Mirvis and C. Cammann, 'The ongoing feedback system: experimenting with a new managerial tool', *Organizational Dynamics*, 4 (Spring 1976): 63–80.

6   F. Mann, 'Studying and creating change' in *The Planning of Change*, eds W. Bennis, K. Benne and R. Chin (New York: Holt, Rinehart and Winston, 1964): 605–15; R. Golembiewski and R. Hilles, *Toward the Responsive Organization: The Theory and Practice of Survey/Feedback* (Salt Lake City: Brighton, 1979); D. Nadler, *Feedback and Organization Development, op. cit.*; J. Wiley, 'Making the most of survey feedback as a strategy for organization development', *OD Practitioner*, 23 (1991): 1–5.

7   G. Ledford and C. Worley, 'Some guidelines for effective survey feedback', (unpublished working paper, Center for Effective Organizations, University of Southern California, 1987).

8   N. Margulies and J. Wallace, *Organizational Change* (Glenville, Ill.: Scott, Foresman, 1973).

9   C. Singh and M. Hart, 'Changing business culture: information is the key', *Australian Accountant*, 68:8:50–52

10 M. Sashkin and R. Cooke, 'Organizational structure as a moderator of the effects of data-based change programs' (Paper delivered at the Thirty-sixth Annual Meeting of the Academy of Management, Kansas City, 1976); D. Nadler, 'Alternative data-feedback designs for organizational intervention' in *The 1979 Annual Handbook for Group Facilitators*, ed. J. Jones and J. Pfeiffer (LaJolla, Calif.: University Associates, 1979): 78–92.

11 S. Seashore, 'Surveys in organizations' in *Handbook of Organizational Behavior*, ed. J. Lorsch (Englewood Cliff, N.J.: Prentice-Hall, 1987): 142.

12 R. Forbes, 'Quo Vadis: the Navy and organization development', (Paper delivered at the Fifth Psychology in the Air Force Symposium, United States Air Force Academy, Colorado Springs, Colo., 8 April 1976).

13 S. Rubenowitz, Goteborg, Sweden: Goteborg Universitet, private communication; D. Eden and S. Shlomo, 'Survey-based OD in the Israel Defense Forces: a field experiment', (unpublished and undated manuscript, Tel Aviv University).

14 D. Bowers, 'OD techniques and their results in 23 organizations: the Michigan ICL Study', *Journal of Applied Behavioral Science*, 9 (January–February–March 1973): 21–43.

15 *Ibid.*, p. 42.

16 W. Pasmore, 'Backfeed, the Michigan ICL Study revisited: an alternative explanation of the results', *Journal of Applied Behavioral Science*, 12 (April–May–June 1976): 245–51; W. Pasmore and D. King, 'The Michigan ICL Study revisited: a critical review', (Working Paper 548, Krannert Graduate School of Industrial Administration, West Lafayette, Ind., 1976).

17 F. Friedlander and L. Brown, 'Organization development' in *Annual Review of Psychology*, eds M. Rosenzweig and L. Porter (Palo Alto, Calif.: Annual Reviews, 1974).

18 J. Porras and P. Berg, 'The impact of organization development', *Academy of Management Review*, 3 (April 1978): 249–66.

19 J. Nicholas, 'The comparative impact of organization development interventions on hard criteria measures', *Academy of Management Review*, 7 (October 1982): 531–42.

20 G. Neuman, J. Edwards and N. Raju, 'Organizational development interventions: a meta-analysis of their effects on satisfaction and other attitudes', *Personnel Psychology*, 42 (1989): 461–83.

21 S. Mohrman, A. Mohrman, R. Cooke and R. Duncan, 'Survey feedback and problem-solving intervention in a school district: "we'll take the survey but you can keep the feedback"' in *Failures in Organization Development and Change*, eds P. Mirvis and D. Berg (New York: John Wiley and Sons, 1977): 149–90.

22 F. Conlon and L. Short, 'An empirical examination of survey feedback as an organizational change device', *Academy of Management Proceedings*, (1983): 225–29.

23 R. Sommer, 'An experimental investigation of the action research approach', *Journal of Applied Behavioral Science*, 23 (1987): 185–99.

24 J. Gavin, 'Observation from a long-term survey-guided consultation with a mining company', *Journal of Applied Behavioral Science*, 21 (1985): 201–20.

Designing interventions

An organisation development intervention is a sequence of activities, actions and events intended to help an organisation improve its performance and effectiveness. Intervention design, or action planning, derives from careful diagnosis and is meant to resolve specific problems and to improve particular areas of organisational functioning identified in the diagnosis. OD interventions vary from standardised programmes that have been developed and used in many organisations to unique programmes tailored to a specific organisation or department.

This chapter describes criteria that define effective OD interventions and then identifies contingencies that guide successful intervention design. Finally, the various types of OD interventions presented in this book are reviewed. Parts 3 to 6 of this book describe fully the major interventions used in OD today.

What are effective interventions?

The term 'intervention' refers to a set of sequenced planned actions or events that are intended to help an organisation increase its effectiveness. Interventions purposely disrupt the *status quo*; they are a deliberate attempt to change an organisation or subunit towards a different and more effective state. In OD, three major criteria define an effective intervention: (1) the extent to which it fits the needs of the organisation, (2) the degree to which it is based on causal knowledge of intended outcomes and (3) the extent to which it transfers competence to manage change to organisation members.

The first criterion concerns the extent to which the intervention is relevant to the organisation and its members. Effective interventions are based on valid information about the organisation's functioning. They provide organisation members with opportunities to make free and informed choices; and they gain members' internal commitment to those choices.[1]

Valid information is the result of an accurate diagnosis of the organisation's functioning. It must fairly reflect what organisation members perceive and feel about their primary concerns and issues. *Free and informed choice* suggests that members are actively involved in making decisions about the changes that will affect them. It means that they can choose not to participate and that interventions will not be imposed upon them. *Internal commitment* means that organisation members will accept ownership of the intervention and take responsibility for implementing it. If interventions are to result in meaningful changes, management, staff and other relevant members must be committed to implementing them.

The second criterion of an effective intervention involves knowledge of outcomes. Because interventions are intended to produce specific results, they must be based on valid knowledge that those outcomes can actually be produced. Otherwise there is no scientific basis for designing an effective OD intervention. Unfortunately, and in contrast to other applied disciplines, such as medicine and engineering, knowledge of intervention effects is in a rudimentary stage of development in OD. Much of the evaluation research lacks sufficient rigour to make strong causal inferences about the success or failure of change programmes. (Chapter 11 discusses how to evaluate OD programmes rigorously.)

Moreover, few attempts have been made to examine the comparative impacts of different OD techniques. This makes knowing whether one method is more effective than another difficult.

Despite these problems, more attempts are being made to systematically assess the strengths and weaknesses of OD interventions and to compare the impact of different techniques on organisation effectiveness.[2] Many of the OD interventions that will be discussed in Parts 3 to 6 of this book have been subjected to evaluative research. This research is explored in the appropriate chapters, along with respective change programmes.

The third criterion of an effective intervention involves the extent to which it enhances the organisation's capacity to manage change. The values underlying OD suggest that organisation members should be better able to carry out planned change activities on their own after an intervention. They should gain knowledge and skill in managing change from active participation in designing and implementing the intervention. Competence in change management is essential in today's environment, where technological, social, economic and political changes are rapid and persistent.

How to design effective interventions

Designing OD interventions requires careful attention to the needs and dynamics of the change situation and to crafting a change programme that will be consistent with the criteria of the effective interventions outlined above. Current knowledge of OD interventions provides only general prescriptions for change. There is little precise information or research about how to design interventions or how they can be expected to interact with organisational conditions to achieve specific results.[3] Moreover, the ability to implement most OD interventions is highly dependent on the skills and knowledge of the change agent. Thus, the design of an intervention will depend to some extent on the expertise of the practitioner.

Two major sets of contingencies that can affect intervention success have been discussed in the OD literature: those having to do with the change situation (including the practitioner) and those related to the target of change. Both kinds of contingencies need to be considered when designing interventions.

Contingencies related to the change situation

Researchers have identified a number of contingencies present in the change situation that can affect intervention success. These include individual differences among organisation members (e.g. needs for autonomy), organisational factors (e.g. management style and technical uncertainty) and dimensions of the change process itself (e.g. the degree of top-management support). Unless these factors are taken into account when designing an intervention, the intervention will have little impact on organisational functioning, or worse, it might even produce negative results. For example, if you are seeking to resolve motivational problems among blue-collar workers in an oil refinery, it is important that you know whether interventions intended to improve motivation (e.g. job enrichment) will succeed with the kinds of people who work there. In many cases, having knowledge of these contingencies might result in modifying or adjusting the change programme to fit the setting. In applying a reward-system intervention to an organisation, the changes might have to be modified according to whether the firm wants to reinforce individual or team performance.

Although knowledge of contingencies is still in a rudimentary stage of development in OD, researchers have discovered several situational factors that can affect intervention success.[4] These include contingencies for many of the interventions reviewed in this book, and they will be discussed in the relevant chapters that describe the change programmes. More generic contingencies that apply to all OD interventions are presented on the next page, including the following situational factors that must be considered when designing any intervention: the organisation's readiness for change, its change capability, its cultural context and the change agent's skills and abilities.

Readiness for change

Intervention success depends heavily on the organisation being ready for planned change. Indicators of readiness for change include sensitivity to pressures for change, dissatisfaction with the *status quo*, availability of resources to support change and commitment of significant management time. When these conditions are present, interventions can be designed to address the organisational issues uncovered during diagnosis. When readiness for change is low, however, interventions need to focus on increasing the organisation's willingness to change.[5]

Capability to change

Managing planned change requires particular knowledge and skills, as outlined in Chapter 10. These include the ability to motivate change, to lead change, to develop political support, to manage the transition and to sustain momentum. If organisation members do not have these capabilities, then a preliminary training intervention may be needed before members can meaningfully engage in intervention design.

Cultural context

The national culture within which the organisation is embedded can have a powerful influence on members' reactions to change. Thus, intervention design needs to account for the cultural values and assumptions held by organisation members. Interventions may need to be modified to fit the local culture, particularly when OD practices developed in one culture are applied to organisations in another culture.[6] For example, a team-building intervention designed for top managers at an Australian firm may need to be modified when applied to the company's foreign subsidiaries. (Chapter 21 will describe the cultural values of different countries and show how interventions can be modified to fit different cultural contexts.)

Capabilities of the change agent

Many failures in OD result when change agents apply interventions beyond their competence. In designing interventions, OD practitioners should assess their experience and expertise against the requirements needed to implement the intervention effectively. When a mismatch is discovered, practitioners can explore whether the intervention can be modified to fit their talents better, whether another intervention more suited to their skills can satisfy the organisation's needs or whether they should enlist the assistance of another change agent who can guide the process more effectively. The ethical guidelines under which OD practitioners operate require full disclosure of the applicability of their knowledge and expertise to the client situation. Practitioners are expected to intervene within their capabilities or to recommend someone more suited to the client's needs.

Contingencies related to the target of change

OD interventions seek to change specific features or parts of organisations. These targets of change are the main focus of interventions, and researchers have identified two key contingencies related to change targets that can affect intervention success: the organisational issues that the intervention is intended to resolve and the level of organisational system at which the intervention is expected to have a primary impact.

Organisational issues

Organisations need to address certain issues to operate effectively. Figure 9.1 lists these issues along with the OD interventions that are intended to resolve them. (The parts and chapters of this book that describe the specific interventions are also identified in the figure.) It shows four interrelated issues that are key targets of OD interventions:

1 *Strategic issues.* Organisations need to decide what products or services they will provide and the markets in which they will compete, as well as how to relate to

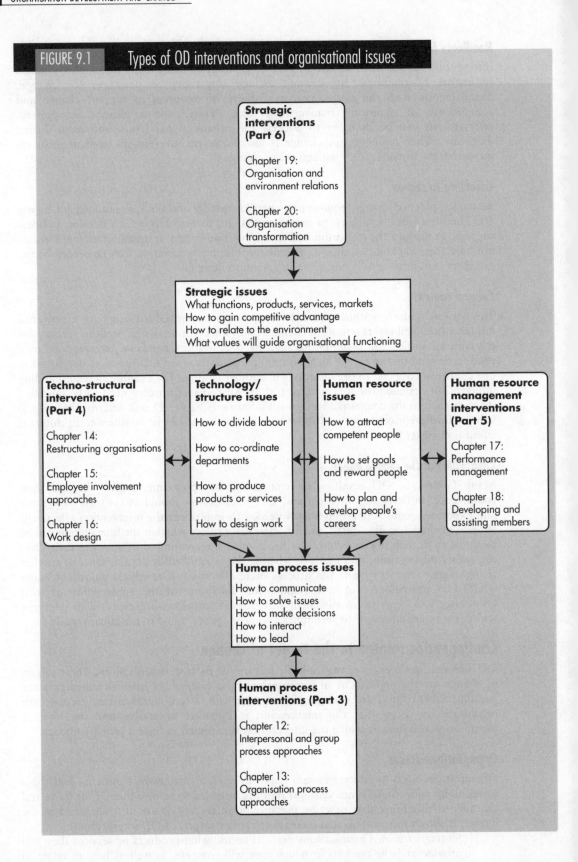

FIGURE 9.1   Types of OD interventions and organisational issues

Strategic interventions (Part 6)

Chapter 19:
Organisation and environment relations

Chapter 20:
Organisation transformation

Strategic issues
What functions, products, services, markets
How to gain competitive advantage
How to relate to the environment
What values will guide organisational functioning

Techno-structural interventions (Part 4)

Chapter 14:
Restructuring organisations

Chapter 15:
Employee involvement approaches

Chapter 16:
Work design

Technology/ structure issues

How to divide labour

How to co-ordinate departments

How to produce products or services

How to design work

Human resource issues

How to attract competent people

How to set goals and reward people

How to plan and develop people's careers

Human resource management interventions (Part 5)

Chapter 17:
Performance management

Chapter 18:
Developing and assisting members

Human process issues

How to communicate
How to solve issues
How to make decisions
How to interact
How to lead

Human process interventions (Part 3)

Chapter 12:
Interpersonal and group process approaches

Chapter 13:
Organisation process approaches

their environments and how to transform themselves to keep pace with changing conditions. These strategic issues are among the most critical facing organisations in today's changing and highly competitive environments. OD methods aimed at these issues are called 'strategic interventions'. They are among the most recent additions to OD and include integrated strategic change, transorganisational development and organisation transformation.

2 *Technology and structure issues.* Organisations must decide how to divide work into departments and then how to co-ordinate them to support strategic directions. They must also make decisions about how to produce products or services and how to link people to tasks. OD methods for dealing with these structural and technological issues are called 'technostructural interventions'. They include OD activities relating to organisation design, employee involvement and work design.

3 *Human resource issues.* These issues are concerned with attracting competent people to the organisation, setting goals for them, appraising and rewarding their performance and ensuring that they develop their careers and manage stress. OD techniques aimed at these issues are called 'human resource management interventions'.

4 *Human process issues.* These issues have to do with social processes occurring among organisation members, such as communication, decision making, leadership and group dynamics. OD methods focusing on these kinds of issues are called 'human process interventions'; included among them are some of the most common OD techniques, such as conflict resolution and team building.

Consistent with system theory as described in Chapter 5, these organisational issues are interrelated and need to be integrated with each other. The double-headed arrows connecting the different issues in Figure 9.1 represent the fits or linkages among them. Organisations need to match answers to one set of questions with answers to other sets of questions to achieve high levels of effectiveness. For example, decisions about gaining competitive advantage need to fit with choices about organisation structure, setting goals for and rewarding people, communication and problem solving.

The interventions presented in this book are intended to resolve these different concerns. As shown in Figure 9.1, particular OD interventions apply to specific issues. Thus, intervention design must create change methods appropriate to the organisational issues identified in diagnosis. Moreover, because the organisational issues are themselves linked, OD interventions need to be similarly integrated with one another. For example, a goal-setting intervention that attempts to establish motivating goals may need to be integrated with supporting interventions, such as a reward system that links pay to goal achievement. The key point is to *think systemically*. Interventions that are aimed at one kind of organisational issue will invariably have repercussions on other kinds of issues. This requires careful thinking about how OD interventions affect the different kinds of issues and how different change programmes might be integrated to bring about a broader and more coherent impact on organisational functioning.

Organisational levels

In addition to facing interrelated issues, organisations function at different levels— individual, group and organisation. Thus, organisational levels are targets of change in OD. Table 9.1 lists OD interventions in terms of the level of organisation they mainly affect. For example, some technostructural interventions affect mainly individuals and groups (e.g. work design), whereas others impact primarily on the total organisation (e.g. structural design).

It is important to emphasise that only the *primary* level affected by the intervention is identified in Table 9.1. Many OD interventions also have a secondary impact on other levels. For example, structural design affects mainly the organisation level but can have an indirect impact on groups and individuals. It sets the broad parameters for designing work groups and individual jobs. Again, practitioners need to think systematically. They must design interventions to apply to specific organisational levels. Moreover, they need to

TABLE 9.1	Types of OD interventions and organisational levels

Interventions	Primary organisational level affected		
	Individual	Group	Organisation
Human process (Part 3)			
Chapter 12:			
T-groups	X	X	
Process consultation		X	
Third-party intervention	X	X	
Team building		X	
Chapter 13:			
Organisation confrontation meeting		X	X
Inter-group relations		X	X
Large-group interventions			X
Grid organisation development		X	X
Technostructural (Part 4)			
Chapter 14:			
Structural design			X
Downsizing			X
Re-engineering		X	X
Chapter 15:			
Parallel structures		X	X
High-involvement organisations	X	X	X
Total quality management		X	X
Chapter 16:			
Work design	X	X	
Human resource management (Part 5)			
Chapter 17:			
Goal setting	X	X	
Performance appraisal	X	X	
Reward systems	X	X	X
Chapter 18:			
Career planning and development	X		
Managing work force diversity	X	X	
Employee wellness	X		
Strategic (Part 6)			
Chapter 19:			
Open systems planning		X	X
Integrated strategic change			X
Transorganisation development			X
Chapter 20:			
Culture change			X
Self-designing organisations		X	X
Organisation learning		X	X

address the possibility of cross-level effects and may need to integrate interventions that affect different levels to achieve overall success.[7] For example, an intervention to create self-managed work teams may need to be linked to organisation-level changes in measurement and reward systems to promote team-based work.

Overview of interventions

The OD interventions discussed in Parts 3 to 6 of this book are briefly described below. They represent the major organisational change methods used in OD today.

Human process interventions

Part 3 of the book presents interventions that focus on people within organisations and the processes through which they accomplish organisational goals. These processes include communication, problem solving, group decision making, and leadership. This type of intervention is deeply rooted in the history of OD. It represents the earliest change programmes characterising OD, including the T-group and the organisational confrontation meeting. Human process interventions derive mainly from the disciplines of psychology and social psychology and the applied fields of group dynamics and human relations. Practitioners applying these interventions generally value human fulfilment and expect that organisational effectiveness follows from improved functioning of people and organisational processes.[8]

Chapter 12 discusses human process interventions that are related to interpersonal relations and group dynamics. These include the following four interventions:

1 *T-group*. This traditional change method is designed to provide members with experiential learning about group dynamics, leadership and interpersonal relations. The basic T-group consists of about 10 to 15 strangers who meet with a professional trainer to examine the social dynamics that emerge from their interactions. Members gain feedback on the impact of their own behaviours on each other in addition to learning about group dynamics.

2 *Process consultation*. This intervention focuses on the interpersonal relations and social dynamics that occur in work groups. Typically, a process consultant helps group members to diagnose group functioning and to devise appropriate solutions to process problems, such as dysfunctional conflict, poor communication and ineffective norms. The aim is to help members to gain the skills and understanding necessary to identify and solve problems themselves.

3 *Third-party intervention*. This change method is a form of process consultation aimed at dysfunctional interpersonal relations in organisations. Interpersonal conflict may derive from substantive issues, such as disputes over work methods, or from interpersonal issues, such as miscommunication. The third-party intervener helps people resolve conflicts through such methods as problem solving, bargaining and conciliation.

4 *Team building*. This intervention is concerned with helping work groups to more effectively accomplish tasks. Like process consultation, team building helps members to diagnose their group processes and to devise solutions to problems. It goes beyond group processes, however, to include an examination of the group's task, member roles and strategies for performing tasks. The consultant may also function as a resource person who can offer expertise that is related to the group's task.

Chapter 13 presents human process interventions that are more system-wide than those described in Chapter 12. They typically focus on the total organisation or an entire department, as well as on relations between groups. These include the following four change programmes:

1 *Organisation confrontation meeting*. This change method is intended to mobilise organisation members to identify problems, to set action targets and to begin working on problems. It is usually applied when organisations are experiencing stress and when management needs to organise resources for immediate problem solving. The intervention generally includes various groupings of employees in identifying and solving problems.

2 *Inter-group relations*. These interventions are designed to improve interactions between different groups or departments in organisations. The microcosm group intervention involves a small group that is made up of people whose backgrounds closely match the organisational problems being addressed. This group then addresses the problem and develops the means to solve it. The inter-group conflict model typically involves a consultant helping two groups to understand the causes of the conflict and to choose appropriate solutions.

3 *Large-group interventions*. These interventions involve a meeting of a broad variety of stakeholders to clarify important values, to develop new ways of working, to articulate a new vision for the organisation or to solve pressing organisational problems. It is a powerful tool for creating awareness of organisational problems and opportunities and for specifying valued directions for future action.

4 *Grid organisation development*. This intervention specifies a particular way of managing an organisation. It is a packaged OD programme that includes standardised instruments for measuring organisational practices as well as specific procedures for helping organisations to achieve the prescribed approach.

Technostructural interventions

Part 4 of the book presents interventions that focus on the technology (e.g. task methods and job design) and structure (e.g. division of labour and hierarchy) of organisations. These change methods are receiving increasing attention in OD, especially in view of current concerns about productivity and organisational effectiveness. They include approaches to employee involvement, as well as methods for designing organisations, groups and jobs. Technostructural interventions are rooted in the disciplines of engineering, sociology and psychology and in the applied fields of socio-technical systems and organisation design. Practitioners generally stress both productivity and human fulfilment and expect that organisation effectiveness will result from appropriate work designs and organisation structures.[9]

In Chapter 14, we discuss technostructural interventions that are concerned with restructuring organisations. These include the following three change programmes:

1 *Structural design*. This process concerns the organisation's division of labour—how to specialise task performances. Interventions aimed at structural design include moving from more traditional ways of dividing the organisation's overall work, such as functional, self-contained-unit and matrix structures, to more integrative and flexible forms, such as process-based and network-based structures. Diagnostic guidelines exist to help determine which structure is appropriate for particular organisational environments, technologies and conditions.

2 *Downsizing*. This intervention seeks to reduce costs and bureaucracy by decreasing the size of the organisation. This reduction in personnel can be accomplished through lay-offs, organisation redesign and outsourcing. Each of these downsizing methods must be planned with a clear understanding of the organisation's strategy.

3 *Re-engineering*. This recent intervention radically redesigns the organisation's core work processes to create tighter linkage and co-ordination among the different tasks. This work flow integration results in faster, more responsive task performance. Re-engineering is often accomplished with new information technology that permits employees to control and co-ordinate work processes more effectively. Re-engineering often fails if it ignores basic principles and processes of OD.

Chapter 15 is concerned with *employee involvement* (EI). This broad category of interventions is aimed at improving employee well-being and organisational effectiveness. It generally attempts to move knowledge, power, information and rewards downward in the organisation. EI includes parallel structures (such as co-operative union-management projects and quality circles), high-involvement plants and total quality management.

Chapter 16 discusses *work design*. These change programmes are concerned with designing work for work groups and individual jobs. It includes the engineering, motivational and socio-technical systems approaches. These approaches produce traditionally-designed jobs and work groups; enriched jobs that provide employees with greater task variety, autonomy and feedback about results; and self-managing teams that can govern their own task behaviours with limited external control.

Human resource management interventions

Part 5 of the book focuses on personnel practices used to integrate people into organisations. These practices include career planning, reward systems, goal setting and performance appraisal. These change methods have traditionally been associated with the personnel function in organisations. In recent years, interest has grown in integrating human resource management with organisation development. Human resource management interventions are rooted in the disciplines of economics and labour relations and in the applied personnel practices of wages and compensation, employee selection and placement, performance appraisal and career development. Practitioners in this area typically focus on the people in organisations, believing that organisational effectiveness results from improved practices for integrating employees into organisations.

Chapter 17 deals with interventions concerning performance management. These include the following change programmes:

1   *Goal setting.* This change programme involves setting clear and challenging goals. It attempts to improve organisation effectiveness by establishing a better fit between personal and organisational objectives. Managers and subordinates periodically meet to plan work, review accomplishments and solve problems in achieving goals.

2   *Performance appraisal.* This intervention is a systematic process of jointly assessing work-related achievements, strengths and weaknesses. It is the primary human resource management intervention for providing performance feedback to individuals and work groups. Performance appraisal represents an important link between goal setting and reward systems.

3   *Reward systems.* This intervention involves the design of organisational rewards to improve employee satisfaction and performance. It includes innovative approaches to pay, promotions and fringe benefits.

Chapter 18 focuses on three change methods that are associated with developing and assisting organisation members:

1   *Career planning and development.* This intervention involves helping people choose organisations and career paths and attain career objectives. It generally focuses on managers and professional staff and is seen as a way of improving their quality of work life.

2   *Managing work-force diversity.* This change programme seeks to make human resource practices more responsive to a variety of individual needs. Important trends, such as the increasing number of women, ethnic minorities and physically and mentally challenged workers in the work force, require a more flexible set of policies and practices.

3   *Employee wellness.* These interventions include employee assistance programmes (EAPs) and stress management. EAPs are counselling programmes that help employees deal with substance abuse and mental health, marital and financial problems often associated with poor work performance. Stress management programmes help organisation members cope with the negative consequences of stress at work. They help managers to reduce specific sources of stress, such as role conflict and ambiguity and provide methods for reducing stress symptoms, such as hypertension and anxiety.

Strategic interventions

Part 6 of the book presents interventions that link the internal functioning of the organisation to the larger environment and transform the organisation to keep pace with changing conditions. These change programmes are new additions to OD. They are organisation-wide and bring about a fit between business strategy, structure, culture and the larger environment. The interventions derive from the disciplines of strategic management, organisation theory, open systems theory and cultural anthropology.

In Chapter 19, we discuss three major interventions for managing organisation and environment relationships:

1   *Open systems planning.* This change method helps organisations and departments to systematically assess their environmental relationships and to plan for improvements in interactions. It is intended to help organisations become more active in relating to their environment.

2 *Integrated strategic change.* This comprehensive OD intervention suggests that the principles of planned change can make a value-added contribution to strategic management. It argues that business strategies and organisational systems must be changed together in response to external and internal disruptions. A strategic change plan helps members to manage the transition from a current strategy and organisation design to the desired future strategic orientation.

3 *Transorganisational development.* This intervention is concerned with helping organisations to join into partnerships with other organisations to perform tasks or to solve problems that are too complex for single organisations to resolve. It helps organisations to recognise the need for partnerships and develop appropriate structures for implementing them.

Chapter 20 presents three major interventions for transforming organisations:

1 *Culture change.* This intervention is aimed at helping organisations to develop cultures (behaviours, values, beliefs and norms) appropriate to their strategies and environments. It focuses on developing a strong organisation culture to keep organisation members pulling in the same direction.

2 *Self-designing organisations.* This change programme involves helping organisations gain the capacity to fundamentally alter themselves. It is a highly participative process that involves multiple stakeholders in setting strategic directions and designing and implementing appropriate structures and processes. Organisations learn how to design and implement their own strategic changes.

3 *Organisation learning.* This intervention involves a process where the organisation systematically examines the way it operates to uncover the patterns in its actions, the assumptions underlying those patterns and the alteration of those patterns. Distinct from individual learning, this intervention helps the organisation move beyond solving existing problems and gain the capability to improve continuously. An organisation that engages in learning over a sustained period of time creates a learning organisation.

Summary

This chapter presented an overview of interventions currently used in OD. An intervention is a set of planned activities intended to help an organisation improve its performance and effectiveness. Effective interventions are designed to fit the needs of the organisation, are based on causal knowledge of intended outcomes and transfer competence to manage change to organisation members.

Intervention design involves understanding situational contingencies such as individual differences among organisation members and dimensions of the change process itself. Four key organisational factors—readiness for change, capability to change, cultural context and the capabilities of the change agent—affect the design and implementation of almost any intervention.

In addition, OD interventions seek to change specific features or parts of organisations. Classification of these targets of change can be based on the organisational issues that the intervention is intended to resolve, and the level of organisational system at which the intervention is expected to have a primary impact. Four types of OD interventions are addressed in this book: (1) human process programmes aimed at people within organisations and their interaction processes, (2) technostructural methods directed at organisation technology and structures for linking people and technology, (3) human resource management interventions aimed at successfully integrating people into the organisation and (4) strategic programmes directed at how the organisation uses its resources to gain a competitive advantage in the larger environment. For each type of intervention, specific change programmes at different organisation levels are discussed in Parts 3 to 6 of this book.

ACTIVITIES

Review questions
1 What is meant by the term 'intervention'?
2 What/who are the primary targets of change programmes?
3 What does 'human resource systems' refer to?
4 Explain the term 'technostructural intervention'.
5 List some key questions to ask when deciding on the appropriate intervention method.
6 How do you best describe 'reward systems'? Give some examples.
7 What is the function of strategic interventions?

Discussion and essay questions
1 Explain what team building is and evaluate its contribution to OD.
2 Contrast employee involvement and QWL with OD.
3 Explain why stress management has come to be a concern to the field of OD.
4 Explain what an 'intervention' is and how it fits into the OD process. What are the key considerations when deciding on an intervention?
5 Explain the role of a human resource management practitioner and contrast it with the role of the 'typical OD practitioner'.

Notes

1   C. Argyris, *Intervention Theory and Method: A Behavioral Science View* (Reading, Mass.: Addison-Wesley, 1970).
2   T. Cummings, E. Molloy and R. Glen, 'A methodological critique of 58 selected work experiments', *Human Relations*, 30 (1977): 675–708; T. Cummings, E. Molloy and R. Glen, 'Intervention strategies for improving productivity and the quality of work life', *Organizational Dynamics*, 4 (Summer 1975): 59–60; J. Porras and P. Berg, 'The impact of organization development', *Academy of Management Review*, 3 (1978): 249–66; J. Nicholas, 'The comparative impact of organization development interventions on hard criteria measures', *Academy of Management Review*, 7 (1982): 531–42; R. Golembiewski, C. Proehl and D. Sink, 'Estimating the success of OD applications', *Training and Development Journal*, 72 (April 1982): 86–95.
3   D. Warrick, 'Action planning' in *Practicing Organization Development*, eds W. Rothwell, R. Sullivan and G. McClean (San Diego: Pfeiffer and Co., 1995).
4   J. Nicholas, 'The comparative impact of organization development interventions', *op. cit.*; J. Porras and P. Robertson, 'Organization development theory: a typology and evaluation' in *Research in Organizational Change and Development*, 1, eds R. Woodman and W. Pasmore (Greenwich, Conn.: JAI Press, 1987): 1–57.
5   T. Stewart, 'Rate your readiness for change', *Fortune* (7 February 1994): 106–10.
6   G. Hofstede, *Culture's Consequences* (Beverly Hills, Calif.: Sage, 1980); K. Johnson, 'Estimating national culture and O.D. values', in *Global and International Organization Development*, eds P. Sorensfen Jr, T. Head, K. Johnson, N. Mathys, J. Preston and D. Cooperrider (Champaign Ill.: Stipes, 1995): 266–81.
7   D. Coghlan, 'Rediscovering organizational levels for OD interventions', *Organization Development Journal*, 13 (1995): 19–27.
8   F. Friedlander and L. Brown, 'Organization development', *Annual Review of Psychology*. 25 (1974): 313–41.
9   E. Lawler III, *The Ultimate Advantage* (San Francisco: Jossey-Bass, 1992).

Managing change

Once diagnosis has revealed the causes of problems or opportunities for development, organisation members can begin planning, and subsequently implementing, the changes necessary for improving organisation effectiveness and performance. A large part of OD is concerned with interventions for improving organisations. The previous chapter discussed the design of interventions and introduced the major ones used in OD today. Chapters 12 to 20 describe these interventions in detail. This chapter addresses the key activities associated with managing organisational changes successfully.

Change can vary in complexity from the introduction of relatively simple processes into a small work group to transforming the strategies and organisation design features of the whole organisation. Although change management differs across situations, in this chapter we discuss tasks that need to be performed when managing any kind of organisational change. (Tasks applicable to specific kinds of changes are examined in the intervention chapters.)

Overview of change activities

The OD literature has directed considerable attention to managing change. Much of this material is highly prescriptive, offering advice to managers about how to plan and implement organisational changes. Traditionally, change management has focused on identifying sources of resistance to change and offering ways of overcoming them.[1] Recent contributions have been aimed at creating visions and desired futures, gaining political support for them and managing the transition of the organisation toward them.[2]

The diversity of practical advice for managing change can be organised into five major activities, as shown in Figure 10.1. The activities contribute to effective change management and are listed in roughly the order in which they are typically performed. The first activity involves *motivating change* and includes creating a readiness for change among organisation members and helping them to overcome resistance to change. This involves creating an environment in which people accept the need for change and commit physical and psychological energy to it. Motivation is a critical issue in starting change, and there is ample evidence to show that people and organisations seek to preserve the *status quo* and are willing to change only when there are compelling reasons to do so. The second activity is concerned with *creating a vision*. The vision provides a purpose and reason for change and describes the desired future state. Together, they provide the 'why' and 'what' of planned change. The third activity involves the *development of political support* for change. Organisations are made up of powerful individuals and groups that can either block or promote change, and change agents need to gain their support to implement changes. The fourth activity is concerned with *managing the transition* from the current state to the desired future state. It involves creating a plan for managing the change activities as well as planning special management structures for operating the organisation during the transition. The fifth activity involves *sustaining momentum* for change so that it will be carried to completion. This includes providing resources for implementing the changes, building a support system for change agents, developing new competencies and skills and reinforcing the new behaviours necessary for implementing the changes.

FIGURE 10.1 Activities contributing to effective change management

Motivating change

- Creating readiness for change
- Overcoming resistance to change

Creating a vision

- Energising commitment
- Describing a desired future state

Developing political support

- Assessing change agent power
- Identifying key stakeholders
- Influencing stakeholders

Managing the transition

- Activity planning
- Commitment planning
- Management structures

Sustaining momentum

- Providing resources for change
- Building a support system for change agents
- Developing new competencies and skills
- Reinforcing new behaviours

Effective change management

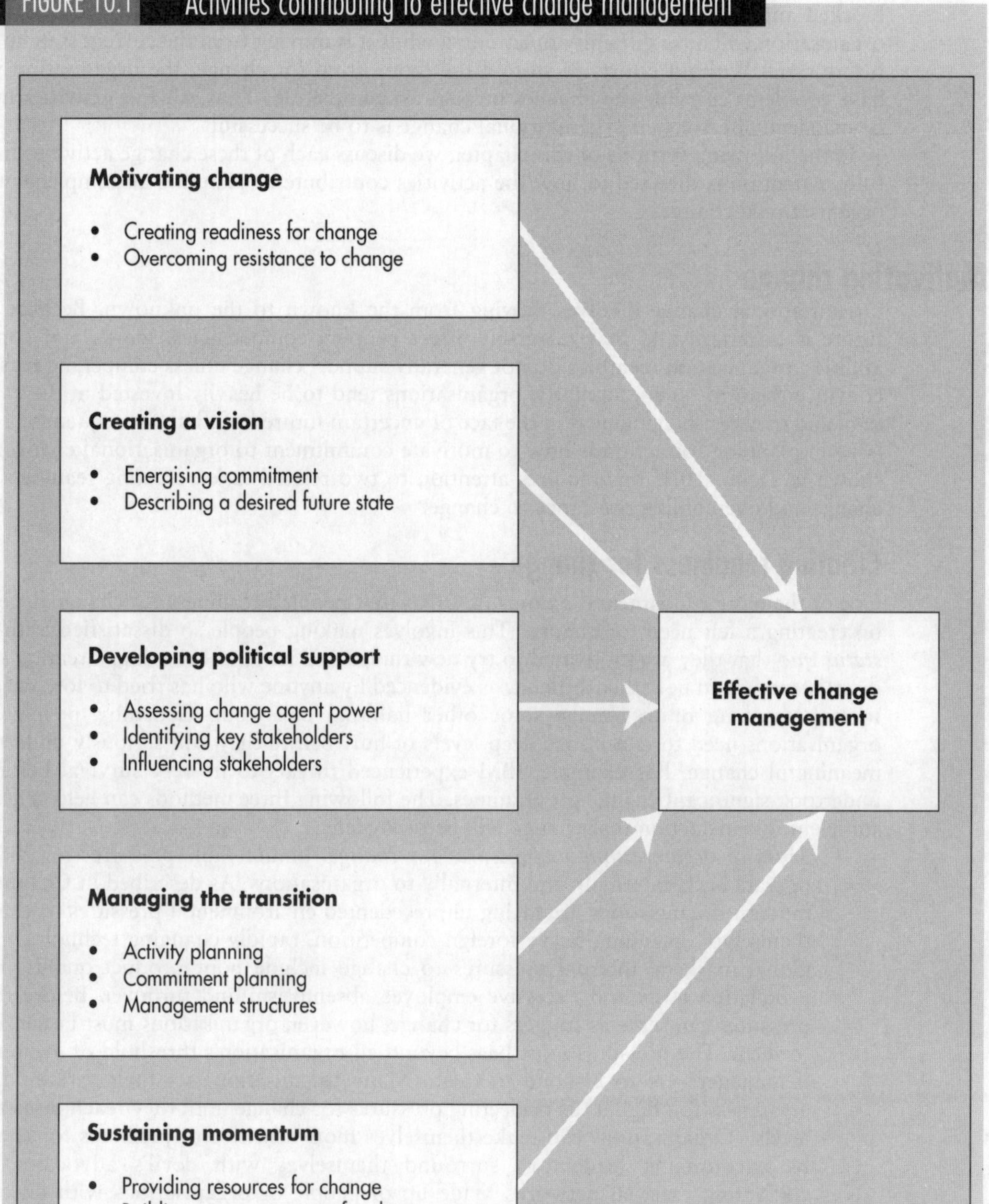

Each of the activities shown in Figure 10.1 is important for managing change. Although little research on their relative contributions to change has been conducted, they all seem to demand careful attention when planning and implementing organisational change. Unless individuals are motivated and committed to change, unfreezing the *status quo* will be extremely difficult. In the absence of vision, change is likely to be disorganised and diffuse. Without the support of powerful individuals and groups, change is likely to be blocked and possibly sabotaged. Unless the transition process is carefully managed, the organisation will have difficulty functioning while it is moving from the current state to the future state. Without efforts to sustain the momentum for change, the organisation will have problems carrying the changes through to completion. Thus, all five activities must be managed effectively if organisational change is to be successful.

In the following sections of this chapter, we discuss each of these change activities more fully. Attention is directed to how the activities contribute to planning and implementing organisational change.

Motivating change

Organisational change involves moving from the known to the unknown. Because the future is uncertain and may adversely affect people's competencies, worth and coping abilities, organisation members do not generally support change unless compelling reasons convince them to do so. Similarly, organisations tend to be heavily invested in the *status quo*, and they resist changing it in the face of uncertain future benefits. Consequently, a key issue in planning for action is how to motivate commitment to organisational change. As shown in Figure 10.1, this requires attention to two related tasks: creating readiness for change and overcoming resistance to change.

Creating readiness for change

One of the more fundamental axioms of OD is that people's readiness for change depends on creating a felt need for change. This involves making people so dissatisfied with the *status quo* that they are motivated to try new things and ways of behaving. Creating such dissatisfaction can be rather difficult, as evidenced by anyone who has tried to lose weight, to stop smoking or to change some other habitual behaviour. Generally, people and organisations need to experience deep levels of hurt before they will seriously undertake meaningful change. For example, IBM experienced threats to its very survival before it undertook significant change programmes. The following three methods can help generate sufficient dissatisfaction that change will be produced:

1 *Sensitise organisations to pressures for change.* Innumerable pressures for change operate both externally and internally to organisations. As described in Chapter 1, modern organisations are facing unprecedented environmental pressures to change themselves, including heavy foreign competition, rapidly changing technology and global markets. Internal pressures to change include poor product quality, high production costs and excessive employee absenteeism and turnover. Before these pressures can serve as triggers for change, however, organisations must be sensitive to them. The pressures must pass beyond an organisation's threshold of awareness if managers are to respond to them. Many organisations set their thresholds of awareness too high, thus neglecting pressures for change until they reach disastrous levels.[3] Organisations can make themselves more sensitive to pressures for change by encouraging leaders to surround themselves with devil's advocates;[4] by cultivating external networks made up of people or organisations with different perspectives and views; by visiting other organisations to gain exposure to new ideas and methods and by using external standards of performance, such as competitors' progress or benchmarks, rather than the organisation's own past standards of performance. A study by Monash University reported that 65% of Australia's top 500 companies believe they will have to benchmark to survive.[5]

2 *Reveal discrepancies between current and desired states.* In this approach to generating a felt need for change, information about the organisation's current functioning is gathered and compared with desired states of operation. (See the section titled *Creating a vision* for more information about desired future states.) These desired states may include organisational goals and standards, as well as a general vision of a more desirable future state.[6] Significant discrepancies between actual and ideal states can motivate organisation members to initiate corrective

changes, particularly when members are committed to achieving those ideals. A major goal of diagnosis, as described in Chapters 5 and 6, is to provide members with feedback about current organisational functioning so that this information can be compared with goals or with desired future states. Such feedback can energise action to improve the organisation. At Honeywell, Chrysler and Imperial Chemical Industries, for example, balance sheets had reached the point at which it was painfully obvious that drastic renewal was needed.

3 *Convey credible positive expectations for the change.* Organisation members invariably have expectations about the results of organisational changes, and those expectations can play an important role in generating motivation for change.[7] The expectations can serve as a self-fulfilling prophecy, leading members to invest energy in change programmes that they expect will succeed. When members expect success, they are likely to develop greater commitment to the change process and to direct more energy into the kinds of constructive behaviour needed to implement change.[8] The key to achieving these positive effects is to communicate realistic, positive expectations about the organisational changes. Organisation members can also be taught about the benefits of positive expectations and can be encouraged to set credible positive expectations for the change programme.

Overcoming resistance to change

Change can generate deep resistance in people and in organisations, making it difficult, if not impossible, to implement organisational improvements.[9] At a personal level, change can arouse considerable anxiety about letting go of the known and moving to an uncertain future. Individuals may be unsure whether their existing skills and contributions will be valued in the future. They may have significant questions about whether they can learn to function effectively and to achieve benefits in the new situation. At the organisation level, resistance to change can come from three sources.[10] Technical resistance comes from the habit of following common procedures and the sunk cost of resources invested in the *status quo*. Political resistance can arise when organisational changes threaten powerful stakeholders, such as top executive or staff personnel, and may call into question the past decisions of leaders. Organisation change often implies a different allocation of already scarce resources, such as capital, training budgets and good people. Finally, cultural resistance takes the form of systems and procedures that reinforce the *status quo*, promoting conformity to existing values, norms and assumptions about how things should operate.

There are at least three major strategies for dealing with resistance to change:[11]

1 *Empathy and support.* A first step in overcoming resistance is to know how people are experiencing change. This can help to identify those who are having trouble accepting the changes, the nature of their resistance and possible ways of overcoming it. Understanding how people experience change requires a great deal of empathy and support. It demands a willingness to suspend judgment and to try to see the situation from another's perspective, a process called 'active listening'. When people feel that those managing change are genuinely interested in their feelings and perceptions, they are likely to be less defensive and more willing to share their concerns and fears. This more open relationship not only provides useful information about resistance but also helps to establish the basis for the kind of joint problem solving that is necessary for overcoming barriers to change.

2 *Communication.* People tend to resist change when they are uncertain about its consequences. Lack of adequate information fuels rumours and gossip and adds to the anxiety generally associated with change. Effective communication about changes and their likely consequences can reduce this speculation and allay unfounded fears. It can help members realistically prepare for change.

However, communication is also one of the most frustrating aspects of managing change. Organisation members are constantly receiving data about current operations and future plans as well as informal rumours about people, changes and politics. Managers and OD practitioners must think seriously about how to break through this stream of information. One strategy is to make change information more salient by communicating through a new or different channel. If most information is delivered through memos and letters, then change information can be sent through meetings and presentations. Another method that can be effective during large-scale change is to deliberately substitute change information for normal operating information. This sends a message that changing one's activities is a critical part of a member's job.

3 *Participation and involvement.* One of the oldest and most effective strategies for overcoming resistance is to involve organisation members directly in planning and implementing change. Participation can lead both to designing high-quality changes and to overcoming resistance to implementing them.[12] Members can provide a diversity of information and ideas, which can contribute to making the innovations effective and appropriate to the situation. They can also identify pitfalls and barriers to implementation. Involvement in planning the changes increases the likelihood that members' interests and needs will be accounted for during the intervention. Consequently, participants will be committed to implementing the changes as it is in their best interests to do so. Implementing the changes will contribute to meeting their needs. Moreover, for people who have strong needs for involvement, the very act of participation can be motivating, leading to greater effort to make the changes work.[13]

Application 10.1 is about Jack Thompson from Walker Manufacturing, who created teams that not only represented various functional departments but also customers and suppliers.[14]

APPLICATION 10.1   Lessons from a leader

Jack L.Thompson is vice-president, operations and engineering, Walker Manufacturing, a division of Tenneco Automotive. He attained that position in the spring of 1992, after having been, since 1990, vice-president of manufacturing for Walker. Prior to joining Walker, he had been with another of the Tenneco Automotive companies, Monroe Auto Equipment Company, for whom he'd worked since 1975. When he left Monroe in 1987, he was the company's executive director of production and process engineering. And he became managing director of Walker Australia Pty Ltd.

Walker is said to be the 'world's largest producer of automotive exhaust systems and components'. To name a few highlights that allowed it to reach this position: the company supplies General Motors, Ford and Chrysler. It supplies GM Opel in Europe, and the Toyota operations in the United Kingdom. In Australia, it is 100% supplier to both Toyota and Mitsubishi; the Australian operations of both Nissan and Ford use Walker as their primary supplier. And so it goes on.

Jack Thompson and his family moved from a community of some 25 000 south of Detroit to, almost literally, the other side of the world in 1987. They moved to Adelaide, Australia. Way down under. Where things are somewhat different from what they are in Monroe. Not just in a superficial sense, but in the way that manufacturing people are managed.

For example, Thompson learned about what's called 'the tall poppy syndrome'. That is, no one really wants to stand out above his or her colleagues. No one wants to receive praise as that might result in their being the target of potshots by their fellow employees.

But Thompson, a firm believer in empowerment and responsibility, decided that it was important that people feel as though he is aware of, and interested in, their accomplishments. And so he gave praise where praise was due. He wanted to get the people to feel that he was concerned.

He spent time with the 680 people who worked in the two plants—one in Adelaide, and the other in Melbourne. He was managing director, responsible for the two operations. He was responsible for a company that was, when he arrived, losing money.

He admits that turning things around—and they did do it, getting to a point where it broke even within 14 months and going from there to a positive return—wasn't easy. 'I worked till I dropped,' he says.

And he needed lots of 'tall poppies' to make things happen, especially as he had to do some significant cost cutting. Overall costs were reduced by 27%

within two years. The number of people was reduced to about 540, yet there was a productivity improvement of 70%.

Jack Thompson got to know the people as best he could. He sent everyone a birthday card. He wrote a personal message on the card; he didn't use a rubber stamp message. This simple act, he says, gave people a reason to come up to him and talk, to have a simple exchange. 'It had an amazing effect,' he states.

Every Wednesday he held a 'lunch with Jack' for the day shift and 'supper with Jack' for the afternoon shift. In both cases, there were eight people from the plants who met with the managing director—who got to know what was going on a bit better than they might have otherwise. 'I always tried to tell them something new,' he recalls, 'and I always asked for rumours back.'

Creating a vision

The second activity for managing change involves creating a vision of what members want the organisation to look like or become. Generally, the vision describes the desired future, towards which change is directed. It provides a valued direction for designing, implementing and assessing organisational changes. The vision can also energise commitment to change by providing a compelling rationale as to why change is necessary and worth the effort. It can provide members with a common goal and challenge. However, if the vision is seen as impossible or promotes changes that the organisation cannot implement, it can actually depress member motivation. For example, Bob Hawke's unfulfilled vision that 'no child will live in poverty ...' was emotionally appealing, but impossible to achieve. In contrast, John Kennedy's vision of 'putting a man on the moon and returning him safely to the earth' was just beyond current engineering and technical feasibility. In the context of the 1960s, it was bold, alluring and vivid; it not only provided a purpose, but a valued direction as well.[15]

Creating a vision is considered a key element in most leadership frameworks.[16] Those leading the organisation or unit are responsible for its effectiveness, and they must take an active role in describing a desired future, and energising commitment to it. In many cases, leaders encourage participation in developing the vision in order to gain wider input and support. For example, they may involve subordinates and others who have a stake in the changes. The popular media include numerous accounts of executives who have helped to mobilise and direct organisational change, including Richard Pratt (Visyboard), Ross Wilson (Tabcorp) and Dennis Eck (Coles-Myer) to name a few.[17] Although these people are at the senior executive level, providing a description of a desired future is no less important for those who lead change in small departments and work groups. At these lower organisational levels, ample opportunities exist to get employees directly involved in the visioning process.

People's values and preferences for what the organisation should look like, and how it should function, heavily drive the process of developing a vision. The vision represents people's ideals, fantasies or dreams of what they would like the organisation to look like or become.

Unfortunately, dreaming about the future is discouraged in most organisations.[18] It requires creative and intuitive thought processes that tend to conflict with the rational, analytical methods prevalent in organisations. Consequently, leaders may need to create special conditions for describing a desired future, such as off-site workshops or exercises that stimulate creative thinking.

To be effective in managing change, creating a vision addresses two key aspects of organisation change: (1) describing the desired future and (2) energising commitment to moving towards it.

Describing the desired future

The visioning process is future oriented. It generally results in a vision statement that describes the organisation's desired future state. Although the vision statement may be detailed, it does not generally specify how the changes will occur. These details are part of the subsequent activity planning that occurs when managing the transition towards the desired future.

A vision statement may include all or some of the following elements that can be communicated to organisation members:

1 *Mission.* Participants often define the mission of their organisation or subunit as a prelude to describing the desired future state. The mission includes the organisation's major strategic purpose, or reason for existing. It may include specification of the following: target customers and markets, principal products or services, geographic domain, core technologies, strategic objectives and desired public image. A study of the mission statements from 218 Fortune 500 companies showed that the higher financial performers prepared written mission statements for public dissemination.[19] The statements included the firms' basic beliefs, values, priorities, competitive strengths and desired public images.

Defining the mission can provide a sound starting point for envisioning what the organisation should look like and how it should operate. In some cases, members may have conflicting views about the mission, and surfacing and resolving those conflicts can help to mobilise and direct energy for the process.

2 *Valued outcomes.* Descriptions of desired futures often include specific performance and human outcomes that the organisation or unit would like to achieve. These valued outcomes can serve as goals for the change process and standards for assessing progress. Valued performance outcomes might include high levels of product innovation, manufacturing efficiency and customer service. Valued human outcomes could include high levels of employee satisfaction, development, safety and job security. These outcomes specify the kinds of values that the organisation would like to promote in the future.

3 *Valued features.* This element of the desired future state specifies what the organisation should look like in order to achieve the valued outcomes. These valued features help to define a desired future state toward which change activities should move. The desired state can be broadly defined, representing a general direction for change, such as having a lean, flexible organisation structure or distributing rewards based on performance. Conversely, valued features can be highly specific and linked to particular valued outcomes. For example, Coles-Myer, a national department store chain, places a high value on customer service and specifies desired methods and behaviours that will help employees become more responsive to customers' needs.

Application 10.2 describes the vision statement for the Commonwealth Handling Equipment Pool (CHEP), with Brambles as its parent company, which has become a national business offering a wide range of products used by most industries in Australia.[20]

APPLICATION 10.2 Commonwealth Handling Equipment Pool (CHEP)

CHEP provides access to an equipment pooling system in which pallets and other load unitisation platforms move between customers with maximum efficiency.

The seamless movement of CHEP pallets and other platforms along customer supply chains, supported by specialist expertise in tracking and control, are key factors that underpin the value provided to customers.

History

The introduction of pallets into Australia can be traced back to 1944 when the US Armed Forces used Australian ports as logistical supply bases for the Pacific. After the US Forces had departed from Australia, they left behind their pallets, forklifts and cranes. These became part of the Commonwealth Handling Equipment Pool (CHEP), which was purchased by Brambles in 1958. With Brambles as parent company, CHEP grew to become a national business offering a wide range of products used by most industries in Australia.

CHEP's success in Australia encouraged Brambles to establish the business in overseas markets, which was done in partnership with GKN plc, a large British-based manufacturing organisation. CHEP is now established on every continent and in over 30 countries.

Product and service offer

The service provided is based around a unique combination of physical products, control systems and depot infrastructure through which the company repairs and relocates to performance standards agreed with its customers.

Vision statement

CHEP is an enterprise of Brambles and part of the global CHEP organisation. The company focuses on adding value for its customers through creative solutions in pallets, product containers and supply chain management.

The company encourages its people to innovate and accept challenges in order to strengthen its position of market leadership. The efforts of its people are directed towards providing benefits to customers, and these benefits include:

- the ability to utilise the most cost-effective and widely-available system of materials handling equipment
- customised solutions in pallets and containers for increased efficiency in moving the customers' products
- providing information to more effectively manage the movement of products
- tracking customer-owned products and assets to improve control.

Energising commitment

In addition to describing a desired future, creating a vision includes energising the commitment to change. This aspect of the visioning process is exciting, connected to the past and present and compelling. It seeks to create a vision that is emotionally powerful to organisation members and which motivates them to change. To achieve excitement for change, organisations often create a slogan or metaphor that captures the essence of the changes. For example, part of Disneyland's return to prominence was guided by the motto 'creating a place where people can feel like kids again'. The metaphor of feeling like a kid provided an important emotional appeal to Disney's change effort.

A vision that is clearly linked to the organisation's past and present can also energise commitment to change. It can provide a realistic context for moving toward the future. It can enable members to develop realistic goals and maintain a temporal perspective of the 'big picture'. Apple's original vision of 'changing the way people do their work' provides a good example. Many employees had experienced the drudgery of a boring job, an uninspired boss or an alienating work place. The notion that they could be a part of an organisation that is changing work into something more challenging, creative or satisfying was naturally alluring to many of them.

Finally, a compelling vision can energise commitment to change. By identifying a powerful reason or purpose for the change, the vision can provide meaning to the change activities that members will need to undertake during the transition. Thus, the words used in the vision can encourage behaviour toward the desired future as well as generate feelings of inclusiveness. Conversely, words can constrain people and leave them feeling controlled or manipulated. For example, 'shrewd' and 'creative' both imply innovative behaviour but have different connotations.

Application 10.3 describes how Griffith University utilised a vision statement to energise commitment to change.[21]

APPLICATION 10.3   Griffith University

Griffith University was established in the early 1970s, which was a period of rapid expansion in higher education. The aim of Griffith University was to respond vigorously to the imperatives of external accountability while at the same time introducing strategies designed to further develop a sustainable concern for quality throughout the university.

Within the context of its mission statement, vision and values, goals and objectives the university's key principles for quality management are expressed in quality-oriented processes and attitudes across the whole range of its activities. These can be summarised as follows:

- the vice-chancellor and senior executive take direct responsibility for leadership of the university's quality advancement programme
- commitment to quality applies to all university elements
- continuous quality improvement is everyone's responsibility
- adequate resources should be deployed to support quality management.

Quality management responsibility is best devolved to operational levels:
- diversity of quality management forms is encouraged
- effective quality management in the university is characterised by
  — efficiency
  — responsiveness
  — planning and innovation

- communication
- the use of standards and criteria to judge performance
- evaluation for improvement
- management information systems
- strategies for implementing change
- cost-effectiveness.

From the quality principles and mission statement, seven critical factors of strategic importance can be identified:
- teaching and learning
- research
- community service
- institutional management
- priority resource allocation
- enhancing technical and information support
- quality advancement procedures.

Implementation of quality plans
Each faculty established its own quality committee to provide leadership, and to increase and facilitate quality improvement at the faculty level. Responsible officers (e.g. deans) are charged with the responsibility of ensuring that performance targets are achieved in the time frame specified. To address the issues that are important in implementation, such as ownership, communication, institutional culture, resources and commitment, the university has also taken the following steps:
- A *loose-leaf portfolio*, incorporating the quality management plan, mission statement, strategic directions, teaching and learning management

plan (TLMP) and the research management plan (RMP), has been circulated to leaders throughout the university and is updated regularly

- As part of staff development, *brainstorming exercises* are also carried out to identify strengths, weaknesses and areas for improvement.

The Griffith experience shows that the quality management plan formed with the involvement of stakeholders is clearly understood by staff who own the plan and who also feel empowered. In addition, Griffith learned that leadership, ownership by staff and their commitment to quality initiatives and staff development are all essential elements of strengthening a quality culture. In the long run, Griffith believes that the professionalism of its staff and their dedication to the students are the factors that will overcome all odds. The progressive enrichment of a quality culture will, in the end, bring its own rewards.

Developing political support

From a political perspective, organisations can be seen as loosely structured coalitions of individuals and groups with different preferences and interests.[22] For example, shop-floor workers may want secure, high-paying jobs, while top executives may be interested in diversifying the organisation into new businesses. The marketing department might be interested in developing new products and markets, and the production department may want to manufacture standard products in the most efficient way. These different groups or coalitions compete with one another for scarce resources and influence. They act to preserve or enhance their self-interest while managing to arrive at a sufficient balance of power to sustain commitment to the organisation and to achieve overall effectiveness.

Given this political view, attempts to change the organisation may threaten the balance of power among groups, resulting in political conflicts and struggles.[23] Individuals and groups will be concerned with how the changes affect their own power and influence, and they will act accordingly. Some groups will become less powerful, while others will gain influence. Those whose power is threatened by the change will act defensively and seek to preserve the *status quo*, e.g. they might attempt to present compelling evidence that change is unnecessary or that only minor modifications are needed. On the other hand, those participants who will gain power from the changes will tend to push heavily for them. They may bring in seemingly impartial consultants to legitimise the need for change. Consequently, conflicting interests, distorted information and political turmoil frequently accompany significant organisational changes.

Methods for managing the political dynamics of organisational change are relatively recent additions to OD. Traditionally, OD has tended to neglect political issues, mainly because its humanistic roots promoted collaboration and power sharing among individuals and groups.[24] Today, change agents are increasingly paying attention to power and political activity, particularly as they engage in strategic change that involves most parts and features of organisations. Some practitioners are concerned, however, about whether power and OD are compatible. A growing number of advocates suggest that OD practitioners can use power in positive ways.[25] They can build their own power base to gain access to other power holders within the organisation. Without such access, those who influence or make decisions may not have the advantage of an OD perspective. OD practitioners can use power strategies that are open and above board to get those in power to consider OD applications. They can facilitate processes for examining the uses of power in organisations and can help power holders devise more creative and positive strategies than political bargaining, deceit and the like. They can help power holders to confront the need for change and can help to ensure that the interests and concerns of those with less power are considered. Although OD professionals can use power constructively in

FIGURE 10.2   Sources of power and power strategies

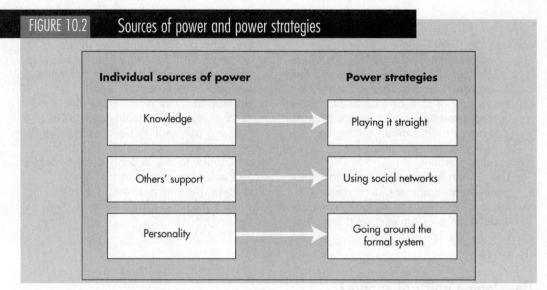

Source: L. Greiner and V. Schein, *Power and Organization Development: Mobilizing Power to Implement Change*, p. 52, copyright © 1988 by Addison-Wesley Publishing Co. Reprinted by permission of Addison-Wesley Publishing Co., Inc., Reading, Mass.

organisations, they will probably always be ambivalent and tense about whether such uses promote OD values and ethics or whether they represent the destructive, negative side of power. This tension seems healthy, and it is hoped that it will guide the wise use of power in OD.

As shown in Figure 10.2, managing the political dynamics of change includes the following activities:

1   *Assessing change agent power.* The first task is to evaluate the change agent's own sources of power. The change agent might be the leader of the organisation or department undergoing change, or he or she might be the OD consultant, if professional help is being used. By assessing their own power base, change agents can determine how to use it to influence others to support changes. They can also identify areas in which they might need to enhance their sources of power.

Greiner and Schein, in the first OD book written entirely from a power perspective, identified three key sources of personal power in organisations (in addition to one's formal position): knowledge, personality and others' support.[26] Knowledge bases of power include having expertise that is valued by others and controlling important information. OD professionals typically gain power through their expertise in organisational change. Personality sources of power can derive from change agents' charisma, reputation and professional credibility. Charismatic leaders can inspire devotion and enthusiasm for change from subordinates. OD consultants with strong reputations and professional credibility can wield considerable power during organisational change. Others' support can contribute to individual power by providing access to information and resource networks. Others may also use their power on behalf of the change agent. For example, leaders in organisational units undergoing change can call on their informal networks for resources and support. They can encourage subordinates to exercise power in support of the change.

2   *Identifying key stakeholders.* Once change agents have assessed their own power bases, they can identify powerful individuals and groups who have an interest in the changes, such as staff groups, unions, departmental managers and top-level executives. These stakeholders can either thwart or support change, and it is important to gain broad-based support to minimise the risk that a single interest

group will block the changes. Identifying key stakeholders can start from the simple question: 'Who stands to gain or lose from the changes?' Once stakeholders have been identified, creating a map of their influence may be useful.[27] The map could show relationships among the stakeholders in terms of who influences whom and what the stakes are for each party. This would provide change agents with information about which individuals and groups need to be influenced to accept and support the changes.

3 *Influencing stakeholders.* This activity involves gaining the support of key stakeholders to motivate a critical mass for change. There are at least three major strategies for using power to influence others in OD: playing it straight, using social networks and going around the formal system.[28] Figure 10.2 links these strategies to the individual sources of power discussed above.

The strategy of *playing it straight* is very consistent with an OD perspective, and so is the most widely used power strategy in OD. It involves determining the needs of particular stakeholders and presenting information as to how the changes can benefit them. This relatively straightforward approach is based on the premise that information and knowledge can persuade people about the need and direction for change. The success of this strategy relies heavily on the change agent's knowledge base. He or she must have the expertise and information necessary for persuading stakeholders that the changes are a logical way to meet their needs. For example, a change agent might present diagnostic data, such as company reports on productivity and absenteeism or surveys of members' perceptions of problems, to generate a felt need for change among specific stakeholders. Other persuasive evidence might include educational material and expert testimony, such as case studies and research reports, demonstrating how organisational changes can address pertinent issues.

The second power strategy, *using social networks*, is more foreign to OD and includes forming alliances and coalitions with other powerful individuals and groups, dealing directly with key decision makers and using formal and informal contacts to gain information. In this strategy, change agents try to use their social relationships to gain support for changes. As shown in Figure 10.2, they use the individual power base of others' support to gain the resources, commitment and political momentum needed for change. This social networking might include, for example, meeting with other powerful groups and forming an alliance to support specific changes. This would probably involve ensuring that the interests of the different parties—e.g. labour and management—are considered in the change process. Many union and management quality-of-work-life efforts involve forming such alliances. This strategy might also include using informal contacts to discover key roadblocks to change and gain access to major decision makers that need to sanction the changes.

The power strategy of *going around the formal system* is probably least used in OD and involves deliberately circumventing organisational structures and procedures to get the changes implemented. Existing organisational arrangements can be roadblocks to change, and, rather than taking the time and energy to remove them, working around the barriers may be more expedient and effective. As shown in Figure 10.2, this strategy relies on a strong personality base of power. The change agent's charisma, reputation or professional credibility lend legitimacy to going around the system and can reduce the likelihood of negative reprisals. For example, managers with reputations as 'winners' can often bend the rules to implement organisational changes. Those needing to support change trust their judgment. This power strategy is relatively easy to abuse, however, and OD practitioners should carefully consider the ethical issues and possible unintended consequences of circumventing formal policies and practices.

Application 10.4 shows how one corporate executive used the personal power bases of expertise and reputation to form social networks with key stakeholders in order to gain support for organisational change.[29]

Using social networks to implement change in a consumer goods company

Wayne, the treasurer and controller of a Fortune 500 consumer products firm, wanted to establish an off-shore trading division. He had been with the company for 18 years, and he believed that the time was right for such a venture. Wayne discusses below how he established alliances with key stakeholders to gain support for the project.

'It was important for me to convince my company's president of the viability of this idea. I have expertise in this area, and my reputation as a winner is well known. I decided that if I could parlay these two assets into gaining the support of others, then the total package would sell to the two top people.'

'I personally visited all of the division vice-presidents overseas, ostensibly to seek support for the project. In my discussions with each of them, I stressed the innovative aspects of the project. I implied that the trading company would be established and hinted strongly that their support would make them part of a successful project.'

'Soon after I returned, I gave a formal presentation to the president, emphasising the benefits of the project. I also stressed the strong support given to the project by the vice-presidents of all the subsidiaries. I was given the go-ahead to establish the off-shore trading company.'

Managing the transition

Implementing organisational change involves moving from the existing organisation state to the desired future state. This movement does not occur immediately but, as shown in Figure 10.3, requires a transition state during which the organisation learns how to implement the conditions needed to reach the desired future. Beckhard and Harris pointed out that the transition state may be quite different from the present state of the organisation and consequently may require special management structures and activities.[30] They identified three major activities and structures to facilitate organisational transition:

1   *Activity planning.* This involves making a road map for change, citing specific activities and events that must occur if the transition is to be successful. Activity planning should clearly identify, temporally orient and integrate discrete change tasks and should link these tasks to the organisation's change goals and priorities. Activity planning should also gain top-management approval, be cost-effective and remain adaptable as feedback is received during the change process.

An important feature of activity planning is that visions and desired future states can be quite general when compared with the realities of actually implementing change. As a result, it may be necessary to supplement them with midpoint goals as part of the activity plan.[31] These represent desirable organisational conditions between the current state and the desired future state. Midpoint goals are clearer and more detailed than desired future states, and so provide more concrete and manageable steps and

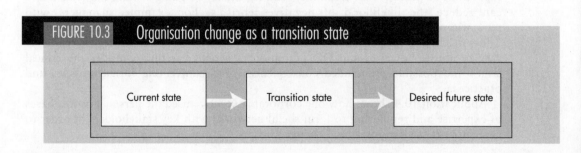

FIGURE 10.3   Organisation change as a transition state

Current state → Transition state → Desired future state

benchmarks for change. Activity plans can use midpoint goals to successfully provide members with the direction and security for embarkation toward the desired future.

2   *Commitment planning.* This activity involves identifying key people and groups whose commitment is needed for change to occur and deciding how to gain their support. Although commitment planning is generally a part of developing political support, discussed above, specific plans for identifying key stakeholders and obtaining their commitment to change need to be made early in the change process.

3   *Management structures.* Because organisational transitions tend to be ambiguous and to need direction, special structures for managing the change process need to be created. These management structures should include people who have the power to mobilise resources to promote change, the respect of the existing leadership and advocates of change and the interpersonal and political skills to guide the change process. Alternative management structures include the following:[32]

- the chief executive or head person manages the change effort
- a project manager is given the temporary assignment of co-ordinating the transition
- the formal organisation manages the change effort in addition to supervising normal operations
- representatives of the major constituencies involved in the change jointly manage the project
- natural leaders who have the confidence and trust of large numbers of affected employees are selected to manage the transition
- a cross-section of people representing different organisational functions and levels manages the change
- a kitchen cabinet representing people in whom the chief executive consults and confides manages the change effort.

Application 10.5 shows how the management and staff of Tubemakers Australia's Yennora plant managed the implementation of total quality management.[33]

APPLICATION 10.5 | Tubemakers Australia's Yennora plant

Private sector organisations in the more developed nations of the West are being exhorted by their governments and leaders of industry to be more productive in order to compete effectively with Japan and the emerging Asian nations. It is often proposed that one way to achieve this is to adopt what is seen to be the Japanese way—to develop a culture of commitment to total quality in every aspect of their industrial and commercial activities, i.e. a total quality culture.

W. Edwards Deming, an American, most comprehensively enunciated the total quality philosophy. In introducing the concepts of statistical process control to post-war Japan, he started the development of an approach to industrial management that has become generally known in the West as *total quality management*, or TQM.

During a visit to Japan in 1981 the management of a cast iron pipe manufacturing plant in Sydney decided that plant safety and plant operations in general could be improved by a new approach to management. Accordingly, they sought a new way of operating that would be compatible with the Australian environment and would provide them with benefits in both safety and general operations. At a plant similar to their own they found the Deming approach, and proceeded over the next few years to implement this approach in their plant.

Since that time, the Deming approach has been systematically introduced through all levels of the plant. Training has been provided, continuous improvement teams have been formed and are functioning, and many changes to processes and procedures have been made. The organisational structure changed, as a result of this approach, from seven hierarchical levels to four, from plant manager to shop floor. Over these years, the programme has had renewed emphasis from time to time through the use of various consultants who provide somewhat different perspectives. These have included programmes such as value-adding management (VAM), and most recently the approach offered by a major American consultant. However, all these approaches have been firmly based on the principles and philosophies laid down by Deming and have reinforced the original direction of change.

The plant has survived the recent recession in the Australian economy and much credit for this has undoubtedly to be given to the effectiveness of the Deming/TQM process. Continuation of the process to encompass *all* employees effectively would appear to be a desirable component of the company's future direction if it is to remain viable and prosper in an increasingly competitive and turbulent environment. The constancy of purpose demonstrated by the general manager of the plant throughout the long period of implementation is worthy of special mention.

Sustaining momentum

Once organisational changes are under way, explicit attention must be directed at sustaining energy and commitment for implementing them. Often, the initial excitement and activity of changing dissipate in the face of the practical problems of trying to learn new ways of operating. A strong tendency exists among organisation members to return to what is well known and learned, unless they receive sustained support and reinforcement for carrying the changes through to completion. In this section, we present approaches for sustaining momentum for change. The subsequent tasks of assessing and stabilising changes are discussed in Chapter 11.

The following four activities can help to sustain momentum for carrying change through to completion:

1 *Providing resources for change.* Implementing organisation change generally requires additional financial and human resources, particularly if the organisation continues day-to-day operations while trying to change itself. These extra resources are needed for such change activities as training, consultation, data collection and feedback, and special meetings. Extra resources are also helpful to provide a buffer as performance drops during the transition period. Organisations can seriously underestimate the need for special resources devoted to the change process. Significant organisational change invariably requires considerable management time and energy, as well as the help of consultants. A separate 'change budget' that exists along with capital and operating budgets can help to identify the resources needed for training members in how to behave differently and for assessing progress and making necessary modifications in the change programme.[34] Unless these extra resources are planned for and provided, meaningful change is not as likely to occur.

2 *Building a support system for change agents.* Organisation change can be difficult and filled with tension, not only for participants but also for change agents.[35] Change agents must often provide members with emotional support, yet they may receive little support themselves. They must often maintain 'psychological distance' from others in order to gain the perspective needed to lead the change process. This can produce considerable tension and isolation, and change agents may need to create their own support system to help them cope with these problems. This typically consists of a network of people with whom the change agent has close

personal relationships. These people can provide emotional support and can serve as a sounding board for ideas and problems. They can challenge untested assumptions. For example, OD professionals often use trusted colleagues as 'shadow consultants' to help them think through difficult issues with clients and to offer conceptual and emotional support. Similarly, a growing number of companies, such as Fisher & Paykel and Heinz-Wattie, are forming internal networks of change agents to provide mutual learning and support.[36]

3 *Developing new competencies and skills.* Organisational changes frequently demand new knowledge, skills and behaviours from organisation members. In many cases, the changes cannot be implemented unless members gain new competencies. For example, employee-involvement programmes often require managers to learn new leadership styles and new approaches to problem solving. Change agents need to ensure that such learning occurs. They need to provide multiple learning opportunities, such as traditional training programmes, on-the-job counselling and coaching, and experiential simulations. This learning should cover both technical and social skills. Because it is easy to overlook the social component, change agents may need to devote special time and resources to helping members gain the social skills needed to implement changes.

4 *Reinforcing new behaviours.* People in organisations generally do those things that bring them rewards. Consequently, one of the most effective ways of sustaining momentum for change is to reinforce the kinds of behaviours needed to implement the changes. This can be accomplished by linking formal rewards directly to the desired behaviours. Desired behaviours can also be reinforced through recognition, encouragement and praise. These can usually be given more frequently than formal rewards, and change agents should take advantage of the myriad of informal opportunities available to recognise and praise changed behaviours in a timely fashion. Perhaps equally important are the intrinsic rewards that people can experience through early success in the change effort. Achieving identifiable, early successes can make participants feel good about themselves and their behaviours, thus reinforcing the drive to change.

Application 10.6 describes how Nally (WA) Pty Ltd, a Western Australian plastics manufacturing company with 60 employees, used various methodologies to gather information, including interviews with a range of people, observation of teams and examination of company documents.[37]

APPLICATION 10.6

Nally (WA) Pty Ltd

Nally (WA) is a small organisation with approximately 60 employees. It produces a range of plastic products (mainly containers) for both the Australian and overseas markets, using modern technology. Production for most of the year involves three shifts per day over a five-day week.

The work force consists of a core of permanent employees and a number of casual staff. Core employees occupy mainly administrative, maintenance and supervisory positions. Casual staff are predominantly factory process workers.

Why TQM?
When the company (formerly Bristile Plastics) was taken over by Viscount in 1987, the new general manager felt the need to develop a new culture, particularly because of the large degree of mistrust and uncertainty between the former Bristile employees and the largely ex-Viscount management. TQM was also based on management's desire to return the company to profitability (both companies had been sustaining losses at the time). This would focus on

high quality service, the use of sophisticated technology and the desire to be market leaders. TQM was seen as a way of helping achieve these goals and developing a team attitude within the company.

Soon after the merger, an off-site three-day residential programme for all managerial employees was held in order to focus on the need to change and be able to respond to continuous change. Several team-building workshops that were designed to help develop co-operation in the new company were also conducted.

A memo from the general manager to all staff in September 1989 signalled the formal commencement of TQM.

Problems and issues

As any organisation that has introduced TQM has discovered, problems and difficulties are encountered. What was noticeable in this company was the flexibility and determination to try to make it work by using new and alternative approaches, such as new team structures. An issue to surface relatively early was management's over-ambitious expectation of the teams. This was perhaps due in part to the limited training that had been provided, particularly in areas like leadership, team building and meeting skills. Furthermore, many employees had a relatively limited understanding of the equipment they were using, making it difficult to identify problems. Participation in teams was also low. To address these issues, an external part-time facilitator was employed, further training provided, an induction programme introduced and increased counselling support for team leaders provided. The production of a videotape for use in employee induction was also considered.

A variety of other issues that required attention included: overcoming the belief that management solves problems, even though employees are aware of them; the feeling that TQM may be a fad and the fear that speaking up about problems at a team meeting could jeopardise one's job. To some extent this is still a problem that management and team leaders need to deal with. One problem with a company of this size with several production shifts is that it cannot afford too much time for employees to be away on training courses. Furthermore, the logistics of organising team meetings is an important issue.

Some felt that inadequate training had taken place initially, particularly for leading hands and supervisors, concerning their role in the TQM process. The generally limited amount of training may have hampered TQM, although some people do not respond well to any amount of training. It has been recognised that people and team-building skills are important. It is also apparent that supervisors, team leaders and leading hands should be well trained prior to embarking on the TQM journey since, if they are not well acquainted with the process, they will be unable to deal with problems when they arise. The question of what to do about those supervisors who are still not fully supportive needs to be addressed at some time.

Other issues that have required attention include authoritarian supervisors who are reluctant to adapt to the new culture of continuous improvement and employee participation and the need for senior management to demonstrate their commitment to factory employees. Their participation in the revised manufacturing team seems to have addressed this problem.

In conclusion, this case demonstrates that TQM is not a package or programme that can simply be installed, as is often suggested by consultants. It is about change and organisational development.

Summary

In this chapter, we described five kinds of activities that change agents must carry out when planning and implementing changes. The first activity is motivating change, which involves creating a readiness for change among organisation members and overcoming their resistance. The second activity is about describing the desired future state, that may include the organisation's mission, valued performance and human outcomes and valued organisational conditions to achieve those results, and creating a vision by articulating a compelling reason for implementing change. The third task for change agents is developing political support for the changes. Change agents must first assess their own sources of power, then identify key stakeholders whose support is needed for change, and devise strategies for gaining their support. The fourth activity concerns managing the transition of the organisation from its current state to the desired future state. This calls for planning a road map for the change activities, as well as planning how to gain commitment for the changes. It may also involve creating special management structures for managing the transition. The fifth change task is sustaining momentum for the changes so that they are carried to completion. This includes providing resources for the change programme, creating a support system for change agents, developing new competencies and skills and reinforcing the new behaviours required to implement the changes.

 ACTIVITIES

Review questions

1 Describe the five activities of change management.
2 Why do people resist change?
3 List the means by which resistance may be managed.
4 What value has 'creating a vision' to the change process?
5 Which power strategy is most closely aligned with OD's traditional humanistic values?
6 How may you develop political support for the change process?
7 What does activity planning involve?
8 Explain some strategies that change agents may use to sustain momentum for a change process.

Discussion and essay questions

1 Why do most change efforts fail? Explain your answer in depth.
2 Describe the key elements of an effective change management programme.
3 If you were developing a change programme, how would you create readiness for change?
4 What political activities might be engaged in to successfully implement change?

Notes

1 J. Kotter and L. Schlesinger, 'Choosing strategies for change', *Harvard Business Review*, 57 (1979): 106–14; R. Ricardo, 'Overcoming resistance to change', *National Productivity Review*, 14 (1995): 28–39.

2 M. Weisbord, *Productive Work places* (San Francisco: Jossey-Bass, 1987); R. Beckhard and R. Harris, *Organizational Transitions: Managing Complex Change*, 2nd ed. (Reading, Mass.: Addison-Wesley, 1987); R. Beckhard and W. Pritchard, *Changing the Essence* (San Francisco: Jossey-Bass, 1991).

3 N. Tichy and M. Devanna, *The Transformational Leader* (New York: John Wiley and Sons, 1986).

4 R. Cosier and C. Schwenk, 'Agreement and thinking alike: ingredients for poor decisions', *Academy of Management Executive*, 4 (1990): 69–74.

5 Reported in 'Briefing', *Business Review Weekly*, 15:7 (26 February 1993): 12.

6 W. Burke, *Organization Development: A Normative View* (Reading, Mass.: Addison-Wesley, 1987).

7 D. Eden, 'OD and self-fulfilling prophesy: boosting productivity by raising expectations', *Journal of Applied Behavioral Science*, 22 (1986): 1–13.

8 *Ibid*, p. 8.

9 Kotter and Schlesinger, 'Choosing strategies', *op. cit.*; P. Block, *Flawless Consulting: A Guide to Getting Your Expertise Used* (Austin, Tex.: Learning Concepts, 1981).

10 N. Tichy, 'Revolutionize your company', *Fortune* (13 December 1993): 114–18.

11 D. Kirkpatrick, ed., *How to Manage Change Effectively* (San Francisco: Jossey-Bass, 1985).

12 V. Vroom and P. Yetton, *Leadership and Decision Making* (Pittsburgh: University of Pittsburgh Press, 1973).

13 T. Cummings and E. Molloy, *Improving Productivity and the Quality of Work Life* (New York: Praeger, 1977).

14 G. Vasilash, 'Lessons from a leader', *Production*, 105:1, (January 1993): 32–38.

15 P. Senge, *The Fifth Discipline,* (New York: Doubleday, 1990).

16 J. Kotter, *Leading Change* (Boston, Mass.: Harvard Business School Press, 1994); W. Bennis and B. Nanus, *Leadership* (New York: Harper and Row, 1985); J. O'Toole, *Leading Change: Overcoming the Ideology of Comfort and the Tyranny of Custom* (San Francisco: Jossey-Bass, 1995); F. Hesselbein, M. Goldsmith and R. Beckhard, eds, *The Leader of the Future* (San Francisco: Jossey-Bass, 1995).

17 J. Kirby, 'Nothing appeals like success', *Business Review Weekly* (20 July 1998): 48.

18 Tichy and Devanna, *The Transformational Leader, op. cit.*

19 J. Pearce II and F. David, 'Corporate mission statements: the bottom line', *Academy of Management Executive 1* (1987): 109–15.

20 http://www.chep.com.au/profile.html

21 K. Tang, 'Benchmarking quality implementation in a service context: a comparative analysis of financial services and institutions of higher education', *Total Quality Management*, 9:7 (1998), 539–52.

22 J. Pfeffer, *Power in Organizations* (New York: Pitman, 1982).

23 D. Nadler, 'The effective management of change', in *Handbook of Organizational Behavior*, ed. J. Lorsch (Englewood Cliffs, N.J.: Prentice–Hall, 1987): 358–69.

24 C. Alderfer, 'Organization development', *Annual Review of Psychology*, 28 (1977): 197–223.

25 T. Bateman, 'Organizational change and the politics of success', *Group and Organization Studies*, 5 (June 1980): 198–209; A. Cobb and N. Margulies, 'Organization development: a political perspective', *Academy of Management Review*, 6 (1981): 49–59; A. Cobb, 'Political diagnosis: applications in organization development', *Academy of Management Review*, 11 (1986): 482–96; L. Greiner and V. Schein, *Power and Organization Development: Mobilizing Power to Implement Change* (Reading, Mass.: Addison-Wesley, 1988).

26 Greiner and Schein, *Power and Organization Development, op. cit.*

27 Nadler, 'The effective management of change'; Beckhard and Pritchard, *Changing the Essence*, both *op. cit.*

28 Greiner and Schein, *Power and Organization Development, op. cit.*

29 *Ibid*, p. 48.

30 Beckhard and Harris, *Organizational Transitions, op. cit.*

31 *Ibid*.

32 *Ibid*.

33 D. Davis and T. Fisher, 'The pace of change: a case study of the development of a total quality organization', *International Journal of Quality and Reliability Management*, 11:8 (1994), 5–18.

34 C. Worley, D. Hitchin and W. Ross, *Integrated Strategic Change: How OD Helps to Build Competitive Advantage* (Reading, Mass.: Addison-Wesley, 1996).

35 M. Beer, *Organization Change and Development: A Systems View* (Santa Monica, Calif.: Goodyear, 1980).

36 R. Hill, T. Bullard, P. Capper, K. Hawes and K. Wilson, 'Learning about learning organisations: case studies of skill formation in five New Zealand organisations', *The Learning Organisation*, 5:4 (1998), 184–92.

37 A. Brown, 'Case study: quality management in the smaller company', *Asia Pacific Journal of Quality Management*, 2:3 (1993), 67–76.

Evaluating and institutionalising OD interventions

This chapter focuses on the final stage of the OD cycle—evaluation and institutionalisation. Evaluation is concerned with providing feedback to practitioners and organisation members about the progress and impact of interventions. Such information may suggest the need for further diagnosis and modification of the change programme, or it may show that the intervention is successful. Institutionalisation involves making OD interventions a permanent part of the organisation's normal functioning. It ensures that the results of successful change programmes persist over time.

Evaluation processes consider both the implementation success of the intended intervention and the long-term results it produces. Two key aspects of effective evaluation are measurement and research design. The institutionalisation or long-term persistence of intervention effects is examined in a framework that shows the organisation characteristics, intervention dimensions and processes that contribute to institutionalisation of OD interventions in organisations.

Evaluating OD interventions

Assessing OD interventions involves judgments about whether an intervention has been implemented as intended and, if so, whether it is having desired results. Managers investing resources in OD efforts are increasingly being held accountable for the results. They are being asked to justify the expenditures in terms of hard, bottom-line outcomes. More and more, managers are asking for rigorous assessment of OD interventions and are using the results to make important resource allocation decisions about OD, such as whether to continue to support the change programme, whether to modify or alter it, or whether to terminate it altogether and perhaps try something else.

Traditionally, OD evaluation has been discussed as something that occurs after the intervention. Chapters 12 to 20, for example, present evaluative research about the interventions after discussing the respective change programmes. This view can be misleading. Decisions about the measurement of relevant variables and the design of the evaluation process should be made early in the OD cycle so that evaluation choices can be integrated with intervention decisions.

There are two distinct types of OD evaluation—one intended to guide the implementation of interventions and the other to assess their overall impact. The key issues in evaluation are measurement and research design.

Implementation and evaluation feedback

Most discussions and applications of OD evaluation imply that evaluation is something done *after* intervention. It is typically argued that, once the intervention has been implemented, it should be evaluated to discover whether it is producing the intended effects. For example, it might reasonably be expected that a job enrichment programme would lead to higher employee satisfaction and performance. After implementing job enrichment, evaluation would involve assessing whether or not it did actually lead to positive results.

This after-implementation view of evaluation is only partially correct. It assumes that interventions have actually been implemented as intended and that the key problem of evaluation is to assess their effects. In many, if not most, OD programmes, however, implementing interventions cannot be taken for granted.[1] Most OD interventions require significant changes in people's behaviours and ways of thinking about organisations; yet interventions typically offer only broad prescriptions for how such changes are to occur. For example, job enrichment calls for adding discretion, variety and meaningful feedback to people's jobs. Implementing such changes requires considerable learning and experimentation as employees and managers discover how to translate these general prescriptions into specific behaviours and procedures. This learning process involves much trial and error and needs to be guided by information about whether behaviours and procedures are being changed as intended.[2] Consequently, we should expand our view of evaluation to include both *during-implementation* assessment of whether interventions are actually being implemented and *after-implementation* evaluation of whether they are producing expected results.

Both kinds of evaluation provide organisation members with feedback about interventions. Evaluation aimed at guiding implementation may be called *implementation feedback*, and assessment intended to discover intervention outcomes might be called *evaluation feedback*.[3] Figure 11.1 shows how the two kinds of feedback fit with the diagnostic and intervention stages of OD. The application of OD to a particular organisation starts with a thorough diagnosis of the situation (Chapters 5 to 8), which helps to identify particular organisational problems or areas for improvement, as well as likely causes underlying them. Next, from an array of possible interventions (Chapters 12 to 20), one or more sets are chosen as a means of improving the organisation. This choice is based on knowledge that links interventions to diagnosis (Chapter 9) and change management (Chapter 10).

In most cases, the chosen intervention provides only general guidelines for organisational change, leaving managers and employees with the task of translating them into specific behaviours and procedures. Implementation feedback guides this process. It

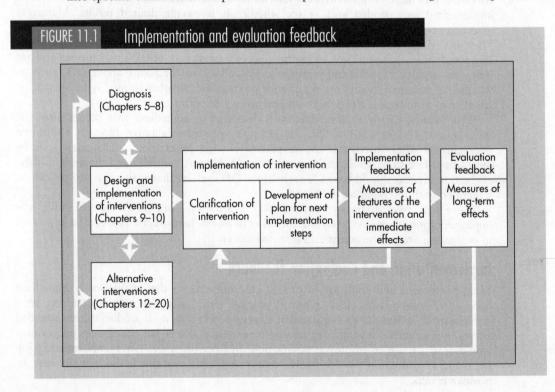

FIGURE 11.1 Implementation and evaluation feedback

consists of two types of information: data about the different features of the intervention itself and data about the immediate effects of the intervention. These data are collected repeatedly and at short intervals. They provide a series of snapshots about how the intervention is progressing. Organisation members can use this information first to gain a clearer understanding of the intervention (the kinds of behaviours and procedures required to implement it) and second to plan for the next implementation steps. This feedback cycle might proceed for several rounds, with each round providing members with knowledge about the intervention and ideas for the next stage of implementation.

Once implementation feedback has informed organisation members that the intervention is sufficiently in place, evaluation feedback begins. In contrast to implementation feedback, it is concerned with the overall impact of the intervention and whether resources should continue to be allocated to it or to other possible interventions. Evaluation feedback takes longer to gather and interpret than implementation feedback. It typically includes a broad array of outcome measures, such as performance, job satisfaction, absenteeism and turnover. Negative results on these measures tell members that either the initial diagnosis was seriously flawed or that the choice of intervention was wrong. Such feedback might prompt additional diagnosis and a search for a more effective intervention. Positive results, on the other hand, tell members that the intervention produced the expected outcomes and might prompt a search for ways of institutionalising the changes, making them a permanent part of the organisation's normal functioning.

An example of a job enrichment intervention helps to clarify the OD stages and feedback linkages shown in Figure 11.1. Suppose the initial diagnosis reveals that employee performance and satisfaction are low and that an underlying cause of this problem lies with jobs that are overly structured and routinised. An inspection of alternative interventions to improve productivity and satisfaction suggests that job enrichment might be applicable for this situation. Existing job enrichment theory proposes that increasing employee discretion, task variety and feedback can lead to improvements in work quality and attitudes and that this job design and outcome linkage is especially strong for employees with growth needs—needs for challenge, autonomy and development. Initial diagnosis suggests that most employees have high growth needs and that the existing job design prevents the fulfilment of these needs. Therefore, job enrichment seems particularly suited to this situation.

Managers and employees now start to translate the general prescriptions offered by job enrichment theory into specific behaviours and procedures. At this stage, the intervention is relatively broad and needs to be tailored to fit the specific situation. To implement the intervention, employees might decide on the following organisational changes: job discretion can be increased through more participatory styles of supervision; task variety can be enhanced by allowing employees to inspect their job outputs; and feedback can be made more meaningful by providing employees with quicker and more specific information about their performances.

After three months of trying to implement these changes, the members use implementation feedback to see how the intervention is progressing. Questionnaires and interviews (similar to those used in diagnosis) are administered in order to measure the different features of job enrichment (discretion, variety and feedback) and to assess employees' reactions to the changes. Company records are analysed to show the short-term effects on productivity of the intervention. The data reveal that productivity and satisfaction have changed very little since the initial diagnosis. Employee perceptions of job discretion and feedback have also shown negligible change, but perceptions of task variety have shown significant improvement. In-depth discussion and analysis of this first round of implementation feedback help the supervisors gain a better feel for the kinds of behaviours needed to move toward a participatory leadership style. This greater clarification of one feature of the intervention leads to a decision to involve the supervisors in leadership training and so help them to develop the skills and knowledge needed to lead participatively. A decision is also made to make job feedback more meaningful by translating such data into simple bar graphs, rather than continuing to provide voluminous statistical reports.

After these modifications have been in effect for about three months, members institute a second round of implementation feedback to see how the intervention is progressing. The data now show that productivity and satisfaction have moved moderately higher than in the first round of feedback and that employee perceptions of task variety and feedback are both high. Employee perceptions of discretion, however, remain relatively low. Members conclude that the variety and feedback dimensions of job enrichment are sufficiently implemented but that the discretion component needs improvement. They decide to put more effort into supervisory training and to ask OD practitioners to provide on-line counselling and coaching to supervisors about their leadership styles.

After four more months, a third round of implementation feedback occurs. The data now show that satisfaction and performance are significantly higher than in the first round of feedback and moderately higher than in the second round. The data also show that discretion, variety and feedback are all high, suggesting that the job enrichment interventions have been successfully implemented. Now evaluation feedback is used to assess the overall effectiveness of the programme.

The evaluation feedback includes all the data from the satisfaction and performance measures used in the implementation feedback. Because both the immediate and broader effects of the intervention are being evaluated, additional outcomes are examined, such as employee absenteeism, maintenance costs and reactions of other organisational units not included in job enrichment. The full array of evaluation data might suggest that one year after the start of implementation, the job enrichment programme is having the expected effects and so should be continued and made more permanent.

Measurement

Providing useful implementation and evaluation feedback involves two activities: selecting the appropriate variables and designing good measures.

Selecting variables

Ideally, the variables measured in OD evaluation should derive from the theory or conceptual model that underlies the intervention. The model should incorporate the key features of the intervention as well as its expected results. The general diagnostic models described in Chapters 5 and 6 meet this criterion, as do the more specific models introduced in Chapters 12 to 20. For example, the job-level diagnostic model described in Chapter 6 proposes several major features of work: task variety, feedback and autonomy. The theory argues that high levels of these elements can be expected to result in high levels of work quality and satisfaction. In addition, as we shall see in Chapter 16, the strength of this relationship varies with the degree of employee growth need: the higher the need, the more that job enrichment produces positive results.

The job-level diagnostic model suggests a number of measurement variables for implementation and evaluation feedback. Whether or not the intervention is being implemented could be assessed by determining how many job descriptions have been rewritten to include more responsibility or how many organisation members have received cross-training in other job skills. Evaluation of the immediate and long-term impact of job enrichment would include measures of employee performance and satisfaction over time. Again, these measures would probably be included in the initial diagnosis, when the company's problems or areas for improvement are discovered.

The measurement of *both* intervention and outcome variables is necessary for implementation and evaluation feedback. Unfortunately, there has been a tendency in OD to measure only outcome variables while neglecting intervention variables altogether.[4] It is generally assumed that the intervention has been implemented, and attention is directed to its impact on organisational outcomes, such as performance, absenteeism and satisfaction. As argued earlier, implementing OD interventions generally takes considerable time and learning. It must be empirically determined that the intervention has been implemented; it cannot simply be assumed. Implementation feedback serves this purpose, guiding the implementation process and helping to interpret outcome data. Outcome measures are ambiguous unless it is known how well the intervention has been implemented. For example, a negligible change in measures of performance and satisfaction could mean that the wrong intervention has been chosen, that the correct intervention has not been implemented effectively or that the wrong variables have been measured. Measurement of the intervention variables helps to determine the correct interpretation of outcome measures.

As suggested above, the choice of what intervention variables to measure should derive from the conceptual framework that underlies the OD intervention. Organisation development research and theory have increasingly come to identify the specific organisational changes that are necessary for the implementation of particular interventions. Much of that information is discussed in Chapters 12 to 20; these variables should guide not only the implementation of the intervention but also choices about what change variables to measure for evaluative purposes. Additional sources of knowledge about intervention variables can be found in the numerous references at the end of each of the intervention chapters in this book and in several of the books in the Wiley Series on *Organisational Assessment and Change*.[5]

The choice of what outcome variables to measure should also be dictated by intervention theory, which specifies the kinds of results that can be expected from particular change programmes. Again, the material in this book and elsewhere identifies numerous outcome measures, such as job satisfaction, intrinsic motivation, organisational commitment, absenteeism, turnover and productivity.

Historically, OD assessment has tended to focus on attitudinal outcomes, such as job satisfaction, while neglecting hard measures, such as performance. There has been a growing number of calls from both managers and researchers, however, for the development of behavioural measures of OD outcomes. Managers are primarily interested in applying OD to change work-related behaviours that have to do with joining, remaining and producing at work. They are increasingly assessing OD in terms of such bottom-line results. Macy and Mirvis have done extensive research to develop a standardised set of behavioural outcomes that can be used to assess and compare the results of OD interventions.[6] Table 11.1 lists these 11 outcomes, including their behavioural definitions and recording categories. The outcomes are in two broad categories: *participation-membership*, including absenteeism, tardiness, turnover, internal employment stability and strikes and work stoppages; and *performance on the job*, including productivity, quality, grievances, accidents, unscheduled machine downtime and repair, material and supply overuse and inventory shrinkage. These outcomes should be important to most managers, and they represent generic descriptions that can be adapted to both industrial and service organisations.

Designing good measures

Each of the measurement methods described in Chapter 7 has advantages and disadvantages. Many of these characteristics are linked to the extent to which a measurement is operationally defined, reliable and valid. These characteristics are discussed below.

1   *Operational definition.* A good measure is operationally defined. That is, it specifies the empirical data needed, how it will be collected and, most importantly, how it will be converted from data to information. For example, Macy and Mirvis developed operational definitions for the behavioural outcomes listed in Table 11.1 (see Table 11.2).[7] They consist of specific computational rules that can be used to construct measures for each of the behaviours. Most of the behaviours are reported as rates adjusted for the number of employees in the organisation and for the possible incidents of behaviour. These adjustments make it possible to compare the measures across different situations and time periods. These operational definitions should have wide applicability across both industrial and service organisations, although some modifications, deletions and additions may be necessary for a particular application.

| TABLE 11.1 | Behavioural outcomes for OD interventions: recording categories |

Behavioral definitions	**Recording categories**
Absenteeism: Each absence or illness over four hours	*Voluntary:* Short-term illness (less than three consecutive days), personal business, family illness
	Involuntary: Long-term illness (more than three consecutive days), funerals, out-of-plant accidents, lack of work (temporary layoff), presanctioned days off
	Leaves: Medical, personal, maternity, military, and other (e.g., jury duty)
Tardiness: Each absence or illness under four hours	*Voluntary:* Same as absenteeism
Turnover: Each movement beyond the organisational boundary	*Involuntary:* Same as absenteeism
	Voluntary: Resignation
	Involuntary: Termination, disqualification, requested resignation, permanent layoff, retirement, disability, death
Internal employment stability: Each movement within the organizational boundary	*Internal movement:* Transfer, promotion, promotion with transfer
	Internal stability: New hires, layoffs, rehires
Strikes and work stoppages: Each day lost due to strike or work stoppage	*Sanctioned:* Union authorized strike, company authorized lockout
	Unsanctioned: Work slowdown, walkout, sitdown
Accidents and work-related illness: Each recordable injury, illness or death from a work-related accident or from exposure to the work environment	*Major:* OSHA accident, illness, or death that results in medical treatment by a medical practitioner or registered professional person under standing orders from a medical practitioner
	Minor: Non-OSHA accident or illness that results in one-time treatment and subsequent observation not requiring professional care
	Revisits: OSHA and non-OSHA accident or illness that requires subsequent treatment and observation
Grievances: Written grievance in accordance with labor–management contract	*Stage:* Recorded by step (first through arbitration)
Productivity: * Resources used in production of acceptable outputs (comparison of inputs with outputs)	*Output:* Product or service quantity (units or $)
	Input: Direct and/or indirect (labor in hours or $)
Production quality: Resources used in production of unacceptable output	*Resource utilised:* Scrap (unacceptable in-plant products in units or $). Customer returns (unacceptable out-of-plant products in units or $). Recoveries (salvageable products in units or $), rework (additional direct and/or indirect labor in hours or $)
Downtime: Unscheduled breakdown of machinery	*Down-time:* Duration of breakdown (hours or $)
	Machine repair: Non-preventative maintenance ($)
Inventory, material, and supply variance: Unscheduled resource utilization	*Variance:* Over- or under-utilization of supplies, materials, inventory (due to theft, inefficiency, and so on)

* Reports only labor inputs.

Source: B. Macy and P. Mirvis, 'Organizational change efforts: methodologies for assessing organizational effectiveness and program costs versus benefits', *Evaluation Review*, 6, pp. 301–72, copyright © 1982 by Sage Publications. Reprinted by permission of Sage Publications.

TABLE 11.2 Behavioural outcomes for OD interventions: computational formulae

Behavioral measures*	Computational formula
Absenteeism rate** (monthly)	$\dfrac{\Sigma \text{ Absence days}}{\text{Average work-force size} \times \text{working days}}$
Tardiness rate** (monthly)	$\dfrac{\Sigma \text{ Tardiness incidents}}{\text{Average work-force size} \times \text{working days}}$
Turnover rate (monthly)	$\dfrac{\Sigma \text{ Turnover incidents}}{\text{Average work-force size}}$
Internal stability rate (monthly)	$\dfrac{\Sigma \text{ Internal movement incidents}}{\text{Average work-force size}}$
Strike rate (yearly)	$\dfrac{\Sigma \text{ Striking workers} \times \Sigma \text{ strike days}}{\text{Average work-force size} \times \text{working days}}$
Accident rate (yearly)	$\dfrac{\Sigma \text{ of accidents, illnesses}}{\text{Total yearly hours worked}} \times 200\,000$***
Grievance rate (yearly)	*Plant:* $\dfrac{\Sigma \text{ Grievance incidents}}{\text{Average work-force size}}$ *Individual:* $\dfrac{\Sigma \text{ Aggrieved individuals}}{\text{Average work-force size}}$
Productivity**** Total	$\dfrac{\text{Output of goods or services (units or \$)}}{\text{Direct and/or indirect labour (hours or \$)}}$
Below standard	Actual versus engineered standard
Below budget	Actual versus budgeted standard
Variance	Actual versus budgeted variance
Per employee	$\dfrac{\text{Output}}{\text{Average work-force size}}$
Quality:**** Total	Scrap + customer returns + rework – recoveries (\$, units, or hours)
Below standard	Actual versus engineered standard
Below budget	Actual versus budgeted standard
Variance	Actual versus budgeted variance
Per employee	$\dfrac{\text{Total}}{\text{average}}$ work-force size
Downtime	Labor (\$) + repair costs or dollar value of replaced equipment (\$)
Inventory, supply, and material usage	Variance (actual versus standard utilization)(\$)

* All measures reflect the number of incidents divided by an exposure factor that represents the number of employees in the organization and the possible incidence of behavior (e.g. for absenteeism, the average work-force size × the number of working days). Mean monthly rates (i.e. absences per workday) are computed and averaged for absenteeism, leaves and tardiness for a yearly figure and summed for turnover, grievances and internal employment stability for a yearly figure. The term *rate* refers to the number of incidents per unit of employee exposure to the risk of such incidences during the analysis interval.

**   Sometimes combined as number of hours missing/average work-force size × working days.

***   Base for 100 full-time equivalent workers (40 hours × 50 weeks).

**** Monetary valuations can be expressed in labor dollars, actual dollar costs, sales dollars; overtime dollar valuations can be adjusted to base year dollars to control for salary, raw material and price increases.

Source: B. Macy and P. Mirvis, 'Organizational change efforts: methodologies for assessing organizational effectiveness and program costs versus benefits,' *Evaluation Review* , 6, pp. 308–9, copyright © 1982 by Sage Publications. Reprinted by permission of Sage Publications.

Operational definitions are extremely important in measurement as they provide precise guides as to what characteristics of the situation are to be observed and how they are to be used. They tell OD practitioners and the client system exactly how diagnostic, intervention and outcome variables will be measured.

2 *Reliability.* Reliability concerns the extent to which a measure represents the 'true' value of a variable—i.e. how accurately the operational definition translates data into information. For example, there is little doubt about the accuracy of the number of cars leaving an assembly line as a measure of plant productivity. Although it is possible to miscount, there can be a high degree of confidence in the measurement. On the other hand, when people are asked about their level of job satisfaction on a scale of 1 to 5, there is considerable room for variation in their response. They may have just had an argument with their supervisor, suffered an accident on the job, been rewarded for high levels of productivity or given new responsibilities. Each of these events can sway the response to the question on a given day. The individual's 'true' satisfaction score from this one question is difficult to discern, and the measure lacks reliability.[8]

Organisation development practitioners can improve the reliability of their measures in four ways. First, rigorously and operationally define the chosen variables. Clearly specified operational definitions contribute to reliability by explicitly describing how collected data will be converted into information about a variable. This explicit description helps to allay the client's concerns about how the information was collected and coded.

Second, use multiple methods to measure a particular variable. As discussed in Chapter 7, the use of questionnaires, interviews, observations and unobtrusive measures can improve reliability and result in more comprehensive understanding of the organisation. Because each method contains inherent biases, several different methods can be used to triangulate on dimensions of organisational problems. If the independent measures converge or show consistent results, the dimensions or problems have probably been accurately diagnosed.[9]

Third, use multiple items to measure the same variable on a questionnaire. For example, in Hackman and Oldham's *Job Diagnostic Survey* for measuring job characteristics (Chapter 16), the intervention variable 'autonomy' has the following operational definition: the average of respondents' answers to the following three questions (measured on a seven-point scale):[10]

- The job permits me to decide *on my own* how to go about doing the work.
- The job denies me any chance of using my personal initiative or judgment when carrying out the work (reverse scored).
- The job gives me considerable opportunity for independence and freedom in how I do the work.

By asking more than one question about 'autonomy', the survey increases the accuracy of its measurement of this variable. Statistical analyses (called psychometric tests) are readily available for assessing the reliability of perceptual measures, and OD practitioners should apply these methods or seek assistance from those who can.[11] Similarly, there are methods for analysing the content of interview and observational data, and OD evaluators can use these methods to categorise such information so that it can be understood and replicated.[12]

Fourth, use standardised instruments. A growing number of standardised questionnaires are available for measuring OD intervention and outcome variables. For example, the Center for Effective Organizations at the University of Southern California and the Institute for Survey Research at the University of Michigan have developed comprehensive survey instruments to measure the features of many of the OD interventions described in this book, as well as their attitudinal outcomes.[13] Considerable research and testing have gone into establishing measures that are reliable and valid. These survey instruments can be used for initial diagnosis, for guiding implementation of interventions and for evaluating immediate and long-term outcomes.

3 *Validity*. Validity concerns the extent to which a measure actually reflects the variable it is intended to reflect. For example, the number of cars leaving an assembly line might be a reliable measure of plant productivity, but it may not be a valid measure. The number of cars is only one aspect of productivity; they may have been produced at an unacceptably high cost. Because the number of cars does not account for cost, it is not a completely valid measure of plant productivity.

OD practitioners can increase the validity of their measures in several ways. First, ask colleagues and clients if a proposed measure actually represents a particular variable. This is called 'face validity' or 'content validity'. If experts and clients agree that the measure reflects the variable of interest, then there is increased confidence in the measure's validity. Second, use multiple measures of the same variable, as described in the section about reliability. In this way, preliminary assessments can be made about the measure's *criterion* or *convergent validity*, i.e. if several different measures of the same variable correlate highly with each other, especially if one or more of the other measures has been validated in prior research, then there is increased confidence in the measure's validity. A special case of criterion validity, called 'discriminant validity', exists when the proposed measure *does not* correlate with measures that it is not supposed to correlate with. For example, there is no good reason for daily measures of assembly-line productivity to correlate with daily air temperature. The lack of a correlation would be one indicator that the number of cars is measuring productivity and not some other variable. Finally, *predictive validity* is demonstrated when the variable of interest accurately forecasts another variable over time. For example, a measure of team cohesion can be said to be valid if it accurately predicts improvements in team performance in the future.

However, it is difficult to establish the validity of a measure until after it has been used. To address this concern, OD practitioners should make heavy use of content validity processes and use measures that have already been validated. For example, presenting proposed measures to colleagues and clients for evaluation prior to measurement has several positive effects. It builds ownership and commitment to the data-collection process and improves the likelihood that the client system will find the data meaningful. In addition, using measures that have been validated through prior research improves confidence in the results and provides a standard that can be used to validate any new measures used in the data-collection process.

Research design

In addition to measurement, OD practitioners need to make choices about how to design the evaluation to achieve valid results. The key issue is how to design the assessment to show whether the intervention did, in fact, produce the observed results. This is called 'internal validity'; the secondary question of whether the intervention would work similarly in other situations is referred to as 'external validity'. External validity is irrelevant without first establishing an intervention's primary effectiveness. Thus, internal validity is the essential minimum requirement for assessing OD interventions. Unless managers can have confidence that the outcomes are the result of the intervention, they have no rational basis for making decisions about accountability and resource allocation.

Assessing the internal validity of an intervention is, in effect, testing a hypothesis—namely, that specific organisational changes lead to certain outcomes. Moreover, testing the validity of an intervention hypothesis means that alternative hypotheses or explanations of the results must be rejected, i.e. to claim that an intervention is successful, it is necessary to demonstrate that other explanations—in the form of rival hypotheses—do not account for the observed results. For example, if a job enrichment programme appears to increase employee performance, other possible explanations, such as the introduction of new technology, improved raw materials or new employees, must be eliminated.

Accounting for these rival explanations is not a precise, controlled experimental process such as might be found in a research laboratory.[14] Organisation development interventions tend to have a number of features that make determining whether they produced observed results difficult. They are complex and often involve several interrelated changes, obscuring whether individual features or combinations of features are accounting for the results. Many OD interventions are long-term projects and take considerable time to produce desired outcomes. The longer the time period of the change programme, the greater are the chances that other factors, such as technology improvements, will emerge to affect the results. Finally, OD interventions are almost always applied to existing work units rather than to randomised groups of organisation members. In the absence of randomly-selected intervention and comparison groups, ruling out alternative explanations for the results is difficult.

Given the problems inherent in assessing OD interventions, practitioners have turned to *quasi-experimental* research designs,[15] that are not as rigorous and controlled as randomised experimental designs, yet still allow evaluators to rule out many rival explanations for OD results other than the intervention itself. Although several quasi-experimental designs are available, those with the following three features are particularly powerful for assessing OD changes:[16]

1 *Longitudinal measurement.* This means measuring results repeatedly over relatively long time periods. Ideally, the data collection should start before the implementation of the change programme and should continue for a period that is considered reasonable for producing the expected results.

2 *Comparison unit.* It is always desirable to compare results in the intervention situation with those in another situation where no such change has taken place. Although it is never possible to get a matching group that is identical to the intervention group, most organisations include a number of similar work units that can be used for comparison purposes.

3 *Statistical analysis.* Whenever possible, statistical methods should be used to rule out the possibility that the results are caused by random error or chance. There are a variety of statistical techniques applicable to quasi-experimental designs, and OD practitioners should apply these methods or seek help from those who can.[17]

Table 11.3 provides an example of a quasi-experimental design that has these three features. The intervention is intended to reduce employee absenteeism. Measures of absenteeism are taken from company monthly records for both the intervention and comparison groups. The two groups are similar, yet geographically separate, subsidiaries of a multi-plant company. Table 11.3 shows each plant's monthly absenteeism rate for four consecutive months both before and after the start of the intervention. The plant receiving the intervention shows a marked decrease in absenteeism in the months after the intervention, whereas the control plant shows comparable levels of absenteeism in both time periods. Statistical analyses of these data suggest that the abrupt downward shift in absenteeism following the intervention was not attributable to chance variation. This research design and the data provide relatively strong evidence that the intervention was successful.

Quasi-experimental research designs that use longitudinal data, comparison groups and statistical analysis permit reasonable assessments of intervention effectiveness. Repeated measures can often be collected from company records without directly involving members of the experimental and comparison groups. These unobtrusive measures are especially

TABLE 11.3	Quasi-experimental research design								
		Monthly absenteeism (%)							
	Sep.	Oct.	Nov.	Dec.		Jan.	Feb.	Mar.	Apr.
Intervention group	5.1	5.3	5.0	5.1	Start of intervention	4.6	4.0	3.9	3.5
Comparison group	2.5	2.6	2.4	2.5		2.6	2.4	2.5	2.5

useful in OD assessment as they do not interact with the intervention and affect the results. More obtrusive measures, such as questionnaires and interviews, are reactive and can sensitise people to the intervention. When this happens, it is difficult to know whether the observed findings are the result of the intervention, the measuring methods or some combination of both.

Multiple measures of intervention and outcome variables should be applied to minimise measurement and intervention interactions. For example, obtrusive measures such as questionnaires could be used sparingly, perhaps once before and once after the intervention. Unobtrusive measures, such as the behavioural outcomes shown in Tables 11.1 and 11.2, could be used repeatedly. These provide a more extensive time series than the questionnaires. When used together, the two kinds of measures should produce accurate and non-reactive evaluations of the intervention.

The use of multiple measures is also important in assessing perceptual changes resulting from interventions. Considerable research has identified three types of change—alpha, beta and gamma—that occur when using self-report, perceptual measures.[18]

Alpha change refers to movement along a measure that reflects stable dimensions of reality. For example, comparative measures of perceived employee discretion might show an increase after a job enrichment programme. If this increase represents alpha change, it can be assumed that the job enrichment programme actually increased employee perceptions of discretion.

Beta change involves the recalibration of the intervals along some constant measure of reality. For example, before-and-after measures of perceived employee discretion can decrease after a job enrichment programme. If beta change is involved, it can explain this apparent failure of the intervention to increase discretion. The first measure of discretion may accurately reflect the individual's belief about the ability to move around and talk to fellow workers in the immediate work area. During the implementation of the job enrichment intervention, however, the employee may learn that the ability to move around is not limited to the immediate work area. At a second measurement of discretion, the employee, using this new and recalibrated understanding, may rate the current level of discretion as lower than before.

Gamma change involves fundamentally redefining the measure as a result of an OD intervention. In essence, the framework within which a phenomenon is viewed changes. For example, the presence of gamma change would make it difficult to compare measures of employee discretion taken before and after a job enrichment programme. The measure taken after the intervention might use the same words, but they represent an entirely different concept. As described above, the term 'discretion' might originally have referred to the ability to move about the department and interact with other workers. After the intervention, discretion might be defined in terms of the ability to make decisions about work rules, work schedules and productivity levels. In sum, the job enrichment intervention changed the way in which discretion is perceived and how it is evaluated.

These three types of change apply to perceptual measures. When other than alpha changes occur, the interpretation of measurement changes becomes far more difficult. Potent OD interventions may produce both beta and gamma changes, which severely complicate interpretations of findings that report change and no change. Further, the distinctions among the three different types of change suggest that the heavy reliance on questionnaires, so often cited in the literature, should be balanced by using other measures, such as interviews and unobtrusive records. Analytical methods have been developed to assess the three kinds of change, and OD practitioners should gain familiarity with these recent techniques.[19]

Application 11.1 describes the evaluation of the effectiveness of an outdoor workshop for team building in an MBA programme.[20]

Institutionalising interventions

Once it has been determined that an intervention has been implemented and is effective, attention is directed at *institutionalising* the changes—making them a permanent part of

Evaluating an outdoor workshop for team building in an MBA programme

This application examines the effectiveness of an outdoor workshop for building study teams (here called 'learning teams') in the MBA programme at the University of Auckland, New Zealand. The workshop described in this research is conducted at the beginning of the MBA degree offered by the Graduate School of Business at the University of Auckland. Some form of this has been run since 1984, but the framework presented here has only been in use since 1989. The workshop is one component of an orientation process for all students entering the first year of the two-year course of study. It is run with two groups: one group called the Management MBA consisting of people aged between 24 and 40 who require a functional specialisation; the other group called the Executive MBA consisting of people aged between 35 and 40 who need more strategic and general management skills.

The introductory exercises serve as icebreakers and begin to develop an atmosphere of group participation that enables a fuller realisation of each individual's potential contribution to group functioning. The class is then split into learning teams that perform different activities. The first two activities are kept secret from other teams as far as possible, enabling each team to undergo its own learning, participation and co-operation. Skits add a further dimension to the workshop, enabling participants to more fully break down their barriers. Although initially daunting to some, they offer the teams a chance to work through an essentially creative problem from conception to production, and help to remove inhibitions that some individuals may have. The hypothesis is that this type of outdoor workshop has a positive effect on team development.

Team functioning is initially measured by questionnaire so as to provide a baseline against which a similar measurement may be made at the completion of the workshop. Mullen's three processes of cognitive, emotional and behavioural learning are used in the design of the workshop activities: team and/or business strategy is used as cognitive material, while outdoor (and some indoor) activities provide the emotional and behavioural learning experience as metaphors for the normal teamworking environment. The workshop should positively influence team process, i.e. how the members interact.

In order to measure both content and process, two similar case studies were used to form the basis of the analysis—Cases X and Y. Both case studies involved the use of teamwork and problem solving and were concerned with business strategy so that the cases had relevance for the participants. One of the two case studies was handed to the team on the first morning of the workshop, the other at the follow-up session two weeks later. A time limit of 60 minutes was placed on each case study, and a questionnaire was completed when the time had elapsed. This questionnaire was given in order to measure the 'process' side of team operation in achieving the task.

In the case of two questions, there was a statistically significant difference between pre- and post-workshop measures. Workshop teams found increased leadership definition in their group functioning after the workshop. It was also evident that the teams that underwent the workshop found that there was less alienation of group members. Combined with the obvious change in their comments in response to the question about leadership and decision-making structure, it could be seen that the outdoor workshop positively influenced the nature of the leadership and participatory nature of group functioning.

the organisation's normal functioning. Lewin described change as occurring in three stages: unfreezing, moving and refreezing. Institutionalising an OD intervention concerns refreezing. It involves the long-term persistence of organisational changes. To the extent that changes persist, they can be said to be institutionalised. Such changes are not dependent on any one person but exist as part of the culture of an organisation. This means that numerous others share norms about the appropriateness of the changes.

How planned changes become institutionalised has not received much attention in recent years. Rapidly changing environments have led to admonitions from consultants and practitioners to 'change constantly', to 'change before you have to' and 'if it's not broke, fix it anyway'. Such a context has challenged the utility of the institutionalisation concept. Why endeavour to make any change permanent, given that it may require changing again soon? However, the admonitions have also resulted in institutionalisation concepts being applied in new ways. Change itself has become the focus of institutionalisation. Total quality management, organisation learning, integrated strategic change and self-design interventions are all aimed at enhancing the organisation's capability for change.[21] In this vein, processes of institutionalisation take on increased utility. This section presents a framework that identifies factors and processes contributing to the institutionalisation of OD interventions, including the process of change itself.

Institutionalisation framework

Figure 11.2 presents a framework that identifies organisation and intervention characteristics and institutionalisation processes affecting the degree to which change programmes are institutionalised.[22] The model shows that two key antecedents— organisation and intervention characteristics—affect different institutionalisation processes operating in organisations. These processes in turn affect various indicators of institutionalisation. The model also shows that organisation characteristics can influence intervention characteristics. For example, organisations with powerful unions may have trouble gaining internal support for OD interventions.

Organisation characteristics

Figure 11.2 shows that three key dimensions of an organisation can affect intervention characteristics and institutionalisation processes.

1 *Congruence*. This is the degree to which an intervention is perceived as being in harmony with the organisation's managerial philosophy, strategy and structure; its

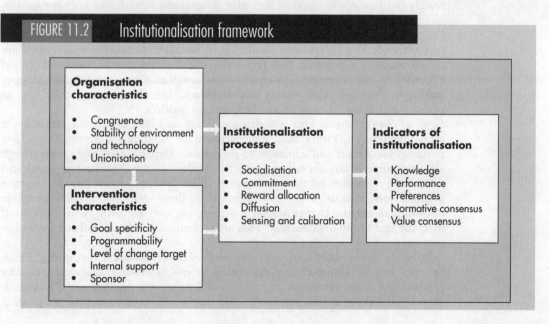

FIGURE 11.2   Institutionalisation framework

current environment; and other changes taking place.[23] When an intervention is congruent with these dimensions, the probability is improved that it will be institutionalised. Congruence can facilitate persistence by making it easier to gain member commitment to the intervention and to diffuse it to wider segments of the organisation. The converse is also true. Many OD interventions promote employee participation and growth. When applied in highly bureaucratic organisations with formalised structures and autocratic managerial styles, participative interventions are not perceived as being congruent with the organisation's managerial philosophy.

2 *Stability of environment and technology.* This involves the degree to which the organisation's environment and technology are changing. Unless the change target is buffered from these changes or unless the changes are directly dealt with by the change programme, it may be difficult to achieve long-term stability of the intervention.[24] For example, decreased demand for the firm's products or services can lead to reductions in personnel, which may change the composition of the groups involved in the intervention. Conversely, increased product demand can curtail institutionalisation by bringing new members on board at a rate faster than they can be effectively socialised.

3 *Unionisation.* Diffusion of interventions may be more difficult in unionised settings, especially if the changes affect union contract issues, such as salary and fringe benefits, job design and employee flexibility. For example, a rigid union contract can make it difficult to merge several job classifications into one, as might be required to increase task variety in a job enrichment programme. It is important to emphasise, however, that unions can be a powerful force for promoting change, especially when a good relationship exists between union and management.

Intervention characteristics

Figure 11.2 shows that five major features of OD interventions can affect institution-alisation processes:

1 *Goal specificity.* This involves the extent to which intervention goals are specific rather than broad. Specificity of goals helps to direct socialising activities (e.g. training and orienting new members) to particular behaviours required to implement the intervention. It also facilitates operationalising the new behaviours so that rewards can be clearly linked to them. For example, an intervention aimed only at the goal of increasing product quality is likely to be more focused and readily put into operation than a change programme intended to improve quality, quantity, safety, absenteeism and employee development.

2 *Programmability.* This involves the degree to which the changes can be programmed. This means that the different characteristics of the intervention are clearly specified in advance, thus facilitating socialisation, commitment and reward allocation.[25] For example, job enrichment specifies three targets of change—employee discretion, task variety and feedback. The change programme can be planned and designed to promote these specific features.

3 *Level of change target.* This concerns the extent to which the change target is the total organisation, rather than a department or small work group. Each level possesses facilitators and inhibitors to persistence. Departmental and group change are susceptible to countervailing forces from others in the organisation, which can reduce the diffusion of the intervention, thus lowering its ability to improve organisation effectiveness. However, this does not necessarily preclude institutionalising the change within a department that successfully insulates itself from the rest of the organisation. This often manifests itself as a subculture within the organisation.[26]

Targeting the intervention to wider segments of the organisation, on the other hand, can also help or hinder change persistence. It can facilitate institutionalisation by promoting a consensus across organisational departments exposed to the change. A shared belief about the intervention's value can be a powerful incentive to maintain the change. But targeting the larger system can also inhibit institutionalisation. The intervention can become mired in political resistance because of the 'not invented here' syndrome, or because powerful constituencies oppose it.

4   *Internal support.* This refers to the degree to which there is an internal support system to guide the change process. Internal support, typically provided by an internal consultant, can help to gain commitment for the changes and help organisation members to implement them. External consultants can also provide support, especially on a temporary basis during the early stages of implementation. For example, in many interventions aimed at implementing high-involvement organisations (see Chapter 15), both external and internal consultants provide support for the changes. The external consultant typically provides expertise on organisational design and trains members to implement the design. The internal consultant generally helps members to relate to other organisational units, to resolve conflicts and to legitimise the change activities within the organisation.

5   *Sponsor.* This concerns the presence of a powerful sponsor who can initiate, allocate and legitimise resources for the intervention. Sponsors must come from levels in the organisation high enough to control appropriate resources. They must have the visibility and power to nurture the intervention and see that it remains viable in the organisation. There are many examples of OD interventions that persisted for several years and then collapsed abruptly when the sponsor, usually a top administrator, left. There are also numerous examples of middle managers withdrawing support for interventions because top management did not include them in the change programme.

Institutionalisation processes

The framework depicted in Figure 11.2 shows five institutionalisation processes operating in organisations that can directly affect the degree to which OD interventions are institutionalised:

1   *Socialisation.* This concerns the transmission of information about beliefs, preferences, norms and values with respect to the intervention. Because implementation of OD interventions generally involves considerable learning and experimentation, a continual process of socialisation is necessary to promote persistence of the change programme. Organisation members must focus attention on the evolving nature of the intervention and its ongoing meaning. They must communicate this information to other employees, especially new members. Transmission of information about the intervention helps to bring new members on board and allows participants to reaffirm the beliefs, norms and values that underlie the intervention.[27] For example, employee involvement programmes often include an initial transmission of information about the intervention, as well as the retraining of existing participants and training of new members. These processes are intended to encourage persistence with the programme, as both new behaviours are learned and new members introduced.

2   *Commitment.* This binds people to behaviours associated with the intervention. It includes initial commitment to the programme, as well as recommitment over time. Opportunities for commitment should allow people to select the necessary behaviours freely, explicitly and publicly. These conditions favour high commitment and can promote stability of the new behaviours. Commitment should derive from several organisational levels, including the employees directly involved and the middle and upper managers who can support or thwart the intervention. In many early employee involvement programmes, for example, attention was directed at gaining the workers' commitment to such programmes. Unfortunately, middle managers were often ignored, resulting in considerable management resistance to the interventions.

3   *Reward allocation.* This involves linking rewards to the new behaviours required by an intervention. Organisational rewards can enhance the persistence of

interventions in at least two ways. First, a combination of intrinsic and extrinsic rewards can reinforce new behaviours. Intrinsic rewards are internal and derive from the opportunities for challenge, development and accomplishment found in the work. When interventions provide these opportunities, motivation to perform should persist. Providing extrinsic rewards, such as money, for increased contributions can further reinforce this behaviour. Because the value of extrinsic rewards tends to diminish over time, it may be necessary to revise the reward system to maintain high levels of desired behaviours.

Second, new behaviours should persist to the extent that employees perceive rewards as equitable. When new behaviours are fairly compensated, people are likely to develop preferences for those behaviours. Over time, those preferences should lead to normative and value consensus about the appropriateness of the intervention. For example, many employee involvement programmes fail to persist because the employees feel that their increased contributions to organisational improvements are unfairly rewarded. This is especially true for interventions that rely exclusively on intrinsic rewards. People argue that an intervention that provides opportunities for intrinsic rewards should also provide greater pay or extrinsic rewards for higher levels of contribution to the organisation.

4 *Diffusion.* This refers to the process of transferring interventions from one system to another. Diffusion facilitates institutionalisation by providing a wider organisational base to support the new behaviours. Many interventions fail to persist because they run counter to the values and norms of the larger organisation. Rather than support the intervention, the larger organisation rejects the changes and often puts pressure on the change target to revert to old behaviours. Diffusion of the intervention to other organisational units reduces this counter-implementation strategy. It tends to lock in behaviours by providing normative consensus from other parts of the organisation. Moreover, the very act of transmitting institutionalised behaviours to other systems reinforces commitment to the changes.

5 *Sensing and calibration.* This involves detecting deviations from desired intervention behaviours and taking corrective action. Institutionalised behaviours invariably encounter destabilising forces, such as changes in the environment, new technologies and pressures from other departments to nullify changes. These factors cause some variation in performances, preferences, norms and values. To detect this variation and take corrective actions, organisations must have some sensing mechanism. Sensing mechanisms, such as implementation feedback, provide information about the occurrence of deviations. This knowledge can then initiate corrective actions to ensure that behaviours are more in line with the intervention. For example, the high level of job discretion associated with job enrichment might fail to persist. Information about this problem might initiate corrective actions, such as renewed attempts to socialise people or to gain commitment to the intervention.

Indicators of institutionalisation

Institutionalisation is not an all-or-nothing concept, but it does reflect degrees of persistence of an intervention. Figure 11.2 shows five indicators that can be used to determine the extent of an intervention's persistence. The extent to which these factors are present or absent indicates the degree of institutionalisation.

1 *Knowledge.* This involves the extent to which organisation members have knowledge of the behaviours associated with an intervention. It is concerned with whether members know enough to perform the behaviours and to recognise the consequences of that performance. For example, job enrichment includes a number of new behaviours, such as performing a greater variety of tasks, analysing information about task performance and making decisions about work methods and plans.

2 *Performance.* This is concerned with the degree to which intervention behaviours are actually performed. It may be measured by counting the proportion of relevant

people performing the behaviours. For example, 60% of the employees in a particular work unit might be performing the job enrichment behaviours described above. Another measure of performance is the frequency with which the new behaviours are performed. In assessing frequency, it is important to account for different variations of the same essential behaviour, as well as highly institutionalised behaviours that only need to be performed infrequently.

3 *Preferences.* This involves the degree to which organisation members privately accept the organisational changes. This contrasts with acceptance that is based primarily on organisational sanctions or group pressures. Private acceptance is usually reflected in people's positive attitudes toward the changes, and can be measured by the direction and intensity of these attitudes across the members of the work unit receiving the intervention. For example, a questionnaire that assesses members' perceptions of a job enrichment programme might show that most employees have a strong positive attitude toward making decisions, analysing feedback and performing a variety of tasks.

4 *Normative consensus.* This focuses on the extent to which people agree on the appropriateness of the organisational changes. This indicator of institutionalisation reflects the extent to which organisational changes have become part of the normative structure of the organisation. Changes persist to the degree that members feel they should support them. For example, a job enrichment programme would become institutionalised to the extent that employees support it and see it as appropriate to organisational functioning.

5 *Value consensus.* This is concerned with social consensus on values that are relevant to the organisational changes. Values are beliefs about how people ought or ought not to behave. They are abstractions from more specific norms. Job enrichment, for example, is based on values promoting employee self-control and responsibility. Different behaviours associated with job enrichment, such as making decisions and performing a variety of tasks, would persist to the extent that employees widely share values of self-control and responsibility.

These five indicators can be used to assess the level of institutionalisation of an OD intervention. The more the indicators are present in a situation, the higher will be the degree of institutionalisation. Further, these factors seem to follow a specific development order: knowledge, performance, preferences, norms and values. People must first understand new behaviours or changes before they can perform them effectively. Such performance generates rewards and punishments, which in time affect people's preferences. As many individuals come to prefer the changes, normative consensus about their appropriateness develops. Finally, if there is normative agreement about the changes reflected in a particular set of values, over time there should be some consensus on those values among organisation members. This developmental view of institutionalisation implies that, whenever one of the last indicators is present, all the previous ones are automatically included as well, e.g. if employees normatively agree with the behaviours that are associated with job enrichment, then they also have knowledge about the behaviours, can perform them effectively and prefer them. An OD intervention is fully institutionalised only when all five factors are present.

Application 11.2 describes Hewlett-Packard's journey to institutionalise a new set of behaviours through structural change. It describes how culture can play a strong role in both supporting and constraining change.[28]

APPLICATION 11.2 — Institutionalising structural change at Hewlett-Packard

Hewlett-Packard (HP) is the eighth-most admired company in the United States, according to Fortune's 1996 ratings, up from number 24 only three years before. Since its founding in 1939, HP has successfully implemented no less than a dozen major organisational changes, including the transition from a high-tech entrepreneurial start-up business to a professionally managed company; from a small instruments business to a leading computer company; from complex instruction set computing technology to a reduced instruction set computing technology base; and from a technology-and-engineering-based company to a market/brand-driven company. It has implemented a number of large-scale structural changes, down-sized, managed two CEO successions, and increased its ability to bring products to market faster. Few organisations have implemented as many major changes and still maintained both their financial performance and corporate reputation. However, implementing and institutionalising structural changes to bring about more co-operation among the computer divisions has been a long and difficult process. The initial structural change was initiated in 1982. By 1992, HP was still trying to reinforce the changes in behaviour that were supposed to result from the re-organisation.

HP operates in the highly volatile electronics and computer industries. Its environment is characterised by high degrees of technological and market change. Just to survive, it must implement a variety of changes, both technological and organisational. HP's traditional and current strategies are built on innovation, differentiation and high quality. In 1993, for example, and before he was officially installed as the new CEO, Lewis Platt announced that HP would be pursuing the convergence of several base technologies, such as wireless communication, printing and measurement, to create whole new products for the converging computer, communication and consumer electronics markets. Implementing such a strategy would require strong co-ordination among HP's product divisions, something HP has always found difficult.

One of the more enduring characteristics of HP is the 'HP Way'. It is a cultural artefact that supports a participative management style and emphasises commonness of purpose and teamwork on the one hand, with individual freedom and initiative on the other. The HP Way is not written down and is therefore difficult to define. As one manager stated in the late 1970s, 'There's something useful in not being too precise—a value to fuzziness. No one can really define the HP Way. If it weren't fuzzy, it would be a rule! This way leaves room for the constant micro-reconciliations needed in a changing world. [HP] is designed as an adaptive company.' However, the HP Way has been both a constraint and a facilitator of change.

For example, the HP Way is at the root of the company's difficulties when trying to institutionalise structural and behavioural changes that ask for co-ordination and co-operation among product divisions. When HP was mainly a producer of high-quality electronic measuring instruments, it was structured into more than 50 highly autonomous and decentralised product divisions focused on specialised niche markets. Individual engineers came up with innovative ideas and 'bootstrapped' new products any way they could. Organisation members were encouraged to work with other engineers in other departments within the same division; but there was little incentive to co-ordinate the development of technologies across divisions. This focus on the individual was supported by a performance management system that measured and rewarded 'sustained contributions'; the key to success for an individual was working with many people in the division. HP prospered by maximising each of its parts.

Former CEO John Young's decision to shift HP's emphasis from small electronic instruments to computers came in 1982, when computers and computer-related equipment accounted for only about a third of its total sales, and most of that was in sales of pocket-sized calculators. As HP went into computers, the keys to success changed. Production of computers required, not the creation of innovative niche products, but the production of products that complemented one another and market shares large enough to encourage software vendors to write programmes for their machines. In a culture that supported individual contributions over divisional co-operation, Young placed all the instrument divisions into one group and all the computer divisions into another. In addition, he centralised research, marketing and manufacturing, which had previously been assigned to the divisions. Problems quickly arose. In one case, the company's new and highly touted graphics printer would not work with its HP3000 minicomputer. The operating software, made by a third HP division, would not allow the two pieces of hardware to interface.

In response, the computer group formed committees to figure out which new technologies to pursue, which to ignore, which of HP's products should be saved and which would be shelved. While the committees came up with recommendations, the committees themselves kept multiplying. The company's entrenched culture, built around the HP Way's philosophy of egalitarianism and mutual respect, promoted consensus. It seems that everyone had to have a hand in making a decision.

By 1988, the organisation chart still showed a predominantly decentralised divisional structure. What it didn't show was the overwhelming number of committees that slowed decision making and product development. In one case, it took seven months and nearly 100 people on nine committees to name the company's new software product. This web of committees, originally designed to foster communication among HP's operating divisions, had pushed up costs and slowed development. In the rapidly changing world of software, personal computers, mini-computers and printers, the culture was hamstringing the organisation's success. The ethic of individual freedom balanced by teamwork had produced an unwieldy bureaucracy.

After a series of delays of important new products, John Young reorganised the computer group. In late 1990, he eliminated most of the committees and removed layers of management by dividing the computer business into two groups: one to handle personal computers and peripherals sold through dealers, and the other to handle sales of work stations and mini-computers to big customers. To match the organisation structure, the previously centralised corporate sales force was split and assigned to a particular division. This change focused HP's computer systems on the market and restored much of the autonomy to the divisions. The balance between individuality and common purpose that characterised the original HP Way was unleashed.

To ensure that the gains in co-operation were not lost as HP embarked on its new strategy, CEO Platt tied division managers' incentive compensation to working co-operatively with other divisions to create new products that use multiple-division technologies. And the lessons learned from the structural changes were not lost. The 1990–91 reorganisation was the result of taking too long to make decisions and getting new products to market. Under the pretence of the HP Way, which encouraged lengthy discussion of ideas, the organisation had become loaded with committees that slowed operations. However, managers realised that it was the implementation of a structure based on the HP Way that was the problem, not the HP Way itself. Thus, newcomers to the organisation are still quickly socialised in the HP Way. In fact, the selection system at HP actually attempts to hire people who will fit the culture of adaptation, innovation and change. By paying close attention to the implementation of structural change, HP has made great strides towards the institutionalisation of individual co-operation and inter-divisional co-ordination.

Summary

We discussed in this chapter the final two stages of planned change—evaluating interventions and institutionalising them. Evaluation was discussed in terms of two kinds of necessary feedback. Implementation feedback is concerned with whether the intervention is being implemented as intended, and evaluation feedback indicates whether the intervention is producing expected results. The former is collected data about features of the intervention and its immediate effects, which are fed back repeatedly and at short intervals. The latter is data about the long-term effects of the intervention, which are fed back at long intervals.

Evaluation of interventions also involves decisions about measurement and research design. Measurement issues focus on selecting variables and designing good measures. Ideally, measurement decisions should derive from the theory that underlies the intervention and should include measures of the features of the intervention and its immediate and long-term consequences. Further, these measures should be operationally defined, valid and reliable and should involve multiple methods, such as a combination of questionnaires, interviews and company records.

Research design focuses on setting up the conditions for making valid assessments of an intervention's effects. This involves ruling out explanations for the observed results other than the intervention. Although randomised experimental designs are rarely feasible in OD, quasi-experimental designs exist for eliminating alternative explanations.

Organisation development interventions are institutionalised when the change programme persists and becomes part of the organisation's normal functioning. A framework for understanding and improving the institutionalisation of interventions identified organisation characteristics (congruence, stability of environment and technology and unionisation) and intervention characteristics (goal specificity, programmability, level of change target, internal support and sponsor) affecting institutionalisation processes. It also described specific institutionalisation processes (socialisation, commitment, reward allocation, diffusion and sensing and calibration) that directly affect indicators of intervention persistence (knowledge, performance, preferences, normative consensus and value consensus).

 ACTIVITIES

Review questions
1 What does 'implementation feedback' try to measure?
2 When should you identify the measurement variables to be used for evaluation and feedback?
3 What do homemade surveys typically have?
4 Which data collection method accurately measures all the variables important to OD?
5 Which indicator represents the highest degree of institutionalisation?
6 List the outcomes that OD consultants should measure.

Discussion and essay questions
1 What are the two kinds of feedback involved in evaluation and what do they tell us?
2 What are the issues involved in measurement?
3 Discuss setting up valid research designs.
4 Define institutionalisation and discuss specific institutionalisation processes.

Notes

1 T. Cummings and E. Molloy, *Strategies for Improving Productivity and the Quality of Work Life* (New York: Praeger, 1977); J. Whitfield, W. Anthony and K. Kacmar, 'Evaluation of team-based management: a case study', *Journal of Organizational Change Management*, 8:2 (1995): 17–28.

2 S. Mohrman and T. Cummings, 'Implementing quality-of-work-life programs by managers' in *The NTL Manager's Handbook*, eds R. Ritvo and A. Sargent (Arlington, Va.: NTL Institute, 1983): 320–28; T. Cummings and S. Mohrman, 'Self-designing organizations: towards implementing quality-of-work-life innovations' in *Research in Organizational Change and Development*, 1, eds R. Woodman and W. Pasmore (Greenwich, Conn.: JAI Press, 1987): 275–310.

3 T. Cummings, 'Institutionalising quality-of-work-life programs: the case for self-design', (paper delivered at the Annual Meeting of the Academy of Management, Dallas, Tex., August 1983).

4 Cummings and Molloy, *Strategies for Improving Productivity and the Quality of Work Life*, op. cit.

5 P. Goodman, *Assessing Organizational Change: The Rushton Quality of Work Experiment* (New York: John Wiley, 1979); A. Van de Ven and D. Ferry, eds, *Measuring and Assessing Organizations* (New York: John Wiley, 1985); E. Lawler III, D. Nadler and C. Cammann, eds, *Organizational Assessment: Perspectives on the Measurement of Organizational Behavior and Quality of Work Life* (New York: John Wiley, 1980); A. Van de Ven and W. Joyce, eds, *Perspectives on Organizational Design and Behavior* (New York: John Wiley, 1981); S. Seashore, E. Lawler III, P. Mirvis and C. Cammann, eds, *Assessing Organizational Change: A Guide to Methods, Measures, and Practices* (New York: John Wiley, 1983).

6 B. Macy and P. Mirvis, 'Organizational change efforts: methodologies for assessing organizational effectiveness and program costs versus benefits', *Evaluation Review,* 6 (1982): 301–72.

7 Macy and Mirvis, 'Organizational change efforts: methodologies for assessing organizational effectiveness and program costs versus benefits', op. cit.

8 J. Nunnally, *Psychometric Theory*, 2nd ed. (New York: McGraw-Hill, 1978); J. Kirk and M. Miller, *Reliability and Validity in Qualitative Research* (Beverly Hills, Calif.: Sage Publications, 1985).

9 D. Miller, *Handbook of Research Design and Social Measurement* (Thousand Oaks, Calif.: Sage Publications, 1991); N. Denzin and Y. Lincoln, eds, *Handbook of Qualitative Research* (Thousand Oaks, Calif.: Sage Publications, 1994).

10 R. Hackman and G. Oldham, *Word Redesign* (Reading, Mass.: Addison-Wesley, 1980): 275–306.

11 Nunnally, *Psychometric Theory,* op. cit.

12 C. Selltiz, M. Jahoda, M. Deutsch and S. Cook, *Research Methods in Social Relations*, rev. ed. (New York: Holt, Rinehart and Winston, 1966): 385–440.

13 J. Taylor and D. Bowers, *Survey of Organizations: A Machine-Scored Standardized Questionnaire Instrument* (Ann Arbor: Institute for Social Research, University of Michigan, 1972); *Comprehensive Quality-of-Work-Life Survey* (Los Angeles: Center for Effective Organizations, University of Southern California, 1981); C. Cammann, M. Fichman, G. Jenkins and J. Klesh, 'Assessing the attitudes and perceptions of organizational members' in *Assessing Organization Change: A Guide to Methods, Measures, and Practices*, eds S. Seashore, E. Lawler III, P. Mirvis and C. Cammann (New York: Wiley-Interscience, 1983): 71–119.

14 R. Bullock and D. Svyantek, 'The impossibility of using random strategies to study the organization development process', *Journal of Applied Behavioral Science*, 23 (1987): 255–62.

15 D. Campbell and J. Stanley, *Experimental and Quasi-Experimental Design for Research* (Chicago: Rand McNally, 1966); T. Cook and D. Campbell, *Quasi-Experimentation: Design and Analysis Issues for Field Settings* (Chicago: Rand McNally, 1979).

16 E. Lawler III, D. Nadler and P. Mirvis, 'Organizational change and the conduct of assessment research' in *Assessing Organizational Change: A Guide to Methods, Measures and Practices*, eds S. Seashore, E. Lawler III, P. Mirvis and C. Cammann (New York: Wiley-Interscience, 1983): 19–47.

17 Cook and Campbell, *Quasi-Experimentation: Design and Analysis Issues for Field Settings*, op. cit.

18 R. Golembiewski and R. Munzenrider, 'Measuring change by OD designs', *Journal of Applied Behavioral Science,* 12 (April–May–June 1976): 133–57.

19 A. Bedeian, A. Armenakis and R. Gilson, 'On the measurement and control of beta change', *Academy of Management Review*, 5 (1980): 561–66; W. Randolph and R. Edwards, 'Assessment of alpha, beta and gamma changes in a university-setting OD intervention', *Academy of Management Proceedings*, (1978): 313–17; J. Terborg, G. Howard and S. Maxwell, 'Evaluating planned organizational change: a method for assessing alpha, beta, and gamma change', *Academy of Management Review*, 7 (1982); 292–95; M. Buckley and A. Armenakis, 'Detecting scale recalibration in survey research', *Group and Organization Studies*, 12 (1987): 464–81; R. Millsap and S. Hartog, 'Alpha, beta, and gamma change in evaluation research: a structural equation approach', *Journal of Applied Psychology*, 73 (1988): 574–84.

20 P. Mazany, S. Francis and P. Sumich, 'Evaluating the effectiveness of an outdoor workshop for team building in an MBA programme', *Team Performance Management*, 3:2 (1997): 97–115.

21 D. Ciampa, *Total Quality: A User's Guide for Implementation* (Reading, Mass.: Addison-Wesley, 1992); P. Senge, *The Fifth Discipline* (New York: Doubleday, 1990); T. Cummings and S. Mohrman, 'Self-designing organizations: towards implementing quality-of-work-life innovations', *op. cit.*; C. Worley, D. Hitchin and W. Ross, *Integrated Strategic Change* (Reading, Mass.: Addison-Wesley, 1996).

22 This section is based on the work of P. Goodman and J. Dean, 'Creating long-term organizational change', in *Change in Organizations*, ed. P. Goodman (San Francisco: Jossey-Bass, 1982): 226–79. To date, the framework is largely untested and unchallenged. Ledford's process model of persistence (see note 23) is the only other model proposed to explain institutionalisation. The empirical support for either model, however, is nil.

23 G. Ledford, 'The persistence of planned organizational change: a process theory perspective' (PhD dissertation, University of Michigan, 1984).

24 L. Zucker, 'Normal change or risky business: institutional effects on the "hazard" of change in hospital organizations, 1959–1979', *Journal of Management Studies*, 24 (1987): 671–700.

25 S. Mohrman and T. Cummings, *Self-Designing Organizations: Learning How to Create High Performance* (Reading, Mass.: Addison-Wesley, 1989).

26 J. Martin and C. Siehl, 'Organizational cultures and counterculture: an uneasy symbiosis', *Organizational Dynamics* (1983): 52–64; D. Meyerson and J. Martin, 'Cultural change: an integration of three different views', *Journal of Management Studies*, 24 (1987): 623–47.

27 L. Zucker, 'The role of institutionalization in cultural persistence', *American Sociological Review*, 42 (1977): 726–43.

28 R. Von Werssowetz and M. Beer, 'Human resources at Hewlett-Packard', *Harvard Business School Case 9-482-125* (Boston: Harvard Business School Press, 1982); B. Buell and R. Hof, 'Hewlett-Packard rethinks itself', *Business Week* (1 April 1991): 76–79; R. Hof, 'Suddenly, Hewlett-Packard is doing everything right', *Business Week* (23 March 1992): 88–89; 'Can John Young redesign Hewlett-Packard', *Business Week* (6 December 1982): 72–78; J. Levine, 'Mild-mannered Hewlett-Packard is making like Superman', *Business Week* (7 March 1988): 110–114; R. Hof, 'Hewlett-Packard digs deep for a digital future', *Business Week* (18 October 1993): 72–75; A. Fisher, 'America's most admired corporations', *Fortune* (4 March 1996): 90–98.

PART 3

HUMAN PROCESS INTERVENTIONS

CHAPTERS

12 Interpersonal and group process approaches

13 Organisation process approaches

Interpersonal and group process approaches

This chapter discusses change programmes relating to inter-personal relations and group dynamics. These change programmes are among the earliest in OD and represent attempts to improve people's working relationships with one another. The interventions are aimed at helping group members to assess their interactions and to devise more effective ways of working together. These interventions represent a basic skill requirement for an OD practitioner.

T-groups, derived from the early laboratory training stem of OD, are mainly used today to help managers learn about the effects of their behaviour on others. Process consultation is another OD technique for helping group members to understand, diagnose and improve their behaviour. Through process consultation, the group should become better able to use its own resources to identify and solve interpersonal problems, which often block the solving of work-related problems. Third-party intervention focuses directly on dysfunctional interpersonal conflict. This approach is only used in special circumstances and only when both parties are willing to engage in the process of direct confrontation.

Team building is aimed both at helping a team to perform its tasks better and at satisfying individual needs. Through team-building activities, group goals and norms become clearer. In addition, team members become better able to confront difficulties and problems and to understand the roles of individuals within the team. Among the specialised team-building approaches presented are interventions associated with ongoing teams as well as temporary teams, such as project teams and task forces.

T-Groups

As discussed in Chapter 1, sensitivity training, or the T-group, is an early forerunner of modern OD interventions. Its direct use in OD has lessened considerably, but OD practitioners often attend T-groups to improve their own functioning. For example, T-groups can help OD practitioners become more aware of how others perceive them and thus increase their effectiveness with client systems. In addition, OD practitioners often recommend that organisation members attend a T-group to learn how their behaviours affect others, and to develop more effective ways of relating to people.

What are the goals?

T-groups are traditionally designed to provide members with experiential learning about group dynamics, leadership and interpersonal relations. The basic T-group consists of about 10 to 15 strangers who meet with a professional trainer to explore the social dynamics that emerge from their interactions. Modifications of this basic design have generally moved in two directions. The first path has used T-group methods to help individuals gain deeper personal understanding and development. This intrapersonal focus is typically called an encounter group or a personal-growth group. It is generally considered outside the boundaries of OD and should be conducted only by professionally-trained clinicians. The second direction uses T-group techniques to explore group dynamics and member relationships within an intact work group. Considerable training in T-group methods and group dynamics should be acquired before attempting these interventions. This group focus has led to the OD intervention called 'team building', which is discussed later in this chapter.

After an extensive review of the literature, Campbell and Dunnette listed six overall objectives common to most T-groups, although not every practitioner need accomplish every objective in every T-group.[1] These objectives are:

1 increased understanding, insight and awareness of one's own behaviour and its impact on others, including the ways in which others interpret one's behaviour
2 increased understanding and sensitivity about the behaviour of others, including better interpretation of both verbal and non-verbal clues, which increases awareness and understanding of what other people are thinking and feeling
3 better understanding and awareness of group and inter-group processes—both those that facilitate and those that inhibit group functioning
4 increased diagnostic skills in interpersonal and inter-group situations. For Campbell and Dunnette, the accomplishment of the first three objectives provides the basic tools for accomplishing the fourth objective
5 increased ability to transform learning into action so that real-life interventions will be successful in increasing member satisfaction, output or effectiveness
6 improvement in individuals' ability to analyse their own interpersonal behaviour, as well as to learn how to help themselves and others with whom they come in contact to achieve more satisfying, rewarding and effective interpersonal relationships.

These goals seem to meet many T-group applications, although any one training programme may emphasise one goal more than the others may. One trainer may emphasise understanding group process as applied to organisations; another may focus on group process as a way of developing individuals' understanding of themselves and others; and a third trainer may choose to focus primarily on interpersonal and intrapersonal learning.

What are the steps?

Application 12.1 illustrates the activities occurring in a typical unstructured strangers' T-group, one of the most popular approaches.

Unstructured strangers' T-group

A typical T-group session for strangers might consist of five or six T-groups of ten to fifteen members who have signed up for a session conducted by the National Training Laboratories, UCLA's Ojai program, a university or a similar organization. The T-group sessions may be combined with cognitive learning, such as brief lectures on general theory, designed exercises or management games.

Each T-group is composed of strangers, i.e. people who have not previously known one another. If several people from the same organization attend, they are put into different T-groups. At the beginning of the training session, the trainer makes a brief and ambiguous statement about either his or her role or some ground rules and lapses into silence. Because the trainer has not taken a leadership role or provided goals for the group, a dilemma of leadership and agenda is created. The group must work out its own methods to proceed further; it must fill the void left by the lack of a leader role or group objectives.

As the group fills the void, the individuals' behaviours become the 'here-and-now' basic data for the learning experiences. As the group struggles with procedure, individual members try out different behaviors and roles, many of which are unsuccessful. One T-group member might make a number of direct, forceful and unsuccessful attempts to take over the leadership role, trying first one style, then another. Finally, he or she conspicuously withdraws from the group, falls silent and appears to be thinking about other things. Group members might observe that this person has two basic styles of working with others; when one style is unsuccessful, he or she adopts the other—withdrawal.

As appropriate, the trainer will make an 'intervention', an observation or comment about the group, its behavior or the activities that are taking place. The type and nature of the intervention will vary, depending on the purpose of the laboratory and the trainer's own style. Usually, the trainer encourages individuals to understand what is going on in the group, their own feelings and behaviors and the impact their behavior has on themselves and others. The primary emphasis is on the here-and-now experience, rather than on anecdotes or 'back at the ranch' experiences.

The emphasis on openness and levelling in a supportive and caring environment allows the participants to gain an insight into their own and others' feelings and behaviours. A better understanding of group dynamics can also make them more productive individuals.

The results of T-groups

T-groups have been among the most controversial topics in organisation development. Probably more has been written about them than any other single topic in OD. A major issue of concern relates to the effectiveness of T-groups—their impact on both the individual and the organisation.

Campbell and Dunnette reviewed a large number of published articles on T-groups and criticised them for their lack of scientific rigor.[2] Argyris, on the other hand, criticised Campbell and Dunnette, arguing that a different kind of scientific rigor is necessary for evaluating T-groups.[3] Although there are obvious methodological problems, the studies generally support the notion that T-group training does bring about change in the individual back in his or her work situation.[4] Among the most frequently found changes are increased flexibility in role behaviour; more openness, receptivity and awareness; and more open communication, with better listening skills and less dependence on others. However, because the goals of many T-group designs are not carefully spelled out, because there are so many variations in design and particularly because many of the research designs do not carefully measure an individual's real work climate and culture, the findings are not highly predictable. Further, some individuals do not attend T-group sessions voluntarily, and little knowledge is available about the differences between those who want to attend and those who are forced to attend.

In considering the value of T-groups for organisations, the evidence is even more mixed. One comparative study of different human process interventions showed that T-groups had the least impact on measures of process (e.g. openness and decision making) and outcome (e.g. productivity and costs).[5] Another comparative study showed, however, that structured T-groups had the most impact on hard measures, such as productivity and absenteeism.[6] The T-groups in this study were structured so that learning could be explicitly transferred back to the work setting. A third comparative study showed that, although T-groups improved group process, they failed to improve the organisational culture surrounding the groups and to gain peer and managerial support in the organisation.[7] Finally, in a meta-analysis of 16 studies, researchers concluded that laboratory training interventions had significant positive effects on overall employee satisfaction and other attitudes.[8]

In his review of the T-group literature, Kaplan concluded that, despite their tarnished reputation, such interventions 'can continue to serve a purpose they are uniquely suited for, to provide an emotional education and to promote awareness of relationships and group process'.[9] To accomplish these purposes, T-groups must be *competently* run so that there is a minimal risk of hurting participants; they must s*electively* include only those people who want to attend; and they need to be *relevant* to the wider organisational context so that participants can apply their learning at work.

Process consultation

Process consultation (PC) is a general model for carrying out helping relationships in groups.[10] It is oriented to helping managers, employees and groups to assess and improve *processes*, such as communication, interpersonal relations, group performance and leadership. Schein argues that effective consultants and managers are good helpers, aiding others to get things done and achieve the goals they have set.[11] Process consultation is an approach to performing this helping relationship. It is aimed at ensuring that those who are receiving the help own their problems and gain the skills and expertise to diagnose and solve them themselves. Thus, it is an approach to helping people and groups to help themselves.

Schein defines process consultation as '*a set of activities on the part of the consultant that helps the client to perceive, understand and act upon the process events which occur in the client's environment*'.[12] The process consultant does not offer expert help in the sense of giving solutions to problems as in the doctor–patient model. Rather, the process consultant observes groups and people in action, helps them to diagnose the nature and extent of their problems and helps them to learn to solve their own problems.

The stages of process consultation follow closely those described for planned change in Chapter 2: entering, defining the relationship, selecting an approach, gathering data and making a diagnosis, intervening, reducing the involvement and terminating the relationship. However, when used in process consultation, these stages are not so clear-cut, because any one of the steps constitutes an intervention. For example, the process consultant has intervened merely by conducting some preliminary interviews with group members. By being interviewed, the members may begin to see the situation in a new light.

Group process

Process consultation deals primarily with five important group processes:
1   communications
2   the functional roles of group members
3   the ways in which the group solves problems and makes decisions
4   the development and growth of group norms
5   the use of leadership and authority.

Communications

One of the process consultant's areas of interest is the nature and style of communication among group members, at both the overt and covert levels. At the overt level, communication issues involve who talks to whom, for how long and how often. One method for describing group communication is to keep a time log of how often and to whom people talk. For example, at an hour-long meeting conducted by a manager, the longest anyone other than the manager got to speak was one minute, and that minute was allotted to the assistant manager. Rather than telling the manager that he is cutting people off, the consultant can decide to give descriptive feedback by citing the number of times others tried to talk and the amount of time they were given. The consultant must make certain that the feedback is descriptive and not evaluative (good or bad), unless the individual or group is ready for that kind of feedback.

By keeping a time log, the consultant can also note who talks and who interrupts. Frequently, certain individuals are perceived as being quiet, when in fact they have attempted to say something and have been interrupted. Such interruptions are one of the most effective ways of reducing communication and decreasing participation in a meeting.

FIGURE 12.1   Johari window

	Unknown to others	Known to others
	2 Known to self, unknown to others	1 Known to self and others
	4 Unknown to self or others	3 Unknown to self, known to others

Source: Adapted by permission of the publisher from J. Luft, 'The Johari Window,' *Human Relation Training News* 5 (1961): 6–7.

Watching body language and other non-verbal behaviour can also be a highly informative way of understanding communication processes.[13] For example, at another meeting conducted by a manager, there was a great deal of discussion at the beginning of the meeting, but soon the second-in-command broke in and said, 'This is a problem-solving meeting, *not* a gripe session'. The manager continued to talk, the 14 other members present all assumed expressions of concentration. But within 25 minutes, all of them had folded their arms and were leaning backward, a sure sign that they were blocking out or shutting off the message. Within ten seconds of the manager's statement, 'We are interested in getting your ideas', those present unfolded their arms and began to lean forward, a clear non-verbal sign that they were now involved.

At the covert or hidden level of communication, sometimes one thing is said, but another meant, thus giving a double message. Luft has described this phenomenon in what is called the *Johari window*.[14] Figure 12.1, a diagram of the Johari window, shows that some personal issues are perceived by both the individual and others (cell 1). Other people are aware of their own issues, but they conceal them from others (cell 2). Persons may have certain feelings about themselves or about others in the work group that they do not share with others unless they feel safe and protected; by not revealing reactions that they feel might be hurtful or impolite, they lessen the degree of communication.

Cell 3 comprises personal issues that are unknown to the individual but that are communicated clearly to others. For example, an individual may shout, 'I'm not angry', as he or she slams a fist on the table, or state, 'I'm not embarrassed at all', as he or she blushes scarlet. Typically, cell 3 communication conveys double messages. For example, one manager who made frequent business trips invariably told his staff to function as a team and make decisions in his absence. The staff, however, consistently refused to do this, because it was clear to them, and to the process consultant, that the manager was *really* saying, 'Go ahead as a team and make decisions in my absence, but be absolutely certain they are the exact decisions I would make if I were here'. Only after the manager had participated in several meetings in which he received feedback was he able to understand that he was sending a double message. Thereafter, he tried both to accept decisions made by others and to use management by objectives with his staff and individual managers.

Cell 4 of the Johari window represents those personal aspects that are unknown to either the individual or others. Because such areas are outside the realm of the consultant and the group, focus is typically on the other three cells. The consultant can help people to learn about how others experience them, thus reducing cell 3. Further, the consultant can help individuals to give feedback to others, thus reducing cell 2. Reducing the size of these two cells helps to improve the communication process by enlarging cell 1, the 'self that is open to both the individual and others'.

The climate of the work group can have a great impact on the size of the quadrants in the Johari window, particularly cell 2. Gibb has outlined two basic types of climate—supportive and threatening.[15] Threatening climates (those that put the receiver on the defensive) can be of several types, and for each there is a corresponding supportive climate.

- *Evaluative versus descriptive.* A listener who perceives a statement as evaluative is put on guard. If, on the other hand, the comment is perceived as descriptive and factual, the receiver is more likely to accept the communication.
- *Control versus problem orientation.* One person's attempt to control another increases the latter's defensiveness. Problem orientation, by contrast, is supportive, as it does not imply that the receiver is somehow inferior.
- *Strategy versus spontaneity.* Strategy implies manipulation, whereas spontaneity reduces defensive behaviour.
- *Superiority versus equality.* To the extent that a person assumes a superior role, he or she arouses defensiveness in the other person. Equality is much more likely to result in joint problem solving.
- *Certainty versus provisionalism.* The more dogmatic a person is, the more that defensiveness will be aroused in others. Provisionalism, on the other hand, allows the other person to have some control over the situation and increases the likelihood of collaboration.

Functional roles of group members

The process consultant must be keenly aware of the different roles that individual members take on in a group. Both upon entering and while remaining in a group, the individual must determine a self-identity, influence and power that will satisfy personal needs while working to accomplish group goals. Preoccupation with individual needs or power struggles can severely reduce the effectiveness of a group, and unless the individual can, to some degree, expose and share those personal needs, the group is unlikely to be productive. Therefore, the process consultant must help the group confront and work through these needs. Emotions are facts, but frequently they are regarded as side issues to be avoided. Whenever an individual, usually the leader, says to the group, 'Let's stick with the facts', it is usually a sign that the emotional needs of group members are not being satisfied and, indeed, are being disregarded as irrelevant.

Two other functions that need to be performed if a group is to be effective are: (1) task-related activities, such as giving and seeking information and elaborating, co-ordinating and evaluating activities; and (2) the group-maintenance function, which is directed toward holding the group together as a cohesive team and includes encouraging, harmonising, compromising, setting standards and observing. Most ineffective groups do little group maintenance. This is a primary reason for bringing in a process observer.

The process consultant can help by suggesting that some part of each meeting be reserved for examining these functions and periodically assessing the feelings of the group's members. As Schein points out, however, the basic purpose of the process consultant is not to take on the role of expert but to help the group share in its own diagnosis and do a better job in learning to diagnose its own processes: 'It is important that the process consultant encourage the group not only to allocate time for diagnosis but to take the lead itself in trying to articulate and understand its own processes.'[16] Otherwise, the group may default and become dependent on the supposed expert. In short, the consultant's role is to make comments and to assist with diagnosis, but the emphasis should be on facilitating the group's understanding and articulation of its *own* processes.

Problem solving and decision making

To be effective, a group must be able to identify problems, examine alternatives and make decisions. The first part of this process is the most important. Groups often fail to distinguish between problems (either task-related or interpersonal) and symptoms. Once the group has identified the problem, an OD consultant can help the group analyse its approach, restrain the group from reacting too quickly and making a premature diagnosis or suggest additional options.

For example, a consultant was asked to process a group's actions during a three-hour meeting that had been taped. The tapes revealed that premature rejection of a suggestion had severely retarded the group's process. When the manager quickly rejected one member's suggestion at the beginning of the meeting, the member repeated his suggestion several times in the next hour, but it was always quickly rejected. During the second hour, he became quite negative, opposing most of the other ideas offered. Finally, toward the end of the second hour, he brought up his proposal again. At this time, it was thoroughly discussed and then rejected for reasons that the member accepted.

During the third hour, this person was one of the most productive members of the group, offering constructive and worthwhile ideas, suggestions and recommendations. In addition, he was able to integrate the comments of others, to modify them and to come up with useful, integrated new suggestions. However, it was not until his first suggestion had been thoroughly discussed (even though it was finally rejected) that he was able to become a truly constructive member of the group.

Once the problem has been identified, a decision must be made. One way of making decisions is to ignore a suggestion. For example, when one person makes a suggestion, someone else offers another before the first has been discussed. A second method is to give decision-making power to the person in authority. Sometimes decisions are made by minority rule, the chairman arriving at a decision and turning for agreement to several people who will comply. Frequently, silence is regarded as consent. Majority rule, consensus or unanimous consent can also make decisions, of course.

The process consultant can help the group understand how it makes decisions and the consequences of each decision process, as well as help diagnose which type of decision process may be most effective in the given situation. Decision by unanimous consent, for example, may sometimes be ideal, but too time-consuming or costly at other times.

Group norms and growth

If a group of people works together over a period of time, it often develops group norms or standards of behaviour about what is good or bad, allowed or forbidden, right or wrong. There may be an explicit norm that group members are free to express their ideas and feelings, whereas the implicit norm is that one does not contradict the ideas or suggestions of certain members (usually the more powerful ones) of the group. The process consultant can be very helpful in helping the group to understand and articulate its own norms and to determine whether those norms are helpful or dysfunctional. By understanding its norms and recognising which ones are helpful, the group can grow and deal realistically with its environment, make optimum use of its own resources and learn from its own experiences.[17]

Leadership and authority

A process consultant needs to understand the processes of leadership and how different leadership styles can help or hinder a group's functioning. In addition, the consultant can help the leader to adjust his or her style to fit the situation. An important step in that process is for the leader to gain a better understanding of his or her own behaviour and the group's reaction to that behaviour. It is also important that the leader become aware of alternative behaviours. For example, after gaining a better understanding of his or her assumptions about human behaviour, the leader may do a better job of testing these assumptions and perhaps changing them.

Basic process interventions

For each of the five group processes described above, a variety of interventions may be used. In broad terms, these interventions may be of the following types:[18]
1 Process interventions, including:
   • questions that direct attention to interpersonal issues
   • process-analysis periods
   • agenda review and testing procedures
   • meetings devoted to interpersonal processes
   • conceptual inputs on interpersonal-process topics.

Process interventions are designed to make the group sensitive to its own internal processes and to generate interest in analysing these processes.
2 Diagnostic and feedback interventions, including:
   • diagnostic questions and probes
   • forcing historical reconstruction, concretisation and process emphasis
   • feedback to groups during process analysis or regular work time
   • feedback to individuals after meetings or data-gathering sessions.

To give feedback to a group, the consultant must first observe relevant events, ask the proper questions, and make certain that the feedback is given to the client system in a usable manner. The process consultant's feedback must be specific, timely and descriptive. The consultant must avoid creating resistance in the client, but at the same time must help the client to use the feedback to learn more about activities that reduce the group's effectiveness or inhibit individual satisfaction.
3 Coaching or counselling of individuals or groups to help them learn to observe and process their own data, accept and learn from the feedback process and become active in identifying and solving their own problems.
4 Structural suggestions pertaining to the following:
   • group membership
   • communication or interaction patterns
   • allocation of work, assignments of responsibility or lines of authority.

Application 12.2 presents an example of process consultation with the top-management team of a manufacturing firm.[19]

APPLICATION 12.2

Process consultation at Apex Manufacturing Corporation

The company was a large manufacturer organized into several divisions. The top-management team, consisting of the president and division managers, was experiencing communication problems after a recent reorganization. The company was expected to grow rapidly in the next few years, and team members felt they should work on group problems now. They sought help from an external consultant who was an expert in process consultation.

An initial meeting set up between one of the key managers in the group and the consultant was intended to acquaint the two parties and to explore the possibility of establishing a consulting relationship.

The manager recounted the group's desire to work on group problems and its need for external help. She also voiced her concerns that the president needed help in handling key people and that the president and his subordinates communicated poorly. The consultant agreed to attend one of the team's weekly meetings. At this time, she would meet the president and other executives and discuss further what could and should be done.

At the initial team meeting, the consultant found a lively interest in having an outsider help the group. Members were willing to enter into an open-ended relationship in which all parties would jointly agree upon each step of process consultation. The consultant explained her approach to process consultation and suggested that she sit in on the weekly team meetings. She also proposed to interview each member over the next few weeks as a way of getting further acquainted with team members. During this initial meeting, the consultant observed that the president was informal yet powerful and confident. He seemed to tolerate process consultation as long as he saw some value in it. The consultant concluded (and subsequently confirmed) that the group's problems resulted mainly from interactions between the president and his subordinates; relationships among the subordinates were less important.

In interviewing team members over the next several weeks, the consultant focused on the president–subordinate relationship. This focus included questions about what went well or poorly with the relationship, how the relationship affected job performance and how members would like to see the relationship changed. This information provided the consultant with a better understanding of the causes underlying the ineffective team meetings. It told her how members viewed the key relationship with the president. During the weekly team meetings, the consultant noticed that the group process was fairly healthy. Members spoke when they felt like it, issues were fully explored, conflict was openly confronted and members felt free to contribute. Although this climate was constructive, it created a major difficulty for the group. No matter how few items were discussed, the team was never able to finish its work. As the backlog of items became longer, members' frustrations grew. Although meetings became longer and more of them were scheduled, there was little success in completing the work.

The consultant suggested that the team was overloaded; the agenda was too large and consisted of a mixture of operational and policy issues without recognizing that each type of issue required a different allocation of time. She asked members to discuss how they might develop a more effective agenda for the meetings. After half an hour of sharing feelings, members decided to sort the agenda into several categories and to devote some meetings exclusively to operating issues and others to policy matters. The operating meetings would be short and tightly run; the policy meetings would last one full day each month at an off-site location, and would explore one or two large questions in depth. It was also decided that the consultant would attend only the full-day policy meetings. Time would be set aside for any theory inputs from the consultant as well as for process analysis of the meetings.

The full-day meetings changed the climate of the group dramatically. It was easier to establish close informal relationships during breaks and meals. Because there was sufficient time, members felt that they could work through their conflicts instead of leaving them dangling. The level of trust in the group increased, and members began to share more personal reactions with each other. In fact, one whole meeting was devoted to giving and receiving feedback from team members, including the president. The consultant suggested that only one person be discussed at a time; that person only listened and did not respond until all the members had had a chance to give feedback. Members were encouraged to discuss the strengths and weaknesses of each member's managerial and interpersonal style. The consultant added her own feedback on points about that member's behavior that she had observed. The exercise was successful in deepening relationships and in exposing areas for future work.

In this example, the consultant worked with the management team for about one year. She helped the group move from chaotic meetings toward a more organized pattern. The group also learned how to manage its own agenda and guide its own process. Members' interactions became more trusting and open, and members learned how to give and receive personal feedback.

When is process consultation appropriate?

Process consultation is a general model for helping relationships, and so has wide applicability in organisations. Because PC helps people and groups to own their problems and learn how to diagnose and resolve them, it is most applicable when:[20]

1   the client has a problem but does not know its source or how to resolve it
2   the client is unsure of what kind of help or consultation is available
3   the nature of the problem is such that the client would benefit from involvement in its diagnosis
4   the client is motivated by goals that the consultant can accept and has some capacity to enter into a helping relationship
5   the client ultimately knows what interventions are most applicable
6   the client is capable of learning how to assess and resolve his or her own problem.

Results of process consultation

Although process consultation is an important part of organisation development and has been widely practised over the past 35 years, only a modest amount of research addresses its effect on improving the ability of groups to accomplish work. The few studies that have been conducted have produced little real evidence of effectiveness. Research findings on process consultation are unclear, especially as these findings relate to task performance.

A number of difficulties arise when trying to measure performance improvements as a result of process consultation. One problem is that most process consultation is conducted with groups that perform mental tasks (e.g. decision making)—the outcomes of such tasks are difficult to evaluate. A second difficulty with measuring its effects occurs because, in many cases, process consultation is combined with other interventions in an ongoing OD programme. Isolating the impact of process consultation from other interventions is difficult.

A review of process consultation studies underscores these problems of measuring performance effects.[21] The survey examined published studies in three categories:

1   reports in which process intervention is the causal variable but performance is measured inadequately or not at all
2   reports in which performance is measured but process consultation is not isolated as the independent variable (the case in many instances)
3   research in which process consultation is isolated as the causal variable and performance is adequately measured. The review suggests that process consultation did have positive effects on participants, according to self-reports of greater personal involvement, higher mutual influence, group effectiveness and similar variables. However, very little, if any, research clearly demonstrates that objective task effectiveness was increased. In most cases, either the field studies did not directly measure performance or the effect of process intervention was confounded with other variables.

A third problem with assessing the performance effects of process consultation is that much of the relevant research has used people's perceptions as the index of success, rather than hard performance measures. Much of this research shows positive results, including the following well-known studies in which the success of process consultation was measured by questionnaires.

Lippitt conducted a series of process-intervention seminars for the top executives of the US Post Office, the General Services Administration and the Small Business Administration.[22] The impact of the seminars was analysed through anonymous, open-ended written questionnaires. The results of the analysis were generally positive, indicating that the seminars had had an impact on both organisational and individual functioning.

Argyris tape-recorded the regular meetings of the board of directors of a consulting organisation over a period of several months.[23] The tapes were analysed and the results fed back to the group. The early results indicated that the board lacked the ability to innovate, to take risks and fully discuss and explore disagreements. After a series of one-day process consultation sessions, board meetings were characterised by members' concern for ideas, openness and helping others; conformity, antagonism and not helping others all decreased as behaviours. Argyris stressed that he was studying changes in behaviour, not changes in the overall effectiveness of the group.

Third-party intervention

Third-party intervention focuses on conflicts arising between two or more people within the same organisation. Conflict is inherent in groups and organisations and can arise from a variety of sources, including differences in personality, task orientation and perceptions among group members, as well as competition over scarce resources. To emphasise that conflict is neither good nor bad *per se* is important. It can enhance motivation and innovation and lead to greater understanding of ideas and views. On the other hand, conflict can prevent people from working together constructively. It can destroy necessary task interactions among group members. Consequently, third-party intervention is used primarily in situations in which conflict significantly disrupts necessary task interactions and work relationships among members.

Third-party intervention varies considerably according to the kind of issues that underlies the conflict. Conflict can arise over *substantive* issues, such as work methods, pay rates and conditions of employment; or it can emerge from *interpersonal* issues, such as personality conflicts and misperceptions. When applied to substantive issues, conflict resolution interventions traditionally involve resolving labour–management disputes through arbitration and mediation. These methods require considerable training and expertise in law and labour relations and are not generally considered to be part of OD practice.

When conflict involves interpersonal issues, however, OD has developed approaches that help to control and to resolve it. These third-party interventions help the parties to directly interact with each other, facilitating their diagnosis of the conflict and how to resolve it. That ability to facilitate conflict resolution is a basic skill in OD and applies to all of the process interventions discussed in this chapter. Consultants, for example, frequently help organisation members to resolve the interpersonal conflicts that invariably arise during process consultation and team building.

Third-party consultation interventions cannot resolve all interpersonal conflicts in organisations, nor should they. Interpersonal conflicts are frequently not severe or disruptive enough to warrant attention. At other times, they may simply burn themselves out without any intervention. Evidence also suggests that other methods may be more appropriate under certain conditions. For example, managers tend to actively control the process and outcomes of conflict resolution when under heavy time pressures, when the disputants are not expected to work together in the future, and when the resolution of the dispute has a broad impact on the organisation.[24] Under these conditions, the third party may resolve the conflict unilaterally with little input from the conflicting parties.

An episodic model of conflict

Interpersonal conflict often occurs in iterative, cyclical stages known as 'episodes'. An episodic model is shown in Figure 12.2. At times, the issues underlying the conflict are latent and do not present any manifest problems for the parties. Something triggers the conflict, however, and brings it into the open. For example, a violent disagreement or frank confrontation can unleash conflict behaviour. Because of the negative consequences of conflict behaviour, the disagreement usually becomes latent again, even though it is still unresolved. Once again, something triggers the conflict, making it overt, and so the cycle continues with the next conflict episode.

Conflict has both costs and benefits for the antagonists and for those in contact with them. Unresolved conflict can proliferate and expand. An interpersonal conflict may be concealed under a cause or issue, serving to make the conflict more legitimate. Frequently, the overt conflict is only a symptom of a deeper problem.

The episode model identifies four strategies for conflict resolution. The first three attempt to control the conflict, and only the last approach tries to change the basic issues

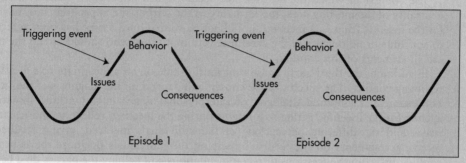

Source: R. G. Walton, *Managing Conflict*, 2nd ed., copyright © 1987 by Addison-Wesley Publishing Company Inc. Reprinted by permission of Addison-Wesley Publishing Company, Reading, Mass.

that underlie it.[25] The first strategy is to prevent the ignition of conflict by arriving at a clear understanding of the triggering factors and thereafter avoiding or blunting them when the symptoms occur. For example, if conflict between the research and production managers is always triggered by new product introductions, senior management can warn them that conflict will not be tolerated during the introduction of the latest new product. However, this may not always be functional and may merely drive the conflict underground until it explodes. As a control strategy, though, this method may help to achieve a temporary cooling-off period.

The second control strategy is to set limits on the form of the conflict. Conflict can be constrained by informal gatherings before a formal meeting or by exploration of other options. It can also be limited by setting rules and procedures that specify the conditions under which the parties can interact. For example, a rule can be instituted that union officials can only attempt to resolve grievances with management at weekly grievance meetings.

The third control strategy is to help the parties cope differently with the consequences of the conflict. The third-party consultant may work with the individuals involved to help them to devise coping techniques, such as reducing their dependence on the relationship, ventilating their feelings to friends and developing additional sources of emotional support. These methods can reduce the costs of the conflict without resolving the underlying issues.

The fourth method is an attempt to eliminate or resolve the basic issues causing the conflict. As Walton points out, 'there is little to be said about this objective because it is the most obvious and straightforward, although it is often the most difficult to achieve'.[26]

Facilitating the conflict resolution process

Walton has identified a number of factors and tactical choices that can facilitate the use of the episode model in resolving the underlying causes of conflict.[27] The following ingredients can help third-party consultants achieve productive dialogue between the disputants so that they examine their differences and change their perceptions and behaviours: mutual motivation to resolve the conflict; equality of power between the parties; co-ordinated attempts to confront the conflict; relevant phasing of the stages of identifying differences and of searching for integrative solutions; open and clear forms of communication and productive levels of tension and stress.

Among the tactical choices identified by Walton are those that have to do with diagnosis, the context of the third-party intervention and the role of the consultant. One of the tactics in third-party intervention is the gathering of data, usually through preliminary interviewing. Group-process observations can also be used. Data gathering provides some understanding of the nature and type of conflict, the personality and conflict styles of the individuals involved, the issues and attendant pressures and the participants' readiness to work together to resolve the conflict.

The context in which the intervention occurs is also important. Consideration of the neutrality of the meeting area, the formality of the setting, the appropriateness of the time for the meeting (that is, a meeting should not be started until a time has been agreed upon to conclude or adjourn) and the careful selection of those who should attend the meeting are all elements of this context.

In addition, the third-party consultant must decide on an appropriate role to assume in resolving conflict. The specific tactic chosen will depend on the diagnosis of the situation. For example, facilitating dialogue of interpersonal issues might include initiating the agenda for the meeting, acting as a referee during the meeting, reflecting and restating the issues and the differing perceptions of the individuals involved, giving feedback and receiving comments on the feedback, helping the individuals diagnose the issues in the conflict, providing suggestions or recommendations and helping the parties do a better job of diagnosing the underlying problem.

The third-party consultant must develop considerable skill at diagnosis, intervention and follow-up. The third-party intervener must be highly sensitive to his or her own feelings and to those of others. He or she must also recognise that some tension and conflict are inevitable and that, although there can be an optimum amount and degree of conflict, too much conflict can be dysfunctional for both the individuals involved and the larger organisation. The third-party consultant must be sensitive to the situation and able to use a number of different intervention strategies and tactics when intervention appears to be useful. Finally, he or she must have professional expertise in third-party intervention and must be seen by the parties as neutral or unbiased regarding the issues and outcomes of the conflict resolution.

Application 12.3 identifies the drivers for change and the potential consequences of these changes on the staff. It also examines the potential for conflict during the period of change.[28]

APPLICATION 12.3 — Cultural change: its effect on the University of Hong Kong estates office

The University of Hong Kong is approximately 90 years old, and Hong Kong's oldest university. Over the last nine decades it has grown considerably in size, now accommodating more than 11 000 full-time and 60 000 part-time students within a 450 000 square metre campus. In the immediate past the university was administered in a very formal manner. Strict rules and regulations, evolved over many years, were applied to obtain and control conformity within the university's management. The administrative model also served to protect the university and its officers from allegations of malpractice or corruption. Typically, power was kept within the upper section of the hierarchical structure and, whether by design or natural evolution, this management style carried many of the hallmarks of Weber's rational-legal or bureaucratic model in its approach.

Within this structure, the estates office evolved within Weber's classical principles, i.e. the 'chain of command' was vertical with clearly defined lines of communication, which were adhered to. In addition, four distinct groups can be identified within the estates office's management structure. These are:

1 Development (architects)
2 Mechanical and engineering (engineers)
3 Building maintenance (surveyors)
4 Administration management.

For many years the university's style of management functioned adequately both within the university and within the estates office. However, being mechanistic, it tended to stifle new opportunities in management styles as staff were programmed in the rigid alignment of the management structure. This was apparent in the four clearly-defined professional disciplines, which functioned autonomously within a strict order and, as Morgan (1996) states, 'one man one boss'. Cross-fertilisation on building projects often came from third parties or facilitators outside the organisation (e.g. outside architects and project managers). From discussions with different officers in the estates office it was apparent that there was professional rivalry. Indeed, conflict was evident, and co-operation between the divisions was sometimes lacking.

Culture change

The university went through dramatic changes in its thinking and methods of management in the mid-1990s. A new vice-chancellor and the changing expectations of customers drove this process. These changes meant that the estates office had to rethink its practice of providing facility management services to the university community at increasingly competitive rates.

With this in mind, the management office embarked on a business process re-engineering (BPR) process of changing the culture and structure of the office. As with any major restructuring, the change did create conflict and uncertainty within the office, which undoubtedly led to increased stress levels within the office.

The management changes took several years to establish. During this period, clear areas of conflict became noticeable and had to be addressed. The major areas of concern included:

- the fear of changing tried and tested work patterns and attitudes
- the fear of failure
- the fear of not being able to produce what is expected of one in the new organisation

- the fear of getting it wrong
- breaking away from traditional tried and tested methods
- the fear of being 'put on' and ending up with a heavy work load
- alienation by sectional colleagues or creating jealousy within departments
- losing one's identity as a professional.

The study indicated that, since the old hierarchical model needed to be totally reshaped, the new organisation could be developed to ensure direct interaction between team members of the various professions. In this way the new structure could be based on a team approach. This in turn challenged some of the fundamental cornerstones of the existing management system and the micro-environment within the office.

In conclusion it is worth noting that any stress created has two directions—the increased stress levels can be advantageous if tapped and used advantageously, while distress is harmful. Looking at job performance, it was found that, within certain limits, an individual's performance actually improves with increased levels of stress. After a point, however, stress clearly results in reduced performance. Finding this limit has been difficult and the office is now in a period of monitoring staff performance.

Undoubtedly, the efficiencies that the office has gained need to be maintained. However, the leaders must be sure that the stress levels of staff are monitored as responsibility and accountability for work are pushed down instead of up.

Further stress causes were also being addressed by training programmes for some staff who were taking up different jobs or responsibility levels, so that the focus was much more on eustress. If managed with this knowledge, the change process could be given extra synergy and any destructive stress levels reduced.

Team building

Team building refers to a broad range of planned activities that help groups to improve the way they accomplish tasks and help group members to enhance their interpersonal and problem-solving skills. Organisations consist of many permanent and temporary groups. Team building is an effective approach to improving teamwork and task accomplishment in these situations. It can help problem-solving groups make maximum use of members' resources and contributions. It can help members to develop a high level of motivation to carry out group decisions. Team building can also help groups overcome specific problems, such as apathy and general lack of interest among members; loss of productivity; increasing complaints within the group; confusion about assignments; low participation in meetings; lack of innovation and initiation; increasing complaints from those outside the group about the quality, timeliness and effectiveness of services and products and hostility or conflict among members.

Equally important, team building can facilitate other OD interventions, such as employee involvement, work design, restructuring and strategic change. These change programmes are typically designed by management teams and implemented by various committees and work groups. Team building can help these groups design high-quality change programmes. It can ensure that the programmes are accepted and implemented by organisation members. Indeed, most technostructural, human resource management and strategic interventions depend on some form of team building for effective implementation.

The importance of team building is well established, and its use is expected to grow even faster in the coming years. Management teams are encountering issues of greater complexity and uncertainty, especially in such fast-growing industries as electronics, entertainment, information technology and processing, and health and financial services. Team building can provide the kind of teamwork and problem-solving skills needed to tackle such issues. As manufacturing and service technologies continue to develop, such as just-in-time inventory systems, manufacturing cells, robotics and service quality concepts, there is increasing pressure on organisations to implement team-based work designs. Team building can facilitate the development of group goals and norms that support high productivity and quality of work life. The globalisation of work and organisations implies that people from different cultures and different geographic locations will increasingly interact over complex management and operational tasks. Team building is an excellent vehicle for examining cross-cultural issues and their impact on decision making and problem solving. When such groups represent the senior management of an organisation, team building can help to establish a coherent corporate strategy and can promote the kind of close co-operation needed to make this new form of governance effective.[29] Finally, in today's business situation, mergers and acquisitions are increasing rapidly. The success of these endeavours depends in part on getting members from different organisations to work effectively together. Team building can facilitate the formation of a unified team with common goals and procedures.

Team building is not clearly differentiated from process consultation in the OD literature. This confusion stems mainly from the fact that most team building *includes* process consultation—helping the group to diagnose and to understand its own internal processes. However, process consultation is a more general approach to helping relationships than team building. Team building focuses explicitly on helping groups to perform tasks and to solve problems more effectively. Process consultation, on the other hand, is concerned with establishing effective helping relationships in organisations. It is seen as being essential for effective management and consultation, and can be applied to any helping relationship, from subordinate development to interpersonal relationships to group development. Thus, team building consists of process consultation *plus* other, more task-oriented, interventions.

Table 12.1 (opposite)

TABLE 12.1   Team-building checklist

I   Problem identification: To what extent is there evidence of the following problems in your work unit?

	Low evidence	Some evidence	High evidence
1 Loss of production or work-unit output	1 2	3	4 5
2 Grievances or complaints within the work unit	1 2	3	4 5
3 Conflicts or hostility between unit members	1 2	3	4 5
4 Confusion about assignments or unclear relationships between people	1 2	3	4 5
5 Lack of clear goals or low commitment to goals	1 2	3	4 5
6 Apathy or general lack of interest or involvement of unit members	1 2	3	4 5
7 Lack of innovation, risk taking, imagination, or taking initiative	1 2	3	4 5
8 Ineffective staff meetings	1 2	3	4 5
9 Problems in working with the boss.	1 2	3	4 5
10 Poor communications: people afraid to speak up, not listening to each other, or not talking together	1 2	3	4 5
11 Lack of trust between boss and members or between members	1 2	3	4 5
12 Decisions made that people do not understand or agree with	1 2	3	4 5
13 People feel that good work is not recognized or rewarded	1 2	3	4 5
14 People are not encouraged to work together in better team effort	1 2	3	4 5

Scoring: Add the score for the 14 items. If your score is between 14 and 28, there is little evidence that your unit needs team building. If your score is between 29 and 42, there is some evidence but no immediate pressure, unless two or three items are very high. If your score is between 43 and 56, you should seriously think about planning the team-building program. If your score is over 56, then team building should be top priority for your work unit.

II   Are you (or your manager) prepared to start a team-building program? Consider the following statements. To what extent do they apply to you or your department?

	Low	Medium	High
1 You are comfortable in sharing organizational leadership and decision making with subordinates and prefer to work in a participative atmosphere	1 2	3 4	5
2 You see a high degree of interdependence as necessary among functions and workers in order to achieve your goals	1 2	3 4	5
3 The external environment is highly variable or changing rapidly and you need the best thinking of all your staff to plan for these conditions	1 2	3 4	5
4 You feel you need the input of your staff to plan major changes or develop new operating policies and procedures	1 2	3 4	5
5 You feel that broad consultation among your people as a group in goals, decisions, and problems is necessary on a continuing basis	1 2	3 4	5
6 Members of your management team are (or can become) compatible with each other and are able to create a collaborative rather than a competitive environment	1 2	3 4	5
7 Members of your team are located close enough to meet together as needed	1 2	3 4	5
8 You feel you need to rely on the ability and willingness of subordinates to resolve critical operating problems directly and in the best interest of the company or organization	1 2	3 4	5
9 Formal communication channels are not sufficient for the timely exchange of essential information, views, and decisions among your team members	1 2	3 4	5
10 Organization adaptation requires the use of such devices as project management, task forces, or *ad hoc* problem-solving groups to augment conventional organization structure	1 2	3 4	5
11 You feel it is important to bring out and deal with critical, albeit sensitive, issues that exist in your team	1 2	3 4	5
12 You are prepared to look at your own role and performance with your team	1 2	3 4	5
13 You feel there are operating or interpersonal problems that have remained unsolved too long and need the input from all group members	1 2	3 4	5
14. You need an opportunity to meet with your people to set goals and develop commitment to these goals	1 2	3 4	5

Scoring: If your total score is between 50 and 70, you are probably ready to go ahead with the team-building program. If your score is between 35 and 49, you should probably talk the situation over with your team and others to see what would need to be done to get ready for team building. If your score is between 14 and 34, you are probably not prepared to start team building.

Dyer has developed a checklist for identifying whether a team-building programme is needed and whether the organisation is ready to start such a programme (Table 12.1).[30] If the problem is a structural or technical one, an inter-group issue, an administrative mistake, or a conflict between only two people, team building would not be an appropriate change strategy.

Team-building activities

A team is a group of interdependent individuals who share a common purpose, have common work methods and hold each other accountable.[31] The nature of that interdependence varies, creating the following types of teams:

- groups reporting to the same supervisor, manager or executive
- groups involving people with common organisational goals
- temporary groups formed to do a specific, one-time task
- groups consisting of people whose work roles are interdependent
- groups whose members have no formal links in the organisation but whose collective purpose is to achieve tasks they cannot accomplish as individuals.

Just as there are various types of teams, so there are a number of factors that affect the outcomes of a specific team-building activity: the length of time allocated to the activity, the team's willingness to look at the way in which it operates, the length of time the team has been working together and the permanence of the team. Consequently, the results of team-building activities can range from comparatively modest changes in the team's operating mechanisms (e.g. meeting more frequently or gathering agenda items from more sources) to much deeper changes (e.g. modifying team members' behaviour patterns or the nature and style of the group's management, or developing greater openness and trust).

In general, team-building activities can be classified as follows:

- activities relevant to one or more individuals
- activities specific to the group's operation and behaviour
- activities that affect the group's relationship with the rest of the organisation.

Usually, a specific team-building activity will overlap these three categories. On occasion, a change in one area may lead to negative results in other areas. For example, a very cohesive team may increase its isolation from other groups, leading to inter-group conflict or other dysfunctional results, which in turn can have a negative impact on the total organisation unless the team develops sufficient diagnostic skills to recognise and deal with such results.

Activities relevant to one or more individuals

Almost all team-building efforts result in one or more of the team members gaining a better understanding of the way authority, inclusion, emotions, control and power affect problem solving and data gathering, and the team can then begin to experiment with different alternatives. For example, in one team, the senior member had some specific, pre-determined agenda items on which she wanted the group to take action. During the team-building process, other members asked whether or not the boss really wanted ideas and contributions from group members. They gave specific examples of the senior member's not-so-subtle manipulation to arrive at preconceived decisions and described how they felt about it. At the end of the discussion, the boss indicated her willingness to be challenged about such preconceived decisions, and the other team members expressed their increased trust and ability to make the challenge without fear of reprisal.

Sometimes, the team-building process generates pressures on individual members, such as requests for better job descriptions. Such requests could have negative results unless accompanied by agreement for further one-to-one negotiations among team members. If these demands are made of the boss, for example, he or she may feel a loss of power and authority unless the team can agree on ways in which the boss can be kept informed about what is happening. Ways of meeting these needs for control and influence without causing feelings of isolation can be explored.

Activities oriented to the group's operation and behaviour

When team-building activities are initiated, members may comment: 'We are not a team, but we want to be one' or 'We are not a team, and we do not want to lose our own autonomy through blind conformity'. Often, clarification of the purpose of the team and rewriting of priorities, goals and objectives precede team-building activities. The first phase of team building may be to establish a framework within which further work can be done. In most team-building activities, groups spend some time on finding ways to improve the mechanisms that structure their approach to work. A group may discuss and modify the balance of the agenda for their regular meetings. In addition, groups often examine their communications patterns and determine ways in which they can be improved. Frequently, this leads to dropping some communications patterns and establishing new ones that are more open and problem solving in nature.

Another issue in group operation is the effective use of time. To improve in this area, the group may examine its present planning mechanisms, introduce better ones, and identify ways of using its skills and knowledge more effectively. In addition, the group may make decisions about reorganising and redistributing the work load. As the group develops over time, it tends to become more aware of the need for action plans about problems or tasks as well as for better self-diagnosis about the effectiveness of its task-accomplishment processes.

Frequently, groups examine and diagnose the nature of their problem-solving techniques. In the earlier stage of team building, specific items are usually diagnosed. But as teams become more mature, they tend to broaden the scope of these diagnostic efforts to include areas that are more directly related to interpersonal styles and their impact on other group members. Throughout this process, group norms become clearer, and the group can provide more opportunity for members to satisfy their individual needs within the group. As a result, the team is much more willing to take risks within both the team and the organisation. Team members become more capable of facing difficulties and problems, not only within their own group but also within the larger organisation. A spirit of openness, trust and risk taking thereby develops.

Activities affecting the group's relationship with the rest of the organisation

As the team gains a better understanding of itself and becomes better able to diagnose and solve its own problems, it tends to focus on its role within the organisation. A group's relationship to the larger organisational context is an important aspect of group effectiveness.[32] As a result, the team may perceive a need to clarify its organisational role and to consider how this role can be improved or modified. Sometimes, the team may recognise a need for more collaboration with other parts of the organisation and may therefore try to establish working parties or project teams that cross the boundaries of existing teams.

As the team becomes more cohesive, it usually exerts a stronger influence on the other substances of the organisation. As this is one area in which team building can have negative effects, the process consultant must help the group to understand its role within the organisation, to develop its own diagnostic skills and to examine alternative action plans so that inter-group tensions and conflicts do not expand.

Types of team building

Family group diagnostic meeting

The family group diagnostic meeting involves the individual 'family group'—where all team members report to the same supervisor, manager or executive. This process, which has been described by a number of authors, is aimed at getting a general 'reading on the overall performance of the group, including current problems that should be worked on in the future'.[33] This technique allows the work group to get away from the work itself in order to gather data about its current performance and to formulate plans for future action. Normally, the immediate supervisor of a work group discusses the concept with the process consultant; if both agree that there is a need for such an approach, the idea is discussed with the group to obtain members' reactions.

If the reactions are favourable, the leader or process consultant may ask the group, before the meeting, to identify those areas in which performance is good and those that need improvement. In addition, group members may be asked to consider their work relationships with one another and with other groups in the organisation. The consultant may, in advance of a general meeting, interview some or all members of the work group to gather preliminary data or merely ask all the members to think about these and similar problems. Then the group assembles for a meeting that may last an entire day.

The diagnostic data can be made public in a number of ways. One method brings the total group together for a discussion, with everyone presenting ideas to the entire group. Another approach breaks the group into smaller groups in which more intensive discussions can take place, and has the subgroups report back to the larger group. A third technique has individuals pair up, discuss their ideas, then report back to the entire group. Finally, the consultant can feed back to the group his or her diagnostic findings that were collected before the meeting so that the total group can process the data and determine whether they are correct and relevant.

After the data have been made public, the issues identified are discussed and categorised. The categories might include, for example, planning, interdepartmental scheduling and tight resources. Next, the group begins to develop action plans, but the primary objective of the family group diagnostic meeting is to bring to the surface problems and issues that need to be worked on. Taking specific action is usually reserved for a later time.

The advantage of the family group diagnostic meeting is that it allows a group to participate in generating the data necessary to identify its own strengths, weaknesses and problem areas. The use of a process consultant is helpful but not essential in this process. A key issue, however, is making certain that the participants recognise that their primary objective is to identify problems rather than to solve them. As Beer has noted, 'All the advantages of direct involvement are inherent in this model, although there may be limited openness if the group has had no previous development and a supportive climate does not exist'.[34]

Family group team-building meeting

The family group team-building meeting occurs with a permanent work group, management team or a temporary, project-type team. It is one of the most widely used OD interventions.

Team development concerns the attempt to help the group learn, with the help of an OD practitioner, to identify, diagnose and solve problems. The problems may involve the *tasks* or *activities* that the group must perform, the process by which it goes about accomplishing the tasks or *interpersonal conflict* between two or more work-team members. French and Bell have defined *team development* as 'an inward look by the team at its own performance, behaviour and culture for the purposes of dropping out dysfunctional behaviours and strengthening functional ones'.[35]

The first intervention is to gather data through the use of questionnaires or, more commonly, interviews. The nature of the data gathered will vary according to the purpose of the team-building programme, the consultant's knowledge of the organisation and its culture and the individuals involved. The consultant may have already obtained data by sitting in as a process observer at staff and other meetings. The data gathered will also depend on what other OD efforts have taken place in the organisation. However they are obtained, the data usually include information on leadership styles and behaviour; goals, objectives and decision-making processes; such variables of organisational culture as trust, communication patterns and interpersonal relationships and processes; barriers to effective group functioning and task and related technical problems.

Frequently, but not always, the data-gathering stage is initiated only after the manager and his or her group have agreed that team development is a process in which they wish to engage and a date has been set for an off-site meeting. This sequence ensures that organisation members have freedom of choice and that the data-gathering stage is conducted as close to the actual meeting as possible. The off-site meeting may last between a day-and-a-half and a week, with the average being about three days. The meeting is held away from the organisation to reduce the number of interruptions and other pressures that might inhibit the process.

At the beginning of the meeting, the consultant feeds back the information that has been collected, which is usually categorised by major themes. The group must establish the agenda by placing priorities on these themes. Based on his or her knowledge of the data and the group, the consultant may help in setting the agenda or may act solely as a process observer, feeding back to the group his or her observations of what the group is doing.

As Beer points out, the consultant can play several different roles during the team-development meeting.[36] One role is that of process consultant, helping the group to understand and diagnose its own group process. The consultant may also function as a resource person, offering expertise as a behavioural scientist, or as a teacher, giving information about such areas as group dynamics, conflict resolution and leadership. However, the primary role of the consultant is to assist the group in learning to identify, diagnose and solve its own problems.

During the meeting, the group should develop action plans for becoming more effective. Frequently, merely discussing the barriers leads to improving the effectiveness of the group. One meeting, however, is rarely enough to effect major change—a series of meetings is usually needed to ensure permanent change.

Application 12.4 outlines the processes and interim outcomes of a cultural change programme in one decentralised area of the Department of Social Security, Victoria. The change was towards teamwork rather than individual performance.[37]

APPLICATION 12.4 — Towards a team-based approach

The Department of Social Security.

During the turbulent years of the 1980s, the Department of Social Security (DSS), part of the Australian Public Service, successfully embraced massive structural, technological, social and cultural change. The challenge has now changed. With the major planks of reform in place, the department began to focus on micro-reform—on continual improvement within a context of diminishing resources.

Area South Victoria was one of 20 geographic areas managing the decentralised regional network. One of the better-performing areas, it was proud of its ability to manage change successfully while maintaining high service standards. Culturally, the organisation had developed a 'can-do' mentality, and was results focused. It had a large core of experienced, hard-working and technically trained staff, but

expansion had dictated the recruitment of some 300 new staff over the preceding three years.

There was growing evidence of a certain jadedness among staff members. The area's overall performance, while still good, was showing early signs of deterioration according to performance indicators. The adrenaline rush of major reform was no longer present as a motivator. And yet, people were working as hard as ever to service their clients. The need for initiating these changes was increasingly falling on operational staff. This was in sharp contrast to the previous reforms, which had been driven primarily from Canberra, the seat of the Australian Federal Government and the Australian Public Service.

The area leaders recognised the problem and consulted widely to determine possible reasons. One of their conclusions was that the culture being replaced had recognised and rewarded individual performance. During the expansion of the 1980s, high-performing individuals had been able to progress rapidly up the corporate ladder. However, in the contracting environment of the 1990s, opportunities for promotion were far fewer. With all this in mind, the management of the area decided to develop a strategy for team development.

Aim

The aim of the strategy was to build a series of interlinking teams across the area. Given that the team structure was already in place, it was decided to work systematically with all these teams, with the objectives of:

- increasing trust among team members
- increasing the understanding of the various strengths of the individuals
- developing processes to capitalise on those strengths
- recognising and rewarding good team performance
- establishing clear strategic objectives for the area
- encouraging all staff members to contribute creatively to the achievement of these objectives.

Methodology

The change process was to occur over a significant period of time and with a large number of teams. It was important that the process be applied consistently and that it should link each team with the others. An agreed theoretical model was required, one which would provide a common language, clear principles and guidelines and be relevant to the diverse array of teams involved.

Team management systems

After considerable research into the wide range of team models available, it was decided to use the Margerison-McCann team management systems. This model identifies eight major types of work that must be done well if a team is to be successful:

- *advising*: obtaining and disseminating information
- *innovating*: creating and experimenting with ideas
- *promoting*: searching for and persuading others of new opportunities
- *developing*: assessing and testing the applicability of new approaches
- *organising*: establishing and implementing ways and means of making things work
- *producing*: operating established systems and practices on a regular basis
- *inspecting*: checking and auditing that systems are working
- *maintaining*: ensuring that standards and processes are upheld.

Using a simple, self-scored questionnaire, the model identifies an individual's team role preferences within this framework. These team roles each have a double-barrelled name, which reflects behavioural and functional aspects of the role.

While many managers carry out all of these work functions, it is likely that there will be some functions that they prefer, and because of this preference they will have developed greater proficiency in them.

The questionnaire (the team management index) generates a team management profile for each individual. This 4000-word report identifies the three strongest team role preferences and provides guidance on how to maximise strengths and compensate for weaknesses in the team environment. The TMS model is dynamic; it provides a snapshot at a point in time, while recognising that people change and develop with training and experience.

By sharing the contents of their team management profile with other team members, each person can learn about the others, and a team profile can be mapped and used to identify the balance of role preferences amongst team members and develop internal strategies to cover any 'gaps'.

It is well known that significant cultural change takes between three and five years to be fully embedded in an organisation. For this reason, it is too early to claim that the team-based strategy has been successful. However, the signs are encouraging. The use of the TMS model proved most effective in fast-tracking the process, allowing team members to deepen their awareness of both their own and others' particular skills quickly, and to develop more co-operative and trusting relationships with the rest of the team.

The model proved crucial in providing a touchstone for assessing the appropriateness of each supporting strategy. Only strategies that were congruent with the TMS model were adopted.

The manager role

Ultimately, the manager is responsible for group functioning, even though the group itself must obviously share this responsibility. Therefore, the development of a work group that can regularly stop to analyse and diagnose its own effectiveness and work process is management's task. The manager has the responsibility of diagnosing (with the group) the effectiveness of the group and taking appropriate action if the work unit shows signs of operating difficulty or stress.

TABLE 12.2	Assessing the need for a consultant

Should you use an outside consultant to help in team building?

Circle the appropriate response

1	Does the manager feel comfortable in trying out something new and different with the staff?	Yes	No	?
2	Is the staff used to spending time in an outside location working on issues of concern to the work unit?	Yes	No	?
3	Will group members speak up and give honest data?	Yes	No	?
4	Does your group generally work together without a lot of conflict or apathy?	Yes	No	?
5	Are you reasonably sure that the boss is not a major source of difficulty?	Yes	No	?
6	Is there a high commitment by the boss and unit members to achieving more effective team functioning?	Yes	No	?
7	Is the personal style of the boss and his or her management philosophy consistent with a team approach?	Yes	No	?
8	Do you feel you know enough about team building to begin a program without help?	Yes	No	?
9	Would your staff feel confident enough to begin a team-building program without outside help?	Yes	No	?

Scoring: If you have circled six or more 'yes' responses, you probably do not need an outside consultant. If you have four or more 'no' responses, you probably do need a consultant. If you have a mixture of 'yes', 'no', and '?' responses, you should probably invite a consultant to talk over the situation and make a joint decision.

Source: W. Dyer, *Team Building*, 2nd ed. © 1988 by Addison-Wesley Publishing Co. Reprinted by permission of Addison-Wesley Co., Inc. Reading, Mass.

However, many managers have not been trained to perform the data gathering, diagnosis, planning and action necessary for them to continually maintain and improve their teams. Thus, the issue of who should lead a team-building session is a function of managerial capability. The initial use of a consultant is usually advisable if a manager is aware of problems, feels that she or he may be part of the problem and believes that some positive action is needed to improve the operation of the unit, but is not exactly sure how to go about it. Dyer has provided a checklist for assessing the need for a consultant (Table 12.2). Some of the questions ask the manager to examine problems and to establish the degree to which the manager feels comfortable in trying out new and different things, the degree of knowledge about team building, whether the boss might be a major source of difficulty, and the openness of group members.

Basically, the role of the consultant is to work closely with the manager (and members of the unit) to a point at which the manager is capable of actively engaging in team-development activities as a regular and ongoing part of overall managerial responsibilities. Assuming that the manager wants and needs a consultant, the two should work together as a team in developing the initial programme, keeping in mind that (1) the manager is ultimately responsible for all team-building activities, even though the consultant's resources are available, and (2) the goal of the consultant's presence is to help the manager to learn to continue team-development processes with minimum consultant help or without the ongoing help of the consultant.

Thus, in the first stages, the consultant might be much more active in data gathering, diagnosis, and action planning, particularly if a one- to three-day off-site workshop is considered. In later stages, the consultant takes a much less active role, with the manager becoming more active and taking on the role of both manager and team developer.

When is team building applicable?

Team building is applicable to a large number of team situations, from starting a new team, to resolving conflicts among members, to revitalising a complacent team. Lewis has identified the following conditions as best suited to team building:[38]

1 patterns of communication and interaction are inadequate for good group functioning
2 group leaders desire an integrated team
3 the group's task requires interaction among members
4 the team leader will behave differently as the result of team building, and members will respond to the new behaviour
5 the benefits outweigh the costs of team building
6 team building must be congruent with the leader's personal style and philosophy.

The results of team building

The research on team building has a number of problems. First, it focuses mainly on the feelings and attitudes of group members. There is little evidence to support the notion that group performance improves as a result of team-building experiences. One study, for example, found that team building was a smashing success in the eyes of the participants.[39] However, a rigorous field test of the results over time showed no appreciable effects on either the team's or the larger organisation's functioning and efficiency. Second, the positive effects of team building are typically measured over relatively short time periods. Evidence suggests that the positive effects of off-site team building are short-lived and tend to fade after the group returns to the organisation. Third, team building rarely occurs in isolation. It is usually carried out in conjunction with other interventions that lead to, or result from, team building itself. For this reason, it is difficult to separate the effects of team building from those of the other interventions.[40]

Studies of the empirical literature present a mixed picture of the impact of team building on group performance. One review shows that team building improves process measures, such as employee openness and decision making, about 45% of the time; it improves outcome measures, such as productivity and costs, about 53% of the time.[41] Another review reveals that team building positively affects hard measures of productivity, employee withdrawal and costs about 50% of the time.[42] Still another review concludes that team building cannot be convincingly linked to improved performance. Of the 30 studies reviewed, only 10 attempted to measure changes in performance. Although these changes were generally positive, the studies' research designs were relatively weak, reducing confidence in the findings.[43] One review concluded that process interventions, such as team building and process consultation, are most likely to improve process variables, such as decision making, communication and problem solving.[44]

Boss has conducted extensive research on arresting the potential 'fade-out effects' of off-site team building.[45] He proposes that the tendency for the positive behaviours developed at off-site team building to regress once the group is back in the organisation can be checked by conducting a follow-up intervention called 'personal management interview' (PMI). This is done soon after the off-site team building and involves the team leader, who first negotiates roles with each member and then holds weekly or biweekly meetings with each member to improve communication, to resolve problems and to increase personal accountability. Boss feels that effective leader and member relationships provide the constant contact and reinforcement necessary for the longer-term success of team building. PMI is a structured approach to the maintenance of effective superior–subordinate relations.

Boss presents evidence to support the effectiveness of PMI in sustaining the long-term effects of off-site team building.[46] He compares the long-term effects of team building in ten teams that had engaged in off-site team building, and a control group with no intervention. The data show that all teams having off-site team building improved their effectiveness as measured soon after the intervention. However, only those teams that subsequently engaged in PMIs were able to maintain those effectiveness levels, while the other teams showed a substantial regression of effects over time. The data further show that PMI can help to maintain the level of group effectiveness over a three-year period.

Buller and Bell have attempted to differentiate the effects of team building from the effects of other interventions that occur along with team building.[47] Specifically, they tried to separate the effects of team building from the effects of goal setting, an intervention aimed at setting realistic performance goals and developing action plans for achieving them. In a rigorous field experiment, Buller and Bell examined the differential effects of team building and goal setting on productivity measures of underground miners. The results show that team building affects the quality of performance, while goal setting affects the quantity of performance. This differential impact was explained in terms of the nature of the mining task. The task of improving the quality of performance was more complex, unstructured and interdependent than the task of achieving quantity. This suggests that team building can improve group performance, particularly on tasks that are complex, unstructured and interdependent. The advantages of combining both interventions were inconclusive in this study, suggesting that there was a need for additional studies on the differential impact of team building and other interventions, such as goal setting.

Summary

In this chapter, we presented human process interventions aimed at interpersonal relations and group dynamics. Among the earliest interventions in OD, these change programmes help people to gain interpersonal skills, to work through interpersonal conflicts and to develop effective groups. The first intervention discussed was the T-group, the forerunner of modern OD change programmes. T-groups typically consist of a small number of strangers who meet with a professional trainer to explore the social dynamics that emerge from their interactions. OD practitioners often attend T-groups themselves to improve their interpersonal skills, or recommend that managers attend a T-group to learn more about how their behaviours affect others.

Process consultation is used not only as a way of helping groups become effective but also as a process whereby groups can learn to diagnose and solve their own problems and to continue to develop their competence and maturity. Important areas of activity include communications, roles of group members, difficulties with problem-solving and decision-making norms and leadership and authority. The basic difference between process consultation and third-party intervention is that the latter focuses on interpersonal dysfunction in social relationships between two or more *individuals* within the same organisation, and is directed more toward resolving direct conflict between those individuals.

Team building is directed toward improving group effectiveness and the ways in which members of teams work together. These teams may be permanent or temporary, but their members have either common organisational aims or work activities. The general process of team building, like process consultation, attempts to equip a group to handle its own ongoing problem solving. Selected aspects of team building include the family group diagnostic meeting and family group team-building meeting.

 ACTIVITIES

Review questions
1 What are the objectives of T-groups?
2 How can you best describe a 'process consultant'?
3 Describe the two major components of group problem solving.
4 What are the basic implications of the model for conflict resolution?
5 In a third party consultation, what skill must the third party develop in order to be successful?
6 The results of team building can be classified into three main areas — what are they?

Discussion and essay questions
1 Evaluate process consultation. When should it be used, and how does it apply to OD?
2 What is a T-group? Discuss the basic objectives of T-groups. What are their strengths and weaknesses?
3 Discuss the role of the third party consultant.
4 Discuss team building and contrast it with a T-group.
5 Discuss the role of 'communications' as it relates to T-groups, team building and process consultation.

Notes

1 J. Campbell and M. Dunnette, 'Effectiveness of T-group experiences in managerial training and development', *Psychological Bulletin*, 70 (August 1968): 73–103.

2 *Ibid.*

3 M. Dunnette, J. Campbell and C. Argyris, 'A symposium: laboratory training', *Industrial Relations*, 8 (October 1968): 1–45.

4 Campbell and Dunnette, 'Effectiveness of T-Group experiences', *op. cit.*; R. House, 'T-group education and leadership effectiveness: a review of the empirical literature and a critical evaluation', *Personnel Psychology*, 20 (Spring 1967): 1–32; J. Campbell, M. Dunnette, E. Lawler III and K. Weick, *Managerial Behavior, Performance, and Effectiveness* (New York: McGraw-Hill, 1970): 292–98.

5 J. Porras and P. Berg, 'The impact of organization development', *Academy of Management Review*, 3 (April 1978): 249–66.

6 J. Nicholas, 'The comparative impact of organization development interventions on hard criteria measures', *Academy of Management Review*, 7 (October 1982): 531–42.

7 D. Bowers, 'OD techniques and their results in 23 organizations: the Michigan IGL Study', *Journal of Applied Behavioral Science*, 9 (January–February 1973): 21–43.

8 G. Neuman, J. Edwards and N. Raju, 'Organizational development interventions: a meta-analysis of their effects on satisfaction and other attitudes', *Personnel Psychology*, 42 (1989): 461–83.

9 R. Kaplan, 'Is openness passe?' *Human Relations,* 39 (November 1986): 242.
10 E. Schein, *Process Consultation II: Lessons for Managers and Consultants* (Reading, Mass.: Addison-Wesley, 1987).
11 *Ibid,* 5–17.
12 *Ibid,* 34.
13 J. Fast, *Body Language* (Philadelphia: Lippincott, M. Evans, 1970).
14 J. Luft, 'The Johari window', *Human Relations Training News,* 5 (1961): 6–7.
15 J. Gibb, 'Defensive communication', *Journal of Communication,* 11 (1961): 141–48.
16 E. Schein, *Process Consultation: Its Role in Organization Development* (Reading, Mass.: Addison-Wesley, 1969): 44.
17 N. Clapp, 'Work group norms: leverage for organizational change, theory and application', working paper (Plainfield, N.J.: Block Petrella Weisbord, no date); R. Allen and S. Pilnick, 'Confronting the shadow organization: how to detect and defeat negative norms', *Organizational Dynamics* (Spring 1973): 3–18.
18 Schein, *Process Consultation; Process Consultation II, op. cit.*
19 Schein, *Process Consultation, op. cit.,* 80–126.
20 Schein, *Process Consultation II, op. cit.,* 32–34.
21 R. Kaplan, 'The conspicuous absence of evidence that process consultation enhances task performance', *Journal of Applied Behavioral Science,* 15 (1979): 346–60.
22 G. Lippitt, *Organizational Renewal* (New York: Appleton-Century-Crofts, 1969).
23 C. Argyris, *Organization and Innovation* (Homewood, Ill.: Richard Irwin, 1965).
24 R. Lewicki and B. Sheppard, 'Choosing how to intervene: factors affecting the use of process and outcome control in third-party dispute resolution', *Journal of Occupational Behavior,* 6 (January 1985): 49–64; H. Prein, 'Strategies for third-party intervention', *Human Relations,* 40 (1987): 699–720.
25 R. Walton, *Managing Conflict: Interpersonal Dialogue and Third-Party Roles,* 2nd ed. (Reading, Mass.: Addison-Wesley, 1987).
26 *Ibid,* 81–82.
27 *Ibid,* 83–110.
28 C. Wilson and J. Wilson, 'Cultural change: its effect on the University of Hong Kong estates office', *Facilities,* 17 (1999), 79–85.
29 T. Patten, *Organizational Development Through Team Building* (New York: John Wiley and Sons, 1981): 2; D. Stepchuck, 'Strategies for improving the effectiveness of geographically distributed work teams,' unpublished Master's thesis, Pepperdine University, Malibu, Calif., 1994.
30 W. Dyer, *Team Building: Issues and Alternatives,* 2nd ed. (Reading, Mass.: Addison-Wesley, 1987).
31 J. Katzenbach and D. Smith, *The Wisdom of Teams* (Boston: Harvard Business School Press, 1993).
32 D. Ancona and D. Caldwell, 'Bridging the boundary: external activity and performance in organizational teams', *Administrative Science Quarterly,* 37 (4, 1992): 634–65; S. Cohen, 'Designing effective self-managing work teams,' paper presented at the Theory Symposium on Self-Managed Work Teams, June 4–5, 1993, Denton, Tex.
33 M. Beer, 'The technology of organization development', in *Handbook of Industrial and Organizational Psychology*, ed. M. Dunnette (Chicago: Rand McNally, 1976): 937–93; W. French and C. Bell, *Organization Development: Behavioral Science Interventions for Organization Improvement* (Englewood Cliffs, N.J.: Prentice-Hall, 1978).
34 Beer, 'The technology of organization development', *op. cit.,* 37.
35 French and Bell, *Organization Development, op. cit.,* 115.
36 Beer, 'Organization development', *op. cit.*
37 R. Rowe, 'Towards a team-based approach', *Career Development International,* 1/2, 1996, 19–24.
38 J. Lewis III, 'Management team development: will it work for you?' *Personnel* (July/August 1975): 14–25.
39 D. Eden, 'Team development: a true field experiment at three levels of rigor', *Journal of Applied Psychology,* 70 (1985): 94–100.
40 R. Woodman and J.Sherwood, 'The role of team development in organizational effectiveness: a critical review', *Psychological Bulletin* 88 (July–November 1980): 166–86.
41 Porras and Berg, 'Impact of organization development', *op. cit.*
42 Nicholas, 'Comparative impact', *op. cit.*
43 Woodman and Sherwood, 'The role of team development', *op. cit.*

44 R. Woodman and S. Wayne, 'An investigation of positive-finding bias in evaluation of organization development interventions', *Academy of Management Journal*, 28 (December 1985): 889–913.

45 R. Boss, 'Team building and the problem of regression: the personal management interview as an intervention', *Journal of Applied Behavioral Science*, 19 (1983): 67–83.

46 *Ibid.*

47 R. Buller and C. Bell Jr, 'Effects of team building and goal setting: a field experiment', *Academy of Management Journal*, 29 (1986): 305–28.

Organisation process approaches

In Chapter 12 we presented interventions that were aimed at improving interpersonal and group processes. This chapter describes system-wide process interventions—change programmes directed at improving such processes as organisational problem solving, leadership, visioning and task accomplishment between groups—for a major subsystem, or for an entire organisation.

The first type of intervention, the organisation confrontation meeting, is among the earliest organisation-wide process approaches. It helps to mobilise the problem-solving resources of a major subsystem or an entire organisation by encouraging members to identify and confront pressing issues.

The second organisation process approach is called inter-group relations. It consists of two interventions: the inter-group conflict resolution meeting, and microcosm groups. Both interventions are aimed at diagnosing and addressing important organisation-level processes, such as conflict, the co-ordination of organisational units and diversity. The inter-group conflict intervention is specifically oriented toward conflict processes, whereas the microcosm group is a more generic system-wide change strategy.

A third organisation-wide process approach, the large-group intervention, has received considerable attention recently and is one of the fastest-growing areas in OD. Large-group interventions get a 'whole system into the room'[1] and create processes that allow a variety of stakeholders to interact simultaneously. A large-group intervention can be used to clarify important organisational values, develop new ways of looking at problems, articulate a new vision for the organisation, solve cross-functional problems, restructure operations or devise an organisational strategy. It is a powerful tool for addressing organisational problems and opportunities and for accelerating the pace of organisational change.

The final section of this chapter describes a normative approach to OD: Blake and Mouton's *Grid® Organization Development*. This is a popular intervention, particularly in large organisations. *Grid Organization Development* is a packaged programme that organisations can purchase and train members to use. In contrast to modern contingency approaches, the *Grid* proposes that there is one best way of managing organisations. Consequently, OD practitioners have increasingly questioned its applicability and effectiveness in contemporary organisations.

Organisation confrontation meeting

The confrontation meeting is an intervention designed to mobilise the resources of the entire organisation to identify problems, set priorities and action targets and begin working on identified problems. Originally developed by Beckhard,[2] the intervention can be used at any time, but is particularly useful when the organisation is in stress and when there is a gap between the top and the rest of the organisation (such as a new top manager). General Electric's 'WorkOut' programme is a recent example of how the confrontation meeting has been adapted to fit today's organisations.[3] Although the original model involved only managerial and professional people, it has since been used successfully with technicians, clerical personnel and assembly workers.

What are the steps?

The organisation confrontation meeting typically involves the following steps:

1 A group meeting of all involved is scheduled and held in an appropriate place. Usually the task is to identify problems about the work environment and the effectiveness of the organisation.

2 Groups are appointed, with representatives from all departments of the organisation. Thus, each group might have one or more members from sales, purchasing, finance, manufacturing and quality assurance. For obvious reasons, a subordinate should not be in the same group as his or her boss, and top management should form its own group. Groups can vary from 5 to 15 members, depending on such factors as the size of the organisation and available meeting rooms.

3 It must be stressed that the groups are to be open and honest and to work hard at identifying problems they see in the organisation. No one will be criticised for bringing up problems and, in fact, the groups will be judged on their ability to do so.

4 The groups are given an hour or two to identify organisation problems. Generally, an OD practitioner goes from group to group, encouraging openness and assisting the groups with their tasks.

5 The groups then reconvene in a central meeting place. Each group reports the problems it has identified and sometimes offers solutions. Because each group hears the reports of all the others, a maximum amount of information is shared.

6 Either then or later, the master list of problems is broken down into categories. Those present can do this by either the individual or manager and his or her staff leading the session. This process eliminates duplication and overlap, and allows the problems to be separated according to functional or other appropriate areas.

7 Following problem categorisation, participants are divided into problem-solving groups, whose composition may, and usually does, differ from that of the original problem-identification groups. For example, people in manufacturing may handle all manufacturing problems. Or task forces representing appropriate cross-sections of the organisation may be used.

8 Each group ranks the problems, develops a tactical action plan and determines an appropriate timetable for completing this phase of the process.

9 Each group then periodically reports its list of priorities and tactical plans of action to management or to the larger group.

10 Schedules for periodic (often monthly) follow-up meetings are established. At these sessions, the team leaders report to either top management, the other team leaders or the group as a whole regarding the progress of their group and plans for future action. The formal establishment of such follow-up meetings ensures both continuing action and the modification of priorities and timetables as needed.

Application 13.1 presents the WorkOut process at General Electric's Medical Systems business. It shows how the basic framework of a confrontation meeting can be adapted to address organisational problems such as productivity and employee involvement.[4]

APPLICATION 13.1

A Work-Out meeting at General Electric's Medical Systems business

Jack Welch and several managers at General Electric, as part of a large-scale change effort, devised a method for involving many organization members in the change process. Work-Out is a process for gathering relevant people together to discuss important issues and develop a clear action plan. There are four goals: to use employees' knowledge and energy to improve work, to eliminate unnecessary work, to build trust through a process that allows and encourages employees to speak out without being fearful and to engage in the construction of an organization that is ready to deal with the future.

At GE's Medical Systems (GEMS), internal consultants conducted extensive interviews with managers throughout the organization. The interviews revealed considerable dissatisfaction with existing systems, including performance management (too many measurement processes, not enough focus on customers, unfair reward systems and unrealistic goals), career development and organizational climate. Managers were quoted as saying:

'I'm frustrated. I simply can't do the quality of work that I want to do and know how to do. I feel my hands are tied. I have no time. I need help on how to delegate and operate in this new culture. The goal of downsizing and delaying is correct. The execution stinks. The concept is to drop the "less important" work. This just didn't happen. We still have to know all the details, still have to follow all the old policies and systems.'

In addition to the interviews, Jack Welch spent some time at GEMS headquarters listening and trying to understand the issues facing the organization.

Based on the information gathered, about 50 GEMS employees and managers gathered together for a five-day Work-Out session. The participants included the group executive who oversaw the GEMS business, his staff, employee relations managers and informal leaders from the key functional areas who were thought to be risk takers and who would challenge the *status quo*. Most of the work during the week was spent unravelling, evaluating and reconsidering the structures and processes that governed work at GEMS. Teams of managers and employees addressed business problems. Functional groups developed visions of where their operations were headed. An important part of the teams' work was to engage in 'bureaucracy busting' by identifying CRAP (Critical Review APpraisals) in the organization. Groups were asked to list needless approvals, policies, meetings and reports that stifled productivity. In an effort to increase the intensity of the work

and to encourage free thinking, senior managers were not a part of these discussions.

By the end of the week, the senior management team listened to the concerns, proposals and action plans from the different teams. During the presentations, senior GEMS managers worked hard to understand the issues, communicate with the organization members and build trust by sharing information, constraints and opportunities. Most of the proposals focused on ways to reorganize work and improve returns to the organization. According to traditional Work-Out methods, managers must make instant, on-the-spot decisions about each idea in front of the whole group. The three choices are approval, rejection with clear reasons and need more data, with a decision to be made within a month.

The five-day GEMS session ended with individuals and functional teams signing close to 100 written contracts to implement the new processes and procedures or drop unnecessary work. The contracts were between individuals, between functional groups and between managers and senior managers, and there were also organizational contracts that affected all members. One important outcome of the Work-Out effort at GEMS was a decision to involve suppliers in its internal electronic-mail network. Through this interaction, GEMS and a key supplier eventually agreed to build new-product prototypes together. Their joint efforts have led to further identification of ways to reduce costs, improve design quality or decrease cycle times.

Work-Out at GE has been very successful, but hard to measure in dollar terms. Since 1988, hundreds of Work-Outs have been held, and the concept has continued to evolve into best practice investigations, process mapping and change acceleration programs. The Work-Out process, however, is clearly based on the confrontation meeting model where a large group of people gather to identify issues and plan actions to address problems.

Results of confrontation meetings

Because organisation confrontation meetings are often combined with other approaches, such as survey feedback, determining specific results is difficult. In many cases, the results appear dramatic in mobilising the total resources of the organisation for problem identification and solution. Beckhard cites a number of specific examples in such varying organisations as a food products manufacturer, a military products manufacturer and a hotel.[5] Positive results were also found in a confrontation meeting with 40 professionals in a research and development firm.[6]

The organisation confrontation meeting is a promising approach for mobilising organisational problem solving, especially in times of low performance. Although the results of its use appear impressive, little systematic study of this intervention has been done, and there is a clear need for evaluative research.

Inter-group relations interventions

The ability to diagnose and understand inter-group relations is important for OD practitioners as:

- groups must often work with and through other groups to accomplish their goals
- groups within the organisation often create problems and demands on each other
- the quality of the relationships between groups can affect the degree of organisational effectiveness.

Two OD interventions—microcosm groups and inter-group conflict resolution—are described here. A microcosm group uses members from several groups to help solve organisation-wide problems. Inter-group issues are explored in this context, and then solutions are implemented in the larger organisation. Inter-group conflict resolution helps two groups work out dysfunctional relationships. Together, these approaches help to improve inter-group processes and lead to organisational effectiveness.

Microcosm groups

A microcosm group consists of a small number of individuals who reflect the issue being addressed.[7] For example, a microcosm group made up of members who represent a spectrum of ethnic backgrounds, cultures and races can be created to address diversity issues in the organisation. This group, with the assistance of OD practitioners, can create programmes and processes targeted on specific problems. In addition to addressing diversity problems, microcosm groups have been used to carry out organisation diagnoses, solve communications problems, integrate two cultures, smooth the transition to a new structure and address dysfunctional political processes.

Microcosm groups work through 'parallel processes', which are the unconscious changes that take place in individuals when two or more groups interact.[8] After two or more groups have interacted, members often find that their characteristic patterns of roles and interactions change to reflect the roles and dynamics of the group with whom they were relating. Put simply, one group seems to 'infect' and become 'infected' by the other groups. An example given by Alderfer helps to clarify how parallel processes work.[9]

An organisational diagnosis team had assigned its members to each of five departments in a small manufacturing company. Members of the team had interviewed each department head and several department members. They had also observed department meetings. The team was preparing to observe their first meeting of department heads and were trying to anticipate the group's behaviour in advance. At first they seemed to have no 'rational' basis for predicting the top group's behaviour because they 'had no data' from direct observation. They decided to role play the group meeting they had never seen. Diagnostic team members behaved as they thought the department heads would, and the result was almost uncanny. Team members found that they easily became engaged with one another in the simulated department-head meeting; emotional involvement occurred quickly for all participants. When the team was actually able to observe a department-head meeting, they were amazed at how closely the simulated meeting had anticipated the actual session.

Thus, if a small and representative group can intimately understand and solve a complex organisational problem for itself, its members are in a good position to recommend action to address the problem in the larger system.

What are the steps?

The process of using a microcosm group to address organisation-wide issues involves the following five steps:

1 *Identify an issue.* This step involves finding a system-wide problem to be addressed. This may result from an organisational diagnosis or may be an idea generated by an organisation member or task force. For example, one microcosm group charged with improving organisational communications was started by a division manager. He was concerned that the information provided by those reporting directly to him differed from the data he received from informal conversations with people throughout the division.

2 *Convene the group.* Once an issue has been identified, the microcosm group can be formed. The most important convening principle is that group membership needs to reflect the appropriate mix of stakeholders related to the issue. If the issue is organisational communication, then the group should contain people from all hierarchical levels and functions, including staff groups and unions, if applicable. If the issue is integrating two corporate cultures after a merger, the microcosm group should contain people from both organisations who understand their respective cultures. Following the initial set-up, the group itself becomes responsible for determining its membership. It will decide whether to add new members and how to fill vacant positions.

   Convening the group also draws attention to the issue and gives the group status. Members also need to be perceived as credible representatives of the problem. This will increase the likelihood that organisation members will listen to, and follow, the suggestions they make.

3 *Provide group training.* Once the microcosm group has been established, training is provided in group problem solving and decision making. Team-building interventions may also be appropriate. Group training focuses on establishing a group mission or charter, working relationships between members, group decision-making norms and definitions of the problem to be addressed.

   From a group-process perspective, OD practitioners may need to observe and comment on how the group develops. Because the group is a microcosm of the organisation, it will tend, through its behaviour and attitudes, to reflect the problem in the larger organisation. For example, if the group is addressing communication problems in the organisation, it is quite likely that it will have its own difficulties with communication. Recognising within the group the problem or issue it was formed to address is the first step toward solving the problem in the larger organisation.

4 *Address the issue.* This step involves solving the problem and implementing solutions. OD practitioners may help the group to diagnose, design, implement and evaluate changes. A key issue is gaining wider organisation commitment to implementing the group's solutions. The following factors can facilitate such ownership. First, a communication plan should link group activities to the organisation. This may include publishing minutes from team meetings; inviting organisation members, such as middle managers, union representatives or hourly workers, into the meetings and making presentations to different organisational groups. Second, group members need to be visible and accessible to management and labour. This can ensure that the appropriate support and resources are developed for the recommendations. Third, problem-solving processes should include an appropriate level of participation by organisation members. Different data collection methods can be used to gain member input and to produce ownership of the problem and solutions.

5 *Dissolve the group.* The microcosm group can be disbanded after the successful implementation of changes. This typically involves writing a final report or holding a final meeting.

Results of microcosm groups

The microcosm group intervention derives from an inter-group relations theory developed by Alderfer and has been applied by him to communications and race-relations problems. A microcosm group that addressed communications issues improved the way in which meetings were conducted, developed a job posting, career development and promotion programme and conducted new employee orientations.[10] In addition, the group assisted in the development, administration and feedback of an organisation-wide employee opinion survey. Alderfer also reported seven years of longitudinal data on a race-relations advisory group in a large organisation.[11] Over time, white members showed significant improvements in their race-relations perceptions; African Americans consistently perceived more evidence of racism in the organisation; and attendance at the meetings varied both over time and by race. In addition to the intra-group data, the case documented several changes in the organisation, including the development of a race-relations competency document, the implementation of a race-relations workshop and the creation of an upward mobility policy.

A dearth of research exists on microcosm groups. This is partly due to the difficulty of measuring parallel processes and associating them with measures of organisational processes. More research on this intervention is needed.

Resolving inter-group conflict

This intervention is specifically designed to help two groups or departments within an organisation resolve dysfunctional conflicts. Inter-group conflict is neither good nor bad in itself. In some cases, conflict among departments is necessary and productive for organisations. This applies in organisations where there is little interdependence among departments. Here, departments are independent, and conflict or competition among them can lead to higher levels of productivity. For example, organisations based on different product lines might want to promote competition among the product groups. This might increase each group's productivity, thus adding to the overall effectiveness of the firm.

In other organisations, especially those with very interdependent departments, conflict may become dysfunctional.[12] Two or more groups may become polarised, and continued conflict may result in the development of defensiveness and negative stereotypes of the other group. Polarisation may be indicated by such statements as: 'Any solution they come up with is wrong'; 'We find that nobody in that group will co-operate with us'; or 'What do you expect of those idiots?' It is particularly the case that, when inter-group communication is necessary, the amount and quality of communication usually drops off. Groups become defensive and begin seeing the others as 'the enemy', rather than in either positive or neutral terms. As the amount of communication decreases, the amount of mutual problem solving also falls off. The tendency increases for one group to sabotage the efforts of the other group, either consciously or unconsciously.

What are the steps?

A basic strategy for improving interdepartmental or inter-group relationships is to change the perceptions (perhaps, more accurately, misperceptions) that the two groups have of each other. One formal approach for accomplishing this consists of a ten-step procedure, originally described by Blake and his associates.[13]

1 A consultant external to the two groups obtains their agreement to work directly on improving inter-group relationships. (The use of an outside consultant is highly recommended because, without the moderating influence of such a neutral third party, it is almost impossible for the two groups to interact without becoming deadlocked and polarised in a defensive position.)

2   A time is set for the two groups to meet—preferably away from their normal work situations.

3   The consultant, together with the managers of the two groups, describes the purpose and objectives of the meeting—the development of better mutual relationships, the exploration of the perceptions the groups have of each other and the development of plans for improving the relationship. The two groups are asked the following or similar questions: 'What qualities or attributes best describe our group?'; 'What qualities or attributes best describe the other group?' and 'How do we think the other group will describe us?' Then the two groups are encouraged to establish norms of openness for feedback and discussion.

4   The two groups are then placed in separate rooms and asked to write their answers to the three questions. Usually, an outside consultant works with each group to help the members become more open and to encourage them to develop lists that accurately reflect their perceptions, both of their own image and of the other group.

5   After completing their lists, the two groups are then brought together again. A representative from each group presents the written statements. Only the two representatives are allowed to speak. The primary objective at this stage is to make certain that the images, perceptions and attitudes are presented as accurately as possible and to avoid the arguments that might arise if the two groups openly confronted each other. Questions, however, are allowed to ensure that both groups clearly understand the written lists. Justifications, accusations or other statements are not permitted.

6   When it is clear that the two groups thoroughly understand the content of the lists, they again separate. By this time, a great number of misperceptions and discrepancies have already been brought to light.

7   The task of the two groups (almost always with a consultant as a process observer) is to analyse and review the reasons for the discrepancies. The emphasis is on solving the problems and reducing the misperceptions. The actual or implicit question is not whether the perception of the other group is right or wrong but rather 'How did these perceptions occur? What actions on the part of our group may have contributed to this set of perceptions?'

8   When the two groups have worked through the discrepancies, as well as the areas of common agreement, they meet to share both the identified discrepancies and their problem-solving approaches to those discrepancies. Because the primary focus is on the behaviour that underlies the perceptions, free and open discussion is encouraged between the two groups, and their joint aim is to develop an overall list of remaining and possible sources of friction and isolation.

9   The two groups are then asked to develop specific plans of action for solving specific problems and for improving their relationships.

10 When the two groups have gone as far as possible in formulating action plans, at least one follow-up meeting is scheduled so that the two groups can report on actions that have been implemented, identify any further problems that have emerged and, where necessary, formulate additional action plans.

In addition to this formal approach to improving interdepartmental or inter-group relationships, there are a number of more informal procedures. Beckhard asks each of the two groups to develop a list of what irritates or exasperates them about the other group and to predict what they think the other group will say about them.[14] A more simplified approach, although perhaps not as effective, is simply to bring the two groups together, dispense with the written lists that have been developed in isolation, and discuss only common problems and irritations.

Different approaches to resolving inter-group conflict form a continuum varying from behavioural solutions to attitudinal change solutions.[15] Behavioural methods are oriented to keeping the relevant parties physically separate and specifying the limited conditions under which interaction will occur. Little attempt is made to understand or to change how members of each group see the other. Conversely, attitudinal methods, such as exchanging group members or requiring intense interaction with important rewards or opportunities clearly tied to co-ordination, are directed at changing how each group perceives the other. Here, it is assumed that perceptual distortions and stereotyping underlie the conflict and need to be changed to resolve it.

Most of the OD solutions to inter-group conflict reviewed in this section favour attitudinal change strategies. However, these interventions typically require considerably more skill and time than the behavioural solutions. Changing attitudes can be quite difficult in conflict situations, especially if the attitudes are deep-seated and form an integral part of people's personalities. Attitudinal change interventions should be reserved for those situations in which behavioural solutions might not work.

Behavioural interventions seem most applicable in situations in which task interdependence between the conflicting groups is relatively low and predictable. For example, the task interaction between the production and maintenance departments might be limited to scheduled periodic maintenance on machines. Here, higher management can physically separate the departments and specify the limited conditions under which they should interact. Where the shared task requires only limited interaction, that interaction can be readily programmed and standardised.

Attitudinal change interventions seem necessary when task interdependence between the conflicting groups is high and unpredictable, such as might be found between the research and production departments during the course of introducing a new product. Here, the two departments need to work together closely, often at unpredictable times and with novel, complex issues. When conflicts arise because of misperceptions, they must be worked through in terms of people's perceptions and attitudes. The shared task does not permit physical separation or limited, specific interaction. It is in these highly interdependent and unpredictable task situations that the conflict resolution interventions discussed in this section are most appropriate.

Application 13.2 uses the example of a small, non-profit organisation, which works in an environment where there is a need for unity, but where conflict between the volunteers and paid workers, and among the volunteers themselves, had become the overriding consideration in all decision making and was paralysing the organisation.[16]

APPLICATION 13.2   A culture of conflict

St B's describes itself as 'a non-school organisation providing post-school educational and social support to students with disabilities by developing, implementing and monitoring individual transition programmes from school to adult life' (St B's *Statement of Commitment*, 1994). It is based in Brisbane, Australia, has a duly-constituted sponsoring body in the Catholic Church, and caters for young people in the 18–21 year age group. Its target group is in the range of mild to moderate level of intellectual disability. Funding comes from the Church, the TAFE (Technical and Further Education) system of the Queensland Government Education Department and from fees paid by the parents and carers of the students enrolled in the courses.

It was obvious from the beginning of the consultancy that St B's was not performing in a manner acceptable to its funding bodies. Student numbers were falling; courses were being offered but not run; marketing of courses was negligible; paid staff were unhappy; there were a number of breakdowns in communication between the committee [voluntary parents/carers] and the paid employees and between the members of Management Committee themselves; there was no negotiation, bargaining or planning; people's individual skills, abilities and values seemed not to be accepted and, overall, members of the

Management Committee were unable to agree on any issues of significance. As a result—and probably most importantly for the future of the organisation—St B's was not meeting TAFE's evaluation criteria for funding.

The consultancy team therefore looked for reasons for what appeared to be an almost complete paralysis of espoused activities. One or more consultants attended six regular monthly meetings of St B's Management Committee, held a number of discussions with individual members of the committee and the two full-time paid staff, had discussions among themselves and made a search of what they felt to be the relevant literature before coming to conclusions about a culture of conflict.

As a result of this research into St B's and the literature relevant to the situation there as it was perceived, they came to a number of conclusions about the culture of conflict. The consultants concluded that the conflict being observing in St B's was partly value dissonance that arose from the accountability and efficiency procedures expected of them by government funding agencies, which were keen to manage and be accountable from an instrumental value paradigm. Certainly Australian Public Service reforms have lauded the values of efficiency, access and equity—of which the literature says that efficiency gets prime position.

The consultants also concluded that St B's was suffering from *affective conflict*, which resulted in an intolerance of others' opinions and motives and consequently was crippling the

organisation's ability to function as it could not set goals or present a coherent, united front when applying for government grants. There was almost total paralysis in decision making. This affective conflict appeared to derive from a combination of the features specific to non-profits and to conflict situations in general.

The overall conclusion was that it was not the lack of management skills that was crippling St B's; it was the amount of affective conflict in the organisation. While needs existed in all areas that had been covered in the training programme, the consultants felt that, if the conflict could be managed, the needs in the other areas would be a long way towards being solved too. However, affective conflict had become endemic at St B's—it was simply part of the culture. And, like most culturally based things, it was not recognised, and certainly not openly and honestly acknowledged.

Therefore, the session that the team conducted on conflict was regarded very warily. The conflict resolution exercise was treated as an interesting, but largely irrelevant time filler. This attitude is typical of something that is deeply ingrained in the culture of an organisation; it is unconscious and non-debatable. Lauer's recommendation that an organisation needs to define its culture to include an articulated respect for differences is very difficult to follow if the differences are not even acknowledged.

In the case of St B's, it would require an entire redefinition of the culture, and, in the light of the covert nature of the conflict, it is doubtful whether this could be done from within the organisation.

Results of inter-group conflict interventions

A number of studies have been done on the effects of inter-group conflict resolution. In his original study, Blake reported vastly improved relationships between the union and management.[17] In a later study, Bennis used Blake's basic design to improve relationships between two groups of State Department officials—high-level administrative officers and officers in the Foreign Service.[18] Initially, there was much mutual distrust, negative stereotyping, blocked communication and hostility between the two groups. 'Each side perceived the other as more threatening than any realistic overseas enemy.'[19] Although no hard data were obtained, the intervention seemed to improve relationships so that the two groups 'at least understood the other side's point of view'.

Golembiewski and Blumberg used a modification of the Blake design that involved an exchange of 'images' among both organisational units and individuals in the marketing division of a large firm.[20] An attitude questionnaire was used to make before-and-after comparisons. The results were found to be different for more or less 'deeply involved' individuals or units. In general, the more deeply involved individuals or units (promotion, regions and divisions and sales) reflected more positive attitudes toward collaboration and had greater feelings of commitment to the success of the entire organisation. Less deeply involved positions or units (such areas as sales training, hospital sales and trade relations) did not show any particular trends in attitudinal changes, either positive or negative.

French and Bell, who used a somewhat similar design, reported that they were able to work successfully with three groups simultaneously.[21] They obtained positive results in their work with key groups in an Indian tribal organisation—the tribal council, the tribal staff and the Community Action Programme (CAP). The researchers asked each group to develop perceptions of the other two, as well as of itself, and to share those perceptions in the larger group. The tribal council developed four lists—both favourable and unfavourable items about the tribal staff, a similar list about the CAP, and predictions as to what the staff and CAP, respectively, would say about the council.

Once each group had developed its lists, the results were shared in a three-group meeting, and the similarities and dissimilarities in the various lists worked through. According to the researchers, the use of this method reduces inter-group problems and friction while increasing communications and interactions.

Huse and Beer have described positive results arising from periodic cross-departmental meetings, whereby personnel within one department would meet, in sequence, with those from other departments to discuss perceptions, expectations and strong and weak points about one another.[22] Interviews indicated that the participants found the meetings extremely helpful. As one engineer said, 'Before we had these meetings, I really wasn't concerned about the people in the other departments except to feel that they weren't doing their job. After we held the interdepartmental meetings, I began to understand some of their problems. I began to listen to them and to work with them.'[23]

In another study, Huse found that bringing representatives of different groups together to work on common work-related problems had a marked effect, not only on relationships among a number of different manufacturing groups, but also on the quality of the product, which increased by 62%.[24] The basic tactic in this study was to ensure that representatives of two or more groups worked jointly on each work-related problem.

Based on their experience at TRW Systems, Fordyce and Weil developed a modified approach whereby each group builds three lists—one containing 'positive feedback' items (those things the group values and likes about the other group), a 'bug' list (those things the group dislikes about the other group) and an 'empathy' list (predictions about what the other group's list would contain).[25] When the groups come together, they build a master list of major concerns and unresolved problems, which are assigned priorities and developed into an agenda. When they have completed the task, the subgroups report the results of their discussions to the total group, which then develops a series of action steps for improving the relations between the groups and commits itself to following through. For each action step, specific responsibilities are assigned, and an overall schedule developed for prompt completion of the action steps.

In conclusion, the technology for improving inter-group relations is promising. A greater distinction between attitudinal and behavioural changes needs to be made in planning effective inter-group interventions. A greater variety of interventions that address the practical difficulties of bringing two groups together is also necessary. Finally, a better background of knowledge must be developed as to when perceptions and behaviour need to be diverse and when they need to be brought more closely together. Growing knowledge and theory suggest that conflict can be either functional or dysfunctional, depending on the circumstances. Further research as to when conflict should be intensified and when conflict should be reduced is needed. In short, conflict should be managed.[26]

Large-group interventions

System-wide process interventions in the third group are called large-group interventions. These change programmes have been variously referred to as 'search conferences', 'open space meetings' and 'future searches'.[27] They focus on issues that affect the whole organisation or large segments of it, such as budget cuts, introduction of new technology and changes in senior leadership. The defining feature of large-group interventions is bringing together large numbers of organisation members, often more than 100, for a two- to four-day meeting or conference. Here, members work together to identify and resolve organisation-wide problems, to design new approaches to structuring and managing the firm or to propose future directions for the organisation. Large-group interventions are among the fastest-growing OD applications. Large-group interventions can vary on several dimensions including purpose, size, length, structure and number. The purpose of these change methods can range from solving particular organisational problems to envisioning future strategic directions. Large-group interventions have been run with groups of less than 50 to more than 2000 participants and have lasted between one and five days. Some large-group processes are relatively planned and structured, although others are more informal.[28] Some interventions involve a single large-group meeting, and others include a succession of meetings to accomplish system-wide change in a short period of time.[29]

Despite these differences, large-group interventions have similar conceptual foundations and methods. Large-group interventions have evolved over the past 25 years and represent a combination of open systems applications and 'futuring' and 'visioning' exercises. Open systems approaches direct attention to how organisations interact with, and are shaped by, their environments. A popular method used in large-group interventions is called 'environmental scanning', which involves mapping the pressures placed on the organisation by external stakeholders, such as regulatory agencies, customers and competitors.[30] This analysis helps members devise new ways of responding to, and influencing, the environment. Futuring and visioning exercises guide members in creating 'images of potential' towards which the organisation can grow and develop.[31] Focusing on the organisation's potential rather than on its problems can increase members' energy for change.

What are the steps?

Conducting a large-group intervention generally involves the following three steps:

1 *Preparing for the large-group meeting.* A design team consisting of OD practitioners and several members from the organisation is convened to organise the event. The team generally addresses three key ingredients for successful large-group meetings: a compelling meeting theme, appropriate members to participate, and relevant tasks to address the theme.

   First, large-group interventions require a compelling reason or focal point for change. Although 'people problems' can be an important focus, more powerful reasons for large-group efforts include impending mergers or reorganisations, responding to environmental threats and opportunities or proposing radical organisational changes. Whatever the focal point for change, senior leaders need to make clear to others the purpose of the large-group meeting. Ambiguity about the reason for the intervention can dissipate members' energy and commitment for change. For example, a large-group meeting that successfully envisioned a hospital's future organisation design was viewed as a failure by a few key managers who thought that the purpose had been to cut costs from the hospital's budget. Their subsequent lack of support stalled the change effort.

   A second issue in preparing for a large-group meeting includes inviting relevant people to participate. A fundamental goal of large-group interventions is to 'get the whole system in the room'. This involves inviting as many people as possible who have a stake in the conference theme, and who are energised and committed to conceiving and initiating change. Senior managers, suppliers, union leaders, internal and external customers, trade group representatives, government and regulatory officials and organisation members from a variety of jobs, genders, races and ages are potential participants.

The third ingredient for successful large-group meetings is to have a range of task activities that enable the participants to fully address the conference theme. As described below, these tasks should be typically assigned to several subgroups, so that each is responsible for examining its own theme and drawing conclusions for action. Generally, participants rely on their own experience and expertise to address system-wide issues, rather than drawing on resources that they have gathered from outside the large-group meeting. This ensures that the meeting can be completed within the allotted time and that members can fully participate as important sources of information.

2   *Conducting the meeting.* The flow of events in a large-group meeting can vary greatly according to its purpose and the framework adopted. These gatherings, however, tend to involve three sequential activities: developing common ground among participants, discussing the issues and creating an agenda for change.

First, participants develop sufficient common ground among themselves to permit joint problem solving. This generally involves team-building activities. One exercise for creating teamwork is called 'appreciating the past'. It asks participants to examine the significant events, milestones and highlights of the organisation's previous 20 years.[32] It demonstrates that participants share a common history, although they may come from different departments, age groups or hierarchical levels. Another exercise asks participants to create a 'market place'.[33] Individuals present to the group their issues, concerns or suggestions around the conference theme. These issues are posted on a wall and grouped into common topics that represent the large group's definition of the key facets of the problem.

Second, members discuss the system-wide issue or theme. To promote widespread participation, members are typically organised into subgroups of eight to ten people, representing as many stakeholder viewpoints as possible. The subgroups may be asked to address a general question, such as 'What are the opportunities for new business in our global market?', or they may be asked to focus on a specific issue, such as 'How can we improve quality but still cut costs on a particular product line?' Subgroup members brainstorm answers to these questions, record them on flipchart paper, and share them with the larger group. The responses from the different subgroups are compared, and common themes identified. Other methods, such as presentations to the large group, small-group meetings on particular aspects of the conference theme or spontaneous meetings of interest to the participants, are used to discuss the conference theme and distribute information to members.

The final task of large-group meetings is creating an agenda for change. Participants are asked to reflect on what they have learned at the meeting and to suggest changes for themselves, their department and the whole organisation. Members from the same department are often grouped together to discuss their proposals and to decide on action plans, timetables and accountabilities.

Action items for the total organisation are referred to a steering committee that addresses organisation-wide policy issues and action plans. At the conclusion of the large-group meeting, the departmental subgroups and the steering committee report their conclusions to all participants and seek initial commitment for change.

3   *Follow-up on the meeting outcomes.* Follow-up efforts are vital if the action plans from large-scale interventions are to be implemented. These activities involve communicating the results of the meeting to the rest of the organisation, gaining wider commitment to the changes, and structuring the change process. In those cases where all the members of the organisation were involved in the large-group meeting, implementation can proceed immediately according to the timetable included in the action plans.

Results of large-group interventions

In the past ten years, the number of case studies describing the methods and results of large-group interventions has increased dramatically. Large-group interventions have been conducted in a variety of organisations, including Hewlett-Packard and Rockport; around a variety of themes or issues, including natural resource conservation, community development and strategic change; and in a variety of countries, including Pakistan, England and India.[34] Despite this proliferation of practice, however, little systematic research has been done on the effects of large-group interventions. Because these change efforts often set the stage for subsequent OD interventions, it is difficult to isolate their specific results from those of the other changes. Anecdotal evidence from practitioners suggests the following benefits from large-group interventions: increased energy toward organisational change, improved feelings of 'community', ability to see 'outside the boxes' and improved relationships with stakeholders. Clearly, systematic research is needed on this important system-wide process intervention.

Application 13.3 describes the experience of Formway Furniture Ltd (NZ) with their concept of delivery windows determined after consultation with stakeholders.[35]

APPLICATION 13.3

Implementation of delivery modes

Formway Furniture Ltd, which was established in 1956, is an engineering firm making chairs and office furniture. In 1969, it was the first company in New Zealand, and among the first in the world, to use gas springs in its chairs. Since the purchase by its current owners in 1981, sales have increased 20 times and the number of employees has grown from nine to ninety. It has been awarded the 'Prince Philip Design Award' for its office chair range. In 1989 it began an assembly and distribution operation in Australia. The owners are working directors and describe themselves as 'innovators at heart, interested in improving both the products they make, the way they do things and enjoying themselves while making the business grow'.

The company discovered that their customers valued delivery reliability much more highly than fast delivery. That is, the customer wanted the product when they said they wanted it and were less concerned about long lead times. Therefore, the company had to find a way of improving their on-time delivery performance and manufacturing flexibility. The firm moved from quoting fixed due dates to ascertaining the customer's delivery window. It helped that the firm's main market consisted of customers who were installing capital items and whose schedules were generally derived from project management requirements.

Many customers found the concept of delivery windows strange and difficult to understand. In such cases, the marketing staff worked closely with the customer to identify what the earliest and latest due dates would be. This kept the company customer-orientated rather than allowing manufacturing to tell marketing what the customer delivery time would be. As a result of the introduction of this concept, some of Formway's customers have been embarrassed by the on-time arrival of the products. They were so accustomed to unreliable delivery performance that they routinely asked for goods earlier than they needed them. Since they are working closely with reliable carriers, the company can achieve delivery to a specified day, and even a specified hour of the day if required, throughout New Zealand.

The company has increased the amount of information going to the shop floor. Workers identify with the customer and the end user, since both names appear on the job sheet. Previously the workers had only a job number. The job sheet also indicates the value of the order, so that workers can measure their performance on a daily basis. This has more meaning for them than hearing sometime later what the previous month's figures had been. The final assembly workers are given a daily dollar value of production to achieve, and the upstream sections respond through the Kanban pull system.

('Kanban' is a manufacturing term that describes materials that are worked upon as they arrive at each work station using visible records or cards. (It is also known as a 'pull' system, which is a basis for Just-In-Time [JIT] management.) The workers have more of the process under their control as they schedule their own production, because they also know the delivery window for the order. So for management, delivery windows are an automatic prioritising approach to production planning which is instantly variable.

Grid® Organization Development: a normative approach

Normative approaches to system-wide process intervention suggest that there is one best way of managing all organisations. This contrasts sharply with modern contingency theory, which proposes that managerial practices should vary according to the organisation's environment, technology and member needs and values. Two interventions represent the primary normative approaches. Likert's System 4 model was discussed in Chapter 1 as an important element in the history of OD, but its application in current organisations has declined substantially.

Blake and Mouton's *Grid® Organization Development*, however, has been extensively applied in organisations and is still used today. Both approaches originated from research about managerial and organisational effectiveness. Over time, instruments for measuring managerial practices, as well as procedures for helping organisations achieve the prescribed objectives, were developed. These instruments and methods evolved into packaged programmes for OD, which are purchased by organisations or practitioners who become trained exclusively in their use.

Probably the most structured intervention in OD, Blake and Mouton's *Grid® Organization Development* derives from research on corporate excellence.[36] It consists of six phases that are designed to analyse an entire business and increase its overall effectiveness.

Blake and Mouton gathered data on organisational excellence from 198 organisations located in the US, Japan and Great Britain.[37] They found that the two foremost barriers to excellence were planning and communication. Rather than accept these barriers at face value, the researchers treated them as symptoms of deeper problems.

For Blake and Mouton, 'planning as a barrier' is a symptom of a deeper problem that results from either organisational strategy based on faulty logic or the absence of a strategy as such.[38] To achieve excellence, the organisation should systematically develop an overall strategic model that contains explicit descriptions of the nature of the organisation and its client or market, clear specifications for the optimum organisational structure and clear descriptions of 20 to 35 major goals or policies that can serve as guidelines for immediate and future decisions and actions. Organisational planning is sound when the properties of the model have been clearly expressed and are well understood throughout the organisation. A primary objective of *Grid® Organization Development* is to improve planning by developing a strategy for organisational excellence based on clear logic.

Like planning as a barrier, 'communications as a barrier' is only a symptom; the cause itself lies deeper. Blake and Mouton believe that the underlying cause of communications difficulties is the character of supervision, which in turn is highly influenced by knowledge (or lack of knowledge) about explicit theories of human behaviour. Although technically competent, a supervisor who does not have a good understanding of human motivation and group dynamics will not be able to generate the best results. Such a supervisor will not be able to establish or work within a climate that provides clear objectives, full commitment and the closeness of co-operation that results from the sound utilisation of people. Consequently, a second primary objective of *Grid® Organization Development* is to help managers gain the necessary knowledge and skills to supervise effectively.

Blake and Mouton developed a grid to help supervisors understand their managerial style and possibly to improve it. The *Leadership Grid®* postulates two basic assumptions about managerial behaviour: (1) *concern for production*, the emphasis on accomplishing productive tasks and (2) *concern for people*, for those who get the work done (compare this to the *Consultant Styles Matrix* in Application 3.1). According to Blake and Mouton, concern for production covers a wide range of considerations, such as the number of creative ideas developed, the quality of policy decisions, the thoroughness and quality of staff services, efficiency and workload measurements or the number of accounts processed or units of output. Concern for production is not limited to things but may also involve human accomplishment within the organisation, whatever the assigned tasks or activities.

Concern for people encompasses a diversity of issues, including concern for the individual's personal worth, good working conditions, a degree of involvement or commitment to completing the job, security, a fair salary structure and fringe benefits and good social and other relationships. The relationship between concern for production and concern for people is shown in Figure 13.1.

Figure 13.1 shows 81 possible variations of the two aspects of management—concern for people and concern for production. Blake and Mouton focus on the four extreme positions, as well as on the middle 5,5 style.[39] These five managerial styles are described below.[40]

The 1,1 managerial style

The manager who has a 1,1 orientation to jobs and people demonstrates little concern for either people or production. The approach is to stay out of trouble. In a sense, the manager has accepted defeat and is primarily concerned with job security and not making waves.

The 1,9 managerial style

The 1,9 manager exhibits a low concern for production but a high concern for people. To the 1,9 manager, people's feelings, attitudes and needs are valuable in their own right, and this type of manager strives to provide subordinates with work conditions that provide ease, security and comfort.

The 9,1 managerial style

This style, which falls in the lower right-hand corner of the grid, is characterised by low concern for people, together with a high concern for production. The 9,1 manager assumes that there must be a conflict between personal needs and the organisation's needs for production. Because it is impossible to satisfy both, the 9,1 manager reduces the dilemma by minimising the attitudes and feelings of subordinates, primarily by arranging work conditions. As a result, little attention is given to individual creativity, conflict and commitment, and the focus is on the work organisation.

The 5,5 managerial style

The 5,5 managerial style, in the middle of the grid, indicates intermediate concern for people and for production. The 5,5 manager assumes conflict between organisational goals and the needs of people in much the same way as the 9,1 or the 1,9 manager. However, the mode of conflict resolution is different. The 5,5 manager seeks compromise among these 'inevitable' conflicts of organisational and personal needs. He or she assumes

FIGURE 13.1   The leadership grid

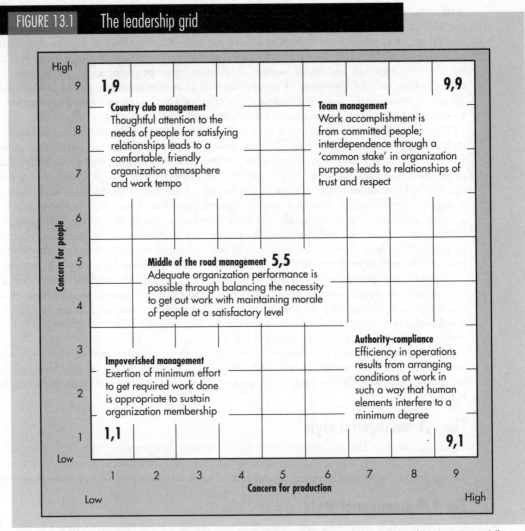

Source: R. Blake and A. Adams McCanse *Leadership Dilemmas—Grid Solutions* (formerly the *Managerial Grid* by R. Blake and J. Mouton). Houston: Gulf Publishing Co., p. 29, copyright © 1991, Scientific Methods, Inc. Reproduced by permission of the owners.

that practical people know they have to work to get the job done and that compromise, trading and paying attention to both job demands and personal needs will allow subordinates to be relatively satisfied.

The 9,9 managerial style

The 9,9 managerial style is located in the upper right-hand corner of the grid. The basic assumptions behind this managerial style are qualitatively and quantitatively different from those underlying the other managerial styles, which assume that there is an inherent conflict between the needs of the organisation and the needs of people. The 9,9 manager, by contrast, believes that the needs of both the organisation and its members can be integrated by involving people in making decisions about the strategies and conditions of work. Therefore, the basic aim of the 9,9 manager is to develop cohesive work teams that can achieve both high productivity and high morale.

Blake and Mouton propose that the 9,9 managerial style is the most effective in overcoming the communications barrier to corporate excellence. By showing a high concern for both people and production, managers allow employees to think and influence the organisation. This results in active support for organisational plans. Employee participation means that better communication is critical; therefore, necessary information is shared by all relevant parties. Moreover, better communication means self-direction and self-control, rather than unquestioning, blind obedience. Organisational commitment arises out of discussion, deliberation and debate over major organisational issues.

The application of *Grid® Organization Development* occurs in the following six phases, which are aimed at overcoming the planning and communications barriers to corporate excellence.

Phase 1—The Grid seminar

In this one-week programme, participants analyse their managerial style and learn team methods of problem solving. First, top management attends the seminar and then returns and takes the next level of management through a similar experience. In addition to assessing themselves through the use of questionnaires and case studies, participants receive feedback on their styles from other group members.

Phase 2—Teamwork development

In this phase of the *Grid* programme, managers are expected to do team development in at least two different groups—with their own boss and with their immediate subordinates. As with the *Grid* seminar itself, the team-building phase is usually conducted in an off-the-job setting so that team members can work without interruption. Usually, as in the seminar, team building starts with top management: the manager and the corporate staff or the manager and the department, division or plant staff. There is usually a steering committee or OD co-ordinator to ensure that the team-building efforts are co-ordinated throughout the organisation, to provide materials, and to establish overall priorities.

Phase 3—Inter-group development

Although an organisation may have various sections or units, each with specialised tasks and different goals, it must still work as a whole if it is to achieve organisational excellence. In most organisations, a fair amount of inter-group or interdepartmental conflict is present. Each group begins to build negative stereotypes of the other groups, which can easily escalate into subtle or not-so-subtle power struggles that result in win–lose situations. Improving inter-group relations involves the following steps:

1 before the sessions, each person involved prepares a written description of the actual working relationship as contrasted with the ideal relationship
2 each group isolates itself for several days to summarise its perceptions of the actual and ideal relationships
3 the two groups meet and, using a spokesperson, limit their interaction to comparing their perceptions
4 the two groups then work on making the relationship more productive. This action phase is completed when both groups have a clear understanding of the specific actions that each group will take and how the actions will be followed up.[41]

Phase 4—Developing an ideal strategic organisation model

In Phase 4, the top managers in the organisation work toward achieving a model of organisational excellence, following six basic rules:

1 clear definitions of minimum and optimum organisational financial objectives
2 clear, explicit definitions of the character and nature of organisational activities
3 clear operational definitions of the character and scope of markets, customers or clients
4 an organisational structure that integrates operations for synergistic results
5 basic policies for organisational decision making
6 approaches to implementing growth capacity and avoiding stagnation or obsolescence.

Phase 5—Implementing the ideal strategic model

Blake and Mouton point out that if the first four phases have been successfully completed, many of the barriers to implementation will already have been remodelled or reduced, managers will have a good understanding of *Grid* theories and communication blocks will have been identified and, one would hope, resolved. Implementing the ideal strategic model thus becomes a matter of keeping certain considerations in mind. First, the nature of the organisation and its market or environment defines business segments that are contained within the ideal organisational strategic model. Second, specific organisational units, such as cost centres or profit centres, are identified. Third, planning teams are appointed for each autonomous unit. The planning team is responsible for preparing and testing the unit's operation in accordance with the specifics of the ideal strategic model for the larger organisation. Fourth, because the units cannot be completely autonomous, an overall headquarters organisation must be established. This organisation must have, at a minimum, the ability to develop executive talent, develop investment capital and provide service to the entire organisation more cheaply or efficiently than can be done by the local decision centres or autonomous units. Finally, the planning co-ordinator and the corporate strategy-implementation committee need to ensure that the implementation strategy is clearly understood while it is in progress, so that enthusiasm for the change can be maintained and resistance to the development and to implementation of the ideal strategic model kept to a minimum.

Phase 6—Systematic critique

The final phase in achieving ideal organisational excellence is the systematic effort to examine the organisation's progress towards that goal, including formal and informal measurement and evaluation of direction, rate, quality and quantity of progress. Phase 6 also allows for the systematic planning of future development activities. Because communication and planning are the greatest barriers to organisational excellence, this critique becomes more important as an organisation goes through the *Grid* process.[42]

Application 13.4 presents an example of *Grid® Organization Development* in a large manufacturing plant.[43]

APPLICATION 13.4 | Organisation development at the Sigma plant

One of the earliest and most extensive applications of the *Grid* occurred at the Sigma plant of a large, multi-plant company. Sigma employed about 4000 employees, including 800 managers and technical staff. A major impetus underlying the program was the merger of the parent company with another firm, which disrupted a long-standing relationship between Sigma and the parent company and required Sigma to operate more autonomously than it had in the past. This new method of operating was especially difficult because of strained relationships among Sigma's departments and between levels of management. A new plant manager experienced difficulty obtaining acceptance and cooperation for suggested improvements.

The *Grid* was considered as a possible method for resolving these problems. Sigma's top managers met with a *Grid* consultant who had been working in other parts of the parent company; they also attended a *Grid* seminar held outside the company. The managers gathered enough positive information about the *Grid* to decide to develop their own program with the consultant's help. The first phase of the *Grid* began with 40 senior managers attending a one-week managerial *Grid* seminar. This phase continued for about eight months until all 800 managers and technical staff had completed the seminar. By that time, the earlier participants had begun later phases of the *Grid*.

These later phases included a number of activities that were intended to solve specific problems:

1   A management team used problem-solving approaches learned in the *Grid* seminar to keep all levels of management informed during union contract negotiations.
2   Management teams were established to work out programs for reducing the costs of utilities and maintenance materials and supplies.
3   A new series of *Grid* programs was extended to lower-level supervisors, including the labor force; union officers were invited to attend the sessions.
4   A safety program based on *Grid* methods was implemented.
5   The plant manager initiated a program in which supervisors and subordinates jointly set performance goals.

An evaluation of the *Grid* program by an external team showed a sharp increase in productivity and a comparably sharp decrease in controllable costs. About 44% of the increase in profitability was due to the reduction in controllable costs, which was primarily traceable to a reduction in labor costs. About 13% of the decrease in controllable costs could be attributed to better operating procedures and higher hourly productivity, which resulted in an increase of several million dollars in profit. Comments by plant personnel showed a favourable response to the program's impact on efficiency.

Other measures also showed the positive impact of the program. The number of meetings (for a sample of managers) increased by 41%, and more emphasis was placed on teamwork and problem solving. *Post hoc* analyses of value and attitude changes showed changes consistent with the norms and values taught in the *Grid* program. One of the most important aspects of this program was that the top managers were instructors for the phase 1 training sessions. These same managers were among those showing the most improvement, as reported by their subordinates.

Grid® *Organization Development* has been adopted in whole or in part by many organisations; phases 1, 2 and 3, which apply mainly to communication barriers, are especially popular.[44] Research about the effectiveness of the *Grid* is mixed, however. On the positive side, Blake and Mouton collected data on two similar organisations; the one that went through the six *Grid* phases improved profitability significantly, while the control organisation did not.[45] An example of a *Grid* failure, on the other hand, is a study that examined the impact of *Grid*® *Organization Development* in six geographic districts of a large federal agency. The researchers assessed the organisational climate of each district to determine the extent to which the organisation was moving toward 9,9 management. The results showed no significant climate changes in any of the six districts. The failure of the *Grid* programme was attributed mainly to the lack of support for the programme by top management.[46]

In conclusion, like Likert's System 4 Management, Blake and Mouton's *Grid*® *Organization Development* is a normative intervention, proposing one most effective way to manage organisations—9,9 management. In recent years, the programme authors have extended the approach to fit different professions, including real estate, social work, nursing and academic administration. As far as Blake and Mouton are concerned, the issue of the effectiveness of the *Grid* is settled. However, both the contingency theory and the mixed research results suggest that the *Grid* can be successful, but not in all situations. More rigorous research is needed to assess under what conditions and in what situations positive results can be expected.

Summary

This chapter described four types of system-wide process interventions: confrontation meetings, inter-group interventions, large-group interventions and *Grid® Organization Development*. *Grid® Organization Development* is a normative programme that proposes a one best way to manage organisations. Although its authors claim that it can be successful in all situations, research assessing normative models is mixed. This suggests that the *Grid* can be successful under certain conditions and that more research is needed to pinpoint what these conditions are.

The other organisation process interventions do not claim universal success; they work best only in certain situations. The organisation confrontation meeting is a way of mobilising resources for organisational problem solving and seems especially relevant for organisations undergoing stress. The inter-group relations approaches are designed to help solve a variety of organisational problems. Microcosm groups can be formed to address particular issues and use parallel processes to diffuse group solutions to the organisation. The inter-group conflict resolution approach involves a method for mitigating dysfunctional conflicts between groups or departments. Conflict can be dysfunctional in situations in which groups must work together. It may, however, promote organisational effectiveness when departments are relatively independent of each other. Large-group interventions are designed to focus the energy and attention of a 'whole system' around organisational processes such as a vision, strategy or culture. It is best used when the organisation is about to begin a large-scale change effort or is facing a new situation.

 ACTIVITIES

Review questions

1 What are the characteristics of a system-wide process intervention?
2 What should be avoided in a confrontation meeting?
3 Describe how a microcosm group intervention succeeds.
4 Identify the characteristics of inter-group conflict resolution methods.
5 What are the two basic assumptions about managerial behaviour in the management grid?
6 Which interventions are successful in all situations?

Discussion and essay questions

1 Describe the similarities and differences between a normative approach, such as *Grid® Organization Development*, and an organisation confrontation meeting.
2 Discuss the similarities and differences between an organisation confrontation meeting and an inter-group conflict resolution intervention.
3 Describe some of the key success requirements for a microcosm group intervention.

Notes

1 M. Weisbord, *Productive Workplaces* (San Francisco: Jossey-Bass, 1987).
2 R. Beckhard, 'The confrontation meeting', *Harvard Business Review*, 4 (1967): 149–55.
3 B. Benedict Bunker and B. Alban, 'What makes large-group interventions effective?' *Journal of Applied Behavioral Science*, 28 (4, 1992): 579–91; N. Tichy and S. Sherman, *Control Your Destiny or Someone Else Will* (New York: HarperCollins Publishers, 1993).
4 This application was adapted from material in Benedict Bunker and Alban, 'What makes large-group interventions effective?' and Tichy and Sherman, *Control Your Destiny or Someone Else Will*, both *op. cit.*

5 R. Beckhard, *Organization Development: Strategies and Models* (Reading, Mass.: Addison-Wesley, 1969).

6 W. Bennis, *Organization Development: Its Nature, Origins, and Prospects* (Reading, Mass.: Addison-Wesley, 1969): 7.

7 C. Alderfer, 'An intergroup perspective on group dynamics' in *Handbook of Organizational Behavior*, ed. J. Lorsch (Englewood Cliffs, N.J.: Prentice-Hall, 1987): 190–222; C. Alderfer, 'Improving organizational communication through long-term intergroup intervention', *Journal of Applied Behavioral Science*, 13 (1977): 193–210; C. Alderfer, R. Tucker, C. Alderfer and L. Tucker, 'The Race Relations Advisory Group: An intergroup intervention' in *Organizational Change and Development*, 2, eds W. Pasmore and R. Woodman (Greenwich, Conn.: JAI Press, 1988): 269–321.

8 Alderfer, 'An intergroup perspective on group dynamics', *op. cit.*

9 *Ibid*, 210.

10 Alderfer, 'Improving organizational communication', *op. cit.*

11 Alderfer, Tucker, Alderfer and Tucker, 'The Race Relations Advisory Group', *op. cit.*

12 D. Tjosvold, 'Cooperation theory and organizations', *Human Relations*, 37 (1984): 743–67.

13 R. Blake, H. Shepard and J. Mouton, *Managing Intergroup Conflict in Industry* (Houston: Gulf, 1954).

14 Beckhard, *Organization Development*, *op. cit.*

15 E. Neilson, 'Understanding and managing intergroup conflict' in *Organizational Behavior and Administration*, eds P. Lawrence, L. Barnes and J. Lorsch (Homewood, Ill.: Richard Irwin, 1976): 291–305.

16 D. Lewis, E. French and P. Steane, 'A culture of conflict', *Leadership and Organization Development Journal*, 18:6 (1997): 275–282.

17 Blake, Shepard and Mouton, *Managing Intergroup Conflict*, *op. cit.*

18 Bennis, *Organization Development*, *op. cit.*

19 *Ibid*, 4.

20 R. Golembiewski and A. Blumberg, 'Confrontation as a training design in complex organizations: attitudinal changes in a diversified population of managers', *Journal of Applied Behavioral Science*, 3 (1967): 525–47.

21 W. French and C. Bell, *Organization Development: Behavioral Science Interventions for Organization Improvement* (Englewood Cliffs, N.J.: Prentice-Hall, 1978).

22 E. Huse and M. Beer, 'Eclectic approach to organizational development', *Harvard Business Review*, 49 (1971): 103–13.

23 *Ibid*, 112.

24 E. Huse, 'The behavioral scientist in the shop', *Personnel*, 44 (May–June 1965): 8–16.

25 J. Fordyce and R. Weil, *Managing WITH People* (Reading, Mass.: Addison-Wesley, 1971).

26 K. Thomas, 'Conflict and conflict management' in *Handbook of Industrial and Organizational Psychology*, ed. M. Dunnette (Chicago: Rand McNally, 1976): 889–936.

27 M. Weisbord, *Productive Workplaces*, *op. cit.*; M. Weisbord, *Discovering Common Ground* (San Francisco: Berrett Koehler, 1993); B. Benedict Bunker and B. Alban, eds, 'Special issue: large-group interventions', *Journal of Applied Behavioral Science*, 28:4 (1992); H. Owen, *Open Space Technology: A User's Guide* (Potomac, Md.: Abbott, 1992).

28 H. Owen, *Open Space Technology, ibid.*

29 D. Axelrod, 'Getting everyone involved', *Journal of Applied Behavioral Science*, 28:4 (1992): 499–509.

30 F. Emery and E. Trist, *Towards a Social Ecology* (New York: Plenum Publishing, 1973); R. Beckhard and R. Harris, *Organizational Transitions: Managing Complex Change*, 2nd ed. (Reading, Mass.: Addison-Wesley, 1987).

31 R. Lippitt, 'Future before you plan' in *NTL Manager's Handbook* (Arlington, Va.: NTL Institute, 1983): 38–41.

32 Weisbord, *Productive Workplaces*, *op. cit.*

33 Owen, *Open Space Technology, op. cit.*

34 Weisbord, *Discovering Common Ground, op. cit.*

35 L. Corbett, 'Delivery windows—a new view on improving manufacturing flexibility and on-time delivery performance', *Production and Inventory Management Journal*, 33(3) (1992): 74–79.

36 R. Blake and J. Mouton, *The Managerial Grid* (Houston: Gulf, 1964); R. Blake, J. Mouton, L. Barnes, and L. Greiner, 'Breakthrough in organization development', *Harvard Business Review*, 42 (1964): 133–55; R. Blake and J. Mouton, *Corporate Excellence Through Grid Organization Development: A Systems Approach* (Houston: Gulf, 1968); R. Blake and

J. Mouton, *Building a Dynamic Corporation Through Grid Organization Development* (Reading, Mass.: Addison-Wesley, 1969).

37 Blake and Mouton, *Corporate Excellence, op. cit.*

38 *Ibid.*

39 R. Blake and A. McCanse, *Leadership Dilemmas—Grid Solutions* (Houston: Gulf, 1991).

40 This discussion is based primarily on Blake and Mouton, *Corporate Excellence, op. cit.*

41 *Ibid.*

42 *Ibid.*

43 Blake, Mouton, Barnes, and Greiner, 'Breakthrough', *op. cit.* 133–55.

44 'Using the managerial grid to ensure MBO', *Organizational Dynamics*, 2 (Spring 1974): 55.

45 Blake and Mouton, *The Managerial Grid, op. cit.*, 178–79. A more complete description is given in R. Blake and J. Mouton, *Organizational Change by Design* (Austin, Tex.: Scientific Methods, 1976): 1–16.

46 L. Greiner, D. Leitch and L. Barnes, 'The simple complexity of organisation climate in a government agency', undated manuscript.

PART 4

TECHNOSTRUCTURAL INTERVENTIONS

CHAPTERS

14 Restructuring organisations

15 Employee involvement

16 Work design

Restructuring organisations

In this chapter, we begin to examine technostructural interventions—change programmes that focus on the technology and structure of organisations. Increasing global competition and rapid technological and environmental changes are forcing organisations to restructure themselves from rigid bureaucracies to leaner, more flexible structures. These new forms of organisation are highly adaptive and cost efficient. They often result in fewer managers and employees, and streamlined work flows that break down functional barriers.

Interventions aimed at structural design include moving from more traditional ways of dividing the organisation's overall work, such as functional, self-contained-unit and matrix structures, to more integrative and flexible forms, such as process- and network-based structures. Diagnostic guidelines help determine which structure is appropriate for particular organisational environments, technologies and conditions.

Downsizing seeks to reduce costs and bureaucracy by decreasing the size of the organisation. This reduction in personnel can be accomplished by lay-offs, organisation redesign and outsourcing, which involves moving functions that are not part of the organisation's core competence to outside contractors. Successful downsizing is closely aligned with the organisation's strategy.

Re-engineering radically redesigns the organisation's core work processes to give tighter linkage and co-ordination among the different tasks. This work flow integration results in faster, more responsive task performance. Business process management is often accomplished with new information technology that permits employees to control and co-ordinate work processes more effectively.

Structural design

Organisation structure describes how the overall work of the organisation is divided into subunits and how these subunits are co-ordinated for task completion. It is a key feature of an organisation's strategic orientation.[1] Based on a contingency perspective shown in Figure 14.1, organisation structures should be designed to fit with at least five factors:

- the environment
- organisation size
- technology
- organisation strategy
- worldwide operations.

Organisation effectiveness depends on the extent to which organisation structures are responsive to these contingencies.[2]

Organisations have traditionally structured themselves into three forms:

- functional departments that are task specialised
- self-contained units that are oriented to specific products, customers or regions
- matrix structures that combine both functional specialisation and self-containment.

Faced with accelerating changes in competitive environments and technologies, however, organisations have increasingly redesigned their structures into more integrative and flexible forms. These more recent innovations include process-based structures that design

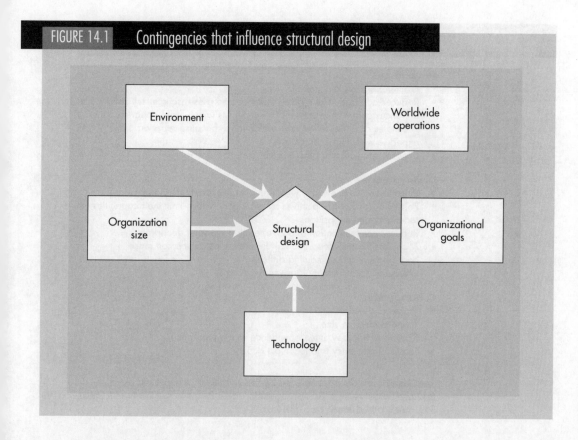

FIGURE 14.1   Contingencies that influence structural design

subunits around the organisation's core work processes and network-based structures that link the organisation to other, interdependent organisations. The advantages, disadvantages and contingencies of the different structures are described below.

The functional organisation

Perhaps the most widely used organisational structure in the world today is the basic hierarchical structure, shown in Figure 14.2. This is the standard pyramid, with senior management at the top, middle and lower managers spread out directly below and

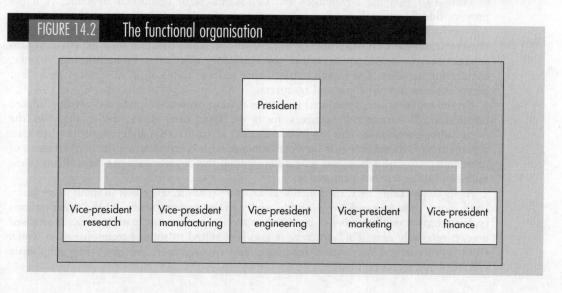

FIGURE 14.2   The functional organisation

TABLE 14.1	Advantages, disadvantages and contingencies of the functional form

Advantages
- Promotes skill specialization
- Reduces duplication of scarce resources and uses resources full time
- Enhances career development for specialists within large departments
- Facilitates communication and performance because superiors share expertise with their subordinates
- Exposes specialists to others within the same speciality

Disadvantages
- Emphasizes routine tasks, which encourages short time horizons
- Fosters parochial perspectives by managers, which limit their capacities for top-management positions
- Reduces communication and co-operation between departments
- Multiplies the interdepartmental dependencies, which can make coordination and scheduling difficult
- Obscures accountability for overall outcomes

Contingencies
- Stable and certain environment
- Small to medium size
- Routine technology, interdependence within functions
- Goals of efficiency and technical quality

Source: Adapted by permission of the publisher from J. McCann and J. Galbraith, 'Interdepartmental relations' in *Handbook of Organisational Design: Remodelling Organisations and Their Environment*, eds P. Nystrom and W. Starbuck, 2 vols. (New York: Oxford University Press, 1981) 2: 61.

workers at the bottom. The organisation is usually subdivided into different functional units, such as engineering, research, operations, human resources, finance and marketing. This organisational structure is based on early management theories regarding specialisation, line and staff relations, span of control, authority and responsibility.[3] The major functional subunits are staffed by specialists in such disciplines as engineering and accounting. It is considered easier to manage specialists if they are grouped together under the same head and if the head of the department has training and experience in that particular discipline.

Table 14.1 lists the advantages and disadvantages of functional structures. On the positive side, functional structures promote specialisation of skills and resources. People who perform similar work and face similar problems are grouped together. This facilitates communication within departments and allows specialists to share their expertise. It also enhances career development within the speciality, whether it be accounting, finance, engineering or sales. The functional structure reduces duplication of services because it makes the best use of people and resources.

On the negative side, functional structures tend to promote routine tasks with a limited orientation. Departmental members focus on their own tasks, rather than on the organisation's total task. This can lead to conflict across functional departments when each group attempts to maximise its own performance without considering the performances of other units. Co-ordination and scheduling among the departments can be difficult when each emphasises its own perspective.

As shown in Table 14.1, the functional structure tends to work best in small to medium-sized firms that face relatively stable and certain environments. These organisations typically have a small number of products or services, and co-ordination across specialised units is relatively easy. This structure is also best suited to routine technologies in which there is interdependence within functions, and to organisational goals that emphasise efficiency and technical quality.

FIGURE 14.3   The self-contained unit organisation

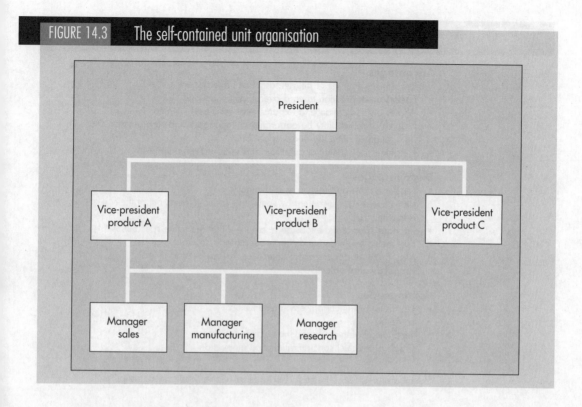

The self-contained unit organisation

The self-contained unit structure represents a fundamentally different way of organising. Also known as a product or divisional structure, it was developed at about the same time by General Motors, Exxon and DuPont.[4] It groups organisational activities on the basis of products, services, customers or geography. All or most of the resources necessary for the accomplishment of specific objectives are set up as self-contained units headed by product or division managers. For example, Southcorp has plants that specialise in manufacturing packaging and others that specialise in wine producing. Each plant manager reports to a particular division or product vice-president, rather than a manufacturing vice-president. In effect, a large organisation may set up smaller (sometimes temporary) special-purpose organisations, each geared to a specific product, service, customer or region. A typical product structure is shown in Figure 14.3. Interestingly, the formal structure within a self-contained unit is often functional in nature.

Table 14.2 provides a list of the advantages and disadvantages of self-contained unit structures. These organisations recognise key interdependencies and promote the co-ordination of resources toward an overall outcome. This strong outcome orientation ensures departmental accountability and promotes cohesion among those contributing to the product. These structures provide employees with opportunities for learning new skills and expanding knowledge, because they can more easily move among the different specialities that contribute to the product. As a result, self-contained unit structures are well suited for developing general managers.

Self-contained unit organisations do, however, have certain problems. There may not be enough specialised work to fully utilise people's skills and abilities. Specialists may feel isolated from their professional colleagues and may fail to advance in their career speciality. These structures may promote allegiance to departmental goals, rather than organisational objectives. They also place multiple demands on people, which may create stress.

The self-contained unit structure works best in conditions that are almost the opposite of those favouring a functional organisation, as shown in Table 14.2. The organisation

TABLE 14.2	Advantages, disadvantages and contingencies of the self-contained unit form

Advantages
- Recognizes sources of interdepartmental interdependencies
- Fosters an orientation toward overall outcomes and clients
- Allows diversification and expansion of skills and training
- Ensures accountability by departmental managers and so promotes delegation of authority and responsibility
- Heightens departmental cohesion and involvement in work

Disadvantages
- May use skills and resources inefficiently
- Limits career advancement by specialists to movements out of their departments
- Impedes specialists' exposure to others within the same specialities
- Puts multiple-role demands upon people and so creates stress
- May promote departmental objectives, as opposed to overall organizational objectives

Contingencies
- Unstable and uncertain environments
- Large size
- Technological interdependence across functions
- Goals of product specialization and innovation

Source: Adapted by permission of the publisher from McCann and Gailbraith, 'Interdepartmental relations', p. 61.

needs to be relatively large to support the duplication of resources assigned to the units. Because each unit is designed to fit a particular niche, the structure adapts well to uncertain conditions. Self-contained units also help to co-ordinate technical interdependencies that fall across functions, and they are suited to goals promoting product or service specialisation and innovation.

The matrix organisation

Some OD practitioners have focused on maximising the strengths and minimising the weaknesses of both the functional and the self-contained unit structures. This has resulted in the matrix organisation.[5] It superimposes the lateral structure of a product or project co-ordinator on the vertical functional structure, as shown in Figure 14.4. Matrix organisational designs originally evolved in the aerospace industry, where changing customer demands and technological conditions caused managers to focus on lateral relationships between functions in order to develop a flexible and adaptable system of resources and procedures, and to achieve a series of project objectives. Matrix organisations are now widely used in manufacturing, service, non-profit, governmental and professional organisations, such as Monsanto Corporation.[6]

Every matrix organisation contains three unique and critical roles: the top manager who heads and balances the dual chains of command; the matrix bosses (functional, product or area) who share subordinates; and the two-boss managers who report to two different matrix bosses. Each of these roles has its own unique requirements. For example, functional matrix bosses are expected to maximise their respective technical expertise within constraints posed by market realities. Two-boss managers, however, must accomplish work within the demands of supervisors who want to achieve technical sophistication on the one hand and meet customer expectations on the other. Thus, a matrix organisation is more than matrix structure. It must also be reinforced by matrix processes, such as performance management systems that get input from both functional and project bosses, by matrix leadership behaviour that operates comfortably with lateral

| FIGURE 14.4 | The matrix organisation |

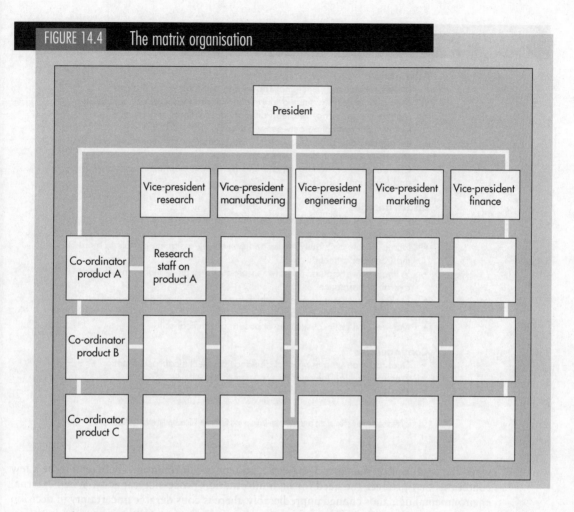

decision making, and by a matrix culture that fosters open conflict management and a balance of power.[7]

Matrix organisations, like all organisation structures, have both advantages and disadvantages, as shown in Table 14.3. On the positive side, matrix structures allow multiple orientations. Specialised, functional knowledge can be applied to all projects. New products or projects can quickly be implemented by using people flexibly and by moving between product and functional orientations as the circumstances demand. Matrix organisations can maintain consistency among departments and projects by requiring communication among managers. For many people, matrix structures are motivating and exciting.

On the negative side, matrix organisations can be difficult to manage. To implement and maintain them requires heavy managerial costs and support. When people are assigned to more than one department, there may be role ambiguity and conflict. Similarly, overall performance may be sacrificed if there are power conflicts between functional departments and project structures. To make matrix organisations work, organisation members need interpersonal and conflict management skills. People can get confused about how the matrix works, which can lead to chaos and inefficiencies.

As shown in Table 14.3, matrix structures are appropriate under three important conditions.[8] First, there must be outside pressures for a dual focus—a matrix structure works best when there are many customers with unique demands on the one hand, and strong requirements for technical sophistication on the other hand. Second, there must be pressures for high information-processing capacity. A matrix organisation is appropriate

TABLE 14.3	Advantages, disadvantages and contingencies of the matrix form

Advantages
- Makes specialized, functional knowledge available to all projects
- Uses people flexibly, since departments maintain reservoirs of specialists
- Maintains consistency between different departments and projects by forcing communication between managers
- Recognizes and provides mechanisms for dealing with legitimate, multiple sources of power in the organization
- Can adapt to environmental changes by shifting emphasis between project and functional aspects

Disadvantages
- Can be very difficult to introduce without a preexisting supportive management climate
- Increases role ambiguity, stress and anxiety by assigning people to more than one department
- Without power balancing between product and functional forms, lowers overall performance
- Makes inconsistent demands, which may result in unproductive conflicts and short-term crisis management
- May reward political skills as opposed to technical skills

Contingencies
- Dual focus on unique product demands and technical specialization
- Pressure for high information processing capacity
- Pressure for shared resources

Source: Adapted by permission of the publisher from McCann and Gailbraith, 'Interdepartmental relations', p. 61.

when the organisation must process a large amount of information. There tend to be a few conditions that produce the need for high information-processing capacity. When external environmental demands change unpredictably, there is considerable uncertainty in decision making. When the organisation produces a broad range of products or services, or offers those outputs to a large number of different markets, there is considerable complexity in decision making. And when there is reciprocal interdependence among the tasks in the organisation's technical core, there is considerable pressure on communication and co-ordination systems. Third, and finally, there must be pressure for shared resources. When customer demands vary greatly and technological requirements are strict, valuable human and physical resources are likely to be scarce. Thus, the matrix works well under these conditions because it facilitates the sharing of these scarce resources. If any of these conditions are not met, a matrix organisation is likely to fail.

Process-based structures

A radically new logic for structuring organisations is to form multi-disciplinary teams around core processes, such as product development, sales generation and customer support.[9] As shown in Figure 14.5, process-based structures emphasise lateral rather than vertical relationships.[10] They group all related functions that are necessary to produce a product or service into a common unit, usually managed by someone called a 'process owner'. There are few hierarchical levels, and the senior executive team is relatively small, typically consisting of the chairperson, the chief operating officer and the heads of a few key support services, such as strategic planning, human resources and finance.

Process-based structures eliminate many of the hierarchical and departmental boundaries that can impede task co-ordination, and slow decision-making and task performance. They reduce the enormous costs of managing across departments and up and

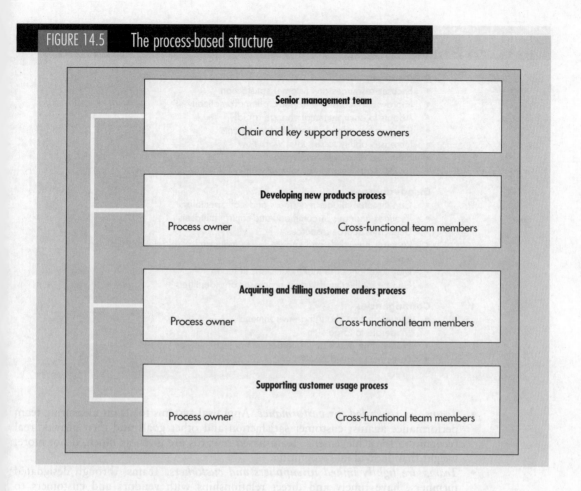

FIGURE 14.5 The process-based structure

Senior management team

Chair and key support process owners

Developing new products process

Process owner   Cross-functional team members

Acquiring and filling customer orders process

Process owner   Cross-functional team members

Supporting customer usage process

Process owner   Cross-functional team members

down the hierarchy. Process-based structures enable organisations to focus most of their resources on serving customers, both inside and outside the firm.

The application of process-based structures is growing rapidly in a variety of manufacturing and service companies. Typically referred to as 'horizontal', 'boundaryless' or 'team-based' organisations, they are used to enhance customer service at such firms as Motorola, Hewlett-Packard, Xerox and Varian Technologies (Australia). Although there is no one right way of designing process-based structures, the following features characterise this new form of organising.[11]

- *Processes drive structure.* Process-based structures are organised around the three to five key processes that define the work of the organisation. Rather than products or functions, processes define the structure and are governed by a 'process owner'. Each process has clear performance goals that drive task execution.
- *Work adds value.* To increase efficiency, process-based structures simplify and enrich work processes. Work is simplified by eliminating non-essential tasks and reducing layers of management. Combining tasks so that teams perform whole processes enriches it.
- *Teams are fundamental.* The key organising feature in a process-based structure is the use of teams, which are used to manage everything from task execution to strategic planning, are typically self-managing and responsible for goal achievement.
- *Customers define performance.* The key goal of any team in a process-based structure is customer satisfaction. Defining customer expectations and designing team functions to meet these expectations command much of the team's attention. The organisation must see this as the primary path to financial performance.

TABLE 14.4	Advantages, disadvantages and contingencies of the process-based form

Advantages
- Focuses resources on customer satisfaction
- Improves speed and efficiency, often dramatically
- Adapts to environmental change rapidly
- Reduces boundaries between departments
- Increases ability to see total work flow
- Enhances employee involvement
- Lowers costs because of lower overhead structure

Disadvantages
- Can threaten middle managers and staff specialists
- Requires changes in command-and-control mindsets
- Duplicates scarce resources
- Requires new skills and knowledge to manage lateral relationships and teams
- May take longer to make decisions in teams
- Can be ineffective if wrong processes are identified

Contingencies
- Uncertain and changing environments
- Moderate to large size
- Non-routine and highly interdependent technologies
- Customer-oriented goals

- *Teams are rewarded for performance.* Appraisal systems focus on measuring team performance against customer satisfaction and other goals and then provide real recognition for achievement. Team-based rewards are given as much, if not more, weight than individual recognition.
- *Teams are tightly linked to suppliers and customers.* Teams, through designated members, have timely and direct relationships with vendors and customers to understand and respond to emerging concerns.
- *Team members are well informed and trained.* Successful implementation of a process-based structure requires team members who can work with a broad range of information, including customer and market data, financial information and personnel and policy matters. Team members also need problem-solving and decision-making skills and abilities to address and implement solutions.

Table 14.4 lists the advantages and disadvantages of process-based structures. The most frequently mentioned advantage is the intense focus on meeting customer needs, which can result in dramatic improvements in speed, efficiency and customer satisfaction. Process-based structures remove layers of management, and consequently information flows more quickly and accurately throughout the organisation. Because process teams are composed of different functional specialities, boundaries between departments are removed, thus affording organisation members a broad view of the work flow and a clear line of sight between team performance and organisation effectiveness. Process-based structures are also more flexible and adaptable to change than traditional structures.

A major disadvantage of process-based structures is the difficulty of changing to this new organisational form. Process-based structures typically require radical shifts in mindsets, skills and managerial roles. These changes involve considerable time and resources and can be resisted by functional managers and staff specialists. Moreover, process-based structures may result in expensive duplication of scarce resources and, if team skills are not present, in slower decision making as teams struggle to define and reach consensus. Finally, implementation of process-based structures relies on the proper identification of key processes needed to satisfy customer needs. If critical processes are mis-identified or ignored altogether, performance and customer satisfaction are likely to suffer.

Table 14.4 shows that process-based structures are particularly appropriate for highly uncertain environments where customer demands and market conditions are changing rapidly. They enable organisations to manage non-routine technologies and to co-ordinate work flows that are highly interdependent. Process-based structures generally appear in medium- to large-sized organisations that have several products or projects. They focus heavily on customer-oriented goals and are found in both domestic and worldwide organisations.

Application 14.1 describes the experience of Liverpool City Council and shows what not to do when attempting a decentralised reform.[12]

APPLICATION 14.1

Liverpool City Council — decentralised reform in local government

Competitive tendering of services in local government is not compulsory in New South Wales. The 1993 *Local Government Act* adopted a voluntaristic approach to reform, allowing individual local authorities to choose a reform methodology suited to their own contextual circumstances in order to encourage more customer-focused and value-for-money services. In response, most councils chose to follow a slow, evolutionary route to reform, based on a succession of small and cautious steps. Decentralised reform has been a rarer occurrence. It involves the creation of a centralised core which determines policy, sets standards and determines and purchases services, in conjunction with a devolved set of autonomous and empowered units that bid for and deliver services in direct competition with external providers.

One of the best known and most notorious attempts at decentralised reform in NSW was that of the Liverpool City Council situated in South West Sydney. The pioneering general manager who initiated changes at Liverpool was John Walker (1992–95). For Walker, it was the 'inappropriate' traditional divisionalised organisational structure of local councils that lay at the root of the problem of local government's archaic culture. Walker attacked the 'archaic and unproductive dominance of local government guilds and the structures adopted to protect these'.

For Walker, a range of problems, including inadequate communication,

professional jealousies, egos, poor people skills, tunnel vision, inadequate strategic planning, fragmented customer service, dominance of centralised functions, insufficient staff involvement and inflexible work practices, lie at the heart of criticisms concerning the professional demarcations inherent in the traditional divisionalised local government structures. These are of two types: problems across divisions and problems within hierarchies.

The end result of this bureaucratic, divisionalised and hierarchical mindset has been the perpetuation of a system that has become notorious for being self-serving, inefficient, ineffective and non-responsive. This has resulted in two major failures: inadequate customer orientation and inadequate competitive orientation.

At Liverpool City Council, the Lord Mayor was credited with initiating the council's vision based on the twin notions of customer service and service contestability, based on a purchaser–provider split. John Walker was appointed as general manager to implement the policy from November 1992.

While developing relationships with major stakeholders, Walker attempted to commence the process of devising a new organisational structure and operational systems to reflect a clear separation of the purchaser and provider functions of council. The departure of old managers and the arrival of new ones provided the opportunity to reorganise the structure.

The objective was to secure a restructured, flat and non-divisional organisational structure based on the concepts of service teams (who decided the type and level of services) and business units (who delivered the services), together with formal provision for public input.

The operation of the new unit structures began to move into full swing during 1994. Responsibility for decision making about the operations of the components of the business was devolved to the respective unit managers. The new structures wrote their own business plans in line with the direction of the strategic plan and operated according to the mindset of performance management—team groupings, non-hierarchical management, customer service guarantees, quality indicators, outcome-focused approaches (data-driven management, key result areas, performance measurements) and rewards for performance. Devolution and empowerment replaced direction and control.

A number of problems emerged. In many cases, the same manager had been asked both to be the purchaser and to prepare for the transition to contestability. This created the conflict that the person who had to give it up determined the pace of change. The new-breed unit managers expected the freedom to deliver on their own business plans and expected to be judged only on their outcomes. Walker's more distant coaching-type relationship with these managers, combined with their local government inexperience, resulted in a situation where such managers became too inward-looking, tending to compete among themselves and creating a scenario of internal rather than external competition. Despite performing well as individual units, the concept of corporate co-ordination became more difficult and the management team struggled to find their role as a group.

Walker had retained the executive directors he had inherited in late 1992. As carriers of the old divisional cultures, these incumbents struggled to come to terms with their new roles in a changed structure, insisting on becoming embroiled in operational matters and unable to adapt to a new role of policy and forward planning. Quite apart from the personalities involved, their roles in relation to the business management roles of the level below them became confused, leading to frustrating clashes between the old-style divisional executives and the new-breed unit managers.

Such issues as the high turnover of staff, which left frequent gaps in the organisation, the bedding-in and socialisation of new personnel compounded these managerial relationship problems, as well as human resource problems associated with staff morale and uncertainty.

In an atmosphere of deteriorating relations between the general manager and the council, the pace of reform stalled during 1995, and Walker resigned in October 1995.

Network-based structures

A network-based structure manages the diverse, complex and dynamic relationships among multiple organisations, each specialising in a particular function or task.[13] As shown in Figure 14.6, the network structure redraws organisational boundaries and links separate organisations to facilitate task interaction. The essence of networks is the relationship between organisations that perform different aspects of work. In this way, organisations do the things that they do well; for example, manufacturing expertise is applied to production and logistical expertise is applied to distribution. Examples of network organisations include joint ventures to design, manufacture and market advanced products, research and development consortia, subcontracting and licensing arrangements across national borders and wholly-owned subsidiaries selling products and services to one another.

FIGURE 14.6   The network organisation

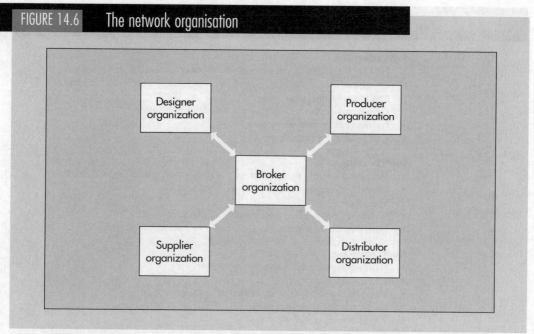

Network-based structures are called by a variety of names, including 'virtual corporations', 'modular corporations' or 'Shamrock organisations'.[14] Less formally, they have been described as 'pizza' structures, spiderwebs, starbursts and cluster organisations. Organisations such as Apple Computers and Bennetton have implemented fairly sophisticated network structures. They are also found in the construction, fashion and entertainment industries, as well as in the public sector.[15]

Network structures typically have the following characteristics:

- *Vertical disaggregation.* Different network members perform different business functions, such as production, marketing and distribution, that are traditionally performed within a single organisation. In the film industry, for example, separate organisations providing transportation, cinematography, music, actors and catering all work together under a broker organisation, the studio. The organisations making up the network represent an important factor in determining its success.[16]
- *Brokers.* Networks are often managed by broker organisations that locate and assemble member organisations. The broker may play a central role and sub-contract for needed products or services, or it might specialise in linking equal partners into a network. In the construction industry, the general contractor typically assembles and manages insulation, mechanical, electrical, plumbing and other specialities to erect a building.
- *Co-ordinating mechanisms.* Hierarchical arrangements or plans do not generally control network organisations. Rather, co-ordination of the work in a network falls into three categories: informal relationships, contracts and market mechanisms. First, co-ordination patterns can depend heavily on interpersonal relationships between individuals who have a well-developed partnership. Conflicts are resolved through reciprocity; network members recognise that each will probably have to compromise at some time. Trust is built and nurtured over time by these reciprocal arrangements. Second, co-ordination can be achieved through formal contracts, such as ownership control, licensing arrangements or purchase agreements. Finally, market mechanisms, such as spot payments, performance accountability and information systems, ensure that all parties are aware of each others' activities.

TABLE 14.5	Advantages, disadvantages and contingencies of the network-based form

Advantages
- Enables highly flexible and adaptive response to dynamic environments
- Creates a 'best of the best' organization to focus resources on customer and market needs
- Each organization can leverage a distinctive competency
- Permits rapid global expansion
- Can produce synergistic results

Disadvantages
- Managing lateral relations across autonomous organizations is difficult
- Motivating members to relinquish autonomy to join the network is troublesome
- Sustaining membership and benefits can be problematic
- May give partners access to proprietary knowledge/technology

Contingencies
- Highly complex and uncertain environments
- All size organizations
- Goals of organizational specialization and innovation
- Highly uncertain technologies
- Worldwide operations

Network structures have a number of advantages and disadvantages, as shown in Table 14.5.[17] They are highly flexible and adaptable to changing conditions. Their ability to form partnerships with different organisations permits the creation of a 'best of the best' company that is better able to exploit opportunities, which may often be global in nature. They allow each member to exploit its distinctive competence. They can enable sufficient resources and expertise to be applied to large, complex tasks in a way that a single organisation could not. Perhaps most important is the fact that network organisations can have synergistic effects, allowing members to build on each other's strengths and competencies.

The major problems with network organisations lie in managing such complex structures. Galbraith and Kazanjian describe network structures as matrix organisations that extend beyond the boundaries of single firms but lack the ability to appeal to a higher authority to resolve conflicts.[18] Thus, matrix skills of managing lateral relations across organisational boundaries are critical to administering network structures. Most organisations, because they are managed hierarchically, can be expected to have difficulties managing lateral relations. Other disadvantages of network organisations include the difficulties of motivating organisations to join such structures and of sustaining commitment over time. Potential members may not want to give up their autonomy to link with other organisations. Once linked, they may have problems sustaining the benefits of joining together. This is especially true if the network consists of organisations that are not the 'best in breed'. Finally, joining in a network may expose the organisation's proprietary knowledge and skills to others.

As shown in Table 14.5, network organisations are best suited to highly complex and uncertain environments where multiple competencies and flexible responses are needed. They seem to apply to organisations of all sizes, and they deal with complex tasks or problems that involve high interdependencies across organisations. Network structures fit with goals emphasising organisation specialisation and innovation. They also fit well in organisations with worldwide operations.

Application 14.2 describes how Emtech International's network structure is configured to align with its strategy and how relationships are managed.[19]

Emtech International — forming business networks

Emtech International, an Australian company founded in 1994, began with great prospects of producing a hazard-warning beacon for the American emergency-services market to replace the open-flame pyrotechnic flare. In 1994, it seemed like a simple process, as pyrotechnic flares are notorious for starting fires. Emergency workers have had uniforms, hands and faces burned, and reports in the US suggest that flares have led to scores of deaths in the past 20 years.

Emtech began with personal contacts in the US but it soon ran into obstacles. The managing director and co-founder says: 'There is no doubt that, whatever you think at the start, it is going to take twice as long and cost twice as much. The process has its moments of exhilaration, and of deep depression.'

Parker and Aylward owned half the company. Parker says the other two partners were too busy to keep up their role in the partnership—to market the beacon. A messy split between the two sides put the company in a spin. Parker turned to RedCentre, a part of the Photonics Co-operative Research Centre (CRC), which helps companies to commercialise products.

Through the Australian Equity Association, Parker found an investor to buy out the other two partners after an agreed reassessment had put their equity share at 25%. The deal did not provide working capital.

RedCentre introduced Parker to other companies to enable it to form a business network. This made Emtech eligible for a grant of just over $100 000 through the Business Networks Programme run by AusIndustry. The network partners are David Flynn, managing director of the industrial designers Niche Design, and Ross Bellesis, managing director of the injection moulding and tooling company, Socobell. Its national manager, Terry Polkinghorn, represents RedCentre.

Getting to the stage of producing the prototype, designed before the network was formed, cost Emtech more than $200 000. Parker says: 'The response from the US market was, "Great. Now can you drop it on its head".' The beacon had to be made tougher.

Back at the drawing board, this time with the network team, Emtech came up with new specifications. Niche designed the product outline and tooling and tested the plastics' performance. The results were impressive but the beacon had to get past US testing authorities (similar to Standards Australia). Parker says: 'It has to be extremely rugged, fully accredited to all the standards for hazardous situations, gas leaks, oil spills. All the components have to comply.'

Emtech's beacon finally passed the test, but sales in the US were slower than expected. Parker planned to sell training videos to keep the 'substantial' marketing budget in check. The beacon was adapted for the Australian safety market and is selling well.

Parker says that working in with RedCentre has made the commercialisation process more ordered. With the business network team, he developed a feasibility plan, then a business plan. Weekly meetings help to keep schedules tight and on target. Flynn says: 'Emtech avoided a classic mistake of start-up companies. They got their product to market. There is a danger of being in continuous R&D mode.'

So far, product development has cost more than $500 000, about 10% going to RedCentre for co-ordinating the process. Niche and Socobell, working on a fee-for-service basis, have accommodated Parker when cash has been tight. RedCentre provided office space. Parker says: 'It is not just the technology input; it is the ability to talk to somebody terribly supportive'. He says the backing of RedCentre also creates substantial credibility overseas.

Parker and Aylward, who now own much less than half of the company and have contributed more than $1 million, have raised about $1.5 million from 17 shareholders and have won a concessional loan from the Industry Research and Development Board. Now they want new shareholders to fund new product development.

Downsizing

Downsizing refers to interventions that are aimed at reducing the size of the organisation.[20] This is typically accomplished by decreasing the number of employees through lay-offs, attrition, redeployment or early retirement, or by reducing the number of organisational units or managerial levels through divestiture, outsourcing, reorganisation or delayering. In practice, downsizing generally involves lay-offs where a certain number or class of organisation member is no longer employed by the organisation. Although traditionally associated with lower-level workers, downsizing has increasingly claimed the jobs of staff specialists, middle managers and senior executives.

An important consequence of downsizing has been the rise of the contingent work force. These less expensive temporary or permanent part-time workers are often hired by the organisations that just laid off thousands of their employees. In many cases, terminated employees become independent contractors or consultants to the organisation that just terminated them. This is because an appropriate reduction in, or redesign of, the work-load does not match the reduced number of workers; fewer workers must accomplish the same amount of work. Overall cost reduction is achieved by replacing expensive permanent workers with a contingent workforce.

Over the past decade, many major corporations and government agencies have engaged in downsizing activities. Among the biggest job-shedders since 1990 are Telstra, who have reduced staff by 15 000 to 66 000; Foster's Brewing Group, down 13 000 to 8304; Westpac Bank down 33 000 from 45 000 and Mayne Nickless, down 11 000 to 29 000.[21] According to the recruitment/outplacement firm DBM, 30 000 banking jobs were abolished between 1991 and 1997. A 1995 study of 1450 organisations in Australia and New Zealand showed that 36% of the surveyed organisations reported permanent reductions in their workforce.[22]

Downsizing is generally a response to several factors, including product or service demand, pressure to focus on short-term profits or budget goals, a major change in organisational strategy and the belief that the slimmer the organisation the better.[23]

John Corrigan, the Technical Support Consultant at ASCPA Management Accounting Centre of Excellence, states that cutting costs has been the mantra of business for the past decade but that there is evidence to suggest that the decimation of middle management ranks in organisations has caused a loss of valuable experience and knowledge.[24] This view is supported by Professor Collins of the Australian Graduate School of Management who says that, in Australia, downsizing has very negative connotations and that, through downsizing, companies have lost a lot of skills that were really needed. Downsizing had very negative social consequences and organisations now find themselves with a new challenge to get commitment from staff. Craig Littler, a visiting Professor at the Melbourne Institute of Economic and Applied Social Research at Melbourne University, states that downsizing was a US concept imported into Australia that was not well managed.

Professor Littler says that, while downsizing plans are still being played out, the phase is over. This view is supported by studies conducted by the Australian Graduate School of Management, which found that the emphasis on cost cutting at 410 big Australian companies had dropped from 68% in 1993 to 56% at the end of 1998.[25]

Application stages

Successful downsizing interventions tend to proceed in the following steps:[26]

1 *Clarify the organisation's strategy.* In this initial stage, organisation leaders specify corporate strategy and clearly communicate how downsizing relates to it. They seek to inform members that downsizing is not a goal in itself, but a restructuring process for achieving strategic objectives. Leaders need to provide visible and consistent support throughout the process. They can provide opportunities for members to voice their concerns, ask questions and obtain counselling if necessary.

2 *Assess downsizing options and make relevant choices.* Once corporate strategy is clear, the full range of downsizing options can be identified and assessed. Table 14.6 describes three primary downsizing methods: workforce reduction, organisation redesign, and systemic changes. A specific downsizing strategy may use elements of all three approaches. Work-force reduction is aimed at reducing the number of employees, usually in a relatively short time frame. It can include attrition, retirement incentives, outplacement services and lay-offs. Organisation redesign attempts to restructure the firm to prepare it for the next stage of growth. This is a medium-term approach that can be accomplished by merging organisational units, eliminating management layers and redesigning tasks. Systemic change is a longer-term option that is aimed at changing the culture and strategic orientation of the organisation. It can involve interventions that alter the responsibilities and work behaviours of everyone in the organisation and that promote continuous improvement as a way of life in the firm.

From around the mid-1980s to today, it has become common for both private and public sector organisations to announce the elimination of thousands of jobs in the quest for quick productivity improvement. For example, in recent years Telstra and the Australian Public Service have each undergone major downsizing efforts involving thousands of employees. Organisations going through such downsizing have to be concerned about managing the effects of these cutbacks, not only for those who are being made redundant, but also for those who 'survive'—albeit with a reduced level of job security.

TABLE 14.6	Three types of downsizing tactics	
Downsizing tactic	**Characteristics**	**Examples**
Workforce reduction	Aimed at headcount reduction Short-term implementation Fosters a transition	Attrition Transfer and outplacement Retirement incentives Buyout packages Lay-offs
Organization redesign	Aimed at organization change Moderate-term implementation Fosters transition and, potentially, transformation	Eliminate functions Merge units Eliminate layers Eliminate products Redesign tasks

Systemic	Aimed at culture change
	Long-term implementation
	Fosters transformation
		Change responsibility
		Involve all constituents
		Fosters continuous
		    improvement and
		    innovation
		Simplification
		Downsizing: a way of life

Source: K. Cameron, S. Freeman and A. Mishra, 'Best practices in white collar downsizing: managing contradictions', *Academy of Management Executive* 5:3 (1991): 62.

Unfortunately, organisations often choose obvious solutions for downsizing, such as lay-offs, that can be quickly implemented. This can produce a climate of fear and defensiveness as members focus on identifying who will be separated from the organisation. It is important to examine a broad range of options and to consider the entire organisation rather than certain areas. This can help to allay fears that favouritism and politics are the basis for downsizing decisions. Moreover, the participation of organisation members in such decisions can have positive benefits. It can create a sense of urgency for identifying and implementing options to downsizing other than lay-offs. Participation can provide members with a clearer understanding of how downsizing will proceed and can increase the likelihood that whatever choices are made will be perceived as being reasonable and fair.

3 *Implement the changes.* This stage involves implementing methods for reducing the size of the organisation. Several practices characterise successful implementation. First, downsizing is best controlled from the top down. Many difficult decisions are required, and a broad perspective helps to overcome people's natural instincts to protect their organisation or function. Second, identify and target specific areas of inefficiency and high cost. The morale of the organisation can be hurt if areas commonly known to be redundant are left untouched. Third, specific actions must be linked to the organisation's strategy. Organisation members need to be consistently reminded that restructuring activities are part of a plan to improve the organisation's performance. Finally, communicate frequently, using a variety of media. This keeps people informed, lowers their anxiety over the process and makes it easier for them to focus on their work.

4 *Address the needs of survivors and those who leave.* Most downsizing eventually involves a reduction in the size of the work force. Consequently, it is important to support not only those employees who remain with the organisation but those who leave. When lay-offs occur, employees are generally asked to take on additional responsibilities and to learn new jobs, often with little or no increase in compensation. This added work load can be stressful, and when combined with anxiety over past lay-offs and possible future ones, it can lead to what researchers have labelled the 'survivor syndrome'.[27] This involves a narrow set of self-absorbed and risk-averse behaviours that can threaten the organisation's survival. Rather than working to ensure the organisation's success, survivors are often preoccupied with whether additional lay-offs will occur, with guilt over receiving pay and benefits while co-workers are struggling with termination, and with the uncertainty of career advancement.

Organisations can address these survivor problems with communication processes that increase the amount and frequency of information provided. Communication should shift from explanations about who left, or why, to clarification of where the company is going, including its visions, strategies and goals. The linkage between employees' performance and strategic success is emphasised so that those remaining feel that they are valued. Organisations can also support survivors through training and development activities that prepare them for the new work they are being asked to perform. Senior management can promote greater involvement in decision making, thus reinforcing the message that people are important to the future success and growth of the organisation.

Given the negative consequences typically associated with job loss, organisations have developed a number of methods to help employees who have been laid off. These include outplacement counselling, personal and family counselling, severance packages, office support for job searches, relocation services and job retraining. Each of these services is intended to help employees in their transition to another work situation.

5 *Follow through with growth plans.* This final stage of downsizing involves the implementation of the organisation renewal and growth process. Failure to move quickly to implement growth plans is a key determinant of ineffective downsizing.[28] (For example, a 1992 study of 1020 human resource directors reported that only

44% of the companies that had downsized in the previous five years had shared details of their growth plans with employees; only 34% had told employees how they would fit into the company's new strategy.[29] These findings suggest that organisations need to ensure that employees understand the renewal strategy and their new roles in it. Employees need to have credible expectations that, although the organisation has been through a tough period, their renewed efforts can move it forward.

Application 14.3 describes the process of strategically-focused downsizing efforts in public and private sector organisations in Western Australia.[30]

APPLICATION 14.3

TQM and downsizing in large organisations

Many organisations are going through periods of downsizing, right-sizing, re-engineering, restructuring or other types of reorganisation with the ultimate goal of reducing staff numbers, developing a leaner organisation and reducing costs. A 1991 study noted that over 85% of the Fortune 1000 firms had downsized their white-collar workforce between 1987 and 1991; more than 50% downsized in 1990 alone. In the public sector, much of this change is driven by the economic rationalist model where the focus is usually on contracting out services, selling parts of the enterprise to the private sector, corporatisation and deregulation.

At the same time, many of these organisations have already invested, or are investing in, continuous improvement activities and adopting the principles of total quality management (TQM). Many are using the quality award models as they strive for business excellence.

Company A manages public sector projects in the state of Western Australia. It has contracted out many functions, including public building maintenance, design and construction. Like many other areas of the public sector, it has undergone downsizing from around 1800 employees to approximately 450 over the past decade.

While the organisation has had process improvement teams operating since about 1990, a more strategic approach to quality management was adopted in 1993, when the strategic

plan was modified to incorporate nine specific directions as a focus for all activities. Specific business directions included delighted customers, strategic asset management, private sector partnerships, motivated and productive employees and continuous improvement.

To support the implementation of quality management and to reinforce the strategic plan, a 'quality ladder' was developed. This was an integrative way of managing quality and comprised a matrix built on seven categories of the Australian Quality Award (AQA), with the addition of one extra—private sector partnership. The ladder has maturity levels extending from 0 to 10, reflecting a state of ignorance (level 0) to excellence (levels 9 and 10). Each cell in the matrix identifies operational indicators and strategies for implementing a quality management approach.

While some restructuring had already taken place before 1994, restructuring further reduced employee numbers to around 450 employees by mid-1996. At the same time it was merged with another government organisation. Despite these significant changes, it was apparent that quality activities were not diminished during this period.

Key features of current quality activities include:
• Ongoing strong commitment to TQM driven by the new CEO (appointed in late 1994) and the executive team who acknowledge the importance of continuing with quality, based on

earlier experiences built up over the years. A strategic business planning workshop in May 1996 confirmed this commitment to quality.

- Strong linkage of quality to an enterprise industrial relations agreement (finalised in January 1995) that includes four areas of performance indicators. These are: external customer satisfaction, commitment to a service charter, use of quality approaches and financial management. Pay bonuses are based on these indicators.
- Strong divisional management linkages through a quality council consisting of the directors of various directorates, and which meets monthly.
- Company A also has cross-organisational strategy groups, which focus on each 'leg' of the quality ladder (quality principle) and aim to stimulate organisational learning. A representative of the top management team sponsors each strategy group.
- Use of a quality matrix to identify achievements to date and action plans based on cells in the matrix and which link back to the corporate plan. The original matrix developed in 1994 is now being reviewed. Attention is now being placed on aligning the cells and principles in the matrix (ladder) with the main strategic goals. In each organisational division the matrix serves as an operational plan where the focus is placed on ascertaining where they are on the matrix and identifying goals from cells in the matrix.

The quality drive within Company A appears not to have diminished during the continued downsizing process. Several reasons may be offered to explain this. First, the CEO is committed to TQM and sees the need to have TQM processes in place during downsizing. Also, while the CEO changed in late 1994, many members of the senior management team have served in the organisation for a number of years, and this has provided a degree of ongoing stability in the senior management ranks. Second, there are still strong linkages between quality principles and the strategic plan that are currently being revised and strengthened. Third, the quality matrix still serves as the basis for organisational divisions to develop operational plans. The cells in the matrix indicate where divisions are and what they need to do to advance to higher levels. Fourth, Company A has retained a driver for quality in the quality manager who has an important input into the strategic planning process. Finally, the industrial relations agreement reinforces the use of quality as part of an employee remuneration system.

Company B operates in the mining industry and has operations throughout Australia and the rest of the world. Quality is incorporated into the organisation's vision, in the quality policy and in their values. Known as 'Excellence through Quality', the vision is built on four foundations—customers (internal and external), employee involvement, continuous improvement and managing for quality.

In 1989, the model of the AQA was introduced for self-assessment at lower levels in the organisation, whereby work units were considered as business units and given the opportunity to define themselves in terms of what the AQA model meant to their activities and to measure where they were on the TQM journey. A cross-functional team developed a quality improvement road map (matrix) that aimed to link all quality activities within the organisation to a comprehensive strategic quality approach.

The road map (in the form of a quality matrix) is referred to as the Company B organisational improvement matrix. Categories in the matrix are:
- leadership
- people management
- planning and deployment
- resource management
- information management

- supplier/customer relations
- process management.

For each category, two or three themes are defined. These are essential elements in relation to the organisation's vision, policy and values. For each theme, concrete and measurable maturity levels are defined. These statements make the matrix an operational tool whereby it is possible for every group within the organisation to define where it is on the maturity ladder and provide direction to the improvement activities to move to higher levels. The matrix was linked to the business planning process, which in turn defines a small number of issues that are really important for the organisation, based on the vision and the values, for the coming planning period.

Company B underwent a somewhat different restructuring exercise during the period 1994–96. Downsizing was less severe and more gradual with employee numbers being reduced over many years through natural attrition. The most significant change in the quality area was the decision to deploy and decentralise the quality specialists from the head office to the various refinery sites in Western Australia. Quality strategies were not considered to be in place until the quality manager reported that the organisation had moved from the entrepreneurial and organisational stage of quality (putting in place all the possible organisational arrangements,

like teams, policies and strategies) to the line responsibility stage (shifting responsibilities from quality staff to line managers), and finally to the ultimate goal of integrating quality into normal day-to-day business.

The focus of quality throughout the company has also been altered so that it is now on process management. Several areas have been selected as major foci, including environmental issues, safety, people and cost. These help to define key result areas (KRA). At the same time, less emphasis is being placed on the 'quality road map' for strategic focus, although it still remains an important educational tool. One reason for the focus on four themes is that this leads to process improvement in a way that attempting to focus on too many activities simultaneously would not.

Deployment of quality is driven primarily from the top and reinforced by the plant manager talking to six employees at a time about quality and the company. The area managers talking to their respective departments and crews follow this. The company has found that it is preferable to use line managers to deploy quality as they have a closer working relationship with their employees. Motorola's cross-functional mapping process has also been used to develop action lists for process improvement.

Results of downsizing

Research on the effects of downsizing has shown mixed results. Many studies have indicated that downsizing may not meet its intended goals, and there is mounting evidence that work force reduction efforts were carried out in piecemeal fashion and failed to meet the objectives of the organisation.[31] Craig Littler, a visiting professor at the Melbourne Institute of Applied Economic and Social Research at Melbourne University, studied 3500 companies across Australia and monitored downsizing patterns; in more than 60% of those companies, the practice of downsizing had not led to any improvement in productivity.[32]

These research findings paint a rather bleak picture of the success of downsizing. The results must be interpreted cautiously, however, as they are subject to at least two major flaws. First, many of the surveys were sent to human resource specialists who might have been naturally inclined to view downsizing in a negative light. Second, the studies of financial performance may have included a biased sample of firms. If the companies selected for analysis had been poorly managed, then downsizing alone would have been unlikely to improve financial performance.

On the positive side, a number of organisations, such as Telstra, General Electric, Motorola, Texas Instruments, Boeing, Chrysler and Hewlett-Packard, have posted solid financial returns after downsizing. Although this evidence contradicts the negative findings described above, recent research suggests that the way in which downsizing is conducted may explain these divergent outcomes. A study of 30 downsized firms in the automobile industry showed that those companies that had effectively implemented the application stages described above scored significantly higher on several performance measures than had firms that had no downsizing strategy or that had implemented the steps poorly.[33] Anecdotal evidence from case studies of downsized firms also shows that organisations that effectively apply the application stages are more satisfied with the process and outcomes of downsizing than are firms that do not. Thus, the success of downsizing efforts may depend as much on how effectively this intervention is applied as on the size of the lay-offs or the amount of delayering.

Re-engineering

The final restructuring intervention is re-engineering—the fundamental rethinking and radical redesign of business processes in order to achieve dramatic improvements in performance.[34] Re-engineering seeks to transform how organisations produce and deliver goods and services. Beginning with the industrial revolution, organisations have increasingly fragmented work into specialised units, each focusing on a limited part of the overall production process. Although this division of labour has enabled organisations to mass-produce standardised products and services efficiently, it can be overly complicated and difficult to manage, as well as being slow to respond to the rapid and unpredictable changes experienced by many organisations today. Re-engineering addresses these problems by breaking down specialised work units into more integrated, cross-functional work processes. This streamlines work processes and makes them faster and more flexible; consequently, they are more responsive to changes in competitive conditions, customer demands, product life cycles and technologies.[35]

As might be expected, re-engineering requires an almost revolutionary change in how organisations design and think about work. It addresses fundamental issues about why organisations do what they do, and why do they do it in a particular way. Re-engineering identifies and questions the often taken-for-granted assumptions that underlie how organisations perform work. This typically results in radical changes in thinking and work methods—a shift from specialised jobs, tasks and structures to integrated processes that deliver value to customers. Such revolutionary change differs considerably from the incremental approaches to performance improvement, such as total quality management (Chapter 15), which emphasise continuous improvement of existing work processes. Because re-engineering radically alters the *status quo*, it seeks to produce dramatic increases in organisation performance.

In radically changing business processes, re-engineering frequently takes advantage of new information technology. Modern information technologies, such as teleconferencing, expert systems, shared databases and wireless communication, can enable organisations to re-engineer. They can help organisations to break out of traditional ways of thinking about work and can permit entirely new ways of producing and delivering products. Amcor is nearing completion of a major restructuring plan that has been underway for two years. According to Amcor's managing director, Russell Jones, the company felt it had to carry out the re-engineering programme if it was going to achieve the financial and strategic objectives that the management had set for the group. Amcor has focused closely on changes designed to improve profitability and help the group regain its corporate credibility through improved earnings. Having embarked on the process to identify core and non-core businesses, and then taken the decision to sell off non-core assets, Amcor now has a far leaner operation. Jones believes that the real benefit to customers and shareholders is that the company is more focused in what it is delivering and will continue to be more efficient in both the short and long term.[36]

Whereas new information technology can enable organisations to re-engineer themselves, existing technology can thwart such efforts. Many re-engineering projects fail because existing information systems do not provide the information needed to operate integrated business processes. The systems do not allow interdependent departments to interface with each other; they often require new information to be entered by hand into separate computer systems before people in different work areas can access it. Given the inherent difficulty of trying to support process-based work with specialised information systems, organisations have sought to develop information technologies that are more suited to business process management work. One of the more promising innovations is a software system called SAP, developed by a German company of the same name. SAP allows firms to standardise their information systems; it can process data on a wide range of tasks and link it all together, thus integrating the information flow among different parts of the business. Not surprising, many of the largest consulting firms that provide re-engineering services, such as Anderson Consulting, ICS Deloitte and Pricewaterhouse Cooper have developed their own SAP consultants. They believe that SAP may be the missing technological link to re-engineering.

Re-engineering is also associated with interventions that have to do with downsizing and work design (Chapter 16). Although these interventions have different conceptual and applied backgrounds, they overlap considerably in practice. Re-engineering can result in production and delivery processes that require fewer people and layers of management. Conversely, downsizing may require subsequent re-engineering interventions. When downsizing occurs without fundamental changes in how work is performed being made, the same tasks are simply being performed by a smaller number of people. Thus, expected cost savings may not be realised because lower productivity offsets lower salaries and fewer benefits.

Re-engineering invariably involves aspects of work design, where tasks are assigned to jobs or teams. It identifies and assesses core business processes and redesigns work to account for key task interdependencies running through them. This typically results in new jobs or teams that emphasise multi-functional tasks, results-oriented feedback and employee empowerment—characteristics associated with motivational and sociotechnical approaches to work design. Regrettably, re-engineering has failed to apply these approaches' attention to differences in individual people's reactions to work to its own work-design prescriptions. It advocates enriched work and teams, without consideration for the considerable research that shows that not all people are motivated to perform such work.

What are the steps?

Re-engineering is a relatively new intervention and is still developing applied methods. Early applications emphasised the identification of which business processes to re-engineer and technical assessment of the work flow. More recent efforts have extended re-engineering practice to address issues of managing change, such as how to deal with resistance to change and how to manage the transition to new work processes.[37] The following application steps are included in re-engineering efforts, although the order may change slightly from one application to another.[38]

1   *Prepare the organisation.* Re-engineering begins with clarification and assessment of the organisation's strategic context, including its competitive environment, strategy and objectives. This establishes the need for re-engineering and the strategic direction that the process should follow. Changes in an organisation's competitive environment can signal a need for radical change in how it does business. In 1994, two North American MNCs decided to re-engineer some of their business processes. One of the companies manufactured electrical instruments in Singapore; the other was operating in petrochemicals in Thailand. An initial

problem in taking such a decision relates to the make-up of the corporate work forces themselves.

It continues to be a problem for MNCs. Decisions about introducing the newest of western techniques may be made by senior expatriate executives to develop local managers, but such development does not help if due regard is not given to cultural differences among both employees in general and local management in particular. The concepts and ideas of management and business developed in the US are not always transferable to other countries in the West, let alone to countries and businesses in Asia-Pacific.[39]

2 *Fundamentally rethink the way work gets done.* This step lies at the heart of business process management and involves these activities:

- identifying and analysing core business processes
- defining their key performance objectives
- designing new processes.

These tasks are the real work of business process management and are typically performed by a cross-functional team that is given considerable time and resources to accomplish them.[40]

a *Identify and analyse core business processes.* Core processes are considered essential for strategic success. They include activities that transform inputs into valued outputs. Core processes are typically assessed through the development of a process map that lists the different activities used to deliver an organisation's products or services.

Analysis of core business processes can include assigning costs to each of the major phases of the work flow. This can help to identify costs that may be hidden in the activities of the production process. Traditional cost-accounting systems do not store data in process terms; they identify costs according to categories of expense, such as salaries, fixed costs and supplies.[41] This method of cost accounting can be misleading and can result in erroneous conclusions about how best to reduce costs.

Business processes can also be assessed in terms of value-added activities—the amount of value contributed to a product or service by a particular step in the process. For example, as part of its invoice collection process, Corky's Pest Control, a small service business dependent on a steady stream of cash payments, provides its customers with self-addressed, stamped envelopes. Although this adds an additional cost to each account, it more than pays for itself in customer loyalty and retention, reduced accounts receivables and late payments handling. Conversely, organisations often engage in process activities that have little if any added value. For instance, a family-owned supermarket introduced a price scanning system at the cash register that was expected to reduce the waiting time for customers at the checkout. But, as their customer base was predominantly a retired community, they also attached visible price labels to each item, thus creating an unnecessary task for employees who could be utilised elsewhere.

b *Define performance objectives.* In this step, challenging performance goals are set. The highest possible level of performance for any particular process is identified, and dramatic goals are set for speed, quality, cost or other measures of performance. These standards can derive from customer requirements or from benchmarks of the best practices of industry leaders (e.g. at the Commonwealth Bank, the teller is also the marketer with specific sales targets to achieve).

c *Design new processes.* The last task in this second step of business process management is to redesign current business processes to achieve breakthrough goals. It often starts with a clean sheet of paper and addresses the question: 'If we were starting this company today, what processes would we need to create a sustainable competitive advantage?' These essential processes are then designed according to the following guidelines:[42]

- begin and end the process with the needs and wants of the customer
- simplify the current process by combining and eliminating steps
- use the 'best of what is' in the current process
- attend to both technical and social aspects of the process
- do not be constrained by past practice
- identify the critical information required at each step in the process
- perform activities in their most natural order
- assume the work gets done right the first time
- listen to people who do the work.

An important activity that appears in many successful business process management efforts is the implementation of 'early wins' or 'quick hits'. Analysis of existing processes often reveals obvious redundancies and inefficiencies. In these cases, appropriate changes may be authorised immediately. These early successes can help to generate and sustain momentum in the business process management effort.

3 *Restructure the organisation around the new business processes.* This last stage in business process management involves changing the organisation's structure to support the new business processes. This typically results in the kinds of process-based structures that were described earlier in this chapter. An important element of this restructuring is the implementation of new information and measurement systems. They must reinforce a shift from measuring behaviours, such as absenteeism and grievances, to assessing outcomes, such as productivity, customer satisfaction and cost savings. Moreover, information technology is one of the key drivers of business process management because it can drastically reduce the cost and time associated with integrating and co-ordinating business processes.

Re-engineered organisations typically have the following characteristics:[43]

- work units change from functional departments to process teams
- jobs change from simple tasks to multi-dimensional work
- people's roles change from controlled to empowered
- the focus of performance measures and compensation shifts from activities to results. Business process management organisations routinely collect and report measures of customer satisfaction, operating costs and productivity to all teams and then tie these measures to pay. In this way, teams and their members are rewarded for working smarter, not harder
- organisation structures change from hierarchical to flat. As described earlier, the favoured structure of the business process management organisation is process-based. Rather than having layers of management, the organisation has empowered, cross-functional and well-educated process teams that collect information, make decisions about task execution and monitor their performance
- managers change from supervisors to coaches; executives change from scorekeepers to leaders. In process-based structures, the roles of management and leadership change drastically. A new set of skills is required, including facilitation, resource acquisition, information sharing, support and problem solving.

Application 14.4 describes the business process management efforts at the Inland Revenue Authority of Singapore. It highlights the importance of focusing on large, strategically important, cross-functional processes and on the enabling role of information technology.[44]

APPLICATION 14.4

Inland Revenue Authority of Singapore — business process management

The scale of transformation accompanying business process re-engineering (BPR) has brought about much challenge to traditional change management practices. Successful implementation of BPR is elusive. Several studies have suggested that as much as 70% of BPR projects failed. The cause has been primarily traced to changed management issues that arise from the paradigmatic shift in work processes, performance measurement and skill requirements.

The re-engineering experience of the Inland Revenue Authority of Singapore (IRAS) reveals that the hard issues in BPR projects are often the soft human issues. The history of tax administration in Singapore goes back to 1947 when the *Income Tax Ordinance* was enacted. Since then, IRAS evolved as the main vehicle through which the government collects revenue and implements economic policies. With Singapore's economic growth, limited resources increasingly strained IRAS. At the end of 1990, the taxman had yet to settle accounts with 35 000, or 50%, of corporate tax cases; 52 000 or 45% of small businesses; and 380 000 or 40% of individual taxpayers. All these amounted to a staggering $1.14 billion revenue in arrears. Backlog creates more backlog. The vicious cycle set IRAS back a few months each year in terms of their assessment efforts. Many taxpayers were unhappy. One telephone survey rated IRAS among the lowest in terms of public satisfaction, which was clearly unacceptable in a government that is obsessed with efficiency and competitiveness. Coupled with other change drivers, IRAS embarked on an enterprise-wide organisational transformation to relook at everything they did and question it.

The re-engineering efforts in IRAS revamped the traditional tax-type organisation into process structures, eliminating 'hands offs' across tax types. Embedded in the heart of the re-engineering is a $69 million Inland Revenue Integrated Systems (IRIS)—an elaborate computer programme that allows the handling of all tax types to be dealt with in an integrated one-stop service manner. All transactions are now fed through IRIS. Only exceptions to the

embedded 600 to 800 rules are thrown out for manual reviews. On average, about 80% of the tax transactions pass through the processing pipeline without any human intervention. The other 20% that require special attention are routed out to specific tax officers according to the required skill levels. The new efficiency offered by the document imaging system also contrasts sharply with the previous system where the 'avalanche of papers' required 'an army of office attendants' simply to move files (as the Senior Deputy Commissioner reported). The application of various technologies—work flow management, intelligent character recognition, three-tier client-server, FCP gateways, super LAN— makes IRAS one of the world's most technologically advanced tax administrators.

Within the business processes, simultaneous changes in the requirements for information, competence, authority and reward were also made. Underlying the re-engineered system were significant changes to the strategic focus of IRAS along the themes of triage (the segmentation of transaction streams), encouraging voluntary compliance and the rebalancing of front-end and back-end procedures.

The above changes in strategic focus have contributed to the organisational effectiveness of IRAS, The results of re-engineering were remarkable. On the negative side, the implementation of IRIS has created a much more stressful and competitive work environment—to the extent that some upstream processes carelessly pushed the work-load downstream, creating another form of hands-offs. IRAS had to fine-tune the performance criteria a few times to align the overall objectives. IRAS is beginning to realise the potential benefits of evolving to a further segmentation by taxpayers' profiles (i.e. both cross-tax type and cross-functional design for different segments of taxpayers) to enable more value-focused tax administration. Given the much greater dependence on IRIS, social interaction among co-workers has reduced significantly, generating some unhappiness among staff. The stability of the computer systems was also erratic. In fact, poor network reliability forced the tax operation to be down on a few occasions.

Overall, however, these negative consequences were tolerable. The Commissioner was presented with the Meritorious Service Medal—one of the highest honours in the 1995 Singapore National Day Awards—for his role in leading the re-engineering efforts in IRAS.

IRAS managed the re-engineering with the involvement of two other major parties, National Computer Board or NCB (quality assurers) and Andersen Consulting or AC (major vendor and consultant). With the facilitation of external consultants, focus groups by functional activities (e.g. collection and assessment) were formed to get an in-depth understanding of the business issues.

Guided by an understanding of the issues on hand and the vision statements, four new focus groups were formed to analyse the changes required in each of the key organisational components, i.e. strategy, people, technology and business processes.

As the project progressed, however, there was little internalisation of the new design as the real impact had yet to be felt. Doubts and uncertainties about the impending change were noted in comments such as 'It won't work for us!' 'We won't know if this high level design will work until we go down to details!' Eventually, IRAS had to extend the user requirement phase by an additional three months, in parallel with actual system-development work, simply to give the people a higher comfort level about the feasibility of the new design and to gather their support.

Various process design and project management issues surfaced during the transition. While technical and rational actions (e.g. objective design validation, incentive bonus) could often be taken for process design/project management matters, handling people issues required greater sensitivity as radical re-engineering brought both psychological and political disruptions to people's turf and jobs. In charting the new organisational structure to support the re-engineered processes, some activities, such as drawing the new boxes and lines generated much controversy. Not all activities fell neatly into the process-organisation structure.

As part of the migration strategy to cope with these uncertainties and iron out potential problems, an interim organisational structure was implemented half a year before the implementation of the IRIS system. The interim structure was essentially the same as the old structure in terms of physical location and system/work supports, except that it now followed the reporting lines of the new organisation structure.

Many of the people issues could be traced to the deeply entrenched bureaucratic culture in IRAS. The results of an anonymous change readiness survey showed that most employees had been with the IRAS for a long time, had little change experience, were loyal only to their functional heads, were narrow in their organisational view and were hesitant to be open/collaborative. Recognising these problems, the new Commissioner set out to change the organisation culture.

The vision that drove the entire re-engineering efforts in IRAS was to be an excellent tax administration, respected for its integrity, fairness and professionalism. IRAS had consistently brought down these high concepts to the operational level in an attempt to clarify the organisational vision. Almost every organisational strategy was articulated along this vision.

The management processes saw a flattening of the hierarchical structure with an expanded span of control. While a supervisor had previously been in charge of 5–7 officers, now he or she supervises 15–20 officers. The shift is towards inculcating individual accountability with clear performance targets. The consistent message from the management is that everyone has a role to play in organisational performance. Extensive mechanisms that build individual accountability exist, applying from the Commissioner right down to the support officers.

The IRAS coped with the essential, yet delicate, people issues by building an information system for change, smoothing the change process, tackling the old entrenched culture, clarifying organisational vision and inculcating a system of accountability and discipline. The major success factor in the IRAS change effort is its recognition that the people resource issue is at the heart of change. Many basic principles of managing change were reiterated in IRAS. However, the applications of these change management principles by IRAS were fragmented and rather haphazard. Clearly, managing the large-scale

transition proved more difficult than IRAS had anticipated. While the experience of IRAS suggests a need for a more integrated change management model, it also highlights the other parts of change management that are simply not predictable. This is particularly so for large-scale projects like IRAS that must take many variables into account over a long implementation time frame.

Reflections on the transformation of IRAS indicate that the reality of large-scale organisational change is highly complex. While part of the complexity can be reduced through an integrated model of change management, the others can only be dealt with by building the internal capabilities for change. At the heart of change, it is the pool of people resources that matters. Organisations planning large-scale change should therefore not treat people issues lightly.

Results from re-engineering

The results from re-engineering vary widely. Industry journals and the business press regularly contain accounts of dramatic business results attributable to re-engineering. On the other hand, the best-selling book on re-engineering reported that as many as 70% of the efforts failed to meet their cost, cycle time or productivity objectives.[45] Despite its popularity, re-engineering is only beginning to be evaluated systematically, and there is little research to help unravel the disparate results.[46]

One evaluation of business process re-engineering examined more than 100 companies' efforts.[47] In-depth analysis of 20 re-engineering projects found that 11 cases had total business unit cost reductions of less than 5% while six cases had total cost reductions averaging 18%. The primary difference was the scope of the business process selected. Re-engineering key value-added processes significantly affected total business unit costs; re-engineering narrow business processes did not.

Similarly, performance improvements in particular processes were strongly associated with changes in six key levers of behaviour, including structure, skills, information systems, roles, incentives and shared values. Efforts that addressed all six levers produced average cost reductions in specific processes by 35%; efforts that affected only one or two change levers reduced costs by 19%. Finally, the percentage reduction in total unit costs was associated with committed leadership.

Summary

This chapter presented interventions aimed at restructuring organisations. Several basic structures, such as the functional structure, the self-contained unit and the matrix configuration, dominate most organisations. Two newer forms, process-based and network structures, were also described. Each of these structures has corresponding strengths and weaknesses, and contingency guidelines must be used to determine which structure is an appropriate fit with the organisation's environment.

Two restructuring interventions were described: downsizing and re-engineering. Downsizing decreases the size of the organisation through workforce reduction or organisational redesign. It is generally associated with lay-offs where a certain number or class of organisation member is no longer employed by the organisation. Downsizing can contribute to organisation development by focusing on the organisation's strategy, using a variety of downsizing tactics, addressing the needs of all organisation members and following through with growth plans.

Re-engineering is the fundamental rethinking and radical redesign of business processes to achieve dramatic improvements in performance. It seeks to transform how organisations traditionally produce and deliver goods and services. A typical re-engineering project prepares the organisation, rethinks how work gets done and finally restructures the organisation around the newly designed core processes.

 ACTIVITIES

Review questions

1 Interventions aimed at structural design include what type of strategies?
2 What should be considered when determining the appropriate technostructural intervention?
3 How would you describe successful downsizing and what are the key success factors?
4 What are the three traditional work structures?
5 Name two more integrative and flexible work structures.
6 What are characteristics of a self-contained unit organisation structure as compared to a process-based structure?
7 What conditions are necessary for the success of a matrix structure?
8 What are the characteristics of re-engineering?
9 Network structures typically have what sort of characteristics?

Discussion and essay questions

1 Compare and contrast the two primary technostructural interventions—downsizing and re-engineering.
2 Describe a functional, self-contained or matrix structure and discuss its advantages and disadvantages.
3 Discuss the differences between process-based and network-based structures. Under what conditions are they appropriate?
4 Describe the short-term, medium- and longer-term approaches to downsizing. What are the key differences between the three?

Notes

1 M. Tushman and E. Romanelli, 'Organizational evolution: a metamorphosis model of convergence and reorientation' in *Research in Organization Behavior*, 7, eds L. Cummings and B. Staw (Greenwich, Conn.: JAI Press, 1985); C. Worley, D. Hitchin and W. Ross, *Integrated Strategic Change* (Reading, Mass.: Addison-Wesley, 1996).

2 P. Lawrence and J. Lorsch, *Organization and Environment: Managing Differentiation and Integration* (Cambridge: Harvard Graduate School of Business, Administration Division of Research, 1967); J. Galbraith, *Organization Design* (Reading, Mass.: Addison-Wesley, 1977): 5.

3 L. Gulick and L. Urwick, eds, *Papers on the Science of Administration* (New York: Institute of Public Administration, Columbia University, 1937); M. Weber, *The Theory of Social and Economic Organization*, eds A. Henderson and T. Parsons (Glencoe, Ill.: Free Press, 1947).

4 A. Chandler, *Strategy and Structure: Chapters in the History of the Industrial Enterprise* (Cambridge: MIT Press, 1962).

5 S. Davis and P. Lawrence, *Matrix* (Reading, Mass.: Addison-Wesley, 1977); H. Kolodny, 'Managing in a matrix', *Business Horizons*, 24 (March–April 1981): 17–35.

6 Davis and Lawrence, *Matrix, op. cit.*

7 W. Joyce, 'Matrix organization: a social experiment', *Academy of Management Journal*, 29 (1986): 536–61; C. Worley and C. Teplitz, 'The use of "expert power" as an emerging influence style within successful US Matrix organizations', *Project Management Journal* (1993): 31–36.

8 Davis and Lawrence, *Matrix, op. cit.*

9 J. Byrne, 'The horizontal corporation', *Business Week*, (20 December 1993): 76–81; S. Mohrman, S Cohen and A. Mohrman, *Designing Team-Based Organizations* (San Francisco: Jossey-Bass, 1995); R. Ashkenas, D. Ulrich, T. Jick and S. Kerr, *The Boundaryless Organization* (San Francisco: Jossey-Bass, 1995).

10 J. Galbraith, E. Lawler and associates, *Organising for the Future: The New Logic for Managing Complex Organizations* (San Francisco: Jossey-Bass, 1993).

11 Byrne, 'The horizontal corporation', *op. cit.*

12 R. Jones, 'Implementing decentralised reform in local government: leadership lessons from the Australian experience', *The International Journal of Public Sector Management*, 12: 1 (1999): 3–76, MCB University Press.

13 W. Halal, 'From hierarchy to enterprise: internal markets are the new foundation of management', *Academy of Management Executive*, 8:4 (1994): 69–83; C. Snow, R. Miles and H. Coleman Jr, 'Managing 21st century network organizations', *Organizational Dynamics*, 20 (1992): 5–19; S. Tully, 'The modular corporation', *Fortune*, (8 February 1993): 106–14.

14 W. Davidow and M. Malone, *The Virtual Corporation: Structuring and Revitalizing the Corporation of the 21st Century* (New York: Harper Business, 1992); J. Bryne, R. Brandt and O. Port, 'The virtual corporation', *Business Week* (8 February 1993); Tully, 'The modular corporation', *op. cit.*; R. Keidel, 'Rethinking organizational design', *The Academy of Management Executive*, 8 (1994): 12–30; C. Handy, *The Age of Unreason* (Cambridge: Harvard Business School Press, 1989).

15 W. Powell, 'Neither market nor hierarchy: network forms of organization' in *Research in Organizational Behavior*, 12, eds B. Staw and L. Cummings (Greenwich, Conn.: JAI Press, 1990): 295–336; M. Lawless and R. Moore, 'Interorganizational systems in public service delivery: a new application of the dynamic network framework', *Human Relations*, 42 (1989): 1167–84; M. Gerstein, 'From machine bureaucracies to networked organizations: an architectural journey' in *Organizational Architecture*, eds D. Nadler, M. Gerstein, R. Shaw and associates (San Francisco: Jossey-Bass, 1992): 11–38.

16 Bryne, Brandt and Port, 'The virtual corporation', *op. cit.*

17 Bryne, Brandt, and Port, 'The virtual corporation', *op. cit.*; G. Dess, A. Rasheed, K. McLaughlin and R. Priem, 'The new corporate architecture', *Academy of Management Executive*, 9 (1995): 7–20.

18 J. Galbraith and R. Kazanjian, *Strategy Implementation: Structure, Systems and Process*, 2nd ed. (St. Paul: West Publishing Company, 1986): 159–60.

19 K. Walters, *Reuters Business Briefing*, 4 May 1998, 60.

20 W. Cascio, 'Downsizing: what do we know? what have we learned?' *The Academy of Management Executive*, 7 (1993): 95–104.

21 J. Kirby, 'Downsizing gets the push', *Business Review Weekly*, 21: 10, 22 March 1999.

22 T. Wagar and C. Gilson, 'Workforce reduction in Australia and New Zealand: A research note', *Human Resource Management Journal*, 6:2 (1996): 88–98.

23 *Ibid.*

24 J. Corrigan, 'Corporate anorexia?' *Australian Accountant*, 67:8 (1997): 50–51.

25 Kirby, 'Downsizing gets the push', *op. cit.*

26 Adapted from Cameron, Freeman and Mishra, 'Best practices …', *op. cit.*; and R. Marshall and L. Lyles, 'Planning for a restructured, revitalized organization', *Sloan Management Review*, 35 (1994): 81–91.

27 J. Brockner, 'The effects of work layoffs on survivors: research, theory and practice' in *Research in Organization Behavior*, 10, eds B. Staw and L. Cummings (Greenwich, Conn.: JAI Press, 1989): 213–55.

28 Marshall and Lyles, 'Planning for a restructured, revitalized organization', *op. cit.*

29 J. Rogdon, 'Lack of communication burdens restructurings', *The Wall Street Journal*, (2 November 1992): B1.

30 A. Brown and T. van der Wiele, 'Insights into TQM and downsizing in large organizations', *Benchmarking for Quality Management and Technology*, 4:3 (1997): 202–12.

31 Kirby, 'Downsizing gets the push', *op. cit.*

32 *Ibid.*

33 Cameron, Freeman and Mishra, 'Best practices …', *op. cit.*

34 M. Hammer and J. Champy, *Reengineering the Corporation* (New York: HarperCollins, 1993); T. Stewart, 'Reengineering: the hot new managing tool', *Fortune*, (23 August 1993): 41–48; J. Champy, *Reengineering Management* (New York: HarperCollins, 1994).

35 R. Kaplan and L. Murdock, 'Core process redesign', *The McKinsey Quarterly*, 2 (1991): 27–43.

36 J. Potter, 'Amcor comes in for an overhaul', *PPI*, 41:6, 69–71 ISSN: 0033409X.

37 M. Miller, 'Customer service drives reengineering effort', *Personnel Journal*, 73 (1994): 87–93.

38 Kaplan and Murdock, 'Core process redesign', *op. cit.*; R. Manganelli and M. Klein, *The Reengineering Handbook* (New York: AMACOM, 1994).

39 S. McKenna, 'The cultural transferability of business and organizational reengineering: examples from Southeast Asia', *The TQM Magazine*, 7:3, 1995, 12–16.

40 J. Katzenbach and D. Smith, 'The rules for managing cross-functional reengineering teams', *Planning Review* (March/April 1993): 12–13; A. Nahavandi and E. Aranda, 'Restructuring teams for the reengineered organization', *The Academy of Management Executive*, 8 (1994): 58–68.

41 M. O'Guin, *The Complete Guide to Activity Based Costing* (Englewood Cliffs, N.J.: Prentice Hall, 1991); H. Johnson and R. Kaplan, *Relevance Lost: The Rise and Fall of Management Accounting* (Cambridge: Harvard Business School Press, 1987).

42 Hammer and Champy, *Reengineering the Corporation, op. cit.*

43 *Ibid.*

44 S. Sia and B. Neo, 'Transforming the tax collector: reengineering the Inland Revenue Authority of Singapore', *Journal of Organizational Change Management*, 11:6 (1998), 496–514.

45 Hammer and Champy, *Reengineering the Corporation, op. cit.*

46 Champy, *Reengineering Management, op. cit.*; K. Jensen, 'The effects of business process management on injury frequency', unpublished Master's thesis, Culver City, Calif.: Pepperdine University, 1993.

47 G. Hall, J. Rosenthal and J. Wade, 'How to make reengineering really work', *Harvard Business Review*, (November–December 1993): 119–31.

Employee involvement

The past decade has witnessed a rapid growth in employee involvement (EI). Faced with competitive demands for lower costs, higher performance and greater flexibility, companies are increasingly trying to enhance the participation, commitment and productivity of their members. This chapter presents OD interventions that are aimed at moving decision making downward in the organisation, closer to where the actual work takes place. This increased employee involvement can lead to quicker, more responsive decisions, continuous performance improvements and greater employee flexibility, commitment and satisfaction.

Employee involvement is a broad term that has been variously referred to as 'empowerment', 'participative management', 'work design', 'industrial democracy' and 'quality of work life'. It covers a diversity of approaches to gaining greater participation in relevant work place decisions. Some organisations, such as Intel, have enhanced worker involvement through enriched forms of work; others, such as Ford, have increased participation by forming employee involvement teams that develop suggestions for improving productivity and quality; Chrysler and Shell Oil have sought greater participation through union–management co-operation on performance and quality-of-work-life issues; and still others, such as Texas Instruments, Glaxo and Motorola, have improved employee involvement by emphasising participation in total quality management.

Current EI approaches have evolved from earlier quality-of-work-life efforts in Europe, Scandinavia and the US. Although the terms 'employee involvement' and 'empowerment' have gradually replaced the designation 'quality of work life', reviewing this historical background provides a clearer understanding of what EI means today. A current definition of EI includes four elements that can promote meaningful involvement in work place decisions: power, information, knowledge and skills and rewards. These components of EI can combine to have powerful effects on productivity and employee well-being.

The following major EI applications are discussed in this chapter:
- parallel structures, including co-operative union–management projects and quality circles
- high-involvement organisations
- total quality management.

Two additional EI approaches, work design and reward system interventions, are discussed in Chapters 16 and 17, respectively.

Employee involvement: what is it?

Employee involvement can be understood against its background in the quality-of-work-life (QWL) movement started in the late 1950s. The phrase 'quality of work life' was used to stress the prevailing poor quality of life at the work place.[1] Over the past 30 years, both the term 'QWL' and the meaning attributed to it have undergone considerable change and development, giving rise to the current emphasis on EI. In this section, the history of QWL and its influence on employee involvement are reviewed. In addition, the important and often misunderstood relationship between EI and productivity is clarified.

Evolution of the quality-of-work-life movement

The present concern with employee involvement can be traced to the 1950s, when Eric Trist and his co-workers at the Tavistock Institute of Human Relations in London conducted a series of studies on work and its human and technical outcomes. This research became the foundation for sociotechnical systems theory—a set of principles that optimises both the social and the technical components of work systems. Many current efforts to enrich work are based on these principles, which are discussed more fully in Chapter 16 on work design. In the US in the 1950s, Davis and his associates began working on ways of changing assembly lines to make them more productive and satisfying places to work.[2] The decade also saw a great deal of research on the causes and consequences of job satisfaction and the beginning of systematic employee attitude surveys.

In the 1960s, the rising concern for civil rights and social responsibility led to a number of US governmental actions, including the *Equal Pay Act (Fair Labor Standards Act*, 1963), the *Civil Rights Act* (1964) and the development of equal opportunity guidelines. From these activist roots sprang two distinct phases of QWL activity. From 1969 to 1974, a widespread interest emerged in improving the quality of experiences that people have at work. The major impetus was the growing concern of a generally affluent society for the health, safety and satisfaction of workers. At the same time, the US was becoming increasingly aware of European efforts to enhance QWL that basically followed a sociotechnical systems perspective.

During this initial burst of QWL activity, concern about the employee and work life relationship developed rapidly. Literature reviews suggest that the number of published references on QWL has doubled each five years since 1955.[3] Although new programmes were starting all the time, many of the early reports were not fully documented. Most of the experiments reviewed had severe deficiencies in both outcome measurement and experimental control. However, a hopeful trend could be seen in the emerging designs of new work systems.[4]

Two definitions of 'QWL' emerged during this first major phase of activity.[5] QWL was first defined in terms of people's reaction to work, particularly individuals' job satisfaction and mental health. Using this definition, QWL focused primarily on the personal consequences of the work experience and how to improve work to satisfy personal needs. The following criteria for QWL characterise this *individual outcome* orientation.[6]

1 *Adequate and fair compensation.* What pay, fringe benefits and other compensation are needed to maintain an acceptable standard of life, particularly in comparison with other work?

2 *Safe and healthy environment.* What is the physical and mental working environment? Are the physical conditions unduly hazardous? What are the conditions that affect employees' health, comfort and convenience when performing their jobs?

3 *Development of human capacities.* To what extent is the work simplified, split up and tightly controlled? To what degree can the job enable the worker to use and develop skills and knowledge and to perform work that is personally meaningful and important?

4 *Growth and security.* To what extent do job assignments contribute to maintaining and expanding capabilities? How can newly acquired or expanded knowledge and skills be used in future work assignments? What is the possibility of furthering one's potential and advancing one's career in organisational terms that associates, peers and family members recognise?

5 *Social integration.* Is there an opportunity to interact with others? Is there freedom from prejudice? Does a sense of interpersonal openness and community or equal opportunity exist? Is there an absence of stratification and the possibility of upward mobility? Is advancement based on merit?

6 *Constitutionalism.* What are the worker's rights, and how are they protected? To what extent does the organisational culture respect personal privacy, tolerate

dissent, adhere to high standards of equity in distributing rewards and provide for due process? How much dignity and respect is there for the individual? Can the worker give honest opinions and be treated as an adult?

7 *The total life space.* Is there a balance between work and life away from the job? Is there absence of undue job stress? What is the employee's state of mind? Is the job or the company causing the employee to be upset or depressed?

8 *Social relevance.* Does the employee see the organisation as being socially responsible in its products, waste disposal, employment practices, marketing techniques and other activities? If employees view the organisation as being socially irresponsible, they can depreciate the value of their own work and careers.

A second, later conception of QWL from this period defined it as an *approach* or *method.*[7] People defined QWL in terms of specific techniques and approaches used for improving work. It was viewed as synonymous with methods such as job enrichment, self-managed teams and labour–management committees. This technique orientation derived mainly from the growing publicity surrounding QWL projects, such as the General Motors–United Auto Workers project at Tarrytown and the Gaines Pet Food plant. These pioneering projects drew attention to specific approaches for improving work.

United States corporations became fascinated with these alternative management styles and with catching up with management developments abroad. Books extolling the virtues of Japanese management practices, such as *Ouchi's Theory Z,*[8] made best-seller lists; adoption of Japan's quality circle concept became widespread almost overnight. At the same time, many of the QWL programmes started in the early 1970s were achieving success, including those of highly visible corporations, such as General Motors, Ford and Honeywell, and unions, such as the United Automobile Workers.

Today, this second phase of QWL activity continues primarily under the banner of 'employee involvement', rather than of QWL. For many OD practitioners, the term 'EI' signifies, more than the name QWL, the growing emphasis on how employees can contribute more to running the organisation so that it can be more flexible, productive, flexible and competitive. Recently, the term 'employee empowerment' has been used interchangeably with the name EI, the former suggesting the power inherent in moving decision making downward in the organisation.[9] The term 'employee empowerment' may be too restrictive, however. Because it draws attention to the power aspects of these interventions, it may lead practitioners to neglect other important elements necessary for success, such as information, skills and rewards. Consequently, EI seems a broader and less restrictive banner for these approaches to organisational improvement than employee empowerment.

There is increasing international concern with productivity and with discovering new approaches for enhancing employee involvement in the work place. For example, at the annual Ecology of Work Conference, co-sponsored by the National Training Laboratories (NTL) Institute and the OD Network, an increasing number of public and private organisations are sharing their EI experiences. In the 1980s, some of the initial fascination with Japanese methods waned, and Americans looked at home for solutions, as evidenced by Peters' and Waterman's *In Search of Excellence*[10] and Peters' and Austin's *A Passion for Excellence,*[11] both of which topped the New York Times non-fiction best-seller list. Extensive plant redesign was undertaken in such well-known companies as Procter and Gamble and Johnson and Johnson, as well as in many smaller organisations.

Research by a number of US organisations that were adopting EI practices has resulted in the most comprehensive, long-term study of EI applications so far. Lawler, Mohrman and Ledford surveyed the *Fortune* 1000 at three time periods: 1987, 1990 and 1993.[12] Their data show positive trends in EI use among these firms over this time period, including both a growing number of firms applying EI and a greater percentage of the workforce included in such programmes. Despite these positive trends, however, this research reveals that the scope and depth of EI interventions are relatively modest. Data from 1993 show that about one-third of the companies surveyed reported no significant involvement efforts and approximately the same percentage revealed limited attempts at getting employees involved in decision making. Thus, although many large organisations are using EI practices, there is considerable room for their diffusion across organisations and throughout the workforce.

Although there are major differences among approaches in different countries, EI has also clearly prospered outside the US, including in Australia. Countries using EI in Western Europe include France, Germany, Denmark, Sweden, Norway, Holland, Italy and Great Britain.[13] Although the tremendous changes currently taking place in countries such as Russia, Czechoslovakia, Hungary, Bulgaria and Yugoslavia may have dampened EI efforts, several programmes are actively underway.[14] Canada, Mexico, India and Japan are also using EI. Internationally, EI may be considered a set of processes directed at changing the structure of the work situation within a particular cultural environment and under the influence of particular values and philosophies. As a result, in some instances, EI has been promoted by unions; in others, by management. In some cases, EI has been part of a pragmatic approach to increasing productivity; in other cases, it has been driven by socialist values.[15]

A working definition of employee involvement

Employee involvement seeks to increase members' input into decisions that affect organisation performance and employee well-being.[16] It can be described in terms of four key elements that promote worker involvement:[17]

- *Power.* This element of EI includes providing people with sufficient authority to make decisions. Such empowerment can cover a diversity of work-related decisions that involve such things as work methods, task assignments, performance outcomes, customer service and employee selection. The amount of power afforded employees can vary enormously, from simply asking them for input into decisions that managers subsequently make, to managers and workers jointly making decisions, to employees making decisions themselves.
- *Information.* Timely access to relevant information is vital to making effective decisions. Organisations can promote EI by ensuring that necessary information flows freely to those empowered to make decisions. This can include data about operating results, business plans, competitive conditions, new technologies and work methods and ideas for organisational improvement.
- *Knowledge and skills.* Employee involvement contributes to organisational effectiveness only to the extent that employees have the requisite skills and knowledge to make good decisions. Organisations can facilitate EI by providing training and development programmes for improving members' knowledge and skills. Such learning can cover an array of expertise having to do with performing tasks, making decisions, solving problems and understanding how the business operates.
- *Rewards.* Because people generally do those things for which they are recognised, rewards can have a powerful effect on getting people involved in the organisation. Meaningful opportunities for involvement can provide employees with internal rewards, such as feelings of self-worth and accomplishment. External rewards, such as pay and promotions, can reinforce EI when they are linked directly to performance outcomes that result from participation in decision making. (Reward systems are discussed more fully in Chapter 17.)

These four elements—power, information, knowledge and skills and rewards—contribute to EI success. They determine how much participation in decision making is possible in organisations. The further that all four elements are moved downward throughout the organisation, the greater the employee involvement in decision making. Moreover, because the four elements of EI are interdependent, they must be changed together to obtain positive results. For example, if organisation members are given more power and authority to make decisions but do not have the information or knowledge and skill necessary to make good decisions, then the value of involvement is likely to be negligible. Similarly, increasing employees' power, information and knowledge and skills but not linking rewards to the performance consequences of changes gives members little incentive to improve organisational performance. The EI methods that will be described in this chapter vary in how much involvement is afforded employees. Parallel structures, such as union–management co-operative efforts and quality circles, are limited in the degree that the four elements of EI are moved downward in the organisation; high-involvement organisations and total quality management provide far greater opportunities for involvement in decision making.

How employee involvement affects productivity

An assumption underlying much of the EI literature is that EI interventions will lead to higher productivity. Until recently, this premise has been based mainly on anecdotal evidence and a good deal of speculation. Today, however, there is a growing body of research findings to support the linkage between EI and productivity.[18] These studies have found a consistent relationship between EI practices and such productivity measures as financial performance, customer satisfaction, labour hours and scrap rates.

Attempts to explain this positive linkage between EI and productivity have traditionally followed the idea that by giving people more involvement in work decisions, they will become more satisfied with their work. Satisfaction, in turn, should improve productivity. There is growing evidence that this satisfaction-causes-productivity premise is too simplistic and sometimes wrong.

A more realistic explanation for how EI interventions can affect productivity is shown in Figure 15.1. EI practices, such as participation in work place decisions, can improve productivity in at least three ways.[19] First, such interventions can improve communication and co-ordination among employees and organisational departments. This can increase productivity by helping to integrate different jobs or departments contributing to an overall task.

Second, EI interventions can improve employee motivation, particularly when they satisfy important individual needs. Motivation is translated into improved performance when people have the necessary skills and knowledge to perform well and when the technology and work situation allow people to affect productivity. For example, some jobs are so rigidly controlled and specified that individual motivation can have little impact on productivity.

Third, EI practices can improve the capabilities of employees, thus enabling them to perform better. For example, attempts at increasing employee participation in decision making generally include skill training in group problem solving and communication.

Figure 15.2 shows the secondary effects of EI. EI practices can increase employee well-being and satisfaction by providing a better work environment and a more fulfilling job. Improved productivity can also increase satisfaction, particularly when it leads to greater rewards. Increased employee satisfaction, deriving from EI interventions and increased productivity, can ultimately have a still greater impact on productivity by attracting good employees to join and remain with the organisation.

In sum, EI interventions are expected to increase productivity by improving communication and co-ordination, employee motivation and individual capabilities. They can also influence productivity by means of the secondary effects of increased employee well-being and satisfaction. Although a growing body of research supports these relationships,[20] there is considerable debate over the strength of the association between EI and productivity.[21] So far, organisations have tended to implement only relatively modest levels of EI, with correspondingly moderate improvements in performance and satisfaction. As greater numbers of organisations experiment with high levels of EI, research should reveal whether these levels produce large improvements in performance and satisfaction.

Employee involvement applications

This section describes five major EI applications that vary in the amount of power, information, knowledge and skills and rewards that are moved downward throughout the organisation (from least to most involvement):

- parallel structures, including co-operative union–management projects and quality circles
- high-involvement organisations
- total quality management.

Parallel structures

Parallel structures are designed to involve members in resolving ill-defined, complex problems and to build adaptability into bureaucratic organisations.[22] Also known as 'collateral structures', 'dualistic structures' or 'shadow structures',[23] parallel structures operate in tandem with the formal organisation. They provide members with an alternative setting in which to address problems and to propose innovative solutions free

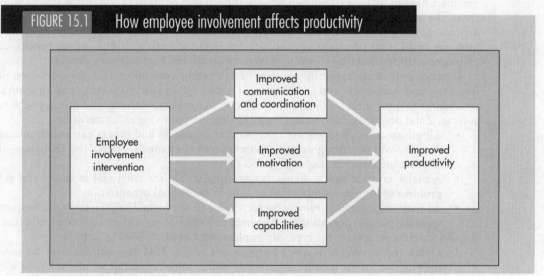

FIGURE 15.1   How employee involvement affects productivity

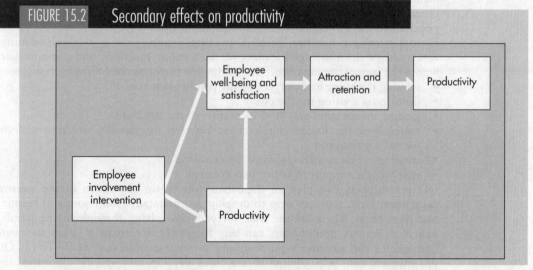

FIGURE 15.2   Secondary effects on productivity

from formal work demands. For example, members may attend periodic off-site meetings where they can explore ways of improving quality in their work area; they may be temporarily assigned to a special project or facility, such as Lockheed's 'skunkworks', to devise new products or solutions to organisational problems. Parallel structures facilitate problem solving and change by providing time and resources for members to think, talk and act in completely new ways. Consequently, norms and procedures for working in parallel structures are entirely different from those of the formal organisation.

Parallel structures fall at the lower end of the EI scale. Member participation is typically restricted to making proposals and to offering suggestions for change. Subsequent decisions about implementing proposals are reserved for management. Membership in parallel structures also tends to be limited, primarily to volunteers and to the numbers of employees for which there are adequate resources. Management heavily influences the conditions under which parallel structures operate. It controls the amount of authority that members have in making recommendations, the amount of information that is shared with them, the amount of training they receive to increase their knowledge and skills and the amount of monetary rewards for participation. Because parallel structures offer limited amounts of EI, they are most appropriate for organisations with little or no history of employee participation, top-down management styles and bureaucratic cultures.

A parallel structure typically consists of a steering committee that provides overall direction and authority and a number of small groups with norms and operating procedures that promote a climate conducive to innovation, learning and group problem solving. Zand describes these structures as having the following characteristics:[24]

- All information channels are open so that managers and others can communicate directly, without using formal communication channels. Thus, the exchange of relevant information is complete and rapid.
- A major norm is that individuals operating within the collateral structure can get problem-solving assistance from anyone in the formal organisation.
- As both organisations remain intact, inputs to the formal organisation are outputs from the parallel organisation. The final decisions occur within the formal structure.

Parallel learning structures are typically implemented in the following steps:[25]

1 *Define the parallel structure's purpose and scope.* This first step involves defining the purpose for the parallel structure as well as initial expectations about how it will function. Organisational diagnosis can help to clarify how a parallel structure can address specific problems and issues, such as productivity, absenteeism or service quality. In addition, management training in the use of parallel structures can include discussions about the commitment and resources necessary to implement them; the openness needed to examine organisational practices, operations and policies and the willingness to experiment and learn.

2 *Form a steering committee.* Parallel structures typically use a steering committee composed of acknowledged leaders of the various functions and constituencies within the formal organisation. This committee performs the following tasks:
   - refining the scope and purpose of the parallel structure
   - developing a vision for the effort
   - guiding the creation and implementation of the structure
   - establishing the linkage mechanisms between the parallel structure and the formal organisation
   - creating problem-solving groups and activities
   - ensuring the support of senior management.

OD practitioners can play an important role in the formation of the steering committee. First, they can help to develop and maintain group norms of learning and innovation. These set the tone for problem solving throughout the parallel structure. Second, practitioners can help the committee create a vision statement that refines the structure's purpose and promotes ownership of it. Third, OD practitioners can help committee members develop and specify objectives and strategies, organisational expectations and required resources and potential rewards for participating in the parallel structure.

3 *Communicate with organisation members.* The effectiveness of a parallel structure depends on a high level of involvement from organisation members. Communicating the purpose, procedures and rewards from participation in the parallel structure can help to gain that involvement. Moreover, employee participation in the development of the vision and purpose for the parallel structure can increase ownership and visibly demonstrate the 'new way' of working. Continued communication about the parallel structure activities can ensure member awareness.

4 *Form employee problem-solving groups.* These groups are the primary means of accomplishing the purpose of the parallel learning structure. Their formation involves selecting and training group members, establishing problems for the groups to work on and providing appropriate facilitation. Selecting group members is important as success is often a function of group membership.[26] Members need to represent the appropriate hierarchical levels, expertise, functions and constituencies that have relevance to the problems at hand. This allows the parallel structure to identify and communicate with the formal structure. It also provides the necessary resources for solving the problems.

Once formed, the groups need appropriate training. This may include discussions about the vision of the parallel structure, the specific problems to be addressed and the way they will be solved. As in the steering committee, group norms promoting openness, creativity and integration need to be established.

Another key resource for parallel structures is facilitation for the problem-solving groups. Although this can be expensive, it can yield important benefits in problem-solving efficiency and quality. Group members are asked to solve problems by cutting through traditional hierarchical and functional boundaries. Facilitators can pay special attention to processes that require disparate groups to co-operate. They can help members identify and resolve problem-solving issues within and between groups.

5 *Address the problems and issues.* Generally, groups in parallel structures solve problems by using an action research process. They diagnose specific problems, plan appropriate solutions and implement and evaluate them. Problem solving can be facilitated when the groups and the steering committee relate effectively to each other. This permits the steering committee to direct problem-solving efforts in an appropriate manner, to acquire the necessary resources and support and to approve action plans. It also helps to ensure that the groups' solutions are linked appropriately to the formal organisation. In this way, early attempts at change will have a better chance of succeeding.

6 *Implement and evaluate the changes.* This step involves implementing appropriate organisational changes and assessing the results. Change proposals need to have the support of the steering committee and the formal authority structure. As they are implemented, the organisation needs information about their effects. This lets members know how successful the changes have been and whether or not they need to be modified. In addition, feedback on changes helps the organisation learn to adapt and innovate.

Parallel structures create a source of involvement beyond that found in most bureaucratic organisations. For many people, especially lower-level employees, this opportunity to influence the formal organisation leads to increased work satisfaction and task effectiveness.[27] Parallel structures can also improve organisational functioning. For example, General Motors adopted Zand's collateral organisation in its Central Foundry Division in December 1974, and the division has continued to evolve and flourish. Division managers may spend up to 20% of their time with the parallel organisation.[28] One study in the division showed that the parallel organisation saved 60 000 labour hours per year in one plant, with similar savings across the entire division. Zand's studies in a bank and a large research and development company reported the use of innovative ideas and approaches. Zand concluded that organisation members learn concepts and methods that enable them to freely invent and use new modes for solving ill-structured problems.[29]

Although parallel structures promise to free up organisations and their members for innovative problem solving and personal development, little controlled research on the approach has been published. The evidence is primarily case study and anecdotal. A recent study of parallel structures composed of employee-involvement teams suggests that, unless these structures are carefully integrated with the formal organisation, they are unlikely to have much impact on the organisation and are likely to be abandoned.[30]

Co-operative union–management projects

Co-operative union–management projects are one of the oldest EI interventions. Typically, these projects seek to improve both worker satisfaction and organisational effectiveness through a parallel organisation. They are mostly associated with the original QWL movement and its focus on work place change. As a result, only moderate increases in power, information, knowledge and skills and rewards are achieved.

Begun in 1973, the series of field experiments (*Quality of Work Programme*) has grown to include a number of different organisations, including a medical centre, a coal mine, a municipal government, a public utility and several manufacturing organisations with different technologies and products. Each project has essentially the same structural characteristics:

- *Quality-of-working life committee.* This committee is a top-level joint union–management committee that serves as the basic centre for planning. The committee, created during the project start-up phase, is composed of key representatives from management, such as a president or chief operating officer, and each of the unions and employee groups involved in the project, such as local union presidents. The committee's mandate is to begin activities that are directed at improving both the quality of working life and the effectiveness of the organisation. The US National Quality of Work Center (NQWC) views increased productivity as proper for an organisation and encourages organisations to be open about it. Unions are told that, because projects are jointly controlled efforts, they need not fear an organisation's productivity motives. Indeed, many unions *distrust* a management philosophy that does not express concern for higher productivity or quality of its product or service.
- *External consultants.* The projects funded by NQWC are designed to be multi-year. Thus, funding is provided (usually for 18 months) for an external consultant to act as third-party facilitator and to provide guidance and assistance to the labour–management committee. The consultant provides QWL training for all participants. In most projects, this committee selects the consultant or consultant group.[31]
- *External researchers.* The original design of NQWC, in conjunction with the University of Michigan's Institute for Social Reseach (ISR), created separate roles for the change agent and the evaluation researcher. It was assumed that keeping these functions separate would allow the consultant to be concerned with client needs and development and would also permit a more objective assessment of change. Therefore, each QWL programme has a separate research team, usually from ISR, which uses a partially standardised package of measurement instruments.[32] The measurement activities are scheduled to last for three years so that long-term effects of the project can be determined.

As experience has increased and the number of projects has grown, the general design has evolved to include the following additional steps:

- *Multiple-level committees.* Clearly a committee that includes persons such as the president of a large organisation and a union vice-president cannot oversee all aspects of a QWL project. It is frequently necessary to establish more than one labour–management committee at a number of selected levels in the organisation to reflect the differing interests and knowledge. The original committee can be amplified and assisted by working committees at the plant level and by core groups at the supervisor and union steward–worker level. These are permanent working committees in departments, plants or work units that deal with day-to-day project activities.

- *Ad hoc committees.* In many instances, the labour–management committee initiates a particular project that involves workers and managers in a specific part of the organisation. At the same time, employees themselves frequently initiate action toward a particular goal. In such cases, an *ad hoc* committee is established to bring about change. Such committees have a specific task and a limited lifetime.

Excellent descriptions of this methodology in action are available in the literature, featuring longitudinal discussions of problems, successes and partial failures. The projects include a large metropolitan hospital,[33] a large international company called the 'National Processing Case',[34] and the Bolivar plant of Harman International Industries.[35]

Application 15.1 presents an example of work restructuring and employee relations at Mobil Adelaide refinery.[36]

APPLICATION 15.1

Work restructuring and employee relations — Mobil Adelaide refinery

The Mobil Adelaide refinery is divided into two business units, the lube refinery and the fuels refinery. The lube refinery has a capacity of 750 000 litres a day of a range of base oils. About 60% of the refinery's lube products are exported to the Australasia South-East Asian region. The other major unit, the fuels refinery, has a daily output of approximately 7 000 000 litres of refined products. This refinery does not export products but supplies nearly all the fuel needed for South Australia.

The Mobil Adelaide refinery operates 24 hours a day, 365 days a year. About half the workforce are process technicians who monitor and regulate every aspect of refinery processing through computer consoles. A quarter of the workforce are maintenance people who check and repair refinery equipment to overcome wear-and-tear problems as well as undertake scheduled maintenance work on equipment. Other technical personnel include chemical, mechanical, electrical and instrument engineers, chemists and laboratory technicians. Administrative staff provide support functions such as accounting, purchasing and personnel.

In 1989, the Adelaide operation was stimulated to change by the results of an International Refinery Competitiveness Survey (the Solomon Survey), which highlighted areas of weakness that threatened the medium-term viability of the refinery. In early 1990, a restructuring process within the operating group of the refinery was created with the objective of improving flexibility, increasing high value speciality products, reducing energy usage and improving yields. In short, work place restructuring through extensive work group involvement and union and management collaboration became the main focus of the Mobil Adelaide refinery renewal programme, and formed the basis of their successful submission for funding under the Australian Best Practice Demonstration Programme.

Prior to the project receiving funding under the Best Practice Programme, the Mobil Adelaide refinery had already embarked on phase one of a major restructuring programme. A major thrust of the change programme centred on refinery technicians, who were the largest group within the refinery (160 employees) and belonged to the National Union of Workers. Undertaken in two phases, the change programme was designed to achieve the following objectives:
- improve employee efficiency and job satisfaction through the redesign of jobs
- achieve greater flexibility, improved work practices and the removal of artificial barriers
- give access to better paid and more meaningful work through structured career paths based on the acquisition and the utilisation of skills and productivity-linked rewards

- improve occupational health, safety and environmental practices in the redesign of work and training
- improve management practices through an ongoing commitment to consultation in the work place.

During the period of the best practice project, an agreement was developed for production group employees. This agreement between Mobil Adelaide Refinery and the National Union of Workers was ratified by the Commission on 17 December 1993. The new Production Group Improvement Plan has been awarded for three years and represents the outcome of restructuring under the best practice project. Some of the key features of the agreement include:

Changes in payment systems

Traditionally, employees were encouraged to increase their overtime loading in order to increase their remuneration. With annualised wages, the overtime component is built into the payment system. The new payment system has created an incentive for employees to work more effectively and reduce the need for overtime. Employees know with certainty what their wages will be over the next few years. This is an improvement over the traditional system where wage fluctuation could be considerable in years when overtime was minimal.

The shift system and the redefinition of supervision

During the process of restructuring, the shift system was changed from a four-shift system to a five-shift system. Each shift team had about eight to ten members and the head of the shift team was called the process area co-ordinator (PAC man). The process area co-ordinators reported to a shift superintendent. Essentially, the role of supervisor or shift superintendent changed from a controlling and policing function to one involving facilitation and communication. The number of supervisors were also reduced from thirteen (one for every shift team) to six, with one superintendent responsible for both plants in every shift. This reduction in the number of supervisory staff was one of the more contentious parts of the change programme. To make this new system work, decision making has been devolved to the shop floor. This change has brought about greater employee ownership for work undertaken at site.

Self-managed teams

The principles of team working has been well received by the workforce, and the company is committed towards the development of work teams. A number of changes that have been made to facilitate this transition further include: shift meetings at the beginning and end of each shift to act as a formal platform for communication between team members, and increased training in group dynamics and interpersonal skills. Other key elements of the self-managed teams included:

- greater mutual dependence through devolution of operational decision making to teams
- the use of multi-skilled teams on benchmarking trips
- team-based reward system that is performance-linked
- product testing
- reliability testing and monitoring
- minor maintenance
- introduction of shift meetings.

The Mobil Adelaide Refinery example highlights a general shift in human resource strategy towards work structures that allow career development, skill enhancement and facilitate greater employee involvement. It is only through consultative processes, which allow real gains for employees as well as management, that long-term changes towards collaborative employee relations can be sustained.

The 1983 Accord between the ruling Australian Labor Party and the Australian Council of Trade Unions created a favourable framework for employee participation, further strengthened by National Wage Decisions. However, the *Workplace Industrial Relations Survey* of 1991 revealed that management–employee consultation remained sporadic on most issues. Although some firms, such as Australia Post, Ford, Lend Lease, Telecom and Woodlawn Mining Co., demonstrated a commitment to information sharing, consultation and a measure of employee participation, they were exceptions rather than the rule. A crucial factor in the extension of employee participation and industrial democracy in the 1990s is the restructuring and development of unions as well as managerial attitudes and approaches.[37]

A few studies raise caution about co-operative union–management programmes. In a study of five plant-level projects, only two of the five plants reported improvements in productivity and union–management relationships. In three of the five plants, relations among managers improved and grievance levels decreased. However, contrary to expectations, the more successful plants had neither clear agreement on the goals of the EI programme nor a jointly developed statement of philosophy, and both union and management leadership tried to subvert the process.[38] Another study covering 25 manufacturing plants showed that involvement in joint union–management programmes had no impact on economic performance.[39]

Studies of unionists' attitudes toward union–management co-operative programmes found a generally positive stance among those directly involved in such programmes.[40] The researchers cautioned, however, that the positive findings may reflect self-justification processes, where respondents assess programmes positively because of the time and effort they have invested. In a study of nine union and nine non-union EI projects, union involvement improved the programme's design and implementation, but there were no differences in the outcomes between the union and non-union efforts.[41] On the other hand, in a longitudinal study of three union–management projects, the union increased its influence over both traditional decisions, such as scheduling and vacations, and non-traditional decisions, such as the implementation of new technology and helping to improve customer service. In addition, when attitudes regarding the programme's success were positive, both management and unionists were viewed as positively contributing to the outcomes. However, when the EI programme was perceived as unsuccessful, management was viewed as the reason for poor performance. The authors concluded that supporting a co-operative union–management effort is a no-lose situation for the union.[42] Still another study suggests that joint EI programmes can inadvertently benefit low-seniority workers at the expense of high-seniority participants.[43] The programmes studied provided easier access to management for junior employees, thus upsetting the time-honoured, benefits-accrue-to-seniority-first tradition of unionised settings.

Quality circles

Quality circles, or 'employee involvement teams' as they are often called in the US, were at one time the most popular approach to EI and represent another example of parallel structure. Originally developed in Japan in the mid-1950s, quality circles represent a participative approach to employee involvement in problem solving and productivity improvement. They consist of small groups of employees who meet voluntarily to identify and solve productivity problems. The group method of problem solving and the participative management philosophy associated with it are natural outgrowths of Japanese managerial practices. The Japanese emphasise decentralised decision making and use the small group as the organisation unit to promote collective decision making and responsibility.[44] Various estimates once put the total circle membership at as many as 10 000 000 Japanese workers.[45]

Quality circles were introduced into Australia in the mid-1970s. Their growth in the late 1970s and early 1980s was nothing short of astounding, with some 4000 companies adopting some version of the circles approach. The popularity of quality circles can be attributed in part to the widespread drive to emulate Japanese management practices and to achieve the quality improvements and cost savings associated with those methods. What may be overlooked, however, is the Japanese philosophy of decentralised, collective

FIGURE 15.3   Quality circles programme structure

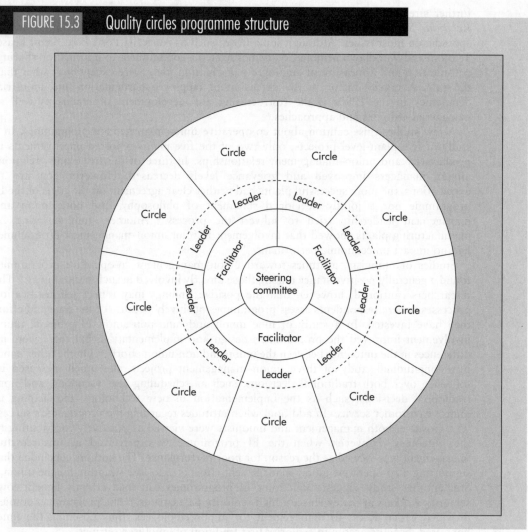

Source: Reproduced by permission of the author from R. Callahan, 'Quality circles: a program for productivity improvement through human resource development' (Unpublished paper, Albers School of Business, Seattle University, 1982), p. 16.

decision making, which supports and nurtures the circles approach. It is questionable whether quality circles will be as successful in the more autocratic, individualistic situations that characterise many Australian companies.[46]

Quality circles require a managerial philosophy and culture that promotes sharing power, information, knowledge and rewards. They require moving some decision making down to employees. Management still retains considerable control, however, because quality circles simply recommend solutions to management. In addition, good recommendations often require training in group problem-solving techniques and information with which to solve problems. Finally, many companies offer rewards to circles that recommend solutions that ultimately result in cost savings or productivity increases.

Although quality circles are implemented in different ways, a typical programme is illustrated in Figure 15.3. Circle programmes are generally implemented with a parallel structure consisting of several circles, each having three to fifteen members. Membership is voluntary, and members of a circle share a common job or work area. Circles meet once a week for about an hour on company time. Members are trained in different problem identification and analysis techniques. Several consulting companies have developed training packages as part of standardised programmes for implementing quality circles. Members apply their training to identify, analyse and recommend solutions to work-related problems. When possible, they implement solutions that affect only their work area and do not require higher management approval.

Each circle has a leader, who is typically the supervisor of the work area represented by circle membership. The leader trains circle members and guides the weekly meetings, which includes setting the agenda and facilitating the problem-solving process.

Facilitators can be a key part of a quality circles programme. They co-ordinate the activities of several circles and may attend the meetings, especially during the early stages of circle development. Facilitators train circle leaders and help them start the different circles. They also help circles obtain needed inputs from support groups and keep upper management apprised of the progress of the programme. Because facilitators are the most active promoters of the programme, their role may be full-time.

A steering committee is the central co-ordinator of the quality circles programme. It is generally composed of the facilitators and representatives of the major functional departments in the organisation. The steering committee determines the policies and procedures of the programme and the issues that fall outside circle attention, such as wages, fringe benefits and other topics normally covered in union contracts. The committee also co-ordinates the different training programmes and guides programme expansion. Large quality circles programmes might have several steering committees operating at different levels.

The popular press is full of glowing reports of quality circles' success. Among the reported results are reductions in costs, improvements in the quality and quantity of production and increased employee skill development, motivation, organisational commitment and satisfaction.[47] These results suggest that circles affect both the organisation, through group ideas that are implemented, and the individual, through membership in a problem-solving group.

Many researchers, however, have raised questions about the rigour of research on quality circles, as well as about the validity of the reported successes.[48] In the most extensive research review to date, covering more than 100 citations, Ledford, Lawler and Mohrman concluded that the existing research evidence shows no clear positive or negative trend in the productivity effects of quality circles.[49] Although the evidence of attitudinal effects was more extensive than that of the productivity effects, the studies reviewed still showed mixed results for attitudinal changes. For example, in one study using a rigorous research design, participation in a quality circle was positively related to measures of personal competence and interpersonal trust, but was not related to an increased sense of participation.[50] Clearly, the effects of quality circles are not nearly as impressive as the popular literature extols them to be.

In an attempt to discover which features of quality circles contribute most to programme success, two researchers conducted a large-scale study of quality circles in nine organisational units of a large, multi-divisional firm.[51] Their findings suggest that quality circles are more successful to the extent that they include, or have access to, the necessary skills and knowledge to address problems systematically; formalise meetings, record keeping and communication channels; integrate themselves both horizontally and vertically with the rest of the company and become a regular part of the formal organisation, rather than a special or extra parallel set of activities. The researchers argued that because quality circles are parallel structures appended to the formal organisation, they have a tendency to wither and die out over time. They tend to have little influence on the formal organisation and are eventually rejected by it. The researchers suggested that careful attention should be devoted to ensuring that quality circles are integrated into the formal organisation. They argued that quality circles are probably best used as a first step toward employee involvement and that eventually their activities should become integrated into the normal functioning of intact work groups.

These findings are consistent with a number of other factors that contribute to programme success.[52] First, quality circles are highly dependent on group members having sufficient group process, problem-solving and presentation skills and adequate task-relevant information.[53] Second, lower-level managers need to support the programme and have participatory leadership styles if employees are to gain the necessary freedom to engage in problem solving. Third, not all people can be expected to react favourably to quality circles. Some workers have low social needs and prefer to work alone, rather than in groups; some do not want greater participation at work. Fourth, top-management support is necessary both to start the programme and to implement many of the subsequent solutions. Unless management is willing to authorise the necessary resources to make suggested improvements, circle members are likely to become disenchanted, seeing the programme more as window dressing than as meaningful participation.

Application 15.2 presents a classic example of a quality circle programme at Reckitt & Colman Foods.[54]

APPLICATION 15.2

Quality circles in Reckitt & Colman's Pharmaceutical Division

In September 1980, as part of a major reorganisation within the Reckitt & Colman group, the newly independent Pharmaceutical Division moved to a new factory and a new managing director, Steve Harris, was appointed. During his initial familiarisation period, Mr Harris was struck by what he saw as the lack of communication on the site between management and the shop floor. The need to redress this perceived deficiency became one of his priorities.

At the same time, the group's training manager, Don Lindsay, was having informal discussions with a firm of management consultants who were promoting quality circles. The managing director was struck by the potential of quality circles as an effective catalyst for the changes he felt were necessary. Specifically, he saw quality circles as having three major advantages.

First, as a means of establishing direct dialogue between senior management and shop floor workers. In the absence of such communication, management–worker dialogue was through the union. It was the wish of the managing director that this not remain the sole channel. The managing director was also looking for a vehicle to serve as a communications channel outside the traditional adversarial grievance procedures.

Second, as a means of developing the skills of supervisors as shop floor

managers. The supervisors were referred to by some in the company as 'cardboard cut-outs', and it was felt desirable that they be encouraged to be more active in areas such as responding to grievances.

Third, as a means of getting the workforce 'creatively engaged' in identifying and solving problems connected with the production process.

The decision to set up the quality circles was the managing director's alone, without any initial discussion with unions, workers or supervisors.

A programme of eight circles commenced in June 1981 after a period of consultation with the site unions, who raised no fundamental objections, and a training period. The site unions were the Australian Workers' Union, the Miscellaneous Workers' Union and the Association of Professional Scientists. The workforce was highly unionised, and award wages were supplemented by annually negotiated site agreements.

The supervisors were initially a little resentful of their compulsory involvement (while workers' involvement was voluntary, the supervisors were required to be the circle leaders). However, most became more enthusiastic when they saw that the introduction of the circles was related to a widespread change in management style.

The workers, with a few exceptions, were enthusiastic about the idea. In particular, they responded well to the intention to encourage worker recommendations for change, since they saw themselves as a resource that management usually ignored.

Within the first two years of the programme there were a number of changes in the division that were clearly associated with the circles. First, there were concrete changes to workplace practices and procedures that developed from quality circle proposals. Most areas of the factory were affected. On the Steradent production line a new wash bay was designed and built, dust extractors installed, the line redesigned for easier access and a noise reduction programme initiated. In the dry mixing area the dispensary was modernised, loading platforms installed and racks altered for ease of access. Similar changes occurred throughout the factory.

Taken individually, these changes rarely appeared to be of great moment. However, their cumulative effect was to convince workers that their ideas were being considered and acted upon in ways that concretely affected their immediate work environment. Both management and workers attested to improved communication throughout the organisation, while management was heartened by the significant improvements in productivity, profitability and industrial relations.

It would be wrong to attribute these improvements entirely to the quality circle programme, but the managing director was in no doubt that it had been a significant catalyst. In this context it is all the more interesting to consider why, by March 1984, only four circles were meeting, and only one after April that year.

There seem to have been a number of factors acting in concert to bring about the demise of the circles:
- the circles ran out of ideas for new projects
- approved projects were not being completed as implementation was usually dependent on the engineers, who had to fit this work in with 'normal' maintenance tasks
- the pressure of production made it difficult for supervisors and workers to fit in quality circle meetings
- the supervisors resigned *en masse* as circle leaders. They were feeling the effect of production pressures and were uncomfortable in a role that required them to act as 'progress chasers'. This was both a practical and symbolic blow to the circles
- the sole facilitator was not given sufficient resources to deal simultaneously with the demands of all eight circles.

Senior management and quality circle members invested the circles with different meaning. For management, stimulating behavioural change was the most important aspect of the programme. Quality circles were merely a convenient catalyst. While they had sought to do something about the declining interest in circles when problems first arose (in mid-1983 a consulting firm was employed to advise on the problems), the cessation of circles was not something that they were unduly concerned about. For the circle members, on the other hand, the most important aspects of the programme were the physical changes that could be made to their work environment and the opportunity to be involved in decisions in this area. For them, the cessation of the circles signalled failure, not success. Unlike management they attached great importance to the form, and not just the function, of quality circles.

The major lesson for management is that quality circles may be treated as a useful catalyst with a transitory existence. They can be very useful. But great care must be taken to see that the decline is managed in a way that does not leave employees with the impression that management has simply dumped the programme. Expectations become established; the disengagement needs to be handled with some subtlety. If, however, the circle programme is to be maintained, support is vital so that resources are available to relieve pressure in problem areas.

TABLE 15.1	Definitions of organisation development

■ *Organizational structure*	■ *Training*
1 Flat	1 Heavy commitment
2 Lean	2 Peer training
3 Minienterprise-oriented	3 Economic education
4 Team-based	4 Interpersonal skills
5 Participative council or structure	■ *Reward system*
■ *Job design*	1 Open
1 Individually enriched	2 Skill-based
2 Self-managing teams	3 Gain sharing or ownership
■ *Information system*	4 Flexible benefits
1 Open	5 All salary
2 Inclusive	6 Egalitarian perquisites
3 Tied to jobs	■ *Personnel policies*
4 Decentralized; team-based	1 Stability of employment
5 Participatively set goals and standards	2 Participatively established through
■ *Career system*	representative group
1 Tracks and counseling available	■ *Physical layout*
2 Open job posting	1 Around organizational structure
■ *Selection*	2 Egalitarian
1 Realistic job preview	3 Safe and pleasant
2 Team-based	
3 Potential and process-skill oriented	

Source: Reproduced by permission of the publisher from Edward Lawler III, 'Increasing worker involvement to enhance organizational effectiveness: design features for a participation system' in P. Goodman and associates, *Change in Organizations*, (San Francisco: Jossey-Bass, 1982), pp. 298–99.

High-involvement organisations

Over the past few years, an increasing number of EI projects have been aimed at creating high-involvement organisations. Typically applied to new industrial plants, this EI intervention attempts to create organisational conditions that support high levels of employee participation. What makes these interventions unique is the comprehensive nature of the design process. Unlike parallel structures that do not alter the formal organisation, almost all organisation features are designed jointly by management and workers to promote high levels of involvement and performance, including structure, work design, information and control systems, physical layout, personnel policies and reward systems.

Design features for a participative system

High-involvement organisations are designed to have features that are congruent with one other. For example, in high-involvement organisations, employees have considerable influence over decisions. To support this decentralised philosophy, employees are given extensive training in problem-solving techniques, plant operation, and organisational policies. In addition, both operational and issue-oriented information is shared widely and is easily obtained by employees. Finally, rewards are closely tied to unit performance, as well as to knowledge and skill levels. These different aspects of the organisation are mutually reinforcing and form a coherent pattern that contributes to employee involvement. Table 15.1 presents a list of compatible design elements characterising a high-involvement organisation.[55] Most such organisations include several, if not all, of these features.

- *Flat, lean organisation structures* contribute to involvement by pushing the scheduling, planning and controlling functions typically performed by management and staff groups toward the shop floor. Similarly, mini-enterprise, team-based structures that are oriented to a common purpose or outcome help to focus employee participation on a shared objective. Participative structures, such as work councils and union–management committees, help to create conditions in which workers can influence the direction and policies of the organisation.

- *Job designs* that provide employees with high levels of discretion, task variety and meaningful feedback can enhance involvement. They allow workers to influence day-to-day work place decisions, as well as to receive intrinsic satisfaction by performing work under enriched conditions. Self-managed teams encourage employee responsibility by providing cross-training and job rotation, which give people a chance to learn about the different functions contributing to organisational performance.
- *Open information systems* that are tied to jobs or work teams provide the necessary information for employees to participate meaningfully in decision making. Goals and standards of performance that are set participatively can provide employees with a sense of commitment and motivation for achieving these objectives.
- *Career systems* that provide different tracks for advancement, and counselling to help people choose appropriate paths can help employees to plan and prepare for long-term development in the organisation. Open job posting, for example, makes employees aware of the availability of jobs that can further their development.
- *Selection of employees* for high-involvement organisations can be improved through a realistic job preview that provides information about what it will be like to work in such situations. Team member involvement in a selection process oriented to potential and process skills of recruits can facilitate a participative climate.
- *Training employees* to gain the necessary knowledge and skills to participate effectively in decision making is a heavy commitment at high-involvement organisations. This includes education in the economic side of the enterprise, as well as inter-personal skill development. Peer training is emphasised as a valuable adjunct to formal, expert training.
- *Reward systems* can contribute to employee involvement when information about them is open and rewards are based on acquiring new skills, as well as on sharing gains from improved performance. Similarly, participation is enhanced when people can choose from different fringe benefits and when reward distinctions between people from different hierarchical levels are minimised.
- *Personnel policies* that are participatively set and encourage stability of employment provide employees with a strong sense of commitment to the organisation. People feel that the policies are reasonable and that the firm is committed to the long-term development of employees.
- *Physical layouts of organisations* can also enhance employee involvement. Physical designs that support team structures and reduce status differences among employees can reinforce the egalitarian climate needed for employee participation. Safe and pleasant working conditions provide a physical environment that is conducive to participation.

These different design features of high-involvement organisations are mutually reinforcing. 'They all send a message to people in the organisation that says they are important, respected, valued, capable of growing and trusted, and that their understanding of, and involvement in, the total organisation is desirable and expected.'[56] Moreover, these design components tend to motivate and focus organisational behaviour in a strategic direction and thus can lead to superior effectiveness and competitive advantage, particularly in contrast to more traditionally designed organisations.[57] A survey of 98 high-involvement organisations showed that about 75% of them perceived their performance, relative to competitors, as better than average on quality of work life, customer service, productivity, quality and grievance rates.[58] For the high-involvement organisations, voluntary turnover was 2%, substantially below the national average of 13.2%; return on investment was almost four times greater than industry averages; and return on sales was more than five times greater. In Australia, the management at the Burswood Resort Hotel in Western Australia recognised that they wanted to develop problem-solving competencies in their employees and embarked on an empowerment programme, acknowledging that achieving an empowered work place was a long-term initiative that required continued management commitment. Their approach was based on management theory and practice, yet remained flexible to the needs of the hotel's employees and customers. A programme was designed and tailored to the hotel's culture and work environment. An empowerment survey was conducted prior to the programme and again 18 months after its completion.[59]

These results cannot be expected in all situations, of course. The following situational contingencies seem to favour high-involvement organisations: interdependent technologies, small organisation size, new plant start-ups and conditions under which quality is an important determinant of operating effectiveness.

At present, there is no universally accepted approach to implementing the high-involvement features described here. The actual implementation process is often specific to the situation, and little systematic research has been devoted to understanding the change process itself.[60] Nevertheless, at least two distinct factors seem to characterise how high-involvement organisations are created. First, implementation is generally guided by an explicit statement of values that members want the new organisation to support. Typically, such values as teamwork, equity, quality and empowerment guide the choice of specific design features. Values that are strongly held and widely shared by organisation members can provide the energy, commitment and direction needed to create high-involvement organisations. A second feature of the implementation process is its participative nature. Managers and employees take active roles in both choosing and implementing the design features. They may be helped by OD practitioners, but the locus of control for the change process resides clearly within the organisation. This participative change process is congruent with the high-involvement design that is being created. In essence, high-involvement design processes promote high-involvement organisations.

Application 15.3 presents an example of personal commitment by the maintenance personnel and commitment to the individual by management, combined with innovative Japanese technology giving Japan Airlines (JAL) one of the highest dispatch-reliability standards in the industry.[61]

JAL and employee involvement

It's called the 'kizuki maintenance engineer system'. Roughly translated, the Japanese word *kizuki* means 'aircraft lover', or more specifically, 'aircraft fanatic'. It's the system that Japan Airlines has established to ensure both the mechanical safety of its aircraft and a smooth, efficient turn-around service. Again more specifically, it assigns individual responsibility for every JAL aircraft to a specific maintenance team.

Established in July 1986, the kizuki maintenance-engineer system is indicative of the JAL's overall maintenance programme, which uses personal commitment and management–employee communications to achieve success.

According to Kimiya Nakazato, managing director, engineering and maintenance, JAL's programme is based on the Japanese management philosophy of 'a group of human beings (working) together in harmony for common ideals'. Nakazato said that this management philosophy is based on 'participation, co-operation, long-term perspective and informative efficiency'.

An example of this is the placement of numerous engineers on the shop floor. This means that technology is easily shared by all the maintenance workers and that the engineers 'can put their valuable experience to practical use, contributing to the company by making proposals for better productivity and solving problems,' Nakazato said.

One engineer, Senior Engineering Mechanic Teizo Watanabe, personally received the Emperor's Award of

Excellence for development of new maintenance methods and the tools to perform them, shown by a long string of personal awards for excellence from JAL.

Also, the shop technicians who are not engineers are trained to think as engineers, said Yoshiki Nakamura, director, maintenance engineering section, Aircraft Systems Maintenance Centre. 'This means that workers not only know what they are doing but why they are doing it and how it works,' he said.

This concept of personal commitment by the maintenance personnel and commitment to the individual by management, combined with innovative Japanese technology, has given JAL one of the highest dispatch-reliability standards in the industry.

Since the tragic loss in 1985 of a 747SR, caused by the improper repair of the aft pressure bulkhead by a Boeing Repair Team, JAL has intensified and accelerated its inspection programmes. As well, JAL is reconstructing its maintenance programme 'to accommodate increasing aircraft ageing counter-measures', the airline said. This includes ageing of the aircraft itself and ageing components. The airline has developed an 'ageing component optimised reliability development' (ACORD) programme designed to ensure that individual components meet all the appropriate standards. Nakamura noted that this attention to detail gives the airline high dispatch reliability and 'not doing it could lead to a flight interruption or a crash'. He is working actively to extend the ACORD programme throughout the industry.

JAL has two primary maintenance centres: Haneda Airport, which also contains the engine-overhaul centre and component-maintenance centre, and Narita International Airport, which also handles aircraft-systems maintenance. These facilities are manned by about 5000 employees, comprising roughly 25% of the total JAL workforce.

A major factor in JAL's highly successful maintenance programme is, as would be expected, advanced state-of-the-art automation. Robotics include an aircraft-washing machine capable of taking any aircraft, including the 747, aircraft window-washing robots, special vehicles to aid mechanics change aircraft wheel and brake drums, and a robot for weighing, identifying and recording jet-engine turbine blades.

All of these automated devices, incidentally, including the massive aircraft-washing machine, were the ideas of JAL employees working on their own time, Nakazato said. The airline actively encourages its employees to develop unique ideas, 'and the ideas don't have to be related to maintenance activity. The ideas could be for a useful machine or a funny toy. We don't mind. This illustrates very clearly the concept that in Japan, an enterprise means its workers,' he said.

The airline's personnel have also developed much of their own automatic testing equipment, both for avionics and components. This includes ATE equipment, software and maintenance simulators.

The aircraft-washing machine is an example of JAL's automation, reducing the cost and staffing requirements from roughly US$2900 and 80 person-hours per aircraft to US$1300 and 6.5 person-hours. A major consideration in the automation of its maintenance facilities is not only for greater efficiency and cost savings but also to reduce the physical labour requirements for its employees, whose average age is mid-40s, according to a JAL spokesperson. An automated measurement system for post-repair engine checks at Narita has reduced personnel by 66%.

Although maintenance personnel account for about a quarter of the workforce, maintenance actually accounts for a relatively small percentage of the airline's total budget. In fiscal 1990, maintenance costs were US$756.69 million out of a US$7.68 billion budget, or 9.8%. This was equal to the 1989 cost and slightly down from 10.1% of the airline's budget in 1988.

Prior to 1989, JAL had four levels of maintenance checks: A check at 250 hours, B at 1000 hours, C at 3000 hours and H for 'hospitalised' at about four years. However, with the advent of the ageing-aircraft problem, the H check was changed to M, or 'major', check. This check has a varied time limitation, according to the age and utilisation of the aircraft, and was designed to shift the centre of maintenance gravity to the older aircraft.

As a key part of its constant monitoring programme, JAL developed the maintenance/engineering system. This programme assigns a specific team of four or five engineers to two or three specific aircraft. Plaques on each aircraft contain the names of its kizuki team. Every incoming aircraft is met by at least one team member, who checks out the log and has primary responsibility for ensuring that mechanical problems are resolved. Nakazato said that the kizuki team members are like 'family doctors', who first see a patient, then either 'heal' the patient or send him on to specialists—line mechanics—as required.

All of these team members are highly experienced, senior maintenance engineers, and normally retire straight from the kizuki team, he said. Key elements to the success of the programme are that it allows an experienced team to concentrate on 'their' aircraft, develop an understanding of it, get to know its peculiarities and follow up on any problems until they are fixed.

The system also serves other purposes, Nakazato said. Along with enhancing operational safety, it 'fosters a deep sense of responsibility that naturally translates into better care', while improving communications between maintenance personnel and flight crews.

With Japan Airlines, as with virtually all Japanese companies, individual responsibility and personal communications are primary elements in getting things done. They give the airline quality maintenance, and according to the philosophy of Kimiya Nakazato, 'quality maintenance means quality airline'.

Total quality management[62]

Total quality management (TQM) is the most recent and perhaps the most comprehensive approach to employee involvement and large systems change. It is a long-term effort that orients all of an organisation's activities around the concept of quality. Total quality is achieved when organisational processes reliably produce products and services that meet or exceed customer expectations. Although it is possible to implement TQM without employee involvement, member participation in the change process increases the likelihood that TQM will become part of the organisation's culture. TQM was very popular in the 1990s, and many organisations, including Morton Salt, the US Postal Service, Weyerhauser, Xerox, Motorola and Analog Devices, implemented total quality interventions.

Like high-involvement designs, TQM pushes decision-making power downward in the organisation, provides relevant information to all employees, ties rewards to performance, and increases workers' knowledge and skills through extensive training. When implemented successfully, TQM is also closely aligned with a firm's overall business strategy and attempts to change the entire organisation towards continuous quality improvement.[63]

The principles underlying TQM can be understood by examining the careers of W. Edwards Deming and Joseph M. Juran, the fathers of the modern quality movement. They initially introduced TQM to American companies during World War II, but in an odd twist of fate after the war, they found their ideas taking hold more in Japan than the US.[64]

Based on the pioneering work of Walter A. Shewhart of Bell Laboratories, Deming applied statistical techniques to improve product quality at defence plants during World

TABLE 15.2	Deming's quality guidelines

The fourteen points	The seven deadly sins
1 Create a constancy of purpose	1 Lack of constancy of purpose
2 Adopt a new philosophy	2 Emphasizing short-term profits and immediate dividends
3 End the practice of purchasing at lowest prices	3 Evaluation of performance, merit rating or annual review
4 Institute leadership	4 Mobility of top management
5 Eliminate empty slogans	5 Running a company only on visible figures
6 Eliminate numerical quotas	
7 Institute on-the-job training	6 Excessive medical costs
8 Drive out fear	7 Excessive costs of warranty
9 Break down barriers between departments	
10 Take action to accomplish the transformation	
11 Improve constantly and forever the process of production and service	
12 Cease dependence on mass inspection	
13 Remove barriers to pride in workmanship	
14 Retrain vigorously	

War II. At the conclusion of the war, US businesses turned to mass-production techniques and emphasised quantity over quality to satisfy post-war demand. General Douglas MacArthur asked Deming, known for his statistical and sampling expertise, to conduct a census of the Japanese population. During his work in Japan, Deming began discussions with Japanese managers about rebuilding their manufacturing base. He advocated a disciplined approach to identifying and improving manufacturing processes affecting product quality. Deming suggested that by minimising deviations from quality standards in the inputs to a manufacturing process, rather than only inspecting finished goods, the Japanese could produce world-class quality products and restore their country. Deming's ideas were eventually codified into the 'Fourteen Points' and the 'Seven Deadly Sins' of quality summarised in Table 15.2. In honour of the ideas that helped rejuvenate the Japanese economy, the Union of Japanese Scientists and Engineers created the Deming Award to distinguish annually the best in quality manufacturing.

At about the same time, Juran's publication of the *Quality Control Handbook* in 1951 identified two sources of quality problems: avoidable and unavoidable costs. Avoidable costs included hours spent reworking defective products, processing complaints, and scrapping otherwise useful material. Unavoidable costs included work associated with inspection and other preventive measures. He suggested that when organisations focused on unavoidable costs to maintain quality, an important opportunity was being missed. Juran advocated that an organisation should focus on avoidable costs that could be found in any organisational process or activity, not just manufacturing.

The current popularity of TQM in the US can be traced to a 1980 NBC documentary titled, 'If Japan can ... why can't we?' The documentary chronicled Deming's work with the Japanese and his concern that American companies would not listen to him after the war. The documentary had a powerful impact on firms that were facing severe competition, particularly from the Japanese, and many companies, including Ford, General Motors, Dow Chemical, and Hughes Aircraft quickly sought Deming's advice. Another important influence on the current TQM movement in the US was Philip Crosby's book *Quality Is Free*.[65] He showed that improved quality can lower overall costs, dispelling the popular belief that high quality means higher total costs for the organisation. With fewer parts reworked, less material wasted and less time spent inspecting finished goods, the organisation's total costs can actually decline. Deming also believed that if the principles of quality were put in place, reduced costs would be a natural by-product of increased quality.

In 1987, the United States Congress established the Malcolm Baldrige National Quality Award. It recognises organisations in services and manufacturing for quality achievement along seven dimensions: leadership, information and analysis, strategic planning, human resource development and management, process management, business results and customer focus and satisfaction. Competition for the award has grown enormously. Many organisations spend millions of dollars to prepare for the contest; others have applied just to receive the extensive feedback from the board of examiners on how to improve quality; and still others feel compelled to apply because customers insist that they show progress in process improvement.

The Australian Quality Awards for Business Excellence are designed to help organisations explore and understand their business systems and processes, benchmark where they stand in terms of the market place and their competitors and develop strategies for continual improvement to ensure their long-term viability and profitability. Winners for 1998 were Australia-New Zealand Direct Line, Building and Construction Industry Authority and South East Water. In 1998 an Award Gold was introduced and given to organisations who had previously been 'winners' as confirmation of their ongoing performance in business excellence (won by Integral Energy).[66]

Total quality management is typically implemented in five major stages:

1   *Gain long-term senior management commitment.* This stage involves helping senior executives understand the importance of long-term commitment to TQM. Without a solid understanding of TQM and the key success factors for implementation, managers often believe that workers are solely responsible for quality. Yet only senior executives have the authority and larger perspective to address the organisation-wide, cross-functional issues that hold the greatest promise for TQM's success.

    The senior managers' role in TQM implementation includes giving direction and support throughout the change process. For example, implementation of organisation-wide TQM generally takes three or more years, although technical improvements to the work flow can take as little as six to eight months. The longer and more difficult parts of implementation, however, involve changes in the organisation's support systems, such as customer service, finance, sales and human resources. Often these systems are frozen in place by old policies and norms that can interfere with TQM. Senior managers need to confront those practices and to create new ones that support TQM and the organisation's strategic orientation.

    Top executives must also be willing to allocate significant resources to TQM implementation, particularly large investments in training. For example, as part of its Baldrige Award preparation, Motorola developed Motorola University, a training organisation that teaches in 27 languages and, so far, has delivered courses to more than 100 000 employees. Departments at Motorola allocate at least 1.5% of their budgets to education, and every employee must take a minimum of 40 hours of training a year. This effort supports Motorola's goals of 'six-sigma' quality (a statistical measure of product quality that implies 99.9997 per cent perfection) and of having a workforce that is able to read, write, solve problems and do maths at the seventh-grade level or above. When several units within Motorola achieved the six-sigma target, the company demonstrated its commitment to continuously improving quality with a new target of tenfold improvement in key goals.

    Finally, senior managers need to clarify and communicate a totally new orientation to producing and delivering products and services throughout the organisation. At Corning, Inc., for example, CEO James R. Houghton, who has been preaching the quality objective since 1983, said, 'If I stop talking about quality now, it would be a disaster.'[67]

2   *Train members in quality methods.* TQM implementation requires extensive training in the principles and tools of quality improvement. Depending on the organisation's size and complexity, such training can be conducted in a few weeks, or up to one or two years. Members typically learn problem-solving skills and simple statistical process control (SPC) techniques, usually referred to as the seven tools of quality. At the South East Queensland Electricity Board (SEQEB), part of the strategy for changing the culture included the establishment of a quality team structure, with customer requirements as the primary focus. This led to the formation of 150 quality teams involving approximately 900 out of 2700 full-time staff. This structure established a framework to align organisational purpose with roles and responsibilities, staff and processes. The quality teams help employees to work together towards improving the quality of products and service; developing the skills and abilities of employees; promoting communication among employees; enhancing the quality of work life and problem-solving using a structured process.[68]

3   *Start quality improvement projects.* In this phase of TQM implementation, individuals and work groups apply the quality methods to identify the few projects that hold promise for the largest improvements in organisational processes. They identify output variations, intervene to minimise deviations from quality standards, monitor improvements and repeat this quality improvement cycle indefinitely. Identifying output variations is a key aspect of TQM. Such deviations from quality standards are typically measured by the percentage of defective products or of customer satisfaction along a set of qualitative and quantitative dimensions.

   TQM is not only concerned with variations in the quality of finished products and services, but also with variations in the steps of a process that produce a product or service and the levels of internal customer satisfaction. For example, by 1991 Hendersons Automotive (SA) was profitable and placed a strong emphasis on consultative management, occupational health and safety, training and quality management. The formulation of policies and their implementation had as their foundation close consultation between management and the shop floor and their representatives. The success of the organisational change programme was demonstrated by the observed outcomes of the process: namely, an increase in shop floor productivity, outside recognition of quality improvements, a reduction in the incidence and severity of injuries, and a reduction in labour turnover and absenteeism.

   Based on the measurement of output variations, each individual or work group systematically analyses the cause of variations using SPC techniques. For example, product yields in a semi-conductor manufacturing plant can go down for many reasons, including a high concentration of dust particles, small vibrations in the equipment, poor machine adjustments and a variety of human errors. Quality improvement projects must often determine which of the possible causes is most responsible. Then using that information, experiments and pilot projects are run to determine which adjustments will cause output variations to drop and quality to improve. Those that do are implemented across the board. Members continue to monitor the quality process to verify improvement and then begin the problem-solving process all over again for continuous improvement.

4   *Measure progress.* This stage of TQM implementation involves the measurement of organisational processes against quality standards. Analysing the competition and knowing their performance are essential for any TQM effort. This sets minimum standards of cost, quality and service and ensures the organisation's position in the industry over the short run. For the longer term, such analytical efforts concentrate on identifying world-class performance, regardless of industry, and creating stretch targets, also known as benchmarks. Benchmarks represent the best in organisational achievements and practices for different processes and are generally accepted as 'world class'. For example, Qantas is often considered the benchmark of airline customer service, while Singapore Airport Terminal Services (SATS) customer-service orientation is considered a world-class benchmark.

The implied goal in most TQM efforts is to meet or exceed a competitor's benchmark. Alcoa's chairman, Paul H. O'Neill, charged all of the company's business units with closing the gap between Alcoa and its competitor's benchmarks by 80% within two years.[69] In aluminium sheet for beverage cans, for example, Japan's Kobe Steel Ltd is the benchmark, and Wall Street estimated that achieving O'Neill's goal would increase Alcoa's earnings by one dollar per share. The greatest leverage for change is often found in companies from unrelated industries, however. For example, Alcoa might look to Integral Energy to get innovative ideas about customer service. Understanding benchmarks from other industries challenges an organisation's thinking about what is possible and compels what is referred to as 'out of the box thinking'.[70]

5 *Rewarding accomplishment.* In this final stage of TQM implementation, the organisation links rewards to improvements in quality. TQM does not monitor and reward outcomes normally tracked by traditional reward systems, such as the number of units produced. Such measures do not necessarily reflect product quality and, because they are ingrained in the organisation's traditional way of doing business, can be difficult to replace. Rather, TQM rewards members for 'process-oriented' improvements, such as increased on-time delivery, gains in customers' perceived satisfaction with product performance, and reductions in cycle time (the time it takes a product or service to be conceived, developed, produced and sold). Rewards are usually designed initially to promote finding solutions to the organisation's key problems—that 20% of the problems that is causing 80% of the firm's poor performance or effectiveness. This linkage between rewards and process-oriented improvements reinforces the belief that continuous improvements, even small ones, are an important part of the new organisational culture associated with TQM. In a survey of 500 firms in four countries by Ernst and Young and the American Quality Foundation, more than half of the US companies studied linked executive pay to improving quality and achieving benchmarks.[70]

TQM has continued to evolve in most industrialised countries. Early adopters of the intervention focused on trying to identify and solve the key problems that faced the organisation in order to improve performance and customer satisfaction. Organisations with mature TQM programmes have shifted their attention from retrospective problem solving to proactive problem anticipation and prevention. For example, the Conference Board's Quality Council II recently held a two-day workshop on using TQM principles to forecast the needs of human resource management. The council, made up of organisations with mature TQM systems, examined how human resource planning could integrate career planning, training and management succession. It also discussed how the human resource function could evolve to a more strategic role in organisation change. This shift from reaction to anticipation seems to be a hallmark of mature, successful TQM programmes.

Application 15.4 describes a TQM intervention at Glaxo Wellcome India, illustrating the programme and concluding with some observations on progress to date and the changes in the organisation's culture as a result.[71]

APPLICATION 15.4 Total quality management at Glaxo India

Glaxo India is the largest pharmaceutical company in India. It has been in existence for more than 75 years and has grown over the years to a maximum of nearly 6000 staff. It has since shed a large foods division, while two voluntary retirement schemes have reduced the staff levels to 4000. It manufactures in its own factories in four locations and uses contractors for approximately 30% of its production. Distribution is through C & F agents throughout India. It is the largest single manufacturing base in the world for Glaxo.

The Indian environment is very varied. India is made up of diverse cultures, each with its own strong ethos. Several dialects are spoken throughout India. The only true common language is English, but training must, of course, be carried out in the local languages. Unions have been both strong and militant but there seems to be a gradual change to a more flexible attitude.

The economy started to open in 1991 but severe price regulations remain in the pharmaceutical industry and competition from rapidly growing Indian companies has threatened Glaxo's leadership in the industry.

Consultants Blythe, Rao and Shahani explain: 'The changed business environment today places high demands on organisations to survive and grow. Globalisation, increased competition, new markets and changed buyer values will allow to survive only those companies that offer excellence in all spheres of business activities. Glaxo Excellence Process (GEP) was an initiative to empower each one of us to consider, contribute, demand and achieve excellence in whatever we do. It has made our work enjoyable, stimulating and challenging. We have begun to take pride and joy in our work and have started to unlock the true potential in all of us.'

There were a number of reasons for starting GEP. Internal reasons included:
- stifled talent within the company and untapped human resources
- divisional and bureaucratic culture
- MBO-driven
- poor teamwork and interpersonal relationships.

Glaxo India's concerns were verified by independent qualitative assessment through interviews and focus groups with employees at various levels in the organisation. Quality of product in the pharmaceutical industry is taken for granted. Glaxo India needed the broad definition of quality to disseminate to all levels and all functions. GEP was seen as a way of transforming the culture. It was believed that the behaviour changes resulting from total quality management (TQM) would automatically give rise to results in the tangibles, which Glaxo India saw as:
- greatly improved product or service
- major decrease in wasted resources
- sustained competitive advantage
- real release of the potential of people
- motivated workforce.

At that stage, the company was going through a major stage of restructuring and was divesting itself of its food division. They had no experience of TQM. Therefore, it was decided they would restrict the exercise to the production and technical areas. These included two smaller marketing companies. The technical division was large enough at approximately 4000 staff and was fairly self-contained.

Glaxo India started the TQM exercise in 1995. 'Each company feels that they are unique and Glaxo India was no exception. We wanted to be able to take advantage of all the work that had gone on in other companies but at the same time we wanted to customise a package to our company.' Helping Glaxo as consultants were John MacDonal Associates, from the UK, and Naresh Shahani of Qualteam Consultants, from India.

The process started with an initial assessment of the existing company culture. The training material was based on the findings of the structured assessment conducted by the consultants. The assessment covered the following points:
- services/products versus the competition
- customers' views
- suppliers' views
- how employees see the company
- how the competition sees the company
- how well managers work together
- how well departments work together
- how good internal competition is
- communication with subordinates and their communication.

Glaxo set up a planning team of the key managers representing all of the functions. Their activities went through six distinct steps:

- planning
- creation of the training package
- training
- communication
- monitoring
- taking the process company-wide.

By the sixth stage, the technical division of the company had demonstrated that the process worked and that there were very real gains to be made. The culture of the company had improved, ownership was very strong in the factories and barriers had fallen in the factories most active in TQM. The decision to take the process company-wide was taken about a year after the process had begun.

Once the work of the planning team was done, it was disbanded and a much smaller steering team formed. It was responsible for making things happen. On each of the company sites, site management teams were set up to manage the activities locally. The site team meets monthly and is the normal management team of the site. Its core role is to plan tactics, promote and manage the implementation. When the process is fully implemented, there is a need for a small, full-time team to keep the momentum going and provide background information. Recognition is key to the success of GEP.

'Although the start was slow, we soon started to see a change in people's attitudes to each other and projects started to come forward, which solved problems we had been living with for years. Apart from significant improvements in all areas of production the process has helped us to change the culture of the company.' The results were obtained through senior management support, agreements on business and cultural goals, routine meetings, reports and other various activities. Factors critical to its success include its customised process, the creation of no separate structure, the speed of implementation and continual communication of what was going on.

The purpose of implementation of GEP in Glaxo Wellcome India was to bring in an attitudinal change in the entire company and to bring in excellence in all spheres of business activities.

'The process works if there is commitment from the top and if you work at it. The simpler the process used, the better it works. The results have to be seen to be believed. We have achieved improved product and service, decrease in wasted resources, sustained competitive advantage, motivated workforce and increased employee involvement. It is very exciting, involves a lot of hard work and has its ups and downs. The basic rules are to determine the starting point, define the destination, map the route, put in place a structured and organised training programme for all staff, set goals and measurables, and launch the recognition system.'

Today, TQM is a popular EI intervention. A recent survey of the *Fortune* 1000 companies showed that about 76% have implemented some form of TQM, and 83% of these firms have increased their use of TQM over the past three years.[72] In addition, 83% of the companies rated their experience with TQM as either positive or very positive. The research also found that TQM is often associated with the implementation of other EI interventions. As organisations implement process improvements, they may need to make supporting changes in reward systems and work design. Finally, the study revealed that TQM was positively associated with performance outcomes, such as productivity, customer service, product/service quality and profitability, as well as with human outcomes, such as employee satisfaction and quality of work life.

TQM is itself a growing industry, with consulting firms, university courses, training programmes and professional associations related to quality improvement diffusing rapidly across industrial nations. In Australia, the quality approach is supported by at least four major associations: the Australian Organisation for Quality (AOQ), the Australian Quality Council (AQC), Quality Assurance Services (QAS) and Standards Australia. These associations actively support TQM by sponsoring quality training workshops and conferences. They also serve as clearing-houses for important information on TQM programmes. For example, the Australian Quality Council is a non-government, not-for-profit, membership-based organisation that co-ordinates the Australian Business Excellence Awards. The Australian Organisation for Quality is Australia's largest supplier of Quality Management training and education and co-ordinates the international Qualcon Conference. Quality Assurance Services is a wholly-owned subsidiary of Standards Australia and involved in the independent assessment and certification services. Standards Australia is the Australian partner responsible for the JASANZ Register (Joint Accreditation System of Australia and New Zealand), which monitors the competence of quality certifiers.

Considerable research into the value of TQM has emanated from such institutions as the Quality Management Research Unit, Monash University, and the Centre for Management Quality Research, RMIT.

A balanced picture of TQM effects is provided by a study of 54 firms representing different sizes and both adopters and non-adopters of TQM. It found that TQM firms significantly outperformed non-TQM firms. The source of the performance advantage was not the tools and techniques of TQM, however, but the culture, empowerment and commitment that came from successful implementation. The study concluded that 'these tacit resources, and not TQM tools and techniques, drive TQM success', and that 'organisations that acquire them can outperform competitors with or without the accompanying TQM ideology'.[73]

Although reports of TQM success are plentiful in the popular literature, there are also reports of problems.[74] Clearly, more systematic research is needed to assess whether these positive outcomes are valid and, if so, whether similar results can be expected across a wide range of organisational applications.

Summary

This chapter described employee involvement interventions. These technostructural change programmes are aimed at moving organisation decision making downward to improve responsiveness and performance and to increase employee flexibility, commitment and satisfaction. Different approaches to EI can be described by the extent to which power, information, knowledge and skills and rewards are shared with employees.

The relationship between EI and productivity can be oversimplified. Productivity can be increased through improved employee communication, motivation and skills and abilities. It can also be affected through increased worker satisfaction, which in turn results in productive employees joining and remaining with the organisation.

Major EI interventions include:
- parallel structures, including co-operative union–management projects and quality circles
- high-involvement designs
- total quality management.

The results of these approaches tend to be positive, and the quality of research supporting these interventions is increasing.

ACTIVITIES

Review questions

1 Employee involvement (EI) is the most recent form of what earlier movement?

2 What are the criteria of the 'individual outcome' orientation for quality of work life (QWL)?

3 A working definition of EI encompasses what characteristics?

4 The power dimension of EI refers to what?

5 How may QWL improve productivity?

6 What are the major applications of EI?

7 What is the value of co-operative union–management projects?

8 Identify some of the limiting factors of Quality Circles.

9 High-involvement plants tend to push certain EI elements down to the lowest levels in the system. Which are they?

10 What is true of high-involvement plants?

11 What are the design features of a participative, high-involvement plant?

12 What are the distinguishing features of the total quality management approach?

Discussion and essay questions

1 Describe, and give examples of, the four elements associated with employee involvement interventions.

2 Compare and contrast the Quality Circle (QC) and Total Quality Management (TQM) applications of employee involvement.

3 Discuss parallel structures and the type of organisation that would benefit most from this structure.

Notes

1 L. Davis, 'Enhancing the quality of work life: developments in the United States', *International Labor Review*, 116 (July–August 1977): 53–65.

2 L. Davis, 'Job design and productivity: a new approach', *Personnel*, 33 (1957): 418–30.

3 J. Taylor, J. Landy, M Levine and D. Kamath, 'Quality of Working Life: An Annotated Bibliography, 1957–1972' (Center for Organizational Studies, Graduate School of Management, University of California at Los Angeles, 1972); J. Taylor, 'Experiments in work system design: economic and human results', *Personnel Review*, 6 (1977): 28–37; J. Taylor, 'Job satisfaction and quality of working life: a reassessment', *Journal of Occupational Psychology*, 50 (December 1977): 243–52.

4 L. Davis, 'Job design: overview and future direction', *Journal of Contemporary Business*, 6 (Winter 1977): 85–102; L. Davis and C. Sullivan, 'A labor–management contract and quality of working life', *Journal of Occupational Behaviour*, 1 (1979): 29–41; P. Gyllenhamer, *People at Work* (Reading, Mass.: Addison-Wesley, 1977); E. Thorsrud, B. Sorensen and B. Gustavsen, 'Sociotechnical approach to industrial democracy in Norway' in *Handbook of Work Organisation and Society*, ed. R. Dubin (Chicago: Rand McNally, 1976): 648–87.

5 D. Nadler and E. Lawler III, 'Quality of work life: perspectives and directions' (Working paper, Center for Effective Organizations, University of Southern California, 1982).

6 R. Walton, 'Improving the quality of work life', *Harvard Business Review*, 52 (May–June 1974): 12; C. McNichols, T. Stanley and M. Stahl, 'Quality of life in the US Air Force: 1977 vs. 1975' (Paper delivered at the Military Testing Association Conference, San Antonio, Tex., October 1978); Organizational Research and Development, *The Quality of Your Work Life in General Motors* (Detroit, Mich.: General Motors, 1976); L. Davis and A. Cherns, eds, *The Quality of Working Life*, 2 vols. (New York: Free Press, 1975).

7 Nadler and Lawler, 'Quality of work life', *op. cit.*

8 W. Ouchi, *Theory Z* (Reading, Mass.: Addison-Wesley, 1981).

9 J. Vogt and K. Murrell, *Empowerment in Organizations* (San Diego: University Associates, 1990).

10 T. Peters and R. Waterman, *In Search of Excellence* (New York: Harper & Row, 1985).

11 T. Peters and N. Austin, *A Passion for Excellence* (New York: Random House, 1985).

12 E. Lawler III, S. Mohrman and G. Ledford, *Creating High Performance Organisations* (San Francisco: Jossey-Bass, 1995).

13 M. Marchington, A. Wilkinson and P. Ackers, 'Understanding the meaning of participation: views from the work place', *Human Relations,* 47:8 (1994): 867–894; C. Goulden, 'Supervisory management and quality circle performance: an empirical study', *Journal of Management Development,* 14:7 (1995): 15–27.

14 D. Welsh, F. Luthans and S. Sommer, 'Managing Russian factory workers: the impact of US-based behavioral and participative techniques', *Academy of Management Journal,* 36:1 (1993): 58–79; D. Jones, 'Employee participation during the early stages of transition: evidence from Bulgaria', *Economic and Industrial Democracy,* 16:1 (1995): 111–35.

15 C. Cooper and E. Mumford, *The Quality of Working Life in Western and Eastern Europe* (Westport, Conn.: Greenwood Press, 1979); P. Sorenson, T. Head, N. Mathys, J. Preston and D. Cooperrider, *Global and Organizational Development* (Champaign, Ill.: Stipes, 1995).

16 D. Glew, A. O'Leary-Kelly, R. Griffin and D. Van Fleet, 'Participation in organizations: a preview of the issues and proposed framework for future analysis', *Journal of Management,* 21:3 (1995): 395–421.

17 E. Lawler III, *High Involvement Management* (San Francisco: Jossey-Bass, 1986).

18 M. Kizilos, 'The relationship between employee involvement and organization performance' (unpublished Doctoral dissertation, University of Southern California, 1995); M. Huselid, 'The impact of human resource management practices on turnover, productivity and corporate financial performance', *Academy of Management Journal,* 38 (1995): 635–72; M. Kizilos, T. Cummings and A. Strickstein, 'Achieving superior customer service through employee involvement', *Academy of Management Best Paper Proceedings* (1994): 197–201; J. Arthur, 'Effects of human resources systems on manufacturing performance and turnover', *Academy of Management Journal,* 37 (1994): 670–87; A. Kallenberg and J. Moody, 'Human resource management and organizational performance', 37 (1994): 948–62; D. Denison, *Corporate Culture and Organisational Effectiveness* (New York: John Wiley & Sons, 1990); G. Hansen and B. Wernerfelt, 'Determinates of firm performance: the relative importance of economic and organizational factors', *Strategic Management Journal,* 10 (1989): 399–411.

19 E. Lawler III and G. Ledford, 'Productivity and the quality of work life', *National Productivity Review,* 2 (Winter 1981–82): 23–36.

20 Glew, O'Leary-Kelly, Griffin and Van Fleet, 'Participation in organizations', *op. cit.*; J. Wagner, 'Participation's effects on performance and satisfaction: a reconsideration of research evidence', *Academy of Management Review,* 19:2 (1994): 312–30.

21 G. Ledford and E. Lawler, 'Research on employee participation: beating a dead horse?' *Academy of Management Review,* 19:4 (1994): 633–36.

22 G. Bushe and A. Shani, 'Parallel learning structure interventions in bureaucratic organisations', in *Research in Organisation Change and Development,* 4, eds W. Pasmore and R. Woodman (Greenwich, Conn.: JAI Press, 1990): 167–94.

23 D. Zand, 'Collateral organization: a new change strategy', *Journal of Applied Behavioral Science,* 10 (1974): 63–89; S. Goldstein, 'Organisational dualism and quality circles', *Academy of Management Review,* 10 (1985): 504–17; V. Schein and L. Greiner, 'Can organization development be fine tuned to bureaucracies?' *Organizational Dynamics* (Winter 1977): 48–61.

24 Zand, 'Collateral organization', *op. cit.*; D. Zand, *Information, Organization and Power: Effective Management in the Knowledge Society* (New York: McGraw-Hill, 1981): 57–88; G. Bushe and A. Shani, *Parallel Learning Structures: Increasing Innovation in Bureaucracies* (Reading, Mass.: Addison-Wesley, 1991).

25 Bushe and Shani, *Parallel Learning Structures, op. cit.,* 123–37.

26 C. Worley and G. Ledford, 'The relative impact of group process and group structure on group effectiveness' (Paper presented at the Western Academy of Management, Spokane, Wash., April 1992).

27 Zand, 'Collateral organization', *op. cit.*

28 E. Miller, 'The parallel organization structure at General Motors—an interview with Howard C. Carlson', *Personnel,* (September–October 1978): 64–69.

29 Zand, 'Collateral organization', *op. cit.* 88; Zand, *Information, Organization and Power, op. cit.* 68–83.

30 E. Lawler III and S. Mohrman, 'Quality circles after the fad', *Harvard Business Review,* 85 (1985): 64–71; S. Mohrman and G. Ledford Jr, 'The design and use of effective employee

participation groups: implications for human resource management', *Human Resource Management*, 24 (Winter 1985): 413–28.

31 M. Duckles, R. Duckles and M. Maccoby, 'The process of change at Bolivar', *Journal of Applied Behavioral Science*, 13 (1977): 387–499. ·

32 D. Nadler, G. Jenkins, P. Mirvis and B. Macy, 'A research design and measurement package for the assessment of quality of work interventions', *Proceedings of the Academy of Management*, New Orleans: Thirty-Fifth Annual Meeting (1975): 87–102.

33 D. Nadler, 'Hospitals, organized labor and quality of work: an intervention case study', *Journal of Applied Behavioral Science*, 14 (1978): 366–81.

34 J. Drexler Jr, 'A union management cooperative project to improve the quality of work life', *Journal of Applied Behavioral Science*, 13: 373–86.

35 Duckles, Duckles and Maccoby, 'The process of change at Bolivar', *op. cit.*, 387–499.

36 P. Dawson, 'Redefining human resource management work restructuring and employee relations at Mobil Adelaide refinery', *International Journal of Manpower*, 16:5/6 (1995), 47–55.

37 R. Lansbury and E. Davis, 'Employee participation: some Australian cases', *International Labour Review*, 131:2 (1992), 231.

38 G. Bushe, 'Developing cooperative labor–management relations in unionised factories: a multiple case study of quality circles and parallel organizations within joint quality of work life projects', *Journal of Applied Behavioral Science*, 24 (1988): 129–50.

39 H. Katz, T. Kochan and M. Weber, 'Assessing the effects of industrial relations systems and efforts to improve the quality of working life on organizational effectiveness', *Academy of Management Journal*, 28 (1985): 509–26.

40 M. Hanlon and D. Nadler, 'Unionists' attitudes toward joint union–management quality of work life programs', *Journal of Occupational Behavior*, 7 (1986): 53–59; D. Collins, 'Self-interests and group interests in employee involvement programs: a case study', *Journal of Labor Research*, 16 (1995): 57–79.

41 J. Thacker and M. Fields, 'Union involvement in quality-of-work life efforts: a longitudinal investigation', *Personnel Psychology*, 40 (1987): 97–111.

42 B. Gilbert, 'The impact of union involvement on the design and introduction of quality of working life', *Human Relations*, 42 (1989): 1057–78.

43 G. Bocialetti, 'Quality of work life: some unintended effects on the seniority tradition of an industrial union', *Group and Organizational Studies*, 12 (1987): 386–410.

44 G. Munchus III, 'Employer–employee based quality circles in Japan: human resource policy implications for American firms', *Academy of Management Review*, 8 (1983): 255–61.

45 R. Callahan, 'Quality circles: a program for productivity improvement through human resource development' (unpublished paper, Albers School of Business, Seattle University, 1982).

46 Munchus, 'Quality circles in Japan', *op. cit.*, 255–61.

47 A. Honeycutt, 'The key to effective quality circles', *Training and Development Journal*, 43 (May 1989): 81–84; E. Yager, 'The quality circle explosion', *Training and Development Journal*, 35 (April 1981): 93–105; 'A quality circle nets a nice round figure', *Supervisory Management*, 40 (1995): 7.

48 M. Barrick and R. Alexander, 'A review of quality circle efficacy and the existence of positive-findings bias', *Personnel Psychology*, 40 (1987): 579–92; J. Vogt and B. Hunt, 'What really goes wrong with participative groups', *Training and Development Journal*, 42 (May 1988): 96–100; R. Steel and G. Shane, 'Evaluation research on quality circles: technical and analytical implications', *Human Relations*, 39 (1986): 449–68.

49 G. Ledford Jr, E. Lawler III and S. Mohrman, 'The quality circle and its variations' in *Enhancing Productivity: New Perspectives from Industrial and Organizational Psychology*, eds, J. Campbell and J. Campbell (San Francisco: Jossey-Bass, 1988): 225–94.

50 R. Steel and R. Lloyd, 'Cognitive, affective and behavioral outcomes of participation in quality circles: conceptual and empirical findings', *Journal of Applied Behavioral Science*, 24 (1988): 1–17.

51 S. Mohrman and G. Ledford Jr, 'The design and use of effective employee participation groups', *Human Resource Management*, 24 (1985): 413–28.

52 Callahan, 'Quality circles', *op. cit.*

53 C. Worley, 'Implementing participation strategies in hospitals: correlates of effective problem-solving teams', *International Journal of Public Administration* (in press).

54 R. Dunford and P. McGraw, 'Abandoning simple recipes and benefiting from quality circles: an Australian Study', *Work & People*, 12:2 (1986), 22–25.

55 Lawler, *High Involvement Management, op. cit.*

56 E. Lawler III, 'Increasing worker involvement to enhance organizational effectiveness' in *Change in Organizations*, ed. P. Goodman (San Francisco: Jossey-Bass, 1982): 299; R. Walton, 'From control to commitment in the work place', *Harvard Business Review*, 63 (1985): 76–84.

57 Lawler, *High Involvement Management, op. cit.*; E. Lawler, *The Ultimate Advantage* (San Francisco: Jossey-Bass, 1992).

58 G. Ledford, 'High involvement organizations', (working paper, Center for Effective Organizations, University of Southern California, 1992).

59 R. Cacioppe, 'Structured empowerment: an award-winning program at the Burswood Resort Hotel', *Leadership & Organization Development Journal*, 19/5 (1998), 264–274.

60 Glew, O'Leary-Kelly, Griffin and Van Fleet, 'Participation in organizations', *op. cit.*

61 D. Nelms, 'JAL: above and beyond', *Air Transport World*, 29:3 (1992), 92–94.

62 The rigour and relevance of this section benefited from the contributions of Dr Miriam Lacey, Associate Professor of Organization Behaviour, Pepperdine University.

63 Y. Shetty, 'Product quality and competitive strategy', *Business Horizons*, (May–June 1987): 46–52; D. Garvin, 'Competing on the eight dimensions of quality', *Harvard Business Review*, (November–December 1987): 101–9; D. Garvin, *Managing Quality: The Strategic and Competitive Edge* (New York: Free Press, 1988).

64 W. Deming, *Quality, Productivity and Competitive Advantage* (Cambridge: MIT Center for Advanced Engineering Study, 1982); W. Deming, *Out of the Crisis* (Cambridge: MIT Press, 1986); J. Juran, *Quality Control Handbook*, 3rd ed. (New York: McGraw-Hill, 1974); J. Juran, *Juran on the Leadership for Quality: An Executive Handbook* (New York: Free Press, 1989).

65 P. Crosby, *Quality is Free* (New York: McGraw-Hill, 1979); P. Crosby, *Quality Without Tears* (New York: McGraw-Hill, 1984).

66 http://www.aqc.org.au/abea_intro.html

67 'The quality imperative', *Business Week*, Special Issue (25 October 1991): 34.

68 K. Navaratnam and B. Hill, 'Customer service in an Australian Quality Award winning public sector service industry', *International journal of Public Sector Management*, 7:2 (1994).

69 'The quality imperative', *Business Week*, 152.

70 *Ibid.*

71 R. Blythe, H. Rao and N. Shahani, 'TQM in Glaxo India—a step-by-step implementation process', *The TQM Magazine*, 9:2 (1997), 98–105.

72 Lawler, Mohrman and Ledford, *Creating High Performance Organizations, op. cit.*

73 T. Powell, 'Total quality management as a competitive advantage: a review and empirical study', *Strategic Management Journal*, 16 (1995): 15.37.

74 D. Waddell, 'The role and responsibilities of quality managers', Department of Management, Monash University, Working Paper 20/98.

Work design

This chapter is concerned with work design—creating jobs and work groups that generate high levels of employee fulfilment and productivity. This technostructural intervention can be part of a larger employee involvement application, or it can be an independent change programme. Work design has been extensively researched and applied in organisations. Recently, organisations have tended to combine work design with formal structure and supporting changes in goal setting, reward systems, work environment and other performance management practices. These organisational factors can help to structure and reinforce the kinds of work behaviours associated with specific work designs. (How performance management interventions can support work design is discussed in Chapter 17.)

This chapter examines three approaches to work design. The engineering approach focuses on efficiency and simplification and results in traditional job and work group designs. Traditional jobs involve relatively routine and repetitive work, requiring little interaction among people to produce a service or product (e.g. telephone operators and data entry positions). Traditional work groups are composed of members performing routine yet interrelated tasks. Member interactions are typically controlled by rigid work flows, supervisors and schedules, such as might be found on assembly lines.

A second approach to work design rests on motivational theories and attempts to enrich the work experience. Job enrichment involves designing jobs with high levels of meaning, discretion and knowledge of results. A well-researched model focusing on job attributes has helped to solve methodological problems with this important intervention.

The third and most recent approach to work design derives from socio-technical systems methods. This perspective seeks to optimise both the social and the technical aspects of work systems. It has led to the development of a popular form of work design called 'self-managed teams'. These teams are composed of multi-skilled members performing interrelated tasks. Members are given the necessary knowledge, information and power to control their own task behaviours with relatively little external control. New support systems and supervisory styles are needed to manage them.

The chapter describes each of these perspectives. Then, a contingency framework for integrating the approaches is presented, based on personal and technical factors in the work place. When work is designed to fit these factors, it is both satisfying and productive.

The engineering approach

The oldest and most prevalent approach to work design is based on engineering concepts and methods. It proposes that the most efficient work designs can be determined by specifying the tasks to be performed, the work methods to be used and the work flow between individuals. The engineering approach is based on the pioneering work of Frederick Taylor, the father of scientific management. He developed ways of analysing and designing work and laid the groundwork for the professional field of industrial engineering.[1]

The engineering approach seeks to scientifically analyse the tasks performed by workers so as to discover those procedures that produce the maximum output with the minimum input of energies and resources.[2] This generally results in work designs with high levels of specialisation and specification. Such designs have several benefits: they allow workers to learn tasks rapidly; they permit short work cycles so that performance can take place with little or no mental effort; they reduce costs as lower-skilled people can be hired and trained easily and paid relatively low wages.

The engineering approach produces two kinds of work design: traditional jobs and traditional work groups. When one person can complete the work, as is the case with bank tellers and telephone operators, traditional jobs are created. They tend to be simplified, with routine and repetitive tasks having clear specifications concerning time and motion. When the work requires co-ordination between people, such as automobile assembly lines, traditional work groups are developed. They are composed of members who perform relatively routine, yet related, tasks. The overall group task is typically broken into simpler, discrete parts (often called jobs). The tasks and work methods are specified for each part, and the different parts are assigned to group members. Each member performs a routine and repetitive part of the group task. Members' separate task contributions are co-ordinated for overall task achievement through external controls, such as schedules, rigid work flows and supervisors.[3] In the 1950s and 1960s, this method of work design was popularised by the assembly lines of Australian automobile manufacturers, such as GM Holden, and was an important reason for the growth of Australian industry after World War II.

The engineering approach to job design is less an OD intervention than a benchmark in history. Critics of the approach argue that the method ignores the social and psychological needs of workers. They suggest that the increasing educational level of the workforce and the substitution of automation for menial labour point to the need for more enriched forms of work, where people have greater discretion and challenge. Moreover, current competitive challenges require a more committed and involved workforce that is able to make on-line decisions and develop performance innovations. Work designed with the employee in mind is more humanly fulfilling and productive than that designed in traditional ways. However, it is important to recognise the strengths of the engineering approach. It remains an important work design intervention as its immediate cost savings and efficiency can easily be measured. It is also well understood and easily implemented and managed.

The motivational approach

The motivational approach to work design views the effectiveness of organisational activities primarily as a function of member needs and satisfaction. It seeks to improve employee performance and satisfaction by enriching jobs. This provides people with opportunities for autonomy, responsibility, closure (doing a complete job) and feedback about performance. Enriched jobs can be found in Australia at such companies as Queensland Golden Circle Limited and Rupnorth Co-operative Limited, among others.

The motivational approach is usually associated with the research of Herzberg, as well as that of Hackman and Oldham. Herzberg's two-factor theory of motivation proposed that certain attributes of work, such as opportunities for advancement and recognition, which he called 'motivators', help to increase job satisfaction.[4] Other attributes, called 'hygiene' factors, such as company policies, working conditions, pay and supervision, do not produce satisfaction but prevent dissatisfaction. Only satisfied workers are motivated to produce.

Although Herzberg's motivational factors sound appealing, increasing doubt has been cast on the underlying theory. For example, motivation and hygiene factors are difficult to put into operation and measure, making implementation and evaluation of the theory difficult. Important worker characteristics that can affect whether or not people will respond favourably to job enrichment were also not included in the theory. Finally, Herzberg's failure to involve employees in the job enrichment process itself does not sit well with most current OD practitioners. Consequently, a second, well-researched approach to job enrichment has been favoured. It focuses on the attributes of the work

FIGURE 16.1   The relationships among the core job dimensions, the critical psychological states and personal and work outcomes

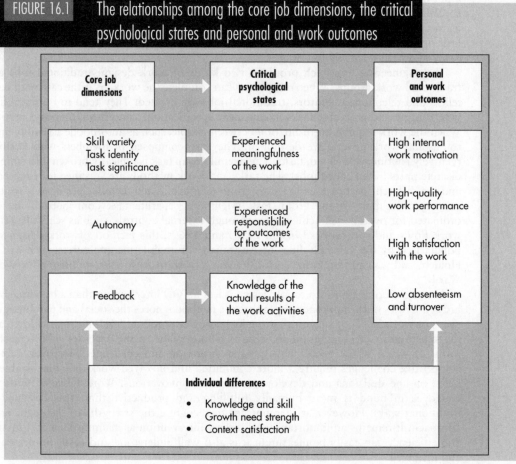

Source: J. Hackman and G. Oldham, *Work Redesign,* copyright © 1980 by Addison-Wesley Publishing Co. Reprinted by permission of Addison-Wesley Publishing Co., Inc., Reading, Massachusetts, p. 90.

itself and has resulted in a more scientifically acceptable theory of job enrichment than Herzberg's model. The research of Hackman and Oldham represents this more recent trend in job enrichment.[5]

The core dimensions of jobs

Considerable research has been devoted to defining and understanding core job dimensions.[6] Figure 16.1 summarises the Hackman and Oldham model of job design. Five core dimensions of work affect three critical psychological states, which in turn produce personal and job outcomes. These outcomes include high internal work motivation, high-quality work performance, satisfaction with the work and low absenteeism and turnover. The five core job dimensions—skill variety, task identity, task significance, autonomy and feedback from the work itself—are described below and associated with the critical psychological states that they create.

Core job dimensions, the skill variety, task identity and task significance

These three core job characteristics influence the extent to which work is perceived as meaningful. *Skill variety* refers to the number and types of skills employed to perform a particular task. Employees at Mono Pumps (Australia), an industrial pump company, can work as warehouse stock clerks, fitters and turners and salespersons. The more tasks an individual performs, the more meaningful the job becomes. Moving an individual from one job to another increases skill variety and a form of job enrichment called *job rotation* is accomplished. However, simply rotating a person from one boring job to another is not likely to produce the outcomes associated with a fully enriched job.

Task identity describes the extent to which an individual performs a whole piece of work. For example, an employee who completes an entire wheel assembly for an aeroplane, including the tyres, chassis, brakes and electrical and hydraulic systems, has more task identity and will perceive the work as more meaningful than will someone who only assembles the braking subsystem. *Job enlargement* is another form of job enrichment that combines increases in skill variety and task identity. Job enlargement blends several narrow jobs into one larger, expanded job. For example, separate machine set-up, machining and inspection jobs might be combined into one. This method can increase meaningfulness, job satisfaction and motivation when employees comprehend and like the greater task complexity.

Task significance represents the impact that the work has on others. In jobs with high task significance, such as nursing, consulting or manufacturing sensitive parts for the space shuttle, the importance of successful task completion creates meaningfulness for the worker.

Experienced meaningfulness is expressed as an average of these three dimensions. Thus, although it is advantageous to have high amounts of skill variety, task identity and task significance, a strong emphasis on any one of the three dimensions can, at least partially, make up for deficiencies in the other two.

Autonomy

This refers to the amount of independence, freedom and discretion that the employee is given to schedule and perform tasks. Salespeople, for example, often have considerable autonomy in how they contact, develop and close new accounts, whereas assembly-line workers often have to adhere to work specifications that are clearly detailed in a policy and procedure manual. Employees tend to experience responsibility for their work outcomes when high amounts of autonomy exist.

Feedback from the work itself

This core dimension represents the information that workers receive about the effectiveness of their work. It can derive from the work itself, as when determining whether an assembled part functions properly, or it can come from external sources, such as reports on defects, budget variances, customer satisfaction and the like. Because feedback from the work itself is direct and generates intrinsic satisfaction, it is considered preferable to feedback from external sources.

Individual differences

Not all people react in similar ways to job enrichment interventions. Individual differences, such as a worker's knowledge and skill levels, growth-need strength and satisfaction with contextual factors, moderate the relationships between core dimensions, psychological states and outcomes. 'Worker knowledge and skill' refers to the education and experience levels that characterise the workforce. If employees lack the appropriate skills, for example, increasing skill variety may not improve a job's meaningfulness. Similarly, if workers lack the intrinsic motivation to grow and develop personally, attempts to provide them with increased autonomy may be resisted. (We will discuss growth needs more fully in the last section of this chapter.) Finally, contextual factors include reward systems, supervisory style and co-worker satisfaction. When the employee is unhappy with the work context, attempts to enrich the work itself may be unsuccessful.

FIGURE 16.2 The JDS profile for a 'good' and a 'bad' job

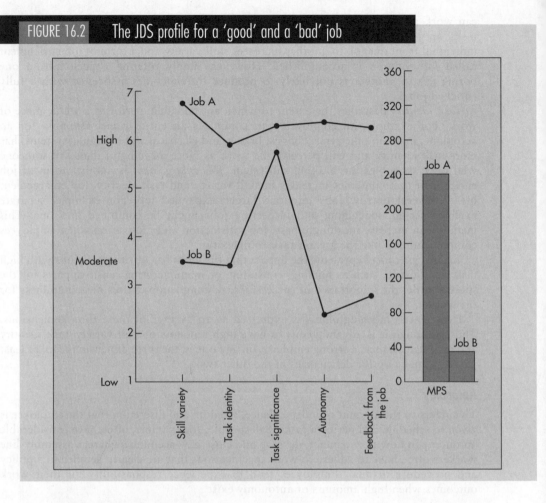

What are the steps?

The basic steps for job enrichment as described by Hackman and Oldham include:

- a thorough diagnosis of the situation
- forming natural work units
- combining tasks
- establishing client relationships
- vertical loading
- opening feedback channels.[7]

Thorough diagnosis

The most popular method of diagnosing a job is through the use of the Job Diagnostic Survey (JDS) or one of its variations.[8] An important output of the JDS is the *motivating potential score*, which is a function of the three psychological states: experienced meaningfulness, autonomy and feedback. The survey can be used to profile one or more jobs, to determine whether motivation and satisfaction are really problems or whether the job is low in motivating potential and to isolate specific aspects of the job that are causing the difficulties. Figure 16.2 shows two different jobs. Job A in engineering maintenance is high on all of the core dimensions. Its motivating potential score is a high 260 (motivating potential scores average about 125). Job B involves the routine and repetitive task of processing cheques in a bank. Its motivating potential score of 30 is well below average and would be even lower were it not for the relatively high task significance of the job. This job could be redesigned and improved.

The JDS also indicates how ready employees are to accept change. Employees who have high growth needs should respond more readily to job enrichment than do those who have low or weak growth needs. Before implementing actual changes, a thorough diagnosis of the existing work system should be completed. The JDS provides measures of satisfaction with pay, co-workers and supervision. If there is high dissatisfaction with one or more of these areas, other interventions prior to work redesign might be more helpful.

Forming natural work units

Natural work units should be formed as far as possible. Although there may be a number of technological constraints, interrelated task activities should be grouped together as much as possible. The basic question when forming natural work units is: 'How can one increase "ownership" of the task?' Forming such natural units increases two of the core dimensions— task identity and task significance—that contribute to the meaningfulness of work.

Combining tasks

Frequently, divided jobs can be put back together to form a new and larger one. Westrail is a government-operated railway service that controls much of the railway system across Western Australia. Maintenance along its extensive system is undertaken by maintenance groups operating within different geographical divisions. Each group is assigned a particular portion of the system that they must maintain. Maintenance refers to a variety of scheduled duties, ranging from the laying of new tracks and upkeep of old sections, to unscheduled emergency work such as that which arises from derailments and repairs stemming from environment-related damage.[9]

Establishing client relationships

When jobs are split up, the typical worker has little or no contact with, or knowledge of, the ultimate user of the product or service. Improvements can often be realised simultaneously on three of the core dimensions by encouraging and helping workers to establish direct relationships with the clients of their work. For example, when a typist in a typing pool is assigned to a particular department, feedback increases because of the additional opportunities for praise or criticism of his or her work. Because of the need to develop interpersonal skills in maintaining the client relationship, skill variety may increase. If the worker is given personal responsibility for deciding how to manage relationships with clients, autonomy is increased.

Three steps are needed to create client relationships:
* the client must be identified
* the contact between the client and the worker needs to be as direct as possible
* criteria and procedures by which the client can judge the quality of the product or service received and relay those judgments back to the worker are needed.

Vertical loading

The intent of vertical loading is to decrease the gap between *doing* and *controlling* the job. A vertically loaded job has responsibilities and controls that were formerly reserved for management. Vertical loading may well be the most crucial of the job-design principles. Autonomy is invariably increased through vertical loading. This approach should lead to greater feelings of personal accountability and responsibility for the work outcomes. For example, at Westrail, the new system granted workers far greater autonomy over scheduling and designation of tasks. A system using scheduling forms was introduced, which enabled thorough work plans to be developed. The forms also serve as a source of feedback for the groups as they are used by upper management to provide direct comparative data about the effectiveness of the group's performance. In addition, the traditional first-line supervisory position was replaced by a trackmaster who acts in the capacity of facilitator and co-ordinator, rather than a traditional supervisor who controls most aspects of the job.[10]

Loss of vertical loading usually occurs when someone has made a mistake. Once a supervisor steps in, the responsibility may be removed indefinitely. In an insurance company, one policy had the notation, 'Before taking any action, check with John'. John had been in a different department and had left five years ago, but the notation was still on the policy. Many skilled machinists complete a form to have maintenance people work on a machine. The supervisor automatically signs the slip rather than allowing the machinist to either repair the machine or ask directly for maintenance.

Opening feedback channels

In almost all jobs, approaches exist to open feedback channels and to help individuals learn whether their performance is remaining at a constant level, improving or deteriorating. The most advantageous and least threatening feedback occurs when a worker learns about performance as the job is performed. In the hot-plate department at Corning Glass, assembling the entire instrument and inspecting it dramatically increased the quantity and quality of information about their performance available to the operators. Frequently, data given to the manager or supervisor can be given directly to the employee. Computers and other automated operations can be used to provide individuals with data not now accessible to them. Many organisations have simply not realised the importance of direct, immediate feedback as a motivator.

Application 16.1 considers the challenge facing an agricultural co-operative operating in a community market, but seeking ways of adding value both to the output of its members and to the service it offers to its members and its customers. Rupnorth Co-operative Ltd highlights the importance of trust and the value of developing close working relationships over time, in order to communicate the need for radical change in strategic focus and implement an effective change management programme.[11]

APPLICATION 16.1 — Managing the linkage with primary producers

In 1995 Rupnorth Co-operative Ltd celebrated 25 years of operation, primarily in the purchase of production inputs to improve the profitability of its 120 grain grower members. Over the last decade, grain growers in the Victorian Wimmera have experienced significant change, both on and off their farms. On-farm production has expanded from the traditional cereal–pasture rotations to include a range of crops such as chick peas, dun peas, lentils, canola and safflower. Off-farm development in grain marketing include the deregulation of the domestic wheat market in 1987 and the marketing of the new crops, which are not regulated.

The directors of Rupnorth realised that the evolution from a buying group to a marketing organisation would involve a fundamental realignment of its relationship with members. As a buying group, the members were the customers of the co-operative with very few tension points and little risk in the relationship. The performance of the co-operative was very easy for members to evaluate by simply comparing input prices. As a marketing organisation, however, the group of growers had to address a number of key relationship issues.

With support from the Department of Primary Industries and Energy's Agribusiness Branch Programmes, the co-operative started to tackle these issues at a two-day strategic planning workshop involving 70 members. Fortunately, the directors had established a regional committee structure 12 months prior to this workshop. Ten regional groups of about 12 members each had been established, with an elected representative from each group providing input to the board. This regional group structure provided a good base for addressing the issues in smaller syndicate teams during the workshop.

In the six months since the workshop the group made a number of critical decisions and successfully developed key relationships with a number of grain customers. Members made the decision to commit a proportion of some of their crops to the co-operative so that marketing activities can commence with an assured supply.

The directors believed that probably the key point to emerge over the previous 12 months had been the level of trust that had been built up over the past 25 years. They believed it would be virtually impossible for a group of grain growers to make the major decisions as quickly as Rupnorth had recently made without some history of working successfully together. Trust is not built overnight.

The Rupnorth growers quickly appreciated that the strength of the group depended on their ability to create customer value, i.e. to differentiate their product and not just sell a commodity. With commodities, the total channel benefits are fixed and the main co-ordination function is to apportion the share between the different players in the channel. In this win–lose game you expect, and find, adversarial relationships. The long-term solution revolves around creating enhanced customer value so that each channel participant has the opportunity to capture some of the benefits. This win–win game provides the context for developing co-operative relationships.

There are two critical underlying issues relating to vertical co-ordination,

as processors try to develop closer relationships with growers. The first is a shift in control, inevitably away from the supplier to the customer. Predicting the establishment of closer vertical co-ordination requires an explicit consideration of the conditions that will allow control to be relinquished. However, Australian farmers generally place a high value on their independence and are extremely reluctant to relinquish any control or independence, especially to another party with whom they have traditionally had an adversarial relationship. Nevertheless, growers could appreciate that when they used auction systems and when their independence was maximised, their risks were also at a maximum. Furthermore, independence and auction systems also meant that they did not receive specific customer feedback and they tended to be isolated from the rest of the food chain. There is a high price to pay for independence.

The second issue involves the implications of the size imbalance between individual growers and processors. Experience suggests that relationships that are unbalanced, in terms of size, are not as effective as balanced relationships. Given the size imbalance between growers and processors we would expect the relationships to exhibit lower levels of co-operation and trust, have higher levels of conflict and to be more unstable. This is usually the case in practice.

At the conclusion of the initial workshop, all parties could appreciate that developing closer relationships would not be easy and would require time and patience.

Barriers to job enrichment

As the application of job enrichment has spread, a number of obstacles to significant job restructuring have been identified. Most of these barriers exist in the organisational context within which the job design is executed. Other organisational systems and practices, whether technical, managerial or personnel, can affect both the implementation of job enrichment and the life span of whatever changes are made.

At least four organisational systems can constrain the implementation of job enrichment:[12]

1 *The technical system.* The technology of an organisation can limit job enrichment by constraining the number of ways in which jobs can be changed. For example, long-linked technology like that found on an assembly line can be highly programmed and standardised, thus limiting the amount of employee discretion that is possible. Technology may also set an 'enrichment ceiling'. Some types of work, such as continuous process production systems, may be naturally enriched, so there is little more that can be gained from a job enrichment intervention.

2 *The personnel system.* Personnel systems can constrain job enrichment by creating formalised job descriptions that are rigidly defined and which limit flexibility in changing people's job duties. For example, many union agreements include such narrowly-defined job descriptions that major renegotiation between management and the union must occur before jobs can be significantly enriched.

3 *The control system.* Control systems, such as budgets, production reports and accounting practices, can limit the complexity and challenge of jobs within the system. For example, a company working on a government contract may have such strict quality-control procedures that employee discretion is effectively curtailed.

4 *The supervisory system.* Supervisors determine to a large extent the amount of autonomy and feedback that subordinates can experience. To the extent that supervisors use autocratic methods and control work-related feedback, jobs will be difficult, if not impossible, to enrich.

Once these implementation constraints have been overcome, other factors determine whether the effects of job enrichment are strong and lasting.[13] Consistent with the contingency approach to OD, the staying power of job enrichment depends largely on how well it fits and is supported by other organisational practices, such as those associated with training, career development, compensation and supervision. These practices need to be congruent with, and to reinforce, jobs that have high amounts of discretion, skill variety and meaningful feedback.

Results of job enrichment

Hackman and Oldham reported using the JDS on more than 1000 people in about 100 different jobs in more than a dozen organisations.[14] In general, they found that employees whose jobs were high on the core dimensions were more satisfied and motivated than those whose jobs were low on the dimensions. The core dimensions were also related to such behaviours as absenteeism and performance, although the relationship was not strong for performance. In addition, they found that responses were more positive for people with high growth needs than for those with weaker ones. Similarly, recent research has shown that enriched jobs are strongly correlated with mental ability.[15] Enriching the jobs of workers with low growth needs or with low knowledge and skills is more likely to produce frustration than satisfaction.

An impressive amount of research has been done on Hackman and Oldham's approach to job enrichment. In addition, a number of studies have extended and refined Hackman and Oldham's approach, including the modification of the original JDS instrument to produce more reliable data[16] and the incorporation of other moderators, such as the need for achievement and job longevity.[17] In general, research has supported the proposed relationships between job characteristics and outcomes, including the moderating effects of growth needs, knowledge and skills and context satisfaction.[18] In regard to context satisfaction, for example, research indicates that employee turnover, dissatisfaction and withdrawal are associated with dark offices, a lack of privacy and high worker densities.[19]

Reviews of the job enrichment research also report positive effects. An analysis of 28 studies concluded that the job characteristics are positively related to job satisfaction, particularly for people with high growth needs.[20] Another review concluded that job enrichment is effective at reducing employee turnover.[21] A different examination of 28 job enrichment studies reported overwhelming positive results.[22] Improvements in quality and cost measures were reported slightly more frequently than improvements in employee attitudes and quantity of production. However, the studies suffered from methodological weaknesses that suggest that the positive findings should be viewed with some caution. Another review of 16 job enrichment studies showed mixed results.[23] Thirteen of the programmes were developed and implemented solely by management. These studies showed significant reduction in absenteeism, turnover and grievances, and improvements in quality of production in only about half of the cases where these variables were measured. The three studies with high levels of employee participation in the change programme showed improvements in these variables in all cases where they were measured. Although it is difficult to generalise from such a small number of studies, employee participation in the job enrichment programme appears to enhance the success of such interventions.

Finally, a comprehensive meta-analysis of more than 75 empirical studies of the Hackman and Oldham model found modest support for the overall model.[24] Although some modifications in the model appear to be warranted, the studies suggested that many of the more substantive criticisms of the model were unfounded. For example, the research supported the conclusion that the relationships between core job characteristics and psychological outcomes were stronger and more consistent than the relationships between core job dimensions and work performance, although these latter relationships did exist and were meaningful. The researchers also found support for the proposed linkages among core job dimensions, critical psychological states and psychological outcomes. Interestingly, the job feedback dimension emerged as the strongest and most consistent predictor of both psychological and behavioural work outcomes. The researchers suggested that of all job characteristics, increasing feedback had the most potential for improving work productivity and satisfaction. The role of growth-need strength as a moderator was also supported, especially between core dimensions and work performance. Clearly, research supporting the job enrichment model is plentiful. Although the evidence suggests that the model is not perfect, it does appear to be a reasonable guide to improving the motivational outcomes of work.

The socio-technical systems approach

The socio-technical systems (STS) approach is the most extensive body of scientific and applied work underlying employee involvement and innovative work designs today. Its techniques and design principles derive from extensive action research in both public and private organisations across a diversity of national cultures. This section reviews the conceptual foundations of the STS approach and then describes its most popular application—self-managed work teams.

Conceptual background

Socio-technical systems theory was originally developed at the Tavistock Institute of Human Relations in London and has spread to most industrialised nations in a little more than 45 years. In Europe and particularly Scandinavia, STS interventions are almost synonymous with work design and employee involvement. In Canada and the US, STS concepts and methods underlie many of the innovative work designs and team-based structures that are so prevalent in today's organisations. Intel and Proctor and Gamble are among the many organisations applying the STS approach to transform how work is designed and performed.

Socio-technical systems theory is based on two fundamental premises:
- that an organisation or work unit is a combined, social-plus-technical system
- that this system is open in relation to its environment.[25]

Socio-technical system

The first assumption suggests that whenever human beings are organised to perform tasks, a joint system is operating—a socio-technical system. This system consists of two independent, yet related, parts: a social part that includes the people performing the tasks and the relationships among them, and a technical part consisting of the tools, techniques and methods for task performance. These two parts are independent of each other by virtue of each following a different set of behavioural laws. The social part operates according to biological and psychosocial laws, whereas the technical part functions according to mechanical and physical laws. Nevertheless, the two parts are related because they must act together to accomplish tasks. Hence, the term 'socio-technical' signifies the joint relationship that must occur between the social and technical parts, and the word system communicates that this connection results in a unified whole.

Because a socio-technical system is composed of social and technical parts, it follows that it will produce two kinds of outcomes: products, such as goods and services, and social and psychological consequences, such as job satisfaction and commitment. The key issue is how to design the relationship between the two parts so that these outcomes are *both* positive (referred to as 'joint optimisation'). Socio-technical practitioners design work and organisations so that the social and technical parts work well together, producing high levels of product and human satisfaction. This contrasts with the engineering approach to designing work, which tends to focus on the technical component and worries about fitting people in later. This often leads to mediocre performance at high social costs. This also contrasts with the motivation approach that views work design in terms of human fulfilment. This approach can lead to satisfied employees, but inefficient work processes.

Environmental relationship

The second major premise underlying STS theory concerns the fact that such systems are open to their environments. As discussed in Chapter 5, open systems need to interact with their environments to survive and develop. The environment provides the STS with necessary inputs of energy, raw materials, and information and the STS, in turn, provides the environment with products and services. The key issue here is how to design the interface between the STS and its environment so that the system has sufficient freedom to function while exchanging effectively with the environment. In what is typically referred to as boundary management, STS practitioners attempt to structure environmental relationships to both protect the system from external disruptions and to facilitate the exchange of necessary resources and information. This enables the STS to adapt to changing conditions and to influence the environment in favourable directions.

In summary, socio-technical systems theory suggests that effective work systems jointly optimise the relationship between their social and technical parts. Moreover, such systems effectively manage the boundary that separates them from, while relating them to, the environment. This allows them to exchange with the environment while protecting themselves from external disruptions.

Self-managed work teams

The most prevalent application of the STS approach is *self-managed work teams*.[26] Alternatively referred to as 'self-directed work teams', 'self-regulating work teams', or 'high-performance work teams', these work designs consist of members performing interrelated tasks.[27] Self-managed work teams are typically responsible for a whole product or service, or a major part of a larger production process. They control members' task behaviours and make decisions about task assignments and work methods. In many cases, the team sets its own production goals, within broader organisational limits, and may be responsible for support services, such as maintenance, purchasing and quality control. Team members are generally expected to learn many, if not all, of the jobs within the team's control and frequently are paid on the basis of knowledge and skills rather than seniority. When pay is based on performance, team rather than individual performance is used.

Self-managed work teams are being implemented at a rapid rate across a diversity of industries and organisations, such as Intel, General Electric and Motorola. A 1993 survey of *Fortune* 1000 companies found that 69% of these firms were using self-managed work teams, an increase from only 28% in 1987 and 47% in 1990.[28] Moreover, 68% of the firms indicated that they were going to increase, or greatly increase, the use of self-managed work teams.

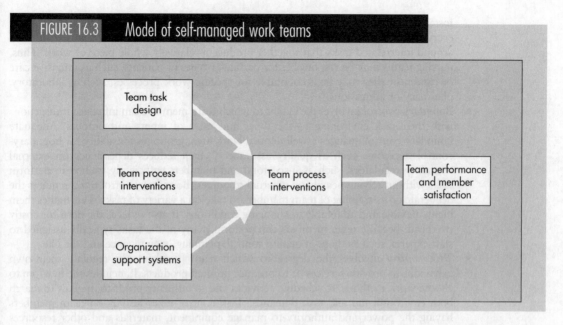

FIGURE 16.3   Model of self-managed work teams

Figure 16.3 is a model explaining how self-managed work teams perform. It summarises current STS research and shows how teams can be designed for high performance. Although the model is mainly based on experience with teams that perform the daily work of the organisation (work teams), it also has relevance to other team designs, such as problem-solving teams, management teams, cross-functional integrating teams and employee involvement teams.[29]

The model shows that team performance and member satisfaction follow directly from how well the team functions. This includes how well members communicate and co-ordinate with each other, resolve conflicts and problems, and make and implement task-relevant decisions. Team functioning, in turn, is influenced by three major inputs:

- team task design
- team process interventions
- organisation support systems.

Because these inputs affect how well teams function and subsequently perform, they are key intervention targets for designing and implementing self-managed work teams.

Team task design

Self-managed work teams are responsible for performing particular tasks. How the team is designed for task performance can therefore have a powerful influence on how well it functions. Task design generally follows from the team's mission and goals, which define the major purpose of the team and provide direction for task achievement. When a team's mission and goals are closely aligned with corporate strategy and business objectives, members can see how team performance contributes to organisation success. This can increase member commitment to team goals.

Team task design links members' behaviours to task requirements and to each other. It structures member interactions and performances. Three task design elements are necessary for creating self-managed work teams: task differentiation, boundary control and task control.[30]

- *Task differentiation* involves the extent to which the team's task is autonomous and forms a relatively self-completing whole. High levels of task differentiation provide an identifiable team boundary and a clearly defined area of team responsibility. Lion Nathan initially had difficulty in introducing self-managed teams at their brewing operation in Khyber Pass, Auckland. The change eventually took three years to implement but was deemed to be beneficial for all. The self-managed team structure fostered a sense of ownership, with improved morale and more enthusiasm among everyone in the company. Also in many hospitals, self-managed nursing teams are formed around interrelated tasks that together produce a relatively whole piece of work. Thus, nursing teams may be responsible for particular types of patients, such as intensive care or cancer, or they may be accountable for specific work processes, such as laboratory, pharmacy or admissions.

- *Boundary control* involves the extent to which team members can influence transactions with their task environment—the types and rates of inputs and outputs. Adequate boundary control includes a well-defined work area; group responsibility for boundary-control decisions, such as quality assurance (which reduces dependence on external boundary regulators, such as inspectors) and members sufficiently trained to perform tasks without relying heavily on external resources. Boundary control often requires the deliberate cross-training of team members to take on a variety of tasks. This makes them highly flexible and adaptable to changing conditions. It also reduces the need for costly overhead, because team members can perform many of the tasks typically assigned to staff experts, such as those in quality control, planning, maintenance and the like.

- *Task control* involves the degree to which team members can regulate their own behaviour to provide services or to produce finished products. It includes the freedom to choose work methods, to schedule activities and to influence production goals to match both environmental and task demands. Task control relies heavily on team members having the power and authority to manage equipment, materials and other resources needed for task performance. This 'work authority' is essential if members are to take responsibility for getting the work accomplished. Task control also requires that team members have accurate and timely information about team performance to allow them to detect performance problems and make necessary adjustments.

Task control enables self-managed work teams to observe and control technical variances as quickly and as close to their source as possible. Technical variances arise from the production process and represent significant deviations from specific goals or standards. In manufacturing, for example, abnormalities in raw material, machine operation and work flow are sources of variance that can adversely affect the quality and quantity of the finished product. In knowledge–work settings, information that is misplaced, incorrect or poorly timed creates variance that can contribute to poor performance. Support staff and managers traditionally control technical variances, but this can take time and add greatly to costs. Self-managed work teams, on the other hand, have the freedom, skills and information needed to control technical variances on-line when they occur. This affords timely responses to production problems and reduces the amount of staff overhead needed.

Team process interventions

A second key input to team functioning involves team process interventions. As described in Chapter 12, teams may develop ineffective social processes that impede functioning and performance, such as poor communication among members, dysfunctional roles and norms and faulty problem solving and decision making. Team process interventions, such as process consultation and team building, can resolve such problems. They can help members address process problems and move the team to a more mature stage of development. Because self-managed work teams need to be self-reliant, members generally acquire their own team process skills. They may attend appropriate training programmes and workshops; they may learn on the job by working with OD practitioners to conduct process interventions on their own teams. Although members' process skills are generally sufficient to resolve most of the team's process problems, OD experts may occasionally need to supplement the team's skills and help members address problems that they are unable to resolve.

Organisation support systems

The final input to team functioning is the extent to which the larger organisation is designed to support self-managed work teams. The success of such teams clearly depends on support systems that are quite different from traditional methods of managing.[31] For example, a bureaucratic, mechanistic organisation is not highly conducive to self-managed teams. An organic structure, with flexibility among units, relatively few formal rules and procedures and decentralised authority, is much more likely to support and enhance the development of self-managed work teams. This explains why such teams are so prevalent in the high-involvement organisations that were described in Chapter 15. Their different features, such as flat, lean structures, open information systems and team-based selection and reward practices, all serve to reinforce teamwork and responsible self-management.

A particularly important support system for self-managed work teams is the external leadership. Self-managed teams exist on a spectrum that ranges from having only mild influence over their work to being almost completely autonomous. In many instances, such teams take on a variety of functions traditionally handled by management. These can include assigning members to individual tasks; determining the methods of work; scheduling; setting production goals and selecting and rewarding members. These activities, however, do not make external supervision obsolete. That leadership role is usually changed to two major functions:

• working with and developing team members
• assisting the team in managing its boundaries.[32]

Working with and developing team members is a difficult process and requires a different style of managing than traditional systems. The team leader (often called 'team facilitator') needs to help team members organise themselves in a way that allows them to become more independent and responsible. He or she must be familiar with team-building approaches and must assist members in learning the skills to perform the job. Recent research suggests that the leader needs to provide expertise in *self-management*.[33] This may include encouraging team members to be self-reinforcing about high performance, to be self-critical of low performance, to set explicit performance goals, to evaluate goal achievement and to rehearse different performance strategies before trying them.

If team members are to maintain sufficient autonomy to control variance from goal attainment, the leader may need to help them manage team boundaries. Teams may have limited control over their task environment, and the leader may need to act as a buffer to reduce environmental uncertainty. This can include mediating and negotiating with other organisational units, such as higher management, staff experts and related work teams. Research suggests that better managers spend more time in lateral interfaces.[34]

These new leadership roles require new and different skills, including a knowledge of socio-technical principles and group dynamics, an understanding of both the task environment and the team's technology and an ability to intervene in the team to help members increase their knowledge and skills. Leaders of self-managed teams should also have the ability to counsel members and to facilitate communication among them.

Many managers have experienced problems trying to fulfil the complex demands of leading self-managed work teams. The most typical complaints mention ambiguity about responsibilities and authority, lack of personal and technical skills and organisational support, insufficient attention from higher management and feelings of frustration in the supervisory job.[35] Attempts to overcome these problems have been made in the following areas:[36]

1   *Recruitment and selection.* Recruitment has been directed at selecting team leaders with a balanced mixture of technical and social skills. Those with extensive technical experience have been paired with more socially adept leaders so that both can share skills and support each other.

2   *Training.* Extensive formal and on-the-job training in human relations, group dynamics and leadership styles have been instituted for leaders of self-managed work teams. Such training is aimed at giving leaders concepts for understanding their roles, as well as hands-on experience in team building, process consultation and third-party intervention (see Chapter 12).

3   *Evaluation and reward systems.* Attempts have been made to tie team leader rewards to achievements in team development. Leaders prepare developmental plans for individual workers and the team as a whole and set measurable

benchmarks for progress. Performance appraisals of leaders are conducted within a group format, with feedback supplied by team members, peers and higher-level management.

4 *Leadership support systems.* Leaders of self-managed work teams have been encouraged to develop peer support groups. Team leaders can meet off-site to share experiences and to address issues of personal and general concern.

5 *Use of freed-up time.* Team leaders have been provided with a mixture of strategies to help them apply their talents beyond the immediate work team. A team leader has more time when the team has matured and taken on many managerial functions. In those cases, team leaders have been encouraged to become involved in such areas as higher-level planning and budgeting, company-wide training and development and individual career development.

Application steps

Socio-technical systems work designs have been implemented in a variety of settings, including manufacturing firms, hospitals, schools and government agencies. Although the specific implementation strategy is tailored to the situation, a common method of change underlies many of these applications. It generally involves high worker participation in the work design and implementation process. Such participative work design allows employees to translate their special knowledge of the work situation into relevant work designs. Because employees have ownership over the design process, they tend to be highly committed to implementing the work designs.[37]

STS applications generally proceed in six steps:[38]

1 *Sanctioning the design effort.* In this stage, workers are provided with the necessary protection and support to diagnose their work system and to design an appropriate work design. In many unionised situations, top management and union officials jointly agree to temporarily suspend existing work rules and job classifications so that employees have the freedom to explore new ways of working. Management may also provide workers with sufficient time and external help to diagnose their work system and to devise alternative work structures. In cases of redesigning existing work systems, normal production demands may be reduced during the redesign process. Also, workers may be afforded some job and wage security so that they feel free to try new designs without fear of losing their jobs or money.

2 *Diagnosing the work system.* This step includes analysing the work system to discover how it is operating. Knowledge of existing operations (or of intended operations, in the case of a new work system) is the basis for designing an appropriate work design. Socio-technical systems practitioners have devised diagnostic models applicable to work systems making products or delivering services. The models analyse the system's technical and social parts and assess how well the two fit each other. The task environment facing the system is also analysed to see how well it is meeting external demands, such as customer quality requirements.

3 *Generating appropriate designs.* Based on the diagnosis, the work system is redesigned to fit the situation. Although this typically results in self-managed work teams, it is important to emphasise that, in some cases, the diagnosis may reveal that tasks are not very interdependent and that an individual-job work design, such as an enriched job, might be more appropriate. Two important STS principles guide the design process.

The first principle, compatibility, suggests that the process of designing work should fit the values and objectives underlying the approach. For example, the major goals of STS design are joint optimisation and boundary management. A work-design process compatible with those objectives would be highly participative, involving those who have a stake in the work design, such as employees, managers, engineers and staff experts. They would jointly decide how to create the social and technical components of work, as well as the environmental exchanges. This participative process increases the likelihood that design choices will be based simultaneously on technical, social and environmental criteria. How well the compatibility guideline is adhered to can determine how well the work design is subsequently implemented.[39]

The second design principle is called 'minimal critical specification'. It suggests that STS designers should specify only those critical features needed to implement the work design. All other features of the design should be left free to vary with the circumstances. In most cases, minimal critical specification identifies what is to be done, not how it will be accomplished. This allows employees considerable freedom to choose work methods, task allocations and job assignments to match changing conditions.

The output of this design step specifies the new work design. In the case of self-managed work teams, this would include the team's mission and goals, an ideal work flow, the skills and knowledge required of team members, a plan for training members to meet those requirements and a list of the decisions the team will make now as well as the ones it should make over time as members develop greater skills and knowledge.

4 *Specifying support systems.* As suggested above, organisational support systems may have to be changed to support new work designs. When self-managed work teams are designed, for example, the basis for pay and measurement systems may need to be changed from individual to team performance to facilitate necessary task interaction among workers.

5 *Implementing and evaluating the work designs.* This stage involves making the necessary changes to implement the work design and evaluating the results. For self-managing work teams, implementation generally requires considerable training to enable workers to gain the necessary technical and social skills to perform multiple tasks, and to control members' task behaviours. It may also entail developing the team through various team-building and process-consultation activities. Organisation development consultants often help team members carry out these tasks with a major emphasis on helping them gain competence in this area. Evaluation of the work design is necessary both to guide the implementation process and to assess the overall effectiveness of the design. In some cases, the evaluation information suggests the need for further diagnosis and redesign efforts.

6 *Continual change and improvement.* This last stage points to the reality that STS designing is never really complete but continues as new things are learned and new conditions encountered. Thus, the ability to continually design and redesign work needs to be built into existing work designs. Members must have the skills and knowledge to continually assess their work unit and to make necessary changes and improvements. From this view, STS designing rarely results in a stable work design, but it does provide a process for continually modifying work to fit changing conditions and to make performance improvements.

Application 16.2 describes an effort by Queensland's Golden Circle Limited to remain competitive by dispensing with its 47-year-old traditional hierarchical management structure and moving towards a less centralised management style. The change process resulted in the creation of self-managed work teams, higher levels of responsibility at lower levels of the organisation and greater job satisfaction.[40]

A break with the old

Golden Circle's Northgate, Brisbane, cannery operates principally as a co-operative to process shareholders' fruit and vegetables. More than 750 growers supply the cannery with more than 170 000 tonnes of fruit and vegetables a year. Golden Circle also manufactures its own cans, cartons, Tetra Paks and cordial bottles. It employs between 600 and 1700 workers, depending on seasonal variations.

The company recognised that its competitors were changing their business practices and, by not following suit, it would be left by the wayside. It also recognised that more ownership, more responsibility and more authority for workers would result in an environment where people worked together to achieve a more productive and competitive Golden Circle. It sees that its employees will benefit by being better trained and, as productivity improves, a pay rise could well follow through an enterprise agreement. Improved communications between workers and management will, the company believes, encourage a feeling of empowerment in workers as they realise that their opinions and views are being listened to.

The new company philosophy accepts that managers may have difficulties with the extra work involved in initially setting up the teams or in delegating their power, but maintains that self-managed teams will make management jobs easier in the long term. Instead of directing staff and giving orders, managers will have the opportunity to delegate the ownership and responsibility for different jobs directly to workers, leading to a democratisation of management style.

Work Improvement Committees (WICs) have existed at Golden Circle for many years but have acted mainly as discussion outlets for work-related issues and have not provided formalised avenues for action. These committees are now playing an important role in the introduction and development of self-managed teams. It was through the committees, and in conjunction with an external business performance consultant, that management and workers were contacted and informed about the self-management concept.

The structure of the WIC was changed so that more shop floor workers would be included in self-managed team deliberations. In addition, several areas wanted to form their own committees, with such names as 'Organisational Change Committee'. It was decided to instigate self-managed teams section by section because of the difficulties of implementing the concept in heavy casual workforce areas.

In December 1993, the first section of the Cannery (Despatch) was approached about implementing teams and the following procedure was used to lay the basis for the development and appointment of self-managed teams in this area:

- An information session lasting about an hour introduced the concept to the 60 employees in the area.
- A seven-member Organisational Change Committee (OCC) participated in a training session to learn the skills needed to look at job redesign.
- A 'Starship Exercise'—a simulated workshop—was conducted for groups of 10–20 workers. The situation was an Origami production line on which employees had to collectively analyse and redesign the hypothetical work situation to make it more effective. The aim of the exercise was to illustrate the many ways in which tasks could be undertaken.
- A Question Raising Session provided a forum for employees to raise any fears, such as job security and pay, that they might have about self-managed teams. All questions asked were recorded, and, together with the answers, later distributed to staff.
- WIC/OCC Meetings averaged one a week for three months. The large number of meetings was required to develop the teams, determine their responsibilities and illustrate how teams would benefit workers and management.
- Once the OCC had evolved the plan by which teams would work, it presented the ideas to employees to obtain their commitment.
- After incorporating any changes that the workforce had suggested, the

OCC presented the concept to a senior management committee to obtain its commitment.

The company found that its biggest problem was the selection of team leaders. Whereas in the past a manager had always appointed group leaders, now the committee wanted to choose its own. After much negotiation and many meetings, all positions were declared vacant and all interested in them were invited to apply. Applicants were interviewed and selected by a panel comprising a warehouse manager, team co-ordinator and a work improvement and human resource representative. Team leaders were appointed for 12 months, after which the teams would decide on procedures for appointing subsequent team leaders.

The next step was the actual organisation of workers into teams. The OCC suggested the development of

seven teams: transport team; loading team; containers team; order assembly team; storage team; training/receivals team and garage team.

Team training, which is currently under way, is being carried out by two TAFE lecturers in liaison with the business performance consultant, following a TAFE leadership and team member training module. The module was developed by Golden Circle in conjunction with Brisbane's North Point TAFE. The programme will run for 20 hours over a five-week period. Workers are introduced to new skills each session and have a week in which to consolidate them and discover any difficulties with them.

The company recognises that the development of self-managed teams will be an ongoing process and follow-up support and training will be provided to anyone who should require it.

Results of self-managed teams

Research on socio-technical systems design efforts is extensive. For example, a 1994 bibliography by researchers at Eindhoven University of Technology in The Netherlands found 3082 English-language studies.[41] And, as with reports on job enrichment, most of the published reports on self-managed teams show favourable results.[42]

A series of famous case studies at General Foods' Gaines Pet Food/Topeka plant, the Saab-Scania engine assembly plant and Volvo's Kalmar and Udevalla plants provide one set of positive findings. The Gaines Pet Food plant operated at an overhead rate some 33% below that of traditional plants.[43] It reported annual variable cost savings of US$600 000, one of the best safety records in the company, turnover rates far below average and high levels of job satisfaction. A long-term, external evaluation of the groups at Gaines plant[44] attributed savings related to work innovation at about US$1 million a year, and, despite a variety of problems, productivity increased in every year but one over a decade of operation. The plant has maintained one of the highest product quality ratings at General Foods since its opening.

Extensive research on self-managing groups has been done by Saab-Scania.[45] The first group was established in 1969, and four years later there were 130 production groups. These groups have generally shown improvements in production and employee attitudes and decreases in unplanned work stoppages and turnover rates. Interestingly, when workers from the US visited Saab's engine assembly plant, they reported that work was too fast and that lunch breaks were too short.[46] A Saab executive commented that the visitors had not stayed long enough to become completely proficient, causing their complaint that the pace was too fast.

The widely publicised use of self-managing groups at Volvo's automotive plant in Kalmar, Sweden, has also shown positive results.[47] The Kalmar factory opened in July 1974, and by the following year it was operating at 100% efficiency. As a reference point, highly productive automobile plants normally operate at about 80% of engineering standards. Interviews with workers and union officials indicated that the quality of work life was considerably better than in assembly jobs that they had had in the past. In addition, Volvo's Udevalla plant reported significant quality improvements and higher productivity than in comparable plants.[48]

A second set of studies supporting the positive impact of socio-technical design teams comes from research comparing self-managed teams with other interventions. For example, probably one of the most thorough assessments of self-managing groups is a longitudinal study conducted in a food-processing plant in the Midwest of the US.[49] Self-managing groups were created as part of an overall revamping of a major part of the plant's production facilities. The effects of the intervention were extremely positive. One year after start-up, production was 133% higher than originally planned, while start-up costs were 7.7% lower than planned. Fewer workers were needed to operate the plant than engineers had projected, with an annual savings in fixed-labour expense of US$264 000. Employee attitudes were extremely positive toward the group design. These positive effects, however, did not result solely from the self-managing design. The intervention also included survey feedback for diagnostic purposes and changes in technology, the physical work setting and management. These kinds of changes are common in self-managing group projects. They suggest that such designs may require supporting changes in other organisational dimensions, such as technology, management style and physical setting in order to facilitate the development of self-managed teams.

This study also permitted a comparison of self-managing groups with job enrichment, which occurred in another department of the company. Both interventions included survey feedback. The self-managing project involved technological changes, whereas the job enrichment programme did not. The results showed that both interventions had similar positive effects in terms of employee attitudes. Only the self-managing project had significant improvements in productivity and costs, however. Again, the productivity improvements cannot be totally attributed to the self-managed teams, but were also the result of the technological changes.

More recently, a rigorous field experiment in a telecommunications company compared self-managed teams with traditionally-designed work groups performing the same types of tasks. The study found significant differences between the two groups in job satisfaction, growth-needs satisfaction, social-needs satisfaction and group satisfaction. Self-managing group members and higher-level managers perceived group performance as superior to traditionally-managed groups. In contrast to these overall findings, however, objective measures of service quality and customer satisfaction did not differ between the two types of groups.[50]

A third set of positive results comes from reviews, or meta-analyses, of other studies. One review examined 16 studies and showed that when productivity, costs and quality were measured, improvements occurred in more than 85% of the cases.[51] Significant reductions in employee turnover and absenteeism rates and improvements in employee attitudes were reported in about 70% of the cases where these variables were measured. Certain methodological weaknesses in the studies suggest, however, that the positive results should be viewed carefully. Another review of 12 studies of self-managing groups showed improvements in hard performance measures in about 67% of the cases where such measures were taken.[52] Both of these reviews also included job enrichment studies, as reported earlier in this chapter. The relative impact of self-managing groups seems about equal to that of job enrichment, especially when the latter includes worker participation in the design process.

Three recent meta-analyses also provide general support for self-managed teams. In a review of all STS work design studies conducted in the 1970s, researchers found a strong positive relationship between the installation of self-managed teams and attitudinal and economic gains.[53] These designs were found to increase employee satisfaction, to reduce production costs through group member innovations and to decrease absenteeism, turnover and accident rates. The researchers found little evidence for claims of increased productivity, primarily because of the lack of sufficient reported data. In a technical and comprehensive meta-analysis, researchers concluded that self-managed teams do produce increases in productivity and reductions in escape behaviour, such as absenteeism, but that these effects varied widely. Higher results were associated with high levels of work group autonomy, supporting changes in the reward system, interventions that did not include technological changes and applications outside the US.[54] Finally, a detailed and comprehensive meta-analysis of 131 US field experiments reported that work innovations, such as autonomous and semi-autonomous work groups, were more likely to impact positively on financial performance measures, including costs, productivity and quality than behavioural or attitudinal variables.[55] Considerable variation in the size of the positive effect, however, led the researchers to suggest that organisation change was risky. Only when other organisational features, such as reward systems, information systems and performance appraisal systems, changed simultaneously was the probability of positive results increased.

Although the majority of studies report positive effects of self-managing groups, some research suggests a more mixed assessment. A field experiment studying the long-term effects of self-managing groups showed improvements in job satisfaction, but no effects on job motivation, work performance, organisational commitment, mental health or voluntary turnover.[56] The company did lower indirect overhead costs, however, by reducing the number of supervisors. This study, which received an award from the Academy of Management for quality research, concluded that the major benefits of self-managed teams are economic, deriving from the need for less supervision.

Designing work for technical and personal needs

This chapter has described three approaches to work design: engineering, motivational and socio-technical. However, trade-offs and conflicts among the approaches must be recognised. The engineering approach produces traditional jobs and work groups and focuses on efficient performance. This approach tends to downplay employee needs and emphasise economic outcomes. The motivational approach strives to design jobs that are stimulating and demanding and highlights the importance of employee need satisfaction. Research suggests, however, that increased satisfaction does not necessarily produce improvements in productivity. Finally, the socio-technical systems approach attempts to optimise both social and technical aspects. Despite this integrative goal, STS has not produced consistent research results. In this final section, we attempt to integrate the three perspectives by providing a contingency framework that suggests that all three approaches can be effective when applied in the appropriate circumstances. Work design involves creating jobs and work groups for high levels of employee satisfaction and productivity. Considerable research shows that achieving such results depends on designing work to match specific factors that operate in the work setting. These factors have to do with the *technology* for producing goods and services and the *personal needs* of employees. When work is designed to fit or match these factors, it is most likely to be both productive and humanly satisfying.

The technical and personal factors affecting work design success provide a contingency framework for choosing among the four different kinds of work designs discussed in the chapter:

- traditional jobs
- traditional work groups
- enriched jobs
- self-managed teams.

Technical factors

Two key dimensions can affect change on the shop floor: technical interdependence, or the extent to which co-operation among workers is required to produce a product or service, and technical uncertainty, or the amount of information processing and decision making that employees must do in order to complete a task.[57] In general, the degree of technical interdependence determines whether work should be designed for individual jobs or work groups. With low technical interdependence and little need for worker co-operation—as,

Work designs that optimise technology

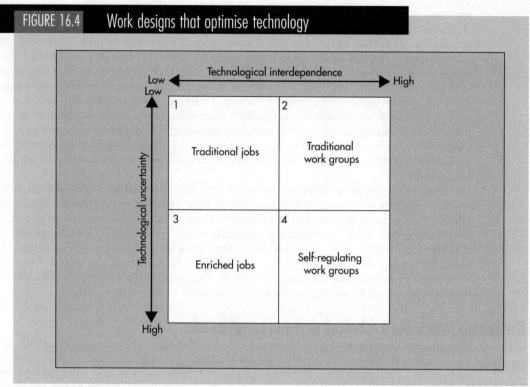

Source: Reproduced by permission of the publisher from T. Cummings, 'Designing work for productivity and quality of work life,' *Outlook* 6 (1982): 39.

for example, in field sales and data entry—work can be designed for individual jobs. Conversely, when technical interdependence is high and employees must co-operate—as in production processes like coal mining, assembly lines and software writing—work should be designed for groups composed of people who perform interacting tasks.

The second dimension, technical uncertainty, determines whether work should be designed for external forms of control, such as supervision, scheduling or standardisation, or for worker self-control. When technical uncertainty is low and little information has to be processed by employees, work can be designed for external control, such as might be found on assembly lines and in other forms of repetitive work. On the other hand, when technical uncertainty is high and people must process information and make decisions, work should be designed for high levels of employee self-control, such as might be found in professional work and troubleshooting tasks.

Figure 16.4 shows the different types of work designs that are most effective, from a purely technical perspective, for different combinations of interdependence and uncertainty. In quadrant 1, where technical interdependence and uncertainty are both low, such as might be found in data entry, jobs should be designed traditionally with limited amounts of employee interaction and self-control. When task interdependence is high yet uncertainty is low (quadrant 2), such as work occurring on assembly lines, work should be designed for traditional work groups in which employee interaction is scheduled and self-control is limited. In quadrant 3, where technical interdependence is low but uncertainty is high, as in field sales, work should be structured for individual jobs with internal forms of control, as in enriched jobs. Finally, when both technical interdependence and uncertainty are high (quadrant 4), such as might be found in a continuous-process chemical plant, work should be designed for self-managed teams in which members have the multiple skills, discretion and information necessary to control their interactions around the shared tasks.

Personal-need factors

Most of the research identifying individual differences in work design has focused on selected personal traits. Two types of personal needs can influence the kinds of work designs that are most effective: social needs, or the desire for significant social relationships, and growth needs, or the desire for personal accomplishment, learning and development.[58] In general, the degree of social needs determines whether work should be designed for individual jobs or work groups. People with low needs for social relationships are more likely to be satisfied working on individualised jobs than in interacting groups. Conversely, people with high social needs are more likely to be attracted to group forms of work than to individualised forms.

The second individual difference, growth needs, determines whether work designs should be routine and repetitive or complex and challenging. People with low growth needs are generally not attracted to jobs that offer complexity and challenge (i.e. enriched jobs). They are more satisfied performing routine forms of work that do not require high levels of decision making. On the other hand, people with high growth needs are satisfied with work offering high levels of discretion, skill variety and meaningful feedback. Performing enriched jobs allows them to experience personal accomplishment and development.

That some people have low social and growth needs is often difficult for OD practitioners to accept, particularly in view of the growth and social values that underlies much OD practice. It is important to recognise that individual differences do exist, however. Assuming that all people have high growth needs or want high levels of social interaction can lead to inappropriate work designs. For example, a new manager of a clerical support unit was astonished to find the six members using typewriters when a significant portion of the work consisted of retyping memos and reports that were produced frequently, but changed very little from month to month. In addition, the unit had a terrible record for quality and on-time production. The manager quickly ordered new word-processors and redesigned the work flow to increase interaction among members. Worker satisfaction declined, interpersonal conflicts increased and work quality and on-time performance remained poor. An assessment of the effort revealed that all six of the staff members had low growth needs and low needs for inclusion in group efforts. In the words of one worker: 'All I want is to come into work, do my job and get my pay cheque.'

It is important to emphasise that people who have low growth or social needs are not inferior to those placing a higher value on these factors. They are simply different. It is also necessary to recognise that people can change their needs through personal growth and experience. OD practitioners need to be sensitive to individual differences in work design and careful not to force their own values on others. Many consultants, eager to be seen on the cutting edge of practice, tend to recommend self-managed teams in all situations, without careful attention to technological and personal considerations.

Figure 16.5 shows the different types of work designs that are most effective for the various combinations of social and growth needs. When employees have relatively low social and growth needs (quadrant 1), traditional jobs are most effective. In quadrant 2, where employees have high social needs but low growth needs, traditional work groups, such as might be found on an assembly line, are most appropriate. These allow for some social interaction but limited amounts of challenge and discretion. When employees have low social needs but high growth needs (quadrant 3), enriched jobs are most satisfying. Here, work is designed for individual jobs that have high levels of task variety, discretion and feedback about results. A research scientist's job is likely to be an enriched one, as is that of a skilled craftperson. Finally, in quadrant 4, where employees have high social and growth needs, work should be specifically designed for self-managed teams. Such groups offer opportunities for significant social interaction around tasks that are both complex and challenging. A team of astronauts in a space shuttle resembles a self-managing work group, as does a group managing the control room of an oil refinery or a group of nurses in a hospital unit.

Work designs that optimise personal needs

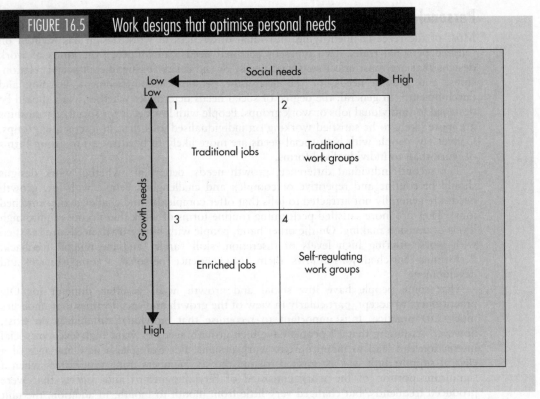

Source: Reproduced by permission of the publisher from T. Cummings, 'Designing work for productivity and quality of work life,' *Outlook* 6 (1982): 40.

Meeting both technical and personal needs

Satisfying both technical and human needs to achieve work-design success is likely to occur only in limited circumstances. When the technical conditions of a company's production processes (as shown in Figure 16.4) are compatible with the personal needs of its employees (as shown in Figure 16.5), the respective work designs combine readily and can satisfy both. On General Motors' assembly lines, for example, the technology is highly interdependent, yet low in uncertainty (quadrant 2 in Figure 16.4). Much of the work is designed around traditional work groups in which task behaviours are standardised, and interactions among workers are scheduled. Such work is likely to be productive and fulfilling to the extent that General Motors' production workers have high social needs and low growth needs (quadrant 2 in Figure 16.5).

When technology and people are incompatible—for example, when an organisation has quadrant 1 technology and quadrant 4 worker needs—at least two kinds of changes can be made to design work to satisfy both requirements.[59] One strategy is to change technology or people to bring them more into line with each other. This is a key point underlying socio-technical systems approaches. For example, technical interdependence can be reduced by breaking long assembly lines into more discrete groups. In Sweden, Volvo redesigned the physical layout and technology for assembling automobiles and trucks to promote self-managed teams. Modifying people's needs is more complex, and begins by matching new or existing workers to available work designs. For example, companies can assess workers' needs through standardised paper-and-pencil tests. The information from these can be used to counsel employees and to help them locate jobs that are compatible with their needs. Similarly, employees can be allowed to volunteer for specific work designs, a common practice in socio-technical systems projects. This matching process is likely to require high levels of trust and co-operation between management and workers, as well as a shared commitment to designing work for high performance and employee satisfaction.

A second strategy for accommodating both technical and human requirements is to leave the two components alone and to design compromise work designs that only partially fulfil the demands of either. The key issue is to decide to what extent one contingency will be satisfied at the expense of the other. For example, when capital costs are high relative to labour costs, such as is found in highly automated plants, work design is likely to favour the technology. Conversely, in many service jobs where labour is expensive relative to capital, organisations may design work for employee motivation and satisfaction at the risk of shortchanging their technology. These examples suggest a range of possible compromises based on different weightings of technical and human demands. Careful assessment of both types of contingencies and of the cost-benefit trade-offs is necessary to design an appropriate compromise work design.

Clearly, the strategy of designing work to bring technology and people more into line with each other is preferable to compromise work designs. Although the latter approach seems necessary when there are heavy constraints on changing the contingencies, in many cases those constraints are more imagined than real. The important thing is to understand the technical and personal factors that exist in a particular situation and to design work accordingly. Traditional jobs and traditional work groups are likely to be successful in certain situations (as shown in Figures 16.4 and 16.5); in other settings, enriched jobs and self-managed teams are more likely to be more effective.

Summary

In this chapter, we discussed three different approaches to work design. In addition, a contingency framework was described to determine the approach most likely to result in high productivity and worker satisfaction, given certain work place characteristics. The contingency framework reconciles the strengths and weaknesses of each approach. The engineering approach produces traditional jobs and traditional work groups. Traditional jobs are highly simplified and involve routine and repetitive forms of work. They do not require co-ordination among people to produce a product or service. Traditional jobs achieve high productivity and worker satisfaction in situations that are characterised by low technical uncertainty and interdependence and low growth and social needs.

Traditional work groups are composed of members performing routine yet interrelated tasks. Member interactions are controlled externally, usually by rigid work flows, schedules and supervisors. Traditional work groups are best suited to conditions of low technical uncertainty, but high technical interdependence. They fit people with low growth needs but high social needs.

The motivational approach produces enriched jobs that involve high levels of skill variety, task identity, task significance, autonomy and feedback from the work itself. Enriched jobs achieve good results when the technology is uncertain but does not require high levels of co-ordination, and when employees have high growth needs and low social needs.

Finally, the socio-technical systems approach is associated with self-managed teams. These groups are composed of members performing interrelated tasks. Members are given the multiple skills, autonomy and information necessary to control their own task behaviours with relatively little external control. Many organisation development practitioners argue that self-managed teams represent the work design of the 1990s. This is because high levels of technical uncertainty and interdependence are prevalent in today's work places and because today's workers often have high growth and social needs.

ACTIVITIES

Review questions
1 Under what conditions would you recommend self-managed work groups?
2 Which quality(ies) is(are) common for people with high growth needs?
3 When the technology and the needs of the employees are incompatible, which changes should be made?
4 What are the characteristics of traditional jobs?
5 When technical interdependence is low and uncertainty is high, and where people have low social needs yet high growth needs, which work design would you recommend?
6 How do self-managed work group supervisors often feel?
7 What are the constraints on job enrichment interventions?
8 List the principles of socio-technical systems design.

Discussion and essay questions
1 Describe the motivational approach to job design. What are the key dimensions that lead to high work quality and internal motivation?
2 What are the technical factors affecting work design success?
3 Discuss socio-technical systems theory and contrast it with the process of OD.
4 Describe self-managed work groups and the best-suited environments for implementation.
5 Discuss why self-managed work groups are more likely to be found in high involvement plants.

Notes

1 F. Taylor, *The Principles of Scientific Management* (New York: Harper and Row, 1911).
2 *Ibid.*
3 T. Cummings, 'Self-regulating work groups: a socio-technical synthesis', *Academy of Management Review,* 3 (1978): 625–34; G. Susman, *Autonomy at Work* (New York: Praeger, 1976); J. Slocum and H. Sims, 'A typology of technology and job redesign', *Human Relations,* 33 (1983): 193–212.
4 F. Herzberg, B. Mausner and B. Snyderman, *The Motivation to Work* (New York: John Wiley and Sons, 1959); F. Herzberg, 'The wise old Turk', *Harvard Business Review,* 52 (September–October 1974): 70–80; F. Herzberg and Z. Zautra, 'Orthodox job enrichment: measuring true quality in job satisfaction', *Personnel,* 53 (September–October 1976): 54–68.
5 J. Hackman and G. Oldham, *Work Redesign* (Reading, Mass.: Addison-Wesley, 1980).
6 A. Turner and P. Lawrence, *Industrial Jobs and the Worker* (Cambridge: Harvard Graduate School of Business Administration, Division of Research, 1965); J. Hackman and G. Oldham, 'Development of the job diagnostic survey', *Journal of Applied Psychology,* 60 (April 1975): 159–70; H. Sims, A. Szilagyi and R. Keller, 'The measurement of job characteristics', *Academy of Management Journal,* 19 (1976): 195–212.
7 Hackman and Oldham, *Work Redesign, op. cit.*; J. Hackman, G. Oldham, R. Janson and K. Purdy, 'A new strategy for job enrichment', *California Management Review,* 17 (Summer 1975): 57–71; R. Walters *et al., Job Enrichment for Results* (Reading, Mass.: Addison-Wesley, 1975); J. Hackman, 'Work design' in *Improving Life at Work: Behavioral Science Approaches to Organizational Change,* eds J. Hackman and L. Suttle (Santa Monica, Calif.: Goodyear, 1977): 96–163.
8 J. Hackman and G. Oldham, *The Diagnostic Survey: An Instrument for the Diagnosis of Jobs and the Evaluation of Job Redesign Projects,* Technical Report No. 4 (New Haven: Yale University, Department of Administrative Sciences, 1974); Sims, Szilagyi and Keller, 'The measurement of job characteristics', *op. cit.*; M. Campion, 'The multimethod job design questionnaire', *Psychological Documents,* 15 (1985): 1; J. Idaszak and F. Drasgow, 'A revision of the job diagnostic survey: elimination of a measurement artifact', *Journal of Applied Psychology,* 72 (1987): 69–74.

9 D. Elloy and A. Randolph, 'The effect of superleader behavior on autonomous work groups in a government operated railway service', *Public Personnel Management*, 26:2 (1997), 257–272.

10 *Ibid.*

11 T. Nitschke and M. O'Keefe, 'Managing the linkage with primary producers: experiences in the Australian grain industry', *Supply Chain Management*, 2:1 (1997), 4–6.

12 G. Oldham and J. Hackman, 'Work design in the organizational context' in *Research in Organizational Behavior*, 2, eds B. Staw and L. Cummings (Greenwich, Conn.: JAI Press, 1980): 247–78; J. Cordery and T. Wall, 'Work design and supervisory practice: a model', *Human Relations*, 38 (1985): 425–41.

13 Hackman and Oldham, *Work Redesign, op. cit.*

14 *Ibid.*

15 M. Campion, 'Interdisciplinary approaches to job design: a constructive replication with extensions', *Journal of Applied Psychology*, 73 (1988): 467–81.

16 C. Kulik, G. Oldham and P. Langner, 'Measurement of job characteristics: comparison of the original and the revised job diagnostic survey', *Journal of Applied Psychology*, 73 (1988): 426–66; J. Idaszak and F. Drasgow, 'A revision of the job diagnostic survey: elimination of a measurement artifact', *Journal of Applied Psychology*, 72 (1987): 69–74.

17 R. Steers and D. Spencer, 'The role of achievement motivation in job design', *Journal of Applied Psychology*, 62 (1977): 472–79; J. Champoux, 'A three sample test of some extensions to the job characteristics model', *Academy of Management Journal*, 23 (1980): 466–78; R. Katz, 'The influence of job longevity on employee reactions to task characteristics', *Human Relation*, 31 (1978): 703–25.

18 R. Zeffane, 'Correlates of job satisfaction and their implications for work redesign', *Public Personnel Management*, 23 (1994): 61–76.

19 G. Oldham and Y. Fried, 'Employee reactions to workspace characteristics', *Journal of Applied Psychology*, 72 (1987): 75–80.

20 B. Loher, R. Noe, N. Moeller and M. Fitzgerald, 'A meta-analysis of the relation of job characteristics to job satisfaction', *Journal of Applied Psychology*, 70 (1985): 280–89.

21 B. McEvoy and W. Cascio, 'Strategies for reducing employee turnover: a meta-analysis', *Journal of Applied Psychology*, 70 (1985): 342–53.

22 T. Cummings and E. Molloy, *Improving Productivity and the Quality of Work Life* (New York: Praeger, 1977).

23 J. Nicholas, 'The comparative impact of organization development interventions on hard criteria measures', *Academy of Management Review*, 7 (1982): 531–42.

24 Y. Fried and G. Ferris, 'The validity of the job characteristics model: a review and meta-analysis', *Personnel Psychology*, 40 (1987): 287–322.

25 E. Trist, B. Higgin, H. Murray and A. Pollock, *Organizational Choice* (London: Tavistock, 1963); T. Cummings and B. Srivastva, *Management of Work: A Socio-Technical Systems Approach* (San Diego: University Associates, 1977); A. Cherns, 'Principles of sociotechnical design revisited', *Human Relations*, 40 (1987): 153–62.

26 Cummings, 'Self-regulating work groups', *op. cit.*, 625–34; J. Hackman, *The Design of Self-Managing Work Groups*, Technical Report No. 11 (New Haven: Yale University, School of Organization and Management, 1976); Cummings and Srivastva, *Management of Work, op. cit.*; Susman, *Autonomy at Work, op, cit.*; H. Sims and C. Manz, 'Conversations within self-managed work groups', *National Productivity Review*, 1 (Summer 1982): 261–69; T. Cummings, 'Designing effective work groups' in *Handbook of Organizational Design: Remodeling Organizations and Their Environments*, 2, eds P. Nystrom and W. Starbuck (New York: Oxford University Press, 1981): 250–71.

27 C. Manz, 'Beyond self-managing teams: toward self-leading teams in the work place' in *Research in Organizational Change and Development*, 4, eds W. Pasmore and R. Woodman (Greenwich, Conn.: JAI Press, 1990): 273–99; C. Manz and H. Sims Jr, 'Leading workers to lead themselves: the external leadership of self-managed work teams', *Administrative Science Quarterly*, 32 (1987): 106–28.

28 E. Lawler, S. Mohrman and G. Ledford, *Creating High Performance Organizations* (San Francisco: Jossey-Bass, 1995).

29 B. Dumaine, 'The trouble with teams', *Fortune* (5 September 1994): 86–92.

30 Cummings, 'Self-regulating work groups', *op. cit.* 625–34.

31 Cummings, 'Self-regulating work groups', *op. cit.*; J. Pearce II and E. Ravlin, 'The design and activation of self-regulating work groups', *Human Relations*, 40 (1987): 751–82; J. Hackman, 'The design of work teams' in *Handbook of Organizational Behaviour*, ed. J. Lorsch (Englewood Cliffs, N.J.: Prentice-Hall, 1987): 315–42.

32 *Ibid.*

33 C. Manz and H. Sims, 'The leadership of self-managed work groups: a social learning theory perspective', (paper delivered at National Academy of Management meeting, New York, August 1982); C. Manz and H. Sims Jr, 'Searching for the "unleader": organizational member views on leading self-managed groups', *Human Relations,* 37 (1984): 409–24.

34 H. Mintzberg, *The Nature of Managerial Work* (New York: Harper and Row, 1973); L. Sayles, *Managerial Behavior: Administration in Complex Organizations* (New York: McGraw-Hill, 1964).

35 R. Walton and L. Schlesinger, 'Do supervisors thrive in participative work systems?' *Organizational Dynamics,* 8 (Winter 1979): 25–38.

36 *Ibid,* 25–38.

37 M. Weisbord, 'Participative work design: a personal odyssey', *Organizational Dynamics* (1984): 5–20.

38 T. Cummings, 'Socio-technical systems: an intervention strategy', in *New Techniques in Organization Development,* ed. W. Burke (New York: Basic Books, 1975): 228–49; Cummings and Srivastva, *Management of Work, op. cit.*; Cummings and Molloy, *Improving Productivity and the Quality of Work Life, op. cit.*

39 Cherns, 'Principles of sociotechnical design revisited', *op. cit.*

40 B. Miles, 'A break with the old', *Work and People.*

41 F. van Eijnatten, S. Eggermont, G. de Goffau and I. Mankoe, 'The socio-technical systems design paradigm' (Eindhoven, The Netherlands: Eindhoven University of Technology, 1994).

42 P. Goodman, R. Devadas and T. Hughson, 'Groups and productivity: analysing the effectiveness of self-managing teams', in *Productivity in Organizations,* eds J. Campbell, R. Campbell and associates (San Francisco: Jossey-Bass, 1988): 295–325.

43 R. Walton, 'How to counter alienation in the plant', *Harvard Business Review,* 12 (November–December 1972): 70–81.

44 R. Schrank, 'On ending worker alienation: the Gaines Pet Food plant', in *Humanizing the Workplace,* ed. R. Fairfield (Buffalo, N.Y.: Prometheus Books, 1974): 119–20, 126; R. Walton, 'Teaching an old dog food new tricks', *The Wharton Magazine,* 4 (Winter 1978): 42; L. Ketchum, *Innovating Plant Managers Are Talking About ...* (International Conference on the Quality of Working Life, Toronto, Canada, 30 August–3 September 1981): 2–3; H. Simon *et al., General Foods Topeka: Ten Years Young* (International Conference on the Quality of Working Life, Toronto, Canada, 30 August–3 September 1981): 5–7.

45 J. Norsted and S. Aguren, *The Saab-Scania Report* (Stockholm: Swedish Employer's Confederation, 1975).

46 'Doubting Sweden's way', *Time* (10 March 1975): 40.

47 P. Gyllenhammär, *People at Work* (Reading, Mass.: Addison-Wesley, 1977): 15–17, 43, 52–53; B. Jönsson, *Corporate Strategy for People at Work—The Volvo Experience* (International Conference on the Quality of Working Life, Toronto, Canada, 30 August–3 September 1981); N. Tichy and J. Nisberg, 'When does work restructuring work? Organizational innovations at Volvo and GM', *Organizational Dynamics,* 5 (Summer 1976): 73.

48 J. Kapstein and J. Hoerr, 'Volvo's radical new plant: the death of the assembly line?' *Business Week* (28 August 1989): 92–93.

49 W. Pasmore, 'The comparative impacts of sociotechnical system, job-redesign and survey–feedback interventions', in *Sociotechnical Systems: A Source Book,* eds W. Pasmore and J. Sherwood (San Diego, University Associates, 1978): 291–300.

50 S. Cohen and G. Ledford Jr, 'The effectiveness of self-managing teams: a quasi-experiment', *Human Relations,* 47 (1, 1994): 13–43.

51 Cummings and Molloy, *Improving Productivity and the Quality of Work Life, op. cit.*

52 Nicholas, 'Comparative impact', *op. cit.*: 531–42.

53 J. Pearce II and E. Ravlin, 'The design and activation of self-regulating work groups', *Human Relations,* 40 (1987): 751–82.

54 R. Beekun, 'Assessing the effectiveness of sociotechnical interventions: antidote or fad?' *Human Relations,* 42 (1989): 877–97.

55 B. Macy, P. Bliese and J. Norton, 'Organizational change and work innovation: a meta-analysis of 131 North American field experiments—1961–1990' in *Research in Organizational Change and Development,* 7, eds R. Woodman and W. Pasmore (Greenwich, Conn.: JAI Press, 1994).

56 T. Wall, N. Kemp, P. Jackson and C. Clegg, 'Outcomes of autonomous workgroups: a long-term field experiment', *Academy Of Management Journal,* 29 (June 1986): 280–304.

57 T. Cummings, 'Self-regulating work groups: a socio-technical synthesis', *Academy of Management Review,* 3 (1978): 625–34; G. Susman, *Autonomy at Work* (New York: Praeger,

1976); J. Slocum and H. Sims, 'A typology of technology and job redesign', *Human Relations*, 33 (1983): 193–212; M. Kiggundu, 'Task interdependence and job design: test of a theory', *Organizational Behavior and Human Performance*, 31 (1983): 145–72.

58 Hackman and Oldham, *Work Redesign, op. cit.*; K. Brousseau, 'Toward a dynamic model of job–person relationships: findings, research questions and implications for work system design', *Academy of Management Review*, 8 (1983): 33–45; G. Graen, T. Scandura and M. Graen, 'A field experimental test of the moderating effects of growth needs strength on productivity', *Journal of Applied Psychology*, 71 (1986): 484–91.

59 T. Cummings, 'Designing work for productivity and quality of work life', *Outlook*, 6 (1982): 35–39.

PART **5**

CHAPTERS

17 Performance management

18 Developing and assisting members

HUMAN
RESOURCE
MANAGEMENT
INTERVENTIONS

Performance management

In this chapter, we discuss human resource management interventions that are concerned with the management of individual and group performance. Performance management involves goal setting, performance appraisal and reward systems that align member work behaviour with business strategy, employee involvement and workplace technology. 'Goal setting' describes the interaction between managers and employees in jointly defining member work behaviours and outcomes. Orienting employees to the appropriate kinds of work outcomes can reinforce the work designs described in Chapter 16 and can support the organisation's strategic objectives. Goal setting can clarify the duties and responsibilities that are associated with a particular job or work group. When applied to jobs, goal setting can focus on individual goals and reinforce individual contributions and work outcomes. When applied to work groups, goal setting can be directed at group objectives and reinforce members' joint actions, as well as overall group outcomes. One popular approach to goal setting is called 'management by objectives'.

Performance appraisal involves collecting and disseminating performance data to improve work outcomes. It is the primary human resource management intervention for providing performance feedback to individuals and work groups. Performance appraisal is a systematic process of jointly assessing work-related achievements, strengths and weaknesses, but it can also facilitate career development counselling, provide information about the strength and diversity of human resources in the company and link employee performance with rewards.

Reward systems are concerned with eliciting and reinforcing desired behaviours and work outcomes. They can support goal-setting and feedback systems by rewarding the kinds of behaviours required, implementing a particular work design or supporting a business strategy. Like goal setting, rewards systems can be oriented to individual jobs and goals or to group functions and objectives. Moreover, they can be geared to traditional work designs that require external forms of control or to enriched, self-regulating work designs requiring employee self-control. Several innovative and effective reward systems are in use in organisations today.

The personnel or human resource departments of organisations traditionally implement performance management interventions, and personnel practitioners have special training in these areas. Because of the diversity and depth of knowledge required to successfully carry out these kinds of change programmes, practitioners tend to specialise in one part of the personnel function, such as performance appraisal or compensation.

Recently, interest in integrating human resource management with organisation development has been growing. In many companies, such as Honeywell, BHP Copper, Colgate Palmolive, Johnson & Johnson and Shell, organisation development is a separate function of the human resource department. As OD practitioners increasingly became involved in organisation design and employee involvement, so they came to realise the need for personnel practices to change in order to bring them more in line with the new designs and processes. Consequently, personnel specialists now frequently help initiate OD projects. For example, a large electronics firm expanded the role of compensation specialists to include the initiation of work-design projects. OD practitioners traditionally

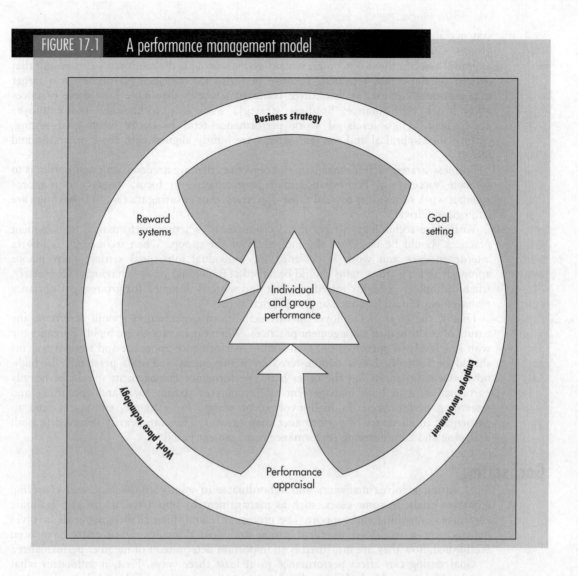

FIGURE 17.1 A performance management model

consulted the compensation people at this firm after the work design had taken place, but the latter were dissatisfied with this secondary role and wanted to be more proactive in work design. In most cases, personnel practitioners continue to specialise in their respective area, yet they become more sensitive to, and competent in, organisation development. Similarly, OD practitioners continue to focus on planned change while becoming more knowledgeable about human resource management.

We begin by describing a performance management model. It shows how goal setting, performance appraisal and rewards are closely linked and difficult to separate in practice. However, each element of performance management is distinct and has its own dynamics. Following the model, each aspect of performance management is discussed and its impact on performance evaluated.

A model of performance management

Performance management is an integrated process of defining, assessing and reinforcing employee work behaviours and outcomes.[1] Organisations with a well-developed performance management process tend to outperform organisations that don't have this element of organisation design.[2] As shown in Figure 17.1, performance management includes practices and methods for goal setting, performance appraisal and reward systems, all of which work together to influence the performance of individuals and work groups. Goal setting specifies the kinds of performances that are desired; performance appraisal assesses those outcomes; reward systems provide the reinforcers that ensure that desired outcomes are repeated. Because performance management occurs in a larger organisational context, at least three contextual factors determine how these practices affect work performance: business strategy, workplace technology and employee involvement.[3] High levels of work performance tend to occur when goal setting, performance appraisal and reward systems are jointly aligned with these organisational factors.

Business strategy defines the goals and objectives that are needed if an organisation is to compete successfully. Performance management needs to focus, assess and reinforce member work behaviours toward those objectives, thus ensuring that work behaviours are strategically driven.

Workplace technology affects the decision as to whether performance management practices should be based on the individual or the group. When technology is low in interdependence and work is designed for individual jobs, goal setting, performance appraisal and reward systems should be aimed at individual work behaviours. Conversely, when technology is highly interdependent and work is designed for groups, performance management should be aimed at group behaviours.[4]

Finally, the level of employee involvement in an organisation should determine the nature of performance management practices. When organisations are highly bureaucratic with low levels of participation, goal-setting, performance-appraisal and reward systems should be formalised and administered by management and staff personnel. In high-involvement situations, on the other hand, performance management should be heavily participative, with both management and employees setting goals and appraising and rewarding performance. In high-involvement plants, for example, employees tend to participate in all stages of performance management. They are heavily involved in both designing and administering performance management practices.

Goal setting

Goal setting involves managers and subordinates in jointly establishing and clarifying employee goals. In some cases, such as management by objectives, it can also facilitate employee counselling and support. The process of establishing challenging goals involves management in the level of participation and goal difficulty. Once goals have been established, how they are measured is an important determinant of member performance.[5]

Goal setting can affect performance in at least three ways. First, it influences what people think and do. It focuses behaviour in the direction of the goals, rather than elsewhere. Second, goals energise behaviour, motivating people to make an effort to reach difficult goals that are accepted. Finally, goal setting leads to persistence in effort over time when goals are difficult but achievable. Goal-setting interventions have been implemented in such organisations as McDonnell-Douglas and 3M.

Characteristics of goal setting

An impressive amount of research underlies goal-setting interventions and practices.[6] This research has resulted in the identification of two major processes that affect positive outcomes:

1 the establishment of challenging goals
2 the clarification of goal measurement.

Goal setting appears to work equally well in both individual and group settings.[7]

Establishing challenging goals

The first element of goal setting concerns the establishment of goals that can be perceived as challenging, but are realistic and for which there will be a high level of commitment. This can be accomplished by varying goal difficulty and the level of employee participation in the goal-setting process. Increasing the difficulty of employee goals, also known as 'stretch goals', can increase their perceived challenge and enhance the amount of effort necessary for their achievement.[8] Thus, more difficult goals tend to lead to increased effort and performance, as long as they can be seen to be feasible. If goals are set too high, however, they may lose their motivating potential, and employees will give up when they fail to achieve them. An important method for increasing the acceptance of a challenging goal is to collect benchmarks or best practice referents. When employees see that other individuals, groups or organisations have achieved a specified level of performance, they are more motivated to achieve that level themselves.

Another aspect of establishing challenging goals is to vary the amount of participation in the goal-setting process. Having employees participate can increase motivation and performance, but only to the extent that members set higher goals than those that are typically assigned to them. Participation can also convince employees that the goals are achievable and so increase their commitment to achieving them.

All three contextual factors play an important role in the establishment of challenging goals. First, there must be a clear 'line of sight' between the business strategy goals and the goals established for individuals or groups. When the group is attempting to achieve goals that are not aligned with the business strategy, performance can suffer and organisation members become frustrated. Second, employee participation in goal setting is more likely to be effective if employee involvement policies in the organisation support it. Under such conditions, participation in goal setting is likely to be seen as legitimate, resulting in the desired commitment to challenging goals. Third, when tasks are highly interdependent and work is designed for groups, group-oriented participative goal setting tends to increase commitment.[9]

Clarifying goal measurement

The second element in the goal-setting process involves the specification and clarification of the goals. When employees are given specific goals, they tend to perform higher than when they are simply told to 'do their best', or when they receive no guidance at all. Specific goals reduce ambiguity about what is expected, and focus the search for appropriate behaviours.

To clarify goal measurement, objectives should be operationally defined. For example, a group of employees may agree to increase productivity by 5%, a challenging and specific goal. But there are a variety of ways of measuring productivity. It is important to operationally define the goal to be sure that employee or group behaviours can influence the measure. For example, a productivity goal defined by sales per employee may be inappropriate for a manufacturing group.

Clarifying goal measurement also requires that employees and supervisors negotiate the resources necessary for their achievement. These resources may include time, equipment, raw materials or access to information. If employees cannot have access to the appropriate resources, the targeted goal may have to be revised.

Contextual factors also play an important role in the clarifying process. Goal specification and clarity can be difficult in high-technology settings. The work is often uncertain and highly interdependent. Increasing employee participation in the clarification of goal measurement can give employees ownership of a non-specific but challenging goal. Employee involvement policies can also impact on how goals are clarified. Employees and work teams can manage the entire goal-setting process, from goal establishment to definition and clarification, when employee involvement policies and work designs favour it. Finally, the process of specifying and clarifying goals is extremely difficult if the business strategy is itself unclear. Under these conditions, attempting to gain consensus on the measurement and importance of goals can lead to frustration and resistance to change.

Application steps

Based on these features of the goal-setting process, OD practitioners have developed specific approaches to goal setting. The following steps characterise those applications:

1 *Diagnosis.* The first step is a thorough diagnosis of the job or work group, employee needs and the three context factors: business strategy, workplace technology and level of employee involvement. This provides information about the nature and difficulty of specific goals, the appropriate types and levels of participation and the necessary support systems.

2 *Preparing for goal setting.* This stage involves the preparation of managers and employees for engagement in goal setting. It typically involves increased interaction and communication between managers and employees, as well as formal training in goal-setting methods. Specific action plans for implementing the programme are also made.

3 *Setting goals.* In this step, challenging goals are established and goal measurement clarified. Employees participate in the process to the extent that contextual factors support such involvement, and because employees are likely to set higher goals than those assigned by management.

4 *Review.* In this final stage the goal-setting process is assessed, so that modifications can be made if necessary. The goal attributes are evaluated to see whether the goals are energising and challenging and whether they support the business strategy and can be influenced by the employees.

Management by objectives

A common form of goal setting used in organisations is management by objectives (MBO). This method is mainly an attempt to align personal goals with business strategy by increasing communications and shared perceptions between the manager and subordinates, either individually or as a group, or by reconciling conflict where it exists.

All organisations have goals and objectives; all managers have goals and objectives. In many instances, however, those goals are not clearly stated, and managers and subordinates have different perceptions as to what those objectives are. MBO is an approach to resolving these differences in perceptions and goals. *Management by objectives* can be defined as systematic and periodic manager–subordinate meetings that are designed to accomplish organisational goals by mutual planning of the work, periodic reviewing of accomplishments and mutual solving of problems that arise in the course of getting the job done.

MBO has its origin in two different backgrounds—organisational and developmental. The organisational root of MBO was developed by Drucker, who emphasised that organisations need to establish objectives in eight key areas: 'market standing; innovation; productivity; physical and financial resources; profitability; manager performance and development; worker performance and attitude and public responsibility'.[10] Drucker's work was expanded by Odiorne, whose first book on MBO stressed the need for quantitative measurement.[11]

According to Levinson,[12] MBO's second root is found in the work of McGregor, who stressed its qualitative nature, and its use for development and growth on the job.[13] McGregor attempted to shift the emphasis from identifying weaknesses to analysing performance in order to define strengths and potentials. He believed that this shift could be accomplished by having subordinates reach agreement with their boss on major job responsibilities, after which they could develop short-term performance goals and action plans for their achievement, thus allowing them to appraise their own performance. Subordinates would then discuss the results of this self-appraisal with their supervisors, thus developing a new set of performance goals and plans. This emphasis on mutual understanding and performance, rather than on personality, would change the supervisor's role from that of judge to helper, thereby reducing both role conflict and ambiguity. The second root of MBO reduces role ambiguity by making goal setting more participative and transactional as it increases communication between role incumbents, and by ensuring that both individual and organisational goals are identified and achieved.

An MBO programme often goes beyond the one-on-one, manager–subordinate relationship to focus on problem-solving discussions that also involve work teams. Setting goals and reviewing individual performance are considered within the larger context of the job. In addition to organisational goals, the MBO process gives attention to individuals' personal and career goals, and tries to make these and organisational goals more complementary. The target-setting procedure allows real (rather than simulated) subordinate participation in goal setting, with open, problem-centred discussions among team members, supervisors and subordinates.

Steps for implementing MBO

There are six basic steps in implementing an MBO process.[14]

1 *Work group involvement.* In the first step of MBO, members of the primary work group define the overall group and individual goals and establish action plans for achieving both organisational and individual goals. If this step is omitted, or if organisational goals and strategies are unclear, the effectiveness of an MBO approach may, over time, be greatly reduced.

2 *Joint manager–subordinate goal setting.* Once the work group's overall goals and responsibilities have been determined, attention is given to the job duties and responsibilities of the individual role incumbents. Roles are carefully examined in terms of their interdependence with those of others outside the work group.

3 *Establishment of action plans for goals.* The subordinates develop action plans for goal accomplishment, either in a group meeting or in a meeting with the immediate manager. The action plans reflect the individual styles of the subordinates, not those of the supervisor.

4 *Establishment of criteria, or yardsticks, of success.* At this point, the manager and subordinates agree on the success criteria for the goals that have been established. These criteria are not limited to easily measurable or quantifiable data. A more important reason for joint development of the success criteria is to ensure that the manager and subordinates have a common understanding of the task and what is expected of the subordinates. Frequently, the parties involved discover that they have not reached a mutual understanding. The subordinates and the manager may have agreed on a certain task, but they find, in discussing how to measure its success, that they have not been communicating clearly. Arriving at joint understanding and agreement on success criteria is the most important step in the entire MBO process.

5 *Review and recycle.* Periodically, the manager reviews work progress, either in the larger group or with the subordinates. There are three stages in this review process. First, the subordinates take the lead, reviewing progress and discussing achievements and the obstacles faced. Next, the manager discusses work plans and objectives for the future. In the third stage, after the action plans have been made, a more general discussion covers the subordinates' future ambitions and other factors of concern. In this final phase, a great deal of coaching and counselling usually takes place.

6 *Maintenance of records.* In many MBO programmes, the working documents of the goals, criteria, yardsticks, priorities and due dates are forwarded to a third party. Although the evidence is indirect, it is likely that the MBO programme, as an OD effort, suffers when a third party, such as higher management or the personnel department, regularly reviews the working papers. Experience shows that when the working papers are routinely passed on, they are less likely to reflect open, honest communication within the supervisor–subordinate pair or the work group. Instead, they often represent an effort to impress the third party or to comply with institutionalised rules and procedures.

Application 17.1 describes how a performance management process was designed at Monsanto Company. It shows how goal-setting processes can be linked with business strategies and performance appraisal processes.[15]

The Chemical Group of the Monsanto Company is a global provider of chemicals, plastics and fibres. Previously the centrepiece of Monsanto's corporate strategy, the Chemical Group's role was changing as Monsanto restructured its business from commodity and speciality chemicals to biotechnology-based products and health care. As part of that role change, the business was asked to become a cash generator with a work force that had been through divestitures, downsizing and other dramatic changes.

In 1991, the human resources department was reorganised into a development group and an administration group. The development group's first assignment was to redesign the performance management system in terms of the Chemical Group's new role and the existing work force. A task force was formed to design a long-range human resource strategy where the new performance management system would be the key implementation vehicle.

Interviews with more than 1500 organisation members, a literature review on performance management and a review of best practices at other firms resulted in several key conclusions. First, human resource management practices can have a major impact on organisation performance. Second, performance management systems typically constrain rather than promote employee contributions to performance. Third, traditional MBO processes are ineffective, contrary to empowerment values and focused more on past accomplishments than on future development. Based on this diagnosis, the task force recommended the adoption of a Performance Enhancement Process (PEP) based on the following design principles:
- focus on development rather than judgment
- focus employee effort on continuous improvement of work processes

- simplify goal setting
- shift the focus from individuals to teams; from supervisory judgment to supervisory coaching
- clarify roles and increase the amount of feedback.

The designed PEP process included direction setting and performance planning, individual development and continual coaching. Direction setting and performance planning initiates the PEP process and occurs at the beginning of each annual performance management cycle. The supervisor and employee meet to establish job accountabilities and goals, and agree on a competency profile that the employee is expected to demonstrate in his or her current job. Job accountabilities are the actual behaviours that directly contribute to the achievement of the organisation's objectives. They define the reason for the job's existence.

Work goals are the specific accomplishments to be achieved during the year. The PEP process suggests that there should be no more than five goals and that one of them should be related to the development of the employee.

Direction setting and performance planning ensure that employees have a clear line of sight between their work and the achievement of the organisation's objectives. In addition, this part of the PEP process is designed to be developmental and future oriented. It tries to avoid the negative dynamics that would prevent a fair appraisal, such as setting low goals that are not challenging, using fuzzy language that allows various interpretations of accomplishments or specifying a long list of assumptions about what might go wrong. Rather, through discussion, the employee and supervisor understand and agree on the direction the employee's work should take.

Finally, a competency expectation profile is developed. The task force defined competency as a combination of knowledge, skills and behaviours that drive performance, and identified 12 core competencies that all employees should develop, such as commitment to task, appreciating differences and customer focus. Each competency was defined differently according to the particular stage in a person's career. Together, the supervisor and employee decide on the competencies that the employee needs to demonstrate during the performance management cycle.

Individual development and continual coaching are the next components of the PEP process. The key to the success of these components is the transformed role of the supervisor from judge to coach. First, the employee evaluates his or her performance according to the stated accountabilities, goals and competencies. The supervisor cannot edit this form, the employee is asked to sign the self-assessment, and it becomes a part of the employee's permanent record. The supervisor's input to the self-assessment is a 'coaching dialogue' that occurs over time and clarifies the

supervisor's view of the employee's performance. Second, the supervisor and employee agree on a list of peers, colleagues, internal customers and others who provide the employee with multiple-viewpoint feedback about the demonstration of his or her competencies. The feedback is summarised and given to the employee, who compares it with the self-assessment and the competency profile developed at the beginning of the cycle. The employee notes discrepancies and uses them to help develop the next competency profile.

The supervisor facilitates the feedback process. He or she helps to identify raters, collects the data and is available to the employee for help in interpretation. The data do not go into the employee's permanent file, and so the supervisor is removed from being the omniscient observer, while a more structured and developmental approach to feedback is achieved.

Effects of goal setting and MBO

Goal setting has been extensively researched and shown to be a particularly effective OD intervention. The research results on MBO are generally positive, but less consistent than the findings on goal setting.

Goal setting appears to produce positive results over a wide range of jobs and organisations. It has been tested on keypunch operators, logging crews, clerical workers, engineers and truck drivers and produced performance improvements of between 11% and 27%.[16] Moreover, four meta-analyses of the extensive empirical evidence that support goal setting conclude that the proposed effects of goal difficulty, goal specificity and participation in goal setting are generally substantiated across studies and with both groups and individuals.[17] Longitudinal analyses support the conclusion that the profits in performance are not short-lived.[18] A recent field study of the goal-setting process, however, failed to replicate the typical positive linear relationship between goal difficulty and performance, raising some concern about the generalisability of the method from the laboratory to practice.[19] Additional research has tried to identify potential factors that might moderate the results of goal setting, including task uncertainty, amount and quality of planning, need for achievement, education, past goal successes and supervisory style.[20] Some support for the moderators has been found. For example, when the technical context is uncertain, goals tend to be less specific and people need to engage in more search behaviour to establish meaningful goals.

The body of research concerning MBO is also large, but provides mixed support. Huse and Kay were among the first to offer statistically documented results when they reported an MBO programme at General Electric.[21] They found consistently positive results in terms of managerial help in performing work, agreement on goals, attitudes toward performance discussions and current and future performance improvements. But they also reported problems when organisational goals were emphasised over developmental goals. Other research has also reported mixed results. Raia, for example, conducted longitudinal studies at Purex and found positive improvements in productivity, communications, performance evaluation and goal awareness.[22] However, many of the managers felt that the MBO programme was not linked to the organisations systems and that it placed too much emphasis on paperwork and production. Carroll and Tosi conducted a long-term study of an MBO programme at Black & Decker.[23] They first evaluated the programme and then used that data to help the company revise and improve it. This resulted in greater satisfaction and use of the programme. The researchers concluded that top-management support of MBO is the most important factor in implementing such programmes. A study of an MBO programme at the College of Business and Economics at Idaho State University showed mixed results.[24] Faculty reported that there were decreases in teaching and research performance and in satisfaction as a result of MBO. However, an examination of the records showed that there had actually been a slight increase in research output and a large improvement in service activities. The researchers explained the discrepancy between faculty assessments and college records as the result of faculty discontent with the programme. The educators perceived that the MBO programme infringed on their academic freedom and autonomy.

The existing research suggests that a properly designed MBO programme can have positive organisational results. However, many programmes are short-lived and wither on the vine because they have been installed without adequate diagnosis of the context factors. In particular, MBO can focus too much on the vertical alignment of individual and organisational goals and not enough on the horizontal issues that exist when tasks or groups are interdependent. The following conditions have been found to promote MBO success:[25]

- installation of the programme must be preceded by adequate diagnosis
- the programme must take the entire organisation into account, including the support and reward systems
- managers must be willing to participate
- the programme must be tailor-made to the specific organisation
- other interventions, such as team building or changes in organisational structure, may need to take place before an MBO programme can be installed.

MBO programmes that overemphasise measurement, do not emphasise the discretionary opportunities open to the individual, lack participation by subordinates (with the manager imposing goals), use a win–lose or reward–punishment psychology and overemphasise paperwork and red tape are doomed to fail.

Performance appraisal

Performance appraisal is a feedback system that involves the direct evaluation of individual or work group performance by a supervisor, manager or peers. Most organisations have some kind of evaluation system that is used for performance feedback, pay administration and, in some cases, counselling and developing employees.[26] Thus, performance appraisal represents an important link between goal-setting processes and reward systems. One survey of more than 500 firms found that 90% used performance appraisal to determine merit pay increases, 87% used it to review performance and 79% used it as the opportunity to set goals for the next period.[27]

Abundant evidence, however, indicates that organisations do a poor job in appraising employees.[28] A recent study found that 32% of managers surveyed rated their performance appraisal process as very ineffective.[29] Consequently, a growing number of firms have sought ways of improving the process. Some innovations have been made in enhancing employee involvement, balancing organisational and employee needs and increasing the number of raters.[30] These newer forms of appraisal are being used in such organisations as Levi-Strauss, Intel and Monsanto.

TABLE 17.1

TABLE 17.1	Performance appraisal elements	
Elements	**Traditional approaches**	**Newer approaches**
Purpose	Organizational, legal Fragmented	Developmental Integrative
Appraiser	Supervisor, managers	Appraised, co-workers and others
Role of Appraised	Passive recipient	Active participant
Measurement	Subjective Concerned with validity	Objective and subjective
Timing	Periodic, fixed, administratively driven	Dynamic, timely, employee- or work-driven

The performance appraisal process

Table 17.1 summarises several common elements of performance appraisal systems.[31] For each element, two contrasting features, representing traditional bureaucratic approaches and newer, high-involvement approaches, are presented. Performance appraisals are conducted for a variety of purposes, including affirmative action, pay and promotion decisions, as well as human resource planning and development.[32] Because each purpose defines what performances are relevant and how they should be measured, separate appraisal systems are often used. For example, appraisal methods for pay purposes are often different from systems that assess employee development or promotability. Employees also have a variety of reasons for wanting appraisal, such as receiving feedback for career decisions, getting a raise and being promoted. Rather than trying to meet these multiple purposes with a few standard appraisal systems, the new appraisal approaches are more tailored to balance the multiple organisational and employee needs. This is accomplished by actively involving the appraised, co-workers and managers in assessing the purposes of the appraisal at the time it takes place and adjusting the process to fit that purpose. Thus, at one time the appraisal process might focus on pay decisions, another time on employee development and still another on employee promotability. Actively involving all relevant participants can increase the chances that the purpose of the appraisal will be correctly identified and understood, and that the appropriate appraisal methods will be applied.

The new methods tend to expand the appraiser role beyond managers to include multiple raters, such as the appraised, co-workers and others having direct exposure to the employee's performance. Also known as 360-degree feedback, it is used more for member development than for compensation purposes.[33] This wider involvement provides a number of different views of the appraisee's performance. It can lead to a more comprehensive assessment of the employee's performance and can increase the likelihood that both organisational and personal needs will be taken into account. The key task is to find an overall view of the employee's performance that incorporates all the different appraisals. Thus, the process of working out differences and arriving at an overall assessment is an important aspect of the appraisal process. This improves the appraisal's acceptance, the accuracy of the information and its focus on activities that are critical to the business strategy.

The newer methods also expand the role of the appraised. Traditionally, the employee is simply a receiver of feedback. The supervisor unilaterally completes a form about performance on predetermined dimensions, usually personality traits, such as initiative or concern for quality. The newer approaches actively involve the appraisee in all phases of the appraisal process. The appraisee joins with superiors and staff personnel in gathering data on performance, and on identifying training needs. This active involvement increases the likelihood that the content of the performance appraisal will include the employee's views, needs and criteria, along with those of the organisation. This newer role for employees increases their acceptance and understanding of the feedback process.

Performance measurement is typically the source of many problems in appraisal as it is seen as subjective. Traditionally, performance evaluation focuses on the consistent use of pre-specified traits or behaviours. To improve consistency and validity of measurement, considerable training is used to help raters (supervisors) make valid assessments. This concern for validity stems largely from legal tests of performance appraisal systems and leads organisations to develop measurement approaches, such as the behaviourally anchored rating scale (BARS) and its variants. In newer approaches, validity is not only a legal or methodological issue but also a social issue; all appropriate participants are involved in negotiating acceptable ways of measuring and assessing performance. Increased participation in goal setting is a part of this new approach. Rather than simply training the supervisor, all participants are trained in methods of measuring and assessing performance. By focusing on both objective and subjective measures of performance, the appraisal process is better understood, accepted and accurate.

The timing of performance appraisals is traditionally fixed by managers or staff personnel and is based on administrative criteria, such as annual pay decisions. Newer approaches now being used increase the frequency of feedback. Although it may not be practical to increase the number of formal appraisals, the frequency of informal feedback can increase, especially when the strategic objectives change or when the technology is highly uncertain. In these situations, frequent performance feedback is often necessary in order to ensure appropriate adaptations in work behaviour. The newer approaches to appraisal increase the timeliness of feedback and allow employees to have more control over their work.

Designing a performance appraisal process

The process of designing or changing performance appraisal processes has received increasing attention. OD practitioners have recommended six steps:[34]

1 *Select the right people.* For political and legal reasons, the design process needs to include human resource staff, legal representatives, senior management and system users. Failure to recognise performance appraisal as part of a complex performance–management system is the single most important reason for design problems. As a result, members representing a variety of functions need to be involved in the design process so that the essential strategic and organisational issues are addressed.

2 *Diagnose the current situation.* A clear picture of the current appraisal process is essential to designing a new one. Diagnosis involves assessing the contextual factors (business strategy, employee involvement and workplace technology), current appraisal practices, satisfaction with current appraisal processes, work design and the current goal-setting and reward-system practices. This information can be used to determine the current system's strengths and weaknesses.

3 *Establish the system's purposes and objectives.* The ultimate purpose of an appraisal system is to help the organisation achieve better performance. Managers, staff and employees can have more specific views about how the appraisal process can be used. Potential purposes can include serving as a basis for rewards, career planning, human resource planning and performance improvement or simply giving performance feedback.

4 *Design the performance appraisal system.* Given the agreed-upon purposes of the system and the contextual factors, the appropriate elements of an appraisal system can be established. These should include choices about who performs the appraisal, who is involved in determining performance, how performance is measured and how often feedback is given. Criteria for designing an effective performance appraisal system include timeliness, accuracy, acceptance, understanding, focus on critical control points and economic feasibility.

First, the *timeliness* criterion recognises the time value of information. Individuals and work groups need to get performance information before evaluation or review. When the information precedes performance evaluation, it can be used to engage in problem-solving behaviour that improves performance and satisfaction. Second, the information contained in performance feedback needs to be *accurate*. Inaccurate data prevent employees from determining whether their performance is above or below the goal targets and discourage problem-solving behaviour. Third, the performance feedback must be *accepted* and owned by the people who use it. Participation in the goal-setting process can help to ensure a commitment to the performance appraisal system. Fourth, information contained in the appraisal system needs to be *understood* if it is to have problem-solving value. Many organisations use training to help employees understand the operating, financial and human resource data that will be fed back to them. Fifth, appraisal information should *focus on critical control points*. The information received by employees must be aligned with important elements of the business strategy, employee performance and the reward system. For example, if the business strategy requires cost reduction but workers are measured and rewarded on the basis of quality, the performance management system may produce the wrong kinds of behaviour. Finally, the *economic feasibility* criterion suggests that an appraisal system should meet a simple cost–benefit test. If the costs associated with collecting and feeding back performance information exceed the benefits derived from using the information, then a simpler system should be installed.

5   *Experiment with implementation.* The complexity and potential problems associated with performance appraisal processes strongly suggest using a pilot test of the new system. The pilot test allows the organisation to spot, gauge and correct any flaws in the design before it is implemented system-wide.

6   *Evaluate and monitor the system.* Although the experimentation step may have uncovered many initial design flaws, ongoing evaluation of the system once it has been implemented is important. User satisfaction, from human resources staff, manager and employee viewpoints, is an essential input. In addition, the legal defensibility of the system should be tracked by noting the distribution of appraisal scores against age, sex and ethnic categories.

Application 17.2 describes the design and development of performance indicators to measure performance in the benchmarked areas of the manufacturing process at Dulux's Clayton plant.[35]

APPLICATION 17.2

Performance appraisal at Dulux, Clayton

In 1991 the Australian Government wanted to encourage Australian enterprises to adopt international best practice strategies. To stimulate the programme the government set up a grant. To receive funds under the programme, the companies must use them to further an existing programme of, among other activities, the study and adoption of international best practice methods; the setting up of reliable performance indicators and the development of training strategies and staff consultative arrangements. Dulux's Clayton, Victorian plant was awarded the government's Best Practice Demonstration Programme grant.

Dulux Australia's mission is to be the leading world-class manufacturer of superior quality coatings and to achieve customer satisfaction through the involvement and commitment of its work force. Dulux had realised that the means to its commercial success lay in benchmarking its operations against the best in the world. This resulted in adopting the best practice methods and safeguarding the future with appropriate performance measurement. Dulux's Best Practice Project aims to accelerate the progress of people, quality and process technological reforms.

Goals set by Dulux were to introduce or enhance manufacturing methods, as well as self-managed work teams, to gain greater involvement and commitment from the work force; the introduction of a comprehensive training and development programme; benchmarking critical success factors to facilitate the introduction of new processes; and to gain the commitment of the work force in continuous improvement. A positive example of these goals has been the strengthening relationship between management and shop floor employees. The company's comprehensive training schedule, development of work teams and the fact that there has been no lost time from disputation since September 1990 are proof of a strong best practices programme.

Dulux consulted with World Class International (WCI), a UK consulting company, which spent five days at the company's Clayton site in mid-1992, after Dulux had begun its best practices programme. The initial benchmarks and associated performance indicators were based on the performance of previous clients of WCI. Dulux developed performance indicators to measure the performance in the benchmarked areas of its manufacturing process, but there were still a few problems, however, as was highlighted during a January 1993 visit by the independent Best Practices Project monitoring team. The representatives noticed that while Dulux was able to show improvements to a range of indicators, they were having difficulty establishing which were vital to the overall business performance of the company and their relationship to bottom-line improvements. Dulux's human resources manager then embarked on a tour of 15 international companies to compare how they established critical success factors (CSFs) and how they developed the performance measures connected with

them. Additionally, the study also included the observation of employee involvement in the workplace, as well as other human resource measures.

The outcome of these visits was that Dulux was able to successfully distinguish what its CSFs are and to decide what other related items were to be measured. These included successful leadership, committed and competent employees, knowledge of customer expectations, knowledge of world class benchmarks, the best possible process and systems and, finally, the commitment to continuous improvement. The process of further developing the performance indicators, or the reworking of existing indicators, will show improvements or decline in the existing CSFs.

A Total Quality Management (TQM) was established in 1988 when Dulux began its reform programme. The company wanted to increase its stature in the export market and had realised that prompt response/delivery, accurate documentation and commitment to supply were the main elements in winning overseas orders. Market research had also shown that consistent customer service and stock availability, plus on-time delivery were its customer's most significant requirements. The reformation of Dulux is evident in the changing structure in their industrial relations. The company now has a site-specific industrial agreement with the FMWU, which includes targeting reforms, such as better consultation between employees and solutions to demarcation issues. The agreement included a site consultative committee of twelve employee representatives, one union official and six management representatives.

This committee meets monthly and is responsible for analysing site performance, reviewing new developments, including changes in the workplace, capital works and employee conditions; and the renewal of agreements. For changes in the workplace, project teams are assembled on an 'as needed' basis.

All employees are divided into work groups that meet weekly to discuss and analyse performance, changing company goals and objectives. Members of these groups are also encouraged to form improvement teams that focus on resolving workplace problems. Work area responsibility has been the flow-on effect from these initiatives. Individuals are taking on more responsibility in such areas as the manufacturing process, production scheduling, interaction between work cells and integration with marketing activities and budgetary responsibilities.

Overall responsibility to co-ordinate change is still placed with the Operations Manager, but there is greater input from the site consultative committee and the individual.

To keep track of changes in the plant, Dulux uses a computer management information system. The company plans to use annual climate surveys of its employees, as well as surveying customers and suppliers to help provide subjective information on the performance.

Effects of performance appraisal

Research strongly supports the role of feedback on performance. One study concluded that objective feedback as a means for improving individual and group performance has been 'impressively effective'[36] and has been supported by a large number of literature reviews over the years.[37] Another researcher concluded that 'objective feedback does not *usually* work, it virtually always works'.[38] In field studies where performance feedback contained behaviour-specific information, median performance improvements were more than 47%; when the feedback concerned less specific information, median performance improvements were over 33%. In a meta-analysis of performance appraisal interventions, feedback was found to have a consistently positive effect across studies.[39] In addition, although most appraisal research has focused on the relationship between performance and individuals, several studies have demonstrated a positive relationship between group performance and feedback.[40] Because these results often vary across settings and even within studies,[41] more research is clearly needed in this area.

Reward systems

Organisational rewards are powerful incentives for improving employee and work group performance. As pointed out in Chapter 16, rewards can also produce high levels of employee satisfaction. OD has traditionally relied on intrinsic rewards, such as enriched jobs and opportunities for decision making, to motivate employee performance. Early quality-of-work-life interventions were mainly based on the intrinsic satisfaction to be derived from performing challenging, meaningful types of work. More recently, OD practitioners have expanded their focus to include extrinsic rewards, such as pay; various incentives, such as stock options, bonuses and profit sharing; promotions and benefits. They have discovered that both intrinsic and extrinsic rewards can enhance performance and satisfaction.[42]

OD practitioners are increasingly attending to the design and implementation of reward systems. This recent attention to rewards has derived in part from research into organisation design and employee involvement. These perspectives treat rewards as an integral part of organisations. They hold that rewards should be congruent with other organisational systems and practices, such as the organisation structure, top-management's human-relations philosophy and work designs. Many features of reward systems contribute to both employee fulfilment and organisational effectiveness. In this section, we describe how rewards affect individual and group performance and then discuss three specific rewards: pay, promotions and benefits.

How rewards affect performance

Considerable research has been done on how rewards affect individual and group performance. The most popular model to describe this relationship is the *value expectancy theory*. In addition to explaining how performance and rewards are related, it suggests requirements for designing and evaluating reward systems.

The value expectancy model[43] posits that employees will expend effort to achieve performance goals that they believe will lead to outcomes that they value. This effort will result in the desired performance goals as long as the goals are realistic, the employees fully understand what is expected of them and they have the necessary skills and resources. Ongoing motivation depends on the extent to which attaining the desired performance goals actually results in valued outcomes. Consequently, key objectives of reward-systems interventions are to identify the intrinsic and extrinsic outcomes (rewards) that are highly valued and to link them to the achievement of desired performance goals.

Based on value expectancy theory, the ability of rewards to motivate desired behaviour depends on six factors:

1 *Availability*. For rewards to reinforce desired performance, they must be not only desired but also available. Too little of a desired reward is no reward at all. For example, pay increases are often highly desired but unavailable. Moreover, pay increases that are below minimally-accepted standards may actually produce negative consequences.[44]

2 *Timeliness*. Like effective performance feedback, rewards should be given in a timely manner. A reward's motivating potential is reduced to the extent that it is separated in time from the performance that it is intended to reinforce.

3 *Performance contingency*. Rewards should be closely linked with particular performances. If the employees succeed in meeting the goal, the reward must be given; if the target is missed, the reward is reduced or not given. The clearer the linkage between performance and rewards, the better able rewards are to motivate desired behaviour. Unfortunately, this criterion is often neglected in practice. Forty per cent of employees believe that there is no linkage between pay and performance.[45] From another perspective, merit increases in a particular year might have been all between 4 and 5%, i.e. almost everyone, regardless of performance level, got about the same raise.

4 *Durability*. Some rewards last longer than others. Intrinsic rewards, such as increased autonomy and pride in workmanship, tend to last longer than extrinsic rewards. Most people who have received a salary increase realise that it gets spent rather quickly.

5 *Equity*. Satisfaction and motivation can be improved when employees believe that the pay policies of the organisation are equitable or fair. Internal equity concerns a comparison of personal rewards to those holding similar jobs or performing similarly in the organisation. Internal inequities typically occur when employees are paid a similar salary or hourly wage regardless of their level of performance. External equity concerns a comparison of rewards with those of other organisations in the same labour market. When an organisation's reward level does not compare favourably with the level of other organisations, employees are likely to feel inequitably rewarded.

6 *Visibility*. To leverage a reward system, it must be visible. Organisation members must be able to see who is getting the rewards. Visible rewards, such as placement on a high-status project, promotion to a new job and increased authority, send signals to employees that rewards are available, timely and performance-contingent.

Reward-systems interventions are used to elicit and maintain desired levels of performance. To the extent that rewards are available, durable, equitable, timely, visible and performance-contingent, they can support and reinforce organisational goals, work designs and employee involvement. The next sections describe three types of rewards—pay, fringe benefits and promotions—that are particularly effective in improving employee performance and satisfaction.

Pay

In recent years, interest has grown in using various forms of payment to improve employee satisfaction and increase both individual and organisational performance. This has resulted in a number of innovative pay schemes, including skill-based pay, all-salaried workforce, lump-sum salary increases, performance-based pay and profit sharing.[46] Each of these systems is described and discussed below.

Skill-based pay plans

Traditionally, organisations design their pay systems by evaluating jobs. The characteristics of a particular job are determined and pay is made comparable to what other organisations pay for jobs with similar characteristics. This job-evaluation method tends to result in pay systems with high external and internal equity. However, it fails to reward employees for all of the skills that they have, discourages people from learning new skills and results in a view of pay as an entitlement.[47]

Some organisations, such as Tubemakers (Australia), have attempted to resolve these problems by designing pay systems according to people's skills and abilities. By focusing on the individual, rather than the job, skill-based pay systems reward learning and growth. Typically, employees are paid according to the number of different jobs that they can perform. For example, Tubemakers' performance management system and its salary package is intended to reinforce team working and a culture of continuous improvement. The salary package consists of three parts: a stable income plan; an improvement share plan; and an individual performance review. The stable income plan is an annualised salary package. This is the guaranteed minimum amount that employees will receive in the year. The annual salary is based on a 44-hour week, which includes a 38-hour base rate plus six hours overtime allowance. According to the representative union official, this has reduced the opportunity for employees to work extra overtime, but new technology is expected to eliminate the need for extensive overtime in the future. The base rate is stable throughout the year and is not tied to productivity profits. The improvement share plan is a profit-sharing process. Employees are given a bonus according to the performance of the entire enterprise on five key criteria: employee hours per tonne of product, percentage of products delivered on time, injury statistics, improvement group activity and the number of suggestions per week. The individual performance review is based on a quarterly review of employee performance and can earn employees up to a 20% salary increase. Their quarterly individual review is labelled 'Goals, actions and measures' (GAM). It was designed to monitor employee and team performance and is tied to the individual performance review. The GAM system focuses on each employee's contribution to the business performance and stresses improvement, and not performance relative to peers. It provides regular feedback and assistance in improving.[48]

Skill-based pay systems have a number of benefits. They contribute to organisational effectiveness by providing a more flexible workforce and by giving employees a broad perspective on how the entire plant operates. This flexibility can result in leaner staffing and fewer problems with absenteeism, turnover and work disruptions. Skill-based pay can lead to durable employee satisfaction by reinforcing individual development and by producing an equitable wage rate.[49]

The two major drawbacks of skill-based pay schemes are the tendency to 'top out' and the lack of performance contingency. 'Top out' occurs when employees learn all the skills there are to learn and then run up against the top end of the pay scale, with no higher levels to attain. Some organisations have resolved this topping-out effect by installing a profit-sharing plan after most employees have learned all relevant jobs. Profit sharing, discussed later in this section, ties pay to organisational effectiveness, allowing employees to push beyond previous pay ceilings. Other organisations have resolved this effect by making base skills obsolete and adding new ones, thus raising the standards of employee competence. Skill-based pay systems also require a heavy investment in training, as well as a measurement system that is capable of telling when employees have learned the new jobs. They typically increase direct labour costs, as employees are paid highly for learning multiple tasks. In addition, because pay is based on skill and not performance, the work force could be highly paid and flexible, but still not productive.

Like most new personnel practices, limited evaluative research exists on the effectiveness of these interventions. Long-term assessment of the Gaines Pet Food plant reveals that the skill-based pay plan has contributed to both organisational effectiveness and employee satisfaction. Several years after the plant opened, workers' attitudes toward pay were significantly more positive than those of people working in other similar plants that did not have skill-based pay. Gaines' workers reported much higher levels of pay satisfaction, as well as feelings that their pay system was fairly administered.[50]

A national survey of skill-based pay plans sponsored by the US Department of Labor concluded that such systems increase work-force flexibility, employee growth and development and product quality and quantity while reducing staffing needs, absenteeism and turnover.[51] These results appear contingent on management commitment to the plan and having the right kind of people, particularly those with interpersonal skills, motivation and a desire for growth and development. This study also showed that skill-based pay is applicable across a variety of situations, including both manufacturing and service industries, production and staff employees, new and old sites and unionised and non-unionised settings. Finally, a 1993 survey of 279 Fortune 1000 companies found that 52% indicated that skill-based pay systems were successful or very successful.[52]

Application 17.3 examines the nature of performance pay schemes introduced by Australian Federal and State governments, and considers how effective they have been.[53]

Pay-for-performance systems: experiences in the Australian public sector

Reform programmes introduced by Australian governments during the 1980s included the appearance of strategic management systems that are now seen to be an integral part of the public sector. Consequently, these practices provided the foundation for the development of performance management strategies. By the mid-1990s, the Commonwealth government had instituted performance appraisal procedures for their employees, plus a range of financial rewards to encourage high achievement. The current programme stands in stark contrast to the situation of little more than a decade ago when staff appraisals were almost unknown, career development remained a matter of individual responsibility and work incentives took the form of permanent tenure and the opportunity to be of service to the public.

The need for public sector reform was instigated by the incoming Federal Labor government in 1983. The *Financial Management Improvement Programme* was introduced into the Australian Public Service from 1984. The goal of the programme was to revise the existing administration into an efficient and effective organisation. The policies that were introduced featured new budgetary measures and the devolution of financial and personnel functions of the line departments. Corporate and programme management, budgeting and performance evaluation was also achieved under an extensive and sophisticated strategic management environment. Corporate management set out the mission and goals of the agency, whereas programme management and budgeting provided the means of operationalising corporate directions and setting expenditure against specific programme aims. The progress section was developed to close the strategic loop and establish whether efficiency and outcome goals had been met. Overall, the programme was designed to give individual organisations a higher degree of autonomy and to individualise and develop their own results-orientated sections. These sections were to be basically self-contained, with only minimal scrutiny from the central agency.

A consequence of the *Financial Management Improvement Programme* was a major structural change, which included reductions in the number of departments from 27 to 16 in 1987, plus a considerable reconstruction of the agencies. Consequently, the human aspect of the programme was largely neglected. Redeployment and redundancies were prevalent and employees were subjected to major changes in their conditions of work. Further, performance appraisals were largely ignored and not focused on until the reform agenda that highlighted performance pay was introduced in 1989/90.

In May 1993, the Senate and the Auditor-General decided to review progress of the scheme. They decided to survey 75 participating organisations, and found that at the end of the 1993 performance appraisal/pay cycle, 94.5% of all officers received a rating of 'fully effective' or better. They were then eligible for a salary bonus. Out of this percentage, they found that 2% were classified as 'outstanding', 30% as 'superior' and 62.5% as 'fully effective'. Only 5.3% were nominated as being 'adequate' and only 0.2% were 'unsatisfactory'. Whereas 90% of agencies rated 90% of their senior officers as eligible for performance pay, 28% of the agencies nominated all their officers as being eligible. Clearly, this was not what the programme had wanted to achieve. Confusion about the guideline directive that 'most' officers should receive a bonus was taken to mean the majority should. Consequently, the programme lost its credibility and motivational value. Monetary payments varied significantly, which did not meet the guidelines standards of suitable gradation between the highest and the lowest amounts paid. The differing payment approaches by the varying agencies resulted in an unfair system.

Lack of confidence in the scheme also created a number of problems. Of the agencies surveyed, 30% reported that they did not believe that the scheme would improve individual performance against corporate goals and more than half did not view the scheme as improving the adaptability and flexibility of officers. An astonishing 60% did not believe that the scheme would have any impact on the management of under-performing staff. The scheme continued on until 1994. At the end of 1994, when the original two-year enterprise agreement between the union and the government expired, the scheme was open for renegotiation. Performance pay was successfully removed by the unions between 1995 and 1996, despite strong resistance from the government. The agreement reached was that there should be a salary increase of 2.6% for all staff in return for initiatives that would lead to productivity increases.

Clearly the Commonwealth performance pay fell short of its expectations. The objectives of the scheme were either not achieved or only partially so. There are many reasons why this scheme was not successful. Initially it had succeeded in its goal of providing a salary increase for its senior officers, but the ratings system quickly overshadowed the benefits of the appraisal system. Secondly, even though most agencies had put in place reliable strategic management practices, a high percentage had experienced difficulty in establishing effective appraisal procedures. In some cases the schemes were put together too quickly, a number of appraisers were not properly trained, some managers were not fully aware of the scheme's objectives and scope and there was uncertainty about the meaning of the guidelines. Finally, a majority of the officers rejected performance pay as a suitable means of increasing productivity. The scheme was largely seen to be undermining the co-operative approach to management that had been cultivated for years. A positive outcome from the scheme is that substantial effort is now being made for all agencies to introduce sound appraisal practices for all employees. Individual career and training needs are emphasised, with the integration of appraisal systems into the agency's corporation plan receiving particular importance.

For a pay-for-performance scheme to work in the Australian public sector, it would seem that a more interventionist stance, such as by co-ordinating agencies, is a necessary requisite for successful implementation. The managerialist framework in which the central agencies have clearly prescribed and understood roles is likely to provide an administrative environment that will facilitate the emergence of performance appraisal and pay. The serious obstacles in the path of successful implementation will be the existence of variables such as organisational trust, union opposition, insufficient government funding and changes in political direction.

All-salaried workforce

An increasing number of companies, such as IBM, Gillette and Dow Chemical, are adopting all-salaried pay systems that treat managers and workers the same in terms of pay administration and some fringe benefits.[54] Typically, such systems pay all employees on a salary basis. People do not punch time clocks or lose pay when they are late and they have generous sick leave and absenteeism privileges. Employees generally prefer all-salaried plans as they allow more freedom about when to start and stop work, and because they treat workers more maturely than do hourly wage systems. All-salaried plans can also improve organisational effectiveness by making the organisation a more attractive place to work, thus reducing turnover.

A major problem with all-salaried workforces is that some employees abuse the plan by chronically staying home or coming late to work. Although there is conflicting evidence about whether all-salaried plans increase or reduce absenteeism and tardiness, negative effects can generally be avoided by combining the plan with a more participative approach to management.

Lump-sum salary increases

Traditionally, organisations distribute annual pay increases by adjusting the regular pay cheques of employees. For example, weekly pay cheques are increased to reflect the annual raise. This tradition has two major drawbacks. It makes employees wait a full year before they receive the full amount of their annual increase. Second, it makes the raise hardly visible to employees, as once it has been added to regular pay cheques, it may mean little change in take-home pay.

Some organisations, such as BF Goodrich, Timex and Westinghouse, have tried to make annual salary increases more flexible and visible.[55] They have instituted a lump-sum increase programme that gives employees the freedom to decide when they receive their annual raise. For example, an employee can choose to receive it all at once at the start of the year. The money that is advanced to the employee is treated as a loan, usually at a modest interest rate. If the person quits before the end of the year, the proportion of the raise that has not been earned has to be paid back.

Lump-sum increase programmes can contribute to employee satisfaction by tailoring the annual raise to individual needs. Such programmes can improve organisational effectiveness by making the organisation more attractive and reducing turnover. They can increase employee motivation in situations where pay is linked to performance. By making the amount of the salary increase highly visible, employees can see a clear relationship between their performance and their annual raise. The major disadvantages of lump-sum programmes are the extra costs of administering the plan and the likelihood that some employees will quit and not pay back the company.

TABLE 17.2	Ratings of various pay-for-performance plans

		Tie pay to performance	Produce negative side effects	Encourage cooperation	Employee acceptance
Salary reward					
Individual plan	Productivity	4	1	1	4
	Cost effectiveness	3	1	1	4
	Superiors' rating	3	1	1	3
Group	Productivity	3	1	2	4
	Cost effectiveness	3	1	2	4
	Superiors' rating	2	1	2	3
Organization-wide	Productivity	2	1	3	4
	Cost effectiveness	2	1	2	4
Stock/bonus reward					
Individual plan	Productivity	5	3	1	2
	Cost effectiveness	4	2	1	2
	Superiors' rating	4	2	1	2
Group	Productivity	4	1	3	3
	Cost effectiveness	3	1	3	3
	Superior's rating	3	1	3	3
Organization-wide	Productivity	3	1	3	4
	Cost effectiveness	3	1	3	4
	Profit	2	1	3	3

* Ratings: 1 = lowest rating, 5 = highest rating

Source: Reproduced by permission of the publisher from E. Lawler III, 'Reward systems' in *Improving Life at Work*, eds J. Hackman and J. Suttle (Santa Monica, Calif.: Goodyear, 1977), p. 195.

Performance-based pay systems

Organisations have devised many ways of linking pay to performance.[56] It is the fastest growing segment of pay-based reward systems development. One study estimated that almost two-thirds of medium and large businesses have some form of performance-based pay system for non-executives. They are used in such organisations as Monsanto, DuPont and American Express.[57] Such plans tend to vary along three dimensions:

- the organisational unit by which performance is measured for reward purposes—an individual, group or organisation basis
- the way performance is measured—the subjective measures used in supervisors' ratings or objective measures of productivity, costs or profits
- what rewards are given for good performance—salary increases, stock or cash bonuses.

Table 17.2 lists different types of performance-based pay systems that vary along these dimensions, and rates them in terms of other relevant criteria.

In terms of linking pay to performance, individual pay plans are rated highest, followed by group plans and then organisation plans. The last two plans score lower on this factor as pay is not a direct function of individual behaviour. At the group and organisation levels, an individual's pay is influenced by the behaviour of others and by external market conditions. Generally, stock and bonus plans tie pay to performance better than salary plans do. The amount of awarded stock may vary sharply from year to year, whereas salary increases tend to be more stable as organisations seldom cut employees' salaries. Finally, objective measures of performance score higher than subjective measures. Objective measures are more credible and people are more likely to see the link between pay and objective measures.

Most of the pay plans in Table 17.2 do not produce negative side-effects, such as workers falsifying data and restricting performance. The major exceptions are individual bonus plans. These plans, such as piece-rate systems, tend to result in negative effects, particularly when trust in the plan is low. For example, if people feel that piece-rate quotas are unfair, they may hide work improvements for fear that quotas may be adjusted higher.

As might be expected, group- and organisation-based pay plans encourage co-operation among workers more than do individual plans. Under the former, it is generally to everyone's advantage to work well together because all share in the financial rewards of higher performance. The organisation plans also tend to promote co-operation among functional departments. Because members from different departments feel that they can benefit from each others' performance, they tend to encourage and help each other to make positive contributions.

From an employee's perspective, Table 17.2 suggests that the least acceptable pay plans are individual bonus programmes. Employees tend to dislike such plans as they encourage competition among individuals and because they are difficult to administer fairly. Such plans may be inappropriate in some technical contexts. For example, technical innovations typically lead engineers to adjust piece-rate quotas upward as the employees should be able to produce more with the same effort. Workers, on the other hand, often feel that the performance worth of such innovations does not equal the incremental change in quotas, thus resulting in feelings of pay inequity. Table 17.2 suggests that employees tend to favour salary increases to bonuses. This follows from the simple fact that a salary increase becomes a permanent part of a person's pay but a bonus does not.

The overall ratings in Table 17.2 suggest that no one pay-for-performance plan scores highest on all criteria. Rather, each plan has certain strengths and weaknesses that depend on a variety of contingencies. As business strategies, organisation performance and other contingencies change, the pay-for-performance system must also change.

When all criteria have been taken into account, however, the best performance-based pay systems seem to be group and organisation bonus plans that are based on objective measures of performance and individual salary-increase plans. These plans are relatively good at linking pay to performance. They have few negative side effects and at least modest employee acceptance. The group and organisation plans promote co-operation and should be used where there is high task interdependence among workers, such as might be found on assembly lines. The individual plan promotes competition and should be used where there is little required co-operation among employees, such as in field sales jobs.

Profit sharing

As the name implies, profit sharing involves paying employees a bonus that is based upon improvements in the operating results of an organisation. Although not traditionally associated with employee involvement, profit sharing has increasingly been included in comprehensive employee involvement projects. Many organisations, such as Polaroid and BHP Copper, are discovering that, when designed correctly, profit-sharing plans can contribute to employee motivation, involvement and performance.

Developing a profit-sharing plan requires making choices about the following design elements:[58]

1 *Process of design.* This factor concerns whether the plan will be designed participatively or in a top-down manner. Because the success of profit sharing depends on employee acceptance and co-operation, it is recommended that a task force composed of a cross-section of employees design the plan and be trained in profit-sharing concepts and practice. The task force should include people who are credible and represent both management and non-management interests.

2 *Organisational unit covered.* The size of the unit included in the plan can vary widely from departments or plants with less than 50 employees to companies with several thousand people. A plan covering the entire plant would be ideal in situations where there is a free-standing plant with good performance measures and

an employee size of less than 500. When the number of employees exceeds 500, multiple plans may be installed, each covering a discrete part of the company.

3 *Determining the bonus.* Profit-sharing plans are based on a formula that generates a bonus pool, which is divided among those covered by the plan. Although most plans are custom-designed, there are two general considerations about the nature of the bonus formula. First, a standard of performance must be developed that can be used as a baseline for calculating improvements or losses. Some plans use past performance to form a historical standard, whereas others use engineered or estimated standards. When available, historical data provide a relatively fair standard of performance; engineer-determined data can work, however, if there is a high level of trust in the standard and how it is set. Second, the costs included in determining the bonus must be chosen. The key is to focus on those costs that are most controllable by employees. Some plans use labour costs as a proportion of total sales, whereas others include a wider range of controllable costs, such as those for materials and utilities.

4 *Sharing profits.* Once the bonus formula has been determined, it is necessary to decide how to share profits when they are obtained. This decision includes choices about what percentage of the bonus pool should go to the company and what percentage to employees. In general, the company should take a low enough percentage to ensure that the plan generates a realistic bonus for employees. Other decisions about dividing the bonus pool include who will share in the bonus and how the money will be divided among employees. Typically, all employees included in the organisational unit covered by the plan share in the bonus. Most plans divide the money on the basis of a straight percentage of total salary payments.

5 *Frequency of bonus.* Most plans calculate a bonus monthly. This typically fits with organisational recording needs and is frequent enough to spur employee motivation. Longer payout periods are generally used in seasonal businesses, or where there is a long production or billing cycle for a product or service.

6 *Managing change.* Organisational changes, such as new technology and product mixes, can disrupt the bonus formula. Many plans include a steering committee to review the plan and to make any necessary adjustments, especially in terms of significant organisational changes.

7 *The participative system.* Many profit-sharing plans include a participative system that helps to gather, assess and implement employee suggestions and improvements. These systems generally include a procedure for formalising suggestions and different levels of committees for assessing and implementing them.

Although profit-sharing plans are tailored to each situation, three major plans are most often used: the Scanlon plan, the Rucker plan and Improshare. The most popular programme is the Scanlon plan, used in such firms as Donnelly Mirrors, De Soto, Midland-Ross and Dana. The Rucker plan and Improshare use different bonus formulae and place less emphasis on worker participation than does the Scanlon plan.[59]

Named after Joe Scanlon, a union leader in the mid-1930s, the Scanlon plan is both an incentive plan and a management philosophy. Scanlon believed in a participative philosophy in which managers and workers share information, problems, goals and ideas. Moreover, he felt that a company's pay system should be tied to that philosophy by rewarding co-operation and problem solving. Based on these beliefs, the Scanlon plan uses a participative suggestion system that involves different levels of worker–management committees. The committees solicit employee suggestions, assess them and see that promising improvements are implemented.

The incentive part of the Scanlon plan generally includes a bonus formula based on a ratio measure comparing total sales volume to total payroll expenses. This measure of labour cost efficiency is relatively responsive to employee behaviours and is used to construct a historical base rate at the beginning of the plan. Savings that result from improvements over this base make up the bonus pool. The bonus is often split equally between the company and employees, with all members of the organisation receiving bonuses that are made up of a percentage of their salaries.

TABLE 17.3	Conditions favouring profit-sharing plans

Organizational characteristic	Favorable condition
Size	Small unit, usually less than 500 employees
Age	Old enough so that the learning curve has flattened and standards can be set based on performance history
Financial measures	Simple, with a good history
Market for output	Good, can absorb additional production
Product costs	Controllable by employees
Organizational climate	Open, high level of trust
Style of management	Participative
Union status	No union, or one that is favorable to a cooperative effort
Overtime history	Limited to no use of overtime in past
Seasonal nature of business	Relatively stable across time
Work floor interdependence	High to moderate interdependence
Capital investment plans	Little investment planned
Product stability	Few product changes
Comptroller/chief financial officer	Trusted, able to explain financial measures
Communication policy	Open, willing to share financial results
Plant manager	Trusted, committed to plan, able to articulate goals and ideals of plan
Management	Technically competent, supportive of participative management style, good communication skills, able to deal with suggestions and new ideas
Corporate position (if part of larger organization)	Favourable to plan
workforce	Technically knowledgeable, interested in participation and higher pay, financially knowledgeable and interested
Plant support services	Maintenance and engineering groups competent, willing and able to respond to increased demands

Source: E. Lawler III, *Pay and Organization Development,* copyright ©1981 by Addison-Wesley Publishing Co. Reprinted by permission of Addison-Wesley Publishing Co. Inc., Reading, Mass., p. 144.

Profit-sharing plans tie the goals of workers to the organisation's goals. It is to the financial advantage of employees to work harder, to co-operate with each other, to make suggestions and to implement improvements. Reviews of the empirical literature and individual studies suggest that when such plans are implemented properly, organisations can expect specific improvements.[60] A study sponsored by the US Government Accounting Office found that plans that had been in place for more than five years averaged annual savings of 29% in labour costs; 61 there is also evidence to suggest that they work in 50 to 80% of the reported cases.[62] A report on four case studies in manufacturing and service settings noted significant increases in productivity (32% in manufacturing and 11% in services), as well as in several other measures.[63] A recent longitudinal field study employing experimental and control groups supports profit sharing's positive effect over time, and even after the group's bonus had been discontinued.[64] Other reported results include enhanced co-ordination and teamwork; cost savings; acceptance of technical, market and methods changes; demands for better planning and more efficient management; new ideas as well as effort; reductions in overtime; more flexible union–management relations and greater employee satisfaction.[65]

Profit-sharing plans are better suited to certain situations than others. Table 17.3 lists the conditions that favour such plans. In general, profit sharing seems suited to small organisations with a good market, simple measures of historical performance and production costs that are controllable by employees. Product and market demand should be relatively stable and employee–management relations should be open and based on trust. Top management should support the plan and support services should be willing and able to respond to increased demands. The workforce should be interested in, and knowledgeable about, profit sharing, and should technically know how to perform tasks.

Promotions

Like decisions about pay increases, many decisions about promotions and job movements in organisations are made in a top-down, closed manner. Higher-level managers decide whether lower-level employees will be promoted. This process can be secretive, with people often not knowing that a position is open, that they are being considered for promotion or the reasons why some people are promoted while others are not. Without such information, capable people who might be interested in a new job may be overlooked. Also, employees may fail to see the connection between good performance and promotions, thus reducing the motivational potential of promotions.

Fortunately, this is changing. Most organisations today have attempted to reduce the secrecy surrounding promotions and job changes by openly posting the availability of new jobs and inviting people to nominate themselves.[66] Although open job posting entails extra administrative costs, it can lead to better promotion decisions. Open posting helps to ensure that interested individuals will be considered for new jobs, thus increasing the pool of available personnel and increasing the likelihood that capable people will be identified. Open posting can also increase employee motivation by showing that a valued reward is both available and contingent on performance.

Some organisations have attempted to increase the accuracy and equity of job-change decisions by including peers and subordinates in the decision-making process. Peer and subordinate judgments about a person's performance and promotability help to bring all relevant data to bear on promotion decisions. Such participation can increase the accuracy of these decisions and can make people feel that the basis for promotions is equitable. In many self-regulating work teams, for example, the group interviews and helps to select new members and supervisors. This helps to ensure that new people will fit in and that the group is committed to making that happen. Evidence from high-involvement plants suggests that participation in selecting new members can lead to greater group cohesiveness and task effectiveness.[67]

Benefits

In addition to pay and promotions, organisations provide a variety of other extrinsic rewards in the form of benefits. Some of these are mandated by law, such as superannuation and workers' compensation; others are a matter of negotiation, such as salary packages; while still others have emerged to keep pace with the needs of the changing labour force, such as retirement plans and child care. Organisations such as Johnson & Johnson and Xerox are increasingly using benefits to attract and retain good employees, to help them better integrate work with home life and to improve the quality of work life. These benefits can translate into economic gains through reduced absenteeism and turnover and greater organisational commitment and performance.

Organisations generally provide equal benefit packages to all employees at similar organisational levels. Employees are essentially treated the same, with major differences usually occurring between hierarchical levels, which therefore tests the equity criterion. This approach also does not account for the kinds of benefits that different people value, and may not pass the availability test. For example, younger workers may want more vacation time, whereas older employees may desire more retirement benefits. By treating employees the same, a company may spend money on benefits that some people do not value. This can also lead to employee dissatisfaction and reduced motivation. Finally, benefits cannot be manipulated during the year and may fail to be timely or contingent on performance.

A flexible salary package programme can contribute to employee satisfaction by providing only those benefits that people value. It can increase organisational effectiveness by making the company an attractive place to work, thus reducing absenteeism and turnover. The plan can also improve employee understanding of the firm's benefits. The Australian Salaried Medical Officers Federation (ASMOF), for example, has negotiated the introduction of a Salary Packaging Scheme for Senior Medical Officers (SMOs) in New South Wales. Employees will have the discretion to determine the mix of salary and benefits (within the approved list) that will constitute their salary package. Benefits may include mortgage repayments, child care expenses or private travel.[68]

The major drawbacks of the plan include the extra costs needed for its administration and the fact that the costs and availability of many fringe benefits are based on the number of people covered by them. For small organisations, this latter difficulty may require special consideration in order to avoid Fringe Benefits Tax or it may entail added risks in implementing the plan.

Reward-system process issues

Thus far, we have discussed different reward systems and assessed their strengths and weaknesses. Considerable research has been conducted on the process aspect of reward systems. Process refers to how pay and other rewards are typically administered in the organisation. At least two process issues affect employees' perceptions of the reward system:

- who should be involved in designing and administering the reward system
- what kind of communication should exist with respect to rewards.[69]

Traditionally, reward systems are designed by top managers and compensation specialists and then simply imposed on employees. Although this top-down process may result in a good system, it cannot ensure that employees will understand and trust it. In the absence of trust, workers are likely to have negative perceptions of the reward system. There is growing evidence that employee participation in the design and administration of a reward system can increase employee understanding and can contribute to feelings of control over, and commitment to, the plan.

Lawler and Jenkins described a small manufacturing plant where a committee of workers and managers designed a pay system.[70] The committee studied alternative plans and collected salary survey data. This resulted in a plan that gave control over salaries to members of work groups. Team members behaved responsibly in setting wage rates. They gave themselves 8% raises, which fell at the fiftieth percentile in the local labour market. Moreover, the results of a survey administered six months after the start of the new pay plan showed significant improvements in turnover, job satisfaction and satisfaction with pay and its administration. Lawler attributed these improvements to employees having greater information about the pay system. Participation led to employee ownership of the plan and feelings that it was fair and trustworthy.

Communication about reward systems can also have a powerful impact on employee perceptions of pay equity and on motivation. Most organisations maintain secrecy about pay rates, especially in the managerial ranks. Managers typically argue that employees prefer secrecy. It also gives managers freedom in administering pay as they do not have to defend their judgments. There is evidence to suggest, however, that pay secrecy can lead to dissatisfaction with pay and to reduced motivation. Dissatisfaction derives mainly from people's misperceptions about their pay relative to the pay of others. Research shows that managers tend to overestimate the pay of peers and of people below them in the organisation, and that they tend to underestimate the pay of superiors. These misperceptions contribute to dissatisfaction with pay because, regardless of the pay level of a manager, it will seem small in comparison to the perceived pay level of subordinates and peers. Perhaps worse, potential promotions will appear less valuable than they actually are.

Secrecy can reduce motivation by obscuring the relationship between pay and performance. For organisations that have a performance-based pay plan, secrecy prevents employees from testing whether the organisation is actually paying for performance;

employees come to mistrust the pay system, fearing that the company has something to hide. Secrecy can also reduce the beneficial impact of accurate performance feedback. Pay provides people with feedback about how they are performing in relation to some standard. Because managers tend to overestimate the pay of peers and subordinates, they will consider their own pay low and thus perceive performance feedback more negatively than it really is. Such misperceptions about performance discourage those managers who are actually performing effectively.

It is important to emphasise that both the amount of participation in designing reward systems and the amount of frankness in communicating about rewards should fit the rest of the organisation design and managerial philosophy. Clearly, high levels of participation and openness are congruent with democratic organisations. It is questionable whether authoritarian organisations would tolerate either one.

Summary

This chapter presented three types of human resource management interventions—goal setting, performance appraisal and rewards systems. Although all three change programmes are relatively new to organisation development, they offer powerful methods for managing employee and work group performance. They also help to enhance worker satisfaction and support work design, business strategy and employee involvement practices.

Principles contributing to the success of goal setting include the establishment of challenging goals and the clarification of measurement. These are accomplished by setting difficult but feasible goals, managing participation in the goal-setting process and being sure that the goals can be measured and influenced by the employee or work group. The most common form of goal setting—management by objectives—depends upon top-management support and participative planning to be effective.

Performance appraisals represent an important link between goal setting and reward systems. As part of an organisation's feedback and control system, they provide employees and work groups with information that they can use to improve work outcomes. Appraisals are becoming more participative and developmental. An increasing number of people are involved in collecting performance data, evaluating an employee's performance and determining how the appraised can improve.

Reward-systems interventions attempt to elicit and maintain desired performance. They can be oriented to both individual jobs or work groups and affect both performance and employee well-being. Three major kinds of reward-systems interventions are the design of pay, promotions and benefits.

The more innovative pay plans include skill-based pay, an all-salaried work force, lump-sum salary increases, performance-based pay and profit sharing. Each of the plans has strengths and weaknesses when measured against the criteria of performance contingency, equity, availability, timeliness, durability and visibility. Interventions regarding promotions include the open posting of jobs and inviting people to nominate themselves for job openings. Involving peers and subordinates in promotion decisions can increase the accuracy and equity of such changes. Flexible benefit programmes give employees some discretion in allocating their total benefit payment. The critical process of implementing a reward system involves decisions about who should be involved in designing and administering it and how much information about pay should be communicated.

ACTIVITIES

Review questions

1 The performance management model includes what parts?

2 What does the goal-setting process involve and how does it work?

3 What is the major premise underlying 'goal setting' as an intervention?

4 Describe the basic steps in the MBO process.

5 What are the design criteria for performance appraisal?

6 Which model relates work performance to rewards?

7 What are reward system processes concerned with?

8 Explain the major drawback of skill-based pay schemes.

9 What is significant about group and organisation-wide pay plans?

10 List the design elements of developing a profit-sharing plan.

Discussion and essay questions

1 Discuss the performance management model. How does performance management relate to employee involvement and work design?

2 What is the rationale for goal setting? Do you agree or disagree?

3 Contrast the effects of various reward systems. Which are most effective?

4 What can be done to improve performance appraisal systems?

Notes

1 A. Mohrman, S. Mohrman and C. Worley, 'High technology performance management' in *Managing Complexity in High Technology Organizations*, eds M. Von Glinow and S. Mohrman (New York: Oxford University Press, 1990): 216–36.

2 D. McDonald and A. Smith, 'A proven connection: performance management and business results', *Compensation and Benefits Review*, 27 (1995): 59–64.

3 J. Riedel, D. Nebeker and B. Cooper, 'The influence of monetary incentives on goal choice, goal commitment and task performance', *Organizational Behavior and Human Decision Processes*, 42 (1988): 155–80; P. Earley, T. Connolly and G. Ekegren, 'Goals, strategy development and task performance: some limits on the efficacy of goal setting', *Journal of Applied Psychology*, 74 (1989): 24–33; N. Perry, 'Here come richer, riskier pay plans', *Fortune*, (19 December 1988): 50–58; E. Lawler III, *High Involvement Management* (San Francisco: Jossey-Bass, 1986); A. Mohrman, S. Resnick-West and E. Lawler III, *Designing Performance Appraisal Systems* (San Francisco: Jossey-Bass, 1990).

4 Mohrman, Mohrman and Worley, 'High technology performance management', *op. cit.*

5 E. Locke and G. Latham, *A Theory of Goal Setting and Task Performance* (Englewood Cliffs, N.J.: Prentice-Hall, 1990).

6 Locke and Latham, *A Theory of Goal Setting, op. cit.*; E. Locke, R. Shaw, L. Saari and G. Latham, 'Goal setting and task performance: 1969–1980', *Psychological Bulletin*, 97 (1981): 125–52; M. Tubbs, 'Goal setting: a meta-analytic examination of the empirical evidence', *Journal of Applied Psychology*, 71 (1986): 474–83.

7 A. O'Leary-Kelly, J. Martocchio and D. Frink, 'A review of the influence of group goals on group performance', *Academy of Management Journal*, 37 (5, 1994): 1285–1301.

8 S. Tully, 'Why to go for stretch targets', *Fortune*, (14 November 1994): 145–58.

9 D. Crown and J. Rosse, 'Yours, mine and ours: facilitating group productivity through the integration of individual and group goals', *Organization Behavior and Human Decision Processes*, 64 (2, 1995): 138–50.

10 P. Drucker, *The Practice of Management* (New York: Harper and Row, 1954): 63.

11 G. Odiorne, *Management by Objectives* (New York: Pittman, 1965).

12 H. Levinson, 'Management by objectives: a critique', *Training and Development Journal*, 26 (1972): 410–25.

13 D. McGregor, 'An uneasy look at performance appraisal', *Harvard Business Review*, 35 (May–June 1957): 89–94.

14 E. Huse and E. Kay, 'Improving employee productivity through work planning' in *The Personnel Job in a Changing World*, ed. J. Blood (New York: American Management Associations, 1964): 301–15.

15 This application was adapted from T. Jones, 'Performance management in a changing context: Monsanto pioneers a competency-based, developmental approach', *Human Resource Management*, 34:3 (1995): 425–42.

16 Locke and Latham, *A Theory of Goal Setting, op. cit.*

17 Tubbs, 'Goal setting', *op. cit.*; R. Guzzo, R. Jette and R Katzell, 'The effects of psychologically based intervention programs on worker productivity: a meta-analysis', *Personal Psychology*, 38 (1985): 275–91; A. Mento, R. Steel and R. Karren, 'A meta-analytic study of the effects of goal setting on task performance: 1966–84', *Organizational Behavior and Human Decision Processes*, 39 (1987): 52–83; O'Leary-Kelly, Martocchio and Frink, 'A review of the influence of group goals on group performance', *op. cit.*

18 C. Pearson, 'Participative goal setting as a strategy for improving performance and job satisfaction: a longitudinal evaluation with railway track maintenance gangs', *Human Relations*, 40 (1987): 473–88; R. Pritchard, S. Jones, P. Roth, K. Stuebing and S. Ekeberg, 'Effects of group feedback, goal setting and incentives on organizational productivity', *Journal of Applied Psychology*, 73 (1988): 337–58.

19 S. Yearta, S. Maitlis and R. Briner, 'An exploratory study of goal setting in theory and practice: a motivational technique that works?' *Journal of Occupational and Organizational Psychology*, 68 (1995): 237–252.

20 R. Steers, 'Task-goal attributes: achievement and supervisory performance', *Organizational Behavior and Human Performance*, 13 (1975): 392–403; G. Latham and G. Yukl, 'A review of research on the application of goal setting in organizations', *Academy of Management Journal*, 18 (1975): 824–45; R. Steers and L. Porter, 'The role of task-goal attributes in employee performance', *Psychological Bulletin*, 81 (1974): 434–51; Early, Connolly and Ekegren, 'Goals, strategy development and task performance', *op. cit.*; J. Hollenbeck and A. Brief, 'The effects of individual differences and goal origin on goal setting and performance', *Organizational Behavior and Human Decision Processes*, 40 (1987): 392–414.

21 Huse and Kay, 'Improving employee productivity', *op. cit.*, 301–15.

22 A. Raia, 'Goal setting and self-control: an empirical study', *Journal of Management Studies*, 2 (1965): 34–53; A. Raia, 'A second look at management goals and controls', *California Management Review*, 8 (1965): 49–58.

23 S. Carroll and W. Tosi Jr, *Management by Objectives* (New York: Macmillan, 1973): 23.

24 D. Terpstra, P. Olson and B. Lockeman, 'The effects of MBO on levels of performance and satisfaction among university faculty', *Group and Organization Studies*, 7 (1982): 353–66.

25 R. Byrd and J. Cowan, 'MBO: a behavioral science approach', *Personnel*, 51 (March–April 1974): 42–50.

26 G. Latham and R. Wexley, *Increasing Productivity Through Performance Appraisal* (Reading, Mass.: Addison-Wesley, 1981).

27 C. Peck, 'Pay and performance: the interaction of compensation and performance appraisal', *Research Bulletin*, 155 (New York: Conference Board, 1984).

28 E. Lawler III, *Pay and Organization Development* (Reading, Mass.: Addison-Wesley, 1981): 113; Mohrman, Resnick-West and Lawler, *Designing Performance Appraisal Systems, op. cit.*

29 D. Antonioni, 'Improve the performance management process before discounting performance appraisals', *Compensation and Benefits Review*, 26:3 (1994): 29–37.

30 S. Mohrman, G. Ledford Jr, E. Lawler III and A. Mohrman, 'Quality of work life and employee involvement' in *International Review of Industrial and Organizational Psychology, 1986*, eds C. Cooper and I. Robertson (New York: John Wiley, 1986); G. Yukl and R. Lepsinger, 'How to get the most out of 360 degree feedback', *Training*, 32:12 (1995): 45–50.

31 Mohrman, Ledford, Lawler and Mohrman, 'Quality of work life and employee involvement', *op. cit.*

32 E. Huse, 'Performance appraisal—a new look', *Personnel Administration*, 30 (March–April 1967): 3–18.

33 S. Gebelein, 'Employee development: multi-rater feedback goes strategic', *HR Focus*, 73:1 (1996): 1,4; B. O'Reilly, '360 degree feedback can change your life', *Fortune*, (17 October 1994): 93–100.

34 Mohrman, Resnick-West and Lawler, *Designing Performance Appraisal Systems, op. cit.*; E. Lawler, 'Performance management: the next generation', *Compensation and Benefits Review*, 26 (3, 1994): 16–19.

35 Anonymous, 'Dulux measures its best practice', *Work & People*, 14:3 (October 1993): 19–21.

36 J. Fairbank and D. Prue, 'Developing performance feedback systems' in *Handbook of Organizational Behavior Management*, ed. L.Frederiksen (New York: John Wiley & Sons, 1982).

37 R. Ammons, *Knowledge of Performance: Survey of Literature, Some Possible Applications and Suggested Experimentation*, USAF WADC technical report 5414 (Wright Patterson Air Force Base, Ohio: Wright Air Development Center, Aero Medical Laboratory, 1954); J. Adams, 'Response feedback and learning', *Psychology Bulletin*, 70 (1968): 486–504; J. Annett, *Feedback and Human Behavior* (Baltimore, Md.: Penguin, 1969); J. Sassenrath, 'Theory and results on feedback and retention', *Journal of Educational Psychology*, 67 (1975): 894–99; F. Luthans and T. Davis, 'Behavioral management in service organizations' in *Service Management Effectiveness*, eds D. Bowen, R. Chase and T. Cummings (San Francisco: Jossey-Bass, 1989): 177–210.

38 R. Kopelman, *Managing Productivity in Organizations* (New York: McGraw-Hill, 1986).

39 Guzzo, Jette and Katzell, 'The effects of psychologically based intervention programs', *op. cit.*

40 D. Nadler, 'The effects of feedback on task group behaviour: a review of the experimental research', *Organizational Behavior and Human Performance*, 23 (1979): 309–38; D. Nadler, C. Cammann and P. Mirvis, 'Developing a feedback system for work units: a field experiment in structural change', *Journal of Applied Behavioral Science*, 16 (1980): 41–62; J. Chobbar and J. Wallin, 'A field study on the effect of feedback frequency on performance', *Journal of Applied Psychology*, 69 (1984): 524–30.

41 F. Luthans, 'The exploding service sector: meeting the challenge through behavioral management', *Journal of Organizational Change Management*, 1 (1988): 18–28; F. Balcazar, B. Hopkins and Y. Suarez, 'A critical objective review of performance feedback', *Journal of Organizational Behavior Management*, 7 (1986): 65–89; R. Waldersee and F. Luthans, 'A theoretically based contingency model of feedback: implications for managing service employees', *Journal of Organizational Change Management*, 3 (1990): 46–56.

42 W. Scott, J. Farh and P. Podsakoff, 'The effects of "intrinsic" and "extrinsic" reinforcement contingencies on task behavior', *Organizational Behavior and Human Decision Processes*, 41 (1988): 405–25; E. Lawler III, *Strategic Pay* (San Francisco: Jossey-Bass, 1990).

43 J. Campbell, M. Dunnette, E. Lawler III and K. Weick, *Managerial Behavior, Performance and Effectiveness* (New York: McGraw-Hill, 1970).

44 C. Worley, D. Bowen and E. Lawler III, 'On the relationship between objective increases in pay and employees' subjective reactions', *Journal of Organization Behavior*, 13 (1992): 559–71.

45 Perry, 'Here come richer, riskier pay plans', *op. cit.*

46 S. Tully, 'Your paycheck gets exciting', *Fortune*, (1 November 1993): 83–98.

47 V. Gibson, 'The new employee reward system', *Management Review*, (February 1995): 13–18.

48 D. Simmons, M. Shadur and A. Preston, 'Integrating TQM and HRM', *Employee Relations*, 17:3 (1995), 75–86.

49 Lawler, *Pay and Organization Development*, op. cit., 66; E. Lawler and G. Ledford Jr, 'Skill-based pay', *Personnel*, 62 (1985): 30–37.

50 Lawler, *Pay and Organization Development*, op. cit., 66.

51 N. Gupta, G. Jenkins Jr and W. Curington, 'Paying for knowledge: myths and realities', *National Productivity Review* (Spring 1986): 107–23.

52 E. Lawler III, S. Mohrman and G. Ledford, *Creating High Performance Organizations: Practices and Results of Employee Involvement and Total Quality Management in Fortune 1000 Companies* (San Francisco: Jossey-Bass, 1995).

53 N. Marshall, 'Pay-for-performance systems: experience in Australia', *Public Productivity & Management Review*, 21:4 (1998): 403–18.

54 Lawler, *Pay and Organization Development*, op. cit., 62–65.

55 *Ibid.*, 69–72.

56 *Ibid.*, 113.

57 'Bonus pay: buzzword or bonanza?' *Business Week*, (14 November 1994).

58 Lawler, *Pay and Organization Development*, op. cit., 134–43; M. Schuster, J. Schuster and M. Montague, 'Excellence in gainsharing: from the start to renewal', *Journal for Quality and Participation*, 17:3 (1994): 18–25; D. Band, G. Scanlon and C. Tustin, 'Beyond the bottom line: gainsharing and organization development', *Personnel Review*, 23:8 (1994): 17.32; J. Belcher, 'Gainsharing and variable pay: the state of the art', *Compensation and Benefits Review*, 26:3 (1994): 50–60.

59 Lawler, *Pay and Organization Development*, op. cit., 146–54.

60 R. Bullock and P. Bullock, 'Garnishing and Rubik's Cube: solving system problems', *National Productivity Review*, 1 (1982): 396–407; J. Ramquist, 'Labor–management cooperation: the

Scanlon plan at work', *Sloan Management Review* (Spring 1982): 49–55; T. Cummings and G. Molloy, *Improving Productivity and the Quality of Work Life* (New York: Praeger, 1977): 249–60; R. Bullock and E. Lawler III, 'Gainsharing: a few questions and fewer answers', *Human Resource Management,* 23 (1984): 23–40; C. Miller and M. Schuster, 'A decade's experience with the Scanlon plan: a case study', *Journal of Occupational Behavior,* 8 (April 1987): 167–74; T. Welbourne and L. Gomez-Meija, 'Gainsharing: a critical review and a future research agenda', *Journal of Management,* 21:3 (1995): 559–609.

61 General Accounting Office, *Productivity Sharing Programs: Can They Contribute to Productivity Improvement?* (Washington, D.C.: US General Accounting Office, 1981).

62 R. Bullock and E. Lawler III, 'Gainsharing: a few questions and fewer answers', *op. cit.*; C. O'Dell, *People, Performance and Pay* (Houston: American Productivity Center, 1987).

63 E. Doherty, W. Nord and J. McAdams, 'Gainsharing and organization development: a productive synergy', *Journal of Applied Behavioral Science,* 25 (1989): 209–29.

64 S. Hanlon, D. Meyer and R. Taylor, 'Consequences of gainsharing: a field experiment revisited', *Group and Organization Management,* 19:1 (1994): 87–111.

65 E. Lawler III, 'Gainsharing theory and research: findings and future directions' in *Organizational Change and Development,* 2, eds W. Pasmore and R. Woodman (Greenwich, Conn.: JAI Press, 1988): 323–44.

66 E. Lawler III, 'Reward systems' in *Improving Life at Work,* eds J. Hackman and J. Suttle (Santa Monica, Calif.: Goodyear, 1977): 176.

67 R. Walton, 'How to counter alienation in the plant', *Harvard Business Review,* 50 (November–December 1972): 70–81.

68 C. Rance, 'Incentive schemes favoured', *The Age* (1 April 1995), Employment Section, 1,3; http://www.cmoa.ican.net.au/ind/nsw/nswsalpackage.html

69 Lawler, *Pay and Organization Development, op. cit.,* 101–11.

70 E. Lawler III and G. Jenkins, *Employee Participation in Pay Plan Development* (unpublished technical report to US Department of Labor, Ann Arbor, Mich.: Institute for Social Research, University of Michigan, 1976).

Developing and assisting members

This chapter looks at three human resource management interventions that are concerned with developing and assisting the well-being of organisation members. First, organisations have had to adapt their career planning and development processes to a variety of trends. For example, there are the different needs and concerns of individuals as they progress through various career stages; technological changes have dramatically altered organisational structures and systems and global competition has forced organisations to rethink how work gets done. These processes and concerns have forced individuals and organisations to re-examine the social contract that binds them together. Career planning and development interventions can help to deal effectively with these issues. Second, increasing work force diversity provides an especially challenging environment for human resource management. The mix of genders, ages, value orientations, thinking styles and ethnic backgrounds that make up the modern work force is increasingly varied. Flexible human resource interventions can help to satisfy the variety of needs posed by this diversity. Finally, wellness interventions, such as employee assistance and stress management programmes, are addressing several important social trends, such as fitness and health consciousness, drug and alcohol abuse and work–life balance.

Career planning is concerned with how people choose their occupations, organisations and work activities. Although organisations have traditionally considered career planning to be a personal matter, a growing number of firms are helping employees to gain the skills, knowledge and information needed to make effective career plans. How people balance their professional and personal lives is an increasingly important part of career planning. Once those plans have been made, career development helps employees to attain their career goals, a process that can include matching people to jobs and helping them to perform and develop. Career planning and development are being applied to employees at widely differing stages of career development, from the initial establishment of a career to retirement and withdrawal from an organisation. Moreover, they are increasingly being used to integrate corporate business objectives and human resource needs with the personal needs of employees.

Work force diversity interventions seek to make human resource policies and practices more responsive to a variety of individual needs. Traditional human resource management is built on a 'one size fits all' model that assumes that all employees want the same things. However, a number of trends, including an increasing percentage of women in the work place, the 'birth dearth' following the baby boomers and increasing ethnic diversity, challenge that assumption. This chapter describes how OD interventions can address the diversity being faced by more and more organisations.

Employee wellness interventions include employee assistance programmes and stress management. Employee assistance programmes are intended to help employees deal with mental health problems, substance abuse and the marital and financial problems often associated with poor work performance. Like most human resource management interventions, wellness programmes are typically carried out by professionals who specialise in this area, such as doctors, psychologists and other health consultants. Recently, some OD practitioners have been gaining competence in wellness programmes, which, like career planning and development, have become a growing part of comprehensive OD programmes. Stress management involves diagnosing and resolving the negative consequences of work-related stress. Stress is neither good nor bad in itself. However, it can reach unhealthy levels or persist for long time periods, causing such problems as headaches, backache, high blood pressure and cardiovascular disease. These problems can result in considerable organisational costs in terms of lost productivity, absenteeism and turnover. Stress management helps employees to recognise stress-related problems and to understand their causes. It is aimed at changing organisational conditions that cause stress and at helping people to cope better with stressful situations.

Career planning and development interventions

Career planning and development have been receiving increased attention in organisations. Growing numbers of managers and professional staff are seeking more control over their work lives. As organisations downsize and restructure, there is less trust in the organisation to provide job security. Employees are not willing to have their careers 'just happen' and are taking an active role in planning and managing them. This is particularly true for women, employees in mid-career and university recruits, who are increasingly asking for career planning assistance.[1] On the other hand, organisations are becoming more and more reliant on their 'intellectual capital'. Providing career planning and development opportunities for organisation members helps to recruit and retain skilled and knowledgeable workers. Many talented job candidates, especially minorities and women, are showing a preference for employers who offer career advancement opportunities.

Many organisations, such as 3M, Ford and Westpac, have adopted career planning and development programmes.[2] These programmes have attempted to improve the quality of work life of managers and professionals, improve their performance, reduce unwanted turnover and respond to equal employment and affirmative action legislation. Companies have discovered that organisational growth and effectiveness require career development programmes if they are to ensure that needed talent will be available. Competent managers are often the scarcest resource. Many companies have also experienced the high costs of turnover among recent college graduates, including MBAs, which can reach 50% after five years. Career planning and development help to attract and hold such highly talented employees, and can increase the chances that their skills and knowledge will be fully utilised.

Recent legislation and court actions have motivated many firms to set up career planning and development programmes for minority and female employees, who are in short supply at the middle- and upper-management levels. Organisations are discovering that the career development needs of women and minorities often require special programmes and the use of non-traditional methods, such as integrated systems for recruitment, placement and development. The restructuring of employment, notably the growth in non-standard employment forms, the implementation of affirmative action and equal employment opportunity legislation and the development of enterprise-based decentralised bargaining, have created a scenario where the central issue is whether or not the employment conditions of women workers have been enhanced, unaffected or regressed by these developments.[3] Similarly, age-discrimination laws have led many organisations to set up career programmes aimed at older managers and professionals. Thus, career planning and development are increasingly being applied to people at various ages and stages of development—from new recruits to those nearing retirement age.

Finally, career planning and development interventions have been increasingly applied to cases of 'career halt', where lay-offs and job losses have resulted from organisation decline, downsizing, re-engineering and restructuring. These abrupt halts to career progress can have severe human consequences, and human resource practices have been developed for helping to cope with these problems.

Career planning is concerned with individuals who are choosing occupations, organisations and positions at each stage of their careers. Career development involves helping employees to attain their career objectives.[4] Although both of these interventions are generally aimed at managerial and professional employees, a growing number of programmes are including lower-level employees, particularly those in white-collar jobs.

Career stages

A career is the sequence of work-related positions occupied by a person during the course of a lifetime.[5] Traditionally, careers have been judged in terms of advancement and upward promotion in the organisational hierarchy. Today, they are defined in more holistic ways to include an individual's attitudes and experiences. For example, a person can remain in the same job, acquiring and developing new skills and having a successful career without ever getting promoted. Similarly, people may move horizontally through a series of jobs in different functional areas of the firm. Although they may not be promoted upward in the hierarchy, their broadened job experiences would constitute a successful career.

Considerable research has been devoted to understanding how ageing and experience affect people's careers. This research has drawn on the extensive work done on adult growth and development[6] and has adapted that developmental perspective to include work experience.[7] Results suggest that employees progress through at least four distinct career stages as they mature and gain experience. Each stage has unique concerns, needs and challenges.

1   *The establishment stage* (age 21–26). This phase is the outset of a career when people are generally uncertain about their competence and potential. They are dependent on others, especially bosses and more experienced employees, for guidance, support and feedback. At this stage, people are making their initial choices about committing themselves to a specific career, organisation and job. They are exploring possibilities while learning about their own capabilities.

2   *The advancement stage* (age 26–40). During this phase, employees become independent contributors who are concerned with achieving and advancing in their chosen careers. They have typically learned to perform autonomously and need less guidance from bosses and closer ties with colleagues. This settling-down period is also characterised by attempts to clarify the range of long-term career options.

3   *The maintenance stage* (age 40–60). This phase involves levelling off and holding on to career successes. Many people at this stage are likely to have achieved their greatest advancements and are now concerned with helping less-experienced subordinates. For those who are dissatisfied with their career progress, this period can be conflictual and depressing, as characterised by the term 'mid-life crisis'. People often reappraise their circumstances, search for alternatives and redirect their career efforts. Success in these endeavours can lead to continuing growth, whereas failure can lead to early decline.

4   *The withdrawal stage* (age 60 and above). This final stage is concerned with leaving a career. It involves letting go of organisational attachments and getting ready for greater leisure time and retirement. The employee's major contributions are imparting knowledge and experience to others. For those people who are generally satisfied with their careers, this period can result in feelings of fulfilment and a willingness to leave the career behind.

The different career stages represent a broad developmental perspective on people's jobs. They provide insight about the personal and career issues that people are likely to face at different career phases. These issues can be potential sources of stress. Employees are likely to go through the phases at different rates; they are likely to experience personal and career issues differently at each stage. For example, one person may experience the maintenance stage as a positive opportunity to develop less-experienced employees; another person may experience the maintenance stage as a stressful levelling off of career success.

Career planning

Career planning involves setting individual career objectives. It is highly personalised and generally includes assessing one's interests, capabilities, values and goals; examining

TABLE 18.1 Career stages and career planning issues	
Stage	**Career-planning issues**
Establishment	What are alternative occupations, organizations and jobs?
	What are my interests and capabilities?
	How do I get the work accomplished?
	Am I performing as expected?
	Am I developing the necessary skills for advancement?
Advancement	Am I advancing as expected?
	How can I advance more effectively?
	What long-term options are available?
	How do I get more exposure and visibility?
	How do I develop more effective peer relationships?
	How do I better integrate career choices with my personal life?
Maintenance	How do I help others to become established and advance?
	Should I reassess myself and my career?
	Should I redirect my actions?
Withdrawal	What are my interests outside work?
	What postretirement work options are available to me?
	How can I be financially secure?
	How can I continue to help others?

alternative careers; making decisions that may affect the current job; and planning how to progress in the desired direction. This process results in people choosing occupations, organisations and jobs. It determines, for example, whether individuals will accept or decline promotions and transfers and whether they will stay in the company or leave it for another job or retirement.

The four career stages can be used to make career planning more effective. Table 18.1 shows the different career stages and the career planning issues relevant at each phase. Applying the table to a particular employee involves first diagnosing the person's career stage—establishment, advancement, maintenance or withdrawal. Next, available career planning resources are used to help the employee address pertinent issues. Career planning programmes include some or all of the following resources:

- communication regarding career opportunities and resources within the organisation and available to employees
- workshops to encourage employees to assess their interests, abilities and job situations and to formulate career development plans
- career counselling by managers or human resource department personnel
- self-development materials, such as books, videotapes and other media, directed toward identifying life and career issues
- assessment programmes that provide various tests on vocational interests, aptitudes and abilities relevant to setting career goals.

Application 18.1 describes the challenge posed by developing managers with regional experience.[8] It provides an example of the range of strategies used to develop a regional culture in Australian companies.

APPLICATION 18.1 Playing the regional game

The greatest challenge for management in a global environment is the development of managers with regional experience, something that Australian companies have not excelled at in the past. Alan Carroll, chairman of Carroll

Partners, a Melbourne-based consultancy, says human resources managers do not have enough authority. He believes that overseas career development has often been short-sighted, but says it is now becoming the key factor for success and can no longer be avoided.

'Whole games were fought in this country in the early 1980s in large companies where the big debate was, "Do I leave head office, because all the politics are played here?" If you went overseas, you either never got back or you came back to a job where no one ever heard of you again. The banks are full of people like that and they are the first to admit it.'

Carroll says the preferred approach for regional development among multi-nationals was the 'cadre' strategy. Staff were recruited from university, admitted to a club where they were expected to work for life and, if considered appropriate, selected at the age of 35 for senior management.

He says this approach, predicated on having one nationality and lifetime employment, does not work for Asia. He cites a Cantonese expression, 'It is better to be the mouth of a rooster than the arse of a bull', which translates as meaning that it is better to be in charge of your own business at 40 than to be in a Western corporate structure playing games for recognition and power. Carroll says: 'It is very difficult to hold good Chinese past 50 (because they leave to start a family company). In fact, the great tradition of Indian and Chinese companies is that they stop growing when they run out of family.'

There is now a realisation that it is imperative to hold on to managers with regional experience. There are four ways, he says, by which companies can develop a regional culture.

The first is the 'egg' strategy: managers who are white on the outside and yellow on the inside. 'They put someone out into the paddock and they stay there and slowly (blend by osmosis) into the terrain. They think Asian and they understand Asia implicitly, but they have the unique advantage of being able to be brought home. There is a certain shared value system that allows you to mix between the two environments without it polluting either one. It is not valued as a (stand-alone) strategy any more.'

Carroll describes the second as a 'banana' strategy, where the company uses headhunters to find people who are yellow on the outside and white on the inside. 'They are tame, they come in bunches, they usually earn $200 000 a year, they will move anywhere else for another $50 000, and they are hired to look local but still not go strange. Most tend not to be there very long.'

The third strategy Carroll describes as typically Australian: the 'goat' strategy, or sending a manager out on a trial basis. 'You strap him to a post and if he is alive in three months you put a fax machine by him and think, 'What a grand strategy'. If he is dead you assume that it would always have happened anyway. If the goat starts to thrive, you take him off his tether and put some grass around him and you check every three months. But then you find you can't bring him home because he is bigger and starting to smell. Within three to five years, the manager has started to go feral; you can't bring him back.'

The fourth strategy Carroll terms the 'mango': a manager who is yellow on the outside and inside. These are local managers who co-ordinate with head office but do not necessarily share its values and cultural assumptions.

Carroll says that it was once possible to run only one strategy, but now all four are required in combination. This necessitates a mentoring system. He says the ladder should start at 28, when the manager has to learn Indonesian, Japanese or Mandarin and gain basic business experience. 'I am the last generation that will be able to work Asia without being fluent in one of the major languages', he says.

At 32, the manager is brought home for three years to work in head office managing a business segment (not a business function or geographical area). 'Business segments are where the politics are played, where the arrangements are made and where the networks really matter,' says Carroll.

At 35, the regional manager is back out again for five years. The manager is at the 'spear-carrying' stage and should 'want to eat the legs off chairs'. He or she should have responsibility for the profit-and-loss side of the business, essential for survival in Asia. 'People who run marketing support jobs or business development jobs typically don't make it,' he says.

At 40, the manager is brought home, usually having lost his or her first marriage and from 40 to 43 they run a major business segment. Between 45 and 50 the regional manager is back in the region again with 20 years of experience. 'You have relationships and the people that matter in Asia.'

At 50, the final cut is made and managers go into a first or second team. The first team runs the company and spends one-third of its time being mentors to those aged between 28 and 35. Carroll says it is essential that managers at this age still have curiosity and energy. 'It is a very tough culling process and what you have at the end of it is someone who can play the monarch-to-monarch game (operate at the highest level). Stuart Hornery from Lend Lease does it well in Indonesia and Percy Barnevik at ABB (ASEA Brown Boveri) is the best.'

According to Table 18.1, employees who are just becoming established in careers can be stressed by concerns for identifying alternatives, assessing their interests and capabilities, learning how to perform effectively and finding out how they are doing. At this stage, the company should provide individuals with considerable communication and counselling about available career paths and the skills and abilities needed to progress in them. Workshops, self-development materials and assessment techniques should be aimed at helping employees to assess their interests, aptitudes and capabilities, and at linking that information to possible careers and jobs. Considerable attention should be directed at giving employees continual feedback about job performance and at counselling them about how to improve performances. The supervisor–subordinate relationship is especially important for these feedback and development activities.

People at the advancement stage are mainly concerned with getting ahead, discovering long-term career options and integrating career choices, such as transfers or promotions, with their personal lives. Here, the company should provide employees with communication and counselling about challenging assignments and possibilities for more exposure and demonstration of skills. It should help to clarify the range of possible long-term career options and provide individuals with some idea about where they stand in achieving them. Workshops, developmental materials and assessment methods should be aimed at helping employees to develop wider collegial relationships, join with effective mentors and sponsors and develop more creativity and innovation. These activities should also help people to assess both career and personal life spheres and to integrate them more successfully.

At the maintenance stage, individuals are concerned with helping newer employees to become established and grow in their careers. This phase may also involve a reassessment of self and career and a possible redirection to something more rewarding. The firm should provide individuals with communications about the broader organisation and how their roles fit into it. Workshops, developmental materials, counselling and assessment techniques should be aimed at helping employees to assess and develop skills in order to train and coach others. For those experiencing a mid-life crisis, career-planning activities

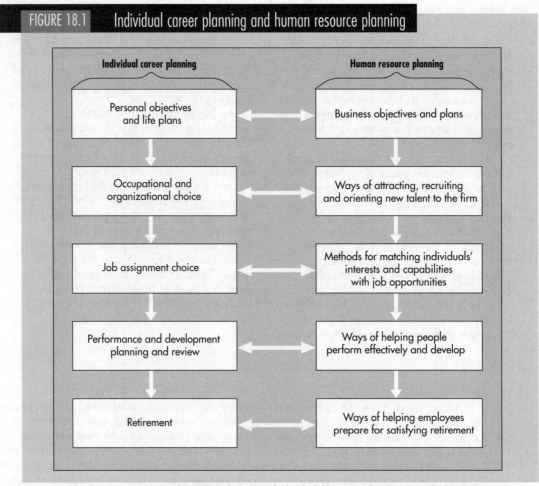

FIGURE 18.1 Individual career planning and human resource planning

Source: Adapted from *Business Horizons* 16, copyright © 1973 by the Foundation for the School of Business at Indiana University. Used with permission.

should be directed at helping them to reassess their circumstances and to develop in new directions. Mid-life crises are generally caused by perceived threats to people's career or family identities.[9] Career planning should help people to deal effectively with identity issues, especially in the context of an ongoing career. This may include workshops and close interpersonal counselling to help people confront identity issues and reorient their thinking about themselves in relation to work and family. These activities might also help employees deal with the emotions evoked by a mid-life crisis and develop the skills and confidence to try something new.

Employees who are at the withdrawal stage can experience stress about disengaging from work and establishing a secure leisure life. Here, the company should provide communications and counselling about options for post-retirement work and financial security, and it should convey the message that the employee's experience in the organisation is still valued. Retirement planning workshops and materials can help employees gain the skills and information necessary for making a successful transition from work to non-work life. They can prepare individuals for shifting their attention away from the organisation to other interests and activities.

Effective career planning and development requires a comprehensive programme that integrates both corporate business objectives and employee career needs. This is accomplished through human resource planning, as shown in Figure 18.1. Human resource planning is aimed at developing and maintaining a workforce to meet business objectives. It includes recruiting new talent, matching people to jobs, helping them develop careers and perform effectively and preparing them for satisfactory retirement. Career planning activities feed into and supports career development and human resource planning activities.

Application 18.2 describes how Colgate-Palmolive, an international consumer-products company, revised career planning to integrate better with business strategy and human resource planning.[10]

APPLICATION 18.2

Linking career planning, human resource planning and strategy at Colgate-Palmolive

Colgate-Palmolive Co. is a global manufacturer and marketer of consumer products, with about 70% of its $8 billion in sales of personal and household-care products deriving from international markets. To support its global business strategy, the company organized into five worldwide business units in 1989: oral care, personal care, hard-surface care, fabric care and pet nutrition. It soon discovered a significant gap between its business strategy and the human resources necessary for its implementation. Consequently, a Global Human Resources Strategy (GHRS) team was formed to devise ways of integrating business strategy with human resource planning and career planning.

The GHRS team's first task was to articulate a human resource vision based on three key values necessary for competing globally: care, teamwork and continuous improvement. This resulted in the following vision statement:

We care about people. Colgate people, consumers, shareholders, and our business partners. We are committed to act with compassion, integrity, and honesty in all situations, to listen with respect to others and to value cultural differences. We are also committed to protect our global environment and enhance the local communities where we work.

We are all part of a global team, committed to working together across functions, across countries and throughout the world. Only by sharing ideas, technologies, and talents can we sustain profitable growth.

We are committed to getting better every day in all we do, as individuals and as teams. By better understanding consumers' and customers' expectations and by continuously working to innovate and improve our products, services and processes, we will 'become the best'.

The GHRS team circulated the vision statement among senior executives throughout the firm. After considerable discussion, they revised and approved it. Based on principles espoused in the vision, the team then worked on crafting a human resource strategy that would align with business objectives. First they interviewed managers from Colgate businesses around the world. 'The line managers provided invaluable perspective and insight as to the needs of the organization and the role of HR in achieving business goals,' said Brian Smith, director of global human resource strategy.

The interviews revealed the need for human resource support in several areas, including career planning, education and training, and strategy implementation. Colgate needed a comprehensive career planning system so that sufficient numbers of managers with the right skills would be available to fill forecast job openings. Employees, on the other hand, needed a meaningful career planning system to help them determine what experiences and skills they would need to achieve their own career objectives. Colgate also needed education and training programmes that could be applied across business units throughout the world. This would reduce the waste and redundancy of the current approach to training where each business unit developed its own, unique programs. Finally, to implement product strategies, the business units needed certain reservoirs of talent, skills and knowledge. This would require career planning and development on a global scale.

Based on the interview data, the GHRS team coordinated the design of human resource practices for each of the major business functions in the firm. This was accomplished through the creation of functional design teams, each chaired by the senior manager of the respective business function. The teams included line managers from the business functions as well as appropriate human resource specialists. They first identified those global competencies that were necessary for performing the different business functions at Colgate and then designed appropriate career paths and training programs that would allow employees to acquire them.

The manufacturing design team, for example, was headed by the manufacturing vice-president. It identified three sets of global manufacturing competencies: functional/technical, managerial and leadership. The functional/technical cluster included skills and knowledge associated with financial analysis, safety, and production management. The managerial competencies included expertise in negotiation, relationship building, and innovation; the leadership skills involved mobilising and inspiring people toward a common vision and strategy. To gain the job experiences necessary to learn these competencies, the manufacturing team identified the following career paths: functional/technical competencies could be learned in entry-level positions; managerial competencies could be acquired through job rotation, promotion, and special job assignments both domestically and globally; leadership competencies could be gained with experience in higher-level director and vice-president positions. To support these career paths, the manufacturing team designed appropriate training programs as well as performance-management processes to monitor and reward learning and performance for each level in the career tracks.

At the conclusion of the functional design teams' efforts in 1992, the GHRS team sponsored a Global Human Resources Conference to launch the implementation of the human resource strategy and practices throughout Colgate. More than 200 human resource leaders from business units around the world attended the week-long conference. Also present were Colgate's chairman, president, chief operating officer, division presidents and global business leaders. The conference articulated the new human resource strategy and practices and linked them directly to business strategy and objectives. It reaffirmed senior management's commitment to the human resource vision and resulted in specific plans to implement the functional career paths, training programs and performance management systems across business units worldwide. Colgate's human resource leaders left the conference with renewed energy for the human resource strategy and with clear directions for implementing it across the global businesses.

Career Development

Career development helps individuals to achieve career objectives. It follows closely from career planning and includes organisational practices that help employees to implement those plans. These may include skill training, performance feedback and coaching, planned job rotation, mentoring and continuing education.

Career development can be integrated with people's career needs by linking it to different career stages. As described earlier, employees' progress through distinct career stages, each with unique issues relevant to career planning: establishment, advancement,

| TABLE 18.2 | Career development interventions | | |

Intervention	Career stage	Purpose	Intended outcomes
Realistic job preview	Establishment Advancement	To provide members with an accurate expectation of work requirements	Reduce turnover Reduce training costs Increase commitment Increase job satisfaction
Job pathing	Establishment Advancement	To provide members with a sequence of work assignments leading to a career objective	Reduce turnover Build organizational knowledge
Performance feedback and coaching	Establishment Advancement	To provide members with knowledge about their career progress and work effectiveness	Increase productivity Increase job satisfaction Monitor human resource development
Assessment centres	Establishment Advancement	To select and develop members for managerial and technical jobs	Increase person–job fit Identify high-potential candidates
Mentoring	Establishment Advancement Maintenance	To link a less-experienced member with a more-experienced member for member development	Increase job satisfaction Increase member motivation
Developmental training	Establishment Advancement Maintenance	To provide education and training opportunities that help members to achieve career goals	Increase organizational capacity
Work–life balance planning	Establishment Advancement Maintenance	To help members balance work and personal goals	Improve quality of life Increase productivity
Job rotation and challenging assignments	Advancement Maintenance	To provide members with interesting work	Increase job satisfaction Maintain member motivation
Dual-career accommodations	Advancement Maintenance	To assist members with significant others to find satisfying work assignments	Attract and retain high-quality members Increase job satisfaction
Consultative roles	Maintenance Withdrawal	To help members fill productive roles later in their careers	Increase problem-solving capacity Increase job satisfaction
Phased retirement	Withdrawal	To assist members in moving into retirement	Increase job satisfaction Lower stress during transition

maintenance and withdrawal. Career development interventions help employees to implement these plans. Table 18.2 identifies career development interventions, lists the career stages to which they are most relevant and defines their key purposes and intended outcomes. It shows that career development practices may apply to one or more career stages. Performance feedback and coaching, for example, are relevant to both the establishment and advancement stages. Career development interventions can also serve a variety of purposes, such as helping members identify a career path or providing feedback on career progress and work-effectiveness. They can contribute to different organisational outcomes such as lowering turnover and costs and enhancing member satisfaction.

Career development interventions have traditionally been applied to younger employees who have a longer time period to contribute to the firm than older members. Managers often stereotype older employees as being less creative, alert and productive than younger workers and consequently provide them with less career development support.[11] Similarly, Table 18.2 suggests that the OD field has been relatively lax in developing methods for helping older members cope with the withdrawal stage. Only two of the eleven interventions presented in Table 18.2 apply to the withdrawal stage—consultative roles and phased retirement. This relative neglect can be expected to change in the near future, however, as the Australian work force continues to grey. To sustain a highly committed and motivated work force, organisations will increasingly need to address the career needs of older employees. They will need to recognise and reward the contributions that older workers make to the company. Work force diversity interventions, discussed later in this chapter, are a positive step in this direction.

Realistic job preview

This intervention provides individuals with realistic expectations about the job during the recruitment process. It provides recruits with information about whether the job is likely to be consistent with their needs and career plans. Such knowledge is especially useful during the establishment stage, when people are most in need of realistic information about organisations and jobs. It can also help employees during the advancement stage, when promotion is likely to cause job changes.

Research suggests that people may develop unrealistic expectations about the organisation and job.[12] They might suffer from 'reality shock' when those expectations are not fulfilled and may leave the organisation or stay and become disgruntled and unmotivated. To overcome these problems, organisations provide new recruits with information about both the positive and negative aspects of the company and the job. They furnish recruits with booklets, talks and site visits showing what organisational life is really like. Such information can reduce the chances that employees will develop unrealistic job expectations, become disgruntled and leave the company.[13] This can lead to reduced turnover and training costs and increased organisational commitment and job satisfaction.[14]

Application 18.3 describes succession planning at AGL.[15]

APPLICATION 18.3   Succession planning at AGL

Many companies struggle with the management of succession. St George's Bank was left in a predicament when their managing director, Jim Sweeny, died suddenly. When CEO, John Prescott left BHP their share price floundered while they were waiting for a replacement. Succession planning initiatives are rarely used. Diligent succession planning that covers all bases can give the company an edge in retaining expertise and stability.

The gas company, AGL, has implemented a succession plan so that it won't be strongly affected by personnel leaving. All managers are encouraged to decide upon at least one short-term and two long-term successors for their jobs. Any manager that fails to do so cannot move on. Len Bleasel, the managing director of AGL, says that at least six employees are selected as possible replacements for each position in the company. There is always someone trained up in the company who can step into any role. Bleasel believes that AGL's approach to succession planning gives the company a strategic advantage in the marketplace. They are able to make acquisitions with relative ease. AGL is able to put people who know the AGL culture into senior roles without having to go into the marketplace to find staff.

Knowledge management is also an integral part of succession management. In the *McKinsey Quarterly*, analysts Jonathan Day and James Wendler wrote that the greatest challenge to any corporation is the co-ordination of knowledge, and that knowledge received very little management attention. Bill McLaughlin, Group Manager of Corporate Affairs, says that the knowledge that staff members have about each other helps breed stability

and expertise. You have to bring people in from outside but you also need to have people with skills and continuity, or else those skills are lost. It is like a form of institutionalised curiosity: formalised interest in the performance and career direction of all people within an organisation. Bleasel says there is nothing especially complex about paying attention to staff interest and promoting their ambitions, but very few organisations do it. Knowing how to take an interest in staff and helping them exploit opportunities for advancement, as well as meeting their obligations to the company, is an integral part of succession planning.

Job pathing

This intervention provides members with a carefully developed sequence of work assignments leading to a career objective. It helps members in the establishment and advancement stages of their careers. Job pathing helps employees develop skills, knowledge and competencies by performing jobs that require new skills and abilities. Research suggests that employees who receive challenging job assignments early in their careers do better in later jobs.[16] Career pathing allows for a gradual stretching of people's talents by moving them through selected jobs of increasing challenge and responsibility. As the person gains experience and demonstrates competence in the job, he or she is moved to another job with more advanced skills and knowledge. Performing well on one job increases the chance of being assigned to a more demanding job.

The keys to effective job pathing are to identify the skills an employee needs for a certain target job and then to lay out a sequence of jobs that will provide those experiences. The different jobs should provide enough challenge to stretch a person's learning capacity without overwhelming the employee or withholding the target job too long. Some banks, for example, have used job pathing to provide employees with a specific series of jobs that teach them how to become a branch manager. A job pathing process was also evident at Colgate-Palmolive (Application 18.2). By identifying the necessary competencies in technical and managerial career tracks, the company was able to provide employees with clear paths to higher-level jobs. Job pathing can reduce turnover by providing members with opportunities for advancement. It can also build organisational knowledge. As employees advance along career paths, they can gain the necessary skills and experience to resolve organisational problems, to assist in large-scale organisation change and to transfer their accumulated knowledge to new members.

Performance feedback and coaching

One of the most effective interventions during the establishment and advancement phases includes feedback about job performance and coaching to improve performance. As was suggested when discussing goal setting and performance appraisal interventions (Chapter 17), employees need continual feedback about goal achievement as well as the necessary support and coaching to improve their performances. Feedback and coaching are particularly relevant when employees are establishing careers. They have concerns about how to perform the work, whether they are performing up to expectations and whether they are gaining the necessary skills for advancement. A manager can facilitate career establishment by providing feedback on performance, coaching and on-the-job training. These activities can help employees to get the job done while meeting their career development needs. Companies such as Monsanto, for example, use performance feedback and coaching for employee career development. They separate the career development aspect of performance appraisal from the salary review component, thus ensuring that employees' career needs receive as much attention as salary issues. Feedback and coaching interventions can increase employee performance and satisfaction.[17] They can also provide a systematic way of monitoring the development of human resources in the firm.

Assessment centres

This intervention was traditionally designed to help organisations select and develop employees with high potential for managerial jobs. More recently, assessment centres have been extended to career development and to the selection of people to fit new work designs, such as self-managing teams.[18] Assessment centres are popular both in Europe and the US; more than 70% of large organisations in the UK and more than 2000 US companies have some form of assessment centre.[19]

When used to evaluate managerial capability, assessment centres typically process 12 to 15 people at a time and require them to spend two to three days on site. Participants are given a comprehensive interview, take several tests of mental ability and knowledge and participate in individual and group exercises that are intended to simulate managerial work. An assessment team consisting of experienced managers and human resource specialists observes the behaviours and performance of each candidate. This team arrives at an overall assessment of each participant's managerial potential, including a rating on several items believed to be relevant to managerial success in the organisation. These results are then fed back to management for use when making decisions about promotions.

Assessment centres have also been applied to career development, where the emphasis is on the feedback of results to participants. Trained staff help participants to hear and understand feedback about their strong and weak points. They help participants to become clearer about career advancement and to identify training experiences and job assignments that will aid that progress. When used for developmental purposes, assessment centres can provide employees with the support and direction necessary for career development. They can demonstrate that the company is a partner rather than an adversary in that process. Although assessment centres can help people's careers at all stages of development, they seem particularly useful at the advancement stage when employees need to assess their talents and capabilities in terms of long-term career commitments. Recent research suggests that assessment centres can facilitate career advancement to the extent that participants are willing to address and work on the centre's recommendations for development.[20] When participants develop themselves in such areas as clarity about career motivation and ability to work with others, their probability of promotion increases.

Assessment centres are increasingly being used to select members for new work designs. They can provide comprehensive information about how recruits are likely to perform in such settings. This can increase the fit between the employee and the job and consequently lead to higher levels of employee performance and satisfaction.

Although common in the US, assessment centres have had limited use in the Asia-Pacific region. Organisations that utilise assessment centres for internal selection (promotion) and employee development include BHP, Cathay Pacific, Coles Myer, Deloitte Haskins and Sells, Hong Kong Shanghai Bank, National Australia Bank and the State Government of New South Wales.[21]

Application 18.4 illustrates that the focus of equality has moved.[22]

APPLICATION 18.4

Work equality in 'phase two', maybe

In 1998, Susan Halliday became the Federal Sex Discrimination Commissioner. Upon her appointment, she declared that the blatant discrimination of the old 'grab and grope' was widely accepted as being inappropriate. Halliday said that Australia has now entered stage two of the process into less obvious forms of discrimination, such as unequal pay and discrimination because of pregnancy.

Responding to Ms Halliday, barrister Dr Jocelyne Scutt was worried that phase two should not be entered into at the expense of tackling blatant harassment and abuse in the work place. That the focus of equality should not shift, as the old attitudes are still prevalent. A year into her job, Halliday has been shocked and surprised at the archaic attitude held in some work-places. It is not just the pervasiveness of sexual harassment that concerns Halliday, but the number of matters that many women assume are just common practice that are creeping back into the work place. Halliday recalls how early in her tenure, she had a man tell her that it had all gone too far, women believed that they had the right to do whatever they wanted. 'We are in the fifteenth anniversary of the Sexual Discrimination Act and there are still a number of people who see the Act as a detriment to the fabric of society,' she says.

The Affirmative Action Agency director, Fiona Krautil, agrees that Australia is in a conservative era. After John Howard became Prime Minister, it was a battle to keep the two roles of Discrimination Commissioner and Affirmative Action Agency Commissioner. The Federal Government had considered merging Sex Discrimination with the Race office after the former commissioner, Sue Walpole, had left. They also considered eradicating the Affirmative Action Agency but feared the electoral backlash from women.

Both Halliday and Krautil come from a business background and both believe that they can use their knowledge gained in business to tackle inequality. They believe that the antagonistic methods used by some feminists would not be productive in the current conservative political environment. It is not a time for complacency but a time to work on existing legislation and a time to consolidate achievements.

In a proactive move, Halliday designed and distributed a friendly leaflet explaining the 15-year-old law and why it made sense to hire a person on ability rather than on preconceived ideas of age or gender. Halliday was not prepared for the backlash against the brochure. Hate mail poured in and she was attacked on radio. One letter she received from a business owner with four companies wrote: 'If I seek a left-handed, blonde-haired, brown-skinned beautiful woman of X dimensions to do a task, I will so seek and so advertise, for it is me who is paying. Your efforts are substantial and permanently damaging Australia. You are doing well—feel proud.' Radio talk-back jockeys, Alan Jones and Steve Price attacked Halliday. Jones said: 'So you mean to tell me that taxpayers are paying for this woman and these rantings? If you want an 18-year-old for a job, you can't advertise for one. If you want a married woman, you can't advertise for one … We're looking for a bubbly receptionist. Not on, that's indirect sexism.' 'The poor employer,' he concluded, 'Why does he bother employing anyone?' Halliday has turned the attacks into a positive experience, using transcripts from Jones and Price when giving talks. She reads them word for word, using them as speech material and at times comic relief.

Halliday also launched a booklet on International Women's Day called *Harsh Realities*, which deals with 28 reports of sex discrimination and harassment in the work place. Phase Two issues are also still being dealt with. A national inquiry has been launched on pregnancy discrimination, which makes up 15% of complaints. Krautil is also adopting a similar conciliatory and education-based programme. They are focusing on forming working relationships with businesses that have previously resisted the agency. A name change from the Affirmative Action Agency to the Equal Opportunity for Women in the Workplace Agency is also taking place.

Another change is the reduction in the eight-step prescriptive form that businesses have to fill out. The new form will be simpler and businesses are being encouraged to report on their own significant issues about what they have achieved, how they got there and the outcomes. Further to this, an incentive scheme of 'best performers' is being instigated to reward companies. Companies that simply comply with the legislation will have to fill out a form every year. Any company that wants to be excluded from the annual reporting must submit to tough guidelines to be exempt. Krautil will still publish the names of companies that do not comply with equal opportunity standards and still exclude them from being eligible to compete for government contracts. However, she also hopes to publish the names of the top 100 family-friendly work places. Krautil wants to encourage employers and get them to create an equal opportunity work place where gender is not an issue.

Mentoring

One of the most useful ways of helping employees advance in their careers is sponsorship.[23] This involves establishing a close link between a manager or someone more experienced and another organisation member who is less experienced. Mentoring is a powerful intervention that assists members in the establishment, advancement and maintenance stages of their careers. For those in the establishment stage, a sponsor or mentor takes a personal interest in the employee's career, and guides and sponsors it. This helps to ensure that an individual's hard work and skill are translated into actual opportunities for promotion and advancement.[24] For older employees in the maintenance stage, mentoring provides opportunities to share knowledge and experience with others who are less experienced. Older managers can be given the responsibility of mentoring younger employees who are in the establishment and advancement career stages. Mentors do not have to be the direct supervisors of the younger employees, but can be hierarchically or functionally distant from them. Other mentoring opportunities include temporarily assigning veteran managers to newer managers to help them gain managerial skills and knowledge. For example, during the start-up of a new manufacturing plant, the plant manager, who was in the advancement career stage, was assisted by a veteran with years of experience in manufacturing management. The veteran was temporarily located at the new plant and was given the responsibility of helping the plant manager develop the skills and knowledge to get the plant operating and to manage it. About once a month, a consultant helped the two managers examine their relationship and set action plans for improving the mentoring process.[25]

In Australia, Lachlan Murdoch and James Packer, both sons of media billionaires, have been through extensive mentoring processes. As protégés of their parents and senior managers, they are preparing to take over the running of some of Australia's largest corporations.

In both Australia and New Zealand, the use of mentors for new advisers is increasing and the companies using this development technique usually compensate mentors. But it is still only a minority of companies that have formal mentoring programmes, with many companies leaving this role to sales managers.

Although research has shown that mentoring can have positive outcomes, it is difficult to artificially create such relationships when they do not occur naturally.[26] Some organisations have developed workshops in which managers are trained to become effective mentors. Others, such as IBM, include mentoring as a key criterion for paying and promoting managers. In a growing number of cases, companies are creating special mentoring programmes for women and minorities who have traditionally had difficulties in cultivating developmental relationships. This is because mentoring is often based on personal relationships built up outside working hours. In addition, some men dislike taking on female protégés because of the sexual innuendos or fear of the sexual harassment claims that often accompany such relationships.[27]

Developmental training

This intervention helps employees to gain the skills and knowledge for training and coaching others. It may include workshops and training materials that are oriented to human relations, communications, active listening and mentoring. It can also involve substantial investments in education, such as tuition reimbursement programmes that assist members in achieving advanced degrees. Developmental training interventions are generally aimed at increasing the organisation's reservoir of skills and knowledge, which enhances the organisational capability to implement personal and organisational strategies.

A large number of organisations offer developmental training programmes, including Honeywell, Procter & Gamble, Alcoa and IBM. Many of these efforts are directed at mid-career managers who generally have good technical skills but only rudimentary experience in coaching others. In-house developmental training typically involves preparatory reading, short lectures, experiential exercises and case studies on such topics as active listening, defensive communication, personal problem solving and supportive relationships. Participants may be videotaped training and coaching others, and the tapes may be reviewed and critiqued by participants and staff. Classroom learning is often rotated with on-the-job experiences and there is considerable follow-up and recycling of learning. Numerous consulting firms also offer workshops and structured learning materials on developmental training, and there is an extensive practical literature in this area.[28]

Work–life balance planning

This relatively new OD intervention helps employees better integrate and balance work and home life. Restructuring, downsizing and increased global competition have contributed to longer work hours and more stress. Baby-boomers in their fifties and others are rethinking their priorities and seeking to restore some balance in a work-dominated life. Organisations, such as Dow Chemical, are responding to these concerns so that they can attract, retain and motivate the best work force. A more balanced work and family life can benefit both employees and the company through increased creativity, morale, effectiveness and lower turnover.

Work–life balance planning involves a variety of programmes to help members better manage the interface between work and family. These include such organisational prac-tices as flexible hours, job sharing and day care, as well as interventions to help employees identify and achieve both career and family goals. A popular programme is called *middlaning*, a metaphor for a legitimate, alternative career track that acknowledges choices about living life in the 'fast lane'.[29] Middlaning helps people redesign their work and income-generating activities so that more time and energy are available for family and personal needs. It involves education in work addiction, guilt, anxiety and perfectionism; skill development in work contract negotiation; examination of alternatives such as changing careers, freelancing and entrepreneuring; and exploration of options for control-ling financial pressures by improving income/expense ratios, limiting 'black hole' worries such as education fees for children and retirement expenses and replacing financial worrying with financial planning. Because concerns about work–life balance are unlikely to abate and may even increase in the near future, we can expect requisite OD interventions, such as middlaning, to proliferate throughout the public and private sectors.

Job rotation and challenging assignments

The purpose of these interventions is to provide employees with the experience and visibility needed for career advancement, or with the challenge necessary for revitalising a stagnant career at the maintenance stage. Unlike job pathing that specifies a sequence of jobs to reach a career objective, job rotation and challenging assignments are less planned and may not be as oriented to promotion opportunities.

Members in the advancement stage may be moved into new job areas once they have demonstrated competence in a particular job speciality. Companies such as Corning Glass Works and Hewlett-Packard identify 'comers' (managers under 40 years old with potential for assuming top-management positions) and 'hipos' (high potential candidates), and provide them with cross-divisional job experiences during the advancement stage. These job transfers provide managers with a broader range of skills and knowledge as well as opportunities to display their managerial talent to a wider audience of corporate executives. Such exposure helps the organisation determine if the member is capable of handling senior executive responsibilities; it helps the member determine whether to seek promotion to higher positions or to particular areas where she or he would like to work. To reduce the risk of transferring employees across divisions or functions, some firms, such as Procter & Gamble, have created 'fallback positions'. These jobs are identified before the transfer and employees are guaranteed that they can return to them without negative consequences if the transfers or promotions do not work out. Fallback positions reduce the risk that employees in the advancement stage will become trapped in a new job assignment that is neither challenging nor highly visible in the company.

In the maintenance stage, challenging assignments can help to revitalise veteran employees by providing them with new challenges and opportunities for learning and contribution. Research on enriched jobs suggests that people are most responsive to them during the first one to three years on a job, when enriched jobs are likely to be seen as challenging and motivating.[30] People who have levelled off and remain on enriched jobs for three years or more tend to become unresponsive to them. They are no longer motivated and satisfied by jobs that have ceased to seem enriched. One way of preventing this loss of job motivation, especially among mid-career employees who are likely to remain on jobs for longer periods of time than people in the establishment and advancement phases, is to rotate people to new, more challenging jobs at about three-year intervals. An alternative is to redesign their jobs at these times. Such job changes would keep employees responsive to challenging jobs and sustain motivation and satisfaction during the maintenance phase.[31]

A growing body of research suggests that 'plateaued employees' (those with little chance of further advancement) can have satisfying and productive careers if they accept their new role in the company and are given challenging assignments with high performance standards.[32] Planned rotation to jobs that require new skills can provide that challenge. However, a firm's business strategy and human resource philosophy need to reinforce lateral (as opposed to strictly vertical) job changes if plateaued employees are to adapt effectively to their new jobs.[33] Firms with business strategies that emphasise stability and efficiency of operations, such as McDonald's, are likely to have more plateaued employees at the maintenance stage than companies with strategies promoting development and growth, such as Shell, BHP and National Bank Australia. The human resource systems of firms with stable growth strategies should be especially aimed at helping plateaued employees lower their aspirations for promotion and withdraw from the tournament mobility track. Moreover, such firms should enforce high performance standards so that high-performing plateaued employees (solid citizens) are rewarded and low performers (deadwood) encouraged to seek help or leave the firm.

Dual-career accommodations

These are practices for helping employees cope with the problems inherent in 'dual careers'—that is, both the employee and a spouse or significant other pursue full-time careers. Dual careers are becoming more prevalent as women increasingly enter the work force. It has been estimated that 58% of Australian married couples now have both partners in the labour force and, by contrast, only approximately 14% of families conform to the traditional family stereotype of male breadwinner with a stay-at-home wife.[34] Although these interventions can apply to all career stages, they are especially relevant during advancement. One of the biggest problems created by dual careers is job transfers, which are likely to occur during the advancement stage. Transfer to another location usually means that the working partner must also relocate. In many cases, the company employing the partner must either lose the employee or arrange a transfer to the same location. Similar problems can occur in recruiting employees. A recruit may not join an organisation if its location does not provide career opportunities for the partner.

Because partners' careers can affect the recruitment and advancement of employees, organisations are devising policies to accommodate dual-career employees. A survey of companies reported the following dual-career accommodations: recognition of problems in dual careers, help with relocation, flexible working hours, counselling for dual-career employees, family day-care centres, improved career planning and policies making it easier for two members of the same family to work in the same organisation or department.[35] Some companies have also established co-operative arrangements with other firms to provide sources of employment for the other partner.[36] General Electric, for example, has created a network of other firms to share information about job opportunities for dual-career couples. (Chapter 19 describes interventions aimed at inter-organisational networking.)

Consultative roles

These provide late-career employees with opportunities to apply their wisdom and knowledge to helping others develop and solve organisational problems. Such roles can be structured around specific projects or problems and they involve offering advice and expertise to those responsible for resolving the issues. For example, a large aluminium-forging manufacturer was having problems developing accurate estimates of the cost of producing new products. The sales and estimating departments did not have the production experience to make accurate bids for potential new business, thus either losing potential customers or losing money on products. The company temporarily assigned an old-line production manager who was nearing retirement to consult with the salespeople and estimators about bidding on new business. The consultant applied his years of forging experience to helping the sales and estimating people make more accurate estimates. In about a year, the salespeople and estimators gained the skills and invaluable knowledge necessary for making more accurate bids. Perhaps equally important, the pre-retirement production manager felt that he had made a significant contribution to the company, something he had not experienced for years.

In contrast to mentoring roles, consultative roles are not focused directly on guiding or sponsoring younger employees' careers. They are directed at helping others deal with complex problems or projects. Similarly, in contrast to managerial positions, consultative roles do not include the performance evaluation and control inherent in being a manager. They are based more on wisdom and experience than on managerial authority. Consequently, consultative roles provide an effective transition for moving pre-retirement managers into more support-staff positions. They free up managerial positions for younger employees while allowing older managers to apply their experience and skills in a more supportive and less threatening way than might be possible from a strictly managerial role.

When implemented well, consultative roles can increase the organisation's problem-solving capacity. They enable experienced employees to apply their skills and knowledge to resolving important problems. Consultative roles can also increase members' work satisfaction in the maintenance or withdrawal career stages. They provide senior employees with meaningful work as they begin to move from the work force to retirement.

Phased retirement

This provides older employees with an effective way of withdrawing from the organisation and establishing a productive leisure life. It includes various forms of part-time work.

Employees gradually devote less of their time to the organisation and more time to leisure pursuits (which to some might include developing a new career). Phased retirement allows older employees to make a gradual transition from organisational to leisure life. It enables them to continue to contribute to the firm while having the necessary time to establish themselves outside work. For example, people may use the extra time off work to take courses, to gain new skills and knowledge and to create opportunities for productive leisure. IBM, for example, offers tuition rebates for courses on any topic taken within three years of retirement.[37] Many IBM pre-retirees have used this programme to prepare for second careers.

Equally important, phased retirement lessens the reality shock often experienced by those who retire all at once. It helps employees to grow accustomed to leisure life and to withdraw emotionally from the organisation. A growing number of companies have some form of phased retirement.

Organisational decline and career halt

In recent years, Australia has experienced an enormous amount of organisation decline, downsizing and restructuring across a variety of smokestack, service, government and high-technology industries. Decreasing and uneven demand for products and services, growing numbers of mergers, acquisitions, divestitures and failures and increasing restructuring to operate leaner and more efficiently have resulted in lay-offs, reduced job opportunities and severe career disruptions for a large number of managers and employees.[38] In the US, between 1991 and 1994, the 25 largest downsizing firms eliminated more than 600 000 jobs.[39] An example in Australia is the ongoing restructuring of the financial services sector that saw one in two banking jobs eliminated by the year 2000 and is still continuing. Some 30 000 banking jobs were abolished between 1991 and 1997.[40]

The human costs of these changes and restructuring are enormous. People inevitably experience a halt in their career development and progression, resulting in dangerous increases in personal stress, financial and family disruption and loss of self-esteem. Fortunately, a growing number of organisations are managing decline in ways that are effective for both the organisation and the employee. One set of human resource practices involves alternatives to the lay-offs that typically occur when firms have to downsize or cut back operations.[41] For example, Polaroid has used job sharing; Hewlett-Packard has experimented with work sharing, in which members take cuts in pay and agree to work fewer hours; 3M has offered early retirement with full pension credit to 20-year employees who are at least 55 years old; Xerox has offered part-time consulting jobs to employees who agree to resign or retire early; and many firms have moved employees from unhealthy to healthy units and businesses within the organisation.

Organisations have also developed human resource practices for managing decline in those situations where lay-offs are unavoidable, such as plant closings, divestitures and business failures. The following methods can help people to deal more effectively with lay-offs and premature career halts:[42]

- *equitable lay-off policies* spread throughout organisational ranks, rather than focused on specific levels of employees, such as shop floor workers or middle managers
- *generous relocation and transfer policies* that help people to make the transition to a new work situation
- *helping people to find new jobs*, including outplacement services and help in retraining
- *treating people with dignity and respect*, rather than belittling or humiliating them because they are unfortunate enough to be in a declining business that can no longer afford to employ them
- *keeping people informed* about organisational problems and possibilities of lay-offs so that they can reduce ambiguity and prepare themselves for job changes
- *setting realistic expectations*, rather than offering excessive hope and promises, so that employees can plan for the organisation's future and for their own.

In today's environment, organisation decline, downsizing and restructuring can be expected to continue. OD practitioners are likely to become increasingly involved in helping people to manage career dislocation and halt. The methods described above can help organisations manage the human resource consequences of decline. However, considerably more research is needed to assess the effects of these strategies and to identify factors that contribute to their success. Because career disruption and halt can be extremely stressful, the interventions described in the section on employee wellness can play an important role in managing the human consequences of organisation decline.

Workforce diversity interventions

Several important trends are profoundly shaping the labour markets of modern organisations. Researchers suggest that workforce characteristics are radically different from what they were just 20 years ago. Employees represent every ethnic background and colour, range from highly educated to illiterate, vary in age from 18 to 80, may appear perfectly healthy or may have AIDS, may be a single parent or part of dual-income, divorced or traditional families and may be physically or mentally challenged.

Workforce diversity is more than a euphemism for cultural or ethnic differences. Such a definition is too narrow and focuses attention away from the broad range of issues that a diverse workforce causes. Diversity results from a mix of people who bring different resources and perspectives to the workplace and who have distinctive needs, preferences, expectations and life styles.[43] Organisations need to design human resource systems that account for these differences if they are to attract and retain a productive workforce and if they want to turn diversity into a competitive advantage.[44]

United States organisations have tended to address workforce diversity issues in a piecemeal fashion; only 5% of more than 1400 companies surveyed thought they were doing a 'very good job' of managing diversity.[45] As each trend makes itself felt, the organisation influences appropriate practices and activities. However, in Australia, the encouragement of more diverse workforces is part of major policy documents such as the Karpin Report and a range of state and federal statutes. The composition of the workforce will continue to change dramatically in the next ten years; specifically, it will continue to become more diverse as women and older workers play greater roles in the workplace.

Workforce diversity interventions are growing rapidly in OD. The number of training experts specialising in diversity quadrupled between 1990 and 1993,[46] and a national survey reveals that 75% of firms either have, or plan to begin, diversity efforts.[47] Research suggests that diversity interventions are especially prevalent in large organisations with diversity-friendly senior management and human resource policies.[48] Although existing evidence shows that diversity interventions are growing in popularity, there is still ambiguity about the depth of organisational commitment to such practices and their personal and organisational consequences. A great deal more research is needed to understand these newer interventions and their outcomes.

Many of the OD interventions described in this book can be applied to managing workforce diversity, as shown in Table 18.3, which summarises different dimensions of workforce diversity, including age, gender, disability, culture, values and sexual orientation.[49] The table also reports the major trends characterising those dimensions, organisational implications and workforce needs and specific OD interventions that can be used to address those implications.

Age

Australia's labour force is getting older. For both men and women the biggest projected increase in labour force numbers will occur in the group aged between 45 and 54. The greatest rate of growth is in the 50–64 age group followed by the 35–49 group.[50] This skewed distribution is mostly the result of the baby boom between 1946 and 1964. As a result, organisations will face a predominantly middle-aged and older workforce. Even now, many organisations are reporting that the average age of their workforce is over 40. Such a distribution will place special demands on the organisation.

TABLE 18.3	Workforce diversity dimensions and interventions		
Workforce differences	**Trends**	**Implications and needs**	**Interventions**
Age	Median age up Distribution of ages changing	Health care Mobility Security	Wellness program Job design Career planning and development Reward systems Job design
Gender	Percentage of women increasing Dual-income families	Child care Maternity/paternity leaves Single parents	Fringe benefit rewards
Disability	The number of people with disabilities entering the workforce is increasing	Job challenge Job skills Physical space Respect and dignity	Performance management Job design Career planning and development
Culture and values	Rising proportion of immigrant and minority-group workers Shift in rewards	Flexible organizational policies Autonomy Affirmation Respect	Career planning and development Employee involvement Reward systems
Sexual orientation	Number of single-sex households up More liberal attitudes toward sexual preference	Discrimination	Equal employment opportunities Fringe benefits Education and training

For example, the personal needs and work motivation of the different cohorts will require differentiated human resource practices. Older workers place heavy demands on health-care services, are less mobile and will have fewer career advancement opportunities. This situation will require specialised work designs that account for the physical capabilities of older workers, career development activities that address and use their experience and benefit plans that accommodate their medical and psychological needs. Research by Bennington and Tharenou indicates that negative stereotypes of the older workers—relating to absence, performance, memory, intelligence, ability to fit in and job satisfaction—are not true.[51] Demand for younger workers, on the other hand, will be intense. To attract and retain this more mobile group, jobs will need to be more challenging, advancement opportunities more prevalent and an enriched quality of work life more common.

Organisation development interventions, such as work design, wellness programmes (discussed below), career planning and development and reward systems will need to be adapted to these different age groups. For the older worker, work designs can reduce the physical components or increase the knowledge and experience components of a job. Younger workers will probably require more challenge and autonomy. Wellness programmes can be used to address the physical and mental health of both generations. Career planning and development programmes will need to recognise the different career stages of each cohort and offer resources tailored to that stage. Finally, reward system interventions can offer increased health benefits, time off and other perks for the older worker while using promotion, ownership and pay to attract and motivate the scarcer, younger workforce.

Unfortunately, older people have not received as much attention as some other disadvantaged groups. But there is a growing realisation that Australia cannot afford to have productive people leaving the workforce at the present rate. Regardless, one employer association has conceded that the prejudiced belief, 'If you are over 50, you are over the hill', persists. Disappointingly, recent research has found that HR managers held the most negative attitudes towards the employment of older workers.[52]

Gender

Another important trend is the increasing percentage of female workers in the labour force. By the year 2005, almost 48% of the US workforce will be women and they will represent about half of the new entrants between 1994 and 2005. In Australia, according to federal government statistics, women make up only 24% of Australia's managers and administrators and, although their participation rate continues to increase, they are predominantly represented in the low-paid occupations.[53] The organisational implications of such trends are sobering. Costs associated with absenteeism and turnover will most likely rise. In addition, demands for child care, maternity and paternity leaves and flexible-working arrangements will place pressure on work systems to maintain productivity and teamwork. From a management perspective, there will be more men and women working together as peers, more women entering the executive ranks, greater diversity of management styles and changing definitions of managerial success.

Work design, reward systems and career development are among the more important interventions for addressing issues that arise out of the gender trend. For example, jobs can be modified to accommodate the special demands of working mothers. A number of organisations have instituted job sharing, where two people perform the tasks associated with one job, to allow their female employees to pursue both family and work careers. Reward system interventions, especially fringe benefits, can be tailored to offer special leaves to both mothers and fathers, childcare options, flexible working hours and health and wellness benefits. Career development interventions help to maintain, develop and retain a competent and diverse workforce.[54] Organisations, such as Polaroid and Hoechst, have instituted job pathing, challenging assignments and mentoring programmes in efforts to retain key female members.

Disability

A third trend is the increasing number of disabled individuals entering the workforce. The workforce of the 21st century will be made up of people with a variety of physical and mental disabilities. More and more organisations will employ physically handicapped individuals, especially as the number of younger workers declines, creating a great demand for labour. According to the Australian Bureau of Statistics, there are approximately two million Australians with a disability. It is claimed that nine out of ten people with disabilities experience difficulty in finding work and are subjected to considerable discrimination.[55]

The organisational implications of the disability trend represent both opportunity and adjustment. The productivity of physically and mentally disabled workers often surprises managers,[56] and training is required to increase managers' awareness of this opportunity. Employing disabled workers, however, also necessitates more comprehensive healthcare, new physical workplace layouts, new attitudes toward working with the disabled and challenging jobs that use a variety of skills.

Organisation development interventions, including work design, career planning and development and performance management, can be used to integrate the disabled into the workforce. For example, traditional approaches to job design can simplify work to permit physically handicapped workers to complete an assembly task. Career planning and development programmes need to focus on making disabled workers aware of career opportunities. Too often, these employees do not know that advancement is possible and they are left feeling frustrated. Career tracks need to be developed for these workers.

Performance management interventions in alignment with the workforce's characteristics, including goal setting, monitoring and coaching performance, are important.

Culture and values

Immigration into Australia from the Pacific Rim, Central Europe, South America, Europe, Africa, the Middle East and the former Soviet states will drastically alter the cultural diversity of the workplace. In addition, these cultures represent a wide range of value orientations. There are more than 200 languages spoken in Australia. Sixteen per cent of Australians speak a language other than English at home.[57] Cultural diversity has broad organisational implications. Different cultures represent a variety of values, work ethics and norms of correct behaviour. Not all cultures want the same things from work, and simple, piecemeal changes in specific organisational practices will be inadequate if the workforce is culturally diverse. Management practices will need to be aligned with cultural values and support both career and family orientations. English is a second language for many people, and jobs of all types (processing, customer contact, production and so on) will need to be adjusted accordingly. Finally, the organisation will be expected to satisfy both extrinsic and monetary needs, as well as intrinsic and personal growth needs.

Several planned change interventions, including employee involvement, reward systems and career planning and development, can be used to adapt to cultural diversity. Employee involvement practices can be adapted to satisfy the needs for participation in decision making. People from certain cultures, such as Scandinavia, are more likely to expect and respond to high-involvement policies; other cultures, such as Latin America, view participation with reservation. (See the discussion of cultural values in Chapter 21.) Participation in an organisation can take many forms, ranging from suggestion systems and attitude surveys to high-involvement work designs and performance-management systems. By basing the amount of power and information that workers have on cultural and value orientations, organisations can maximise worker productivity.

Reward systems can focus on increasing flexibility. For example, flexible working hours allow employees to meet personal obligations without sacrificing organisational requirements by arriving and leaving work within specified periods. Many organisations have implemented this innovation,[58] and most report that the positive benefits outweigh the costs.[59] Work locations can also be varied. Many organisations allow workers to work at home by telecommuting part of the time. Other flexible benefits, such as floating holidays, allow people from different cultures to match important religious and family occasions with work schedules. Child-care and dependent-care assistance also support different lifestyles.

Finally, career planning and development programmes can help workers identify advancement opportunities that are in line with their cultural values. Some cultures value technical skills over hierarchical advancement, whereas others see promotion as a prime indicator of self-worth and accomplishment. By matching programmes with people, job satisfaction, productivity and employee retention can be improved.

Sexual orientation

Finally, diversity in sexual and affectionate orientation, including gay, lesbian and bisexual individuals and couples, is increasingly affecting the way that organisations think about human resources. Accurate data on the number of gays and lesbians in the workforce are difficult to obtain because laws and social norms do not support self-disclosure of a person's sexual orientation. However, related data suggest that this dimension of workforce diversity is gaining in significance.[60]

The primary organisational implication of sexual orientation diversity is discrimination. People tend to have strong emotional reactions to sexual orientation. When these feelings interact with the gender and culture and values trends described above, the likelihood of discrimination, both intended and unconscious, is high. An important aspect to this discrimination is the misperceived relationship between sexual preference and AIDS/HIV.

Interventions aimed at this dimension of workforce diversity are relatively new in OD and are still being developed, as organisations encounter sexual orientation issues in the workplace. The most frequent response is education and training. This intervention increases members' awareness of the facts and decreases the likelihood of overt discrimination. Human resource practices having to do with equal employment opportunity and fringe benefits can also help to address sexual orientation issues.

According to one recruitment consultant, some companies are targeting gay and lesbian personnel as they tend to be highly educated, mobile and have a reputation for honesty, loyalty and being conscientious, organised and well-presented.[61] Some organisations have modified their equal employment opportunity (EEO) statements to address sexual orientation. Firms such as Fujitsu and Dow Chemical have communicated strongly to members and outsiders that decisions with respect to hiring, promotion, transfer and so on cannot (and will not) be made with respect to an individual's sexual orientation. Similarly, organisations are increasingly offering 'domestic partner benefit' plans. Companies such as Microsoft and Apple have extended healthcare and other benefits to the same-sex partners of their members. A 1992 *Newsweek* poll found that 78% of the respondents favoured extending employee benefits to domestic partners of gays and lesbians.

Application 18.5 describes a prominent workforce diversity intervention at Denny's restaurants. After a series of embarrassing news reports and lawsuits over discriminatory practices, the company moved swiftly to make system-wide changes in its policies and practices.[62]

APPLICATION 18.5　　Denny's diversity turnaround

In the US, Denny's operates a national chain of restaurants positioned between quick-service outlets, like McDonald's and Taco Bell, and more up-scale restaurants, like Chile's and TGI Friday's. Not only has Denny's been struggling to survive in a highly competitive industry, it has been fighting to reverse a history of racism and other discriminatory policies that permeated the organization and were embedded in its culture, systems and structure. A consulting report in 1990 identified lack of diversity in top management as a key strategic issue. Denny's primary customers and many of its workers were not white; yet almost all its managers were white males. Although Denny's CEO acknowledged the report, he admitted that he had not really thought about it. Soon after, the company recruited its first female senior executive to run human resources, an institutional response that gave the appearance of change.

But the problems at Denny's were far deeper and more widespread than affirmative action quotas; they extended beyond the firm's employees to its customers. In one infamous incident, Denny's was accused of leaving six black Secret Service agents waiting nearly an hour for breakfast while white customers received prompt attention. In another, a white waitress who worked at several Denny's outlets in California was told by management to discourage black customers from staying in the restaurant too long. A white manager confirmed the problem: '"Blackout" was used by Denny's management to refer to a situation where too many black customers were in the restaurant.' When he tried to discontinue this discriminatory policy, his district manager threatened to fire him.

Adverse media attention and mounting legal problems finally forced Denny's to confront the magnitude of its problems and to seek significant changes. On 1 April 1 1993 the company settled a federal lawsuit for discriminating against African-American customers, eventually paying more than US$54 million to 295 000 customers and their lawyers. As part of the consent decree, Denny's promised to treat all customers equally in the future, to publicise its nondiscriminatory policies and to train employees in diversity issues. An independent civil-rights monitor was appointed to supervise Denny's for seven years and to investigate any further charges of discrimination.

Within months of the incident with the Secret Service agents, Ron Petty, former head of Burger King USA, arrived to repair Denny's image. He was subsequently joined by another Burger King executive, Jim Adamson, who was named CEO of Denny's parent company, Flagstar. Together, Petty and Adamson set out to transform Denny's culture and business practices, including management hiring, supplier policies, training, performance management, and employee selection and retention.

Adamson quickly assembled a dedicated team to address Denny's and Flagstar's culture. In his first meeting with members, he stated emphatically that he was 'going to do everything possible to provide better jobs for women and minorities. And I will fire you if you discriminate. Anyone who doesn't like the direction this train is moving had better jump off now.' Within months, all but four of the Company's top twelve officers left. Among their replacements were a Hispanic man and an African-American woman. Strategic personnel changes further down in the company included hiring Rachelle Hood-Phillips as head of diversity affairs; Norm Hill, a black male, as leader of human resources; and Magaly Peterson, a black female, as manager of minority development.

One of Peterson's first tasks was to change supplier policies about minority vendors. Flagstar had been nearly as insensitive to minority business people as it had been to its customers. Minority vendors were often ignored or given scant bidding information by the Company's buyers who claimed that the market did not contain qualified minority suppliers. After Peterson took over, purchasing agents were suddenly glad to give minority suppliers the information they needed to make competitive bids. Today, there is considerably more supplier co-operation and Peterson notes that she has had no problem locating nonwhite vendors for Denny's and its sister chains.

Under Petty and Adamson's leadership, Denny's also created a fast-track program to help minorities become franchisees. Applicants enrol in a training program for one to three years according to their experience. During this time, they gain skills, know-ledge and experience and are given the opportunity to show that they can successfully operate a restaurant. Every applicant who completes the training can buy a franchise with a loan guaranteed by Denny's. The first spot on the fast-track program went to a black man, previously a market manager at Kentucky Fried Chicken with responsibility for more than a dozen restaurants. Because of his experience, he raced through the basic thirteen-week management course in eight weeks. After spending a month working as an assistant restaurant manager, he asked to manage one of the least-profitable Denny's in the system. Despite management reluctance, he turned the restaurant around in a little over four months, producing profit margins of 17.2%, which are near the company average. With a loan guarantee from Denny's, he bought the franchise and hopes to own 20 more. 'I was skeptical about Denny's at first. But after a few months I knew that this company was really committed to helping minorities.'

As with most diversity interventions, Denny's developed training programs to give minorities entrance to the executive ranks and to improve members' responsiveness to diversity issues. This training played a significant role in raising awareness, allowing members to work on their attitudes and behaviors and providing support to new policies. Denny's diversity training reinforced the requirements of the consent decree forbidding discrimination. It combined legal information with customer-service guidelines, because the best way to avoid complaints is to treat everyone equally. Employees were required to attend the training sessions and refusal to do so was considered insubordination. 'We have fired people who have resisted the training,' says Norm Hill.

In addition to righting bad policies from the past, Denny's implemented hiring practices to ensure that the future workforce is more tolerant of diversity issues. It created a computerised interviewing technique called 'HR Easy' that seeks to screen job applicants for racial bias. Prospective employees dial an 800 number to answer a series of questions, including 'Have you ever used drugs?' 'Do you like dealing with people of different races?' 'Do you have a problem working with people of different races?' The program works on the assumption that it takes longer to tell a lie than to tell the truth. If the interviewee hesitates too long, a follow-up, face-to-face interview is scheduled.

So far, Denny's diversity efforts have helped to slow declining performance. Since 1993, the year of the worst racial incidents and performance results, operating income and customer traffic have both improved. Revenue growth has been slow, however, mainly because about 45 company-owned restaurants were sold to franchisees, many of them minorities. Says Adamson: 'When I leave, I want it said that I made Flagstar a much more inclusive, user-friendly company.' Trends in relevant data suggest that his wish may come true. The percentage of minority officers, vice-presidents and above, has risen from zero in 1993 to 11% in 1996. Minorities now hold 20% of the jobs directly below vice-president—no non-whites were in those positions in 1993. Of Denny's 512 franchisees, 27 are now owned by African-Americans, in contrast to one in 1993.

Employee wellness interventions

In the past decade, organisations have become increasingly aware of the relationship between employee wellness and productivity.[63] The estimated cost for medical treatment and loss of worker productivity for all diseases is more than \$150 billion per year.[64] Employee assistance programmes (EAPs) and stress management interventions have grown as organisations take more responsibility for the welfare of their employees. Companies such as Yahoo! and FAI Home Security, are sponsoring a wide variety of fitness and wellness programmes.[65]

In this section, we discuss two important wellness interventions—EAPs and stress management. EAPs are primarily reactive programmes. They identify, refer and treat employee problems, such as drug abuse, marital difficulties or depression, which impact on worker performance. Stress management is both proactive and reactive. It is concerned with helping employees alleviate or cope with the negative consequences of stress at work.

Employee assistance programmes

Forces affecting psychological and physical problems at the work place are increasing. In 1985, 8% of mayors, governors and CEOs of the *Fortune* 1000 said that substance abuse was a very significant problem. By 1989, that percentage had risen to 22%. More recently, a study suggested that one out of ten workers abuse drugs or alcohol and that each of those workers costs an employer about one-quarter of the worker's salary in lost productivity.[66] Britain's Royal College of Psychiatrists suggested that up to 30% of employees in British companies would experience mental health problems and that 115 million work days were lost each year due to depression.[67] Other factors, too, have contributed to increased problems. Altered family structures, the growth of single-parent households, the increase in divorce, greater mobility and changing modes of child rearing are all fairly recent phenomena that have added to the stress experienced by employees. These trends indicate that an increasing number of employees need assistance for a variety of personal problems. In response, the number of EAPs in *Fortune* 500 companies doubled between 1976 and 1986.[68] In addition, the research suggests that EAP use increases during downsizing and restructuring.[69]

FIGURE 18.2   An employee assistance programme (EAP)

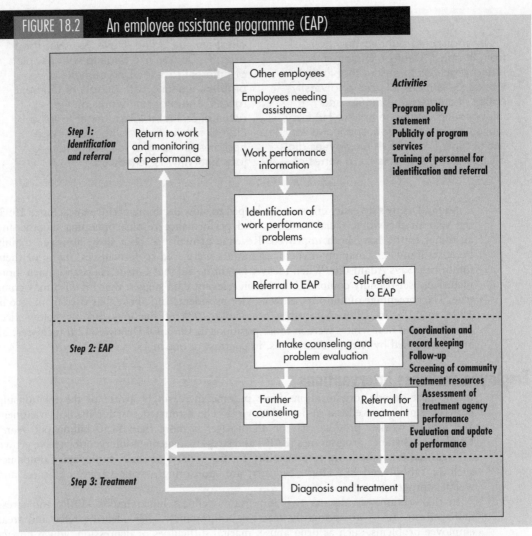

Employee assistance programmes help to identify, refer and treat employees whose personal problems affect their performance.[70] Initially started in the 1940s to combat alcoholism, these programmes have expanded to deal with emotional, family, marital and financial problems and, more recently, drug abuse. EAPs can be either broad programmes that address a full range of issues, or they can focus on specific problems, such as drug or alcohol abuse.

Central to the philosophy underlying EAPs is the belief that, although the organisation has no right to interfere in the private lives of its employees, it does have a right to impose certain standards of work performance and to establish sanctions when these are not met. Anyone whose work performance is impaired because of a personal problem is eligible for admission into an EAP programme. Successful EAPs have been implemented at General Motors, Johnson & Johnson, Motorola, BHP, Lendlease and Qantas. Although limited, some research has demonstrated that EAPs can positively affect absenteeism, turnover and job performance.[71]

The employee assistance programme model

Figure 18.2 displays the components of a typical EAP programme, including the identification and referral of employees into the programme, the management of the EAP process and diagnosis and treatment.

1 *Identification and referral.* The first step in an EAP is entry into the programme. This can occur through formal or informal referral. In the case of formal referrals, the process involves the identification of those employees who are having work performance problems and getting them to consider entering the EAP. Identification of problem employees is closely related to the performance management process discussed in Chapter 17. Performance records need to be maintained and corrective action taken whenever performance falls below an acceptable standard. During action planning to improve performance, managers can point out the existence of support services, such as the EAP. A formal referral takes place if the performance of an employee continues to deteriorate and the manager decides that EAP services are required. An informal referral occurs when an employee initiates admission to an EAP programme, even though performance problems may not exist or may not have been detected.

As shown in Figure 18.2, several organisational activities support this first step in the EAP process. First, a written policy with clear procedures regarding the EAP is necessary. Second, top management and the human resources department must publicly support the EAP, and publicity about the programme should be well distributed throughout the organisation. Third, training and development programmes should help supervisors to effectively identify and document performance problems, to carry out performance improvement action planning and to develop appropriate methods for suggesting and referring employees to the EAP. Finally, the confidentiality of employees using the programme must be safeguarded if it is to have the support of the workforce.

2 *EAP office.* The second component of an EAP is the work performed in the programme office, where people with problems are linked with treatment resources. The EAP office accepts the employee into the programme; provides problem evaluation and initial counselling; refers the employee to treatment resources and agencies; monitors the employee's progress during treatment; and reintegrates the employee into the workforce. In some EAPs, especially in large organisations, the actual counselling and treatment resources are located in-house. In most EAPs, however, the employee is referred to outside agencies that contract with the organisation to perform treatment services. In all cases, a clear procedure for helping the employee to return to the workforce is important and needs to be managed so as to maintain confidentiality.

The EAP programme itself needs to be managed if it is to be effective. For example, the programme's relationship to disciplinary procedures must be clear. In some organisations, corrective actions are suspended if the employee seeks EAP help. In others, the two processes are not connected. Maintaining confidential records and treatment information is also essential. In-house resources have the disadvantage of appearing to compromise this important programme element but may offer some cost savings. If external treatment resources are used, care must be taken to screen and qualify these resources.

3 *Treatment.* The third component is the treatment of the employee's problem. Potential resources include in-patient and out-patient care, social services and self-help groups. The resources tapped by EAPs will vary from programme to programme.

Implementing an employee assistance programme

EAPs can be flexible and customised to fit with a variety of organisational philosophies and employee problems. Practitioners have suggested seven steps to follow when establishing an EAP.[72]

1 *Develop an EAP policy and procedure.* Specific guidelines concerning the EAP and its availability to employees and their families need to be established. Policies concerning confidentiality, disciplinary procedures, communication, training and overall programme philosophy should be included. Senior management and union involvement (where appropriate) should be used in the development of the guidelines in order to gain commitment.

2 *Select and train a programme co-ordinator.* An individual should be designated by the organisation as the EAP co-ordinator. This person is responsible for the overall co-ordination of programme activities. This may include training, handling programme publicity, evaluating programme activities, troubleshooting to ensure the quick resolution of problems and providing ongoing programme support.

3 *Obtain employee/union support for the EAP.* It is critical for programme effectiveness to obtain employee or union support for EAP implementation. This can include meeting with key employee or union representatives to obtain their input into determining significant features of the EAP, including office location, staffing, participation in an EAP Advisory Committee and employee/union attendance at EAP training; to review significant policy and/or procedural components to ensure support; and to share endorsements from other organisations where EAPs have been implemented.

4 *Publicise the programme.* Communications about the EAP's availability and an increase in employee awareness of its procedures, resources and benefits should receive high priority. Both formal and informal referrals to the programme assume that managers and employees are aware of the programme's existence. If it is not well publicised, or if people do not know how to contact the programme office, then participation may be below expected levels.

5 *Establish relationships with healthcare providers and insurers.* All applicable health insurance policies should be reviewed to determine coverage for mental health and chemical dependency treatment. Although most policies include this coverage, reimbursement procedures often vary. This information needs to be summarised for EAP users so that all parties are aware of potential costs and responsibilities. EAP staff should be prepared to advise employees seeking treatment about the expected insurance coverage and any personal expenses related to treatment that may be incurred. Potential providers of EAP treatment services should be interviewed, screened and selected. Appropriate procedures need to be developed for making referrals and maintaining confidentiality.

6 *Schedule EAP training.* The legal climate surrounding EAPs, referrals and employee discipline requires that EAP training methods and materials be up-to-date and accurate. Training should include role-plays about handling difficult employees, as well as methods for referring workers to the programme.

7 *Administrative planning and management.* A plan should be developed for reviewing programme effectiveness. This typically involves auditing procedures, measuring system user satisfaction and determining whether treatment options need to be added or deleted. Ongoing training of EAP staff should also occur. This training needs to emphasise the changing legal requirements of EAPs, new counselling or treatment options, organisational changes that may impact on programme use and behaviours that focus on service quality.

Application 18.6 describes the evolution of an EAP and wellness programme at Johnson & Johnson.[73] It also demonstrates how such programmes can be implemented in large, decentralised organisations.

APPLICATION 18.6   Johnson & Johnson's employee assistance and Live for Life programmes

Johnson & Johnson (J&J) is the most diversified healthcare corporation in the world. It grosses more than US$6.5 billion a year and employs some 75 000 people at 165 companies in 56 countries. Its philosophy is embodied in a document called 'Our Credo'. A section of this document makes a commitment to the welfare of its employees.

The J&J companies are decentralized and directly responsible for their own operation. Corporate management is committed to this structure because of the many proven advantages to the businesses and people involved, such as the development of general managers, faster product development and a closer connection to the customer.

Based on a successful pilot project in the Ethicon division of J&J, top management decided to implement EAPs throughout the rest of the company. The J&J EAPs are in-house treatment programs that offer employees and family members confidential, professional assistance for problems related to alcohol and drug abuse, as well as marital, family, emotional and mental health problems. Treatment of the whole person underlies the counseling effort. The major goal is to help clients assume responsibility for their own behavior and, if it is destructive to themselves or others, to modify it. This process is supported with a variety of therapies that clearly recognize that any one method is not a panacea for the resolution of the client's problems. Employees can enter an EAP by self-referral or by counseling from their supervisor. The program emphasizes the necessity of maintaining complete confidentiality when counseling the employee or family member to protect both the client's dignity and job.

Johnson & Johnson's employee assistance program is publicly committed to resolving the major health problem in the country—substance abuse and addiction. The program is specifically designed to identify, intervene and treat substance abuse and addiction, as well as the family problems associated with this disease.

The implementation of EAPs throughout J&J was accomplished in three phases. The first phase consisted of contacting the managers and directors of personnel for each of the decentralized divisions. The EAP needs of the division were assessed and an educational process initiated to inform managers and directors about the employee assistance program. This EAP training was then conducted in each of the personnel departments of the divisions. The second phase included a formal presentation to the management board of each division. Information about the employee assistance program and about an alcohol and drug component for executives was presented. The third phase involved the development of cost estimates for EAP use and the employment of an EAP administrator to implement the program in each division. In addition, the corporate director of assistance programs established a quality assurance program to review all EAP activities biennially.

The EAPs were implemented between 1980 and 1985. More than 90% of all domestic employees have direct access to an EAP and the remaining employees have telephone access. There are employee assistance programs at all major J&J locations throughout the US, Puerto Rico and Canada. Programs are also operating in Brazil and England. A study of J&J's EAP in the New Jersey area showed that clients with drug, emotional or mental health problems who availed themselves of EAP services were treated at substantial savings to the company.

More recently, the employee assistance programs have been integrated with J&J's wellness program known as 'Live for Life'. This program was initiated by the chairman of the board in 1977. He committed to provide all employees and their families with the opportunity to become the healthiest employees of any corporation in the world. The Live for Life program offered classes in nutrition, weight reduction and smoking cessation. In addition, small gymnasiums with workout equipment, aerobics rooms and swimming pools were made available. Now known as 'Live for Life Assistance' programs, health, safety, benefits, wellness and employee assistance programs work together to promote employee well-being in the work place.

Stress management programmes

Concern has been growing in organisations about managing the dysfunction caused by stress. There is increasing evidence that work-related stress can contribute to a variety of ailments, such as tension headaches, backaches, high blood pressure, cardiovascular disease and mental illness. It can also lead to alcoholism and drug abuse, two problems that are reaching epidemic proportions in organisations and society. For organisations, these personal effects can result in costly health benefits, absenteeism, turnover and low performance. A recent study reported that one in three workers said they have thought about quitting because of stress; one in two workers said job stress reduces their productivity; and one in five workers said they had taken sick leave in the past month because of stress.[74] Another study estimates that each employee who suffers from a stress-related illness loses an average of 16 days of work per year.[75] Finally, the Research Triangle Institute estimated the cost to the US economy from stress-related disorders at US$87 billion per year. Other estimates are more conservative, but they invariably run into the billions of dollars.[76]

Like the other human resource management interventions, stress management is often carried out by practitioners who have special skills and knowledge in this area. These typically include psychologists, doctors and other health professionals specialising in work stress. Recently, some OD practitioners have gained competence in this area and there has been a growing tendency to include stress management as part of larger OD efforts. The concept of stress is best understood in terms of a model that describes the organisational and personal conditions contributing to the dysfunctional consequences of stress. Two key types of stress-management interventions may be employed: those aimed at the diagnosis or awareness of stress and its causes and those directed at changing the causes and helping people to cope with stress.

Definition and model

Stress refers to the reaction of people to their environments. It involves both physiological and psychological responses to environmental conditions, causing people to change or adjust their behaviours. Stress is generally viewed in terms of the fit between people's needs, abilities and expectations and environmental demands, changes and opportunities.[77] A good person–environment fit results in positive reactions to stress, whereas a poor fit leads to the negative consequences already described. Stress is generally positive when it occurs at moderate levels and contributes to effective motivation, innovation and learning. For example, a promotion is a stressful event that is experienced positively by most employees. On the other hand, stress can be dysfunctional when it is excessively high (or low) or persists over a long period of time. It can overpower people's coping abilities and exhaust them physically and emotionally. For example, a boss who is excessively demanding and unsupportive can cause subordinates undue tension, anxiety and dissatisfaction. These factors, in turn, can lead to withdrawal behaviours, such as absenteeism and turnover; to ailments, such as headaches and high blood pressure and to lowered performance. Situations like this one, where there is a poor fit between employees and the organisation, produce negative stress consequences.

A tremendous amount of research has been conducted on the causes and consequences of work stress. Figure 18.3 presents a model that summarises stress relationships. It identifies specific occupational stresses that may result in dysfunctional consequences. The individual differences among people determine the extent to which the stresses are

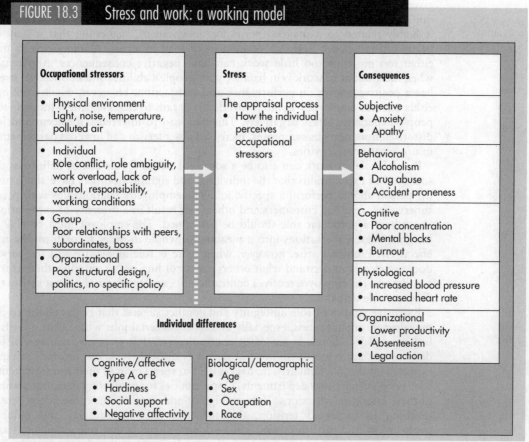

| FIGURE 18.3 | Stress and work: a working model |

Source: Reproduced by permission of the publisher from J. Gibson, J. Ivancevich and J. Donnelly Jr, *Organizations: Behaviours, Structure, Processes*, 8th ed. (Plano, Texas: Business Publications, 1994): 266.

perceived negatively. For example, people who have strong social support experience the stresses as less stressful than those who do not have such support. This greater perceived stress can lead to such negative consequences as anxiety, poor decision making, increased blood pressure and low productivity.

The stress model shows that almost any dimension of the organisation (e.g. working conditions, structure, role or relationships) can cause negative stress. This suggests that much of the material covered so far in this book provides knowledge about work-related stresses. Moreover, it implies that virtually all of the OD interventions included in the book can play a role in stress management. For example, process consultation, third-party intervention, survey feedback, inter-group relations, structural design, employee involvement, work design, goal setting, reward systems and career planning and development can all help to alleviate stressful working conditions. Thus, to some degree, stress management has been under discussion throughout this book. Here, the focus is upon those occupational stresses and stress-management techniques that are unique to the stress field and that have received the most systematic attention from stress researchers.

1 *Occupational stresses.* Figure 18.3 identifies several organisational sources of stress, including structure, role on the job, physical environment and relationships. Extensive research has been done on three key organisational sources of stress: the individual items related to work overload, role conflict and role ambiguity.

Work overload can be a persistent source of stress, especially among managers and white-collar employees who have to process complex information and make difficult decisions. Quantitative overload consists of having too much to do in a given time period. Qualitative overload refers to having work that is too difficult for one's abilities and knowledge. A review of the research suggests that work overload is highly related to managers' needs for achievement, suggesting that it may be partly self-inflicted.[78] Research relating work load to stress outcomes reveals that either too much or too little work can have negative consequences. Apparently, when the amount of work is in balance with people's abilities and knowledge, stress has a positive impact on performance and satisfaction. However, when workload either exceeds employees' abilities (overload) or fails to challenge them (underload), people experience stress negatively. This can lead to lowered self-esteem and job dissatisfaction, nervous symptoms, increased absenteeism and lowered participation in organisational activities.[79]

People's roles at work can also be a source of stress. A role can be defined as the sum total of expectations that the individual and significant others have about how the person should perform a specific job. The employee's relationships with peers, supervisors, vendors, customers and others can result in a diversity of expectations about how a particular role should be performed. The employee must be able to integrate these expectations into a meaningful whole in order to perform the role effectively. Problems arise, however, when there is role ambiguity and the person does not clearly understand what others expect of him or her, or when there is role conflict and the employee receives contradictory expectations and cannot satisfy the different role demands.[80]

Extensive studies of role ambiguity and conflict suggest that both conditions are prevalent in organisations, especially among managerial jobs where clarity is often lacking and job demands are often contradictory.[81] For example, managerial job descriptions are typically so general that it is difficult to know precisely what is expected on the job. Similarly, managers tend to spend most of their time interacting with people from other departments. Opportunities for conflicting demands abound in these lateral relationships. Role ambiguity and conflict can cause severe stress, resulting in increased tension, dissatisfaction and withdrawal and reduced commitment and trust in others. Some evidence suggests that role ambiguity has a more negative impact on managers than role conflict. In terms of individual differences, people with a low tolerance for ambiguity respond more negatively to role ambiguity than others; introverts and individuals who are more flexible react more negatively to role conflict than do others.[82]

2 *Individual differences.* Figure 18.3 identifies several individual differences that affect how people respond to occupational stresses. These include hardiness, social support, age, education, occupation, race, negative affectivity and Type A behaviour pattern. Much research has been devoted to the Type A behaviour pattern, which is characterised by impatience, competitiveness and hostility. Type A personalities (in contrast to Type Bs) tend to invest long hours working under tight deadlines. They put themselves under extreme time pressure by trying to do more and more work in less and less time. Type B personalities, on the other hand, are less hurried, aggressive and hostile than Type As. Considerable research shows that Type A people are especially prone to stress. For example, a longitudinal study of 3500 men found that Type As had twice as much heart disease, five times as many second heart attacks and twice as many fatal heart attacks as Type Bs.[83] Researchers explain Type A susceptibility to stress in terms of an inability to deal with uncertainty, such as might occur with qualitative overload and role ambiguity. To work rapidly and meet pressing deadlines, Type As need to be in control of the situation. They do not allocate enough time for unforeseen disturbances and consequently experience extreme tension and anxiety when faced with unexpected events.[84]

Unfortunately, the proportion of Type A managers in organisations may be quite large. One study showed that 60% of the managers were clearly Type A and only 12% were distinctly Type B.[85] In addition, a short questionnaire measuring Type A behaviours and given to members of several MBA classes and executive programmes has found that Type As outnumber Type Bs by about five to one. These results are not totally surprising, because many organisations (and business schools) reward aggressive, competitive, workaholic behaviours. Indeed, Type A behaviours can help managers to achieve rapid promotion in many companies. Ironically, those behaviours may be detrimental to effective performance at top organisational levels. Here, tasks and decision making require the kind of patience, tolerance for ambiguity and attention to broad issues often neglected by Type As.

Diagnosis and awareness of stress and its causes

Stress management is directed at preventing negative stress outcomes by either changing the organisational conditions that cause stress or by enhancing employees' abilities to cope with them. This preventive approach starts from a diagnosis of the current situation, including the employees' self-awareness of their own stress and its sources. This provides the information necessary to develop an appropriate stress-management programme.[86] Two methods for diagnosing stress are the following:

1 *Charting stresses.* This involves identifying organisational and personal stresses that operate in a particular situation. It is guided by a conceptual model like that shown in Figure 18.3 and measures potential stresses that affect employees negatively. Data can be collected through questionnaires and interviews about environmental and personal stresses. Researchers at the University of Michigan's Institute for Social Research have developed standardised instruments for measuring most of the stresses shown in Figure 18.3. It is important to obtain perceptual measures, as people's cognitive appraisal of the situation makes a stressor stressful. Most organisational surveys measure dimensions that are potentially stressful to employees, such as work overload, role conflict and ambiguity, promotional issues, opportunities for participation, managerial support and communication. Similarly, there are specific instruments for measuring the individual differences, such as hardiness, social support and Type A or B behaviour pattern. In addition to perceptions of stresses, it is necessary to measure stress consequences, such as subjective moods, performance, job satisfaction, absenteeism, blood pressure and cholesterol level. Various instruments and checklists have been developed for obtaining people's perceptions of negative consequences, and these can be supplemented with empirical data taken from company records, medical reports and physical examinations. Once measures of the stresses and consequences have been obtained, it is necessary to relate the two sets of data. This will reveal which stresses contribute most to negative stress in the situation under study. For example, a relational analysis might show that qualitative overload and role ambiguity are highly related to employee fatigue, absenteeism and poor performance, especially for Type A employees. This kind of information points to specific organisational conditions that need to be improved to reduce stress. Moreover, it identifies the kinds of employees who may need special counselling and training in stress management.

2 *Health profiling.* This method is aimed at identifying stress symptoms so that corrective action can be taken. It starts with a questionnaire asking people for their medical history, personal habits, current health and vital signs, such as blood pressure, cholesterol and triglyceride levels. It may also include a physical examination if some of the information is not readily available. Information from the questionnaire and physical examination is then analysed, usually by a computer that calculates a person's health profile. This compares the individual's characteristics with those of an average person of the same sex, age and race. The profile identifies the person's future health prospect, typically by placing her or him in a health-risk category with a known probability of fatal disease, such as cardiovascular. The health profile also indicates how the health risks can be reduced by personal and environmental changes, such as dieting, exercising or travelling.

Many firms cannot afford to do their own health profiling and contract with health firms to do it on a fee basis per employee. Other firms have extensive in-house health and stress-management programmes. At one programme, health profiling was an initial diagnostic step. Each participant first went through a rigorous physical and medical history examination, which determined their health risks and was used to prescribe an individualised health programme. Company officials reported that the programme had positive results: 'It has generated good public interest, helped recruiting efforts and provided better all-around fitness for participants in the programme. Individual health screening has uncovered six cases of early-stage cancer and a number of cases of high blood pressure and heart disease.'[87]

Alleviating stresses and coping with stress

After diagnosing the presence and causes of stress, the next stage of stress management is to do something about it. Interventions for reducing negative stress tend to fall into two groups: those aimed at changing the organisational conditions that cause stress and those directed at helping people to cope better with stress. Because stress results from the interaction between people and the environment, both strategies are necessary for effective stress management.

This section first presents two methods for alleviating stressful organisational conditions: role clarification and supportive relationships. These are aimed at decreasing role ambiguity and conflict and improving poor relationships, key sources of managerial stress. Then, two interventions aimed at helping people to better cope with stress are discussed: stress inoculation training and health facilities. These can help employees alleviate stress symptoms and prepare themselves for handling stressful situations.

1 *Role clarification.* This involves helping employees better understand the demands of their work roles. A manager's role is embedded in a network of relationships with other managers; each has specific expectations about how the manager should perform the role. Role clarification is a systematic process for finding out others' expectations and arriving at a consensus about the activities constituting a particular role. There are a variety of role-clarification methods, such as job-expectation (JET)[88] and role-analysis techniques (RAT).[89] They follow a similar strategy. First, the people relevant to defining a particular role are identified (e.g. members of a managerial team, a boss and subordinate and members of other departments relating to the role holder) and brought together at a meeting, usually away from the organisation.

Second, the role holder is given the opportunity to discuss his or her perceived job duties and responsibilities. The other participants are encouraged to comment and to agree or disagree with the perceptions. An OD practitioner may be present and may act as a process consultant to facilitate interaction and reduce defensiveness. Third, when everyone has reached consensus on defining the role, the role holder is responsible for writing a description of the activities that are now seen as constituting the role. A copy of the role description is distributed to the participants to ensure that they fully understand and agree with the role definition. Fourth, the participants periodically check to see whether the role is being performed as intended and make modifications if necessary.

Role clarification can be used for defining a single role or the roles of members of a group. It has been used in such companies as Alcoa, Johnson & Johnson and Honeywell to help management teams arrive at agreed-upon roles for members. The process is generally included as part of initial team-building meetings for new management teams starting high-involvement plants. Managers share perceptions and negotiate about one another's roles as a means of determining areas of discretion and responsibility. Role clarity is particularly important in new plant situations where managers are trying to implement participative methods. The ambiguity of such settings can be extremely stressful and role clarification can reduce stress by helping managers translate such ambiguous concepts as 'involvement' and 'participation' into concrete role behaviours.

Research on role clarification supports these benefits. One study found that it reduced stress and role ambiguity and increased job satisfaction.[90] Another study reported that it improved interpersonal relations among group members and contributed to improved production and quality.[91] These findings should be interpreted carefully, however, as both studies had weak research designs and used only perceptual measures.

2 *Supportive relations.* This involves establishing trusting and genuinely positive relations among employees, including bosses, subordinates and peers. Supportive relations have been a hallmark of organisation development and are a major part of such interventions as team building, inter-group relations, employee involvement, work design, goal setting and career planning and development. Considerable research shows that supportive relations can buffer people from stress.[92] When people feel that relevant others really care about what happens to them and are willing to help, they can better cope with stressful conditions. The pioneering coal mining studies that gave rise to the sociotechnical systems theory found that miners needed the support from a cohesive work group to deal effectively with the stresses of underground mining.

Recent research on the boss–subordinate relationship suggests that a supportive boss can provide subordinates with a crucial defence against stress. This research suggests that organisations need to become more aware of the positive value of supportive relationships in helping employees to cope with stress. They may need to build supportive, cohesive work groups in situations that are particularly stressful, such as the introduction of new products, solving emergency problems and handling customer complaints. For example, firms such as Procter & Gamble and Alcoa have recognised that internal OD consultation can be extremely stressful and they have encouraged internal OD practitioners to form support teams to help each other better cope with the demands of the role. Equally important, organisations need to direct more attention to ensuring that managers provide the support and encouragement necessary to help subordinates cope with stress.

3 *Stress inoculation training.* Companies have developed programmes to help employees gain the skills and knowledge to better cope with stresses. Participants are first taught to understand stress-warning signals, such as difficulty in making decisions, disruption in sleeping and eating habits and a greater frequency of headaches and backaches. Then they are encouraged to admit that they are over-stressed (or under-stressed) and to develop a concrete plan for coping with the situation. One strategy is to develop and use a coping self-statement procedure. Participants verbalise a series of questions or statements each time they experience negative stress. The following sample questions or statements address the four stages of the stress-coping cycle: preparation ('What am I going to do about these stresses?'), confrontation ('I must relax and stay in control'), coping ('I must focus on the present set of stresses') and self-reinforcement ('I handled it well').[93]

Stress inoculation training is aimed at helping employees cope with stress, rather than at changing the stresses themselves. Its major value is sensitising people to stress and preparing them to take personal action. Self-appraisal and self-regulation of stress can free employees from total reliance on others for stress management. Given the multitude of organisational conditions that can cause stress, such self-control is a valuable adjunct to interventions that are aimed at changing the conditions themselves.

4 *Health facilities.* A growing number of organisations are providing facilities for helping employees cope with stress. Elaborate exercise facilities are maintained by such firms as Xerox and Pepsico. Similarly, more than 500 companies (e.g. Exxon, Mobil and Chase Manhattan Bank) operate corporate cardiovascular fitness programmes. Before starting such programmes, employees are required to take an exercise tolerance test and to have the approval of either a private or a company doctor. Each participant is then assigned a safe level of heart response to the various parts of the fitness programme. Preliminary evidence suggests that fitness

programmes can reduce absenteeism and coronary risk factors, such as high blood pressure, body weight, percentage of body fat and triglyceride levels.[94] A recent review of the research, however, suggests that fitness programmes primarily result in better mental health and resistance to stress, and that organisational improvements, such as reduced absenteeism and turnover and improved performance, are more questionable.[95]

In addition to exercise facilities, some companies, such as McDonald's and Equitable Life Assurance, provide biofeedback facilities. Managers take relaxation breaks, using biofeedback devices to monitor respiration and heart rate. Feedback of such data helps managers to lower their respiration and heart rate. Other companies provide time for employees to meditate. Still other firms have stay-well programmes.

Application 18.7 presents an example of utilising the Stress Arousal Checklist (SACL) at Melbourne Water Corporation.[96]

Dealing with stress at Melbourne Water Corporation

The Corporation, a semi-government body, which in the early 1990s had undergone major reorganisation into three regional businesses, had seen staff reduced from 9000 to 2400 in five years.

One of the regional businesses recognised that its staff had undergone considerable pain as a result of the change processes. What is of particular interest is that employees experienced stress in different ways and that there were different experiences of stress in different parts of the organisation. The investigation of these experiences, while they were facilitated by consultants, involved bringing senior management into direct contact with staff as the project proceeded.

It began with the administration of a simple (voluntary and confidential) test, which assumed that workers might

respond to change situations within two kinds of emotional range—arousal (or excitement) and stress. Combinations of these states could be represented on a grid of the kind set out below.

Scoring on the *Stress Arousal Checklist* (SACL) allowed workers, and those supporting them, some insights into the way they had been dealing with the changes in the Corporation. Individuals with special needs could seek help from medical or counselling staff who had been made available.

In addition to individual assistance, focus groups were set up in each branch of the business to identify the sources of pressure and how they might be dealt with. Not unexpectedly, those dealing with customers on a day-to-day basis were under the greatest stress. Even within groups some individuals acted as

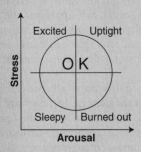

Source: *HR Monthly*, March 1995.

'buffer zones' that protected other members of the group. What kind of programmes should a responsive HR manager implement, once groups such as these identify problems? Perhaps not as high-powered as one might expect, if we follow the suggestions of one of the consultants, Patrick Farrell:

'In the majority of instances, what was not done was the traditional programme focus. A small number of skills-based stress management sessions were conducted, but the most effective responses were simple, human-scale interventions that addressed the people dimension of the experience of work. These included such things as more effective recognition schemes, social events and opportunities to interact more with peers. Perhaps the most important step was putting the whole issue on the table as a valid source of enquiry and concern for managers ... A repeat of the SACL tests and focus groups four months later revealed a significant lowering of stress levels and increased arousal levels.'

Summary

This chapter presented three major human resource interventions: career planning and development, workforce diversity interventions and employee wellness programmes. Although these kinds of change programmes are generally carried out by human resource specialists, a growing number of OD practitioners are gaining competence in these areas and the interventions are increasingly being included in OD programmes.

Career planning involves helping people choose occupations, organisations and jobs at different stages of their careers. Employees typically pass through four different career stages—establishment, advancement, maintenance and withdrawal—with different career planning issues relevant to each stage. Major career planning practices include communication, counselling, workshops, self-development materials and assessment programmes. Career planning is a highly personalised process that includes assessing one's interests, values and capabilities; examining alternative careers; and making relevant decisions.

Career development helps employees achieve career objectives. Effective career development includes linking corporate business objectives, human resource needs and the personal needs of employees. Different career development needs and practices exist and are relevant to each of the four stages of people's careers.

Workforce diversity interventions are designed to adapt human resource practices to an increasingly diverse workforce. Demographic, gender, disability and culture and values trends all point to a more complex set of human resource demands. Within this context, OD interventions such as job design, performance management and employee involvement practices have to be adapted to a diverse set of personal preferences, needs and lifestyles.

Employee wellness interventions, such as employee assistance programmes and stress management, recognise the important link between worker health and organisational productivity. EAPs identify, refer and treat employees and their families for a variety of problems. These include marital problems, drug and alcohol abuse, emotional disturbances and financial difficulties. EAPs preserve the dignity of the individual, but also recognise the organisations' right to expect certain work behaviours. EAPs typically include these activities:

- identifying and referring an employee to the programme
- accepting the employee into the programme, monitoring the employee's progress in treatment and reintegrating the employee into the workforce
- diagnosis and treatment.

Stress management is concerned with helping employees to cope with the negative consequences of stress at work. The concept of stress involves the fit between people's needs, abilities and expectations and environmental demands, changes and opportunities. A good person–environment fit results in positive reactions to stress, such as motivation and innovation, whereas a poor fit results in negative effects, such as headaches, backache and cardiovascular disease. A model for understanding work-related stress includes occupational stresses; individual differences, which affect how people respond to the stresses and negative stress outcomes. Occupational stresses include work overload and role ambiguity and conflict. People with a Type A behaviour pattern, which is characterised by impatience, competitiveness and hostility, are especially prone to stress. The two main stages of stress-management are diagnosing stress and its causes and alleviating stresses and helping people to cope with stress. Two methods for diagnosing stress are charting stresses and health profiling. Techniques for alleviating stressful conditions include role clarification and supportive relationships; stress inoculation training and health facilities are ways of helping employees better cope with stress.

 ACTIVITIES

Review questions
1 Define career planning and explain the basic methods used.
2 Implementing a career planning program includes what strategies?
3 What are the trends indicative of increasing workforce diversity?
4 Which OD intervention is most appropriate when addressing a diverse workforce?
5 What is the underpinning philosophy of EAPs, and what are the key steps in implementation?
6 What is(are) the characteristic(s) of stress? Explain the organisational sources of stress.
7 What is stress management primarily concerned with?
8 What are the strategies for role clarification?

Discussion and essay questions
1 Compare and contrast career development and career planning.
2 Describe and discuss the impact of increasing diversity on organisations and OD.
3 What are the costs and benefits of implementing an employee assistance programme?

Notes

1 J. Fierman, 'Beating the mid-life career crisis', *Fortune* (6 September 1993): 52–62; L. Richman, 'How to get ahead in America', *Fortune* (16 May 1994): 46–54.
2 Anonymous, 'Catalysts for career development: four case studies', *Training & Development*, 47:11 (1993), 26.
3 G. Strachan and J. Burgess, 'Towards a new deal for women workers in Australia? Growing employment share, enterprise bargaining and the "family friendly" workplace', *Equal Opportunity International*, 17:8 (1998), 1–13.
4 D. Hall and J. Goodale, *Human Resource Management: Strategy, Design and Implementation* (Glenview, Ill.: Scott, Foresman, 1986): 392.
5 D. Feldman, *Managing Careers in Organizations* (Glenview, Ill.: Scott Foresman, 1988).
6 E. Erikson, *Childhood and Society* (New York: Norton, 1963); G. Sheehy, *Passages: Predictable Crises of Adult Life* (New York: E.P. Dutton, 1974); D. Levinson, *Seasons of a Man's Life* (New York: Alfred A. Knopf, 1978); R. Gould, *Transformations: Growth and Change in Adult Life* (New York: Simon and Schuster, 1978).
7 D. Super, *The Psychology of Careers* (New York: Harper and Row, 1957); D. Hall, *Careers in Organizations* (Santa Monica, Calif.: Goodyear, 1976); E. Schein, *Career Dynamics: Matching Individual and Organizational Needs* (Reading, Mass.: Addison-Wesley, 1978); L. Baird and K. Kram, 'Career dynamics: the superior/subordinate relationship', *Organizational Dynamics*, 11 (Spring 1983): 46–64; J. Slocum and W. Cron, 'Job attitudes and performance during three

career stages', (working paper, Edwin L. Cox School of Business, Southern Methodist University, Dallas, 1984).

8 D. James 'Playing the regional game' in R. Stone, *Readings in Human Resource Management*, 3 (Jacaranda Wiley 1998): 154

9 M. McGill, 'Facing the mid–life crisis', *Business Horizons,* 16 (November 1977): 5–13.

10 D. Anfuso, 'Colgate's global HR unites under one strategy', *Personnel Journal,* 74 (10, 1995): 44–48; D. McNamara, 'Developing global human resource competencies', presentation to the Conference Board Quality Council II, 11 April, 1996, Chicago, Ill.

11 B. Rosen and T. Jeered, 'Too old or not too old', *Harvard Business Review,* 55 (November–December 1977): 97–106.

12 J. Wanes, 'Realistic job previews for organizational recruitment', *Personnel,* 52 (1975): 58–68.

13 J. Wanes, 'Effects of a realistic job preview on job acceptance, job attitudes and job survival', *Journal of Applied Psychology,* 58 (1973): 327–32; J. Wanes, 'Realistic job previews: can a procedure to reduce turnover also influence the relationship between abilities and performance?' *Personnel Psychology,* 31 (Summer 1978): 249–58; S. Premark and J. Wanes, 'A meta–analysis of realistic job preview experiments', *Journal of Applied Psychology,* 70 (1985): 706–19.

14 B. Merlin, A. Dennis, S. Youngblood and K. Williams, 'Effects of realistic job previews: a comparison using an enhancement and a reduction preview', *Journal of Applied Psychology,* 73 (1988): 259–66; J. Vandenberg and V. Scarpello, 'The matching method: an examination of the processes underlying realistic job previews', *Journal of Applied Psychology,* 75 (1990): 60–67.

15 D. James, 'Managing', *Business Review,* 24 August 1998, 68.

16 D. Bray, R. Campbell and D. Grant, *Formative Years in Business: A Long Term AT&T Study of Managerial Lives* (New York: John Wiley and Sons, 1974).

17 F. Balcazar, B. Hopkins and Y. Suarez, 'A critical objective review of performance feedback', *Journal of Organizational Behaviour Management,* 7 (1986): 65–89; J. Chobbar and J. Wallin, 'A field study on the effect of feedback frequency on performance', *Journal of Applied Psychology,* 69 (1984): 524–30; R. Waldersee and F. Luthans, 'A theoretically based contingency model of feedback: implications for managing service employees', *Journal of Organizational Change Management,* 3 (1990): 46–56.

18 G. Thornton, *Assessment Centres* (Reading, Mass.: Addison-Wesley, 1992); A. Engelbrecht and H. Fischer, 'The managerial performance implications of a developmental assessment center process', *Human Relations,* 48:4 (1995): 387–404.

19 Thornton, *Assessment Centres, op. cit.*; P. Griffiths and P. Goodge, 'Development centres: the third generation', *Personnel Management,* 26:6 (1994): 40–43.

20 R. Jones and M. Whitmore, 'Evaluating developmental assessment centres as interventions', *Personnel Psychology,* 48 (1995): 377–88.

21 M. Lawson, 'Assessing 'real' coordination', *Australian Financial Review,* 2 August 1996, 15.

22 A. Gome, 'Work equity in 'phase two', maybe', *Business Review Weekly,* 18 June 1999, 40.

23 J. Clawson, 'Mentoring in managerial careers' in *Family and Career,* ed. C.Derr (New York: Praeger, 1980); K. Kram, *Mentoring at Work* (Glenview, Ill.: Scott, Foresman, 1984); A. Geiger–DuMond and S. Boyle, 'Mentoring: a practitioner's guide', *Training and Development* (March 1995): 51–54.

24 E. Collins and P. Scott, 'Everyone who makes it has a mentor', *Harvard Business Review,* 56 (July–August 1978): 100.

25 Anonymous, 'Mentoring, recruiting and financing in New Zealand and Australia', *Limra's Marketfacts,* 16(3):5, 1997.

26 Hall and Goodale, *Human Resource Management, op. cit.,* 373–74.

27 B. Ragins and J. Cotton, 'Jumping the hurdles: barriers to mentoring for women in organizations', *Leadership & Development Journal,* 17:3 (1996), 37–41.

28 See, for example, D. Kolb, D. Rubin and J. McIntyre, *Organizational Psychology: Readings on Human Behavior in Organizations,* 4th ed. (New York: Prentice-Hall, 1984).

29 D. Hitchin, 'Midlaning: a method for work–life balance planning', (working paper, Pepperdine University, Culver City, Calif., 1996).

30 R. Katz, 'Time and work: towards an integrative perspective', in *Research in Organizational Behavior,* 2, eds B. Staw and L. Cummings (New York: JAI Press, 1979): 81–127.

31 K. Brousseau, 'Toward a dynamic model of job–person relationships: findings, research questions and implications for work system design', *Academy of Management Review,* 8 (January 1983): 33–45.

32 J. Carnazza, A. Korman, T. Ference and J. Stoner, 'Plateaued and non-plateaued managers: factors in job performance', *Journal of Management,* 7 (1981): 7–27.

33 J. Slocum, W. Cron, R. Hansen and S. Rawlings, 'Business strategy and the management of the plateaued performer', *Academy of Management Journal,* 28 (1985): 133–54.

34 J. Pierce and B. Delahaye, 'Human resource management implications of dual–career couples', *The International Journal of Human Resource Management,* 7:4 (1996), 905–23.

35 D. Hall and M. Morgan, 'Career development and planning' in *Contemporary Problems in Personnel,* 3rd ed., eds K. Pearlman, F. Schmidt and W. Hamnek (New York: John Wiley and Sons, 1983): 232–33.

36 M. Bekas, 'Dual-career couples—a corporate challenge', *Personnel Administrator* (April 1984): 37–44.

37 J. Ivancevich and W. Glueck, *Foundations of Personnel/Human Resource Management,* 3rd ed. (Plano, Tex.: Business Publications, 1986): 541.

38 J. Nocera, 'Living with lay-offs', *Fortune* (1 April 1996): 69–71.

39 J. Byrne, 'The pain of downsizing', *Business Week* (9 May 1994).

40 Anonymous, 'Job pressure for finance sector executives continues', *Australian Accountant,* 68(11):13, 1998.

41 L. Perry, 'Least-cost alternatives to lay-offs in declining industries', *Organizational Dynamics,* 14 (1986): 48–61; J. Treece, 'Doing it right, till the last whistle', *Business Week* (6 April 1992): 58–59.

42 D. Cook and G. Ferris, 'Strategic human resource management and firm effectiveness in industries experiencing decline', *Human Resource Management,* 25 (Fall 1986): 441–58; R. Sutton, K. Eisenhardt and J. Jucker, 'Managing organizational decline: lessons from Atari', *Organizational Dynamics,* 14 (Spring 1986): 17–29; K. Cameron, S. Freeman and A. Mishra, 'Best practices in white–collar downsizing: managing contradictions', *The Academy of Management Executive,* 5 (1991): 57–73; K. Cameron, 'Strategies for successful organizational downsizing', *Human Resource Management,* 33 (1994): 189–212.

43 D. Jamieson and J. O'Mara, *Managing Workforce 2000: Gaining the Diversity Advantage* (San Francisco: Jossey-Bass).

44 F. Rice, 'How to make diversity pay', *Fortune* (8 August 1994): 78–86; R. Thomas Jr, 'From affirmative action to affirming diversity', *Harvard Business Review* (March–April 1990): 107–17.

45 Rice, 'How to make diversity pay', *op. cit.,* 79.

46 K. Murray, 'The unfortunate side effects of diversity training', *The New York Times* (1 August 1993): Section 3, 5.

47 P. Towers, *Workforce 2000 Today: A Bottom-line Concern—Revisiting Corporate Views on Workforce Change* (New York: Author, 1992).

48 S. Rynes and B. Rosen, 'A field survey of factors affecting the adoption and perceived success of diversity training', *Personnel Psychology,* 48 (1995): 247–70.

49 The statistics cited in support of each trend and the organizational implications are derived from a variety of sources, including: Thomas Jr, 'From affirmative action to affirming diversity', *op. cit.*; C. Trost, 'New approach forced by shifts in population', *Wall Street Journal* (22 November 1989): B1, B4; M. Greller, 'The changing workforce and organization effectiveness: an agenda for change', *Journal of Organization Change Management,* 3 (1990): 4–15; M. Graddick, E. Bassman and J. Giordano, 'The changing demographics: are corporations prepared to meet the challenge?' *Journal of Organization Change Management,* 3 (1990): 72–79; Jamieson and O'Mara, *Managing Workforce 2000, op. cit.*; 'Human capital: the decline of America's work force', *Business Week* (19 September 1988): 100, 141; 'Managing now for the 1990's', *Fortune* (26 September 1989): 46; F. Chessman and associates, *Leadership for Literacy: The Agenda for the 1990s* (San Francisco: Jossey-Bass, 1990). In addition, this section benefited greatly from the advice and assistance of Pat Pope, president of Pope and Associates, Cincinnati, Ohio.

50 B. Holmes and S. Linder-Plez, 'Managing your ageing baby boomers', *HR Monthly* (October 1996): 10–13.

51 L. Bennington and P. Tharenou, 'Older workers: myths, evidence and implications for Australian managers', *Asia Pacific Journal of Human Resources,* 34:3 (1986): 63–76.

52 S. Wilson, 'Encouraging an age neutral culture', *Management* (April 1996): 13–16.

53 A. Ferguson, 'Karpin criticisms add weight to affirmative action push', *Business Review Weekly,* 17:18 (1995): 66.

54 M. Galen, 'Equal opportunity diversity: beyond the numbers game', *Business Week* (14 August 1995).

55 D. Stone, 'More opportunities sought for disabled', *Weekend Australian* (8 September 1990): 34.

56 Jamieson and O'Mara, *Managing Workforce 2000, op. cit.*

57 S. Baskett, 'Our changing face', *Herald Sun* (19 January 2000): 28.

58 S. Nollen and V. Martin, *Alternative Work Schedules: Part 1: Flexitime* (New York: American Management Association, 1978).

59 T. Cummings and J. Jaeger, 'Flexible workhours: a survey of 139 European countries', (paper presented at the Western Academy of Management, Monterey, Calif., 1981); D. Ralston, W. Anthony and D. Gustafson, 'Employees may love flexitime, but what does it do to the organization's productivity?' *Journal of Applied Psychology,* 70 (1985): 272–79.

60 H. Kahan and D. Mulryan, 'Out of the closet', *American Demographics* (May 1995): 40–47.

61 J. Segal, 'The unprotected minority?' *HR Magazine,* 40:2 (1995), 27–33.

62 F. Rice, 'Denny's changes its spots', *Fortune* (13 May 1996): 133–42.

63 J. Blair and M. Fotter, *Challenges in Health Care Management* (San Francisco: Jossey-Bass, 1990).

64 K. Warner, T. Wickizer, R. Wolfe, J. Schildroth and M. Samuelson, 'Economic implications of the workplace health promotion programs: review of the literature', *Journal of Occupational Medicine,* 30 (1988): 106–12.

65 H. Hawkes, 'Nice perk if you can get it', *Sunday Life, Sunday Age Magazine* (23 May 1999): 12–14.

66 S. Savitz, 'Mental health plans help employees, reduce costs', *Best's Review,* 96:3 (1995): 60–62.

67 C. Hodges, 'Growing problem of stress at work alarms business', *People Management,* 1:9 (1995): 14–15.

68 Hall and Goodale, *Human Resource Management, op. cit.*: 558.

69 W. Lissy and M. Morgenstern, 'Employees turn to EAPs during downsizing', *Compensation and Benefits Review,* 27:3 (1995): 16.

70 Hall and Goodale, *Human Resource Management, op. cit.*: 554.

71 M. Shain and J. Groenveld, *Employee Assistance Programs: Philosophy, Theory and Practice* (Lexington, Mass.: D.C.Heath, 1980).

72 J. Spicer, ed., *The EAP Solution* (Center City, Minn.: Hazeldon, 1987).

73 Adapted from T. Desmond, 'An internal broadbrush program: J&J's Live for Life Assistance Program' in *The EAP Solution,* ed. J. Spicer (Center City, Minn.: Hazeldon, 1987): 148–56.

74 T. O'Boyle, 'Fear and stress in the office take toll', *Wall Street Journal* (6 November 1990): B1, B3; A. Riecher, 'Job stress: what it can do to you', *Bryan–College Station Eagle* (15 August 1993): D1.

75 D. Allen, 'Less stress, less litigation', *Personnel* (January 1990): 32–35; D. Hollis and J. Goodson, 'Stress: the legal and organizational implications', *Employee Responsibilities and Rights Journal* 2 (1989): 255–62.

76 D. Ganster and J. Schaubroeck, 'Work stress and employee health', *Journal of Management,* 17 (1991): 235–71; T. Stewart, 'Do you push your employees too hard?' *Fortune* (22 October 1990): 121–28.

77 T. Cummings and C. Cooper, 'A cybernetic framework for studying occupational stress', *Human Relations,* 32 (1979): 395–418.

78 J. French and R. Caplan, 'Organization stress and individual strain' in *The Failure of Success,* ed. A. Morrow (New York: AMACOM, a division of American Management Associations, 1972).

79 *Ibid.*

80 R. Kahn, D. Wolfe, R. Quinn, J. Snoek and R. Rosenthal, *Organizational Stress* (New York: John Wiley and Sons, 1964).

81 C. Cooper and J. Marshall, 'Occupational sources of stress: a review of the literature relating to coronary heart disease and mental ill health', *Journal of Occupational Psychology,* 49 (1976): 11–28; C. Cooper and R. Payne, *Stress at Work* (New York: John Wiley and Sons, 1978).

82 Cooper and Marshall, 'Occupational sources', *op. cit.*

83 R. Rosenman and M. Friedman, 'The central nervous system and coronary heart disease', *Hospital Practice,* 6 (1971): 87–97.

84 D. Glass, *Behavior Patterns, Stress and Coronary Disease* (Hillsdale, N.J.: Lawrence Erlbaum, 1977); V. Price, *Type A Behavior Pattern* (New York: Academic Press, 1982).

85 J. Howard, D. Cunningham and P. Rechnitzer, 'Health patterns associated with Type A behavior: a managerial population', *Journal of Human Stress,* 2 (1976): 24–31.

86 See, for example, the Addison-Wesley series on occupational stress: L. Warshaw, *Managing Stress* (Reading, Mass.: Addison-Wesley, 1982); A. McClean, *Work Stress* (Reading, Mass.: Addison-Wesley, 1982); A. Shostak, *Blue-Collar Stress* (Reading, Mass.: Addison-Wesley, 1982); L. Moss, *Management Stress* (Reading, Mass.: Addison-Wesley, 1982); L. Levi, *Preventing Work Stress* (Reading, Mass.: Addison-Wesley, 1982); J. House, *Work Stress and Social Support* (Reading, Mass.: Addison-Wesley, 1982).

87 J. Ivancevich and M. Matteson, 'Optimizing human resources: a case for preventive health and stress management', *Organizational Dynamics*, 9 (Autumn 1980): 7–8.

88 E. Huse and C. Barebo, 'Beyond the T–Group: increasing organizational effectiveness', *California Management Review*, 23 (1980): 104–17.

89 I. Dayal and J. Thomas, 'Operation KPE: developing a new organization', *Journal of Applied Behavioral Science*, 4 (1968): 473–506.

90 Huse and Barebo, 'Beyond the T–Group', *op. cit.*: 104–17.

91 Dayal and Thomas, 'Operation KPE', *op. cit.*: 473–506.

92 House, *Work Stress and Social Support, op. cit.*

93 Ivancevich and Matteson, 'Optimizing human resources', *op. cit.*: 19.

94 J. Zuckerman, 'Keeping managers in good health', *International Management*, 34 (January 1979): 40.

95 L. Falkenberg, 'Employee fitness programs: their impact on the employee and the organization', *Academy of Management Review*, 12 (1987): 511–22.

96 J. Griffiths, B. Lloyd–Walker and A. Williams, 'HRM and the responsive organization— dealing with stress at Melbourne Water Corporation' in *Human Resource Management*, (Prentice Hall Australia 1999): 726.

PART 6

STRATEGIC INTERVENTIONS

CHAPTERS

19 Organisation and environment relationships

20 Organisation transformation

Organisation and environment relationships

This chapter is concerned with interventions that are aimed at organisation and environment relationships. These change programmes are relatively recent additions to the OD field that focus on helping organisations to relate better to their environments, and to achieve a better fit with those external forces that affect goal achievement and performance. Practitioners are discovering that additional knowledge and skills, such as competitive strategy, finance, marketing and political science, are necessary to conduct such large-scale change.

Because organisations are open systems, they must relate to their environments if they are to gain the resources and information needed to function and prosper. These relationships define an organisation's strategy and are affected by particular aspects and features of the environment. Organisations have devised a number of responses for managing environmental interfaces. The responses vary from creating special units to scan the environment to forming strategic alliances with other organisations.

The interventions described in this chapter help organisations to gain a comprehensive understanding of their environments and to devise appropriate responses to external demands. Open systems planning is aimed at helping organisation members to assess the larger environment and to develop strategies for relating to it more effectively. The intervention results in a clear strategic mission for the organisation, as well as action plans for influencing the environment in favoured directions.

Integrated strategic change is a comprehensive OD intervention. It suggests that business strategies and organisational systems must be changed together in response to external and internal disruptions. A strategic change plan can help members to manage the transition state between the current strategic orientation and the desired future strategic orientation.

Transorganisational development is concerned with helping organisations to enter into partnerships with other organisations in order to perform tasks or to solve problems that are too complex and multi-faceted for them to resolve on their own. These multi-organisation systems abound in today's environment and include joint ventures, strategic alliances, research and development consortia and public–private partnerships. They tend to be loosely coupled and non-hierarchical and, consequently, require different methods from those of most traditional OD interventions that are geared to single organisations. These methods involve helping organisations to recognise the need for partnerships and developing co-ordinating structures for carrying out multi-organisation activities.

Organisation and environment framework

This section provides a framework for understanding how environments affect organisations and, in turn, how organisations can impact on environments. The framework is based on the concept described in Chapter 5 that organisations and their subunits are open systems existing in environmental contexts. Environments provide organisations with the necessary resources, information and legitimacy, and organisations must maintain effective relationships with suitable environments if they are to survive and grow. A manufacturing firm, for example, must obtain raw materials so that it can produce its products, and then use appropriate technologies to efficiently produce them, induce customers to buy them and satisfy the laws and regulations that govern its operations. Because organisations are dependent on environments, they need to manage all the external constraints and contingencies, while at the same time taking advantage of external opportunities. They also need to influence the environment in favourable directions through such methods as political lobbying, advertising and public relations.

In this section, we first describe the different environments that can affect organisations, and then identify those environmental dimensions that tend to influence the organisational responses to those external forces. Finally, we review the different ways in which an organisation can respond to the environment. This material provides an introductory context for describing the various interventions that concern organisation and environment relationships—open systems planning, integrated strategic change and transorganisational development.

Environments

Organisational environments consist of everything outside organisations that can affect, either directly or indirectly, their performance and outcomes. This could include external agents (such as suppliers, customers, regulators and competitors) and the cultural, political and economic forces in the wider societal and global context. These two classes of environments are called the 'task environment' and the 'general environment', respectively.[1] We will also describe the enacted environment, which reflects members' perceptions of the general and task environments.

The *general environment* consists of all external forces that can influence an organisation or department, and includes technological, legal and regulatory, political, economic, social and ecological components. Each of these forces can affect the organisation in both direct and indirect ways. For example, economic recessions can directly impact on the demand for a company's product. The general environment can also impact indirectly on organisations by virtue of the linkages between external agents. For example, an organisation may have trouble obtaining raw materials from a supplier because a consumer group has embroiled the supplier in a labour dispute with a national union, a lawsuit with a government regulator or a boycott. These members of the organisation's general environment can affect the organisation, even though they have no direct connection to it.

The *task environment* consists of those specific individuals and organisations that interact directly with the organisation and can affect goal achievement. The task environment consists of customers, suppliers, competitors, producers of substitute products or services, labour unions, financial institutions and so on. These direct relationships are the medium through which organisations and environments mutually influence one another. Customers, for example, can demand changes in the organisation's products, but the organisation can attempt to influence customers' tastes and desires through advertising.

The *enacted environment* consists of the organisation's perception and representation of its environment. Weick suggested that environments must be perceived before they can influence decisions as to how to respond.[2] Organisation members must actively observe, register and make sense of the environment before their decisions as to how to act can be made. Thus, only the enacted environment can affect which organisational responses are chosen. The general and task environments, however, can influence whether those responses are successful or ineffective. For example, members may perceive customers as relatively satisfied with their products and may decide to make only token efforts at new-product development. If those perceptions are wrong and customers are dissatisfied with the products, the meagre efforts at product development can have disastrous consequences for the organisation. Consequently, an organisation's enacted environment should accurately reflect its general and task environments if members' decisions and actions are to be based on external realities.

Environmental dimensions

Organisational environments can be characterised along a number of dimensions that can influence organisation and environment relationships. One perspective views environments as information flows and suggests that organisations need to process information in order to discover how to relate to their environments.[3] The key feature of the environment to affect information processing is *information uncertainty* or the degree to which environmental information is ambiguous. Organisations seek to remove uncertainty from their environment so that they know how best to transact with it. For example, they try to discern customer needs through focus groups and surveys and they attempt to understand competitor strategies by studying their press releases and sales force behaviours, and by learning about their key personnel. The greater the uncertainty, the more information processing is required to learn about the environment. This is particularly the case when environments are *dynamic* and *complex*. Dynamic environments change abruptly and unpredictably; complex environments have many parts or elements that can affect organisations. These kinds of environments pose difficult information-processing problems for organisations. Global competition, technological change and financial markets, for example, have made the environments of many multinational firms highly uncertain and have severely strained their information-processing capacity.

Another perspective sees environments as consisting of resources for which organisations compete.[4] The key feature of the environment is *resource dependence*, or the degree to which an organisation relies on other organisations for resources. Organisations seek to manage critical sources of resource dependence, while remaining as autonomous as possible. For example, firms may contract with several suppliers of the same raw material so that they are not overly dependent on one vendor. Resource dependence is extremely high for an organisation when other organisations control critical resources that cannot easily be obtained elsewhere. Resource criticality and availability determine the extent to which an organisation is dependent on other organisations and must respond to their demands, as the 1970s oil embargo by the Organisation of Petroleum Exporting Countries (OPEC) clearly showed many Australian firms.

FIGURE 19.1	Environmental dimensions and organisational transactions

		Resource dependence	
		Low	High
Information uncertainty	Low	Minimal environmental constraint and need to be responsive to environment	Moderate constraint and responsiveness to environment
	High	Moderate constraint and responsiveness to environment	Maximal environment constraint and need to be responsive to environment

Source: Adapted from H. Aldrich, *Organizations and Environments* (New York: Prentice-Hall, 1979): 133.

These two environmental dimensions—information uncertainty and resource dependence—can be combined to show the degree to which organisations are constrained by their environments and consequently must be responsive to their demands.[5] As shown in Figure 19.1, organisations have the most freedom from external forces when information uncertainty and resource dependence are both low. In this situation, organisations do not need to be responsive to their environments and can behave relatively independently of them. United States automotive manufacturers faced these conditions in the 1950s and operated with relatively little external constraint or threat. As information uncertainty and resource dependence become higher, however, organisations are more constrained and must be more responsive to external demands. They must accurately perceive the environment and respond to it appropriately. As described in Chapter 1, modern organisations, such as financial institutions, high-technology firms and healthcare facilities, are facing unprecedented amounts of environmental uncertainty and resource dependence. Their very existence depends on their recognition of external challenges and their quick and appropriate responses to them.

Organisational responses

Organisations employ a number of ways of responding to environmental demands. These help to buffer the organisation's technology from external disruptions and to link the organisation to sources of information and resources. Referred to as 'external structures', these responses are generally carried out by administrators and staff specialists who are responsible for setting corporate strategy and managing the environment. Three major external structures are described below.

Scanning units

Organisations must have the capacity to monitor and make sense of their environment if they are to respond to it appropriately. They must identify and attend to those environmental parts and features that are highly related to the organisation's own survival and growth. When environments have high information uncertainty, organisations may need to gather a diversity of information in order to comprehend external demands and opportunities. For example, they may need to attend to segmented labour markets, changing laws and regulations, rapid scientific developments, shifting economic conditions and abrupt changes in customer and supplier behaviours. Organisations can respond to these conditions by establishing special units for scanning particular parts or aspects of the environment, such as departments of market research, public relations, government relations and strategic planning.[6] These units generally include specialists with expertise in a particular segment of the environment, who gather and interpret relevant information about the environment, communicating it to decision makers who develop appropriate responses. For example, market researchers provide information to marketing executives about customer tastes and preferences. Such information guides choices about product development, pricing and advertising.

Proactive responses

These involve attempts by organisations to change or modify their environments. Organisations are increasingly trying to influence external forces in favourable directions.[7] For example, they engage in political activity to influence government laws and regulations; seek government regulation to control entry to industries; gain legitimacy in the wider society by behaving in accordance with valued cultural norms; acquire control over raw materials or markets by vertical and horizontal integration; introduce new products and services and advertise to shape customer tastes and preferences. Although the range of proactive responses is almost limitless, organisations tend to be highly selective when choosing them. The responses can be costly to implement and can appear aggressive, thus evoking countervailing actions by powerful others, such as competitors and the government. For example, Microsoft's dominance in the software industry has drawn heavy scrutiny from the US Justice Department and from competitors. Moreover, organisations are paying increased attention to whether their responses are socially responsible and contribute to a healthy society. The Body Shop, for example, views its business as an important arm of society and devotes a considerable amount of time and corporate resources to charity and pressing social issues. Today, there is much global attention to the ethical and moral implications of organisational behaviours.

Collective structures

Organisations can cope with problems of environmental dependence and uncertainty by increasing their co-ordination with other organisations. These collective structures help to control interdependencies among organisations and include such methods as bargaining, contracting, co-opting and creating joint ventures, federations, strategic alliances and consortia.[8] Contemporary organisations are increasingly turning to joint ventures and partnerships with other organisations in order to manage environmental uncertainty and perform tasks that are too costly and complicated for single organisations to perform. These multi-organisation arrangements are being used as a means of sharing resources for large-scale research and development, for reducing risks of innovation, for applying diverse expertise to complex problems and tasks and for overcoming barriers to entry into foreign markets. For example, defence contractors are forming strategic alliances to bid on large government projects; firms from different countries are forming joint ventures to overcome restrictive trade barriers and high-technology firms are forming research consortia to undertake significant and costly research and development for their industries. Major barriers to forming collective structures in Australia are the organisations' own drive to act autonomously and government policies that discourage co-ordination among organisations, especially in the same industry. Japanese industrial and economic policies, on the other hand, promote co-operation among organisations, thus giving them a competitive advantage in their responses to complex and dynamic global environments.[9] For example, starting in the late 1950s, the Japanese government provided financial assistance and support to a series of co-operative research efforts among Japanese computer manufacturers. The resulting technological developments enabled the computer firms to reduce IBM's share of the mainframe market in Japan from 70% to about 40% in less than 15 years.

The interventions discussed in this chapter derive from this organisation and environment framework. They help organisations to assess their environments and make appropriate responses to them.

Open systems planning

Open systems planning (OSP) helps an organisation to systematically assess its task environment and to develop strategic responses to it. Like the other interventions in this book, OSP treats organisations or departments as open systems that must interact with a suitable environment in order to survive and develop. It helps organisation members develop a strategic mission for relating to the environment and influencing it in favourable directions. The process of applying OSP begins with a diagnosis of the existing environment and how the organisation relates to it. It then develops possible future environments, and action plans to bring about the desired future environment. A number of practical guidelines exist to apply this intervention effectively.

Assumptions about organisation-environment relations

Open systems planning is based on four assumptions about how organisations relate or should relate, to their environment.[10] These include the following:

1 *Organisation members' perceptions play a major role in environmental relations.* Members' perceptions determine which parts of the environment are attended to or ignored, as well as what value is placed on those parts. Such perceptions provide the basis for planning and implementing specific actions in relation to the environment.

For example, a production manager might focus on those parts of the environment that are directly related to making a product, such as raw-material suppliers and available labour, while ignoring other, more indirect parts, such as government agencies. These perceptions would probably direct the manager toward talking with the suppliers and potential employees, while possibly neglecting the agencies. The key point is that organisation and environment relations are largely determined by how members perceive the environment and choose to act toward it.

2   *Organisation members must share a common view of the environment to permit co-ordinated action toward it.* Without a shared view of the environment, organisation members would have trouble relating to it. Conflicts would arise about what parts of the environment are important and what value should be placed on different parts. Such perceptual disagreements make planning and implementing a coherent strategy difficult. For example, members of a top-management team might have different views on the organisation's environment. Unless those differences are shared and resolved, the team will have problems developing a business strategy for relating to the environment.[11]

3   *Organisation members' perceptions must accurately reflect the condition of the environment if organisational responses are to be effective.* Members can misinterpret environmental information, ignore important forces or attend to neg-ligible events. Such misperceptions can render organisational responses to the environment inappropriate, as happened to American car makers during the energy crisis of the mid-1970s. They believed that consumers wanted large automobiles and petroleum producers had plentiful supplies of relatively inexpensive petrol. The traditional strategy of manufacturing large numbers of large-sized cars was quickly shown to be inappropriate to the actual environment, i.e. the consumer's growing preference for small, fuel-efficient cars and the decision of OPEC member nations to raise the price of crude oil. Such misperceptions typically occur when the environment exhibits high levels of complexity and unpredictable change. Such turbulence makes understanding the environment or predicting its future difficult.

4   *Organisations cannot only adapt to their environment but also proactively create it.* Organisation and environment relations are typically discussed in terms of organisations adapting to environmental forces. Attention is directed to understanding and predicting environmental conditions so that organisations can better react to them. A more proactive alternative is for organisations to plan for a desired environment and then to take action against the existing environment so as to move it in the desired direction. This active stance goes beyond adaptation, because the organisation is trying to create a favourable environment rather than simply reacting to external forces. For example, when Alcoa first started to manufacture aluminium building materials, there was little demand for them. Rather than wait to see whether the market developed, Alcoa entered the construction business and pioneered the use of aluminium building materials. By being proactive, the company created a favourable environment.

Implementation process

Based on these premises about organisation and environment relations, open systems planning can help organisation members to assess their environment and plan a strategy for relating to it. After OSP, they may value differently the complexity of their environment and may generate a more varied range of response strategies.[12] OSP is typically carried out by the top management of an entire organisation, or by the management and key employees of a department. This group initially meets off-site for a two- to three-day period and may have several follow-up meetings of shorter duration. The OD practitioner helps to guide the process. Members are encouraged to share their perceptions of the environment and to collect and examine a diversity of related data. Considerable attention is directed to the communication process itself. Participants are helped to establish sufficient trust and openness to share different views and to work through differences.

OSP starts from the perspective of a particular organisation or department. This point of reference identifies the relevant environment. It serves as the focus of the planning process, which consists of the following steps:[13]

1 *Assess the external environment in terms of domains and the expectations that those domains have for the organisation's behaviour.* This step maps the current environment facing the organisation. First, the different parts or domains of the environment are identified. Listing all the external groups that directly interact with the organisation, such as customers, suppliers or government agencies usually does this. Then, each domain's expectations of the organisation's behaviour are assessed.

2 *Assess how the organisation responds to the environmental expectations.* This step assesses the organisation's responses to the environmental expectations identified in step one.

3 *Identify the core mission of the organisation.* This step helps to identify the underlying purpose or core mission of the organisation, as shown by how it responds to external demands. Attention is directed at discovering the mission as it is evidenced in the organisation's behaviour, rather than by simply accepting an official statement of the organisation's purpose. This is accomplished by examining the organisation and those environment transactions identified in steps one and two, and then assessing the values that seem to underlie those interactions. These values provide clues about the actual identity or mission of the organisation.

4 *Create a realistic future scenario of environmental expectations and organisation responses.* This step asks members to project the organisation and its environment into the near future, assuming that there are no real changes in the organisation. It asks what will happen in steps one, two and three if the organisation continues to operate as it does at present.

5 *Create an ideal future scenario of environmental expectations and organisation responses.* Here, members are asked to create alternative, desirable futures. This involves going back over steps one, two and three and asking what members would ideally like to see happen in both the environment and the organisation in the near future. People are encouraged to fantasise about desired futures without worrying about possible constraints.

6 *Compare the present with the ideal future and prepare an action plan for reducing the discrepancy.* This last step identifies specific actions that will move both the environment and the organisation toward the desired future. Planning for appropriate interventions typically occurs in three time frames: tomorrow, six months from now and two years from now. Members also decide on a follow-up schedule for sharing the flow of actions and updating the planning process.

Application 19.1 presents an example of how open systems planning worked at a large community hospital.[14] The example underscores the complexity of information that OSP can generate. It also shows how OSP can help organisation members develop a strategic mission of guiding future environmental relationships.

APPLICATION 19.1   Open systems planning at Seaside Hospital

Seaside Hospital is a 700-bed community hospital located in a city of about 500 000 persons. It is the main teaching hospital of a nearby medical school and enjoys both an excellent reputation and the support of a large endowment. For the five years preceding the open systems planning intervention, Seaside had been using its endowment to fund a recurrent budget deficit, which resulted from a continual conflict over priorities and budget among the three key groups running the hospital. The administrators, headed by the hospital director, were mainly concerned with regulations and cost containment. The doctors, under the leadership of the chief of the medical executive committee, were primarily interested in medical technology and modernizing equipment. The board of trustees, headed by the chairman of the board, was mainly concerned with inflation and protecting the endowment.

The hospital director contacted an external consultant for help in getting the three diverse groups to come together to set realistic budgets that would not dip into the endowment. The initial diagnosis suggested that the lack of budget co-ordination was a symptom of the failure to set hospital priorities in terms of its changing environment. Each group was acting on what it thought to be the best interests of the hospital. Given this conclusion, the chairman of the board of trustees asked the hospital director to chair an *ad hoc* planning committee made up of members of all three groups to clarify priorities, and to develop a more effective planning process. The consultant suggested, and the planning committee agreed, that open systems planning be used to achieve these goals.

Initial meetings of the planning committee revealed disagreements about the hospital's core mission. Because this contributed to the conflicting priorities that were hindering the planning process, the committee decided that developing a shared core mission would be a major output of open systems planning.

The committee then proceeded with the intervention. The first step was to analyze the hospital's external environment in terms of the key forces that were placing demands or constraints on its functioning. These included the federal government, the state health planning association, the nearby medical school, third-party payers, the medical profession and medical science and the hospital workers' union. To determine the demands of these forces, both now and in the near future, experts representing each external force were invited to two

full-day workshops to share their views with the planning committee and selected members of the hospital. After the workshops, all participants were given a questionnaire that asked for their opinions about the critical environmental concerns facing the hospital in the next five years. The results were summarized and distributed to the participants for their review and written comments. Excerpts from the questionnaire report are outlined in Table 19.1.

The planning committee next considered each external force in terms of:
1 Seaside's current response
2 the likely effect if that response were continued
3 alternative responses
4 issues raised by items one to three.
The administrative staff conducted most of this analysis; the planning committee spent most of its time reviewing that material and getting the opinions of the participants who had attended the two earlier workshops. As might be expected, the committee quickly found itself buried in information and impatient with examining environmental responses. Members were anxious to resolve the issues facing Seaside. At this point, the external consultant reminded the committee members of the need for thorough diagnosis before setting policy and resolving issues. He also worked with committee members on enhancing listening skills, identifying conflict and managing time. Shown in Table 19.2 is an example of this time-consuming internal-response analysis for one external force: state and federal government planning.

The next step of open systems planning was to examine the internal-response data to discover the key issues facing Seaside. The planning committee examined all of the issues raised in the previous step in terms of overlap, inter-relatedness and temporal order. It arrived at a coherent subset of issues and asked hospital administrators and doctors to respond to them separately. These responses further reduced the issues to five key questions that needing to be answered in order to define Seaside's

| TABLE 19.1 | External forces outline |

Forces	Example demands
Federal Government	
SSA[a]	Take low cost from high-cost systems
	Increased comparison of hospital costs and more demands for justification of high costs and/or lowering of costs
	Limit health expenditures—less than 1% real growth for foreseeable future hospital expenditures
HHS[a]	
Staffing	More primary care MDs
	Increase in hospital residencies (nationally)
	Decrease in speciality residencies (nationally)
Planning	New legislation—but unpredictable postponements/moratoriums
State government	
Department of Health	Increasing pressure to plan *with* other hospitals/community agencies
State Budget Office	Will set caps—similar to federal government
Local medical school program	Wants Seaside Hospital to be in a multihospital system
	Wants Seaside Hospital to assume primary responsibility for paediatrics, radiation oncology, radiology and surgical subspecialties
Health insurance funds	Likely to become more aggressive in order to protect selves
Community	Use Seaside Hospital resources to rehabilitate southern area of community
	Have more neighborhood health centers—may require our future support
Other hospitals/HMOs[a]	Seaside Hospital should not get any bigger
Organized labor	Pay certain categories of employees more (in relation to other hospital contracts)
	Pressure for more say for professionals—even without unionization
External review agencies	
PRSO[a]	Pressure from PRSO to reduce length of stay and possibly ancillary service volume
JCAH[a]	Pressure from JCAH and others for upkeep of physical plant and employee safety

[a] SSA—Social Security Administration; HHS—Department of Health and Human Services; HMO—Health Maintenance Organisation; PSRO—Professional Standards Review Organisation; JCAH—Joint Commission on the Accreditation of Hospitals.

Source: Reproduced by permission of the publisher from R. Fry, 'Improving trustee, administrator and physician collaboration through open systems planning' in *Organization Development in Health Care Organizations*, eds N. Margulies and J. Adams (Reading, Mass.: Addison-Wesley, 1982): 286.

core mission in relation to health care, education and research:

- What should be our role at primary, secondary and tertiary care levels?
- What residencies should be offered here?
- What undergraduate education should be offered here?
- Which departments should be developed as academic (as opposed to clinical) departments?
- What kinds of basic or clinical research should we support?

The planning committee next asked the administrative and doctor groups to respond separately to the questions. The issues were highly conflictual and implied making trade-offs, such as whose department would be enlarged and whose would be cut back. The involvement of these larger groups helped to sustain wider interest and

TABLE 19.2	Analysis of state and federal government planning as an external force

A *How is Seaside Hospital responding today?*
Little, if any, joint planning. Some planning with community agencies and University, e.g., Home Care Association, alcoholism program; not, however, through our initiation.
Cooperating in committee on future planning. Outcome of this committee's discussions unknown at present.
Outcome of planning with others is regionalized or 'dividing the pie'. Present process of examining our role is a response to that pressure.
Actively conversant with federal and state regulations and supporting efforts to monitor Health Department activities.
Increasing awareness of the importance of planning on our part, e.g., current process.

B *Effect if Seaside Hospital continues present response*
Lack of response in planning with others may influence the Health Department to take a more active, aggressive role in planning for the system.
Lacking a coordinated interinstitutional plan, available limited resources may be utilised by other institutions, which may not be consistent with our objectives.

C *Preliminary optional responses*
Become more aggressive in developing corporate affiliations with other institutions.
Support planning arm of the state hospital association to coordinate/integrate the plans of various institutions.
Individually coordinate Seaside Hospital plans with others having mutual interests and develop agreements for sharing resources or services.
Continue to plan individually.
Support the formation and development of a consortium of the university-affiliated hospitals.
Continue to develop internal planning capabilities to keep abreast.
Allow the Health Department to create plans without input and minimize changes for successful implementation.

D *Issues*
What should be the relationship for planning/resource allocation between Seaside Hospital and other health care providers?
Should the objectives of other institutions be integrated in some way into the process of determining our own objectives and if so, how?
What should be our role in various service levels, i.e. primary, secondary and tertiary, for the region?

Source: Reproduced by permission of the publisher from R. Fry, 'Improving trustee, administrator and physician collaboration through open systems planning' in *Organization Development in Health Care Organizations*, eds N. Margulies and J. Adams (Reading, Mass.: Addison-Wesley, 1982): 287.

commitment in what the planning committee was trying to do. The committee then took the various inputs and over the course of several meetings arrived at position statements for each question. The trustee members of the planning committee were the most active at these meetings, offering compromises, making finalized statements and supporting the committee's work in general. The following solutions came out of these meetings:

- primary care would become more central in the future
- tertiary standing would be maintained by keeping certain residencies and academic departments and dropping others
- only two of the clinical departments would ever become academic if funds were available for their growth
- the hospital's primary care services would actively compete with private doctors' surgeries in the community.

The next step was to sell the proposals to the different constituencies and implement them. A 60-page report summarizing the committee's work and solutions was distributed to all participants of the first two workshops. Then a one-day workshop was held to field concerns, solicit responses and sell the solutions. Shortly thereafter, the committee submitted a final report, which was approved by the board of trustees. To implement and monitor the policy decisions, a permanent joint planning committee with trustee, administrator and clinical members was formed. It replaced planning sub-committees that had existed in each group. This new joint committee was made responsible for continually interpreting Seaside's core mission, recommending programme changes, informing staff of the rationale for program decisions and determining guidelines to enforce the core mission. The committee took immediate action to review each department's resource allocation in terms of the new core mission and to examine requests for exemptions and for capital funds of more than $50 000.

The entire open systems planning intervention at Seaside took about 15 months. It resulted in a core mission statement that was accepted and supported by administrators, trustees and doctors. The common priorities would guide the budget process and reduce troublesome conflicts among the different constituencies. Moreover, the intervention led to the creation of the joint planning committee to guide the growth and development of the hospital and to settle future disputes.

Guidelines for implementing open systems planning

Practitioners who have applied open systems planning offer a number of suggestions for its effective use.[15] These rules of thumb include the following:

1 *Devote sufficient time and resources.* Open systems planning is time-consuming and requires considerable effort and resources. There is much preparatory work in collecting environmental information, analysing it and drafting reports for group discussion. Also, participants must be given sufficient time to develop healthy inter-personal relationships so that they can discuss the information openly, resolve conflicting viewpoints and arrive at a sufficient consensus to proceed effectively.

2 *Document all steps.* OSP generates considerable information and people can easily lose track of the data. Written reports of the various steps help to organise the diverse information. They can also keep other organisation members informed of the process and can provide them with a concrete focus for reacting to it.

3 *Deal only with key parts of the environment.* The tendency is to collect and examine too much information, losing track of what is important for organisational effectiveness. Mapping out the existing environment should start with an initial scanning that defines broad environmental domains. Only those domains considered important to organisational or departmental functioning are used for the remaining steps of the process.

4 *Follow the steps in order.* In using OSP, people tend to confuse the existing environment with the future environment. They also tend to mix the realistic future with the ideal future. If the steps are systematically followed, the process will logically lead from the present to the realistic future environment and then to the desired future environment.

5 *View planning as process, not outcome.* Probably the key value of OSP is helping organisation members develop an ongoing process for assessing and relating to the environment. While specific plans and action steps are important, they should be viewed as periodic outcomes of a larger process of environmental management.

Integrated strategic change

Integrated strategic change (ISC) is a recent intervention that brings an OD perspective to traditional strategic planning. It was developed in response to managers' complaints that good business strategies often never get implemented. The research suggested that too little attention was being given to the change process and to those human resource issues that were necessary to execute the strategy.[16] For example, the predominant paradigm in strategic planning, formulation and implementation artificially separates strategic thinking from operational and tactical actions; it ignores the contributions that planned change processes can make to implementation. In the traditional process, senior managers and strategic planning staff prepare economic forecasts, competitor analyses and market studies. These studies are then discussed and the firm's strengths and weakness are rationally aligned with the environmental opportunities and threats to form the organisation's strategy.[17] Implementation occurs as middle managers, supervisors and employees hear about the new strategy through memos, restructuring announcements, changes in job responsibilities or new departmental objectives. As a result, there is little understanding of the need for change and little ownership of the new behaviours, initiatives and tactics required to achieve the objectives.

ISC, in contrast, was designed to be a highly participative process. It has three key features:[18]

1 The relevant unit of analysis is the organisation's *strategic orientation* or the constellation of strategy, structure and process. A business strategy and the organisation design that supports it must be considered as an integrated unit.

2 Creating the strategic plan, gaining commitment and support for it, planning its implementation and executing it is treated as one integrated process. The ability to conduct such a process over and over again when conditions warrant it represents a sustainable competitive advantage.[19]

3 Individuals and groups throughout the organisation are integrated into the analysis, planning and implementation process to create a more achievable plan, to maintain the firm's strategic focus, to focus attention and resources on the organisation's key competencies, to improve co-ordination and integration within the organisation and to create higher levels of shared ownership and commitment.

Application stages

The ISC process is applied in four steps:
- performing a strategic analysis
- exercising strategic choice
- designing a strategic change plan
- implementing the plan.

The four steps are discussed sequentially here but actually unfold in overlapping and integrated ways. Figure 19.2 displays the steps in the ISC process and its change components. An organisation's existing strategic orientation, identified as its current strategy (S_1) and organisation design (O_1), is linked to its future strategic orientation (S_2/O_2) by the strategic change plan.

1 *Performing a strategic analysis.* The ISC process begins with a diagnosis of the organisation's readiness for change and its current strategy and organisation (S_1/O_1). The most important indicator of readiness is senior management's willingness and ability to carry out strategic change. Greiner and Schein suggest that the two key dimensions in this analysis are the leader's willingness and commitment to change and the team members' willingness and ability to follow the leader's initiative.[20] Organisations whose leaders are not willing to lead and whose

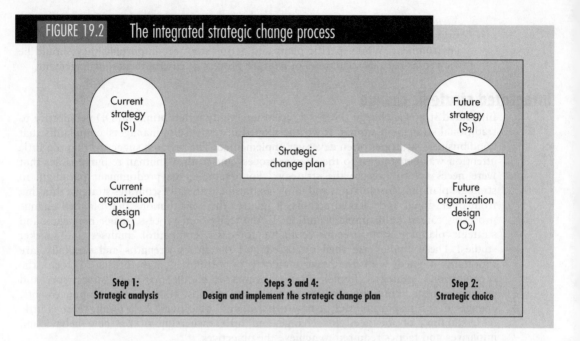

FIGURE 19.2 The integrated strategic change process

senior managers are not willing and able to support the new strategic direction when necessary should consider team-building processes to ensure their commitment.

The second stage in strategic analysis is understanding the current strategy and organisation design. The process begins with an examination of the organisation's industry as well as its current financial performance and effectiveness. This information provides the necessary context to assess the current strategic orientation's viability. Porter's models of industry attractiveness[21] as well as the environmental framework introduced at the beginning of this chapter are the two most relevant models for analysing the environment. Next, the current strategic orientation is described to explain current levels of performance and human outcomes. Several models for guiding this diagnosis exist.[22] For example, the current strategic orientation can be assessed according to the model and methods introduced in Chapter 5. The organisation's mission, goals and objectives, intent and business policies represent the strategy. The structure, work, information and human resource systems describe the organisation design. Other models for understanding the organisation's strategic orientation include the competitive positioning model[23] and other typologies.[24] These frameworks assist in assessing customer satisfaction, product and service offerings, financial health, technological capabilities and organisational culture, structure and systems.

Strategic analysis actively involves organisation members in the process. Search conferences, employee focus groups, interviews with salespeople, customers, purchasing agents and other methods allow a variety of employees and managers to participate in the diagnosis and increase the amount and relevance of the data collected. This builds commitment to, and ownership of, the change effort; should a strategic change effort be initiated, members are more likely to understand why and be supportive of it.

2 *Exercising strategic choice.* The strategic analysis often points out misfits among the organisation's environment, strategic orientation and performance. As the process unfolds, alternative strategies organisation designs and member preferences will emerge. Based on this analysis, senior management visions the future and broadly defines two or three alternative sets of objectives and strategies for achieving them. Market forecasts, employees' readiness and willingness to change, competitor

analyses and other projections can be used to develop these alternative future scenarios.[25] The different sets of objectives and strategies also include projections about the organisational design changes that will be necessary to support each alternative. Although participation from other organisational stakeholders is important in the alternative generation phase, choosing the appropriate strategic orientation ultimately rests with top management and cannot be easily delegated. Senior managers are in the unique position of being able to view strategy from a general management position. When major strategic decisions are given to lower-level managers, the risk of focusing too narrowly on a product, market or technology increases.

This step determines the content, or 'what', of strategic change. The desired strategy (S_2) defines the products or services to offer, the markets to be served and the way these outputs will be produced and positioned. The desired organisation design (O_2) specifies the organisational structures and processes necessary to support this new strategy. The alignment of an organisation's design with a particular strategy can be a major source of superior performance and competitive advantage.[26]

3 *Designing a strategic change plan.* The strategic change plan is a comprehensive agenda for moving the organisation from its current strategy and organisation design to the desired future strategic orientation. It represents the process, or 'how', of strategic change. The change plan describes the types, magnitude and schedule of change activities, as well as the costs associated with them. It also specifies how the changes will be implemented, given power and political issues, the nature of the organisational culture and the current ability of the organisation to implement change.[27]

4 *Implementing a strategic change plan.* The final step in the ISC process is the actual implementation of the strategic change plan. The implementation of the change plan draws heavily on knowledge of motivation, group dynamics and change processes. It deals continuously with such issues as alignment, adaptability, teamwork and organisational and personal learning. Implementation requires senior managers to champion the different elements of the change plan, which they do by initiating action and allocating resources to particular activities, setting high but achievable goals and providing feedback on accomplishments. In addition, leaders must hold people accountable to the change objectives, institutionalise each change that occurs and be prepared to solve problems as they arise. This final point recognises that no strategic change plan can account for all of the contingencies that emerge. There must be a willingness to adjust the plan as implementation unfolds in order to address unforeseen and unpredictable events and to take advantage of new opportunities.

Application 19.2 examines the experience of Australian industrial collaborative projects. It uses the CSIRO's Division of Manufacturing Technology, General Motors-Holden's Automotive Ltd, James Hardie Irrigation and the Hoover Press Shop in Sydney to illustrate the political nature of collaborative projects and to highlight the processes involved in transferring research innovation into programmes of organisational change.[28]

APPLICATION 19.2

Research design and shop floor practice: the CSIRO-Holden collaboration

The Commonwealth Scientific and Industrial Research Organisation's (CSIRO) Division of Manufacturing Technology (DMT) has been conscious of the importance of organisation and political issues in the design of technology and the implementation of new forms of work organisation. The main aim of this government-funded group is to work closely with companies for the purpose of increasing the competitiveness of Australian industry. A major aim of DMT is to develop and apply integrated manufacturing technologies for enhanced productivity in the manufacturing sector. An agreement was reached with General Motors-Holden's Automotive Limited (GM) on the design and development of cellular forms of work organisation in February 1986.

DMT's goal was to develop a computer-aided design system, which would establish appropriate plant layouts that were based on group technology principles, as well as a shop floor programme for use by cell employees to help them in the complex task of setting acceptable short-term plans in multi-product batch manufacture. In the early stages of the project, DMT realised that there was a problem with shop floor consistency. The materials data and the manufacturing data were in separate databases. The major problem with this was that the files did not match and so it was possible to have manufacturing routeing information for parts that had not been made for five years. CSIRO had to then develop a software scheduler that would be able to carry out consistency checks between both files, and then highlight the errors so that GM could take appropriate action.

Once data validity could be assured, the next step was to develop software for cellular design. Two related versions of a PC scheduler were developed. The first one simulated a design cell and provided various statistics on how good the design would be in meeting various load requirements. The programme works on a time line by looking at the current time and at what jobs have a minimum amount of time between now and when they are due, and then ordering them in priority. The second programme was for actual shop floor operational use.

There were many organisational constraints on the design process during the course of this project. In the early stages of the project GM put considerable pressure on CSIRO to produce 'real' results. GM was under financial constraints and did not want to wait 18 months for the cell design. The company wanted to see practical changes early in the project,

and so it was decided that, instead of preparing a total design prior to implementation, implementation should take place in parallel with cell design.

Consequently, this put CSIRO under considerable pressure to plan, implement and operate a pilot cell parallel with the development of the relevant software. Originally, the submission had set a series of stages from the identification of the type of change through to the initial implementation and operation. CSIRO had to convince the senior GM management of the value of the change programme. Due to the organisational funding of the project and the comparatively junior managerial positions of the GM personnel directly involved, the need for the local plant managers to show initial return on the investment became paramount. This led to the local plant managers putting pressure on CSIRO to provide a cell design that they could implement quickly. The pilot cell came into being by a partial match between a sub-group of parts being identified by GM with a sub-group of parts being analysed by CSIRO. Subsequent to the pilot cell design, the CSIRO team applied their process flow analysis (PFA) software to plant data and regrouped the equipment into isolated sets that could exist independently. There were a number of design restraints given to CSIRO by the plant manager that they had to consider. Working within these restraints, CSIRO delivered a first draft of the cell design to the local management. Guidance was needed on how the cells should be re-arranged to take into account the detailed workings of the shop floor. The plant personnel were then required to closely examine the manufacturing operations in relation to the proposed design. Alterations were made and then sent back to CSIRO, who made amendments and then resubmitted the design. This process went on for nearly 12 months.

The last step in the process occurred in May 1986 when data collection was stopped and two potential areas for the location of manufacturing cells were recognised. The costs of establishing cell one were $18 000 and for cell two $35 000. GM was concerned with the costs involved and asked CSIRO to concentrate on finding a cheaper option. In late June, CSIRO submitted a new cell option to GM and later to the consulting firm Arthur Anderson, who confirmed that savings of up to $2 million per annum could be achieved by undergoing the suggested changes. By September, the work cell was approved after much discussion and consultation between GM and CSIRO. Phase one of the project was formally reported as being completed in January 1987.

The activities that were necessary to achieve this change were not only technological, but also involved how organisations, politics and occupational groups, managers, systems designers and individual employees responded and participated in the transformation. This was particularly relevant in the design and developmental cycles when GM was reacting to both inside and outside pressures. For CSIRO, it was not simply a question of integrating technology, people and organisational structures, but of managing the political collaborative process in the design, development and implementation of the manufacturing advanced technology.

Transorganisational development

Transorganisational development (TD) is an emerging form of planned change aimed at helping organisations develop collective and collaborative strategies with other organisations. Many of the tasks, problems and issues facing organisations today are too complex and multifaceted to be addressed by a single organisation. Multi-organisation strategies and arrangements are increasing rapidly in today's global, highly competitive environment. In the private sector, research and development consortia allow companies to share resources and risks associated with large-scale research efforts. For example, Sematech involves many large organisations, such as Intel, AT&T, IBM, Xerox and Motorola, that have joined together to improve the competitiveness of the US semi-conductor industry. Joint ventures between domestic and foreign firms help to overcome trade barriers and to facilitate technology transfer across nations. For example, the New United Motor Manufacturing, Inc. in Fremont, California is a joint venture between General Motors and Toyota to produce automobiles, using Japanese teamwork methods. In the public sector, partnerships between government and business provide the resources and initiative to undertake complex urban renewal projects, such as Baltimore's Inner Harbor Project and Pittsburgh's Neighborhood Housing Services. Alliances among public service agencies in a region, such as the Human Services Council of Grand River, Michigan and OuR TOWN, a co-operative project between local governments to promote rural tourism, can help to co-ordinate services, promote economies and avoid costly overlap and redundancy.

Transorganisational systems and their problems

Cummings has referred to these multi-organisation structures as transorganisational systems (TSs)—groups of organisations that have joined together for a common purpose.[29] TSs are functional social systems midway between single organisations and societal systems. They are able to make decisions and perform tasks on behalf of their member organisations, although members maintain their separate organisational identities and goals. In contrast to most organisations, TSs tend to be under-organised: relationships among member organisations are loosely coupled; leadership and power are dispersed among autonomous organisations, rather than hierarchically centralised; and commitment and membership are tenuous as member organisations attempt to maintain their autonomy while jointly performing.

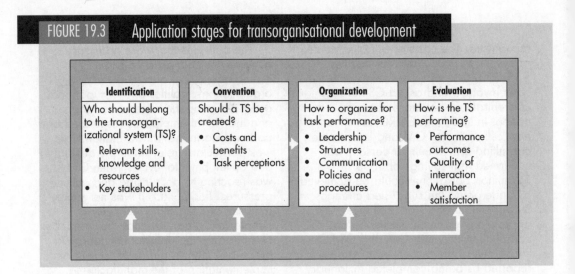

FIGURE 19.3 Application stages for transorganisational development

These characteristics make creating and managing TSs difficult.[30] Potential member organisations may not see the need to join with other organisations. They may be concerned with maintaining their autonomy or have trouble identifying potential partners. Australian firms, for example, are traditionally 'rugged individualists' preferring to work alone, rather than to join with other organisations. Even if organisations do decide to join together, they may have problems managing their relationships and controlling joint performances. Because members are typically accustomed to hierarchical forms of control, they may have difficulty managing lateral relations among independent organisations. They may also have difficulty managing different levels of commitment and motivation among members, and sustaining membership over time.

Application stages

Given these problems, transorganisational development has evolved as a unique form of planned change aimed at creating TSs and improving their effectiveness. In laying out the conceptual boundaries of TD, Cummings described the practice of TD as following the stages of planned change appropriate for under-organised systems (see Chapter 2).[31] These stages parallel other process models that have been proposed for creating and managing joint ventures, strategic alliances and inter-organisational collaboration.[32] The four stages are shown in Figure 19.3, along with key issues that need to be addressed at each stage. The stages and issues are described below.

Identification stage

This initial stage of TD involves the identification of potential member organisations of the TS. It serves to specify the relevant participants for the remaining stages of TD. Identifying potential members can be difficult, because organisations may not perceive the need to join together or may not know enough about each other to make membership choices. These problems are typical when trying to create a new TS. Relationships among potential members may be loosely coupled or non-existent, and so, even if organisations see the need to form a TS, they may be unsure about who should be included.

The identification stage is generally carried out by one or a few organisations who are interested in exploring the possibility of creating a TS. Change agents work with these organisations to specify criteria for membership in the TS and identify organisations meeting those standards. Because TSs are intended to perform specific tasks, a practical criterion for membership is how much organisations can contribute to task performance. Potential members can be identified and judged in terms of the skills, knowledge and resources that they can bring to bear on the TS task. TD practitioners warn, however, that identifying potential members should also take into account the political realities of the situation.[33] Consequently, key stakeholders who can affect the creation and subsequent performance of the TS are identified as possible members.

During the early stages of creating a TS, there may be insufficient leadership and cohesion among participants to choose potential members. In these situations, participants may contract with an outside change agent who can help them to achieve sufficient agreement on TS membership. In several cases of TD, change agents helped members to create a special leadership group that could make decisions on behalf of the participants.[34] This leadership group comprised a small cadre of committed members and was able to develop enough cohesion among themselves to carry out the identification stage.

Convention stage

Once potential members of the TS have been identified, the convention stage is concerned with bringing them together to assess whether creating a TS is desirable and feasible. This face-to-face meeting enables potential members to mutually explore their motivations for joining, and their perceptions of the joint task. They seek to establish sufficient levels of motivation and of task consensus to form the TS.

Like the identification stage, this phase of TD generally requires considerable direction and facilitation by change agents. Existing stakeholders may not have the legitimacy or skills to perform the convening function and change agents can serve as conveners if they are perceived as legitimate and credible by the different organisations. In many TD cases, conveners came from research centres or universities with reputations for neutrality and expertise in TD.[35] Because participating organisations tend to have diverse motives and views and limited means for resolving differences, change agents may need to structure and manage interactions to facilitate the airing of differences and arriving at consensus about forming the TS. They may need to help organisations work through differences and reconcile self-interests with those of the larger TS.

Organisation stage

When the convention stage results in the decision to create a TS, members begin to organise themselves for task performance. This involves establishing structures and mechanisms to facilitate communication and interaction among members and to direct joint efforts to the task at hand.[36] For example, members may create a co-ordinating council to manage the TS and they might assign a powerful leader to head that group. They might choose to formalise exchanges among members by developing rules, policies and formal operating procedures. In cases in which members are required to invest large amounts of resources in the TS, such as might occur in an industry-based research consortium, the organising stage typically includes voluminous contracting and negotiating about members' contributions and returns. Here, corporate lawyers and financial analysts play key roles in structuring the TS. They determine how costs and benefits will be allocated among member organisations, as well as the legal obligations and contractual rights of members.

Evaluation stage

This final stage of TD involves assessing how the TS is performing. Members need feedback so that they can identify problems and begin to resolve them. Feedback data generally include performance outcomes and member satisfaction, as well as indicators of how well members are jointly interacting. Change agents, for example, can periodically interview or survey member organisations about various outcomes and features of the TS and feed that data back to TS leaders. Such information can enable leaders to make necessary modifications and adjustments in how the TS is operating. It may signal the need to return to previous stages of TD to make necessary corrections, as shown by the feedback arrows in Figure 19.3.

Application 19.3 describes how senior management at the Christchurch, New Zealand-based PDL Group of companies has settled into the task of improving flat company fortunes and a newly formed strategic alliance with Australian electrical goods distributor Avatar Industries.[37]

APPLICATION 19.3

A new strategic alliance for PDL Electronics

The mammoth effort of restructuring a full board and management during the middle of the year was 'horrendous', according to Mark Stewart, the chief executive of PDL, although the effort will be worth it. PDL Industries specialises in a diverse range of electrical product manufacture. The company designs and manufactures electrical wiring accessories, as well as industrial switchgear and electrical consumer appliances. Two basic commitments were the results of PDL's 1998 strategic review, when the group's business was scrutinised. The first commitment was to take on a more aggressive stance towards costs and overheads and second, to ensure that technology and production development was to remain the company's dominant focus. To further this, PDL formed a strategic alliance with Avatar Industries, an Australian electrical goods manufacturer and distributor in 1999.

The association with Avatar is a long-term project and will operate throughout New Zealand, Australia and the UK. The alliance opens doors for PDL to Australia's retail electrical product market—an in-demand market for PDL, as previously they had only been involved in Australia's trade sector. Australia's retail market is being targeted as a long-term priority as substantial growth is expected in PDL's market share in certain product areas.

Richard Hall, PDL's general manager of marketing, said that they expected new sales revenue to amount to several million dollars under the new deal. They were already getting positive support from large retail hardware chains in Australia. PDL sees the alliance as being complementary rather than overlapping. The two companies complement each other in that PDL is a technological company, whereas Avatar's basic strength lies in its distribution channels in the Australian marketplace.

The alliance would also further export opportunities in Britain through Avatar's British subsidiary, DETA Electrical. Avatar has an extensive range of international sources, which will be to PDL's advantage. One of PDL's main strengths lies in its research and development of electrical products for the international markets. PDL will be used as a development base to strengthen Avatar's products and technology. Together, PDL and Avatar are in a strong market position.

Finally, another positive result of the alliance is that no significant expansion will be required for the manufacturing plant to fulfil the growing supply to the international markets. It is also expected that, with the increase in manufacturing levels, more staff will be required. However, PDL are being hesitant about employing more people until they are sure of what impact the present efficiency drive will have on production.

Roles and skills of the change agent

Transorganisational development is a relatively new application of planned change and practitioners are still exploring appropriate roles and skills. They are discovering the complexities of working with under-organised systems made up of multiple organisations. This contrasts sharply with OD, which has traditionally been applied in single organisations that are heavily organised. Consequently, the roles and skills relevant to OD need to be modified and supplemented when applied to TD.

The major role demands of TD derive from the two prominent features of TSs: their under-organisation and their multi-organisation composition. Because TSs are under-organised, change agents need to play *activist* roles in creating and developing them.[38] They need to bring structure to a group of autonomous organisations that may not see the need to join together or may not know how to form an alliance. The activist role requires a good deal of leadership and direction, particularly during the initial stages of TD. For example, change agents may need to educate potential TS members about the benefits of joining together. They may need to structure face-to-face encounters aimed at sharing information and exploring interaction possibilities.

Because TSs are made up of multiple organisations, change agents need to maintain a *neutral* role, treating all members alike.[39] They need to be seen by members as working on behalf of the total system, rather than as being aligned with particular members or views. When change agents are perceived as neutral, TS members are more likely to share information with them and to listen to their inputs. Such neutrality can enhance the change agents' ability to mediate conflicts among members. It can help them uncover diverse views and interests and forge agreements between different stakeholders. Change agents, for example, can act as mediators, assuring that members' views receive a fair hearing and that disputes are equitably resolved. They can help to bridge the different views and interests and achieve integrative solutions.

Given these role demands, the skills needed to practise TD include *political* and *networking* abilities.[40] Political competence is needed to understand and resolve the conflicts of interest and value dilemmas inherent in systems that are made up of multiple organisations, each seeking to maintain autonomy while jointly interacting. Political savvy can help change agents to manage their own roles and values in respect to those power dynamics. It can help them to avoid being co-opted by certain TS members, thus losing their neutrality.

Networking skills are also indispensable to TD practitioners. These include the ability to manage lateral relations among autonomous organisations in the relative absence of hierarchical control. Change agents must be able to span the boundaries of diverse organisations, link them together and facilitate exchanges among them. They must be able to form linkages where none existed and to transform networks into operational systems capable of joint task performance.

Defining the roles and skills of TD practitioners is still in a formative stage. Our knowledge in this area will continue to develop as more experience is gained with TSs. Change agents are discovering, for example, that the complexity of TSs requires a team consulting approach, involving practitioners with different skills and approaches working together to facilitate TS effectiveness. Initial reports of TD practice suggest that such change projects are both large-scale and long-term.[41] They typically involve multiple, simultaneous interventions that are aimed at both the total TS and its constituent members. The stages of TD application are protracted, requiring considerable time and effort to identify relevant organisations, to convene them and to organise them for task performance.

Summary

In this chapter we presented interventions aimed at improving organisation and environment relationships. Because organisations are open systems that exist in environmental contexts, they must establish and maintain effective linkages with the environment in order to survive and prosper. Three environments impact on organisational functioning: the general environment, the task environment and the enacted environment. Only the last of these can affect organisational choices about behaviour, but the first two impact on the consequences of those actions. Two key environmental dimensions affect the degree to which organisations are constrained by their environments and need to be responsive to them: information uncertainty and resource dependence. When both dimensions are high, organisations are maximally constrained and need to be responsive to their environment.

Open systems planning helps an organisation to systematically assess its environment and develop strategic responses to it. OSP is based on assumptions about the role of people's perceptions in environmental relations and the need for a shared view of the environment that permits co-ordinated action toward it. It begins with an assessment of the existing environment and how the firm relates to it and progresses to possible future environments and action plans to bring them about. A number of guidelines exist for effectively applying this intervention.

Integrated strategic change is a comprehensive intervention for addressing organisation and environment issues. It gives equal weight to the business and organisational factors that affect organisation performance and effectiveness. In addition, these factors are highly integrated during the process of assessing the current strategy and organisation design, selecting the desired strategic orientation, developing a strategic change plan and implementing it.

Transorganisational development is an emerging form of planned change that is aimed at helping organisations create partnerships with other organisations to perform tasks or to solve problems that are too complex and multifaceted for single organisations to carry out. Because these multi-organisation systems tend to be under-organised, TD follows the stages of planned change relevant to under-organised systems: identification, convention organisation and evaluation. TD is a relatively new application of planned change, and appropriate change-agent roles and skills are still being formulated.

 ACTIVITIES

Review questions
1 What constitutes the organisation's general environment?
2 What is the key dimension of task environment?
3 Organisations gain 'control' over their environments through what strategies?
4 What is associated with a transorganisational system? Describe its stages.
5 Explain open systems planning and identify what undermines its effectiveness.
6 What is the assumption that underlies the integrated strategic change process and what are the steps for implementation?

Discussion and essay questions
1 How does integrated strategic change differ from traditional strategic planning and traditional planned organisation change?
2 What is open systems planning and what assumptions is it based on?
3 How do environmental factors affect the types of interventions that might be carried out in an organisation?
4 What is the role of the change agent in transorganisational development?

Notes

1   R. Miles, *Macro Organization Behavior* (Santa Monica, Calif.: Goodyear, 1980); D. Robey and C. Sales, *Designing Organizations*, 4th ed. (Homewood, Ill.: Irwin, 1994).

2   K. Weick, *The Social Psychology of Organizing*, 2nd ed. (Reading, Mass.: Addison-Wesley, 1979).

3   J. Galbraith, *Competing with Flexible Lateral Organizations*, 2nd ed. (Reading, Mass.: Addison-Wesley, 1994).

4   J. Pfeffer and G. Salancik, *The External Control of Organizations: A Resource Dependence Perspective* (New York: Harper and Row, 1978).

5 H. Aldrich, *Organizations and Environments* (New York: Prentice-Hall, 1979); L. Hrebiniak and W. Joyce, 'Organizational adaptation: strategic choice and environmental determinism', *Administrative Science Quarterly,* 30 (1985): 336–49.

6 Pfeffer and Salancik, *The External Control of Organizations, op. cit.*

7 Aldrich, *Organizations and Environments, op. cit.*

8 *Ibid.*

9 W. Ouchi, *The M-Form Society: How American Teamwork Can Recapture the Competitive Edge* (Reading, Mass.: Addison-Wesley, 1984); L. Thurow, *Head to Head: The Coming Economic Battle Among Japan, Europe and America* (New York: William Morrow, 1992).

10 T. Cummings and S. Srivastva, *Management of Work: A Socio-Technical Systems Approach* (San Diego: University Associates, 1977): 112–16.

11 L. Bourgeois, 'Strategic goals, perceived uncertainty and economic performance in volatile environments', *Academy of Management Journal,* 28 (1985): 548–73; C. West Jr and C. Schwenk, 'Top management team strategic consensus, demographic homogeneity and firm performance: a report of resounding nonfindings', *Academy of Management Journal,* 17 (1996): 571–76.

12 J. Clark and C. Krone, 'Towards an overall view of organisation development in the seventies', in *Management of Change and Conflict,* eds J. Thomas and W. Bennis (Middlesex, England: Penguin Books, 1972): 284–304.

13 C. Krone, 'Open systems redesign' in *Theory and Method in Organization Development: An Evolutionary Process,* ed. J. Adams (Arlington, Va.: NTL Institute for Applied Behavioral Science, 1974): 364–91; G. Jayaram, 'Open systems planning' in *The Planning of Change,* 3rd ed., eds W. Bennis, K. Benne, R. Chin and K. Corey, (New York: Holt, Rinehart and Winston, 1976): 275–83; R. Beckhard and R. Harris, *Organizational Transitions: Managing Complex Change,* 2nd ed. (Reading, Mass.: Addison-Wesley, 1987); Cummings and Srivastva, *Management of Work, op. cit.*

14 R. Fry, 'Improving trustee, administrator and physician collaboration through open systems planning' in *Organizational Development in Health Care Organizations,* eds N. Margulies and J. Adams (Reading, Mass.: Addison-Wesley, 1982): 282–92.

15 Jayaram, 'Open systems planning', *op. cit.,* 275–83; Cummings and Srivastva, *Management of Work, op. cit.*; Fry, 'Improving collaboration', *op. cit.,* 82–92.

16 M. Jelinek and J. Litterer, 'Why OD must become strategic' in *Organizational Change and Development,* 2, eds W. Pasmore and R. Woodman (Greenwich, Conn.: JAI Press, 1988): 135–62; A. Bhambri and L. Pate, 'Introduction—the strategic change agenda: stimuli, processes and outcomes', *Journal of Organization Change Management,* 4 (1991): 4–6; D. Nadler, M. Gerstein, R. Shaw and associates, *Organizational Architecture* (San Francisco: Jossey-Bass, 1992); C. Worley, D. Hitchin and W. Ross, *Integrated Strategic Change: How Organization Development Builds Competitive Advantage* (Reading, Mass.: Addison-Wesley, 1996).

17 H. Mintzberg, *The Rise and Fall of Strategic Planning* (New York: The Free Press, 1994).

18 Worley, Hitchin and Ross, *Integrated Strategic Change, op. cit.*

19 P. Senge, *The Fifth Discipline* (New York: Doubleday, 1990); E. Lawler, *The Ultimate Advantage* (San Francisco: Jossey-Bass, 1992); Worley, Hitchin and Ross, *Integrated Strategic Change, op. cit.*

20 L. Greiner and V. Schein, *Power and Organization Development* (Reading, Mass.: Addison-Wesley, 1988).

21 M. Porter, *Competitive Strategy* (New York: The Free Press, 1980).

22 R. Grant, *Contemporary Strategy Analysis,* 2nd ed. (Cambridge, Mass.: Basil Blackwell, 1995).

23 M. Porter, *Competitive Advantage* (New York: Free Press, 1985).

24 R. Miles and C. Snow, *Organization Strategy, Structure and Process* (New York: McGraw-Hill, 1978); M. Tushman and E. Romanelli, 'Organizational evolution: a metamorphosis model of convergence and reorientation' in *Research in Organization Behavior,* 7, eds L. Cummings and B. Staw (Greenwich, Conn.: JAI Press, 1985).

25 J. Naisbitt and P. Aburdene, *Reinventing the Corporation* (New York: Warner Books, 1985); A. Toffler, *The Third Wave* (New York: McGraw-Hill, 1980); A. Toffler, *The Adaptive Corporation* (New York: McGraw-Hill, 1984); M. Weisbord, *Productive Workplaces* (San Francisco: Jossey-Bass, 1987).

26 E. Lawler III, *The Ultimate Advantage* (San Francisco: Jossey-Bass, 1992); M. Tushman, W. Newman and E. Romanelli, 'Convergence and upheaval: managing the unsteady pace of organizational evolution', *California Management Review,* 29 (1987): 1–16; Nadler, Gerstein, Shaw and associates, *Organizational Architecture, op. cit.*; R. Buzzell and B. Gale, *The PIMS Principles* (New York: Free Press, 1987).

27 L. Hrebiniak and W. Joyce, *Implementing Strategy* (New York: Macmillan, 1984); J. Galbraith and R. Kazanjian, *Strategy Implementation: Structure, Systems and Process*, 2nd ed. (St. Paul: West Publishing Company, 1986).

28 P. Dawson, 'Advanced technology design, people and organisation: experience of Australian industrial collaboration', *Integrated Manufacturing Systems*, 7:5 (1996): 5–11.

29 T. Cummings, 'Transorganizational development' in *Research in Organizational Behavior*, 6, eds B. Staw and L. Cummings (Greenwich, Conn.: JAI Press, 1984): 367–422.

30 B. Gray, 'Conditions facilitating interorganizational collaboration', *Human Relations*, 38 (1985): 911–36; K. Harrigan and W. Newman, 'Bases of interorganization co-operation: propensity, power, persistence', *Journal of Management Studies*, 27 (1990): 417–34; Cummings, 'Transorganizational development', *op. cit.*

31 Cummings, 'Transorganizational development', *op. cit.*

32 C. Raben, 'Building strategic partnerships: creating and managing effective joint ventures' in *Organizational Architecture*, eds D. Nadler, M. Gerstein, R. Shaw and associates (San Francisco: Jossey-Bass, 1992): 81–109; B. Gray, *Collaborating: Finding Common Ground for Multiparty Problems* (San Francisco: Jossey-Bass, 1989); Harrigan and Newman, 'Bases of interorganization cooperation', *op. cit.*; P. Lorange and J. Roos, 'Analytical steps in the formation of strategic alliances', *Journal of Organizational Change Management*, 4 (1991): 60–72.

33 D. Boje, 'Towards a theory and praxis of transorganizational development: stakeholder networks and their habitats', (working paper 79–6, Behavioral and Organizational Science Study Center, Graduate School of Management, University of California at Los Angeles, February 1982); B. Gricar, 'The legitimacy of consultants and stakeholders in interorganizational problems', (paper presented at annual meeting of the Academy of Management, San Diego, August 1981); T. Williams, 'The search conference in active adaptive planning', *Journal of Applied Behavioral Science*, 16 (1980): 470–83; B. Gray and T. Hay, 'Political limits to interorganizational consensus and change', *Journal of Applied Behavioral Science*, 22 (1986): 95–112.

34 E. Trist, 'Referent organizations and the development of interorganizational domains', (paper delivered at annual meeting of the Academy of Management, Atlanta, August 1979).

35 Cummings, 'Transorganizational development', *op. cit.*

36 Raben, 'Building strategic partnerships', *op. cit.*

37 M. Stewart, 'New strategic alliance for PDL', *New Zealand Manufacturer* (February 1999): 1–23.

38 Cummings, 'Transorganizational development', *op. cit.*

39 *Ibid.*

40 B. Gricar and D. Brown, 'Conflict, power and organization in a changing community', *Human Relations*, 34 (1981): 877–93.

41 Cummings, 'Transorganizational development', *op. cit.*

Organisation transformation

This chapter presents interventions that are aimed at transforming organisations and describes activities designed to change the basic character or culture of the organisation. These interventions bring about important alignments among the organisation strategies, design elements and culture and between the organisation and its competitive environment.[1] These frame-breaking and sometimes revolutionary interventions are mostly directed at the culture or dominant paradigm within the organisation and typically go beyond improving the organisation incrementally, instead focusing on changing the way it views itself and its environment.

Organisation transformations can occur in response to, or in anticipation of, major changes in the organisation's environment or technology. In addition, these changes are often associated with significant alterations in the firm's business strategy, which, in turn, may require modifying corporate culture as well as the internal structures and processes in order to support the new direction. Such fundamental change entails a new paradigm for organising and managing organisations. It involves qualitatively different ways of perceiving, thinking and behaving in organisations. Movement toward this new way of operating requires top managers to take an active leadership role. The change process is characterised by considerable innovation and learning, and continues almost indefinitely as organisation members discover new ways of improving the organisation and adapting it to changing conditions.

Organisation transformation is a recent advance in organisation development and there is some confusion about its meaning and definition. This chapter starts with a description of several major features of transformational change. Against this background, three kinds of interventions are discussed: culture change, self-design and organisation learning.

Organisation culture is the pattern of assumptions, values and norms shared by organisation members. A growing body of research has shown that culture can affect strategy formulation and implementation, as well as a firm's ability to achieve high levels of performance. Culture change involves helping senior executives and administrators to diagnose existing culture and make necessary alterations in the basic assumptions and values that underlie organisational behaviours.

Self-designing organisations are those that have gained the capacity to fundamentally alter themselves. Creating them is a highly participative process involving multiple stakeholders in setting strategic directions, designing appropriate structures and processes and implementing them. This intervention includes considerable innovation and learning as organisations design and implement significant changes. Organisation learning refers to the capacity of an organisation to change and improve.[2] Distinct from individual learning; this intervention helps the organisation move beyond solving existing problems to gain the capability to improve continuously. It results in the development of a learning organisation, where empowered members take responsibility for strategic direction.

Characteristics of transformational change

During the 1990s a large number of organisations radically altered the way they operated and related to their environment. Increased foreign competition forced many industries to downsize and to become leaner, more efficient and flexible. Deregulation pushed organisations in the financial services, telecommunications and airline industries to rethink business strategies and to reshape how they operate. Public demands for less government and lowered deficits forced public-sector agencies to streamline operations and to deliver more for less. Rapid changes in technologies rendered many organisational practices obsolete, pushing firms to be continually innovative and nimble.

Organisation transformation implies radical changes in the way members perceive, think and behave at work. These changes go far beyond making the existing organisation better, or fine-tuning the *status quo*. They are concerned with fundamentally altering the assumptions that underlie how the organisation relates to its environment and functions. Changing these assumptions entails significant shifts in corporate philosophy and values and in the numerous structures and organisational arrangements that shape members' behaviours. Not only is the magnitude of change greater, but the change fundamentally alters the qualitative nature of the organisation.

Organisation transformation interventions are recent additions to OD and are still in a formative stage of development. For example, organisation learning was originally discussed in the late 1950s, but did not reach prominence until the early 1990s. Examination of the rapidly growing literature on the topic suggests, however, the following distinguishing features of these revolutionary change efforts.

Triggered by environmental and internal disruptions

Organisations are unlikely to undertake transformational change unless significant reasons to do so emerge. Power, sentience and expertise are vested in existing organisational arrangements and when faced with problems, members are more likely to fine-tune those structures than to drastically alter them. Thus, in most cases organisations must experience or anticipate a severe threat to survival before they will be motivated to undertake transformational change. Such threats generally arise when environmental and internal changes that threaten the very existence of the organisation as it is presently constituted render existing organisational strategies and designs obsolete.

In studying a large number of organisation transformations, Tushman, Newman and Romanelli showed that transformational change occurs in response to at least three kinds of disruption:[3]

- *industry discontinuities*: there are sharp changes in legal, political, economic and technological conditions that shift the basis for competition within industries
- *product life cycle shifts:* changes in product life cycle that require different business strategies
- *internal company dynamics:* changes in size, corporate portfolio strategy, executive turnover and the like.

These disruptions severely jolt organisations and push them to alter business strategy and, in turn, their mission, values, structure, systems and procedures.

Systemic and revolutionary change

Transformational change involves reshaping the organisation's culture and design elements. These changes can be characterised as systemic and revolutionary as the entire nature of the organisation is fundamentally altered. Typically driven by senior executives, change may occur rapidly so that it does not get mired in politics, individual resistance and other forms of organisational inertia.[4] This is particularly true of changes to such features of the organisation as structure, information systems, human resource practices and work design, which tend to reinforce one another, thus making it difficult to change them in a piecemeal manner.[5] They need to be changed together and in a co-ordinated fashion so that they can mutually support each other, as well as the new cultural values and assumptions.[6] Transformational change, however, is distinguished from other types of strategic change by its attention to the people side of the organisation. For a change to be labelled 'transformational', a majority of individuals in an organisation must change their behaviour.[7]

Long-term studies of organisational evolution underscore the revolutionary nature of transformational change.[8] They suggest that organisations tend to move through relatively long periods of smooth growth and operation. These periods of convergence or evolution are characterised by incremental changes. At times, however, most organisations experience severe external or internal disruptions that render existing organisational arrangements ineffective. Successful firms are able to respond to these threats to survival by transforming themselves to fit the new conditions. These periods of total system and quantum changes represent abrupt shifts in the organisation's structure, culture and processes. If successful, they enable the organisation to experience another long period of smooth functioning until the next disruption signals the need for another drastic change.[9]

These studies of organisation evolution and revolution point to the benefits of implementing transformational change as rapidly as possible. The faster the organisation can respond to disruptions, the quicker it can attain the benefits of operating in a new way. Rapid change enables the organisation to reach a period of smooth growth and functioning sooner, thus providing it with a competitive advantage over those firms that change more slowly.

New organising paradigm

Organisations undertaking transformational change are, by definition, involved in second-order or gamma types of change.[10] Gamma change involves discontinuous shifts in mental or organisational frameworks.[11] Creative metaphors, such as 'organisation learning' or 'continuous improvement', are often used to help members visualise the new paradigm.[12] During the 1980s, increases in technological change, concern for quality and worker participation led to at least one shift in the organising paradigm. Characterised as the transition from 'control-based' to 'commitment-based' organisations, the features of the new paradigm included leaner, more flexible structures; information and decision making pushed down to the lowest levels; decentralised teams and business units accountable for specific products, services or customers; and participative management and teamwork. This new organising paradigm is well suited to changing conditions.

Driven by senior executives and line management

A key feature of organisation transformation is the active role of senior executives and line managers in all phases of the change process.[13] They are responsible for the strategic direction and operation of the organisation and actively lead the transformation. They decide when to initiate transformational change, what the change should be, how it should be implemented and who should be responsible for directing it. Because existing executives may lack the talent, energy and commitment to undertake these tasks, they may be replaced by outsiders who are recruited to lead the change. Research on transformational change suggests that externally recruited executives are three times more likely to initiate such change than existing executive teams.[14]

The critical role of executive leadership in transformational change is clearly emerging. Lucid accounts of transformational leaders describe how executives such as Ziggy Switkowski at Telstra, John McFarlane at ANZ and Philip Aiken at BHP actively manage both the organisational and personal dynamics of transformational change. Nadler, Tushman and others point to three key roles for executive leadership of such change:[15]

1 *Envisioning.* Executives must articulate a clear and credible vision of the new strategic orientation. They must set new and difficult standards for performance and generate pride in past accomplishments and enthusiasm for the new strategy.

2 *Energising.* Executives must personally show their excitement about the changes, and model the behaviours that they expect of others. They must communicate examples of early success in order to mobilise energy for change.

3 *Enabling.* Executives must provide the resources necessary for undertaking significant change and use rewards to reinforce new behaviours. Leaders must also build an effective top-management team to manage the new organisation and develop management practices to support the change process.

Continuous learning and change

Transformational change requires considerable innovation and learning.[16] Organisation members must learn how to enact the new behaviours that are required in order to implement new strategic directions. This typically involves a continuous learning process of trying new behaviours, assessing their consequences and modifying them if necessary. Because members must usually learn qualitatively different ways of perceiving, thinking and behaving, the learning process is likely to be substantial and to involve much unlearning. It is directed by a vision of the future organisation and by the values and norms necessary for supporting it. Learning occurs at all levels of the organisation, from senior executives to lower-level employees.

Because the environment itself is likely to be changing during the change process, transformational change rarely has a delimited time frame, but is likely to persist as long as the firm needs to adapt to change. Learning how to manage change in a continuous manner can help the organisation keep pace with a dynamic environment. It can provide the organisation with the built-in capacity to continually fit into its environment.

Culture change

The topic of organisation culture became extremely important to Australian companies during the 1990s and culture change is now the most common form of organisation transformation. The number of culture change interventions has grown accordingly. Organisation culture is also the focus of growing research and OD application, and has spawned a number of best-selling management books starting with *Theory Z, The Art of Japanese Management, In Search of Excellence* and, more recently, *Built to Last, Corporate Culture and Performance* and *Beyond the Boundaries*.[17] Organisation culture is seen as a major strength of such companies as AMP, Lend Lease, Ansett Airlines and Arnotts. A growing number of managers have come to appreciate the power of corporate culture in shaping employee beliefs and actions. A well-conceived and well-managed organisation culture, closely linked to an effective business strategy, can mean the difference between success and failure in today's demanding environment.

Concept of organisation culture

Despite the increased attention and research devoted to corporate culture, there is still some confusion about what the term 'culture' really means when applied to organisations.[18] Examination of the different definitions suggests that *organisation culture* is the pattern of basic assumptions, values, norms and artefacts shared by organisation members. These shared meanings help members make sense of the organisation. The meanings signal how work is to be done and evaluated, and how employees are to relate to each other and to significant others, such as customers, suppliers and government agencies.

Organisation culture includes four major elements existing at different levels of awareness, as shown in Figure 20.1.[19]

1 *Artefacts*. Artefacts are the highest levels of cultural awareness. They are the visible manifestations of the deeper levels of culture, such as norms, values and basic assumptions. They include observable behaviours of members, as well as the structures, systems, procedures, rules and physical aspects of the organisation. At Mono Pumps, a pump manufacturing firm in Melbourne, all members of the organisation are encouraged to believe that they have a valuable contribution to make to the organisation. There is an implied sense of 'Have a go', which results in employees being encouraged to discuss directly with the customer the development of particular products to suit their needs, or to arrange maintenance or service for their pumps. Although this may not be specifically stated, it is, nevertheless, a generally accepted procedure.

2 *Norms*. Just below the surface of cultural awareness are norms guiding how members should behave in particular situations. These represent unwritten rules of

FIGURE 20.1   Levels of corporate culture

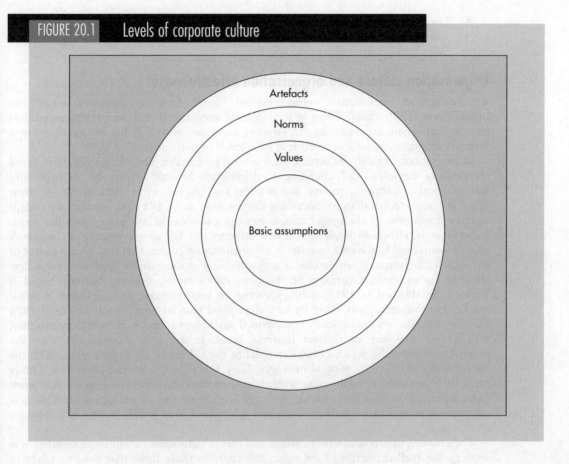

behaviour. At Mono Pumps, norms dictate that employees are allowed to go beyond their normal job description in order to satisfy customer requirements.

3 *Values.* The next deeper level of awareness includes values about what *ought* to be in organisations. Values tell members what is important in the organisation and what they need to pay attention to. Obviously, the norms and artefacts support this value.

4 *Basic assumptions.* At the deepest level of cultural awareness are the taken-for-granted assumptions about how organisational problems should be solved. These basic assumptions tell members how to perceive, think and feel about things. They are the non-confrontable and non-debatable assumptions about how to relate to the environment, about human nature, human activity and human relationships. For example, the basic assumption at Mono Pumps is that all the employees are skilled and competent in their tasks. The consequence is that customers are happy about the service they receive and remain loyal to the organisation.

Corporate culture is the product of long-term social learning and reflects what has worked in the past.[20] It represents those basic assumptions, values, norms and artefacts that have worked well enough to be passed on to succeeding generations of employees. For example, the cultures of many companies (including BHP, CSR and Pacific Dunlop) are deeply rooted in the firm's history. They were laid down by a strong founder and have been re-inforced by successive top executives and corporate success into customary ways of perceiving and acting. These customs provide organisation members with clear and widely shared answers to such practical issues as the following:[21]

- 'Who's who and who matters around here?'
- 'Who's "us"? Who's "them"? How do we treat them and us?'

- 'How do we do things around here and why?'
- 'What constitutes a problem and what do we do when one arises?'
- 'What really matters here and why?'

Organisation culture and organisation effectiveness

The interest in organisation culture derives largely from its presumed impact on organisation effectiveness. There is considerable speculation and increasing research to suggest that organisation culture can improve an organisation's ability to implement new business strategies, as well as to achieve high levels of performance.

Organisations in many industries, such as energy, banking and electronics, have faced increasingly complex and changing environments brought about by deregulation, technological revolutions, foreign competition and unpredictable markets. Many firms (e.g. Telstra, the Australian Broadcasting Corporation and CSR) have attempted to adapt to those conditions by changing business strategy and moving into new, unfamiliar areas. Unfortunately, efforts to implement a new strategy can fail simply because a company's culture is unsuited to the new business.[22] An organisation culture that was once a source of strength for a company can become a major liability in successfully implementing a new strategy. For example, Castricum Brothers is a major meat-processing business based in Victoria. Established in 1958, it has survived an unpredictable and turbulent external market environment, more often by luck than good management. It was not until 1994 that the organisation dramatically transformed itself from a Tayloristic work organisation into a new structure of distinct business units. In order to dramatically turn the organisation around it was necessary to redefine the culture of the organisation. With the appointment of a young general manager, Gary Castricum, a second-generation family member, it was possible to do away with antiquated work practices and create a new work place environment that was conducive to participative forms of management. This new culture was unique in an industry described as unglamorous, tough, macho and resistant to change.[23]

The growing appreciation that culture can play a significant role in implementing new strategy has fuelled interest in the topic, especially in those firms that need to adapt to turbulent environments. A number of independent consultants and consulting firms have increasingly focused on helping firms to implement new strategies by bringing culture more in line with the new direction.[24] Indeed, much of the emphasis in the 1970s on formulating business strategy shifted to organisation culture in the 1980s as firms discovered cultural roadblocks to implementing strategies. Along with this emerging focus on organisation culture, however, came the sobering reality that cultural change is an extremely difficult and long-term process. Some experts doubt whether large firms can even bring about fundamental changes in their cultures; those who have accomplished such feats estimate that the process takes between six and 15 years.[25] For example, Telstra has struggled for years to change from a service-oriented telephone company to a market-oriented communications business. Its recent industrial conflict is thought to be partly the result of a dramatic shift in culture from a 'public sector' mindset to one that is more conducive to a market competitive environment.

Evidence suggests that, in addition to affecting the implementation of business strategy, corporate culture can affect organisation performance. Comparative studies of Eastern and Western management methods suggest that the relative success of Japanese companies in the 1980s could be partly explained by their strong corporate cultures that emphasise employee participation, open communication, security and equality.[26] One study of American firms showed a similar pattern of results.[27] Using survey measures of culture and Standard & Poor's financial ratios as indicators of organisational effectiveness, the research examined the relationship between culture and effectiveness for 34 large American companies over a five-year period. The firms represented 25 different industries, and more than 43 000 people responded to the survey instrument. The results show that firms whose cultures support employee participation in decision making, adaptable work methods, sensible work designs and reasonable and clear goals perform significantly better (financial ratios about twice as high) than companies scoring low on these factors. Moreover, the employee participation element of corporate culture only showed differences in effectiveness among the firms after three years; the other measures of culture showed differences in all five years. This suggests that changing some parts of corporate culture, such as participation, needs to be considered as a long-term investment.

More recently, a study of 207 firms in 22 different industries between 1987 and 1991 examined the relationship between culture and performance.[28] The researchers examined relationships between financial performance and the strength of a culture, the strategic appropriateness of a culture and the adaptiveness of a culture. First, there were no significant performance differences between organisations with widely shared values and those with little agreement around cultural assumptions. Second, there was a significant relationship between culture and performance when the organisation emphasised the 'right' values—values that were critical to success in a particular industry. Finally, performance results over time supported cultures that emphasised anticipation of, and adaptation to, environmental change.

These findings suggest that the strength of an organisation's culture can be both an advantage and a disadvantage. Under stable conditions, widely shared and strategically appropriate values can significantly contribute to organisation performance. However, if the environment is changing, strong cultures can be a liability. Unless they also emphasise adaptiveness, the organisation may experience wide swings in performance during transformational change.

Diagnosing organisation culture

Culture change interventions generally start by diagnosing the organisation's existing culture so as to assess its fit with current or proposed business strategies. This requires uncovering and understanding the shared assumptions, values, norms and artefacts that characterise its culture. OD practitioners have developed a number of useful approaches for diagnosing organisation culture, which fall into three different, yet complementary, perspectives: the behavioural approach, the competing values approach and the deep assumption approach. Each diagnostic perspective focuses on particular aspects of organisation culture and together the approaches can provide a comprehensive assessment of these complex phenomena.

The behavioural approach

This method of diagnosis emphasises the surface level of organisation culture—the pattern of behaviours that produce business results.[29] It is among the more practical approaches to culture diagnosis because it assesses key work behaviours that can be observed.[30] The behavioural approach provides specific descriptions about how tasks are performed and how relationships are managed in an organisation. For example, Table 20.1 summarises the organisation culture of an international banking division as perceived by managers. The data were obtained from a series of individual and group interviews asking managers to describe 'the way the game is played', as though they were coaching a new organisation member. Managers were asked to give their impressions in regard to four key relationships (company-wide, boss–subordinate, peer and interdepartment) and in terms of six managerial tasks (innovating, decision making, communicating, organising, monitoring and appraising/rewarding). These perceptions revealed a number of implicit norms for how tasks are performed and relationships managed at the division.

Cultural diagnosis derived from a behavioural approach can also be used to assess the *cultural risk* of trying to implement the organisational changes that are necessary for supporting a new strategy. Significant cultural risks result when changes that are highly important to the implementation of a new strategy are incompatible with the existing patterns of behaviour. Knowledge of such risks can help managers determine whether implementation plans should be changed to manage around the existing culture, whether the culture should be changed or whether the strategy itself should be modified or abandoned.

TABLE 20.1	Summary of corporate culture at an international banking division

Relationships	Culture summary
Companywide	Preserve your autonomy
	Allow area managers to run the business as long as they meet the profit budget
Boss–subordinate	Avoid confrontations
	Smooth over disagreements
	Support the boss
Peer	Guard information; it is power
	Be a gentleman or lady
Interdepartment	Protect your department's bottom line
	Form alliances around specific issues
	Guard your turf

Tasks	Culture summary
Innovating	Consider it risky
	Be a quick second
Decision making	Handle each deal on its own merits
	Gain consensus
	Require many sign-offs
	Involve the right people
	Seize the opportunity
Communicating	Withhold information to control adversaries
	Avoid confrontations
	Be a gentleman or lady
Organizing	Centralize power
	Be autocratic
Monitoring	Meet short-term profit goals
Appraising and rewarding	Reward the faithful
	Choose the best bankers as managers
	Seek safe jobs

Source: Reprinted by permission of the publisher from H. Schwartz and S. Davis, 'Matching corporate culture and business strategy', *Organizational Dynamics*, 10 (Summer 1981): 38, American Management Association, New York. All rights reserved.

The competing values approach

This perspective assesses an organisation's culture in terms of how it resolves a set of value dilemmas.[31] The approach suggests that an organisation's culture can be understood in terms of four important 'value pairs'; each pair consisting of contradictory values placed at opposite ends of a continuum, as shown in Figure 20.2. The four value pairs are internal focus vs external focus, organic processes vs mechanistic processes, innovation vs stability and people orientation vs task orientation. Organisations continually struggle to satisfy the conflicting demands placed on them by these competing values. For example, when faced with the competing values of internal vs external focus, organisations must choose between attending to internal operations or their external environment. Too much emphasis on the environment can result in the neglect of internal efficiencies. Conversely, too much attention to the internal aspects of organisations can result in their missing important changes in the competitive environment.

The competing values approach commonly collects diagnostic data about the four sets of competing values, using a survey that has been specifically designed for the purpose.[32] It provides measures of where an organisation's existing values fall along each of the four competing values continua. When taken together, these data identify an organisation's culture as falling into one of the four quadrants shown in Figure 20.2: group culture, adhocracy culture, hierarchical culture and rational culture. For example, if an

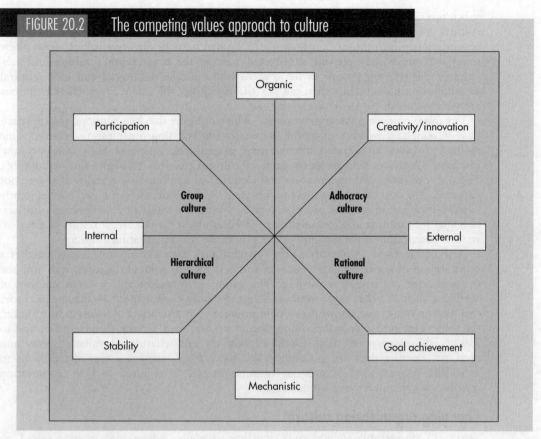

FIGURE 20.2   The competing values approach to culture

Source: Reproduced by permission of the publisher from D. Denison and G. Spreitzer, 'Organizational culture and organizational development: a competing values approach' in *Research in Organizational Change and Development*, 5, eds R. Woodman and W. Posmore (Greenwich, Conn.: JAI Press, 1991): 4.

organisation's values are internally focused and emphasise people and organic processes, it manifests a group culture. On the other hand, a rational culture characterises values that are externally focused and emphasises task achievement and mechanistic processes.

The deep assumptions approach

This final diagnostic approach emphasises the deepest levels of organisation culture—the generally unexamined assumptions, values and norms that guide member behaviour and which often have a powerful impact upon organisation effectiveness. A diagnosis of culture from this perspective typically begins with the most tangible level of awareness, and then works down to the deep assumptions.

Diagnosing organisation culture at the deep assumptions level poses at least three difficult problems for collecting pertinent information.[33] First, culture reflects shared assumptions about what is important, how things are done and how people should behave in organisations. People generally take cultural assumptions for granted and rarely speak of them directly. Rather, the company's culture is implied in concrete behavioural examples, such as daily routines, stories, rituals and language. This means that considerable time and effort must be spent observing, sifting through and asking people about these cultural outcroppings in order to understand their deeper significance for organisation members. Second, some values and beliefs that people espouse have little to do with the ones they really hold and follow. People are reluctant to admit this discrepancy, yet the real assumptions underlying idealised portrayals of culture must somehow be discovered. Third, large, diverse organisations are quite likely to have several subcultures, including countercultures that go against the grain of the wider organisation culture. Assumptions may not be widely shared and may differ across groups in the organisation, which means that focusing on limited parts of the organisation or on a few select individuals may provide a distorted view of the organisation's culture and sub-cultures. All relevant groups in the organisation must be discovered and their cultural assumptions sampled. Only then can practitioners judge the extent to which assumptions are widely shared.

Organisation development practitioners who emphasise the deep assumptions approach have developed a number of useful techniques for assessing organisation culture.[34] One method involves an iterative interviewing process that involves both outsiders and insiders.[35] Outsiders help members uncover cultural elements through joint exploration. The outsider enters the organisation and experiences surprises and puzzles that were not expected. The outsider shares these observations with insiders and the two parties jointly explore their meaning. This process involves several iterations of experiencing surprises, checking for meaning and formulating hypotheses about the culture. It results in a formal written description of the assumptions that underlie the organisation's culture.

A second method for identifying the organisation's basic assumptions brings together a cross section of senior management, old and new members, labour leaders, staff and line managers for a two-day workshop. The group first brainstorms a large number of artefacts, such as behaviours, symbols, language and physical space arrangements. From this list, the values and norms that would produce such artefacts are deduced. In addition, the values espoused in formal planning documents are listed. Finally, the group attempts to identify the assumptions that would explain the constellation of values, norms and artefacts. Because they are generally taken for granted, these are typically difficult to articulate. A great deal of process consultation skill is required to help organisation members see the underlying assumptions.

Changing organisation culture

There is considerable debate over whether changing something as deep-seated as organisation culture is possible.[36] Those advocating culture change generally focus on those elements of culture that are nearer to the surface, such as norms and artefacts. These elements are more changeable than are the deeper elements of values and basic assumptions. They offer OD practitioners a more manageable set of action levers for changing organisational behaviours. Some would argue, however, that unless the deeper values and assumptions are changed, organisations have not really changed the culture.

Those arguing that implementing culture change is extremely difficult, if not impossible, typically focus on the deeper elements of culture (values and basic assumptions). Because these deeper elements represent assumptions about organisational life, members do not question them and have a difficult time envisioning anything else. Moreover, members may not want to change their cultural assumptions. The culture provides a strong defence against external uncertainties and threats.[37] It represents past solutions to difficult problems. Members may also have vested interests in maintaining the culture—they may have developed personal stakes, pride and power in the culture and may strongly resist attempts to change it. Finally, cultures that provide firms with a competitive advantage may be difficult to imitate, thus making it hard for less successful firms to change their cultures to approximate the more successful ones.[38]

Given the problems with cultural change, most practitioners in this area suggest that changes in corporate culture should be considered only after other, less difficult and less costly, solutions have either been applied or ruled out.[39] Attempts to overcome cultural risks when strategic changes are incompatible with culture might include ways of managing around the existing culture. Consider, for example, a single-product organisation with a functional focus and a history of centralised control that is considering an ambitious product-diversification strategy. The firm might manage around its existing culture by using business teams to co-ordinate functional specialists around each new product. Another alternative to changing culture is to modify strategy to bring it more in line with culture. The single-product organisation just mentioned might decide to undertake a less ambitious strategy of product diversification.

Despite problems in changing corporate culture, large-scale cultural change may be necessary in certain situations: if the firm's culture does not fit a changing environment; if the industry is extremely competitive and changing rapidly and frequently; if the company is mediocre or worse; if the firm is about to become a very large company; or if the company is smaller and growing rapidly.[40] Organisations facing these conditions need to change their cultures in order to adapt to the situation or to operate at higher levels of effectiveness. They may have to supplement attempts at cultural change with other approaches, such as managing around the existing culture and modifying strategy.

Although knowledge about changing corporate culture is in a formative stage, the following practical advice offers guidelines for cultural change:[41]

1   *Clear strategic vision.* Effective cultural change should start from a clear vision of the firm's new strategy and of the shared values and behaviours needed to make it work.[42] This vision provides the purpose and direction for cultural change. It serves as a yardstick for comparing the firm's existing culture and for deciding whether proposed changes are consistent with new values. A useful approach to providing clear strategic vision is development of a statement of corporate purpose, listing in straightforward terms the basic values that the organisation believes in. For example, the task set by ANZ's CEO John McFarlane to make dealing with the bank 'an enjoyable customer experience' is a big ask in a country where 'bank bashing' has become a national sport.[43]

2   *Top-management commitment.* Cultural change must be managed from the top of the organisation. Senior managers and administrators need to be strongly committed to the new values and need to create constant pressures for change. They must have the staying power to see the changes through.[44] For example, Bob Ansett, the former CEO of Budget Rent-a-Car, famed for his practice of 'management by walking around', now has a successful career on the management lecture circuit.

3   *Symbolic leadership.* Senior executives must communicate the new culture through their own actions. Their behaviours need to symbolise the kinds of values and behaviours being sought. In the few publicised cases of successful culture change, corporate leaders have shown an almost missionary zeal for the new values; their actions have forcefully symbolised the values.[45] For example, Toyota Australia's implementation of '360-degree performance appraisal' began at the top—giving even the most junior workers a chance to assess the performance of their bosses.[46]

4   *Supporting organisational changes.* Cultural change generally requires supporting modifications in organisational structure, human resource systems, information and control systems and management styles. These organisational features can help to orient people's behaviours to the new culture.[47] They can make people aware of the behaviours required to get things done in the new culture and can encourage the performance of those behaviours. For example, when Peter Kirby became managing director of building materials and commodity conglomerate CSR in 1998, he had a clear brief: fix up the company and its share price. He realised that focusing on numbers and balance sheets was not enough; what the company needed was a cultural change: more women, more local nationals in overseas businesses and more accountability in divisions—all changes that reinforce the importance of challenges and being proactive.[48]

5   *Selection and socialisation of newcomers and termination of those with different views.* One of the most effective methods of changing corporate culture involves changing organisational membership. People can be selected and terminated in terms of their fit with the new culture. This is especially important in key leadership positions, where people's actions can significantly promote or hinder new values and behaviours. For example, the arrival of new CSR managing director Peter Kirby in 1998 led to the departure of two senior managers and changes amongst the executive group.[49] Another approach involves socialising new hires into the new culture. People are most open to organisational influences during the entry stage,

when they can be effectively indoctrinated into the culture. For example, companies with strong cultures like Amcor, CSR and Westpac attach great importance to socialising new members into the company's values.

6   *Ethical and legal sensitivity.* Cultural change can raise significant tensions between organisation and individual interests, resulting in ethical and legal problems for practitioners. This is particularly pertinent when organisations are trying to implement cultural values that promote employee integrity, control, equitable treatment and job security—values often included in cultural change efforts. Statements about such values provide employees with certain expectations about their rights and how they will be treated in the organisation. If the organisation does not follow through with behaviours and procedures that support and protect these implied rights, it may breach ethical principles and, in some cases, legal employment contracts. Recommendations for reducing the chances of such ethical and legal problems include setting realistic values for culture change and not promising what the organisation cannot deliver; encouraging input from throughout the organisation in setting cultural values; providing mechanisms for member dissent and diversity, such as internal review procedures; and educating managers about the legal and ethical pitfalls inherent in cultural change and helping them to develop guidelines for resolving such issues.

Application 20.1 presents an example of culture change at Yakka. The example illustrates the importance of a vision statement and the executive commitment required to bring about transformational change in an organisation.[50]

APPLICATION 20.1

Yakka devises a service that imports could not match

A contemporary Australian myth is that the manufacturing industry became moribund after World War II because of over-protection. At best this was an incomplete analysis, considering that countries such as Japan have become internationally competitive while heavily protecting their domestic markets; it also contains a strategic trap: the cultural cringe.

It invites Australian managers to think they have to 'catch up' with the competition, when proper strategy is better seen as competing with oneself. Rather than imitating what competitors do well, the challenge is to do something competitors cannot.

American management theorist Gary Hamel says the aim is to imagine a new future, usually by looking outside the industry in which the company is operating. He says companies often fail to do this because they think that whoever takes the lead is likely to make mistakes, and that trying to implement it is more risky.

Neither assumption, he says, holds true. Companies that take the lead often do not fail and even when they experience difficulties, what they learn usually proves to be valuable. And, properly managed, innovation need not be more risky.

Hamel believes that management must balance under- and over-commitment. He calls this 'maximising the ratio of learning over investment'. He defines the aim as being 'to learn one day earlier than my competitors about the technology and the demand etc., while betting one dollar less to get that insight. I don't believe you can wait and let others make mistakes. Neither do I think getting to the future first is about betting the farm.'

Industrial clothing company Yakka is attempting to adopt this approach to strategy. Its managing director, Andrew Edgar, says that the trigger has been falling levels of protection for the textile, clothing and footwear industries. Although less protected than other areas of the industry (industrial clothing was never protected by quotas) tariffs have been falling by 3% annually and the company has not increased prices since July 1995.

During the same period, Yakka's average wage costs rose by more than $80 a month—more, Edgar notes, than the entire monthly wages of a Chinese worker. Wage costs are a relatively low proportion of overall costs—the raw material content of industrial clothing is 65–70% of total costs—but the pressure is on to achieve significant productivity improvements and to prepare for what might be hyper-competition from overseas.

Fourteen months ago, management set out to examine the company's 'core competencies', the characteristics that make it unique. Edgar says that what he found most useful was examining 'the whole concept of a company like Yakka remaining and being internationally competitive'.

'We realised it's not about all the time ... catching up with the competition, whether it be Chinese or Malaysian or Indian; or price competition from domestic competitors sourcing from China and Fiji,' he says. 'I think people cottoned on that it is a good objective to get ahead of competition. A lot of what we are dealing with is a perceived threat of what is out there. It has not yet turned into reality in terms of the quantum of imports.'

The core competencies, management decided, were the business's 60-year history, its financial stability, its existing market presence and its brand-name presence. Edgar says the company is also seeing a unique advantage in the way it adds a service component to the products:

'The garment-management system that has been developed in the business enables us to service major corporate accounts, whereby we can service the requirements of each individual in an organisation the size of Telstra, dealing directly with each individual's requirements. We can take an order, process that order and deliver it to that person's place of work.'

Des Blake, director of Blake Strategic Planners, says two core competencies stood out: Yakka's expertise in the work wear market and its development of information technology that allowed it to individually tailor the wardrobe requirements of employees of large organisations. 'It is an example of how the boundaries between markets and products are becoming very blurred,' he says. 'The new product is work wear with service customised to the individuals in the organisation.'

Edgar says: 'Other garment manufacturers will all claim to have some sort of garment-management system. But we have had a long involvement in its development and the resources to tailor-make the computer software to be able to deliver a service package. We have also been able to work very closely with other corporations to work with their computer systems, including establishing EDI invoicing and order links.'

Yakka is a medium-sized company with $200 million annual turnover. The executive chairman is part-owner John Laidlaw. New management initiatives are not unusual for the company: ten years ago it introduced just-in-time manufacturing and multi-skilled teams to replace individual piecework. The hierarchy was also flattened.

Edgar says that the strategic planning initiatives so far have only involved the first and second level of management, but it is intended that eventually everyone will participate. He says: 'I have no reason to believe that this type of concept cannot be pushed further down into the organisation. In so doing, we will increase people's levels of understanding of the real challenges facing the company, which will in turn result in their jobs being regarded as internationally competitive. The most important thing is being able to communicate an understanding of the process, to get people to think a bit differently.'

Edgar has established cross-functional management teams—including accountants, manufacturers and marketers—as a means of breaking down traditional barriers. The greatest problem, he says, is encouraging people to think ahead, as well as attending to the problems of the day.

'Inevitably, today's problems win out, but I don't think it is very different from any strategic planning process,' he says. 'The difference with this is that it has resulted in a change in thinking and in people's approach to day-to-day decision making, because they are measuring it against a slightly different benchmark. Just by getting people to be internationally aware, for example, has created a sort of thought process that has influenced some decisions made by the company.'

Blake says that Yakka is fiercely Australian and the shift to thinking about the international context carries more weight than it would in a company that has had global activities for a long time. He says Yakka management is likely to succeed because it is willing to take an 'intellectual' approach to management and keep up-to-date with latest management thinking.

'In my view, management is a profession and should be regarded as a profession,' he says. 'If you go to a doctor or a lawyer, you expect them to be up-to-date in their knowledge. Managers have the responsibility for a lot of people's welfare in their hands. So why should they not be expected to maintain their knowledge and self-education?'

Edgar says that management is no more difficult than it has been; it is simply that expectations have risen. Yakka is not a large exporter and Edgar acknowledges that international recognition of the brand is low. But he says that in a low-tariff environment, the challenge is to think in international terms, even when most operations are domestic.

Self-designing organisations

A growing number of researchers and practitioners have called for self-designing organisations that have the built-in capacity to transform themselves to achieve high performance in today's competitive and changing environment.[51] Mohrman and Cummings have developed a self-design change strategy that involves an ongoing series of designing and implementing activities carried out by managers and employees at all levels of the firm.[52] The approach helps members to translate corporate values and general prescriptions for change into specific structures, processes and behaviours that are suited to their situations. It enables them to tailor changes to fit the organisation and helps them to continually adjust the organisation to changing conditions.

The demands of transformational change

Mohrman and Cummings developed the self-design strategy in response to a number of demands that were facing organisations engaged in transformational change. These strongly suggested the need for self-design, in contrast to more traditional approaches to organisation change that emphasise ready-made programmes and quick fixes. Although organisations prefer the control and certainty inherent in programmed change, the five requirements for organisational transformation reviewed below argue against this strategy:

1 Transformational change generally involves altering most features of the organisation and achieving a fit among them and with the firm's strategy. This suggests the need for a *systemic* change process that accounts for these multiple features and relationships.

2 Transformational change generally occurs in situations where heavy change and uncertainty is being experienced. This means that changing is never totally finished,

as new structures and processes will continually have to be modified to fit changing conditions. Thus, the change process needs to be *dynamic* and *iterative*, with organisations continually changing themselves.[53]

3   Current knowledge about transforming organisations provides only general prescriptions for change. Organisations need to learn how to translate that information into specific structures, processes and behaviours appropriate to their situations. This generally requires considerable on-site innovation and learning as members learn by doing—trying out new structures and behaviours, assessing their effectiveness and modifying them if necessary. Transformational change needs to facilitate this *organisational learning*.[54]

4   Transformational change invariably affects many organisation stakeholders, including owners, managers, employees and customers. These different stakeholders are likely to have different goals and interests related to the change process. Unless these differences are surfaced and reconciled, enthusiastic support for change may be difficult to achieve. Consequently, the change process must attend to the interests of *multiple stakeholders*.[55]

5   Transformational change needs to occur at *multiple levels of the organisation* if new strategies are to result in changed behaviours throughout the firm. Top executives must formulate a corporate strategy and clarify a vision of what the organisation needs to look like if they are to support it. Middle and lower levels of the organisation need to put those broad parameters into operation by creating structures, procedures and behaviours to implement the strategy.[56]

Self-design change strategy

The self-design strategy accounts for these demands of organisation transformation. It focuses on all features of the organisation (e.g. structure, human resource practices and technology) and seeks to design them to mutually support the business strategy. It is a dynamic and an iterative process aimed at providing organisations with the built-in capacity to continually change and redesign them as the circumstances demand. The approach promotes organisational learning among multiple stakeholders at all levels of the firm, providing them with the knowledge and skills necessary for transforming the organisation and continually improving it.

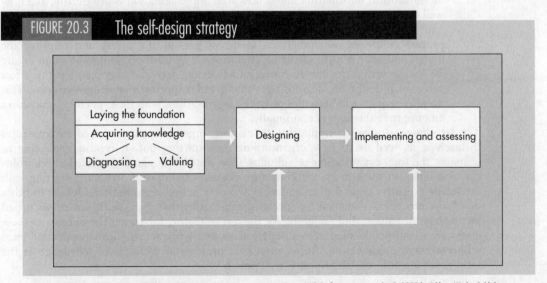

FIGURE 20.3   The self-design strategy

Laying the foundation
Acquiring knowledge
Diagnosing — Valuing

Designing

Implementing and assessing

Figure 20.3 outlines the self-design approach. Although the process is described in three stages, in practice the stages merge and interact iteratively over time. Each stage is described below:

1 *Laying the foundation.* This initial stage provides organisation members with the basic knowledge and information needed to get started with organisation transformation. It involves three kinds of activities. The first is to *acquire knowledge* about how organisations function, about organising principles for achieving high performance and about the self-design process. This information is generally gained through reading relevant material, attending in-house workshops and visiting other organisations that have successfully transformed themselves. This learning typically starts with senior executives or with those managing the transformation process and cascades to lower organisational levels if a decision to proceed with self-design is made. The second activity in laying the foundation involves *valuing*—determining the corporate values that will guide the transformation process. These values represent those performance outcomes and organisational conditions that will be needed to implement the corporate strategy. They are typically written in a values statement that is discussed and negotiated by various stakeholders at all levels of the organisation. The third activity is to *diagnose* the current organisation to determine what needs to be changed in order to enact the corporate strategy and values. Organisation members generally assess the different features of the organisation, including its performance. They look for incongruities between the organisation's functioning and its valued performances and conditions. In the case of an entirely new organisation, members diagnose constraints and contingencies in the situation that need to be taken into account when designing the organisation.

2 *Designing.* In this second stage of self-design, organisation designs and innovations are generated to support corporate strategy and values. Only the broad parameters of a new organisation are specified; the specifics are left to be tailored to the different levels and groupings within the organisation. Referred to as *minimum specification design*, this process recognises that designs need to be refined and modified as they are implemented throughout the firm.

3 *Implementing and assessing.* This last stage involves implementing the designed organisation changes. It includes an ongoing cycle of action research: changing structures and behaviours, assessing progress and making the necessary modifications. Information about how well implementation is progressing and how well the new organisational design is working is collected and used to clarify design and implementation issues and to make necessary adjustments. This learning process continues indefinitely as members periodically assess and improve the design and alter it to fit changing conditions. The feedback loops shown in Figure 20.3 suggest that the implementing and assessing activities may lead back to affect subsequent designing, diagnosing, valuing and acquiring knowledge activities. This iterative sequence of activities provides organisations with the capacity to transform and improve themselves continually.

The self-design strategy is applicable to existing organisations that need to transform themselves, as well as to new organisations just starting out. It is also applicable to changing the total organisation or subunits. The way self-design is managed and unfolds can also differ. In some cases, it follows the existing organisation structure, starting with the senior executive team and cascading downward across organisational levels. In other cases, the process is managed by special design teams that are sanctioned to set broad parameters for valuing and designing for the rest of the organisation. The outputs of these teams are then implemented across departments and work units, with considerable local refinement and modification. Application 20.2 presents an example of self-design at the local government level—the Knox City Council.[57]

Walking the talk pays off in Knox

Americans call it 'walking the talk'— management getting out of the executive suite, meeting employees and encouraging them to have a say in how work is done. At Knox Council, chief executive Terry Maher and his team believe that good communications, within the organisation and with local residents, is vital for effective local government. Knox managers are encouraged to walk the talk formally, through a number of programmes, and informally, by knowing staff and what they do.

Late in 1997, the council hosted a one-day conference on internal communications sponsored by the Australian Quality Council. Mr Maher says it was a milestone in efforts to foster a culture of communication that officially began with participation in a national AQC benchmarking study.

'It benchmarked areas such as supportiveness of management, honesty among employees and management, genuine listening skills, recognition of employee ideas, reliability of information, distribution of information about goals, feedback on staff performance, communication between departments and staff involvement in the change process,' Mr Maher said.

'Our business services received terrific results, identifying that the council had a strength in people skills. One service unit was ranked second in the study for its communication processes. We decided to build on this strength.' Knox went on to become the first municipal council in Australia to implement the AQC's self-assessment programme.

'I guess some people would see it as a management fad but it's not,' Mr Maher says. He believes the programme has the potential to foster business excellence and continuous improvement beyond the process mapping required to comply with international standard series ISO 9000.

Service areas and management are being assessed in terms of leadership, strategic policy and planning, analysis, customer focus, people, processes and other areas of performance. Action plans for improvement are being developed and findings sent to the AQC for analysis and comparison with other organisations that are undertaking the programme.

Mr Maher says Knox will continue participating in the Australian Centre for Local Government Research surveys of community satisfaction that have, for the past two years, shown that the council leads participating Victorian municipalities on a range of measures. He believes keeping abreast of internal and external attitudes to council performance is one of the keys to maintaining Knox's reputation as a local government leader.

Organisation learning

The third organisational transformation intervention is called 'organisation learning' (OL), change processes aimed at helping organisations develop and use knowledge to change and improve themselves continually. Organisation learning is crucial in today's rapidly changing environments as it can enable organisations to acquire and apply knowledge more quickly and effectively than competitors, and so can provide a competitive advantage. Organisation learning is one of the fastest-growing interventions in OD and has been used by such firms as BHP, NEC Australia and AMP to facilitate transformational change.

Organisation learning interventions draw heavily on similarities between individual learning and OL. It is possible for individual members to learn while the organisation does not. For example, a member may learn to serve the customer better without ever sharing such learning with other members. Conversely, it is possible for the organisation to learn without individual members learning. Improvements in equipment design or work procedures, for example, reflect OL, even if individual members do not understand these changes. Moreover, because OL serves the organisation's purposes and is embedded in its structures, it stays with the organisation, even if members change.

Processes of organisational learning

Organisation learning consists of four interrelated processes: discovery, invention, production and generalisation.[58] Learning starts with discovery when errors or gaps between desired and actual conditions are detected. For example, sales managers may discover that sales are falling below projected levels and set out to solve this problem. Invention is aimed at devising solutions to close the gap between desired and current conditions. It includes diagnosing the causes of the gap and inventing appropriate solutions to reduce it. The sales managers may learn that poor advertising is contributing to the sales problem and may devise a new sales campaign to improve sales. Production processes involve implementing solutions, while generalisation includes drawing conclusions about the effects of the solutions and applying that knowledge to other relevant situations. For instance, the new advertising programme would be implemented and, if found successful, the managers might apply variations of it to other product lines. Thus, these four learning processes enable members to generate the knowledge necessary to change and improve the organisation.

Levels of organisation learning

Organisations can apply the learning processes described above to three levels of learning.[59] The lowest level is called 'single-loop' (or 'adaptive') learning and is focused on learning how to improve the *status quo*. This is the most prevalent form of learning in organisations, and it enables members to reduce errors or gaps between desired and existing conditions. It can produce incremental change in how organisations function. The sales managers described above engaged in single-loop learning; they sought to reduce the difference between desired and current levels of sales.

'Double-loop' (or 'generative') learning is aimed at changing the *status quo*. It operates at a more abstract level than single-loop learning because members learn how to change the existing assumptions and conditions within which single-loop learning operates. This level of learning can lead to transformational change, where the *status quo* itself is radically changed. For example, the sales managers may learn that sales projections are based on faulty assumptions and models about future market conditions. This knowledge may result in an entirely new conception of future markets with corresponding changes in sales projections and product-development plans. It may lead the managers to drop some products that had previously appeared promising, develop new ones that had not been considered before and alter advertising and promotional campaigns to fit the new conditions.

The highest level of OL is called 'deuterolearning', which involves learning how to learn. Here learning is directed at the learning process itself and seeks to improve how organisations perform single- and double-loop learning. For example, the sales managers might periodically examine how well they perform the processes of discovery, invention, production and generalisation. This could lead to improvements and efficiencies in how learning is conducted in the organisation.

The learning organisation

Organisation learning interventions are aimed primarily at designing and implementing what is commonly referred to as 'the learning organisation', a term used to describe organisations that are capable of effective OL.[60] Much of the literature on the learning organisation is prescriptive and proposes how organisations should be designed and managed to promote effective learning. Although there is relatively little systematic research to support these premises, there is growing consensus among researchers and practitioners about specific organisational features that characterise the learning organisation.[61] These qualities are mutually reinforcing and fall into five interrelated categories:

1 *Structure*. Learning organisations are structured to facilitate OL. Their structures emphasise teamwork, strong lateral relations and networking across organisational boundaries, both internal and external to the firm. These features promote the information sharing, systems thinking and openness to information that are necessary for OL. They help members scan wider parts of the organisation and its environment and reduce barriers to shared learning. Learning organisations also have relatively flat managerial hierarchies that enhance opportunities for employee involvement in the organisation. Members are empowered to make relevant decisions and to significantly influence the organisation, thus nurturing the personal mastery and efficacy that are essential to OL.

2 *Information systems*. Organisation learning involves gathering and processing information and, consequently, the information systems of learning organisations provide an infrastructure for OL. Organisations traditionally rely on information systems for control purposes. They focus on single-loop learning, where information is used to detect and correct errors in organisational functioning. In today's environments where learning is increasingly directed at transformational change, organisations require more sophisticated information systems to support these higher levels of OL. They need systems that facilitate the rapid acquisition, processing and sharing of rich, complex information and that enable knowledge to be managed for competitive advantage. Examples of information systems that facilitate OL include Monsanto's 'knowledge management architecture', which uses 'Lotus Notes', now renamed 'Domino', to link salespeople, account managers and competitor analysts to shared customer and competitor data bases that are updated continually. Motorola's process of 'Total Quality Management', which relies heavily on external benchmarks and continuous measurement to improve quality, is another example.[62]

3 *Human resource practices*. Because organisation members are the ultimate creators and users of OL, the human resource practices of learning organisations are designed to promote member learning. These include appraisal and reward systems that account for long-term performance and knowledge development; they reinforce the acquisition and sharing of new skills and knowledge. For example, Toyota Australia uses skill-based pay to motivate employees to use multiple skills and diverse jobs. Similarly, the training and development programmes of learning organisations emphasise continuous learning and improvement. They are directed at enhancing human capital and opportunities for OL. AMP, one of Australia's largest insurance organisations, has developed a special relationship with the University of Technology in Sydney in order to undertake the high quality training of staff.

4 *Organisation culture*. The shared assumptions, values and norms that comprise an organisation's culture can have a strong influence on how members carry out the learning processes of discovery, invention, production and generalisation. Learning organisations have strong cultures that promote openness, creativity and experimentation among members. These values and norms provide the underlying social support needed for successful learning. They encourage members to acquire, process and share information; they nurture innovation and provide the freedom to try new things, to risk failure and to learn from mistakes. The Wesley Hospital in Brisbane takes this concept even further through the HealthWise project—a computer-based information centre in which patients can interactively research diseases and treatment.[63] Members are encouraged to think and behave differently. Mistakes and errors are treated as a normal part of the innovation process and members actively learn from their failures how to change and improve both themselves and the organisation.

5 *Leadership*. Like most interventions aimed at organisation transformation, OL depends heavily on effective leadership throughout the organisation. The leaders of learning organisations are actively involved in OL. They model the openness, risk taking and reflection necessary for learning. They communicate a compelling vision of the learning organisation and provide the empathy, support and personal advocacy needed to lead others in that direction.

Organisation learning and organisation performance

A key premise underlying much of the OL literature is that OL interventions will lead to higher performance. Although the positive linkage between OL and performance is widely assumed, the mechanisms through which OL translates into organisation performance are rarely identified or explained, but an understanding of this is essential when applying this intervention in organisations.

Based on the integration of existing theory and exploratory field research, Figure 20.4 explains how OL affects organisation performance.[64] This framework suggests that specific

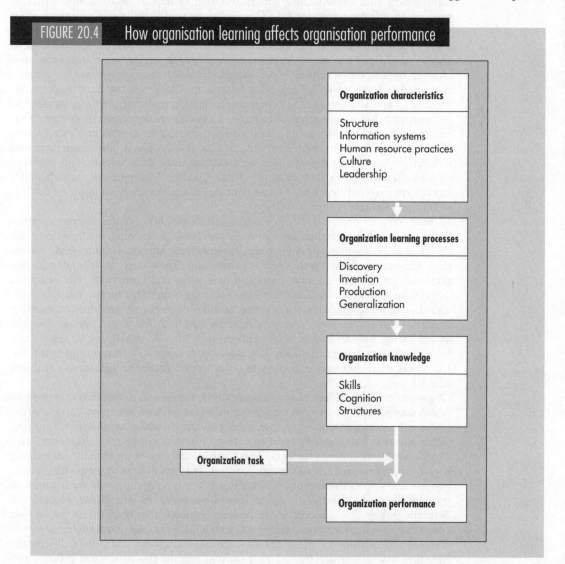

FIGURE 20.4 How organisation learning affects organisation performance

Source: Reproduced with permission from W. Snyder and T. Cummings, 'Organization learning disorders: conceptual model and intervention guidelines,' working paper, School of Business, University of Southern California, 1996.

organisational characteristics, like those described above for the learning organisation, influence how well the OL processes of discovery, invention, production and generalisation are carried out. These OL processes affect organisation performance through their impact on organisation knowledge—the skills, cognitions and systems that comprise the organisation's core competencies. Specifically, the OL processes influence the amount and kind of knowledge that an organisation possesses; that knowledge, in turn, directly influences performance outcomes, such as product quality and customer service. As depicted in Figure 20.4, the linkage between organisation knowledge and performance depends on the organisation's task or technology. Organisation knowledge will lead to high performance insofar as it is both relevant and applied effectively to the organisation's task. For example, customer-service tasks generally require good interpersonal and listening skills as well as information about customer needs. Successful task performance relies heavily on members having this knowledge and applying it effectively to customers.

Because organisation knowledge plays a crucial role in linking OL processes to organisation performance, increasing attention is being directed at how organisations can acquire and use it effectively. Two of the more popular books on innovation and global competition include the term 'knowledge' in their titles: Leonard-Barton's *Wellsprings of Knowledge: Building and Sustaining the Sources of Innovation*[65] and Konaka and Takeuchi's *The Knowledge-Creating Company: How Japanese Companies Foster Creativity and Innovation for Competitive Advantage*.[66] They show how many Japanese companies and such firms as Hewlett-Packard and Motorola achieve competitive advantage through building and managing knowledge effectively. These knowledge capabilities have been described as 'core competencies',[67] 'invisible assets',[68] and 'intellectual capital',[69] suggesting their contribution to organisation performance. There is growing emphasis both in the accounting profession and in many industries on developing accounting measures that capture knowledge capital. In knowledge-intensive firms, such as Anderson Consulting and Microsoft, the value of knowledge may far exceed the value of capital assets.[70] Moreover, the key components of cost in many of today's organisations are research and development, intellectual assets and services rather than materials and labour, which are the focus of traditional cost accounting. For example, NEC Australia has developed a world-leading approach to knowledge—teams that foster knowledge and cross-disciplinary knowledge—across all divisions of the company.[71]

Organisation knowledge is particularly valuable when it is unique and cannot easily be obtained by competitors.[72] Thus, organisations seek to develop or acquire knowledge that distinctly adds value for customers, and that can be leveraged across products, functions, business units or geographical regions. For example, Target excels at managing its unique distribution systems across a diversity of regional stores. Honda is particularly successful at leveraging its competence in motors across a number of product lines, including automobiles, motorcycles and lawn mowers.

Change strategies

Organisation learning is a broad phenomenon that can be influenced by a variety of structures, processes and performances occurring in organisations. Consequently, many of the interventions described in this book can help organisations develop more effective learning capabilities. Human resource management interventions, such as performance appraisal, reward systems and career planning and development, can reinforce members' motivation to gain new skills and knowledge. Technostructural interventions, such as process-based and network structures, self-managing work teams and re-engineering, can provide the kinds of lateral linkages and teamwork needed to process, develop and share a diversity of information and knowledge. Human process changes, such as team building, search conferences and inter-group relations interventions, can help members develop the kinds of healthy interpersonal relationships that underlie effective OL. Strategic interventions, such as integrated strategic change and open systems planning, can help organisations gain knowledge about their environment and can help them develop values and norms that promote OL.

In addition to these broader interventions, change strategies designed specifically for OL have been developed. Although these interventions are relatively new in OD and do not follow a common change process, they tend to focus on cognitive aspects of learning and how members can become more effective learners. In describing these change strategies, we draw heavily on the work of Argyris and Schon and of Senge and his colleagues, as well as many Australian researchers like Hearn and Candy, because they are the most developed and articulated in OL practice.[73]

From this perspective, OL is not concerned with the organisation as a static entity but as an active process of sense making and organising. Members socially construct the organisation as they continually act and interact with each other and learn from those actions how to organise themselves for productive achievement. This active learning process enables members to develop, test and modify mental models or maps of organisational reality. Called 'theories in use', these cognitive maps inform member behaviour and organising.[74] They guide how members make decisions, perform work and organise themselves. Unfortunately, members' theories in use can be faulty, resulting in ineffective behaviours and organising efforts. They can be too narrow and fail to account for important aspects of the environment; they can include erroneous assumptions that lead to unexpected negative consequences. Effective OL can resolve these problems. It can enable members to learn from their actions how to detect and correct errors in their mental maps and so promote more effective organising efforts.

The predominant mode of learning in most organisations is ineffective, however, and may even intensify errors. Referred to as Model I learning, it includes values and norms that emphasise unilateral control of environments and tasks and the protection of oneself and others from information that may be hurtful.[75] These norms result in a variety of defensive routines that inhibit learning, such as withholding information and feelings, competition and rivalry and little public testing of theories in use and the assumptions that underlie them. Model I is limited to single-loop learning where existing theories in use are reinforced.

A more effective approach to learning, called Model II, is based on values that promote valid information, free and informed choice, internal commitment to the choice and continuous assessment of its implementation.[76] This results in minimal defensiveness with greater openness to information and feedback, personal mastery and collaboration with others and public testing of theories in use. Model II applies to double-loop learning where theories in use are changed, and to deuterolearning where the learning process itself is examined and improved.

Organisation learning interventions are aimed at helping organisation members learn how to change from Model I to Model II learning. Like all learning, this change strategy includes the learning processes of discovery, invention, production and generalisation. Although the phases are described linearly below, in practice they form a recurrent cycle of overlapping learning activities.

1 *Discover theories in use and their consequences.* This first step involves uncovering members' mental models, or theories in use, and the consequences that follow from behaving and organising according to them. Depending on the size of the client system, this may directly involve all members, such as a senior executive team or it may include representatives of the system, such as a cross-section of members from different levels and areas.

   Organisation learning practitioners have developed a variety of techniques to help members identify their theories in use. Because these theories are generally taken for granted and are rarely examined, members need to generate and analyse data to infer the theories' underlying assumptions. One approach is called 'dialogue', a variant of the human-process interventions described in Chapter 12.[77] It involves members in genuine exchange about how they currently address problems, make decisions and interact with each other and relevant others, such as suppliers, customers and competitors. Participants are encouraged to be open and frank with each other, to treat each other as colleagues and to suspend individual assumptions as far as possible. Organisation learning practitioners facilitate dialogue sessions, using many of the human-process tools described in Chapter 12, such as process consultation and third-party intervention. Dialogue can result in a clearer understanding of existing theories in use and their behavioural consequences. It can enable members to uncover faulty assumptions that lead to ineffective behaviours and organising efforts.

A second method of identifying theories in use involves the construction of an action map of members' theories and their behavioural consequences.[78] Organisation learning practitioners typically interview members about recurrent problems in the organisation, explanations of why they are occurring, actions that are taken to resolve them and outcomes of those behaviours. Based on this information, an action map is constructed, showing interrelationships among the values underlying the theories in use, the action strategies that follow from them and the results of those actions. This is fed back to members so that they can test the validity of the map, assess the effectiveness of their theories in use and identify factors that contribute to functional and dysfunctional learning in the organisation.

A third technique for identifying theories and surfacing assumptions is called the 'left-hand, right-hand column'.[79] It starts with each member selecting a specific example of a situation where he or she was interacting with others in a way that produced ineffective results. The example is described in the form of a script and is written on the right side of a page. For instance, it might include statements such as: 'I told Larry that I thought his idea was good.' 'Joyce said to me that she did not want to take the assignment because her work load was too heavy.' On the left-hand side of the page, the member writes what he or she was thinking but not saying at each phase of the exchange. For example: 'When I told Larry that I thought his idea was good, what I was really thinking was that I have serious reservations about the idea, but Larry has a fragile ego and would be hurt by negative feedback.' 'Joyce said she didn't want to take the assignment because her work load is too heavy, but I know it's because she doesn't want to work with Larry.' This simple yet powerful exercise can reveal hidden assumptions that guide behaviour. It can make members aware of how erroneous or untested assumptions can undermine work relationships.

A fourth method that helps members identify how mental models are created and perpetuated is called the 'ladder of inference', as shown in Figure 20.5.[80] It demonstrates how far removed from concrete experience and selected data are the assumptions and beliefs that guide our behaviour. The ladder shows vividly how members' theories in use can be faulty and lead to ineffective actions. People may draw invalid conclusions from limited experience; their cultural and personal biases may distort meaning attributed to selected data. The ladder of inference can help members understand why their theories in use may be invalid and why their behaviours and organising efforts are ineffective. Members can start with descriptions of actions that are not producing intended results and then back down the ladder to discover the reasons that underlie those ineffective behaviours. For example, a service technician might withhold valuable yet negative customer feedback about product quality from management, resulting in the eventual loss of business. Backing down the ladder, the technician could discover an untested belief that upper management does not react favourably to negative information and may even 'shoot the messenger'. This belief may have resulted from assumptions and conclusions that the technician drew from observing periodic lay-offs and from hearing widespread rumours that the company is out to get trouble makers and people who speak up too much. The ladder of inference can help members understand the underlying reasons for their behaviour and can help them confront the possibility that erroneous assumptions are contributing to ineffective actions.

2 *Invent and produce more effective theories in use.* Based on what is discovered in step one, members invent and produce theories in use that lead to more effective actions and are more closely aligned to Model II learning. This involves double-loop learning as they try to create and enact new theories. In essence, members

FIGURE 20.5   The ladder of inference

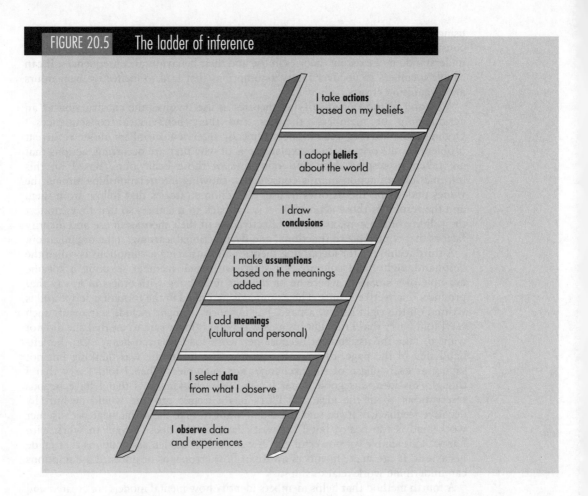

I take **actions** based on my beliefs

I adopt **beliefs** about the world

I draw **conclusions**

I make **assumptions** based on the meanings added

I add **meanings** (cultural and personal)

I select **data** from what I observe

I **observe** data and experiences

learn by doing; they learn from their invention and production actions how to invent and produce more effective theories in use.

As might be expected, learning how to change theories in use can be extremely difficult. There is a strong tendency for members to revert to habitual behaviours and modes of learning. They may have trouble breaking out of existing mindsets and seeing new realities and possibilities. OL practitioners have developed both behavioural and conceptual interventions to help members overcome these problems.

Behaviourally, practitioners help members apply the values that underlie Model II learning—valid information, free choice and internal commitment—to question their experience of trying to behave more consistently with Model II.[81] They encourage members to confront and talk openly about how habitual actions and learning methods prevent them from creating and enacting more effective theories. Once these barriers to change have been discussed openly, members typically discover that they are changeable. This shared insight often leads to the invention of more effective theories for behaving, organising and learning. Subsequent experimentation with trying to enact those theories in the work place is likely to produce more effective change because the errors that invariably occur when trying new things are now discussible and hence correctable.

Conceptually, OL practitioners teach system thinking to members in order to help them invent more effective theories in use.[82] It provides concepts and tools for detecting subtle yet powerful structures that underlie complex situations. Learning to see such structures can help members understand previously unknown forces that operate in the organisation. This information is essential for developing effective theories for organising, particularly in today's complex, changing world.

Systems thinking generally requires a radical shift in how members view the world: from seeing parts to seeing wholes; from seeing linear cause–effect chains to seeing interrelationships, from seeing static entities to seeing processes of change. Practitioners have developed a variety of exercises and tools to help members make this conceptual change, including system diagrams for displaying circles of influence among system elements; system archetypes describing recurrent structures that affect organisations; computerised micro-worlds where new strategies can be tried out under conditions that permit experimentation and learning; and games and experiential exercises demonstrating systems principles.[83]

3 *Continually monitor and improve the learning process.* This final stage involves deuterolearning—learning how to learn. Here, learning is directed at the learning process itself and at how well Model II learning characteristics are reflected in it. This includes assessment of OL strategies and of the organisational structures and processes that contribute to them. Members periodically assess how well these elements facilitate single- and double-loop learning (as described in steps 1 and 2). They generalise positive findings to new or changing situations and make appropriate modifications to improve OL. Because these activities reflect the highest and most difficult level of OL, they depend heavily on the members' capability to do Model II learning. Members must be willing to question openly their theories in use about OL; they must be willing to test publicly the effectiveness of their learning strategies and of the wider organisation.

Application 20.3 describes the initiation of an OL process at BHP. It demonstrates one method for discovering an organisation's theories in use and shows how identifying them can be a threatening part of organisation transformation.[84]

APPLICATION 20.3

BHP management school will nurture new leadership style

As part of management's move to emphasise the importance of knowledge, BHP is about to open a $30-million in-house management school at Yuroke, 12 minutes from Melbourne airport. The school will run what it calls global leadership courses for more than 5000 staff a year, representing a large portion of BHP's 65 000 staff.

Ern Prentice, corporate manager of BHP's organisation and management development, says the intention is to encourage employees to take greater initiative and responsibility, which he defines as leadership. Ultimately the company will be made up of 'leaders'— people who 'own' their work—rather than staff controlled and directed by management. Prentice says some dramatic structural changes are coming. He says: 'We will see the company

more in terms of internal networks. Informal networks have been set up throughout BHP for various reasons. They have a lot of *de facto* power, saying, for example, "We will run the engineering part this way." The normal line management has to come to grips with that.'

Prentice says: 'Over the next ten years this virtual organisation thing will emerge, whereby BHP will be a strong network blessed with certain capabilities, rather than a company having a certain type of technical hierarchy.' He says this will allow the company to be flexible and adaptive. 'You can react very quickly because you don't have all this normal strong policy and process business in between,' he says.

The conversion of BHP into a knowledge organisation began four years ago when it established a task group of line managers and human resource managers to define what it was trying to achieve. The conclusion was that it was essential to encourage employees to have more ownership of their work and to predicate much of the company's strategic capability on the employees' ability to learn and share knowledge.

The leadership training programmes have already started and are concentrating as much on the personal attributes of the staff as on transmitting technical information. Staff are being subjected to personality tests and encouraged to work on personal weaknesses, especially in how they relate to other staff. The intention is to create what management consultant Peter Senge, in his book *The Fifth Discipline*, describes as a 'dialogue'. He says: 'The purpose of dialogue is to go beyond any one individual's understanding. A new kind of mind comes into being, which is based on the development of a common meaning.'

Prentice says: 'The whole question of the leveraging of knowledge and experience is in very early days. A lot of organisations are yet to come to grips with it. We will look more at the talent and the training than at saying we have spent $5 million—which is not easy to do. It is not easy to get people to understand we are talking about capability. The "learning organisation" is a misnomer and it is a pity people call it that. But we have got to be in the learning business and that means asking how many networks and centres of excellence there are and how do you leverage that knowledge and expertise.'

Outcomes of organisation learning

There is little hard evidence of OL's effect on organisations and more evaluative research is needed. For example, Argyris and Schon state that they are unaware of any organisation that has fully implemented a double-loop learning (Model II) system.[85] Even more troubling, they describe and analyse several case studies of change that are not typically labelled as organisation learning examples. As a result, they appear to suggest that organisation learning is equivalent to concepts such as organisation adaptation, innovation and strategic change. This exacerbates confusion about what OL is and is not.

ASTOLg stands for the Australian Systems Thinking and Organisational Learning group. This group was formed in April 1993 by a small group of staff from the Department of Business Management interested in the concepts of systems thinking and organisational learning at Monash University, Melbourne. The ASTOLg is dedicated to the understanding and application of systems thinking, systems dynamic modelling and ongoing personal and organisational learning in Australian organisations and the community at large. It aims to provide a focus and networking point for interested persons and organisations from Australia, New Zealand and further afield. It has strong linkages with major centres of research and activity in both the US and Europe. Activities already under way or planned include: the publishing of a regular members' newsletter; development of a resource centre; developing and maintaining international linkages; providing networking and learning opportunities for members and for those members of the public who support research and teaching activities.

Summary

In this chapter we presented interventions for helping organisations transform themselves. These changes can occur at any level in the organisation, but their ultimate intent is to change the total system. They typically happen in response to, or in anticipation of, significant environmental, technological or internal changes. These changes may require alterations in the firm's strategy, as described in Chapter 19, but are mostly aimed at altering corporate culture, vision and mental models within the organisation.

Corporate culture includes the pattern of basic assumptions, values, norms and artefacts shared by organisation members. It influences how members perceive, think and behave at work. Corporate culture affects whether firms can implement new strategies and whether they can operate at high levels of excellence. Culture change interventions start with diagnosing the organisation's existing culture. This can include assessing the cultural risks of making those organisational changes needed to implement strategy. Changing corporate culture can be extremely difficult and requires clear strategic vision, top-management commitment, symbolic leadership, supporting organisational changes, selection and socialisation of newcomers and termination of people who do not support the changes and sensitivity to legal and ethical issues.

A self-design change strategy helps a firm to gain the built-in capacity to design and implement its own organisational transformation. Self-design involves multiple levels of the firm and multiple stakeholders and includes an iterative series of activities: acquiring knowledge, valuing, diagnosing, designing, implementing and assessing.

Organisation learning refers to a process whereby the organisation systematically inquires into the way it operates in order to uncover the patterns in its actions, the assumptions underlying those patterns and the alteration of those patterns. The primary focus of an organisation's learning activities is to increase organisation members' awareness of their theories in use, and then challenge and change their basic assumptions for taking action. An organisation that engages in learning over a sustained period of time creates a learning organisation.

 ACTIVITIES

Review questions

1 What is transformational change?
2 What does the behavioural approach to diagnosing culture propose?
3 Describe the three approaches to diagnosing culture. Which is the most difficult to interpret?
4 Define organisational culture.
5 How does the competing values approach view culture?
6 What are the key roles of leadership in transformational change?
7 List the criteria for organisation learning.
8 What is the focus of a self-designing organisation and how would you lay its foundations?

Discussion and essay questions

1 Under what conditions are transformational changes necessary?
2 How would an OD practitioner attempt to change an organisation's culture?
3 How can an OD practitioner help an organisation become self-designing?
4 Describe how an organisation can use 'double-loop learning' to improve performance.
5 Is it a current management strategy to treat chaos with chaos?

Notes

1 C. Lundberg, 'On organizational learning: implications and opportunities for expanding organizational development' in *Research in Organizational Change and Development*, 3, eds W. Pasmore and R. Woodman (Greenwich, Conn.: JAI Press, 1989): 61–82.

2 M. Fiol and M. Lyles, 'Organizational learning', *Academy of Management Review*, 10 (1985): 803–13; J. March and H. Simon, *Organizations* (New York: John Wiley, 1958).

3 M. Tushman, W. Newman and E. Romanelli, 'Managing the unsteady pace of organizational evolution', *California Management Review*, (Fall 1986): 29–44.

4 *Ibid.*

5 A. Meyer, A. Tsui and C. Hinings, 'Guest coeditors introduction: configurational approaches to organizational analysis', *Academy of Management Journal*, 36:6 (1993): 1175–95.

6 D. Miller and P. Friesen. *Organizations: A Quantum View* (Englewood Cliffs, N.J.: Prentice-Hall, 1984).

7 B. Blumenthal and P .Haspeslagh, 'Toward a definition of corporate transformation', *Sloan Management Review*, 35 (3, 1994): 101–7.

8 Tushman, Newman and Romanelli, 'Managing the unsteady pace', *op. cit.*; L. Greiner, 'Evolution and revolution as organizations grow', *Harvard Business Review*, (July–August 1972): 37–46.

9 M. Tushman and E. Romanelli, 'Organizational evolution: a metamorphosis model of convergence and reorientation' in *Research in Organization Behavior*, 7, eds L. Cummings and B. Staw (Greenwich, Conn.: JAI Press, 1985): 171–222.

10 J. Bartunek and M. Louis, 'Organization development and organizational transformation' in *Research in Organizational Change and Development*, 2, eds W. Pasmore and R. Woodman (Greenwich, Conn.: JAI Press, 1988): 97–134.

11 R. Golembiewski, K. Billingsley and S. Yeager, 'Measuring change and persistence in human affairs: types of changes generated by OD designs', *Journal of Applied Behavioral Science*, 12 (1975): 133–57.

12 J. Sackmann, 'The role of metaphors in organization transformation', *Human Relations*, 42 (1989): 463–85.

13 A. Pettigrew, *The Awakening Giant: Continuity and Change in Imperial Chemical Industries* (Oxford: Blackwell, 1985); A. Pettigrew, 'Context and action in the transformation of the firm', *Journal of Management Studies*, 24 (1987): 649–70; Tushman and Romanelli, 'Organizational evolution', *op. cit.*

14 M. Tushman and B. Virany, 'Changing characteristics of executive teams in an emerging industry', *Journal of Business Venturing*, (1986): 37–49; L. Greiner and A. Bhambri, 'New CEO intervention and dynamics of deliberate strategic change', *Strategic Management Journal*, 10 (Summer 1989): 67–86.

15 M. Tushman, W. Newman and D. Nadler, 'Executive leadership and organizational evolution: managing incremental and discontinuous change' in *Corporate Transformation: Revitalizing Organizations for a Competitive World*, eds R. Kilmann and T. Covin (San Francisco: Jossey-Bass, 1988): 102–30; W. Bennis and B. Nanus, *Leaders: The Strategies for Taking Charge* (New York: Harper and Row, 1985); Pettigrew, 'Context and action in the transformation of the firm', *op. cit.*

16 T. Cummings and S. Mohrman, 'Self-designing organizations: towards implementing quality-of-work-life innovations' in *Research in Organizational Change and Development*, 1, eds R. Woodman and W. Pasmore (Greenwich, Conn.: JAI Press, 1987): 275–310.

17 W. Ouchi, *Theory Z: How American Business Can Meet the Japanese Challenge* (Reading, Mass.: Addison-Wesley, 1979); R. Pascale and A. Athos, *The Art of Japanese Management* (New York: Simon and Schuster, 1981); T. Deal and A. Kennedy, *Corporate Cultures* (Reading, Mass.: Addison-Wesley, 1982); T. Peters and R. Waterman, *In Search of Excellence* (New York: Harper and Row, 1982); T. Peters and N. Austin, *A Passion for Excellence* (New York: Random House, 1985); J. Pfeffer, *Competitive Advantage Through People* (Cambridge: Harvard Business School, 1994); J. Collins and J. Porras, *Built to Last* (New York: Harper Business, 1994); J. Kotter and J. Heskett, *Corporate Culture and Performance* (New York: The Free Press, 1992): D. Dunphy and D. Stace, *Beyond the Boundaries* (Sydney: McGraw Hill, 1994).

18 D. Meyerson and J. Martin, 'Cultural change: an integration of three different views', *Journal of Management Studies*, 24 (1987): 623–47; D. Denison and G. Spreitzer, 'Organizational culture and organizational development: a competing values approach' in *Research in Organizational Change and Development*, 5, eds R. Woodman and W. Pasmore (Greenwich, Conn.: JAI Press, 1991): 1–22; E. Schein, *Organizational Culture and Leadership*, 2nd ed. (San Francisco: Jossey–Bass, 1992).

19 Schein, *Organizational Culture and Leadership*, *op. cit.*; R. Kilmann, M. Saxton and R. Serpa, eds, *Gaining Control of the Corporate Culture* (San Francisco: Jossey-Bass, 1985).

20 Schein, *Organizational Culture and Leadership*, *op. cit.*

21 M. Louis, 'Toward a system of inquiry on organizational culture', paper delivered at the Western Academy of Management Meeting, Colorado Springs, Colo., April 1982.

22 E. Abrahamson and C. Fombrun, 'Macrocultures: determinants and consequences', *Academy of Management Journal*, 19 (1994): 728–55.

23 A. Bodi, G. Maggs and D. Edgar, 'When too much change is never enough', *Business & Professional Publishing*, Australia, 1997.

24 B. Uttal, 'The corporate culture vultures', *Fortune*, (17 October 1983): 66–72.

25 *Ibid.*, p. 70.

26 Ouchi, *Theory Z*; Pascale and Athos, *Japanese Management*, both *op. cit.*

27 D. Denison, 'The climate, culture and effectiveness of work organizations: a study of organizational behavior and financial performance', PhD dissertation, University of Michigan, 1982.

28 Kotter and Heskett, *Corporate Culture and Performance, op. cit.*

29 D. Hanna, *Designing Organizations for High Performance* (Reading, Mass.: Addison-Wesley, 1988).

30 H. Schwartz and S. Davis, 'Matching corporate culture and business strategy', *Organizational Dynamics*, (Summer 1981): 30–48; S. Davis, *Managing Corporate Culture* (Cambridge, Mass.: Ballinger, 1984).

31 Denison and Spreitzer, 'Organizational culture and organizational development', *op. cit.*; R. Quinn, *Beyond Rational Management: Mastering the Paradoxes and Competing Demands of High Performance* (San Francisco: Jossey-Bass, 1988).

32 R. Quinn and G. Spreitzer, 'The psychometrics of the competing values culture instrument and an analysis of the impact of organizational culture on quality of life' in *Research in Organization Change and Development*, 5, eds R. Woodman and W. Pasmore (Greenwich, Conn.: JAI Press, 1991): 115–42.

33 Schein, *Organizational Culture and Leadership, op. cit.*

34 R. Zammuto and J. Krakower, 'Quantitative and qualitative studies of organizational culture' in *Research in Organizational Change and Development*, 5, eds R. Woodman and W. Pasmore (Greenwich, Conn.: JAI Press, 1991): 83–114; Quinn and Spreitzer, 'The psychometrics of the competing values culture instrument', *op. cit.*

35 Schein, *Organizational Culture and Leadership, op. cit.*

36 P. Frost, L. Moore, M. Louis, C. Lundberg and J. Martin, eds, *Organizational Culture* (Beverly Hills, Calif.: Sage, 1985): 95–196.

37 Meyerson and Martin, 'Cultural change', *op. cit.*

38 J. Barney, 'Organizational culture: can it be a source of sustained competitive advantage?' *Academy of Management Review,* (1986): 656–65.

39 Uttal, 'Corporate culture vultures', *op. cit.*

40 *Ibid.*, 70.

41 Schwartz and Davis, 'Matching corporate culture and business strategy'; Uttal, 'Corporate culture vultures'; Davis, *Managing Corporate Culture*; Kilmann, Saxton and Serpa, *Gaining Control*; Frost, Moore, Louis, Lundberg and Martin, *Organizational Culture*, all *op. cit.*; V. Sathe, 'Implications of corporate culture: a manager's guide to action', *Organizational Dynamics*, (Autumn 1983): 5–23; B. Drake and E. Drake, 'Ethical and legal aspects of managing corporate cultures', *California Management Review*, (Winter 1988): 107–23.

42 C. Worley, D. Hitchin and W. Ross, *Integrated Strategic Change,* (Reading, Mass.: Addison-Wesley, 1996); R. Beckhard and W. Pritchard, *Changing the Essence* (San Francisco: Jossey-Bass, 1992).

43 S. Flint, *The Age*, (20 November 1997): 1.

44 Dumaine, 'Creating a new company culture', *op. cit.*; C. O'Reilly, 'Corporations, culture and commitment: motivation and social control in organizations', *California Management Review,* 31 (Summer 1989): 9–25; Pettigrew, 'Context and action', *op. cit.*

45 Dumaine, 'Creating a new company culture', *op. cit.*

46 K. McGhee, *Sydney Morning Herald*, (1997).

47 Tichy and Sherman, *Control Your Destiny, op. cit.*

48 *The Age* (26 April 1998): 25.

49 *Australian Financial Review* (10 June 1998): 21.

50 *Business Review* (17 March 1997): 72.

51 B. Hedberg, P. Nystrom and W. Starbuck, 'Camping on seesaws: prescriptions for a self–designing organization', *Administrative Science Quarterly,* 21 (1976): 41–65; K. Weick, 'Organization design: organizations as self–designing systems', *Organizational Dynamics,* 6 (1977): 30–46.

52 S. Mohrman and T .Cummings, *Self–Designing Organizations: Learning How to Create High Performance* (Reading, Mass.: Addison-Wesley, 1989); Cummings and Mohrman, 'Self–designing organizations', *op. cit.*

53 P. Lawrence and D. Dyer, *Renewing American Industry* (New York: Free Press, 1983).

54 C. Argyris, R. Putnam and D. Smith, *Action Science* (San Francisco: Jossey-Bass, 1985); C. Lundberg, 'On organizational learning: implications and opportunities for expanding

organizational development' in *Research on Organizational Change and Development*, 3, eds R. Woodman and W. Pasmore (Greenwich, Conn.: JAI Press, 1989): 61–82; P. Senge, *The Fifth Discipline* (New York: Doubleday, 1990).

55 M. Weisbord, *Productive Workplaces* (San Francisco: Jossey-Bass, 1987); R. Freeman, *Strategic Management* (Boston: Ballinger, 1984).

56 Miller and Friesen, *Organizations, op. cit.*

57 C. Rance, *The Age*, (14 March 1998): 36.

58 J. Dewey, *How We Think* (Boston: D.C. Heath & Company, 1933).

59 C. Argyris and D. Schon. *Organizational Learning: A Theory of Action Perspective* (Reading, Mass.: Addison-Wesley, 1978); C. Argyris and D. Schon, *Organizational Learning II: Theory, Method and Practice* (Reading, Mass.: Addison-Wesley, 1996); Senge, *The Fifth Discipline, op. cit.*

60 Senge, *The Fifth Discipline, op. cit.*; S. Chawla and J. Renesch eds, *Learning Organizations: Developing Cultures for Tomorrow's Workplace* (Portland, Oreg.: Productivity Press, 1995).

61 M. McGill, J. Slocum and D. Lei, 'Management practices in learning organizations', *Organizational Dynamics*, (Autumn 1993): 5–17; E. Nevis, A. DiBella and J. Gould, 'Understanding organizations as learning systems', *Sloan Management Review*, (Winter 1995): 73–85.

62 Nevis, DiBella and Gould, 'Understanding organizations as learning systems', *op. cit.*

63 *Australian Financial Review*, (22 May 1998): 67.

64 W. Snyder and T. Cummings, 'Organization learning disorders: conceptual model and intervention guidelines', working paper, School of Business, University of Southern California, 1996.

65 D. Leonard–Barton, *Wellsprings of Knowledge: Building and Sustaining the Sources of Innovation* (Boston: Harvard Business School Press, 1995).

66 X. Konaka and X. Takeuchi, *The Knowledge-Creating Company: How Japanese Companies Foster Creativity and Innovation for Competitive Advantage* (New York: Oxford University Press, 1995).

67 C. Prahalad and G. Hamel, 'The core competencies of the corporation', *Harvard Business Review*, 68 (1990): 79–91.

68 H. Itami, *Mobilizing for Invisible Assets* (Cambridge: Harvard University Press, 1987).

69 T. Stewart, 'Intellectual capital', *Fortune*, (3 October 1994): 68–74.

70 *Ibid.*

71 P. James, *Business Review Weekly*, (29 October 1997): 82.

72 J. Barney, 'Looking inside for competitive advantage', *Academy of Management Executive*, 9:4 (1995): 49–61; M. Peteraf, 'The cornerstones of competitive advantage', *Strategic Management Journal*, 14:3 (1993): 179–92; Worley, Hitchin and Ross, *Integrated Strategic Change, op. cit.*

73 Argyris and Schon, *Organizational Learning II*; Senge, *The Fifth Discipline*, both *op. cit.*; P. Senge, C. Roberts, R. Ross, B. Smith and A. Kleiner, *The Fifth Discipline Fieldbook: Strategies for Building a Learning Organization* (New York: Doubleday, 1995); Hearn and Candy in *Management Development in Australia*, ed. B. Smith (New South Wales, Harcourt Brace Jovanovich)

74 Argyris and Schon, *Organizational Learning II, op. cit.*

75 *Ibid.*

76 Argyris and Schon, *Organizational Learning II, op. cit.*; C. Argyris, *Intervention Theory and Method* (Reading, Mass.: Addison-Wesley, 1970).

77 Senge, *The Fifth Discipline, op. cit.*

78 Argyris and Schon, *Organizational Learning II, op. cit.*

79 Argyris and Schon, *Organizational Learning II*; Senge, Roberts, Ross, Smith and Kleiner, *The Fifth Discipline Fieldbook*, both *op. cit.*

80 Senge, Roberts, Ross, Smith and Kleiner, *The Fifth Discipline Fieldbook, op. cit.*

81 Argyris and Schon. *Organizational Learning II*; Argyris, *Intervention Theory and Method*, both *op. cit.*

82 Senge, *The Fifth Discipline, op. cit.*

83 *Ibid.*

84   D. James, *Business Review*, (10 February 1997): 44.

85 Argyris and Schon, *Organizational Learning II, op. cit.*, 112.

PART 7

SPECIAL APPLICATIONS OF ORGANISATION DEVELOPMENT

CHAPTER

21 Organisation development in global settings

Organisation development in global settings

This chapter discusses the practice of organisation development in international settings. It describes the contingencies and practice issues associated with OD in foreign organisations, worldwide organisations and in global social change organisations. The increasing applicability and effectiveness of OD in some countries and cultures is debatable, however. Because OD was predominantly developed by American and Western European practitioners, its practices and methods are heavily influenced by the values and assumptions of industrialised cultures. Thus, the traditional approaches to planned change may promote management practices that conflict with the values and assumptions of other societies. There are many practitioners, however, who believe that OD can result in organisational improvements in any culture. Despite different points of view on this topic, the practice of OD in international settings can be expected to expand dramatically. The rapid development of foreign economies and firms, along with the global marketplace, are creating organisational needs and opportunities for change.

When designing and implementing planned change for organisations operating outside Australia, OD practitioners needs to fit two important contingencies: the cultural values of the host country and its level of economic development. Preliminary research suggests that failure to adapt OD interventions to these cultural contingencies can produce disastrous results.[1]

In worldwide organisations, OD is applied to help firms operate in multiple countries. Referred to as global, multinational or transnational corporations, they must suit their organisational methods and procedures to different cultures. Here, OD can help members gain the organisational skills and knowledge necessary for operating across cultural boundaries. It can enhance organisational effectiveness through better alignment of people and systems with international strategy.

Organisation development is playing an increasingly important role in global social change. Organisation development practitioners, using highly participative approaches, are influencing the development of evolving countries, providing a voice for under-represented social classes and bridging the gap between cultures that face similar social issues. The application of planned change processes in these settings represents one of the newest and most exciting areas of OD.

International organisation development

Organisation development is increasingly being practised internationally within organisations.[2] The Weili Washing Machine Factory in Zhongshan, China, for example, implemented a new reward system that linked pay with productivity, a major change from the guaranteed income policies of the past. In addition, plant managers, who had been elected by employees, were given considerable autonomy by city officials to operate the plant.[3] This international diffusion of OD derives from three important trends: the rapid development of foreign economies, the increasing worldwide availability of technical and financial resources and the emergence of a global economy.[4]

The dramatic restructuring of socialist economies and the rapid economic growth of developing countries are numbing in scope and impact. Between 1987 and 1992, the industrial output of Taiwan, Korea, Hong Kong, Singapore, Thailand, the Philippines and Malaysia accounted for more trade with the US than did Japan's. In Europe, Italy is one of the fastest-growing economies and the local and foreign investment in Spain is unprecedented. The transformation of the former Soviet Union and of Eastern European countries, such as Poland and East Germany, is producing new growth-oriented economies. The abolishment of apartheid has placed South Africa on a progressive development path.

Organisations operating in these rejuvenated or newly emerging economies are increasingly turning to OD practices to solve problems and to improve effectiveness. In Germany, for example, industrial expansion following reunification was fuelled in part by immigrants filling factory jobs. The '*Learnstatt*' concept, a form of quality circles, developed from courses where immigrants were being taught to speak German. In such organisations as Kraftwerk Union AG and BMW, new ideas about work processes were introduced during the language training to make the classes more interesting and applicable. Eventually, these groups began to discuss ways of improving manufacturing efficiency.[5] Other interventions, such as co-determination, work councils and extensive apprenticeship programmes, represent efforts to increase employee empowerment in German organisations.

The second trend contributing to OD applications in global settings is the unprecedented availability of technological and financial resources. Foreign governments and organisations now have access to worldwide resources and use them to fuel growth and development. The increased availability of capital and technology, for example, was cited as a major reason for the rise of Chilean firms in the 1980s.[6] Information technology, in particular, is making the world 'smaller' and more interdependent. As international organisations adopt new technology, the opportunity to apply techniques that facilitate planned change increases. Organisation development interventions can smooth the transition to a new reporting structure, clarify roles and relationships and reduce the uncertainty associated with implementing new techniques and practices.

The final trend to fuel international OD applications is the emergence of a global economy. Many foreign organisations are maturing and growing by entering the global business community. This international expansion is facilitated by lowered trade barriers, deregulation and privatisation. The established relationships and local knowledge that once favoured only a small number of worldwide organisations are no longer barriers to entry into many countries.[7] As organisations expand globally, they are faced with the need to adapt structures, information systems, co-ordinating processes and human resource practices to suit worldwide operations in a variety of countries. This has led to OD interventions geared to planned change across different cultures and economies.

The success of OD in international settings depends on two key contingencies: cultural context and economic development. Organisation development interventions need to be responsive to the cultural values and organisational customs of the host country if the changes are to produce positive results.[8] For example, team-building interventions in Latin American countries can fail if there is too much emphasis on personal disclosure and interpersonal relationships. Latin Americans typically value masculinity, paternalism and status-consciousness. They may be suspicious of human-process interventions that seek to establish trust, openness and equality, and consequently may actively resist them. A country's economic development can also affect the success of OD interventions.[9] For example, organisations operating in countries with moderate levels of economic development may need business-oriented interventions rather than OD changes. There is little to be gained from addressing interpersonal conflict in a top-management team, for instance, if the organisation has difficulty getting products shipped or delivering service.

Cultural context

Researchers have suggested that applying OD in different countries requires a 'context-based' approach to planned change.[10] This involves fitting OD to the organisation's cultural context, including the values held by members of the particular country or region.

| TABLE 21.1 | Cultural values and organisation customs | | |

Values	Definition	Organization customs when the value is at one extreme	Representative countries
Context	The extent to which words carry the meaning of a message; how time is viewed	Ceremony and routines are common Structure is less formal; fewer written policies People are often late for appointments	High: Asian and Latin American countries Low: Scandinavia, US
Power distance	The extent to which members of a society accept that power is distributed unequally in an organization	Autocratic decision making Superiors consider sub-ordinates as part of a different class Close supervision of subordinates Employees not likely to disagree Powerful people are entitled to privileges	High: Latin American countries; Eastern European countries Low: Scandinavian countries
Uncertainty avoidance	The extent to which members of an organization tolerate the unfamiliar and unpredictable	Experts have status/authority Clear roles preferred Conflict is undesirable Resistance to change Conservative	High: Asian countries Low: European countries
Individualism	The extent to which people believe they should be responsible for themselves and their immediate families	Personal initiative encouraged Time is valuable to individuals Competitiveness is accepted Autonomy is highly valued	High: US Low: Latin American countries; Eastern European countries
Masculinity	The extent to which organization members value assertiveness and the acquisition of material goods	Achievement reflected in wealth and recognition Decisiveness is valued Larger and faster is better Sex roles clearly differentiated	High: Asian and Latin American countries; South Africa Low: Scandinavian countries

These beliefs inform people about what behaviour is important and acceptable in the host country's culture. Cultural values play a major role in shaping the customs and practices that occur within organisations as well. They influence how members react to organisational phenomena having to do with power, conflict, ambiguity, time and change.

There is a growing body of knowledge about cultural diversity and its effect on organisational and management practices.[11] Researchers have identified five key values that describe national cultures and influence organisational customs: context orientation, power, uncertainty avoidance, masculinity and individualism (Table 21.1).[12]

Context orientation

This value describes how information is conveyed and time valued in a culture. In low-context cultures, such as Scandinavia and Australia, information is communicated in words and phrases. By using more specific words, more meaning is expressed. In addition, time is viewed as discrete and linear—something that can be spent, used, saved or wasted.

In high-context cultures, on the other hand, the medium reflects the message more than the words, and time is a fluid and flexible concept. For example, in Japan and Venezuela, social cues provide as much, if not more, information about a particular situation than words alone. Organisations in high-context cultures emphasise ceremony and ritual. How one behaves is an important signal of support and compliance with the way things are done. Structures are less formal in high-context cultures; there are few written policies and procedures to guide behaviour. Because high-context cultures view time as fluid, punctuality for appointments is less a priority than maintaining relationships.

Power distance

This value concerns the way people view authority, status differences and influence patterns. People in high power distance regions, such as Latin America and Eastern Europe, tend to favour unequal distributions of power and influence and, consequently, autocratic and paternalistic decision-making practices are accepted. Organisations in high power distance cultures tend to be highly centralised with several hierarchical levels and a large proportion of supervisory personnel. Subordinates in these organisations represent a lower social class. They expect to be supervised closely and believe that power holders are entitled to special privileges. Such practices would be inappropriate in low power-distance regions, such as Scandinavia, where participative decision making and egalitarian methods are prevalent.

Uncertainty avoidance

This value reflects a preference for conservative practices and familiar and predictable situations. People in high uncertainty avoidance regions, such as Asia, prefer stable routines, resist change and seek to maintain the *status quo*. They do not like conflict and believe that company rules should not be broken. In regions where uncertainty avoidance is low, such as in many European countries, ambiguity is less threatening. Organisations in these cultures tend to favour fewer rules, higher levels of participation in decision making, more organic structures and more risk taking.

Individualism

This value is concerned with looking out for one's self as opposed to one's group or organisation. In high-individualism cultures, such as Australia, the US or Canada, personal initiative and competitiveness are strongly valued. Organisations in individualistic cultures often have high turnover rates and individual, as opposed to group, decision-making processes. Employee empowerment is supported when members believe that it improves the probability of personal gain. These cultures encourage personal initiative, competitiveness and individual autonomy. Conversely, in low-individualism countries, such as Taiwan, Japan and Peru, allegiance to one's group is paramount. Organisations in these cultures tend to favour co-operation among employees and loyalty to the company.

Masculinity

This value concerns the extent to which the culture favours the acquisition of power and resources. Employees from masculine cultures, such as Asia and Latin America, place a high value on career advancement, freedom and salary growth. Organisations in these cultures tend to pursue aggressive goals and to have high levels of stress and conflict. Organisational success is measured in terms of size, growth and speed. On the other hand, workers in feminine cultures, such as those in Scandinavia, tend to prize the social aspects of work, including working conditions and supervision. They typically favour opportunities to learn and grow at work.

Economic development

In addition to cultural context, an important contingency affecting OD success internationally is a country's economic development, which can be judged from social, economic and political perspectives.[13] For example, economic development can be reflected in a country's management capability as measured by information systems and skills; decision-making and action-taking capabilities; project-planning and organising abilities; evaluation and control technologies; leadership, motivational and reward systems; and human selection, placement and development levels. Similarly, the United Nation's Human Development Programme has developed a *Human Development Index* that assesses a country's economic development in terms of life expectancy, educational attainment and income.

Subsistence economies

Countries such as Bangladesh, Nepal, Afghanistan, India and Nigeria have relatively low degrees of development and are agriculturally based. Their populations tend to consume most of what they produce and any surplus is used to barter for other necessary goods and services. A large proportion of the population is unfamiliar with the concept of 'employment'. Working for someone else in exchange for wages is not common or understood, and so there are few large organisations outside the government. In subsistence economies, OD interventions emphasise global social change; they focus on creating conditions for sustainable social and economic progress. These change methods are described in the last section of this chapter.

Industrialising economies

These countries, which include South Africa, the Philippines, Brazil, Iran and the People's Republic of China, are moderately developed and tend to be rich in natural resources. Economic growth is fuelled by an expanding manufacturing base that accounts for increasing amounts of the country's gross domestic product. The rise of manufacturing also contributes to the formation of a class system that includes upper-, middle- and low-income groups. Organisations operating in these nations generally focus on efficiency of operations and revenue growth. Consequently, OD interventions address strategic, structural and work-design issues.[14] They help organisations to identify domestic and international markets, to develop clear and appropriate goals and to structure themselves to achieve efficient performance and market growth.

Industrial economies

Highly developed countries, such as Scandinavia, Japan, Germany and the US, emphasise non-agricultural industry. In these economies, manufactured goods are exported and traded with other industrialised countries; investment funds are available both internally and externally; the work force is educated and skilled; and technology is often substituted for labour. Because the OD interventions described in this book were developed primarily in industrial economies, they can be expected to have their strongest effects in these contexts. Their continued success cannot be assured, however, as these countries are rapidly advancing to post-industrial conditions. Here, OD interventions will need to fit into economies that are driven by information and knowledge, where service outpaces manufacturing and where national and organisational boundaries are more open and flexible.

How cultural context and economic development affect OD practice

The contingencies of cultural context and economic development can have powerful effects on the way in which OD is carried out in different countries.[15] They can determine whether change processes proceed slowly or quickly, involve few or many members, are directed by hierarchical authority or by consensus and focus on business or organisational issues.

When the two contingencies are considered together, they reveal four different international settings for OD practice, as shown in Figure 21.1. These different situations reflect the extent to which a country's culture fits with traditional OD values of humanising organisations and improving their effectiveness (poor vs good) and the degree to which the

FIGURE 21.1	The cultural and economic contexts of international CD practice

		Cultural fit	
		Poor	Good
Economic development	Industrializing	Latin America, Indonesia, Philippines, Arab Region	South Africa
	Industrial	Eastern Europe, Asia, Latin America	Scandinavia, UK

country is economically developed (industrialising vs industrial). There is a relatively good fit between OD values and countries where cultural values favour low levels of context orientation and power distance and moderate levels of uncertainty avoidance, individualism and masculinity.[16] The more the cultural context differs from this values profile, the more the OD process will need to be modified to fit the situation. In Figure 21.1, the degree of economic development is restricted to industrialising and industrial nations. Subsistence economies are not included because they afford little opportunity to practise traditional OD; a more appropriate strategy is global social change, discussed later in this chapter. Generally, the more developed the economy, the more OD is applied to the organisational issues described in this book. In less developed situations, OD focuses on business issues, such as procuring raw materials, producing efficiently and marketing successfully.[17]

Poor fit, industrialising settings

This context is least suited to traditional OD practice. It includes industrialising countries with cultural values that align poorly with OD values, including many Arab nations, such as Iraq, Iran and the United Arab Republic; the South Pacific region, including Malaysia, Indonesia and the Philippines; and certain Latin American countries, such as Brazil, Ecuador, Guatemala and Nicaragua. These regions are highly dependent on their natural resources and have a relatively small manufacturing base. They tend to be high-context cultures with values of high power distance and masculinity and of moderate individualism and uncertainty avoidance.

These settings require change processes that fit local customs and that address business issues. As might be expected, little has been written about the application of OD in these countries and there are even fewer reports of OD practice. Cultural values of high power distance and masculinity are inconsistent with OD activities that emphasise openness, collaboration and empowerment. Moreover, executives in industrialising economies frequently equate OD with human-process interventions, such as team building, conflict management and process consultation. They perceive OD as too soft to meet their business needs. For example, Egyptian and Filipino managers tend to be autocratic, engage in protracted decision making and focus on economic and business problems. Consequently, organisational change is slow paced, centrally controlled and aimed at achieving technical rationality and efficiency.[18]

Not all organisations are influenced by these contextual forces in the same way. In an apparent exception to the rule, Ricardo Semler, the president of Semco S/A (Brazil), has designed a highly participative organisation.[19] Most Semco employees set their own working hours and approve hires and promotions. Information flows down through a relatively flat hierarchy and strategic decisions are made participatively by company-wide vote. Brazil's cultural values are not as strong on power distance and masculinity as are other Latin American countries. This may explain the apparent success of this high-involvement organisation. It suggests that OD interventions can be implemented within this cultural context when strongly supported by senior management.

Application 21.1 describes a work design intervention in a plant in Egypt. It demonstrates some of the difficulties associated with planned change in industrialising countries whose cultural context does not fit with traditional OD values. It also demonstrates some of the ingredients for successful OD in these situations.[20]

APPLICATION 21.1　　　　Job enrichment in an Egyptian organisation

Plant A, in Cairo, Egypt, produces electrical and communications equipment for both the government and the public markets. It is the largest factory of its kind in Egypt and works closely with its government customers to produce what is needed and to co-ordinate its actions. This particular facility's development over the years had been based on a foreign model of how a factory of this type should be designed. As one of the many government-owned factories built in the last 20 years, its form has also been strongly affected by the Egyptian social and legal environment. For example, the factory was functionally organized, but it also has a few matrix project groups reporting to the chairman of the board. The board is composed of a politically appointed chairman, a vice-chairman for finance and administration and one for commerce. It also consists of a technical vice-chairman, a representative of the user governmental agency and three members elected from the workers and employees. Though the influence of these elected board members is nearly nil, legislation does exist in Egypt to call for workers' elections for board members. The chairman serves as the chief executive officer and the vice-chairmen serve as operating executives. The factory falls under the authority of the technical vice-chairman, as do all the other production units except the special matrix groups.

The primary consultant to the factory had been a member of its board of directors for five years, but at the time of the research his relationship was informal, existing primarily through his friends and associates still at the factory. As a result of discussions with the consultant, management agreed to focus on a particular unit in the factory to carry out action research on work design and job enrichment. Management believed that this unit had an atmosphere of low morale, high absenteeism, turnover percentages higher than desired and an evident need for improving productivity and reducing reject rates. The focus unit contained 176 employees including a manager and his assistant, 20 engineers and 36 supervisors (17 males and 19 females). There were 96 assembly workers on a one-shift operation and of these, only 18 were men. The 14 clerks and cleaning personnel were all male.

The plant's organization and job design were heavily influenced by the English manufacturing firms whose products it was producing and assembling. The work design had come directly from the production specifications and, without any significant alteration, it had been set up to operate the same way in Egypt. The production process in the plant consisted of 52 separate, specialized and inspected operations, each one done by one worker and taking six to nine minutes to complete. The work flowed through two U-shaped facilities with assembly and inspection completed in one section, then loading and packing completed nearby in another. Individuals only interacted when they moved an assembled piece from one stage to the next. Technical advisors from the foreign firms were present in the factory, but they did not take an active part in this project or the job redesign effort.

The overall design of the research followed an action research approach that involves the organization in identifying its own problems and opportunities, designing solutions to these and then testing and modifying the solutions as appropriate. The board proposed and approved a step-by-step strategy. The first step was to train designated personnel about the concepts of OD and the action research process. These programs were conducted in Arabic and covered the basic theories of work motivation, job design, group leadership, problem analysis and evaluation techniques.

The second step consisted of diagnostic activities. Complete data were collected about the organization's structure and its production rates over the previous six months. In addition, pre-intervention data were collected from the unit that had been chosen to receive special attention for comparison with data to be collected after the intervention. These data included reject rates, damaged parts costs and turnover and absenteeism rates. Observations and interviews were used to generate information about the climate of the organization and also about how work was being performed and the related morale factors. An oral questionnaire, given to a sample group of members of the test unit, asked about work conditions and attitudes about work. Four special meetings of members from all levels of the organization and led by the consultant, the vice-chairman and the research and development manager were held to collect ideas and suggestions about the research; the results were tabulated and then discussed with the research team and the chairman of the board.

From all of this information, a problem statement and a research hypothesis were developed as follows: 'At present in the test unit, there is an atmosphere of low morale and job dissatisfaction. It is hypothesized that this is resulting from the boredom and fatigue associated with the nature of the work in the test unit.' (This is a direct quotation from the consultant's report, translated into English.) Based on these conclusions, problem-solving meetings were set up in the test unit with the managers and the research team. A brainstorming design was used to generate ideas. The agreed-upon solution was that 'restructuring the work functions and positions in the test unit in order to decrease work fatigue and monotony would lead to an increase in job satisfaction and raise morale, thus reducing absenteeism, turnover, and improving productivity' (another quotation from the consultant's report). This solution was then reviewed and agreed upon by higher-level management. Through this process, all levels of the organization became involved in the project and although management had a chance to review the suggestions from the research team, the workers felt that the solutions were a result of their own participation. After a solution to the identified problems had been decided upon, the next step was to design the implementation procedures.

A training program was used to explain the principles of a job enrichment process. A force-field analysis (see Chapter 7) provided guidance to the implementation process. The objective of the job enrichment program was to let each individual accomplish, as far as possible, a complete operation. Where this was not feasible, the objective was to design the job so that it could be completed in full by a small group of workers under the leadership of one supervisor. Of the test unit's 52 operations, the first 26 were combined and placed with a group of six employees working together with one foreman. Other assembly and test operations were combined to give a person a whole job, and job rotation and job sharing were also introduced to reduce the boredom of certain tasks. In addition, an inspection operation was redesigned to eliminate continuous operation of a piece of equipment that exposed personnel to harmful radiation.

The implementation plan called for a two-week pilot test to address the morale and productivity problems. After two days, the results were so negative that the experiment was stopped and the sources of the poor results investigated. Three issues required attention. First, more training in the new work procedures was proposed for the experimental unit. Second, the active interest of everyone in the plant interfered with, and in some cases actually interrupted, the work. In response, a special location was provided where interested employees could observe the new project, but they could not interfere or offer 'helpful' recommendations. Third, it was discovered that two supervisors' opposition to the project had never been dealt with effectively. They were actively sabotaging the project. These two supervisors were disciplined and moved away from the test unit, thus

effectively solving that problem. The high level of worker commitment made it easy to address these issues and another two-week pilot test was initiated.

After the operators had been retrained and the test redesigned, the second trial run produced both hard and soft results. First, the production rate at the beginning of the test period was slightly lower than normal but soon climbed above the previous rate and in only two weeks showed an 11% improvement. In addition, the proportion of rejected to accepted parts decreased by 6% and the costs of damaged parts decreased by 25%. Second, the duration of the test was not long enough to determine significance in the absenteeism or turnover statistics, but there was much evidence of increased interest and involvement in the job. Moreover, employee morale and work attitudes improved and interviews with, and observations of, the workers revealed that they were reacting positively to being a part of an effort to improve their jobs.

Good fit, industrialising settings

This international context includes industrialising countries with cultures that align with traditional OD values. Such settings support the kinds of OD processes described in this book, especially techno-structural and strategic interventions that focus on business development. According to data on economic development and cultural values, relatively few countries fit this context. South Africa is close, and recent political and cultural changes make it one of the most interesting settings in which to practise OD.

South Africa is an industrialising economy. Its major cities are the manufacturing hubs of the economy, although agriculture and mining still dominate in rural areas. South African values are in transition and may become more consistent with OD values. South Africans have customarily favoured a low-context orientation and moderate levels of power distance, individualism, uncertainty avoidance and masculinity. Organisations have tended to be bureaucratic with authoritarian management, established career paths and job security primarily for Caucasian employees.[21] These values and organisational conditions are changing, however, as the nation's political and governance structures are being transformed. Formerly, apartheid policies reduced uncertainty and defined power differences among citizens. Today, free elections and the abolishment of apartheid have drastically increased uncertainty and established legal equality among the races. These changes are likely to move South Africa's values closer to those that underlie OD.[22] If so, OD interventions should gain increasing relevance to this nation's organisations.

A recent study of large South African corporations suggests the directions that OD is likely to take in this setting.[23] The study interviewed internal OD practitioners about key organisational responses to the political changes in the country, such as the free election of Nelson Mandela, abolishment of apartheid and the *Reconstruction and Development Programme*. Change initiatives at Spoornet, Eskom and Telkom (railways, electricity and telecommunications providers, respectively), for example, centred around two strategic and organisational issues. First, the political changes opened up new international markets, provided access to new technologies and exposed these organisations to global competition. Consequently, these firms initiated planned change efforts to create corporate visions and to identify strategies for entering new markets and acquiring new technologies. Second, the political changes forced corporations to modify specific human resource and organisational practices. The most compelling change was mandated affirmative action quotas. At Spoornet, Eskom and Telkom, apartheid was thoroughly embedded in the organisations' structures, policies and physical arrangements. Thus, planned change focused on revising human resource policies and practices. Similarly, organisational structures that had fitted well within the stable environment of apartheid were outmoded and too rigid to meet the competitive challenges of international markets. Planned changes for restructuring these firms were implemented as part of longer-term strategies to change corporate culture towards more egalitarian and market-driven values.

Poor fit, industrial settings

This international setting includes industrialised countries with cultures that fit poorly with traditional OD values. Many countries in Latin America, Asia and Eastern Europe fit this description. Reviews of OD practice in these regions suggest that planned change includes all four types of interventions described in this book, although the change process itself is adapted to local conditions.[24] For example, Venezuela, Chile, China, Japan and Korea are high-context cultures where a knowledge of local mannerisms, customs and rituals is required to understand the meaning of communicated information.[25] To function in these settings, OD practitioners must not only know the language but the social customs as well. Similarly, cultural values emphasising high levels of power distance, uncertainty avoidance and masculinity foster organisations where roles, status differences and working conditions are clear, where autocratic and paternalistic decisions are expected and where the acquisition of wealth and influence by the powerful is accepted. OD interventions that focus on social processes and employee empowerment are not naturally favoured in this cultural context and consequently need to be modified to fit these situations.

Asian organisations, such as Matsushita, Nissan, Toyota, Fujitsu, NEC and Hyundai, provide good examples of how OD interventions can be tailored to this global setting. These firms are famous for continuous improvement and TQM practices; they adapt these interventions to fit the Asian culture. Roles and behaviours required to apply TQM are highly specified, thereby holding uncertainty to a relatively low level. Teamwork and consensus decision making associated with quality improvement projects also help to manage uncertainty. When large numbers of employees are involved, information is spread quickly and members are kept informed about the changes taking place. Management controls the change process by regulating the implementation of suggestions made by the different problem-solving groups. Because these interventions focus on the work process, teamwork and employee involvement do not threaten the power structure. Moreover, TQM and continuous improvement do not radically alter the organisation but produce small, incremental changes that can add up to impressive gains in long-term productivity and cost reduction.

In these cultures, OD practitioners also tailor the change process itself to fit local conditions. Latin American companies, for example, expect OD practitioners to act as experts and to offer concrete advice on how to improve the organisation. To be successful, OD practitioners need to have sufficient status and legitimacy to work with senior management and to act in expert roles.[26] Status is typically associated with academic credentials, senior management experience, high-level titles or recommendations by highly placed executives and administrators. As might be expected, the change process in Latin America tends to be autocratic and driven downward from the top of the organisation. Subordinates or lower-status individuals are not generally included in diagnostic or implementation activities because this might equalise power differences and threaten the *status quo*. Moreover, cultural norms discourage employees from speaking out or openly criticising management. There is relatively little resistance to change as employees readily accept those changes that are dictated by management.

In Asia, OD tends to be an orderly process. It is driven by consensus and challenging performance goals.[27] Organisational changes are implemented slowly and methodically, which helps to build trust and to reduce uncertainty associated with change. Changing too quickly is seen as arrogant, divisive and threatening. Because Asian values promote a cautious and somewhat closed culture that prizes consensus, dignity and respect, OD tends to be impersonal and to focus mainly on work flow improvements. Human-process issues are rarely addressed because people are expected to act in ways that do not cause others to 'lose face' or to bring shame to the group.

Good fit, industrial settings

This last setting includes industrialised countries with cultural contexts that fit well with traditional OD values. Much of the OD practice described in this book was developed in these situations, particularly in the US.[28] To extend our learning, we will focus on how OD is practised in nations other than the US in this global setting.

Scandinavians enjoy a high standard of living and strong economic development.[29] Because their cultural values most closely match those traditionally espoused in OD, organisational practices are highly participative and egalitarian. Organisation development practice tends to mirror these values. Multiple stakeholders, such as managers, unionists and staff personnel, are actively involved in all stages of the change process, from entry and diagnosis to intervention and evaluation. This results in a change process that is heavily oriented to the needs of shop-floor participants. Norwegian labour laws, for example, give unionists the right to participate in technological innovations that can affect their work lives. Such laws also mandate that all employees in the country have the right to enriched forms of work.

Given this cultural context, Scandinavian companies pioneered sociotechnical interventions to improve productivity and quality of work life.[30] Sweden's Saab-Scania and Volvo restructured automobile manufacturing around self-managed work groups. Denmark's Patent Office and Norway's Shell Oil demonstrated how union–management co-operative projects can enhance employee involvement throughout the organisation. In many cases, national governments were heavily involved in these change projects; they sponsor industry-wide improvement efforts. The Norwegian government was instrumental in introducing industrial democracy to that nation's companies. It helped union and management in selected industries to implement pilot projects aimed at enhancing productivity and quality of work life. The results of these sociotechnical experiments were then diffused throughout the national economy. In many ways, the Scandinavian countries have gone further than other global regions in linking OD to national values and policies.

Countries associated with the UK tend to have values that are consistent with a low-context orientation, moderate to high individualism and masculinity and moderate to low power distance and uncertainty avoidance. For example, a British subordinate who is told to think about a proposal is really being told that the suggestion has been rejected. These values also promote organisational policies that are steeped in formality, tradition and politics. The UK's long history tends to reinforce the *status quo* and, consequently, resistance to change is high.

Organisation development practice in the UK parallels the cultural pattern described above. In Great Britain, for example, sociotechnical systems theory was developed by practitioners at the Tavistock Institute for Human Relations.[31] Applications such as self-managed work groups have not readily diffused within British organisations, however. The individualistic values and inherently political nature of this culture tend to conflict with interventions that emphasise employee empowerment and teamwork. In contrast, the Scandinavian cultures are far more supportive of sociotechnical practice and have been instrumental in diffusing it worldwide.

The emergence of the European Common Market has served as a catalyst for change in many British organisations. Companies such as Imperial Chemical Industries, British Aerospace, International Computers Ltd. (ICL) and Reuters are actively engaged in strategic change interventions. At British Petroleum, chairman Robert B. Horton is implementing a flexible organisation to compete better in the emerging economy. He is reducing the number of levels in the structure, discontinuing long-standing committees, eliminating staff and empowering employees in teams.[32] More limited interventions, such as team building, conflict resolution and work redesign, are being carried out in such organisations as Unilever and SmithKline Beecham.

Worldwide organisation development

An important trend facing many business firms is the emergence of a global market place. Driven by competitive pressures, lowered trade barriers and advances in telecommunications, the number of companies offering products and services in multiple countries is increasing rapidly. The organisational growth and complexity associated with worldwide operations pose challenging managerial problems. Executives must choose appropriate strategic orientations for operating across cultures, geographical locations and governmental and environmental requirements. They must be able to adapt corporate policies and procedures to a diversity of local conditions. Moreover, the tasks of controlling and co-ordinating operations in different nations place heavy demands on information and control systems and on managerial skills and knowledge.

Worldwide organisation development applies to organisations that are operating across multiple geographic and cultural boundaries. This contrasts with OD in organisations that operate outside Australia but within a single cultural and economic context. This section describes the emerging practice of OD in worldwide organisations, a relatively new, yet important, area of planned change.

What is a worldwide organisation?

Worldwide organisations can be defined in terms of three key facets. First, they offer products or services in more than one country and consequently must relate to a variety of demands, such as unique product requirements, tariffs, value-added taxes, transportation laws and trade agreements. Second, worldwide firms must balance product and functional concerns with geographic issues of distance, time and culture. Australian textile and footwear companies, for example, face technological, moral and organisational issues in determining whether to produce their products in less-developed countries and, if they do, they must decide how to integrate manufacturing and distribution operations on a global scale. Third, worldwide companies must carry out co-ordinated activities across cultural boundaries, using a wide variety of personnel. Workers with different cultural backgrounds must be managed in ways that support the goals and image of the organisation. The company must therefore adapt its human resource policies and procedures to fit the culture and accomplish operational objectives. From a managerial perspective, the problem of selecting executives to head foreign operations is also an important decision in worldwide organisations.

Worldwide strategic orientations

A key question in designing OD interventions in worldwide organisations is how products, organisational units and personnel are arranged to form strategic orientations that enable firms to compete in the global market place.[33] Worldwide organisations can offer certain products or services in some countries and not others; they can centralise or decentralise operations; and they can determine how to work with people from different cultures. Despite the many possible combinations of characteristics, researchers have found that worldwide organisations tend to implement one of three types of strategic orientations: global, multinational and transnational. Table 21.2 presents these orientations in terms of the diagnostic framework described in Chapter 5. Each strategic

| TABLE 21.2 | Characteristics and interventions for worldwide strategic interventions | | | | |

Worldwide strategic orientation	Strategy	Structure	Information system	Human resource	OD interventions
Global	Standardized products Goals of efficiency through volume	Centralized, balanced and coordinated activities Global product division	Formal	Ethnocentric selection	Career planning Role clarification Employee involvement Senior management team building Conflict management
Multinational	Tailored products Goals of local responsiveness through specialization	Decentralized operations; centralized planning Global geographic divisions	Profit centres	Regiocentric or polycentric selection	Intergroup relations Local management team building Management development Reward systems Strategic alliances
Transnational	Tailored products Goals of efficiency and responsiveness through integration	Decentralized Worldwide coordination Global matrix or network	Subtle, clan-oriented controls	Geocentric selection	Extensive selection and rotation Cultural development Intergroup relations Building corporate vision

orientation is geared to specific market, technological and organisational requirements. Organisation development interventions that can help organisations to meet these demands are also included in Table 21.2.

The global orientation

This orientation is characterised by a strategy of marketing standardised products in different countries. It is an appropriate orientation when there is little economic reason to offer products or services with special features or locally available options. Manufacturers of office equipment, computers, tyres and containers, for example, can offer the same basic product in almost any country.

The goal of efficiency dominates this orientation. Production efficiency is gained through volume sales and large manufacturing plants, while managerial efficiency is achieved by centralising all product design, manufacturing, distribution and marketing decisions. Tight co-ordination is achieved by the close physical proximity of major functional groups and formal control systems that balance inputs, production and distribution with worldwide demand. Many Japanese firms, such as Honda, Sony, NEC and Matsushita, used this strategy in the 1970s and early 1980s to grow in the international economy. In Europe, Nestlé exploits economies of scale in marketing by advertising well-known brand names around the world. The increased number of microwaves and two-income families allowed Nestlé to push its Nescafé coffee and Lean Cuisine low-calorie frozen dinners to dominant market share positions in Europe, North America, Latin America and Asia.

In the global orientation, the organisation tends to be centralised with a global product structure. Presidents of each major product group report to the CEO and form the line organisation. Each of these product groups is responsible for worldwide operations. Information systems in global orientations tend to be quite formal, with local units reporting sales, costs and other data directly to the product president. The predominant human resource policy integrates people into the organisation through ethnocentric selection and staffing practices, which seek to fill key foreign positions with personnel or expatriates from the home country where the corporation headquarters is located.[34] All managerial jobs at Volvo and Michelin, for example, are occupied by Swedish and French citizens, respectively.[35] Ethnocentric policies support the global orientation because expatriate managers are more likely than host-country nationals to recognise and comply with the need to centralise decision making and to standardise processes, decisions and relationships with the parent company. Although many Japanese automobile manufacturers have decentralised production, Nissan's global strategy has been to retain tight, centralised control of design and manufacturing, ensure that almost all of its senior foreign managers are Japanese and have even low-level decisions come out of face-to-face meetings in Tokyo.[36]

Several OD interventions can be used to support the global strategic orientation, including career planning, role clarification, employee involvement, conflict management and senior management team building. Each of these interventions can help the organisation to achieve improved operational efficiency. For example, role clarification interventions, such as job enrichment, goal setting and conflict management, can formalise and standardise organisational activities. This ensures that each individual knows specific details about how, when and why a job needs to be done. As a result, necessary activities are described and efficient transactions and relationships created.

Senior management team building can improve the quality of decisions made at that level. Centralised policies make the organisation highly dependent on this group and can exaggerate decision-making errors. In addition, interpersonal conflict can increase the cost of co-ordination or cause significant co-ordination mistakes. Process interventions at this level can help to improve the speed and quality of decision making and improve interpersonal relationships.

Career planning can help home-country personnel develop a path to senior management by including foreign subsidiary experiences and cross-functional assignments as necessary qualifications for advancement. At the country level, career planning can emphasise that advancement beyond regional operations is limited for host-country nationals. Organisation development can help here by developing appropriate career paths within the local organisation or in technical, non-managerial areas. Finally, employee empowerment can support efficiency goals. It can involve members in efforts at cost reduction, work standardisation and minimisation of co-ordination costs.

The multinational orientation

This strategic orientation is characterised by a product line that is tailored to local conditions. It is best suited to markets that vary significantly from region to region or country to country. At American Express, for example, charge card marketing is fitted to local values and tastes. The 'Don't leave home without it' and 'Membership has its privileges' themes seen in Australia are translated to 'Peace of mind only for members' in Japan.[37]

The multinational orientation emphasises a decentralised, global division structure. Each region or country is served by a divisional organisation that operates autonomously and reports to headquarters. This results in a highly differentiated and loosely co-ordinated corporate structure. Operational decisions, such as product design, manufacturing and distribution, are decentralised and tightly integrated at the local level. For example, laundry soap manufacturers in the 1980s offered product formulas, packaging and marketing strategies that conformed to the different environmental regulations, types of washing machines, water hardness and distribution channels in each country. On the other hand, planning activities are often centralised at corporate headquarters to achieve important efficiencies necessary for worldwide co-ordination of emerging technologies and of resource allocation. A profit-centre control system allows local autonomy as long as profitability is maintained. Examples of multinational corporations include Hoechst and BASF of West Germany, IBM, NCR and Merck of the

US and Honda of Japan. Each of these organisations encourages local subsidiaries to maximise effectiveness within their geographic region.

People are integrated into multinational firms through polycentric or regiocentric personnel policies because these firms believe that host-country nationals can best understand native cultures.[38] By filling positions with local citizens who appoint and develop their own staffs, the organisation seeks to align the needs of the market with the ability of its subsidiaries to produce customised products and services. The distinction between a polycentric and regiocentric selection process is one of focus. In a polycentric selection policy, a subsidiary represents only one country. In the regiocentric selection policy, a slightly broader perspective is taken and key positions are filled by regional citizens (i.e. people who might be called 'Europeans', instead of 'Germans' or 'Italians').

The decentralised and locally co-ordinated multinational orientation suggests the need for a complex set of OD interventions. When applied to a subsidiary operating in a particular country or region, the OD process described above for foreign organisations is relevant. The key is to tailor OD to fit the specific cultural and economic context where the subsidiary is located.

When OD is applied across different regions and countries, interventions must account for differences in cultural and economic conditions that can affect OD success. Appropriate interventions for multinational corporations include inter-group relations, local management team building, sophisticated management selection and development practices and reward systems changes. Team building remains an important intervention. Unlike team building in global orientations, the local management team requires attention in multinational firms. This presents a challenge for OD practitioners as polycentric selection policies can produce management teams with different cultures at each subsidiary. Thus, a programme for one subsidiary may not work with a different team, given the different cultures that might be represented.

Inter-group interventions to improve relations between local subsidiaries and the parent company are also important for multinational companies. Decentralised decision making and regiocentric selection can strain corporate–subsidiary relations. Local management teams, operating in ways appropriate to their cultural context, may not be understood by corporate managers from another culture. Organisation development practitioners can help both groups to understand these differences by offering training in cultural diversity and appreciation. They can also help smooth parent–subsidiary relationships by focusing on the profit-centre control system or other criteria as the means for monitoring and measuring subsidiary effectiveness.

Management selection, development and reward systems also require special attention in multinational firms. Managerial selection requires finding technically and managerially competent individuals to run local or regional subsidiaries, who also possess the interpersonal competence needed to interface with corporate headquarters. Because these individuals may be hard to find, management development programmes can teach these cross-cultural skills and abilities. Such programmes typically involve language, cultural awareness and technical training; they can also include managers and staff from subsidiary and corporate offices to improve communications between these two areas. Finally, reward systems need to be aligned with the decentralised structure. Significant proportions of managers' total compensation could be tied to local profit performance, thereby aligning reward and control systems.

The transnational orientation

The transnational strategy combines customised products with both efficient and responsive operations. This is the most complex worldwide strategic orientation because transnationals can manufacture products, conduct research, raise capital, buy supplies and perform many other functions wherever in the world the job can best be done. They can move skills, resources and knowledge to regions where they are needed.

The transnational orientation combines the best of the global and multinational orientations and adds a third attribute: the ability to transfer resources both within the firm and across national and cultural boundaries. Otis Elevator Inc., a division of United Technologies, developed a new programmable elevator using six research centres in five countries: a US group handled the systems integration; Japan designed the special motor drives that make the elevators ride smoothly; France perfected the door systems; Germany handled the electronics; and Spain took care of the small-geared components.[39] Other examples of transnational firms include General Electric, Electrolux, Unilever and Hewlett-Packard (HP).

Transnational firms organise themselves into global matrix and network structures that are especially suited for moving information and resources to their best use. In the matrix structure, local divisions similar to the multinational structure are crossed with product groups at the headquarters office. The network structure treats each local office, including headquarters, product groups and production facilities, as self-sufficient nodes that co-ordinate with each other to move knowledge and resources to their most valued place. Because of the heavy information demands needed to operate these structures, transnationals tend to have sophisticated information systems. State-of-the-art information technology is used to move strategic and operational information throughout the system rapidly and efficiently. Organisational learning practices (Chapter 20), such as knowledge-management systems, are used to gather, organise and disseminate the knowledge and skills of members who are located throughout the world.

People are integrated into transnational firms through a geocentric selection policy that staffs key positions with the best people, regardless of nationality.[40] This staffing practice recognises that the distinctive competence of a transnational firm is its capacity to optimise resource allocation on a worldwide basis. Unlike global and multinational firms that spend more time training and developing managers to fit the strategy, the transnational firm attempts to hire the right person from the beginning. Recruits at any of Hewlett-Packard's foreign locations, for example, are screened not only for technical qualifications but for personality traits that match the cultural values of HP.[41]

Transnational companies require OD interventions that can improve their ability to achieve efficient worldwide integration under highly decentralised decision-making conditions. These interventions include extensive management selection and development practices in support of the geocentric policies described above, inter-group relations and development and communication of a strong corporate vision and culture.

Effective transnational firms have well developed vision and mission statements. These documents communicate the values and beliefs that underlie the firm's culture and guide its operational decisions. OD processes that increase member participation in the construction or modification of these statements can help members to gain ownership of them. Research into the development of corporate credos at the British computer manufacturer ICL, SAS and Apple Computer showed that success was more a function of the heavy involvement of many managers than the quality of the statements themselves.[42]

Once vision and mission statements have been crafted, management training can focus on clarifying their meaning, the values they express and the behaviours required to support those values. This process of gaining shared meaning and developing a strong culture provides a basis for social control. Because transnationals need flexibility and co-ordination, they cannot rely solely on formal reports of sales, costs or demand to guide behaviour. This information often takes too much time to compile and distribute. Rather, the corporate vision and culture provide transnational managers with the reasoning and guidelines for why and how they should make decisions.

This form of social control supports OD efforts to improve management selection and development, inter-group relationships and strategic change. The geocentric selection process can be supplemented by a personnel policy that rotates managers through different geographical regions and functional areas to blend people, perspectives and practices. At such organisations as GE, Coca-Cola and Colgate, a cadre of managers with extensive foreign experience is being developed. Rotation throughout the organisation also improves the chances that when two organisational units must co-operate, key personnel will know each other and make co-ordination more likely. The corporate vision and culture can also become important tools in building cross-functional or interdepartmental processes for transferring knowledge, resources or products. Moreover, they can provide guidelines for formulating and implementing strategic change. They can serve as a social context for designing appropriate structures and systems at local subsidiaries.

Changing worldwide strategic orientations

In addition to implementing planned changes that support the three basic worldwide strategic orientations, OD can help firms to change from one orientation to another. At first, OD can help organisations make the transition from a domestic to a worldwide strategic orientation. Researchers have found that many organisations that sell products or services to other countries start with either global or multinational orientations. They have also suggested that global and multinational organisations tend to evolve into a transnational orientation.[43] This evolution occurs because of changes in the organisation's environment, markets or technologies. In the global orientation, for example, environmental changes can reduce the need for centralised and efficient operations. The success of Japanese automobile manufacturers employing a global strategy caused employment declines in the US auto industry and overall trade imbalances. Consumer and government reactions forced Japanese firms to become more responsive to local conditions. Conversely, for the multinational orientation, environmental changes can reduce the need for tailored products and locally responsive management. The typical response is to centralise many decisions and activities.

Thus, the evolution to a transnational orientation is a complex strategic change effort requiring the acquisition of two additional capabilities. First, global orientations need to adapt multinational policies, whereas multinational orientations need to become more global. Second, the organisation needs to acquire the capacity to transfer resources efficiently around the world. Much of the difficulty in evolving to a transnational strategy lies in developing these additional capabilities.

From domestic to global or multinational

Change from a domestic to a worldwide organisation represents a dramatic shift in scope for most firms. The direction this change takes depends largely on the degree to which the worldwide market is homogeneous. Success in a homogeneous market depends on a global orientation of delivering standardised products or services to different countries in the most efficient manner. In more heterogeneous markets, success relies on a multinational orientation of customising products and services to fit local conditions. Domestic organisations typically gain their knowledge of worldwide markets through initial efforts to export products abroad. This can be accomplished by giving worldwide markets increased importance in the operating structure of the firm. For example, the company may create a special international division to handle all foreign sales of its products. The international division is primarily responsible for marketing and distribution, although it may be able to set up joint ventures, licensing agreements, distribution territories/ franchises, sales offices and, in some cases, manufacturing plants. This initial movement into the international arena enables domestic organisations to learn about the demands of the global market place, thus providing knowledge about whether a global or multinational orientation is needed to compete.

In addition to information about the market, organisations take into account their distinctive competencies when choosing an international strategy. They assess whether their culture and core competencies are more suited for centralised or decentralised decision making. Centralisation favours a global orientation and decentralisation favours a multinational strategy.

Once companies develop a strategic orientation for competing internationally, they create an organisation design to support it. Information like that found in Table 21.2 is useful for designing structures, information systems and personnel practices for specific strategic orientations.

OD can help domestic organisations become international. Team building and large group interventions, such as search conferences, can facilitate the process through which senior executives gather appropriate information about international markets, distinctive competencies and culture, and choose a strategic orientation. Based on that decision, OD interventions can help the organisation to implement it. For instance, members can use integrated strategic management to design and manage the transition from the old strategic orientation to the new one. They can apply technostructural interventions to design an appropriate structure, to define new tasks and work roles and to clarify reporting relationships between corporate headquarters and foreign-based units. Managers and staff can apply human resource management interventions to train and prepare managers and their families for international assignments and to develop selection methods and reward systems that are relevant to international operation.[44]

Application 21.2 examines the human resource practices of Samsung, one of the largest conglomerates in Korea.[45]

APPLICATION 21.2 — Globalisation and a new human resource policy in Korea

The remarkable growth of the Korean economy over the last three decades has received much attention from Western academics and business people. During this period Korea achieved a real annual growth rate of about 8% in gross national product (*Asian Wall Street Journal*, 1995). In 1996, Korea was formally invited to join the Organisation for Economic Co-operation and Development (OECD), confirming and at the same time enhancing Korea's status as a major global player.

Samsung was founded by the legendary tycoon, Byung-Chull Lee in 1938. In 1995, Samsung's sales rose to $87 billion and its assets totalled $87 billion. Samsung is the second largest *chaebol* (Korean term for a large conglomerate), composed of 35 enterprises, which employ 233 000 employees in 66 countries. Samsung is a major global competitor in electronics, machinery, chemicals and finance. Other areas of Samsung's operations include the auto manufacturing, newspaper, hotel and entertainment industries.

Samsung has been one of the most important vehicles for Korea's remarkable economic growth and has received numerous awards from the government for its contributions.

Samsung's leadership in effective human resource management (HRM), however, has been seriously challenged as the *chaebol* has begun to compete with the world's most competitive firms in both its domestic and global markets. The success and pride of Samsung largely stemmed from being the best in Korea — where foreign competition was almost non-existent because of trade barriers maintained by the government. However, these trade barriers are being reduced due to pressures from the USA, the beginnings of the World Trade Organisation (WTO) and the General Agreement on Tariffs and Trade (GATT), as well as the requirements to join the OECD. As Samsung increasingly competes with foreign firms, it has begun to realise that it must build competitiveness into its management and HRM practices in order to succeed in the global marketplace.

In response to these challenges, Samsung felt the need to create a new management paradigm to guide itself into the future. Under the 'New Management Initiative' by Chairman Lee, Samsung drafted a new vision.

In the old paradigm, the growth of the Korean economy and Samsung was very fast and, in a sense, automatic. Therefore, Samsung just needed hard-working people and did not pay much attention to providing individuals with incentives to excel. However, the new business environment, characterised by slower growth and increased competition, requires Samsung to adopt a new paradigm where it is much more important to have creative and innovative people as well as industrious people, and to develop world-class specialists in each area in which Samsung competes.

Following the guidance of the new management paradigm, Samsung introduced the 'New HR Policy (*Shin In Sa*)' in 1995. The goal of the New HR Policy was to create the maximum possible value for the employees and the organisation. Samsung believes this is possible through an HRM system which puts greater emphasis on performance rather than on seniority, and properly rewards individual performance. The New HR Policy thus brought sweeping changes to the core components of Samsung's HRM system: the job hierarchy, promotion, compensation and performance appraisal.

Increased competition in domestic and international markets has forced Samsung to review its management paradigm and resulting HRM system critically. The traditional HRM system emphasised group harmony (*In Hwa*) and age norms for compensation and promotions. Promotion was primarily based on seniority, and the incentive pay scheme (bonus) was linked to group

performance. This made the performance appraisal an unimportant paper exercise for the employees and their supervisors.

Samsung determined that, to succeed in the global market, it needed to utilise its people more effectively. To shed old traditions, Samsung launched the New HR Policy in 1995 to tighten the links between performance, promotion and compensation in the attempt to recognise and encourage efforts towards development of greater individual creativity and excellence. Samsung introduced individual incentives into the compensation system and adopted a more effective appraisal system to support promotion and compensation decisions.

Like Samsung, most *chaebols* are in the process of transforming their HR systems in response to increased competition in the domestic and international markets. These conglomerates also face challenges similar to those that Samsung encounters. Whether Korea's *chaebols* can effectively overcome these challenges and transform their HR systems will significantly affect not only their performance but also the economic growth of Korea in the future.

From global to transnational

In the transition from a global to a transnational orientation, the firm must acquire the know-how to operate a decentralised organisation and to transfer knowledge, skills and resources among disparate organisational units operating in different countries. In this situation, the administrative challenge is to encourage creative over centralised thinking and to let each functional area operate in a way that best suits its context. For example, if international markets require increasingly specialised products, then manufacturing needs to operate local plants and flexible delivery systems that can move raw materials to where they are needed, when they are needed. OD interventions that can help this transition include:

* training efforts that increase the tolerance for differences in management practices, control systems, performance appraisals and policies and procedures
* reward systems that encourage entrepreneurship and performance at each foreign subsidiary
* efficient organisation designs at the local level.

The global orientation strives to achieve efficiency through the centralisation and standardisation of products and practices. In the case of organisational systems, this works against the establishment of highly specialised and flexible policies and resists the movement of knowledge, skills and resources. Training interventions that help managers develop an appreciation for the different ways that effectiveness can be achieved will aid the global organisations move toward transnationalism.

Changes in reward systems can also help the global firm evolve. By changing from the highly quantitative, centralised, pay-for-performance system characteristic of a global orientation, the organisation can reward individuals who champion new ideas and provide incentives for decentralised business units. This more flexible reward system promotes co-ordination among subsidiaries, product lines and staff groups. In addition, the transition to a transnational orientation can be facilitated by having OD practitioners work with individual business units, rather than with senior management at headquarters. Working with each subsidiary on issues relating to its own structure and function sends an important message about the importance of decentralised operations.

Finally, changing the staffing policy is another important signal to organisation members that a transition is occurring. Under the global orientation, an ethnocentric policy supported standardised activities. By staffing key positions with the best people, rather than limiting the choice to just parent-country individuals, the symbols of change are clear and the rewards for supporting the new orientation are visible.

From multinational to transnational

When an organisation moves from a multinational to a transnational orientation, products, technologies and regulatory constraints can become more homogenous and require more efficient operations. The competencies required to compete on a transnational basis, however, may be located in many different geographic areas. The need to balance local responsiveness against the need for co-ordination among organisational units is new to multinational firms. They need to create interdependencies among organisational units through the flow of parts, components and finished goods; the flow of funds, skills and other scarce resources; or the flow of intelligence, ideas and knowledge. For example, as part of Ford's transition to a transnational company, the redesign of the Tempo automobile was given to one person, David Price, an Englishman. He co-ordinated all features of the new car for both sides of the Atlantic and used the same platform, engines and other parts. To accomplish the co-ordination between Detroit and Europe, Ford used teleconferencing and computer links, as well as considerable air travel, to manage the complex task of meshing car companies on two continents.[46]

In these situations, OD is an important activity, because complex interdependencies require sophisticated and non-traditional co-ordinating mechanisms.[47] Organisation development interventions, such as inter-group team building or cultural awareness and interpersonal skills training, can facilitate development of the communication linkages necessary for successful co-ordination. In addition, the inherently 'matrixed' structures of worldwide firms and the cross-cultural context of doing business in different countries tend to create conflict. Organisation development interventions, such as role clarification, third-party consultation and mediation techniques, can help to solve such problems.

The transition to being a transnational firm is difficult and threatens the *status quo*. Under the multinational orientation, each subsidiary is encouraged and rewarded for its creativity and independence. Transnational firms, however, are effective when physically or geographically distinct organisational units co-ordinate their activities. The transition from independent to interdependent business units can produce conflict as the co-ordination requirements are worked through. Organisation development practitioners can help to mitigate the uncertainty associated with the change by modifying reward systems to encourage co-operation and clearly spelling out the required behaviours for success.

Global social change

The newest and perhaps most exciting applications of organisation development in international settings are occurring in global social change organisations (GSCOs).[48] These organisations tend to be not-for-profit and non-governmental. They are typically created at the grass-roots level to help communities and societies address important problems, such as unemployment, race relations, homelessness, hunger, disease and political instability. In international settings, GSCOs are heavily involved in social change, particularly in developing nations. Examples include the World Conservation Union, the

Hunger Project, the Nature Conservancy, International Physicians for the Prevention of Nuclear War, International Union for the Conservation of Nature and Natural Resources and the Asian Coalition for Agrarian Reform and Rural Development. Many practitioners who help to create and develop these GSCOs come from an OD background and have adapted their expertise to fit highly complex, global situations. This section describes global social change organisations and how OD is practised in them.

Global social change organisations: what are they?

Global social change organisations are part of a social innovation movement to foster the emergence of a global civilisation.[49] They exist under a variety of names and include development organisations, international non-governmental organisations (INGOs), international private voluntary organisations and bridging organisations.[50] They exist to address complex social problems, including overpopulation, ecological degradation, the increasing concentration of wealth and power, the lack of management infrastructures to facilitate growth and the lack of fundamental human rights. The efforts of many GSCOs to raise awareness and mobilise resources toward the solution of these problems culminated in the United Nations Conference on Environment and Development in Rio de Janeiro in June 1992, where leaders from both industrialised and less-developed countries met to discuss sustainable development.[51]

GSCOs differ from traditional for-profit firms on several dimensions.[52] First, they typically advocate a mission of social change—the formation and development of better societies and communities. 'Better' typically means more just (Amnesty International, Hunger Project), peaceful (International Physicians for the Prevention of Nuclear War) or ecologically conscious (Nature Conservancy, Greenpeace). Second, the mission is supported by a network structure. Most GSCO activity occurs at the boundary or periphery between two or more organisations. Unlike most industrial firms that focus on internal effectiveness, GSCOs are directed at changing their environmental context. For example, World Vision co-ordinated the efforts of more than 100 organisations in an effort to address the human consequences of Ceausescu's Romanian government.[53] Third, GSCOs generally have strong values and ideologies that are used to justify and motivate organisation behaviour. These 'causes' provide intrinsic rewards for GSCO members and a blueprint for action. The ideological position that basic human rights include shelter has directed Habitat for Humanity to erect low-cost homes in Tijuana, Mexico and other under-developed communities. Fourth, GSCOs interact with a great range of external and often conflicting constituencies. To help the poor, GSCOs must often work with the rich; to save the ecology, they must work with developers; to empower the masses, they must work with the powerful few. This places a great deal of pressure on GSCOs to reconcile pursuit of a noble cause with the political reality of power and wealth. Fifth, managing these diverse external constituencies often creates significant organisational conflict. On the one hand, GSCOs need to create specific departments to serve and represent particular stakeholders. On the other hand, GSCOs are strongly averse to bureaucracy; they desire collegial and consensus-seeking cultures. The conflicting perspectives of the stakeholders, the differentiated departments and the ideological basis of the organisation's mission can produce a contentious internal environment. For example, the International Relief and Development Agency was created to promote self-help projects in Third World countries using resources donated from First World countries. As the agency grew, departments were created to represent different stakeholders: a fund-raising group handled donors, a projects department worked in the Third World, a public relations department directed media exposure and a policy information department lobbied the government. Each department adapted to fit its role. Fund-raisers and lobbyists dressed more formally, took more moderate political positions and managed less participatively than did projects department staff. These differences were often interpreted in political and ideological terms, creating considerable internal conflict.[54] Sixth, GSCO membership is often transitory. Many people are volunteers and the extent and depth of their involvement varies over time and by issue. Turnover is quite high.

Application stages

Global social change organisations are concerned with creating sustainable change in communities and societies. This requires a form of planned change where the practitioner is heavily involved in the change, many stakeholders are encouraged and expected to participate and 'technologies of empowerment' are employed.[55] Often referred to as 'participatory action research',[56] planned change in GSCOs typically involves three types of activities:

- building local organisation effectiveness
- creating bridges and linkages with other relevant organisations
- developing vertical linkages with policy-makers.

Building the local organisation

Although GSCOs are primarily concerned with changing their environment, a critical issue in development projects is recognising the potential problems inherent in the GSCO itself. Because the focus of change is their environment, members of GSCOs are often oblivious to the need for internal development. Moreover, the complex organisational arrangements of a network make planned change in GSCOs particularly challenging.

Organisation development practitioners tend to focus on three activities when helping GSCOs build themselves into viable organisations: using values to create the vision, recognising that internal conflict is often a function of external conditions and understanding the problems of success. For leadership to function effectively, the broad purposes of the GSCO must be clear and closely aligned with the ideologies of its members. Singleness of purpose can be gained by tapping into the compelling aspects of the values and principles that the GSCO represents. For example, the Latin American Division of the Nature Conservancy holds an annual two-day retreat. Each participant prepares a 'white paper' concerning his or her area: the issues, challenges, major dilemmas or problems and ideas for directions that the division could take. Over the course of the retreat, participants actively discuss each paper. They have considerable freedom to challenge the *status quo* and to question previous decisions. By the end of the retreat, discussions have produced a clear statement about the course that the division will take for the following year. People leave with increased clarity about, and commitment to, the purpose and vision of the division.[57]

Developing a shared vision results in the alignment of individual and organisational values. Because most activities occur at the boundary of the organisation, members are often spread out geographically and are not in communication with each other. A clearly crafted vision allows individuals in disparate regions and positions to co-ordinate their activities. At the Hunger Project, for example, OD practitioners asked organisation members, 'What is your job or task in this organisation?' The GSCO president responded, 'That is simple. My work is to make the end of hunger an idea whose time has come.' A receptionist answered, 'My task in this organisation is to end hunger. I don't just answer phones or set up meetings. In everything I do, I am working to end hunger.'[58] Because of the diverse perspectives of the different stakeholders, GSCOs often face multiple conflicts. In working through them, the organisational vision can be used as an important rallying point for discovering how each person's role contributes to the GSCO's purpose. The affective component of the vision is what allows GSCO members to give purpose to their lives and work.[59]

Another way of managing conflict is to prevent its occurrence. At the Hunger Project, the 'committed listener' and 'breakthrough' processes give GSCO members an opportunity to seek help before conflict becomes dysfunctional. Every member of the organisation has a designated person who acts as a committed listener. When things are not going well or someone is feeling frustrated in his or her ability to accomplish a goal, he or she can talk it out with this colleague. The role of the committed listener is to listen intently, to help the individual to understand the issues and to think about framing or approaching the problem in new ways. This new perspective is called a 'breakthrough'—a creative solution to a potentially conflictual situation.

Finally, a GSCO's success can create a number of problems. The very accomplishment of its mission can take away its reason for existence, thus causing an identity crisis. For example, a GSCO that creates jobs for under-privileged youth can be dissolved because its funding is taken away, its goals change or simply because it accomplished its purpose. During these times, the vital social role that these organisations play needs to be emphasised. GSCOs often represent bridges between the powerful and powerless, between the rich and poor and between the elite and oppressed. They may need to be maintained as a legitimate part of the community.

Another problem can occur when GSCO success produces additional demands for greater formalisation. New people may need to be hired and indoctrinated into the culture; greater control over income and expenditures may need to be developed; new skills and behaviours may have to be learned; and so on. The need for more formal systems often runs counter to ideological principles of autonomy and freedom and can produce a profound resistance to change. Employee participation during diagnosis and implementation can help them to commit to the new systems. In addition, new employment opportunities, increased job responsibilities and improved capabilities to carry out the GSCO's mission can be used to manage commitment and resistance to the changes.

Alternatively, the organisation can maintain its autonomy through structural arrangements. The Savings Development Movement (SDM) of Zimbabwe was a grass-roots effort to organise savings clubs, the proceeds of which helped farmers to buy seed in volume. Its success in creating clubs and helping farmers lower their costs caused the organisation to grow very rapidly. Leaders chose to expand SDM not by adding staff but by working with the Ministry of Agriculture to provide technical support to the clubs and with the Ministry of Community Development and Women's Affairs to provide training. The savings clubs remained autonomous and locally managed. This reduced the need for formal systems to co-ordinate the clubs with government agencies. The SDM office staff did not grow, yet the organisation remained a catalyst, committed to expanding participation, rather than providing direct services.[60]

Creating horizontal linkages

Successful social change projects often require a network of local organisations with similar views and objectives. Such projects as transforming the community of Maliwada, India,[61] developing relief distribution systems in Bangladesh[62] or teaching leadership skills in South Africa[63] require multiple organisations to interact. Consequently, an important planned change activity in GSCOs is the creation of strong linkages to organisations in the community or society where the development project is taking place. For example, GSCOs aimed at job development must not only recruit, train and market potential job applicants but must also develop relationships with local job providers and government authorities. The GSCO must help these organisations to gain commitment to the GSCO's vision, to mobilise resources and to create policies to support development efforts.

The ability of GSCOs to sustain themselves depends on their establishing linkages with other organisations whose co-operation is essential to preserving and expanding their efforts. Unfortunately, members of GSCOs often view local government officials, community leaders or for-profit organisations as part of the problem. Rather than interacting with these stakeholders, GSCOs often 'protect' themselves and their ideologies from contamination by these outsiders. Planned change efforts to overcome this myopia are similar to the transorganisational development interventions discussed in Chapter 19. GSCO members are helped to identify, convene and organise these key external organisations. For example, following the earthquakes in Mexico City in 1985, the Committee of Earthquake Victims was established to prevent the government and landlords from evicting low-income tenants from their destroyed housing. The committee formed relationships with other GSCOs concerned with organising the poor or with responding to the disaster. The committee also linked up with local churches, universities, charitable organisations and poor urban neighbourhood organisations. It bargained with the government and appealed to the media to scuttle attempts at widespread eviction proceedings. This pressure culminated in agreement around a set of principles for reconstruction in Mexico City.[64]

Developing vertical linkages

GSCOs must also create channels of communication and influence upward to governmental and policy-level decision-making processes. These higher-level decisions often affect the creation and eventual success of GSCO activities. For example, the Society for Participatory Research in Asia (PRIA) is a non-governmental organisation that provides research information and educational services for grass-roots activists on issues of land alienation, women and work and occupational safety and health. PRIA has used its capacity for research and policy analysis to identify national policy initiatives that affect GSCOs in India. As a result, its staff participates with other GSCOs concerned with influencing government policies. When the Indian government proposed new regulations and tax policies, PRIA helped to assess the proposed legislation, advised the GSCOs of its implications and became involved in making modifications that were favourable to the GSCOs' activities.[65]

Vertical linkages can also be developed by building on a strong record of success. The Institute of Cultural Affairs (ICA) is concerned with the 'application of methods of human development to communities and organisations all around the world'. With more than 100 offices in 39 nations, ICA trains and consults to small groups, communities organisations and voluntary associations, in addition to providing leadership training for village leaders, conducting community education programmes and running ecological preservation projects. Its reputation has led to recognition and credibility: it was given consultative status by the United Nations in 1985 and it has category II status with the Food and Agriculture Organisation, working relation status with the World Health Organisation and consultative status with UNICEF.[66]

Application 21.3 describes the beginning of a global social change organisation in South Africa before the abolishment of apartheid.[67] The 'keynote address' contributed to the development of a strong vision and the subsequent work identified the needs to build the horizontal and vertical linkages that would provide the GSCO with the legitimacy to influence non-violent change.

APPLICATION 21.3 — Building global social change organisations in South Africa

A meeting of the Community Development and Management Association of Africa (CDMMA) was held in August 1986 in Johannesburg, South Africa. A South African OD consultant, Louw DuToit, had established the group, believing that change needed to occur in his country and that traditional top-down approaches were not working. Although having a meeting in which both black and white individuals participate was legal, there were obvious social ramifications for encouraging a group of South Africans to confront the issue of apartheid. DuToit invited two other OD practitioners to deliver a participative opening address to the group.

The purpose of the keynote address was to introduce the concept of cultural synergy to the 300 members attending the opening banquet, as well as to establish the climate for creative problem solving. This situation was difficult because, in addition to CDMAA members, also present were non-members who funded DuToit's larger project 'Leaders for the Future'. Because some of these sponsors came from large Afrikaner-dominated companies, many

CDMAA members felt uneasy about the opening session. In addition, many CDMAA members did not know each other before this meeting.

The rest of the conference was open only to CDMAA members. The consultants believed that some team-building activities were necessary in order to build a cohesive group of CDMAA members with superordinate goals that could confront the problem of a nonviolent solution to apartheid. The keynote address, given before the banquet, was nontraditional in that it modelled the action research methods of organization development.

The authors began the keynote address with an overview of the action research process and then explained the idea of cultural synergy. The group brainstormed for 20 minutes on the following question: 'I want you to vision this group in the future. Go beyond your individual selves, race, tribe, or religion. What can you do that will enable your group to become culturally synergistic?' The authors suggested that individuals form the smaller groups with acquaintances instead of friends. This meant individuals would have to move physically to another part of the room. Each group recorded its answers on a flip chart.

In minutes, the energy level in the room rose dramatically. Group members were leaning closely together to hear without disturbance from other groups. As the 20 minutes passed, the noise level increased to a roar. The consultants had to stop the groups because of the time limit, not because they had finished their work.

Before the eight groups made their reports, the facilitators warned the participants to listen carefully to the final summary because they would be asked if it included the major elements from all groups. Each group left their flip chart notes in front of the room for all to see. Seven statements summarized the groups' beliefs about what was necessary to achieve cultural synergy, including actions to build trust,

acceptance, honesty, more interaction, and hope for a better future and getting to know each other personally.

The summary statements caused participants to realise that they were a united 'community' now, no longer individuals or fragmented groups. At the conclusion of the keynote event, the consultants expressed their appreciation to the group for its enthusiastic co-operation and encouraged it to bring its energy back the following day when follow-up work would begin. The group then adjourned to the banquet.

This first data-gathering process provided information about the group for the group. It created the common ground on which to build a vision for the future that was compelling to all members. The very process of collecting the data began the team-building and organization development process. It was a mini-intervention that began the creation of a new culture by establishing norms of working together, trusting each other, brainstorming, sharing data, and celebrating success. The evening provided a positive experience and a working model on which to build organization action.

The next morning when the large group reconvened, it was given the task of generating ideas about 'the factors involved in peaceful change in South Africa'. Members decided that working in small groups and reporting back to the larger group was the way they wanted to handle this new task. They worked in small groups during the morning and, in the afternoon, reported on their work to the large group. The results of the first day's work were a rough list of ideas that would help cause peaceful change.

During the second day, the groups refined the first day's list by focusing on the question: 'What are the helping factors or existing resources that would encourage peaceful change in South Africa?' The outcomes of the entire meeting were summarized after the second day. The groups endorsed these factors as facilitators of peaceful change for South Africa and committed themselves to action plans. The large group adopted the following principles for changes:

- *Participation and representation in decision making for all (both politically and educationally).* Politically, the CDMAA saw no black voice in the central government. It expressed concern that there was no 'bill of rights' for South Africans and it asked, 'Without such a guarantee of rights, how far can we go?' The group felt that the problem with education rested in the way that funds were inequitably distributed. The group believed that, if blacks participated in decision making, there would be more equality in the distribution of funding and the quality of teacher training and education would improve.
- *Equal practical education for all to train the future leaders.* The group believed that quality education was essential for peaceful change in South Africa. Initially the organization appeared to focus on education for blacks, but others argued persuasively that the masses, despite race, needed to be educated. Additionally, practical education that would ensure jobs for all people trained was emphasized. It was important to all attending that politics should not influence education and that the educational system needed to be nonracial if it was to be of benefit to all South Africans.
- *Freedom from restrictions for all.* It was the group's belief that, without this freedom, there could not be peaceful change. The group expressed the belief that the freedoms of speech, movement and the vote were basic to peaceful change in South Africa.
- *Equal opportunities (housing/jobs/education/health).* The group believed that the government should allow equal opportunity for everyone across a wide range of issues. It felt that current inequalities around housing, rent, employment, healthcare,

distribution of wealth, bus availability, and the justice system existed. Both blacks and whites at this meeting agreed that equality was an important issue for peaceful change in South Africa.
- *Dissolve political rifts within and between political groups.* The group recognized political rifts throughout South Africa in both the tribes and homelands and even among white Afrikaners. The participants believed that nonracial political parties would eliminate this problem through the system of one person, one vote.
- *The future lies with our children who can work and play together now without prejudice.* Several members talked about how their children play together now without any problems. They acknowledged that the children learn hostility. One member pointed out, 'There is an international school where the children don't see black and white, they just see Sacred Heart College. When they meet in the shopping centre, they go out of their way to talk to each other. The children have the future unless we take it away from them.'
- *The people must join on common ground as one team; together we can solve our own problems.* The group mentioned, 'We are always comparing ourselves with the other side, not facing our problems. We, the people, need to form a team like the soccer team against Rhodesia [Zimbabwe]. There is hugging and encouraging in a multiracial team. We must forget black and white and look toward victory!' The group also agreed that fragmentation of the moderates, the largest percentage of the population, is a problem and that peace will come when moderates, the right and the left become a team.
- *Let the moderates unite the frustrated blacks and the insecure whites so that together we can change the cultural attitudes of the masses and unify the people through trust, honesty, and forgetting our differences.* Group

members identified themselves as moderates with a responsibility to pull together the fighting groups. They said, 'The extreme left and right don't trust us because they think we are weak. It is our job to create the grey area so that we can work together. Then we can pull them into our group.'

- *Bring the extreme political positions closer to the moderate stance by focusing on common elements with communication, decisions, and*

education. The left, the right and moderates all have some areas of concern in common. The moderates make up 80% of the population. This group of moderates felt that 'it is our job to point out to the others that we all care about justice, education, security, health, economy, and waste. The emphasis needs to be on common elements and not the differences. It is these differences that cause the barriers and stop us from uniting.'

Change agent roles and skills

Planned change in development organisations is a relatively new application of organisation development in international settings. The number of practitioners is small but growing, and the skills and knowledge necessary to carry out OD in these situations are being developed. The grass-roots, political and ideological nature of many international GSCOs requires change agent roles and skills that are quite different from those in more formal, domestic settings.[68]

GSCO change agents typically occupy stewardship and bridging roles. The steward role derives from the ideological and grass-roots activities associated with GSCOs. It asks the change agent to be a co-learner or co-participant in achieving global social change. This type of change is 'sustainable', or ecologically, politically, culturally and economically balanced. Change agents must therefore work from an explicit value base that is aligned with GSCO activities. For example, change agents are not usually asked, 'What are your credentials to carry out this project?' Instead, practitioners are asked, 'Do you share our values?' or 'What do you think of the plight of the people we are serving?' Stewardship implies an orientation toward the development of sustainable solutions to local and global problems.

The second role, bridging, derives from the grass roots and political activities of many GSCOs. Bridging is an appropriate title for this role because it metaphorically reflects the core activities of GSCOs and the change agents who work with them. They are both mainly concerned with connecting and integrating diverse elements of societies and communities toward sustainable change. They are also concerned with transferring ideas between individuals, groups, organisations and societies.

Carrying out the steward and bridging roles requires communication, negotiation and networking skills. Communication and negotiation skills are essential for GSCO change agents because of the asymmetrical power bases extant in grass-roots development efforts. GSCOs are relatively powerless compared to governments, wealthy upper classes and formal organisations. Given the diverse social systems involved, there is often no consensus about a GSCO's objectives. Moreover, different constituencies may have different interests and there may be histories of antagonism between groups that make promulgation of the development project difficult. The steward and bridging roles require persuasive articulation of the GSCO's ideology and purpose at all times, under many conditions and to everyone involved.

The change agent must also be adept at political compromise and negotiation. Asymmetrical power contexts represent strong challenges for stewardship and bridging. To accomplish sustainable change, important trade-offs must often be made. The effective change agent needs to understand the elements of the ideology that can and cannot be sacrificed and when to fight or walk away from a situation.

Networking skills represent a significant part of the action research process as applied in GSCO settings. Networking takes place at two levels. First, in the steward role, practitioners bring specific knowledge of problem-solving and appreciative inquiry to the GSCO.[69] The participants bring local knowledge of political players, history, culture and ecology. A 'co-generative dialogue' or 'collective reflection' process emerges when these two frames of reference interact to produce new ideas, possibilities and insights.[70] This process was clearly demonstrated in Application 20.3 when the participants addressed cross-cultural synergy to develop the actions necessary for bringing about peaceful change in South Africa. When both the practitioner and the participants contribute to sustainable solutions, the stewardship role is satisfied.

Second, in the bridging role, networking skills are necessary to create conditions that allow diverse stakeholders to interact and solve common problems or issues. Change agents must be able to find common ground so that different constituencies can work together. Networking requires the capability to tap multiple sources of information and perspective, often located in very different constituencies. Through these networks, action becomes possible.

But bridging also implies making linkages between individual, group, GSCO and social levels of thought. Ideas are powerful fuel in international grass-roots development projects. Breakthrough thinking by individuals to see things in new ways can provide the impetus for change at the group, GSCO, social and global levels. This was demonstrated in the Live Aid rock concerts in 1988, the culmination of one man's concern over famine relief in Africa.[71]

The change agent in international GSCO settings must play a variety of roles and use many skills. Clearly, stewardship and bridging roles are important in facilitating GSCO accomplishment. Other roles and skills will probably emerge over time. Change agents, for example, are finding it increasingly important to develop 'imaginal literacy' skills—the ability to see the possibilities, rather than the constraints, and the ability to develop sustainable solutions by going 'outside the boxes' to create new ideas.[72]

Summary

This chapter has examined the practice of international organisation development in three areas. In organisations outside Australia, the traditional approaches to OD need to be adapted to fit the cultural and economic development context in which they are applied. This adaptation approach recognises that OD practices may be culture-bound; what works in one culture may be inappropriate in another. The cultural contexts of different geographical regions were examined in terms of five values: context orientation, power distance, uncertainty avoidance, masculinity and individualism. This approach also recognises that not all OD interventions may be appropriate. The prevailing economic situation may strongly favour business-oriented over process-oriented interventions. The process of OD under different cultural and economic conditions was also described. These descriptions are, however, tentative. As OD matures, its methods will become more differentiated and adaptable.

OD activities to improve global, multinational and transnational strategic orientations are in increasing demand. Each of these strategies respond to specific environmental, technological and economic conditions. Interventions in worldwide organisations require a strategic and organisational perspective on change to align people, structures and systems.

Finally, the OD process in global social change organisations was discussed. This relatively new application of OD tries to promote the establishment of a global civilisation. Strong ideological positions regarding the fair and just distribution of wealth, resources and power fuel this movement. By strengthening local organisations, building horizontal linkages with other similar-minded GSCOs and developing vertical linkages with policy-making organisations, a change agent can help the GSCO become more effective and change its external context. To support roles of stewardship and bridging, change agents need communication, negotiation and networking skills.

ACTIVITIES

Review questions
1 What are the reasons for an increase in OD practice in international settings?
2 Which economic and cultural context tends to be most difficult for traditional OD processes?
3 What will be the focus of an OD intervention in an organisation implementing a global strategic orientation?
4 A regiocentric personnel selection and recruitment policy is most likely to be associated with what type of strategic orientation?
5 What activities are associated with OD in a global social change organisation?

Discussion and essay questions
1 Describe how OD interventions need to be adapted to fit different cultural contexts.
2 With global strategic orientations, describe how OD can improve the implementation of those strategies.
3 How do global social change organisations differ from traditional organisations? How does the process of planned change differ?

Notes

1 L. Bougeois and M. Boltvinik, 'OD in cross–cultural settings: Latin America', *California Management Review*, 23 (Spring 1981): 75–81; L. Brown, 'Is organization development culture bound?' *Academy of Management Newsletter*, (Winter 1982); P. Evans, 'Organization development in the transnational enterprise' in *Research on Organization Change and Development*, 3, eds R. Woodman and W. Pasmore (Greenwich, Conn.: JAI Press, 1989): 1–38.

2 P. Sorensen Jr, T. Head, K. Johnson, N. Mathys, J. Preston and D. Cooperrider, eds, *Global and International Organization Development* (Champaign, Ill.: Stipes, 1995); D. Berlew and W. LeClere, 'Social intervention in Curacao: a case study', *Journal of Applied Behavioral Science*, 10 (1974): 29–52; B. Myers and J. Quill, 'The art of O.D. in Asia: never take yes for an answer', proceedings of the O.D. Network Conference, Seattle (Fall 1981): 52–58; R. Boss and M. Mariono, 'Organization development in Italy', *Group and Organization Studies*, 12 (1987): 245–56.

3 P. Engardino and L. Curry, 'The fifth tiger is on China's coast', *Business Week*, (6 April 1992): 43.

4 T. Peters, 'Prometheus barely unbound', *Academy of Management Executive*, 4 (1990): 70–84; Evans, 'Organization development in the transnational enterprise', *op. cit.*, 3–23.

5 R. Pieper, 'Organization development in West Germany' in *Global and International Organization Development*, eds P. Sorensen Jr, T. Head, K. Johnson, N. Mathys, J. Preston and D. Cooperrider (Champaign, Ill.: Stipes, 1995): 104–21.

6 C. Fuchs, 'Organizational development under political, economic and natural crisis' in *Global and International Organization Development*, eds P. Sorensen Jr, T. Head, K. Johnson, N. Mathys, J. Preston and D. Cooperrider (Champaign, Ill.: Stipes, 1995): 248–58.

7 'A survey of multinationals: big is back', *The Economist*, 24 (June 1995).

8 Evans, 'Organization development in the transnational enterprise', *op. cit.*: 8–11; Brown, 'Is organization development culture bound?' *op. cit.*; Bourgeois and Boltvinik, 'OD in cross–cultural settings', *op. cit.*; W. Ouchi, *Theory Z* (Reading, Mass.: Addison-Wesley, 1981).

9 T. Head, 'The role of a country's economic development in organization development implementation' in *Global and International Organization Development*, eds P. Sorensen Jr, T. Head, K. Johnson, N. Mathys, J. Preston and D. Cooperrider (Champaign, Ill.: Stipes, 1995): 18–25; W. Woodworth, 'Privatisation in Belarussia: organizational change in the former USSR', *Organization Development Journal*, 3 (1993): 53–59.

10 E. Schein. *Organization Culture and Leadership*, 2nd ed. (San Francisco: Jossey-Bass, 1992); Evans, 'Organization Development in the Transnational Enterprise', *op. cit.*:11.

11 G. Hofstede, Culture's Consequences (Beverly Hills, Calif.: Sage, 1980); A. Jaeger, 'Organization development and national culture: where's the fit?' *Academy of Management Journal*, 11 (1986): 178–90; N. Margulies and A. Raia, 'The significance of core values on the

theory and practice of organizational development', *Journal of Organizational Change and Management,* 1 (1988): 6–17; R. Knotts, 'Cross–cultural management: transformations and adaptations', *Business Horizons,* (January–February 1989): 29–33.

12 Hofstede, *Culture's Consequences, op. cit.*; E. Hall and M. Hall, *Understanding Cultural Differences* (Yarmouth, Maine: Intercultural Press, 1990); F. Trompenaars, *Riding the Waves of Culture* (London: The Economist Press, 1993).

13 K. Murrell, 'Management infrastructure in the Third World' in *Global Business Management in the 1990s,* ed. R. Moran (New York: Beacham Publishing, Inc., 1990); The United Nations Development Program, *Human Development Report* (New York: Oxford University Press, 1994); P. Kotler, *Marketing Management,* 9th ed. (Englewood Cliffs, N.J.: Prentice-Hall, 1997).

14 B. Webster, 'Organization development: an international perspective' (unpublished Master's thesis, Pepperdine University, Culver City, Calif., 1995).

15 Jaeger, 'Organization development and national culture', *op. cit.*

16 K. Johnson, 'Estimating national culture and O.D. values' in *Global and International Organization Development,* eds P. Sorensen Jr, T. Head, K. Johnson, N. Mathys, J. Preston and D. Cooperrider (Champaign, Ill.: Stipes, 1995): 266–81; Jaeger, 'Organization development and national culture', *op. cit.*

17 Woodworth, 'Privatization in Belarussia', *op. cit.*

18 A. Shevat, 'The practice of organizational development in Israel' in *Global and International Organization Development,* eds P. Sorensen Jr, T. Head, K. Johnson, N. Mathys, J. Preston and D. Cooperrider (Champaign Ill.: Stipes, 1995): 180–83; W. Fisher, 'Organization development in Egypt' in *Global and International Organization Development,* eds P. Sorensen Jr, T. Head, K. Johnson, N. Mathys, J. Preston and D. Cooperrider (Champaign Ill.: Stipes, 1995): 184–90.

19 R. Semler, 'All for one, one for all', *Harvard Business Review,* (September–October 1989): 76–84.

20 This application is adapted from K. Murrell and M. Wahba, 'Organization development and action research in Egypt', *Organization Development Journal,* 5:1 (1987): 57–63. A large amount of material is pulled directly from the article in an attempt to retain the language and tone of the intervention, which provides important evidence about how the basic action research process and its underlying values were adapted to fit the Egyptian context.

21 J. Preston, L. DuToit and I. Barber, 'A potential model of transformational change applied to South Africa' in *Research in Organization Change and Development,* 9, eds R. Woodman and W. Pasmore (Greenwich, Conn.: JAI Press, in press); G. Sigmund, 'Current issues in South African corporations: an internal OD perspective' (unpublished Master's thesis, Pepperdine University, Culver City, Calif., 1996).

22 Johnson, 'Estimating national culture and O.D. values', *op. cit.*

23 Sigmund, 'Current issues in South African corporations', *op. cit.*

24 Webster, 'Organization development' *op. cit.*; I. Perlaki, 'Organization development in Eastern Europe', *The Journal of Applied Behavioral Science,* 30 (1994): 297–312; J. Putti, 'Organization development scene in Asia: the case of Singapore' in *Global and International Organization Development,* eds, P. Sorensen Jr, T. Head, K. Johnson, N. Mathys, J. Preston and D. Cooperrider (Champaign Ill.: Stipes, 1995): 215–23; M. Rikuta, 'Organizational development within Japanese industry: facts and prospects' in *Global and International Organization Development,* eds P. Sorensen Jr, T. Head, K. Johnson, N. Mathys, J. Preston and D. Cooperrider (Champaign Ill.: Stipes, 1995): 231–47; J. Reeder, 'When West meets East: cultural aspects of doing business in Asia', *Business Horizons,* (January–February 1987): 69–74; Myers and Quill, 'The art of O.D. in Asia', *op. cit.*; I. Nonaka, 'Creating organizational order out of chaos: self–renewal in Japanese firms', *California Management Review,* (Spring 1988): 57–73; S. Redding, 'Results-orientation and the Orient: individualism as a cultural determinant of Western managerial techniques', *International HRD Annual,* 1 (Alexandria, Va.: American Society for Training and Development, 1985); K. Johnson, 'Organizational development in Venezuela' in *Global and International Organization Development,* eds P. Sorensen Jr, T. Head, K. Johnson, N. Mathys, J. Preston and D. Cooperrider (Champaign Ill.: Stipes, 1995): 259–64; Fuchs, 'Organizational development under political, economic and natural crisis', *op. cit.*; R. Babcock and T. Head, 'Organization development in the Republic of China (Taiwan)' in *Global and International Organization Development,* eds P. Sorensen Jr, T. Head, K. Johnson, N. Mathys, J. Preston and D. Cooperrider (Champaign Ill.: Stipes, 1995): 224–30; R. Marshak, 'Training and consulting in Korea', *OD Practitioner,* 25 (Summer 1993): 16–21.

25 Babcock and Head, 'Organization development in the Republic of China' *op. cit.*; Johnson, 'Organizational development in Venezuela', *op. cit.*

26 Johnson, 'Organizational development in Venezuela' *op. cit.*; A. Mueller, 'Successful and unsuccessful OD interventions in a Venezuelan banking organization: the role of culture' (unpublished Master's thesis, Pepperdine University, Culver City, Calif., 1995).

27 Rikuta, 'Organizational development within Japanese industry', *op. cit.*

28 Webster, 'Organization development', *op. cit.*; B. Gustavsen, 'The LOM program: a network–based strategy for organization development in Sweden' in *Research in Organization Change and Development*, 5, eds R. Woodman and W. Pasmore (Greenwich, Conn.: JAI Press, 1991): 285–316; P. Sorensen Jr, H. Larsen, T. Head and H. Scoggins, 'Organization development in Denmark' in *Global and International Organization Development*, eds P. Sorensen Jr, T. Head, K. Johnson, N. Mathys, J. Preston and D. Cooperrider (Champaign Ill.: Stipes, 1995): 48–64; A. Derefeldt, 'Organization development in Sweden' in *Global and International Organization Development*, eds P. Sorensen Jr, T. Head, K. Johnson, N. Mathys, J. Preston and D. Cooperrider (Champaign Ill.: Stipes, 1995): 65–73; J. Norsted and S. Aguren, *The Saab–Scania Report* (Stockholm: Swedish Employer's Confederation, 1975); B. Jonsson, 'Corporate strategy for people at work—the Volvo experience', paper presented at the International Conference on the Quality of Working Life, Toronto, Canada, 30 August–September 3, 1981.

29 Johnson, 'Estimating national culture and O.D. values', *op. cit.*

30 Norsted and Aguren, *The Saab–Scania Report*; Jonsson, 'Corporate strategy for people at work', both *op. cit.*

31 E. Trist, 'On socio–technical systems' in *The Planning of Change*, 2nd ed., eds W. Bennis, K. Benne and R. Chin (New York: Holt, Rinehart and Winston, 1969): 269–72; A. Cherns, 'The principles of sociotechnical design', *Human Relations*, 19 (1976): 783–92; E. Jacques, *The Changing Culture of a Factory* (New York: Dryden, 1952).

32 P. Nulty, 'Batman shakes BP to bedrock', *Fortune* (19 November 1990): 155–62.

33 C. Bartlett and S. Ghoshal, 'Managing across borders: new strategic requirements', *Sloan Management Review*, (Summer 1987): 7–17; C. Bartlett and S. Ghoshal, 'Managing across borders: new organizational responses', *Sloan Management Review*, (Fall 1987): 43–53; D. Heenan and H. Perlmutter, *Multinational Organization Development* (Reading, Mass.: Addison-Wesley, 1979); Evans, 'Organization development in the transnational enterprise', *op. cit.*: 15–16; Y. Doz, *Strategic Management in Multinational Companies* (Oxford: Pergamon Press, 1986); C. Bartlett, Y. Doz and G. Hedlund, *Managing the Global Firm* (London: Routledge, 1990).

34 Heenan and Perlmutter, *Multinational Organization Development*, *op. cit.*, 13.

35 A. Borrus, 'The stateless corporation', *Business Week*, (14 May 1990): 103.

36 *Ibid.*, 105.

37 J. Main, 'How to go global—and why', *Fortune*, (28 August 1989): 76.

38 Heenan and Perlmutter, *Multinational Organization Development*, *op. cit.*: 20.

39 Borrus, 'The stateless corporation', *op. cit.*: 101.

40 Heenan and Perlmutter, *Multinational Organization Development*, *op. cit.*: 20.

41 Evans, 'Organization development in the transnational enterprise', *op. cit.*

42 *Ibid.*

43 C. Bartlett and S. Ghoshal, 'Organising for world-wide effectiveness: the transnational solution', *California Management Review*, (Fall 1988): 54–74.

44 R. Tung, 'Expatriate assignments: enhancing success and minimizing failure', *Academy of Management Executive*, (Summer 1987): 117–26; J. Roure, J. Alvarez, C. Garcia–Pont and J. Nueno, 'Managing internationally: the international dimensions of the managerial task', *European Management Journal*, 11 (1993): 485–92; A. Mamman, 'Expatriate adjustment: dealing with hosts—attitudes in a foreign assignment', *Journal of Transitional Management Development*, 1 (1995).

45 S. Kim and D. Briscoe, 'Globalization and a new human resource policy in Korea', *Employee Relations*, 19:4 (1997), 298–308.

46 Main, 'How to go global', *op. cit.*: 73.

47 Evans, 'Organization development in the transnational enterprise', *op. cit.*

48 L. Brown and J. Covey, 'Development organizations and organization development: toward an expanded paradigm for organization development' in *Research in Organizational Change and Development*, 1, eds R. Woodman and W. Pasmore (Greenwich, Conn.: JAI Press, 1987): 59–88; P. Tuecke, 'Rural international development' in *Discovering Common Ground*, ed. M. Weisbord (San Francisco: Berrett–Koehler, 1993).

49 P. Freire, *Pedagogy of the Oppressed* (Harmondsworth, England: Penguin, 1972); H. Perlmutter and E. Trist, 'Paradigms for societal transition', *Human Relations*, 39 (1986): 1–27; F. Westley, 'Bob Geldof and Live Aid: the affective side of global social innovation', *Human Relations*, 44 (1991): 1011–36; D. Cooperrider and W. Pasmore, 'Global social change: a new agenda for social science', *Human Relations*, 44 (1991): 1037–55; H. Perlmutter, 'On the rocky road to the first global civilization', *Human Relations*, 44 (1991): 897–920; E. Boulding, 'The old and new transnationalism: an evolutionary perspective', *Human Relations*, 44 (1991): 789–805; P. Johnson and D. Cooperrider, 'Finding a path with a heart: global social change organizations and their challenge for the field of organizational development' in *Research in Organizational Change and Development*, 5, eds R. Woodman and W. Pasmore (Greenwich, Conn.: JAI Press, 1991): 223–84.

50 D. Cooperrider and T. Thachankary, 'Building the global civic culture: making our lives count' in *Global and International Organization Development*, eds P. Sorensen Jr, T. Head, K. Johnson, N. Mathys, J. Preston and D. Cooperrider (Champaign Ill.: Stipes, 1995): 282–306; Brown and Covey, 'Development organizations and organization development', *op. cit.*

51 E. Smith, 'Growth vs. environment', *Business Week*, (11 May 1992): 66–75.

52 L. Brown, 'Bridging organizations and sustainable development', *Human Relations*, 44 (1991): 807–31; Johnson and Cooperrider, 'Finding a path with a heart'; Cooperrider and Thachankary, 'Building the global civil culture', both *op. cit.*

53 W. Pasmore, 'OD and the management of global social change: implications and opportunities', *ODC Newsletter*, (Winter 1994): 8–11.

54 Brown and Covey, 'Development organizations and organization development', *op. cit.*

55 Johnson and Cooperrider, 'Finding a path with a heart'; Cooperrider and Thachankary, 'Building the global civic culture', both *op. cit.*

56 W. Whyte, *Participatory Action Research* (Newbury Park, Calif.: Sage, 1991).

57 Johnson and Cooperrider, 'Finding a path with a heart', *op. cit.*, 240–41.

58 *Ibid.*, p. 237.

59 P. Vaill, 'The purposing of high performing organizations', *Organisation Dynamics*, 11 (Autumn 1982): 23–39.

60 M. Bratton, 'Non–governmental organizations in Africa: can they influence public policy?' *Development and Change*, 21 (1989): 81–118.

61 Tuecke, 'Rural international development', *op. cit.*

62 Pasmore, 'OD and the management of global social change', *op. cit.*

63 L. DuToit, 'Leadership for the future: a large systems OD intervention in South Africa' in *Global and International Organization Development*, eds P. Sorensen Jr, T. Head, K. Johnson, N. Mathys, J. Preston and D. Cooperrider (Champaign Ill.: Stipes, 1995): 203–14; L. DuToit, 'Large systems change: corporate reaction to transnational demands in South Africa', presentation to the 1995 OD Network, Seattle, Wash., 1995.

64 S. Annis, 'What is not the same about the urban poor: the case of Mexico City' in *Strengthening the Poor: What Have We Learned?* ed. J. Lewis *et al.* (Washington, D.C.: Overseas Development Council, 1988): 138–43.

65 Brown, 'Bridging organizations', *op. cit.*, 815.

66 Johnson and Cooperrider, 'Finding a path with a heart', *op. cit.*

67 J. Preston and T. Armstrong, 'Team building in South Africa: cross cultural synergy in action', *Public Administration Quarterly*, 15 (1991): 65–82; J. Preston, L. DuToit, D. Van Zyl and F. Holscher, 'Endemic violence in South Africa: An OD solution applied to two educational settings', *International Journal of Public Administration*, 16 (1993): 1767–91.

68 L. Brown and J. Covey, 'Action research for grassroots development: collective reflection and development NGOs in Asia', presentation at the Academy of Management, Miami, 1990.

69 D. Cooperrider and S. Srivastva, 'Appreciative inquiry in organizational life' in *Research in Organizational Change and Development*, 1, eds R. Woodman and W. Pasmore (Greenwich, Conn.: JAI Press, 1987): 129–69.

70 Brown and Covey, 'Action research for grassroots development', *op. cit.*; M. Elden and M. Levin, 'Cogenerative learning: bringing participation into action research' in *Participatory Action Research*, ed. W. Whyte (Newbury Park, Calif.: Sage, 1991): 127–42.

71 Westley, 'Bob Geldof and Live Aid', *op. cit.*

72 E. Boulding, *Building a Global Civic Culture: Education for an Interdependent World* (Syracuse, N.Y.: Syracuse University Press, 1988).

PART 8

CASE
STUDIES

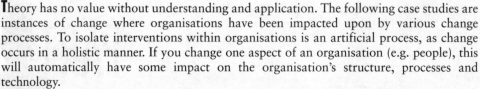

Introduction to the case studies

Theory has no value without understanding and application. The following case studies are instances of change where organisations have been impacted upon by various change processes. To isolate interventions within organisations is an artificial process, as change occurs in a holistic manner. If you change one aspect of an organisation (e.g. people), this will automatically have some impact on the organisation's structure, processes and technology.

To help you to categorise the change process, consider each case in the context of the type of change (whether it is structural, behavioural, process and/or technical) in relation to the impact of change (interpersonal, group, inter-group and/or organisational). Remember that a change can often be the result of a combination of many factors, but the task in case analysis is to isolate what is the dominant consequence of change, construct hypothetical scenarios and recommend or suggest alternative responses.

Remember that there is never just one 'correct' answer. It all depends on 'the moment in time'.

Case study analysis

A case study, in the context of this text, is a description of a particular organisation and the problem (or set of problems) it encounters while operating in a competitive environment. The case study may give a brief history of the organisation over a period of time, describe the environment in which it exists, problems it may have already dealt with and past managerial responses. Information as to how it conducts its business and manages its internal environment is also often included. The main intention of the case study is to identify a problem being experienced by the organisation and to offer enough information to allow thorough analysis and the formation of a solution.

Case studies are often useful tools for practitioners as well as for students, as they are mostly based on real-life scenarios. Existing organisations may allow certain information to be published as a case study, but, in situations where a typical problem cannot be identified in an existing organisation, a fictional scenario may be presented. It is the process of analysis that is important, not just the outcome.

The main purpose of the case study is to place individuals in positions where they can make best use of their knowledge of management theory while being exposed to the reality of organisational problem solving. The reality often involves dealing with a group of people, some of whom may be more vocal and opinionated than others, in order to arrive at a solution that can be implemented. Hence, a group discussion and presentation is the usual way of assessing an individual's ability to tackle a case study.

In this text, the case studies are deliberately provided towards the end of the book. Good case study analysis relies on a knowledge of change management theory and research. So, trying to attempt an analysis without full comprehension of the underlying principles may result in a simplistic, rather than a holistic, solution to the problem.

Case studies are one major step on the path from being a student to being a practitioner in a chosen field. Quite often the case study may not include all the information needed by a student. This does not necessarily mean that there is a need to acquire the missing information elsewhere. It is actually an example of how a manager in a real organisation may have to deal with problems. The ability to recognise what information is missing is a particularly useful skill. Everyone can draw upon his or her experience in one form or another. By discussing this with the group, the student is able to demonstrate his or her capacity for critical analysis. The group may then be able to discuss possible solutions, or ways in which it can work around the lack of information. This offers an experiential approach for team building, which itself is a fundamental organisation-development intervention. Outlined below are some steps that may be of use when analysing a case study.

Read the information carefully

Read and re-read the case study. Gain an understanding of the problem(s) and where it exists within the context of the organisation. Be able to succinctly define the problem that needs solving. Being aware of the history of the company and its development may be useful when presenting a solution to the class as these factors define a company and its ability to implement the changes involved in a proposed solution.

With most case studies, you are really only given the good news, so feel free to 'read between the lines' and play 'devil's advocate'.

Analyse and ask questions

An analysis is really a critical evaluation of the information given. It is not simply a re-working of the narrative of the case study. Questions must be asked in order to identify issues that are related to the existing knowledge of relevant theory. Look for evidence that may not be immediately apparent, and identify the strengths and weaknesses of the organisation. If unfamiliar issues have been raised, it would be wise to clarify them by revisiting the appropriate part of this text. It is important to remember that a case study is supposed to be as real as possible. Therefore, part of the analysis is to define what information is necessary and whether there are any inconsistencies.

Diagnose

A thorough analysis and collation of evidence should make it possible to diagnose the problem that needs a solution. However, the problem will often not be apparent on the first reading, or even on the second. Knowing that there is a problem, and knowing what the problem is are two quite different things. Remember that you have a problem if you do not have a problem! Your questions that were asked in the analysis, and those posed at the end of most case studies, now need answers. Try to support every answer with both evidence from the case study and theory derived from prior learning. Even if the questions have been supplied with the case study, as has been done in a number of cases, it is not sufficient to only consider answers to those particular questions. All questions arising from a thorough analysis must be asked and answered.

Develop a solution

Even after a thorough analysis, the solution may not be immediately apparent. There is never a 'right' answer, as the case study is supposed to be based on a real-life organisation. In reality, problems are solved, and the solution deemed 'right', only after it has been implemented and supported by the results. The solution may have been incorrect, but this will only become apparent after it has been implemented. Therefore, the students' role in analysing a case study is to generate alternatives and put forward a solution that is the result of research and constant questioning. They will not know, nor will they be told, if they are 'right'. The solution needs to be presented as an action plan, and will involve the recommendation of a number of workable actions to be taken.

Present the solution

Many case studies are tackled by groups and their responses presented to the class in order to encourage discussion and debate. When this happens, the analysis needs to be carefully planned and the solution clearly supported by evidence that is strong enough to withstand class analysis and questioning. Class discussion can often be beneficial in that it provides alternatives or constructive criticisms that should be taken into account by the group or individual analysing the case study. Think of the discussion as a real-life meeting of business colleagues, where alternative opinions are regularly expressed.

In the real-life scenario, differences in group dynamics are often evident, as some individuals are loud in voicing their opinions, while others are very quiet. Presenting a class discussion can give the student a great deal of practice for later work place meetings. In terms of written responses to case studies, consulting class members before writing the final report is advantageous in that it allows the student to gain critical insight from others.

The following cases are a collation of studies done by various people in Australia and New Zealand. They are examples of what is happening every day, and as soon as they are written, they become history. It is important, therefore, that you observe, take notes and write your own case study—then you will be part of the process. The next edition of this text might include your contribution.

Changing HR practices in China — CableCo

By **Cherrie Jiuhua Zhu**

Background

CableCo is a joint venture between an Australian corporation, AuzCo, and two Chinese organisations—the Municipal Post and Telecommunications Bureau (Post Bureau) and a subsidiary company of China National Postal and Telecommunications Appliances Corporation (PTA). Both organisations are located in the city of Tianjing, a well-developed industrial city that is directly under the control of the central government. The main products of the joint venture are telecommunications and various other kinds of communication cables. The registered capital of CableCo was initially A$11.5 million, of which 70% was invested by AuzCo, while the remaining 30% was contributed by the Post Bureau and PTA.

AuzCo is a multinational corporation and one of the top 50 companies in Australia. It has had a long trading history with China and was among the first Australian companies to set up joint ventures in China. The Cable Group of AuzCo possesses the latest advanced technology in cable production, together with a 50-year history of successful cable manufacturing. Both the Post Bureau and PTA are state-owned organisations with more than 40 years' experience in operating and administrating telecommunications in China. The co-operation between the Chinese and Australian parties that was demonstrated at the initial stage laid a solid foundation for the establishment and future development of the venture.

The first contact regarding a joint venture was made in June 1990, and was followed by both parties signing a contract in October and obtaining local government approval and a business license for the joint venture in late November 1990. It took less than six months for CableCo to be established after the initial contact. In January 1991, the company began factory construction, and selection and purchasing of equipment. The site was located in an Economics and Technology Development Zone, 47 kilometres from the downtown area of Tianjing. With the support of the local government, and through close co-operation between the two parties, CableCo produced its first telecommunication cable in March 1992, only 15 months after it had commenced factory design and construction.

Before the establishment of CableCo, preparation work was the responsibility of a senior manager from AuzCo and six Chinese managerial and technical staff from TeleCo, a state-owned enterprise under both the Post Bureau and PTA. Among the six Chinese was the deputy director in charge of technical work at TeleCo, who later became the executive manager of the joint venture. The other five were from TeleCo's Administration office, Production Department and Accounting Department, and they all became senior managers in the joint venture.

Organisational size and structure

CableCo's total output in 1993 was worth 75 million yuan (about A$12.5 million, at an exchange rate of 6 yuan to to the Australian dollar), and it had a total of 184 employees by the end of October 1994. The annual output per head in 1993 was about 410 000 yuan. Since AuzCo contributed 70% of the total investment, it maintained four directors on the board of CableCo, while the Chinese party had two members. The chairman of the board was an Australian from AuzCo while the vice-chairman was a Chinese from the Post Bureau. To encourage localisation of the management team in China, AuzCo only sent two 'long-term' expatriates, the general manager and the finance/accounting manager, to work in the joint venture on a full-time basis. Other expatriates, such as production and quality control engineers, worked at CableCo on a short-term basis.

The general manager of CableCo was also the general manager of AuzCo's other cable joint venture in China. Because of his commitment to the other joint venture, the general manager could only visit CableCo once a month for a few days. During his short stays, he would inspect the work completed and deal with problems or issues that were beyond the control of the executive manager. The general manager was an overseas Chinese from Taiwan selected by AuzCo, as one of AuzCo's expatriate selection criteria specified bilingual skills. The executive manager had day-to-day managerial responsibility for the whole company. When CableCo was set up, it had five departments—Production, Finance and Accounting, Personnel and Administration, Marketing and Technical. With the development of production in March 1994, the company set up three new departments— Quality control, Materials and Import and export.

The current organisational chart is depicted in Figure A.1. It is clear from this that the Production Department is the largest and most important functional unit in the company, with more than 60% of the employees (113 out of 184). In this department, the position of head of department was vacant, and so the deputy HOD was responsible for all the work, with assistance from the executive manager when necessary. This department had three workshops, and each workshop had its own chief head, deputy head and assistant head. Within each workshop there were two to three production lines. The line managers were also process engineers who were responsible for both the management and technical aspects of production. Each production line consisted of two or three groups of seven to nine employees, one of whom was the supervisor.

The HOD of the Finance and Accounting Department was an Australian Chinese expatriate sent by AuzCo, who could speak fluent Mandarin. This manager was concurrently the HOD of the Personnel and Administration Department because it was felt that a foreigner could deal better with difficult personnel management issues in China. For example, Chinese managers often found it hard to reject a candidate who did not satisfy the job requirement but was introduced or strongly recommended by friends, relatives or superiors. Nepotism is criticised but still widely practised in China. By contrast, a foreigner would feel much less obligated in this regard and could refuse to accept this connection-based practice. Because of their relatively small size, each of the other departments had only one deputy HOD and a small number of staff. A senior manager from AuzCo who had been responsible for preparation work prior to the venture's establishment often came to the joint venture to help co-ordinate contact between AuzCo and CableCo.

Following his appointment, the Executive Manager was given the power to form a management team, which consisted of his colleagues who had been involved in the establishment of CableCo. The management team preferred to recruit employees for the joint venture from the open labour market rather than from the Chinese partner's enterprise, TeleCo, because of the concern that employees from state-owned enterprises were used to 'eating from a big rice pot' (egalitarian pay regardless of performance). However, the joint venture law required that selection priority should be given to employees from the Chinese partner, and the contract signed by both parties stipulated that 60% of CableCo's employees should be recommended by the Chinese partner. Therefore, of the staff initially employed in the joint venture, 60% came from TeleCo while the remaining 40% were recruited from the general community through open advertisement.

Among the 70 managerial and production workers who left TeleCo and joined CableCo, 21 later returned to TeleCo, as it had been guaranteed that they could whenever they resigned from the joint venture. Their reasons for leaving CableCo included personal reasons, difficulties in meeting the requirements of efficiency and work intensity in the joint venture, and dissatisfaction with the pay system (to be discussed later). However, the remainder became key employees of the joint venture, performing roles such as

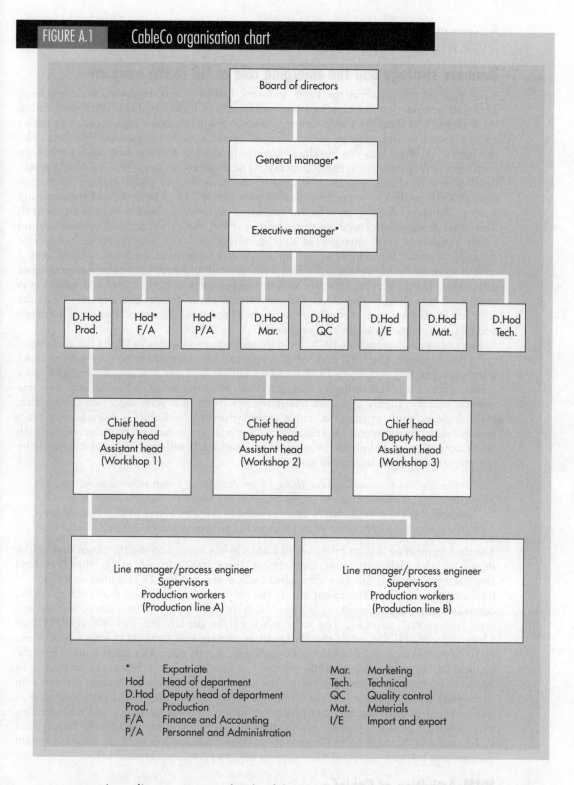

FIGURE A.1   CableCo organisation chart

*	Expatriate		Mar.	Marketing
Hod	Head of department		Tech.	Technical
D.Hod	Deputy head of department		QC	Quality control
Prod.	Production		Mat.	Materials
F/A	Finance and Accounting		I/E	Import and export
P/A	Personnel and Administration			

supervisors, line managers or heads of departments. Thirty per cent of the 184 employees had completed tertiary education. Employees were classified into two groups, managerial and non-managerial, rather than into cadres and workers as was the custom in state-owned enterprises. The former group included managers and administrative staff, while the latter mainly referred to operation workers. This distinction was based solely on their current job position.

Business strategy and the emerging role of HR in the company

As a modern enterprise in the cable industry, CableCo was equipped with the most advanced machinery and technology and had a team of highly qualified employees. Using the trademark of AuzCo's Cable Group, CableCo soon attained a high reputation for its quality products and prompt service within domestic and international markets. The company's mission was 'to produce quality products, provide first-class service to customers and guarantee reliable delivery'. The business strategy was to continuously develop new products, improve the quality of goods, reduce costs, manage its human resources efficiently and strengthen management control. Implementation of the company strategy depended heavily on effective employee performance and management control. This was strongly influenced by three factors. First, the production of communication cables requires a large quantity of raw materials, and any wastage greatly increases production costs. Second, being an information transmission medium, quality was a critical issue as cables were usually laid underground and problems caused maintenance difficulties. Third, AuzCo's standard in terms of production, cost control and quality was used as a benchmark. Therefore, throughout the entire production process, from the selection of raw materials through to the finished products, efficient utilisation of materials and quality products was always emphasised.

Since economic reforms in 1978, the telecommunication sector in China has undergone rapid development. The total number of telephones has increased from 3.69 million (0.43 telephones per 100 people) in 1978 to 38.02 million (3.2 per 100 people) in 1994. As a consequence, the cable industry has attracted investors from domestic and overseas markets and the supply of cables has outstripped demand. With increased competition from domestic and international cable manufacturers, the CableCo management team realised that improvements in efficiency and effectiveness had to be achieved through better utilisation of its human resources. This was clearly reflected in comments made by the executive manager during the interview:

> People are the most important thing in an enterprise when other conditions, i.e. technology, market and government policies, are more or less the same as in other companies in the same industry. How to manage our employees so they remain loyal to the company and become more efficient in their work is a challenge we now face.

The management of human resources of CableCo has hence become the major task of the Personnel and Administration Department (hereafter referred to as the Personnel Department), which is not an independent budget unit but has 26 full-time staff (14% of total employees). This department also fulfils miscellaneous functions that are beyond the control of other departments, such as public relations, employees' grievance, welfare and even recreational activities. The daily work of the department was managed by two Chinese deputy HODs, while the HOD, an expatriate sent by AuzCo who was also the HOD of the Finance and Accounting Department, mainly acted as a figurehead to help the Chinese managers to tackle subtle personal relationship issues whenever necessary. In addition to the administrative work, the Personnel Department became involved in developing the company's business strategy and in various other HRM activities, such as human resource planning and compensation, including wage packages and welfare. This was somewhat unusual, as wage administration is normally controlled by the Department of Finance and Accounting in Chinese enterprises. CableCo followed the Chinese system for one year before integrating this function into its Personnel Department.

HRM Activities at CableCo

Before discussing HRM at CableCo, HRM at AuzCo's Cable Group needs to be addressed briefly as the Group helped the joint venture to establish its HRM system. AuzCo had a well-established HRM system with an HR director at corporate level, a general manager

(HR) at group level, and an HR manager at company level. The Cable Group practised major HRM activities as defined in the West. It executed HR planning, although the significance of this activity had only been recognised for some two to three years. This activity was used with merit-based recruitment and selection to increase the company's competitiveness by having the right people at the right time. It was also used with training to maintain a high level of performance by updating employees' knowledge and skills. The company had job analysis to clarify job responsibilities and authorities, to establish individual performance standards, and to manage performance, compensation and employment planning. Managers also conducted performance appraisal interviews with their staff members, mainly for performance feedback but sometimes for promotion and transfer. The Group also offered on- and off-the-job training programmes to its employees. However, the Cable Group did not include a bonus system in its HRM practices, and was weak in employee career planning as it had no formal career-counselling programme. Performance appraisal was conducted more for white-collar employees than for blue-collar ones. The concepts of HRM that were used in the Cable Group were introduced to CableCo, and some practices, such as merit-based recruitment and selection and performance appraisal, were also transferred to the joint venture.

Human resource planning

Human resource planning was conducted annually at CableCo under the control of the general manager. Its focus was on the overall control of employee numbers. The demand for employees was generally based on production needs, which was greatly influenced by AuzCo as the Australian practice was used as a standard. Within the limit of a planned total number of employees, each department could put forward its staffing needs according to its production plans and number of positions available. The Personnel Department would either employ or transfer employees to meet staffing needs. Planning was mainly regulated by top management, and the role played by the Personnel Department was primarily co-ordination and administration.

According to the executive manager, the reason behind short-term oriented planning was that both parties held different ideas and approaches to business development. For example, the Chinese party strongly suggested investment in the project for producing optical fibre cable because they believed that the domestic market for such a product held great potential. Accordingly, they deliberately selected and employed some new graduates for preliminary work on this project. However, their suggestion was ignored by AuzCo, as the Australian party did not want to further expand its business before it had identified a market in China. When a long-term business strategy could not be accepted by both parties, the joint venture had difficulty making long-term human resource plans, and staff were then recruited on a short-term, or even *ad hoc*, basis.

Human resource planning was affected not only by the company's business strategy but also by the employee turnover rate. The turnover rate was closely related to employee background and commitment. At CableCo, employees from the Chinese partner's company, TeleCo, showed more loyalty and commitment to the joint venture and had a much lower turnover rate than new employees recruited from local rural areas. The employees from TeleCo all lived in downtown accommodation supplied by TeleCo. They were all at least 35 years old, with some ten years of working experience with TeleCo. Being a state-owned enterprise, TeleCo offered lifetime employment to its employees, even when they joined CableCo. This meant they could return to TeleCo if they resigned from the joint venture. With regard to accommodation, the joint venture paid the housing allowance (20% of employees' average salary) in two different ways. One was to pay the allowance individually to those who supplied their own accommodation. The other was to pay collectively to TeleCo as compensation for the dormitories it supplied to those employees working at CableCo. Therefore, those joint venture employees from TeleCo could still live in their original dormitories and wait in a queue along with other TeleCo's employees for housing adjustment (to move into a larger flat). This was one of the major reasons that employees from TeleCo felt obligated to the joint venture. They showed more willingness to devote themselves to the development of CableCo and most of them became committed and key employees of the company.

By contrast, the turnover rate of locally recruited employees was much higher for two reasons: the nature of their job and the availability of employment opportunities in the local area. As CableCo did not supply accommodation to its employees as did many other foreign joint ventures, its employees, except those from TeleCo, were primarily recruited from the local area. CableCo was located in a recently developed coastal region, which had previously been rural farmland. Between 1984, when the Economics and Technology Development Zone was set up, and 1994, more than 2000 enterprises with varying types of ownership (foreign joint ventures, wholly foreign-owned and privately owned companies) had been established in the area. The local farmers had many employment opportunities, even though they had less education than did workers from the city. As these employees were usually offered low-skill jobs and money was often their highest priority, they showed little commitment to the company and were always ready to leave for a better paid job elsewhere.

In order to keep a stable work force, CableCo had to consider issues such as the source of employees and the turnover rate in its human resource planning. In dealing with these issues, as the executive manager noted, the supply of accommodation was a critical factor. In the mid-1990s it was impossible for employees to purchase their own accommodation. The executive manager believed that solving employees' accommodation problem by supplying a dormitory or flat would attract the right people from wider sources and help to retain them as planned. If it did not provide accommodation, the company would continue to suffer from an unstable workforce. Nevertheless, AuzCo refused to supply any kind of accommodation to Chinese employees, as they had never supplied accommodation in Australia. Furthermore, AuzCo refused to increase the housing allowance (currently 20% of its wage bill), and this made it impossible for CableCo to supply any kind of accommodation. This prevented the joint venture from recruiting employees outside the local area unless employees could find accommodation for themselves. With many new companies in the area, the local labour market was competitive and the turnover rate unpredictable, making HR planning even more difficult.

Apart from the accommodation issue, the lack of participation by managers, especially line managers, also affected human resource planning. CableCo's line managers and other managerial staff, such as supervisors, were involved chiefly in the implementation of the plan rather than in the planning itself. This was partly due to the direct control exerted on the overall human resource planning by the general manager, and partly because the managerial staff lacked an understanding of human resource planning, as this activity had not existed at their level in the centrally planned economy.

Performance appraisal

CableCo formally adopted a performance appraisal system in June 1993, with the intention of linking performance with compensation so as to break the iron rice bowl practice prevalent in Chinese state-owned enterprises. As the company had not set up a bonus system by late 1994, the major purpose of performance appraisal was wage administration—to increase or decrease employee wage scales according to annual assessment results.

The Personnel Department designed an appraisal form with the same criteria for both managerial and non-managerial employees. However, the weighting given to each criterion varied between different groups. For example, items that related more to managerial skills would be weighted more heavily for managerial employees, while items related to technical competencies would be weighted more heavily for production workers. There were ten major criteria in conducting appraisals, including knowledge of the job, quality and quantity of work completed, supervisory potential, reliability, awareness of cost reduction, occupational safety, adaptability, co-operation and communication. Each item had a brief definition, e.g. knowledge of the job was defined as 'the degree to which the employee has learned and understood the objectives and procedures of the job'.

Each criterion was assessed on a five-grade scale ranging from 'outstanding' to 'marginal'. For example, the five grades for 'quality of work' were classified as:

5 *exceptionally high quality*—consistently accurate, precise, quick to detect errors in the work

4 *work sometimes superior but usually accurate*—negligible amount needs to be redone and work regularly meets standard

3 *a careful worker*—a small amount of work needs to be redone, corrections made in reasonable time, and usually meets average standards

2 *work frequently below standard*—inclined to be careless, and small amount of work needs to be redone

1 *work often below standard*—seldom meets normal standards, and excessive amount needs to be redone.

According to the job position, any available quantified standards were incorporated into each grade.

The appraisal at CableCo was conducted annually from the top to the bottom, which meant that the executive manager evaluated the performance of department managers, while department managers assessed line managers, and line managers assumed responsibility for evaluating supervisors and production workers. The appraisal was conducted without the appraisees' knowledge and the rating was totally dependent upon the appraiser's daily observation and individual judgment. The appraisal ratings were kept confidential from appraisees as required by the Personnel Department. After appraisers at each level had completed the evaluations, the appraisal forms were handed over to the Personnel Department. The personnel staff would then check each employee's personal records to see whether he or she had received any rewards or penalties during the year, as these results would also be incorporated into the final assessment. The final marks of the appraisal were calculated by the Personnel Department and would be used to determine a wage increase or reduction.

The managers at CableCo valued this kind of appraisal, as they believed it was not time-consuming, and could encourage people to work harder. They were also in favour of keeping the appraisal results confidential so as to avoid possible conflicts with employees. However, the fact that the appraisal form and the results were confined to the Personnel Department and the managers who had conducted the appraisal aroused strong dissatisfaction among many employees. During the research interviews, production workers expressed their concerns about the way that the appraisal was conducted. First, they were denied access to the appraisal form and were thus ignorant of the contents and criteria of assessment. Second, they questioned the appraiser's ability to make a fair and unbiased judgment of subordinates, and they raised doubts about the influence of personal relationships on assessment results. Finally, they were concerned about the consistency and reliability of the appraisal results as they were so obviously subjective.

Although the company's intention in conducting performance appraisal was to break traditional egalitarian practices by linking performance to individual pay so as to offer employees more incentives, defects in the system reduced its effectiveness. First, without the knowledge of appraisal criteria and their measurement, employees were denied the opportunity to clearly understand the company's requirements for high performance. Second, the confidentiality of appraisal results distanced managers from employees because of the distrust that arose from this privately conducted assessment, which also failed to achieve other appraisal purposes such as communication and development. Without the feedback from assessment, employees had difficulty in identifying deficiencies in their work and thus did not know how to improve their performance, or even if they needed to. Further, the lack of participation by employees in the formulation of appraisal criteria diminished initiatives and reduced enthusiasm towards the appraisals.

In addition to performance appraisal, the company had penalty policies. The Personnel Department issued a list of prohibited behaviours and their corresponding penalties, including verbal or written warnings, suspension from work and dismissal. Any kind of penalty would result in a one-off fine or a reduction of wage scale. However, the company did not have a policy for rewarding or encouraging particularly satisfying behaviour, except that those who performed well were rated higher in the performance appraisal, and might receive a wage increase after the annual performance assessment.

Compensation and welfare

The compensation and welfare system at CableCo was quite different to those of the state-owned enterprises. The differences were chiefly reflected in the unpredictability and confidentiality of the design and the distribution of its wage packages. From the first day of its operation, CableCo eliminated the fixed wage scale that had been used over four decades in China, especially in state-owned enterprises. The initial wage package for different job positions was determined by factors such as the relevant wage level in both local and domestic markets, wage levels in other foreign joint ventures and the inflation rate. While the government required that the wage scale in joint ventures should be at least 20% higher than that in state-owned enterprises, the company kept its wage level more than 50% higher than state-owned enterprises. For example, CableCo production workers with the same education and work experience as their counterparts in a state-owned enterprise could be paid more than 700 yuan per month in 1994. The payment in an equivalent state-owned enterprise such as TeleCo would be less than 500 yuan (the payment here refers to take-home-pay, including allowances and bonuses). Managers at CableCo were paid at an even higher level than their counterparts at TeleCo. Given the intense competition in the local labour market, CableCo kept its wage scale in the upper middle range among local foreign-invested enterprises in order to retain its key employees.

After employees had started work, wages were adjusted solely on the basis of performance or changes in position, rather than on seniority. Therefore, the wage package for each individual became relatively unpredictable because it was no longer fixed by the job position or length of service. Employees who achieved high marks in the annual performance appraisal would have their wage increased. Although the validity and reliability of performance appraisal was questioned by employees, it still helped to link pay to performance.

Each individual's wage package was kept confidential as required by company regulation. The *Employee Handbook* stated that employees were not allowed to reveal their own wage scales or inquire about others' wage packages. If they did, they would either be warned or penalised. The reason for the confidentiality of wage packages, as explained by the deputy HOD of the Personnel Department, was to abolish the old iron wage system (fixed wage scales regardless of employee performance) and to avoid unnecessary jealousy or dissatisfaction among employees. This manager further noted that, although employees favoured performance-linked pay, many people still had difficulty accepting that high performers would earn more than low performers, regardless of their age, position or length of service.

During the interviews conducted by the researcher, the interviewees were asked about their attitudes towards the company's unpredictable and confidential wage packages. The managers generally responded positively, because most of them were satisfied with the pay they received and the way it was distributed. This wage system gave them incentives to perform well, and also reduced the chances of colleagues or subordinates who might be paid less discussing wages, which might cause unnecessary resentment or envy. However, the managers were strongly dissatisfied about the absence of a bonus system within the company, as they all believed that annual wage increases could not offer timely rewards to employees. Similarly, production workers considered this wage system to be acceptable—apart from the uncertainty about the criteria for wage increases and the lack of a bonus system. The first issue could be addressed by reforming the performance appraisal system, while the second needed to be considered by the company. Although both managers and workers considered that a bonus system could further differentiate high and low performers and link reward more closely to individual performance, their belief was not supported by the company.

The company had not set up a bonus system because of concern expressed by both partners of the venture. From the Australian parent company's point of view, bonuses could not be considered until the joint venture had repaid all its loans and started to make profits. The Chinese partner thought the bonus system should not be established until other supporting activities were in place, such as job analysis and performance appraisal. Since the bonus system was generally introduced in 1979, it has become a significant part of wage packages in Chinese enterprises, with the aim of offering incentives to employees. However, bonuses were often equally distributed among employees in order to avoid potential disputes or conflicts, and thus lost any function as a motivational tool. In the absence of an effective way to closely link bonuses to performance, the company preferred not to set up a bonus system. However, after more than two years of operation, both managers and employees, and especially those in the Production and Marketing Departments, were expressing a strong desire for the establishment of a bonus system. They maintained that a bonus system would better link performance with compensation, and that it would be a move towards remaining competitive in a tight labour market.

Although the company used performance appraisal results to help adjust wages, this method had its limitations. First, as CableCo's managers pointed out during interviews, the wage adjustment normally occurred only once a year and hence often delayed the company's recognition of individual employees' performance and their contribution to the enterprise. Second, as wage scales were usually set up for long-term purposes, it was inappropriate to substantially enlarge wage differences between high and low performers working in similar positions. Third, a person's wage level was not easy to reduce, as employees in China were accustomed to wage increases. By contrast, bonuses would be more flexible and could be easily adjusted, offering rewards when appropriate. The gap between high and low level bonuses could be broadened to better encourage high performers. Finally, a bonus could be more closely linked to the company's total performance. CableCo did not have a profit-share plan, and managers and workers felt that a bonus system would be an adequate substitute for the time being.

In mid-1994, 11 production workers resigned from the joint venture and returned to their positions at TeleCo. The executive manager used this as an illustration of the need for a bonus system. The 11 people were all experienced and key workers in production lines and were all high performers at CableCo. However, because of the significantly higher requirements at CableCo in terms of product quantity and quality, work intensity and a stronger management control, they had to work much harder at CableCo than at TeleCo. In addition, they spent more than two extra hours in travel time every day, because CableCo was nearly 50 km away from their homes. Although their wages were some 50% more at CableCo than at TeleCo, they did not feel that their efforts were adequately compensated. Two of the workers who resigned told the researcher (during a case study at TeleCo) that CableCo's wage system without bonuses did not really differentiate between high and low performers, as the wage differences were small (some workers told the researcher that they knew their close friends' wages, and that people working in similar positions could usually find out the 'secret' wages of others through 'gossip'). When the company lost these 11 workers, the production lines nearly collapsed and it took some two months to train new workers to work independently on the lines.

In late 1994, the executive manager submitted a report to the general manager about the establishment of a bonus system. He suggested that monthly bonuses should be adopted in order to encourage the achievement of production or sales objectives and a reduction in material wastage. He provided detailed measurements to determine the amount of bonus and recommended a method of bonus distribution. During the interview, the executive manager emphasised that the bonus system should be used in conjunction with performance appraisal. However, he agreed that the appraisal system should be revised first to enable employee participation in criteria-setting and thus allow a more objective reflection of employee performance. However, at the time of writing the company is still waiting for approval from the general manager to alter the appraisal system and establish a bonus system.

Apart from compensation in the form of wages, the company also made efforts to meet the welfare needs of its employees. It offered transportation between home and work, and supplied free meals during working time. It also purchased health and social insurance for employees' medical treatment and superannuation purposes. However, CableCo did not supply its employees with any accommodation, which was one of the major welfare items offered by many Chinese enterprises. In China, due to low wages, few employees are able to buy their own apartments or flats. For example, in 1994 in the area where CableCo was located, a two-bedroom apartment with total living space of 50 square meters cost 200 000 yuan. A line manager in the joint venture could only earn about 12 000 yuan per year. Although banks were starting to offer home loans to individuals with the guarantee of their employing companies, individuals had to pay 30% of the purchase price as a deposit. The 60 000 yuan required at the initial stage was an impossible sum for most ordinary wage earners. The accommodation problem reduced CableCo's sources of labour. The executive manager was very concerned, especially as the situation was bound to worsen when production expanded further and more modern technology was introduced. However, the Australian partner showed little understanding of the significance of this issue.

In summary, this case study has outlined how human resources are currently managed in CableCo, a foreign-invested enterprise, with respect to three HR activities—human resource planning, performance appraisal and compensation and welfare.

Recruitment and selection

The practice for recruitment and selection at CableCo was for the functional department to submit its recruitment application to the Personnel Department and then to select candidates with assistance from the Personnel Department (using internal documentation).

There were four steps in the selection procedure. First, the department with a staffing need would submit an application to the Personnel Department detailing both the overall quotas of employees as fixed by the company each year and the departmental production needs. Each application would include a brief job description and the candidate specifications needed to enable the Personnel Department to start recruiting.

Second, the Personnel Department would recruit candidates according to the department's specifications through three channels. The first channel involved renting a stand in the local labour market, where the personnel staff could place job advertisements and hand out application forms. This was the cheapest way to recruit candidates (usually 300 yuan per day per stand), and it was mainly used for employing workers and technicians. The second was to advertise the job in local or national newspapers. This was used for recruiting experienced, middle to senior level managers or highly skilled professionals. It could cost thousands of yuan—one advertisement in the *Economic Daily* (*Jingji Ribao*, a widely circulated Chinese national newspaper) would cost 5000 to 8000 yuan per day. The last method was to recruit new graduates from universities. This required paying 10 000 yuan (1994 price) by CableCo to the relevant university for each new graduate employed by the company (university education in the mid-1990s was nearly free to students, with the state paying most of the cost).

The third step was for the Personnel Department and the department that submitted the application to short-list and select candidates. The Personnel Department would conduct general checks first, including the verification of the applicant's qualifications, previous performance in political and professional areas, family background and social connections. After this stage, the applicant's file would be sent to the relevant department for further examination, especially in the technical area. The department would set written tests and/or conduct interviews by managers and professional staff. Candidates applying for managerial work were interviewed by the personnel manager and a manager from the relevant department. The Personnel Department designed a standardised interview assessment sheet for all departments that included items such as general impression (e.g. manner, attitude, appearance); verbal skills (e.g. logical thinking, synthesis of ideas, clarity of expression); understanding of the company and the knowledge required; the match between the applicant's experience and the requirements of the job ; determination shown by the applicant to work in the company; and proficiency in English. The interviewee was evaluated on a five-point scale that ranged from 'excellent', through 'good', 'average' and 'pass' to 'poor'. Total marks made up one determinant in the final decision.

Finally, after the department had chosen a candidate, it would inform the Personnel Department, which would then make an offer of employment to the applicant. The applicant could refuse the offer without any negative consequences. However, the company had not experienced any rejections of employment offers. Once the applicant had accepted the offer, the Personnel Department would be responsible for all the necessary administrative work, which included signing a probationary labour contract with the recruit, setting up a personal file card and conducting a brief orientation session in which the *Employee Handbook* was given to the new employee. There was also a general introduction to the company. The Personnel Department kept a record of unsuccessful applicants with the intention of setting up a databank in the future. However, by 1994 the Personnel Department had still not been computerised and many records, including personal file cards, were still handwritten.

CableCo's approach to staffing offered each department an opportunity to select recruits according to its own specifications, and this was particularly important as formal job descriptions were not available for many positions within the company. CableCo had written job descriptions only for production workers, and these specified the nature of the job, operation process and requirements for product quality and quantity. The descriptions set up criteria for selection and also enabled workers to follow production instructions and perform self-monitoring. No other positions in CableCo had such formal descriptions. Supervisors in charge of other positions were required to verbally explain their work to new employees, covering details such as the type of work involved and the method used to complete the work. The verbal descriptions depended heavily on the supervisor's understanding of the job and interpersonal communication skills. Although the department had to offer a job description for advertising purposes, this was not based on a formal job analysis. In addition, the transfer of a supervisor could result in inconsistencies. Thus, the involvement of relevant department or line managers in the selection process helped to match candidates with the job, which helped to improve the selection success, as shown by the reduced number of dismissals. CableCo dismissed only five employees during their probationary period on grounds of incompetence in a period of more than two years.

Nevertheless, this selection method had its shortcomings as it relied heavily on individuals in each department. This could result in a lack of consistent and objective standards within the company or poor adherence to the company's business strategy because of an individual manager's ignorance or negligence. For example, the company planned to computerise the whole management system, including accounting and finance, in late 1994, but accountants hired in 1993 were not computer-literate. Errors of this kind could have been avoided if the selection criteria had been tied to the company's strategy for development and human resource planning, and if the Personnel Department had offered active guidance to departments rather than merely administrative assistance.

Generally, new employees were given a six-month probationary period. During this period, the company could discontinue an employee's contract at any time if the person was found to be unsuitable for the job. Similarly, the employee was free to resign without any legal obligation. After this period, employees would be given a formal labour contract. The contract system applied to everyone in the company and the duration of the contract was generally two years. If both parties were satisfied, the contract could be renewed for another two years. Employees who undertook training overseas (and graduates who cost the company 10 000 yuan per head to employ) had to sign five-year contracts. Anyone who resigned during the contractual period had to compensate the company for the training fee or for costs incurred in the duration of employment.

If any department wanted to dismiss an employee for incompetence, the department had to submit a report to the Personnel Department, which then sent staff to talk with the recruit involved. Instead of immediate dismissal, the personnel staff usually encouraged the individual to resign to save face and also to reduce the negative impact on the morale of the remaining employees. Only when someone had seriously violated the company's regulations or contract would the Personnel Department support immediate dismissal of the person concerned.

Managing strategic change at Energize

By **Michael Duncan and V. Nilakant**

In the summer of 1998/99, CEO John Forfar looked back with pride on the achievements of Energize Limited.[1] One of New Zealand's smallest electricity companies, Energize had come a long way in five years. Despite being a comparative minnow in an industry where size mattered, Energize had succeeded in a period of ongoing uncertainty where other electricity companies continued to struggle. It hadn't been a painless process and many decisions had been hard to make. However, the tough times had hardened Forfar's team into a tight unit and had created an organisation that industry and non-industry observers alike heralded as an exemplary model for change management.

Stirring his coffee before his first meeting of the day, Forfar smiled as he looked around the open-plan facility, listening to chatter echoing from each of the team work stations. In less than five years Energize's strategy of total quality management had transformed the organisation. Organisational barriers, both psychological and physical, had been broken down to create a new organisation from the old one. As he returned to his own team's work station Forfar knew that they had all travelled so far and achieved so much that it was difficult to imagine this to be the same organisation as it had been in years gone by.

Energize of old

Energize in the summer of 1998 was far removed from its predecessor, the Central Power Board (CPB). As was the case with all New Zealand electricity companies, Energize's forebear had been only one of more than 40 administrative bodies called 'power boards' that had been created in the 1920s to develop and manage New Zealand's electricity supply. The CPB and all other power boards in New Zealand had operated in close conjunction with local government authorities—either regional or city councils—and had been charged with overseeing the development of the electricity infrastructure to ensure that every household had access to electricity. As a national priority during this period in New Zealand's history, the central government had helped power boards to meet this obligation by protecting them in two ways. First, substantial subsidies had been made available to power boards, thus ensuring that physical, labour and financial resources were both affordable and readily available, guaranteeing the sustainability of each organisation. Second, legislation had been enacted to establish protected franchise boundaries around each board's operating areas. With high entry barriers and the possibility of any form of competition eliminated by government protection, an extraordinarily stable environment had developed. Unimpeded by the restraints of commercial pressures, all power boards, including the CPB, had been able to concentrate solely on the construction and maintenance of local electricity networks, irrespective of the expense. As a result, by the late sixties, most New Zealanders had been connected to an electricity supply, placing the country among world leaders. For more than 65 years the CPB and power board system had maintained the supply of electricity to New Zealand households and businesses unchallenged. With such proven effectiveness in the implementation of the government's development strategy there seemed to be little need or desire for change at either a national, regional or organisational level. Power boards and the industry's operating environment were well established, and a sense of stability and permanence had developed.

The old culture and structure

Thinking about how some of Energize's older employees had referred to that period as 'the good old days', Forfar remembered his first experiences in the CPB. They really had been the dark ages; a job-for-life mentality, the frustrations of bureaucracy, a formalised hierarchy, closed doors and whispers in corridors. How times had changed! In retrospect, he knew that these embedded characteristics were symptomatic of the monopolistic operating environment of the time—after all, every power board that he had dealt with had exhibited a structure and culture similar to that of the CPB.

CPB's structure was fundamentally identical to those of all New Zealand electricity power boards. Despite the apparently simplicity of the organisation's function—to distribute electricity—the monopolistic and protected environment had allowed power boards to develop structurally complex and highly bureaucratic organisations. Until the mid-eighties, the CPB had been top heavy with five levels of administration and 15 departments under the charge of six area heads, a chief engineer and a chief financial officer. This structure emphasised a strict command and control hierarchy with clearly-bounded roles and responsibilities. With its engineering focus the CPB had structured itself around functional areas, placing value and emphasis on task specialisation. Despite functional specialisation, the traditional cost-plus environment had seen little importance placed on infrastructural support. The consequent lack of budgetary, accounting and information systems had meant that the CPB had had no reliable source of financial or organisational information. As in other government departments, all operational and non-operational CPB functions had remained 'in-house'. This saw the likes of painters, gardeners and cleaners being permanently employed by the CPB on a permanent payroll that, at its height, had included more than 160 employees.

The operating environment not only influenced the structure, but also shaped the culture of the CPB. A unique power board culture had developed as certain skills, abilities and behaviours were valued and rewarded. This culture had been dominated by engineering values. With legislative protection, one product, one consumer population and a steady revenue stream, the CPB had developed a monopolistic culture, which valued job security, with many individuals working for the organisation for their entire careers. It also emphasised the physical maintenance of the electricity network above all else, as employees identified with, and took pride in, 'their network'. An engineering bias and environmental protection had led the culture to adopt a highly bureaucratic tendency. Communication had been formal and generally indirect. Official signatures had been required on all documents, and all purchases had had to be approved by the board. People had hidden away in their offices, with large titles on the doors. When customers had come to pay their bills or ask for specific services, it was difficult for anyone to answer questions without referring to each divisional specialist—if they could be found.

Environmental change

In 1992 electricity industry policy makers shifted their attention away from delivering an effective service to offering an efficient one. This marked a significant change in government policy. The focus moved from ensuring the ongoing development of electricity infrastructure to the reduction of electricity costs so that New Zealand's competitiveness in the international arena could be enhanced. With this intent, legislation was passed that radically transformed the rules of the operating environment. The electricity market was liberalised and competition encouraged as all protective measures and forms of subsidy were removed. For the first time in more than 60 years the CPB and all electricity companies faced legal and competitive pressures that forced them to change the way they did business.

CPB responds

As Forfar looked over the proof of the latest customer newsletter, he once again mused that the decisions made in those early days had been fundamental to Energize's development.

Although legislation had redefined the norms and values of the operating environment, he knew that the CPB could have followed a 'wait-and-see' strategy, which would have allowed the CPB time to establish physical and economic barriers to protect its traditional businesses and markets and watch other companies test the limits and opportunities of the new environment. However, in 1992 a defensive stance had been far from the mind of CPB's governing board. Instead, as new board members took the reins, it was soon clear that the CPB was going to take an aggressive stance. The CPB would not only survive a new competitive environment, but would embrace the spirit of reform as an opportunity to realign its operations for growth and prosperity. The changing environment had set in motion a series of events that would radically reinvent the CPB.

The first step in the change process had been to appoint a CEO. This was a new position and title for the CPB—traditionally all power board operations had been headed by a general manager (GM), typically a tenured position held by an engineer. General managers had been responsible solely for overseeing the day-to-day operation of electricity companies, while issues of a strategic nature had been left to the board. CPB's last GM had been no different; an engineer with the CPB since leaving school, he had grown up within the organisation and was highly qualified when selected for the GM position. However, as the environment changed to emphasise commercial competencies, the CPB re-evaluated its requirements as far as its most senior office-holder was concerned. It was clear to the board that the incumbent GM's profile and hands-on style was no longer suited to current needs. They now needed a CEO who was capable of leading the organisation through change and preparing it for a competitive environment without interference from the board. Consequently, they negotiated an amicable early retirement with the GM, and advertised the position of CEO in mid-1992. By the end of that year, Paul Wilkinson had been appointed to the top job on a strict three-year contract to oversee the development of CPB. With an international background in management consulting and specialist knowledge of the computer industry, Paul was well versed in the demands of change management. He was charged with sole responsibility for effecting radical change.

It was at that stage that Forfar first became involved with Energize. He had talked to Wilkinson many times about the similarity of their initial experiences with the organisation. Wilkinson's early frustration with the hierarchy and bureaucracy had meant that he had quickly seen that his vision for the organisation would never be achieved without change at the top.

One of Paul's first moves was to require all managers to reapply for their positions, granting him the freedom to review and renew the CPB's operation and skills base. By March 1993, Wilkinson had personally selected a new management team—one that he believed shared his vision of growth. Although a small number of incumbent managers remained, people from outside the firm and industry were serving as managers in the CPB for the first time. Selected on the basis of their skills and abilities, the new managers broke forever the traditional hierarchical progression associated with the power board, and their appointments telegraphed the urgency for change to the wider organisation.

Forfar recalled that Wilkinson's agenda had always been clear and concise—the organisation was to undergo total strategic, structural and cultural redevelopment in a consultative manner. However, in Forfar's eyes the first concern had seemed cosmetic. Wilkinson had wanted to immediately disassociate the new organisation from the old power board and to this end he had called the management team together. Arguing that the company needed a fresh new image and brand name in a competitive environment, Wilkinson charged his management team with the task of devising a new name and corporate image for the company. For the first time, help was sought from a marketing company and, through a brainstorming exercise, the name 'Energize' was devised. This name had seemed to capture the freshness that Wilkinson and his team wanted to inject into the organisation. Accompanied by widespread publicity for the 'new' business, a new wardrobe for customer service staff and soon-to-be redesigned service areas, both staff and customers now visibly dealt with a new organisation. Over time Forfar had come to appreciate that this seemingly cosmetic change was actually a significant step in a process that would fundamentally alter the organisation's strategy, structure and culture.

TABLE B.1	Energize's short-, medium- and long-term objectives

Short-term objectives—value creation
- To ensure competitive and secure sources of electricity.
- To achieve outstanding management performance.
- To create strong financial stability and resources.

Medium-term objectives—Target '95
- Short-term goals were translated into a medium-term (two-year) strategy called 'Target '95'. This strategy aimed for Energize to be a 'healthy business, meeting the needs and desires of its owners, satisfying its customers, motivating its employees and remaining safe from predators'.

Long-term objectives—Target 2000
- Finally a long-term strategy called Target 2000 was created to aim at 'industry leadership in systems and processes, being the best overall team in the industry, providing the highest level of customer satisfaction in the New Zealand industry and showing a track record of value creation'.

Mapping out a strategy for change

With the onset of a competitive environment Wilkinson had made it clear to his management team that Energize needed to strengthen its position. It was decided to survey their market and use the findings to help direct the strategic and structural redesign of Energize. The sheer scope of this exercise, and Wilkinson's desire for Energize's rapid transformation, saw the CEO seek the assistance of a major international consulting company. The consultants were to recommend changes that would enable Energize to become an industry leader. All businesses, processes and procedures were comprehensively reviewed in terms of the survey findings. In October 1993, the consulting organisation submitted its final report, which called for a total commitment to Business Process Re-engineering (BPR) with a focus on growth and strength through customer satisfaction and retention. Outlining the strengths and weaknesses of each of Energize's operating areas, the report provided the guidance necessary for the CEO to drive Energize's transformation.

The entire management team shared Forfar's high opinion of the consultant's findings and recommendations. The review process had offered a clear strategy that was fundamental in turning the CPB around. First, it clarified the strategic objectives of the firm and defined short-, medium- and long-term organisational objectives.

Second, those objectives allowed Energize's strengths and weaknesses to be identified and compared with external benchmarks. Third, a course of action for structural and cultural change to improve on these benchmarks could be prescribed. With the consultant's guidance the senior management team set in motion a two-year course of action for Energize, whose objective was to:
- replace 95% of routine, repetitive business activities with automated systems by 31 March 1995
- be process-focused in management and organisation
- invest significantly in training staff to work as effective teams with no less than ten days training per employee per year
- have fewer dissatisfied and more satisfied customers than any other electricity company, with a target of 1% dissatisfied and 20% delighted customers by 31 March 1995.

The Energize Concept

Wilkinson rallied his team around him and, in a brainstorming session, devised a way to create cultural change. What finally emerged was the *Energize Concept*—a plan that would see the organisation reach its long-term objectives through the development of its people. By investing in staff training and development, it was envisioned that the *Energize Concept* would create within the organisation a pool of skilled managers capable of meeting and exceeding international best-practice benchmarks. This would allow Energize to sell their management skills, organisational processes and philosophy to other companies, thus creating growth and value at every stage.

The process of change

In early 1994, it was time for Wilkinson and his team to take the first step and lead the organisation to change.

Changing the structure

Energize radically restructured the organisation around core organisational processes and created four task areas—Task Management, Sales and Service, Resourcing and Infrastructure. In each of these task areas 12 key processes were identified and categorised, while non-core processes were outsourced. All personnel were assessed, irrespective of their position in the old hierarchy, and placed within one of seven skills groups. From these skills groups, five member cross-functional teams could be formed. Made up of members from all task areas and led ('coached') by any member considered to be highly competent in the problem's area, these teams would form and have the authority to address problems in any one of Energize's 12 process categories. With the benefit of hindsight, Forfar now realised that this process had essentially been a skills audit. It had forced the organisation's culture away from the strict task management philosophy of old and given Energize access to a pool of people organised, not by tenure or position, but according to individual strengths and abilities.

The development of a team culture was taken further when Wilkinson took a radical step and, on his own initiative, moved the entire organisation to a new 'open plan' facility. In place of the closed doors, walls and rumour that typified the old power board, Wilkinson created team-sized open work cells that he envisioned would minimise the physical and psychological barriers to communication. Forfar remembered the positive feedback that replaced the negative perception of this change when Wilkinson led by example and included himself in a work team, working as the others did in a cell.

Infrastructure development

Forfar had seen the organisation change more in the space of six months than it had in the past six decades. A new name, new premises, new strategy and the creation of work teams had opened up and energised the organisation. However, the team creation process had revealed that top-quality customer service could only develop with massive investment in infrastructure and human resources. Without that development, Wilkinson acknowledged that the changes necessary for Energize to realise its potential would be met with resistance that would jeopardise the entire strategy. Over a period of 18 months, Energize followed the recommendations of the consulting company, undergoing a massive process of infrastructural redevelopment, which included:

- *documentation of procedures*: documentation teams were set up specifically to capture and standardise processes and procedures. Once developed, these documents were passed to the operational areas concerned, who became responsible for their maintenance and review. The entire documentation review took less than a year from its inception.
- *asset management plans*: each process area developed a plan that would best see the resources of the company utilised to achieve strategic ends. Network contracting (maintenance and construction) was for the first time made contestable, allowing other companies the opportunity to competitively tender for work in Energize's former franchise area.
- *investment in technology*: Energize heavily invested in new computer technology—primarily in the installation of a $2 million local area network (LAN) and despatch

system. The LAN linked each member of Energize, from the CEO to the front office staff, and made information on network status and customer details available to all. The use of LAN, intra- and internet technologies was central to meeting the challenge of Energize's new strategy and changing the culture of the firm. The consultation, learning and support associated with the introduction of the new technology also strengthened the developing team culture, offered new opportunities to learn and develop with the organisation and motivated and raised the morale of most people.

- *call centre:* one of the strongest forces for change was the creation of a centralised customer inquiry call centre. The CEO focused on creating an efficient and effective customer service facility. Under the guidance of a Sales and service team, call centre staff were employed and trained in customer service, the history and operation of the electricity industry and use of the LAN. The call centre's value as a communicative and cultural change tool was emphasised by the CEO, who required all staff, including himself, to answer enquiries for one day each month.

Changing the culture

Forfar now knew that, although structural and procedural development was central to the change process, staff development had been fundamental in the creation and development of Energize.

A formal strategy that addressed the need for ongoing individual development was implemented. Policies included the introduction of aptitude testing, compulsory regular training and standardised performance review procedures, but also left room for more informal recognition of achievements. Aptitude testing that was implemented at all levels of the organisation allowed the audit and assessment of skills and ability, while ensuring alignment of competencies with organisational roles. Investment in training and development ensured that individuals could develop the ability to participate in Energize's change process and offer a high level of customer service. Formal training in specific functions (electricity network operations, accounting, customer service protocols, computer operation) was reinforced by less formal 'on the job' training provided by the interaction within cross-functional teams. For the first time, individual and teams performance was formally measured against set criteria. The primary method was a quarterly performance review that, under the guidance of team coaches, examined individual and group achievements based on goals and objectives established at the beginning of the quarter. This process allowed an examination of problems and their causes, and also provided a means of reviewing strengths and weaknesses at a group and personal level. At the end of the process individuals with their coach would have refocused and recorded personal objectives, and teams would have set the next quarter's objectives while being aware of organisational expectations. Although a small bonus system had been established, a more influential informal teams reward system had developed. Called the 'Bloody Amazing Awards', team members that met or exceeded expectations were held up as role models and rewarded with bottles of wine or mystery weekends, thus positively reinforcing a change in behaviour.

The outcome

An independent competitor analysis that had been commissioned in late 1994 revealed that Energize was recognised within the industry as having advanced beyond the development of any other electricity company, and wide interest in Energize's development process and the *Energize Concept* quickly mounted. With its focus on growth and expansion, CEO Wilkinson sought to establish strategic partnerships with other electricity companies keen on embracing change, and marketed the advantages of utilising the competencies of Energize's change and asset management teams. However, by mid-1995, the operating environment had begun to stagnate. Although competition had entered the industry, political apathy, legal issues and general industry resistance halted the Government's development of a competitive market. As the pressure for ongoing change towards a free and potentially privatised industry decreased, electricity companies became increasingly defensive. The energy that had been injected into the industry slowly began to fade as companies retreated to more cautious 'wait and see' strategies.

Energize continues to change

Forfar recalled Wilkinson's meeting with the entire organisation in mid-1995. He had told them that, irrespective of the lack of environmental development, the strategies associated with the *Energize Concept* remained valid. Wilkinson had reiterated that competition was a reality and that they would remain true to the *Energize Concept* vision of efficient and effective customer service. Energize would lead the industry and so prove itself advanced through its continuous technological and procedural improvement and low prices. Although the environment wasn't going to be competitive, Energize would be.

Energize's senior management, the marketing team and the governing board took a three-tiered approach to ensuring that Energize's strategy and competitiveness was communicated to customers. First, bimonthly customer newsletters, with specific domestic and commercial versions, were distributed in order to keep customers informed of organisational improvements and operational movements. Second, Energize established an accredited business partner scheme. The accreditation scheme offered Energize customers a range of endorsed products and services that were directly related to electricity use. Third, savings made as a result of efficiency gains were not directly put into the final electricity price, but instead were offered as quarterly discounts with comparisons to 'competitors' prices'. This strategy, in tandem with the ongoing support of the call centre and community sponsorship schemes, meant that Energize maintained a stable and loyal customer base to the detriment of potential competitors.

At the end of 1995, CEO Wilkinson's three-year contract was coming to an end. With Energize structurally, strategically and culturally transformed and capable of meeting the challenges of the future, his job as change manager was complete. In early 1996, John Forfar took the reins as CEO. With the support of the Energize team and his inside knowledge, he continued the momentum of the *Energize Concept*.

One of John's first acts involved further separating the organisation into specialised functions. This process had begun early in 1993 with divisionalisation, a process that had granted operational autonomy to each function. However, with the substantial changes to the industry, it had become clear that the nature of contracting (network maintenance and construction) and appliance retailing was changing. Appliance retailing was no longer regarded as a core service and, because it was a highly competitive sector, Energize no longer had the competencies or networks to successfully compete with specialised retail outlets. In early 1996, this operation was sold to the joint venture partner. Contracting services, on the other hand, was a strategically valuable venture. With competition slowly beginning to encroach on the former monopoly franchise area, Energize moved to capitalise on the financial and competitive opportunities that contracting presented by creating a fully separate subsidiary 'NETwork'. ISO accredited in 1994, 'NETwork', as a stand-alone entity, was freely able to compete for line maintenance and construction work on Energize's and other electricity companies' networks. With only corporate links to its subsidiary, Energize could concentrate exclusively on asset management and customer service.

Forfar also capitalised on the call centre and technological competencies that had developed within Energize over the previous four years. In 1998, Energize went into a joint venture to create a centralised billing and call centre service. The joint venture was the first move towards the conglomeration of the industry that had been forecast by CEO Wilkinson some six years previously.

The appropriateness of the changes that Energize had made were recognised at that time when it was announced as one of four winners of the New Zealand national award for service excellence. Recognising the strengths in Energize's business performance, complaints procedure, despatch system and call centre, the award acknowledged that Energize was ahead of all other New Zealand electricity companies. The government's commitment to change was finally enacted with the passing of the *Energy Industry Reform Act* (1998). Forcing electricity companies to separate physical network and electricity retail functions, the Act opened up the entire industry to the competition and conglomeration that the *Energize Concept* had envisioned years earlier. With the systems, procedures and culture in place to deal with a competitive environment, Energize was ideally positioned to exploit new opportunities. Energize's future had arrived.

QUESTIONS

1 How would you characterise the change at Energize?
2 Assume that you had been hired as a consultant by Wilkinson to advise him on change. What would you have done differently?
3 How would you evaluate the outcome of change at Energize?
4 What lessons about organisational change can one learn from the Energize experience?

Note

1 'Energize' is the disguised name of a real company. Names of people have been changed to conceal their identity.

Employee relations at Centrelink

By **Sarah Turberville and Rowena Barrett**

Introduction

> *Governments must strive to do things better, with fewer resources, and above all, differently.*

OECD, 1995:6

In an effort to increase the efficiency and effectiveness of both the management and delivery of public services, many Western democratic governments have implemented public sector reform programmes.[1] Underlying the emerging model of public sector management, known broadly as the 'new public management',[2] is an emphasis on individual choice, performance and competition.[1] Changes to employment relations in the public sector are critical if reform is going to lead to the development of a new results-based, performance-oriented 'culture'.[1,3]

Changing employee relations in the Australian Public Service

In November 1996 the *Workplace Relations Act 1996* replaced the *Industrial Relations Act 1988* and, in so doing, introduced the ability for individual employment agreements to regulate workplace industrial relations in the Federal industrial relations jurisdiction. Individual agreements sit alongside collective agreements, all of which are underpinned by awards stripped back to contain only 20 minimum conditions. The underlying rationale for these changes is 'freedom of choice', the platform on which the Liberal/National Coalition went to the Federal election on 2 March 1996. As far as agreements were concerned, the thrust of the *Workplace Relations Act 1996* was that the parties concerned should choose the most appropriate type of agreement to regulate their workplace relations (see section 3c of the Act). This meant that the parties need not formalise their workplace agreement at all. If they do choose to formalise their agreement, the *Workplace Relations Act 1996* provided for collective union and non-union certified agreements and individual Australian workplace agreements.

Also in November 1996, Peter Reith, Minister for Small Business and Workplace Relations, released the discussion paper, *Towards a Best Practice Australian Public Service*. This document was clearly part of the push to encourage the development of a performance culture in the Australian Public Service (APS), as was evident in the statement: 'the culture of the APS does not sufficiently promote high performance or drive innovation, and the important contribution of individual public servants is often overlooked or stifled by process and unnecessary regulations'.[4] There were three key features of reform outlined in the document. The first was legislative change via a major overhaul of the *Public Service Act 1922*.[5] The second was reform to workplace relations and the devolution of agreement making, under-pinned by a simplified award (with the phasing out of paid rates awards).[6] The third feature of reform was the strengthening of APS management and leadership, thus facilitating the development of a performance culture in APS workplaces based on a clear vision and the communication of future directions. With respect to performance-related pay (PRP) the following was stated:

The government believes that agency heads should decide, and be publicly accountable for, the application of PRP arrangements within their agencies subject to overall budget parameters set by government. There is a need for greater flexibility in the way agencies recognise and reward performance, both through tangible and non-pay rewards. The government supports greater experimentation and sharing of experience in how best to reward outstanding team performance or individual goal achievement.[4]

Operationally, agreement making was devolved to agencies. However, the government maintained control of the process by specifying the parameters in which agencies could bargain. *Policy Parameters for Agreement Making* was released by the Department of Employment, Workplace Relations and Small Business (DEWRSB) on 23 May 1997 in order to provide agencies with guidelines for the process of agreement making (Advice 1997/29). Number four of the twelve parameters specifically referred to performance and performance pay in the context of classification structures. This policy parameter essentially required that salary movements be guided by performance management (Advice 1998/4). Further, it gave agencies some flexibility to base pay on the job, with scope for a component to be paid as a supplement, one-off bonus or as an allowance.

In March–April 1997 the Community and Public Service Sector Union (CPSU) had initiated service-wide and agency bargaining periods. By December 1998, 86 agreements (covering around 95% of APS staff) had been certified by the Australian Industrial Relations Commission. Another one was awaiting certification. Thirty-eight were made under s. 170LK of the *Workplace Relations Act 1996* (non-union certified agreements); and another 42 were stand-alone. In total, agencies employing almost all APS staff were currently involved in (or had completed) negotiating certified agreements. As agencies were not required to have Australian Workplace Agreements (AWAs) cleared by DEWRSB, there are no clear figures available as to their spread. However, according to the Office of the Employment Advocate, at the end of October 1998 there were about 2500 AWAs in the APS.[7]

The bargaining process in the APS has produced a diversity of outcomes. Working conditions and pay arrangements now vary between agencies, while agreements range across time-scales. The lack of uniformity in bargaining outcomes became an issue after the 1998 federal election, when a wave of restructuring occurred across the APS. The key problem lay in determining under which terms and conditions personnel in merged departments were employed. Despite these problems, Dr Kemp, Minister assisting the Prime Minister on the Public Service, avowed that agreement making has transformed the culture of the APS.[8]

These large-scale changes, which have been undertaken across the APS in such a short period, have been driven by the desire to create 'a high-performance APS'. Further changes are proposed in order to increase the devolution of 'people management' to agencies. These include making revisions to the policy parameters with a view to their reduction; further reform to the *Workplace Relations Act*, seeking to make agreements more accessible; spreading AWAs down from the SES level to all APS personnel; and enabling agencies to include redundancy, leave and superannuation in agreements.[8]

Centrelink

As one of the most significant reforms to Australian public administration in the post-war-period, Centrelink aims to apply world's best practice in service delivery to over five million customers across Australia.

Senator Jocelyn Newman, 26 July 1998

Background

The Commonwealth Services Delivery Agency—Centrelink—is 'a dynamic new organisation' established through legislation in July 1997 and opened on 24 September 1997 as a statutory authority to link a range of government services. Through area and national support offices, call centres and customer services centres, Centrelink delivers a range of social security and employment services to some 6.2 million customers (with

$43.4 billion per year in payments).[9] Service agreements have been signed with a range of Commonwealth agencies, including the Departments of Social Security; Education, Training and Youth Affairs; Health and Family Services; and Primary Industry and Energy, as well as State housing authorities. Centrelink employs approximately 23 750 full-time equivalent staff, spread over 432 work sites, including:

- customer service centres
- student services centres
- career reference centres
- call centres
- area and national support offices
- youth services
- retirement service centres
- family service centres.[10,11]

This diverse range of services entails 'processing 8.4 million on-line transactions per day', made up of 78 classes of payment, which over one year amounts to dealing with 5.1 million customers and 300 million contracts.[10] These services had previously been provided by the various government departments. Corporate governance of Centrelink, as a statutory authority, is controlled by a board of seven members, whose legislative remit is to:

- decide Centrelink's goals, priorities, policies and strategies
- ensure that functions are properly, efficiently and effectively performed.[10,11]

This governing board is made up of two departmental secretaries, the CEO, an independent chair with experience in both the public and private sector and four members representing the private sector. The board, via the chair, reports directly to the Minister for Social Security,[10] and is perceived as a guiding hand that promotes strategic direction, accountability, quality and cost-effective service.[11]

Centrelink is funded by its one-year service agreements (or performance contracts), representing purchaser–provider relationships, with the government departments listed above. It is intended that these agreements be extended to three years, and to other departments, including the Australian Taxation Office, Departments of Employment, Workplace Relations and Small Business; Immigration and Multicultural Affairs; and Transport and Regional Development. As performance contracts, the purchasing department can rescind the agreement if Centrelink does not deliver the required level of service.[10] The provision of social security and employment services is in partnership with the Department of Social Security (DSS). Centrelink and the DSS proportionally share three main responsibilities that represent the different levels of service policy and delivery.

This new Government service delivery structure attracted overseas research interest in July 1998, when the Kennedy School of Government at Harvard University prepared a case study that 'will highlight both the innovative structure of Centrelink and the service delivery and customer relations strategies which it has adopted'.[12] The Kennedy School of Government researcher states:[12]

> We at the Kennedy School are deeply interested in the many efforts, through the world, to make government more responsive to the needs and expectations of citizens ... Centrelink clearly represents a dramatic effort in that direction and, as such, has attracted our attention.

TABLE C.1	Responsibilities shared by Centrelink and the DSS	
Function	**Centrelink proportion**	**DSS proportion**
Policy development	10% (As customer service feedback and statistics)	90%
Product design	50%	50%
Service delivery style	90%	10%

TABLE C.2	Drivers as forces for change

Broad driver	Specific drivers and description
Global change	**Competition:** Pressure on public service to deliver quality at competitive price
	Separation of purchaser and provider: Department's move to policy formulation and contracting out functional responsibilities
	Need for responsiveness: Customer service based on private sector model
	Change of expectations: Desire for customer choice, quality and personalised service, access to information, and flexible service delivery locations
	Technological change: Opportunities for alternative service delivery via new technology, e.g. Internet access and cashless transactions (as in other sectors)
Reforms to labour market and social security	**Reform to labour market assistance:** Assistance to job seekers to be based on outcomes and choice; registration and referral provided by one agency; choice of employment placement services from both public and private sector
	Savings in social security payments: Savings to be achieved by targeting of income support payments; stricter compliance measures; work process redesign and increasing reliance on customer self-provision
Political commitment	**Government:** Prime ministerial and ministerial desire to reform public sector service delivery
	Public service: Department secretaries' desire to create one agency to provide social security and employment services

Adapted from S. Vardon, 'Centrelink' in eds C. Clark and D. Corbett *Reforming the Public Sector: Problems and Solutions* (Sydney: Allen and Unwin, 1999): 178–79.

Drivers for change at Centrelink

The creation of 'one-stop shopping for government human services'[10] is seen as the culmination and expression of a long-held desire to fundamentally change the provision of public services in Australia, where the delivery model has shifted from a series of transactions to solving problems for individual customers. This change has been effected by a series of broad 'drivers' that have created a 'unique model of public administration in human services in the world'.[10] These forces for change are summarised in Table C.2.

Strategic success

A central priority at Centrelink has been to set the 'Strategic directions and strategic plan', published in the *Centrelink Strategic Framework 1997–2002*. Centrelink's mission, vision and goals fit well with the ideals of 'new public management'. For example, the vision is about 'making a difference to the Australian community through responsive high quality government services and opportunities and giving value for money'.[13]

TABLE C.3	Centrelink's five-year strategic plan	
Time frame	**For the customer**	**Positioning Centrelink**
Within 6–18 months	Personalised service	Gain customer loyalty and get community involvement and respect for outcomes
Within 2–3 years	Help customers find solutions during periods of transition	As a virtual organisation delivering quality services at a competitive price
Within 3–4 years	Centrelink as a key part of a community that finds solutions for customers	Premier broker of information and solutions and excellence in service
Within 4–5 years	Access to the full range of government services in one site consistent with the mission	Recognised internationally and a partner in global service development

Adapted from C. Zanetti, 'Managing change: focus on improving service quality and information management', *Australian Journal of Public Administration*, 57:4, pp. 3–13, and S. Vardon, 'Centrelink' in eds C. Clark and D. Corbett *Reforming the Public Sector: Problems and Solutions* (Sydney: Allen and Unwin, 1999).

This five-year strategic plan and the scale of change places a heavy emphasis on customer service and, therefore, has particular consequences for managing employee relations and work organisation at Centrelink. Centrelink has consequently sought to 'embed' the strategic plan at the workplace[11] through the introduction of:
- a point of decision making (the initial customer service officer, who has contact with the customer, can make a final decision)
- the use of appointments
- employees titled 'customer service officers' rather than administrative officers
- open office layouts
- establishing teams
- extended opening hours, e.g. Saturday morning interviews
- customer segment teams (rather than the older structure based on which payment system was applicable).[11]

To a large extent, these changes to workplace organisation and practices have been reflected and codified in the provisions of the certified enterprise agreement.

Managing employee relations at Centrelink

Introduction

Since 1993, workplace wages and conditions in Australia have become increasingly decentralised, with less reliance being placed on industry-based awards and the promulgation of enterprise bargaining as a means of determining salary increases and conditions of employment, contingent on the particular workplace circumstances or environment. In the first instance, the *Industrial Relations Reform Act 1993* began the process of decentralisation, but latterly these changes to the industrial regulation have been reinforced and extended by the *Workplace Relations Act 1996*.

A major aim of the Liberal–National government has been to reform employee relations in the Australian public service, and agreement making at a local departmental level is seen as a powerful vehicle for achieving this. Formerly 'our enterprises, both private and public, abdicated their responsibility for ensuring that employment conditions and working arrangements were actually geared to the needs of the enterprise'.[8] This 'abdication' is perceived to have led to 'disempowered' and 'disinterested' employees, a problem that can now be overcome by 'strategically managing people'.[8] Historically, there has been a multiplicity of trade unions representing employees in the public service, whereas today the Community and Public Sector Union (CPSU) is, for the most part, the 'bargaining agent' with the remit to represent APS employees. Provisions in the *Workplace Relations Act 1996* do, notably, open up opportunities for other 'bargaining agents' to represent employees, either individually or collectively, in the process of determining employment conditions.

Centrelink Development Agreement 1997–98

As a case study for our people management strategies, I think our workplace agreement is a powerful demonstration of what can be achieved.

Vardon 1998:5

'Our workplace agreement'

The *Centrelink Development Agreement (CDA) 1997–98*, with the additional attachment incorporating the *Centrelink Call Centres Agreement 1997*,[13] was certified by the Australian Industrial Relations Commission in November 1997 under s. 170LJ of the *Workplace Relations Act 1996*. Centrelink and the CPSU at the time of writing were in the process of renegotiating a new certified agreement, after the CPSU had served Centrelink management with a log of claims on 14 August 1998. Both documents, detailing wages, conditions and other workplace practices, are a public expression of the rights and responsibilities of employees and employers. Put simply, the certified agreement outlines the negotiated provisions that apply to managing employees at Centrelink.

The CEO of Centrelink perceives the certified workplace agreement as 'form(ing) one of the cornerstones of our organisations' strategic success' and as a means to 'meet our corporate goals and adapt to reposition our organisation'.[10] The agreement is seen as a mechanism for organisational change that promotes a customer-driven culture through a customer service strategy. It allows for performance to be improved by offering monetary rewards to staff in workplaces who introduce customer service improvement plans (for both internal and external customers). Further, provisions in the agreement allow local managers more discretion (rather than a 'rules'-based approach) and flexibility as to office opening and working hours.

There is a stated desire to 'empower' staff to 'have more confidence in solving problems and adding value in a more direct and creative way', but simultaneously 'doesn't want complacent people in our organisation'.[10] This will be encouraged by:

- encouraging managers to recognise and reward excellence
- establishing customer service teams with much greater control over their own work environment and performance
- recognising staff who have a high level of competence in customer service (known as 'customer service champions')
- providing a monetary bonus to staff for developing a customer service improvement plan within every work team
- a 2% pay rise on the basis of performance improvements.

According to the CEO of Centrelink, the certified enterprise agreement can be characterised by the following main themes:

- the introduction of teams as the main form of work organisation
- customer service and quality as underlying principles of the agreement (e.g. the capacity for extending opening hours)
- management prerogative in decision making maintained
- prescriptive rules to be replaced by guiding principles
- improvements to be made in order to promote more family-friendly work environments.[10]

Provisions within the agreement

Team-based work

> *The move to teams is likened by staff to a journey—a journey where managers progressively let go and staff gradually take on new roles and responsibilities as their skills, knowledge and confidence grows.*

PSMPC, 1999

The move to team-based working for employees at Centrelink is seen as a vital component if their *Quality First* policy is to work, and as a key mechanism for 'empowering' staff as Centrelink evolves into a 'learning organisation'. Team work is used to promote employee self-management, and capitalise on employees' skills, in the context of a high commitment to public service with a lessened role for middle management. All employees were expected to be working as part of a team by the end of 1998. This participative approach to managing Centrelink's activities was not only intended to promote employee satisfaction, but was recognised as being crucial to meeting strategic objectives, improving performance and, therefore, gaining a competitive advantage.[14]

Various mechanisms and support services will facilitate the implementation of teams at Centrelink:

- the team-based work policy implementation will be aided and facilitated by commitment and support from managers
- specialised training packages (to enhance problem solving and decision making) have been developed for team leaders
- specialised team advisers will provide ongoing advice and support for team leaders and local managers
- the move to team-based working (along with performance-based bonus pay) is to be formally incorporated as a provision in Centrelink's certified agreement.

The certified agreement contains provisions extending team-based working, in the interests of improved customer service and job satisfaction, with the stated intention that staff will evolve into genuine self-managing teams.[13] The existing work groups will move to team-based work 'with the relevant managers defining the responsibilities, authority to make decisions and purpose of the team'. Ideally, a team will have:

- responsibility for a clearly distinguishable area of work
- a common understanding and shared responsibility for the final product or service
- responsibility for planning, implementing and evaluating their work
- responsibility for the day-to-day operations and problem solving
- responsibility for longer-term improvement to the work
- consensual decision making and accountability for their decisions
- a team manager with a leading and coaching role.[13]

So, while there is a stated intention to move to self-managing teams, there remains a controlling and facilitating role for managers. It is acknowledged, however, that this evolution could have repercussions for managerial roles and responsibilities, and that 'managers need to recognise that in moving to teams there will be significant changes in their roles and responsibilities'. If the 'ideals' for team work listed above are successfully implemented, there should be important ramifications for salary levels and group-based performance-related pay. For example, with increasing responsibilities, will non-managerial employees enjoy parallel pay increases and will group-based contingency pay be implemented? At present, performance-related pay for non-SES staff is distributed at an enterprise level.

Recognition and remuneration

Employees at Centrelink received a 1.5% salary increase, backdated three months prior to certification of the agreement. There were to be further bonuses and ongoing pay rises after the agreement and the *Quality First* strategy had been implemented. This included a $300 bonus (based on employees' pay) to all employees (full-time, part-time and temporary—at the time of certification) for the development of agreed plans to improve internal and external customer service. A further 2% salary increase that took effect on 30 June 1998 was accompanied by the proviso that all workplaces should have commenced their implementation of the customer service development plans and that there has been an overall improvement in Centrelink's performance.

Improvement in performance will be considered to have happened if two of the following measures (without reduction in the remainder) constitute 'overall improvement' (i.e. a 'balanced scorecard'):[13]

- overall customer satisfaction measured by customer survey
- call waiting times in call centres averaged over three months, and compared to previous three months
- debt recovery (compared with preceding three months)
- improvement in safety measures and employee satisfaction
- accuracy of decisions (compared with preceding three months).

If the improvements were not achieved by 1 July 1998 (for the purpose of the 2% salary increase), there was to be an assessment by both parties of all possible barriers to improvement, with a view to the increase being implemented on 30 November 1998. Legislation or policy changes that may be seen to affect the performance of Centrelink would not necessarily delay or nullify the 2% pay rise.

Centrelink Call Centres Agreement 1997

The *Centrelink Call Centres Agreement 1997* is attached to the *Centrelink Development Agreement 1997–98* and has been developed 'in recognition of the particular conditions which operate in Centrelink call centres'.[13]

The *Call Centres Agreement* retains the language of customer service, and notes that a *Centrelink Call Centre Customer Charter* was to be developed by no later than 30 June 1998 for adoption by all call centre employees.[13] Further, the Centrelink Call Centre Steering Committee was to be the means of advancing the call centre's objectives and initiatives.[13]

Performance improvement and technological innovation in call centres

Performance improvement 'initiatives' were to be promoted in the call centres by a series of interventions in their work organisation, e.g.

- standardisation of operations
- key performance indicators
- on-phone time
- role specialisation
- standard queue configuration
- extended and varied Centrelink call centre opening hours
- employee attendance arrangements
- change management
- identification of learning needs.

These performance improvement interventions were also to be supported by technological 'innovations', such as:

- common telecommunications platforms
- load switching between centres
- support tools
- automated call handling.

Making Advancement Towards Excellence (MATE) programme

The Centrelink call centres are developing and introducing key performance indicators (KPIs) by collecting individual employee data sets. These KPIs are intended to identify learning needs and are a means of developing appropriate skills. It is stressed in the certified agreement that they will not be used for assessing and comparing, for setting individual targets for employees, or for probation or disciplinary purposes. Nevertheless, it is the case that performance is being measured on an individual rather than a workplace basis, and that there is no provision stating that individual data will remain anonymous. If, as stated, the *MATE* programme aims to improve the performance of call centres to meet call traffic,[13] is it necessary to collect individual data sets, with the advent of tailored new technology?

There has also been recent and continuing industrial action in connection with the job losses proposed under the banner of the 'special efficiency dividend', a new service delivery model. Centrelink announced that 2700 staff would be made redundant in 1998, together with a further 2315 staff losses planned for 1999–2000. This restructuring aimed to save $149 million over the following three years.[15]

Challenges for the future

Centrelink's challenges for the future lie primarily in its ability to provide a high quality service at a competitive price as it moves away from the regulated environment of the Australian Public Service. This 'journey' will require Centrelink to 'exploit its financial and intellectual assets' to ensure that its products and services are not easily replicated. The 'unique' quality of Centrelink's service provision, skills and assets should ensure that 'Centrelink positions itself as a premier broker of information and solutions, and excellence in service'.[11]

Nevertheless, there are indications that employee relations and workplace issues are a key concern at Centrelink. Challenges arising from this include:

- developing the leadership of the organisation
- maintaining staff engagement and interest in being part of a learning environment, while being unafraid of the competitive environment in which Centrelink operates
- developing as a knowledge-based organisation with strong intellectual capital
- answering the difficult questions of how to do business with the private sector (to what extent should there be an interface between the private and public services?)
- maintaining staff commitment.[11]

Put simply, senior managers at Centrelink will need to address human resource management issues that tackle problems of employee satisfaction and commitment, training and development in the new model of service delivery, the introduction of new technology, and the leadership skills of the senior and front-line managers during a period of turbulence and uncertainty.

Conclusion

Embracing the new public management in Australian Public Service:

- partial, unsuccessful implementation during phase 1: too many problems
- lack of autonomy and the devolution of decision making to agency heads in connection with the terms and conditions of employment (especially performance-related pay that only related to senior officers and senior executive services)
- second attempt in phase 2, with PRP being extended further and driven by ideological agenda. There was certainly more scope for adopting PRP within policy parameters, but these are very broad and open to interpretation.
- greater devolution through the *Workplace Relations Act* and various types of enterprise agreements. But it is too early to say how successful this devolution is going to be.

Performance-related pay

- PRP in the APS, and particularly Centrelink as a government business enterprise, represents a duality between a return to contracts and an extension of status.
- The rhetoric of the strategic plans is resonant of extension of status (or soft HRM), as is the *Certified Agreement 1997*, which is seen as a vehicle for implementing cultural change. The CEO talks about empowering staff (extension of status), but

does not want complacent staff, who can only be identified through performance management (appraisal and performance pay).
- Team work has been introduced, to evolve into self-managing teams (extension of status), but the teams will be controlled and facilitated by management (return to contract).

Key themes in the agreement
- Teamwork
- Customer service
- Management prerogative retained
- The devolution of 'rules' from service-wide to local managers, but management prerogative retained at enterprise/workplace level—'centralised decentralism'
- Contingent pay increase at Centrelink, and contingent 'bonus' based on Centrelink-wide performance (not just at local level)
- Individual PRP still only at senior levels. However, PRP applies to all, with no increment movement if performance standards are not met Centrelink-wide.
- Openings for return to contract via the *MATE* programme at Centrelink call centres. Performance management evolving along 'team Taylorist' principles: performance data is not to be used for individual performance assessment—but then for what purpose?
- Call centre operations overseen by Centrelink Steering Committee, which is not a joint employee–management consultative committee. Employees are provided with reasons for any particular discussion, but are not involved.

Finally
- Individual performance-related pay is not extensive and still at senior officer level
- But there may be an evolutionary process at work in Centrelink—especially with the prospect of privatisation.

Notes

1 O. Hughes, *Public Management and Administration: An Introduction*, 2nd ed. (London: Macmillan, 1998).
2 C. Hood, 'A public management for all seasons?' *Public Administration*, 69:1 (1991): 3–19.
3 I. Kessler and J. Purcell, 'Performance related pay: objectives and application', *Human Resource Management Journal*, 2:3 (1992): 16–33.
4 P. Reith, *Towards a Best Practice Australian Public Service* (Canberra: Australian Government Publishing Service, 1996).
5 In June 1998 the new *Public Service Bill* was introduced into Parliament, but it has since twice been refused passage through the Senate.
6 The options for agreements included AWAs and CAs, with or without union involvement, as provided for under the *Workplace Relations Act*, 1996.
7 DEWRSB, *Australian Government Employment: Developments to Date* (Canberra: Australian Government Publishing Service, 1998). (http://www.dwrsb/gov.au/ageg)
8 D. Kemp, 'A high performance public service', address to 'Building the Momentum of APS Reform', PSMPC Lunchtime Seminar, Canberra, 3 August, 1998.
9 Centrelink, *Annual Report, 1997–98*, (Canberra: Australian Government Publishing Service, 1998).
10 S. Vardon, 'Commitment from the top: using agreements and strategic people management to achieve business goals' in *Agreement Making and Achieving Corporate Goals* (Canberra: Department of Workplace Relations and Small Business, 1998). http://www.dwrsb/gov.au/ageg
11 C. Zanetti, 'Managing change: focus on improving service quality and information management', *Australian Journal of Public Administration*, 57:4 (1998): 3–13.
12 J. Newman, *Harvard University Case Study on Centrelink* (Canberra: Minister for Family and Community Services, media release, 26 July 1998).
13 *Centrelink Development Agreement 1997–98* (Community and Public Sector Union, Media, Entertainment and Arts Alliance and Centrelink) (Sydney: Australian Industrial Relations Commission, 18 November 1997).

14 Public Sector Merit Protection Commission (1999) 'Moving to teams at Centrelink', *Better Practice Online*. http://www.psmpc.gov.au/spmonline/ teamscentrelink.htm
15 K. Murphy, 'Centrelink cuts raise fears of secret agenda to privatise', *Australian Financial Review*, 10 November 1998.

Other references

CPSU, 'Pressure leads to government meeting', *Centrelink News*, 24 November 1998. http:/www.cpsu.org.au/

CPSU, 'Positive action', *Centrelink News*, 20 November 1998. http:/www.cpsu.org.au/

CPSU, 'Centrelink job cuts and media speculation', *Centrelink News*, 6 November 1998. http:/www.cpsu.org.au/

CPSU, 'Centrelink development agreement up for renegotiation: CPSU call centre specific part of log', *Social Security Section*, 28 July 1998. http:/www.cpsu.org.au/

CPSU, 'What you want in our log of claims', *Centrelink Agreement—Bulletin No. 1: Social Security Section*, 15 July 1998. http:/www.cpsu.org.au/

DEWRSB, *Human Resource Management Framework for Corporatisation and Privatisation. Advice No. 1998/19*, 29 May 1998. http://www.dwrsb/gov.au/ageg

DEWRSB (1998) *Monitoring the Workplace Relations Act 1996: Developments.* http://www.dwrsb/gov.au/ageg

I. Kessler, 'Performance related pay: contrasting approaches', *Industrial Relations Journal*, 25:2 (1994): 122–35.

S. Vardon, 'Centrelink' in *Reforming the Public Sector: Problems and Solutions*, eds C. Clark and D. Corbett (Sydney: Allen and Unwin, 1999).

B. Yates, 'Workplace relations and agreement making in the Australian Public Service', *Australian Journal of Public Administration*, 57:2 (1998), 82–90.

World Vision Australia: a not-for-profit organisation

By **Rowan Lewis and Di Waddell**

Introduction

Overseas aid organisations are part of a larger sector referred to as the not-for-profit (NFP) sector. The NFP sector is made up of a myriad of organisations, some community-based and some sponsored by churches or philanthropic bodies, which deliver a wide range of human services to Australia and other overseas countries. It is a vast and complicated sector with many distinctive characteristics.

Presently, there are around 11 000 NFP organisations operating in Australia who receive government funding, and an unknown number of similar organisations who operate without government support.[1] The sector employs around 100 000 paid staff, while an additional 95 million hours of unpaid work is contributed by people volunteering their time and talents.[2]

The sector's size is also significant in terms of expenditure. The combined annual expenditure of NFPs in 1993–94 was $4.8 billion dollars. Its income was derived from a number of different sources, including government funding ($2.7 billion), commercial activity ($1 billion), and fund raising ($580 million).[2]

The predominant services provided include aged care, disability care, crisis accommodation, emergency relief, employment and training services, advocacy and overseas aid. These activities indicate the ideological perspective that forms the foundation of NFP organisations. NFPs are essentially stewards. Their place in society is to be the medium through which individuals, families and whole communities can gain resources (contributed by the public and private sectors) toward their betterment.[3]

Overseas aid sub-sector

Overseas aid organisations are an influential part of the greater NFP sector and are commonly referred to as non-government development organisations (NGDOs). This group of organisations is principally concerned with providing emergency relief and developmental assistance to Australia and overseas countries, as well as advocating human rights and environmental issues.[4] There are around 120 NGDOs operating in Australia, appropriating a combined income of $285 million (1993–94).[2] Worldwide, NGDOs are described as a 'significant force of international development',[2] who are contributing an estimated US$9 billion to developing countries.[5]

NGDOs differ greatly in terms of size and influence. Some NGDOs are quite large, commanding multi-million dollar budgets and employing hundreds of employees, while others are quite small, operating with less than five staff. In relation to the wider sector, four NGDOs are rated among the 50 largest NFPs in Australia.[2] World Vision Australia and CARE Australia, for example, are the two largest Australian NGDOs, achieving incomes in 1993–94 of $89 million and $44 million respectively.[2]

These larger organisations are mainly involved in long-term development projects, such as irrigation, clean water supplies, farming and community education. Because of their sheer size, networks and infrastructure, they are also able to effectively lobby international corporations and overseas governments and assist in emergency relief when disasters occur. Smaller scale organisations generally specialise in just one area of developmental assistance or advocacy, and often focus on particular countries (e.g. Sudan Interior Mission), regions (e.g. Asian Aid Organisation) or specific issues (e.g. Leprosy Mission Australia).

Funding is also a significant feature of the sub-sector. NGDOs derive their income from a number of sources, including Commonwealth Government funding ($71 million), public donations ($173 million), and other sources including international bodies and commercial operations (totalling $41 million). By international standards, the public contribution of $173 million dollars to development work rates Australia as one of the more generous countries. On the other hand, the Australian Government, with a 1993–94 budget of $1.4 billion, is only a medium-sized participant in the overseas aid arena, though its regional significance is quite important to surrounding countries like Papua New Guinea.[2,4,7]

Drivers of change

> *In the last five to ten years, the sector has been subjected to many pressures on a rapidly increasing basis which literally prejudice much of its future existence.*
>
> Wesley Central Mission, Melbourne[2]

Ideology

Aid and development work has been the focus of NGDOs for more than half a century, but there is little evidence to suggest that there has been an overall improvement in the standard of living, incidence of poverty or income distribution.[6] This lack of success has driven NGDOs to explore different approaches to aid and development work, resulting in the emergence of alternative ideologies.

Funding

Public donations and government funding are notoriously parochial.[1] Aid policies tend to change as each new government is installed, and interim alterations occur with every new budget. Public giving tends to rise and fall around significant international crises and is also influenced by the degree of media involvement

This erratic nature of funding places NGDOs in a difficult position. They are not in a position to scale down projects as funding declines, because development is a drawn-out process requiring a long-term commitment. As a consequence, many NGDOs have developed professional marketing groups aimed at 'better mobilising the donor dollar'.[1]

Accountability

The increased requirements of accountability are driving change in the aid sub-sector. This can be seen in two ways: the ethical accountability required by the public in return for their donations; and the legal obligations to the government for their funding arrangements.

Professionalism

Finally, many of the activities that are driving change also require increasing degrees of professionalism. High-level advocacy, for example, calls for a well-organised effort, carried out by a reputable organisation in a competent manner. Professional accountants are required to manage million-dollar budgets that must conform to the requirements of government accountability. Other employees are finding that they are advantaged if they work towards an MBA or come to the organisations with a number of years' private sector management experience.

Case study: World Vision Australia

World Vision Australia is part of World Vision International, a global partnership of organisations that encompass 65 national entities, established with the expressed purpose of working amongst the 'poor and oppressed', applying Christian values to promote 'human transformation'. The international partnership is made up of support offices that raise funds and co-ordinate the administration of relief programmes, as well as field offices that carry out the relief and development work. The distinction is becoming increasingly superficial as a number of field offices (e.g. Thailand, India and Philippines) are now able to raise significant funds of their own.

World Vision Australia (WVA) was established in 1966 and in the first year of operations witnessed a modest beginning, with four staff handling an income of $50 203, and a sponsorship base of 307 people. Since then, WVA has grown substantially. In the first 20 years of operations, regional offices were established in Sydney, New Zealand,[8] South Australia, and Western Australia. By the end of 1985—a year in which the Ethiopian crisis heightened international awareness of aid and development issues—WVA was appropriating an income of $30.8 million. The years spanning the 1980s and early 90s witnessed a number of tragedies and international crises. WVA, like many other NGDOs, grew steadily over this period as it worked hard to mobilise resources and respond to the needs of developing countries. In addition to the variety of emergency relief efforts co-ordinated during the period (Rumanian Child, Project Lebanon, Africa Crisis Action, Cambodian Child Survival), WVA also became quite vocal on a number of advocacy and human rights issues (paedophilia, land mines, child prostitution). Today, WVA is the largest NGDO operating in Australia, with an annual income of $98 million, 340 paid employees, more than 5000 active volunteers and many thousands of child sponsors and donors.

Background to the change

The change that occurred at World Vision is described as both a 'restructure' and 'process re-engineering' effort by interview participants. It represents the culmination of events spanning some three years. Consensus points to early 1995 as the starting point, when WVA began what was described as an 'internal drive for greater effectiveness'.

To WVA's credit, the majority of staff recognised the need for change, and were willing to actively participate. Both employees and volunteers spoke of increased competition over aid funding, diminishing domestic donations, pressure toward increased accountability (from the government and the general public), and the need for development work to maintain a multiple emphasis on community, regional, national and international issues. There was a general understanding that development is 'not what it used to be' and WVA will have to change in order to stay relevant and remain in the forefront of effective aid and development work.

In early 1995, under its former CEO, WVA embarked on a 'Future Search' programme. This was a participatory, vision-forming process, intended to prepare the WVA for the twenty-first century by identifying a picture of what the organisation needed to become. WVA identified that, in many respects, they had reached a plateau and were in danger of

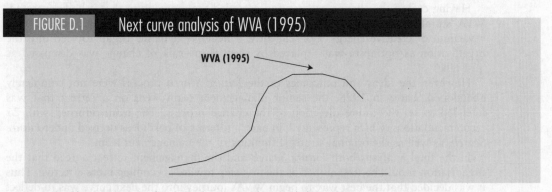

FIGURE D.1   Next curve analysis of WVA (1995)

WVA (1995)

Source: Adapted from C. Handy, *The Age of Paradox* (Paradox, Mass: Harvard Business School Press, 1994)

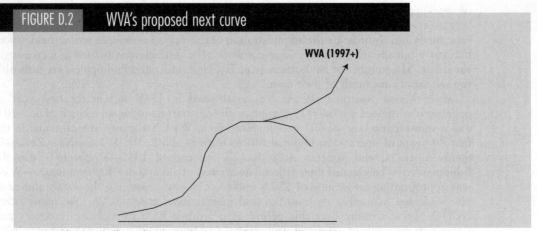

FIGURE D.2   WVA's proposed next curve

WVA (1997+)

Source: Adapted from C. Handy, *The Age of Paradox* (Paradox, Mass: Harvard Business School Press, 1994)

moving into decline (see Figure D.1). Certain fund-raising initiatives had become mature and processes were so established that no one questioned them any more. One group executive described the situation succinctly, commenting that 'the radical, thinking-at-the-fringes, questioning spirit that is the essence of 'NGO-ness' had gone from World Vision'.

The *Future Search* programme was derived from the work of Charles Handy,[9] an author who describes a process called 'next curve analysis'.[10] *Future Search* became a 'revolutionary, bottom up, participatory process' of working out how WVA can begin a new journey, on a new curve, as a new organisation (see Figure D.2). The process consisted of a variety of meetings, focus groups and retreats, all designed to encourage the staff to think creatively and adventurously about the future. What made the process unique was that, while the former CEO played an integral role, the initiative largely bypassed the senior management team and focused on middle management and staff. *Future Search* reflected the former CEO's particular vision of the future of development work. This vision described a process where the people on the ground were the voice behind the issues, and the task of management was to co-ordinate this bottom-up process.

The whole process came to a 'sticky end' in early 1996. There was a feeling among some members of the senior management team (and the Board), that the *Future Search* process was 'out of control'. While the thinking was very creative and ideas abounded, there was an opinion that expectations were too high. Many of the ideas generated were unrealistic— WVA did not have the technical or professional background to achieve some of these ideas, and others completely disregarded the business realities of public accountability and the bottom line. As a result, the senior management team, in conjunction with the Board, saw fit to resume a more directive stance of change management.

Having ceased the change process and curtailed the momentum that it had generated, WVA 'stumbled through 1996'. *Future Search* was not replaced by a new initiative, leaving a vacuum of creative energy. Consequently, a negative dynamic began to seep into the organisation as optimism was replaced by scepticism—talk of change was dismissed as 'just talk'.

However, the ideas and outcomes of the *Future Search* process were not completely abandoned. Later in 1996, the senior management team went on a retreat that was intended to set the future direction of the change process. The team returned with 21 recommendations, which represented, in part, a filtering of past ideas derived under *Future Search*, as well as the original strategic thinking of the management team.

In the final analysis, both *Future Search* and the management retreat agreed that the organisation should be streamlined as the first step towards becoming more effective. Thus it was decided that the best way to begin WVA's journey into the next curve was to deflect attention to the organisation's structure and process. To this end, a team of staff from across the organisation was established to work with external consultants on the 'restructuring' and 're-engineering' effort. This team reviewed the operations of the organisation with a mandate to improve effectiveness, efficiency, service and quality. During this time (late 1996 to early 1997) the former CEO accepted an overseas position and was replaced externally. The new CEO assumed his position with the review nearly complete, and thus began the process of implementing the change as his first major task.

Change activity

Restructure

Interview participants largely took issue with certain inefficiencies in the restructuring process that had evolved into the past structure of WVA, which had become disparate and unbalanced. There were nine key activities represented on the senior management team (including the CEO), and the marketing group in particular had grown too large and unwieldy. There was a feeling among managers that WVA was not presenting a unified front, and the present structure was stifling energy rather than releasing it.

The streamlining process began by grouping similar activities together and centralising the organisation's administrative aspects. Consequently, the senior management team was reduced from nine to six. The marketing department was essentially split three ways, with communications being linked to the bureau and the state offices co-ordinated by the operations group. Marketing has, therefore, taken on more of a corporate focus. In addition, a number of activities were rationalised or disbanded, including education services.

In line with the new structure, the review concluded that WVA could reduce its staffing levels by 45 full-time positions and still remain equally effective. This recommendation was accepted with the understanding that, as far as possible, this target should be reached through natural attrition. To date, the target has not been reached and management has made 25 staff redundant in the months subsequent to the restructuring. These redundancies were normally linked with areas that were disbanded, or projects that had reached completion and were not renewed.

In order to combat the negativity and uncertainty that can be associated with 'down-sizing', WVA have embarked on a unique exercise called 'Motivate and Move'. *Motivate and Move* is a career development programme that is designed to encourage staff to think about what they can achieve as part of their career, either inside WVA or outside in another place of employment. Through this programme (which employees join voluntarily), WVA is attempting to mobilise staff, filling out the new structure internally, and if some people find work outside the organisation, then WVA is able to downsize through attrition and not redundancy. From a management perspective, the idea is to invest heavily in the 'front end' of downsizing, equipping and developing staff now, in lieu of redundancy pay-outs at the end if targets are not met through attrition.

Re-engineering

The re-engineering process focused on a number of areas that could be automated, or treated as cost-centres. Processes such as donor support management and receipting were targeted as manual activities that could be automated. Non-value-adding areas such as publications were similarly marked for rationalisation, or reoriented so that they could prove their financial contribution to the organisation. Updating the computer system was also recommended to reduce inefficiencies as well as facilitating compatibility with other World Vision partners.

At the time of interview, this aspect of the change was still being implemented, as attention had initially been focused on structural issues. However, the apparent commercial flavour of many of the recommendations has caused some contention in the organisation. Staff who argue that it has no place in NFP organisations have objected to the bottom-line mentality.

Modular Transformation

A modular transformation is a scale of change where the organisation seeks to gain the voluntary commitment of employees to a radical new vision that requires significant re-interpretation or revision of core values. This degree of change described the experience of WVA for three reasons:

1 the restructuring process was quite large and traumatic
2 the process was handled very quickly and decisively
3 fundamental values were affected by the change.

First, the restructuring was quite large and affected almost all aspects of the organisation. There was hardly a job or person that did not feel the effects of the change, as reporting relationships were altered, budgets reallocated and offices moved. Second, WVA's change was also transformational by virtue of its decisive nature.

This decisive implementation of change was chosen by the senior management team because they perceived the organisation as being 'sick' of change. The demise of *Future Search* had left the organisation sapped of energy and cynical of change. By acting quickly and decisively, it was hoped that the change could be implemented, and the organisation achieve closure on the preceding three years.

Finally, the scale of change was considered to be modular because the core values of the organisation were affected by the change. WVA is firmly grounded on seven core values, which, according to one group executive, are 'sacred and will never be altered'. However, the emphasis placed on the restructuring and re-engineering has certainly led to a re-interpretation of these core values, particularly with respect to matters of 'efficiency' and the 'bottom line'. In particular, the core value of 'people' has become the object of considerable contention, given the downsizing undertaken by WVA and the subsequent redundancies that occurred. While one perspective argues that the process of downsizing is definitely contradictory to this core value, others suggest that the value has simply been reinterpreted. This later perspective points out that the increasing demands of accountability require that the core value of 'people' be interpreted in a wider context. WVA is accountable for 'valuing' not only the employees who work in Australia, but also the various donors who contribute funds, not to mention the overseas recipients of these resources. This split accountability creates a need for values to be prioritised and hard decisions made.

Directive

Analysis of the style of change management indicates that it was handled in a directive manner by senior management through a process that was top-down and which largely excluded employees from participation. Even though the review was intended to be participative in nature (insofar as it involved middle management and line staff), the feeling across the organisation was that staff were neither 'involved nor engaged in the process'. While WVA did utilise some participative mechanisms, such as circulating a summary of the review's recommendations and encouraging response, middle management and staff felt that, despite these measures, they were still not able to effectively influence the final outcomes.

Senior management acknowledged the directive style with which the change was handled and indicated that it was a deliberate choice. They point out that part of the change process was making some very difficult decisions that did not lend themselves to collaborative decision making. If they did handle the process in a more participative manner, it would probably have drawn out the change process even further, and that would have been untenable.

In many ways, the last three years has witnessed WVA come full circle in its management of change. From the vision-finding participative nature of *Future Search*, the organisation has finally implemented structural change in a top-down manner. The process, however, continues, as the organisation settles and consolidates into its new structure. Both management and staff recognise this process as more participative in nature, with both parties actively contributing to the process.

Evaluation

WVA's method of change management would be classified by the operational definition as directive and transformational, which is the opposite of the method suggested by such authors as Dunphy and Stace.[11,12] Similarly, the organisation does not provide a great deal of support for the result derived from the data analysis, which found that NFP organisations prefer to manage change participatively, regardless of whether the change is transformational or incremental.

The interviews at WVA were being conducted at the time of restructuring and six months afterwards. The earlier interviews conveyed a positive feeling of anticipation. Staff members spoke of the 'change process going on for long enough' and the loss of momentum was keenly felt. It was time to have a decision made that would 'get the organisation moving once again'. Six months later, the 'mood' of the organisation was substantially different. Morale was variously described as 'flat', 'uncertain' and 'patchy'. One group executive described it as 'low ... perhaps the lowest ever'. Such a stark change in morale can be interpreted in a number of ways. One could conclude that the change process was poorly managed, or alternatively that the organisation had not really had enough time to settle and redevelop routines. Either way, managers and employees alike have levelled a number of criticisms at the change process.

Employee participation

The strongest criticism surrounds the lack of employee participation allowed by senior management during the change process. In part, this criticism is not justified. The management team did put in place a number of structures that allowed employees to participate in the process. Apart from the review team, made up of employees from across the organisation, a summary of the recommendations of the review process was circulated, comments and feedback invited and each was responded to individually. However, the criticism does point out, and management (to their credit) recognises, that these participative structures were not enough. The process failed to be participatory as employees felt themselves to be neither engaged nor able to influence outcomes.

Interestingly, when this kind of criticism was raised, it was clear that employees were not objecting to the fact that final decisions were made by senior management. The comments seemed to indicate that the participation sought was simply involvement in the overall process. There was an understanding in the organisation that, given the size of WVA, not all decisions can be made collaboratively, and that there are occasions when it is appropriate for the leadership of the organisation to step in and make decisions.

Efficiency

Another contentious issue for WVA was the drive for efficiency, and the resultant bottom-line orientation of many of the changes. While certain members of the management team stand by this developing commercial orientation, others have described it as 'fundamentally flawed'. In part, the debate is philosophically based. One manager considered this commercial orientation as being incompatible with the values of NFPs, and especially NGDOs. The manager strongly disagreed with the incessant drive to attach performance indicators to every aspect of the organisation, thereby only evaluating activities in terms of costs and value. These sentiments were echoed by a number of people who were concerned that the change may disaffect the 'NGDO-ness' of WVA, even though it may improve its overall effectiveness.

However, those who stand by these changes contend that they are not at odds with the fact that WVA is an NGDO, but rather that they are a necessary reinterpretation of core values, given the demands of the present environment. An example of this reinterpretation applies to the core value of stewardship, which has been a foundation of WVA's work and is one of the organisation's core values. A critical function of the organisation is its role as a medium through which resources are redirected from those who have plenty to those who are in need. However, the growing demands for NGDO accountability have led to a certain reinterpretation of WVA's role as a steward. It is no longer enough simply to work towards the achievement of basic rights for individuals. Accountability requirements now demand that they be championed as efficiently as possible. While some would argue that it is inappropriate to attach a dollar value to human dignity, others point out that the ends justify the means—it is not such a bad thing to be required to achieve the most good for the least amount of money.

The outcome of this drive toward greater efficiency and effectiveness has led to the trimming down, and streamlining of, the organisation. However, 'getting to the fat' has proved to be difficult, as NGDOs traditionally operate with a lean administrative structure and WVA is no exception. There is a mixed evaluation of this particular issue. There is some agreement that, in terms of the overall structure, the change was effective, as non-core activities were dropped. Most contention arose from the issue of staffing levels.

The review process had identified that the organisation could still remain effective with 45 fewer staff. WVA's response to this recommendation was to accept this target, but aim to achieve it through natural attrition and the *Motivate and Move* programme. The response to this has been mixed. The organisation is obviously benefiting from staff going through this development programme, and it is also encouraging staff to think bigger than just WVA. However, the programme does present an ambiguous message that can be misunderstood by staff.

Interestingly, the decision to downsize this way did not lead to more confidence in senior management. Rather, it caused a degree of uncertainty in the organisation as employees wondered whether their jobs were among those targeted for reduction. Furthermore, natural attrition and the *Motivate and Move* programme tend to encourage the most skilled and mobile staff members to leave, potentially leaving behind the 'fat'. Thus, it seems that by trying to downsize humanely, the process backfired and WVA retains an uncertain working environment that has not effectively removed the pockets of inefficiency.

Vision

Aside from these streamlining issues, restructuring also has a number of subtle implications, which the WVA management is only now beginning to realise. One is that, restructuring either confirms or denies where various activities rate in the organisation's future vision.

Such was the case with the review's treatment of the Education and advocacy section. It recommended that this section be disbanded, mainly because it could not be justified as a value-adding aspect of the organisation. The recommendation was accepted, implemented and, needless to say, caused much disputation amongst staff. Some consider public education to be an integral part of development, as, in their view, the task of any NGDO is to balance advocacy and education so that the public's thinking about issues of poverty and injustice are challenged. The outcome of the restructuring process, however, suggested that WVA is trying to effect change by focusing on high-level advocacy instead of community education. Thus, it is apparent that, although the restructuring process focuses directly on practical issues, it implicitly affects matters of vision and ideology. Given that the visions and missions of NGDOs are based on an ideological or moral position, restructuring can influence the scale of change because, by implication, it can alter this position.

In the case of WVA, this point is critical. Essentially, the whole process began with the question, 'What is WVA, and what do we need to become in order to thrive in the twenty-first century?'. This is a question of ideology and vision, but the change process answered it in pragmatic terms, redefining the organisation's ideology and vision through changes in structure and process. If this method of change is likened to building a house, then the process effectively designed and built the dwelling without giving prior thought to the foundation. Interestingly, vision was identified (in retrospect) by a number of managers as the missing ingredient in the change process, and perhaps the crucial element that might once again get WVA 'moving'.

It seems that WVA has difficulty in restoring stability and momentum to the organisation because it has handled the change directively, without first clarifying its vision. Further, the commercial nature of the re-engineering process has introduced a new dynamic that has met with mixed support. As a result, the original question, 'What is World Vision?', has not been clarified, and the subsequent question, 'What do we need to become in order to thrive in the twenty-first century?' also remains unresolved.

Further, it should be kept in mind that WVA has barely completed its change process and is currently consolidating the new structure. However, the highlighted criticisms are still pertinent. With the benefit of hindsight, almost all the senior management team commented that they would have done some things differently, and some wonder what would have happened if the *Future Search* process had been followed through to fruition.

Discussion

The participation dilemma

The degree of employee participation is more of a defining factor in NGDO change management than is the scale of change. It was apparent that employee participation was the most problematic aspect of change. This alludes to a common problem—setting the 'boundaries of participation'. By 'participation boundaries' is meant the limitations set in place by management to circumscribe the discretion of employees.

The three-year process of change at WVA witnessed the use of very different types of boundaries. The *Future Search* programme had been almost unbounded, with very few parameters being defined. Employees had been actively encouraged to think adventurously about the future and disregard present realities. This process never reached fruition as it was replaced by a review and restructuring process with strict boundaries. The employees' only opportunity for participation was an invitation to comment on the overall recommendations derived from the review process.

Whether or not this directive management style came as a direct response to the collaborative nature of *Future Search* is irrelevant. What is pertinent is that, in retrospect, a number of senior managers now consider the boundaries to have been too high. They recognise that the employees were not given enough opportunity to contribute to the review and, consequently, were not engaged in the change process. This is now seen to be a key factor leading to today's low morale.

Employee participation is something of a balancing act. If the process is too closely circumscribed, employees are not engaged and perceive the result as a foregone conclusion. By leaving the process unbounded, employees may act in ignorance and contribute irrelevantly. Consequently, boundary setting forms one aspect of the participation dilemma.

A second aspect concerns the dynamic nature of the participation process. Interestingly, members from both organisations indicated that they did not want a collaborative process. Rather, they agreed that it was appropriate for senior management to make the final decisions on the outcomes of change. Those interviewed spoke of dual management requirements—of leading from the front and leading from behind. Each was seen to be appropriate, according to the situation. This is perhaps responsible for the position that WVA is now in. It is struggling to leave the change behind, demonstrating the dynamic nature of participation.

In summary, the task of managing participation requires:

- setting appropriate boundaries in order to maximise the potential of employee participation (not necessarily the degree of employee participation). This aspect is relative to the organisation in question, and will be discussed later in this section.
- ensuring that the process of review and change is sensitive to these boundaries. This ensures that any contribution made by employees is appropriate and able to be fully utilised by those making the final decision for change.
- treating these boundaries as dynamic, adjusting them across the change process as managers are variously required to lead from the front and from behind. Again, this

must be treated as relative to each organisation's situation. For example, it may be necessary for a strong lead on the part of management in the initial stages of the change process, so that staff members appreciate the need to change and consequently contribute to the process.

The role of vision, mission and ideology

The struggles encountered by an organisation in regard to its vision, mission and ideology is another key issue highlighted by this study. The case study described how WVA disregarded these matters in the process of change, possibly to its detriment. There appears to be a curious dynamic between the restructuring/re-engineering process and the organisation's vision, mission and ideology[13] that warrants further discussion.

Managers identify questions of philosophy as the driving force behind the eventual change. Much of the activity of the last two to three years can be viewed as attempts to answer the two classic questions: 'What kind of organisation are we?' and 'What kind organisation do we need to become?'

Initially, WVA addressed these questions directly through *Future Search*. In the end, however, it achieved change through the reverse process, defining processes and structures first and worrying about philosophy second. This link between organisational structure, process and philosophy becomes clearer when the definition of NGDOs is taken into consideration—NGDOs can only be clearly identified by the values that form their foundation. Structures and processes are the means by which these values are attained. If a NGDO changes its structures and processes, it changes the means by which it achieves its founding values, implicitly emphasising one philosophy and de-emphasising another. While the link is indirect, the evidence gathered during this study suggest that it is quite strong. Consequently, managers must be aware that even the most practical of changes may carry implications that reach far deeper, and which greatly elevate the scale of change. An organisation must be sensitive to this in order to avoid contention, or at least utilise it effectively.

Employee participation and organisational philosophy

It is the opinion of the authors that this structure-process-philosophy link also impacts on the participation dilemma. In essence, it provides a mandate that change in NGDOs be managed participatively. The reasoning behind this assertion, which is largely derived from the case study, is as follows.

The majority of employees found in NGDOs work there because they identify with the values for which the organisation stands. Money is not the sole motivating factor as was indicated by a number of interviewees. Given this orientation, the worker is greatly affected by a restructuring process that alters the compatibility of values that had previously existed. If the dissonance between the employee's values and the organisation's new philosophy is too great, it may be reason to leave the organisation and seek employment or volunteer work elsewhere.

This factor greatly increases the importance of carefully managing employee participation in an NGDO change process. People do not change their values overnight. The values may evolve over time, but their development is gradual, and participation can play an integral part in this development. Through the process of discussion and debate, new insight can be attained and a consensus possibly reached. Arguably, this process offers a better chance of ensuring success than does a directive style that gives employees no opportunity to influence the values of the new organisation.

Change management evaluation

The change effort at WVA represented a process that went against the social orientation of NGDOs. Management chose to directively lead from the front, while the commercial nature of the change subordinated (or 'reinterpreted') many of the core values to matters of efficiency. These aspects cannot be ignored as they would have influenced the resultant low morale, and help to explain the organisation's current difficulties.

WVA now has the common problem of operating with an ill-defined vision, mission and ideology simply because they were ignored during the change process, and had consequently evolved by implication.

Without the benefit of specific information with which to evaluate the organisation (e.g. business performance indicators or measures of job satisfaction), it is difficult to make a reliable assessment. What can be observed, however, is that WVA members now comment that if they had their time over again, they would manage the change process differently.

QUESTIONS

1 How would World Vision Australia compare with a 'profit' organisation?
2 Categorise and discuss WVA's change management against Dunphy and Stace's (1990) *Change Matrix*[11] and operational definitions.

Notes

1 ACOSS, *ACOSS Response to Industry Commission Inquiry Into Charitable Organisations Draft Report* (Sydney: ACOSS, 1995).
2 A. McNair, 'Charitable organisations in Australia' in *Industry Commission Inquiry Into Charitable Organisations Draft Report* (Melbourne: Australian Government Printing Service, 1994)
3 M. McAllister, 'The non-government sector: roles and future roles' in *NGOs Facing Tomorrow* (Sydney: ACOSS, 1981).
4 AusAID, *Review of the Effectiveness of NGO Programmes* (Canberra: Goanna Print, 1995).
5 I. Smillie and H. Helmich, *Non-Governmental Organisations into Development Agencies* (Paris: OECD, 1993).
6 ACOSS, *Australian Attitudes to Overseas Aid* (Canberra: ACFOA, 1997).
7 Government funding is carried out through the Australian Agency for International Development (AusAID). It comes under the auspice of the Department of Foreign Affairs and forms part of the portfolio of the Minister of Development Co-operation and Pacific Island Affairs. Prior to 29 March 1995 the agency was called the Australian International Development Assistance Bureau (AIDAB).
8 The New Zealand office became an independent entity in 1974.
9 C. Handy, *The Age of Paradox* (Massachusetts: Harvard Business School Press, 1994).
10 The process is very similar to product life-cycle mapping, and has been transferred to organisational strategic planning by such authors as Handy (1994:49) and Robbins and Mukerji (1990:97).
11 D. Dunphy and D. Stace, *Under New Management* (Sydney: McGraw Hill, 1990).
12 D. Dunphy and D. Stace, *Beyond the Boundaries* (Sydney: McGraw Hill, 1994).
13 For the sake of simplicity, vision, mission and ideology will be collectively referred to as the organisation's 'philosophy'.

Other references

B. Burnes, *Managing Change* (London: Pitman, 1996).
K. Feinstein, 'Innovative management in turbulent times: large scale agency change', *Administration in Social Work*, 9:3 (Fall, 1985): 35–46.
J. Henderson-Loney, 'Shared leadership: a new model for the next century', *Nonprofit World*, 14:5 (1996): 40–42.
Industry Commission, *Charitable Organisations in Australia* (Melbourne: Australian Government Printing Service, 1995).
A. Kadushin, *Supervision in Social Work* (New York: Columbia University Press, 1976).
R. Kay, 'Leadership in voluntary organisations' in *Voluntary Agencies,* eds D. Billis and M. Harris (London: MacMillan, 1996).
R. Maurer, 'Using resistance to build support for change', *Journal for Quality and Participation*, 19:3 (June 1996): 56–63.
S. Robbins and D. Mukerji, *Managing Organisations: New Challenges and Perspectives* (Sydney: Prentice Hall, 1994).

R. Weinbach, *The Social Worker as Manager* (Needham Heights, MA: Allyn & Bacon, 1994).

D. Wilson, 'How do voluntary agencies manage organisational change?' in *Voluntary Agencies*, eds D. Billis and M. Harris (London: MacMillan, 1996).

World Vision Staff Manual (World Vision Australia).

D. Young, *Casebook of Management for Nonprofit Organizations* (New York: Haworth Press, 1985).

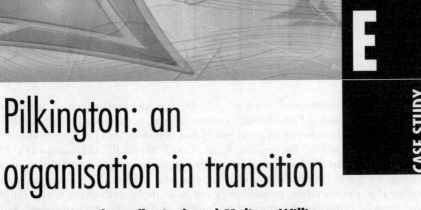

Pilkington: an organisation in transition

By **Brendan Barrett, Chantelle Cook and Melissa Williams**

Introduction

Pilkington is a multinational glass manufacturer, known worldwide for its superior quality. The organisation is divided into three specialised areas—automotive, building and corporate. Even though Pilkington has traditionally dominated the float glass process, a number of internal problems and pressures from overseas competitors has given rise to the need for change.

Pilkington's change process involved three distinct phases. Phase 1 was initiated partly because of the changes in Australia's wage policies. Despite good intentions, Pilkington's first enterprise agreement, which provided employees with increases of $30–$35 over 12 months,[1] eventually failed because 'both parties become fed up with fighting each other'. However, the initial change process also resulted in a significant redesign of Pilkington's formal structure, which indirectly affected other elements of the organisation. For example, the introduction of teams led to the creation of a more co-operative environment and organisational culture.

Although substantial progress was made in the initial change process, there were still many 'problems' that continued to obstruct the implementation of the proposed changes, and these resulted in a second round of changes in November 1995 and finally a third attempt at organisational change in November 1996. Not surprisingly, in the 1998 *Annual Report*,[2] the chairman of Pilkington, Sir Nigel Rudd, stated that the costs of the organisational change had been significant (£225 million), because the 'rationalisation programmes were more widespread and the job redundancies greater than originally expected'.

Brief history

Pilkington Australasia is a wholly owned subsidiary of the British Pilkington plc, known as one of the oldest and most respected glass makers in the world.[3] Pilkington glass was first sold on the Australian market in 1858. The introduction of Pilkington's float glass plant at Dandenong (Victoria) in 1972 began a revolution in glass manufacturing. The float process eliminated the distortion that had been characteristic of the traditional plate and sheet glass. Despite the extensive operations in Australia, it was not until 1988 that Pilkington Australia severed its ties with Pilkington ACI and became a wholly owned subsidiary of Pilkington plc.[3]

The industry

The glass industry has developed significantly since Pilkington first arrived in Australia. Today there is a range of glass products (such as clear and tinted float glass, wired and decorative glass and mirror glass). Consequently, Pilkington has expanded its operations to include value-added products and services, such as the supply, merchandising and installation of glass for a multitude of domestic and commercial markets. The predominant markets that Pilkington serve are the building and automotive industries, although this is expanding to include the special energy and electronic markets. The demand for glass is so intense that production occurs at Pilkington 24 hours a day, seven days a week.[4]

Business policies

Pilkington has implemented various policies that demonstrate its commitment to a broader range of issues. These include environmental, occupational health and safety and quality policies. Their environmental policy has demonstrated the respect that Pilkington has for all elements of the environment. Geoff Marshall, the company's Managing Director, stated that environmental issues are regularly discussed at all levels of the group in order to maintain high standards of business ethics.[3] The environmental policy specifies that the recycling programmes are to comply with plant waste minimisation plans, thereby reducing the amount of landfill and natural gas consumed in the float glass factories.[5]

The occupational health and safety policy reflects Pilkington's concern for workplace safety. This policy has emphasised workplace reforms that originated as a result of the fatal accident of an employee.[6] As a result of the accident, the policy states that safety in the workplace is a 'shared responsibility' between management and employees, and that in order to maintain a safe environment there must be mutual respect for one another.[3]

The third policy relates to the quality of all Pilkington products. A number of technological advancements have been made over the past decades, and all staff have been encouraged to commit themselves to Pilkington's quality programmes. As a result Pilkington's quality certification standard, AS 3092, is adhered to at all times, thus ensuring that the organisation consistently performs at a high standard and uses reliable work methods. In 1993, Geoff Marshall made it clear that quality would be a prime consideration in all managerial decisions. The fact that Pilkington currently supplies glass for all Australian-manufactured Toyotas suggests that their underlying quality initiatives have and will continue to pay off.[7]

The need for change

Up until the late 1980s, Pilkington enjoyed a virtual monopoly in the glass manufacturing arena. For years the Dandenong site provided a 'cash cow' for both management and employees.[1]

A combination of both external (environmental) and internal (organisational) forces moved Pilkington towards widespread organisational change. Externally, the increasing levels of foreign competition primarily highlighted the need for change. The reduction of tariffs and import quota levels, as part of the *General Agreement on Tariffs and Trade* (GATT), had suddenly allowed countries such as Germany, China and India to compete effectively in the global marketplace.[8] Glass manufacturers in these countries were producing at low costs, causing Pilkington difficulties in meeting international price levels.

A number of internal factors also encouraged management to consider the implementation of widespread organisational change. Traditionally Pilkington had employed a work force that was relatively old (the average age prior to the change was between 48 and 50). In addition, these workers had created a culture of 'expected overtime'. Consequently, overtime accounted for a massive 70% of payroll in some departments.[1] Thus, although most of the workers thought that Pilkington was a good place to work, management could see that such practice could not continue if the organisation was going to continue to produce 'world class glass'[3] and be profitable at the same time.

Culture

Organisational culture refers to the core values that are shared by the majority of organisational members.[9] As in many organisational changes, one of Pilkington's greatest challenges was to re-create its organisational culture.

A major concern for management was the tendency for employees to 'go slow', so that they would be required to stay back, work overtime and get paid more.[4] By doing this, Pilkington employees were not only restricting the plant's output, but also drawing larger pay packets for work that should have been completed in much less time.

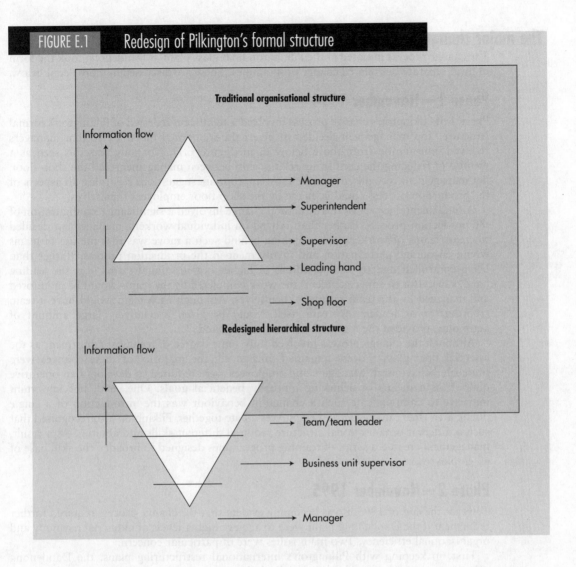

FIGURE E.1 Redesign of Pilkington's formal structure

This 'overtime' culture was strengthened by strong group norms. It is well known that groups of workers exert, at least to some degree, pressure on individuals who do not conform to the majority view.[10] Thus, it is likely that the employees who were accumulating overtime hours actively encouraged other workers to do the same.

Organisational structure: the underlying problem

The cultural characteristics of Pilkington prior to the change represented a 'symptom' of a deeper underlying 'problem'. From an extremely simplistic viewpoint, Pilkington's essential problem lay in its organisational structure. Traditionally the Dandenong float glass plant had relied on a hierarchical structure where top management set performance standards and objectives and disseminated them down the 'ranks' to the shop floor (Figure E.1). This type of organisational structure promoted downward communication only and, as a result, many employees felt as though they were being instructed by managers who knew little or nothing about day-to-day operations. Such an autocratic management stance encouraged the development of a conflictual relationship between management and employees. As a result there was a strong 'them vs us' culture that contributed to low levels of employee morale and commitment.[4]

The major change processes

The change process initiated at the Pilkington float glass plant at Dandenong took the form of three separate but related change programmes. These are discussed in more detail below.

Phase 1—November 1994

Phase 1 of Pilkington's change process involved a significant redesign of Pilkington's formal structure. Top management decided to invert the traditional hierarchy so that managers received information from those below them (Figure E.1). Not only was this seen as a method of reducing the conflicting relationship between management and the shop floor, but management recognised that the most appropriate suggestions regarding all aspects of the production process could be made by the shop floor employees themselves.

A fundamental aspect of this structural change involved a significant reconfiguration of the production process. Rather than relying on individual workers, management decided to create teams of workers.[4] The thinking behind such a move was that the use of teams would encourage participation and involvement in the production process. Rather than being controlled directly by individuals of higher organisational status (e.g. the leading hand, supervisor or superintendent) the work completed by the teams would be monitored and managed by the team members themselves. Although each team would have a team co-ordinator or leader, the team itself would be given a relatively large amount of autonomy, provided the required work was completed.

Although the change process involved only some degree of technical adjustment as the essential float glass process remained unchanged, the majority of these changes were primarily behavioural. Managers and employees were required to develop a co-operative outlook as a means of achieving mutually beneficial goals. One small but important initiative to communicate such a change in behaviour was the introduction of a single dining area where managers and employees all ate together. Pilkington also recognised that such a different organisational structure required different skills and abilities. As a result, management created a series of training programmes designed to broaden the skill base of all employees.[3]

Phase 2—November 1995

Towards the end of 1995 it was becoming evident that the change process required further refinement if the Dandenong plant were to achieve higher levels of industrial harmony and organisational efficiency. Two main issues were of particular concern.

First, in keeping with Pilkington's international restructuring plans, the Dandenong plant was required to implement a radical change programme in a short period of time. Due to their time constraint, management saw little scope for employee involvement in the change process. However, while such 'directive approach'[11] proved relatively successful, it was met with widespread employee resistance. To combat employee grievances, Pilkington formulated the *Stage II Enterprise Agreement* which, among other things, recommended moves towards a more consultative process between management and employees.

The second issue of concern related to the training programmes. Under the initial change programme, employees had been required to undertake training in order to become multi-skilled. The main problem with this initiative was that employees were being trained in areas that were not relevant to their positions as they already had the required skills to operate the production equipment.[12] Consequently, under the second *Enterprise Agreement*, management removed many of the training programmes that had been established under the initial change programme.

As time progressed, employees became more and more disgruntled with the approach adopted by management. In late 1995 the Australian Workers Union organised a staff strike in order to protest against management's 'bulldozer' attitude to organisational restructuring. Employees caused the entire Dandenong plant to shut down for ten consecutive days, costing the organisation an estimated $10 million dollars in lost sales.[12]

Phase 3—December 1996

The strike caused management great concern. At the beginning of 1996 a group of six management staff embarked on a comprehensive review of Pilkington's overseas glass plants.[12] At the conclusion of this exercise, the 'World Best Practice Group' produced a report labelled 'The need for change' (April 1996). This report formed the basis of Pilkington's *Enterprise Bargaining Agreement III*.[5]

The objective of this agreement was to 'fundamentally change the work place environment through introducing work practices ... and remuneration systems which remove barriers and obstacles to change and positively encourage work place reforms and continuous improvement'.[5] The third *Enterprise Agreement* was therefore more comprehensive than any of the previous agreements, and introduced a wider variety of changes.

The main focus of the report was to clarify the organisational structure at the Dandenong plant. The 1996 *Enterprise Agreement* specifically:

- provided that float glass operations would be conducted by a total of 17 different teams, all of which were to be organised under one of three business unit groups (glass making, on-line cutting and stacking and warehousing). Communication would flow from the team leaders to the team supervisors, through the business group managers and finally onto the plant manager.
- outlined general business unit goals and targets
- defined team activities, goals and performance measures and related these to the business requirements of the group
- specified the objectives of each business unit, the number of people required in each business unit, the physical boundaries for each team and the required inputs and outputs.

A number of organisational processes were further developed by the agreement. The report reinforced the *Total Productive Maintenance* (TPM) concept, whereby those people who operate the equipment are presumed to know it best. In addition, the agreement rescinded all previous limitations placed on training programmes. Thus, management agreed to reintroduce employee training in an effort to develop a more highly skilled work force that could better satisfy the needs of the business.

Finally, the new agreement also introduced a number of policies regarding the behaviour of employees. A comprehensive disciplinary procedure was formulated[5] and all employees were informed of the types of behaviour that would result in instant dismissal. Furthermore, a formal Pilkington Safety Policy[5] was established and distributed among the workers.

Evaluation of the change process

Pilkington designed evaluation criteria at the beginning of each change phase as part of its aim of continuous improvement.[4] A mixture of both humanistic and financial indicators were established to measure these criteria and, hence, the effectiveness of the change.

Employee morale

As part of the changes made in Phase 1, performance in this area was to be determined by the indicators of industrial harmony (number of strikes), absenteeism and labour turnover.[4] In terms of results, these indicators portrayed mixed signals. Labour turnover was stable with only one small strike in the year prior to 1995.[4] However, over the period from 1995 to 1997 employee numbers were reduced by 27%. In view of this, Pilkington maintained a relatively good level of industrial harmony. However, management was concerned with the high rate of absenteeism, which stood at 5.8%.[4]

Productivity

This criterion was to be measured by taking into account factors such as the cost of manufacturing, market prices, return on investment and profit levels. Results for these indicators present a deceiving picture. A 31% turnaround in profits was achieved,[4] but this figure may well have been assisted by 'falling prices', which were brought about by a reduction in manufacturing costs. Thus, return on investment, which at that time was approximately 6%, was clearly falling well short of the projected 25% ROI figure.[4]

Quality

Pilkington uses regular customer satisfaction surveys to gauge the quality standard of its products. Results after assessment of the first change showed an impressive customer satisfaction rate of 97%.[4] This customer satisfaction rate clearly shows that Pilkington was adhering strictly to its internal quality policy, which listed in detail the quality practices to be employed throughout the entire manufacturing process.

Safety

In Phase 2 of the change process, Pilkington improved its evaluation criteria to include measurable targets and outcomes.[12] Safety performance was simply measured by lost time due to work place injuries. At the beginning of the change in November 1995, the float section had recorded an average of 3.8 injuries that resulted in three or more lost workdays.[13] A subsequent target of one lost work day was set for the 1997/98 period, but to the surprise of management not one employee was injured at work over that period. On the process side, the results were also positive. In the 1997/98 period the average time lost due to injury was 1.6 days, whereas in the 1995/96 period lost time due to injury had been 5.5 days.[13] These figures indicate that Pilkington was taking its safety policy more seriously and that it was obviously communicating these policies more effectively to all employees.

Cost per tonne

In order to maximise profits, Pilkington decided to reduce the cost per tonne of the product. Manufacturing, distribution and administration costs were all used to indicate Pilkington's performance in this area. Since 1995/96 Pilkington had managed to lower manufacturing costs from $463 to $413 per tonne in 1997/98. Distribution costs were also reduced from $35 to $27 per tonne, as were the associated administrative costs (from $24 to $12 per tonne). These figures show that Pilkington had managed to lower both manufacturing and distribution costs to better than targeted levels.[13]

Employee productivity

Output per employee was the indicator for this criterion and the results were very positive for Pilkington. There was an improvement of 46.5% in 1996/97 over the 1995/96 figures and a further 42% increase in 1997/98 over the 1996/97 statistics.[13] With current employee productivity hovering on 51.7 units per employee, Pilkington is well above its target of 46.7 units per employee.[13]

Conclusion

Widespread corporate reorganisation has definitely made Pilkington Australia a much stronger international glass manufacturer. Many procedural inefficiencies, brought about by the different practices, processes and standards introduced into the group's operations by the large number of acquisitions made in the years prior to the 1980s,[2] have been minimised or removed altogether. The roles of managers and employees have been clarified, and improvements are already evidenced by the standardised manufacturing equipment and centralised purchasing functions.

Nevertheless, the future for Pilkington still holds many challenges. Budgetary constraints, which have become particularly tight during the change process, mean that management, the union and all employees will have to concentrate on establishing and maintaining co-operative agreements. Although the plant is coming to the final stages of the change process, all the staff members are still adjusting to the massive structural amendments that have been made since 1994. While it is clear that the organisational culture has shifted from a conflicting to a co-operative one, it will be many years before the cultural environment truly reflects the structural characteristics of the organisation.

QUESTIONS

1 What type of change is being introduced at Pilkington?

2 What factors moved Pilkington towards change?

3 Explain how Pilkington can ensure that the changes made remain in place.

4 What role did organisational structure play in the change process? Could Pilkington have fixed its 'problems' without changing the structure of the organisation?

5 Describe the methods or techniques that Pilkington's change agents used to implement the change process.

6 What criteria did Pilkington set up to evaluate the change process? In hindsight were they appropriate?

7 Why was there initial resistance to change, and how was this overcome?

8 How does the Action Research Model[14] apply to the change process at Pilkington?

9 Can you identify any issues that Pilkington should consider in the future? Will Pilkington have to make any other organisational changes?

Notes

1 L. Simonelli, 'The changing of a 'cash cow' culture to one of a competitive business', *IRM*, (May 1997).

2 Pilkington, *Annual Reports* (1997, 1998).

3 Pilkington, *Information Pack* (1995).

4 D. Patton (Human resources manager at the Dandenong plant), interview, 24 May 1995.

5 Pilkington (Australia) Operations Ltd, *Glass Operations Float (Dandenong) Enterprise Bargaining Agreement Stage III* (Australian Industrial Relations Commission, 1996): 27.

6 V. Trioli, 'Dying at work—Victoria's cheap justice', *The Age* (11 September 1995): 1.

7 R. Gottliebsen, 'First glimpses of the new era', *Business Review Weekly*, (11 September 1995): 6.

8 D. Mahoney, M. Trigg, R. Griffin and M. Putsay, *International Business: A Management Perspective* (Sydney: Longman Australia, 1998).

9 S. Robbins and N. Barnwell, *Organisational Theory In Australia*, 2nd ed. (Sydney: Prentice Hall, 1994): 376.

10 See, for example, D. Feldman, 'The development and enforcement of group norms', *Academy Of Management Review*, 9:2 (1984); S. Asch, 'Studies of independence and conformity: a minority of one against an unanimous majority', *Psychological Monographs*, 70:9 (1956).

11 D. Dunphy and D. Stace, *Under New Management: Australian Organisations In Transition*, (Roseville, NSW: McGraw Hill, 1990): Chapter 4.

12 D. Cook (Employee relations manager at the Dandenong plant), interview, 7 October 1998.

13 Pilkington, *Presentation Slides* (1998).

14 D. Harvey and D. Brown, *An Experimental Approach To Organization Development*, 5th ed., (USA: Prentice Hall, 1996), 46.

Other reference

http://www.pilkington.com

Water industry reform — stopping the leaking tap?

By **Amanda Pyman, Ivan Mathieson, Alec Craig and Kathleen Doherty**

Introduction

In 1995, the Victorian State Government, under statute, amalgamated 21 water and waste water authorities in the Wimmera-Mallee region of Victoria to form Grampians Water. Acting independently of the government, most of the original authorities had been run by boards of locally elected volunteers. In some instances this had occurred for up to 80 years. Therefore, the amalgamation in 1995 was a dramatic and abrupt change to what the community were accustomed. As the sole shareholder, the government appointed eight directors to the board to run the newly formed entity on its behalf.

More recently, in 1997, further changes at Grampians Water have resulted in the negotiation of an enterprise bargaining agreement with staff, and the development of a memorandum of understanding with the government. The memorandum of understanding covers the future direction of capital works within the region in which Grampians Water operates. The government is contributing $26 million towards these works.

The characteristics of Grampians Water

Grampians Water operates as a public sector organisation within the Victorian Water Industry, providing water and waste water services to the community. The authority operates in a wide and diverse area, serving a population of approximately 60 000 people, providing water to 67 towns and waste water services to 21 towns. The area serviced by Grampians Water is geographically the largest region in the state, covering almost the entire Wimmera Mallee region. The three main sources of water supply are from the Wimmera Mallee Water's open channel network, water from separate systems in the Grampians and at Mt Cole, and groundwater.

Grampians Water is the only supplier of urban services in this region at present, and so there is currently no competition. However, there is a need for Grampians Water to be a leader in this industry in order to avoid further government intervention. Such interventions may result in further amalgamations with other regional authorities in the State, or privatisation, leading to fierce competition.

The authority currently operates from a corporate office in Horsham, district offices in Ararat and Stawell and three operational depots. The corporate office in Horsham is generally central to all parts of the region, being at the intersection of major north-south and east-west highways that run through the area.

The chief executive officer, Lachlan Campbell, provides the central focus for the management of the board. The executive management team includes the CEO, secretary and representatives from four separate departments; Customer Services, Service Delivery, Business Performance and Major Works. This team provides further management expertise regarding the authority's operations. Figure F.2 provides specific details.

The Customer Services Department aims to ensure that the authority provides high levels of customer service to all urban communities, and that the needs of customers are met in the most efficient and effective manner. This department has a further role in that it provides legal, administrative and other corporate services to Grampians Water.

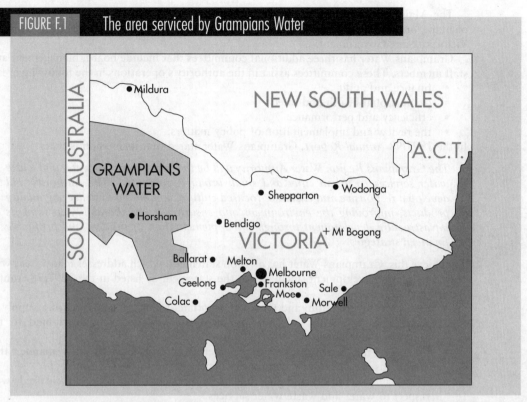

The area serviced by Grampians Water

The Service Delivery Department seeks to ensure that the authority delivers quality service to its customers, including adequate bulk water supplies, adequate water pressure, service reliability and rapid response to service emergencies.

The Business Performance Department's goals are to ensure that the authority meets customers' operational needs, and the financial demands of its shareholder. As such, it aims to implement prudent financial strategies focused on service and product quality. Further, it is required to provide an agreed per assessment return to the shareholder, while also meeting the authority's future infrastructure funding requirements.

FIGURE F.2 Organisational chart of Grampians Water

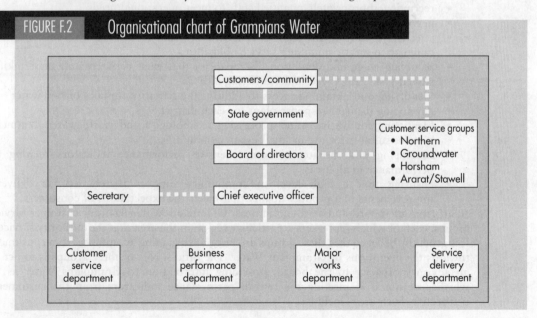

The Major Works Department was established to be responsible for capital works planning and construction, as detailed in the memorandum of understanding with the Victorian State Government.

Grampians Water has three additional committees that include board, management and staff members. These committees assist in the authority's operations in the following areas:

- finance and audit
- occupational health and safety
- efficiency and performance
- the review and implementation of policy matters.

In the 1997/98 *Annual Report*, Grampians Water stated that its mission is that:

> *The Grampians Region Water Authority will be the best supplier of water and waste water services to urban cities and small urban communities. The Authority will develop a responsive and customer-focused culture, committed to delivering quality products, improving the environment and ensuring it has the ability to fund its infrastructure development through the implementation of prudent and profitable financial strategies.*

To achieve this, Grampians Water has a vision statement, which addresses many areas with regard to future development. Elements of the statement as listed in the 1997/98 Annual Report include:

- that after investigation, and where appropriate, to ensure provision of a supply of water safe in quality, adequate in quantity and effectively distributed to the authority's customers
- to ensure the provision of waste water treatment facilities in a manner that safeguards the health of the authority's customers and the environment
- to identify community and government requirements, and address their needs with respect to water and waste water services
- to create and observe high safety standards
- to be a good corporate citizen and gain the respect of customers through empathy and good customer service
- to encourage all staff to continue to develop skills by further training and education.

Grampians Water's 1997/98 *Annual Report* states that it is committed to a core strategy 'to be the best provider of water and waste water services to urban cities and small urban communities'. It is suggested that the critical success factors pertinent to achieving this core strategy include:

- recruiting appropriately qualified staff to meet operational needs
- negotiating and securing the essential facilities required for operation
- effectively lobbying the state government in order to achieve a revenue positive outcome to meet community service obligations
- rectifying wage and condition discrepancies that exist between staff undertaking similar tasks, employed under differing awards
- identifying and obtaining access to additional alternative supplies of raw water
- developing drought response plans for each district
- identifying innovative water processing technologies and waste water treatment systems suitable for use in small urban communities
- developing and monitoring comprehensive performance indicators relating to performance in all areas
- ensuring that a high level of community support is retained via delivery improvements in a product quality that meets the expectations of consumers.

Apart from the board and staff committees, Grampians Water has four customer service groups, each of which represents a particular region in the area that the authority services. It is generally believed that these groups are integral to gaining acceptance from consumers towards the operations of Grampians Water. The official role of these groups is to act in an advisory capacity to the board, providing information to Grampians Water as to whether or not it is meeting the overall performance indicators from the customers' perspective. Such areas include:

TABLE F.1	Grampians Water: Financial results—balance sheet	
	1997/98	**1996/97**
Current assets	$31 683	$19 637
Non-current assets	$138 838	$132 726
Total assets	**$170 521**	**$152 363**
Current liabilities	$2154	$7553
Non-current liabilities	$932	$8517
Equity	$167 435	$136 293
Total liabilities and equity	**$170 521**	**$152 363**

- highlighting concerns that the customers may have about any aspect of the business of Grampians Water
- providing feedback to the directors on customer expectations and the perceived performance levels in areas such as service, environmental quality, and handling customer complaints
- offering suggestions about how Grampians Water could best meet the needs and expectations of the community
- assisting in the review of major capital works programmes for the area
- discussing and advising from a customer's viewpoint, the likely implications of Grampians Water policies
- acting as a link between Grampians Water and its customers.

Grampians Water's annual business plans establish the monetary goals of the authority, quantifying the financial costs of any change processes. Figure F.3 and Table F.1 are contained in the 1997/98 *Annual Report*. They indicate Grampians Water's statement of assets and liabilities, main revenue-raising components and major areas of expenditure.

The major change processes and reasons

Stage 1—the amalgamation of 21 water and waste water authorities

Beginning in 1994, this change was driven by external pressure from the Victorian State Government. The government, represented by staff from the Department of Water Resources, met with 21 individual authorities to outline the government's objectives.

FIGURE F.3	Analysis of revenue and expenditure 1997/98

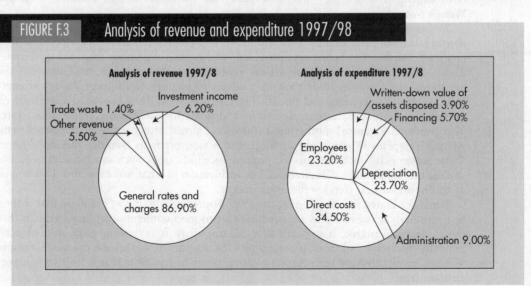

Analysis of revenue 1997/8

Trade waste 1.40%
Other revenue 5.50%
Investment income 6.20%
General rates and charges 86.90%

Analysis of expenditure 1997/8

Written-down value of assets disposed 3.90%
Financing 5.70%
Employees 23.20%
Depreciation 23.70%
Direct costs 34.50%
Administration 9.00%

Subsequently, the government decided to establish Grampians Water and appointed a board of directors. The government selected these directors on the basis of the perceived needs of the organisation. The government changes were based on the need to:

- introduce competition into the industry with the aim of reducing consumer costs
- redirect the water industry focus from public service provider to customer service
- allow authorities to concentrate on their core business of distributing water and treating waste water, as for many this had previously been a role undertaken by local government
- achieve economies of scale in the industry
- increase the ability of authorities to undertake necessary capital works to improve service quality. In a number of areas Grampians Water had inherited ageing infrastructure, which required major capital works to ensure that water quality is guaranteed and effluent discharge environmentally managed (see also stage 3).
- improve the ability of authorities to attract and retain skilled people within the industry
- reduce the state's indebtedness.

This change should be considered in the light of the major changes that were occurring in the Victorian public sector at the time. Many public sector authorities were being corporatised to compete with private enterprise, or in preparation for privatisation. As such, most changes were commercially driven, with the objective of reducing staffing levels in the Public Service, without compromising the level of services provided. The Victorian government considered the services provided by many of the original water and waste water authorities in the state as less than satisfactory, requiring immediate and drastic changes to meet government objectives.

Given the Victorian government's approach, Grampians Water faced a monumental task in establishing their credibility with staff and customers. Yesterday they had been part of a local water authority; today they were part of a regional water authority, Grampians Water. The change ran counter to the internal culture and stable environment of the original 21 authorities who had adopted, in the main, a public service provider attitude. After establishment, Grampians Water's external environment was relatively stable, as the government did not threaten further amalgamations. This contrasted dramatically with their internal environment. Internally, changes were constant and rapid, as the organisation attempted to change the culture from a local to a regional perspective, and from a public service provider focus to a customer focus. Comments from participants in the change process indicate that it took a long time to convince some staff that a change in culture was possible, as they resisted the need for change. By examining the new and changing environment in which they were operating, the board set out to establish Grampians Water's own identity.

To assist in establishing Grampians Water's identity, the directors had a *Director's Briefing Manual* produced by a transitional group of former authorities' elected members and staff. Further, the board was provided with general directions from the government. These directions quantified the action expected by the government. Following these directions, the directors undertook an analysis to identify Grampians Water's strengths, weaknesses, opportunities and threats. From this analysis, they produced a strategic plan outlining a mission statement, directions and goals for Grampians Water. The strategic plan provided a general motherhood statement, aimed at achieving a framework within which Grampians Water could develop, and action plans to quantify this development. These action plans included specific performance indicators, such as time lines as to when specific tasks were to be completed and quantification of what was expected. This was seen as an important first step for the organisation.

While the Board was developing the *1995 Strategic Plan*, it was planning that it should be continually reassessed and adjusted in order to meet contemporary requirements. From the evidence available, it appears that the authority is reviewing goals and objectives annually through its strategic planning process. As part of this review process, Grampians Water is re-establishing the necessary action plans to ensure that it is able to achieve its core strategy.

While these were the written objectives and plans, Grampians Water also had to contend with the underlying need to manage the change process, in order to maximise the benefits for customers, staff and its shareholder. Therefore, rather than make drastic changes, Grampians Water initially decided to establish district offices at Ararat, Birchip, Nhill, Stawell and Warracknabeal, in addition to the corporate office in Horsham. As such, those individuals transferred from former water and waste water authorities to Grampians Water remained in the location to which they were accustomed. In adopting the transitions groups' recommendation, the board's objectives appear to be aimed at:

- a drive for the acceptance of Grampians Water across the region, with the least possible disruption to previous operations
- limiting the possible alienation of staff and customers as a result of the change.

In 1995, the board identified in the strategic plan that the quality of staff was a strength. These staff were said to possess high levels of systems and operational knowledge, and were pleased to belong to Grampians Water, hence being dedicated to its success. In order to maintain this, the authority states that it is committed to the principles of merit and equity in relation to personnel practices. This includes a commitment to providing employees with education and training, taking into account potential experience and past performance to promote both organisational and personal development. While opportunities for training and education during this change process significantly increased motivation and reduced the stress levels of those employees involved, it was apparent that such opportunities were neither promoted nor offered to all members of staff. Further, observation suggests that what the board optimistically identified in its strategic plan was not necessarily the case, due to:

- a loss of people with skills and knowledge, who left as a response to the changes, partly as a result of the lack of career prospects within the organisation
- a loss of dedication and effectiveness of staff due to the stress of increased workloads and responsibilities.

This was highlighted when outdoor staff indicated that they faced an increase in the skills required, while indoor staff suggested that they were required to become more specialised as a result of the change. This suggests that while such rapid changes to work roles were necessary, they negatively affected morale.

In addition to the issues facing individuals, information gathered indicates that group problems also existed. Grampians Water's indoor and outdoor staff were two groups in fundamental conflict in this change process. This was a result of their physical location in the organisation. Outdoor staff suggested that they experienced a lack of information about the change process. Initial proposed changes were communicated to the outdoor staff by management, but a degree of distrust of the information given saw them use the more familiar grapevine. Information conveyed through the grapevine was often misconstrued, and there was a belief that secrets existed. Outdoor staff also believed that the indoor staff possessed superior knowledge and understanding of the change processes. Furthermore, the outdoor staff did not associate themselves with the new organisation, leading to an 'us vs them' mindset and a lack of trust regarding the entire change process.

Furthermore, contrasting mindsets also existed between the various towns encompassing Grampians Water, as a result of the different cultures that existed in different offices prior to and after amalgamation. This made the achievement of a single corporate culture for Grampians Water almost impossible. Facing this dilemma, Grampians Water believed that it was necessary to be proactive in their operations.

Stage 2—negotiation and introduction of the enterprise bargaining agreement

The negotiation of an enterprise bargaining agreement between Grampians Water and its work force took place during 1997. The agreement was attained through an adversarial approach, which pitted the board and management against staff and unions. The union's involvement was said to slow the process, but the enterprise bargaining agreement was signed in December 1997. The objective was to create a more responsive and flexible workforce in relation to the needs of Grampians Water, from both cost and operational perspectives. Measurement of cost flexibility for Grampians Water occurs through meeting employee and operations budget targets.

The negotiation of the enterprise bargaining agreement meant that Grampians Water was able to introduce specific performance indicators into their operations for the first time. The performance indicators used to evaluate individuals include:

- response time to customer complaints, call-outs, letters and other enquiries
- meeting individual goals established through performance appraisals.

Performance indicators used to evaluate groups include:

- measurement of the number of complaints that are received about the group's work. An example might be the number of complaints from ratepayers about incorrect rate notices having been sent to them
- time limits set on certain tasks, such as the Rates and charges area sending rate notices out on time
- meeting the budgetary requirements of the group.

It is noted that these group and individual performance indicators combine to reflect the overall operation and public image of Grampians Water.

The enterprise bargaining agreement has also allowed for a rationalisation of hours and payment methods to provide some uniformity of conditions. In return, staff covered by the enterprise bargaining agreement received a wage increase of 4% on the signing of the agreement. Individuals may receive a further 2% wage increase after nine months, if individual performance appraisals indicate that they have achieved agreed performance indicators. At the end of the first nine months, Grampians Water and the workforce were being appraised and renegotiating performance indicators to cover a greater range of factors with the possibility of this leading to a further 2% wage increase if performance levels were met when an evaluation of the revised performance indicators was undertaken nine months later. Given that these performance indicators are now part of the evaluation process under the enterprise bargaining agreement, they provide a recognised reward system for the individual.

Results indicate that, while it was the intention that the enterprise bargaining agreement should deliver a more flexible spread of hours, this has been difficult to achieve, as former work practices are preferred. Uniformity of conditions for all employees is also still to be achieved, although it is recognised that wage and salary relativities are now more equitable.

Stage 3—negotiation of the memorandum of understanding with the Victorian government

As its sole shareholder, the Victorian government's influence on the activities of Grampians Water is significant. This limits the options available to Grampians Water when considering appropriate responses to change and how and when it should occur, especially as the government is able to make further radical change whenever it considers it to be necessary. Given this scenario, the Victorian government announced further reforms to the water industry in October 1997, as a result of concerns related to:

- the speed of progress by the water industry in improving water quality and in treating waste water
- the general cost of water and waste water services to the customer.

To attain these reforms, the Government indicated that it was willing to make a financial contribution towards the costs involved.

In the six weeks following the October 1997 announcement, Grampians Water negotiated with the government the terms to be incorporated in a memorandum of understanding. Signed in December 1997, the memorandum of understanding is a legal agreement between Grampians Water and the government, which requires Grampians Water to achieve the terms of the agreement in return for financial assistance from the government. The final terms of the memorandum of understanding require Grampians Water to:

- rewrite the 1997/98 business plan to cover the 1998/99 financial year. In doing this, Grampians Water budgeted for an 18% reduction in revenue from rates and charges until 30 June 1999.
- undertake capital works in more than 40 towns to provide water that meets World Health Organisation Drinking Water Quality guidelines. This had to be completed prior to the state government election in 2000, and was to be assessed by Grampians Water testing water samples on a quarterly basis, following the completion of capital works. Samples had to meet the guidelines, and a report of sample results had to be provided to the government as verification that compliance was occurring.
- undertake capital works to sewer four towns with populations greater than 500 that have reticulated water supplies. This work had to be completed by 2001.
- undertake capital works to ensure that all waste water treatment plants discharge effluent to standards consistent with the *State Environment Protection Policy (Waters of Victoria)* by 2001.
- undertake necessary dam improvement works on Grampians Water storage dams by 2003 to ensure compliance with safety standards, and to protect water supplies.

In return the Victorian government provided $26 million to assist Grampians Water's capital works programme. This level of funding is far less than the estimated cost of the programme, which is $80 million. Further, the $26 million is to be kept in a special account by Grampians Water, who must provide details of transactions within the account to the government on a quarterly basis. The achievement of the ambitious capital works programme has seen the targets above included in the Board's revised business and strategic plans.

Further, in response to the memorandum of understanding, Grampians Water took the following actions:

- reviewing its operations to assess how best to meet the needs of customers, given the new budgetary constraints. This includes reassessing the strategic plan to make it relevant to the objectives of the memorandum of understanding by scanning the external environment and comparing Grampians Water with other water authorities in Victoria
- reviewing the staff structure in regards to organisational needs
- reviewing the business plan and capital works programme to meet memorandum of understanding requirements.

This resulted in:

- updating the strategic plan. Considered for adoption in February/March 1998 was downsizing through voluntary redundancy and having staff reapply for a lesser number of positions within Grampians Water.
- reducing the number of district offices, apart from Horsham, from five to two. This resulted in some staff relocations, predominantly affecting office staff, with the purpose of achieving economies of scale and promoting unity within the organisation.
- developing work teams to undertake various tasks throughout Grampians Water, particularly in the operations area.
- developing a business plan and capital works programme to take advantage of the latest technologies. This included telemetry, which reduces the need for operations staff to actually attend asset locations to undertake maintenance.
- holding a series of public meetings throughout the area to discuss the options available in upgrading the water and waste water infrastructure in the cities and towns identified in the memorandum of understanding.
- re-evaluating performance indicators within the enterprise bargaining agreement structure.

The memorandum of understanding provides Grampians Water with an external mechanism for evaluating its overall performance in regards to water and waste water services. In addition, the government requirement of an 18% reduction in revenue from rates and charges for the 1997/98 and 1998/99 financial years acted as an external financial evaluation. The reduction of revenue was partly delivered through the reissue of 1997/98 rate notices and revision of 1997/98 and 1998/99 business plans.

Throughout stage 3, there was evidence of a greater level of support for change, or at least acknowledgment, from staff of the need for radical change. Although partial support and acknowledgement of change had developed, psychosocial problems continued to exist in response to the change. As a result, Grampians Water attempted to introduce several measures to deal with these problems. During the change process, it established opportunities for staff to consult with church-based counsellors. In many instances this approach proved to be effective in reducing stress and in dealing with personal issues. However, this did not act as a panacea to all interpersonal problems, and only suited the needs of some staff members. For instance, it was identified that the outdoor staff viewed the concept of counselling as unnecessary and in contrast with their personal images socially.

It was also noted that Grampians Water had recently introduced teams throughout their operations as part of this particular change process. The aim of team development is to foster co-operation among all staff. Teams comprise individuals from most levels across the organisation, with the objective of providing all staff with a particular member of management whom they can approach with questions and problems. This was a positive step towards resolving the problems that exist, but evidence suggested that the objectives of team development were not being achieved in every case. This might have been because some at management level viewed this role as being of little importance, given their heavy workloads.

What of the future?

It is generally acknowledged that change will continue as the government proceeds with reducing its public commitments. This was illustrated by the sale of other corporatised government activities, such as power generation and distribution, and the then still proposed sell-off of transport and gas assets and operations.

Many of the actions taken under the memorandum of understanding were directed towards upgrading the standard of assets to a level that provided:

- a quality level of service that meets internationally recognised health standards
- infrastructure that is state-of-the-art and therefore saleable.

The continuing corporatisation of public sector organisations, such as Grampians Water, suggested that the Victorian government might still have been considering the possible sale of the water industry to private concerns. While the then currently stated government policy did not include privatisation of the water industry, in the event of current organisations failing to meet jointly agreed goals, or even if such goals were met, it did not stop the government from scanning the market to ascertain the profitability of such a sale. If, in the future, privatisation were to eventuate, the result might have seen Grampians Water acting as a caretaker organisation in an overall government privatisation scheme.

QUESTIONS

1 List the problems at the individual, group and organisation levels. What were the causes of these?

2 How could the problem of skilled staff leaving for better opportunities have been approached? Discuss the advantages and disadvantages.

3 Discuss three means of dealing with stress resulting from increased workloads and responsibilities. Discuss the advantages and disadvantages.

4 Suggest ways of handling the different inter-group conflicts. Discuss the advantages and disadvantages.

5 List some advantages and disadvantages of the performance indicators used, and make suggestions for further improvements.

6 What should Grampians Water have done to ensure its survival when facing future pressures from the government? Discuss the advantages and disadvantages.

7 What macro-level OD interventions could have been used to implement the changes occurring at Grampians Water? Discuss the advantages and disadvantages.

8 Using the model for adaptive orientation[2], characterise Grampians Water's management style in each of the three stages.

9 How could the strategies for planned organisational change as outlined by Dunphy and Stace[3], be used to describe the strategies used by Grampians Water? What strategy could have been used then, or be used in the future, with regards to the management of change?

Notes

1 *Grampians Water Annual Report* (1997/8).
2 D. Harvey and D. Brown, *An Experiential Approach to Organization Development*, 5th ed. (New Jersey 1996: Prentice Hall International).
3 D. Dunphy and D. Stace. 'Transformational and coercive strategies for planned organizational change beyond the OD model', *Organizational Studies*, 9 (1988): 317–34.

Other references

Grampians Water: *Annual Reports* (1995/6 and 1996/97).
Grampians Water: *Newsletters*.
Grampians Water: *Strategic Plan* (1995).
Grampians Water: *Director's Briefing Manual* (Transition Group 1994).
C. Granrose and J. Portwood, 'Matching individual career plans and organizational career management', *Academy of Management Journal*, 30 (1987): 699–720.
L. Hansen, *Integrative Life Planning: Critical Tasks for Career Development and Changing Life Patterns,* (California 1997: Jossey-Bass).
M. Matteson and J. Ivanevich, *Controlling Work Stress: Effective Human Resource and Management Strategies,* (California 1987: Jossey-Bass).
M. McGill, *Organization Development for Operating Managers,* (New York 1977: AMACOM)
N. Norvell, *Stress Management Training: A Group Leader's Guide,* (New York 1990: Professional Resource Exchange).

The acquisition of Heatane by Elgas

By **Renae Richards and Natalie Smith**

On 1 July 1993, Elgas, a specialist in liquified petroleum gas (LPG), purchased Heatane, the LPG and appliance division of the Gas and Fuel Corporation of Victoria.[1] LPG is naturally occurring propane and butane gases that produce an environmentally friendly form of energy.

Background: Elgas

Elgas was created in 1984 by the joining of Portagas, the LPG division of the Australian Gas Light Company, with CIG energy (now BOC) in equal partnership to share infrastructure and resources.[1] The resultant private company's primary areas of operation were New South Wales, South Queensland, South Australia and Victoria.

The Elgas philosophy is one of customer service, well-trained staff, safety and security and, most importantly, profit.[2] The Victorian business grew as it took on the existing Heatane customers.[1] Elgas provides LPG for commercial, industrial, automotive and domestic purposes. Commercially, LPG is used for power generation, heating, hot water and cooking. Elgas clients include Warner Brothers Movie World, ski resorts, hospitals and the Sydney Olympics.[2] Industrial uses include boilers, power generation, as a forklift fuel, flame hardening and furnaces.

Elgas was appointed the Australian agent for 'Razorgas', a flame-hardening form of LPG that had been developed in the UK.[2] A substantial portion of Elgas' business can be attributed to 'Autogas', the automotive LPG that can be used in cars. This is an economical and environment-friendly alternative to petrol. To support the sales of Autogas, Elgas offers the 'Autocard', which offers credit terms to individuals and companies.[2]

For domestic purposes, Elgas provides gas for barbecues, gas lighting, heating, refrigerators and cooking. Delivery can be by one of two methods. 'Easygas' involves the company monitoring a household's usage of gas and automatically topping up the supply when necessary.[2] The exchange cylinder process involves the customer having two vessels on site. Once one has been depleted, they switch to the reserve. A phone call to Elgas will result in the replacement of the original cylinder.

Background: Heatane

Prior to the takeover, Heatane's profits had been diminishing. To prevent the division draining the balance sheet of the entire Gas and Fuel Corporation, Heatane was made an autonomous division, whose concept of success was purely one of profit. The sole aim was to maintain its position as a market leader and expand its sales base. However, ongoing profit loss forced Heatane to appoint consultants, which resulted in staff being reduced from 240 to 120.[1] When the poor performance continued, the government aborted the changes proposed by the consultants and instead decided to privatise Heatane.

The major change process

The acquisition of Heatane by Elgas began with a tendering process that lasted three months and saw Elgas, Kleenheat and Boral reply to the tender. During this time, all bidders were allowed to preview all documentation relating to Heatane, subject to a confidentiality agreement. Elgas developed a plan to either buy Heatane (Plan A) or attack the customer base of the successful tenderer (Plan B).[3]

Plan A: successful tender

In the event that Elgas successfully acquired Heatane, a plan was developed to facilitate the merging of the two companies' resources, while ensuring that Kleenheat and Boral could not take advantage of the company's vulnerable position and poach customers. Predictions of these competitors' future actions were made and contingency plans put into place. It was anticipated that Boral and Kleenheat would plan any attack to commence on 1 June 1993 to allow one month of Heatane defending and Elgas having no access to Heatane resources.[3] To counteract this, customer contact and reassurance was planned to commence on 17 May—just seven days after the announcement.

The merger facilitation plans effectively consisted of a list of basic priorities for Elgas employees to follow. Of major importance was the continuation of existing contracts that came up for renewal during the initial stages of the acquisition. Elgas developed a policy that allowed employees to offer customers a price that matched that of any competitor, provided that a five-year agreement was made.[3] The policy further stated that employees should promise to deliver more localised services and, if any customer was hesitant about renewing a contract, the pretext of misfiling and time delays should be used to persuade the customer.[3]

Plan B: unsuccessful tender

It was decided that, if Kleenheat or Boral won the tender, the initial priorities for either company would be the same, so that only one contingency plan needed to be developed. Elgas predicted that, as both competitors would pursue a critical branch network across Victoria, the company priority should be to strengthen the existing EasyGas network of dealers. The first step was documented as presenting an 'above odds' proposal to the three key dealerships in Ballarat, Geelong and Bairnsdale to ensure that they signed to Elgas.[3]

The second step was to acquire an agent in each regional town where gas usage was in excess of 100 tonnes.[3] The gas exchange component of the agency would be utilised to inhibit profitable return by competitors, while the EasyGas component would be the vehicle for market share erosion and profitability.

At this stage, separate plans were formulated in the event of either a Kleenheat or Boral takeover, because of their different strengths and weaknesses. As Kleenheat was expected to maintain a centralised truck transport focus in Melbourne and Geelong, Elgas planned to minimise returns on localised business and sign five-year contracts to ensure that the unit rate of transport would rise significantly.[3] Industrial relations was seen to be Kleenheat's most vulnerable area. Elgas proposed that approaching TWU on a 'fair competition' basis would compel TWU and FGEIU to fight for membership, and so develop conflict between drivers and subcontractors. This early industrial unrest would generate significant market opportunities.[3]

Boral's success in tendering would induce Elgas to exploit the company's lack of both resources and familiarity with the market. Elgas predicted that Boral would need to bring in staff from interstate, thus unsettling human resources. It was planned that Elgas would take out large bulk and autogas, but this would only unbalance Boral with excess truck capacity. Dealers were considered to be the key as their volumes and margins were needed to establish the branch network. By localising sales activity and maximising local density in the branch areas, Elgas planned a future of breaking up the Victorian market.[3]

The announcement

During the tender period, Elgas had many discussions with the Australian Consumer Competition Commission (ACCC) about the possible monopoly power that Elgas would have within Victoria. After clearance from the ACCC, Elgas won the right to serve

Heatane's customers, assets and supplier agreements from Esso and BHP through the Dandenong terminal.[1] This allowed Elgas to have an economical and reliable supply of LPG. It was conditional upon Elgas employing 80 of the existing 120 staff, as well as honouring any existing agreements.[1]

Elgas senior management had three weeks' notice of their success before the official announcement. Although staff were not told until the day of the announcement, employees stated that informal communication had leaked the news almost as soon as senior management knew.[4] The day after the announcement, Elgas managers met with the Heatane distributor councils to convey their intentions and were received with a very high level of mistrust.[1] Two days later, off-site sessions were held with Heatane staff informing them that all would be interviewed to work for Elgas if they desired, and that those who were unsuccessful or did not wish to be interviewed would be offered positions within the Gas and Fuel Corporation.[1] At the time these sessions were being conducted, Elgas staff were moving into the Heatane building.

The change process

According to the definitions of organisation development (OD) and organisation transformation (OT), the Elgas takeover could be described as OD on an OT time frame. The Elgas takeover of Heatane is consistent with the concept of organisational development, except for the time frame. Because of the highly competitive nature of the company's market, the change process was conducted fairly rapidly in order to prevent loss of market share. In this context, 'change process' refers to the time between the announcement and amalgamation of the two companies. The reasoning behind this expedient implementation was that the quicker the integration, the lower the fear factor among employees, contractors and customers.[5]

It must be recognised that the changes experienced by existing Elgas employees were minor when compared to those of the former Heatane employees. Their change process was more consistent, with organisation transformation due to the shift in framework, assumptions, people, processes, technology and corporate culture. To assist this progression, intra-group and inter-group training was introduced—the former aimed at teaching former Heatane employees the skills required to perform within the Elgas company, the latter aimed at building bridges between the two groups of employees.[1] In this way, inter-group training was used as a guise for building teamwork, motivation and trust and decreasing resistance to change.[6]

During the initial stages of the takeover, Elgas kept a tight control over security so that former Heatane staff had no opportunity to sabotage the company.[1] Employees that chose or were compelled to take positions at Gas and Fuel were moved from Elgas as soon as a position became available.

In an attempt to regroup after the takeover, Elgas introduced regular meetings between employees and management and often mixed teams of workers to facilitate a more friendly work environment.[1] To motivate teams to exceed quotas, group incentives such as additional annual leave were introduced. Any opportunity for communication was utilised, including a two-day 'Outward Bound' course aimed at improving the camaraderie among the workers and a weekly newsletter for employees.[1] Elgas continued their existing employee appraisal programme to ascertain employee satisfaction, productivity and skill development, and these resulted in some employees changing jobs, being made redundant or sacked due to incompetence.[1] As the majority of those removed were former Heatane staff, mistrust compounded until an Elgas manager was sacked, primarily for his poor treatment of former Heatane staff.[1]

Elgas employees' perspective

From the perspective of Elgas employees, the takeover of Heatane was a positive achievement. As long-time competitors, the acquisition of their biggest rival led to high group cohesion among Elgas employees.[4] High levels of formal and informal communication from management to employees created a relaxed and trusting environment. While there was no fear of job loss, some employees were concerned that the family atmosphere at Elgas would be lost when the number of employees increased.[4]

After the takeover, morale dropped slightly among the existing Elgas employees, when many traditional perks of the job were abolished as a result of cost cutting.[4] Furthermore, management gave Elgas staff the impression that former Heatane employees 'could do no wrong', and were asked to 'tread lightly' around the newcomers.[4] This bred resentment among Elgas employees, which took some time to resolve.

Heatane employees' perspective

Before the announcement by the government that Heatane would be sold, consultants assessed the company in an attempt to save it from privatisation. However, the notification was made while the consultants' recommendations were still in the formative stages of implementation, and this unsettled the staff.[7] Between this news and the announcement of the successful tender were six weeks of uncertainty. Then there was more bad news: not only were they getting a new owner, but it was none other than their arch-rival. Immediately after the announcement, Heatane staff waited for some information about their future, before conducting a two-week strike when none was forthcoming.[7]

When Elgas officially took over Heatane they were met with a justifiably suspicious and uncertain group of people—many of whom had lost work mates in the acquisition. Heatane staff were well aware of how public servants are perceived by private business, and were determined to avoid the lazy stereotype.[7] Former Heatane staff state that Elgas took four years for the two companies to fully amalgamate.[7]

Action plans, strategies and techniques

Team building

Elgas tried to instil a team-based atmosphere within the new company. Previously, Heatane had had a very segregated work place with an 'us vs them' mentality.[7] Many clerical staff had not visited the Dandenong or Williamstown depots, and many tanker drivers had never been inside head office at Mulgrave. To overcome these problems, team development was fostered through the use of site visits, administration conferences, outdoor training and social functions.

Elgas has a philosophy of organisation team work.[4] There is an emphasis on one organisation, with no clear divisions in regard to occupations. Therefore, drivers are classified as being a part of the same team as clerical staff. All new and existing clerical staff experienced a day in a tanker making deliveries, and all tanker drivers spent a day within head office.[1] Further, all metropolitan staff were taken to country branches to see how they operated.

Administration conferences were conducted for all employees. Groups that incorporated a cross-section of job descriptions were created.[1] While the primary goal of these conferences was training in the new systems, philosophies, operations, safety and product knowledge, getting-to-know-you activities were included.[4] Social functions were organised for evenings, providing further opportunities for the staff to interact.

All staff were expected to attend outdoor training.[1] Both Elgas and Heatane staff were again mixed together to participate in problem-solving and trust activities. Middle managers attended training conducted by external consultants at Mt Baw Baw to improve their skills in communicating with subordinates and resolve any issues that might result from the merger.[1] Initially, Heatane employees were resistant to the idea of 'such extravagance', but resistance diminished with time.[7] Elgas employees had experienced a similar type of training before. Some problems arose from some individuals not being able to handle the pressure, which Elgas viewed as not being related to the merger, but as individual personality characteristics.[1]

This aspect of the training programme is questionable as the employees were forced to attend. Although, in this instance, the training succeeded in developing some cohesion in the group, the initial resistance reported is cause for alarm. Kramar, McGraw and Schuler criticise the notions behind outdoor training activities, as there are difficulties in transferring acquired skills to the work place.[8] Furthermore, the ethical question of risking the health of unfit participants has seen the popularity of these programmes dwindle over recent years. In retrospect, such a programme should have been offered to employees, with alternatives available to the less adventurous. Other experiential techniques include case studies, business games, role playing and simulations.[9]

Social functions were held within a short time of the merger announcement. The night after the announcement, a welcome dinner at a convention centre in Dandenong was held for employees of the new organisation.[1] No expense was spared, with all employees being invited to bring their partners along. The senior managers (from Sydney) and the board of Elgas also attended to meet the new staff.[1]

Delivering the message

On the Friday that the Victorian Government announced that Elgas was the successful tenderer, both company's staff were being informed of the decision.[1] Elgas provided their metropolitan staff with an informal drinks session, and senior and middle management discussed the implications of the takeover with staff. The managing director, from Sydney, attended after completing the formal paperwork at the government chambers. A formal letter was sent to all staff stating that, as a result of the privatisation process, Elgas was the successful tenderer and that, in the long term, this would result in a powerful company. The broad requirements of the merger with Heatane were detailed and all staff were assured of their jobs.[1] Furthermore, the time frame for forthcoming events and the resulting impact on existing Heatane staff was detailed. However, Elgas employees were not told how many employees from Heatane would be retained.[4] Elgas country branches were rung by senior management and told of the success of the tender, and were sent a supplementary message through the internal computer system.[1]

It is believed that Heatane staff were informed only through the public announcement and mail.[7] The details of the letter informing them of Elgas' success are unknown. Former Heatane dealers were informed through the dealer council the next day, when Elgas management detailed the plans for the new company and the Elgas philosophies.[1]

Resistance to change

General

Elgas employees, while their jobs were guaranteed, were still uncertain about the takeover. They were concerned about a potential change in the organisation culture, from one of a small company where the senior manager knew everyone's name to one of a large hierarchical organisation where they would be in danger of losing their identity.[4]

Naturally, Heatane staff resisted the takeover. It was an outward symptom of their failure as an organisation. They became preoccupied with defending their share of the LPG market rather than with developing a new customer base.[1] Thus, staff harboured anger and resentment towards the privatisation process. They had previously encountered the change management consultants who had restructured the organisation and reduced staffing levels by 100.[7] Furthermore, Heatane staff had not been kept well informed by their own management of the progress of privatisation, resulting in the involvement of the unions. A two-week strike ensued as staff tried to gain more information.[7] Competitors of Heatane who were involved in the tender process could not attack during this period because of the confidentiality agreement that they had signed.

Heatane's major customers demanded to meet with Elgas management about the plans for the company. The distributors were very mistrusting as, over the years, Elgas had already taken much of their business.[1] In addition, Elgas distributors viewed their Heatane competitors as being inferior. In effect, Heatane employees were moving from a highly regulated, closed-door government division to an open-door private company, with new technology and a different working environment.[7] This meant that a high degree of resistance was probable, which threatened the success of the acquisition. Although theory offers a variety of forces that drive acceptance of a change programme and break down resistance, none of these appeared to apply to Elgas. There was no dissatisfaction with the existing situation, external pressure, momentum or motivation. In the case of Elgas, it seems that the resistance simply burnt out over time as employees realised that, in order to keep their jobs, they had to accept the change.

Operating

Resistance to the operating procedures came to a head when Heatane employees were forced to utilise Elgas' operating systems. Slight disagreements flared when comparisons were made between the systems, and naturally each group supported its own system. This was overcome by Elgas management examining both systems and adapting positive aspects of the Heatane system to fit the existing Elgas one.[1] This appeared to satisfy both groups of employees.

Heatane tanker drivers, known for their militancy, were not supportive of the takeover. However, Elgas was prepared to take them on and eventually personality clashes were overcome through individual counselling. Most drivers eventually adapted to the new system.[1] Nevertheless, middle management at Elgas state that there is still some mistrust.[7]

Culture

Corporate culture consists of the shared values, beliefs and behaviours that members of an organisation have formed over time. Elgas tried to create a shared vision of the new organisation through the *Elgas People Magazine*, policies and procedures manuals and the involvement of employees in the developing of budgets and market plans each year.[1] All employees are involved in the decision-making process through empowerment. Employees are encouraged to make decisions on their own and to assume more responsibility.

One key vision that had to be inculcated in Heatane employees was the Elgas emphasis on profit.[1] Heatane's own vision had involved an increase in volume. The *Elgas People Magazine*, a glossy monthly magazine, was used as a tool to communicate the company's philosophies and detail all excellence awards to all employees and distributors.

Middle management found that Heatane employees naturally followed the lead of existing Elgas employees in regard to work hours and how hard they should work.[1] Heatane staff were provided with employee manuals detailing the company's philosophy and operating processes and attended administration conferences and social functions. Initially, Heatane staff were fearful of losing their jobs, which may have contributed to their acceptance of the new culture.[7] It was the belief of Elgas management that the 'Purple G' rewards programme eventually led to staff seeing the rewards of working hard.[1]

Some Elgas managers handled the differences in culture far better than others. Those that struggled to integrate their subordinates were counselled and received training in problem-solving and communication skills. An attrition rate of 20% showed that some employees failed to adjust to the new conditions and chose to move on. This rate was expected and allowed for in initial redundancies, so that few employees needed to be replaced. The belief is that attrition was due to an increase in organisation size rather than to a conflict between employees' work ethics.[1]

In the post-takeover days, former Elgas staff believed that too much emphasis was being placed on who their former employer had been, but former Heatane employees believed that Elgas staff were being favoured.[7] Thus, everyone and everything was classified according to whether they were an old Heatane employee or an old Elgas employee. Employees noticed that group cohesion eventually increased as the Heatane label was gradually replaced with Elgas. It seems that, as former Heatane cylinders and tankers were relabelled Elgas, so were the people.

The vastly different cultures of Heatane and Elgas were bound to cause some problems. As Heatane staff gradually adopted the values, beliefs and associated behaviours of Elgas employees, they went through a process termed 'sharing the vision'. Elgas management successfully handled this culture change by guiding the Heatane employees from the initial stage of adopting a clear vision, through empowerment, developing trust to finally rewarding their performance.[1] Due to the relative ease with which this transition was accomplished, it can be inferred that Heatane had had a comparatively weak corporate culture.[10]

Evaluation of the change process

The initial plan

Elgas developed a three-year operational plan that had been approved by the board prior to the purchase. This included projections of sales volume, cost of sales, overheads, debtors, debtors' targets, staffing levels, suitability of organisational structure, staff competency, return on assets, asset recovery, customers lost and gained and distributor losses and the cost of rebranding and imaging.[1]

Senior management reviewed the operational plan monthly. Adjustments were made to day-to-day operations when there were major deviations from the original plan.[1] Projections had been based on a period of high inflation that would have enabled prices/rentals to be increased. However, a period of low inflation occurred, thus limiting the opportunity to bring pricing up to market levels. Gas prices also increased to record levels as a result of changes in gas prices in the Middle East, and these were unable to be recovered in the market. All the above adjustments resulted in a review of the company's profit predictions.[1]

Human resources

An acquisition can adversely affect employees, especially in the short run. To deal with the problems that result from the announcement and implementation of a merger, several possible solutions have been advanced: more frequent communication with employees; enhanced, responsive training programmes; tracking systems to monitor employee attitudes and concerns and increased specialisation.[11] By adopting these solutions, managers may be able to alleviate some of the confusion and conflict created during a merger. Frequent communication with employees is critical in reducing merger-related problems.[12] Unfortunately, effective communication has become a popular buzzword with such a broad definition that it has all but lost its significance.[11]

Management must ensure that some system is in place to check employees' reactions to the merger. Are the staff unhappy or overly worried about job security or new policies? Are the new employees meshing well with the more seasoned veterans? The Human Resources Department of the post-merger organisation should develop and implement an employee survey to measure and quantify answers to these types of questions.[10]

When a company acquires another company, it runs the risk of losing the new employees' motivation and commitment if it fails to address their unique needs.[13] To monitor such conditions, the human resources of the company were evaluated on an ongoing basis. Line managers and the personnel department were given prime responsibility for this task, which included the evaluation of technology competency, the effectiveness of training programmes, attitude to fellow employees, attitude to customers and mystery shopper results.[1] The bulk tankers were measured on the number of litres delivered, customer run outs, percentage of gas delivered into the vessel and deliveries where no gas was required. Sales representatives were evaluated according to the number of outgoing calls, new business gained or lost, retention of margins and customer resignations.[1]

Individuals were counselled on a regular basis to gauge their attitude to the restructured organisation. Any ideas were welcomed and implemented where practical. Formal staff appraisals were conducted every six months, giving the employee and line manager the opportunity to discuss the employees' performance on a one-to-one basis.[1]

Employees were asked to complete an anonymous 'how was your boss' survey. This evaluated the effectiveness of the manager from an employee point of view. Surveys were reviewed by the general manager of each department in conjunction with the manager being evaluated.[1] This enabled the company to develop managers by reviewing their strengths, weaknesses and management style. The relevant training was then provided.

One novel form of evaluation involved the 'Elgas Competition', whereby all aspects of the customer centre were judged on a points system that led to financial bonuses for each member of the team.[2] The points system depended upon return on assets, sales growth, outstanding debtors, control of costs, customer surveys, new business gained, tanker and depot inspections and the achievement of outstanding leave and training budgets.[1] This encouraged all employees to focus on all aspects of the successful business.

Some of the lessons learned during the course of the acquisition were that the same core message must be released to all staff at the same time and that senior executives must walk-the-job more than normal, preferably by attending team briefings with those levels of staff that they would not normally meet.[5] The biggest challenge was working with line management to ensure that the staff, drawn from many different parts of the group, now worked well, together with common goals and priorities—looking forward positively, not forever comparing conditions with 'how we used to do it'.[5]

Customers' and contractors' response

The overall customer satisfaction was measured through the use of an external agent. Anonymous telephone surveys and face-to-face interviews were conducted to determine the overall level of satisfaction with customer service, employee attitude and knowledge.[1] Overall customer reaction to the takeover was also evaluated.

External suppliers and contractors were also questioned about their reaction to the takeover. Issues raised included the disadvantages and advantages of the new organisation and any particular strengths and weaknesses.[1] Internal line managers, in their day-to-day dealings with suppliers, had the opportunity to discuss any problems.

General

Overall, the effectiveness of Elgas in Victoria had considerably increased by the end of the takeover process. Volume increased by 4% per annum, profit increased by 8% per annum and costs were reduced by 15% per annum.[1] As a result, Elgas Victoria moved from bottom position in a ranking of all Australian states to equal first with New South Wales. Elgas Victoria now provides half of the total organisation's profit for Australia.[2]

During the first few months of the merger, it was anticipated that Elgas would lose 10% of its sales volume as a result of competition from unsuccessful tenderers. However, neither Boral and Kleenheat had contingency plans in place and were slow off the mark, resulting in only a 4% loss of volume.[1]

Experiences such as the Longford gas disaster in August 1998 and a fire in Elgas' state office in March 1999 were also used as opportunities to evaluate the takeover. These emergency situations proved that the staff had become a team and could work well together. While Elgas employees were not directly involved in the Longford disaster, many natural gas customers wanted to change to LPG.[1] Staff dealt with thousands of hostile customers while working long hours under extreme pressure. It was Elgas' policy to service the existing customers and then distribute the remaining gas needed for essential services.[1] Staff were rewarded with a dinner provided by management.[4]

Criticisms

The handling of the takeover can be critically examined in several key areas. First, Elgas did not consider hiring an external change agent to conduct the takeover process. External change agents offer numerous advantages, including objectivity, greater leverage and greater power. Thus, an external change agent might have viewed the takeover process differently to Elgas management and so might have provided alternative ways of conducting the process. When Elgas management were questioned about the use of a change agent, cost factors and industry knowledge were reasons cited for not doing so.[1]

During the diagnostic phase, Elgas did not consider the implications of 'people issues' when gathering information in regard to the desirability of the takeover. Key documents examined, while listing staffing numbers, did not highlight the strengths and weaknesses of existing Heatane staff. Although Elgas management had considered the implications of a private company taking over a public entity, an examination of the various staff members' cultural practices was not carried out.

As mentioned earlier, Elgas utilised Outward Bound team-building activities to foster a joint sense of culture. The suitability of this type of activity must be questioned. It is easy to get caught up in the excitement of the exercises and not pay attention to the experiential learning that should be taking place. There are also ethical and legal issues in relation to placing individuals in stressful outdoors environments without their 'true' consent. The question of whether it is 'above and beyond' the job description must be asked. Furthermore, what was initially intended as a team-building exercise may well have created a more divided work force. According to company culture, Elgas employees viewed the exercise as exciting and worthwhile, unlike the Heatane employees who saw it as a waste of time.[1]

Resistance to change within the organisation may have been better overcome by examining the theoretical reasons for resistance to change and applying formal organisational development techniques to counteract this. Suggested reasons include uncertainty regarding the change; loss of existing benefits and threats to power. To reduce the resistance, Elgas could have allowed employees greater participation in the change process. Employees would therefore have ownership of the change process. All other techniques used by Elgas support theoretical models through the use of communication, leadership and reward systems in the form of the 'Purple G' programme.

It is the authors' belief that, despite the earlier criticisms, the Elgas takeover process of Heatane was highly effective and consistent with most OD research. While initial resistance did occur, it is now four years since the takeover and former Heatane staff are reporting no animosity or resentment.[7] Natural attrition has provided a change in the mix of employees, with many new staff members being unaware of the previous turmoil.

Conclusion

Elgas conducted a successful takeover of Heatane during 1994. The change process followed the conventional OD model. The logistics of the takeover were examined during the diagnostic phase. Heatane documents were examined in regard to the suitability of the company and plans made for the tender process. During the action, strategy and plans phase, Elgas management sought to implement a team-based culture through the use of Outward Bound activities, conferences, magazines and social activities. The evaluation phase examined both hard data in regard to sales and volume as well as performance appraisals, surveys and interviews. Overall, the Elgas takeover of Heatane has been judged to have been highly successful, but this evaluation process is still continuing.

QUESTIONS

1 The change process has been described as 'OD on an OT time frame'. Explain the different approaches and how they relate to Elgas.

2 Management had different perceptions of resistance by Elgas and Heatane employees. Why was this the case?

3 What recommendations would you make to Kleenheat and Boral for future takeover attempts?

4 How does an acquisition, such as Elgas acquiring Heatane, differ from a strategic merger of two companies on equal terms, and which do you think is more likely to be successful?

Notes

1 Personal communication from B. Richards, regional manager, Victoria (29 September 1999). The authors wish to sincerely thank Mr Richards for his invaluable assistance in completing this assignment.
2 *Elgas Company Overview* (Mulgrave: Elgas, 1998).
3 B. Broadhurst, *Memo to Staff: Plan A and Plan B* (Mulgrave: Elgas, 1993).
4 Personal communication from K. Francis, casual customer service officer (29 September 1999).
5 C. Kerr, 'Human resourcing following a merger', *International Journal of Career Management*, 7:2 (1995), 7–9.
6 R. Conroy, 'Managing mergers', *Executive Excellence*, 9:6 (1992), 14–15.
7 Personal communication from C. Dineen, supervisor, Melbourne Office (29 September 1999).
8 R. Kramar, P. McGraw and R. Schuler, *Human Resource Management in Australia*, (Melbourne: West Publishing Company and Addison Wesley Longman, 1997).
9 R. DeSimone and D. Harris, *Human Resource Development*, (Orlando: Dryden Press, 1998).
10 S. Cartwright and C. Cooper, *Mergers and Acquisitions: The Human Factor*, (Oxford: Butterworth-Heinemann 1992).
11 E. Schatz, 'New people, policies, and places: how to manage a credit department merger', *Journal of Commercial Lending*, 76:6 (1994), 26–31.
12 G. Vinten, 'Employee relations in mergers and acquisitions', *Employee Relations*, 15:4 (1993) 47–64.
13 L. Capozzi, 'Retaining the human potential of corporate acquisitions', *HR Magazine*, 39:8 (1994), 76–79.

Self-managed work teams as a management tool

By **Peter Benazic, Judy Pool and Cathy Williams**

Introduction

As a result of changes in state government legislation, compulsory competitive tendering (CCT), council amalgamations and the introduction of the National Competition Policy, the Maribyrnong City Council made the decision to introduce self-managed work teams in the Parks and Gardens business unit.

The central themes of this case study will be how self-managed work teams (SMWT) have been implemented at a time when the second round of CCT was to be submitted, the concept of *Gainshare* and what the key issues are for team members in the future.

Characteristics of the Maribyrnong Council

The Maribyrnong City Council is a relatively new small municipality, lying to the west of Melbourne's central business district. It is a synthesis of the former cities of Footscray and Sunshine. Maribyrnong City Council, in relation to other municipal areas, is smaller in both geographic size and in its capacity to generate income. Generally speaking, the city incorporates some of Melbourne's most impoverished suburbs, such as Braybrook and Maidstone. However, within the city boundaries, there are also suburbs where the 'upwardly mobile' are choosing to live, such as Yarraville and Seddon. Reclaiming of industrial sites in recent times has also created opportunity for developers to provide access to river frontage properties—development that will probably lead to further future gentrification of the region.

Historically the city grew as a result of industrialisation.[1] People settled in the area because it is close to industry, which provided employment. A transformation occurred in the eighties when there was a significant influx of migrants, particularly Vietnamese.[1]

It is important to understand the external environment that impacts upon the service delivery responsibility of the Parks and Gardens business unit. The municipality is not affluent, it is steeped in 'blue-collar' working-class values, has a diverse population of more than 65 nationalities, and is undergoing a process of gentrification that is creating a demand for increased standards in service delivery. In addition, in line with the current (at the time of writing) Victorian Liberal government policy, the council services are under pressure from the state government to reduce the cost of overall operations, in a time of reduced funding to local government, increased competition and diminishing resources.

Goals of the Parks and Gardens business unit

The Parks and Gardens business unit's goals are to:

- optimise contracts' specifications for the benefit of Council, customers and City Services
- develop service level agreements in conjunction with corporate and internal services, and to ensure their implementation to everyone's satisfaction
- strengthen the constructive relationships with the Culture and Public Spaces Department, Urban Environment Department, Assets and Infrastructure Department, Community Support Services and Council

- market the advantages of the forum of the Parks and Gardens business unit and the synergised in-house teams partnership approach to the provision of quality, competitive services to all stakeholders
- develop a programme for continuous quality improvement and the education and training of Parks and Gardens business unit staff
- exceed the obligations to Council as a business owner
- promote the development of alternative models for the sustainable delivery of services.

In its *1999–2001 Corporate Plan*, the Maribyrnong City Council outlined its commitment to:

- providing responsive and accountable leadership for the diverse communities of Maribyrnong
- facilitating and encouraging sustainable development in the best interests of the community
- providing value-for-money services and facilities that increasingly meet community expectations
- strengthening community life
- managing, improving and developing the resources of the municipality.

Maribyrnong City Council states that it has refined and developed its thinking about the environment and its relationship to the economic and social landscape. In striving to integrate environmental, economic and social factors it has developed a focus on sustainability.

Sustainability refers to fora of development and activity, which improve the quality of life and enhance the quality of the natural and social environment. It embraces social, economic and environmental issues.

The Maribyrnong City Council recognises that sustainability depends upon developing equilibrium between social and community priorities, economic realities and possibilities and good environmental management.

Introduction to self-managed work teams

Why SMWTs were introduced at Parks and Gardens

The decision to move to SMWTs within the Parks and Gardens business unit was based on many factors. One was a response to the Victorian Liberal government policy and the introduction of CCT. SMWTs made good economic sense as they maximised profit while minimising expenditure. CCT could result in low morale due to downsizing and the possibility of in-house bids not being successful. Rapid downsizing in the Maribyrnong City Council between 1994 and 1996 meant that the introduction of teams could absorb the duties that were once performed by many supervisors, as they were now shared among a flatter structure and fewer employees.

The reform process of local government saw the appointment of a new CEO and a new senior management team made up of external people who had not been part of the previous two city councils. The new director of physical services, who would previously have been a technical expert, came from a human resource management background. This was a great departure from the traditional engineering influences that had typically managed physical services. Almost immediately the new director moved into a process of consultation, explaining the challenges ahead and endeavouring to plan, as a team, for the change process.

How SMWTs were introduced—structure

The local government reform process at the Maribyrnong City Council gave the newly appointed CEO the opportunity to establish a structure that was free from earlier personnel constraints. Most councils typically adopted Mintzberg's 'Divisionalised Form' as depicted by Bolman and Deal.[2] The Maribyrnong City Council moved to a model of

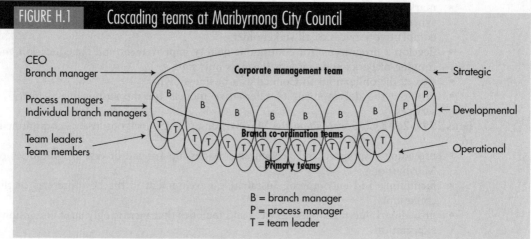

FIGURE H.1 Cascading teams at Maribyrnong City Council

B = branch manager
P = process manager
T = team leader

Source: Maribyrnong City Council internal document

cascading teams (Figure H.1) from its original divisional structure. The level of acceptance and the manner in which teams have developed within the Maribyrnong City Council varies from branch to branch. The City Services branch, which consists of all the Councils' 'tested' business units (including Parks and Gardens), is seen to be committed to the implementation of SMWTs.

The self-managed team model was invoked in the Park and Gardens business unit as a mechanism to achieve greater outputs and improve response rates to those requesting service output. One of the main drivers for this process was the need to become competitive in an era of open market and reduced resources. Prior to the introduction of CCT the business unit had consisted of 65 personnel, of whom only 40 now remain. The challenge for management was to develop a high-performing, flexible structure. Self-managed work teams appeared to be one way of achieving this and so were implemented. Prior to the self-management model, staff had operated in a hierarchical structure that perpetuated the 'X theory'.[3] Argyris[3] contends that organisations operating in the X paradigm have an inherent belief that people are lazy and constantly require supervision if they are to achieve high outputs. The self-management model requires an organisation to move away from the 'X theory' if it is to be successful.

The Park and Gardens business unit is made up of six teams with no formally-prescribed leaders. The membership of each team varies from two staff in the smallest team to nine in the largest team. Research conducted by Natale, Libertella and Rothschild[4] suggests that team sizes should be between two and twenty-five for optimal performance, so the Parks and Gardens business unit is currently operating with team membership numbers that, if the research is correct, will achieve optimal performance!

The decision process in the team is based on a consensus model. Each team member is required to hold a portfolio that reflects a core management function, such as finance or quality control. Team members are designated a specific portfolio and are required to deal with issues pertaining to that portfolio on behalf of the team.

Implementing the change to self-managing work teams — the HR approach

Although there was much anxiety during the amalgamation process, there seemed to be little resistance or open hostility towards the management team during this phase. This can be attributed to the director's ability to operate within a human resource perspective, rather than a structural one. Whether this was strategically decided by the CEO or simply occurred by chance is uncertain. It appears, however, through discussions with the Parks and Gardens business unit managers, that the process was handled well. This reinforces an assertion of Purser and Cabana[5] that strategic decision making should be people-inclusive, not people-exclusive.

The new philosophy introduced by senior management was the catalyst for the move to self-managing teams, and resulted in major change, not just in operating but also in thinking, for the staff of the Parks and Gardens business unit. Traditionally they had operated in a highly structural environment, with a culture of little trust with high levels of resentment towards the five layers of hierarchy.

Downsizing

The newly-appointed business unit manager was instructed to place the staff in teams. With the CCT process looming, it was recognised that there was a need for a reduction in staff numbers for the sake of economic competitiveness. All staff were given the option of taking voluntary departure packages. In hindsight, it is the view of many within the Parks and Gardens business unit that this was processed in an uncontrolled manner, and that good staff left the organisation at this time. Pfeffer[6] contends that 'selective recruitment is crucial for the development of successful teams, particularly as it results in a reduction of expensive training costs.' Unfortunately, many valuable people who had had a team focus left the organisation during this turbulent period.

The staff within the Parks and Gardens Unit at the Maribyrnong City Council had little choice about 'choosing' to become involved in a team. While it may be argued that staff had the choice to leave, as they could have accepted a voluntary departure package, one could also argue that this was not a viable decision for blue-collar workers in their mid- to late-forties, many of whom had left school at an early age and had subsequently only worked for the one organisation.

Effects of the changes on employees

The introduction of CCTs, downsizing and the move to SMWTs brought about considerable changes in the employees' work place. The employees of the Parks and Gardens business unit at Maribyrnong City Council found themselves working in a far more complex organisation than previously. Staff members are now required to respond to a changing community with increased expectations. At the same time, they are required to develop a range of key interpersonal skills, work effectively in teams, continue to refine work processes and deal with the ambiguity of a changing organisation.

Gainshare Scheme

One of the most significant changes for employees was the introduction of the *Gainshare Scheme*. The principles of the *Gainshare Scheme* are:
- all employees in each participating group will receive an equal share of any gain if they work equal ordinary hours
- all participating employees will be involved in the design of each gainsharing plan
- the design of gainsharing plans may differ between business units and the design and effectiveness of gainsharing plans will be reviewed at least once a year.

The aim of the *Gainshare Scheme* are to create additional funds for the ongoing development of the Public Works Provider Group and to reward staff for achieving the following outcomes:
- constant improvement in operations based on innovation and better, smarter, more cost-effective ways of doing things
- develop a viable sustainable business with the best staff, best systems, best plant and equipment and best quality outputs
- increase staff skills and knowledge
- high levels of safety performance with the aim of zero injuries
- service delivery beyond customer expectations
- public works provider operations working together as a team and providing mutual support.

The Maribyrnong City Council scheme will be reviewed not later than 12 months from the commencement of the *Local Area Work Place Agreement*, and each 12 months thereafter. The scheme is administered by a committee that is made up of a representative from each work team, plus management representatives who oversee the operation of the scheme. Grievance procedures pertaining to the scheme have been established under each team's *Local Area Work Agreements*.

The implementation and effect of the Gainshare Scheme

The 'selling' of the SMWT concept to employees is one that any salesperson could be proud of. The big winner in the 'sell' appears to be the concept of *Gainshare*. Whilst the survey results indicated that staff did not believe *Gainshare* had improved the operation of their team, the discussions with individuals certainly indicated that *Gainshare* was a prime motivator. However, the distribution of the *Gainshare* is an issue that requires further discussion with management and amongst the teams themselves.

Employees demonstrated a shift in values. Team members have the opportunity to make a lot of money through the *Gainshare* process if they perform well and secure the right project. Emphasis is placed on making the maximum amount of money through their work with the team.

The tender process creates work place stress for employees. As the teams approach the time for new tenders to be submitted, their stories become negatively focused on the process, the Council and external competitors that are likely to put in bids. This reflects the feelings of fear and insecurity felt by team members who have to compete for their livelihood every three to five years. From the authors' survey of employees, it became clear from the data compiled that team members were no longer feeling a sense of security in their jobs, which demonstrates the value that team members place on winning the next tender.

The workers' stories demonstrate their new 'survivor' mentality.[7] Once, working for the Maribyrnong City Council had meant a secure and stable job, but the new tender structure and *Gainshare* meant that their positions became unstable, insecure and focused on competition.

From the survey data collated, the *Gainshare* scheme has created a great deal of tension and competition between teams. A response from the survey indicated that team members do not believe that *Gainshare* has improved the operations of their team.

SMWTs and empowerment

Having the power to make decisions is one of the most talked-about issues within organisations. In some respects SMWTs and tendering empowered employees, as their introduction led to the teams having a good deal of power as to how the resources are used, and how the money is expended. This has come about by the delegation of authority, especially financial.

Some difference of opinion as to who were the real key stakeholders at the Council meant that many of the SMWTs felt it difficult to build and establish links with management. They felt they had little influence on decisions in relation to the tendering out of the services within the unit. At the Maribyrnong City Council it is still the case that the 'Town Hall' holds and controls the information, and this impacts significantly on the teams' ability to be self-managing and having a feeling of being in control.

Perhaps one could conclude that one of the key motivators for individuals within the SMWTs is that they felt empowered to undertake their new work practices. The teams do have clear goals and are motivated by the *Gainshare* initiative. However, on the other hand, as the life of the tender draws to a close, they feel disempowered and many now believe that they are no longer able to influence decisions in the tender process.

The tender process

Commitment to the Maribyrnong City Council

The results of the survey and discussions with staff within the SMWTs seemed to indicate that they had had a strong commitment to the Maribyrnong City Council. The impact of the tender process was disheartening for the staff, who for many years had been committed to the organisation, yet may well be unemployed in the new millennium. A perceived lack of long-term strategic direction and commitment by the 'Town Hall bureaucracy' as to the services provided by the SMWTs is an area that we believe should be further investigated and acted upon by management.

Being familiar with the politics of the Council and having a need to build upward coalitions were not things that the team members felt to be of great importance. This was interesting, as one would think that by building these coalitions, one could go some way towards influencing the decision by the Maribyrnong City Council in the next tender round.

With the current tender, it is perceived that, for the first round, the Maribyrnong City Council had been inclined to go with the system, staff and networks that they knew, rather than establish new coalitions with an external tender bidding party. The second tender round may not result in the same outcome, and this will have a huge impact on the individuals who have shown such commitment to the Parks and Gardens business unit.

The various SMWTs have differing views as to who are the players in the Maribyrnong City Council, yet all are extremely aware that there will be winners and losers with the second tender process. Interestingly, a sound majority was confident they would again win the next tender bid.

Job satisfaction

There are seven factors that increase employee acceptance of change. One of these factors is job satisfaction. In the case of the SMWTs, the satisfaction that staff indicate that they get from their job is positive—21 out of 33 respondents agreed or strongly agreed that they were satisfied with their job. Although staff surveyed were of the view that their team and individual roles had had a positive effect on the operations of the Parks and Gardens unit, the constant knowledge that the second tender round was hanging over their heads was, in our view, affecting their ability to be and feel effective. The energies of all, managers and team members alike, is being spent on putting together the next tender, supporting staff, continuing the commitment to training and allowing staff the chance to participate in the process—all at a time when staff futures are uncertain.

From the data received, both verbally and written through the survey, one could conclude that the Parks and Gardens staff are generally satisfied in their job. The survey requested a response to the statement ' I am satisfied with my job', but unfortunately did not explicitly compare this with job satisfaction prior to the introduction of SMWTs. However, the survey did investigate if working in teams is better than working in the old system. Whilst there were some extremes in the response, the majority were positive. We are not able to state conclusively that employees have greater job satisfaction as a result of the introduction of SMWTs. From discussions with individuals at the work site, we observed that there was a general 'go with the flow' attitude. Work was not 'the be-all and end-all' of their existence.

This judgment is based on data that suggested that staff felt in general that they were well paid for their skills, that there was a strong preference to remain in their existing teams and that more than half were confident that the in-house bid in the next CCT round would be successful. Fifteen responses were in the upper range, twelve responses were in the middle range, while only six staff said they were not confident that the next in-house bid would be successful.

Conflict within teams

We are of the view that scarce resources and the *Gainshare* initiative have had an even greater impact on escalating some of the unspoken conflict within teams. The decision made by the Minister to merge local governments was made to streamline resources. Winning the next tender round is not spoken about confidently by managers within the business units; the loss of the next tender bid may not only bring home a loss of meaning and purpose for the individuals and teams who have worked hard over the life of the tender, but increase the unemployment rate within the state of Victoria.

Outcomes of the tender process

The Parks and Gardens unit has successfully won three of the four areas tendered to date. The move to teams, coupled with a review of work practices, has resulted in the development of competitive bids. The tendering process has delivered savings to the Maribyrnong City Council, as services are delivered for considerably less than had previously been the case. In some cases, half the staff deliver a more consistent and higher quality service.

The development of service specifications as a result of the tendering process has provided a clear requirement of activities for service provision. To date, the Parks and Gardens teams are delivering the requirements of the specifications and in some cases exceeding expectations.

The tendering process provided a catalyst for the move towards self-managed teams. As a result, teams have been given the authority to control expenditure related to the delivery

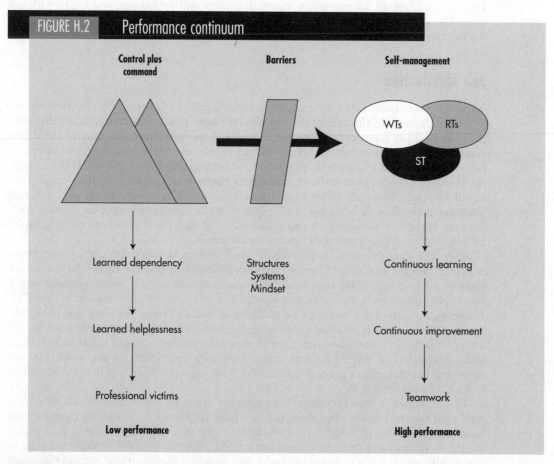

FIGURE H.2   Performance continuum

Source: G. Donovan, 'Serendipity,' *Self Managed Work Team Global Network*, (1997) Perth, Australia: 3.

of services. Teams have improved purchasing practices and developed financial management skills to monitor expenditure. A generous *Gainshare* system was introduced to encourage each team to be frugal with budgets. Although there are examples of teams becoming overzealous in an endeavour to generate savings, there has overall been positive behavioural change in the way that teams manage plant, equipment and material—a process that had traditionally been abused.

The outcome for teams has been the acquisition of greater scope for decision making, the development of new skills and a capacity to generate additional income. The Parks management is able to focus on future bids, as the teams now have independent accountability for the delivery of the service. The Maribyrnong City Council is receiving the service at a competitive market rate.

Summary

In conclusion, the implementation of self-managed work teams has been successful according to the broadest indicators. The Maribyrnong City Council Physical Services area, of which the Parks and Gardens business unit is part, is delivering services two million dollars cheaper than that prior to tender. This has been achieved with half the number of staff, no industrial disputation and in a municipality that has doubled in geographic area.

From this, it can be concluded that the implementation of the self-managed work team model appears to have been successful from a structural and economic perspective. Teams have successfully won tenders and are currently delivering services more efficiently and effectively than was previously the case. The challenge is to continue the move towards high performance as illustrated by Donovan in Figure H.2, in order to remain competitive and viable.

The Maribyrnong City Council is committed to continuous learning, continuous improvement and the concept of teams, yet this could be viewed as being only for the life of the current tender.

It is the view of the authors that the concept of tendering out services that are to be delivered to the community is fraught with imminent failure—the need for this process is short-sighted and not desirable in the longer term. However, the introduction of SMWTs has, in our view, been a successful change management strategy.

The difficulty in drawing a conclusion about the success or otherwise of the introduction of self-managed work teams at the Parks and Gardens business unit is that, along with the introduction and implementation, comes the large 'CCT guillotine' hanging over each team's head, which is about to fall again in mid-2000. The signs are there for a positive second bid, as long as the business unit managers do not get bogged down in the structural and staffing issues, but take the time to reflect on the achievements of the past tender period, and, more importantly, the achievements of the teams. They should celebrate those achievements before the announcement of the next tender bid results.

QUESTIONS

1 What effects do you think tendering will have on local government services in the future?

2 Describe the administrative procedures involved in applying for local government tenders.

3 Explain the concept of *Gainshare*. How useful is this as a change management tool? What are its limitations/advantages/disadvantages?

4 Explain Mintzberg's 'divisionalised form'. How did the Maribyrnong City Council's new structure differ from this?

5 In what circumstances are SMWTs an effective change management strategy? List the advantages and disadvantages.

6 What are the indicators of a successful SMWT?

7 How might successful SMWTs be developed in a local government setting such as at the Maribyrnong City Council Parks and Gardens business unit?

8 How might managers better deal with employees who are forced to undergo similar work place change to those at the Maribyrnong City Council?

9 Discuss ways by which employees might be helped to deal with the stress associated with winning.

Notes

1 J. Lack, *The History of Footscray* (Victoria, Australia: Hargeen Publishing Company, 1991): 93, 407.

2 L. Bolman and T. Deal, *Reframing Organizations*, 2nd edn (San Francisco: Jossey-Bass, 1997).

3 C. Argryris, *Management and Organisational Development: The Path from XA to YB*, (Sydney: McGraw-Hill Inc.): 7.

4 S. Natale, A. Libertella and B. Rothschild, 'Team performance management', *Team Performance Management: an International Journal*, 1:2 (New York, 1995): 10.

5 R. Purser and S. Cabana, 'Involve employees at every level of strategic planning', *Quality Progress*, 30 (May 1997): 66.

6 J. Pfeffer, 'Successful organization', *Executive–Excellence*, 15:3 (March 1998): 11–12.

7 S. Appelbaum, C. Delage, N. Labib and G. Gault, 'The survivor syndrome: aftermath of downsizing', *Career Development International*, 2 (MCB University Press, 1997): 279–86.

Other references

L. Bolman and T. Deal, *Organization Dynamics*, (Fall 1992): 21, 34–44 .

G. Donovan and J. Cluer, '100 Lessons from self-managed work teams', *Self-Managed Work Team Global Network* (Perth, Australia, 1994): 7.

G. Donovan, 'Serendipity', *Self-Managed Work Team Global Network* (Perth, Australia, 1997): 3.

Call centre relocation: Advantage Credit Union

By **Paul Bolton, Philip Carr, Kylie Davenport, Kent Hansen and Theo Tolkis**

Introduction

Advantage Credit Union was formed by the merger of Advantage Credit Union Ltd and Piccol Credit Co-operative Ltd, both of which had been in business for more than 30 years and had grown as the result of numerous mergers.

In response to the growing demand by its members to do business over the phone, and its vision of becoming a national direct credit union by the year 2003, the former Piccol Credit Co-operative had established a call centre at its head office. This call centre, Member Direct, originally had had a staff of four and took between 3000 and 4000 calls a month. Over time the number of calls increased, as did the number of staff.

This rapid expansion strained the ability of Member Direct to continue to handle the growing number of calls effectively and efficiently. The call management system was showing signs of not being able to cope with the volume, and was in need of an upgrade. However, the area could only accommodate one or two more staff members before a major upgrade to the facilities was required.

Average wait times, a measure of call centre effectiveness and efficiency, were six times the industry average, which was around 20 to 30 seconds. It was evident that, if Piccol was to continue to develop its direct strategy, it would need to redevelop the call centre. As a result of the rapid growth, a decision was made to move the call centre from Melbourne to Dandenong.

Industry profile

In the customer service desert that is the financial services industry, the credit union is becoming an oasis from economic rationalisation.

The financial services industry is dominated by the 'Big 4' banking institutions, whose sole objective is to provide a return to shareholders via dividends and share value growth.

As the market 'reacts' to any announcements, it is not unusual to read of massive sackings, closures or sale of non-performing assets immediately before or after a profit announcement is made. As an example, the NAB announced a disappointing $900 million net profit for the half-year just ended, which was followed immediately by an announcement that fees were to be increased on a range of products.

Is it any wonder that people, disenchanted by the 'Big 4', are deserting them in favour of smaller, customer-focused institutions, such as Advantage Credit Union and the like?

The lengths to which the Advantage Credit Union went to provide benefits for the affected staff illustrated the difference between a big bank and the Advantage Credit Union. An article in *The Age* in March 1998 stated that total employment in the banking industry has dropped by 17% since 1991, with almost 40 000 bank employees retrenched due to closures, mergers and new technology. An example is Westpac, who retrenched 270 people from around Australia to set up its centralised mortgage settlement department in Adelaide.

Advantage Credit Union is a part of the Australian finance industry and the wider International Co-operative Movement. Advantage Credit Union is a financial co-operative created under the framework of the Australian Financial Institutions Code. As a financial co-operative, Advantage Credit Union operates under a mutual structure whereby members are both owners and customers.

On 1 October 1997, Advantage Credit Union and Piccol Credit Union ceased trading independently and emerged as a new entity, Advantage Credit Union Ltd.

In October 1995, Piccol had merged with a large community-based credit union, the Dandenong Community Credit Union. Dandenong Credit Union did not have a call centre, but it had installed an Interactive Voice Response Unit (IVR) to handle basic member enquiries, such as balances, statement requests and transfers. The IVR was taking some 6000 calls a month. In planning for the merging of the two databases, which occurred on 31 December 1995, it was decided that the IVR system would be upgraded to cope with the number of calls expected to come from the merged entity. It was also decided that Member Direct's staff numbers would be increased to cope with the extra enquiries. At the time of the database merger, Member Direct had ten staff.

In the ensuing months, the number of calls handled by Member Direct increased, as did the number of calls handled by the IVR. During the period from January 1996 to March 1997, various other changes relating to how calls into Piccol were handled were instigated. One of these was the installation of a national 13 number, 13 11 40, which was advertised to members as the way to contact Piccol. Callers to this number were given three options. Option 1 connected them to the IVR for balances, transaction enquiries, transfers and statements. Option 2 transferred them to an operator for loan enquiries and option 3 transferred them to a Member Direct consultant for any other type of enquiry.

By February 1997, Piccol was receiving approximately 80 000 calls per month. Some 22 000 were transferred to options 2 or 3. By this stage there were 14 staff handling the calls and it was evident that this area would continue to grow rapidly.

In March 1997 a task group was formed, consisting of the retail services manager, Member Direct manager and Member Direct supervisor. The purpose of the group was to review the options available and recommend an outcome. They were to also take into account the need to provide a contingency plan for the call centre operation should the Collins Street site lose communications, as had been the case in early February when there had been a bomb hoax.

The recommendation of the task group was to develop the first floor of the Dandenong office into a second call centre. Piccol, through its merger with Dandenong Credit Union, owned the building at Dandenong. The idea was that Member Direct would be split into two, with staff working within Member Direct being given the opportunity to nominate to work either in the city or at Dandenong. Over time it was envisaged that the Dandenong site would grow in numbers to become the predominant site. However, the Collins Street site would continue to 'house' a portion of Member Direct, and calls would be split evenly between the two sites. This recommendation was accepted.

Staff in the call centre were notified of the proposed changes and given the opportunity to request a transfer to the Dandenong site, which five did. They were also told that, at least initially, any new staff recruited for the call centre would be advised that they were to work at Dandenong. Approval was given to employ two new staff members.

In June 1997, agreement for the merger between Piccol and Advantage Credit Unions was reached. The official merger date was to be 1 October 1997, but the databases were not to merge until 31 March 1998. To co-ordinate the implementation of the database merger, a Merger Implementation Committee (MIC) was formed, made up of the Advantage general manager, Advantage IT manager and the Piccol retail services manager. It was the responsibility of the team to coordinate a review of all aspects of the operation, and, ultimately, after consultation with the internal stakeholders, decide on which aspects of both organisations would be kept in the merged entity. It was through this review process that the following recommendations on the operation of the call centre were approved.

- The Piccol IVR would be kept and upgraded to cope with the combined entities calls, once the databases had been merged.
- The Piccol national 13 number 13 11 40 would become the new Advantage Credit Union advertised phone number.

- Due to space restrictions at head office, the call centre was to relocate to Dandenong. The Dandenong site would be developed to accommodate 40 staff in the call centre.
- The new site would be fully operational by 1 February 1998.

Management realised that this change would affect a number of staff from the current Piccol call centre who lived far from Dandenong. Before announcing the change to staff the management team formulated an offer that included a compensation package for the affected staff and a communications package for the rest of the organisation.

The 15 staff members in Member Direct were called to a meeting on Thursday 28 August 1997, when the CEO, human resources manager and retail services manager advised them of the impending changes and their options.

In fairness to the Member Direct manager, he was notified of the change before the meeting. While staff were aware that Dandenong would eventually become the major site, no one had expected the change to be as sudden. Staff members were given the opportunity to discuss the change and ask any immediate questions.

Staff were encouraged to talk it through and to speak to the CEO, retail services manager or human resources manager over the ensuing few days. They were advised that the retail services and human resources managers would be in constant touch over the next few weeks. The rest of the organisation was advised once the meeting had finished.

Many questions were asked over the ensuing weeks as staff internalised the change and considered their options. While they were not obliged to notify the organisation of their intentions immediately, it became evident that up to eight or nine staff would require redeployment. With this in mind, and with the expected extra calls as a result of the database merger at the end of February 1998, it was decided to employ an additional 12 staff early in November in order to allow time for induction and training.

Member Direct personnel were encouraged to have input into the design of the new call centre. Those who wished were taken out to Dandenong by the retail services manager, initially to allow them to get their bearings and later, nearer the time of the call centre's completion, to see their almost completed new 'home'.

A year after the announcement, in January 1998, the call centre moved to Dandenong. There were then twenty-five staff and a further six were to be employed early in 1999. Of the original staff, five are still there. Of that five, all but one was expected to move to Dandenong. Of those who tried the move to Dandenong, one left due to pregnancy (but was due to return) and one requested to be moved back to Collins Street after three months. This request was accommodated. Another transferred to Dandenong, but resigned six months later to go to another company. One was dismissed due to an indiscretion, while another staff member chose to take the package offered after three months.

The other staff members who chose not to go were all accommodated with positions at Collins Street. The Member Direct manager resigned to take up a new position at a company in Mulgrave in November 1997.

One of the major issues to be addressed as a result of the change and the influx of new staff was the loss of knowledge from those who left. New staff require six months to fully understand all the products and services offered by the Credit Union. The 13 number now handles more than 200 000 calls a month, of which some 37 000 to 40 000 are transferred to the call centre at Dandenong. The average hold time is now around 20 to 25 seconds.

Managements' perspective on the change

From a management perspective, the move to Dandenong was seen as a relatively painless and successful move. The management team philosophy had been to foresee any obstacles that might have occurred in a bid to achieve the goal of a smooth transition of the call centre from the city to the outer suburb of Dandenong. The human resources manager was quite adamant that the transition went according to plan, without any major problems. This was due to the establishment of a 'guiding committee', which ensured that all facets of the move were competently handled. This 'guiding committee' was made up of the CEO, human resources manager and retail services manager.

In the interview conducted with the HR manager, the underlying mentality was that the move was inevitable and the associated 'grieving or that type of stuff' was merely a typical consequence of the move that was being implemented. It was interesting to note that, although the organisational co-ordination was quite professional, the emotional ramifications were not addressed. In fact it was surprising to learn that they had not been foreseen as a major obstacle.

In the change process, we witness the professional efficiency of the management team's approach to the relocation of the call centre. Establishing a sense of urgency, forming a powerful guiding coalition, creating a vision and communicating that particular vision were all predominant in the transition process. Immediately after the decision to relocate the call centre had been made, it was promoted as an urgent requirement, due to the increasing number of calls and the strains they were placing on the Member Direct department.

The staff members were notified four months before the proposed operational date of 1 February 1998, and their options outlined to them. The establishment and introduction of a 'guiding committee' helped to ensure that all possible difficulties or adverse issues were foreseen and procedures implemented in the process to address these particular issues.

In his communication to the staff, the CEO outlined the justifications for the move and the potential benefits to the organisation. He also offered his services, as well as those of the human resources and retail services managers, to further address any personal issues that might arise. It comes as no surprise that most, in fact nearly all, management–employee discussions that took place involved the independent 'approachable' human resources manager.

Although staff were encouraged to voice their ideas on the aesthetics of the new call centre, they were not given any say in the decision-making process as to how the transition would take place.

The human resources department chose to address the 'touchy–feely' issues on an individual basis as they arose. Even then, it was left to the discretion of the individual to voice their opinions on any feelings, of mistreatment, grief or loss, rather than openly discuss these matters in a counselling type environment.

Management's goal was to develop a facility that would effectively handle the expected increase in call volume, while at the same time reducing average wait times to acceptable industry levels. In this regard management achieved its goal.

The staff members' perspective of the change

As was to be expected, all surveyed expressed shock and disbelief when they heard the announcement that the call centre would be moved. This reaction did not change significantly in the following fortnight.

All respondents were able to recall the reasons given for the move and all agreed that the move made sense. In this case it is to be questioned why the attitude of the staff did not progress from their initial reaction of shock and disbelief. The reasons for the move were not just economic, but also service-oriented in that it would enable the Advantage Credit Union, through a state-of-the-art call centre, to better serve its members well into the future.

The staff who were surveyed indicated that management had been up-front with the reasons for the change, but had not reinforced the vision of expanding the company to its members. The staff members indicated that they were not happy about how the announcement had been made, but they been unable to recommend alternatives, apart from first advising the Member Direct supervisor.

The use of metaphors in the change process

An examination of the metaphors used by staff members to describe their organisation highlighted that management may have been able to use metaphors as a useful tool in the change process.

The overwhelming metaphor used by respondents was that of a family, reflecting on the culture of the organisation, which is based upon the principles of 'co-operation, moral integrity, trust, financial prudence, caring for members and social responsibility'.[1] One of the goals of the organisation is to 'create a people-focused culture'.

There is a child–parent type relationship between the staff and management. An example of this was to be seen on the day that the managers took the staff to see the facility at Dandenong. It was like a family outing, including a trip to Hungry Jacks and an ice-cream on the way home. The CEO is considered to be the father figure, and, when the change was announced, the staff surveyed did not feel that the CEO was approachable about the issue.

It is noteworthy that various staff spoke about the family being broken up and likened the move to a divorce. The staff members that were happy with the change were disturbed by the fact that other staff members were unhappy. This indicated the strong bonds between staff members.

Other metaphors used to describe the change included a school, which may also indicate a child–adult type relationship. The oldest staff member described the organisation as a well-oiled machine, which may have been influenced by this staff member's age, having been brought up through the industrial revolution. This staff member also described herself as a mother to the other staff members in the organisation, once again implying a family relationship. A staff member, who had not been directly involved in the call centre before the change, described the city call centre as a time-bomb waiting to go off because of the work overload and the system's inability to cope adequately with the call volume.

One staff member, who had initially been happy with the change, felt left out because management was not paying attention to those who were happy, and the staff member also felt isolated from the team members who were unhappy. She commented that there was almost a feeling of resentment towards her because she was happy with the change, which made her feel even more isolated.

Due to the distance from the city to Dandenong, the staff members were concerned that a part of the family would now be isolated from the head office. It was as though social contacts were being severed, which was very difficult for the staff to come to terms with.

A high degree of psychological ownership was evident between the staff members and the team. The change threatened both self-continuity and the staff members' ability to control what was happening to the team, and this led to considerable resistance. The metaphor of the family and divorce, where the children have no control over the inevitable separation of the family unit, has some relevance here.

The 'family home' was no longer able to cope with the growth and maturity of the organisation. The staff members felt as though they were being pushed out of the 'nest'— and they had no control over this situation. The change in the environment had created a feeling that the psychological contract had been violated.

Conclusion

The move was regarded by management as a success, especially as, after only a few months, the call centre was fully operational and performance had improved. What should be of concern to the management, however, is the residual resistance toward the organisation.

The financial services industry is one of the most competitive segments. As such, future changes are to be expected. The continued neglect of this residual resistance to change could undermine the strategic competitive advantage of the Advantage Credit Union—its staff's commitment to the organisation. The management might feel that they 'got away with it' this time, but unless they are aware of, and attempt to combat the residual resistance, it will grow to become a larger resisting force against change that may affect the success of any future transitions.

QUESTIONS

1 Using Kotter's framework, describe the strengths and weaknesses of management's implementation of the change.[2]

2 'When a metaphor in use is known, it is easier for those in charge to communicate with those that may be affected.'[3] Discuss this statement in relation to this case.

3 The financial industry is dynamically changing. What are the lessons to be learnt from this change?

4 Using Lewin's *Force-field Analysis*, depict both the driving and resisting forces of change. Discuss what effect the understanding of this theory would have on the change process in this case.[4]

5 What recommendations do you suggest could have further enhanced this change process?

6 Discuss the change as related to Bridge's 'Three Stage Theory'.[5]

Notes

1   *Advantage Credit Union Plan 1998–2003.*

2   J. Kotter, *Leading Change*, (Massachusetts: Harvard Business School Press, 1996).

3   I. Palmer and R. Dunford 'Understanding organisations through metaphor' in *Organisation Development. Metaphorical Explorations*, eds C. Oswick and D. Grant (London: Pitman, 1996).

4   K. Lewin, *Field Theory in Social Science* (New York: Harper and Row, 1951).

5   W. Bridges, 'Managing organizational transitions', *Organizational Dynamics*, 15 (1986): 24–33.

CASE STUDY J

Melbourne City Parking and Traffic

By **Olivia Tsen and Chulanga Jayawardanai (with contributions by Paul Wilson)**

Description of the organisation

The following case study concerns a government sector service organisation within the Department of Development and Statutory Services of the Council of the City of Melbourne, one of the largest capital cities in Australia, situated on the south-east coast.

The City of Melbourne has practised by-laws enforcement since 1922. In that year, during a police strike, the By-Laws and Traffic branch was formed by recruiting police officers who had had their positions abolished. From then until 1985 this branch was part of the town clerk's office, which eventually amalgamated with the Traffic Engineer's branch. In 1985, after the branch had undergone restructuring, it became part of the Regulatory Services Group.

Parking and Traffic, as it has since been renamed, now consists of a labour force of 150 personnel. The organisation stems from the principal officer and branches out to the co-ordinator of parking and traffic regulations and the co-ordinator of correspondence and payments. Over 80% of the employees are under the management of the co-ordinator of parking and traffic regulations, whose group is made up of two project officers, eight staff in the communications centre, 20 school supervisors and 102 traffic officers.

The organisation is proactive in the provision of on-street parking turnover, traffic flow, road safety and information services. The major activities performed by Parking and Traffic are: traffic management and administration, parking management and parking enforcement and administration.

Traffic management and administration

As far as traffic management and administration are concerned, the foremost tasks encompass traffic administration, traffic signals, traffic installations and street lighting. In an effort to satisfy these concerns, Parking and Traffic provide services such as the investigation, design and supervision of traffic management systems, supervision of school crossings, investigation and design and review of road-markings for traffic control and production and the construction and maintenance of traffic signs. They also maintain safety zones and pedestrian crossings, provide and set up temporary road barriers when required, and are responsible for the level of street lighting in all locations around Melbourne.

Parking management

In terms of parking management, Parking and Traffic are responsible for on-street parking, off-street parking, and the management of sports centre car parks. Therefore, their services include the investigation of parking requirements, the provision, construction and maintenance of parking signs, control of all meter parking zones and collection of all revenues. Services also include the management and provision of off-street parking facilities and short-term parking facilities in various locations, as well as ensuring that there is adequate car parking facilities in place for functions at the various sporting venues in Melbourne.

Parking enforcement and administration

Parking enforcement and administration activities include the enforcement of all traffic and parking by-laws, monitoring and taking appropriate actions in relation to abandoned vehicles, as well as the processing and control of all parking infringement notices throughout the City of Melbourne.

Apart from the activities normally expected in parking and traffic management, the organisation has recently extended its duties. New activities involve co-ordinating and liaising with the police and the sheriff's office on special operations that relate to stolen vehicles and other criminal matters. Staff of the organisation co-ordinate and liaise with the Victorian Taxi Association (VTA), VicRoads, state agencies and industry groups; and play a crucial role in information dissemination and special events. This is especially important as Melbourne thrives on tourism, business and entertainment. Parking and Traffic are also involved in planning and participating in the state's 'Displan', which involves preparations for emergency situations that may range from small-scale state emergency plans to natural disasters.

Parking and Traffic have recognised that they should play a fundamental role in customer service. One of the most urgent corporate goals is to deliver quality services that are responsive to business and community expectations, demonstrably cost-effective and subject to public accountability.[1] The main customers are the residents, businesses, motorists, schools, pedestrians, visitors and delivery agents of the City of Melbourne.

The change processes at Parking and Traffic

Parking and Traffic has been experiencing what could be termed as 'evolutionary changes' ever since it was first created. In the early stages of its operation, traffic officers had police type duties, and over the years their duties have been predominantly focused on the issuing of infringement notices. Now their occupation includes a host of varied duties, as already mentioned.

Parking and Traffic has experienced changes in many areas and their impact has affected the organisation in different degrees. Some of the changes that Parking and Traffic have undergone are:

- the introduction of women to carry out duties that had been the preserve of men for years
- the introduction of staff of various nationalities and cultures
- the introduction of computerised technology
- the adoption of a customer-oriented approach
- amendments to work practices and policies
- the introduction of new management approaches and objectives.

At the beginning of 1990 there was a great push for change, instigated by the Victorian state government and the Council of the City of Melbourne. Evidence of this was the introduction of enterprise bargaining in 1993, a large investment in technology in 1994, the formulation of a five-year contingency plan in 1997 and the introduction of programmes such as *QUALITAS* and *Best Value* during 1996 and 1997.

The aim of Parking and Traffic was to improve the quality of work through efficiency and effectiveness, through a culture that promoted continuous improvement and learning, and through a customer-oriented approach. In essence, Parking and Traffic wanted to create an organisation that would benchmark working practices in the industry, both at a national and international level.

This being Parking and Traffic's largest and most challenging change process, it was imperative for the organisation to manage this transition and evaluate its progress. Therefore, this case study will focus on the three main areas that were the most significant to the change process:

- technological change
- teams
- cultural change.

Technological change at Parking and Traffic

Technology has brought about changes to many organisations, regardless of size, sector or industry. In Parking and Traffic, technology has had an immense impact on the organisation and its employees. As in most organisations, the introduction of personal computers has considerably changed the working environment, administration and processing. However, the greatest technological change to affect the work of traffic officers was the introduction of the hand-held AutoCite in 1994.

Before 1994, infringement notices were all handwritten. At the time, this process of issuing infringement notices was acceptable, simply because there were no other comparable methods. It was only in 1994, when an American company approached Parking and Traffic about their innovative product called the AutoCite, that it became obvious that the method being used was inefficient.

The handwritten tickets were inefficient because writing them was time-consuming, they involved a lot of paperwork, were prone to a high incidence of inaccuracies, were difficult to write out in adverse weather conditions and, consequently, the number of tickets issued was too low. The AutoCite had the potential to eliminate these problems, offering both efficiency and safety, as it enabled the traffic officers to quickly issue a ticket in dangerous areas of Melbourne. After the capabilities of the AutoCite had been demonstrated, the machines were 'road-tested' in the City of Melbourne. Machines were assessed by users for qualitative factors such as ease of use, suitability for the parking layout of the City of Melbourne, the speed of processing and the reduction of other problems associated with the issuing of handwritten parking infringements (e.g. the accuracy of recorded information). After these preliminary tests, Parking and Traffic embarked on the process of introducing the machine.

Implementation of the AutoCite technology

As management set out to meet the objectives of increasing efficiency and cost-effectiveness, the main target was to successfully implement the new technology. Management first consulted the team leader and the assistant team leaders about AutoCite. Having gained their confidence in the benefits of the new hand-held machine, they proceeded to communicate the benefits to the employees, who were given the opportunity to voice their opinions and express any concerns they might have had about the AutoCite.

There was also a strong union involvement in this change process. Officers and the union were involved in group discussions about the usability of the AutoCite machines. Areas of discussion included problems with the machines, improvements in the actual issuing of the tickets, increased interaction with other officers and departments (due to shorter processing time) and changes in job satisfaction and morale.

Management also actively involved staff in software design so that the imported technology would be suitable for local use. Similarly, basic modifications to the machine were only made after the staff had experimented with the device. Such participation increased their acceptance of the new technology, as each individual was given an opportunity to participate at each stage of the change process. Furthermore, it was seen that staff involvement was likely to lead to increased employee commitment and motivation as each individual had interest and ownership of the change process.[2] Management provided training under the guidance of a qualified trainer, so that staff could effectively use the device with minimal error.

Outcome of the change to AutoCite technology

Despite an overall acceptance of the introduction of the AutoCite, it was apparent that there was still some resistance from the traffic officers. As the co-ordinator of parking and traffic observed, they felt as though a 'big brother was watching over them', since the AutoCite recorded information about the location and the time when tickets were issued. In this way, it was possible to observe if they were working consistently. Some officers felt

TABLE J.1	Parking revenue 1993–97				
	1993	**1994**	**1995**	**1996**	**1997**
Parking revenue ($m)	24.8	26.2	18.5	23.4	30.14

Source: Melbourne City Council, *Annual Review 1996–1997* (Melbourne, September 1997): 88.

threatened by the machine, as they thought it implied they would have to meet higher targets, and the older members of the workforce were worried that they would find the AutoCite difficult to operate. In the most extreme cases, a few workers opposed it so much that they left the organisation. However, management was tolerant of the opposition and the AutoCite was accepted by nearly all members. Acceptance was aided by the fact that management trained the employees for three to four months with the new machines, using training officers from the American company. To minimise any pressures felt by the officers when faced with the new technology, management chose not to set performance targets, instead using past performance data, which served as a guide to improve performance. After a trial period, periodic tests were conducted to assess the performance of staff, and to offer feedback so that each worker was aware of his or her progress.

After the installation of the AutoCite, it was observed that the new device enabled staff to process an infringement notice expediently. As a result of this, each officer was able to improve parking turnover and traffic flow by detecting more offenders during their shift. While it might have seemed that this device was employed to raise revenue, staff were not threatened with having to penalise more offenders in order to justify the cost of the technology. Although an increase in parking revenue was recorded in 1994 (Table J.1), this trend is mainly attributed to the escalating value of each infringement notice, which was set externally by the state government and Road Traffic Authority (RTA). Despite the efficiency of the new device, it was observed that over time the number of recorded offences decreased, as greater emphasis was placed upon improving customer service and public safety.

The new technology also improved the accuracy of each infringement notice. As some officers were required to attend court and justify their actions when removing or impounding a vehicle, the new device helped both management and staff as information about each infringement was lodged into the information management system. Consequently, over time the proportion of cases withdrawn decreased as the accuracy of processing each infringement notice improved. As a result, the organisation saved considerable time and money, as fewer cases were dismissed when taken to court.

Another benefit of the new technology was increased managerial control. As data pertaining to each offence was stored in the device and later entered into the information management system, management could identify high and low performers. While allowing for differences in ability and other situational factors, management was able to compare the performance of one employee against another (assuming that both officers covered the same geographical route) by referring to data stored in the information system. In addition, the new device enabled management to co-ordinate staff more effectively by identifying areas in which there were likely to be more or fewer offenders, thereby increasing detection and improving traffic flow and public safety.

Various data were entered into the device so that an officer could retrieve information from other departments. These data were used to carry out tasks that would otherwise have been performed by other departments. For example, if an officer suspected that a vehicle had been abandoned, relevant information could be verified by the retrieval of data contained in the unit. Besides this, general information was also inserted into the unit so that each officer could help the public with tourist and street information. Hence, the change process led to each worker being required to perform a wider variety of tasks.

Work redesign and the use of teams at Parking and Traffic

In October 1993, enterprise bargaining pressured organisations to improve working conditions, e.g. to increase decision making, responsibility and skill formation. Unions, management and employees were all involved in the negotiation process. An outcome of this was the introduction of teams in Parking and Traffic, which were considered to be vital to instigating a more efficient and effective workforce. Prior to this, traffic officers worked individually.

The workforce was divided into eight teams, each team having a team leader and an assistant team leader. In conjunction with team formation, working hours of the employees were changed. Shifts ranged from a seven-day spread with a week off every ten weeks, to four days on, four days off. Shifts encompassed day shifts, night shifts and weekend shifts with compensation and penalty rates complementing the type of shift and the range of hours worked. These changes in shifts had implications for individuals as their working hours affected their private, family and working life. However, management found overall that employees were generally supportive and understanding of the new shifts and of the change to working in teams. Parking and Traffic did not encounter much resistance to the team approach. As the co-ordinator of parking and traffic explained, 'A few employees found it difficult to work as a team, but we have hardly had any problems once the employees settled into their new work routine.'

The objective of the team orientation approach was to create a sense of belonging, increase cohesiveness, motivation, safety and, overall, to increase productivity. With the types of shifts that were available, it was required that traffic officers work in pairs to enhance their personal safety. Teams were rotated every week between the different geographical locations. Management was able to place an individual officer at a certain location and given time because of the detailed shifts, colour-coded areas on city maps, radio and mobile communications. This information was particularly useful, for example, in times of emergency. Traffic officers were able to respond and be located faster than previously. The rotation system also enabled officers to experience different locations, duties and responsibilities. The composition of the teams was determined by the workers themselves in order to avoid any disagreements.

Team meetings were conducted on a weekly basis, with each team being given an opportunity to host the meeting. Each team member was encouraged to participate in the conduct of the meeting. The objectives of the team meetings were to monitor the progress of teams, address any issues or concerns, provide information updates and obtain feedback or put forward ways of improving team functioning. Another significant outcome from the introduction of team working was the opportunity for promotion. Individuals were able to fulfil and carry out some of their superiors' duties, and through recognition of their capabilities and experience, given opportunities to progress through the organisation.

Teams also enabled particular staff (team leaders and assistant team leaders) to improve their interpersonal skills (such as communication, negotiation and conflict resolution) through training, so that the team could function more effectively. As observed by management, improving the competencies and skills of particular workers appeared to enhance worker commitment and job satisfaction. Training also improved the organisational skill base, and gave some workers an incentive to seek advancement within the organisation.

Cultural change at Parking and Traffic

In 1997 the City of Melbourne Council formulated a five-year contingency plan, which affected all the departments in the council. This included a commitment to delivering quality services to about 1.5 million customers, increased responsiveness to business and community expectations, and the avowed intention to become more cost-effective and publicly accountable.[3] The main aim was to place the council in a very secure financial position, that would ensure that better administration could be achieved, and so allow the council to improve its performance.

The first step that the council initiated was the development of the corporate plan, which documented the vision, mission and values of the council. It also outlined the projects and strategies that would be undertaken to achieve this vision. The corporate plan placed pressures on the Parking and Traffic division to also adopt this customer-oriented approach. It was apparent that customer service needed to be improved within Parking and Traffic. A customer satisfaction survey conducted in late 1996 showed that improvements in on-street parking and traffic management were being demanded by residents.[3]

Parking and Traffic recognised the need not only for individual attitudinal and behavioural changes, but also for continually improving its work practices in the pursuit of their new corporate culture. The formation of the City of Melbourne's quality strategy called *QUALITAS*, together with the organisation's *Enterprise Bargaining Agreement*, meant that quality achievement was necessary throughout all the organisation's activities. Through *QUALITAS*, Parking and Traffic has started a process of continuously developing the professional skills of all employees and making the organisation a more enjoyable place to work.[3]

Implementation of the cultural change

Management embarked on the task of distributing information about the change process to staff. They then communicated to staff the importance of this change, and offered workers an opportunity to discuss any issue that might have been of particular concern to them. As a result, management perceived that such discussions increased the acceptance of change, as most employees understood the purpose and intended outcomes of this shift in culture. Employees were invited to identify inefficient practice so that management and staff could take whatever action was necessary to improve the quality of customer service.

Training also helped to foster the customer service culture. Staff were educated through training programmes such as stress management, legislation classes, verbal judo courses, interpersonal skills development and body language. They were also required to have a general knowledge of various tourist sites, places of interest and public transport in Melbourne as they were now to play a significant role as information officers for the public and tourists. National exchange programmes were also set up, so that staff were able to expand their knowledge of work practices in other states, cities and suburbs. They were required to conduct presentations on their research and express their opinions, and were encouraged to propose recommendations.

This training and development was particularly important as many had not participated in this type of training before, and it reinforced the new customer-oriented approach of the organisation. While enabling staff to perform their task effectively, the provision of training also improved the organisational skill base.

Outcome of the cultural change

Overall, the cultural change had a dramatic impact on the staff. In the beginning it was perceived that the staff of Parking and Traffic held fears of conformity. It was not in their existing culture to be so involved, accountable and constantly evaluated. Some of the staff struggled to adopt this customer-service approach. Some found it a disruption of their routine. Previously, they had not had to perform more than the minimal task of issuing parking tickets at their discretion. There remained after some time a few members of the work force who still had not accepted the cultural change. However, the majority of the staff of Parking and Traffic embraced it with enthusiasm. In recognition of this, Parking and Traffic received an award by the Council of City of Melbourne for their achievements.

It also appeared that some officers were unclear about their role and function within the organisation during the change process. The message from management that customer service was paramount led some to become confused as to whether this goal was more important than other established organisational goals. Another perceived problem with the change was that several workers failed to internalise the shift in culture. Some appeared unwilling to give up the familiar for the unknown, whereas others opposed the change because of the potential disruption to routine and habit.

Continuous change at Parking and Traffic

Overall, there is evidence to suggest that service quality and organisational performance improved after the change processes that had taken place at Parking and Traffic over the previous five years. Changes to the AutoCite system enabled an increase in the level of parking turnover, increased the detection of offenders and improved information accuracy. Customer feedback and public fora aided Parking and Traffic in evaluating the success of their change in culture. The responses indicated notable improvement, and also highlighted where further progress was required. Employee surveys showed that employees generally understood the goals of the organisation and what was expected of them. Furthermore, despite some instances of resistance and opposition to change, surveys and feedback in team discussions seem to indicate general increases in communication, employee participation and, as a whole, an acceptance of the change in culture.[4]

Although there are obvious improvements in quality and performance, it is difficult to draw sound conclusions as change is still taking place. Parking and Traffic's continual drives for change stem primarily from the City of Melbourne's recent adoption of various quality strategies. In particular, two major policies have placed pressures on the Parking and Traffic division to maintain their customer-service orientation and increase quality through the promotion of creativity and skills development.

1 The quality strategy for Melbourne City, called *QUALITAS*, which was implemented in 1996–97, encourages the continual professional development of staff and increased quality of work life. This has the ultimate objective of improved customer and quality service.[3]

2 The '*Best Value*' approach, which was also recently introduced by Melbourne City to ensure the delivery of cost-effective yet quality services. This policy encompasses several requirements:

- proof that services and activities are of the best quality and price
- proof that the whole organisation demonstrates *Best Value*
- a clear indication of the future activities and services that will be undertaken to maintain *Best Value*
- that Melbourne City will retain its reputation as a leader in progressive reform.[5]

In line with these policies, developments in progress at Parking and Traffic at the time of inquiry include a more efficient and information-rich technology (called 'Ticket Man') that will eventually replace the AutoCite. The organisation is also in the process of formally outlining parking and traffic standards in a training manual that will serve as a benchmark for other councils in Australia and overseas.

Another concept that has recently been adopted by Parking and Traffic is the use of the learning organisation to instil a culture that encourages employees to develop new concepts and insights and to share knowledge. In essence, Parking and Traffic will continue to recognise contributions, ideas and suggestions for new projects to facilitate improvements in quality and the retention of industry leadership.

QUESTIONS

1 In the facilitation of technological change, management consulted extensively with staff. What are the benefits of a consultative approach, and are there any disadvantages? What other management methods could Parking and Traffic have used to facilitate changes to technology and work design?

2 What are some of the perceived factors that caused employee resistance to technological and work design and cultural change in this case?

3 The organisation conducted meetings with unions to help reduce resistance in those opposed to change, and to involve the members who were positive towards change. What other methods could have been employed to use resistance to benefit the organisation?

4 How could the organisation avoid the problem of Parking and Traffic officers being assigned to mundane and repetitive tasks, given the nature of their work?

5 The adoption of teams can have the benefits of improving employee participation and increasing job satisfaction. However, the use of teams can also be problematic. Identify some of these problems and offer suggestions as to how they might be resolved.

6 In what ways can rewards and recognition programmes encourage both acceptance of change and a work environment that embraces continuous improvement? Consider the types of rewards that might be used in the Parking and Traffic organisation, including individual, team, intrinsic and extrinsic motivators.

7 After the cultural change, some officers appeared to be unclear as to their main task. In particular, officers were confused as to whether their job should focus on customer service or whether it was primarily about the issuing of parking infringement notices. How could this be clarified to staff?

8 Parking and Traffic are striving to become a learning organisation in order to retain industry leadership and continually improve work processes and service quality. What elements are necessary when creating a learning organisation? What methods and processes could be used to facilitate a learning organisation?

Notes

1   Melbourne City Council, *Corporate Plan 1997–2002*, (Melbourne: Melbourne City Council, 1997).

2   W. Burke, *Organizational Development: A Process of Learning and Changing*, 2nd ed., (Massachusetts: Addison-Wesley, 1994): 150; D. Harvey and D. Brown, *An Experiential Approach to Organization Development*, 5th ed., (New Jersey: Prentice-Hall, 1996): 164.

3   Melbourne City Council, *Annual Review 1996–1997*, (Melbourne: Melbourne City Council, 1997).

4   Melbourne City Council, *Employee Survey 1998*, (Melbourne: Melbourne City Council, 1998).

5   Melbourne City Council, *Mercury Staff Journal*, (June), (Melbourne: Melbourne City Council, 1998).

Changes in Telstra's field workforce

By **Warrick Coad, Susan Foley, Libby Hanson, Sue McConnell and David Vickers**

Introduction

An institution devoted to the installation and maintenance of telegraph and/or telephone networks has existed in Australia for almost 100 years. Until 1975 the Postmaster-General's department (PMG) of the Australian government controlled and managed the Post Office, telegraph and telephone networks. In 1975, the PMG was broken up to form two government enterprises known today as Australia Post and Telstra (née Telecom). Telstra is Australia's principal telecommunications company, and until recently operated in a monopolistic environment.

The telecommunications industry has undergone significant change in recent years as the Australian market has moved towards open competition. Telstra has been subject to competition since 1991, when Optus was formed to compete in the long-distance and international telephone service arenas. On 1 July 1997, Australia's telecommunication markets were opened to full competition with no limit on the number of telecommunication carriers that may enter the market.

In November 1997, Telstra was partly privatised to help drive a new culture across the company in this new competitive environment. According to Telstra's 1998 *Annual Report*, Telstra's vision is 'to enhance its position as the leading telecommunications and information services company in Australia and to become a leading provider of such services in the Asia-Pacific region'.[1]

Earlier, to realise this vision, increase shareholder value and prepare for competition, Telstra adopted a four-part growth strategy, which has been in place since 1992. Part of this strategy is 'transforming corporate culture and improving productivity', suggesting that Telstra is transforming its corporate culture to improve productivity with the objective of lowering its cost base relative to revenue loss as a direct result of competition. The 1998 *Annual Report* states:

> ... this involves continuing to change to meet evolving customer requirements, making major changes to work practices and improving management accountability and commercial discipline. The Company is also redeploying and reducing its workforce and outsourcing where appropriate. Telstra has invested substantial resources over the past several years to develop technologically advanced infrastructure and systems. This is expected to result in reduced labour costs, and improve operating flexibility and service reliability.

The Customer Field Workforce Agreement

In 1998, Telstra management decided to introduce an initiative named the 'Customer Field Workforce Agreement' (CFWA). The aim of this initiative was to improve operating flexibility, control costs and improve the career structure and prospects of the Telstra field workforce. Altogether, the CFWA affected some 18 000 Telstra staff. This report will concentrate specifically on 10 000 of these staff, namely the field workforce of the Commercial and Consumer Business Unit. This workforce is responsible for the installation and ongoing maintenance of the telephone network for all residential and small business customers across Australia. These staff are itinerant workers, working from Telstra vans or station wagons to which their jobs are dispatched via a computerised despatch system.

Traditionally, the field workforce had three distinct roles:

- *installation and maintenance technicians* (approximately 1500 staff—15% of the workforce). These staff work exclusively in customers' premises, completing installations or maintenance jobs
- *network technicians* (approximately 1500 staff—15% of the workforce). These staff work exclusively in exchange buildings completing installations or proactive and reactive maintenance procedures
- *installation and maintenance linemen* (approximately 7000 staff—70% of the workforce). These staff work on external installation and maintenance work, repairing and upgrading the telephone cables that run between the exchange buildings and the customer's premises.

Demarcation has always existed between these three roles. For example, a customer reports a fault on their telephone line. An initial test conducted by the fault-reporting section of Telstra considers that the fault is most probably located in the customer's premises. A technician is therefore sent to correct the fault. On arrival the technician concludes that the fault is located outside the customer's premises, and so the technician can only log the fault back into the system, whereupon a lineman will be allocated to fix the fault. This is a result of the technician and lineman carrying different tools, having different competence sets, and of the historical demarcation that has existed between technicians and linemen. The CFWA removed these instances of unproductive work.

The objective of the CFWA was to integrate the work of each of these groups so that a single staff member from this workforce possesses the skills and competence to perform all facets of the required work within the installation and maintenance regime. The broader an individual's skills kit, the more flexible that management can be in the allocation of job assignments, allowing more staff to be more productive more of the time.

CFWA will deliver cost savings through simplification

Telstra has had to carry a substantial amount of bureaucratic baggage from its past. The CFWA delivered Telstra cost savings through the simplification of the award structure. By introducing a simple 10-tier pay structure, it also removed clutter and duplication that had built up over 100 years from the award. The new pay structure replaced 114 individual designations and 350 separate salary points. An external consulting company was employed to ensure that the new salary levels were consistent with similarly skilled employees in other industries.

Finally, the CFWA removed salary allowances, most of which were no longer relevant in today's market.

The benefits that CFWA delivered to employees

The incentive for employees to accept the CFWA were many:

- a more secure future
- a broader skill set
- formal recognition of skills by the telecommunications industry
- a minimum 4% pay increase, although the average lineman will receive approximately 9%
- a one-off lump sum payment as compensation for the abolition of allowances.

Subcultures of the workforce

From a cultural perspective, linemen had traditionally been viewed as construction workers. In a male-dominated occupation, the average lineman wears overalls, is typically of European extraction, is an outdoors type of man—a man's man. From the authors' viewpoint, the underlying values for linemen may include having a sense of freedom that comes from working in the outside environment.

The technician is viewed as a professional, wears a shirt and tie, is typically Anglo-Saxon male, qualified, a detail-orientated individual—in some aspects the IT 'nerd' of the seventies. Both groups have been with Telstra for a long time and so their current cultures are very entrenched. The demographics tell us both groups are, on average, 47 years old and have been with Telstra for 22 years. They are people who share a culture of lifetime employment with Telstra.

CFWA implementation

The CFWA was conceptualised in December 1996. For the first 18 months Telstra management and the Communication, Electrical and Plumbers Union (CEPU) negotiated the specifics of the CFWA, with little communication being sent to the field workforce. During this period, external consultants were also employed to ensure that salary levels of the new CFWA positions were at external market rates, and to aid in the definition of the positions.

The CFWA is a Workplace Agreement and a legal requirement of the *Workplace Relations Act 1996* is that the affected staff 'vote in' the new agreement.

Once an understanding had finally been reached with CEPU, an intensive communications strategy was launched three months prior to the ballot. The communications strategy consisted of:

- team briefings by senior management, briefing up to 200 people at a time. One of the senior managers interviewed suggested that this part of the strategy was crucial if staff were to receive a consistent message early in the transition stage.
- documentation regarding the CFWA was posted to every affected employee's home address
- meetings between supervisors and individuals to explain the impact that CFWA would have on a personal basis. Salary calculation statements were provided at this time.
- a help desk was set up to address employees' issues and questions
- weekly communication briefs were disseminated to all affected employees
- ballots were conducted, and votes forwarded to, an external company for counting.

The outcome

The CFWA returned a positive vote, with approximately 70% of staff accepting the change. Overall costs of the project were unavailable, but the average employee's salary increased by 7.3% per annum with a further 4% to follow in December 1999.

The change process at Telstra was handled reasonably well on some levels and not very well on others. From the perspective of management the removal of the demarcation line between the technicians and the linemen created the opportunity for a far more flexible workforce. The linemen, being the majority of staff, have committed to the changes, and so management is of the opinion that the change was successful.

The resistance to the change from a number of staff, mostly technicians, has not subsided and management is of the view that some staff, especially many of the network technicians, will never change or 'cross-skill'. All senior managers and team leaders interviewed indicated that they had given up any thought of imposing the change on these staff. From this perspective, the change process has been unsuccessful.

Changing the culture

The culture within Telstra is one of the major resistance factors to the change. Changing culture means changing people's minds and behaviours. It shapes a person's actions and attitudes to change, their readiness to accept change and the speed with which change will be adopted. Turner and Crawford say that 'if culture is to change it has to be through the actions and interactions of members of the culture'.[2] In Telstra's case, most of the people issues were not realised until after the change had been implemented. Although managers were briefed before the change, the front-line people were not included until just before the changes were 'imposed'.

As discussed, the technicians and linemen come from vastly different cultures, even though they have always worked in close proximity to each other. This second factor has given management the incorrect signals that merging the two groups would be a straightforward, simple fix to alleviate ˜some efficiency issues and continue with the company's cost-reduction strategies.

With such long tenure (the average age being 47 years and average length of service 22 years), psychological ownership of the current roles and responsibilities must exist. Psychological ownership is defined as 'the state where an individual feels as though the target of ownership (or a piece of that target) is his or hers'.[3] Ownership can include material items, as well as immaterial objects such as jobs. Psychological ownership will engender commitment, involvement and job satisfaction and link the staff to the organisation.

It is not unreasonable to suggest that the linemen are the less skilled and educated group of individuals of the two, and that this change will improve their overall skill sets. One of management's selling points to the linemen was that they would have an opportunity to gain external qualifications as well as salaries that match those of technicians. Prior to the change, linemens' salaries were approximately 10% lower than those of technicians.

With the amalgamation of two different cultures, one could argue that two types of changes are occurring. The lineman will be experiencing evolutionary change,[4] even though it may be an imposed change. Evolutionary change is an incremental change to a job that adds to a person's sense of self and feelings of competence. It is also an imposed change as management has issued the directive to change.

Dirks *et al.* would suggest this would involve a sense of losing control over the psychological ownership of the job and therefore have a negative impact.[4] However, while this may be true, the evolutionary change, the gaining of more, should negate the impact of who has actually instituted the change, especially in such a traditionally hierarchical organisation. In this instance of change, the role of the linemen is expanding. Assuming psychological ownership, the linemen should be displaying a positive disposition towards the change.

Conversely, although the technicians are broadening their range of activities, they are substituting higher-level technical expertise with a lower-level skill set. As Victor and Stephens suggest, 'any far-reaching organisational change involves destruction as well as creation'.[5]

For the technician, the exact opposite type of change is occurring—the destructive side to this change initiative. Again, it is an imposed change, but more importantly, a subtractive change.[4] The technicians will be feeling a sense of loss insofar as the skills they have acquired through education are no longer required, and are not being utilised. They have moved from an educated technician's role to one that involves the barest of technical know-how to achieve the desired ends. Dirks *et al.* suggest that individuals will feel 'cast down' when possession of psychological ownership 'dwindles'.[4]

A response to this destructive and subtractive change may see the technician vigorously fight to maintain the *status quo*. If this fight to retain status does not succeed, Maslow's hierarchy of needs would suggest that the technician will lose self-esteem and the motivation to perform.[6] This, in turn, will negate the sought-after productivity gains and most probably have a detrimental effect on current performance levels. The interviews conducted clearly demonstrate this was the case with technicians, thereby reinforcing this theory.

With continued external pressure, particularly from Telstra's competitors, consolidation of resources, process improvement and a shift in people's attitudes are essential for change. Kotter and Heskett's model conclusively show the components of corporate culture (see Figure K.1).[7]

Behaviour and shared vision among people form the culture in the organisation. This behaviour, in turn, is shaped by the shared vision and is referred to as shared values. At Telstra this model is indicative of the issues faced by senior management. Many staff,

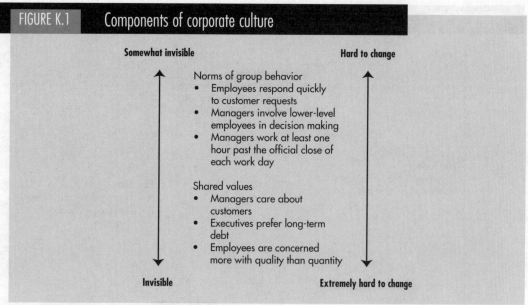

FIGURE K.1   Components of corporate culture

Somewhat invisible   **Hard to change**

Norms of group behavior
- Employees respond quickly to customer requests
- Managers involve lower-level employees in decision making
- Managers work at least one hour past the official close of each work day

Shared values
- Managers care about customers
- Executives prefer long-term debt
- Employees are concerned more with quality than quantity

Invisible   **Extremely hard to change**

Source: J. Kotter and J. Heskett, *Corporate Culture and Performance* (New York: The Free Press, 1992).

particularly the network technicians, are still resisting the change. They have not been given the opportunity to receive counselling or offered a forum to work through their fear and other issues with the CFWA. In reality, until many of the longer-serving staff leave the organisation, existing work patterns are not expected to change to a great extent. It is unlikely that a complete cultural shift will occur until resistant staff leave the organisation or change their 'mental models'.[8]

Fear

From the questionnaires completed by the front-line staff, a feeling of fear was clearly evident in their conceptualising of the prospective change. *The Fear Cycle* by Kriegel and Brandt illustrates this process from a network technician's point of view (see Figure K.2).[9]

As this cycle illustrates, the fear initially built during the preceding 18-month-period, where communication was not forthcoming from the company, resulted in staff showing resistance through industrial action and cynicism. This, in turn, can result in a vicious cycle where the company is not really interested in the concerns of these individuals, in the belief that they can be replaced by people more willing to accept the CFWA.

Resistance to the CFWA arose mostly through human resistance in the form of cynicism, mistrust of management and perceived loss of status. A long history of employment in a particular role predisposed this workforce to obstinacy. Listed below are some of the factors of resistance:
- training of technicians and linemen was traditionally segregated
- the physical gulf between roles reinforced animosity
- the differences in training levels
- bureaucratic resistance (structural)
- job insecurity
- loss of status.

Bearing this in mind, it is of utmost importance to involve key individuals early in the process to ensure their 'buy-in'. This, in particular, is where Telstra handled the CFWA change process poorly. Although incentives were provided to staff through pay increases and job security was offered through cross-skilling, no involvement in the change process or behavioural counselling was offered. Involving those most likely to resist earlier may have resulted in staff moving through the phases of acceptance more quickly: denial, resistance, exploration and commitment, as illustrated in Figure K.3.[10]

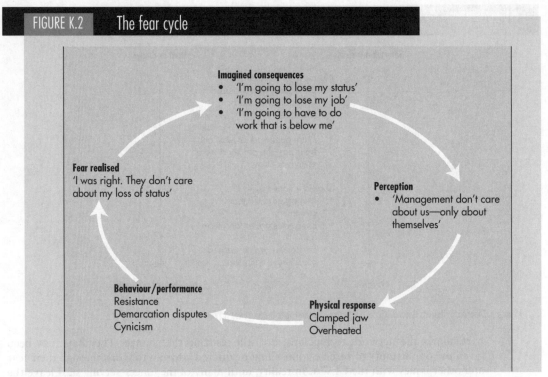

FIGURE K.2 The fear cycle

Source: R. Kriegel and D. Brandt, *Sacred Cows Make the Best Burgers* (Australia: Harper Collins Publishers, 1996).

Cynicism

A degree of cynicism can usually be expected when organisational change occurs, and this is often healthy. However, prolonged cynicism can be counterproductive and can hinder the change process to such an extent that the change is wholly unsuccessful. Reichers, Wanous and Austin note that cynicism 'can become a self-fulfilling prophecy (and) lack of support

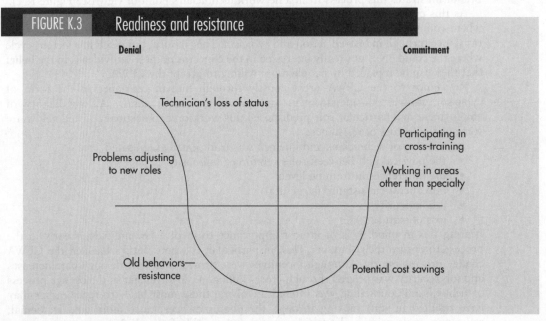

FIGURE K.3 Readiness and resistance

Source: C. Scott and D. Jaffe, *Managing Organizational Change* (California: Crisp Publications, 1989).

may bring about failure or very limited success'.[11] As noted earlier, cynicism prevailed within the technician groups.

Reichers *et al.*[11] also assert that such cynicism can be a consequence of other historical change efforts. While this may have affected the technicians' reaction to change, the primary issue was loss of status. This initially manifested itself as distrust, but has moved to apathy as evidenced by the fact that many technicians are currently not willing to perform duties that are extraneous to their previous role.

Further, the technicians could feel that a psychological contract has been broken. Andersson states that 'Psychological and implied contracts between individuals and organisations can be a powerful lens for the study of individual attitudes in the work place.'[12] Perhaps a new 'contract' would facilitate progression to the acceptance phase of the change process. Given the demographics of this workforce, this is likely to be a long-term proposition. 'Cynics are not active in progressing the change and, in fact, would prefer to keep the old ways.'[13]

The technicians' ability to satisfy a customer's needs by completing all aspects of a job should, theoretically, provide a sense of achievement. The CFWA was intended to achieve this end. 'In particular, it is important for people to experience progress, to see that their day-to-day tasks make a difference.'[14]

Common change errors

In 1996 Kotter determined a number of errors that are common to organisational change efforts and the consequences resulting from these.[15] What is interesting to note is that, in the majority of cases, Telstra went down the path of avoiding all these errors, obviously with greater levels of success in some than others. The errors include:

- *allowing too much complacency:* due to the monumental change that Telstra has endured since deregulation of the industry in 1991, the internal change agent was determined to prevent complacency. This was particularly crucial given the investment and expected performance improvement that the CFWA was designed to produce.
- *failing to create a sufficiently powerful guiding coalition:* by utilising team leaders in the communications team in the final process, they were able to gain further confidence in the changes by the staff affected, than if they had used senior management as the sole means of communication. Hence, the use of team leaders was important in the communication process. The change agent indicated that this was successful in some areas and not as successful in others, depending on the level of 'buy-in' of individual team leaders and their background within the company.
- *underestimating the power of vision:* at a senior management level there was a clearly defined mission, although the collective vision was not communicated early enough to the field workforce. This certainly could have been useful in obtaining employee 'buy-in'.
- *declaring victory too soon:* the change agent stated that he believed the changes introduced to Telstra would take approximately three years to bring significant benefit to the company. There has certainly been some initial benefits due to the fact that the majority of linemen are now performing a combined role. However, a large number of jobs are still being handled by multiple Telstra staff. Real benefits are a long-term proposition.

On a less positive note, however, a number of consequences have arisen from the changes that were either not expected or have not been addressed at this stage.

- *management and team leaders still see the two roles as being differentiated:* terminology used by managers and team leaders interviewed was that of 'lineys' and 'techs' rather than the all-encompassing 'field workforce'.
- *cross-training has only been completed by staff who have embraced the change process:* team leaders do not expect resistant staff to cross-train (partly due to the next point). Furthermore, no action is being taken by management to address this issue.

- technicians are being allocated to traditional technician jobs and linemen to linemen jobs: it is only when there is an overflow of work in one area that staff are cross-skilling. This, in turn, ensures slower development of the skills required to complete the work.
- lack of measurement of the change is preventing revision; Telstra lacks a formal monitoring process to determine the success, or otherwise, of the change.

Conclusion

The CFWA has brought benefits for Telstra in that it achieved a more flexible workforce, resulting in cost savings through the number of staff required to respond to a single customer's complaint. It has resulted in increased pay for all staff and increased job security for the majority of affected workers.

However, Telstra senior management need to ensure that staff who are still in the resistance stage are provided with support and coaching to ensure that there is some sort of adoption of the changes if they are to prevent the cynicism built up during this change process from negatively affecting future change.

Although the process has been acknowledged by senior management to be a long-term proposition, feedback needs to be introduced so that adequate reviews can be undertaken to ensure that the best gains are achieved from the considerable investment already made through implementing the CFWA. Nothing can be learnt for future change if reviews are not conducted on present-day change.

Notes

1 Telstra, *Annual Report* (1998).
2 D. Turner and M. Crawford, *Change Power* (Warriewood, Australia: Business and Professional Publishing, 1998).
3 J. Pierce, S. Rubenfeld and S. Morgan, 'Employee ownership: a conceptual model of process and effects', *Academy of Management Review*, 16 (1991): 121–44.
4 K. Dirks, L. Cummins and J. Pierce, 'Psychological ownership in organizations: conditions under which individuals promote and resist change', *Research in Organizational Change and Development*, 9 (1996): 1–23.
5 B. Victor and C. Stephens, 'The dark side of the new organizational form: an editorial essay', *Organizational Science*, 5:4 (1994): 479–82.
6 'Maslow's hierarchy of needs' in S. Robbins, B. Millett, R. Cacioppe and T. Waters-Marsh, *Organisational Behaviour* (Australia: Prentice Hall, 1998).
7 J. Kotter and J. Heskett, *Corporate Culture and Performance* (New York: The Free Press, 1992).
8 P. Senge, *The Fifth Discipline* (Australia: Random House, 1990).
9 R. Kriegel and D. Brandt, *Sacred Cows Make the Best Burgers* (Australia: Harper Collins Publishers, 1996).
10 C. Scott and D. Jaffe, *Managing Organizational Change* (California: Crisp Publications, 1989).
11 A. Reichers, J. Wanous and J. Austin, 'Understanding and managing cynicism about organizational change', *Academy of Management Executive*, 11:1 (1997): 48–59.
12 L. Andersson, 'Employee cynicism: an examination using a contract violation framework', *Human Relations*, 49 (1996): 1395–498.
13 K. Hackman, 'Understanding and managing resistance to change', *HR Monthly* (1999): 8–9.
14 F. Barrett, 'Creating appreciative learning cultures', *Organizational Dynamics*, 24(1995):36–49.
15 J. Kotter, *Leading Change* (Boston, Massachusetts: Harvard Business School Press, 1996).

Other references

S. McClelland, *Organizational Needs Assessments: Design, Facilitation and Analysis* (Westport, CT: Quorum Books, 1995).
R. McLennan, *Managing Organizational Change* (New Jersey: Prentice-Hall, 1989).

Guardian Pharmacies Australia Limited

By **Anthony Paula, Alex Bradilovich, Bernadette Ivkovic and David Lyster**

Background

Sigma Company Ltd is an Australian-owned pharmaceutical manufacturer and major wholesaler that bought Guardian Pharmacies Australia Ltd in April 1997 as part of its vision for its Retail Services division. A process to change the corporate identity of Guardian was begun in mid-1997, being officially completed in June 1998.

Guardian currently has 25 employees. Pharmacies displaying the Guardian name pay a membership fee, are classed as members and are considered to be part of the organisation. Guardian increased its membership base by approximately 22% over two years, while future projections indicate a potential for substantial growth.

Guardian Family Care Chemists was formed by a group of pharmacists on 19 March 1975 in order to enable competitive buying and shared advertising costs. In 1983 Guardian chemists amalgamated with Guild Family Care, creating the 212-strong Guardian Family Care Chemist group, which placed its emphasis on family health care and professional pharmacy. Guardian was portrayed as the professional health care adviser to the community.

The membership was expanded in May 1989 when Guardian was launched in Western Australia. A peak was reached in October 1989, when membership totalled 230, but dropped in both 1990 and 1992 as a result of the ongoing rationalisation of pharmacy numbers. An all-time low of 164 was reached in 1992, at which time pharmacists were secluding themselves in the dispensary.

Competition came for all pharmacies in the early 1990s as new legislation allowed some pharmaceutical products to be sold by other retailers. Pharmacies struggled to hold on to their share of the retail trade.

Why did Sigma, a large pharmaceuticals manufacturer, want to be involved in the retail sector? In the mid-1980s the face of retail was changing. Organisations needed buying power as independent retailers were squeezed by larger organisations. People were living longer and needing more health support at the same time as health care costs were increasing and pharmacists leaving the profession. This increased competition and led to lower margins for pharmacies, while consumers were becoming more price- and value-conscious. Sigma saw these changing economic and social conditions as an opportunity for growth and expansion.

The years 1995 and 1996 saw the Guardian division regain its market share, and its membership grow steadily. Consumer health care information became a major theme, while the group's sales were boosted by the use of bigger catalogues that also showed gift products. March 1996 saw sales having increased by 6.8% in 1995. More extensive sales growth occurred in April 1996 when Guardian experienced a sales increase of 30%.

In 1996 Sigma purchased two small technology companies—the Melbourne-based POS Solutions and Canberra-based Professional Connections, which were used to create an Australia-wide UNIX-based computer system that gave Sigma and all its subsidiaries, including Guardian Pharmacies, up-to-date stock and purchasing information in a way that competitors did not then have. This was a very valuable asset for the organisation, and helped Sigma to attract and lock in potential members.

In trying to become the nation's largest pharmaceuticals group, Sigma purchased a New South Wales-based wholesaler, Andrews Laboratories, in March 1997, giving the organisation 20% of the New South Wales pharmaceutical market.

Sigma purchased Guardian Family Care Chemists Australia Ltd in May 1997, giving Sigma the largest national group of pharmacies. The organisation had exclusive distribution rights with both Guardian and Amcal across Australia.

Highly successful presentations of the new Guardian strategy were conducted in 22 locations around Australia in the second half of 1997. June 1998 saw Guardian roll out its new concept road show, supported by a $2 million television advertising campaign that was aimed at getting consumers to support the new Guardian promotion package and product branding.

In mid-1998 Sigma introduced the Guardian banner into New Zealand, when it acquired the Auckland-based Russell Pharmaceuticals. In February 1999 Sigma finalised a takeover of Pharmacy Wholesalers, which was based in Wellington, New Zealand. After a pre-Christmas takeover bid, it had received acceptances representing 93.2% of the issued shares by the start of February, giving Sigma a 24% stake in the New Zealand wholesale market and leading to the organisation reaching sales of A$171 million.

Securing a strong wholesale base in New Zealand was part of a larger strategy, as it allowed them to supply the Amcal and Pharmacy-care networks. It also allowed Sigma to launch Guardian into the New Zealand market in September 1998.

Guardian's change of identity

With the acquisition of Guardian Pharmacies, Sigma Pharmaceuticals obtained a well-established distribution channel, 'an avenue that could be used to funnel innovative methods of health care delivery to the broader community', while Guardian obtained the strong backing of a parent company.

The vision of Sigma was 'to develop a uniquely positioned banner group equipped to meet the requirements of pharmacy in the next century while delivering better health outcomes to pharmacy's consumer client base'. The group was aiming at becoming the future leader in pharmaceuticals.

The change was essential for Guardian's survival, and it affected all three branches of its pharmacy business:
- lifestyle: health and beauty
- medicine and wellness-related items
- information and knowledge (the forgotten category).

Guardian members had indicated before the change that Guardian was 'not going anywhere', was 'treading water' and was 'not progressive'. Now it was recognised that customer needs had changed considerably over the years and that research 'showed that today's customers demand a pharmacy that offers a different environment to shop in to that of 10–15 years ago'. Obtaining value for money was now more important to consumers than brand name. To survive, pharmacies had to adapt to the changing needs of the customer or become outdated. 'Pharmacists have a choice of remaining dinosaurs or moving into the next millennium.'

Under current law, only qualified and registered pharmacists may wholly or mostly own a pharmacy. With the threat of deregulation looming in the pharmacy industry, it was foreseen that pharmacy needed to prepare for a more competitive environment in the retail sector. Guardian aimed to benchmark the industry, and in October 1997 set out to change the corporate identity. This involved 'a reinvention of pharmacy: not simply a fit-out'. The new Guardian identity was a total concept that integrated many elements, including store layout, store presentation (interior and exterior), in-store graphics, packaging and wardrobe. In the new public identity:
- The name 'Guardian' stands for caretaker, protector and minder. The word 'pharmacy' was used (instead of 'chemist') to represent a more healthcare-oriented business.
- The symbol of the mortar and pestle was used as it is one of the symbols that consumers identify with a pharmacy. It is used in the Guardian icon as a strong

memorable image that links the old values of apothecary, medicine and hands-on caring with the new values of being bold, modern, confident and professional.

- The typeface is now a handcrafted serif as opposed to the old machine-made sans serif one.
- The colours were carefully chosen to create the right mood for both staff and customers. They linked the previous corporate colour scheme to the concept of positive health that was the organisation's basic philosophy.
- The Guardian shape—the unique curve in the logo—is used in all signs, stationery and interiors. It links the whole concept together, ensuring that the message communicated to the customer is consistent.

The change process

An external consultant (Design Portfolio—a specialist retail and commercial design company) was brought in to design the new Guardian concept, taking into account key considerations that Sigma considered essential for Guardian's new look.[1]

Design Portfolio began by performing a needs analysis on Guardian through a combination of pharmacy visits, executive interviews, questionnaires (internal and customer-based) and competition analysis. This, combined with open research on customer behaviour resulting from pharmacy format, layout and signage, resulted in several strategies that moved the emphasis away from a product and price to a patient-integrated process, designed to enhance Guardian's position as a force and set a 'new benchmark for pharmacy'.[1]

The entire change process took approximately nine months to complete. It began with the needs analysis on Guardian by 'Design Portfolio'. Technological research was also undertaken, looking at the resources available to pharmacies. This analysis involved visits to 61 pharmacies in Victoria, Tasmania, South Australia, Western Australia, New South Wales and Queensland.

Executive interviews were performed within Sigma, Guardian, the Pharmaceutical Society of Australia, the Guild and industry suppliers. Finally, a pharmacist needs analysis questionnaire was distributed, which attracted 178 replies. As Guardian at that time had pharmacy memberships of 217, the response rate was more than adequate. The competitor analysis performed by Guardian in consultation with Design Portfolio revealed a need for a totally new organisational philosophy and business concept.

To guarantee the success of any change process, the *status quo* must be altered or unfrozen if individuals are to change their present attitudes and current beliefs. Within Guardian, employees feared that they would lose their jobs through this phase. Such resistance to change had to be eliminated, or utilised correctly, for the change process to be effective.

Throughout the change process, Guardian encouraged suggestions for change from both management and employees. This proved to be an effective approach that stemmed from the two-way relationship that existed between management, who were attempting to implement the change, and the employees, who were affected by the change.

As most employees were convinced that the change was in their own, and the organisation's, best interest, the change process proceeded smoothly. All concerned believed that the changes would be beneficial.

For the new corporate identity to be successful, Design Portfolio identified the following:

- *a new corporate identity package*, including full internal and external graphics, stationery and uniforms
- *a retail design concept*, which was the main focus of the change
- *a national promotions strategy*, including a comprehensive calendar that promoted national and house brands
- *a house brand strategy*, which featured an extensive range of house brand products, leading to good margins and repeat business, and ongoing research and development into new lines

- *a consistent advertising strategy*. Funds for a national advertising campaign, with particular emphasis on television, were to be used to promote the new image of Guardian. A new theme was to be: 'Someone to watch over you'.
- *retail services*. Being part of the wider Sigma family gave Guardian the opportunity to use Sigma's resources to develop new services, such as *Mystery Shopper* programmes.
- *a category management programme*, which was one of the most valuable services Sigma had to offer. The new Guardian version of store category management encompassed a world-class standard that allowed Guardian to go beyond normal space management programmes.
- *training programmes*—featuring comprehensive training for both pharmacists and pharmacy assistants
- *a loyalty programme* that is unique to Guardian, and is a worldwide pioneer for any marketing group within the pharmacy industry
- *local area marketing* was a specialised service introduced to provide for individual customers' needs within differing market segments. The programme worked particularly well to lock in customer loyalty as it delivered a complementary service.
- *professional services* are the cornerstone of Guardian's reputation and so a strong emphasis is placed on additional professional services within pharmacy. Part of Guardian's vision was to make these services revenue generating, while also enhancing the pharmacist's professional role.
- *a new nursing service* was introduced in June 1999 as part of a programme for healthcare services in the home. This was seen as a way of serving a specific group of customer's needs. By performing this role, Guardian would not only be customer-responsive, but also show leadership in developing new market segments.
- *a community public relations campaign* was one of the key strategies for raising the public awareness of the Guardian banner. This aimed to associate the organisation with a worthwhile and emotive community project—the *Guardian Angels*, a volunteer knitting drive that supported World Vision.

The final result of the analysis conducted with Design Portfolio, and the concomitant need to change, was communicated to the staff and the membership by the general manager in a roadshow style presentation. The general manager highlighted the successes and failures of the past and specified point-by-point the proposed changes. Much of the content was familiar to listeners as many stakeholders had participated in the developmental stage.

In order to minimise employee misconceptions about the change process, significant time and attention was dedicated to informative/consultative discussion before any change took place. A video format of the change presentation is now used when introducing prospective members to the group, as it is an invaluable tool for showing how Guardian's past has led to it becoming the pharmacy marketing group of the future.

Management at Guardian took advantage of the informal communications between people who work together, such as staff and members. In Guardian's case, this is seen to be very important as the nature of the pharmaceuticals industry creates a number of informal and formal networks.

Cultural aspects of the organisation were seen to be relevant to the change process, and are incorporated into the organisation's new image as symbols in the corporate identification package. Bolman and Deal suggest that the correct formal arrangements can minimise problems while increasing quality and performance.[2] A most notable research finding in Guardian's case was that this whole change process was performed without formal follow-up analysis to measure its success or failure.

The financial figures and membership numbers suggest that Guardian's objectives are being met. Guardian acknowledges they are in a retail environment, which has become very competitive, particularly with deregulation and the introduction of pharmacy-only product lines into supermarkets. Therefore, Guardian provides full retail support to help member pharmacists build better businesses. The organisation has since created new markets and set a standard that is regarded by other pharmaceutical organisations as providing market leadership.

Store presentation initiatives resulted in the forward dispensing concept that Guardian considers to represent the future in pharmacy. By this initiative, supported by the creation of entirely new services such as nursing, Guardian has become the industry leader.

The forward dispensing concept is flexible enough to serve different pharmacists and different pharmacies without compromising its integrity. At the same time, all marketing and promotional strategies work in unison to advertise and promote the 'new pharmacy' in the industry. In addition, the new Guardian house brand products help to build a strong Guardian brand.

Impact of change

The effect of change

The degree of business success is directly related to the level of ability to change. Resistance was low in Guardian, but there was some, causing people at varying levels to leave the organisation. In the initial phase, some smaller pharmacies dropped their membership, partly because of the 80% increase in membership fees plus the cost involved in refitting the stores in order to adopt the new image. Once the change process was underway, there were few political or power issues, but people continued to leave the organisation.

The culture changed to be more profit-driven than previously, even though the basic philosophy within the vision/mission statement was becoming more patient-orientated. This was probably due to the current world-wide trend toward organisational rationalism.

At Guardian, continued evaluation appears to be virtually non-existent, apart from personal performance appraisals and some performance indicators, such as financial figures and pharmacy membership numbers. From these measurements, the changes initially appeared to be successful. Guardian membership rose by 25% and financial figures placed Sigma at number eight in turnover of all retail organisations within Australia. However, this rise later stagnated and concern by management became apparent.

Obstacles to the change process were the cost of the changes and the increase in membership fees. To address these issues, 'value for money fit-outs' were a key consideration, and marketing of the new concept involved presentations of the new concept in various locations around Australia.[3] Response was extremely positive, and was expected to have a significant long-term impact on total membership numbers.

The combined strategies ranged from marketing through professional services, retail design, loyalty programmes, home branding and training to advertising and improved corporate imaging. The result is a complete 'new corporate concept' programme for pharmacies that is designed to improve customer satisfaction and trust in the organisation.[4] The financial figures and membership numbers shown in monthly management reports formed the basis for an ongoing analysis of the change process.

Guardian management needs to consider the effect of methods of work organisation on the behaviour and performance of members within the organisation. Its new work organisation is definitely more productive, as is shown by the higher membership numbers while it remains a lean organisation. This is reflected in its financial statements.

Impact on individuals

Current Guardian members feel that individual attitudes towards Guardian have changed. Initially, employees felt that Guardian was outdated and lacking direction, resulting in a lack of staff confidence. Generally, they felt that Guardian did not have a strong presence in the community and that it was not capitalising on what presence it did have. Long-term employees describe the environment as a very pleasant family experience. However, employees who joined the company shortly before the change found the environment confusing, as there was a lack of direction.

There were significant staff movements prior to the changes, and the environment was unsettled for a while. However, employees soon realised that this was a means to an end, and most were willing to ride out the storm.

Once the change in corporate identity had taken place, employees felt confident and highly motivated. Guardian had taken on an achievement-oriented environment with a strong sense of direction. There is a look of professionalism, and employees believe it to be very dynamic. Short-term employees considered the culture to be progressive, friendly and positive. Long-term employees found it an 'everyone for themselves' environment, and they used the term 'compliance' when asked to describe the culture.

Most individuals felt that they were finally able to get on with the job at hand—something they had been waiting for. The change in corporate identity finally gave them the opportunity to expand their roles at Guardian. Having previously felt stifled and imprisoned in their roles, the change was seen as offering a fresh lease on life. Along with the acceptance of change, there was an increase in work load as Guardian acquired more memberships. This increase in workload was initially seen as an indication of the public's acceptance of the change in corporate identity, and was viewed with excitement and vigour. However, in time the increase in membership and subsequent workloads, along with no perceived increase in resources, placed existing Guardian staff under enormous pressure to perform with little apparent support. One manager noted that if the processes were in the same way, many staff members, including managers, were in danger of burnout.

Impact on groups

The change in corporate identity resulted in major changes at pharmacy level. It led to altered customer demographics, involving an increase in over-the-counter (OTC) sales and customers purchasing products that they would not previously have bought.[3]

Change in processes

Before the change there had been a sense of complacency and 'band-aid practices'. There were no formal procedures in place to deal with problems, resulting in a confused environment. Delegation was at times the only way to solve a problem. No one seemed to be responsible for solving problems. As part of the change, formal procedures were introduced, but interview responses indicate that these procedures are hindering future progress. Most of the respondents consider the procedures in place to be letting the 'achievers and team-oriented people down', while the 'big picture strategists' were overlooking local issues.

The biggest change involved the concept of 'forward pharmacy', which brings the pharmacist out from behind the counter to give advice to, and communicate with, customers, instead of keeping the traditional two counters and staff between the customer and pharmacist.[1] It requires a change in thinking by pharmacists, as well a change in how they allocate their time and work.

Change in the department

Staff who were uncomfortable with the change resigned. Some areas expanded as new roles became necessary. All respondents to the questionnaire commented on the marked increase in work load in their department. This increase placed a new dimension on working relationships within departments, sometimes positive and productive, but at other times negative and counter-productive. Possible reasons given were the increased number of tasks arising from the increased membership, and differing levels of service standards between people in the same department.

Impact on the organisation—Guardian

Research has shown an underlying and generalised feeling that the change had led to certain inadequacies, including management and leadership issues, as well as the levels of skilled and trained personnel. It was noted that a lack of trained and skilled staff was a major hindrance to achieving the vision of Guardian.

As soon as they have been initiated, new employees are required to follow the organisation's vision. This allows the organisation to develop a positive attitude in all staff members. An area of concern that became evident through research, was the new 'attitude' within the organisation. It is felt among staff that some employees, while delivering excellent service to members, were overlooking their fellow employees.

Financial impact

The change in identity had a positive impact on finances. An indication of this is in the 1998–99 midyear report,[5] which shows a steady climb in monthly figures (well over projected budgets) coinciding with an increased membership. Overall, the general manager believed that Sigma's capacity to deliver increased return on investment (ROI) was mainly due to the concept banner being better promoted within the corporate environment.

Technology

The lack of technology prior to the change was mentioned throughout the interview process. People from almost all areas noted inadequacies and room for improvement in the IT support systems. Many of the highly motivated and enthusiastic employees felt that Guardian would fall if it did not do something very soon about its lack of office technology. It was felt that it would be a 'real shame' if all the hard work of staff went to waste because the larger the membership base became, the slower the output from staff. The introduction of the 'Unix' computer systems by Sigma alleviated much of this problem and staff generally felt that their needs were being serviced.

Human resources

Another area of great concern for both management and staff was the lack of human resources. Some felt that there needed to be more staff, others felt that there needed to be a more efficient way of utilising the skills of the present staff, possibly through training and development. This would enable Guardian to meet its promises to the market more efficiently than was being done at present.

Financial statistics and evaluation of the membership acquisition and numbers provided Guardian with a constant reflection of the effect of change on the organisation. The overall perception of the market place by staff members is positive, and they are loyal and dedicated to the cause, but they like to know where Guardian is going, so that they can be involved in recommending ongoing development.

Conclusion

The structure of Guardian has changed little, with the change process mostly being limited to marketing concepts and a shift in the general orientation of the organisation from product and price to family and health care. Overall, the change process has been positive for Guardian. Increased gross earnings and membership numbers provide quantitative evidence of the positive outcome to change. Staff members in general feel that change was necessary and those changes that have occurred are mostly for the better. It is interesting to note how longer-term employees state that the new culture is an 'everyone for themselves' environment, while short-term employees consider it to be progressive, friendly, positive and family-oriented. From the responses received, Guardian did very well to communicate the reason for the need to change and the subsequent change process. This success can be attributed to the employees feeling that, although the time was stressful, they had always been aware of the end result and were comfortable dealing with the short-term stresses attributable to the change process. Guardian has succeeded in changing its corporate identity at all levels of the organisation. It's biggest challenge lies in its future.

Recommendations

The following recommendations are based on information obtained from interview responses as well as on academic literature:

- Guardian will find its future growth a challenge because of its lean human resource capacity and its limited information technology skills. Though these two areas are very different and can be looked at separately, in this case it would be highly beneficial to look at them both together.

- It is recommended that Guardian invest into its 'intellectual capital'. Using a resource-based view (RBV), it is recommended that Guardian conduct a profile of its performance and the capabilities of its resources (i.e. a skills audit). As Guardian's building blocks are its resources, it is timely to analyse these resources and their capabilities. Guardian's success will rest on its ability to meet its pressures from the external environment by ensuring that its internal resources are capable of meeting the strategic objectives.[6]

- One of the recurring issues was the fear that Guardian would be unable to sustain internal service levels to members should the membership increase and the number of individuals servicing the membership remain the same. Another issue was the need to upskill staff to meet the future needs of the organisation. Much of this employee development rests on Guardian's ability to provide more advanced information technology opportunities. It is recommended that, should Guardian choose to take this path in organisational development, the high level of communication that led to the successful change in corporate identity be maintained.

Notes:

1 'Format embraces forward pharmacy', *Inside Retailing*, (July 1998): 10.
2 L. Bolman and T. Deal, *Reframing Organizations*, 2nd ed. (San Francisco: Jossey-Bass Publishers, 1997).
3 Sigma, *Profit Track*, (March/April 1999).
4 Guardian, *January Board Reports for February 1999* (Guardian–Sigma Group, 1999).
5 Sigma, *Annual Report* (Sigma 1997/98).
6 M. Taylor, 'A feedforward and feedback framework for analysing an organization's resources, capabilities and development needs', *Health Manpower Management*, 24:6 (1998): 196–205.

Stanley Australia

By **Christopher Andrews, Lee O'Mahoney and John Bourke**

Introduction

This paper focuses on the management of an ongoing change process undertaken by the Australian subsidiaries of the US multinational corporation, The Stanley Works. The changes are in response to the parent corporation's worldwide strategy, adopted as a response to increasing competitive pressures and which involved significant changes in culture and strategy.

The Stanley Works

Background: The Stanley Works (USA)

The Stanley Works was founded in 1843 in Connecticut, USA, as a manufacturer of hinges, bolts and other hardware. After meeting with early success, Stanley began exporting in the 1870s, and shortly after the turn of the century established its first overseas production site. Over time, Stanley has diversified its product lines and expanded its international operations to the extent that it now produces more than 50 000 different products, ranging from hand, mechanical, air and hydraulic tools to hardware, fastening systems, doors and automatic doors. It describes itself as 'a global manufacturer and marketer of tools, hardware, doors and home decor products for professional, industrial, consumer and home improvement purposes'.[1] Despite describing itself as 'global', Stanley could perhaps be more accurately labelled as a US-owned-and-operated multinational corporation. Its many subsidiaries—some operating under the Stanley name, others (usually well-known acquisitions) retaining their identity—are quite tightly controlled by the US headquarters.

Stanley has built an international reputation as a manufacturer of quality tools and hardware. It is present in every major region in the world, and sales revenue in 1997 was more than US$2.67 billion. Despite this, the corporation has been under increasing pressure since the late 1980s. Traditionally, Stanley had been able to differentiate its products from the much cheaper tools manufactured throughout Asia by virtue of quality and brand recognition. However, in the 1980s Asian manufacturers began to improve the quality of their products and by the early 1990s the quality of some Asian products was approximating that of Stanley. This improvement, coupled with much lower costs, created immediate problems for the corporation. With competitive pressures increasing, Stanley began to lose market share and customers. In January 1997, a new CEO of the US Corporation, John Trani, was appointed, with the specific task of addressing these problems. He decided to institute sweeping changes in the way the corporation operated. The world-wide manufacturing and distribution sites would be decreased from 123 to 70, with two sources for each product category (one third-world, one first-world country). Additionally, the organisational structure would be changed from divisional to matrix. The effects that this would have on the Australian operations were to be profound and immediate.

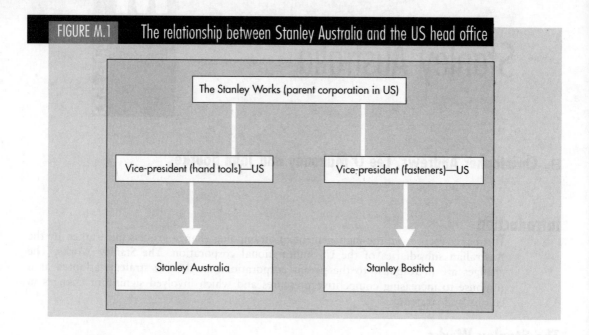

FIGURE M.1   The relationship between Stanley Australia and the US head office

Stanley in Australia

The Stanley Works owned and managed two independent companies in Australia at this time. Stanley Australia manufactured hand tools and reported to a US vice-president (hand tools). Stanley Bostitch manufactured fastening tools and fasteners and reported separately to a US vice-president (fasteners). Stanley Australia employed some 400 employees, while Stanley Bostitch employed 150, mainly at its Sydney operations.

These two firms had felt the effects of the hostile market place even more than the American parent because of the Australian tariff structure, as compared to that of the US. Increasing competition from imports had been coupled with the loss of business from crucial customers who had decided to import their own mechanics' tools from Asia (e.g. J. Blackwood and Son and Repco).

The change process

The changes to be instituted

In the first half of 1997, the decisions of the US parent corporation were communicated to the Australian office. The US parent company had asked for some input regarding costing, but otherwise the Australian divisions had given very little input to the diagnosis. Stanley Australia management was charged with the preparation of cost justifications and developing the implementation process, including alternative product sourcing and plant closures. Bob Andrews, vice-president (human resources), when asked what goals management wanted to achieve, mentioned increased profitability and market share.

The major effects of the changing global strategy were to be felt in Australia in two ways: manufacturing operations in the country would cease, and the two subsidiary companies, Stanley Australia and Stanley Bostich, would be combined. The demise of manufacturing meant the closure of four plants and the sale of a fifth (making vices). This was top management's response to the assessment of the viability of the current strategies and the threats from external environments—better quality and cheaper tools from Asian countries. Following detailed investigation of alternative product sourcing, it soon became apparent that some products enjoying market leadership in Australia were not available elsewhere within the Stanley world. Accordingly, some product lines (screwdrivers and hacksaw blades, along with the world-competitive Stanley knife production) were given a reprieve, thereby saving some 90 jobs in manufacturing.

The closure of manufacturing operations

Despite the limited reprieve in manufacturing, the transformation was to be major. There were to be changes in all areas of the company's operations. Closures were to occur at plants in Hobart, Wangaratta, Sydney, as well as the West Heidelberg headquarters, while the vices and clamps plant in Coburg, which 'did not fit' the company's product lines, was to be sold off.

Changes — people

The most obvious part of the change process was the elimination of superfluous jobs in manufacturing. Even taking into account the reprieve of certain manufacturing operations, Stanley Australia still needed to make some 300 employees redundant. The changes were not all at the lower levels, either. At this time the CEO of Stanley Australia, John Francis, retired and was replaced by Mark Parow, a former senior sales executive with the Dulux organisation. The purpose of this appointment was to give the Australian operation a solid sales and marketing orientation. Additionally, the sales/marketing department was to be increased (to heighten company focus on this area) and restructured to remove those employees whose skills did not align with the new requirements.

The process of informing the workers and the world of the cutbacks was a story in itself. The strategy adopted by Stanley to minimise internal resistance was formed by management, and was described by Bob Andrews, vice-president (human resources), as an attempt to allow people to 'depart with dignity', Helping the workers take the next step in their employment or towards retirement was also considered important. The central plank of this approach was a commitment to openness and honesty. The workers were informed of the decision on 16 October 1997, half an hour before the media, the unions and the Commonwealth Employment Service (CES), ensuring that they were the first to know. This honoured a commitment by the corporation's CEO that employees would be the first to learn of decisions that vitally affected them, such as plant closures. The next day, unions were advised of a sophisticated outplacement programme.

Stanley made certain that employees knew what the changes were and why they had to occur. This enabled the employees to understand and accept the impact of the changes. There was no participation and involvement of employees because of the considerable time constraints that had been imposed by the US parent company. To address the natural fears of the employees, Stanley adopted a range of measures. Again, the emphasis was on openness and honesty, but this was supplemented with a number of programmes. The 'over 50s' section of the work force was given special consideration. Professional firms provided outplacement and financial advisory services in the earliest stages in recognition that the job market would be toughest for this group. Similarly, a wide-ranging 'grief-counselling' network, involving the CES, the Department of Social Security (DSS) and professional private services, was implemented. To maintain continuity, the unofficial tradition of giving departing workers a card (signed by their colleagues) and a gift was retained, but altered. Instead of fellow workers contributing to the gift—which would leave the last to depart in the cold—Stanley gave these workers a gift voucher, on condition that no collection be taken up.

In May 1996, a three-year redundancy agreement had been negotiated with the three major unions, forestalling potential major disaffection in the course of negotiations. Both sides had expressed satisfaction with the outcome.

Another tool that Stanley had used to minimise resistance following the announcement was negotiation. Management negotiated with employees on incentives to remain at work and to maintain production schedules. Since the workers were still needed for up to nine months after the initial announcements, the company also had to discourage people from 'cashing in' their accrued sick leave and attempt to maintain morale and loyalty. The redundancy agreement was one method used to address these issues and was explained in detail (along with the superannuation package) to the workers. For example, printouts of estimated entitlements were provided to employees. Additionally, a bonus of two weeks' sick leave payment was included, on condition that the individual's attendance record stayed within acceptable limits. Additionally, a volunteer programme meant that redundancy was held open to all employees. Thus, even those who would still have jobs with the restructured firm could apply. The jobs that successful applicants left open could then be applied for by those whose positions were scheduled to become redundant. Throughout the entire process, meetings with employee representatives were held at fortnightly intervals, and it was stressed that the company would keep them advised of any developments. In return it was asked that the employees be honest and up-front with their concerns. Outplacement facilitators provided these meetings with feedback on ongoing programmes.

To evaluate the success of this programme, Stanley looked at such factors as industrial disruption, unfair dismissal cases and absenteeism. Also, each step in the process had a budget, costed in detail and approved at a senior level, with a continual review of costs. Management was pleased to note that all budget targets were met. Similarly, although inevitably present in such a situation, absenteeism was blunted by an estimated 3%— meaning that all incentives programmes paid for themselves abundantly.

Although the Australian plants had reacted reasonably well to the changes, extra pressure from the US to meet profitability goals resulted in further unscheduled downsizings.

Cultural changes

Concurrent with the operational transformations, Stanley Australia began a process of far-reaching cultural change. Management stated that they wished to give employees a greater role in decision making, subject to them accepting accountability for their actions and results. They also recognised the need to implement a process of communication and involvement in teams and for individuals. This transition was perceived as necessary for the integration of all employees, to increase employee satisfaction, to reduce waste costs and to improve overall efficiency.

While divesting itself of manufacturing skills and people, the company increased its numbers and skills in logistics and sales and marketing. This resulted in a slightly changed company demographic. The workforce was now younger and more skilled. Almost immediately, a greater preparedness to spend became apparent. This was enabled by the increased margins achieved from importing, rather than manufacturing, and necessary because of the need for competitive marketing, closure and clean-up of activities and the need for a new modern National Call Centre.

Stanley had few industrial relations problems during the process. The company was concerned that it might spend valuable time on legal issues relating to the redundancies. This did not eventuate. In fact, there was only one claim for unfair dismissal from the 300 redundancies, and the Industrial Relations Commission rejected this claim. Stanley saw this as a good evaluation mechanism, showing that the strategies implemented were a success. Indeed, it generated plaudits from Head Office in the US and officers of the company's employer association.

Processes

The virtual elimination of manufacturing has had significant impacts on the processes of Stanley Australia. For example, ISO 9001 became ISO 9002 as the design function was removed from Australia. This meant that procedures for processes throughout the organisation had to be rewritten, if only to reflect organisational change. The focus on overseas purchasing, rather than domestic manufacturing, led to increased lead times and storage space with an initial concomitant reduction in market responsiveness. This placed increased pressure on the computer systems, coinciding with, and complicated by, steps taken to remove the Year 2000 Bug.

At the individual level, the process changes opened new career opportunities for people in logistics, sales and marketing. Unfortunately, this was far outweighed by a reduction in the number of opportunities in other areas. The new technologies introduced (for example, the national call centre) resulted in some job loss, but there was no overt resistance as they were seen to be vital to the company's survival.

These changes impacted at the organisational level. The increased levels of stock taken in to counter the higher lead-time reduced the amount of space available for the company. This placed pressure on the occupational health and safety systems. For example, in 1998 a forklift ran over a worker's foot, causing severe injury. It was the first such incident at Stanley for many years.

In general, the organisational processes became more technologically advanced. The increased emphasis on IT systems enabled the company to plan to become more responsive to its markets. Given the skilled workforce now employed, management planned a greater reliance on self-managed teams, although this was still a long way off. Additionally, to operate the new systems, workers hired in the future will need to be more highly skilled. This will create a more professional, skilled and diverse organisation at all levels and will assist in the process of increasing worker autonomy.

Changes: structure

Structural changes resulting solely from the demise of manufacturing were easily identifiable. Firstly, manufacturing was divested, as were certain support staff. There was increased emphasis on the purchasing, forecasting and planning functions. Additionally, the marketing manager position was divided into two, one manager being responsible for mechanics' (Sidchrome and Stanley) tools, the other for builders' tools (mainly under the Stanley brand). As stated previously, the sales and marketing departments experienced greatly-increased prestige, remuneration and strategic influence.

The merging of Stanley Australia and Stanley Bostitch

The merger of two related, but different, subsidiaries of the American corporation was always going to create a host of problems for those managing it. On 16 October 1997 the integration of Stanley Bostitch into Stanley Australia was announced. At the individual level, the goal was to keep the two groups in a position of visible equality. It was hoped that this would help alleviate any resentment and resistance from the Stanley Bostitch employees, who might otherwise perceive the change as a 'takeover'. Much had to be done to reassure and motivate Bostitch personnel—primarily in sales and services departments.

Effects: people

This strategy was only partially successful. Since the new amalgamated company had initially planned to utilise virtually all of the Stanley Australia systems and processes, the former Stanley Bostitch employees faced a great deal of change. Fear of impending adverse change and new challenges prompted a variety of reactions, not always positive in character. Perhaps some mitigation of the tensions came from the recognition that Stanley Australia systems and processes were often more advanced and efficient.

At the group level, the former Stanley Bostitch employees initially struggled to adjust to the new situation. For example, their typical customers had previously been fencing contractors, builders and the like. Now they were expected to sell to major retailers. Inevitably there was some reluctance to embrace the transformation. As time went on, however, they became increasingly inculturated. Management expect that they will continue to adjust as they increase their familiarity with the Stanley Australia systems and gain some 'ownership' over them.

The organisation as a whole is now in a state of cultural flux. Stanley Bostitch had been operating in a *laissez faire*, even *ad hoc* fashion. An analysis of its former environment reveals a 'support culture',[2] where there was high trust and harmony with a sense of belonging.

Stanley Australia, by contrast, had been run on traditional lines—though it was in the process of being 'opened up'. It could, therefore, be described as a 'power' culture focusing on strength, direction, control and loyalty. There were strict processes, rules, regulations and procedures. Additionally, management had the long-term goal of moving towards an achievement-orientated culture, with everything assessed in terms of the ultimate, super-ordinate goals.

The combination of these two contradictory cultures in the two organisations caused dissonance for many employees. The problems were exacerbated by an ongoing transformation of the Stanley Australia culture, which initially placed the employees in a state of uncertainty.

Processes

The processes and procedures undertaken by the amalgamated company are still being resolved. In general, the operative principle is that the most appropriate processes will be used. This contrasts with the initial decision to utilise, in areas of duplication, the Stanley Australia processes over those of Stanley Bostitch. The effects of this policy are yet to be seen in full. At an individual level, the Stanley Bostitch employees have suffered from increased uncertainty and decreased morale in the short term. The salespeople were expected to take responsibility for geographical areas, and sell all Stanley products within their areas. It has been difficult for the former Stanley Bostitch employees to sell what had previously been Stanley hand-tool products to the more sophisticated major retail outlets.

At a group level, it is hoped and expected that, in time, the shared problems experienced by the sales staff will mould them into a close unit. At the organisational level the only real change that was expected was the different skill mix, which could have had an impact on future strategies and performance. Stanley has subsequently modified its approach, allowing more specialisation back to Bostitch products by those who possess only this knowledge and skill.

Performance management processes, based on the Stanley leadership qualities and preset goals, have been upgraded and will be supplemented by consequent succession and training plans. Self-managed teams are on the agenda and will be implemented when stability returns to the organisation.

Changes: structure

The structural changes necessitated by the merging of the two firms were as follows:
- the sales, marketing, finance and logistics departments were to be unified, with the central base in Melbourne. The structure was still to be divisional, based on the existing structure of Stanley Australia
- the former CEO of Stanley Bostitch would become redundant, the position being absorbed within the role of managing director, Stanley Australia
- human resources was to be outsourced to a consultancy on a two-days-per-week basis.

Effects: structure

At the individual level, the structural changes mean that career opportunities have increased. There will be new chains of command with the concomitant problems of adjusting to new expectations and management. Already, with the process still very much under way, there have been some shakeouts. Another noticeable effect has been the fear of Stanley Bostitch employees that they will be swamped and lost in the Stanley Australia structure. To combat this, every effort has been made to give the Stanley Bostitch people equality in the organisation.

At the group level, teams now often consist of a mix of Stanley Bostitch and Stanley Australia employees. As an organisation, there was some difficulty in reconciling the HR policies of the two groups, but it was expected that this would be achieved as the new structure coalesces.

At the time of writing, there are many hopeful signs of a successful transition from a manufacturing to sales and marketing ethos within the organisation. The success of the plant closures is measured by their achievement within budget, free of industrial disruption, unfair dismissal claims and spurious Workcover claims. The managing director is committed to quarterly expositions of company results and forecasts. Key performance indicators, such as sales, inventory turn-overs and safety, are posted daily throughout the establishment, including interstate branches. The Managing Director has joined the Safety Committee. Profitability and sales are at satisfactory levels, which decrease the level of focus upon the Australian operation from the US headquarters.

Summary

Due to competitive global pressures, The Stanley Works in Australia has undergone comprehensive changes in strategy and culture. The strategic change affected a large number of employees over the entire organisation, and the pervasiveness was such that all levels of the organisation were impacted upon. The merger of Stanley Works and Stanley Bostich involved far-reaching cultural changes for all employees, based primarily on increased decision making for employees, and communication and involvement in teams.

With the pace of change involving much more than just the departure of some 300 employees over an 18-month period, some facets of organisational change suffered neglect. The time pressures and expectations of the US headquarter led to, at times, insufficient communication and less direct involvement in the change processes by the people affected.

Notes

1 www.stanleyworks.com
2 D. Harvey and D. Brown, *An Experiential Approach to Organization Development*, 5th ed. (New Jersey: Prentice-Hall, 1996): 411.
3 R. DeSimone and D. Harris, *Human Resource Development* (Orlando: Dryden Press, 1998).

Qenos: The Kemcor–Orica joint venture

By **Steven Coulton, Anne Duncan, Jague Lee and Sari Sitalaksmi**

Synopsis

The study provided valuable insights into the real issues relating to mergers, transformation and transition that are all part of the challenges associated with change management in the corporate world. It considers the creation of a virtual monopoly within the Australian plastics industry with the proposed merger of the Kemcor and Orica polythene businesses. The merger was well thought through in terms of business rationale in that it considered the available synergistic benefits and the economy of scale that the joint venture company would bring. In many areas the human asset was considered and a great deal of work went into the preparation and communication of the announcement in order to manage the people issues associated with the fear and uncertainties of such a transformation.

The research undertaken by way of interviews and surveys shows that, in the initial stages, the levels of preparation and communication were both well presented and well received. However, the employee perception of the way in which the two companies managed the transition phase indicated that the level of communication diminished shortly after the merger announcement. This was evidenced by the lack of visibility of senior management (particularly with respect to people management), the lack of communication regarding the selection process, ongoing delays and, most importantly, the lack of one-on-one dialogue.

Introduction

This paper examines the formation of Qenos, which was created by a merger between two of Australia's largest petrochemical companies, Kemcor and Orica (formerly ICI) Plastics Group. As the only two Australian manufacturers of polyethylene, the antecedent companies traditionally competed aggressively against each other for a share of the local market, and have operated under distinct organisational cultures. Radical transformations, such as merging with an arch-rival, inevitably entail dramatic changes in all aspects of the organisation, including the content and definition of jobs, the shape of the organisational structure and the values and beliefs that people hold about what is important to the organisation. This precipitates the introduction of people barriers that must be addressed. Radical change is based on discontinuous thinking and requires a paradigm shift in recognising and breaking away from outdated rules and assumptions. Discontinuous thinking is what gives transformational change the power to generate radical breakthroughs. For the same reason it is also what raises a vast number of barriers.

The purpose of the study was to examine two companies in the process of merging for their mutual benefit and survival. The Kemcor–Orica merger was selected because it was imminent, accessible and particularly relevant to the subject of managing change. It was expected that this study would reveal some of the classic problems and issues as suggested in theories related to transformational change, and particularly the transition process.

Background

In the late 1980s, a government-sponsored study was conducted by the Department of Industry, Technology and Regional Development (DITARD) to evaluate the viability of the

Australian plastics industry. Similar to the Button Automotive Industry plan, the DITARD report concluded that, in order to survive the globalisation of industry into the next millennium, the Australian plastics industry needed to rationalise from several competing, undersized, local manufacturers into focused, streamlined, integrated, world-scale organisations that could compete on the international market. This was driven by planned reductions in tariff barriers that would expose the previously protected local manufacturing industry to the razor-sharp claws of competition from the aggressive and predatory Asian tigers.

To date the plastics industry in Australia has already rationalised significantly:

- *polystyrene (PS):* Dow and Huntsman marketing joint venture; Australian Polystyrene Co.
- *polyvinyl chloride (PVC):* Auseon and ICI Vinyls joint venture; Australian Vinyls Co.
- *polypropylene (PP):* Shell (Montell) acquisition of ICI PP business and the Kemcor acquisition of Hoechst PP business
- *high density polyethylene (HDPE):* Kemcor acquisition of the Hoechst HDPE plant.

The sole remaining large-volume, locally produced polymer that had not yet seen any rationalisation was low-density polyethylene (LDPE). This product was produced by two manufacturers, Kemcor at Altona in Victoria and Orica at Botany in New South Wales. While both companies have a diverse product range, the market in which they competed most aggressively was the flexible packaging market, where LDPE and linear low-density polyethylene (LLDPE) are used extensively in blown film production for packaging.

Tariff reductions, down from 40% in the 1980s to the current level of 5%, together with the dumping of excess product from giant overseas suppliers, in some cases below the cost of manufacture, brought about the situation where the two local competitors finally agreed to work together. Their aim was to form a polyolefin manufacturing and marketing joint venture company to include PP, HDPE, LDPE, LLDPE, elastomers and plastic compounds, with a total capacity of approximately 500 000 tonnes per annum. This capacity would result in the joint venture company being the eighth-largest producer in the Asia-Pacific region.

Kemcor itself is a joint venture company involving Mobil and Exxon. The current Kemcor organisation is a formation of several fully-integrated businesses at the Altona petrochemical site, including:

- the former Petroleum Refineries Australia (PRA)
- Commercial Polymers (Compol)—previously owned by Union Carbide, manufacturers of high- and low-density polyethylene
- Hoechst HDPE and PP reactors
- ASR—manufacturer of rubber latex.

Orica is the new name of the former ICI Australia, which was divested by its British parent company, ICI plc, in 1997. This sell-off enabled Orica to focus on other core business areas such as explosives, paint, chemicals and fertilisers. Due to the cyclical volatility of such base commodities as polyethylene, Orica had stated that it would either divest, merge or shut down any non-strategic or under-performing businesses that did not generate the return on investment (ROI) that its shareholders expected.

While the DITARD report and several industry precedents involving mergers provided a compass for some direction in this joint venture, a catalyst or change agent was required to lead the way forward in what was considered to be uncharted waters. The statements issued by the Orica Managing Director, declaring that Orica intended to divest all remaining investments in plastics and concentrate on the revised core business growth platforms of chemicals, fertilisers, explosives and consumer effects (paint), prompted the need to consider a joint venture or complete divestment of the polythene division.

The possibility of a joint venture was raised with Kemcor, and in July 1998 the two companies announced that, subject to certain conditions, Orica Polyethylene Division and Kemcor were to merge to form a joint venture company with a target commencement date of 1 October 1998.

The merger was subject to three specific criteria:

- approval by the ACCC with respect to anti-competitive activity and the reduction of competition, as the joint venture would be the only Australian producer of polyethylene. An important criteria in this decision would be the 10% minimum level of competition from imports, but as the current level of imports was 20%, this was deemed not be an obstacle.
- approval by the Foreign Investment Review Board (FIRB), as both Mobil and Exxon were foreign-owned companies.
- the mutual due diligence process, which allows the parties to investigate each other's records, contracts, commitments, environmental status of production sites and balance sheets in order to determine the final ownership ratios, any ongoing implications and the projected profitability of the proposed 'Joint Venture Company' that was later to become known as Qenos.

Both Orica and Kemcor faced tremendous competition in the marketplace. An interview with the commercial director of the joint venture revealed that the merger initiative was part of the separate strategic plan of both companies for their very survival, and in order to become the market leader in the Asia-Pacific region. The companies expected that the merger would bring better economies of scale, operational synergies and greater competitiveness with overseas producers. This was reinforced by the DITARD report, which recommended the rationalisation of the plastics industry in order for Australian manufacturers to remain competitive. External catalysts included such factors as market share loss, rapid environmental changes and deregulation. It was considered that both companies would contend with a higher risk if the merger were not undertaken.

The joint venture executives initially created a sense of urgency, but this mostly focused on the 'hard' issues as a matter of priority—tasks and processes, such as engineering, logistics and information technology issues. However, it did not seem to treat the 'soft' human issues with the same degree of urgency. Consequently, the executives often found difficulty in responding to employees' questions in the predetermined time frame. This heightened some employees' concerns, and was exacerbated by the announcement of a second formal delay of the commencement date. An outplacement programme was initially provided only for Kemcor employees and an interviewee indicated that this programme was prematurely terminated because of the ongoing delays in the merger negotiations. This withdrawal or absence of the outplacement programme was seen to illustrate the lack of appreciation for employees' feelings. At this juncture in the merger process, the leaders' communication skills were considered to be critical.

There had been rumours about the merger within the industry and at both companies since early 1998. These rumours may have served to fill the gap in the inadequate information about the merger provided to employees. A definite decision and internal statement on the merger was announced at Kemcor earlier than at Orica, where people continued to hear only rumours. The reaction by some long-term employees was that the companies had broken their unwritten, mutual psychological contract:

'Some long-term employees who are to be made redundant feel cheated because they had expected to be employed by the company until they retired.'

Failure to predict a post-merger culture clash could deal a death blow to any anticipated benefits. Interviews with Kemcor and Orica personnel showed that there are cultural commonalities between the companies, but they also acknowledge the cultural differences between the companies. A simple example lies in the language differences, one company using the term 'manager', while the other uses the term 'team leader' for the same position.

The change process

1 Creating the guiding coalition

Six key executives were initially selected to develop a number of transition teams made up of people from Orica and Kemcor. The teams included human resources, information systems, supply chain and finance transition. In order to move forward, the executive team facilitated team building throughout the company in an attempt to achieve a successful start-up for the merger.

Although management appeared to lack an understanding of the employees' psychological ownership of Orica and Kemcor as separate entities, it had a greater awareness of the need to develop a strong psychological ownership of the future company. The process of building a new team continued by selecting the most appropriate candidates from the antecedent companies for each horizontal layer of management. The new team would meet to decide on the design of the next layer of structure, followed by the appointment of selected candidates, and so on. This was an excellent example of generating ownership and psychological contract—at least at middle management levels. The joint venture management team preferred to use internal change agents, rather than external consultants, although an external facilitator was used for the management team's initial three-day team-building exercise. The change agents for the joint venture were senior managers who had had previous successful merger and acquisition experiences, and appeared to be concerned mostly with the emergent structure and technology.

'We're doing it all ourselves, we're not using anybody, not using any external organisation; we've done these sorts of things before, so it's the management team and myself.'

2 Developing a vision and strategy

The joint venture management team planned to invite all employees' participation in developing the new entity's vision after the merger commenced. The result may be a cohesive and strong team, but there was a long time gap between the announcement of the merger and the official joint venture opening. In the interim there was no communicated vision at all. Delaying the development of a vision for the new entity until after its commencement put the joint venture at risk of trying to steer a rudderless ship into the future. The transition manager claimed that an interim vision had been developed, but this appeared to be a set of objectives and tasks to be achieved prior to the commencement of the joint venture, rather than a statement that motivates people to rethink what is possible.

The executive team did not seem to give adequate attention to developing the joint venture vision. 'It is perceived as a secondary task.' In addition, there was no definite timetable for developing a vision for the new entity, and, as a result, employees remained uncertain about the future. Employees' fears for future job availability within the joint venture were not managed well, and many were confused about their loyalties and uncertain future.

'Now we have confusion over who we are working for!'

The joint venture may lose key personnel for the following reasons:
- employee uncertainty regarding their future at the company
- a lack of communication, and the tardiness in providing certainty
- increased employee mistrust of the company.

3 Communicating the change vision

The most critical part of transformational change lies within a courageous leadership that is able to drive widespread acceptance of the merger. Senior leaders may have to dismantle the organisational structure that they helped create and worked hard to make successful; they may have to convince other senior managers effectively to go back to square one. The company had been communicating the need for the merger, but this still remained unclear to many employees. Based on the survey results, this might have been due to a lack of intensive ongoing, and repeated, communication.

- *'The rumour mill was a better source of information than management, and this was disgraceful.'*
- *'They could have dispelled fears quicker.'*

While some attempts at presentations and discussion groups were made, they were minimal and might not have reached the target groups. Formal updates were provided through newsletters and e-mail, but their effectiveness in getting feedback from employees is questionable. These tools were perceived as a one-way street, answers often being delayed, or not appearing at all, and not all individuals had personal access to a computer.

The joint venture team had not yet begun to develop a vision for the new entity, this being perceived as something to be done once the merger was up and running, when everyone could be involved in its development. Meanwhile, this situation caused a degree of uncertainty among employees, with the potential for generating fear, role conflict, stress, labour turnover, resistance, negativity and sabotage. It was apparent that some of the senior managers involved in the transition process were themselves somewhat resistant to unwilling change. Management were reluctant to conduct feedback surveys, endorse the name change or involve external consultants, and they relied mostly on previous experience with mergers as the only source of success. While the managers appeared to be unaware of their own reactions, they were aware of the probability of the employees' resistance to change and perceived this as a common and understandable reaction to the uncertainty they would feel about the future. In order to avoid a clash with the unions and to overcome their fear and resistance, management declared that no line worker would be affected by the merger. Both Orica and Kemcor claimed that there would be ongoing downsizing, whether or not the merger went ahead, simply because the level of competition in the industry would force rationalisation within the two separate companies.

From interviews with senior managers, it was found that management had not noted any unusual behaviour and felt that all the employees were diligently going about their business pending the merger. However, from discussions and survey feedback from other employees, what was interpreted as employees' commitment to the merger may, in fact, have been a case of denial at all levels within the organisation.

The repeated delays in commencing the merger had an adverse effect on cynicism, morale and trust. The strong presence of cynicism was noted during interviews, particularly amongst non-management employees:

- 'Feedback mismanaged.'
- 'HR issues mismanaged.'
- 'Not enough attention to individuals who will not go with the joint venture.'
- 'It appears that the (job) selections were prejudged.'
- 'All of the top people were given or found jobs in other areas, while the rest must cope as best they can.'

Such statements were redolent with cynicism and anger.

The termination of the outplacement programme negated any message that the companies cared about their employees, and appeared to exacerbate the level of cynicism and distrust that had already been incensed by the repeated postponements of the merger commencement date. The syndicate group found, from the survey and interviews, that in the exploration and commitment stages people had been optimistic about the merger. However, optimism among most of the employees then began decreasing, coinciding with an increasing level of cynicism, as typified by the following quote:

> Not only could we not achieve an optimistic deadline; we couldn't even achieve a pessimistic deadline.

4   Generating short-term wins

Many mergers fail for a number of reasons, such as the degree of employee co-operation and resistance. Between two-thirds and three-quarters of all mergers are ultimately regarded as failures. Insights gained from interviews with Kemcor and Orica personnel, together with a study of the relevant literature, identified several implications that might have adversely affected the merger if not addressed:

- disruption of the organisation culture
- loss of key employees
- unexpected costs
- lack of information for planning purposes
- excessive optimism
- failure to prepare properly for change
- disparities of preparation between the two companies.

The importance of communication and a clear vision are demonstrated by the fact that employee uncertainty about the future after a merger can lead to adverse consequences, such as fear, role conflict and stress, labour turnover, resistance to change, and non-cooperation. The postponement of the merger for the second time resulted in a significant increase in distrust and all the above adverse behavioural responses.

Subject to the final, drawn-out contract negotiations between the two main parties being concluded quickly and satisfactorily, the merger should proceed without any insurmountable resistance due to 'people issues' or other such obstacles. This is not to say that there will not be any further concerns, fears and HR issues. In fact, it is likely that there will be an increase in 'people issues' as more people transfer from the two antecedent companies to the joint venture company, and as the official commencement date draws nearer. This will probably be due to the physical dislocation, the upheaval of desks, offices and totally different work environments, formation of new teams, new bosses, new colleagues and, tragically, for some the final realisation of job losses. Some of this is inevitable, but if the commencement date is further postponed, the implications for a positive and successful merger will be severe. This is borne out by the increasingly negative trend depicted in the survey results. The stated excuse or reason for the lack of focus on people issues, such as communication and feedback, was that there were many more important and urgent issues to attend to, as was highlighted during the interviews:

- 'Which miracle do we perform first?'
- 'We are all engineers and scientists here, and when under pressure we tend to revert to type and concentrate on tasks rather than on people issues.'

If this attitude continues and if the human asset is overlooked for much longer, morale, and subsequently productivity, will plummet. While this weakness is clearly recognised, a greater effort is required to overcome this mechanistic outlook and to focus on the human element. The antecedent companies must now focus on finalising the negotiations and dealing with the human issues that have arisen from the joint venture.

Conclusion

The transition to the joint venture has been reasonably well managed, due in part to previous experience by all parties in continuous long-term change, transformational change and recent experience in mergers and acquisitions. This has led to an over-reliance on previous experience to achieve success, rather than on integrating new theories or better change models.

However, it became apparent that the senior and middle management were focused on the 'task issues' at the expense of the human element. One reason given for this was that most of the management were 'engineers and scientists and when we're under pressure we revert to type'.

Of the two indicators most commonly used to measure mergers and acquisitions—financial performance and behavioural indices, the joint venture management seemed to be mostly interested in financial measurement. The transition manager stated:

'The joint venture will be considered a success when it has delivered the $40 million of synergies that have been identified. Anything less will be considered a failure!'

Should the joint venture continue to ignore these issues, there will be a decrease in morale and productivity and increased dissatisfaction, culminating in the eventual loss of further essential personnel and the ultimate failure of the joint venture company to deliver its promises.

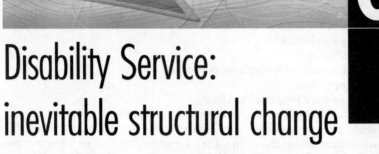

Disability Service: inevitable structural change

By **David Brett, Wendy Cox, Suzanne Diprose, Cynthia Loquet and Robert Moore**

Introduction

Until 1 February 1999, Disability Service (DS) had a functional structure made up of four service divisions and support and development divisions. Since 1 February 1999, DS has effected planned structural change and begun to operate with three regionalised divisions and the same support and development divisions.

DS is a provider in the disability services industry. It is both a company limited by guarantee and a public benevolent institution. It has a volunteer Board as its governing body. The CEO, the general management, plus the support and development divisions in their entirety, are located at Head Office. Other managers and all direct service employees work at facilities located throughout metropolitan and country areas. Today DS delivers services to around 3500 adults and children in their homes, in day facilities and in community centres. DS also runs eight small manufacturing businesses.

The government is the primary source of DS funding. In the past, the organisation seemed insulated from both the industry and its external environment. While funds were prevalent, the client was the paramount concern; competitors and the outside world were incidental. The external environment, however, has subsequently had a significant impact on DS (and the government-funded disability services industry, generally) in various ways, including:

- accountability is now based on demonstrable outcomes for clients against government expenditure per hour of service delivered
- incipient awareness that organisations will need to develop strategic partnerships with other disability service providers and with commercial sponsors
- an ageing population of disabled with a concomitant need for long-term residential care
- continuing de-institutionalisation and a trend towards the integration of people with disabilities into the broader community
- globalised networking increasing knowledge exchange.

DS has numerous competitors in the industry, and the rivalry for funding is intense. Moreover, non-profit, charitable institutions not only compete for funding from state and Commonwealth governments, but also seek to attract the same, shrinking pool of fund-raising dollars from the community. Nevertheless, DS market share is to some extent assured—none of the other service providers has the expertise or resources to meet the high support needs of many DS clients.

In recent years, DS has operated under difficult financial circumstances. While DS recorded a net surplus in 1997/98, this included interim transitional funding. This funding was provided on the condition that DS submitted to an external review of its operations by B6 Consulting. The review was completed in November 1997, although the Board contested the factual basis of much of the final report and rejected some of the recommendations. As a result, DS negotiated a further government-funded consultancy. B6 Consulting performed this consultancy, and they in turn engaged CC Consulting to examine specific and unique issues.

The final report from CC Consulting was delivered to the Board in May 1998. One of the key recommendations of the report, as it had been in the B6 Consulting report, was that DS should restructure on a regional basis, which would duplicate the regionalised funding model adopted by government. At this time, there was a reshuffle in the membership of the Board, establishing new affiliations with government. Soon after the CC Consulting report was accepted by the Board, significant staff reductions were made in direct care positions.

DS was compelled to operate within a purchaser–provider framework. The restructure was an effort to address discontinuities in the environment, and specifically the move to compulsory tendering, user-pays services and new levels of accountability. The government is now a customer and does not allocate the block grants it once did. Naturally, the government now also evaluates DS services more critically, and compares the quality, efficiency and effectiveness of its services with other disability service providers. DS, however, did not have a firm grasp of its competitor competencies and the organisation had not defined its core business. Indeed, B6 Consulting recommended that DS benchmark against other disability service providers—a difficult task given the lack of uniform accounting standards among disability service providers.

The move to a regional structure was preceded in September 1998 by a spill of senior and upper middle management positions in service delivery. This affected four general managers and seven other managers. In the regional structure, there would be three general managers and a maximum of eight regional managers. Each of the general management positions was advertised both externally and internally; the regional management positions were initially made available only to internal applicants.

Two of the four incumbent general managers were appointed in November 1998 to roles that were comparable to those they had previously held. An outside candidate was appointed to the third general management position, which was, in effect, a combination of two of the previous general management positions. Once the general management appointments had been confirmed, recruitment to the regional management positions commenced. Four of the five managers from the old structure were appointed as regional managers; the fifth manager chose to resign rather than apply for a new position. The remaining four appointments were from middle management ranks in direct service. Each of the eight appointments took effect on 1 February 1999.

In April 1999, the reporting structure was again modified: the nine government regions were to be divided among the eight regional managers along lines specific to DS. In addition, three of the regional managers were to have responsibility for still unspecified state-wide portfolios.

There are no measures in place at DS to evaluate the effectiveness of the restructure, which may be because the CEO and the Board had already committed DS to the change. To evaluate the restructure might be interpreted as the CEO lacking resolve; in a sense, the decision to implement the change was an unqualified endorsement of a regional structure. Moreover, there are key performance indicators enmeshed in the regional structure: DS must perform to government expectations, and without a decisive commitment there was the possibility that the culture could undermine the change.

Culture was fundamental to how the change process unfolded at DS. The culture at DS was not easily discerned. As the organisation evolved at the community level and by functional discipline, there were a number of subcultures in existence. The geographical spread of DS, while it added richness and vitality to the organisational mix, also provoked divisiveness as some facilities and functional areas saw themselves as separate entities. While there was commonality between subcultures, they each had established and sustained different basic assumptions about the organisation. To restructure on a regional basis, in a manner that negated the importance of functional areas, therefore endangered the continued existence of various subcultures.

The defining characteristic of DS culture was derived from the philanthropic origins of the organisation. There was an overriding belief that DS must be engaged in 'worthy', or client-related, pursuits; any expenditure that subtracted from funds for clients was not 'worthy' and could be disparaged. However, the recent recruitment of staff with business management backgrounds had led to a gradual move towards a problem-solving culture with a corporate outlook. This was also a source of potential conflict, as tension between the cultures was prevalent.

The sentient value system of the organisation—and of the individuals within the organisation—was compromised by the restructure. A significant level of attachment, variously expressed as passion and immutable client focus, was evident within DS. More profoundly, this dedication manifested as martyrdom and an identification with clients so powerful that some staff considered themselves as vulnerable, misunderstood and under-valued as clients. In these cases, change was perceived as a personal criticism and strenuously resisted; to accept change would be to reject the self.

Some staff used metaphors to describe how they were informed about the restructure. The simple notion that staff were treated like 'schoolchildren' carried with it the suggestion that staff were talked down to, and that attendance at meetings was compulsory. There was a suggestion in comments like this that scepticism was hardening into cynicism at DS. Over the previous ten years there had been a number of failed restructures, and this had created a seen-it-and-survived-it-all-before attitude among staff who had been with DS for more than five years.

DS repeatedly downsized for short-term economic gain throughout the nineties. As a result, there was a sense of powerlessness and thwarted potential and wariness about new appointments. DS also discovered, however, that its corporate memory was being eroded, and downsizing carried with it long-term systemic consequences. The disbandment of programmes, for example, meant that networks were lost and fundraising dollars diminished. Similarly, when replacement staff were hired (or redundant staff re-hired at consultant rates) there was scepticism about why staff were retrenched in the first place. It was therefore, in part, a pragmatic decision to restructure on a regional basis as an alternative to downsizing. This way DS would operate more efficiently and in accordance with government expectations.

Staff also expressed cynicism about the pre-Christmas timing of the change. At year's end people were tired, distracted, with no energy for change and no fight or time to act. Management, however, expressed optimism and relief that there was finally action after two years of speculation about a regional restructure. This gap between cynicism and optimism might have been closed had senior management improved the communication process.

Disability Service did not provide any official communication about the restructure between a general staff meeting in September 1998 and a memorandum notifying general management appointments in November 1998. There were two subsequent memoranda: one dated January 1999 announcing the appointment of regional managers and one dated April 1999 describing the finalised structure. The fact that communication was restricted to memoranda alone led to covert communication, rumour and speculation. Indeed, the DS was described as dark, in that the personality of the organisation was murky and secretive.

The CEO did not publicly articulate the future direction of the organisation. Staff described the CEO as unassuming and bland. But her style in implementing the restructure was also considered by staff to be heavy-handed. This apparent paradox left staff confused, and they noted that:

- the two more extroverted general managers from the old regime were 'rolled', forming a team that was inwardly focused and complementary to the CEO. This meant that her decision making was not questioned as thoroughly as it had been by the two retrenched general managers, allowing her to introduce her ideas more readily. With a team loathe to disagree with the CEO, however, there was a concomitant decline in the vigour of the debate among the executive.

- despite enacting tough decisions, the CEO retained control. Some staff considered that she adopted a coercive approach in shedding staff. The thinking here was that because of her timidity, or perhaps because she was a woman, she needed to act strongly. This also gave the impression of being able to implement her decisions, whether or not she did so successfully.

- poor people maintenance skills and an inability to motivate and inspire were displayed. Change seemed to descend upon the organisation rather than being managed. As a result, staff, who had been told they were the lifeblood of the organisation, did not find the evidence to back that up. The clerical and administrative staff, in particular, regarded the CEO as remote and uncommunicative.

- true consultation did not occur, discussion was avoided and challenges quietly crushed. For many staff, the restructure was something to be endured. The reasons why it was happening were never clearly expressed and the personal losses that staff experienced were not acknowledged. Meanwhile the CEO was seen as being instrumental in the process, but somehow disconnected from it all. This lessened her chances of being able to salvage the loyalties of the staff who survived.
- outcomes were apparently achieved with no regard for personal fallout. Again, the wholesale retrenchments conditioned the way that staff viewed the CEO. She was widely considered to be unaware of the pain that she was causing others.

The CEO was working with a vision and mission that had been formulated by her immediate predecessor. He had created this vision and mission in isolation and, as a result, there was no sense of ownership by staff at that time, let alone to the same vision and mission in a new regime. Moreover, there was disparity between the values espoused by DS and the abrupt manner in which change was accomplished. While the organisation purported to involve stakeholders at all stages of the change process, this never occurred.

Staff input was always restricted to management level and, for the most part, to senior management. There was no attempt to harness the energies of middle management and lower level staff. The manner in which staff cuts were made was never a matter for negotiation. Despite the protracted length of the restructure, there was no time lag during which natural attrition was allowed to account for the numbers who were cut.

Perhaps a fresh vision and mission, introduced by the CEO and driven down deep into the organisation, would have engendered genuine enthusiasm and ownership of the change. The DS vision and mission, if they contributed to change at all, engendered compliance rather than commitment. It was a simple case of most of the staff being told how things were going to be.

The change to a regional structure at DS was:

- inevitable and necessary for the survival of the organisation
- a planned response to discontinuities in the environment
- driven by government, the CEO and the Board.

Index

A-groups 7
Aboriginal health workers 8–9
accounting organisations, codes of
  practice 65–6
action research 7–10, 11, 27,
  28–31
Adamson, Jim 388, 389
Advantage Credit Union 577–82
AGL 374–5
AIG Insurance 7
Alderfer, C 222, 224
all-salaried workforce 352
analysis of data 119–25, 496
  content analysis 120
  difference tests 124–5
  force-field analysis 120–1
  means 121
  qualitative 119–21
  quantitative 121–5
  scattergrams 122–4
Andrews, Christopher 607
Ansett, Bob 441
ANZ Bank 12–13, 61
Apex Manufacturing Corporation
  199
Argyris, Chris 16, 61, 194, 201,
  202, 452, 456
Austin, N 274
Australian Council for Educational
  Research 113
Australian Public Service 350–2,
  518–27
Avatar Industries 426

Barnevik, Percy 369
Barrett, Brendan 541
Barrett, Rowena 518
Beckhard, R 1, 2, 7, 15, 16, 162,
  219, 222, 225
Beer, M 1, 2, 210, 211, 228
Bell, C 210, 215, 228
Bellesis, Ross 255
Benazic, Peter 568
benefits, employee 357
Bennington, L 384
Bennis, Warren 16, 227
Bethesda Hospital 133–4
BHP 455–6
Blake, Des 443–4

Blake, Robert 7, 219, 224, 227,
  232–8
Bleasel, Len 374
Block, Peter 17, 73
Blumberg, A 228
Boland, Ann 46
Bolton, Paul 577
Boss, R 215
Bourke, John 607
Bowers, D 135
BP Kwinana refinery 99–100
Bradilovich, Alex 599
Brambles 157
Brett, David 620
Brown, Dave 17
Buller, R 215
Burke, W 1, 2, 16
Byung–Chull, Lee 479

Cable Co. 499–509
call centres 577–81
Caltex-Ampol 10
Campbell, J 193, 194
career halt 382–3
career planning and development
  147, 365–83
Carr, Philip 577
Carroll, Alan 367–9
Carroll, S 342
case studies 496–623
case study analysis 496–8
Centrelink 518–27
change agents 426–7, 488–9,
  521, 530
change management 150–67
  creating a vision 155
  developing support 159
  evaluation 538
  momentum 164
  motivation 152–5, 164
  power sources and strategies
    160
  resistance to 153, 562
  transitions 161–7
change practitioners 45–63
  careers of 56–7
  contracts 68–76
  diagnosis of organisations 78–93
  ethics 58–62

professional values 57–8
role of 51–7
selection of 70
skills of 46–51
support for 164
training of 46, 56, 58, 92
change strategies 451–6
Chenall, R 8
Clark, Tom 88
Clarke, David 15, 16
Coad, Warrick 591
Coch, Lester 8
Coles Supermarkets 57
Colgate-Palmolive Co. 371–2
Collier, John 7
Collins, Professor 256
Community Development and
  Management Association of
  Africa 485–8
compensation 147, 347–59, 506
competing values and culture 438
continuous learning 434
Cook, Chantelle 541
Cooperrider, David 17
Corrigan, John 256
Coulton, Steven 614
Cox, Wendy 620
Craig, Alec 541
Crosby, Philip 239
CSIRO 421–3
cultural change 148, 434–44,
  515, 516, 542, 563,
  587, 593, 610
cultural diagnosis 437–40, 511
cultural diversity 386, 464
Cummings, Thomas 17, 112, 423,
  424, 444

data collection 108–19
  analysis 119–25
  interviews 111, 113–14
  observations 111, 114–15
  questionaires 110–13
  sampling 115–19
  unobtrusive measures 111,
    115–16
Davenport, Kylie 577
Davis, L 273
Day, Jonathon 375

Deming, W E 14, 163–4, 292–4
Dennys Restaurants 387–9
Department of Social Security
   (Commonwealth) 211
diagnosis 78–93, 96–106
   analysis of data 119–25
   boundaries 81
   collection of data 108–19
   definition 78
   feedback 80–1, 12–36, 170
   groups 96–101
   jobs 101–6
   open systems model 80–2
   organisational levels 82–3
   organisation culture 437–40
diagnostic models 79–93
   open systems 80–2
disabled workers 385
Disability Service 620–3
Diprose, Suzanne 620
Doherty, Kathleen 548
double-learning 448
downsizing 146, 256–62, 571
Drucker, P 338
dual-career accommodation 380
Dulux Australia Ltd 130–1, 345–7
Duncan, Anne 614
Duncan, Michael 510
Dunnette, M 193, 194
Dunphy, D 1, 2, 38, 39, 40
DuToit, Louw 485
Dyer, W 208, 214

Eck, Dennis 155
economic development 465–6
Edgar, Andrew 442–3
Elden, Max 17
Elgas 558–67
employee assistance programs
   389–94
employee involvement 272–99,
   537, 538
employee wellness 147, 389
Emtech International 255–6
Energise Ltd 510–17
environment of organisations
   408–57
Esso 87
evaluation 169–79, 535
   measurement 172–7
   research design 177

feedback 9–11, 153
   content of 127–9
   effects of 128
   implementation and evaluation
      169–72
   in open systems 80–1
   interdependant groups 134
   limitations of 135
   of diagnostic information 80–1,
      127–36
   performance 375
   results of 135–6

Flynn, David 255
Foley, Susan 591
Ford Motor Co. 14
Fordyce, J 228
Forfar, John 510, 511, 512, 516
Formway Furniture Ltd 231–2
French, John 8
French, W 1, 2, 210, 228
functional organisation structure
   243–5

Gainshare Scheme 571–2
Galbraith, J 244, 246, 248, 254
GEM Co 103–5
gender and workplace 385
General Electric Medical Systems
   220–2
General Motors-Holden 422–3
Gibb, J 197
Gilbert, Alan 34
Glaxo India 296-8
global orientation 474–5
global social change 481–9
globalisation 4
goal-setting 147
Golden Circle Ltd 319–21
Golembiewski, R 228
Grampians Water 548–57
Greiner, Larry 16, 160
grid organisation development 146
Grid® Organisation Development
   146, 232–8
Griffith University 158
group design 96–101
   diagnosis model 97
   inputs 96
   outputs 98
Guardian Pharmacies Australia Ltd
   599–606

Hackman, J 96, 101, 176, 305,
   306, 307, 312–3
Hall, Richard 426
Halliday, Susan 377
Hamel, Gary 442
Handy, Charles 532
Hansen, Kent 577
Hanson, Libby 591
Harris, R 162
Harris, Steve 286
Hart, M 8
Herzberg, F 101, 305, 306
Hewlett Packard 185–7
high involvement organisations
   288–92
horizonal linkages 484
Hornery, Stuart 369
Horton, Robert 473
Houghton, J 294
human resource management
   interventions 146, 502
human resource planing 503
Huse, E 228, 341

implementation feedback 169–72
   measurement of 172–7
Improshare 355
industrial economies 466
industrialising economies 466
information technology 4
institutionalising interventions
   179–88
integrated strategic change
   419–23
inter-group relations 145
international organisation
   development 462–73
interventions 139–48, 169–88
   career planing 365–83
   definition 139
   design of 140–4
   employee involvement 272–99
   evaluation 169–79
   human processes 145–6,
      191–238
   human resource management
      146–7, 334–401
   institutionalising 179–88
   organisation and environment
      408–57
   organisation transformation
      431–57
   process consultation 145,
      195–202
   process interventions 219–38
   strategies 147, 408–57
   T-group 145, 192–5, 215
   team building 145, 206–15
   techno-structural 146, 242–327
   third party 145, 202–5
   workforce diversity 383–9
Investors in People 10–11
Ivkovic, Bernadette 599

JAL 290
James, Ted 91
Jayawardanai, C 583
Jenkins, G 358
job design 101–6, 304–27
job pathing 375
job rotation 380
Johari Windows 196–7
Johnson, A 56
Johnson & Johnson 392–4
Jones, Russell 262
Juran, Joseph 14, 292, 293

Kaplan, R 194
Kay, E 341
Kazanjian, R 254
Kelman, H 60
Kemp, Dr 519
Kirby, Peter 441
Knight, Phil 88, 89
Knox City Council 447
Konaka, X 451
Kotter, J 83, 597
Krautil, Fiona 377, 378

Langfield-Smith, K 8
large-group interventions 146
Lawler, Edward III 16, 96 112, 274, 358
Learnstatt Concept 463
Ledford, Gerry 17, 96, 274
Lee, Jague 614
Lend Lease Corporation 4, 15, 283, 369, 434
Leonard-Barton, D 451
Levinson, H 338
Lewin, Kurt 6,7, 8, 9, 26–8, 120, 121, 181
Lewin's Model 26–8, 32, 41
Lewis, Rowan 529
Likert, Rensis 6, 9, 10, 11, 12, 232
Likert Scale 9
Lindsay, Don 286
linking pin 12
Lippitt, G 61, 70, 201
Lippitt, R 28
Littler, Craig 256, 261
Liverpool City Council 251–2
Loquet, Cynthia 620
Ludekens, H 91, 92, 93
Luft, J 196
lump sum salary increases 352–3
Lundberg, Craig 16
Lyster, David 599

McCann, D 116, 212, 214, 246, 248
McConnell, Sue 591
McFarlane, John 12, 13, 441
McGregor, Douglas 7, 338
McLaughlin, Bill 375
Macy, B 173–5
Maher, Terry 447
Mallen, David 46
management by objectives 338–42
management systems 11, 534
managerial innovation 4
Mann, Floyd 9, 10
Margerison, C 116, 212
Margulies, Newton 16
Maribyrnong City Council 568–75
Marsh, D 52
Mathieson, Ivan 548
matrix organisation 246–8
Melbourne City Parking and Traffic 583–9
Melbourne Water Corporation 400–1
mentoring 378-9
Mercer, Don 12
microcosm groups 222–4
Mirvis, P 173–5
MLC 15
Mobil Adelaide refinery 281–2
modular transformation 534
Mohrman, Sue 17, 96, 112, 274, 444
Mono Pumps 38

Monsanto Company 340–1
Moore, Robert 620
Morgan, Hugh 4
Morris, C 96
Mouton, J 219, 232-8
multinational orientation 475–6
Murdoch, Lachlan 378
Murrell, Ken 17

Nadler, D 83, 108, 111, 128
Nakamura, Yoshiki 291
Nakazato, Kimiya 290
Nally (WA) Pty Ltd 165–6
National Training Laboratories 6, 7
NEC Australia 90-3
network-based structures 252–6
Nganampa Health Council 9
Nike 87–90
Nilakant, V 510

Odiorne, G 338
Oldham, G 106, 176, 305, 306, 307, 312–13
O'Mahoney, Lee 607
O'Neill, Paul 296
open systems planning 147, 412–19
organisation confrontation meeting 145
organisation culture 86, 434–44
organisation learning 148, 447–56
organisation transformation 431–57
organisational change 3, 4
    action research model 27, 28–31, 32
    case studies 496–623
    common errors 597
    critics of planned change 37–41
    cultural change 440–44, 587, 593, 610
    evaluation of 564
    impact of 603, 604, 611–12
    Lewin's model 26–8, 32, 41
    management of 150–67
    model of 32–4
    motivating change 152-5
    resistance to 153, 562
    strategies 39–40, 513
    theories of 26–32
organisational design 84–6, 88, 96
    performance measurement 86
    strategy 84, 89
organisational development
    action research 7–10, 11, 27, 28–31
    careers in 5, 45–63
    courses on 16
    culture and 463–73
    definition 1–3
    evolution in 16–17
    goals of 1
    history of 6–17
    in global settings 461–90
    international 462–73

interventions 139–48, 169–88
    management of 150–67
    participative management 11, 12–13, 537, 538
    practitioners of 45–63, 68–76
    process of 68–76
    quality of work life 13–14, 272–5
    special applications 461–90
    strategic change 15–16
    structural design 242–56
    trends shaping change 4
    world-wide 473–81
organisations, diagnosing of 78–93, 96–106
    analysis of data 119–25
    collection of data 108–119
    group level 96–101
    job level 101-6
overseas aid organisations 529–30

Packer, James 378
participative management 11, 12–13, 537, 538
Pasmore, William 17
Paula, Anthony 599
pay 349-57
PDL Electronics 426
Peregrine Corporate Training 7
performance appraisal 147, 342–7, 504
performance feedback 375
performance management 334–59
    goal setting 336–42
    model of 335–6
performance appraisal 147, 342–7, 504
    reward systems 347–59
performance-based pay 353–4, 526
Peters, T 274
Petty, Ron 388
phased retirement 381
Pilkington Australasia 541–7
Platt, Lewis 186, 187
Pocknee, Graeme 92, 93
Pool, Judy 568
Porras, Jerry 17, 37
Porter, Michael 83, 420
Pratt, Richard 155
Prentice, Ern 455, 456
Prescott, John 374
Preston, Joanne 17
process-based structures 248
process consultation 145, 195–202
process interventons 219–38
    confrontations 219–22
    Grid® Organisation development 232–8
    intergroup relations 222–8
    large-group 229–32
productivity 13–14
profit sharing 354–7
promotions 357
Proust, Elizabeth 13
Pyman, Amanda 548

Qenos 614–19
quality circles 14, 274, 283–8
quality of work life 13–14, 272–5
questionnaires 110–13

Raia, Anthony 16, 342
Reckitt and Coleman 286
recruitment 508
redundancy 609
re-engineering 146, 262–8, 533
Reith, Peter 518
Research Centre for Group
  Dynamics (MIT) 6, 9
restructure 533
reward systems 147, 347–59
Rhodeback, M 59
Richards, Renae 558
Robertson, P 37
Rucker plan 355
Rupnorth Co-operative Ltd 310–11

Samsung 479-80
Scanlon, Joe 355
Scanlon plan 355
scanning units 411
scattergrams 122–4
Schein, Edgar 16, 29, 160, 197
Schmidt, W 56
Schon, D 452, 456
Scutt, Dr J 377
Seaside Hospital 414-18
self-contained unit 245–6
self-designing organisations 148,
  444–7
self-managing work groups 13,
  314–23, 568–75
Semler, R 467
Senge, P 452, 456
sexual orientation and workforce
  diversity 386–9
Shepard, Herbert 7
Shewhart, W 292
Shop Distributive and Allied
  Employees Association 5
Sigma Co Ltd 236–7, 599–606
Singapore Inland Revenue Authority
  265–8
Singh, C 8
Sitalaksmi, Sari 614
skill-based pay 349–52
Smith, Natalie 558
Snell, Alan 10
Southcorp 245
Stace, D 1, 2, 38, 39, 40

St Andrew's War Memorial Hospital
  71–2
Stanley Australia 607–13
statutory authorities case study
  116–18
St B's 226–7
Stewart, Mark 426
strategic interventions 147, 408–57
stress management programs
  394–401
structural design 146, 242–56
subsistence economies 466

T-groups 6–7
  interventions 145, 192–5, 215
  results of 194
Takeuchi, X 451
Tannenbaum, Robert 16, 50
Taylor, F 304
team building 7, 145, 193,
  206–16, 561
  activities 208
  checklist 207
  consultants on 213
  results of 214
types of 209–13
team performance index 116–18
  techno-structural interventions
    146, 242–327
  employee involvement 272–99
  restructuring 242–69
  work design 304–27
Telstra 591–8
Tharenou, P 384
third party interventions 145
Thompson, Jack 154–5
Tolkis, Theo 577
Toohey, John 7
Tosi, W 342
total quality management 163–6,
  259–61, 292–9
Trani, John 607
transformational change 431–4
transnational orientation 476–8
transorganisational development
  148, 423–7
Trist, Eric 13, 273
Tsen, Olivia 583
Tubemakers 163, 349
Turberville, Sarah 518
Tushman, M 83

University of Auckland MBA
  programme 180

University of Hong Komg 204–5
University of Queensland 31

Vaill, Peter 16
Van Deur, C 61
Vickers, David 591

Waddell, Di 529
Walker, John 251
Walker Manufacturing 154–5
Walpole, Sue 377
Walton, R 203
Watanabe, Teizo 290
Waterman, R 274
Watson, J 28
Weick, K 409
Weil, R 228
Weisbord, M 83
Welch, Jack 220
Wendler, James 375
Westley, B 28
Westrail 14
White, L 59
Whyte, William 7
Wilkinson, Paul 512-16
Williams, Alan 5
Williams, Cathy 568
Williams, Melissa 541
Williams, Stuart 17
Wilson, Paul 583
Wilson, Ross 155
Work design 304–27, 587
  engineering approach 304–5
  motivational approach 305–13
  socio-technical systems approach
    313–23
  technical personal needs design
    323–7
work-life balance 379
workforce age 383–5
workforce diversity 147, 383–9
workplace agreements 523–6,
  591
World Vision Australia 529–39
world-wide organisation
  development 473–81
world-wide strategic orientation
  478–81
Wunder, Bob 104

Yakka 442–4
Young, John 186, 187

Zand, D 278, 279